The Breakdown
of Democratic Regimes

The Breakdown of Democratic Regimes, edited by Juan J. Linz and Alfred Stepan, is available in separate paperback editions:

The Breakdown of Democratic Regimes:
Crisis, Breakdown, and Reequilibration
by Juan J. Linz

The Breakdown of Democratic Regimes: Europe
edited by Juan J. Linz and Alfred Stepan

The Breakdown of Democratic Regimes: Latin America
edited by Juan J. Linz and Alfred Stepan

The Breakdown of Democratic Regimes: Chile
by Arturo Valenzuela

The Breakdown
of Democratic Regimes

Edited by Juan J. Linz and Alfred Stepan

The Johns Hopkins University Press
Baltimore and London

Manufactured in the United States of America

The Johns Hopkins University Press, Baltimore, Maryland 21218
The Johns Hopkins Press Ltd., London

Library of Congress Catalog Card Number 78–584
ISBN 0-8018-2008-1

Library of Congress Cataloging in Publication data
will be found on the last printed page of this book.

Contents

PART III.   LATIN AMERICA

Juan J. Linz and Alfred Stepan, editors

PART IV.   CHILE

Arturo Valenzuela

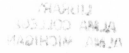

Editors' Preface
and Acknowledgments

How and why democratic regimes break down are the central questions addressed by the contributors to this volume.[1] Such breakdowns have long preoccupied social scientists. However, much of the existing literature on the subject has focused attention on the emergence of nondemocratic political forces or the underlying structural strains that lead to the collapse of democratic institutions.[2] Implicitly if not explicitly, the impression often given by such works is that of the virtual inevitability of the breakdown of the democratic regimes under discussion. While recognizing the scholarly legitimacy and analytic utility of studying antidemocratic movements and structural strains, we have addressed a somewhat different aspect of the breakdown of democratic regimes.

Given the tragic consequences of the breakdown of democracy in countries such as Germany, Spain, and Chile, we believed it intellectually and politically worthwhile to direct systematic attention to the dynamics of the political process of breakdown. In particular, we felt it important to analyze the behavior of those committed to democracy, especially the behavior of the incumbent democratic leaders, and to ask in what ways the actions or nonactions of the incumbents contributed to the breakdown under analysis. Did the prodemocratic forces have available to them other options that might have alleviated the crisis of democracy? Was the breakdown of democracy indeed inevitable? A closely related concern of the participants was the endeavor to abstract from the historical record recurrent patterns, sequences, and crises involved in the dynamic process of breakdown.

This publication has a long and complex history. Juan J. Linz's involvement with the question of the breakdown of democracy began with his concern with the fate of Spanish democracy, a fate that affected him as a child in Spain and as a citizen. Linz's reading of the monumental work on the breakdown of the Weimar Republic by Karl Dietrich Bracher led him to ask broad theoretical questions, which he explored with Daniel Bell at Columbia University in the mid-1960s. Linz and Alfred Stepan met at Columbia during this period, when Stepan was beginning to write a dissertation on the breakdown of democracy in Brazil, a process he had seen at first hand while writing articles in Latin America for the *Economist*. Other contributors who were at Columbia University at the same time included Paolo Farneti, Peter Smith, Arturo Valenzuela, and Alexander Wilde.

In order to encourage scholarly exchange on the political aspects of the breakdown of democracy, a panel was organized under the auspices of the Committee on Political Sociology. This panel met at a number of sessions at the Seventh World Congress of Sociology, held at Varna, Bulgaria, in 1970. Before the congress, Linz circulated a short paper titled "The Breakdown of Competitive Democracies: Elements for a Model," which became the focus of discussion by the members of the panel engaged in studies of individual countries and attending the congress. Among the contributors to the complete hardcover edition of this volume presenting initial drafts of the papers at Varna were Erik Allardt on Finland, Paolo Farneti on Italy, Rainer Lepsius on Weimar Germany, Juan Linz on Spain, Walter Simon on Austria, Peter Smith on Argentina, Alfred Stepan on Brazil, and Alexander Wilde on Colombia. Arend Lijphart was a stimulating commentator.[3]

After fruitful exchanges at Varna, we dispersed, with the firm commitment to continue working on the project and to hold a conference in a few years focusing on the comparative and theoretical aspects of our work. In order to introduce other important cases and different perspectives, Stepan encouraged Guillermo O'Donnell to write on the crisis of democracy in Argentina in the decade after the fall of Perón, and Julio Cotler and Daniel Levine to discuss the Peruvian and Venezuelan cases. After the overthrow of Allende in Chile, the editors invited Arturo Valenzuela to analyze the tragic events leading to the end of democracy in Chile.

With the generous support of the Concilium of International and Area Studies of Yale University, and the Joint Committee on Latin America of the Social Science Research Council and the American Council of Learned Societies, the augmented group met at Yale University in December 1973, at a conference chaired by Linz and Stepan, by then both members of the Yale faculty. At this meeting the papers presented benefited from the able suggestions of Douglas Chalmers, Edward Malefakis, and Eric Nordlinger, who acted as discussants. At the end of the conference the participants decided to revise their work in the light of one another's findings and the collective discussion of areas of similarity and dissimilarity. A year at the Institute for Advanced Study in Princeton allowed Linz to revise his introduction and maintain contact with the co-authors.

Despite the group's interest in underlying, recurrent patterns of breakdown, there has been no attempt to force individual contributors into the procrustean bed of the editors' own thinking. The reader will discover important differences in the authors' intellectual orientations, which grew in part out of the diversity of the democracies studied and reflect in part genuine differences of opinion on the relative weight to be attached to political forces, even after these forces had been given due consideration by all contributors.

It should be stressed that this volume is an initial social scientific effort at middle-level generalizations about complex historical reality. Such a work is, of course, never a substitute for fundamental historical studies of individual cases; rather, it builds upon such studies and, we hope, draws the attention of historians to more generalized propositions, propositions they can in turn pursue further in their own work. Although we are concerned with middle-level generalizations, it is the editors' view that the historicity of macro-political processes precludes the highly abstract generalizing of ahistorical social scientific models of the type susceptible to computer simulations and applicable to all past and any future cases. It is our hope, nevertheless, that scholars interested in developing more formal models may build on our work and incorporate into their models the complex realities here discussed. At this stage of the analysis our collective attention to the political dynamics of the breakdown of democracies has brought to light a number of recurring elements which are discussed at length in Linz's introductory essay. The independent contributions made to breakdowns by political incumbents is a theme that emerges in almost all the papers and has justified our attention to this aspect of the problem, an aspect all too often overlooked. Indeed, in reference to the democratic breakdown in many if not most of the cases analyzed, the editors concur with the remark made by the great German historian, Friedrich Meinecke, upon hearing of the appointment of Hitler to the chancellorship: "This was not necessary."

The individual studies shed new light on some of the most historically important cases of breakdown of democracy, such as Germany, Italy, Spain, and Chile. In addition, some of the less well-known cases forcefully illustrate hitherto neglected aspects of the question of the survival of democracy. Daniel Levine's study of Venezuela examines a fascinating case of political learning. Ten years after the breakdown in Venezuela in 1948, many of the institutional participants in the breakdown—the church, the army, the political parties—consciously and successfully devised strategies to avoid such a breakdown when a new attack on democratic institutions began in 1958. Alexander Wilde's discussion of the reequilibrium of Colombian democracy in the 1950s also shows how political learning was crucial for the construction of a consociational democracy. The chapter by Risto Alapuro and Erik Allardt discusses the little-known case of Finland, in which, despite intense conflict, the process of breakdown described in other chapters was avoided. The analysis of nonoccurrence as well as of occurrence increased our understanding of the breakdown process.

With the publication of this project, many of the contributors are turning their attention to closely related issues that loom large on the scholarly agenda. High priority for further work along these lines should now be given to the analysis of the conditions that lead to the breakdown of authoritarian regimes, to the process of transition from authoritarian to democratic regimes, and especially to the political dynamics of the consolidation of postauthoritarian democracies.

The editors want to thank The Johns Hopkins University Press for its help in publishing a project of such large intellectual scope and sheer physical size as this one. We want to give special thanks to Henry Tom, the social sciences editor of the Press, for his great assistance. The project would not have arrived in the reader's hands without extensive copy editing. Jean Savage and Victoria Suddard helped in the early stages of copy editing.

Yale University   JUAN J. LINZ
                                                                     ALFRED STEPAN

NOTES

1. An extensive discussion of the definition of democracy and the criteria for the selection of cases is found in Juan Linz's introductory essay, entitled "Crisis, Breakdown, and Reequilibration." This essay is also available separately as a Johns Hopkins University Press paperback.
2. Much of this literature is discussed in the work by Linz just cited.
3. The crisis of democracy in Portugal in the 1920s, France in the 1950s, Peru and Greece in the 1960s, and the continuing conflict in Northern Ireland were also discussed in papers presented by Herminio Martins, Steven Cohn, David Chaplin, Charles Moskos, and Richard Rose, respectively. Conflicting obligations did not permit them to continue with the project. Richard Rose developed his paper in a somewhat different direction and published it separately as a book, *Governing without Consensus: An Irish Perspective* (Boston: Beacon Press, 1971).

I.

The Breakdown
of Democratic Regimes

CRISIS, BREAKDOWN,
& REEQUILIBRATION

Juan J. Linz

The Breakdown
of Democratic Regimes
CRISIS, BREAKDOWN,
& REEQUILIBRATION

1.

Introduction

A change of political regime affects millions of lives, stirring a spectrum of emotions from fear to hope. The March on Rome, the *Machtergreifung* by Hitler, the Spanish civil war, Prague in February of 1948, the coup against Allende—such dramas, symbolizing the transfer of power, become fixed in the memory of people as pivotal dates in their lives. Yet the events themselves are in truth the culmination of a longer process, an incremental political change that has evolved over a more or less prolonged period. Is there a common pattern in the processes that have led to changes of regime, or is each a unique historical situation? Is it possible to construct a descriptive model of the process of the breakdown of democracy that could ultimately contribute to a better understanding of its elements and dynamics? If it were possible to construct such a model, which would be an explanatory model, would we know more about the conditions for stability of democracy?

Certainly the problem of the stability and overthrow of political systems has long occupied the minds of those who study politics. In recent years social scientists have devoted considerable attention to the study of the prerequisites for political stability, particularly in democracies.[1] Analyses, however, have tended to be static, with more emphasis on the social, economic, and cultural correlates of stable regimes in a given moment of time than on the dynamic processes of crisis, breakdown, and reequilibration of existing regimes or the consolidation of new ones. This emphasis has resulted primarily from the availability of systematic and quantitative data on a large number of polities and of new techniques in statistical analysis.[2] It has also reflected postwar optimism about the durability of democracies, once established. At the same time, however, historians have provided detailed records of the events and the social, economic, and political changes leading to those dramatic moments that brought Mussolini, Hitler, and Franco to power or, as in France, led to a turnabout in the battle of a democracy to survive. Further perspectives on events and situations are available to us in the wealth of personal writings by those who helped shape history.[3]

It would seem fruitful, therefore, to combine the knowledge of the events themselves, derived from the accounts of historians and the records of participants, with the problem formulations derived from contemporary social sci-

3

ence in our effort to construct a descriptive model—and perhaps ultimately an explanatory model—of the processes operating in a change of regime.[4] Analysis of many seemingly unique historical situations suggests the possibility of common patterns—certain sequences of events that recur in country after country. In fact, the participants often seem aware of such chains of events, and express such awareness in widespread attitudes of resignation, tragedy, inevitability, or hubris.[5]

In these analyses, social scientists, particularly sociologists (especially those with a Marxist orientation), tend to emphasize the structural characteristics of societies—socioeconomic infrastructures that act as a constraining condition, limiting the choices of political actors. They focus on the underlying social conflicts, particularly class conflicts, that in their view make the stability of liberal democratic institutions unlikely, if not impossible. They contend that breakdown is sufficiently explained by great social and economic inequity, concentration of economic power, economic dependency on other countries, and the inevitable antidemocratic reaction of the privileged against the institutions that allow the mobilization of the masses against the existing socioeconomic order. We would be the last to deny the importance of those factors and their considerable effect in particular cases.[6] Yet even if sociological analyses or those based on culture, national character, or psychological variables could explain *why* the breakdown occurs, we still would have to ask *how*.

In our view, one cannot ignore the actions of either those who are more or less interested in the maintenance of an open democratic political system or those who, placing other values higher, are unwilling to defend it or even ready to overthrow it. These are the actions that constitute the true dynamics of the political process.[7] We feel that the structural characteristics of societies—their actual and latent conflicts—constitute a series of opportunities and constraints for the social and political actors, both men and institutions, that can lead to one or another outcome. We shall start from the assumption that those actors have certain choices that can increase or decrease the probability of the persistence and stability of a regime.[8] Undoubtedly, the resulting actions or events tend to have a cumulative and reinforcing effect that increases or decreases the probability of survival of democratic politics. Certainly, in the last stages before the denouement, the opportunities to save the system might be minimal. Our model, therefore, will be probabilistic rather than deterministic.

In this context, the analysis of cases in which a democracy in crisis managed to reequilibrate becomes particularly interesting, since it would prove *a contrario* some of the hypotheses we shall develop. The special merit of Karl Dietrich Bracher's brilliant description of the fall of the Weimar Republic was his emphasis on the patterned and sequential character of the breakdown process through the phases of loss of power, power vacuum, and takeover of power.[9] We shall focus on those more strictly political variables that tend to be neglected in many other approaches to the problem of stable democracy, because in our view political processes actually precipitate the ultimate breakdown.[10] We shall do so without ignoring the basic social, economic, and cultural conditioning variables. It also would seem that without attention to the historical political process, it would be difficult to explain why political institutions in different societies do not suffer the same fate on experiencing similar strains. In crisis situations like those we shall be discussing, leadership, even the presence of an individual with unique qualities and characteristics—a Charles de Gaulle, for instance—can be decisive and cannot be predicted by any model.[11] Even so, we hope to show that certain types of individual and institutional actors confronted with similar situations have a high probability of responding in ways that contribute to the breakdown of regimes. It is our task to describe and, as far as possible, account for those actions on the road toward breakdown or reequilibration of democracies.

We do not hesitate to admit that our problem formulation seeks to point out opportunities that democratic leaders might use to assure the consolidation, stability, persistence, and reequilibration of their regimes, as well as the pitfalls likely to be encountered in the process. We would hope that our knowledge will help them in their efforts, even though our insights, if valid, should also be useful to those who want to attend a "school for dictators."[12]

Breakdown of Competitive Democracies

The focus of our analysis and of the essays in this book is on competitive democracies,[13] with no attempt here to extend the study to authoritarian, totalitarian, or traditional political systems.[14]

To avoid any misunderstanding of our intellectual effort, it is necessary to define with some precision the type of regime whose breakdown we are analyzing. Our criteria for a democracy may be summarized as follows: legal freedom to formulate and advocate political alternatives with the concomitant rights to free association, free speech, and other basic freedoms of person; free and nonviolent competition among leaders with periodic validation of their claim to rule; inclusion of all effective political offices in the democratic process; and provision for the participation of all members of the political community, whatever their political preferences. Practically, this means the freedom to create political parties and to conduct free and honest elections at regular intervals without excluding any effective political office from direct or indirect electoral accountability. Today "democracy" implies at least universal male suffrage, but perhaps in the past it would extend to the regimes with property, taxation, occupational, or literacy requirements of an earlier period, which limited suffrage to certain social groups.

The exclusion from political competition of parties not committed to the legal pursuit of power—which in reality is limited to enforceable exclusions (of minor parties or of individuals on a temporal and partial basis, as in political screening for civil service)—is not incompatible with the guarantee of free competition in our definition of a democracy.[15] It is the legal equal opportunity for the expression of all opinions and protection by the state against arbitrary and above all, violent interference with that right, rather than an unconditional opportunity for the expression of opinions, that distinguishes a democratic regime. Our definition of democracy would not include regimes that might once have received the genuine support of a majority but have since become unwilling to submit their power to revalidation by the society. It does not require a turnover of parties in power, but the possibility of such a turnover, even when such alternation is prima facie evidence of the democratic character of a regime.[16]

There can be no doubt that social and political realities in countries included in our analysis have sometimes led them to deviate from even our minimal definition. This is particularly true for the Latin American states and also for rural Italy south of Rome during the first decades of the century, when administrative, social, and economic pressures imposed limits on political civil liberties to the point that even the counting of ballots was suspect. Deviation from the democratic ideal does not necessarily constitute its denial, however, and the regimes under consideration all satisfied our minimal criteria. Only the inclusion of Peru and Colombia might be questioned. That few additional countries—notably Japan in the interwar years, Czechoslovakia, Latvia, Lithuania, perhaps some Balkan countries, and Greece after World War II—might have been included in our analysis indicates how small a number of democracies qualifies even under our minimal definition.

We have deliberately omitted from our definition any reference to the prevalence of democratic values, social relations, equality of opportunities in the occupational world, and education, as our focus here is the breakdown of political democracy, not crisis in democratic societies. The influence of political democracy on nonpolitical aspects of a society—or conversely, the effect of a nondemocratic culture on the persistence or failure of a democratic regime—is clearly worth studying; to include in our definition, however, such elements as the democratization of the society and the degree of equality would not ònly prevent us from asking many relevant questions but would reduce the number of cases in our analysis.

Given this definition, neither the transformation of a postdemocratic into a totalitarian system, the internal changes leading to posttotalitarian regimes (as in the de-Stalinization of Communist regimes), the breakdown of authoritarian regimes (Portugal in 1974), nor the transition to democracy of traditional monarchical rule fall within our purview. No doubt there are processes common to the breakdown of any regime, and processes distinctive to the fall of democracies, but it would be difficult, without a comparative study of regime changes in both democratic and nondemocratic systems, to isolate the variables and identify them as one or the other. This is not to overlook some general patterns. No system that could be called totalitarian in any meaningful sense of the term has broken down through internal causes, even those systems that have experienced sufficient transformation to be described as post-totalitarian authoritarian regimes.[17] The Nazi system, and even Fascist rule in Italy—which might be considered an arrested totalitarianism—were overthrown only by external defeat. The breakdown of most authoritarian regimes has led not to the establishment of democracy but to the estalishment of another authoritarian regime—perhaps in the case of Cuba, a totalitarian system—after a coup or a revolution. Study of the few cases in which an authoritarian regime transformed itself into a democracy, or was overthrown to give place to one, could contribute to our understanding of the common variables. Although that number is small, there are several cases in which democracies were succeeded by authoritarian regimes and in turn by the reestablishment of democracy. The contributors to this volume who deal with such cases have used the opportunity to explore how one fatal crisis of democracy helped later democratic rulers to avoid some of the errors of their predecessors.[18]

We have not included a number of postcolonial democracies that had little time to become institutionalized, whose form of government was largely a transplant from the mother country, and whose consolidation of political institutions usually coincided with the process of state-building. We doubt that our analysis would be applicable to the breakdown of postindependence democratic institutions in Africa and Asia, as in Nigeria or Pakistan, for it is limited in almost every case to states whose existence was consolidated before they became democracies. (Only Finland acquired statehood after World War I, and Austria emerged as a separate state out of the Austrian-Hungarian Empire by the *diktat* of the victors.)

The democracies to which our model applies are all nation-states, even Spain, which, though it has a multinational character for some Spaniards, is regarded by most as a nation-state. Only in Austria, where a significant number of citizens identified with Germany, was the existence of the nation-state questioned. Undoubtedly, including Czechoslovakia in the interwar years and a multinational country like Yugoslavia in our analysis would have highlighted the importance of cultural and linguistic conflicts in the crisis of democracy—though in the case of Czechoslovakia it would be difficult to isolate the internal strains from the external pressures that led to Munich and the secession of Slovakia, and subsequently the end of democracy and independence as well.[19]

Should the regimes on which our analysis is based properly be considered competitive democracies, or should they be classified as a special type of democratic regime? The chapters on some of the Latin American countries will quickly establish characteristics in their democratic institutions, especially in operational aspects, that differentiate them from the old established democracies of Western Europe and even from the unstable "democracies in the making" of Europe. In fact, Alexander Wilde suggested that we should use a modified and less demanding definition of democracy in terms of some common characteristics of competitive political institutions and the peculiar forms that those institutions might take. Unfortunately, there is no meaningful, accepted typology of competitive democracies, nor any accepted measure of the degree of democracy. Only the distinction between democracies based on majority rule and those that Lijphart calls "consociational" has gained wide acceptance.[20] Our analysis includes no democracies that could properly be classified as consociational; in fact, none of those so characterized has experienced a breakdown of its institutions. This leads us to suspect that the very political mechanisms described by the term "consociational democracy" might be very effective in handling the strains that might otherwise endanger their democratic institutions. Certainly, the democracies normally considered consociational—the Netherlands, Belgium, Switzerland, post–World War II Austria, and, until its recent breakdown, Lebanon—share many other characteristics favorable to democratic stability.

In summary, our analysis is applicable only to democratic regimes in consolidated nation-states that had achieved independence or a measure of political autonomy a considerable time before the crisis of the regime. In addition, all the democracies analyzed are based on majority rule rather than on complex consociational mechanisms.

Stillborn or Embattled New Democracies

The question of whether our model of the breakdown process might not be based on regimes established only shortly before the crisis that triggered their downfall, and that we might, therefore, be dealing with a failure of consolidation rather than the breakdown of a democratic regime, is an important one.[21] Such a model, it could be argued, would not be applicable to regimes satisfying the requirement of persistence of patterns elaborated by Harry Eckstein, and particularly not to those that had enjoyed a stable existence of a more than one generation, like the United Kingdom, Switzerland, the Scandinavian countries, Belgium, the Netherlands, and even France.[22]

This point cannot be ignored, and we shall return to it when we emphasize the importance of the belief in the legitimacy of democratic institutions as a factor increasing the likelihood of stability in a democracy. Undoubtedly, stability breeds stability, to put it tautologically. Old democracies were once new, beset by the risks facing all new democracies, even in those cases in which it could be argued that the historical evolution was slower and more involved with continuity of traditional institutions and elites, thus confronting rulers with fewer and more manageable problems. Furthermore, some of the older democracies had the advantage of being small and relatively prosperous countries—those in certain parts of Europe, for example.[23] Historians and sociologists have drawn attention to the unique circumstances under which the transformation of traditional political systems into modern democracies took place in such cases. It could be argued that whenever those slow and unique developments leading to democracy were absent, even before the French Revolution, the probability for the consolidation of democracy was considerably lower.

However, while the specific regimes that were overthrown in such countries as Portugal, Germany, Austria, and Spain had only recently been established, liberal democratic processes had in each case gained ascendancy over half a century, if not longer, under constitutional or semiconstitutional monarchies. In Italy the constitutional monarchy had been instituted simultaneously with the building of the nation in the Risorgimento and had undergone a process of democratization that accelerated, along with that of many more stable democracies, in the first decades of the century, particularly after World War I. In spite of deviations from the ideal represented by oligarchy, limited democracy, and authoritarian periods, the Latin American countries were strongly committed ideologically to liberal democracy, and no other legitimacy formula had wide appeal. It is true that a number of countries had significant intellectual minorities that defended other political formulas, but large majorities favored a legal, rational, democratic legitimacy formula. Only in Germany did the conservative antidemocratic ideologies gain wide and organized acceptance in important sectors of society before the breakthrough of democracy in 1918.

In summary, in the countries analyzed here democracy per se was not new, nor did it in most cases have to contend with widespread hostility before the onset of the crisis, though certain specific regimes and the regime-building forces established only a few years before their demise did come under such attack. It could be argued that in many cases the attack was not initially directed against democracy itself but against the particular content that the regime-building and sustaining forces wanted to give it. In fact, willingness to offer those favoring a different political and social order a more effective role and some guarantees within the democratic process might have prevented their disaffection. Obviously, it is not always possible to distinguish the form of democracy from its substantive content. What is initially conceived as an attack on particular governing forces, therefore, turns quickly into an overthrow of democratic institutions by force or manipulation that makes reestablishment of such institutions impossible for almost a generation.

A somewhat different but related question is raised by those who contend that the democracies that failed or were overthrown had been instaured under conditions that made their success extremely unlikely. To put it more graphically, they were stillborn. Certainly historians can argue that the circumstances surrounding the birth of a new regime—the underlying social structure, the latent social conflicts, and the institutional and ideological heritage from previous regimes—were such that, unless the new democratic rulers were able in an initial phase to transform the society, any serious crisis would inevitably have a destructive outcome. This point of view has often been argued in connection with the Weimar Republic and can be sustained with even more cogency in many Latin American cases.[24] In fact, the theorists of the *dependencia* tend to consider the solution of social problems the prerequisite of a stable regime. On a broad historical scale, Barrington Moore has advanced the thesis that unless societies have experienced a basic socioeconomic revolution, particularly in the agrarian power relations and the economic systems associated with the great political revolutions of the West, democracy has no chance of survival.[25]

Without ignoring the insights that can be derived from these approaches, we contend that a large part of the breakdown process cannot be accounted for by those variables. Indeed, there are countries whose democracies have enjoyed considerable periods of stability in spite of those identical initial handicaps.[26] Therefore, we would not say that such democracies were stillborn, even granting that some may have had genetic defects or an aborted period of consolidation. Precedent conditions may, as we shall see, limit the capacity of a regime to handle crises, but breakdown itself cannot be explained without paying attention to political processes taking place after its instauration. The elements favorable to democracy under precedent authoritarian or semidemocratic constitutional regimes, the discrediting and failure of the predemocratic regimes, and the enthusiasm and hope created by the new regimes should not be underestimated. No regime enjoys the full support or compliance of all of its citizens. According to Richard Rose's typology of regime authority, few regimes are fully legitimate or coercive, and most function in a range of intermediate categories.[27] The question is, then, what causes a regime to move beyond its functional range to become a disrupted or semicoercive regime that ends in repudiation by large or critical segments of the population?

To phrase the question otherwise would be to say that only democracies enjoying high support and high compliance over long periods of time have a significant chance of avoiding breakdown and repudiation, a hypothesis that would be almost tautological, in addition to being unduly pessimistic. Our hypothesis is that the democratic regimes under study had at one point or another a reasonable chance to survive and become fully consolidated, but that certain characteristics and actions of relevant actors—institutions as well as individuals—decreased the probability of such a development. Our analysis makes the assumption that those actions show a pattern repeated with variations in a number of societies. The repetition of the same or similar patterns in the breakdown process might give rise to a deterministic interpretation. We want to emphasize, however, the probabilistic character of our analysis and to stress that at any point in the process up to the final point chances remain, albeit diminishing chances, to save the regime. One is reminded of the great German historian Meinecke's comment, upon hearing the news of Hitler's appointment as chancellor: "This was not necessary."[28] It would be tempting to try to define at each juncture and for each regime what the odds were in favor of its survival, but our guess is that even after the most painstaking comparative research, few scholars would agree on the probability to be assigned to each case.

Socioeconomic Change as a Factor

Another assumption of our analysis that is open to question is that the distinctive political processes common to competitive democracies are valued in and of themselves by significant sectors of society. The contrary assumption is that democratic institutions are valued only insofar as they produce policies satisfactory to their supporters. Put another way, allegiance to any political system exists only insofar as it guarantees the persistence of, or the opportunity to change, a certain social, normally socioeconomic, order. According to that view, democracy is only a means to an end. Once people realize that their goals cannot be achieved through democratic institutions, the democratic system will be discarded. Those taking this position generally have in mind a certain socioeconomic order, but the same sequence could be postulated for a cultural, religious, or international order.

Obviously, these are extreme formulations of two positions that do not correspond to any concrete historical reality. While legal, rational, democratic authority in the Weberian sense in theory demands allegiance irrespective of the content that the democratic political process would give it,[29] both the "natural law" tradition and the more sociological Schumpeterian analysis underline the fact that no democracy can be based exclusively on such an abstract claim of legitimacy.[30] Yet we also decidedly reject the assumption that any type of regime is simply the expression and defense of a particular socioeconomic, cultural, or religious order. In fact, democracy is the type of political institutionalization that allows change in those orders without immediate changes in the political sphere, as well as permitting considerable independent influence by the political leadership on those other sectors of the social order. Certainly, *hinc et nunc* and in the short run, it is only analytically possible to separate the political regime from a given social order or from particular processes of politically imposed change. In a longer time perspective, democracy can serve many and changing ends, and can defend and contribute to the creation of different social and economic orders. Therefore, in principle, a democratic system should be able to rally legions of people pursuing widely varying goals over time. Only in the short run and with a zero-sum, either/or view of conflicts in society—both stances characteristic of extremist positions—does support for democracy as distinct from support for a particular conception of the social order become impossible and meaningless.

Extremist politics are the result of structural strains, and in certain societies, in certain historical situations, they engage large segments of the population. However, their capacity to do so is generally a reflection of a failure of the democratic leadership. The democratic system itself is not the generator. In our view, a democracy is unlikely to be supported unconditionally, irrespective of policies and outcomes for different social groups, but neither is it supported or challenged just because of its identification with a particular social, specifically socioeconomic, order.[31] Analytically, four different situations can be distinguished, depending on the degree of legitimacy granted by majorities of the population to the democratic political institutions and to the socioeconomic system they defend or are in the process of creating. Certainly, the ideal situation occurs when very large majorities grant legitimacy to both political institutions and the socioeconomic system, and when the social order is not perceived as unjust nor is reasonable change seen as threatening to those who enjoy a privileged position in the existing order. When both are considered illegitimate, little stability can be expected either of the regime or of the society, except through use of large-scale coercion. Most societies that have experienced changes of regime have fallen in the two intermediary situations in the typology, when one's or the other's loss of legitimacy obtains. In those cases a complex set of interrelationships and feedbacks exists between the political and social systems.

To say precisely how much the hostility to, or rigid defense of, the social order contributed to the crisis of the political system, and how much the weakening or loss of legitimacy of the political order exacerbated economic and social problems, would be difficult and would have to be determined in each particular case. For our theoretical purposes, however, it is important to emphasize that the two processes can be kept analytically distinct, though in reality both are likely to occur.[32] Making these assumptions, our political analysis of the historical process of breakdown might have greater or lesser relevance to each, but in neither case would it be irrelevant. The constraints imposed on significant segments of society by the illegitimacy of the existing social order or the changes it is undergoing will affect the degree of freedom to institutionalize and defend democratic political institutions, perhaps limiting—though never obliterating—the range of choice for the political actors. In fact, in those situations the consolidation of legitimate political institutions becomes more important in assuring continued, slow, but nonviolent social change. Rapid revolutionary social change in such circumstances is probably incompatible with democracy; as both radicals and conservatives might agree, the option is one or the other, whether explicitly or implicitly. It is no accident that political actors who are highly indignant about the injustice of the social order are often ready to risk the stability of democracy, which for them is a lesser value than social change. This is the source of the ambivalence of many Socialists, particularly Marxists, toward political democracy.[33] The resultant ambivalent and indecisive policies of their leaders have been a major factor in the breakdown of democracy in many countries—Italy, Austria, Spain, Chile, and to a lesser extent, Germany. The radical critic of the existing social order or, for that matter, of the cultural or religious order, might maintain that if in the short run democracy cannot serve as an instrument for decisive social change, it does not deserve his loyalty. What he might not realize is that the alternative is not revolutionary change, imposed in authoritarian fashion, but the reversal of slow processes of change under conditions of freedom and compromise, by counterrevolutionary authoritarian rule.

Analysis focused largely on actions by democratic rulers that increase or decrease the probability of a breakdown is not unrelated to the assumption that such leaders, at least in the short run, should value the persistence of democratic institutions as highly if not more highly than other goals. Not everyone will (or should) agree with that assumption, but irrespective of such agreement, we feel that it is intellectually legitimate to study the problem of breakdown from this perspective.[34]

2.
Elements of Breakdown

Revolution and Regime Breakdowns

Those who accede to power after the breakdown of a democracy often speak of their "revolution," thereby claiming for themselves the aura of legitimacy attached to that word and what it symbolizes. Most of these so-called revolutions, however, have been military coups d'état or semi- or pseudo-legal transfers of power rather than violent takeovers: *Machtüber-nahme* rather than *Machtergreifung*.[1] There are exceptions, however; in Spain, the civil war of 1936–39 bears closer resemblance to the aftermath of the fall of the czarist regime, traditional rule in China, or colonial rule in Vietnam and other Third World countries. If the term "revolution" is used in another sense—radical change of the social structure—it cannot be applied, since most of the breakdowns have been counterrevolutionary, in that they have aimed at preventing radical changes in the social structure, even though they often culminated in decisive changes. "Revolution" in the more restrictive sense of association with changes guided by leftist ideologies is inapplicable as well, since none of the relatively stabilized democracies has fallen under the onslaught of the left, although revolutionary attempts by the Left, or more often just the talk of revolution, contributed decisively to the crisis and breakdown of democracy in Italy, Spain, Chile, and to a lesser extent, Germany. The success of the great revolutions in the twentieth century against traditional, authoritarian, and colonial regimes owes much to the disorganization and the delegitimation of the so-called Establishment due to external wars and defeat.[2] Probably only the ultimate changes after the breakdown of German democracy in 1933 and the subsequent totalitarian transformation of society under the Nazis can in some sense of the word be called revolutionary.[3] The Spanish revolution of the Left that was initiated after the military uprising against the Republic was finally defeated by counterrevolutionary forces. Thus, despite some overlap between breakdown of democratic regimes and revolutions, the two phenomena can and must be studied separately, lest we stretch the concept of revolution beyond recognition.

As we shall see, political violence is both an important indicator and a contributing cause of breakdown, but the line between cause and effect is blurred. In a number of cases in the present study, the amount of politically significant violence was relatively minor, even when a distorted perception of that violence and a low threshold of tolerance for violence in the society contributed to the breakdown. Undoubtedly, the study of political and social violence is central to our problem, but the theories advanced to explain the amount and character of violence are not sufficient to account for the breakdown of regimes and will be treated as explanations of one of the contributing factors.[4] Research on the beginnings, patterns, and causes of collective and individual violence in democracies in crisis is needed, but the need is even greater for research on the contemporary perception of that violence and the responses of different elites to it. The techniques of collective history developed by French historians should be applied to the study of these elites, particularly the activists on the right, who often are neglected in such analyses.[5]

In the past, when democratic regimes had acquired a certain stability they could be threatened by challengers, who would persuade important sectors of the population to switch allegiance from government to challenger. They would then undermine the regime's authority by demonstrating its inability to maintain order, forcing it to resort to an unwarranted, arbitrary, and indiscriminate use of power that often led to further withdrawal of support. In modern societies, however, governments faced with such threats can generally count on the compliance of many citizens, their staff, bureaucrats, policemen, and the military if they decide to activate their commitments to legitimate authority. Therefore, disloyal oppositions have tended increasingly to avoid direct confrontation with governments and their agents and have aimed instead at combining their illegal actions with a formally legal process of transfer of power. In that process the neutrality, if not the cooperation, of the armed forces or a sector of them has become decisive. The twentieth century has seen fewer revolutions started by the populace than the nineteenth, and their fate in modern states has generally been defeat. The Communists and Nazis learned that lesson. Mussolini's combination of illegal action and legal takeover became the new model for overthrow of democracies.[6] Only the direct intervention of the military seems to be able to topple regimes in modern stabilized states. This probably explains why, despite the revolutionary mobilization of the masses by leftist parties and their partial successes, none of the democracies whose breakdown we can study was toppled by a revolution or takeover by the parties of the Left. The Czechoslovakia of 1948 was the only democracy taken over by the Communists, but in that case it is difficult to separate the internal processes that have some similarity to the breakdowns we shall study from the presence of the Soviet army and the influence of the Soviet Union.[7] The outcome of the breakdown of democratic regimes generally seems to be the victory of political forces identified as rightists, even when that term might not exactly describe their policies in power. This does not mean that in many cases the Left did not play a decisive role in weakening democratic governments and provoking their overthrow.

Legitimacy, Efficacy, Effectiveness, and the Breakdown of Democracy

Our analysis starts with the existence of a government that has attained its power through a democratic process of free elections and claims the obedience of the citizens within its territory on that basis, with a relatively high probability that they will comply. That obedience may spring from a wide range of motives, from fear of the sanctions that could be imposed to positive support based on the belief in the government's right to demand obedience.[8] Most people, of course, obey out of habit and rational calculation of advantage. In principle, however, democratic regimes are based on much more. More than any other type of regime, they depend for support on the activation of commitments for the implementation of decisions binding on the collectivity. In normal times, habit and rational calculation of advantage might assure compliance, but in crisis situations, when the authority of the government is challenged by some group in the society, or when decisions affect many citizens negatively, this is not sufficient. It becomes even less so when those in authority must make use of force, asking others to risk their lives and to take the lives of fellow citizens in the defense of the political order.

Weber formulated it as follows: "Custom, personal advantage, purely affectual or ideal motives of solidarity do not form a sufficiently reliable basis for a given domination. In addition there is normally a further element, the belief in *legitimacy*."[9] In the words of a democratic political leader: " . . . the most effective means of upholding the law is not the state policemen or the marshals or the national guard. It is you. It lies in your courage to accept those laws with which you disagree as well as those with which you agree."[10] This belief in legitimacy assures the capacity of a government to enforce decisions. Obviously no government is accorded legitimacy in this sense by all its citizens, but no government can survive without that belief on the part of a substantial number of citizens and an even larger number of those in control of the armed forces. Democratic governments require that belief, with more or less intensity, at least within the ranks of the majority. Normally a democratic government should enjoy that legitimacy even among those who constitute its opposition. This is what is meant by the expression "loyal" opposition. At the very least, legitimacy is the belief that in spite of shortcomings and failures, the existing political institutions are better than any others that might be established, and that they therefore can demand obedience. Ultimately it means that when the rulers who hold power constitutionally demand obedience, and another group questions that demand in the name of alternative political arrangements, citizens will voluntarily opt for compliance with the demands of those in authority. More specifically, the legitimacy of a democratic regime rests on the belief in the right of those legally elevated to authority to issue certain types of commands, to expect obedience, and to enforce them, if necessary, by the use of force. "In a democracy, citizens are free to disagree with the law, but not to disobey it, for in a government of laws, and not of men, no one, however prominent or powerful, and no mob, however unruly or boisterous, is entitled to defy them."[11] That belief does not require agreement with the content of the norm or support for a particular government, but it does require acceptance of its binding character and its right to issue commands until changed by the procedures of the regime. In democracies such change implies gaining control of the government without the use of force, according to constitutional procedures such as free competition for the peaceful support of the majority of citizens, legitimate forms of influence, and the use of constitutional mechanisms to control the decisions of the rulers. That belief is based on the expectation that the rulers, if challenged and required to abandon power by legitimate means, will not attempt to retain power by illegitimate means. Democratic legitimacy, therefore, requires adherence to the rules of the game by both a majority of the voting citizens and those in positions of authority, as well as trust on the part of the citizenry in the government's commitment to uphold them.

In every society, there are those who deny legitimacy to any government and those who believe in alternative legitimacy formulae.[12] Regimes vary widely in the amount and intensity of citizen belief in their legitimacy. In the case of a democracy, however, belief in its legitimacy by a majority of the population or even a majority of the electorate is insufficient for stability. Belief in that legitimacy on the part of those who have direct control of armed forces is particularly important. However, it seems unlikely that military leaders would turn their arms against the government unless they felt that a significant segment of the society shared their lack of belief and that others were at least indifferent to the conflicting claims for allegiance.[13]

Legitimacy is granted or withdrawn by each member of the society day in and day out. It does not exist outside the actions and attitudes of individuals. Regimes therefore enjoy more or less legitimacy just by existing. Gains and losses of support for governments, leaders, parties, and policies in a democracy are likely to fluctuate rapidly while the belief in the legitimacy of the system persists. There is clearly an interaction between the support for the regime and that for the governing parties, which in the absence of other indicators leads to the use of electoral returns and public opinion responses as indirect evidence of the legitimacy of the system. Consequently, the loss of support for all political actors in a democratic regime is likely to lead to an erosion of legitimacy, just as widespread support for a government, particularly beyond those supporting it with their votes, is likely to contribute to the strength of legitimacy.[14]

Why do people believe in the legitimacy of democratic institutions? Answering this question is almost as difficult as explaining why people believe in particular religious dogmas, for, as is the case with religious beliefs, the degree of understanding, of skepticism and faith, varies widely across the society and over time.[15] Undoubtedly, political socialization plays a decisive role, and this is an advantage for long-established democratic regimes whose educational system, mass media, and high culture have made democratic ideals pervasive and understandable. As in the case of other social beliefs, the major role in formulating, elaborating, and transmitting the legitimacy formulae is played by the intellectuals. There is also what the Germans would call a *Zeitgeist,* a feeling shared across national boundaries, that a particular type of political system is the most desirable or the most questionable. This feeling tends to be reinforced or weakened by the positive or negative perception of other more powerful states or nations that are successful with a particular type of regime. In the interwar years the *Zeitgeist* was deeply affected by the success of Fascist Italy, and later Nazism, and this helped weaken the commitment to democratic legitimacy in many countries. As Weber noted, no type of legitimacy is found in pure form in any society. Most people give allegiance to a regime on the basis of a complex set of beliefs. Democratic legitimacy, therefore, is often reinforced by becoming a form of tradition, and the personal charisma of democratic leaders committed to the regime tends to reinforce its institutions.[16]

Our minimal definition of legitimacy, then, is a relative one: a legitimate government is one considered to be the least evil of the forms of government. Ultimately, democratic legitimacy is based on the belief that for that particular country at that particular historical juncture no other type of regime could assure a more successful pursuit of collective goals.[17]

At this point two other dimensions characterizing a political system become relevant—its efficacy and its effectiveness.[18] In the course of time both can strengthen, reinforce, maintain, or weaken the belief in legitimacy. However, the relationships between these variables are far from fully transitive and lineal, since perception of the efficacy and effectiveness of a regime tends to be biased by the initial commitments to its legitimacy. Legitimacy, at least for a time, operates as a positive constant that multiplies whatever positive value the efficacy and effectiveness of the regime might achieve. It insures effectiveness even in the absence of desirable efficacy, and contributes to the ultimate outcome: persistence and relative stability of the regime. Should the value of legitimacy (the result of positive minus negative values among different sectors of the population or for key sectors) be close to zero, or negative, the failures of efficacy and effectiveness would be compounded. We might represent the relationship as follows:

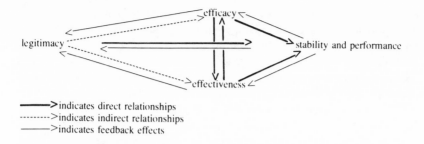

——————>indicates direct relationships
-------->indicates indirect relationships
——————>indicates feedback effects

The more positive the values on each of the relations, over time, the greater the stability and performance of the regime. What we do not know is how much each of those direct, indirect, and feedback relationships contributes. To express it graphically, we do not know how thick or thin the connecting arrows would be. Regimes that, to an outside observer, appear to be attaining the same levels of success or failure in handling problems, but that initially enjoyed different levels of legitimacy, do not seem to suffer the same consequences. Because of this, the circumstances surrounding the instauration of a regime and its initial consolidation become very important when and if it faces serious crises. Seen in this light, the particular historical origins of the Weimar Republic and its initial failures might account for its final breakdown in spite of its considerable success in the mid-1920s. Unfortunately, we have neither developed the systematic indicators nor collected the data over time on the legitimacy of regimes that would test hypotheses of this type.

Members of society, and today this implies a large collectivity, grant political power to the authority in a regime to pursue the satisfaction of their material and ideal interests. No one can deny that the ruling group is likely to pursue its own material and ideal interests, but they are unlikely to retain legitimacy if they pursue them exclusively or at too heavy a cost to broader segments of the society. Accountability, introduced by elections in democratic politics, makes it necessary for the leadership to demonstrate that they are pursuing collective goals acceptable to the majority without representing excessive deprivations for their opponents, even when they might represent a heavy burden to particular minorities. The response of society at large to the policies of its rulers is obviously not the same as that of an objective expert observer, and the success of a ruler might be based more on convincing society that the goals pursued are in its interest than in their actually being so. However, there is evidence that the people can be fooled some of the time but not all of the time.

While in theory the interests of the collectivity, or at least of a majority, constitute the yardstick for measuring the performance of the regime, the level of organization and consciousness of different sectors in the society varies considerably, as Mancur Olson has shown.[19] This makes the interests and perception of the more organized sectors particularly relevant. In addition, governments, like enterprises, are not necessarily judged by their short-run performance—particularly when the institutions and the leadership enjoy trust, i.e., legitimacy. The Paretian analysis of utility has emphasized that the utility of the collectivity does not coincide with the utility of its individual members, that there are direct and indirect utilities to be taken into account, and that long-term and short-term utilities do not coincide, etc. Considerations like these make it very difficult for even an objective outside observer to judge to what extent a democratic government is efficacious and at the same time responsive to an electorate. In addition, the problem is often compounded by the debate over whether it should be responsive to the electorate or should comply with the democratically taken decisions of the members of the governing party, in view of the pressures for internal party democracy. In addition to being responsive to the demands of a broad electorate and to the party membership, democratic governments cannot ignore the demands of key well-organized interests whose withdrawal of confidence can be more decisive than the support of the electorate. To give one example: policies that produce the distrust of the business community and lead it to an evasion of capital, even when those policies are supported by a majority of the electorate, might create a serious threat to a regime.

Given the interdependence, and in many cases, the dependence, of societies and states, the response of leading actors in the international political and economic system becomes another factor in judging the efficacy of policies. All this points to the complexity of a theoretical and empirical definition of the efficacy of a government or regime. Certainly, regimes and governments must serve collective goals, but as an already extensive literature on the functions of the state shows, those goals are far from being a fixed object of agreement.[20] They are historically conditioned and defined at each point in time by the political leadership and the society, particularly its organized forces. They represent constantly changing challenges. It is in clarification of these goals that the literature on the revolution of rising expectations (i.e., the increasing diffusion of institutions from one to another society or the internationally established standards of performance) becomes relevant. Social scientists impressed by the undeniable importance of economic and social policies in contemporary societies have, however, neglected consideration of some of the basic functions of any political system, past or present, particularly the problems of maintenance of civil order, personal security, adjudication and arbitration of conflicts, and a minimum of predictability in the making and implementation of decisions. Many of the regimes that failed because of a loss of efficacy did so because of difficulties at this level rather than because of their handling of more complex problems.

Efficacy, therefore, refers to the capacity of a regime to find solutions to the basic problems facing any political system (and those that become salient in any historical moment) that are perceived as more satisfactory than unsatisfactory by aware citizens. Many people, however, are likely to be neutral or indifferent toward many policies, and thus the total evaluation of the perceived efficacy of a regime is complicated by ignorance of the full significance of those responses for the stability of regimes. And further, contrary to the democratic dogma of one man/one vote, as Robert Dahl has already emphasized, the intensity of responses to policies cannot be ignored.[21] This becomes particularly important on considering the response of key, strategically located social groups or institutions, which in pure democratic theory should not be a consideration for the politician but in fact are central to his decision-making. Fortunately, the efficacy of a regime is judged not by the actions of a particular government over a short span of time, but as the sum of its actions over a longer period of time compared to the performance of different governments likely to be more satisfactory to one or another segment of the society.

This represents a special disadvantage for new regimes facing serious problems during the period of consolidation, since their governments cannot point to past achievements as proof of the regime's efficacy in the face of their presumably temporary failures. The problem becomes even more serious when the preceding regime has considerable efficacy to its credit, efficacy to which its remaining supporters can point.[22] Newness is a disadvantage that must be overcome, although the dynamics of regime change suggest that regime breakdown results from loss of legitimacy, and that the fall in and of itself enhances the legitimacy of the new regime. In the short run, however, the process of establishment may lead to a loss of efficacy or at least a discrepancy with the expectations created, and therefore a considerable drop in legitimacy before consolidation is achieved. If we were to draw the curves of these changes for different societies, we would find quite variable patterns within this general mode. In this regard, it is important to keep in mind, as Otto Kirchheimer has stressed, that a new regime's constituent acts in terms of policy are decisive for its consolidation.[23]

This leads to the importance of the formulation of the initial agenda of a new regime, the implications of its output for different sectors of society, and the consequent shifts in amount and intensity of legitimacy granted to it. That initial agenda is by and large in the hands of the leadership. The leadership can also delineate the conditions for solutions that will avoid both otherwise inevitable disappointments and the mobilization of intensive opposition, which in the consolidation phase will not be limited to the government but will extend to the regime. An adequate analysis of the means-ends relationships (the compatibility of the use of certain means with other ends and conflicts between possible ends) becomes crucial. This requires political intelligence, adequate information, and honesty in the perception of conflicts of ultimate values. In any case, outcomes beneficial to particular groups in society are likely to be delayed because of the difficulty of implementation at this stage. While efficacy is likely to be judged by outputs, sometimes the neutralization of potential opponents of the regime is of equal or more importance than the immediate satisfaction of those who have granted legitimacy to the new regime on the basis of their expectations.

Democratic regimes face more difficult problems in this respect than nondemocratic regimes: the implications of their policies are visible to everyone, because of the freedom for criticism and information, which limits the regime's manipulation of the perceptions of society. It is in the area of "reform mongering," to use Hirschman's phrase, that democratic leadership must prove its ability.[24] If regime change were associated inevitably with a widespread revolution of rising expectations, the problems for a new regime might prove almost unsolvable. This result is generally modified by the "tunnel effect" (again a description by Hirschman), in which satisfaction of the expectations of some sectors of the society gives hope to others who do not see immediate outputs to satisfy their demands.[25] In sum, an intelligent formulation of the agenda, adroit management of the process of reform mongering, and immediate achievements in a particular sector that may serve as constituent acts for the new regime can make the problem of efficacy more manageable than seems possible at first.

We shall return to the issue of regime efficacy when we take up the solvability of problems confronting a regime and how they can become unsolvable, thereby contributing to the process of breakdown.

Legitimacy and efficacy, therefore, are analytically distinguishable dimensions that in reality are closely interrelated in ways about which we know very little. In what way does legitimacy facilitate efficacy, and to what extent, in different types of regimes and with different levels of legitimacy, does efficacy contribute to legitimacy? These are central questions in the study of the dynamics of regimes, but until recently they have received little comparative research.[26]

The effectiveness of regimes is still another dimension, though it is not often treated separately from efficacy, probably because it is a dimension at a lower level of generality and is therefore more difficult to distinguish empirically from legitimacy. "Effectiveness" is the capacity actually to implement the policies formulated, with the desired results. The fact that even the best laws are worthless if unenforceable falls within this concept. Despite widespread consensus about the goals to be pursued, and even about the means to be used, those goals, and above all, the means, can actually turn out to be unavailable, inefficient, and subject to delay and resistance in the process of implementation. At this point, perhaps more than at the point of policy formulation, discrepancies between expectations and satisfactions emerge, and dissatisfaction arises. Such ineffectiveness weakens the authority of the state and, as a result, weakens its legitimacy. Ineffectiveness also raises questions about policies that had been perceived as efficacious. Here again, new regimes face particular problems, since they have not yet assembled the administrative staff necessary to implement policies. During the initial phase, leaders are not in full command of the necessary information. The initial surge of support for the regime, plus the disorganization and weakness of the opposition, leads them to underestimate the resistance their policies are likely to e.icounter. Further, their self-righteousness as successors to a despised regime leads them to disregard even the valid arguments of the opposition, thereby increasing such resistance. As exemplified by the Socialist response to the agrarian reform failures of the leftist bourgeois-Socialist government in Spain in 1931–33, ineffectiveness is likely to split the regime-building coalition. Ineffectiveness is also likely to encourage illegitimate resistance to the decisions of the government. In this context, the maintenance of order in the implementation of decisions becomes central for the authority of regimes. Later we shall turn to a particular type of ineffectiveness, the inability to impose order or legal sanctions against those turning to private violence for political ends.[27] As all theorists have emphasized, the *ultima ratio* of legitimate authority is the use of force. A democratic leader—in fact, any leader—must be able to say: "My obligation under the Constitution and the statutes was and is to implement the orders of the legitimate authority with whatever means are necessary and with as little force and civil disorder as the circumstances permit and to be prepared to back them up with whatever other civil or military enforcement might have been required."[28]

All theorists of revolution, particularly the revolutionaries themselves, agree that the inefficient use of force, or reluctance to use it, is decisive in the transfer of legitimacy to the opponents of the regime.[29] At this point the decisive question posed by Pareto becomes relevant: "How can one incline people who would otherwise be neutral in the struggle to condemn resistance on the part of the governing powers and so to make the resistance less vigorous; or at a venture to persuade the rulers themselves in that sense, a thing for that matter that is not likely to have any great success in our day, save with those whose spinal columns have utterly rotted from the bane of humanitarianism."[30] Ineffectiveness of governments makes the question of legitimacy salient, particularly to those in charge of enforcing the law and defending the regime. This is an extremely complex problem in the process of breakdown of regimes and will be discussed at length later on.

The combination of these three dimensions produces an eight-fold typology of situations, the consequences of which should be analyzed in detail in the light of empirical situations. The realization that in any particular case we would need the aggregate patterns not only for the whole society but for particular segments of it, and, in some cases, the perception of these dimensions by key actors and political institutions, indicates how complex the analysis of the dynamics of regimes and their breakdowns can become.

Party Systems and the Instability of Democracy

Party systems in Western democracies are the result of long-term, complex historical developments, and therefore it is difficult to define the extent to which the same factors account for the emergence of different types of party systems and durable democracies. Undoubtedly, the same structural factors that account for crisis-ridden democracies also account in large part for extreme, polarized, centrifugal multiparty systems. However, party systems are the result not only of structural factors but of institutional factors like electoral laws, the actions of political and social elites, the diffusion of ideologies, or *Zeitgeist* at the time of the instauration of democracy; they can also be considered as an independent or at least an intervening factor in the crisis of democracy. It is in this context, the character of party systems and party competition, that the consequences for democratic stability of electoral systems—in particular, proportional representation—have become the subject of scholarly debate.

Two-party systems (to use an operational definition like that provided by Giovanni Sartori), could and can be found in only a small number of democracies.[31] Historically, the United States, the United Kingdom—with the exception of some periods of transition—and New Zealand, strictly defined, are the only extant two-party systems. (One might add Australia and Canada, which function as such.) In twentieth-century continental Europe, only pre-1923 Spain could be considered a two-party system at the parliamentary level (but not at the electoral level, particularly regionally). A number of smaller European democracies might have developed into two-party systems, had they retained single-member majority voting, but the introduction of proportional representation prevented such a development. Austria, which today functions as a two-party system, could not be considered as such in the period between wars, particularly around 1930. In Latin America, Colombia and Uruguay could be considered two-party systems, even though the latter has features that should qualify that statement. Outside the West, only the Philippines and Iran might at some time have qualified.

If we ask to what extent the pattern of political competition in two-party systems has contributed to democratic stability, our first impression is clearly positive, even though Spain in 1923 (with the reservations noted), Colombia in recent decades, and more recently, Uruguay and the Philippines, would suggest that such a party system does not prevent breakdown. It should be noted that in the case of these and other Latin American democracies, another factor might have to be taken into account: the presidential system.

It is perhaps no accident that when a two-party format is subject to maximal ideological distance and centrifugal competition, it is either destroyed or paves the way to a confrontation that takes the shape of civil war. This was the case in Colombia and perhaps in other Latin American countries. Republican

Spain, thanks to an electoral system that gave a heavy advantage to the largest pluralities and therefore to two major electoral coalitions, tended toward the two-party format, with the consequences, noted by Sartori, for highly ideological polities. In such a context, extreme multipartism, with all its costs, is the survival solution. It is no accident that fear of polarization inclined the Spanish Cortes to opt for proportional representation, rather than a single-member district system, in 1976, despite the fear of party fragmentation.

Continental European countries and Chile—the most stable Latin American democracy—were multiparty systems, albeit of very different sorts. A number of them have been, since the freeze in the party systems around World War I, moderate multiparty systems; that is, in Sartorian terms, they have fewer than five parties (which count to form coalitions or have blackmail potential). Specifically, they are Belgium and Ireland (three-party format); Sweden, Iceland, and Luxembourg (four-party format); Denmark (four-party until the 1950s, five afterward); and Switzerland, the Netherlands, and Norway (five-party format). (Norway and Sweden have had long periods of social democratic predominance, since 1935 and 1932, respectively.) All are systems with governing coalitions within the perspective of alternating coalitions, without sizable or relevant antisystem parties (except Belgium in the 1930s), with all their relevant parties available for cabinet coalitions or able to coalesce as oppositions, and with unilateral oppositions. They are characterized by 1) relatively small ideological distance among their relevant parties; 2) a bipolar coalitional configuration; and 3) centripetal competition.

This was not the case in the Portuguese Republic, Italy after World War I, Weimar Germany, France under the Third and Fourth Republics, the Republic in Spain, Finland, Czechoslovakia, the Baltic states, Eastern European and Balkan countries in the intermittent democratic periods, or Chile before the fall of Allende.

Certainly, comparison between countries with moderate nonpolarized multiparty systems and those having extreme multiparty systems suggests that moderate multiparty systems are associated with stability of democracy. Only in Belgium (at a moment when one could speak of a five-party system, with 11.5 percent of the vote going to the Fascist Rex and 7.1 to the Flemish nationalists) was democracy close to being endangered.

Of the thirteen relatively institutionalized democracies with extreme multiparty systems (leaving out Poland, Hungary, and the Balkan countries), seven were victims of a breakdown due to internal causes; one (Czechoslovakia) succumbed to a mixture of external and internal factors in 1938; two (Finland in 1930–32 and France in 1934) came close to a breakdown; and in 1958 the Fourth Republic escaped that fate through reequilibration. To these cases we could add Chile in 1973. There is, however, Italy, which since 1945 has been the archetypical case of multiparty system that has not experienced a breakdown, though it may be described as "surviving without government."

It seems clear that the two main types of multiparty systems distinguished by Sartori are not unrelated to the problem of democratic stability. Sartori rightly notes that segmented extreme multiparty systems whose parties locate themselves on more than one dimension, not competing between themselves since they have assured ethno-cultural, territorial, or religious electorates—Israel, Switzerland, and the Netherlands for example—constitute special cases. If they are not considered, the relationship between instability and extreme multipartism becomes even more salient. (It is impossible and unnecessary to present here his sophisticated analysis of the dynamics of extreme, centrifugal, polarized, ideological multiparty systems.)

Polarized pluralism is a system of five or more relevant parties (that is, with "coalition use" or "power of intimidation") characterized by the following:

1) The presence of antisystem parties (which undermine the legitimacy of the regime)

2) Bilateral oppositions (counteroppositions that are, in constructive terms, incompatible)

3) The central placement of one party (the DC in Italy) or of a group of parties (Weimar)

4) Polarization, or the positioning of the lateral poles literally two poles apart, due to ideological distance

5) The prevalence of centrifugal rather than centripetal drives in the electorate

6) Ideological patterning as a *forma mentis* rather than a pragmatic mentality differentiating parties

7) The presence of irresponsible oppositions, due to peripheral turnover rather than alternative coalitions, persistent opposition of antisystem parties, and semiresponsible opposition of those flanking parties forced to compete with them

8) The politics of outbidding.

It is the dynamic characteristics that account for the potential for breakdown in these systems: specifically, the polarization, the centrifugal drives, and the tendency toward irresponsibility and outbidding.

Another way to clarify the problem would be to study those extreme multiparty systems (in Sartori's sense) that resisted or have continued to resist their course toward breakdown for a prolonged time; specifically, the Third French Republic, the Fourth for many years, and Italy after 1945. Both Giuseppe Di Palma and Sartori himself have pointed out some of the factors involved.[32]

Undoubtedly, the experience of nondemocratic rule and the fear of it lead a large proportion of the voters to continue to give their support to the "Center" as a safe position, the one that best assures the survival of existing democracy, despite their disillusionment with its performance.

Is there a way out of the dynamics of extreme, polarized, multiparty systems? Sartori points—with skepticism—to a process of relegitimation of the antisystem parties. This process requires the antisystem parties to relegitimate, among their own followers, the system and the system parties. Such a process, he argues, would need to be visible, not based merely on invisible understandings (a point also made by Giuseppe Di Palma). Even if an antisystem party makes an effort in this direction, it is still not assured that it will be credible to both its opponents and its own followers, since it follows a long period of reciprocal delegitimation. A centripetal convergence at the invisible level of parliamentary cooperation, local politics, interest-group compromise, clientelism, and patronage can counteract the centrifugal systemic characteristics and insure "surviving without governing." Ultimately, however, it might not prevent a continuing process of deterioration, particularly in the context of violent antisystem activities of groups on both sides of the spectrum and in the face of "unsolvable problems." Let us retain for our analysis the idea that extreme multipartism alone does not determine the breakdown of democracy, but it does increase its probability. The case of Italy shows that such a system can last many years without resulting in that fatal outcome.

To approach the breakdown, the antisystem parties must act clearly as a disloyal opposition, and those flanking them must act as semiloyal parties when the Center (party or parties) loses strength when confronted with electoral defeat, faces "unsolvable" problems, or loses the will to govern. Sartori has analyzed *why,* in extreme multiparty systems, such situations are likely to develop (in part due to the dynamics of party competition), but it is our task to show more concretely *how* the process takes place.

Disloyal, Semiloyal, and Loyal Oppositions

Changes in regime occur with the transfer of legitimacy from one set of political institutions to another.[33] They are brought on by the action of one or more disloyal oppositions that question the existence of the regime and aim at changing it.[34] Such oppositions cannot be repressed or isolated; in a crisis they can mobilize intense, effective support; and by a variety of means they can take power or at least divide the allegiance of the population, which can lead to civil war. In certain unique circumstances, rulers selected by democratic means, faced with what they perceived as massive disloyal opposition, have been able to modify the democratic rules of the game and reequilibrate democracy by themselves, thus creating a new regime. Such a modification occurred during the transition from the Fourth to the Fifth Republic in France, and in Finland in the thirties. (For an analysis of the latter, see the chapter by Allapuro and Allardt in this volume.) It is not unlikely, as the case of Estonia shows, that they might try to save the regime from the immediate threat of a disloyal opposition by changing it in an authoritarian direction.

No regime, least of all a democratic regime, which permits the articulation and organization of all political positions, is without a disloyal opposition. On the other hand, in most societies, the existing regime tends to have the benefit of the doubt, or at least the neutrality, of large sectors of the society. Except in crisis situations, this allows it to isolate and otherwise discourage disloyal oppositions, which are usually minorities and assume importance only in the process of breakdown. These facts give semiloyal oppositions a decisive role in the process of the loss of power by democratic regimes and implementation of a semi- or pseudo-legal takeover. Semiloyalty is particularly difficult to define, even *a posteriori*. The borderline between loyalty and ambivalent or conditional loyalty is not easy to draw, particularly since the democratic process strives to incorporate outsiders into the system as a participating loyal opposition. In a political system characterized by limited consensus, deep cleavages, and suspicion between leading participants, semiloyalty is easily equated with disloyalty by some of the participants, while others dismiss or underrate such fears and emphasize the potential for loyalty of those suspected of ambivalence. This ambiguity contributes decisively to the crisis atmosphere in the political process. But to understand this concept fully, we must first define disloyal opposition.

Certain parties, movements, and organizations explicitly reject political systems based on the existence of the authority of the state or any central authority with coercive powers. An example would be the pure anarcho-syndicalists, who certainly consider themselves disloyal to any democratic parliamentary regime and await the historical opportunity for their utopian revolution.

Another obvious source of disloyal opposition would be secessionist or irredentist nationalist movements whose goal is the establishment of a separate new state or union with another neighboring nation-state.[35] However, it is not always easy to identify a secessionist party, since such groups generally start out by claiming to advocate cultural, administrative, or political autonomy within state or federal institutions. It is sometimes difficult to distinguish the rhetoric of nationalism compatible with a multinational state from appeals to create a separate nation-state, particularly when this rhetoric is propagated by parties that operate in both the regional and national political arena and employ a different style and a division of roles in their leadership. Such parties are often exposed to outbidding by extremists and activists, who seize upon the rhetoric of the broader movement and major parties to force them, in crisis situations, into actions that are, or appear to be, disloyal to the state rather than the regime. They are certainly likely to be perceived as disloyal even when they are only semiloyal. Principled commitment to a single overriding goal or the interest of a minority nation or a cultural and linguistic minority population leads such parties to be extremely opportunistic in relation to the regime-sustaining forces, which contributes to the distrust with which they are often perceived. The cooperation of such parties with the democratic regime, given their obvious ambivalence toward the state and the regime and their long-range commitment, grants those disloyal opponents of the regime who are strongly committed to the persistence of the state an opportunity to question the loyalty of the regime parties cooperating in these efforts to reach consociational solutions. In crisis situations, extremist ultraloyalists who are opposed to the regional nationalists' demands for autonomy find an opportunity to ask embarrassing questions, quoting nationalist rhetoric and demanding public declarations of loyalty to the state, which they conceived as a nation-state. Refusal becomes an argument against the regime parties cooperating with the nationalists. It also pushes the ambivalent nationalist into more disloyal, or apparently disloyal, positions.

Small extremist parties can be allowed a principled opposition, even a radical and violent one; but when such parties gain widespread support, infiltrate or control major interest groups, and begin to be perceived as serious contenders for power, they are likely to convey equivocal messages in order to maintain their radical opposition to the system while claiming to aim at a legal access to power. A plebiscitarian conception of democracy, identification with a latent majority, and disqualification of the majority as being illegitimate allow these parties to assert their ultimate claim to power, and the boundary between disloyalty and semiloyalty becomes confusing for many participants. In this sense, Fascist and particularly Communist parties after World War II were disloyal in a very different way from the anarchists, the antiliberal and antidemocratic monarchists in the nineteenth century, and some national liberation movements. This ambivalence of antisystem parties, which were at one point or another defined as disloyal, has made possible the legal takeover of power and destruction of democracy as well as the slow, complex process of integration into a competitive democratic system. The Fascist parties in interwar Europe and the Communists in the limited competitive democracies of Eastern Europe after World War II are prime examples of disloyal oppositions that protested against accusations of disloyalty while advocating destruction of the system as rightfully legal participants. And certain Socialist parties in the late nineteenth century and pre–World War I Europe were perceived at the time as disloyal oppositions because of their Marxist ideology, while they were in fact being slowly integrated into democratic politics.[36] Similarly, some of the political movements identified with the Catholic church and inspired by the fulminations against the liberal democratic state of the *Syllabus* were to become the strongest supporters of various democratic political systems in the second half of the twentieth century.

What would be an effective "litmus test" of loyalty to a democratic regime? An obvious possibility is public commitment to legal means for gaining power, and rejection of the use of force. Ambiguities in such public commitment are certainly prima facie evidence of semiloyalty, but not always, as we shall see, of disloyalty.

Under certain circumstances, when the authority of the state is unable to impose the disarmament of all participants in the political process and to defend all parties against the violence of any other, it becomes easy to claim that paramilitary organizations and threats of force are purely defensive or preventive measures. In societies in which the armed forces traditionally act as the moderating power and intervene in the political process, parties may claim that some of their mobilizational measures are only defensive and supportive of the regime. Again, this blurs the distinction between disloyalty and semiloyalty, as various participants define the actions of the parties quite differently.

Another basic test might be rejection of any "knocking at the barracks" for armed forces support. Again, in an unstable situation in which a number of participants in the political process are perceived as disloyal, even loyal, regime-supporting parties would be tempted to establish such contacts with the army command or factions in the army close to them. In that case, the criterion is somewhat ambiguous, since even the system's supporting parties are likely to seek out support in the event of a crisis that might strain the expected normal loyalty of the army to the regime.

Another criterion would be denial of legitimacy as participants in the political process to parties that claim to be loyal participants, parties that have the right to rule thanks to the support they received from the electorate. One example of this would be the *retraimiento,* a traditional pattern of opposition behavior in Spanish and Latin American politics that involves a withdrawal from the legislature and a refusal to participate in parliamentary debates or in free elections, and results in delegitimation. The use of mass pressure by trade unions, taxpayers, or citizens in the form of strikes or mass protests disrupting the operation of government would be another indicator of disloyalty. But again, such actions are not unambiguous, since even system-supporting parties may turn to such tactics when they feel that there is no opportunity for fair and open competition in the elections. System parties, when faced with a formal, legal takeover of power by what they fear is an antisystem party, find such tactics the last recourse for defense of the system. How are we to judge such behavior without a judgment about the loyalty of those against whom those actions are directed?

Another closely related indicator would be the readiness to curtail the civil liberties of the leaders and supporters of parties attempting to exercise constitutionally guaranteed freedoms. To interpret that criterion rigidly would deprive democratic regimes of many legitimate defense measures. Certainly many of the measures, like the prohibition of uniforms, limitations on huge mass rallies in public places, strict control of the right to own weapons, and censorship of incitement to violence, can be construed as an illegitimate limitation of civil liberties and will make governments imposing them vulnerable to accusations of slowly eliminating democratic freedoms.

Obviously, blanket attacks on the political system rather than on particular parties or actors, systematic defamation of politicians in the system parties, constant obstruction of the parliamentary process, support for proposals made by other presumably disloyal parties with disruptive purposes, joint actions with other presumably disloyal parties for disruptive purposes, and joint actions with them in crisis situations and in toppling governments without any possibility of constituting a new majority are all typical actions of disloyal oppositions.[37] However, some of this behavior is occasionally characteristic of parties that we would not go so far as to label disloyal.

Strife between parties, efforts to discredit opponents, and the characterization of other parties as representatives of narrow interests in conflict with the public interest are normal, natural, and legitimate actions within the democratic process. Style, intensity, and fairness in conducting these actions mark the distinction between loyal and disloyal oppositions. Typically, disloyal oppositions picture their opponents collectively as instruments of outside secret and conspiratorial groups—communism, the Masons, international capitalism, the Vatican, or foreign powers.[38] Since corruption is likely to become particularly visible in democratic politics, oppositions have an opportunity to discredit as corrupt not only the leaders (and their associates) but the whole party, and in the case of a disloyal opposition, the whole system. When system parties turn to that style of politics, it is prima facie evidence of the shift toward semiloyalty. A significant correlation exists between the image of politicians or the political class as a whole as dishonest and the readiness to turn to violent means, as table 1, showing responses to survey questions by those supporting non-Communist parties under the Fourth Republic, shows.[39]

Table 1. Survey Questions: Are Politicians Honest? Should Your Party Seize Power by Force?

	Should Take Power by Force	Should not Take Power by Force	No Answer	(N)
Majority of honest men	3.6%	74.8%	21.6	329
Minority of honest men	7.1	58.8	34.1	364
No honest men at all	16.1	22.3	61.6	112

NOTE: Those asked these questions were supporters of parties other than the Communists in France.

Public scandals involving system party leaders, if intelligently exploited by a disloyal opposition, provide an opportunity to establish bridges between other system parties and the disloyal opposition on the legitimate claim of exposing the corruption of the system. They contribute in this way to the drift into semiloyalty.

We have listed a number of criteria for disloyalty, none of which appears as necessary and sufficient, since opposition groups that might ultimately be integrated into the system as loyal supporters occasionally engage in them, particularly when faced with political forces they perceive as disloyal. Certainly, disloyalty in parties that do not publicly commit themselves to the overthrow or total transformation of the system if elected is not unambiguous. It is this basic ambiguity of the definition of disloyalty, except in the case of small, highly ideological and principled antisystem antidemocratic parties, that makes it so difficult to defend an embattled democracy and to prevent the silent takeover by antidemocratic parties. The combination of a number of such indicators would allow us to describe the syndrome that defines political forces disloyal to democracy. Even if it is not disloyal, a political force with such characteristics can reasonably be perceived by some of the participants as disloyal to competitive democracy and by many more as semiloyal.[40] When a party that has engaged in one or several of the patterns described is in power, its opponents will seize upon those actions to label it a threat to democracy, even when it has refrained from taking power undemocratically or suspending the democratic electoral process and the necessary civil liberties. In such a situation, who is to decide whether that label is an alibi for the antidemocratic ambitions of the opponents or the basis for an *ademocratic* defense of democracy? The outcome of the conflict would seem an obvious test, but unfortunately, a defense of democracy by ademocratic means is not likely to bring about its reequilibration.

The intermittent presence, in attenuated or ambivalent form, of some of the characteristics we have used to define political forces disloyal to a democratic system, is characteristic of semiloyal parties and actors as well. In addition, certain other characteristics define semiloyalty, foremost of which is the willingness of political leaders to engage in secret negotiations to search for the basis of cooperation in government with parties they themselves (and others acting with them) perceive as disloyal. This indicator does not imply the intent to overthrow the system or change it radically, since it might be motivated by the desire to integrate into the system forces that can be coopted, moderated, or sometimes split through such negotiations. There is evidence that more often than not such efforts contribute to the demise of democratic institutions. But there are also cases in which they have helped to neutralize and ultimately defeat antidemocratic forces, sometimes, as in Finland, at the cost of some deviation from pure liberal democracy.[41]

An indicator of semiloyal behavior, and a source of perceptions leading to questions about the loyalty of a party to the system, is a willingness to encourage, tolerate, cover up, treat leniently, excuse, or justify the actions of other participants that go beyond the limits of peaceful, legitimate patterns of politics in a democracy. Parties become suspect when, on the basis of ideological affinity, agreement on some ultimate goals, or particular policies, they make a distinction between means and ends. They reject the means as undignified and extreme, but excuse them and do not denounce them publicly because of agreement with the goals so pursued. Such agreement in principle and disagreement on tactics is a frequent indicator of semiloyalty. Political violence, assassination, conspiracies, failed military coups and unsuccessful revolutionary attempts provide the test situations for semiloyalty. Unequal application of justice to the illegal acts of different disloyal oppositions contributes decisively to the image of semiloyalty. The granting and refusal of amnesty to opponents of a democratic system provides another test situation. Governments that face disloyal opposition at either end of the spectrum, or have gained support from parties who acted disloyally against a previous government, are in a difficult position when forced simultaneously to assert their authority and expand the basis of support for their rule. In such circumstances, the suspicion of semiloyalty becomes almost unavoidable. Parties of heterogeneous composition, recruited by the fusion of different elements, inheriting leaders and supporters from a previous regime, and divided by factional conflicts, find themselves divided and in ambiguous positions when faced with such situations. Because the lack of discipline in parties makes it difficult for the leaders to disavow the statements and actions of their lieutenants and subleaders, their own public statements might not be sufficient to gain confidence. A frequent pattern (one seen during the interwar years in Europe) is the radicalization of the youth and student organizations of parties that the mature party leadership cannot disown without losing some of its most active and enthusiastic followers. The same sometimes holds for special-interest groups closely tied with political parties.

Ultimately, semiloyalty can be identified by a basically system-oriented party's greater affinity for extremists on its side of the political spectrum than for system parties closer to the opposite side. Unfortunately, in a highly polarized society, when extremist parties engage in violence and have the power to attract segments of the system parties or their electorate, system parties are likely to behave in such a way that they seem semiloyal even if they are not. One characteristic of the final stage of the breakdown process is that to one degree or another the parties whose main aim should be to defend the authenticity of the constitutional, democratic, political process engage in actions that justify other participants' perception of them as semiloyal.

The crisis situation, provoked by unsolvable problems and by the presence of a disloyal opposition, with its voluntarism and sense of historical mission, promising *hinc et nunc* a solution to all those problems without feeling obliged to spell out specific policies that could gain majority support, creates the conditions for the emergence of semiloyal political forces. The antecedents of that development, however, can often be found in earlier, more stable periods. One that often characterizes newly established democratic regimes is the tendency of its supporters to identify democracy with their own particular social and cultural policies. The majority, in setting up a new democratic regime, is impressed by its own strength and by the weakness of the social strata identified with the preceding regime. It often feels that its task is not only to establish an institutional framework for democratic processes but to anchor in the constitution many very specific policy decisions. On that basis, any opposition to those policies is perceived as antidemocratic action rather than as an effort to change the decisions of the temporary majority. Such an exclusionary definition of democracy pushes what could have been a loyal opposition into semiloyalty as we have defined it. The Spanish Republicans' expression "A Republic for the Republicans," meaning by "Republicans" those who supported unconditionally the policies enacted by the founders of the regime, certainly had that effect. Many democratic reform parties tend to misperceive any opposition to a particular constitution or to basic social, economic, and religious changes as antidemocratic, when there would be room for such opposition in a democratic constitutional framework.[42] Democracy, particularly in its difficult early years, requires mechanisms that allow the opposition, if willing to abide by the law, to have a significant share of power. The inclusion of the opposition could be accomplished by offering them an opportunity to participate in the legislative process through committee work, by granting the interest groups linked with them access to those in power, and sometimes allowing them representation in corporative institutions. Decentralization, or local and regional self-government, can reduce the feeling of those not participating in the foundation of the new regime that they have been excluded. The systematic exclusion or discrimination against the partisans of the opposition in many realms of public life, such as the bureaucracy, the armed forces, or the administration of interventionist economic policies, might push those ready to become a loyal opposition into semi- and disloyal positions. Such elements might easily become the active supporters of semiloyal positions that could contribute years later to the breakdown of the regime.

Much sophistication is needed in the initial stage to discern which groups and individuals from the opposition, especially the latter, can become loyal or honestly neutral but compliant citizens. The temptation of *ressentiment* politics is often too strong to allow such a process of integration. Undoubtedly, unnecessary personality conflicts within the political elite tend to hamper the future cooperation of government and loyal opposition. Those conflicts are not so great when the democratic political system has evolved slowly out of a more restricted political system like a semiconstitutional monarchy with representative institutions, an oligarchic democracy in which democratic reformers had already participated in a minority role, or a system of dual authority like that of India before independence. They are exacerbated when the instauration of democracy follows a prolonged period of authoritarian rule that provided no opportunity for the emergence of counterelites, and the interaction in certain political arenas such as legislatures, municipal governments, or interest-group bargaining.

Instauration of democracy after an authoritarian regime allows its founders to question the credentials of many interests in the society, among them opposition leaders who collaborated with the fallen regime. In this respect, regimes succeeding highly ideological and exclusionary totalitarian regimes that possessed a well-defined political elite of the activists of a single party face a less difficult situation than those succeeding amorphous authoritarian regimes. If the founders of a new regime label any person who has been connected with the previous regime unfit to participate in the democratic process unless he denies his past, they contribute to a self-fulfilling prophecy of creating a semiloyal or even a disloyal opposition. In a democracy, loyalty to a new regime cannot be applied retroactively, except in extreme cases when the general consensus of the society rejects the previous regime almost unanimously on moral grounds. In this respect, the posttotalitarian democracies in Germany and Italy after World War II found themselves in a situation quite different from that of the post–Primo de Rivera Republic in Spain or the post-Perón democracy in Argentina. In both latter cases the authoritarian regime had been welcomed by a large part of the population; and despite the errors that led to its breakdown, its legitimacy, rejected according to widely shared liberal democratic standards, was not rejected on moral grounds by large segments of the population. The understandable exclusion of the regime's former supporters did not allow them to become a semiloyal opposition with a chance of integration, much less part of the loyal opposition.

Spain's return to democracy in 1976–77, after the death of Franco and almost forty years of authoritarian rule, presents special characteristics. Like Turkey's return to democracy in 1945, the change is unique in that it has taken place not through a breakdown of the regime but through the intiative of the rulers, under internal and external pressure. To date (after the 1977 election), it has led not to a transfer of power to the main opposition forces but to a power-sharing process legitimated by a free competitive election. The change through *reforma* rather than *ruptura* poses special problems for new democratic institutions. These institutions were born according to the formal constitutional amendment procedures of the Franco constitution, yet they countervened the spirit of the fundamental laws in a process that has much in common with the antidemocratic perversion of democratic constitutions, but with the opposite result. Some of the problems for the cases of instauration and restoration noted above in the Spanish case acquire new and unexpected complexity.

One of the central characteristics of a crisis democracy is that even the parties that have created the system tend to deviate from the ideals of a loyal system party when they encounter hostility among extremists on either side of the spectrum. The constraints of the situation push everyone toward some form of semiloyalty, even semiloyalty to the democratic system.

Certainly the actors in the political process of a crisis-ridden democracy are even less able than the historians or social scientists who follow them to agree on which other participants are loyal, semiloyal, or disloyal. This ambiguity ultimately makes the defense of the democratic political process very difficult and contributes a great deal to the slow but apparently inevitable process of breakdown. The presence of one, but particularly two, polarized disloyal oppositions with significant support tends to lead to the emergence of semiloyal political actors, to their polarization, and to the increased isolation of those unequivocally loyal to a democratic competitive political system.

It is this inherent ambiguity of the political process in crisis situations that so often makes simple moral judgment after the fact so dangerous and sometimes unjust. At the time, only intensive interaction and communication within the elites interested in the survival of the system on a basis of mutual trust can create a consensus on loyalty and disloyalty. Only under those conditions can the willingness to put loyalty to the system before other commitments, ideological affinities, and interests be achieved.

What emerges at this point is a definition of political forces constituting the loyal opposition to a democratic regime. Ideally, such forces would be characterized by:

1) An unambiguous public commitment to achievement of power only by electoral means and a readiness to surrender it unconditionally to other participants with the same commitment.

2) A clear and uncompromising rejection of the use of violent means to achieve or maintain power except by constitutionally legitimate means when faced with an illegal attempt to take power.

3) A rejection of any nonconstitutional appeal to the armed forces to gain power or to retain it against a loyal democratic opposition.

4) An unambiguous rejection of the rhetoric of violence to mobilize supporters in order to achieve power, to retain it beyond the constitutional mandate, or to destroy opponents, including even ademocratic or antidemocratic opponents. The defense of democracy must be carried out within a legal framework, more or less narrowly construed, without arousing popular passions and political vigilantism.

5) A commitment to participate in the political process, elections, and parliamentary activity without setting up conditions beyond the guarantee of the necessary civil liberties for reasonably fair democratic political processes. Requiring an agreement on substantive rather than procedural policies is in principle incompatible with the assumptions that the minority must respect *pro tempore* the decisions of the majority and that the majority in turn must respect the right of the minority to reverse its policies, except in the realm of requirements for competitive politics, should it become the majority.

6) A willingness in principle to assume the responsibility to govern or be part of the majority when no alternative government by system parties is possible. An even more stringent but not unreasonable requirement would be the willingness to participate in government when it might otherwise be weakened in face of crisis.

7) The willingness to join with opponents ideologically distant but committed to the survival of the democratic political order. (This requirement is more stringent and perhaps unreasonable.) It might apply even against parties that are closer ideologically but are committed to helping to undermine the democratic political process by the use or the rhetoric of violence and an effort to curtail the civil liberties of a legitimate opposition.

8) A rejection of secret contacts with the disloyal opposition and a rejection of its support when offered in exchange for tolerance of its antidemocratic activities. In principle, an effort to make the boundary between the system party, broadly defined, and antisystem parties as clear as possible both publicly and privately is a major characteristic of system-loyal parties or political forces.

9) The readiness to denounce to a legitimate democratic government the activities of opposition forces or the armed forces aiming at the overthrow of that government. This criterion is certainly stringent, and is more difficult to apply, since it goes beyond the unwillingness to participate in such conspiratorial activities to requiring support for political opponents facing a threat.

10) A commitment in principle to reduce the political role of neutral powers, like presidents and kings, the judiciary, and the armed forces, to narrow limits to assure the authenticity of the democratic political process.

If those ten requirements had to be unambiguously satisfied, the number of loyal participants in the democratic political process in most societies undergoing a serious crisis would be greatly reduced. In fact, in some of the cases we shall analyze, like that of Spain in the 1930s, the reader of the detailed historical record might come to the conclusion that there were *no* major parties and key leaders that would fully satisfy that ideal definition. In any democracy in crisis we will discover taints of semiloyalty even in the parties most committed to democratic stability, parties which under normal circumstances would satisfy our criteria.

It might clarify the distinctions we have made to link them with Richard Rose's analysis of the authority of regimes.[43] System parties and the loyal opposition contribute, through high support and high compliance, to the full legitimacy of the regime authority. The open and sincere disloyal opposition is characterized by low support and low compliance. Their aim is the repudiation of the regime, but failing in this, their actions make it semicoercive. When the opposition is strong and is faced with a strong regime, its actions tend to make the regime coercive. Modern disloyal oppositions, however, in the ambiguities of their appeal, give the impression of mixed support, and they vary their degree of compliance in accordance with the strength of the regime parties, the cohesion of government forces, the opportunities presented by the situation, and the unsolvable problems. Their presence results in partially legitimate, divided, or disrupted regimes, terms coined by Richard

Rose that convey a sequence in the loss of control faced by the system parties confronted with the refusal of the disloyal opposition to comply, as regime authority becomes less efficacious and effective. It is, however, the semiloyal opposition, with its relatively high, or at least mixed, compliance, rather than the disloyal opposition, that pushes regimes into the partially legitimate and divided authority situation. The regimes we shall study in this volume found themselves in these intermediary situations, moving from partial to divided legitimacy, sustained as coercive or semicoercive, and finally becoming disrupted and repudiated or isolated as in the Rose typology. It is our contention that the conditions leading to semiloyalty, or even suspicion of semiloyalty, by leading participants in the political game, opposition and government parties alike, account for the breakdown process almost as much as the role of the disloyal oppositions.

Crisis, Loss of Power, Breakdown, and Takeover

We have attempted to underline the probabilistic and changing character of legitimacy, efficacy, and effectiveness of a political system at any moment in its development. We have also characterized the loyal and disloyal oppositions to a regime, particularly a democractic regime, as well as the type of opposition that we call semiloyal, which will play a decisive role in our description of the process of breakdown. We have not yet mentioned the sequences of events, the dynamic processes that serve to explain why these dimensions display different characteristics at different times in a democratic political system.

The kinds of events that contribute decisively to destabilization, overthrow, and in some cases reequilibration of a democracy have in recent years been the object of considerable theoretical discussion and empirical research concerned particularly with the onset and characteristics of violence and resultant governmental reactions. Cabinet stability as both an indicator and a cause of the crisis of regimes has been studied empirically, but not in connection with the broader problem of the stability of regimes.[44] Other aspects, like the implication for democratic stability of different party systems and the links between party systems and electoral systems, have, since the important work by Hermens, been the object of much debate.[45] Unfortunately, there has been relatively little research on the links between economic and political crises, despite the importance assigned in the Marxist theoretical tradition to the economic crisis under capitalism, the resultant breakdown of democracies, and rise of fascism to power.[46] There is no lack of theoretical or empirical research on these and other processes contributing to the breakdown of democratic regimes. However, the insights derived from such analyses have not been integrated into a more complex descriptive model. That, in our view, can only be derived from an inductive analysis of at least some of the paradigmatic cases that historical research has so thoroughly documented for us. In this respect, the work of Bracher has broken new ground.[47] The fascination with political violence, expressed most notably by American social scientists in response to recent events in the United States, and the concentration of intellectual efforts on the study of the unstable polities of the Third World have led to an unfortunate neglect of other aspects of the process of crisis, breakdown, and reequilibration. Let us not forget that while civil strife and political violence have caused the overthrow of government and regimes in many countries, the relatively stabilized democracies, which are the object of our study, have fallen in a more complex process in which the violence was but one contributing factor. Perhaps violence triggered those other processes, but only in cases of direct military intervention has the use of organized violence sealed the fate of regimes. Even in those cases, as more sophisticated recent analyses of the role of the military in politics have shown (see Alfred Stepan's study of the Brazilian military), military action was the result of the complex process of decay of the existing regime.[48]

The one-sided focus on the actions of the opponents of the regime, particularly radical and violent movements, the frustrated segments of the population, and military intervention, has tended to overlook the actions of those interested in the survival of the democratic regime, and the many organized social forces and institutions that might have been favorable or at least neutral toward the regime but finally withdrew their support from it. Social scientific analysis seems to alternate between an emphasis on the ultimate structural strains (particularly social-economic conflicts, inequality and rapid social economic change, and dependency) and on the period of open strife that immediately precedes the breakdown. This dual emphasis neglects the political process itself, functioning under constraints and often contributing to the conditions that generate rebellion and violent conflict. We agree with Charles Tilly when he writes:

Despite the many recent attempts to psychologize the study of revolution by introducing ideas of anxiety, alienation, rising expectations, and the like, and to sociologize it by employing notions of disequilibrium, role conflict, structural strain, and so on, the factors which hold up under close scrutiny are, on the whole, political ones. The structure of power, alternative conceptions of justice, the organization of coercion, the conduct of war, the formation of coalitions, the legitimacy of the state—these traditional concerns of political thought provide the main guides to the explanation of revolution. Population growth, industrialization, urbanization, and other large-scale structural changes do, to be sure, affect the probabilities of revolution. But they do so indirectly, by shaping the potential contenders for power, transforming the techniques of governmental control, and shifting the resources available to contenders and governments.[49]

Our main focus, therefore, will be on the incumbents and their actions, their formulation of the agenda for the regime, their way of defining problems and their capacity to solve them, the ability of the pro-regime forces to maintain sufficient cohesion to govern, the willingness of the democratic leaders to assume the responsibilities of power, the rejection of the temptation to turn to ademocratic political mechanisms to avoid making political decisions, the readiness to turn to nonpartisan sources of legitimacy, the willingness to coopt or enter coalitions with the disloyal opposition rather than turn to the defense of the regime, the narrowing of the political arena after the loss of power and the onset of a power vacuum, as well as such inadequate responses to the crisis atmosphere as badly timed elections and inadequate use of the coercive resources of the state. It is such political processes that give rise to, strengthen, and embolden the disloyal opposition and contribute to the emergence and wavering actions of the semiloyal opposition. It is also in such political processes, initiated by the incumbents, that we must search for an explanation of the processes of reequilibration or transformation of democratic regimes that allow them to overcome serious crises. They also contribute much to explaining the results of the breakdown process and the reasons the succeeding regime takes one or another configuration.

The Instauration and Consolidation of Democratic Regime and Its Future Stability

The history of the democracies whose fate concerns us here highlights the importance of the inauguration and initial consolidation of the regime for its future capacity to confront a serious crisis. It is no accident that constitutional debates use so much energy in building new democracies and that politicians and traditional political science devote so much attention to the virtues and defects of the subsequent constitutions. In retrospect it is easy to blame certain constitutional provisions, such as the famous Article 48 of the Weimar constitution, for consequences that were not intended and probably could not have been foreseen when the provision was being drafted. The same could be said of the electoral law of the Spanish Republic, hastily enacted without much discussion by the provisional government, or the absence of a real executive in the Estonian constitution.

The drafting of a constitution, however, is not the only process in democratic regime-building that has long-term implications. Equally important, or more so, and not just for the provisional or first government but for the regime itself, is the initial agenda adopted at that stage. For that agenda often creates expectations that cannot be satisfied within the existing framework and soon become the source of semiloyalty on the part of forces involved in the regime-building process. In fact, the initial agenda can contribute to consolidation of basic positions toward the legitimacy of the regime, particularly when that agenda is defined not as a government program but as a substantive part of the constitution that is difficult to reverse by simple majorities. Furthermore, when a regime changes, a large proportion of the population is expectant or neutral, rather than strongly committed to those who have established it or loyal to the regime that has fallen. This is particularly true when the party system of the new regime was not able to crystallize under its predecessor, as is the case when a preceding authoritarian regime did not allow organized opposition to participate in any way in the political process. In such an event, attitudes toward the legitimacy and efficacy of the new regime are quite likely to be permanently shaped by its initial steps. At this stage the new rulers can enact policies that have a socially constituent character, creating a solid basis of support among those benefiting from them. It is also a moment when they can minimize the concerns of those neutral to the change of regime but worried about its implications.

The leaders of a new democratic regime are likely to be tempted to place all unsolved problems of the society on their agenda simultaneously, presumably to maximize support, without realizing that in doing so they also maximize the number of persons likely to be affected negatively by their reforms. The simultaneous placement on the agenda of many complex problems whose solution has been protracted for decades is likely to overtax the resources of a leadership with little administrative experience, limited information, and scarce financial resources. Even assuming that the solutions proposed were all efficacious, the regime might be equally damaged by lack of effectiveness in implementing them quickly. In the process it would have raised unduly the expectations of its supporters and aroused the fears of those who expected to be negatively affected by the reforms without reaping the support of those intended as beneficiaries.

Why should this be the recurrent pattern in new democratic regimes? In our view, there are multiple causes. One is the tendency to blame the accumulation of problems on neglect by a previous regime rather than on the intractability of social reality. The initial euphoria and the image of widespread support, measured more by the crowds on the street and the festive mood than by votes, often give rise to the feeling that with good will all problems can be solved, particularly after a long dictatorial period. The leaders of the democratic regime have usually had time to think about the problems of the society and their solutions, but have not confronted the task of formulating them in precise terms and linking the solutions with specific facts in the face of the resistance they are bound to encounter. New democracies generally are instituted by coalitions in which even minor groups whose strength is still unknown might be represented and want a hearing. In multinational societies, the crisis of the previous regime and the unsettled future tend to weaken the central government and activate autonomist or even secessionist demands that have to be put on the agenda. The new leaders also might feel somewhat uncertain about their future strength, should the social forces identified with the previous regime recover their organizational capabilities, and therefore wish to legislate and even add their programmatic aspirations to the new constitution.

This desire to achieve fundamental changes in a society by legislative fiat is not matched by the resources to implement such changes. Any change of regime is likely to have some disturbing effects on the economy, and not infrequently this leads to a withdrawal of public credit, evasion of capital, and reduction of investment. Combined with the limitations in the attention span of government leaders absorbed in constitutional and legislative debates, who are coping with an unfamiliar bureaucratic machinery assisted by an unqualified staff, implementation of such a broad agenda tends to become practically impossible. The resulting disappointments and frustrations are likely to lead to conflict within the initial regime-building coalition.

Many of the changes that new regimes introduce are of a symbolic character: the change of flags, for example, is generally deeply felt only by a minority, but is hurtful to those attached to tradition.[50] Such changes may arouse enthusiasm at first, but since they do not represent tangible advantages for the supporters of the new regime, they do not constitute the kind of breakthrough or policies that might attach large sectors of society to the new order. They do become, however, an important rallying point for the disloyal opposition and contribute to a semiloyal attitude on the part of political groups hoping to win supporters from the disloyal opposition.

The new rulers also have a tendency, probably based on their feeling of moral superiority, to waste energy in what might be called *ressentiment* politics against persons and institutions identified with the old order.[51] This would consist in petty attacks on their dignity and their sentiments. Such measures are likely to be echoed at lower level, in administration and local government, particularly in the rural societies, and may even be used in settling personal accounts.[52]

Bitterness over symbolic changes and the emotional costs of *ressentiment* politics are not easily forgotten.[53] In such policies lodge the roots of disloyal opposition and latent ambivalence toward the regime that may become manifest years later at the time of serious crisis. Often the psychological shock that accompanies a regime change is greater than the actual social changes, and this accounts for the intensity of the hostility on the one side and the disillusion with the actual changes on the other.

In the consolidation phase of the democratic regime, therefore, an intelligent analysis of the political costs and benefits of each policy is particularly important. What is at stake is not the success or failure of a particular government but the formation of basic predispositions toward the regime. Much can be gained by selecting a limited number of problems and instituting at a relatively rapid pace reforms that will benefit and reassure a significant number of people at the cost of disappointing small and sometimes highly visible minorities. This is not easy, but some regimes have been fortunate. For example, in some Eastern European countries large-scale agrarian reform was possible because the large landowners were members of a foreign ethnic minority.

Foreign policy issues very often represent a heavy load for a new regime, which might at first find itself in relations of dependency with other countries. This was a particularly acute problem for Germany, Austria, and other successor states after World War I. The formation of the German Republic and full democratization accompanied defeat and the acceptance of the Versailles treaty, which led many Germans to deny legitimacy to the new regime and to feel a nostalgic loyalty to the old order.[54] This was particularly true among army officers and civil servants, and even among Protestant clergymen and professors. The statehood imposed on Austria, and the Allied prohibition of any unification with Germany, restated whenever the Republic found itself in economic difficulties, contributed to the illegitimacy of democracy among those with strong pan-German sentiments. As Paolo Farneti shows in his analysis of the Italian crisis, the cleavages created in all camps by interventionism, the cost of the war, and disappointment with the fruits of victory contributed much to the inability of Italian democracy-in-the-making to face the difficult readjustments in its economy and social structure after the war.[55] Dependency and economic nationalism in Latin America after World War II played a similar role.

Such issues seem to be particularly intractable in the consolidation phase because the identity of the state is at stake. Foreign commitments cannot be as easily reversed as internal policies, since they depend on outside powers not under the control of any future government, and a disloyal opposition can easily blame the system rather than a particular government for the constraints. In addition, the process of international negotiation is likely to lead to contradictory and ambiguous positions. Statements made for home consumption may differ from those made at the conference table, compromises are accepted with mental reservations, and expectations of revision begin to develop. An extreme example of such ambivalence can be found in the Fiume policies of Italian governments and the German rearmament in contravention of the Versailles treaty, policies that contributed to the emergence of highly politicized paramilitary groups that were tolerated by the authorities despite their protestations to the contrary.

Incorporation of Those outside the Regime-Founding Coalition

In our view, a new democratic regime can count on the intense loyalty of those who opposed the previous regime and first assumed power to create the new institutions. Contrary to what many analysts in sympathy with them believe, the number of those continuing to accord legitimacy to a fallen regime generally tends to be small. After all, the fall of the previous system is usually the result of a shift in loyalty by citizens of weak commitment, by the apolitical, as a result of a crisis of legitimacy, efficacy, or effectiveness. If these citizens had not shifted their allegiance, the previous rulers would have been able to resist the change and to rally at least enough support for a violent conflict with the challengers; this in turn would probably have led to a period of dictatorship rather than to a democracy. The period of consolidation, there-fore, is largely a struggle for the allegiance of those relatively uncommitted sectors of the population.

Unorganized, disoriented, even fearful at first, the uncommitted might join, or at least vote for, the more moderate sectors of the new regime-building coalition (in Germany, this was expressed as support for the Deutsche De-mokratische Partei). But given the opportunities for political organization provided by democracy, the growing awareness of their distinct interests, and the almost inevitable failure of governments in this phase, these unattached sectors may regroup behind new parties or even political figures from the previous regime. These new political forces are likely to question the deci-sions made in the name of a temporary majority and to win considerable support in subsequent elections. The problem for the builders of a new democ-racy is whether these challengers should be admitted as fully legitimate partic-ipants in the political process, or if their participation should be conditional upon their full acceptance of the changes introduced by the regime founders. This issue can divide the founding coalition and the political elite. Setting a high threshold for participation beyond the electoral level and excluding the principled opposition from many arenas is likely to make future cooperation in a crisis situation difficult. In some cases potentially loyal democrats, who do not support the substantive content that others want to assign to the regime, are pushed into a principled opposition and cooperation with the disloyal opposition, a tendency sometimes reinforced by the electoral system. An image of semiloyalty might result, and those parties at the other end of the spectrum in the regime-founding coalition will veto the entry of such forces into the government and violently criticize more centrist parties who are ready to incorporate them into the system. The result is a strong centrifugal tendency on the part of all participants and the fragmentation of parties (in extreme cases this becomes the "impossible game" as described by O'Donnell in Argentina after Perón).[56] The immediate result is deep personal antagonism between parties and the impossibility of forming a broad, shifting center coalition against extremists on both sides of the spectrum. Ultimately, the result is a weakening of the legitimacy of democratic institutions and the growth of both disloyal and semiloyal oppositions; if a serious crisis were to require a regrouping of the democratic forces, it might prove impossible.

We must emphasize the importance of defining the disloyal opposition clearly and at some stages isolating it politically, but this process can be successful only if there is concomitant readiness to incorporate into the system those who are perceived as at least semiloyal by some sectors of the regime-building coalition. Statesmanship, flexibility, and timing are badly needed at this stage, because the process of incorporation, which does not always represent a gain in efficacy, can be very important in the process of legitimation of an open, competitive democratic system.

Here again, continuity between the democracy and its predecessor regime is important. Political elites that have become known to each other, even developed a certain trust over years of parliamentary life, are more likely to accept such an incorporation than are adversaries who have no shared experiences in politics. The contrast between the relative stability gained by the Weimar Republic and Austrian democracy in the mid-twenties, and postwar Italy and Spain in the thirties, can be explained in part by the relative continuity of parliamentary personnel.[57] The emergence of two new parties, the Populari and the CEDA in the Latin democracies, representing a new form of Catholic participation in political life under a young, unknown leadership, was upsetting to the bourgeois liberals, while the effect of the Zentrum in Germany and the Christian Social Party in Austria was just the opposite.

Legitimation as a Problem for Democratic Leadership

In our introduction we advanced the proposition that, the higher the commitment in numbers and intensity to the legitimacy of the regime, the greater its capacity to survive serious crises of efficacy and effectiveness when confronted with unsolvable problems. Faced with problems of equal dimensions, a regime with a high commitment to its legitimacy has a higher probability of survival than a regime without such commitment. Legitimation, therefore, becomes the primary task of democratic leadership. Establishing the initial agenda in the period of consolidation, the negative consequences of *ressentiment* politics or foreign policy liabilities, and the difficulties of incorporating potentially loyal forces not in the regime-building coalition are all clearly relevant to this problem. There are, however, other dimensions that should be analyzed in the study of the consolidation of new democracies in order to account for their later weakness.

Democracies build their legitimacy on the basis of loyalty to the state or the nation. In fact, certain sectors of society, particularly army officers, civil servants, and sometimes intellectual leaders, feel a stronger identification with the state or the nation than with a particular regime and reject in principle the partisan identification of the state. Unless the regime is the result of widespread social mobilization of a revolutionary type that allows it to reject the idea of continuity of the state, this represents a serious problem.

One solution that can be successful is a purge of those unwilling to make a clear and public commitment to the new political order. In fact, many analyses of the breakdown of democratic regimes blame the founders for not having carried out democratization (or penetration in terms of democratic loyalty) of such institutional sectors. However, to do so in modern societies that recognize acquired rights, and in liberal democracies that guarantee freedom of opinion, is far from easy. It is likely to result in ambivalent and contradictory policies that, instead of achieving the desired result, arouse the indignation of those affected.

In this area symbolic discontinuities that force public expression of otherwise unarticulated beliefs about the legitimacy of the system become crucial. Minor issues, like the changes of flag, national anthem, or ritual invocations, can often create incidents and bitter feelings, and help to crystallize a disloyal opposition. Supporters of the new regime sometimes find satisfaction in those symbolic changes, but in our view, stabilization requires the maximum continuity in the symbols of the state and the nation as a consensual basis between those committed to the new regime and those they intend to incorporate into it. Such symbolic continuity will make regime acceptance easier by avoiding emotion-laden choices in the initial stages.

Another serious problem faced by regimes, particularly democracies, in building legitimacy is posed by failure to define the boundaries of the state and the nation. In situations like that in Northern Ireland, any form of democratic majority rule will be perceived by the minority as oppression, and the loyalty of part of that minority to another nation-state makes even consociational solutions difficult. The question is not one of the legitimacy or instability of a democracy, but of a state. The problem exists, though in less extreme forms, for many multinational states, particularly when the state or the regime has been built largely by one nationality, like the Serbs in pre–World War II Yugoslavia, the Czechs in Czechoslovakia, and, historically, Castile in Spain. In these cases, full democracy must allow the expression of the nationalism of the periphery, and it permits not only autonomist or federalist demands, but secessionist demands. Tolerance for these demands, which is sometimes imposed by the international situation, creates almost unsolvable problems for democratic leadership.

The same is true when the nation is conceived as a broader entity than the state, including people across the borders. Such a conception accounts for the ambivalent loyalty of nationalistic pan-movements to democratic institutions, because these movements question the regime leadership's acceptance of the existing state boundaries. As the experiences in Italy, Austria, Weimar Germany, and to some extent Finland, show, the democratic leadership, with its ambivalence imposed by international pressure as well as its own policy commitments, contributes to the delegitimation of the system or at least some of its participants. Perhaps the democratic leadership in these situations ought to emphasize the state as a source of legitimacy, rather than the nation.

Let us not forget that Fascist appeal is based on the need to affirm national solidarity against a system that allowed cleavage and conflict of interest within the society. That democratic forces could, generally through gross distortion, be relabeled as anational because of their international links was important in the process of delegitimation of many democracies. This would apply to socialism with its heritage of internationalism and pacifism; the Catholic parties' links with the Vatican and an international church; the bourgeois business parties and their links with international capitalism; and obviously international communism, which, without sharing in power, was a beneficiary of democratic freedom.

All studies of revolutions and of the intelligentsia have pointed out the latter's role as legitimizers and delegitimizers of authority. As Pareto noted, ideological formulations by the clergy, and by intellectuals in the modern world, have been extremely influential in convincing the subject classes of their right to rebel and the ruling classes of their moral right to use force to defend an existing order.[58] Given the role of universities in the training of government officials, judges, and lawyers, and the role of journalists and writers in shaping public opinion in societies that guarantee freedom of thought and expression, the distribution of attitudes toward the legitimacy of the regime and the various sources of attack on it is bound to depend to a large extent on the climate created by these different sectors of the intelligentsia and the academic community. It could be argued that each political and social movement has the support of its own intellectuals, who therefore play only a secondary role, but Karl Mannheim, with his idea of the free-floating intelligentsia, would argue the contrary.[59] In spite of the partisan attachments of its intellectuals, every society includes some intellectuals whose standing, on account of their creativity or their literary, aesthetic, or scientific achievements, is special, and whose critiques of the political order play an important role in any legitimacy crisis. Freedom of expression, the rejection of censorship, the right to cultural, religious, and political heterodoxy, and the freedom of dissent have been and continue to be central concerns for intellectuals and artists. No political system today gives greater scope to those freedoms than democracies, even without discounting the occasional deviations from those norms, and certainly the regimes whose breakdown concerns us here allowed intellectuals to pursue their creative role. It should follow that a liberal democratic system would find widespread support in the intellectual community, but the evidence on the political role of intellectuals in many democracies in crisis shows that few took upon themselves the public defense of democratic liberal institutions against opponents from either the Right or the Left.

There are obviously important national differences resulting from the cultural, religious, and institutional traditions as well as differences between the academic, the literary, and the artistic sectors, and there are also differences that reflect changing historical situations. However, many of those differences account more for the Left/Right orientation of the intellectual critique of liberal democratic politics, their sympathies for one or another type of extremism, than for their identification with regime-supporting parties. The paradox of the ambivalence of intellectuals toward liberal democracy is not easy to explain,[60] although the following factors might account for it: the elitism of intellectuals and their hostility to the average man, who is, after all, the average voter; their dislike for politics based on self-interest rather than on ideas of a better society; their dislike for the professional politician, whom they often consider their inferior and whose lack of understanding and respect for their ideas they resent; and their unwillingness to accept the bureaucratic discipline and *cursus honorum* of modern mass parties, which reduces their influence as compared to that of trade union officials, men with experience in local government, or leaders of interest groups. Additional factors might be the frustration of intellectuals with the unwillingness of mass electorates and their representatives to devote resources to either high or avant-garde culture; their hostility to the influence exercised by powerful interests through the use of money for advantages in and through mass parties, in contrast to their own influence as men with creative ideas; the frustration of the expert with the pragmatic distortion of his best proposals; and last but not least, the bitter hostility against other intellectuals ready to serve those in power and subverting the critical role of the intelligentsia.

Even when intellectuals support the creation of democratic regimes, they soon adopt critical positions and withdraw from the political process. The literati, particularly artists, tend to become indignant with the banality of the routine political process. The second rank leaders of parties, the petty party officials, and the low-level rhetoric and demagoguery of electoral campaigns become the object of their ridicule. The *alltag* character of democratic politics contrasts with the potential for great historical transformations realized in other societies that serve as utopian points of reference. All such responses find an echo among students, and certain sectors of the educated and half-educated will simplify them to mobilize support against the system, which they feel has betrayed or failed to realize higher spiritual values, be they conservative or revolutionary. Those predispositions created by an intellectual climate are likely to reemerge for other reasons when the leaders of the regime fail in their tasks.

The ambivalence of many intellectuals toward competitive pluralistic liberal democracy has perhaps an even more profound origin. It is the basic moral ambiguity of a political system that legitimizes decisions on the basis of formal, procedural, legal correctness without distinction of content except respect for civil liberties and the equality before the law of all citizens, with no reference to substantive justice and no link to a system of ultimate values. In societies suffering from serious injustices and deep cultural cleavages, it is difficult to accord intellectual justification to a system in which the will of the electorate, the technicalities of the law-making process, and the decision of the courts can serve to maintain a social order that arouses moral indignation or, conversely, can allow a reformist majority to question an inherited value system. Democracy can be justified only by a particular turn of mind, founded, as Kelsen has already noted, on a certain relativism or on a pragmatism grounded in an empirical processing-coding based on an open cognitive structure, flexible elements, and weak affect, to use Sartori's expression.[61] It is far from evident that such an outlook will prevail when a society confronts difficult problems that cannot wait.

3.
The Process
of Breakdown

Unsolvable Problems and Crisis

Any political system, once established with a certain amount of legitimacy, can count on the passive obedience of most citizens and the more or less effective repression of violent challenges from a disloyal opposition by the forces of order. As long as the electoral strength or even the parliamentary representation of the disloyal oppositions does not constitute an absolute majority, and if the loyal parties agree on the desirability of the system's continuity, a democratic regime can survive. But before that point is reached, one or a number of crises will probably have undermined the consensus of the democratic parties and their capacity to cooperate. Such crises are the result of a lack of efficacy or effectiveness of successive governments when confronted with serious problems that require immediate decisions. In the last analysis, breakdown is a result of processes initiated by the government's incapacity to solve problems for which disloyal oppositions offer themselves as a solution. That incapacity occurs when the parties supporting the regime cannot compromise on an issue and one or the other of them attempts a solution with the support of forces that the opposition within the system perceives as disloyal. This instigates polarization within the society that creates distrust among those who in other circumstances would have supported the regime.

It is only a slight exaggeration to label such problems unsolvable, for a solution acceptable to a majority among the regime-supporting parties cannot be found, and meanwhile a large part of the politically and socially mobilized population becomes less willing to wait for effective action. This means that increasing numbers of the population withdraw legitimacy from the system and support disloyal oppositions, or at least advocate collaboration with them in search of a solution. In this context it is irrelevant that the problem might have reached such intensity because of the activities, particularly the violent activities, of the disloyal oppositions. In fact, the antidemocratic oppositions' strongest argument is their claim to be able to solve the problem and to obstruct any solution they find unsatisfactory. This process leads from the unsolvable problem to the loss of power, the power vacuum, and ultimately to the transfer of power or the polarization of society and civil war. There can be

no doubt that a polarized, centrifugal, multiparty system is both a consequence and a cause of such a process.

Given the constraints of the system, how does it happen that regimes come
to face problems that are unsolvable—or are at least perceived as such by a
majority? There are many reasons, and it would be presumptuous to attempt to
analyze them here in detail. Some are structural problems that perhaps no
regime can solve. Others might exceed the capacity of a regime trying not to
compromise democratic freedoms and processes. Still others might simply
become unsolvable because of the way in which the democratic leadership has
formulated them and its ability to implement certain solutions or overcome
certain constraints that should not be insuperable.[1] In societies, particularly
European societies, in which democratic regimes gained considerable stability, relatively few problems were of the structural type; many of the difficulties arose following decisions by the democratic leadership that made solutions
within the democratic framework impossible. Oversimplifying somewhat, we
can say that a regime's unsolvable problems are often the work of its elites.

Obviously some problems are caused by an absolute imbalance between a
society's needs and its resources that perhaps no government could resolve
without outside support. This is certainly the case in the poor, overpopulated
countries of the Third World, and no government committed to full respect for
democratic freedoms would be able to tackle them. These problems may
worsen if the structural difficulties are not recognized, if problems are blamed
on others, and if false hopes are created by the leadership. Intractable structural problems inherited from the past, however, might prove intractable only
in the short run, especially if the desired solutions are measured with reference
to other, more developed societies rather than with respect to the starting
point. Hirschman has rightly noted how a structural view of progress tends
toward a pessimism that discounts any relative progress and rejects anything
but an integrated, comprehensive, and simultaneous solution of all basic
problems.[2] Another fallacy would be the belief that no specific problem can or
should be tackled until power relations in the society have been completely
restructured and the groups perceived as obstacles to solutions have been
dispossessed or destroyed, without even exploring the possibility of solutions
bypassing or affecting those groups without destroying them. Ultimately this
is the position of maximalist marxist Socialism, convinced of the impossibility of cooperation with other parties within a democratic framework, unwilling to enter into the government and formulate specific solutions to pressing
problems, and even less willing merely to safeguard democratic institutions as
instruments of future solutions.

In an increasingly economically interdependent world, the solution of certain problems is beyond the decision-making capacity of many national governments. This has led and will increasingly lead to ultranationalistic and
voluntarist responses, which are likely to be associated with authoritarian
politics. There have been, and there will probably continue to be, conflicts

between states that might not be susceptible to immediate revision by peaceful means, or at least without the kind of mobilization of resources that would make a military threat credible. Democratic political processes make that kind of solution difficult and therefore expose a government committed to a revision of its international position and the boundaries of the state to principled attack by a nationalistic disloyal opposition.

A realistic appraisal of the situation and an unambiguous commitment to peaceful revision of the status quo, rather than the creation of ambiguous expectations through other solutions, might prevent many difficulties. Undoubtedly, as Clausewitz has emphasized in his classic analysis of war as the continuation of politics with other means, success depends on defining goals for the military leadership for which the political leadership can provide the necessary means, as defined by the military. If those means cannot be provided, pursuit of those goals must be renounced.[3] In fact, unless there is overwhelming consensus on the goals to be pursued by military means and success is relatively rapid, a democracy will face considerable questioning of methods like conscription, high casualties, and expenditures used to pursue a certain goal as well as increasing doubts about the value of the goal. In such a situation, democratic leaders may be tempted not to abandon the goal but to pursue it without demanding the necessary means from the society in the hope of reducing the opposition caused by the demands. This unwillingness to recognize the internal logic of the military instrument, to admit the impossibility of achieving military goals with the available means, is likely to have serious consequences for the stability of the regime. It means the inevitable alienation of the military leadership from the political leadership, because the military feels it has been made responsible for the failures of the politicians, who are unwilling to confront the society with the real choices.

Some of the most serious crises of democratic regimes have been caused by this kind of problem, particularly since democratic regimes must tolerate pacifists and even treasonous opposition to war. It was certainly a major contributing factor in the breakdown of the constitutional monarchy in Spain in 1923, in the final crisis of the Third Republic, which was provoked by the unwillingness of the army command to continue the war under a government moving outside metropolitan France, and in the rebellion that fortunately only led to the transformation of the Fourth into the Fifth Republic in 1958. This type of problem is not unique to democratic political systems, as recent events in Portugal show, but is particularly salient for them. It should be noted that the military challenge to civil authority is not necessarily based on a commitment to continue the war, but might in fact favor abandoning it in view of the impossibility of victory with the available means.

This example derived from the Clausewitz analysis exemplifies the basic source of unsolvable problems in our sense of the term—the setting by the political leadership of goals for which it is unable to provide the necessary means, and its unwillingness to renounce those goals once it becomes apparent that the means cannot be provided. That incapacity is often caused by the incompatibility of certain means with other goals that the leaders are either unable or unwilling to relinquish. In some cases, the leaders might be unaware of the impossibility of simultaneously pursuing incompatible objectives or values. Max Weber, in his *Science as a Vocation,* suggested that a central task for social scientists was to contribute to the rationality in human life by making explicit such conflicts between values and improving knowledge of the means-ends relations as well as of the indirect and often unanticipated consequences of using certain means.[4] The blindness of political leadership to some of these relationships springs from many causes, including ignorance and incapacity, although ideological rigidity, dependence on subleaders, expectations created in the electorate, and the constraints imposed by interest groups are the main causes. They can force the democratic leadership to face the difficult choice of pursuing ends and values to which it is committed, or to give them up, in part or temporarily, for the sake of the survival of democratic institutions.[5] Who is to argue that political leaders should sacrifice staunchly held policy goals, the interests of their followers, or their image of a good society for the sake of the persistence of political institutions that do not seem to serve the pursuit of those aims?

In view of this discussion, it should be no surprise that political leaders with strong commitment to an ideology or those identified with specific social interests are least able to give foremost consideration to the persistence of institutions. When ideological and social motivations become fused, as in the case of many Marxist Socialist leaders deeply concerned with the interests of the working class and the trade unions, or Catholic politicians combining an ideological view of society with an unquestioned loyalty to the church, unwavering commitment to a political system per se becomes extremely unlikely. The impossibility of solving a pressing problem within such confines leads easily to withdrawal from responsibility and semiloyalty to the system.

In a democracy, the leaders depend, particularly in a crisis, on the support of party organizations rather than the electorate. This often means responsiveness to the middle-level cadres (likely to be the most highly ideological) and leaders of special-interest groups, which makes the problem particularly difficult.[6] In some cases the increasing infiltration of interest groups at the grass-roots level by emerging leaders identified with one of the disloyal oppositions tends to further limit the political leadership's freedom of action in terms of system interests.[7]

Complex problems, particularly when faced by a fragmented leadership, lead to inaction or ambivalent solutions and afford the disloyal opposition the opportunity to attack the system and demand the power to implement simple solutions. Hitler stated it quite well when he said: "I will disclose to you what has raised me to my position. Our problems seemed complicated. The German people did not know what to do about them. In these circumstances the people preferred to leave them to the professional politicians. I on the other hand have simplified the problems and reduced them to the simplest formula. The masses recognized this and followed me.''[8]

The capacity of governments to handle problems is obviously limited; it depends on alternative strategies in contriving reforms, as described by Hirschman, and most governments can handle only particular types of problems successfully.[9] In fact, it could be argued that shifting coalitions, and consequently unstable governments, in a crisis-ridden society might build up a better record for the regime than would the same political forces facing all the problems. However, government instability, irrespective of some of the positive consequences it might have in terms of efficacy, is perceived by the society as both a sign and cause of regime crisis.[10] Success in handling difficult problems sequentially with changing coalitions within the regime is largely a question of timing.

Unsolved structural problems, therefore, undermine the efficacy and, in the long run, the legitimacy of the regime, but they are rarely the immediate cause of the breakdown. It is only when they become acute and demand an immediate response that they can become unsolvable. This can be brought on by rapid and massive changes in economic conditions, such as a deep depression, rampant inflation, or a negative turn in the balance of payments, defeat or stalemate in war, or when dissatisfaction is expressed in more than anomic violence, generally under the leadership of a disloyal opposition and accompanied by mass mobilization. The most serious crises are those in which the maintenance of public order becomes impossible within a democratic framework: when the regime needs to be reassured of the loyalty of the forces of repression, when the use of such forces against one or another group becomes impossible without endangering the regime-sustaining coalitions, and when the disloyal opposition is perceived as capable of mobilizing large parts of the population, or strategically located sectors of it, unless the problem is solved.

In the last analysis the breakdown is precipitated by what the constitutional tradition calls "states of emergency"—the need for extraordinary powers, the state of exception. As Carl Schmitt noted, with considerable exaggeration but also with insight, the sovereign is the one who can decide in the state of emergency.[11] At this point, when the problems are beyond the democratic sovereign, the transfer of loyalties to another sovereign takes place. And in Tilly's view, this transfer, broadly speaking, defines revolution.[12] Either a regime change or a change within the regime that implies a decisive reequilibration must take place.

The capacity of the regime-sustaining forces to handle such situations, however, derives from the accumulation of the resources of legitimacy over time and the record of its efficacy in previous crises.

Albert Hirschman's theory of loyalty unexpectedly parallels the Weberian concept of legitimacy and our application of it to the problem of stability.[13] Hirschman notes how demand of a product—in this case, support for a regime—is always likely to be a function not only of current but also, to some extent, of previous quality, because of inertia and lags in perception. In our terms, legitimacy is a function not only of current performance but of previous performance. As he writes, "Loyalty strongly reinforces this influence of past performance of the firm or organization on present behavior of the customers or members." Where Hirschman says "loyalty," "organization," and "members" we would say "legitimacy," "regime," and "citizens." The central theme of his analysis is that as the result of loyalty, members will stay on longer than they would otherwise do, in the hope, or rather the reasoned expectation, that improvement or reform can be achieved "from within." In our context, they will not shift their support to the disloyal opposition, but will continue to support the regime-sustaining parties and hope for a recovery of efficacy or effectiveness. This gives them a chance to implement adequate policies or, if nothing else, to gain time, allowing circumstances beyond the control of the government to improve. In this instance, regimes with a long history of stability have an advantage over new regimes.

Different regimes might be equally unable to find adequate solutions to such problems as unemployment caused by depression. But the initial strength of the disloyal opposition's blaming the problem not on a particular government, but on the system, the difference in degree of mobilization and violence expected, and the extent of trust in the unconditional loyalty of the forces of order against any challenger can make the problem unsolvable in one case and just a crisis in another. In sum, it is not the technical characteristics of the problems but the political context in which they are placed, the constraining conditions on the regime, and the alternatives offered by the existence of one or more disloyal oppositions that ultimately trigger the process of breakdown.

Crisis Strata and Their Location in Society and Politics

The extent to which individuals can be mobilized for either mass movement or violent action against the regime in a crisis varies widely from one society to another. The recent literature on why men rebel has assembled considerable empirical evidence, using the theory of mass society and research on the psychological processes underlying aggressive responses as a starting point. Sociological analysis and descriptive studies have focused on the facilitating conditions, particularly those legitimizing violent action and those enabling the organization and the success of such action. Unfortunately for our purposes, the research has been either on historical cases like the French Revolution and its nineteenth century counterparts or on agrarian unrest in Third World countries.

There are no systematic comparative data on the role of crisis strata and their impact in the democracies included in our analysis.[14] We have some basic statistics on unemployment that permit cross-national comparisons, but no similar data on the social impact of the Great Depression on the independent middle classes or the peasantry and even less systematic data linking those economic and social changes with the rates of political mobilization, particularly in the form of paramilitary partisan organizations. While it is possible to use biographical data to trace the impact of World War I, civil strife in the postwar years, and nationalist mobilization to defend the borders and to fight the Ruhr occupation in creating the core of activists of the Nazi movement, particularly those engaging in violent actions, we have no comparable analysis for the origin of North Italian squadrismo.

The presence in the crisis-stricken social groups of individuals who have leadership qualities, free time, experience with discipline, and skills in the use of violence is particularly important in accounting for the nature of the disloyal opposition and its possible course of action. In this context, a crisis affecting the Spanish upper and middle classes including important sectors of the landowning peasantry under the Republic did not produce a political movement like Nazism or even Italian Fascism. In Spain, the lack of participation in World War I and the resulting absence of a veterans' generation and reserve officers of middle-class backgrounds, as well as the smaller number of students who had not completed their educations and were under- or unemployed, limited the size of the potential leadership cadres for a Fascist movement. Consequently, social classes affected by the crisis of the Republic and threatened by the mobilization of the working class could not rely on a large number of Fascist activists and therefore had to turn to the army to defend their interests.

Political Violence and Its Impact

Except for the intervention of the armed forces, the takeover of power from democratic leaderships has rarely been the result of a direct attack like that described in the manual on coup d'état by Curzio Malaparte.[15] Hitler did not move into the Reichskanzlei as the result of a putsch. And Mussolini did not march into Rome to storm the Quirinal at the head of the Fascist legions, but, summoned by the king, traveled in a sleeping car. Violence did, however, play a major role in the breakdown of these democracies, not so much in the actual takeover as in the process of limiting their efficacy, contributing to their loss of legitimacy, and creating a loss of power and power vacuum. Unfortunately, the rich body of research on patterns and causes of violence fails to link such patterns with their consequences for regime stability.[16] In fact, countries that typologies classify as unstable because of the amount of political violence that characterizes them have not suffered regime change, while others characterized by less violence have gone through deep crisis and even change. What is more, not infrequently the violence erupts only as a result of an attempted regime change.

The literature makes even less effort to analyze to what extent the growing violence or fear of it is the result of the actions of the authorities, except for exploring the now-popular thesis that the repressive actions of government tend to make more victims than do the actions of the challengers, and that this might contribute to the mobilization for further violence. Perhaps because the literature has concentrated on cases in which violence for political purposes or with political consequences was the expression of grievances that scholars have been ready to consider justified, attention has centered on the dysfunction of attempts to repress it. Little attention has been paid to situations in which the authorities, the police, and the judiciary, even though disapproving of violent political acts, dealt leniently with them because they felt sympathetic to the motives of those engaging in them or hostile to their victims.[17] Nor has the literature focused much on the impact of decisions concerning violence and its punishment on the political process and the relationships between parties and actors in the political system. In our view, some of the delegitimizing consequences of violence can be found in the area of decisions made in response to violence.

We refer to such complex decisions as whether an act is considered to be political or to represent social grievances, or as one conceived by irresponsible madmen or common criminals, irrespective of their claims and the perception of particular sectors of society; judgment about whether to stop the first outbreaks of violence or to allow its perpetrators recognition by negotiating with them; and decisions about the amount and type of force to be used to repress violence, in particular the use of police, armed forces, and paramilitary groups supporting the government. Further complex decisions involve the degree and type of recognition to be given to the representatives of forces of order who died in the performance of their duty; responses in terms of declaring various levels of emergency and restrictions of civil liberties; actions to be taken against leaders who may have allied themselves with those engaged in violence, particularly if they hold parliamentary immunity; and decisions about whether recourse should be to the ordinary or special jurisdictions in particular military courts when the events took place under states of emergency granting powers to the military. Decisions must be made as to readiness to pursue individual actors whose guilt can be easily established and who sometimes are responsible for real atrocities, but inability or unwillingness to pursue political leaders who supported the guilty parties but whose guilt cannot be proven; as to pardon or execution of sentences in such situations and resolutions of internal conflicts within the government coalition and between government and head of state in such matters; actions and legislation limiting the freedom of parties to engage in activities that are likely to produce situations of violence, like certain types of demonstrations, provocative marches, or the wearing of uniforms, and the right of civil servants, particularly members of the police and armed forces, to belong to certain parties; and ultimately, as to whether to outlaw certain organizations and even political parties because of their illegal acts and their threat to civil peace.

All these decisions can undermine or strengthen the legitimacy, efficacy, and effectiveness of a government in relation to different sectors of the society and the political spectrum. But the capacity to make such decisions with positive results depends largely on the previous legitimacy, efficacy, and effectiveness of both the government and the regime. This constant interaction in a changing situation makes it equally difficult for social scientists to advance general propositions and for the politicians to face such ambiguous situations.

What is most important is that when the violation of the laws and violence is intended for political purposes, is condoned by a leadership with considerable following, and is not condemned by large sectors of society (even when not approved by them), a regime, particularly a centralized government, must respond; and it cannot, as in private crimes or even anomic social violence, ignore the political implications of its decision. For in a society with disloyal opposition at either end of the spectrum, the regime-supporting forces can be sure that whatever decision they take will be exploited by one side or the other, or even both, to undermine regime legitimacy. In these situations the semiloyalty of some political groups or leaders is likely to manifest itself and contribute further to an atmosphere of distrust and polarization.

The individual chapters in this volume will give considerable evidence of how decisions in this area, in one way or another, have contributed to the loss of authority of democratic regimes and their ultimate breakdown, not always to the benefit of those who created those crises.

Loss of the Monopoly on Organized Political Force

A chief characteristic of the modern state is the monopoly of legitimate force in the hands of the police and the military under the direction of the political authorities. When the decision to use force cannot be made by the political authorities alone, but requires the consultation or agreement of those in control of that armed force, then the government is faced with a serious loss of legitimacy. The same holds true when a government allows organized groups with paramilitary discipline whose purpose is to use force for political ends to emerge in the society. Such groups are likely to become more and more autonomous, to develop their own ideology and purposes, and in general to be unresponsive to democratically elected governments. Not even paramilitary organizations, created with government approval by parties identified as supporters of the democratic regime in order to oppose a disloyal opposition and support the government in an emergency, seem to be either effective or desirable in a democratic political system. Certainly the tolerance of a democratic regime for the creation of paramilitary organizations by disloyal oppositions creates a most serious threat to its existence. This tolerance constituted a decisive factor in the disintegration of democratic rule in Italy, Germany, Austria, and to some extent, Spain.[18]

Unique historical circumstances contributed to the emergence of paramilitary groups in the Europe of the interwar years.[19] For example, in Germany, Austria, Finland, and the Baltic countries the defense of border areas, particularly those of mixed ethnic composition, was taken over by citizen guards, created more or less spontaneously under the leadership of volunteer, demobilized reserve or retired officers. The fact that some of those countries were new nations without a professional army accounts for this pattern. In northeastern Europe the borders were to be defended against the Soviet Union, a fact of importance in understanding the political orientation of the groups so formed and the veterans' organizations that maintained their traditions. In the case of Austria and Germany the defeat and disintegration of the army, the limits imposed by the victors on the army, and its role and size were other factors.[20] Those groups were directed not only against border threats but also against more or less successful revolutionary or pseudorevolutionary attempts, like the short-lived Kurt Eisner reign in Bavaria.[21] They were organized as a result of the fears aroused by the Russian and Hungarian revolutions.

Given their weak resources, these new democratic states had to tolerate and, in a number of cases, rely on the support of such irregular organizations. These groups, however, developed a spirit of their own and became the core of ultranationalist and rightist paramilitary groups that led the hostility against not only the Communists but also the regime-founding moderate Socialists. Their members were to become National Socialists, active in the paramilitary SA and SS. In addition, in later years the high command of the army, with some support from the government, decided that these organizations and the militant veterans' organizations could form both the core of a reserve army for internal and external emergencies and an instrument to circumvent the limitations on military training imposed by the Versailles treaty.

The same was true in Italy, where many army commanders and some governments closed their eyes to or even encouraged nationalistic paramilitary organizations, like those involved in D'Annunzio's Fiume expedition or the Fascists in the disputed Italo-Yugoslav border area, bypassing involvement of the armed forces in order to avoid the wrath of allies who opposed Italian demands. That ambivalence toward politically organized violence was later extended to the Fascists in their struggle against domination by leftist organizations in the countryside in the red belt of the Po Valley.

In all these cases, government tolerance of the violent acts of the disloyal opposition increased as a result of the ambivalence of the authorities, the potential cost of suppressing the opposition, the links between the opposition and the regular army due to the presence of many former officers among their leadership, and the fear of the organization of paramilitary groups by the Left in response to their actions. Furthermore, if the regime-supporting parties were to create their own paramilitary organizations, the decision to outlaw such organizations fully would have had to be applied to them too, and this was another policy that encountered resistance. In addition, in Germany the differences in the political composition of the governments of the German states and their policies toward such organizations impeded the development of a single unified policy. One of the most serious consequences of the government's loss of the monopoly over the armed forces was its resultant dependence on the army in matters of internal order. The army high command was thus included in decision-making concerning armed disloyal oppositions.

Another case in point occurs when democratic governments or party leaders question the loyalty of the state's armed forces or even of lower government units. They then attempt to combat that threat by creating, encouraging, tolerating, or even talking about the creation of nongovernmental armed forces like the workers' guards, the *grupos de onze* in Brazil, or the *cordones industriales* in Chile. It would seem that in a democratic framework, the capacity of political groups and nonrevolutionary governments to create such forces is limited. Before they can be organized, the military establishment, realizing the threat, will strike against such governments, probably with greater unity than would otherwise be the case. The same is probably true for any policy encouraging the politicization of soldiers or noncommissioned officers as a preventive policy against a military putsch. Such measures are a clear indication of the government's or the regime's loss of legitimacy among the armed forces and are only likely to accelerate and reinforce that loss. In a modern society with a well-organized, professional military, defeat and repression of such forces is the most likely outcome, if not civil war, should the police or sectors of the army remain loyal to the government.

Little of the analysis of violence in recent literature has considered this twilight zone of encouraged or tolerated paramilitary organizations that become political factors, probably because the amount of violence as measured by the usual indicators might be small. Even though systematic data are lacking, the standard indicators of civil violence for the last years of the Weimar Republic probably would be lower than for the early years, but the visibility of political armies and the inability of the government to reestablish its monopoly over organized force boded ill for democracy.

In this context it should also be emphasized that the political significance of violence by both challengers and government agents depends very much on the response to violence by the institutions that must sanction it: parliament, respected organs of public opinion, and spokesmen of the elite. One-sidedness in excusing or condemning such acts is both an indicator and a cause of loss of legitimacy of participants in the political process. Our chapter on the Spanish case illustrates how such a process creates unsolvable problems for a regime, and how intelligent participants realized that this would accelerate the process of breakdown unless drastic decisions were made by the regime's supporters to stop it.

Paradoxically, a democratic regime might need a larger number of internal security forces than a stabilized dictatorship, since it cannot count on the pervasive effect of fear. Its reactions to violence require massive but moderate responses; only numerical superiority can prevent the deadly reactions of overpowered agents of authority. It needs to protect not only government leaders but opposition leaders and even one group of extremists against another. Reequilibration of democratic regimes probably requires intelligent responses to such challenges, including in some cases a redefinition of the tolerable limits of civil liberties.

Democratic Crisis and Multinational States

One assumption of any working democratic political system is that the loyalty of the citizens to the state, irrespective of regime or government in power, should be greater than their loyalty to another state either existing or in the making.[22] The legitimacy of the state within its territorial boundaries is a prior condition to the legitimacy of any regime and is particularly important in the case of a democracy that must guarantee civil liberties to all citizens. In a multinational state, when across the border lies another state and that considers them irredenta with which a significant number of its citizens identify, stability is seriously threatened. In such a case, especially should a strong nationalist movement with more or less veiled secessionist aims exist, democracy and perhaps even the state may lose viability. A stable political system assumes that citizens in all parts of the country should feel bound by the decision of the authorities and not give their loyalty to another state.[23]

The basic assumption of the democratic political process is that today's minority might in the future either become a majority by convincing those in the present majority to agree with them, or hope to become a majority as a result of slow changes in the social structure. That was the case of the labor parties whose hopes were pinned on the growing class consciousness of the workers and/or the growing number of proletarians in the Marxist sense of the word, i.e., those without ownership of the means of production. The same would be true for ideological parties of one or another character. The situation is quite different in the case of ethnic, cultural, or linguistic minorities, unless they can hope to assimilate the majority or unless decisions on the policies affecting them are delegated to self-governing local bodies, where they would constitute the majority. Unfortunately, even that might not be a solution in societies in which the national minority that is a majority at the local level faces a large-scale minority in its own region without any hope of assimilating it. Consociational mechanisms can reduce the inevitable tensions in this case, but as any reader of the growing literature on consociational democracies will realize, the preconditions established for their success are not always present and are not easily achieved.[24]

In fact, we would say that the principle of nationality—cultural and linguistic nationalism in multinational states, particularly those with a dominant national culture and identity and without a clear territorial separation of the different communities—is not likely to lead to stable democracies. Perhaps constant renegotiation of the processes of assimilation that assure homogeneity of political subunits might allow the creation of a multinational state in which the basic sentiment would be one of loyalty to a state rather than a national identification.[25] Unfortunately, in the modern world the aim seems to be to build nations rather than states, a task that is probably beyond the capacity of any state that has not achieved the characteristics of a nation-state before the era of nationalism. In an age in which all national cultures or languages are in principle considered equal, in which all occupational roles are increasingly linked with the use of language in writing, and in which people increasingly live in large, heterogeneous urban centers in constant communication with public and private bureaucracies, mass media, etc., it is impossible to build a nation on the basis of cultural homogeneity. The federalists and advocates of regional or local community self-government would say that this is no major problem if the central authorities are ready to devolve many matters, if not most, to subunits. Without entering into the question of whether a modern industrial economy and state organization can function effectively and equitably with such decentralization, the problem remains unsolved if this devolution means only a transfer of the problem from a national level to a lower unit of government. Certainly, decentralization can make possible the coexistence of multiple nationalities within the territory of one state and avoid the permanent minority status of a particular group by making it the majority in its territory. The trouble starts when such a policy makes another group a permanent minority within that autonomous territory, as it frequently does. This is likely to be the case in most multinational states, since centuries of coexistence, internal migrations, assimilation to dominant culture, loss of cultural identity of important segments of the population, and the advantage of more powerful languages are likely to have destroyed the cultural homogeneity of the subunits. Furthermore, the processes of rapid economic development, industrialization, and the differentials in birthrate between the developed and less-developed regions are likely to produce large-scale internal migrations from the less-developed to the more highly developed parts of the country, further reducing the homogeneity of the sub-units. This inevitably means that in any subunit to which autonomy is granted there will be permanent minorities who will feel the same way about their status as the former minority felt in the national political unit. The democratic process with its civil liberties cannot itself guarantee, either de jure or de facto, the rights of such a minority against subtle discrimination and efforts at assimilation. If the majority is committed to increasing the national cultural homogeneity in its territory, and the minority is committed to retaining its distinctive cultural heritage, a large number of policy issues are likely to become sources of conflict. Prosperity permits certain solutions—the multi-plication of all public services in different languages, for example—but in a poor country some of those solutions are not available. In addition, as the sociolinguists have stressed, there is likely to be a ranking of the languages, a segregation of spheres of use, that ultimately implies an inequality that is likely to be intolerable for one or another group and will lead to efforts to redress the situation by political means.[26] A permanent minority of this type has no redress against a majority committed to its own values except appeal to the power of outside authorities, with the inevitable consequence of political and constitutional conflicts that will be extremely difficult to solve. If, in addition, that minority can call on the support of a power outside the state, its actions will be particularly threatening and will probably lead to legal and illegal actions incompatible with the free society. Secession, either to join another state or to transform the nation into a nation-state, is the likely con-sequence. The coexistence of different populations in the same territory, how-ever, is likely to leave the new state with the same heritage.

It is clear that democracy does not provide an easy answer to the question of under what conditions secession is legitimate, inevitable, and viable. Who is to define the territorial boundaries of the unit to secede, what sort of majorities are to be required, and what guarantees should be given to the remaining new minorities? Sometimes history provides boundaries in which the decision-making process can take place, but those historical borders are often far removed from the cultural and linguistic borders and the feelings of identity that have developed over time. Shall the units in which a majority for seces-sion should be allowed to carry the day be the whole region, provinces, municipalities, or neighborhoods? The larger the unit, the larger the number of minorities that will be tempted to secede from the new state; the smaller the unit used in making the decision democratically, the less likely it is that this newly emerging state will be viable in terms of geographic boundaries, eco-nomic resources, communications, and historical identity. What should be done about the geographical enclaves in the midst of the new state or in its large, heterogeneous cities that have resulted from assimilation and/or internal migrations? One answer has been the transfer and exchange of populations that has been done on a massive scale after wars of conquest and defeat in Eastern Europe and between Greece and Turkey after World War I. However, with minor exceptions, such transfers have been carried out without asking the people involved if they wanted to move or stay where they had always lived. It does not seem very democratic to impose such a decision by force even when it appears legitimate to make people choose. The realities of modern developing economies, however, are unlikely to allow large-scale relocation as a permanent solution, and commitment to the equality of languages and cultures is not likely to allow a policy of discrimination in favor of assimilation.

In a world rife with nationalism there are no easy solutions, and perhaps no solutions at all, to these dilemmas within the context of a liberal society. This accounts for the instability of the democracies in multinational states.[27] It also accounts for the likelihood that one or another group will turn to outside intervention to protect its interests, to the imposition by authoritarian regimes, or at best to the coordination of multinational units by an elite identified with a larger political unit and not responsive to nationalistic demands from the people. Any of those likely responses to the problems of a multinational state means the end of democracy, if democracy is taken to mean rule by the majority with respect for the rights of the minority and opportunities for the latter to participate in the decision-making process.

Even when the nationalistic sentiments of the majority do not favor such exclusivistic and ultimately secessionist solutions, the problem is far from easy to handle within the framework of a multinational democratic state. In such a state, even when it is supported by majorities, both in the subunit and the larger political unit, who are making reasonable compromises on policy issues, there are likely to be powerful minorities questioning, sometimes violently, any solution except full independence. There are likely to be other minorities ready to maintain the larger unit as a state or to engage in nation-building by assimilation and even force. Unfortunately, when such extremist minorities are repressed by one or another political unit, they are likely to find varying degrees of support even among those opposed to maximalist solutions, particularly when an effort is made to repress them as well. The interplay between a secessionist ultranationalist minority and moderate nationalist movements, accommodating parties at the center and extremist unitary parties at the center, imposes a heavy strain on a democratic state. The secessionist and the unitary centralist minorities have an easy target in the moderates at the periphery and at the center, and their attempts to find compromise solutions will be considered illegitimate, if not treasonable, by the extremists. That interaction is likely to be even more complicated when any of those four political alignments is divided by other issues like class or the religious-secularist cleavage, a division that is likely to occur in economically advanced countries. In that case, cooperation on the national question between the moderates at the center and those on the periphery, who take opposite sides on other issues, is likely to be difficult, and the temptation to collaborate with moderates and even extremists in the opposition in one or the other unit increases. This would be only natural for democratic political parties, but it acquires a different significance when a regional nationalist government of one political coloring allies itself with an opposition at the center, or the central government allies itself with a regional opposition supporting its demands against the regional government. In such a context, normal conflicts of interest and ideology acquire an additional intensity and meaning through interpretation either as secessionist threats or as an effort to undermine regional autonomy. Tempers are likely to flare, and normal constitutional conflicts may be perceived as threats to a regime, if not the state. The normal democratic mechanism of decision by shifting majorities is not likely to enjoy a particular legitimacy in such a context.

If we add appeals to neighboring countries sympathetic to the peripheral nationalisms for their own reasons—linguistic or ethnic affinity, or just plain power politics—the instability is likely to increase, and the predisposition to take repressive measures against minorities perceived as semi- or disloyal will be reinforced. Such measures are likely to intensify the tension. The presence of mixed populations with divided loyalties complicates the picture even further. Defense of their interests and their manipulation by the central government offers an opportunity to challenge the democratic representativeness of the regional government and parties.

It is no accident, therefore, that few multinational states have been stable democracies. This, in addition to many other factors, accounts for the lack of consolidation of Eastern European and Balkan democracies in the interwar years and those of many Third World countries outside Latin America after independence. Our decision to limit the cases to be included in this volume to relatively stable states that were, for most of their citizens, nation-states, does not allow us to pursue this complicated problem. The chapter on Spain provides some evidence of the contribution of multinationalism to the crisis of a democracy, although class and ideological conflicts were ultimately more decisive in that case. The ambiguity of statehood versus nation was, as Walter Simon has shown, one of the problems of the First Republic of Austria.[28] Even without a specifically nationalistic component, the conflicts between the Länder and the Reich in the Weimar Republic, particularly the rightist stronghold in Bavaria, and the memory of secessionist efforts after World War I, like those in Rhenania, contributed to the worsening of the political climate in Germany.[29] From this perspective it would have been very desirable to analyze the Czechoslovakian case as a combination of internal and external pressures endangering democratic stability; in fact, in view of such problems the relative stability of that new Central European democracy appears even more worthy of study from a theoretical point of view.

Crisis, the Democratic Party System, and Government Formation

Inability of the regime-sustaining forces to find solutions to pressing problems when faced with disloyal oppositions and increasing violence is reflected in government instability and growing difficulty in forming coalitions; in the fractionalization and subsequent fragmentation of parties; and in shifts in the electorate toward the extremes. These three processes tend to be interrelated and mutually reinforcing, and therefore the acts of the regime leaders aimed at preventing them can be essential steps in the process of reequilibration in the face of crisis.

The three processes often inaugurate a new phase, characterized by loss of power and a transfer of authority to ademocratic elements in the constitution. This is a result of the abdication of responsibility by democratic leaders and their growing dependence on the support of state structures that are more permanent or less immediately dependent on the electorate. Ultimately, the sequence of events is likely to lead to a reduction of the political arena and the growing influence of small, ill-defined groups. In these later phases different political forces begin to consider the possibility of coopting disloyal oppositions, as they are unable or unwilling to isolate and repress them.[30] In this stage even regime-supporting parties attempt to act semiloyally to the regime. This sequence of events that we have described is not inevitable, but becomes increasingly probable; it represents a downward road, a narrowing of alternatives, a funneling process that ultimately must be resolved by a change of regime or, in the best of cases, a solution within the regime.

Let us focus on the more immediate consequences of the crisis for the party system and its capacity to produce stable, efficacious governments and consequently to retain the loyalty of a sufficiently large segment of the electorate.

Problems that fit our characterization of being unsolvable put the government on the defensive. Parliamentary debates require increased attention, while other issues are likely to be neglected. Those members most responsible for policy failures are likely to resign. Latent tensions within and between government parties become explicit, and cabinet reorganization follows. Such problems may be more serious and visible in the case of multiparty coalition governments. Certain component members, particularly minor parties on the extremes of the spectrum within the coalition, begin to reconsider their commitment and explore alternative coalitions or a temporary withdrawal from responsibilities of government. The same would hold for one of the major parties if its interests and expectations were negatively affected. Concern for the electoral consequences of continuing in government might lead such parties to withdraw from direct governmental responsibility. Whenever the head of state has the constitutional power to dissolve parliament and call new elections, he faces a choice between a realignment of coalitions, a minority government of lowered efficiency, or dissolution.

What we have been describing is a normal process in parliamentary democracies, and the outcome might well be a realignment of forces within the spectrum of democratic parties as has occurred so often in the Third and Fourth French Republics and postwar Italy. The existence of a real political force in the center, with *Koalitionsfähigkeit* on both sides of the spectrum and sufficient parliamentary strength, can make it workable even for prolonged periods of time. It may lead, however, to limited efficacy of the system and internal erosion of the dominant Center party.[31]

For many reasons, the impossibility of such a solution in extremely fragmented, centrifugal, multiparty systems without elections on fixed dates leads to dissolution and a shift of the decision to the electorate. In societies where the parties have penetrated the whole electorate and created subcultures that allow only minor shifts of independent voters, and where there is widespread consensus that certain extremist parties constitute a disloyal opposition and should remain isolated, the outcome might not differ much from that of the elections preceding the crisis. In these situations the voters realize that there is no real alternative, and the appeal of the democratic parties is based on the rejection of both extremes more than on the accomplishments of the regime-supporting parties. The more or less minor realignments that result can keep the system going. The situation changes decisively, however, when the disloyal oppositions make considerable electoral gains. As a result, the system parties may feel that they should stay out of the government in order to be better able to compete with disloyal oppositions and to be free to join the opposition to the weakened government coalition.

If the cycle just described takes place several times in relatively rapid succession, without a reequilibration effort through formation of a regime-supporting coalition at the governmental or electoral level, a loss of efficacy and ultimately of the legitimacy of the regime may result. The last three years of the Weimar Republic exemplify this process, even though Hindenburg's electoral success, founded on the support of the democratic parties against the extremist candidates, indicated a certain potential for reequilibration. A good example of the opposite response to what might have become a regime crisis occurred in Belgium in 1936, when parties rallying behind Van Zeeland in a byelection caused a setback to the Rex party.[32]

The causes of extreme multipartism with centrifugal tendencies have been the subject of considerable study. Obviously, the complexity of the social structure and the multiple cleavages that result, the persistence of ideological traditions, and the divisive consequences of ideological politics are the main factors. A feeble electoral system, particularly one with pure proportional representation, exercises no restraint on the voters, and in the case of a feeble party system it furthers the persistence of fragmentation. In the case of a fragmented and polarized multiparty system with an electoral law that does not reward efforts at cooperation by the system parties, but fosters competition among them in addition to their activities against the disloyal oppositions, the calling of new elections is not likely to be of much help in solving the crisis. After all, electoral competition will probably bring out the differences in interests and ideological commitments of the regime-supporting parties, making their collaboration afterward even more difficult. Furthermore, by blaming the regime rather than a particular party, and by offering simplistic solutions that they will not be called upon to implement, the antisystem parties can benefit from the discontent of the electorate and make the system even more unworkable. They can ultimately achieve a negative majority that makes parliamentary government based on a majority principle almost impossible, and they can make governments dependent on the confidence of extra parliamentary powers. All the evidence points to the conclusion that in a crisis situation democratic parties are subject to very special strains that lead to fragmentation, withdrawal from responsibility, and mutual vetoes.

Fragmentation can become manifest in increased factionalism within parties that becomes visible at party congresses and leads to successive splits that increase the number of parties. The decisions necessary in a crisis situation force latent cleavages based on ideology, interest-group linkages, and personalities into the open. Crises impose decisions running counter to ideological commitments of the parties and sacrifices by closely linked interest groups, and they open up opportunities for struggles among leaders. Uncertainty about the reaction of a discontented electorate encourages such responses, as well as competition with neighboring parties, and creates among the leaders expectations of forming alternative coalitions. Even when this political fluidity might allow a disaggregated sequential solution of problems with shifting coalitions (as was the case in the Fourth Republic in France), it also creates in the public's mind an image of instability, lack of principle, dependence of parties on interest groups, opportunism, and struggle for personal power among leaders.

Events that would have a limited impact under normal circumstances serve to crystallize such tensions in crisis situations. Among them the historical record signals the importance of problems of public order and the indecisive or excessive responses to them by the agents of the government for which its leadership is made responsible; financial or personal scandals affecting the image of parties and leaders; the highly loaded issues of amnesty or execution of sentences, particularly death sentences, for political crimes; and the complex issues created by the division of power between executive, legislative, and judicial branches—in parliamentary systems, the relationship with the president or king. These problems in and of themselves might not be unsolvable in our sense, but they provide a dramatic scenario for the political rhetoric and moral indignation likely to divide the political class. To them we might add the suspicions created by alliances between leaders or parties with forces or institutions that can interfere with the political process, often called indirect powers, such as the church, the Vatican, Masonry, big business, high finance, and foreign powers.

Some readers may be surprised that our analysis does not deal with external intervention—overt or covert—in the breakdown process, particularly in view of the recent emphasis on this factor in the cases of Greece and Chile. In response to such criticism we would argue that without internal processes leading to a crisis of a regime, such interventions—short of military invasion—would not occur, much less be successful, in established nation-states. They might contribute to some extent to the final outcome, but they are not the cause of the crisis, nor are they likely to be the main variable in the process. Furthermore, the classic cases, like the rise of Fascism to power, the breakdown of the Weimar Republic, and the events leading to the military uprising in Spain in 1936 (not the prolonged Civil War), were unrelated to any foreign intervention.

Abdication of Democratic Authenticity

One not infrequent consequence of the loss of cohesion in regime-supporting coalition parties is the effort to remove highly conflictive issues from the arena of partisan politics by transforming them into legal or technical questions. The aim is to gain time, since legal solutions are notoriously slow. Typically, questions of constitutionality are raised about certain laws and decisions, and issues are referred to constitutional courts. The legitimacy of having judicial bodies make what are essentially political decisions in a democracy is always doubtful, and in countries where judicial bodies have been established only recently, their judgment is even less likely to be considered binding. Another device is to substitute experts and high-ranking civil servants for representatives of the parties in politically exposed positions and to take refuge behind the technical nature of the decisions. Economic policy may be left in the hands of a presumably apolitical director of a central bank, and more and more cabinet posts are assigned to nonparty ministers or civil servants, allowing the politicians and the parties to avoid responsibility. Party leaders might participate in government as individuals without the mandate of their parties, which accordingly are not obliged to support their initiatives. The most powerful party leaders refuse to accept the prime ministership or to help form coalition governments. They delegate their responsibilities to second-level leaders, who are presumably ready to do their bidding, generally without independent authority or prestige, and are sometimes of limited ability.[33] The ambiguous relations between those second-level leaders and the men for whom they stand in, and their difficulties in communicating, plus the nurturing of their ambitions by other leaders, further complicate the political process. The result is a lessening of the authenticity of democratic institutions, particularly the power and responsibility of parliament.

In such situations the influence of the head of state, be it president or king, increases. He will be tempted to use his own judgment, which will lead to more government instability and often the calling of new elections. The growing influence of the head of state, the judiciary, the higher civil service, and sometimes the heads of the armed forces represents a shift of power from the democratically accountable leadership—a shift to what Carl Schmitt calls the neutral powers: nonpartisan, above party sources of authority—and with it the denaturation and loss of substance of the democratic process.[34]

In societies where important institutions—particularly the army, but also the civil service and other groups—feel a strong identification with a continuing center of authority identified as the "state" and distinct from the parties, these changes justify authoritarian tendencies. Rainer Lepsius, in his chapter, has shown how the possibility of interpreting Article 48 of the Weimar Constitution broadly facilitated the abdication of responsibility by the leading democratic parties, created the "impossible game" of presidential cabinets and emergency legislation, and encouraged ideological tendencies toward antidemocratic, authoritarian, bureaucratic rule consistent with the pre-1918 tradition. In Germany this solution proved too unstable to withstand a dynamic disloyal opposition led by a charismatic figure capable of rallying broad support for a silent revolution early in 1933.

A unique transition to authoritarian rule took place in Estonia and Latvia in the thirties. These were two of the smaller European democracies, born in 1918 on the border of the Soviet Union, close to Finland culturally, and oriented toward the West. Both had attained relatively homogeneous social structures after successful agrarian reforms, which reduced the initial radicalization of the Russian Revolution.[35] It was not the challengers of the extreme Right or the extreme Left who interrupted the normal functioning of their democratic institutions, nor was it the armed forces. Rather, it was the democratically elected leaders: President Päts in Estonia and President Ulmanis in Latvia. There seemed to be two main alternatives: instability with a democratic framework, due to the presence of important Fascist movements and governmental instability, due to the large number of small parties (multiplied, particularly by Latvia, by those representing ethnic minorities, and by proportional representation) and the impact of the world economic crisis; *or* an authoritarianism with roots outside the established political framework, which would probably have resulted in a Fascist regime. The leaders of the democratic parties, using the prestige they had gained during the struggle for independence, overcame the threat posed by a nonparliamentary right wing by establishing authoritarianism in order to thwart it. The last democratic cabinet, executing a bloodless palace coup, presided at the autodemise of democracy in 1934.

A particular case of abdication and loss of democratic authenticity, sometimes suffered in an effort to reequilibrate a system in crisis, is the effort by political leaders to seek the support of military command by offering cabinet posts or even the prime ministership to leading officers. This is a way of asking for an explicit pledge of support, but it indicates that the normal, implicit loyalty of the armed forces is in doubt. This will inevitably lead to a heightened politicization of the officer corps and will ultimately force it to decide whether it is willing to continue supporting the regime in the same way that a party gives support through the participation of its ministers in a coalition. This will heighten the internal ideological divisions within the officer corps and will ultimately force a decision about the legitimacy of the government, and perhaps the regime.[36]

Salvador Allende's decision to persuade the three armed forces chiefs to enter the cabinet in response to the crisis in the commercial supply system and the first truckers' strike is a good example. They defined their participation as nonpolitical, designed merely to defuse the situation and guarantee honest congressional elections. General Prats insisted that their presence be only temporary, since he felt it was "dangerous for the armed forces to appear linked to a government where ideologies are so defined." A majority of the officers opposed that political role which they felt compromised their professional character.

These processes are all more likely in a crisis situation, but in our view, they are not inevitable. They are generally chosen as temporary devices, as delaying actions, without full awareness of their long-term implications. Leaders of democratic parties who are ready to formulate policies and confront their followers with the real alternatives, to demand obedience and pose the question of confidence, to confront powerful interests even within their own constituency and overcome ideological rigidities and personal feuds, can gain a broad base of public support. Even at this stage the process of loss of authenticity of democracy is often a question of failure of leadership.

Excursus on Presidential and Parliamentary Democracies

Our emphasis on the role of "neutral" powers, based on the roles of King Victor Emmanuel and Hindenburg, but also of Shinfrud in Finland and Coty in France, rests on the European experience. Rereading our analysis, we realize that there is an obvious difference between parliamentary or semiparliamentary regimes like the Weimar Republic and presidential systems like the United States and the Latin American republics. The directly elected presidents, with their own democratic legitimacy and strong executive powers, who are free to appoint a cabinet that does not require a vote of confidence from the legislature, obviously occupy a totally different position in the political system. In a sense, the Reichspräsident in the Weimar constitution and the current French president occupy an intermediate and hybrid position.

Impressed by the stability of the paradigmatic presidentialist democracy in the United States, and the recurrent crises and critiques of parliamentarism, scholars have asked few questions about the relationship between these two major constitutional types of democracy and political stability. The almost automatic commitment to presidentialism within the Latin American constitutional tradition, and the more recent predominance of behavioralist sociological analyses of Latin American politics, has led to an almost total neglect of the role of presidentialism in political instability south of the Rio Grande. The earlier literature in particular is full of references to "caudillismo," "personalism," and "continuismo," but those phenomena are interpreted in historical and cultural terms rather than linked to institutional arrangements and constraints. The hispanic cultural tradition, the negative image of European, particularly French, parliamentarism held by Spanish-speaking intellectuals, and for a long time, their admiration for the United States constitution, did not encourage questions about the virtues of presidentialism. On the other hand, Americans, satisfied, on the whole, with their constitution, were not likely to attribute any share in the recurrent crises of most presidential regimes (which happen to be Ibero-American or African) to the institution of the presidency. This dual outlook is also reflected in the contributions to this volume.

However, when reviewing the cases included in our purview, a question came to mind: Does presidentialism have something to do with the political instability of Latin American democracies? The question was triggered in part by a comparison—admittedly a very superficial one—between Italy and Argentina. In both we find antisystem parties, the Communists and the Peronists, with relatively similar proportions of the vote (at least in the years following the fall of Perón). Both are linked with powerful trade unions and are distrusted by large sections of the society and by the Establishment, but the consequences of their presence have long been very different. It would be too much to say that the ideological distance between the Peronists and other parties and social groups was larger (at least until recently) than that between the PCI and the Christian Democrats or the Liberals, to say nothing of the neo-Fascists. Reading Guillermo O'Donnell's description in this volume of the "impossible game," particularly in the Frondizi period, one might ask oneself: Why has the Italian political game been less "impossible"?

In answer, we might consider the following hypothesis. The presidential election "game" has a zero-sum character, whereas a parliamentary system offers the possibility of dividing the outcomes. Parliamentary elections present many options: formation of coalition governments; cooperation between government and opposition in the legislative process, either overtly or covertly; and the potential for gains by opposition parties in successive elections (particularly in centrifugal multiparty systems). This reduces the frustrations of the loser, creates expectations for the future, and often allows the loser a share in the power. In a presidential system, in which the winner of a plurality of 33.1 percent gains control of the executive office for a fixed period in time and dispenses relatively freely the power to appoint all high officers, to introduce legislation, and to veto the proposals of the legislature, the opposition is likely to feel impotent and even enraged. An opposition that was divided in the election has many reasons to come together after defeat; in turn, the incumbent is likely to fear frustration of his program and feel that at the end of his term he might well face defeat. The unipersonal magistracy, the plebiscitarian character of the election, and even the contrast between the national scope of issues debated in the presidential contest and the localism, clientelism, and possible corruption of legislative elections—all these factors are likely to give the president a sense of power, of having a mandate that is likely to exceed his real support, and will exacerbate his irritation when he is faced with a legislature unwilling to respond to his leadership. Some of the factors we have just mentioned were certainly present in the crises of Brazil under Goulart and Chile under Allende.

"But why not in the United States?" one might ask. However, we should not forget the fragmentation of the U.S. political arena between federal and state governments, the strong institutional position of the Supreme Court, the prestige of the Senate, and—a factor often ignored—the bipartisan recruitment of many officials (including the Cabinet) and the bipartisan formulation of certain policies in the United States. After all, political scientists have called for "responsible party government" because, to a large extent, American government is not party government.

In the case of polarization of ideology or interest, the zero-sum character of the presidential game undoubtedly introduces pressures to limit its consequences: no reelection, the attempt of the legislature to veto or filibuster the decision-making process, efforts to use the courts to limit the power of the president, the resistance of state governments (particularly when headed by powerful governors who are popularly elected and belong to a different party), often even the separate election of presidents and vice presidents of different parties or coalition, and finally, the intervention of the armed forces as "poder moderador." All those devices lead to constitutional conflicts that weaken the system, endanger its legitimacy, and frustrate presidents who feel that they have a direct, popular, plebiscitarian mandate. (Of course, this mandate is often only a plurality that in a parliamentary regime would oblige them to work with the opposition or act as a "tolerated" minority government.) On the other hand, a large segment of the electorate, identified with a popular president, understanding little about all those maneuvers or legal constitutional battles, is likely to feel frustrated by those it perceives as a "minority" identified with vested interests. In view of all this, even when the ideological distance between supporters of a president and his opposition might be the same or smaller than the distance between government parties and the opposition in a parliamentary system, the conflict might be more intense.

Another difference between presidential and parliamentary systems, be they constitutional monarchies or republics, is that there is—with the exception of the courts, who are often weak—no moderating power. A king or president in Europe can respond to a change in the constellation of political forces in parliament; the power of dissolution or the threat of its use can lead to a restructuring of the government in a critical situation; and a government leader who has failed can generally be replaced, with his cooperation. A president, in contrast, is elected for a fixed period, and his ouster involves a constitutional crisis. This helps to explain why the military frequently assume the "moderating" function. They are often encouraged by a frustrated opposition and feel "legitimated" by constitutional provisions making them the defenders of the constitution.

The differences we have noted may contribute to an understanding of why there were a number of transitions from democracy to nondemocratic rule in Europe that took place semi- or pseudo-constitutionally, and even at the time were not perceived as a break in democratic legitimacy. Let us not forget how many observers viewed the advent of Mussolini to the premiership. A manifesto of the Partito Communista Italiano issued on 28 October (*L'Ordine Nuovo*, 29 October)—a day before the arrival of Mussolini in Rome as premier designate—reaffirmed the equivalence of the Fascist and a democratic solution. Two days later, *Rassegna Communista* wrote: "We deny that the coming to power has any revolutionary character or any remote similarity to a coup d'état. . . . A coup d'état overthrows one leading class and changes the fundamental laws of a state; until today the Fascist victory has renewed the cabinet." Nenni, the Socialist leader, reminiscing in 1964, wrote: "Everyone in Italy agreed in not taking Fascism seriously."

In the case of presidential regimes, such a *Machtübergabe*—like those in Germany and Austria at the end of World War I, the appointments of Mussolini and Hitler, or the change from a Labour government to a National government under MacDonald—would not have been possible. To change the government in a presidential regime when the president is unwilling—and few are likely to be willing to relinquish the office—requires a break with the rules of democratic election of the chief executive: government crises almost by definition become regime crises. And although some political scientists might be ready to say that military intervention of the "poder moderador" is the functional alternative to reshuffling a parliamentary coalition, the two are not equivalent in terms of democratic legitimacy and the stability and legitimation of institutions of popular government.

In view of these considerations, perhaps the consequences of the "presidential" versus the "parliamentary" game in democracies deserves further and more systematic analysis.

4.

The End
of Democracy

Loss of Power, Power Vacuum, and the Preparation for a Transfer of Power or Confrontation

Unsolvable problems, a disloyal opposition ready to exploit them to challenge the regime, the decay of democratic authenticity among the regime-supporting parties, and the loss of efficacy, effectiveness (particularly in the face of violence), and ultimately of legitimacy, lead to a generalized atmosphere of tension, a widespread feeling that something has to be done, which is reflected in heightened politicization. This phase is characterized by the widespread circulation of rumors, increased mobilization in the streets, both anomic and organized violence, toleration or justification of some of those acts by some sectors of society, and above all, increased pressure from the disloyal opposition. The readiness to believe in conspiracies and the rapid diffusion of rumors, sometimes encouraged by limits imposed on the news media in an attempt to control the situation, contribute to the uncertainty and unpredictability that may lead to worsening of economic crises.

In this atmosphere the leading actors may decide not to confront the basic problems of the government but to try to overcome the political crisis. Typically, efforts are made to strengthen the power of the executive, sometimes by proposing constitutional amendments, granting emergency powers, suspending the sessions of the legislature, intervening, suspending, or interfering with regional or local governments, or reshuffling the top-level military command. If such measures were combined with a growing cohesion of the regime-supporting parties, a clear assumption of responsibility by their most outstanding leaders, a capacity and willingness to maintain order without bias in favor of those closer to the parties in power, and rejection of any collaboration with a disloyal opposition, they might lead to a reequilibration process.

A second alternative would be an attempt to expand the bases of the regime by incorporating at least part of the disloyal opposition or coopting its leadership for a new coalition. As we shall see, this leads at best to a transformation of the regime, and more often to a transfer of power, a *Machtübergabe*, which the disloyal opposition might transform quickly into a *Machtübernahme*. This was the case in Italy in 1922, Germany in 1933, and Czechoslovakia in 1948.

A third alternative would be to allow the process of polarization to continue and ignore the threats coming from disloyal oppositions and semiloyal elements in a pre–civil war situation until one of the disloyal forces attempts to assume power. The democratic leadership then has only two options: to withdraw, turning over its power to the armed forces, sometimes under the cover of apolitical institutions like the supreme court, in the hope that the moderating power will not introduce a regime change but will only suspend normal democratic processes temporarily; or to appeal to the nation and to mobilize organized forces (like the trade unions), including those considered disloyal or semiloyal, in an effort to broaden its authority. In a highly polarized society this second option (taken by the Spanish minority bourgeois Republican government after it failed to reach a compromise with a military pronunciamento) means civil war. Only with a rapid victory could the government continue to claim democratic legitimacy rather than become the legitimizer of a revolutionary transformation of the regime or proceed with the transfer of power. French politicians, particularly Guy Mollet, were certainly aware of these possibilities in May 1958 when they rejected the chance to resist the military coup in Algiers by appealing to mass mobilization in which the Communists would have played a leading role.[1] They were haunted by the memory of the Spanish government in July 1936 and its dependence on the militias of the proletarian revolutionary parties, particularly the Anarcho-Syndicalists and the maximalist Socialists.

In a society in which the democratic leadership has experienced such a loss of power, if the army is not apt to assume the role of a moderating power and the disloyal oppositions convey ambiguous signals that combine a willingness to participate in a solution with the capacity to present a revolutionary threat, the pattern of transfer of power is the most likely. In fact, it might appear to be the best possible solution, should the neutral powers provide it with a stamp of legitimacy, the armed forces tolerate or even welcome it, and at least some of the regime-supporting parties believe that they have enough bargaining power to protect their interests and certain institutional arrangements.

Legal revolution was first attempted in the defeated states after World War I and opened the door to the establishment of democratic republics in Germany and Austria.[2] Mussolini, however, perfected the process in favor of a disloyal opposition and an antidemocratic regime. After the failure of the Beer Hall Putsch, Hitler realized that power could be gained only with the appearance of legality, and in 1933 he succeeded in much less time than the Italian Fascists. Although there are undeniable differences, the 1948 coup in Prague shows some similarities. The situation in late May 1958 in Paris again showed some similarities, even though the unique personality of de Gaulle and his commitment to democracy changed what appeared to be a threat to a democratic regime into a transformation that can be considered a reequilibration of democracy as well. Since the process of "legal" takeover was so successful in those cases, analysis seems relevant even when the historical record makes it difficult to apply the same formula today. We might note that legal revolution—using constitutional institutions against their clear intent or what the Germans would call *verfassungswidrige Verfassungsänderung*—has been used by the Suárez government in Spain (1976–77) to make possible the transition from an authoritarian regime to democracy. In this case, the pressure brought to bear by the opposition, its mobilization of the street, and the rising cost of repression convinced the rulers to inaugurate the transition to democracy. They did this without coopting the opposition leaders into the government, and without a breakdown of the institutional framework (*ruptura*), but with a clear discontinuity.

This situation occurs when a democratic regime that has experienced a serious loss of power and legitimacy is confronted with a disloyal opposition possessing considerable striking power due to its capacity for mass mobilization and its readiness to use the threat of force, but also due to its presence in parliament which enables it to facilitate a formal constitutionally legal assumption of power with the cooperation of other parties. A disloyal opposition that has gained power bases through mobilizing the streets and employing organized paramilitary groups, but whose leader is prepared to talk sensibly and to declare, albeit ambiguously, his readiness to respect at least some key institutions and to moderate his extremist supporters, if granted a share in power, finds itself in the best position for a takeover. Opportunistic concessions to a variety of interests and institutions are aimed at neutralizing their opposition to the entry into the government. Perhaps the ability to control a heterogeneous following and the absence of lieutenants who might question the compromises being made on the road to power is another condition for the success of this tactic. It was certainly a decisive asset to Hitler that none of his opponents in the NSDAP could command any following in the party.

To succeed, however, this tactic requires certain responses both on the part of some of the parties and leaders not previously linked with the disloyal opposition and on the part of the neutral powers of the state. The process of formally legal or semilegal takeover is initiated when some of the parties or leaders who are far from committed to an overthrow of democracy feel that the antiregime leadership could be coopted without danger to the system or at the cost of such transformations as a strengthened executive, the outlawing of a party, or the curtailment of some civil liberties. Their actions tend to be based on the assumption that they might be senior partners in the new coalition, as was the case when von Papen thought that he had engaged Hitler, rather than the other way around. At one point or another, leaders of the regime may agree with some of the objectives of the disloyal opposition, if not its methods, and will be tempted to explore the conditions under which they might reach an agreement that would bring the disloyal opposition, or a sector of it, into the system. One obvious strategy is an attempt to split the disloyal opposition, as when Schleicher dreamed of exploiting the divergence between Strasser and Hitler.

Arguments for this action are as follows: the leader might be more amenable to compromise than many of his followers; a share in responsibility will moderate extremist positions; participation in power will stop unmanageable street violence; and cooptation will effect suppression of another disloyal opposition perceived as more dangerous. These hopes are encouraged by the ambiguous statements of the disloyal opposition's leader and seem to be confirmed by internal tensions within his own movement. The initiatives for such negotiations are often handled by intermediaries who have their own reasons for favoring such a solution; they tend to be taken in secret and are broken off when they become public. At this stage regime-supporting parties or factions in them and individual leaders move into positions we might call semiloyal. Often the neutral powers look favorably on such a solution, or at least, careful of their own survival, do not reject it outright. The result is a growing atmosphere of suspicion in the political class that often leads to further fragmentation within the parties, including the disloyal opposition itself, and provokes the accusation that the leadership is ready to sell out the movement, its more radical goals, and its leaders for a cabinet post. This accelerates the pace of events toward denouement.[3]

Secret negotiations, the need to get the approval of the neutral powers, the benevolent neutrality of the armed forces, and the desire of interest groups to solve the crisis are all factors leading to a transfer of the political process from the parliamentary arena to another, invisible and much more restricted. The narrowing of the arena and the important role played by small groups of individuals is characteristic of this final phase in the process of breakdown. (By a strange coincidence, as Daniel Bell has pointed out, these groups— conspiracies, clubs, committees, cabals, courts, *camarillas,* caucuses—all begin with a small "c.") Their presence explains why the breakdown process has been so often analyzed in terms of a conspiracy theory. These groups may have an important role in the immediate process of transfer of power, but they are a product of the entire process.

Another consequence of this slow, but mounting, exploration of an opening to the disloyal opposition is that the more important and permanent institutions of society begin to realize that extremists, formerly regarded with hostility or at least considerable ambivalence, might come into power.[4] Consequently, these institutions slowly but perceptibly disengage from the democratic regime and from those parties to whom they had entrusted their political interests. Typically, business organizations will begin to contribute to such parties; the churches will lift their injunctions against supporting or joining such parties and tend to become less identified with a religious party like the Populari or the Zentrum; the trade unions might reconsider their ties with political parties like the Social Democrats; and the army will insist on its loyalty to the state and its leader with the implicit message that its loyalty is not to a particular government or regime.[5] The leaders of a disloyal opposition will, of course, encourage these trends by an adroit use of expressions of respect for the institutions, specific promises and guarantees, and more or less veiled threats to prevent institutions from casting their lot with the existing regime.

The less politically committed segments of the population also begin to accept cooptation of the disloyal opposition, in the hope that it will lead to a more stable government, greater efficacy, and above all, an end to the politically inspired violence that they suffer as bystanders. Paradoxically, a disloyal opposition that has been a major contributor to the atmosphere of civil disorder can appear at this stage as offering a chance for order. This weakens the capacity of the more militant, prodemocratic forces to mobilize their supporters against their opponents' entry into the government, since at that stage they might be blamed for the outbreak of violence and civil war.

The discovery of what the Nazis would call legal revolution has increased the difficulty of bringing into the regime members of any opposition whose loyalty to the democratic system is suspect. Offering cabinet seats to representatives of such a party, which allows it to overcome the last threshold on the road to full legitimacy as a participant in democratic politics, might lead to an escalation of demands, bolstered by such pressures as well-orchestrated mass support on the streets. A slight shift in control of the state's power of coercion toward legitimating the actions of party militias could spell the inevitable doom of democracy.

But *Machtergreifung* and the subsequent consolidation of authoritarian or totalitarian rule is not the only threat to democracy in this case. The entry into the government of a party perceived by a large sector of the population or by key institutions like the army as semiloyal or disloyal to the institutions, even when it is not intent on a takeover, is likely to produce an "anticipated" reaction in the form of revolutionary protest, legitimized as the defense of democracy or a preventive military putsch. This was the case in Spain in 1934, when the CEDA's entry into the government served to justify the Asturian proletarian revolution, the secessionist putsch by the Catalan Generalitat government, and the withdrawal from participation in the institutions by the liberal Left bourgeois parties. Democracy managed to survive, but it had been mortally wounded. We must emphasize that macrohistorical political models of processes like the power takeovers by Mussolini and Hitler are never repeated according to the same script, largely because the participants in new but similar situations are likely to take into account, rightly or wrongly, what they think are the lessons of the past. In fact, it is surprising that some of the patterns are nevertheless repeated in macrosociological processes. For this reason model-building is not so feasible in macrosociology as in microsociology.

The model of the legal conquest of power—revolution from the top—

makes the Communist party's transition from negative integration to full participation in a democracy much more risky and difficult than that of the Socialist labor parties in the early decades of this century. The moral stance of early revolutionary movements did not allow their members to participate in government unless they constituted the democratically elected majority. When they did accept participation, it was under the assumption that this would help them build such a majority rather than use power to subvert the system. They would have rejected as immoral such a statement as: "The Constitution prescribes only the arena of the struggle; it does not specify the goal. We shall enter the legitimate organizations and in this way make our party the decisive factor. Once we possess the constitutional right to do so, we shall, of course, cast the state in the mold that we consider to be the right one"[6]—even if that mold required a change of regime. When democratic Socialists first entered democratic government, they did not expect (as rereading Harold Laski would show) that their opponents would allow them to pursue their policies legally.[7] In many cases they were wrong. But the fact that they were sometimes right gave new life to the maximalist interpretation of the Marxist heritage, a position well expressed in this text:

This permits us to do what the Third International [then] does not allow. That is to participate in a government with the Republicans and still recognize the transitory revolutionary dictatorship of the proletariat as the ineluctable postulate of scientific socialism.

What did the bourgeois newspapers suppose? Undoubtedly they supposed us to be inoffensive social democrats, full of pseudo-democratic prejudices, and so foolish that if it were necessary to prevent a fascist dictatorship, we would merely ask for new elections.[8]

The ambiguity of this position has had fateful consequences for democracy in many countries: Italy, Austria, Spain, and Chile.

The questions we have just raised are not academic when we consider the possibility of the participation of Italian and French Communists in government and their role in the Portuguese developments in 1975.

The End of a Democratic Regime and Its Aftermath

The death of a democracy is often recorded in the history books as associated with the date of a particular event: the March on Rome, Hitler's appointment as chancellor, the outbreak of the Spanish civil war, the attack on La Moneda and the death of Allende. But in fact, those fateful days or hours preceding the events that marked the end of a regime were only the culmination of a long and complex process. When they occurred, many of the actors probably did not realize or intend the fateful consequences. In many cases, the nature of the regime being born in such moments was not known even to those whose intent was to overthrow the existing political order. The transition to a new regime was often possible only because so many of the participants were unaware of the ultimate implications of their actions and, even more often, were mistaken in their analysis of the situation. In retrospect, it is possible to identify points at which opportunities existed for alternative courses of action that might have reduced the probability of the fall of the regime.

At the latter stages of the process that leads from the loss of power to the power vacuum, the question of the timing of decisions and actions becomes particularly relevant. The responses of the rulers and participants can be characterized (unfortunately, more often than not, *a posteriori*) as premature, timely, delayed, "eleventh-hour," or taken when time has run out. Reequilibration would require timely actions, while extrapolation from other crises might lead to premature responses that would accelerate rather than halt the breakdown. (The October revolution in Spain may be seen in this light.) But most examples are of belated actions (like those of the reformist Socialists of Turati in the Italian crisis of the twenties). The intellectual value of our analysis should consist, therefore, in that it should enable leaders of democracies facing serious crisis to be more conscious of the choices and risks they face.

One might wonder whether analysis of the circumstances of the final dénouement, while relatively uninteresting from the point of view of accounting for the death of democracy, might not be of great importance in understanding the nature of the regime that is emerging: its process of consolidation, its future stability, the possibilities of its transformation, its effect on the future of the society.

Depending on that transition, the difficulties and opportunities for the reestablishment of democracy are in some measure the result of that final stage of breakdown process and perhaps of the interpretations that the society and different actors give to those dramatic events. The end of a democratic regime, even when it can be dated symbolically, is also the beginning of the building of a new regime, a process that we see as having distinctive problems and patterns that require descriptive models.

We have focused on cases in which it was not possible in the final stage for those committed to the survival of democracy to prevent its demise. However, their options in that stage have decisive consequences for how the challengers of the democratic order can and will act. Certainly the end of a democracy shows a number of different patterns that deserve further research. The main patterns seem to be:

1. An unconstitutional displacement of a democratically elected government by a group ready to use force, whose action is legitimated by institutional mechanisms planned for emergency situations. Interim rule is set up

with the intent to reestablish the democratic process with certain deviations at a later time.

2. The assumption of power by a combination of ademocratic, generally predemocratic, authority structures that coopt part of the political class of the previous democratic regime and integrate elements of the disloyal opposition, but undertake only limited changes in the social structure and most institutional realms.

3. The establishment of a new authoritarian regime, based on a realignment of social forces and the exclusion of all the leading political actors of the preceding democratic regime, without, however, creating new political institutions or any form of mass mobilization in support of its rule.

4. The takeover of power by a well-organized disloyal opposition with a mass base in the society, committed to the creation of new political and social order, and unwilling to share its power with members of the political class of the past regime, except as minor partners in a transition phase. The outcome may range from the establishment of a self-confident authoritarian regime to a pretotalitarian regime.

5. The takeover of power that does not succeed even against a weakened regime and requires a prolonged struggle (civil war). Such a conflict can be the result of one of two variables, or more likely a combination of them: the willingness of the democratic government to resist the pressures to relinquish power by demanding the obedience of the coercive instruments of the state and the support of the population, combined with the inability to defeat its opponents; and the existence in the society of a high level of political and social mobilization, which may or may not be with the democratic government but is ready to challenge the takeover by its opponents.

The first of these five patterns was the traditional model of military intervention, the *poder moderador*, in nineteenth century Spain and Latin America. It was only possible in societies with relatively low levels of political mobilization, parties that were the personal following of leaders or coalitions of notables or caciques, and an army without its own political aims. Given the corruption of the electoral process under oligarchic democracy, and the readiness of large segments of the political class to encourage or accept such interventions, the result for the society was not too different from a rigged election replacing one group of politicians with another group similar in social composition and aims. Since the democracies fitting our definition (and studied in this volume) were, or were beginning to be, a different type, even when some of the participants in the military coups conceived their role in these terms and some of the politicians encouraged them to play the old role of the moderating power, the outcome was closer to the second and third patterns.

The second pattern would be the model of the transition to royal dictatorships in a number of Balkan countries. Rumania under King Carol and Yugoslavia in the interwar years provide interesting examples. The residues of traditional or semitraditional monarchical legitimacy for the army and some sectors of the population, combined with the problems of unsuccessful democratic regimes and conflicts between nationalities, make authoritarian regimes of a military-bureaucratic character possible. These regimes coopt large numbers of professional politicians who had been elected thanks to their local bases of power or the influence they were able to exercise by using the access to government. Semi- or pseudodemocratic mechanisms could be maintained by excluding minor activist groups ready to challenge the social or political order from political life and ignoring the demands of nationalities challenging the privileged status of a dominant nationality. The alternative to a ''halfway'' democracy was a semiauthoritarian regime, in which the main difference was loss of freedom for an opposition whose chances of gaining power democratically were already limited, but whose freedom might in the long run have represented a threat.

The breakdown of a democracy that has gained considerable legitimacy, whose parties have roots in the society representing various interests and distinctive ideologies, and whose leaders enjoy considerable appeal, is more likely to lead to the final three patterns, which represent a greater discontinuity and a real change of regime. Of these, the fourth on our list is unlikely to be the most frequent, since a disloyal mass political movement only rarely gains power in a democracy as the Fascists did in Italy and Germany. The unique circumstances that allowed such mass movements to challenge the state's monopoly of armed force combined with electoral successes and, aided by semiloyalty of other political forces and the neutrality of the armed forces, to proceed to a pseudolegal transfer of power without encountering popular resistance, are unlikely to be repeated in modern societies. Fascism as a mass movement, with its ideology, style, organizational inventiveness, and heterogeneous social basis, was a result of a unique historical situation after World War I.[9] Conservative interests, frightened by the Russian Revolution and local pseudorevolutions or revolutionary rhetoric, looked upon the Fascists as potential allies. The democratic liberal leaders, particularly in Italy, did not perceive the serious threat to their position that the new movement represented. Today they are not likely to put their hope for a defense against the threat of possible leftist revolution in an antidemocratic mass movement that could easily provoke a civil war. They will make a greater effort to work within the democratic framework, using the coercive resources of the state to defend it against radical challenges, confident that their interests can be protected within it, in the knowledge that the opponents on the left are not too likely to win power electorally and are unable to take it by force. Should they come to the conclusion that democracy does not guarantee an acceptable social order, they are more likely to turn to a preventive coup by the armed forces, with considerable active or passive support from the sectors of society being threatened. The outcome then would be an authoritarian regime with many of the characteristics of Fascist regimes, but bureaucratic-technocratic in nature, not based on the mass mobilization that precedes the breakdown of democracy. If the leaders were unsuccessful, the result would be a civil war whose outcome would be decided largely by military means and probable international intervention.

In spite of the high level of politicization of society, the mobilization of the masses, and the polarization that preceded the breakdown of a number of democracies, the takeover of power in a number of cases was not particularly bloody, even when the subsequent terror and repression of opponents were as great as they were in Germany. Breakdown leading to a real civil war has been the exception; undoubtedly, the pattern of legal revolution invented by Mussolini was unexpected and poorly understood, so that the Left was unable to initiate the sort of violent reaction that might have led to a civil war. Defeat without struggle was abetted by the Communist interpretation of Fascism in the interwar years: it was seen as a temporary phenomenon that would exhaust itself as the last stand of monopolistic capitalism revealed its failure to the masses and led to their disillusionment with social democracy, particularly when Moscow was advocating the theory of social Fascism.[10] The semilegal takeover of power, made possible by the semiloyal opposition legitimized by the neutral powers, the coerced decision of democratic parties, and the benevolent neutrality of the armed forces, together with the self-deception of many leaders about the consequences of the *Machtergreifung*, made any reaction impossible until it became too late to challenge the rapidly consolidating power of the Nazi state. The pattern was not to be repeated.

In Austria, a less threatening authoritarian alternative required a short civil war to consolidate itself in power, and in Spain, a few months later, a misperceived comparable situation led to the October revolution. In the middle thirties the situation had changed; democrats of various persuasions were more ready to cooperate to save democratic regimes against the Fascist danger; the Communists, after considerable hesitation, changed their line toward Socialist parties. In relatively stable societies the revolutionary rhetoric that had pushed many potential democrats into the arms of Fascism was abandoned, and conservatives were probably less enthusiastic about the Fascist mass movement. Only in Spain did a crisis of democracy, coming after its defeat in so many countries, produce a militant response by both the democrats and the proletariat. Both groups saw their gains threatened and at the same time saw an opportunity for revolution when the authority of the state was challenged by the army and its supporters on the right. Since the government felt confident of its democratic legitimacy and enjoyed the support of important sectors of the population, even among the army, police, and civil servants (a fact that is often ignored), it decided to resist the military uprising. Simultaneously, the working class, which had been organized for revolution, or at least organized to exercise pseudorevolutionary pressures on the government, was ready to respond to the threat and the appeal of the government. The loyalty, or at least the ambivalence, of some segments of the army, the mobilization of the masses by the proletarian organizations, and the hostility of regional nationalists to a centralist Right created resistance to the army and its civilian supporters in many parts of Spain. In other parts of the country, action by the military could mobilize widespread civilian support, making a quick defeat of the rebels by the loyalists impossible and therefore making a civil war, prolonged by foreign intervention, inevitable. The two political systems that fought each other for almost three years ended having little in common with the one existing in July 1936, and even less with the one established in 1931.

Although the model of the rise to power of a Mussolini or a Hitler will not be repeated, the possibility of the combined resistance of a democratic government with a leftist orientation and a mobilized working class, as in Spain, cannot be ignored in contemporary democracies. Unfortunately those who expect to combine democratic rule with rapid social and economic change, a combination perceived by both its supporters and its opponents as revolutionary, seem unlikely to succeed without a civil war if their opponents can gain the support of the armed forces. Even if the loyalists were to win, it would be a considerable time after a civil war before a government could function as a democracy, granting to the defeated the same political rights as the victors. Civil war, whatever the outcome, means the death of democracy and the establishment of some type of dictatorship.

Contrary to the beliefs and hopes of democrats, a democratic regime should never be allowed to approach the point at which its survival will depend on the readiness of its supporters to fight for it in the streets. Few citizens, even in a crisis, are ready to support those who might want to overthrow democracy, but in a modern society they feel unable to do anything in such a situation.[11] Only those on the extremes of the political spectrum are prepared to fight or are likely to have the organizational resources to do so. To resist the disloyalty of minorities, a democratic government must prevent their access to the means of violence by keeping them disarmed and politically isolated from mass support. Should such minorities be able to gain support from the levels of power that would allow them to command the loyalty or neutrality of the instruments of coercion of the state, the fate of the regime is in serious danger. A primary requirement of a stable democratic regime is retention of its legitimacy among those in direct control of the instruments of coercion. Any policy that would so deeply alienate them that they would be willing to rebel is not viable. In certain respect the armed forces in a modern society are a concurrent minority, in the sense that Calhoun uses the term. However, a government that enjoys legitimacy beyond its own electoral support is unlikely to encounter the disloyalty of more than a sector of the armed forces in a modern democracy. Its chances of survival depend on the response to its claim of legitimacy by those officers who are not committed to a coup. The loyalty of conscripts as citizens, the population irrespective of party in that context, and the mobilization of those committed to partial political goals (including those who for other reasons have questioned democracy's legitimacy) might not produce the most efficient response, and might in fact be counterproductive. Perhaps the only hope for a regime so threatened is to compromise with the insurgents, if they are too strong, or to seek the support of the armed forces not involved in the pronunciamento; that is, they should turn to certain organized sectors of the society rather than hope to defeat the insurgents by "arming the people." This solution, even at the cost of changes in policy, institutional changes, the curtailment of some civil liberties, or the cooptation of some semiloyal leaders, offers more hope for the future of democracy than do resistance and civil war. These considerations and the availability of the charisma of de Gaulle, who won considerable legitimacy far beyond his own partisan support, allowed the democratic leadership of the Fourth Republic to make the transition to the Fifth—a rare case of reequilibration.

Reequilibration can be the outcome of near-breakdown in a democratic regime. Unfortunately, few of the crises of democracy have been studied from this perspective. In fact, it could be argued that several of the democracies that ultimately failed had overcome previous crises, and that scholars should therefore place more emphasis on the positive aspects of the way those crises were surmounted.[12]

5.

The Process of Reequilibration

Reequilibration of Democratic Systems as a Problem

Reequilibration of a democracy is a political process that, after a crisis that has seriously threatened the continuity and stability of the basic democratic political mechanisms, results in their continued existence at the same or higher levels of democratic legitimacy, efficacy, and effectiveness.[1] It assumes a severe jolting of those institutions, a loss of either effectiveness or efficacy, and probably legitimacy, that produces a temporary breakdown of the authority of the regime. Reequilibration is compatible with changes of regime within the genus *democratic* (broadly defined); that is, it includes changes like those from the Fourth to the Fifth French Republic, or from a *régime censitaire* to modern mass democracy, or from a system based on majority rule to one based on consociational mechanisms. Reequilibration can be, even when it does not need to be, a breakdown or profound transformation of one regime, but not of democratic legitimacy and basic institutions.

Breakdown followed by reequilibration of democracy can be effected by anti- or aconstitutional means, by the interference in the normal democratic processes of a political actor (like a charismatic leader) whose initial legitimation is ademocratic, or by the use of force, as in a military putsch. Reequilibration, therefore, might be accompanied by a disjunction between what the German political scientists of the twenties called "legality" and "legitimacy." The new regime might be established illegally, but it must be legitimated by the democratic process afterward, and above all, it must operate thereafter according to democratic rules. It undoubtedly represents a violation of the condition of regime continuity, the continuous functioning of the established rules, and the mechanisms institutionalized to change them. In this sense de Gaulle's ascent to power in 1958 is unlike a change of government from Conservative to Labor in the United Kingdom or even Nixon's succession by Ford after impeachment proceedings started. The question we ask and will answer hypothetically at this point is, "Under what conditions is a reequilibration possible?"

The first condition would seem to be the availability of a leadership uncompromised by the loss of efficacy and legitimacy of the existing regime in crisis and committed to the creation of a new regime with new institutions to be

87

legitimated by future democratic procedures. Secondly, that leadership must be able to gain the acceptance of those who remained loyal to the existing regime as well as those who opted for disloyalty in crisis and therefore are potential supporters of a nondemocratic regime. Third, the leadership of the regime that has lost power, efficacy, effectiveness, and probably considerable legitimacy must be able to accept that fact and facilitate rather than oppose the transfer of power. Closely related to this requirement is the willingness of the former leadership, with its commitment to certain policy goals, ideologies, and interests, to subordinate the realization of these goals in order to save the substance of democracy, even at the cost of temporary discontinuity. Such willingness and ability presuppose confidence in the democratic commitment of the leadership to whom power will be transferred. Since no regime and its leadership are likely to have lost all their authority and legitimacy, the temptation and justification to resist illegal challenge exists. But as their opponents can also have a powerful claim to legitimacy, the outcome can only be the establishment of authoritarian rule or civil war, if that opposing claim is used to mobilize a sector of the population to resist the transfer of power and transformation of the regime. At a somewhat different level of significance, there is a fifth condition: a certain level of indifference and passivity in the bulk of the population must exist during the final denouement of the crisis. Furthermore, the reequilibration model is only possible when the semiloyal opposition to a particular regime is capable of controlling and neutralizing a disloyal opposition that questions not only the particular regime or government but the democratic system. It is a game in which the semiloyal actors in one regime consciously deceive the disloyal political forces whose challenge may have precipitated the breakdown and brought them to power.

The requirements of reequilibration would seem to be a unique constellation of factors. Reequilibration originates in a leadership outside of the regime in crisis but acceptable to many of its supporters; at the same time, this leadership is capable of bringing into a new regime many of its challengers and isolating diehard opponents. It is also committed to legitimizing the new regime by democratic means and continuing afterward with democratic institutions. Reequilibration occurs in the presence of the readiness of the electorate to approve the regime transformation or change, an approval conditioned by trust in the new regime's capacity to solve the unsolvable problem that precipitated the final crisis. These are requirements aptly fulfilled by the transition from the Fourth to the Fifth French Republic. De Gaulle's availability, his personal charismatic legitimacy, his commitment to democracy as he understood it, and the willingness of leading political figures of the Fourth Republic to cooperate, as well as the passivity of most of the metropolitan population of France in the crisis days, made it possible.[2] Low-keyed mobilization by the Communist party, facilitated by the unwillingness of most democratic leaders to counter the threat on the right by asking for Communist support, was another factor.

Albert Hirschman considers the problem of recuperation of a firm or organization whose performance has lapsed, and calls attention to some of the same requisites we have noted for the reequilibration process.[3] When he writes that it is generally best for a firm to have a mixture of *alert* and *inert* customers—alert ones to provide the firm with a feedback mechanism which starts the effort at recuperation, and inert customers to provide it with the time and dollar cushion for this effort to come to fruition—he is referring to sectors comparable to those we mentioned in the process of reequilibration. The parallel is with the disloyal opposition, which has left the democratic system, and the large number of passive supporters of democracy who are not ready to give it their support, who wait for an effort of the political class to solve the crisis, or remain unaware of, or unperturbed by, decline in quality. Those tolerant of the failures of democracy, unwilling to join the disloyal opposition, but not ready to demand total conformity with democratic principles, make the reequilibration process possible, even at the cost of democratic legality.

The question can be raised as to whether some of the nondemocratic regimes that were established through a combination of illegal, violent pressures and the formally legal investiture of the new government, particularly after a certain pacification of the country and some signs of efficacy, might not have developed into a new democratic regime in which the challengers would have become the hegemonic basis of a coalition. Perhaps Mussolini did not rule out such a possibility in 1922. The entry into the government of representatives of other parties, the vote of confidence he obtained, the benevolent neutrality of the General Confederation of Labor, which was ready to distance itself from the Socialist party, the attempt to curtail the violence of the squads, the initial successes in the economic field, and above all, the transformistic traditions of Italian politics, would have favored such a development. In this sense, it might seem that the Matteoti murder and its aftermath, which made Mussolini appear responsible for the violence of Fascist extremists and led to their pressure on him to protect them, caused him to opt for a fully authoritarian, if not totalitarian, alternative.

The concept of reequilibration in the Paretian tradition does not mean that the new equilibrium of forces within the constraints of the democratic process would be the same as before. Nor does it mean that within certain limits the rules of the game would not be modified, particularly the electoral laws, which can contribute so much to shaping the party system, or the relationships between executive and legislature. In fact, the changes required may reach the borderline between democracy and semiauthoritarian solutions if the new regime imposes certain limits on civil liberties or outlaws particular parties, as in the case of the Communist party in Finland in the 1930s. But might not a less democratic democracy, particularly if an opposition considered disloyal by large segments of the polity is outlawed, be a better alternative than risking civil war or an authoritarian regime in defense of democratic authenticity?

We have deliberately started our discussion of reequilibration with an emphasis on the most advanced stage in which change of regime occurs within the genus *democratic*, but patterns that are more likely, more viable, and less risky might be considered at an earlier stage of the breakdown process. In principle, all require parties committed to the democratic order to sacrifice their particular goals, the interests of many of their followers, and their ideological commitments, as well as accepting limits on the most libertarian interpretation of civil liberties, for the sake of stabilizing the situation and insuring survival of the system. In a sense they involve an oligopolistic solution that deviates from pure competition but avoids monopoly of power. Such solutions are characterized by national unity coalition governments, temporary postponements of elections, agreement between the parties not to compete in elections, and prearranged formulas to assure the parties rotation in office or proportional representation in key government posts. They reflect the actions of democracies in time of war, but the cases of Austria after World War II and Colombia after the Rojas Pinilla dictatorship are interesting examples of such efforts in post-crisis democracies. (For the latter, see the chapter by Alexander Wilde in part 3 of this project.)

These cases, as well as the proposals made for such solutions in crisis periods, would make interesting studies. In this context, the idea of a Spanish Republican dictatorship, advanced by democratic politicians uncommitted to either the Popular Front or the moderate Right in the spring of 1936, is particularly interesting. Could Azaña, aided by his considerable personal prestige, with the cooperation of CEDA moderates and the more moderate sectors of the Socialist party led by Prieto and supported by the bulk of the army, have succeeded in such a solution, thereby avoiding civil war or reducing it to local revolutions and pronunciamentos? Our qualified answer would be "probably." However, the cost of such extreme solutions might be too high for the participants, since they might involve a restructuring of the party system—a splitting of major parties and readiness to use considerable force. In fact, the greatest cost would be psychic, and the politicians faced with such a choice would be unlikely to take the risks involved. To betray lifetime commitments and loyalties is not easy, even for politicians, particularly when success is far from assured.

Our analysis of the extreme models of reequilibration has, among other purposes, aimed at highlighting the degrees of freedom open to the political leadership even in extreme situations. It is only the execution of such mental experiments, combined with the effort to understand (*verstehen*) the actors, that will advance our knowledge about processes of political change, even when that process might be an obstacle to the building of elegant causal models.[4]

Restoration and Reinstauration of Democracy

Founding a new democracy and consolidating it after a relatively short period of nondemocratic rule, with many leaders of the earlier democratic regime playing major roles, is not strictly a case of reequilibration.[5] It differs decisively from those cases in which the autocratic period has lasted many years and its persecution of democratic leaders has been so thorough that few have returned to political life. The passing of time implies that new generations who have no identification with the predictatorship parties and leadership will have entered political life. New leaders will then found a new regime that might see little reason to claim to be a legitimate continuation of the previous regime and thus to represent a case of instauration rather than restoration.[6] Most cases of the return to democracy might be somewhere in between.

The restoration situation poses some special problems, created by the need to overcome tension between the parties that contributed to the breakdown, to eliminate suspicion of past semiloyal actions, and to avoid reaffirmation of policies and ideological positions that contributed to the crisis. This will all be influenced by the extent to which the leadership of the reestablished regime has learned from past experience. Will it reaffirm the positions of the past, raise again the divisive issues of that time, and unearth past recriminations against opponents to blame them for the breakdown? In this respect, the instauration of a new regime by new men may have some advantages for the consolidation of democracy. On the other hand, those who lived through a fateful crisis are likely to better understand the types of action that lead to the downfall of democracy, have more experience in democratic political procedures, and make better parliamentarians. They may be able to contribute knowledge and greater pragmatism to the consolidation of the regime, thereby avoiding some of the difficulties that occur in the consolidation stage of new democratic regimes and that contributed to the crisis of the previous one.

The reestablishment process will vary depending on the nature of the regime established after the fall of democracy. Certainly, totalitarian rule, by persecuting almost all the democratic leaders, is likely to have created considerable solidarity among them. To have been together in jails and concentration camps can create a readiness to work together among even the most bitter opponents. Such a regime also poses less ambiguity about the identity of leaders and supporters—particularly the identity of members of the single mobilization party. The principled exclusion of the old political class, even if some of its members would have been ready to collaborate with a new regime, makes it easy to define those who shall be allowed to play an active role in the restoration of democracy. Perhaps this has been one of the advantages in the process of rebuilding the democracies in Germany, Austria, and even Italy after World War II. Restoration after an authoritarian regime that coopted politicians active in the preceding regime, that persecuted some opponents and tolerated others, poses more serious problems. This is particularly true when some of the emerging parties use the past record of political leaders and parties as an argument to disqualify them from participating in political life. The Communists in Eastern Europe after World War II, particularly in Czechoslovakia, were very adroit in using this tactic.

This is not the place to pursue this problem, which will be touched upon in other chapters. It is important, however, to see that it underlines a problem central to macropolitical sociological analysis: continuity and discontinuity in the political process.

The Right to Disobedience, and Rebellion and Partisanship in Defense of Democracy

Can it be that our analysis itself is shaped by the conflict we are analyzing? Are our theories embedded in a tradition of both scientific inquiry and political discourse not made explicit? Are the terms we use consciously or unconsciously biased in favor of the regime against its opponents? A recent essay by Terry Nardin, the literature on civil disobedience, and recent analyses of violence in America raise such questions, which could be safely ignored in an analysis of the breakdown of democracies based on the paradigmatic case of the Weimar Republic, but not in that of other cases.[7]

It is important to keep in mind that the rebellion against democratic regimes is ultimately a conflict about legitimacy formulas. The rebels claim that the democratic authorities have forfeited their right to rule and that they have become illegitimate even within their own system of values.[8] The Weberian analysis of legitimacy emphasizes that limits are built in in each type of regime and that the transformation of regimes beyond them is a source of their delegitimation and their ultimate breakdown.[9] De Tocqueville warned especially of the dangers of oppression by the majority in a democracy.[10] Violation of constitutional norms, abuse of power, disregard of civil liberties, and excessive violence by the authorities cannot be ignored as cause for the breakdown of democracies. Certainly those overthrowing a regime will claim such abuses, and it is this claim that convinces many moderate nonpartisan citizens to support, or at least accept, the overthrow of a regime. In our terms it could be said that the actors disloyal to a democratic regime are those accorded power by democratic procedures: the legally elected government is the source of danger to the continuity and normal functioning of democratic institutions.

In the cases in our purview, that argument may be dismissed as self-serving, in view of the unwillingness of those who have used it to attain power to reestablish free democratic political processes, despite their claim of having overthrown a particular democratic government to save democracy. It is also belied by the willingness of such groups to enter into coalition with political groups that were disloyal to a democratic regime even before it allegedly violated the democratic trust. It could be argued, therefore, that such arguments have validity only when the overthrow of a particular government, the temporary crisis of a democratic regime, leads to the reestablishment of democracy. But this is an easy way out of a serious question, because it is unlikely that this disruption by violent means, even in the defense of democracy, can lead to the establishment or reequilibration of a democratic regime, irrespective of the intentions of the actors. Therefore, the outcome does not prove that the arguments used at the time were hypocritical or the allegations false.

From this perspective, the breakdown of democracy is caused not by the actions of a disloyal opposition, but by rulers who, though they have acquired power by constitutional democratic means, exercise it in such a way that the normal methods open to a loyal opposition for exercising its critique—the use of the constitutional mechanism for control of the government, the exercise of democratic liberal freedoms and waiting for the next election to make the rulers accountable for their abuse of power—begin to seem inadequate to assure the continuity of a democratic regime. European political theorists have formulated this situation in terms of the conflict between legality and legitimacy—in this case, democratic legitimacy.

It differs from situations in which the opposition to a regime is based on other legitimacy formulas. These might include the defense of traditional authority in the counterrevolutionary attacks on democracy in the nineteenth century, the charisma of a leader, the historical mission of a revolutionary movement or a class represented by its most conscious members, though they are an electoral minority, or a conception of the national community expressed by plebiscite rather than through the representation of interests in the society. In those cases, two conceptions of legitimacy conflict, both claiming the allegiance of the people. In the last analysis, citizens must decide to which side they will grant the right to use force, in view of their ultimate values, placing those values higher than values sustaining a democratic regime, if they cannot be permanently assured within the framework of the regime. No democratic regime can guarantee any set of ultimate values forever, since democracy is based on the assumption that from time to time the majority of citizens might favor different values. In fact, in stable democracies the compromises acceptable to most citizens on such ultimate values tend to be protected against rapidly changing majorities by the requirement that only qualified majorities can change them and, in some extreme cases of conflict, by giving the veto right even to a minority. As Schumpeter emphasized, a condition for the success of democracy, in contrast to the classical theory of democracy, is that the effective range of political decision should not be extended too far, and that not every function of the state should be subject to a democratic political method.[11]

Another question is whether one of the causes of breakdown of democracy is the anti- or ademocratic behavior of formally democratic rulers. This would mean a situation different from that in the final crisis of the Weimar Republic or in Italian democracy in the early twenties, when disloyal opposition and the loss of efficacy and effectiveness combined to produce a transfer of power to what was to be a new regime. Certainly, disloyal oppositions will always claim that the democratic authorities have betrayed their own principles, will always be among the most vocal defenders of civil liberties for themselves while denying them to others, and will always claim, sometimes with good reason, to be the victims of discrimination, persecution, and even illegal acts by the authorities. No one should be surprised to learn, in reading the autobiographies of Nazi activists collected by Abel, that they felt like an oppressed minority suffering police actions and social pressures brought to bear at the workplace, by excommunication from the church, and by family and friends.[12] At the same time, let it be noted, they boasted of readiness to use violence against their opponents. In fact, most democratic governments, faced with a disloyal opposition using violence and with leaders who publicly justify its use against a regime they define as illegitimate, are likely to use measures that would be and should be unacceptable against a loyal opposition. They may enact legislation banning the carrying of arms, wearing of uniforms, and organization of paramilitary units, forbidding membership in such organizations by police or army officers and civil servants, and banning demonstrations whose clear purpose is to provoke violence.[13]

Such measures taken in defense of democracy, even when legally enacted by democratic majorities in the legislatures, can be and have been questioned from a strict civil libertarian point of view.[14] Their adoption undoubtedly involves the risk of what Continental legal theorists call *abus du droit*, that is, the use of legal norms for purposes for which they were not intended. It occurs when these stringent measures are extended to opponents who cannot be considered to constitute a violent disloyal opposition. At this point the defense of democracy might become delegitimizing for those who do not support the disloyal opposition. In this twilight zone it begins to be difficult to distinguish between those who question the authority on grounds legitimate within the democratic framework and those who are semiloyal because, while disapproving of the methods of the disloyal opposition, they agree with its ultimate goals. Indeed, they might even consider a coalition with it in view of their own aims or some shared goals. Then the struggle begins for the minds of those without strong commitment to the existing political or social order and those committed to its overthrow.

That struggle is well described by Pareto in this classic text:

Theories designed to justify the use of force by the governed are almost always combined with theories condemning the use of force by the public authority. A few dreamers reject the use of force in general, on whatever side; but their theories either have no influence at all or else serve merely to weaken resistance on the part of people in power, so clearing the field for violence on the part of the governed. In view of that we may confine ourselves to considering such theories, in general, in the combined form.

No great number of theories are required to rouse to resistance and to the use of force people who are, or think they are, oppressed. The derivations therefore are chiefly designed to incline people who would otherwise be neutral in the struggle to condemn resistance on the part of the governing powers, and so to make their resistance less vigorous; or at a venture, to persuade the rulers themselves in that sense.[15]

In a democratic regime and in a society where many people have accepted democratic legitimacy, the most telling argument in that ideological battle will be an effort to distinguish formal democratic legitimacy reduced to legality from genuine democracy, which may be defined as the responsiveness of the rulers to the real will of the people. That will cannot be manifested through formal democracy. Radical critics, including the Fascists, have argued that civil liberties are insufficient, given the inequalities in resources of different groups in the society, particularly in view of the control of economic means necessary for political action. Partisans of this position use as evidence the private ownership of mass media or their control by the government, the informal sanctions of the society against radical supporters at the workplace, for example, the commitment of all established institutions to the existing social and political order, the essentially conservative bias of the whole culture, and most recently, the pervasive influence of the consumption-oriented society that promotes individual aspirations rather than collective action, and material goals rather than the transformation of power relations.[16] The radicals undoubtedly have a point. But who can say whether their failure to mobilize democratically those whom they claim to represent is a result of those constraints or of the lack of attractiveness of their program and leadership?

There are enormous differences between societies in this respect. We would be the last to argue that the introduction of liberal democratic institutions and political processes in underdeveloped countries, or in traditional societies where the cultural and social relations support an existing social order, could lead to a rapid and peaceful transformation through the political mobilization of the underprivileged. It is tempting to substitute the decisive action of minorities, confident in their interpretation of the "real" needs of the people, for the slow process of mobilization through political parties and mass organizations. Barred from access to power through electoral means and the influence on public opinion, a self-conscious elite, claiming to speak for the silent masses, is likely to reject political democracy in the name of its identification with inarticulate majorities. In the ideological arsenal, the concept of false consciousness offers such a minority an easy way out. The inevitable consequence is the rejection of political democracy and the advocacy of dictatorship by the conscious minority—presumably dictatorship aiming to create the preconditions for *real* democracy: that is, one giving the people a real opportunity to participate. It was in this sense that Marx understood the dictatorship of the proletariat as the emergency organization of the revolutionary act, as an instrument to destroy the state, which was as the tool of the ruling class, as an instrument that would itself wither away. Sartori has rightly noted that in Marx's own time, the term, which he incidentally uses only in three places, did not have the derogatory meaning attached to it today.[17] It was Lenin who changed the emphasis and argued that the dictatorship of the proletariat is more democratic than bourgeois democracy, in this classic text:

The dictatorship of the proletariat, i.e., the organization of the vanguard of the oppressed as the ruling class for the purpose of suppressing the oppressors, cannot result merely in an expansion of democracy. *Simultaneously* with an immense expansion of democracy, *which for the first time* becomes a democracy for the poor, democracy for the people, and not democracy for the money bags, the dictatorship of the proletariat imposes a series of restrictions on the freedom of the oppressors, the exploiters, the capitalists. We must suppress them . . . their resistance must be crushed by force; and it is clear that where there is suppression, where there is violence, there is no freedom and no democracy.[18]

The point is not to discuss Leninist theory and the relationship between democracy and the Communist society, but to recognize that Lenin's analysis argues that the Marxist-Leninist is always automatically democratic, whereas all others are always automatically nondemocratic. We do not have to turn to anti-Marxist critics to appreciate the dangerous implications of his thought; Rosa Luxemburg did it brilliantly in her analysis of the Russian revolution when she wrote:

Yes, dictatorship! But this dictatorship consists in the *manner of applying democracy,* not in its *elimination,* in energetic, resolute attacks upon the well-entrenched rights and economic relationships of bourgeois society, without which a socialist transformation cannot be accomplished. But this dictatorship must be the work of the *class* and not of a little leading minority in the name of the class—that is, it must proceed step by step out of the active participation of the masses; it must be under their direct influence, subjected to the control of complete public activity; it must arise out of the growing political training of the mass of the people.[19]

And she continues her eloquent testimony:

Freedom only for the supporters of the government, only for the members of one party—however numerous they may be—is no freedom at all. Freedom is always and exclusively freedom for the one who thinks differently. Not because of any fanatical concept of "justice" but because all that is instructive, wholesome and purifying in political freedom depends on this essential characteristic, and its effectiveness vanishes when "freedom" becomes a special privilege.[20]

Let us be clear, therefore, that political democracy does not necessarily assure even a reasonable approximation of what we would call a democratic society, a society with considerable equality of opportunity in all spheres, including *social* equality, as well as opportunity to formulate political alternatives and mobilize the electorate for them. We should also be clear that dictatorships by a minority, a party self-appointed as spokesmen for a class, or the "people" assumed to be the majority, has never led to a regime that would satisfy a formulation like Rosa Luxemburg's.

There is, however, considerable evidence that slowly, over time, political democracy as we have defined it has led to considerable progress in the direction of a democratic society. It has not reached it, but it has approached it in a few cases.

There can be little argument with those who reject political democracy, in view of its slow progress toward a democratic society.[21] They should be free to consider the problems we have discussed and the analyses in this book basically irrelevant. From their perspective, it probably makes little difference if some of the countries studied were ruled by a democracy inching toward a democratic society or by an authoritarian regime.[22] In fact, some of the goals they consider worth pursuing might be achieved as well or better by authoritarian regimes than by oligarchic or stalemated democracies. Authoritarian regimes, however, have other costs that we might not be ready to pay, and in our view they leave the problem of building legitimate and stable political institutions in the twentieth century unsolved. From this perspective, which we would not argue to be value-free, the problem of the breakdown of even imperfect political democracies seems relevant. The danger lies in indifference to the crises of democracies and in willingness to contribute to their acceleration, in the hope that crisis will lead to a revolutionary breakthrough toward a democratic society rather than mere political democracy. The vain hope of making democracies more democratic by undemocratic means has all too often contributed to regime crises and ultimately paved the way to autocratic rule.

Notes

CHAPTER 1

1. For a good review of the literature, see John D. May, *Of the Conditions and Measures of Democracy* (Morristown, N.J.: General Learning Press, 1973). The discussion was initiated by a seminal article by Seymour M. Lipset, "Some Social Requisites of Democracy: Economic Development and Political Legitimacy," *American Political Science Review* 53 (1959):69–105. Other major contributions to the debate were Harry Eckstein, "A Theory of Stable Democracy," appended to his *Division and Cohesion in Democracy: A Study of Norway* (Princeton, N.J.: Princeton University Press, 1966); and Robert A. Dahl, *Polyarchy: Participation and Opposition* (New Haven: Yale University Press, 1971). For a critical analysis, see Brian M. Barry, *Sociologists, Economists, and Democracy* (London: Collier-Macmillan, 1970), chap. 3. See also the collection of papers in the reader edited by Charles F. Cnudde and Deane E. Neubauer, *Empirical Democratic Theory* (Chicago: Markham, 1969).

2. In addition to the already quoted efforts of Lipset and Dahl, we can mention those of Phillips Cutright, "National Political Development: Its Measurement and Social Correlates," in *Politics and Social Life*, ed. Nelson W. Polsby, Robert A. Dentler, and Paul A. Smith (New York: Houghton Mifflin, 1963); and Deane E. Neubauer, "Some Conditions of Democracy," *American Political Science Review* 61 (December 1967):1002–9. On the much broader problem of the stability of political systems, democratic or not, the essay by Ted Robert Gurr, "Persistence and Change in Political Systems, 1800–1971," *American Political Science Review* 68 (December 1974):1482–1504, deserves special notice. See also Leon Hurwitz, "Democratic Political Stability: Some Traditional Hypotheses Reexamined," *Comparative Political Studies* 4 (January 1972):476–90; and idem, "An Index of Democratic Political Stability: A New Methodological Note," *Comparative Political Studies* 4 (April 1971):41–68.

3. In this respect the work of the historian-political scientist Karl Dietrich Bracher, beginning with his theoretical-historical essay "Auflösung einer Demokratie: Des Ende der Weimarer Republik als Forschungsproblem," in *Faktoren der Machtbildung*, ed. Arkadij Gurland (Berlin: Duncker and Humblot, 1952), pp. 39–98, has been pathbreaking. Our analysis has been inspired by and owes much to his thinking and monumental work.

4. Let us warn the reader that he will not find in this essay or in the chapters in this volume any formal model susceptible to computer simulation. Neither our training, the state of our knowledge, nor the complexity of the problem warranted it, but we would certainly welcome other scholars to try such a formulation of our efforts. For an example of how less formal analyses can be translated into a quite different language and scientific style, see Roland F. Moy, *A Computer Simulation of Democratic Political Development: Tests of the Lipset and Moore Models*, Comparative Politics Series, no. 01–019, vol. 2 (Beverly Hills, Ca.: Sage Professional Papers, 1971).

5. It would be interesting to study comparatively and systematically to what extent different participants, particularly the democratic leaders, were or were not aware of the dangers to the system at critical junctures before the final breakdown. For example, the statement of SPD (German Social-Democratic party) leader Breitscheid at the party congress in Magdeburg in 1929 about the implications of a breakup of the great coalition (which took place in March 1930) reveals both awareness of the threat to democracy and parliamentarianism and

unwillingness to make any sacrifice to save them. See Werner Conze, "Die Krise des Parteienstaates in Deutschland, 1929–30," in Gotthard Jasper, *Von Weimar zu Hitler, 1930–1933* (Cologne: Kiepenheuer and Witsch, 1968), p. 44. Even more foreboding were the pleas of Indalecio Prieto, the Spanish Socialist leader, in the spring of 1936, quoted in my chapter on Spain.

6. See the chapters on Latin American cases.

7. Our basic starting point is Max Weber's formulation, "methodological individualism." It is well stated in a 1920 letter quoted by Wolfgang J. Mommsen, "Diskussion über 'Max Weber und die Machtpolitik,'" in *Verhandungen des 15 deutschen Soziologentages: Max Weber und die Soziologie heute* (Tübingen: J. C. B. Mohr [Paul Siebeck], 1965), p. 137, as follows: "Sociology can be pursued only by starting from the actions of the one, few or many individuals [einzelnen]; strictly individualistic in the method.... The State in its sociological meaning is nothing but the probability [chance] that certain forms of specific actions shall take place. Actions of specific individual human beings. Nothing else.... the subjective in it that the actions are oriented by specific conceptions. The objective is that we the observers feel that there is a probability that these actions oriented by those conceptions will take place. If there is no such probability the State does not exist any more."

8. Our view of the social and political process conceives of historical situations as "... a relatively delicate balance between the forces working in radically opposed directions, so that the difference made by a war, a political movement, or even the influence of a single man may be of very far-reaching consequences.... It is not that such a factor 'creates' the result. It is rather that, in addition to the other forces working in that direction, it is sufficient to throw the total balance in favor of the one possible outcome rather than the other." Max Weber, in Reinhard Bendix, *Max Weber: An Intellectual Portrait* (London: Heinemann, 1960), p. 269. Incidentally, Sir James Jeans uses the same image: "The course of a railway train is uniquely prescribed for it at most points of its journey by the rails on which it runs. Here and there, however, it comes to a junction at which alternative courses are open to it, and it may be turned on to one or the other by the quite negligible expenditure of energy involved in moving the points." Quoted by Albert Speer in *Inside the Third Reich* (New York: Avon, 1971), p. 55.

9. Bracher, "Anflösung einer Demokratie."

10. For a stimulating discussion of the role of precipitating causes, see Robert McIver, *Social Causation* (Boston: Ginn and Co., 1942), esp. chap. 6, pp. 161–94.

11. Leadership is, for our purposes, a residual variable that ultimately—as the preceding text by Weber noted—cannot be ignored; but it should not be introduced before the explanatory power of other variables has been exhausted. In some cases, however, its contribution is so obvious that it should be given its due: For example, in our discussion of the reequilibration of French democracy in the transition from the Fourth to the Fifth Republic. The outcome there without de Gaulle would probably have been quite different. The problem of leadership and its quality—particularly in crisis situations—as an independent variable has tended to be neglected due to an overreaction against "great men in history" approaches and an overemphasis on sociological factors. See Lewis Edinger, "The Comparative Analysis of Political Leadership." For recent studies, see Lewis J. Edinger, ed., *Political Leadership: Studies in Comparative Analysis* (New York: John Wiley and Sons, 1967), and the Summer 1968 issue of *Daedalus*, entitled "Philosophers and Kings: Studies in Leadership."

12. The expression was coined by Ignazio Silone and serves as title to his book *The School for Dictators* (London: Jonathan Cape, 1939), a witty and insightful work that is very relevant for the readers of this volume. (Perhaps someone should write a "School for Democrats.")

13. On the problem of defining political democracy in terms that are both meaningful and operational, see Giovanni Sartori, *Democratic Theory* (Detroit, Mich.: Wayne State University Press, 1962); Dahl, *Polyarchy;* and the classic statements by Hans Kelsen, *Vom Wesen und Wert der Demokratie* (Tübingen: J. C. B. Mohr, 1929), and "Foundations of Democracy," *Ethics* 66 (October 1955), pt. 2.

14. See Juan J. Linz, "Totalitarian and Authoritarian Regimes," in *Handbook of Political Science,* ed. Fred I. Greenstein and Nelson W. Polsby (Reading, Mass.: Addison-Wesley, 1975), vol. 3, pp. 175–411, for a characterization of those different types of regimes and some considerations about the dynamics of change in and of them. The problem of decay, breakdown, and its aftermath in Iberian authoritarian regimes is discussed in Juan J. Linz,

"Spain and Portugal: Critical Choices," in *Western Europe: The Trials of Partnership*, ed. David S. Landes (Lexington, Mass: D. C. Heath, 1977), pp. 237–96.

15. The question of freedom for antidemocratic parties, particularly those advocating the use of force to overthrow democratic regimes, is a complex one. The question of legal repression of political organizations while upholding liberal institutions is discussed in Otto Kirchheimer, *Political Justice: The Use of Legal Procedures for Political Ends* (Princeton, N.J.: Princeton University Press, 1961), chap. 4, pp. 132–72, with particular emphasis on the West German application of constitutional provisions to the KPD and the right-wing SRP. For an analysis of the situation in the thirties, see Karl Loewenstein, "Legislative Control of Political Extremism in European Democracies," *Columbia Law Review* 38, no. 4 (April 1938), and no. 5 (May 1938), pp. 725–74.

16. The idea that at least one successful alternation in power at the national level between the democratic regime-instauring party or coalition and the opposition would be required to define a regime as democratic seems to us too stringent. Certainly, alternation of government and opposition at the national level is not frequent, even in two-party democracies. See Giovanni Sartori, "Il caso italiano: Salvare il pluralismo e superare la polarizzazione," *Revista Italiana di Sciènza Politica* 3 (1974):675–87 and 676–78. It is even less likely in multiparty systems, where shifting coalitions are frequent occurrences.

17. See Linz, "Totalitarian and Authoritarian Regimes," pp. 336–50. To get a sense of the limited change that the Dubček reforms represented in principle, see Alex Pravda, "Reform and Change in the Czechoslovak Political System: January–August 1968," Sage Research Papers in the Social Sciences (Beverly Hills, Ca.: Sage, 1975).

18. See the chapters on Venezuela and Colombia in this volume. The extensive literature on Austrian politics after World War II makes constant reference to this "learning."

19. Victor S. Mamatey and Radomir Luza, eds., *A History of the Czechoslovak Republic, 1918–1948* (Princeton, N.J.: Princeton University Press, 1973).

20. There is by now an extensive literature on this type of democracy. See, for example, Arend Lijphart, *Democracy in Plural Societies: A Comparative Exploration* (New Haven, Yale University Press, 1977). For a bibliography and selection of texts, see Kenneth D. McRae, ed., *Consociational Democracy: Political Accommodation in Segmented Societies* (Toronto: McClelland and Stewart, 1974). The concept, however, has not remained unchallenged. See Brian Barry, "Review Article: Political Accommodation and Consociational Democracy," *British Journal of Political Science* 5, no. 4 (1975):477–505.

21. The Weimar Republic lasted only from 1918 to 1933, if we include the period before the approval of the constitution and the presidential rather than parliamentary governments of the early thirties. However, it would be a mistake to ignore the largely liberal and incipiently democratic period under the Empire, in which the parties organized and free elections, both to the Reichstag and Länder legislatures, took place regularly. Even the Spanish Republic, proclaimed on 14 April 1931 and doomed on 18 July 1936, came after a century in which liberalism and democracy had imposed itself—with more or less success—and after forty-seven years of peaceful constitutional (or at least semiconstitutional) monarchy (1876–1923). The Italian liberal and increasingly (with the expansion of suffrage) democratic state had even deeper roots in the Risorgimento and unification periods.

22. The problem of durability has been analyzed in Harry Eckstein, *The Evaluation of Political Performance: Problems and Dimensions* (Beverly Hills, Ca.: Sage, 1971), pp. 21–32, and in Ted Robert Gurr and Muriel McClelland, *Political Performance: A Twelve-Nation Study* (Beverly Hills, Ca.: Sage, 1971), pp. 10–17.

23. Robert A. Dahl and Edward R. Tufte, in *Size and Democracy* (Stanford, Ca.: Stanford University Press, 1973), analyze thoroughly the hypotheses advanced on the ways in which small size might contribute to democracy.

24. See Klaus Epstein's review of books by Joseph Berlau, Peter Gay, and Carl Schorske in *World Politics* 11 (1959):629–51, and the concluding chapter in Guenther Roth, *The Social Democrats in Imperial Germany: A Study in Working-Class Isolation and National Integration* (Totowa, N.J.: Bedminster Press, 1963).

25. In this context, the book by Barrington Moore, *Social Origins of Dictatorship and Democracy* (Boston: Beacon Press, 1966), deserves mention. His deliberate neglect of the smaller states is compensated for in the following works: Dahl, *Polyarchy*; Hans Daalder, "Building Consociational Nations," in *Building States and Nations*, ed. S. N. Eisenstadt and Stein

Rokkan (Beverly Hills, Ca.: Sage, 1973), vol. 2, *Analyses by Region*, pp. 15-31; Dankwart Rustow, "Sweden's Transition to Democracy: Some Notes toward a Genetic Theory," *Scandinavian Political Studies* 6 (1971): 9-26; and Francis G. Castles, "Barrington Moore's Thesis and Swedish Political Development," *Government and Opposition* 8, no. 3 (1973): 313-31.

26. Austria in the twenties saw periods in which the main "camps" were able to overcome their differences; the Baltic republics, after gaining their independence and enduring short civil wars followed by thorough agrarian reforms, seemed destined for stability; and even the Weimar Republic at one point seemed on the way to stabilization. On the other hand, we have countries like Belgium, which have experienced serious political crises without experiencing any serious danger to their democratic institutions. Our analysis, therefore, should be complemented by the study of periods of consolidation and stabilization of democracy, and of successful weathering of crises.

27. Richard Rose, "Dynamic Tendencies in the Authority of Regimes," *World Politics* 21, no. 4 (July 1969):602-28.

28. Friedrich Meinecke, *The German Catastrophe: Reflections and Recollections* (Cambridge, Mass.: Harvard University Press, 1950), p. 63. He writes: "I said to myself with the deepest consternation not only that a day of misfortune of the first order had dawned for Germany, but also, 'This was not necessary.' Here existed no pressing political or historical necessity such as had led to the downfall of William II in the Autumn of 1918. Here it was no general tendency, but something like chance, specifically Hindenburg's weakness, that had turned the scales."

29. In his classic typology of authority, Weber does not explicitly discuss the distinction between democratic (or "polyarchic," to use Dahl's terminology) and nondemocratic regimes, but there is an obvious overlap between his type of legal-rational authority and democratic regimes as we have defined them. As he deliberately avoided the problems posed by the natural law critics—emphasizing considerations of substantive justice rather than "formal" justice—we have avoided the question of responsiveness in democracies in favor of a criterion of formal accountability that has the advantage of relatively easy empirical verification. On this distinction, see Juan J. Linz, "Michels e il suo contributo alla sociologìa polìtica." Introduction to Roberto Michels, *La sociologia del partito politico nella democrazia moderna* (Bologna: Il Mulino, 1966), pp. lxxxi-xcii.

30. The natural law tradition inevitably places justice above formal legality and "general principles of law" above enacted laws, but offers no unequivocal means of ascertaining what they are, unless we would turn to the claims made by the Catholic church to define what is "natural," *sive recta rationis*. Such a claim has been used by Catholic thinkers to justify tyrannicide and the right to rebellion, and in the American Protestant and secular tradition of "civil disobedience." For Catholic thought, see Heinrich A. Rommen, *The State in Catholic Thought: A Treatise in Political Philosophy* (St. Louis, Mo.: Herder, 1945), pp. 473-76. Both can also serve minorities who want to challenge, even violently, the actions of legally elected authorities acting constitutionally when these authorities are perceived as threatening ultimate values. This was the argument used by some Catholics to justify the uprising against the Republican government in Spain; see the influential book by Aniceto de Castro Albarrán, *El derecho a la rebeldía* (Madrid: Imp. Gráfica Universal, 1934).

31. The distinction between a denial of legitimacy to the political system and its denial to the socioeconomic system is basically analytical. In reality the two are difficult to distinguish. Certainly a deep hatred toward a socioeconomic order almost inevitably leads to denial of legitimacy to the political system should the system sustain that social order or even allow its reestablishment. Since a democracy (as we have defined it) assures the survival of such a hated order if the majority supports it, or allows the temporarily defeated minority to argue freely for its restoration, the rejection of democracy in that case would be a logical consequence. Similarly, those who value a socioeconomic order so highly that the prospect of even a temporary democratically imposed change would be unacceptable will turn against democracy. A more serious question arises if we argue that free competition in regular elections for the power to implement alternative programs requires organizational and economic resources, and a degree of personal independence, which can only be guaranteed by a free disposal of resources by groups and individuals escaping the control of the government

and its supporters. More concretely, if the socialization of property and income beyond basic individual needs, and the integration into single-interest organizations privileged by and dependent on the government, would deprive the opposition of any opportunity to organize its appeal, we would conclude that the establishment of such a socioeconomic and institutional order is incompatible with political democracy. Paradoxically, the liberals fearful of socialism and those who argue that in a classless Socialist society there is no need for competition between parties agree in their ultimate conclusion.

32. Meinecke, *German Catastrophe,* pp. 63–65, rightly stresses the importance of this point in the interpretation of the historical process. It is also decisive in determining whether the defense of democracy is possible, since the alternative view, which links the outcome of the conflict inevitably with underlying structural problems, external factors, cultural traditions, etc., undermines the defenders' faith in their success, and therefore their will. It also contributes to the willingness of others to pursue their goals "preventively," without waiting for change within a democratic framework that is ultimately doomed.

33. The ideological ambiguity of maximalist Marxist socialism in contrast to social-democratic reformism—first formulated by Bernstein—has often been noted but not systematically studied. A good analysis of one of its variants is Norbert Leser, *Zwischen Reformismus und Bolschewismus: Der Austromarxismus als Theorie und Praxis* (Vienna: Europa, 1968). Another is Erich Matthias, "Kautsky und der Kautskyanismus: Die Funktion der Ideologie in der deutschen Sozialdemokratie vor dem ersten Weltkrieg," in *Marxismusstudien,* ed. Iring Fetscher, (Tübingen: J. C. B. Mohr, 1957), vol. 2., pp. 151–97. Even in Harold Laski's *Democracy in Crisis* (Chapel Hill, N. C.: University of North Carolina Press, 1933), we find this ambiguous formulation applied to the United Kingdom in the thirties: "I believe, therefore, that the attainment of power by the Labour Party in the normal electoral fashion must result in a radical transformation of parliamentary government. Such an administration could not, if it sought to be effective, accept the present forms of its procedure. It would have to take vast powers, and legislate under them by ordinance and decree; it would have to suspend the classic formulae of normal opposition. If its policy met with peaceful acceptance, the continuance of parliamentary government would depend upon its possession of guarantees from the Conservative Party that its work of transformation would not be disrupted by repeal in the event of its defeat at the polls."

34. Obviously there will be those who sincerely feel that other human values rank higher, and who, if democracy cannot insure those values because an "unenlightened" electorate lacks the proper "consciousness of its interests," will be prepared to bend democracy and the civil liberties it presupposes to their wishes or threaten revolutionary action should it be an obstacle to them. Certainly in the face of poverty, inequality, economic stagnation, and national dependency on foreign powers accepted by democratic rulers (for example, the Weimar politicians accepting with reservations an *Erfüllungspolitik*), such a response is understandable. However, those who think this way should be very sure that the odds in a nonelectoral struggle are in their favor; they should remember that for each successful revolution there have been more victorious counterrevolutions that have represented not only the maintenance of the status quo but often a loss of gains already made and terrible costs for those advocating such radical changes.

CHAPTER 2

1. This point is well developed in M. Rainer Lepsius, "Machtübernähme und Machtübergäbe: Zur Strategie des Regimewechsels," in *Sozialtheorie und Soziale Praxis: Homage to Eduard Baumgarten,* Mannheimer Sozialwissenschaftliche Studien, vol. 3, ed. Hans Albert et al. (Meisenheim: Anton Hain, 1971), pp. 158–73.

2. Popular revolutions (*strictu sensu*), particularly Marxist-inspired revolutions, have not succeeded in countries with liberal and relatively democratic institutions. The attempts made in Germany and Finland at the end of World War I and the October revolution in Asturias

(Spain) failed; the revolutionary climate in northern Italy in 1919 came to nothing. Even some of the attempts in more autocratic countries, such as Hungary, have also failed. The successful revolutions of the twentieth century have been against nondemocratic regimes: Mexico, Russia, Yugoslavia, China, and Cuba, and in colonial countries in the process of gaining independence, such as Vietnam and Algeria. In the case of Russia, China, and Yugoslavia, war was a major contributing factor. Nine of the peasant-based revolutions in Mexico, Russia, China, Vietnam, Algeria, and Cuba studied by Eric Wolf in *Peasant Wars of the Twentieth Century* (New York: Harper and Row, 1969) were directed against minimally established democratic regimes. As Edward Malefakis has noted, the Spanish peasantry in the revolutionary civil war was divided between the two sides and did not constitute the core of the revolutionary forces. In addition, its revolutionary mobilization during the Republic was limited, and it had no role in the October revolution. See "Peasants, Politics, and Civil War in Spain, 1931–1936," in *Modern European Social History*, ed. Robert Bezucha (Lexington, Mass.: D. C. Heath, 1972), pp. 192–227.

3. Whether or not to consider the Nazi impact on German society revolutionary depends on one's concept of revolution. Obviously, if only changes in the ownership of the means of production define revolution, Hitler's rule was not revolutionary. If we consider radical changes in the status structure, the position of the army and the churches, control of the economy, and above all, the values of the society as being the defining factors, it certainly was a revolution. Even if we consider changes toward equality as the defining factor, the leveling of traditional German status distinctions by inverting the social hierarchies in and by the party, even the equality before despotic arbitrary power, we could argue that it was revolutionary.

    The changes in German society that were planned and, in part, realized, which are described by David Schoenbaum in *Hitler's Social Revolution: Class and Status in Nazi Germany, 1933–1939* (Garden City, N.Y.: Doubleday, 1963), are different from those resulting from most breakdowns of democracy in Europe. See also Ralf Dahrendorf, *Society and Democracy in Germany* (Garden City, N.Y.: Doubleday, 1969), pp. 381–96, for an insightful discussion of the "unintended" modernizing effect of the National Socialist revolution on German society.

4. In this context see Eckstein, *Evaluation of Political Performance*, pp. 32–50. Even where political violence contributes ultimately to the breakdown of a regime, the peak of the violence does not necessarily coincide with the final phase. Civil war, putsches, and assassinations characterized the early years of the Weimar Republic and were followed by a phase of consolidation, but they left a legacy of disloyalty and skepticism about the regime. In Spain, the revolution of October 1934 did not produce a breakdown but wounded the system deeply. For an example of the time series needed to relate both phenomena and the different components of violence, see "Political Protest and Executive Change," Section 3 of Charles L. Taylor and Michael C. Hudson, *World Handbook of Political and Social Indicators* (New Haven: Yale University Press, 1972), pp. 59–199. One of the more sophisticated comparative analyses is Ivo K. Feierabend, with Rosalind L. Feierabend and Betty A. Nesvold, "The Comparative Study of Revolution and Violence," *Comparative Politics* 5, no. 3 (April 1973):393–424 (with bibliographic references). It was initiated by the earlier work of Ted Robert Gurr, including (with Charles Ruttenberg) *The Conditions of Civil Violence: First Tests of a Causal Model*, Princeton University, Center of International Studies, Research Monograph no. 28 (Princeton, N.J., 1967). See also Douglas A. Hibbs, Jr., *Mass Political Violence: A Cross-National Causal Analysis* (New York: Wiley, 1973). Unfortunately, there are no comparable cross-national studies of internal violence in the interwar years to contrast the rates of violence in countries experiencing a breakdown of regimes, those not experiencing a breakdown, and contemporary rates. Nor is it easy, as we shall note, to relate the different measures of violence—rate, intensity, type, location—with the problem of stability of regimes. Certainly, northern Italian violence was high before 1922, but the south was relatively quiescent; the pervasive threat of violence caused by the Nazi SA presence is difficult to compare with the more deadly actions of the *squadristi*, etc. This would be an interesting area for comparative historical research.

5. An excellent example is Peter Merkl, *Political Violence under the Swastika: 581 Early Nazis* (Princeton, N.J.: Princeton University Press, 1975). There is no comparable study of Italian

squadrismo. The reaction of the authorities and the courts toward political violence also deserves study. For Weimar Germany we have the work of Emil J. Gumbel, *Vom Fememord zur Reichskanzlei* (Heidelberg: Lambert Schneider, 1962), based on his studies in the twenties, like *Zwei Jahre Mord* (Berlin: Neues Vaterland, 1921), but there are no comparable analyses of judicial treatment of violence in Italy, Austria, or Spain in the crisis period.

6. The ambiguities in the German case are well discussed in Hans Schneider, "Das Ermächtigungsgesetz vom 24, März 1933," in *Von Weimar zu Hitler: 1930-1933*, ed. Gotthard Jasper (Cologne: Kiepenheuer and Witsch, 1968) pp. 405–42, which quotes the relevant literature. See also Hans Boldt, "Article 48 of the Weimar Constitution: Its Historical and Political Implications," in *German Democracy and the Triumph of Hitler*, ed. Anthony Nicholls and Erich Matthias (London: Georg Allen and Unwin, 1971), pp. 79–98. This is one of the few cases in which legality came into conflict with democratic legitimacy, one in which legal procedures were used to achieve ends in clear conflict with the basic assumptions of democratic legitimacy. The bureaucracies and the armed forces—particularly in the German/Prussian tradition—were more bound to legality, positivistically understood, than committed to liberal-democratic values, which facilitated the Nazi *Machtergreifung* and consolidation in power enormously. It assured the new rulers the loyalty of many who would be far from being their supporters.

7. We regret that we have not included an analysis of the breakdown or overthrow of democracy in Czechoslovakia in 1948. Obviously the pressures and the more or less direct intervention of the Soviet Union make this a special case. See Josef Korbel, *Communist Subversion of Czechoslovakia, 1938-1948: The Failure of Co-existence* (Princeton, N.J.: Princeton University Press, 1959) and Pavel Tigrid, "The Prague Coup of 1948: The Elegant Takeover," in *The Anatomy of Communist Takeovers*, ed. Thomas T. Hammond and Robert Farrell (New Haven: Yale University Press, 1975), with bibliographic references to Western and recent Czech sources. The same can be said for the sequence of events leading to the secession of Slovakia after the Munich *diktat* and the internal transformation of the Czech remainder state before its incorporation into Germany as the *Reichsprotektorat*.

8. Max Weber, in *Economy and Society*, ed. Guenther Roth and Claus Wittich (New York: Bedminster Press, 1968), pp. 212-13 stated:

> Domination was defined above (ch. I:16) as the probability that certain specific commands (or all commands) will be obeyed by a given group of persons. It thus does not include every mode of exercising "power" or "influence" over other persons. Domination ("authority") in this sense may be based on the most diverse motives of compliance: all the way from simple habituation to the most purely rational calculation of advantage. Hence every genuine form of domination implies a minimum of voluntary compliance, that is, an *interest* (based on ulterior motives or genuine acceptance) in obedience. Normally the rule over a considerable number of persons requires a staff (cf. ch. I:12), that is, a *special* group which can normally be trusted to execute the general policy as well as the specific commands. The members of the administrative staff may be bound to obedience to their superior (or superiors) by custom, by affectual ties, by a purely material complex of interests, or by ideal (*wertrationale*) motives. The quality of these motives largely determines the type of domination. *Purely* material interests and calculations of advantages as the basis of solidarity between the chief and his administrative staff result, in this as in other connexions, in a relatively unstable situation. Normally, other elements, affectual and ideal, supplement such interests. In certain exceptional cases the former alone may be decisive. In everyday life these relationships, like others, are governed by custom and material calculation of advantage.

9. Ibid., p. 213.
10. John F. Kennedy, during the Oxford, Mississippi, crisis, as quoted in the *New York Times*, 1 October 1962, p. 22.
11. Ibid.
12. "Multiple sovereignty is the identifying feature of revolutions. A revolution begins when a government previously under the control of a single, sovereign polity becomes the object of effective, competing, mutually exclusive claims on the part of two or more distinct polities; it ends when a single sovereign polity regains control over government." Charles Tilly,

"Revolutions and Collective Violence," in Greenstein and Polsby, *Handbook of Political Science*, vol. 3, p. 519. This excellent essay coincides in many points with our analysis and complements it in other respects. Tilly's critical review of other approaches saves us from the need to do such a review here.

13. This is not the place to quote the extensive bibliography on military interventions in politics. See Linz, "Totalitarian and Authoritarian Regimes," for a brief review of the problem and references to the literature. A recent addition to the growing literature on the subject is William R. Thompson, "Regime Vulnerability and the Military Coup," *Comparative Politics* 7, no. 4 (1975):459–87, which has extensive bibliographic references. Alfred Stepan, in *The Military in Politics: Changing Patterns in Brazil* (Princeton, N.J.: Princeton University Press, 1974), and in his chapter in this volume, shows how military intervention must be seen in the light of the actions of democratic rulers along the lines suggested in this essay, and not just from a perspective centered almost exclusively on the military.

14. On this point, see Juan J. Linz, "The Bases of Political Diversity in West German Politics" (Ph.D. diss., Columbia University, 1959). See also the chapter entitled "Cleavage and Consensus in West German Politics: The Early Fifties," in *Party Systems and Voter Alignments: Cross-National Perspectives*, ed. Seymour M. Lipset and Stein Rokkan, (New York: Free Press, 1967), pp. 305–16.

A fascinating set of data deserving further, sophisticated analysis is the long time series with identical or largely comparable questions on the overall support for prime ministers in different social groups and across party lines. Such diffuse support, tolerance, or rejection is one component and indicator of the willingness to grant legitimacy to a regime. See, for example: Pierpaolo Luzzato Fegiz, *Il volto sconosciuto dell' Italia: Dièci anni di sondagi Doxa* (Milan: Giuffrè, 1956), pp. 534–47; idem, *Il volto sconosciuto dell' Italia: Seconda serie, 1956–1965* (Milan: Giuffrè, 1966), pp. 865–99; and Elisabeth Noelle and Erich Peter Neumann, ed., *Jahrbuch der Öffentlichen Meinung, 1965–1967*, Allensbach, Institut für Demoskopie, 1967, Ib. *Jahrbuch der Öffentlichen Meinung 1968 bis 1973*, ib. 1974.

15. This point has been made with incomparable irony by Vilfredo Pareto in *The Mind and Society: A Treatise on General Sociology*, 2 vols. (New York: Dover, 1965), no. 585.

16. The mixed character of the bases of legitimacy of any actual democracy was emphasized by Max Weber in the course of his work, particularly in his political writings. In his view, the charisma of the statesman-political leader could contribute to the authority of democratic institutions. In this respect Harry Eckstein's thesis of congruence of authority patterns and the contribution that an authoritative leadership can make in a more authoritarian society— he refers specifically to the Kanzlerdemokratie in the German Federal Republic—is in the Weberian tradition.

17. The hypothesis that "the stability of a democratic system depends on both its *effectiveness* and its *legitimacy*, although these two concepts have often been confused in the concrete analysis of the crisis of a given political system," an elaboration of that distinction, and an application to some examples was first made by Lipset, emerging out of discussions with the author, in his essay "Political Sociology," in *Sociology Today: Problems and Prospects*, ed. Robert K. Merton, Leonard Broom, and Leonard S. Cottrell, Jr. (New York: Basic Books, 1959), pp. 81–114, esp. pp. 108–9. Lipset reiterated the point in *Political Man: the Social Bases of Politics*, (Garden City, N.Y.: Doubleday, 1960), chap. 3, pp. 77–98.

18. Leonardo Morlino, building on Eckstein, arrives at formulations very close to ours. He notes the need to distinguish decision-making efficacy from the capacity to implement decisions overcoming constraining conditions—to distinguish outputs from outcomes. In a footnote he even says: "The necessity to take into account [in the analysis] the outputs instead of the outcomes is another reason why we prefer decisional efficacy to effectiveness; effectiveness [effetività] tends to put the emphasis on the results. Our analysis makes efficacy and effectiveness separate variables in relation to the breakdown process, since they are not interchangeable or two dimensions of a single concept." See "Stabilità, legittimita e efficàcia decisionale nei sistèmi democràtici," *Rivista Italiana di Sciènza Polìtica* 3, no. 2 (August 1973):247–316, particularly pp. 280 ff.

Some time after I had written this analysis, someone called to my attention that Chester I. Barnard, in *The Functions of the Executive* (Cambridge, Mass.: Harvard University Press, 1947), pp. 19–20, used the terms "efficiency" and "effectiveness" to refer to a distinction similar to the one I had made between efficacy and effectiveness. I had read Barnard but was unaware of the following passage linking his work with mine:

> When a specific desired end is attained we shall say that the action is "effective." When the unsought consequences of the action are more important than the attainment of the desired end and are dissatisfactory, effective action, we shall say, is "inefficient." When the unsought consequences are unimportant or trivial, the action is "efficient." Moreover, it sometimes happens that the end sought is not attained, but the unsought consequences satisfy desires or motives not the "cause" of the action. We shall then regard such action as efficient but not effective. In retrospect the action in this case is justified not by the results sought but by those not sought. These observations are matters of common personal experience.
>
> Accordingly we shall say that an action is effective if it accomplishes its specific objective aim. We shall also say it is efficient if it satisfies the motives of that aim, whether it is effective or not, and the process does not create offsetting dissatisfactions. We shall say that an action is inefficient if the motives of that aim are not satisfied, or offsetting dissatisfactions are incurred, even if it is effective. This often occurs; we find we do not want what we thought we wanted.

19. Mancur Olson, *The Logic of Collective Action: Public Goods and the Theory of Groups* (Cambridge, Mass: Harvard University Press, 1965), pp. 132–33, 165–67, and 174–78.
20. The "function" or "purpose" of the state was a central theme in traditional political science—as the German literature on the *Staatszweck* shows. For a critical discussion, see Hermann Heller, *Staatslehre* (Leiden: A. W. Sijthoff's Uitgeversmaatschappij N.V., 1934). In a sense, the literature on "outputs" of the political system and on the role of the state in developing countries has replaced that approach, not always improving on earlier formulations.

   Since this essay was written, a new interest in problems close to our discussion of "unsolvable" problems has emerged around the questions of "overload of government" and "ungovernability." See the papers presented at the Colloquium on Overloaded Government, European University Institute, Florence, December 1976; Richard Rose, "Governing and Ungovernability: A Skeptical Inquiry," *Studies in Public Policy*, Centre for the Study of Public Policy, University of Strathclyde, Glasgow, 1977; and Erwin K. Scheuch, *Wird die Bundesrepublik unregierbar* (Cologne: Arbeitgeberverband der Metallindustrie, 1976).
21. Robert A. Dahl, *A Preface to Democratic Theory* (Chicago: University of Chicago Press, 1956), chap. 4, "Equality, Diversity, and Intensity," pp. 90–123.
22. Unfortunately, we have little data on how electorates and key elites perceive past regimes at different moments in time—immediately after their fall, in the course of the consolidation of a new regime, and with the passing of time—and how the performance of preceding regimes serves as frame of reference in the evaluation of new regimes. Social science should pay much more attention to what Maurice Halbwachs called *La Mémoire collective* (Paris: Presses universitaires de France, 1950).

   Since World War II, German survey research and an isolated study of Italian opinion have explored the image of past regimes. See G. R. Boynton and Gerhard Loewenberg, "The Decay of Support for Monarchy and the Hitler Regime in the Federal Republic of Germany," *British Journal of Political Science* 4 (1975):453–88, which relates those responses to satisfaction with the present regime.
23. Otto Kirchheimer, "Confining Conditions and Revolutionary Breakthroughs," *American Political Science Review* 59 (1965):964–74; the article has been anthologized in *Politics, Law and Social Change*, ed. Frederic S. Burin and Kurt L. Shell (New York: Columbia University Press, 1969).
24. Albert O. Hirschman, *Journeys toward Progress: Studies of Economic Policy-Making in Latin America* (Garden City, N.Y.: Doubleday, 1965), chap. 5, "The Continuing of Reform," pp. 327–84.
25. Albert O. Hirschman, "The Changing Tolerance for More Inequality in the Course of Economic Development; With a Mathematical Appendix by Michael Rothschild," *Quarterly Journal of Economics* 87 (November 1973):544–66.

26. Gabriel A. Almond and Sidney Verba, *The Civic Culture: Political Attitudes and Democracy in Five Nations* (Princeton, N.J.: Princeton University Press, 1963), is one of the outstanding exceptions. Steven F. Cohn, "Loss of Legitimacy and the Breakdown of Democratic Regimes: The Case of the Fourth Republic" (Ph.D. diss. Columbia University, 1976), is the first effort to test the questions raised here systematically with survey data collected over time under the Fourth Republic.

27. On this point see the discussion of "governmental inaction" by Charles Tilly in "Revolutions and Collective Violence," pp. 532–33, and Ted Robert Gurr, *Why Men Rebel* (Princeton, N.J.: Princeton University Press, 1969), pp. 235–36.

28. John F. Kennedy, in his speech on the Oxford, Mississippi, crisis. *New York Times,* 1 October 1962, p. 22.

29. Harry Eckstein, "On the Etiology of Internal Wars," *History and Theory* 4, no. 2 (1965):133–63, quotes Trotsky's list of the three elements necessary for revolution: "the political consciousness of the revolutionary class, the discontent of intermediate layers, and a ruling class which has lost faith in itself." Tilly, in "Revolutions and Collective Violence," in a list of four proximate conditions of revolution lists "incapacity or unwillingness of the agents of the government to suppress the alternative coalition or the commitment to its claims" (p. 521), and proceeds (pp. 532–37) to analyze "governmental inaction." The fate of the liberal state in Italy was certainly sealed when it tolerated—for whatever reasons (complicity or incapacity)—situations like those described by Renzo De Felice in *Mussolini il fascista, i Vol. I, La conquista del potere: 1921–1925* (Turin: Einaudi, 1966), pp. 25–30, 88–89, and 129. It was Fascist, Nazi, proletarian violence, which governments were partly unwilling and partly unable to check, that created a power vacuum leading to the breakdown. The Italian politician Salandra formulated it well when he wrote in a letter on 15 August 1922: "As you know I am, as you, both admiring and worried about fascism. Six years of weak and absent government, on occasion treasonous, have led us to put the hopes of the saving of the country in a force armed and organized outside of the powers of the State. This is a profoundly anarchic phenomenon in the strict sense of the word." See p. 286.

    On the other hand, Mussolini could comment to a fellow Fascist, G. Rossi: "If in Italy there were a government deserving that name today, without further delay it should send its agents and carabinieri to seal and occupy our offices. An organization armed with both cadres and a *Regolamento* [disciplinary code for its members] is inconceivable in a State that has its Army and its police. Therefore there is no state in Italy. It is useless; therefore, we have necessarily to come to power. Otherwise the history of Italy will become a *pochade* [an unfinished draft]." Ibid., p. 317. This was his response to the Facta government's failure to react to the provocation of institutionalizing a private army. Authority that is unwilling or unable to use force when challenged by force loses its claim to the obedience of even those not ready to question it. For them, authority may be prior to coercion, but for opponents like the *squadristi* the only resource left is effective coercion.

30. Pareto, *Mind and Society*, vol. 2, pp. 1527–28, no. 2186. To avoid the dangerous misinterpretation of Pareto as a mindless advocate of force, this text should be read in conjunction with numbers 2174 and 2175 (pp. 1512–13). In the context of our discussion it should be clear that those responsible for the maintenance of a democratic political order should be given, by those believing in the legitimacy of that order, the right to use adequate force to thwart opponents ready to use force to overthrow or to dislocate that order. The issue of coercion on the authorities or other citizens by political groups, the preparedness to do so, is not part of civil liberties, nor is the advocacy of such use by political leaders. Obviously such a rule must be applied without partisanship. A modern state cannot tolerate political groups, even those committed to democracy, defending themselves rather than being protected by the state.

31. Our excursus about the relationship between party systems and democratic stability is based on the extraordinarily insightful and stimulating typology of party systems and the analysis of their dynamics found in Giovanni Sartori, *Parties and Party Systems: A Framework for Analysis* (Cambridge: Cambridge University Press, 1976), vol. 1, chaps. 5 and 6, pp. 119–216.

32. Giuseppe Di Palma, *Surviving without Governing: The Italian Parties in Parliament* (Berkeley and Los Angeles: University of California Press, 1977), chaps. 6 and 7, pp. 219–86. For

the debate provoked by Sartori's application of his model of polarized multiparty systems to contemporary Italy, see his "Il caso italiano"; and Luciano Pellicani, "Verso il superamento del pluralismo polarizzato," in idem, pp. 645–74, where the reader will find other writings on the subject.

33. The idea of "dual sovereignty" implicit in Pareto's analysis was articulated by Leon Trotsky but also stated by Mussolini. On 4 October (less than a month before the March on Rome), he quoted with approval a newspaper analysis: "There are two governments in Italy today—one too many." Quoted in Christopher Seton-Watson, *Italy from Liberalism to Fascism: 1870–1925* (London: Methuen, 1967), p. 617. For an intelligent use of this notion of multiple sovereignty in the study of revolutions, see Tilly, "Revolutions and Collective Violence."

34. The whole problem of different types of opposition in democracies has been discussed in Robert A. Dahl's contributions to *Political Oppositions in Western Democracies* (New Haven: Yale University Press, 1966), and his *Polyarchy*.

35. Richard Rose, *Governing without Consensus: An Irish Perspective* (Boston: Beacon Press, 1971). See particularly chap. 5, "How People View the Regime," pp. 179–202, and chap. 7, "Party Allegiance," pp. 218–246. See also Arend Lijphart, "The Northern Ireland Problem: Cases, Theories, and Solutions," *British Journal of Political Science* 5 (1975):83–106. See also Richard Rose, *Northern Ireland: Time of Choice* (Washington, D.C.: American Enterprise Institute, 1976), and idem, "On the Priorities of Citizenship in the Deep South and Northern Ireland," *Journal of Politics* 38 (1976):247–91.

When permanent, numerically weak minorities of distinctive cultural, racial, national, and religious characteristics are confronted with a majority that rejects cooperation with them, then the rights of that minority are not likely to be protected, nor are its interests taken into account by the rule "one man, one vote." (This is particularly true with single-member, majority representation.) In this case all the formal elements of democracy may exist, but the spirit may be violated or absent. Rose argues that in such a situation equality before the courts, and the enforcement of legal rights by them, might be a better avenue than the vote to the benefits of citizenship.

36. In this context, Roth, *Social Democrats in Imperial Germany*, is particularly relevant. For the concept of negative integration, see pp. 311–22.

37. A prime example would be the convergence of the Nazis and the Communists in parliamentary opposition to the Weimar parties, which made the "system" unworkable. A more concrete example would be the strike of the Berlin city transport workers in 1932, initiated, against the decision of the trade unions, by the Nazis and Communists, who turned to sabotage and violence. This strike had an important psychological impact on the thinking of the *Reichswehr* and its planning for a two-pronged attack. See Hans Otto Meissner and Harry Wilde, *Die Machtergreifung: Ein Bericht über die Technik des Nationalsozialistischen Staatsstreiches* (Stuttgart: Cotta'sche Buchhandlung, 1958), pp. 11–20, for an account of those events. On the policy of the KPD, see Hermann Weber, *Die Wandlung des deutschen Kommunismus: Die Stalinisierung der KPD in der Weimarer Republik* (Frankfurt: Europäische Verlagsanstalt, 1969). On the *Reichswehr* reaction, see Francis L. Carsten, *Reichswehr und Politik, 1918–1933* (Cologne: Kiepenheuer and Witsch, 1964), pp. 429 ff.

38. This is not to deny that such forces do not play a role in politics, but they certainly do not operate to the extent and in the way they are alleged to do in such simplified conspiratorial interpretations of politics. For an outstanding analysis of this style of politics, see Seymour M. Lipset and Earl Raab, *The Politics of Unreason: Right-Wing Extremism in America, 1790–1970* (New York: Harper and Row, 1970). Extremists, themselves prone to conspiratorial activities, infiltration, manipulation of causes, and untruthful propaganda, are likely to project their behavior onto their opponents. The danger point is reached when such beliefs become shared by more moderate, Establishment types, as when Attorney General Brownell abetted the labeling of the Democratic party with treason in the heyday of McCarthyism.

39. On the French crisis in 1958, see Cohn, "Losses of Legitimacy," which developed ideas originally presented at the World Congress of Sociology in Varna, Bulgaria, in 1970. This monograph tests many of the hypotheses of this chapter, including a sophisticated analysis of the available survey data collected by the IFOP.

Scandals occupy a special place in French politics and have contributed considerably to the delegitimation of politicians, parties, Parliament, and the Third and Fourth Republics. For an insightful analysis of the functions and dynamics of scandals (very applicable to the Spanish crisis in 1935), see Philip Williams, "The Politics of Scandal," in *Wars, Plots, and Scandals in Post-War France* (Cambridge: Cambridge University Press, 1970), pp. 3–16. For a review of the literature on the May 1958 crisis, see idem, pp. 129–66.

40. On the Italian perception of the Communist party, see Juan J. Linz, "La democrazìa italiana di fronte al futuro," in *Il caso italiano: Italia anni 70*, ed. Fabio Luca Cavazza and Stephen R. Graubard (Milano: Garzanti, 1974), pp. 124–62. See esp. p. 161, which also refers to comparable French data. Also see Giacomo Sani, "Mass Constraints on Coalition Realignments: Images of Anti-System Parties in Italy," *British Journal of Political Science* 5, (January 1976):1–32, and "Mass Level Response to Party Strategy: The Italian Electorate and the Communist Party," in *Communism in Italy and France*, ed. Donald L. Blackmer and Sidney Tarrow (Princeton, N.J.: Princeton University Press, 1975), pp. 456–544.

41. See chapter by Risto Alapuro and Erik Allardt, "The Lapua Movement: The Threat of Rightist Takeover in Finland, 1930–32," in this volume.

42. The danger of identifying the regime with the policies of the first majority that instored it is well stated by Gil Robles:

> Against whom has national opinion voted? Has it voted against the regime or against its policy? For me, honestly, at least today, the Spanish people has voted against the policy of the Constituent Assembly. However, if you, who have in your hands the governing of the state, you who militate in the opposition, insist in identifying, as until now, the policy followed with the regime; if you attempt to convince the Spanish people that socialism, sectarianism and Republic are consubstantial, then you can rest assured that the people will vote against the Republic and the regime. In that hypothesis it shall not be us who shall oppose the sweeping march of Spanish opinion.

Quoted in Carlos Seco Serrano, "La experiencia de la derecha posibilista en la Segunda república española: Estudio preliminar," in José María Gil Robles, *Discursos parlamentarios* (Madrid: Taurus, 1971), xxxiii–xxxiv.

43. Rose, "Dynamic Tendencies in the Authority of Regimes."

44. The relationship between government-cabinet stability or instability and regime stability needs further exploration. Recently, considerable attention has been paid to a more systematic measurement of cabinet instability and the analysis of its causes. See, for example, Hurwitz, "An Index of Democratic Political Stability," and Michael Taylor and V. M. Herman, "Party Systems and Government Stability," *American Political Science Review* 65 (1971):28–37. Klaus von Beyme, *Die parlamentarischen Regierungssysteme in Europa* (Munich: R. Piper, 1970), presents data on cabinet instability in a number of European countries since the nineteenth century and its causes; see pp. 875–84 and 901–67. An excellent monograph on the subject is A. Soulier, *L'instabilité ministériele sous la Troisième République (1871–1938)* (Paris: Recueil Sirey, 1939).

We have some systematic evidence that cabinet instability is closely related to the breakdown of European parliamentary democracies in the interwar years, and to the intensity of the crises. Obviously, this is not a cause-and-effect relationship, since government instability is a reflection of the political and social crisis, but we have little doubt that frequent changes in government also contribute to that crisis. Data to support this contention are found in the table on p. 111. Taking the average duration of interwar cabinets before the depression and after it (a measure that has its limitations and could be refined), we see that in only one of the countries in which governments lasted less than nine months on the average did democracy survive, and that was France. On the other hand, within that group of countries in which governments lasted longer than nine months, only one experienced a regime change. That was Estonia, with its preemptive authoritarianism in which a democratically elected leader broke with democratic legality in a crisis situation. In most of the countries that had stable governments before the depression—the Netherlands, the United Kingdom, Denmark, Sweden, Norway, and Ireland—all of whom had governments with an average duration of one year or more, the postdepression governments were more stable. (This did not hold true for the Netherlands, the second most stable, where the duration dropped from 996 days to 730.) Even in Finland, which faced a serious crisis, stability

Cabinet Instability in European Parliamentary Systems between World War I and World War II or the Breakdown of Democracy

Country	Dates Covered	Average Duration (in days)
	Predepression	
Portugal	16 May 1918–28 May 1926 30 cabinets, 19 prime ministers	117
Yugoslavia	? December 1918–? January 1929 24 cabinets, 7 prime ministers	154
Spain	21 March 1918–13 September 1923 12 cabinets, 7 prime ministers	166
Germany	9 November 1918–27 March 1930 18 cabinets, 9 prime ministers	210
France	16 November 1917–3 November 1929 18 cabinets, 8 prime ministers	239
Italy	30 October 1917–30 October 1922 7 cabinets, 5 prime ministers	260
Austria	30 October 1918–30 September 1930 16 cabinets, 6 prime ministers	267
Finland	17 April 1919–4 July 1930 14 cabinets, 12 prime ministers	294
Estonia	25 January 1921–2 July 1929 10 cabinets, 7 prime ministers	306
Czechoslovakia	14 September 1918–7 December 1929 12 cabinets, 7 prime ministers	340
Ireland	? January 1919–? March 1932 10 cabinets, 5 prime ministers	368
Belgium	31 May 1918–6 June 1931 11 cabinets, 7 prime ministers	432
Norway	31 January 1913–12 May 1931 9 cabinets, 8 prime ministers	441
Sweden	19 October 1917–7 June 1930 10 cabinets, 8 prime ministers	461
Denmark	30 March 1920–30 April 1929 6 cabinets, 5 prime ministers	533
United Kingdom	10 January 1919–5 November 1931 7 cabinets, 4 prime ministers	668
Netherlands	9 September 1918–10 August 1929 4 cabinets, 3 prime ministers	996
	Postdepression	
Portugal	—	—
Yugoslavia	—	—
Spain	14 April 1931–18 July 1936 19 cabinets, 8 prime ministers	101
Germany	30 March 1930–30 January 1933 4 cabinets, 3 prime ministers	258
France	3 November 1929–16 June 1940 22 cabinets, 13 prime ministers	165
Italy	—	—
Austria	30 September 1930–20 May 1932 4 cabinets, 4 prime ministers	149
Finland	4 July 1930–27 March 1940 6 cabinets, 6 prime ministers	592
Estonia	9 July 1929–17 October 1933 6 cabinets, 5 prime ministers	260

Cabinet Instability in European Parliamentary Systems between World War I and World War II or the Breakdown of Democracy (cont.)

	Predepression	
Country	Dates Covered	Average Duration (in days)
Czechoslovakia	7 December 1929–5 October 1938 6 cabinets, 4 prime ministers	537
Ireland	? March 1932–? June 1938 3 cabinets, 1 prime minister	750
Belgium	6 June 1931–22 February 1939 11 cabinets, 11 prime ministers	285
Norway	12 May 1931–25 June 1945 4 cabinets, 4 prime ministers	469
Sweden	7 June 1930–13 December 1939 5 cabinets, 5 prime ministers	694
Denmark	30 April 1929–4 May 1942 1 cabinet, 1 prime minister	4750
United Kingdom	5 November 1931–28 May 1940 3 cabinets, 3 prime ministers	1035
Netherlands	10 August 1929–9 August 1939 5 cabinets, 2 prime ministers	730

NOTE: The number of days cannot be considered exact, since it is not always clear precisely when a government falls and another is constituted. Another measure of instability would be the number of days taken to form a new government.

increased. It was only in Belgium that the duration dropped closer to the danger point: from 432 days to 285.

45. The question of the relationship between democratic stability and electoral systems has been the object of prolonged and intense debate since Ferdinand A. Hermens launched his blistering attack on the destructive implications of proportional representation with *Democracy or Anarchy?* (Notre Dame, Ind.: Notre Dame University Press, 1941). Maurice Duverger, with his classic work, *Political Parties* (New York: John Wiley, 1963), Anthony Downs, with *The Economic Theory of Democracy* (New York: Harper, 1957), and the numerous writings of Giovanni Sartori (see nn. 13, 16, and 68) and the polemics surrounding them, have all contributed to the argument. The most important monograph is Douglas W. Rae, *The Political Consequences of Electoral Laws* (New Haven: Yale University Press, 1971). Stein Sparre Nilson, "Wahlsoziologische Probleme des Nationalsozialismus," *Zeitschrift für die gesamte Staatswissenschaft* 60, no. 2 (1954): 282–83, illustrates the complexity of the problem. The case of Weimar has been analyzed in great detail in Hans Fenske's monograph, *Wahlrecht und Parteiensystem: Ein Beitrag zur deutschen Parteiengeschichte* (Frankfurt: Athenäeum, 1972). See also Friedrich Schäfer, "Zur Frage des Wahlrechts in der Weimarer Republik," in *Staat, Wirtschaft, und Politik in der Weimarer Republik: Festschrift für Heinrich Brüning*, ed. Ferdinand A. Hermens and Theodor Schieder (Berlin: Duncker and Humblot, 1967), pp. 119–40, particularly on the debates and proposals for election law reform in the face of the impending crisis. The theoretical refinements and empirical analysis of different cases make it questionable to put all the blame on proportional representation, since a majority system can lead to equally destructive consequences in a polarized society with large extremist minorities. Much depends on the point in the crystallization of the party system at which one or another electoral system is introduced.

46. Werner Kaltefleiter, *Wirtschaft und Politik in Deutschland: Konjunktur als Bestimmungfaktor des Parteiensystems* (Cologne: Westdeutscher Verlag, 1968). See also Heinrich Bennecke, *Wirtschaftliche Depression und politischer Radikalismus, 1918–1938* (Munich: Olzog, 1970), who, in addition to Germany, refers to Austria and the Sudetenland.

47. Karl Dietrich Bracher, "The Technique of the National Socialist Seizure of Power," in *The Path to Dictatorship, 1918–1933: Ten Essays by German Scholars* (Garden City, N.Y.: Doubleday, 1966), pp. 113–32. See esp. p. 117. See also idem, *Die Auflösung der Weimarer Republik: Eine Studie zum Problem des Machtverfalls in der Demokratie* (Stuttgart: Ring 1957); idem, *The German Dictatorship* (New York: Praeger 1970); and idem, with Wolfgang Sauer and Gerhard Schulz, *Die nationalsozialistische Machtergreifung: Studien zur Errichtung des totalitären Herrschaftssystems in Deutschland, 1933–34* (Cologne: Westdeutscher Verlag, 1960).

48. See also his contribution to this work; *The Military in Politics*; "The New Professionalism of Internal Warfare and Military Role Expansion," in *Authoritarian Brazil: Origins, Policies, and Future*, ed. Alfred Stepan (New Haven: Yale University Press, 1973), pp. 47–65; *The State and Society: Peru in Comparative Perspective* (Princeton, N.J.: Princeton University Press, 1978). See also John S. Fitch, *The Military Coup d'Etat as a Conservative Political Process: Ecuador, 1948–1966* (Baltimore: Johns Hopkins University Press, 1977).

49. Charles Tilly, "Does Modernization Breed Revolution?" *Comparative Politics* 3 (April 1973):447.

50. The change of the national flag by the German and Spanish republics provided an opportunity for such conflicts. Another example is the substitution of *Viva la República* for *Viva España* in official and army ceremonies.

51. *Ressentiment* has been the object of an interesting monograph by the philosopher-sociologist Max Scheler, entitled *Ressentiment* (New York: Free Press of Glencoe, 1961) (edited and with an Introduction by Lewis A. Coser). The term was derived from Nietzsche, in whose work it occupies a central place and is the object of a phenomenological description. Coser's summary follows (to retain the distinctive meaning of the word, the French spelling used by Nietzsche and Scheler has been used rather than the English word "resentment"):

> It denotes an attitude which arises from a cumulative repression of feelings of hatred, revenge, envy and the like. When such feelings can be acted out, no *ressentiment* results. But when a person is unable to release the feelings against the persons or groups evoking them, thus developing a sense of impotence, and when these feelings are continuously re-experienced over time, then *ressentiment* arises. *Ressentiment* leads to a tendency to degrade, to reduce genuine values as well as their bearers. As distinct from rebellion, *ressentiment* does not lead to an affirmation of countervalues since *ressentiment*-imbued persons secretly crave the values they publicly denounce (p. 24).

Typically, ressentiment politics is more anti-something than pro-something.

52. For examples, see Carmelo Lisón-Tolosana, *Belmonte de los Caballeros: A Sociological Study of a Spanish Town* (Oxford: The Clarendon Press, 1966), pp. 45, 289–90.

53. Robert E. Lane, *The Regulation of Businessmen: Social Conditions of Government Economic Control* (New Haven: Yale University Press, 1954), has emphasized the psychological rather than material cost of regulation and resistance to it. See pp. 19–35.

54. It is obviously difficult to gauge the impact of the Versailles treaty, its different provisions, the reparation agreements, and the interventions of the Allies, particularly the Ruhr occupation, on internal political developments, but they cannot have been negligible. See Erich Matthias, "The Influence of the Versailles Treaty on the Internal Development of the Weimar Republic," in *German Democracy and the Triumph of Hitler*, ed. Anthony Nicholls and Erich Matthias (London: Georg Allen and Unwin, 1971), pp. 13–28. For evidence in the autobiographies of Nazi activists, see Merkl, *Political Violence under the Swastika*, passim.

55. See the chapter by Paolo Farneti in this volume.

56. See Guillermo A. O'Donnell, *Modernization and Bureaucratic-Authoritarianism: Studies in South American Politics* (Berkeley, Ca.: Institute of International Studies, 1973), chap. 4, "An Impossible 'Game': Party Competition in Argentina, 1955–1966," pp. 166–99.

57. The implications of different degrees of continuity or discontinuity in the political elite after changes in regime, particularly democratization, have not been studied. See Juan J. Linz, "Continuidad y discontinuidad en la elite política española: De la Restauración el Régimen actual," in *Estudios de Ciencia Política y Sociología: Homenaje al Profesor Carlos Ollero* (Madrid: Carlavilla, 1972), pp. 361–424.

58. Pareto, *Mind and Society*.

59. We are referring to his development of the concept, coined by Alfred Weber, of "socially unattached intelligentsia" [freischwebende Intelligenz]. Karl Mannheim, Ideology and Utopia: An Introduction to the Sociology of Knowledge (New York: Harcourt Brace Jovanovich, n.d.), pp. 153–64.

60. There has been no comparative study of the role of intellectuals in the crises of pluralistic democracies; and it is often assumed, in view of their persecution or rejection by authoritarian or totalitarian regimes succeeding them, that they must have been identified with the overthrown democratic state. Only in the case of Germany has the role of intellectuals—those influential among both the elites and the mass public—been the object of considerable research and polemic. See Peter Gay, Weimar Culture: The Outsider as Insider (New York: Harper and Row, 1968), and the issue of Social Research entitled Germany 1919–1932: The Weimar Culture (vol. 39, no. 2, Summer 1972). George Mosse, The Crisis of German Ideology: Intellectual Origins of the Third Reich (New York: Grosset and Dunlop, 1964), has rightly paid special attention to the broad penetration of völkisch antiWeimar ideologies through a multitude of channels. Nor should we forget the debunking of the Weimar system and the Social Democrats by the leftist intelligentsia. See Istvan Deak, Weimar Germany's Left-Wing Intellectuals (Berkeley and Los Angeles: University of California Press, 1969). No similar analyses exist for Italy and Spain. Certainly the intellectual critique, as Salvemini recognized in his Foreword to William Salomone, Italian Democracy in the Making, contributed to the alienation from Giolittian Italy. In Spain, leading intellectuals like Ortega y Gasset, Unamuno, and others had a short honeymoon with the Republic, then turned highly critical (see my chapter on Spain in this volume). Fortunately, the work by Alastair Hamilton, The Appeal of Fascism (New York: Avon, 1971) (with a Foreword by Stephen Spender), has corrected the misleading impression that only second-rate intellectuals and writers could be found supporting or toying with Fascism even when anti-Fascists predominated at later stages. Unfortunately, cultural critics of both the Right and the Left contributed, often irresponsibly, often by expressions of sympathy for movements they did not know well, to the undermining of imperfect, but nevertheless civil democratic, polities.

Few texts reveal the ambivalence toward freedom of many intellectuals as well as these words written in 1931:

The notion of liberty such as it is taught us, seems to me false and pernicious in the extreme. And if I approve Soviet constraint I must also approve Fascist discipline. I believe ever more firmly that the idea of liberty is nothing but a hoax. I would like to be sure that I would think the same if I were not free myself, I who value my own liberty of thought above all else: but I also believe more and more firmly that man does nothing valid without constraint, and that those capable of finding this constraint within themselves are very rare. I believe, too, that the true color of a particular thought only assumes its full value when it is thrown into relief against an unperturbed background. It is the uniformity of the masses which enables certain individuals to rise up and stand out against it. The "Render unto Caesar the things which are Caesar's; and unto God the things that are God's" of the Gospel seems to me wiser than ever. On God's side we have liberty—the liberty of the spirit; on Caesar's side there is submission—the submission of our acts. (André Gide, Journal, 1889–1939, quoted in Hamilton, Appeal of Fascism, p. 24.)

A perfect example would be Oswald Spengler, writing "Hitler is a fool, but one must support his movement," voting for him and displaying Swastika flags with the explanation that "When one has a chance to annoy people, one should do so." Hamilton, Appeal of Fascism, p. 174.

61. Kelsen, Vom Wesen und Wert der Demokratie, and "Foundations of Democracy." There is certainly a tension between "ideology" as a belief system based on fixed elements, and characterized by strong affect and closed cognitive structure, and its converse, "pragmatism," as these terms are defined by Giovanni Sartori in "Politics, Ideology, and Belief Systems," American Political Science Review 63 (June 1969):398–411. It might be argued that the unconditional commitment to democratic constitutional procedures, defense of the civil liberties required for their continuous operation, and the rejection of extra-legal violence against legitimate authorities are also ideological.

CHAPTER 3

1. The emphasis on confining conditions is Otto Kirchheimer's contribution to our analysis. See his "Confining Conditions and Revolutionary Breakthroughs."
2. Albert Hirschman has highlighted those social and psychological processes, particularly in *Journeys toward Progress* (Garden City, N.Y.: Doubleday, Anchor Books, 1965) chap. 4, "Problem-solving and Policy-making: A Latin American Style?" pp. 299–326.
3. Karl von Clausewitz, *War, Politics, and Power*, ed. Edward M. Collins (Chicago: Regnery, 1962), pp. 83, 92–93, and 254–63. (This volume consists of selections from *On War* and *I Believe and Profess*.)
4. Max Weber, "Science as a Vocation," in *From Max Weber: Essays in Sociology*, ed. Hans H. Gerth and C. Wright Mills (New York: Oxford University Press, 1958), pp. 129–56; see esp. pp. 156–62.
5. The bind in which Social Democrats found themselves was well described by Fritz Tarnow, deputy and head of the Woodworker's Union, in the key address at the last SPD party convention (1931) before the rise of Hitler, when he said: "Do we stand . . . at the sick-bed of capitalism merely as the diagnostician, or also as the doctor who seeks to cure? Or as joyous heirs, who can hardly wait for the end and would even like to help it along with poison? . . . It seems to me that we are condemned both to be the doctor who earnestly seeks to cure and at the same time to retain the feeling that we are the heirs, who would prefer to take over the entire heritage of the capitalist system today rather than tomorrow." Quoted in Franz Neumann, *Behemoth: The Structure and Practice of National Socialism, 1933–1944* (New York: Octagon, 1963), p. 31. It was characterized by the Italian Claudio Treves in March 1920 in these words: "This is the tragedy of the present crisis: you can no longer impose your order on us, and we cannot yet impose ours on you." Quoted by Seton-Watson in *Italy from Liberalism to Fascism*, p. 560. See also the quote from Turati on p. 559.
6. Max Weber noted that German parties in the Bismarckian empire, excluded from actual control of the executive and therefore from full responsibility, tended to be highly ideological or closely identified with specific interest groups. Many parties therefore got into the habit, which continued in the Weimar Republic, of acting more like pressure groups than parties. The leadership struggle in the German DNVP between Hugenberg and Graf Westarp and of Lord Beaverbrook and Baldwin in the British Conservative party had different outcomes that reflect this difference. See Weber, "Parliament and Government in a Reconstructed Germany," in *Economy and Society*, ed. Guenther Roth and Claus Wittich (New York: Bedminster Press, 1968), vol. 3, pp. 1381–1469. See esp. pp. 1392, 1409, 1424–30, and 1448.
7. This process was decisive in weakening German bourgeois and rural-based parties in the last years of the Weimar Republic and in the success of Nazism both electorally and in gaining access to the Establishment. Another aspect is the veto by interest groups—business or trade unions—of decisions of parties and party leaders running counter to their interests even when *political* considerations—the concern for the stability of the system—demanded sacrifices. The rigidity of the trade unions in relation to the SPD and of business interests in relation to the DVP contributed decisively to the fall of the Müller cabinet, the last parliamentary government of Weimar. See Helga Timm, *Die deutsche Sozialpolitik und der Bruch der Grossen Koalition im März 1930*, Beiträge zur Geschichte des Parlamentarismus und der politischen Parteien, no. 1 (Düsseldorf: Droste, 1953).
8. Quoted in Joachim C. Fest, *The Face of the Third Reich: Portraits of Nazi Leadership* (New York: Pantheon Books, 1970), n. 25.
9. See Hirschman, *Journeys toward Progress*, pt. 2, "Problem-solving and Reformmongering," which is one of the most stimulating analyses of policy-making I know. Rather than review here many of its propositions—directly relevant to our analysis—I urge the reader to turn to this work.
10. Philip M. Williams, *Crisis and Compromise: Politics in the Fourth Republic* (Hamden, Conn.: Archon, 1964), pp. 426–27, notes that, "obliged to face the facts they hoped to dodge, politicians repeatedly conceded to a new premier the very demands on which they had overthrown his predecessor.... All too frequently a year with no crisis meant a year of no policy, and the continued presence of a group of ministers distracted attention from the

absence of government." The crisis was also a decision-making device," a method of government by shock treatment."

11. This is a central theme in the work of this political scientist, who was an insightful observer of and participant in the breakdown of Weimar democracy. In his decisionistic view of the political process and in his 1927 definition of politics in terms of the *Freund-Feind* ("friend-enemy") distinction, he reflected the "incivil" politics of his time. See Mathias Schmitz, *Die Freund-Feind-Theorie Carl Schmitts* (Cologne: Westdeutscher Verlag, 1965), for a discussion and references to Carl Schmitt's writings and secondary sources.

12. See nn. 46 and 83.

13. Albert O. Hirschman, *Exit, Voice, and Loyalty* (Cambridge, Mass: Harvard University Press, 1970), p. 91.

14. The term "crisis strata" was coined by Sigmund Neumann in *Permanent Revolution: Totalitarianism in the Age of International Civil War* (New York: Praeger, 1965) pp. 30–32, 106–11. This is not the place to refer to the extensive literature on social movements and the conditions for their emergence and success. For a recent review, see Anthony Oberschall, *Social Conflict and Social Movements* (Englewood Cliffs, N.J.: Prentice-Hall, 1973). Since Fascist movements played a major role in the breakdown or crises of democracies studied here, but a sociologico-historical analysis of Fascism falls outside of the scope we have set to our essay, the reader is referred to Juan J. Linz, "Some Notes toward a Comparative Study of Fascism in Sociological Historical Prespective," in *A Reader's Guide to Fascism*, ed. Walter Laqueur (Berkeley and Los Angeles: University of California Press, 1976), pp. 3–121, as well as other essays in that volume.

15. Curt Erich Suckert [Curzio Malaparte], *Coup d'Etat: The Technique of Revolution* (New York: E. P. Dutton, 1932).

16. Gurr, *Why Men Rebel*, Hugh Davis Graham and Ted Robert Gurr, eds. *Violence in America: Historical and Comparative Perspectives* (Washington, D.C.: National Commission on the Causes and Prevention of Violence, 1969); Robert M. Fogelson, *Violence as Protest: A Study of Riots and Ghettos* (Garden City, N.Y. Doubleday, 1971); and H. L. Nieburg, *Political Violence: The Behavioral Process* (New York: St. Martin's Press, 1969).

17. This was particularly true under the Weimar Republic, where acts of violence and assassinations by rightist patriotic "idealists" were treated with incredible leniency, while similar actions by leftist "revolutionaries" were harshly punished. This certainly undermined the legitimacy of the legal order and the political system. See Gumbel, *Vom Fememord zur Reichskanzlei*; Heinrich E. Hannover and Elisabeth Hannover, *Politische Justiz, 1918–1933* (Frankfurt: Fischer, 1966); and Bracher, *Die Auflösung der Weimarer Republik*, pp. 191–98. This attitude of the judiciary was also reflected in its decisions in constitutional matters in favor of authoritarian solutions.

In Italy, too, the authorities, particularly the lower echelons of the police, were far from neutral in their response to political violence. This point is well documented by reports of prefects like Mori, who wanted to preserve the authority of the state; it is also reflected in the statistics compiled by the Ministry of the Interior. For example, of 1073 acts of violence committed on 8 May 1921, 964 had been denounced to the judicial authority by the parties. But the most telling fact is that 396 Fascists had been arrested and 878 allowed to go free, while 1421 Socialists were arrested and 617 allowed to go free. See De Felice, *Mussolini il fascista*, vol. 1, pp. 35 and passim. The great Socialist historian Gaetano Salvemini has effectively described the resultant climate of violence and its origins.

We have no systematic data on the behavior of the judiciary in the Spanish crisis, but the fact that both the Right and later the Left had plans to introduce reforms making it more dependent on the government suggests that it might have been more impartial. Even so, the slowness of proceedings contributed indirectly to political tension, since it meant unnecessary detentions, as Joaquín Chapaprieta, who was prime minister in 1935, noted in *La paz fue posible* (Esplugues de Llobregat: Ariel, 1971), pp. 378–80. In this case we find the complaint that the courts tended to be lenient with "social crimes."

18. To capture the atmosphere created by the presence of paramilitary organizations of parties, see the excellent monograph by William Sheridan Allen, *The Nazi Seizure of Power: The Experience of a Single German Town, 1930–1935* (Chicago: Quadrangle, 1965), and the

many local histories of the rise to power of the Italian Fascists and the struggle against them. For a "collective biography" of such activists and streetfighters, see Merkl, *Political Violence under the Swastika*, based on autobiographies volunteered by Nazis in response to an appeal by sociologist Theodor Abel.

19. On the paramilitary organizations emerging in the period after World War I, their variety, ideologies and transformation in the course of the Republic, see Bracher, *Die Auflösung der Weimarer Republik*, chap. 5, and the older studies by Ernst H. Posse, *Die politischen Kampfbünde Deutschlands* (Berlin, 1931), and Robert G. L. Waite, *Vanguard of Nazism: The Free Corps Movement in Postwar Germany, 1918–1923* (Cambridge, Mass: Harvard University Press, 1952). See also Wolfgang Abendroth, "Zur Geschichte des Roten Frontkämpferbundes," in *Dem Verleger Anton Hain Zum 75: Geburtstag am 4. Mai 1967*, ed. Alwien Diemer (Meisenheim: Glan, 1967). For Italy, see Giovanni Sabbatucci, *I combattènti nel primo dopoguerra* (Bari: Laterza, 1974), and Fernando Cordova, *Arditi e Legionari d' annunziani*, (Padova: Marsilio, 1969). For a general analysis, see Michael A. Ledeen, "The War as a Style of Life," in *The War Generation*, ed. Stephen Ward (New York: Kennikat, 1975).

20. For Austria, see Bruce Frederick Pauley, "Hahnenschwanz and Swastika: The Styrian Heimatschutz and Austrian National Socialism, 1918-1934" (PH.D. diss., University of Rochester, 1967), and Ludwig Jedlicka, "The Austrian Heimwehr," *Journal of Contemporary History* 1, no. 1 (1966):127–44.

21. See Allan Mitchell, *Revolution in Bavaria 1918–1919: The Eisner Regime and the Soviet Republic* (Princeton, N.J.: Princeton University Press, 1965). Werner T. Angress, *Stillborn Revolution: The Communist Bid for Power in Germany, 1921–1923* (Princeton, N.J.: Princeton University Press, 1963), is another monograph on the early assaults of the Left against German democracy.

22. Since democracy and nationalism were "born" together in the historical sense, and the first successful democracies were nation-states (with the exception of the Swiss confederation of democratic cantons), theorists made little effort to deal with the possible conflict between national aspirations and democratic politics. Democracy was in fact identified with national sovereignty. Only with the democratization of the Austro-Hungarian Empire and the application of Wilsonian principles of national self-determination did the problem become visible, but the anti- or ademocratic politics in Eastern Europe soon obscured it again. Even the appearance of multinational states in the Third World and the resurgence of primordial ethnic identities in recent years in Western Europe have not yet led to a systematic analysis, except in the framework of the literature on consociational democracies. The renewed interest in linguistic and cultural conflict has led to interesting analyses of individual countries but no systematic studies of how to guarantee the rights of minorities and how to handle the problems of secession, which received some attention in the twenties and thirties.

The tension had already been recognized by Lord Acton when he wrote:

> The greatest adversary of the rights of nationality is the modern theory of nationality. By making the State and the nation commensurate with each other in theory, it reduces practically to a subject condition all other nationalities that may be within the boundary. It cannot admit them to an equality with the ruling nation which constitutes the State, because the State would then cease to be national, which would be a contradiction of the principle of its existence. According, therefore, to the degree of humanity and civilization in that dominant body which claims all the rights of the community, the inferior races are exterminated, or reduced to servitude, or outlawed, or put in a condition of dependence. *(Essays on Freedom and Power* [Boston: Beacon, 1948], p. 192.)

23. This is not the place to refer to the extensive literature on communal conflict and civil wars of secession. A case where formal democratic institutions have not worked rather than broken down is that of Northern Ireland. At the Varna sessions Richard Rose presented a paper on that case that has not been included in this volume, since he published an extensive analysis in *Governing without Consensus*. See also Lijphart, "The Northern Ireland Problem."

For evidence on the small number of multilingual democracies, see Joshua A. Fishman,

"Some Contrasts between Linguistically Homogeneous and Linguistically Heterogeneous Polities," in *Language Problems of Developing Nations*, ed. Joshua A. Fishman, Charles A. Ferguson, and Jyatirindra das Gupta (New York: Wiley, 1968). See also Eric Nordlinger, *Conflict Regulation in Divided Societies*, Harvard University Center for International Affairs, Occasional Paper no. 29 (Cambridge, Mass., 1972), which focuses on the most constructive attempts to regulate conflict. Alvin Rabushka and Kenneth A. Shepsle, *Politics in Plural Societies: A Theory of Democratic Instability* (Columbus, Ohio: Charles E. Merrill, 1972), is a most pessimistic account, with reference to many countries, of the possibility for stable democracy in plural societies.

24. K. D. McRae *Consociational Democracy;* idem, "The Concept of Consociational Democracy and Its Application to Canada," in *Les états multilingues: Problèmes et solutions*, ed. Jean-Guy Savard and Richard Vigneault (Quebec: Université Laval, 1975), pp. 245–301.

25. It is significant that in our time social scientists have been writing about "nation-building" when the task in most parts of the world is "state-building." Similarly, the idea of patriotism, which did not imply a nationalistic sense of identity, has disappeared from our language. In this context the work of Robert Michels, *Der Patriotismus: Prolegomena zu seiner soziologischen Analyse* (Munich: Duncker and Humblot, 1929), still deserves attention.

26. Joshua Fishman, "Bilingualism with and without Diglossia: Diglossia with or without Bilingualism," *Journal of Social Issues* 23 (1967):29–38.

27. See Savard and Vigneault, *Les états multilingues*, for a number of papers relevant to the problem. There is obviously one notable exception: Switzerland. See Jürg Steiner, *Amicable Agreement versus Majority Rule: Conflict Resolution in Switzerland* (Chapel Hill: University of North Carolina Press, 1974). Other exceptions are Belgium, Canada, possibly India, and until recently, Lebanon.

28. See Walter Simon's chapter on Austria in *The Breakdown of Democratic Regimes: Europe.*

29. The imbalances in power between Prussia and the Reich, the particularistic policies of Bavaria that contributed to a crisis like the Beer Hall Putsch, the opportunity for the Nazis to enter Land governments like Thuringia, and the divergent policies of Land authorities in the defense of the state against paramilitary organizations all contributed to the exacerbation of the crisis. See, for example, Ernst-August Roloff, *Bürgertum und Nationalsocialismus, 1930–1933: Braunschweigs Weg ins Dritte Reich* (Hannover: Verlag für Literatur und Zeitgeschehen, 1961.)

30. The Germans even invented a term for those attempts—*Zähmungskonzept* [conceptions of domestication]. Those attempts at the cooptation of a well-organized opponent, one who is often in control of the street, inevitably led the opposition to "ask for more and more." In this case Clemenceau's statement that "Every man or every power whose action consists solely in surrender can only finish by self-annihilation. Everything that lives resists..." (quoted by Eckstein in "Etiology of Internal Wars," p. 157) became only too true. What was conceived as containment led to appeasement and finally to surrender. Examples of this process of negotiation, generally covert and done through intermediaries, can be found in De Felice, *Mussolini il fascista*, Vol. 1, pp. 255–60, 282–85, 300–305, and 345–46. Such negotiation was based on the growing conviction among the elite that "Contra il fascismo oggi non si governa" [Today one does not govern against the Fascists]. Such efforts are sometimes perceived as dangerous by the disloyal opposition when it considers the partner capable of reasserting authority, as was the case with Giolitti in Italy. In Germany we have the tentative attempts of Brüning and Schleicher, and finally the "successful" cooptation of Hitler by von Papen that made the Führer chancellor and master of Germany.

In such attempts at cooptation it is characteristic of the disloyal opposition to bargain initially for only a limited share in power, perhaps a few ministries; but as the regime parties withdraw from a position of strength and resistance to its claims, the disloyal opposition increases its demands. In the case of the "March on Rome" the demands escalated from some cabinet seats to the premiership. We should not forget that the Fascists in the first Mussolini cabinet had only six of the sixteen portfolios, or that Hitler and the other three Nazi cabinet members were "flanked" by eight conservatives in addition to von Papen as vice-chancellor. The nature of the portfolios claimed is also significant: If those in control of the police and armed forces (and today, the mass media) are transferred to the opposition, any defense of democracy becomes impossible. On the other hand, as Salandra notes in his memoirs about negotiations with Mussolini, when the opposition controls the violence in the streets and its leader does not enter the government, the entry into the cabinet of some ministers and the exclusion of the ministry of interior would leave the government in a weak position. De Felice, *Mussolini il fascista*, vol. 1, p. 346.

31. This is a central theme in Sartori "European Political Parties," pp. 137–76, which contains his analysis of the dynamics of such party systems. The analysis is confirmed by electoral returns in Germany after 1928, in Austria and Spain in 1936, and in Italy since 1948. (However, some observers want to read the Italian returns differently, considering not the parties but the distance between parties—concretely, the growing PCI—and the Center in terms of ideology, policy actions, and the perceptions of the electorate.)

32. In May 1936 the Rex party had polled 11.5 percent of the vote, and its leader, aroused by mass rallies, sought a plesbiscitarian election in Brussels by ordering one of the Rexist deputies to resign. This forced a by-election. The democratic parties—Catholics, Liberals, and Socialists—realizing that their division might prove fatal, agreed on a single candidate: the prime minister. The vote would be thus for or against the regime. Everyone, including the Cardinal-Archbishop of Malines, mobilized to condemn the movement. The 19 April 1937 poll totaled 175,000 for Van Zeeland, and 69,000 for Degrelle, including the votes of the Flemish Nationalist UNV. Rex did not recover from the defeat produced by the unity of the democratic parties.

33. The Facta government, welcomed by the Fascists for its weakness, blocking other alternatives, is a prime example. Facta himself had little desire to assume the burdens of office and considered himself a stand-in for Giolitti, who was waiting for the right moment to return to power. Schleicher and von Papen before the Machtergreifung were also leaders of this sort, as were several of the prime ministers and ministers imposed by Alcalá Zamora between 1933 and 1936 and Casares Quiroga Azaña's prime minister after his elevation to the presidency of the Spanish Republic.

34. Building on a complex tradition in constitutional theorizing (linked mainly with the name of Benjamin Constant) Carl Schmitt in his influential *Der Hüter der Verfassung* (Tübingen: J. C. B. Mohr [Paul Siebeck], 1931) developed the idea of *neutrale Gewalt* [neutral power], and its "independence" from the pluralistic party-state (pp. 132–59). See also his "Das Zeitalter der Neutralisierungen und Entpolitisierungen" (October 1929), reprinted in *Positionen und Begriffe in Kampf mit Weimar-Genf-Versailles: 1923–1939* (Hamburg: Hanseatische Verlagsanstalt, 1940), pp. 120–32, and "Übersicht über die verschiedenen Bedeutungen und Funktionen des Begriffes der innerpolitischen Neutralität des Staates" (1931), in the same volume, pp. 158–161.

35. Tönu Parming, *The Collapse of Liberal Democracy and the Rise of Authoritarianism in Estonia*, Contemporary Political Sociology Series, no. 06–010 (Beverly Hills, Ca.: Sage, 1975); Georg von Rauch, "Zur Krise des Parlamentarismus in Estland und Lettland in den 30er Jahren," in *Krise des Parlamentarismus in Ostmitteleuropa zwischen den beiden Welkriegen*, ed. Hans-Erich Volkmann (Marburg/Lahn: J. G. Herder Institut, 1967), pp. 135–55; and Jürgen von Hehn, *Lettland zwischen Demokratie und Diktatur*, Jahrbücher für die Geschichte Osteuropas, Supplement 3 (Munich: Isar Verlag, 1957). For a history of these short-lived, smaller European democracies, see Georg von Rauch, *The Baltic States: The Years of Independence. Estonia, Latvia, Lithuania, 1917–1940* (London: C. Hurst, 1974).

36. One of the signs of crisis of a regime and ultimately one of the contributing factors in its breakdown is the tendency of the military leadership to take an "attentist" position, to identify itself publicly with the "State" or the "nation," and to avoid committing itself to the regime. This was the position of von Seeckt and many high-ranking Spanish office's', including Franco. It allowed them not to confront their more politicized colleagues, with whom they did not fully disagree, and to attempt to maintain a semblance of unity in the armed forces under the cloak of neutrality. Such a position eventually became untenable, and younger officers increasingly felt that in a polarized society they had to take sides. An army like the Italian, which, confronted with the Fascist assault on power, "would do its duty but would prefer not to have to do it," obviously limits the decision-making capacity of the political leadership when it is confronted with political violence. Certainly no regime can allow officers or even ex-officers to have any relationship whatsoever with political paramilitary groups. (For bibliographic references, see other chapters in this volume.)

CHAPTER 4

1. See, for example, Jules Moch, "De Gaulle d'hier à demain," *La Nef* 19 (July–August 1958):9–15. Remembering his role as minister of the interior in May 1958, he writes of "The Fear . . . that on account of the balance of forces and their dynamics, the disorders, if they should explode, would benefit the Communists exclusively. Prague in 1948 haunted my sleepless nights as much as Madrid in 1936." Guy Mollet came back to the same theme, in *13 mai 1958–13 mai 1962* (Paris: Plan, 1962), pp. 11–13, when he argued in favor of de Gaulle, saying: "The government of colonels would have come to power almost without 'coup ferir'. I know that possibly one or two thousand courageous men would have been sent to slaughter, but that would have been the Spanish [Civil] War without the republican army. In that hypothesis, I believed that it [the government of colonels] would have lasted twenty or thirty years." Here Guy Mollet perceives, with brilliant insight, the sad fact that breaks with democratic legitimacy are not easily reversed.
2. See Lepsius, "Machtübernahme und Machtübergabe: Zur Strategie des Regimewechsels."
3. This sense of urgency is reflected in Mussolini's expression "O ora o mai piú" [Either now or never]. Once this stage of serious negotiations for cooptation is reached, the leaders of the antisystem forces also start feeling an urgency to attain power, and to fail to do so is risky for them. Recriminations among leaders about a willingness to sell out for a "minister's seat" might split the party between revolutionaries and pragmatists; the masses, now mobilized for action, might not be available on another occasion; the opportunistic supporters (particularly financial backers) might feel that the movement is a "bad investment," since it does not have the drive to power; and the regime-supporting forces might regain confidence and unite.

   In spite of his negotiations with Giolitti, Mussolini said: "It is necessary to put the masses into action, to create an extraparliamentary crisis and to get into the government. It is necessary to prevent Giolitti from getting into the government. As he has fired against D'Annunzio, he would give the order to fire against the fascists." De Felice, *Mussolini il fascista*, vol 1, pp. 304–5. It was at that point that Pareto, in a letter to Pantaleoni, perceived the danger of "domestication" of Fascism by the "fox," Giolitti, and he and leading Fascists felt the urgency of "revolution" before abandoning the drive and losing their following. Ibid., p. 304. The texts quoted by De Felice, and many analyses of the time, illustrate that even at the eleventh hour a "real statesman" with authority over the army and the civil service who is "willing to shoot" can be a threat to the breakdown or overthrow of democracy.
4. An opposition confident of its chance to seize power will devote considerable attention to establishing contacts and using a mixture of reassurances and more-or-less veiled threats to neutralize the opposition of institutions like the churches (in the case of the Catholic countries, the Vatican), business groups, Freemasonry, the monarchy, even the trade unions, and to encourage them to withdraw their support from the political parties of the democratic regime. In some cases this involves the manipulation of factional cleavages within those institutions. This is also true for those aiming to displace an authoritarian regime in crisis, as any reader of the statements of the Spanish Communist party today would know.

   In *Mussolini il fascista* De Felice gives evidence of the increasing intensity of such moves by Mussolini between the Naples party congress and the March on Rome.
5. There are numerous examples, but let us mention a few. In Italy, the Catholic church, particularly the Vatican, foreseeing the prospect of a Mussolini government started having secret contacts with him. What is more important, the church began withdrawing its identification with the Popolari party, particularly by disapproving of clerical activity in politics. This undermined Sturzo's position. In Germany, the relationship between the Zentrum party, the church, and the Vatican at the time of the Nazi *Machtergreifung* has been the object of scholarly polemic. The debate has centered around the contributions of Rudolf Morsey ("Die deutsche Zentrumspartei," in *Das Ende der Partein 1933*, ed. Erich Matthias and Rudolf Morsey), and Ernst-Wolfgang Böckenförde ("Der deutsche Katholizismus im Jahre 1933," in Gotthard Jasper, *Von Weimar zu Hitler, 1930–1933* [Cologne: Kiepenheuer and Witsch, 1968], pp. 317–43; and "Das Ende der Zentrumspartei und die Problematik des politischen Katholizismus in Deutschland," ibid., pp. 344–76). A similar Vatican policy has

been noted in Ricardo de la Cierva, *Historia de la Guerra Civil Española* (Madrid: San Martín, 1969), pp. 478–79, in relation to the Republic shortly before its advent in 1931. Even the trade unions, so closely tied to the Socialists and other radical parties, sometimes begin following a strategy separate from that of the parties, become available for semiauthoritarian alternatives, affirm their own identities, and, as the policies of D'Aragona and Leipart after the Fascist and Nazi takeovers show, hope to survive under the new regime.

In Italy, the CGL (Confederazione Generale del Lavoro) showed an increasing tendency to act independently of the Socialist party, particularly at the time of the "pacification pact." On 6 October 1922, before Mussolini became prime minister, it had already denounced its pact with the Socialist party to "maintain itself free from any ties with whatever political party, considering such an act indispensable to maintain the trade union unity." This policy was encouraged by Mussolini and continued until the Matteoti murder with renewed vigor. See De Felice, *Mussolini il fascista*, vol. 1, pp. 380–85, 598–618.

On the growing distance between the positions of trade unions and the Social Democratic party in Germany, see Erich Matthias, "Der Untergang der Sozialdemokratie 1933," in Jasper, *Von Weimar zu Hitler, 1930–1933*, pp. 298–301, and Karl Dietrich Bracher, Wolfgang Sauer, and Gerhard Schulz, *Die Nationalsozialistische Machtergreifung: Studien zur Errichtung des totalitären Herrschaftssystems in Deutschland 1933–1934* (Cologne: Westdeutscher Verlag, 1960), pp. 175–86. The German developments in 1933 are all the more surprising in view of the Italian experience.

Business interests are even more cautious in relation to an opposition that might take over a regime. They are ready to include such parties among those receiving a share (whose size depends on the party's prospects and "reasonableness") of their contributions, in order at least to maintain access to party leadership, if not to influence or shape policy. Sometimes the social position of leading businessmen allows them to act as go-betweens in the "politics of the small c's," often in the interest of the "pacification" so important for business.

6. Adolf Hitler, in his famous "oath of legality" at the Leipzig Reichswehr trial in 1930, when he spoke with impunity before the court. Quoted in Bracher, *Path to Dictatorship, 1918–1933*, p. 117.

7. Laski, *Democracy in Crisis*, passim.

8. Editorial in *El Socialista*, 16 August 1933, quoted in Stanley G. Payne, *The Spanish Revolution: A Study of the Social and Political Tensions That Culminated in the Civil War in Spain* (New York: Norton, 1970), pp. 108–9. For other expressions of the same thought, see pp. 108, 111, 137. Largo Caballero, leader of the maximalist wing of the PSOE and ex-cabinet member, put it in these terms just before the 1933 election:

> I say to you that if we win on the 19th we shall make the capitalists change their minds. But if we lose, it seems to me that we will enter a new period in which electoral activity will not be enough. It will be necessary to do something more powerful—anything but renounce our ideals. There will be no justice so long as socialism does not triumph. Only when we can hoist the red flag of revolution on the official buildings and towers of Spain will there be justice.

For a further discussion of the tragic conflict in the Spanish Socialist party, see my chapter on Spain in this volume.

9. This is not the place for an analysis of the Fascist phenomenon and its role in the interwar crisis in Europe. For references to the constantly growing literature see Laqueur, *A Reader's Guide to Fascism*. In that volume the reader will find also our own definition of Fascism and an analysis of its appeal and of the social bases of Fascist movements (pp. 3–121).

10. Theodore Draper, "The Ghost of Social Fascism," *Commentary*, February 1969, pp. 29–42. See also Weber, *Die Wandlung des deutschen Kommunismus*, vol. 1, pp. 232–47.

11. Even in more solidly established regimes than France in 1958, we would not expect a distribution of responses different from that shown in the table on p. 122.

12. From that perspective, the history of the Weimar Republic from its birth to the late twenties offers interesting examples: the Kapp Putsch, the Beer Hall Putsch, and the attempts made by leftist extremists. We might also mention the February 1934 crisis in Paris, when the Leagues threatened Parliament, and the May 1968 threat to the Gaullist Fifth Republic. On the latter, see Bernard E. Brown, *Protest in Paris: Anatomy of a Revolt* (Morristown, N.J.:

Response to Questions: What Would You Do in the Case of a Communist Uprising? In the Case of a Military Uprising?

Military Uprising	Communist Uprising				
	Support the Regime	Do Nothing	Support Uprising	No Answer	Total
Support the regime	4.6%	1.4%	2.4%	0.5%	8.9%
Do nothing	11.0	59.2	2.4	1.6	74.2
Support uprising	3.0	2.2	0.5	0.1	5.8
No answer	0.8	0.8	0.3	9.3	11.2
Total	19.4	63.6	5.6	11.5	100.1 (2624)

For a detailed analysis, see Cohn, "Losses of Legitimacy and the Breakdown of Democratic Regimes."

General Learning Press, 1974); and Philippe Benéton and Jean Touchard, "Les interprétations de la crise de mai-juin 1968," *Revue Française de Science Politique* 20, no. 3 (June 1970), 503–44.

The case of Finland is particularly interesting, since the dangers of extreme multipartism, the presence of the third-largest Communist party in the West, and its proximity to the USSR would have made the stability of its democracy dubious. See Kevin Devlin, "Finland in 1948: The Lesson of a Crisis," in Hammond and Farrell, *Anatomy of Communist Takeovers*; and C. Jay Smith, "Soviet Russia and the Red Revolution of 1918 in Finland," idem, pp. 71–93.

Another interesting case in which conditions for a stable democracy seemed absent but a regime managed to consolidate itself is studied in Frank Munger, *The Legitimacy of Opposition: The Change of Government in Ireland in 1932*, Contemporary Political Sociology series, vol. 2 (Beverly Hills, Ca.: Sage, 1975).

CHAPTER 5

1. The idea of treating a social system as a "state of equilibrium" was one of the contributions of Vilfredo Pareto. See *The Mind and Society*, 122–25, and esp. chap. 12, numbers 2060–70 ff. It was further developed by L. J. Henderson, and through his teaching and the work of Parsons it has entered the mainstream of sociology. Let us quote Pareto's formulation: "We can take advantage of the peculiarity in the social system to define the state we choose to consider and which for the moment we will indicate by the letter X. We can then say that we state X is such a state that if it is artificially subjected to some modification different from the modification it undergoes normally, a reaction at once takes place tending to restore it to its real, its normal, state" (2068). In Pareto's view all states of equilibrium have such a dynamic aspect, are not inherently incompatible with change ("progress"), and are obviously not always desirable or valuable from everyone's perspective. All "states" of a social (or political) system in a Paretian view are in a constant process of adjustment. Here we are dealing with those situations—to which he refers in his discussion—in which there is not merely a small, continuous, imperceptible alteration of the system, but a major disruption after which elements in the system are capable of responding without changing some of their basic relationships (in this case, democratic institutions) and reaching a new stable situation.

2. An important source for understanding the unique role of de Gaulle in French politics is Institut Français d'Opinion Publique, *Les français et de Gaulle*, with an Introduction by Jean Charlot (Paris: Plon, 1971), which brings together the survey data on the general from 1945

until after his death. Innumerable tables give evidence of the charisma that surrounded him at many points in his career and of the retrospective approval of his role as a statesman. On the response of politicians to him at the time of the 1962 election, see Mattei Dogan, "Le personnel politique et la personnalité charismatique," *Revue Française de Sociologie* 6 (1965):305–24, and the essays on de Gaulle in Stanley Hoffman, *Decline or Renewal: France Since the 1930s* (New York: Viking, 1974), pt. 3.

3. Hirschman, *Exit, Voice, and Loyalty*, p. 24.

4. See Max Weber's discussion of "objective possibility" in "Critical Studies in the Logic of the Cultural Sciences: A Critique of Eduard Meyer's Methodological Views," in *The Methodology of the Social Sciences*, trans. and ed. E. A. Shils and H. A. Finch (New York: Free Press, 1949), pp. 113–88; see esp. pp. 180–85.

5. There is a basic difference between the return to democracy after German occupation, particularly when exiled governments insured the continuous legitimacy of institutions, and return to democracy after the establishment of nondemocratic regimes—in Italy, Germany, Austria, Japan, and even Vichy France, for example. It should not be forgotten that in the latter cases democracy was only reestablished by the victors. (See Robert A. Dahl, "Governments and Political Oppositions," in Greenstein and Polsby, *Handbook of Political Science*, vol. 3, pp. 115–74, esp. pp. 155–58.) In addition, in those cases nondemocratic rule had not lasted long: seventeen years in Italy (1926–45), twelve in Germany, eleven in Austria, and eight in Japan. This alone should differentiate those cases from that of Portugal, in which democracy was restored after forty-eight years, and Spain, in which the process took thirty-seven. In Portugal, it was the military, after colonial defeat, rather than internal pressures, that overthrew the authoritarian regime, and the reestablishment of competitive democracy is still seriously in doubt. Of the overthrown democracies, only Greece and some Latin American countries (Venezuela, Colombia, Argentina, Brazil, and Chile) have returned to more or less unstable democratic rule as a result of internal developments after periods of authoritarian rule. Gianfranco Pasquino, in "L'Instaurazione di regimi democràtici in Grècia e Portogallo," *Il Mulino* 238 (March–April 1975):217–37, underlines the difference in duration of those two regimes in accounting for the different outcomes.

6. Robert A. Kann, *The Problem of Restoration: A Study in Comparative Political History* (Berkeley and Los Angeles: University of California Press, 1968).

7. Terry Nardin, *Violence and the State: A Critique of Empirical Theory* (Beverly Hills, Ca.: Sage, 1971).

8. This is the classic distinction of the scholastic political theorists between legitimacy of origin or title and of exercise. While democratically legitimate in origin—that is, freely elected—such governments exercise their power in ways contradictory to the values underlying democratic politics.

9. This point is emphasized in Bendix, *Max Weber*, p. 300, and in Johannes Winckelmann, *Legitimität und Legalität in Max Webers Herrschaftssoziologie* (Tübingen: J. C. B. Mohr, 1952).

10. Alexis de Tocqueville, *Democracy in America* (London: Oxford University Press, 1946), chap. 34, pp. 583–84.

11. Joseph A. Schumpeter, *Capitalism, Socialism, and Democracy* (New York: Harper and Brothers, 1950), pp. 291–93, emphasized, as a second condition for the success of democracy, that "the effective range of political decision should not be extended too far." In fact, Schumpeter noted "democracy does not require that every function of the State be subject to its political method."

12. Merkl, *Political Violence under the Swastika*.

13. Karl Loewenstein, "Legislative Control of Political Extremism in European Democracies," pp. 591–622 and pp. 725–74, is an excellent review of those efforts.

14. Clinton L. Rossiter, *Constitutional Dictatorship: Crisis Government in the Modern Democracies* (Princeton, N.J.: Princeton University Press, 1948), is a detailed analysis of the functions and dangers of emergency rule in democracies, including the multiple uses of Article 48 of the Weimar Constitution and French, British, and American laws and practices. A final section, setting up eleven criteria of *constitutional* dictatorship, is particularly interesting in connection with the problem of reequilibration of democracy (pp. 297–306).

15. Pareto, *Mind and Society*, number 2186.

16. See the influential formulation by Herbert Marcuse, "Repressive Tolerance," in *Critique of Pure Tolerance* (Boston: Beacon Press, 1965). For a critique, see Alastair MacIntyre, *Herbert Marcuse: An Exposition and a Polemic* (New York: Viking, 1970).
17. Sartori, *Democratic Theory*, chap. 16, pp. 418–19 and 444–45.
18. *State and Revolution*, quoted in ibid., pp. 421–22.
19. Rosa Luxemburg, in her essay "The Russian Revolution," written in prison (1917–1918). That essay is included in *Rosa Luxemburg Speaks*, ed. Mary-Alice Waters (New York: Pathfinder, 1970), pp. 365–95; see esp. p. 394.
20. Ibid., pp. 389–90.
21. We do not enter into the question of "how" democratic those regimes, which according to our definition can be considered democratic, actually are. We enter even less into the somewhat different problem of how far "social" and "economic" democracy has been achieved in the "political" democracies. Indeed, political democracies differ in their "democraticness," and there have been attempts to measure that degree. For an interesting discussion, see May, *Of the Conditions and Measures of Democracy*.
22. This was, let us remember, the Communist position when the theory of social-fascism was formulated, at the time the Nazi flood was rising. The KPD (Kommunistische Partei Deutschlands), in a resolution by its Central Committee in May 1931, declared: "The fascist dictatorship does not in any way represent a contrast in principle to bourgeois democracy under which the dictatorship of the finance capital is also carried out. [It is] simply a change in the forms, an organic transition." In February 1932 the committee noted that "democracy and fascist dictatorship are only two forms that harbor the same class content.... They approach each other in their external methods as well...." The practical implications of this ideological position were formulated by a KPD parlamentarian as follows: "When the fascists come to power, then the united front of the proletariat will come into being and sweep everything away. To starve under Brüning is not better than under Hitler. We are not afraid of the fascists. They will mismanage faster than any other government." Quoted by Richard Hamilton in a forthcoming book on the social bases of Nazism.

II.
The Breakdown of Democratic Regimes

EUROPE

Edited by
Juan J. Linz and Alfred Stepan

The Breakdown
of Democratic Regimes
EUROPE

1.

Social Conflict, Parliamentary Fragmentation, Institutional Shift, and the Rise of Fascism: Italy

Paolo Farneti

Introduction

The working of a parliamentary system can be viewed as based on a "division of labor" between civil society, political society, and institutional set. By the first we mean the set of cleavages such as Center-periphery, city-countryside, etc., including class cleavages and their political expressions, that give rise to conditions of interest or solidarity. By the second we mean those groups (from clubs to mass parties and labor unions) that are based on the principles of association or organization. By the third we mean those structures, mostly regulated by legal order, that can be analyzed primarily in terms of consent or force.

To be sure, while these three structures define the complexity of any political system, they are particularly visible as determinants of the complexity of parliamentary systems. As such, they are the results of distinct historical processes. The civil society is the outcome of the industrial revolution; the institutional set is the outcome of the bureaucratic rationalization and centralization performed by the monarchies of the *ancien régime*. The political society is the outcome of the democratic revolution, that is, the democratic development of the principles stated in 1789, through the 1848 revolution and the political and social struggles of the second half of the nineteenth and the first decades of the twentieth centuries.

For many states, especially in Europe, the process of state building has been one through which the tensions and the conflicts arising from the basic cleavages of nineteenth-century societies found a provisional mediation, if not a

3

solution. With the progressive democratization of politics, with the institution of elected parliaments, and with the entrance of new groups into the political arena, this basic function of conflict mediation was taken over by the political society and by an elected political elite composed of professional politicians rather than state functionaries. This process meant the emancipation of the realm of politics and policy-making from both civil and institutional forces. And in effect the "division of labor" stems from the relationships between mutually emancipated structures: civil, political, and institutional.[1] As a relatively emancipated structure, the political society finds its basic resource in redefining the cleavages emerging from the civil society—transforming them into specifically political cleavages and political issues. In fact, an issue becomes political when it is able to aggregate the society into a basic cleavage of *pro* and *contra* the alternative solutions. Of course, it is also part of the art of politics to prevent issues from becoming political. This means that the relationships between civil, political, and institutional structures are in continuous tension. In fact, civil and institutional structures tend to become "politicized," that is, to become part of political society and to transform their own cleavages into political cleavages. The political society tends to monopolize the practice of politics and political issue-making, thereby absorbing into its own structure and logic of performance both civil and institutional forces. In all these cases there is a disruption of the division of labor of the political system in general, and of parliamentary systems in particular.

A crisis of parliamentary system can therefore be analyzed as a failure of the political society to maintain the rules of this division of labor, a balance that demands a restraint on itself and a systematic effort to deter the civil and institutional forces from any attempt at disrupting this balance. When this does not happen, a loss of autonomy of the political society marks the initial stage of a crisis process, together with a polarization of politics and issue-making to civil and institutional forces; this polarization results in the "politics of the streets" and the "politics of the barracks."

Neither the first nor the second kind of politics, however, is a long-term political project, unless it is a "planned" revolution or coup d'état. When neither revolution nor coup d'état is the outcome, the loss of autonomy of the political society is followed by a stalemate situation or a "power vacuum"[2]: the situation is defined by small groups and few persons. The diffusion of the political arena that characterizes the first crisis phase is followed by a shrinking of the political arena during this second phase. Any political project able to aggregate enough forces to resolve the loss of autonomy and overcome the stalemate is likely to take over the political power.

In the case of Italian fascism, this aggregation of forces happened neither through revolutionary outbreak nor purely institutional force (coup d'état), but essentially through the use of private violence.

Political and Socioeconomic Structure

In the framework of a diffusion of the political arena, loss of autonomy of the political society, and a consequent reduction in the number of workable solutions within the rules of the division of labor, we can verify the existence of critical elements that have been suggested in the introductory essay by Juan Linz. In the process of the political society's loss of autonomy we can understand the emergence of issues that cannot be solved within the rules of the division of labor (Linz's "unsolvable problems") but demand a new arrangement of relationships between civil, political, and institutional forces. We can also understand the tendency of the political forces in the existing alignment to lose their identities in favor of civil and institutional forces and therefore to question both their "loyalty" toward the existing arrangement ("semiloyalty" and open "disloyalty") and their own willingness to assume responsibility in it.

In the reduction of the political arena, and above all in the number of possible solutions within the rules of the game, we see the "fragmentation" of the political forces and their "polarization" around one dominant cleavage: for or against the existing institutional arrangement. When one pole of the alignment is supported through private violence, "crisis strata" become decisive for the political balance. It must be emphasized that the use of violence cannot be considered to be at the same level as the other critical elements. It is much more essential to and decisive in fostering the crisis, for at least two reasons. First, if the modern state is defined by the achievement of internal pacification and the reduction of maintenance of public order to a function performed by professional administrators, then the use of private violence and its acceptance is a break with an essential element. Second, if the political alignment is polarized, and one pole of the alignment has the capacity for the use of violence, then the weight of that one pole is such that no contractual relationship is any longer feasible.

This focus on a specific political mechanism should not make us overlook the economic and social determinants of the crisis process, and in particular, their timing. They are significant in a market economy when powerful minority interests succeed in aggregating a larger and larger part of the population—in a word, when the crisis fosters a solidarity otherwise very difficult to achieve. In particular, this happens when the traditional cleavage between "property classes"—based on rent—and "acquisition classes"—based on profit—is blurred by the rise of a common interest on the part of both classes in the dismissal of the existing institutional arrangement, and whenever the "safety of contracts" is threatened.[3] From this point of view, changes in the structure of the property classes and the acquisition classes are of momentous importance, because they can contribute to the formation of this common interest. Therefore, economic crises are of little importance as long as they do not bring about a change within and between the two class systems of a partially industrialized market economy. This change can be a rearticulation of interest in which the role of political forces, as much as political emergency procedures (such as early elections and so forth), can be decisive.

There is, however, in the framework of the model proposed here, a slightly different way to consider the relationship between socioeconomic structure and political structure in a critical situation. We defined the model of relationships between civil, political, and institutional structures as a division of labor because in effect it is based on differentiated role performances. From this point of view, a crisis, i.e., a redefinition of roles, can be seen as paralleled by the introduction of a new technical discovery in the technical division of labor, which also demands a redefinition of roles. A new piece of machinery or a new technical device creates new jobs and eliminates old jobs. Similarly, a profound economic and social crisis can be seen as creating and eliminating jobs in a system of division of labor between civil, political, and institutional tasks. The result is, as in the case of the introduction of a new device, not necessarily a further differentiation of roles: it can very well be a consolidation of roles and therefore a return to a less differentiated condition in the relationship between the three structures, depending on the nature of the socioeconomic crisis and the specific historical situation.

The two perspectives do not contradict each other. The first one is, in effect, a case of the second one, because it depends on at least two conditions: a market economy with a sizable business class, and a partially industrialized economy with the consequent coexistence of acquisition classes and property classes. It is one of the tasks of this discussion to verify the hypothesis in the Italian case of the early twenties.

An Outline of the Italian Crisis of the Early Twenties

In the pages to follow we will try to give evidence of the three phases as they existed in postwar Italy: *loss of autonomy* of the political society ("loss of power," "power deflation," and "fragmentation," are used as synonyms); *exhaustion of legitimate political alternatives* (or "reduction of the political arena," "stalemate situation," etc.); and *takeover of power*. We start from one major assumption: the reshuffling of political cleavages as a result of the issue of participation in the war, and the crisis of relationships between property and acquisition classes consequent to the war mobilization. In the specific Italian case, therefore, the war is accountable for (1) the potential for political and social crisis and (2) for their *convergence* and consequent disruption of an already shaky parliamentary system.

During the first phase the old alignment of Right, Center, and Left is broken up by the dual cleavage of interventionism and neutralism, the international situation being, at least in part, accountable for the persistence of this cleavage after the end of the war. The loss of autonomy of the political society, i.e., of the political parties in the postwar Parliament, is made visible by a diffusion of the political arena in the politics of the streets (the wave of strikes of 1919 and 1920) and in the political mobilization of institutions, namely the army, during the Fiume adventure (also 1919–20). In this phase the aggregation of old interventionist liberalism begins, in a political space soon to be filled by the Fascist movement.

During the second phase, the game seems to be in the hands of the old Neutralist alignment: Giolittian Liberals, Socialists, particularly the Reformist wing of the Socialists—led by Filippo Turati—and the Popolari—led by Luigi Sturzo. Internal contradictions prevent an aggregation of these forces, thereby creating a stalemate: a visible exhaustion of political alternatives within the framework of the existing institutional structure. The silence of the streets at this point encourages the exercise of political violence on the side of the Fascist squads. The silence is paralleled by the withdrawal of the army and the police forces, whose loyalty toward the existing arrangement is more and more questionable.

During the third phase, starting with the resignation of Giovanni Giolitti from the cabinet in the twenties, the political alignment is in effect displaced both by the politics of the Fascist parliamentary group and by the restless Fascist violence all over the country. Step by step, the issue becomes the exercise of force and violence on two sides: the institutional side (represented by the army and the crown) and the Fascist side. Late attempts to control the situation, through last-minute agreements on the side of the political forces loyal to the parliamentary system, are ineffective, and end on the night of 27–28 October 1922.

The fragmentation of political forces, as the result of the war and the war-commitment of the country, is in sharp contrast with the aggregation of social forces consequent to the war mobilization. There are at least three key factors that in our view account for a joining of property and acquisition classes in a common struggle and for their political relevance. The wave of strikes in the first postwar years (1919–20) marked, for the first time in the history of the country, a common and relatively homogeneous mobilization of both industrial workers and peasants (agricultural daily workers and small peasants).[4] This meant a mobilization of "negatively privileged classes," according to Weber's definition, both in the system of acquisition classes (industrial workers) and in the system of property classes (peasants).[5]

The energy mobilized by the strikes was finally exhausted, but considerable improvements in labor legislation had been achieved, both for industrial workers and agricultural workers, including the obligatory hiring of labor in the fields ("imponibile di mano d'opera"). It had not achieved—but the slogan remained as a threat—"the land to the peasants."

In this situation the possibility of an alliance between "positively privileged classes" in the two systems was created: property-owners in the countryside (including small property-owners), and industrialists and financiers in the urban-industrial areas. The alliance was formed on the grounds of a common feeling that the government was "in the hands of the subversives," i.e., the Socialists. This feeling was supported by Turati's policy, which blocked the government without participating in it, and thus gave way to collective reactions.

The result was the aggregation of the interests of a social minority with the interests of a social majority, that of the property classes. It was a social novelty that soon became a political novelty: the Fascist movement became a mass party (section 1).

The second phase—which we have defined as the stalemate of the traditional political alignment (mostly coinciding with the old, Neutralist forces)—was characterized by the Giolittian attempt at coopting fascism at a parliamentary level together with the social and political effects of Fascist violence, by then massive and systematic. Last but not least, the final attempt of the Bonomi government to find a workable solution incorporating both the inclusion of the Popolari in the cabinet and the "pacification pact" between the Fascists and the Socialist labor unions will be considered as the last step in the exhaustion of the legitimate alignment and of the stalemate that preceded the final breakdown of the political system (section 2).

With the first and second Facta governments, the political arena had shifted from the legitimate political alignment, and therefore the representation of the political society, to a different political axis, based on the show of force. The institutional setting, represented by the crown and the army (the latter with its questionable loyalty) was on one side, and the Fascist movement, with its show of force and goal of dividing the last forces of the traditional alignment, on the other. The failure of the "legalitarian strike" and the silence of the streets before and after the March on Rome can be considered as further evidence of the desert, social and political, in which the final destruction of the parliamentary system took place (section 3).

1. The Loss of Autonomy of the Political Society

New Political Cleavages

World War I had the effect of reshuffling political cleavages, especially for the Liberals. Democrats and Socialists were split by the interventionism-neutralism cleavage, and so were the Popolari, even if opposition to intervention in the war was expressed only by the minority in their group. However, those most affected by this division belonged to the old Liberal ruling group.[6] We can summarize the two cleavages in the following way:

	Left	Right
Interventionists	Democrats (Francesco Nitti) Social Reformists (Leonida Bissolati, Ivanoe Bonomi) Independent Socialists (Arturo Labriola)	Liberals (Antonio Salandra, Sidney Sonnino, Vittorio Emanuelle Orlando) Popolari (Filippo Meda) Nationalists (Luigi Federzoni)
Neutralists	Socialists (Filippo Turati) Leftist Popolari (Guido Miglioli)	Liberals (Giovanni Giolitti)

The new cleavage weakened the Giolittian Liberals on both the right and the left: on the right, by the split with men like Salandra and the moderate Catholics such as Meda and his followers; on the left, the gap between Giolitti's group and the Democrats and Social Reformists was deepened. Yet this split did not draw Giolitti's liberalism, Turati's socialism, or Sturzo's Popolari nearer to each other. They had all inherited ancient aversions, and their neutralism had radically different roots, both ideological and pragmatic. On the contrary, interventionism could serve as an aggregating force for the Right: divided, until then, into the major political forces of the Giolittian alignment, it finally found a common ground of action. Its practice, as indicated by the way the Salandra-Sonnino cabinet forced the Chamber of Deputies into the declaration of war, was extraparliamentary.

Interventionism had a political space with potential for expansion and reaggregation, notwithstanding the crisis of the *Fascio Parlamentare di Difesa Nazionale*. The political space of neutralism, on the contrary, was occupied by forces that tended to neutralize each other: Socialists, Popolari, and the Giolitti group. In this situation issues had a divisive rather than an aggregating function. In particular, the issues of the immediate postwar period raised the possibility that the alignment would be immobilized by "unsolvable problems."

The elections at the end of 1919 increased rather than simplified these divisions, because they increased the internal articulation of interventionism and neutralism and, while keeping neutralism and interventionism as a significant cleavage, made any coalition government more and more difficult at a time in which coalition was increasingly indispensable.

The remarkable institutional innovations of the 1919 electoral system (proportional representation, reduction of the voting age from thirty to twenty-one and from twenty-one to eighteen for those who had been drafted during the war) did not bring about any solution to the already complicated alignments that had survived the war. In fact, these innovations fragmented the old alignment (Liberals, Democrats, etc.) without aggregating the new one (Socialists and Popolari).

If we compare the data from 1913–19 to 1919–21 (table 1), a number of things become apparent: the enormous increase in neutralism (the Socialist group is larger than any other political group in the Chamber of Deputies); the even more conspicuous increase of the Popolari group; the weakened condition of the Giolittian group and the reduction of rightist liberalism (Salandra Liberals, the Economic party, the Agrarian party, etc.); and finally, the fragmentation of "leftist interventionism," i.e., Radicals, Republicans, Independent Socialists, and Reform Socialists.

The change from the Orlando cabinet to the Nitti cabinet meant a change from a coalition led by conservative interventionism to one led by Democratic interventionism: both alternatives became more difficult after the 1919 elections as the two groups were weakened. Coalitions with Neutralist groups

Table 1. **Political Cleavages, Old and New, in the Chamber of Deputies for 1913–19 and 1919–21**

1913–19

	Left		*Right*	
Interventionists	Radicals	73	Constitutional Democrats	29
	Republicans	17	Democrats	11
	Independent Socialists	8	Liberals (non-Giolitti)	70
	Social Reformists	19	Catholics	20
			Conservative Catholics	9
		N=117		N=139
Neutralists	Socialists	52	Giolitti Liberals	200
		N=52		N=200
		N=508		

1919–21

	Left		*Right*	
Interventionists	Republicans	9	Salandra Liberals	23
	Radicals	57	"Economic Party" and	
	Independent Syndicalists and Social		"Agrarians"	15
	Reformists	22		
	"Rinnovamento"	33		
		N=121		N=38
Neutralists	Socialists	137	Giolitti Liberals	
	Communists	17	("Democrazia Liberale")	91
		N=154		N=91
	"Right" and "Left" Popolari		99	
			N=99	
		N=503		

SOURCE: Ugo Giusti, *Dai plebisciti alla costituente* (Rome: Faro, 1945), pp. 47 and 75.

became a necessity: the only logical alternative in this situation was a Socialist-Popolari government aided by some leftist Interventionists. But the self-exclusion of the Socialists on one side and of the Popolari on the other brought the choice toward Giolitti's group, the oldest group of Neutralists. Giolitti could not turn to right-wing interventionism because of his old Neutralist attitudes, nor to the Socialists without having them face a split, nor to the Catholic Popolari, because they considered him an old anti-clerical. The result was the early election of 1921. In other words, the war, as long as it lasted, had forged an emergency coalition; once it was finished, new cleavages appeared without erasing the old ones. There accumulation made cabinet formation more and more difficult, i.e., neither the Parliament nor the country could bring about a solution. It is no wonder, therefore, that political society, under the pressure of the mobilization of the streets and the mobilization of the army, at least at the beginning of the Fiume adventure, was losing its relative autonomy and control.

After 1919 we see the exhaustion of three possible alternatives: a coalition led by Democratic interventionism; a coalition led by Democratic neutralism—namely the Socialists—that had not yet been tried, but was already exhausted with the exhaustion of the mass mobilization in the streets; and a coalition led by centrist neutralism, namely Giolitti. Three major governmental chances were exhausted during the one and one-half years between the end of 1919 and the middle of 1921. The fourth possibility, a full-fledged coalition with the Popolari, was actually tried after the fall of Giolitti, led by Bonomi, but it faced: (1) a Fascist movement that was already a massive force and (2) a developing political space precisely in the area of right-wing interventionism. The following analysis of the internal cleavages of the mass parties of the alignment should validate this contention.

The Socialist forces had mobilized since the end of the war, and their success in the 1919 elections seemed to be a validation of this practice. However, the Socialists were divided by a double cleavage: (1) reformism versus revolutionarism, and (2) political versus strictly syndicalist practice in the labor unions. These cleavages resulted in a set of contradictory consequences. The revolutionary wing of the PSU (Partito Socialista Ufficiale)— the *Massimalisti*—had been the majority in the party since the Rome convention of September 1918. (They got 74 percent of the vote, while 13 percent went to the Reformist wing led by Turati, Treves, and Modigliani and 13 percent to an undecided "Center.") The result was that the secretariat of the party was in the hands of the Massimalisti, and the parliamentary group was in the hands of Turati's *Riformisti*, the two groups checking and finally paralyzing each other. It was the other way around inside the leading group of CGI: (Confederazione Generale del Lavoro) at the end of the 1920s the "syndicalist" group led by Buozzi had 54 percent of the votes, while 37 percent went to the Massimalisti and 9 percent were abstentions. This was enough to impose both syndicalist and political mobilization and enough to maintain the mobilized masses' expectations beyond the achievements obtained by the governments (and within an inflationary economy), with the result that the resource of political mobilization was exhausted.[7]

A parallel cleavage appeared to divide the Popolari. Their tremendous increase in membership after the war reinforced their domestic contradiction, thereby making attempts at coalition difficult if not impossible, and in any case always subordinate to the initiatives of other political forces. The leadership of the party, in fact, was centered in Sturzo's line and ideology, both anti-Socialist and anti-Liberal: this excluded most of the major forces of the political alignment. It did not prevent the Popolari from cooperating even with the last Giolitti cabinet, albeit with diffidence and despite profound tensions. But the parliamentary group (Meda and De Gasperi) was certainly more moderate, and for this reason was on several occasions in disagreement with the party leadership. It was in any case more bound to the Vatican, which had followed with unconcealed distrust the development of a Catholic party.

Parliamentary groups in both parties (the PSU and the PPI, or Partito Popolari Italiano) were expressions of the electorate; both parties' leaderships were expressions of their active participants. The gap between and the contradictions within the two major mass parties of the alignment were therefore *both* in the country and in the Parliament. The cleavage that divided the party leadership and the parliamentary leadership in both parties was not subject to bargaining; this is one more reason to believe in the formation, *a contrario,* of a political space in which the old interventionist forces, the discontent of property classes and acquisition classes, the disarray of the young officers' generation, and the demands of some institutional personnel for "order" could find a political expression through a fast, almost emergency-like aggregation.

If we turn to the other side of the alignment, we find equivalent cleavages, namely, liberalism and radicalism. The Liberal side was numerically enfeebled (it declined from 300 representatives in 1913 to about 100 in 1919) and divided between neutralism and interventionism. But even within neutralism there were two opposite tendencies toward the Socialists: cooptation versus thorough rejection. Radicalism, both "leftist" and "interventionist," was also numerically enfeebled and politically fragmented around personalities like Bissolati, Nitti, and Bonomi; this eliminated any possibility of mediation between the two mass parties, the Socialists and the Popolari. Radicalism turned out to be no alternative to Giolitti's liberalism.

New Social Aggregations

There is some evidence to support the hypothesis that a convergence between property classes and acquisition classes (both positively and negatively privileged) led to their consequent mobilization, which initiated the loss of autonomy of the political society. In the first place, workers and peasants were able to mobilize simultaneously in a way unprecedented in the country's social history (table 2). It is true that the political leadership of the Massimalisti, their dream of an Italian October Revolution, was initially responsible for the wave of strikes that allied the middle and upper classes against socialism. However, the readiness of the population to mobilize on purely political issues remains to be explained. There is little question that this postwar mobilization was a consequence of the impact of wartime mobilization, especially on the peasants and agricultural workers who were the rank and file of the army. From this point of view, the war had the effect of dissolving the traditional regional divisions that had prevented the Socialist party from becoming a modern, centralized, mass party with an available *masse de maneuvre*. The political leadership of the Socialist party inherited a condition of unity and a capacity for social and ideological mobilization of the electorate that, had it not been for the war—and *that* war—would have taken many years of painstaking organizational and political activity to achieve.

In the second place, the convergence might have been favored by the postwar industrial demobilization consequent to the conversion of war industries to a normal market economy. For instance, the number of industrial workers in a city like Turin, in which the war industry was particularly important, had returned, during 1919, to 1914 levels. Demobilized workers, provisional industrial workers returned to the fields, are a mobilizable force, and in any case constitute a force that contributes to the simultaneous mobilization of city and countryside. The same observation can be extended to the large industrial cities of the north, Milan and Genoa, both of which suffered from the first steps toward a return to a "normal" market economy. The government's early commitment to a return to a market economy, which was encouraged by Liberal economists, can be seen as a further cause of political instability. In fact, the discontent that this return produced in the working classes could have had an immediate impact on a political structure that had undergone a rapid democratization. The dismissal of the controls over the division of labor—controls appropriate to a wartime economy—was coupled with the sudden increase of mass parties in Parliament consequent to the introduction of proportional representation and the lowering of the voting age. Two things happened simultaneously: the expulsion of part of the population from the labor market (i.e., social citizenship) and input of the whole adult population into the political society (i.e., political citizenship). It overloaded the political society and, to some extent, the labor unions, and posed the dilemma of the whole postwar period, i.e., whether to follow the mobilization of the social classes or perform the control function that had been relinquished by the institutional structure.

A second and most important variable in the aggregation of the property and acquisition classes was the enormous increase, right after the war, in the

Table 2. Number of Strikers in Industry and Agriculture, by Region: 1913 and 1919–21 (in percentages)

Regions	1913		1919		1920		1921	
	Industry	Agriculture	Industry	Agriculture	Industry	Agriculture	Industry	Agriculture
Piedmont, Liguria, and Lombardy	65	9	65	51	56	18	58	38
Veneto	2	3	3	14	4	10	6	8
Total—north	*67*	*12*	*68*	*65*	*60*	*38*	*64*	*46*
Emilia	6	50	3	13	4	26	2	25
Tuscany	10	—	5	10	9	25	6	—
Rest of center	9	19	5	11	6	9	9	5
Total—center	*25*	*69*	*13*	*34*	*19*	*60*	*17*	*30*
Campania	3	—	13	—	13	—	9	—
Apulia	1	8	1	4	2	8	1	21
Sicily	3	1	3	—	5	3	8	1
Rest of south	1	—	2	—	1	2	1	2
Total—south	*8*	*9*	*18*	—	*21*	*13*	*18*	*24*
Total industrial strikers	384,725		993,558		858,133		589,259	
Total agricultural strikers	79,842		487,208		1,045,732		79,298	
Total strikers	464,567		1,480,766		1,903,865		668,557	

SOURCE: *Annuario statistico italiano, 1913* (Rome: Bertero, 1914); *Annuario statistico italiano, 1919–1921* (Rome: Librèria dello Stato, 1925).

agricultural middle class, small landowners, and tenants (table 3). Favored by the inflation in the payment of debts, many peasants had hurried to purchase the land made available by large landowners who were both frightened by Socialist strikes and attracted by the possibility of speculation. This "new class" was limited and often threatened by the mobilization of salaried workers in the fields (*braccianti*) and their powerful leagues. It is plausible to guess that these millions of new landowners and their families, about five million people altogether, could become a mass of support for agrarian fascism. They were interested not only in defending their new property against the collectivization of the land proposed by the *leghe braccianti* and therefore against the salaried workers' mobilization, but also in regular functioning of the market, in order to pay the debts incurred in buying the land. There is no social force as interested in law and order as an agricultural middle class of small landowners. These landowners were ready to see any government grant of rights to the leagues, including the compulsory hiring of daily workers, as a betrayal and a concession to "red subversivism."

Apparently, the government effectively protected the Socialist leagues. The protection of the workers' wages was pursued thoroughly, and the wages themselves were kept relatively high in relation to the progress of inflation. This was the outcome of the joint effort of leagues and cooperatives. The cooperatives, which were organizations that had not merely a syndical purpose, like the leagues, but shared products, tools, and working personnel, claimed "the land for the peasants," while the leagues insisted upon collectivization of the land. The appeal was double and contradictory and, combined with the agrarian reform promised during the war but not delivered afterward, may have resulted in in a wide disaffection of salaried agricultural workers with their labor organizations and the Socialist party.

While the political cleavages had the cumulative effect of fragmenting the political elite and complicating the possibility of an effective and stable government, these social cleavages underwent a powerful trend toward aggrega-

Table 3. Occupations in Agriculture, 1871–1936 (in percentages)

Census Year	Land- owners	Managers	Share- croppers	Workers	Other	Total
1871	18.0	7.7	17.0	56.9	.4	100 (5,616,482)
1881	18.1	6.6	13.7	61.2	.4	100 (5,450,127)
1901	24.9	8.5	19.8	46.4	.4	100 (6,411,001)
1911	18.3	9.3	18.7	53.3	.4	100 (6,052,623)
1921	32.4	7.2	15.4	44.7	.3	100 (7,085,124)
1931	36.7	12.7	19.7	30.5	.4	100 (6,544,663)
1936	32.9	18.4	20.0	28.4	.3	100 (6,306,742)

SOURCE: Arrigo Serpieri, *La struttura sociale dell-agricoltura italiana* (Rome: Edizione italiana, 1947), p. 123.

tion, thereby increasing their pressure over the political society. Social classes, until 1919, were sharply divided by the traditional cleavage of country and city, industry and agriculture. Property-owning classes were dominant in the countryside and acquisition-oriented classes were dominant in the city. The two sectors now joined and split according to a class cleavage: salaried workers and small peasants and industrial workers were aligned on one side, small and large property and business owners on the other. With the war, class society had taken a leap forward.

This new situation divided a political elite into new cleavages that overlapped with the old ones. Moreover, this elite was bound to a way of looking at politics and society that belonged to the Giolittian era: personalities rather than groups, clienteles rather than organized parties, and patronage rather than mass politics. Therefore, the loss of autonomy of the political society can also be seen as a *lag* between political and civil societies following the war. The political society failed to anticipate the reshuffling of social divisions that followed the war and did not adapt to them once they became manifest. Once again, the political society laid the groundwork for an alternative mobilization: that of the institutions.

New Institutional Cleavages

The Fiume enterprise revealed a potential cleavage in the institutional personnel, mainly in the army: nationalism, victorious war, crown, and expansion of Italy in the Mediterranean were arrayed on one side; internationalism, subversion, redistribution of wealth to labor, and last but not least, republic on the other. The career officers, the veterans, and their associations were politicized on the first side of the cleavage, and this group found its hero in D'Annunzio and his slogan of the "betrayed victory." To be sure, the Fiume adventure remained a partial mobilization of the army against the orders of the legitimate government, and from this point of view it was a break with the century-old tradition of an army loyal to political power. Yet it failed to become a mobilization of the whole army and therefore it failed to make the army the backbone of a Nationalist "block" to overthrow the institutions through a coup d'état. However, it became a rallying point for the radical Right in the country and paved the way for consent to fascism.

Part of this picture is the slowness in the demobilization of the army itself, kept on duty mainly for reasons of public order. Yet this delay in the return of noncareer officers to the labor market did not prevent them from feeling the frustrations of readjusting to civilian bourgeois life in an atmosphere of hostility—from the Socialists and the mobilized masses—toward the war, the soldiers, and the officers.

Against this background we have the first assaults against Socialist headquarters such as that against the offices of the "Avanti!" in Milan, led by

Futurist crackpots and above all by the "Arditi" officers. They, together with the Fiume mobilization, set the style for the exercise of private violence against both the Opposition forces and the legitimate institutional forces.

The weakness shown by the Nitti government against the protagonists of the Fiume adventure had momentous consequences for the creation of a political space for the extreme Right.[8] In fact, if it is true that the Fiume mobilization failed to become a general mobilization of the army, it is also true that it died more from its own exhaustion than from effective governmental reaction, at least until Giolitti's return to power. The government failed to involve the crown with its full responsibility, and this surprising pattern of leniency was probably based on a lack of communication between the two constitutional powers necessary to restore order.

In this way, the yielding of the political society to the "politics of the streets," which we have identified as the first element of its loss of autonomy and of crisis of the political system, finds its counterpart in the government's failure to restore order in the face of a partial essentially minimal mobilization of the army for purposes that were clearly illegal and clearly ran counter to the international commitment of the whole country to its allies.

The Fiume adventure failed in its stated goals, but it set the stage for a series of concessions by legal authorities and abuses by those who saw the possibility of unpunished systematic violence that led to the final overthrow of an incipient democracy.

The Political Space of Fascism

There are two key issues in the development of fascism as a political force, and they are both bound to the process of "loss of autonomy" of the political society. The first is the monopolization of the rightist space of the political-ideological alignment through antisocialism. This allies, at least provisionally, rightist Liberals, Arditi, Nationalists, and Dannunziani. The second is the entrance of facism into the social movement, which resulted from the convergence between property and acquisition classes, "positively privileged," as they were defined. This second phase is called also "agrarian fascism."

The process of monopolization of a political space implies two tasks: the precise identification of a constant enemy and the aggregation and hegemonization of friends or allies.[9] In the case of fascism, the constant enemy was, beyond any doubt, socialism. If the beginnings of fascism, the foggy ideological statements of the meeting of 23 March 1919 and of the October convention in the same year, can give the impression of being "leftist," they must be seen as components of a search for political space. This search, in order to maintain its constant antisocialism, obliged the Fascists to borrow some weapons from the enemy, particularly ideological weapons.

Fascism borrowed its whole ideology from the Nationalists, who combined populism and expansionism ("imperialism"). Nationalists were, to some extent, "respectable," and rejected violence as a political practice; fascism combined the Nationalist motive with the practice of violence, on the grounds of provocation (but the technique of violence came directly from the collaboration with the Arditi, few and fragmented though they were). The lesson of Fiume and the Dannunziani was that a rightist upheaval based on the army was impossible, and therefore it was necessary to coopt the moderate opinion; second, the most important, was that locally limited violence was being tolerated, particularly when it was directed against the Socialists. Finally, if liberalism—and especially Giolitti—was the real and most frightening enemy, its public support showed the necessity and importance of the moderate opinion, the importance, therefore in insisting repeatedly on the motive of the restoration of law and order.

It was of crucial importance for fascism to show that the exhaustion of Socialist mobilization and the failure of the Fiume mobilization, both threats to the order of the state, could not be followed by the restoration of legitimate political order. It was not a "victory" of the legitimate alignment; on the contrary, it could be settled once and for all with the victory of fascism itself.

It is in this framework of a double technique, the result of two years' experience at claiming to support order and attacking it at the same time, that we must see the decision to participate in the 1921 early elections. Mussolini used the entrance into the Parliament for two equally important purposes: to appear as a legitimate force, and to have a position from which to maneuver in the Parliament itself. They are both part of the same fundamental project: to use as a resource the fact that the threats to the parliamentary regime, from both Left and Right, had failed.

Mussolini himself expressed the difficulty of an aggregation of the electorate on this political space in reference to the 1921 elections:[10]

. . . in any case who would vote for us? Not the mass of the workers, because it is indoctrinated by Leninism [*leninizzata*]. The middle class reads the "Avanti!" as you can see it everywhere. Therefore it will never vote for the lists of the "Electoral Blocks," which include the class of the small merchants [*esercenti*], the homeowners, or other categories of this kind!

There was only one way to turn the apparent defeat of any system-breaking attempt, Left or Right, into a political resource: continue the threat through the systematic use of violence based precisely on the exhaustion or failure of the other attempts, and on the leniency of the government toward such violence.

That is why, on purely political grounds, 1921 marks the period of the toughest Fascist violence against not only the Socialists and their organizations, both leagues and cooperatives, but against decentralized bureaucratic authorities like the prefects. Fascist violence found a precise political location at the very end of two alternative attacks against the legal order: the mobilization of the streets and the mobilization of the institutional personnel, mainly the army. And in this way "law and order" could become not only a slogan but a bloody banner.

2. The Stalemate of the Political Alignment

We can find a number of reasons to account for Giolitti's failure to reestablish the legitimate game of politics from 1920 to 1921, i.e.: the unquestionable worsening of the economic situation; his inability to turn the failure of the occupation of the factories and the Fiume mobilization into a successful parliamentary alignment; the decision to coopt fascism on an electoral level rather than face a frontal engagement with a party that was increasing in violence and number of adherents; the confusion, rather than clarification, of the political horizon that resulted from the 1921 early elections.

Economic Difficulties

There are those who insist, rightly but perhaps excessively, on the purely political determinants that led fascism to power, but the economic difficulties that marked the whole postwar period were a powerful determinant of the success of fascism. The period 1920–21 was marked by increasing unemployment, but the government continued to make provisions for the employed working class, both in industry and agriculture, under the pressure of social mobilization.

As any Liberal leader would have done, Giolitti in effect oriented his policies toward a rigid balance of the public budget (*pareggio del bilancio*). This, however, could neither eliminate the commitments of previous governments nor go against organized labor's demands, particularly in view of a possible split and subsequent alliance between Giolitti and the Reform Socialists.

Most important was the decrease in units employed in industry (from 4.36 in 1920 to 4.35 in 1921)[11] and the "rigidity" of the number of units employed in the tertiary sector (from 3.40 in 1920 to 3.45 in 1921).[12] This meant that in a period of conversion from a war to a market economy, there was an increase in nonproductive labor that overloaded the distribution of the GNP.

In this situation, if a social policy of "squeeze" was needed, it demanded a stability that these cabinets lacked. Nor had they the courage to declare an emergency (as the situation in fact was), because the emergency theme had already been monopolized by fascism.

The Giolitti cabinet, even from the economic point of view, concluded the phase of "loss of autonomy" of the political society. In the fall of 1920, two important bills were passed by this cabinet: the conversion of all bonds and securities, both private and public, to the name of the possessor (until then they had been held by the bearer) and a favorable solution of collective contracts for the *Federterra*, the union of the agricultural workers. In a sense this was the farthest point that a "liberal" economy could reach at that point, and Giolitti's insistence on balancing the budget, as we have seen, was the indication of a turning point in the economic and social policies not only of that government but of the governments to come, as long as no Socialist alternative was in view.

Giolitti's project, therefore, was particularly difficult because it passed bills favorable to the Socialists in order to gain Socialist support in the Parliament, but the social and economic resources needed to lead a joint government with the Socialists had been exhausted. The Socialists were being rewarded for entering the cabinet, but not for staying in it, as there were no resources to carry on basic reforms. Yet, this was inevitable, given the resources of the economy and the political isolation of Italy in the international setting, which precluded international financial help.

On one side the period of favorable concessions to the working classes, both industrial and agricultural, was being concluded: it had been a blank check, so to speak, to the leftist members of the alignment, social and political. But at the same time that the Left was once more invited to enter a coalition in order to achieve a stable government, the resources for social policies were exhausted. It was objectively difficult to make a leftist political move and a rightist economic move. Inflation was the last, but dangerous, resort, and in fact between 1920 and 1921 there was an increase of nearly 50 percent in the prices of such necessary goods as bread (from Lit. 0.83 to Lit. 1.41), pasta (from Lit. 1.24 to Lit. 2.14), and meat (from Lit. 9.64 to Lit. 12.96). But inflation arouses the discontent of all the strata of the society: working classes and middle classes together, urban and rural strata, property and acquisition classes (except, of course, speculators, who represent a politically irrelevant minority).

Missed Chances and Missed Collision

The failure of the cabinet to use the end of the strikes and Fiume as a resource was coupled with its avoidance of a frank acknowledgment of the breakup of public order by the Fascist squads. Both failures became a paradoxical legitimation of fascism.

The occupation of the factories marked the final stage of Socialist and working-class mobilization. Giolitti had a crucial role in avoiding a bloody conclusion to the occupation by keeping the police outside the factories, despite the pressures from the newly organized *Confindustria*.[13] He had a role also, when the movement was exhausted, in reaching an agreement favorable to the *maestranze* by providing some commitment, on the side of the management, to workers' control of the factories. In a word, Giolitti helped to save the symbolic value of the movement for the occupation of the factories, while it was evident to the main actors that the movement had failed and that in general working-class politics in Italy had taken a step backward. But this symbolic *sauvetage* was exactly what prevented the government from using the end of the factory-councils as a victory and a symbol of the restoration of order. At least it did not succeed in giving the public the sense that the Socialist upheaval and turmoil were over and that order was being restored under the banner of the traditional forces of the political alignment. In this way, the whole affair turned from a chance at increased credibility into a loss of credibility for the last workable cabinet.

The Fiume enterprise was ended by the signing of the Rapallo treaties, and the consequent demobilization of the Dannunziani from Fiume by the navy. This showed that the army, in general, was loyal to the government, and the whole issue could have been used to demonstrate the success of the government in restoring normal relationships, inside and outside the country, even if, in the whole issue of dismissing Fiume, Giolitti had the silent help of Mussolini.[14] But precisely as in the case of the occupation of the factories, the end of the Fiume enterprise was not used by the government as a resource to increase its credibility if not its legitimacy.

Legitimation, during a period of crisis and public disorder fomented by the Left and the Right, would have required deeper roots, namely, the concentration of public commitment on the issue of public order and the repression of violence. In fact, the issue of order would have had two different destinies according to which political force decided to monopolize and use it. Faced with two alternatives—monopolization of the issue of public order and identification of fascism as "disorder," or cooptation of fascism into the political arena and permitting violence as long as it was directed against the Socialists—Giolitti and his group chose the second, thereby leaving to fascism the possibility of causing civil disorder and using that disorder as an excuse to overthrow the parliamentary system.

According to some historians, this "electoral cooptation" of fascism by Giolitti was due to his disappointment in the results of the Socialist convention at Leghorn in the fall of 1920.[15] There the Socialist party split, not on the right, thereby leaving the moderates free for a coalition with Giolitti (despite all the difficulties that have been just pointed out), but on the left, thereby creating a further element of fragmentation because of the inevitable isolation of the newly formed Communist party. However, this can hardly be an explanation for such a momentous decision on the part of Giolitti and his group. His decision in fact was based on the erroneous idea that Fascist violence could neutralize Socialist violence, without thinking that if one of the two groups had won, it would have demanded all the power in exchange for its "services."

Fascist violence, which was in fact directed mostly against the strongholds of socialism, as Szymanski has shown, increased tremendously during 1921.[16] At the same time, its electoral cooptation in the lists of the Liberals compensated the Fascist movement, which, during the same year, increased its membership by more than 50 percent (see table 4).

It was necessary for fascism to prevent a return to normality in any case by directing violence against the structures created by the Liberal and Socialist traditions. Fascism in fact directed violence against the Parliament (thrashing and killing deputies), the municipalities (breaking up municipal councils), and the labor unions (burning down the *camere del lavoro*).

If the ebb of liberalism and socialism explains both the numerical force of fascism and the speed with which this size was reached, violence explains its internal articulation and geographic distribution. Fascism increased particularly in regions bordering on Yugoslavia, which had been most involved in the Fiume enterprise and in which nationalism meant an expansion into the Dalmatian coast. Fascism increased in central Italy as well, where socialism was strongest and where the Socialist postwar mobilization had been not only deeply felt but also rewarded in terms of governmental measures.

Therefore, fascism monopolized *de facto* anti-Socialist resentment. As an anti-Socialist mass movement using violence (until then identified with So-

Table 4. Increase in Fascist Membership during 1921 and Early 1922, by Region

Regions	March 1921	December 1921	Change (in percentages)	May 1922	Change (in percentages)
Piedmont	2,411	9,618	+75	14,526	+34
Lombardy	13,968	37,939	+63	79,329	+52
Liguria	2,749	7,405	+63	8,841	+16
Veneto	23,549	44,740	+47	46,078	+3
Northern Italy	*42,677*	*99,702*	*+57*	*148,774*	*+33*
Emilia	17,652	35,647	+50	51,637	+31
Tuscany	2,600	17,768	+85	51,372	+65
North Central Italy	*20,252*	*53,415*	*+62*	*103,009*	*+48*
Umbria	485	4,000	+88	5,410	+26
Marches	814	2,072	+61	2,311	+10
Latium	1,480	4,163	+64	9,474	+57
Abruzzi	1,626	6,166	+74	4,763	−22
South Central Italy	*4,405*	*16,401*	*+73*	*22,231*	*+26*
Campania	3,550	13,423	+73	13,944	+4
Apulia and Lucania	4,211	19,619	+78	20,683	−5
Calabria	*712*	*2,406*	*+70*	*2,066*	*−14*
Sicily	3,569	10,110	+65	9,546	−5
Sardinia	1,100	3,372	+67	2,057	−39
Southern Italy	*13,142*	*48,930*	*+73*	*48,296*	*−1*
Italy	80,476	218,448	+63	332,310	+32

Source: Computed from Renzo de Felice, *Mussolini il fascista,* vol. 1, *La conquista del potere, 1921–1925* (Turin: Einaudi, 1966), pp. 8–11.

cialist "street politics"), it gained for its cause the industrial management, a group with little or no penchant for veterans, Nationalists, and middle-class mobilization.[17] With this, fascism constituted a block that could replace the political alignment on one condition: that it operated quickly, precisely because it was a provisional aggregation.

We have seen that the Giolitti government, the last government with a chance to stabilize parliamentary democracy, had missed its chance to acquire credibility. This failure is the origin of Giolitti's failure to face a direct confrontation with the Fascists. Lost chances of restoring the government's credibility brought about an evaded confrontation with a movement that systematically destroyed public order. The appearance of Fascists in the 1921 electoral lists of the Liberals signifies the Liberals' surrender of their responsibility to rule the country.

Further Political Fragmentation in the Parliament

The early elections had three basic effects on the political scene. First, both by presenting their candidates together with those of the Liberals, Nationalists, Democrats, and Social Reformists in the *Blocchi Nazionali,* and by obtaining a parliamentary group, Fascists became "respectable" in the eyes of moderate public opinion. Second, the elections increased the fragmentation of the political alignment, which was further exacerbated by fragmentation of the parliamentary groups. Finally, consequent to this stand of the political forces, Giolitti resigned, thereby leaving the scene at the very moment in which a strong hand was needed. In fact, one can date the takeover of fascism from mid-1921, precisely after these elections.

Giolitti's parliamentary force, in effect, was less than half that of the same group of *Democrazia Liberale* in 1919: the distinction, if not the split, was on the right, the splinter group being headed by De Nava. The *Democrazia Sociale* group, was split on the Right: Nitti, prime minister during the immediate postwar period, was left with forty-two representatives, about half the membership of his group in 1919, and the splinter group was headed by the Sicilian, Duke Colonna di Cesarò, who was not only a Rightist but sympathized with fascism. The fragmentation of the Socialist group is known; its overall decrease was minimal when the loss of power of the Socialists in the country as early as 1921 is taken into consideration. The Salandra group remained the same and represented the destiny of right-wing liberalism, torn between its allegiance to existing institutions and its sympathy toward fascism. The disappearance of Bonomi's group, i.e., the supporters of the man who was to become prime minister after Giolitti's departure, was evidence of the further deterioration of "leftist interventionism" (table 5).

The outcome of Giolitti's early elections highlighted two negative aspects of the overall situation in the country: the fragmentation of the Left and of neutralism, and the consistency and potential solidarity of the Right, of the old interventionism.

In the 1922 Chamber of Deputies, the Liberal group of Democrazia numbered forty-two representatives and was chaired by Giolitti. It was a very heterogeneous group, as the different political destinies of its members later showed. Nitti's *Democrazia Italiana* (thirty-six representatives) had more or

Table 5. Fragmentation of Parliamentary Groups from 1919 to 1922

1919–21

Seats Corresponding to the Electoral Slate		Seats Corresponding to the Later-formed Parliamentary Groups	
Liberals	41	Liberal Democracy (Giolitti)	91
Democrats	60	Radical group (Nitti)	57
Radicals	12	Liberal group (Salandra)	23
Lists of Liberal, Radical,		Social Reformists (Bissolati)	21
Democratic candidates	96	"Gruppo Misto" (including	
Front-fighters	20	Republicans)	24
Economic party	8	Renewal group (Bonomi)	33
Social Reformists	6	Popolari	99
Republicans	4	Official Socialist party	137
Lists of other candidates	5	Communist party	17
Popolari	100		
Official Socialist party	156		
Total	508	*Total*	508

1921–24		1921		1922	
Liberals	43	Liberal Democracy		Democrats	
Liberal Democrats	68	(Giolitti)	78	(Giolitti)	42
Demo-Socials	29	Demo-Socials		Liberal Democrats	
Social Reformists	25	(Nitti)	64	(De Nava)	23
National blocks	105	Social Reformists	24	Italian Democrats	
Republicans	6	Liberal democratic		(Nitti)	36
Official Socialist		group (Salandra)	17	Demo-Socials	
party	123	"Gruppo Misto"	28	(Di Cesarò)	41
Communist party	13	Agrarians	27	Social Reformists	26
Popolari	106	Fascists	35	Liberal democratic	
Others	17	Nationalists	10	group (Salandra)	21
		Official Socialist		"Gruppo Misto"	32
		party	123	Agrarians	23
		Communist party	14	Fascists	32
		Popolari	107	Nationalists	11
				Official Socialist	
				party (Turati)	83
				Socialist group	
				(Serrati)	40
				Communist party	14
				Popolari	106
Total	535	*Total*	527	*Total*	530

SOURCE: Ugo Giusti, *Dai plebisciti alla costituente* (Rome: Faro, 1945), pp. 75, 85–86.

less the same structure as the Giolitti group but a less lenient attitude toward fascism, as did Bonomi's group of Social Reformists (twenty-six representatives); both were hardly relevant, either politically or intellectually. These three groups, by and large, made up the Center of the political alignment of 1921. Without the Popolari, the Center amounted to 104 representatives, one-fifth of the Chamber. Even combined with the 106 representatives of the Popolari, it could not constitute the majority needed to form a cabinet. The Center needed help that, once again, could not come from the Left (Socialists and Communists), but rather from the Right, with all its equivocal consequences, including the thirty-two Fascists of the National Block.

The Center, composed of the right-wing of neutralism (Giolitti's group) and the left-wing of interventionism (Nitti and Bonomi) was less equipped to run the government than it had been in 1919. Once again, interventionism and neutralism had irrevocably split the old Liberal Center, and the consequences of this split were evident in each electoral test.

The Center, the old Liberal Center, was split more than it had been in 1919. In fact, to the cleavages Left and Right, Neutralism-Interventionism, the more subtle cleavage of the attitude pro and contra Fascism, with numberless nuances, had been added. The Center needed the help of other forces, no matter who those other forces were, since it would not have been able to reach a majority even if it had been more homogeneous. Moving toward the right wing of the alignment, we find the twenty-three representatives of De Nava's Democrazia Liberale and the forty-one representatives of Colonna di Cesarò's Democrazia Sociale, both "liberal" in their origins, both to the right of Giolitti's group, and both willing to cooperate with the Fascists.

The Right is clearly defined as composed of the Salandra group, labeled "Liberal democratic," with twenty-one (a year earlier, seventeen) members; the most conspicuous representation of the *Confindustria* (Benni, Celesia di Vegliasco, De Capitani d'Arzago, etc.); the Agrarians (twenty-three representatives, earlier, twenty-seven); the Fascists (thirty-two, earlier, thirty-five); and eleven Nationalists (earlier, ten). In 1919 the clearly defined Right amounted to thirty-five representatives, in 1922 eighty-seven.

The Left, Socialists and Communists together, decreased, although it remained a numerically powerful group. However, it could not be counted upon in any parliamentary "combination" to form a government (see table 5).

The Socialists were not disposed to enter the cabinet. Had they split they would have sustained a substantial loss: forty *Massimalisti* and fourteen Communists, besides all the consequences to the party, including the relationship with the CGL. But even if they had not split, they would enter the government, any government, not on a cresting wave, so to speak, as would have been the case two years or even one year earlier; they would enter at a time when their influence, both political and moral, was ebbing.

The Popolari—whose numbers slightly increased—became of crucial importance. However, the old clerical-anticlerical cleavage, plus the personal idiosyncrasies of Sturzo and Giolitti, prevented any agreement between the Popolari and the only group that could take the initiative inside the old Liberal Center—that is, the group supporting Giolitti, and in particular Giolitti himself. Without the "old man," this group counted for very little, and in fact the Popolari's support for a member of this group, such as Facta (according to the naive politics of having a "Giolittiane" but not Giolitti), was disruptive. The Popolari then could take the initiative, but the only acceptable man of that group was the moderate (and ex-interventionist) Meda, who represented a tiny minority inside the Popolari's parliamentary group. The result was that the Popolari did not take the initiative in forming a cabinet, at least a seriously feasible one, but prevented the formation of a large political support for the Giolitti group.

In this situation, the only "disposable" forces were those of the Right; they were small and contradictory, but they were "disposable." One was practically dominating the streets and could therefore bargain on a different table than that of all the other forces, the table of force, i.e., in a location practically above any contractual relationship. In fact, sooner or later, that force would have to deal with the only real "opponent" who could mobilize the army against it: the crown.

From a purely parliamentary point of view, with this situation of the Left, the Center, and the Right of the alignment, there was a visible reduction of the political arena to groups of the old Liberal Center and groups of the Right.

3. The Takeover of Power

The Fascist takeover of power was essentially political, not military, and from this point of view the March on Rome was the conclusion of a strategy based on the exercise of violence and, above all, on the enfeeblement and division of the forces of the political alignment. This division insured that the issue of order as a basic one able to aggregate political and social forces into an anti-Fascist front would be avoided, and resulted in a weak political leadership being made the arbitrator among forces that were both weakened and willing to be the "gate-keepers" of power for fascism.

In this perspective, we can consider a sequence of events in the Parliament and in the country, but the starting point of the analysis is no longer the Parliament or the sociopolitical forces in the country, but fascism itself. From the fall of Giolitti to the March on Rome, fascism defined the situation.

The "pacification pact" (August 1921) between Fascists and Socialist unions must be seen as an attempt to detach the Socialist party from its syndicalist basis, thereby disconnecting political socialism from labor socialism. The reaction of the squadristi leaders (concluded at the Augusteo Theater in November 1921) was not merely in terms of a "class struggle"; they reacted against the useless salvage of an organization already in critical condition, particularly since such salvage would only have put obstacles in the way of the squadristi's planned violence.

The Bonomi government fell because of the failure of the pacification pact that it had supported: one more indication that fascism defined the political situation, its stability, and its recurrent crises. The story that followed is one that, at the level of analysis, appears as the exhaustion of possible combinations and alternatives, but in none of these failures (when success might have endangered the chance for fascism to take over power), was fascism (or Mussolini) absent.

It is worth reviewing the several possible combinations, all alternatives to a Fascist takeover and sometimes even to Fascist participation in the government, and all containing one basic element: street violence by the Fascists, now prompted by the prospect of certain political combinations in the Parliament. In this sense, Parliament was subjugated to the streets.

Failure of Alternative Arrangements

Parliamentary life comprises all the occasions for political alliances: issues, events, and critical situations. Consideration of a few of them should make clear the contradictions among the political forces of the legitimate alignment and the Fascist technique of dividing the forces from one another and all of them from the country.

The fall of Bonomi's cabinet opened two possibilities. The first was an alliance between Giolitti, De Nicola, and Orlando (the Center-Right), with a program to reintroduce majority rule in the elections. This arrangement failed because of Sturzo's opposition (this was Sturzo's first "veto" to Giolitti). The veto was in the obvious interest of mass parties, including the Fascists, so it therefore blurred the cleavage between fascism and antifascism. The second arrangement was an alliance between Facta (a member of Giolitti's group) and the Popolari party. (This resulted in the first Facta government, which lasted until the end of July 1922). Facta and the Popolari party agreed on the promise of a favorable consideration of the statewide exam in public schools, which was granted by a Popolari member (Anile) in the Ministry of Public Education. The issue of church versus state blurred the basic cleavage that was breaking up the country.

During the first Facta cabinet, a Socialist attempt at isolating the Fascists in Parliament (as a consequence of a series of eruptions of violence), supported by the Popolari (the *mozione Longinotti* of 19 July 1922), met the opposition of rightist Liberals, particularly Salandra. This group permitted the Fascists to join the *mozione* as a vote of no confidence against the cabinet. A political victory for Mussolini resulted, though it was based on the presence of allies.

The fall of Facta's cabinet opened another series of alternative arrangements that are worth being compared with the first ones after Bonomi's fall. Orlando's design of assembling a grand coalition of Liberals, Fascists, and

Popolari met the opposition of the Popolari (Sturzo in particular) to having either Fascists or Giolitti in the government. The king tried to appoint Ivanoe Bonomi a second time (the first Bonomi cabinet had fallen on 2 February 1922). But Bonomi, who had the support of the Popolari, faced the opposition of Salandra Liberals, Demosocials (Nitti), Giolittians, and of course, Fascists.

At this stalemate there was an attempt by the Socialists and Popolari to respond, "patronized" by Bonomi. The task of canceling this alternative, the only feasible and anti-Fascist course of action, was performed by Giolitti: the newspaper *La Tribuna* published a letter by Giolitti in which the old leader cast many doubts over "a union of Sturzo, Treves, and Turati." Giolitti was the only figure who still had enough power—by himself—to veto such an important initiative, and he did it solely to return the veto to Sturzo.

When Bonomi gave up his attempts to form a cabinet, a series of impossible appointments followed, which showed the impotence of the traditional alignment of forces: Meda (Popolari), De Nava (rightist Liberal), and a projected appointment to Orlando, which was again interrupted by the news about the "legalitarian strike." Turati was consulted by the king on 29 July 1922, and a legalitarian strike was declared. This had disastrous consequences, including the second, definite appointment of Facta ("from facta to facta" while the storm was gathering), which passed in the emergency situation.

It was this atmosphere of division and fragmentation that prevented the Socialist-Popolari coalition, the only alliance with any hope of stability, from forming. The gains made by fascism during this period are manifested by an episode that took place when Orlando was first appointed. Shortly after he announced his design for a grand coalition (21–23 July 1922), Orlando had a talk with Mussolini, who, in order not to be isolated, asked for a cheap exchange: three undersecretaries (one to the presidency) for three inconspicuous Fascists. At the time of his second, prospective appointment, Orlando had another talk with Mussolini (28 July 1922). During that one-week interval Mussolini's price had risen to two ministries, including one for himself, the Ministry of the Interior. It was only a short step from this demand to the demand for total power, as Mussolini declared in the newspaper *Il Mattino* (11 August 1922) after the week of Fascist violence in retaliation for the "legalitarian strike" (1–3 August 1923).

The great victory for fascism resulted from the failure of the coalition between the Socialists and the Popolari. If it was a logical coalition, it was also immature in 1919, and during the three crucial years it had apparently deteriorated, rather than matured. In fact, it is difficult to believe that an agreement as important as that between the Socialists and Popolari turned out to be so vulnerable that it could be broken up by a simple column inspired by an old man.

The second Facta government, the one that fell with the March on Rome, witnessed a further reduction of the political arena and the entrance of new actors into the politically decisive arena, such as the king or even the Masons. Socialists and Popolari did not enter the last game, and the streets were silent, after the noise and violence. Violence was, however, being performed by the squads. Even the Vatican (as opposed to the leftist leadership of Sturzo) took a position in the game. The political parties were on the way out.

Reduction of the Political Arena

The failure of workable alternative arrangements further reduced the political arena and created a power vacuum that made the possibility of a government "imposed by the streets" more and more feasible. The streets, after the failure of the legalitarian strike, were monopolized by the Fascists; they could, however, be controlled by the army. As the "army" meant the "crown," in the middle of September 1922 Mussolini approached the monarchy in the well-known talk at Udine.

The power vacuum was not solely the result of the reduction of the political arena to four actors: the cabinet, the crown, Giolitti, and Mussolini. It was created in part by their internal relations, which gave the last-minute alternative of Giolitti versus Mussolini a complex aspect that resulted in the "lack of drama" with which the takeover was carried through.

The self-exclusion of the political forces from the arena reduced the situation to the alternative of Giolitti or Mussolini. The cabinet was quasi-paralyzed; the crown, according to the formal procedures, could come into the picture only on the initiative of the cabinet. There is sufficient evidence that Facta was negligent in contacting the king, for largely conjectural reasons that are of no interest here.[18] However, from the analysis of the government's decisions and nondecisions it appears that it was divided by two contrasting lines that neutralized each other: the Taddei line, which favored strong intervention against mounting Fascist violence, and the Facta line, which favored letting things go, based on the provisional task of paving the way for the return of Giolitti.

The lack of any reaction to the constant civil disorder gives, of course, a different weight to the two last-minute competitors and to their projects, but it is not the only reason for the difference in bargaining power.

Mussolini made no secret of his project of a dictatorship. As early as August of the same year in the interview to *Il Mattino* he had posed the dilemma of "either Parliament or seizure of power" and had stated that "it is out of the question that fascism wants to become the state." This kind of statement made the attempts by Salandra, Nitti, and of course by Giolitti himself to coopt fascism seem grotesque.

We have no evidence that Giolitti had a definite project in mind, unless we consider the scuttling of the tentative Socialist-Popolari agreement that we have mentioned and later the demand for a "strong government" led by a "prestigious man" that appeared as an editorial in *La Stampa* on 13 September 1922 but is considered a self-proposal by Giolitti.

The difference in "weight" in fact resulted from several elements, most of them in favor of fascism. First, Giolitti planned to include the Fascists in the government, while Mussolini carefully avoided any mention of Giolitti for a parallel project. Second, Giolitti had uncertain allies, if not enemies, in Salandra and other representatives of the old Liberal alignment. In other words, the old cleavages and the old hostilities did not melt away in this emergency situation, partially because there was no dramatization on the side of Giolitti or of the Giolittiani of the situation in terms of "*sauvetage* of democracy" versus "the end of democracy." This happened, however, precisely because a basic element of Giolitti's program was the inclusion of Fascists in the government.

The frontal collision, already repeatedly avoided in order to maintain public order, was avoided even at the last minute, thereby giving Mussolini a monopoly to define the political situation. There is also the question of "style," which becomes important during crises, because groups are replaced by personalities and therefore the whole existing arrangement is more vulnerable. Given his uncertain allies, Giolitti should have remained in Rome, physically present, in order to aggregate his existing forces. However, his absence from the arena of the match, the aloofness with which he responded to the pressures to come and start talks concerning the formation of a new cabinet, all make the observer think that his strategy was opposite to the one demanded by the situation. Giolitti employed the traditional parliamentary tactic of playing the role of the indispensable man—a tactic used by those who

Table 6. Progressive Absenteeism in Parliament for the "Vote of Confidence" in the Government, 1919–22

Cabinets	Date	Confidence	No Confidence	Abstentions	Present	Absent
Orlando	23 June 1919	78	262	—	340	168
Nitti	11 May 1920	112	191	4	307	201
Nitti	21 May 1920	146	264	—	410	98
Giolitti[a]	26 June 1921	234	200	6	440	95
Bonomi	2 February 1922	368	11	3	382	153
Bonomi[b]	2 February 1922	127	295	1	423	112
Facta	19 June 1922	103	288	—	391	144
Facta	1 July 1922	122	247	—	369	166
Mussolini	30 October 1922	215	80	—	295	240

SOURCE: Computed from data in Francesco Bartolotta, *Parlamenti e governi d'Italia dal 1848 al 1970* (Rome: Vito Bianco, 1971), vol. 2.

[a]From 1921 on, the total number of deputies rose from 508 to 535 due to inclusion of the provinces previously under Austrian-Hungarian rule.

[b]The *ordine del giorno* that caused the resignation of the Bonomi cabinet had two different parts that were voted on separately. Here we have the results of the two votes.

resign the minute they think of themselves as being irreplaceable. It is, however, a tactic that often has proved to be wrong.

The self-exclusion of Giolitti left the field open to the leader of fascism. The technique of waiting was paralleled by the Fascist decision to anticipate the showdown of the march, which they were sure would have failed had the army seriously intervened. The rest is known, as the dilemma of Victor Emmanuel reproduced the dilemma that the political forces had refused, with different degrees of intensity, to face thoroughly.

The quasi-progressive absenteeism from the sessions of the Parliament (table 6) is also an indication of the final reduction of the political arena, to the point that Mussolini presented his first cabinet, with the well-known "Bivouac speech," to a semideserted House.

Fascism and Crisis

What was the relationship between the crisis of the Liberal state and the takeover of fascism? In these pages we have tried to illustrate the thesis that fascism was more the outcome of the crisis of the parliamentary state than an irresistible force. We have tried to identify those elements of the crisis of the Liberal-parliamentary state in Italy that are common to other parliamentary systems undergoing rapid transformation and mobilization. (The war caused this transformation in Italy; today it could result from serious economic crisis.) In such cases the rules of the "division of labor" between civil, political, and institutional elements of society—the rules on which the European parliamentary system is based—are turned upside down. Since the political society is the "protagonist" of the parliamentary system, because it maintains the rules of the game of this division of labor, our attention was inevitably directed to the contradictions within the political elite in general and the Liberal political elite in particular.

Fascism was finally able to exploit the confused reaction to the process of democratization of Italian society, when the Liberal, Socialist, and Catholic political forces renounced their role of redefining the tensions arising from the contradictions of the society and the state. In particular, Italian fascism was an answer to two political elites: the Liberals, who were not willing to accept the passage from liberalism to democracy, and the Socialists, who were equally unwilling to forgo the passage from democracy to socialism. Fascism grew out of the crisis of both the governing and the opposition forces of Giolittian Italy. As the crisis of the governing force was decisive, a few points are worth considering. A part of the Liberal elite was unwilling to accept passage from a political system managed by a social minority that, because of the electoral system it had given to itself, was overrepresented as a political majority, to a political system in which social and political majorities tended to coincide, both in numbers and in power. There is a statement by Antonio Salandra, one of the stauncher supporters of fascism within the group of the Liberals, in a letter written to the Liberal philosopher Benedetto Croce, that clearly reveals the mood of Liberals (and also of the so-called Democrats), i.e., of the basic political forces of Italy before World War I: "The victory of Giolitti and his associates over Pelloux and his government marked a turning point not from Reaction to Liberalism, but from Liberalism to Democracy. Italy was profoundly immature and badly adjusted to Democracy. From this came all the events that later followed."[19]

This was precisely the mood of the Liberals, of the force that, whether interventionist or neutralist (it did not really matter), was the continuous loser during and after the World War I. In this sense we can say that fascism was the outcome of the incapacity (or unwillingness) of liberalism to turn into liberal democracy based on universal suffrage and proportional representation. In the same sense we can say that fascism was also the outcome of the incapacity (or unwillingness) of socialism to become social democracy, rather than turning into a rather wishful revolutionarism. Fundamentally, fascism exploited the incapacity of political forces of the Liberal state to aggregate and organize themselves as a mass party capable of coopting the middle classes. Italian liberalism, and above all, its most able representative, Giolitti, failed to aggregate the interests and the solidarities of the Italian middle class, both industrial and rural. It failed to coopt the increasing Italian middle class in a liberal democratic project of government, as Franklin D. Roosevelt succeeded in doing with his "New Deal," once in power.

Giolitti would probably have succeeded in this project of social and political cooptation had Italy not entered the great European conflict that brought out the most irrational feelings of the Italian middle class, especially that petty "humanism"—made of rhetoric, resentment, and low income—that a careful observer of his own contemporary politics had rightly identified as a fundamental matrix of that climate of opinion that contributed to the Fascist takeover of power.[20]

However, there is little doubt that the Fascist regime marks the beginning of that upward trend of the middle classes, their political and economic expansion, that was interrupted by neither World War II nor its aftermath. This phenomenon constitutes one of the most interesting problems of our modern political systems.

NOTES

1. Paolo Farneti, "Introduzione," in *Il sistèma politico italiano*, ed. Paolo Farneti (Bologna: Il Mulino, 1973), pp. 12–26.
2. Karl Dietrich Bracher, *Die Auflösung der Weimarer Republik* (Stuttgart: Ring Verlag, 1955).
3. Max Weber, *Wirtschaft und Gesellschaft: Grundriss der Verstehenden Soziologie*, vol. 1 (Cologne and Berlin: Kiepenheuer and Witsch, 1964), pp. 223–26.
4. A. F. K. Organski, "Fascism and Modernization," in *The Nature of Fascism*, ed. J. S. Woolf (London: Weidenfeld and Nicolson, 1968), pp. 9–14.
5. Weber, *Wirtschaft und Gesellschaft*, pp. 224–25.
6. Roberto Vivarelli, *Il dopoguèrra in Italia e l'avvènto del fascismo, 1918–1922*, vol. 1, *Della fine della guèrra all'impresa di Fiume* (Naples: Istituto Italiano per gli Studi Storici, 1967); Giampiero Carocci, *Stòria del fascismo* (Milan: Garzanti, 1972); Axel Kuhn, *Das Faschistische Herrschafts-system und die Moderne Gesellschaft* (Hamburg: Hoffman and Conze, 1973); Adrian Lyttelton, *The Seizure of Power: Fascism in Italy, 1919–1929* (London: Weidenfeld and Nicolson, 1973); Nicola Tranfaglia, *Dallo stato liberale al regime fascista* (Milan: Feltrinelli, 1974); Giovanni Sabbatucci, ed., *La crisi italiana del primo dopoguèrra: La stòria e la crìtica* (Bari: Laterza, 1976).
7. R. Frank, "Les classes moyennes en Italie," in *Inventaires III: Classes moyennes*, ed. Charles Bougle (Paris: Alcan, 1939), pp. 82 ff.; N. Tranfaglia ed., *Fascismo e capitalismo* (Milan: Feltrinelli, 1976) (see in particular the essay by Valerio Castronovo); Paolo Farneti, "La classe politica italiana dal suffragio allargato al suffragio universale," in *Sistèma Politico e società civile* (Turin: Giappichelli, 1971); Giampiero Carocci, *Stòria d'Italia dall'unità ad òggi* (Milan: Feltrinelli, 1975); Giorgio Rochat, *L'esèrcito italiano da Vittorio Veneto a Mussolini* (Bari: Laterza, 1967), pp. 26–66.
8. Nino Valeri, *Da Giolitti a Mussolini: Momenti della crisi del liberalismo* (Florence: Parenti, 1956).
9. Carl Schmitt, *Der Begriff des Politischen* (Berlin: Duncker and Humblot, 1932).
10. Renzo De Felice, *Mussolini il rivoluzionàrio* (Turin: Einaudi, 1966), p. 636.
11. *Annuario statìstico italiano, 1919–1921* (Rome: Librerìa dello Stato, 1925), p. 400.
12. Paolo Ercolani, "Documentazione statìstica di base," in *Lo sviluppo econòmico in Italia*, vol. 3, *Studi di settore e documentazione di base*, ed. Giorgio Fua (Milan: Angeli, 1969), p. 413.
13. Alfredo Frassati, *Giolitti* (Florence: Parenti, 1959), pp. 29–30.
14. Renzo De Felice, *Mussolini, il fascista*, vol. 1, *La conquista del potere: 1921–1925* (Turin: Einaudi, 1966), pp. 276 ff.
15. Gabriele De Rosa, *Stòria del Partito Popolare italiano* (Bari: Laterza, 1966), pp. 27–37.
16. Alfred Szymanski, "Fascism, Industrialism, and Socialism: The Case of Italy," *Comparative Studies in Society and History* 15 (1973): 400.
17. Piero Melograni, *Gli industriali e Mussolini: Rappòrti tra confindustria e fascismo dal 1919 an 1929* (Milan: Longanesi, 1972); Roland Sarti, *Fascism and the Industrial Leadership in Italy, 1919–1940* (Berkeley and Los Angeles: University of California Press, 1971).
18. Efrem Ferraris, *La marcia su Roma vista dal Viminale* (Rome: Leonardo, 1946); Antonino Repaci, *La Marcia su Roma* (Milan: Rizzoli, 1972).
19. Quoted in Paoll Alatri, *Le orìgini del fascismo*, 2nd ed. (Rome: Editori Riuniti, 1971), p. 36, n. 3.
20. Luigi Salvatorelli, *Nazionalfascismo* (Turin: Piero Gobetti, 1923).

2.

From Fragmented Party Democracy to Government by Emergency Decree and National Socialist Takeover: Germany

M. Rainer Lepsius

The breakdown of the Weimar Republic was more than the collapse of a government or the dissolution of a political system. The seizure of power by the National Socialist party and the dictatorial regime of Adolf Hitler demonstrated the possibilities for self-destruction of a modern society. This change, revolutionary in its consequences, happened in a nonviolent way, observing the legal provisions of a democratic constitution in an economically developed, socially tightly organized, and culturally highly diversified country.

Since its occurrence, more than forty years ago, a great many attempts have been made to analyze the breakdown of the Weimar Republic. However, as a historian of that period recently said: "Despite the plethora of studies dealing with Nazism and the Third Reich, those phenomena in no sense belong to a closed chapter of history. Instead, they remain the focus of a vigorous and ongoing body of international scholarship. Historians and social scientists have as yet far from plumbed the full depths of the sea of documentation they generated."[1] One could add that the social sciences are still struggling to develop adequate systematic categories to analyze this event in theoretical terms.

This essay will not attempt to give a systematic analysis or a general interpretation, nor will it give an account of the sequence of events that led to the breakdown. The former would not be possible because of the lack of theoretical analysis that has still to be done, the latter is unfeasible because of space and is unnecessary in view of the available literature.[2] The following paragraphs will attempt to discuss some dimensions of the complex process and propose a number of analytical accounts that will be neither exhaustive nor evaluated in regard to their relative weight for the explanation of the total historical phenomenon.

1. The Democratic Potential

The strength of a democratic regime rests with the popular support of a democratic conception of government. The Weimar Republic, it has often been stated, was a republic without republicans and a democracy without democrats. While both statements are too rigid, they certainly point toward one of the basic hazards of the Weimar Republic: a very narrow democratic potential.

With the term "democratic potential" we do not refer to theories of a peculiar authoritarian German modal personality nor to conceptualizations of a specific German value system. In this context the democratic potential is defined by democratic conceptions of the political order institutionalized in the party system. The institutionalization of democratic and nondemocratic concepts of political order in the political system does not need to correspond with the distribution of personality types. Democratic personalities may have an identification with authoritarian parties, just as authoritarian personalities may have acquired a political affiliation with parties committed to democratic institutions. The institutionalization of social behavior cannot be reduced to underlying motivations or attitudes; it makes social action to a certain degree independent of them and defines legitimated alternatives of behavior for people with all kinds of personality structures.[3] The strength of the democratic potential of a political system, hence, can be measured by the votes for parties committed to democratic institutions. The more components of the political process are committed to democratic institutions, the greater is the institutionalized democratic potential. The more homogeneously the part system is oriented toward a democratic political order, the less the democratic regime becomes endangered by shifts in party identification and by sudden disaffections with a particular government. If, however, competing conceptions of the basic political order are firmly institutionalized in the party system, changes in the respective strength of the parties may have repercussions on the nature of the political regime. The more the strength of the institutionalized democratic potential is based on some parties only, the more risks a democratic regime runs by changes in voter alignments or protest movements in times of crisis.

In the Weimar Republic one can distinguish three major conceptions of political order firmly institutionalized in the party system: the democratic, the authoritarian, and the Communist. To these we will add a fourth residual category comprising splinter parties organized along particularistic regional and economic interests with ambivalent or undefined conceptions of the national political order. Table 1 shows the general distribution of votes along those groupings for the period of 1907 to 1933 according to the results of the national elections.

The democratic camp was formed by a coalition of the Social Democrats, the Catholics, and the Left liberals, who were striving for a democratization of the *Kaiserreich* and proposed peace negotiations in 1917 (the Interfraktionelle Ausschuss). This "Weimar coalition" took responsibility for the armistice in 1918, established the democratic constitution of the new Republic in 1919, and defended a democratic political order in the years of turmoil from 1918 to 1920. It founded the Republic, but it was a coalition of parties with very divergent political interests and lacked a homogeneous political platform. It had a unique strength in the National Assembly of 1919 that it never regained. This was partly due to the fact that at the time of the election, 19 January 1919, only two months after the armistice, the demission of the Kaiser, and the collapse of traditional order and imperial illusions, the authoritarian camp found itself in a state of organizational and political weakness. However, it soon recovered and by July 1920, at the first *Reichstag* elections, it had regained its prewar strength. The second factor, leading to the majority for the democratic camp in 1919, was the organizational unity of the Socialist party. The radical wing of the Socialists had not yet established an organization throughout the country, and only by the end of 1920 did the Communist party become a party with mass support. The permanent institutionalization of the Communist conception of a political order became an uncompromising opposition to the democratic order and drew its support from strata that formerly had voted for the democratic camp; this, then, weakened it below its prewar strength.

The authoritarian conception of political order was not only a carry-over from imperial times, a nostalgic resentment against the present state of affairs, believed to be caused by Allied reparations and political mismanagement, and anxieties of the middle classes toward Socialist reforms. It was deeply rooted in a widespread intellectual conviction that there was a distinctly German road to modernity, which was not to follow the lines of the West. This conception had a number of long-standing leitmotifs: power should be wielded by an elite of virtue and competence, not by functionaries of the impersonal parliamentary mechanisms; social conflicts should be solved by reason of the public good rather than settled by compromises of conflicting interests; integration should be achieved by national commitment and a quest for community, not by particularistic interest mediation and institutionalized procedures; and the state should have ultimate authority and moral dignity in regard to the autonomous forces of society and the individual pursuit of goals. These ideas coalesced in a distrust of democracy and the free organization of social interests and in the belief in state intervention and constitutionally secured elite author-

Table 1. National Elections in Germany, 1907–33 (*Reichstagswahlen*)

Percentage of Votes in National Elections

Conceptions of Political Order	1907	1912	1919	1920	1924_1	1924_2	1928	1930	1932_1	1932_2	1933
Authoritarian[a]	33	27	15	30	36	35	26	30	45	42	55
Democratic[b]	59	63	76	47	46	50	49	43	38	36	33
Communist[c]	—	—	7	20	13	9	11	13	14	17	12
Particularistic[d]	8	10	2	3	5	6	14	14	3	5	2

[a]For the elections in 1907 and 1912 these are the Deutsche Konservative Partei, Reichspartei, National-Liberale Partei, Bund der Landwirte, and the Deutsche Reformpartei. For the elections in 1919 and after they are the Deutschnationale Volkspartei, Deutsche Volkspartei, Nationalsozialistische Deutsche Arbeiterpartei, and the Landbund.

[b]For the elections in 1907 and 1912 these are the Fortschrittliche Volkspartei, Zentrum, Sozialdemokratische Partei. For the elections in 1919 and after they are the Deutsche Demokratische Partei (Staatspartei), Zentrum and Bayerische Volkspartei, and Sozialdemokratische Partei.

[c]Unabhängige Sozialdemokratische Partei and Kommunistische Partei.

[d]Regional protest parties of ethnic minorities and splinter parties of peasant and middle-class economic organizations.

ity. It should be made clear that such a concept of political order was neither totalitarian nor Fascist: it did not call for a unitarian mass movement but for a cooperation of social units in their own right (*berufständische Ordnung*); it did not believe in a military policing of society but in the authority of welfare-oriented paternalism; it did not advocate an uncontrollable charismatic leader bound only by his fortune and his idiosyncratic judgments but an open elite committed to the public good and responsible to publicly shared values of honor and individual virtues subject to law. These ideas were formed in the course of the nineteenth century under the impact of industrialization and the French Revolution. They were directed toward a double goal: to overcome the backwardness of Germany rapidly and at the same time to avoid the negative consequences of modernization clearly evident in the Western countries. The German way to modernity was believed to be superior in terms of efficiency as well as in terms of humanitarian values.[4]

The democratic concept of political order was in a precarious situation. However, its potential support was not so weak that democracy had no chance to survive. In 1919 it had a unique strength, and in 1932 it still had not lost a chance for a majority. The democratic potential could increase under favorable conditions.

To substantiate this argument, it is useful to analyze two presidential elections: 1925 and 1932. The presidential elections forced a polarization and concentration, as an absolute majority (in the second ballot, a relative majority) was necessary. They also led to a symbolic dramatization by the personalization of the election. While in the parliamentary elections numerous parties provided many and often indistinct alternatives, the presidential elections restricted the choices and mobilized the democratic and authoritarian potential more clearly. Table 2 condenses the voting results according to the different conceptions of political order in the two ballots for *Reichspräsident* and adds the results of the preceding national parliamentary election.

There is a two-step process of concentration and polarization. The first occurs between the parliamentary elections and the first ballot for the presidential elections, where the alternatives are reduced from about fifteen parties to five or seven candidates for the presidency. Thereby, the voters of the particularistic parties have to make a choice between the major orientations of the national party system.

In the second ballot a further reduction of alternatives takes place, with three candidates representing the three basic conceptions of political order. While the Communists can retain their hard-core support, despite having no chance to win, the ambivalent situation between the democratic and the authoritarian orientations becomes clearly apparent. The victorious candidate in both elections was Field Marshal von Hindenburg, who was the candidate for the authoritarian camp in 1925 and the candidate of the democratic camp in 1932. In 1925 his candidacy pulled 12.8 percent of the electorate toward an

Table 2. Relative Strength of Basic Orientations in the Elections for
Reichspräsident in 1925 and 1932 Compared to the Parliamentary
Elections of 1924 and 1930

	Percentage of Votes		
Conceptions of *Political Order*	*Reichstag* *7 December 1924*	*Reichspräsident 1925*	
		1st ballot	*2d ballot*
Authoritarian	35.5	39.9	48.3
Democratic	49.5	53.0	45.3
Communist	9.2	7.0	6.4
Particularistic	5.8	0.1	—
Turnout	77.7	68.9	77.6
Conceptions of *Political Order*	*Reichstag* *14 September 1930*	*Reichspräsident 1932*	
		1st ballot	*2d ballot*
Authoritarian	30.3	36.9	36.8
Democratic	42.9	49.6	53.0
Communist	13.1	12.2	10.2
Particularistic	13.7	0.3	—
Turnout	81.4	86.2	83.5

authoritarian orientation; in 1932, however, it pulled 10.1 percent toward the democratic orientation. In contrast to these effects, there was a comparatively good economic situation in 1925, which should have favored the democratic forces, while in 1932 the economic crisis was at its peak, which should have favored a radical protest vote. It seems that the polarizing effect of the candidacy of Hindenburg, in both elections, could not break up the basic strength of the authoritarian and the democratic potential; it could, however, swing the ambivalent electorate to either one or the other. In rough calculations on the aggregate election results—with all its known fallacies—it seems to be safe to conclude that the three major institutionalized conceptions of political order had a respective potential throughout the Weimar Republic of about 45 percent for a democratic political order, 35 percent for an authoritarian political order, and 10 percent for a Communist political order. It was for the remaining 10 percent of the electorate, which was undecided between the democratic and the authoritarian camp, to decide the fate of the democratic order.

The democratic potential of the Weimar Republic rested on the coherence and integrative capabilities of its intermediary organizations, parties, and interest groups to safeguard its basic core and to win support from segments of the population that were ambivalent or attached to the other conceptions of order. The coherence between the organizations was by and large maintained throughout the period. There were important breakups, particularly when the

Bavarian branch of the Catholic party decided to desert the democratic camp in the second ballot in the election of the Reichspräsident in 1925, which made Hindenburg the winner rather than the Catholic candidate, Wilhelm Marx, and caused the first major symbolic shift to the right in the political structure. But despite great internal differences and struggles, the organizations of the democratic camp maintained close connections and formed the government of Prussia continuously until its enforced dissolution of Chancellor von Papen on 20 July 1932.[5] The integrative abilities of the parties and intermediary organizations of the Catholic and Socialist segments of the democratic camp lasted until the Nazi seizure of power in 1933. In the end, the democratic camp lost because the liberal and Protestant segments had already disintegrated in the late twenties.

The democratic potential could have grown through the disintegration of either the authoritarian or the Communist camps. The Communists, however, became more and more uncompromising during the Weimar period.[6] In the course of its internal Stalinization during the years 1924 to 1928, the Communist party moved further away from the Socialists and made them their main target after 1929. Ideologically as well as organizationally, the Communist camp was tightly integrated and ready to absorb the protest vote of the unemployed working class.

The authoritarian camp compromised on occasion between 1925 and 1927. Altogether it lost popular support, but many of its followers moved toward the ambivalent group of regional or economic particularism rather than toward the democratic camp. The authoritarian camp returned to a course of system opposition in 1928–29; but it was not the traditional forces that regained popular support. It became completely reorganized and energetically strengthened by the Nazi party, which not only unified different groupings but was able to attract most of the ambivalent segments, and by the end of the period it had also made some inroads into the solid basis of the democratic camp, thereby creating a relative majority for the authoritarian camp.

The democratic potential remained stagnant. It might have been enlarged by integrating the ambivalent sector or by destroying the two other camps. This could have been achieved by the successful performance of democratic governments or by expanding the integrative capability of the respective intermediary organizations. The first was hard to achieve, given the basic differences of the political forces inside the democratic camp on major issues of internal policy and the general obstacles created by the war and the economic development. The second possibility was not pursued because of the subcultural fixation of the organizations, parties as well as interest groups. The Catholic Zentrumspartei was enclosed by religious boundaries, the Sozialdemokratische Partei by class boundaries. The disintegration of the authoritarian potential in 1919 and 1928 could not be utilized for a permanent growth of the democratic camp. It rather enlarged the ambivalent segments from 1928 to 1930 and provided an unstructured reservoir for recruitment by the Nazis. It was their vigorous campaigning and unscrupulous tactical agitation that restructured the authoritarian camp, moving it beyond the boundaries of Protestant middle-class conservatism into a highly politicized mass movement. This process, of course, was enormously aided by the disruptive effects of the economic crisis. The democratic regime was not doomed by the weakness of the democratic potential, but by its internal fragmentation and overall stagnation. The authoritarian potential did not win because of its traditionally institutionalized concepts of political order and organization but through its renewed internal cohesion and the vitality provided by the Nazi movement. The basic weakness of the democratic potential, however, limited the elasticity of the democratic regime in times of severe crisis because it did not allow for a change of government and coalition of political forces within a common democratic conception of political order. Change of government always implied the danger of a change of regime. A stable democratic regime should allow for a change of government without a threat to the regime. In this sense the Weimar Republic was not a stable democracy.

Parliamentary democracy, established during the turmoil of the German defeat in 1918–19, remained an "improvised democracy."[7] Legitimacy rested less on value commitments than on instrumental considerations. As perceived efficiency declined during the economic crisis after 1929, so did the legitimacy of the parliamentary regime. A substantial part of the population shared what Thomas Mann expressed in 1918: "I don't want politics. I want objectivity, order, and decency."[8] Mounting difficulties led to new improvisations during the period of presidential cabinets (1930–33) and to an erosion of parliamentary procedures. The political system did not satisfy the quest for leadership and symbolic integration so prominent in Nazi agitation.

2. The Party System

The German party system was formed in the Kaiserreich from 1870 to 1890 and carried over into the Weimar Republic without basic changes. This had two major consequences for the political process in the Weimar Republic. Firstly, the party system was based on the social and cultural cleavages of the seventies and eighties, and preserved them over a period of fifty years, while fundamental changes in the social structure took place. Second, in the Bismarckian political culture and within the imperial constitution with its pseudo-parliamentary government, the parties became used to acting as representatives of their respective sociocultural milieus rather than as responsible units of government. This traditional attitude led, within the parliamentary regime of the Weimar Republic, to an unconstructive inclination to regard uncompromising representation of traditional goals more highly than participation in government.

The basic fragmentation of the German party system consisted of four major groupings: a conservative political formation resting on the Protestant, agrarian segments of the population, located primarily in north and east Germany and oriented toward premodern authoritarian values; a liberal political grouping resting on Protestant urban and agrarian populations and organized along the influence patterns of local *Honoratioren*, divided into a nationalist right wing and a democratic left wing; the Center party, binding together the Catholic population in agrarian, middle class, and industrial areas primarily in west and south Germany; and the Socialist labor movement, integrating the secularized working class in the industrialized urban centers, dedicated to democratic and Socialist emancipation. The party system was structured along religious, class, regional, and ideological lines in a complex way that did not lead to a clear grouping of opposing coalitions; it evoked within any coalition high sensitivity on issues of firmly instutionalized interests.[9] In the course of the Weimar Republic the fragmentation grew further, thereby weakening the traditional party system. The Socialists split into the Social Democratic and the Communist parties. In the Catholic camp, the Bavarian branch became independent. The conservative and liberal milieus, however, experienced the greatest disintegration in numerous splinter parties of particularistic orientation.[10] Figure 1 tries to represent the party system of 1928 in a two-dimensional space. One dimension is a democratic-authoritarian continuum, the other dimension is a capitalist-socialistic continuum. The placement of the parties within this property space is, of course, always somewhat difficult to decide. The sketch should be used as an indication of the relative standing of the parties to one another and not as an indication of their absolute standing on questions of the political or the socioeconomic order. The percentages in the sketch refer to votes obtained in the elections of 20 May 1928 and are used to define the relative size of the parties.

The party system of the Weimar Republic offered two main alternatives for broad coalitions. Each, however, had to overcome a major internal cleavage. The democratic dimension united the parties of the Weimar coalition, the Social Democrats, the Catholic parties, and the liberal Democratic party. They could compromise on constitutional issues, as they endorsed the democratic regime, and on foreign policy, as they agreed on a revisionist strategy toward the Versailles treaty. They could not compromise on social issues, particularly when the Deutsche Volkspartei was included in a coalition, as they were too heterogeneous along the capitalist-socialistic dimension. The other coalition of forces was structured along homogeneity on the capitalist dimension and could include the Deutschnationale Volkspartei, the Deutsche Volkspartei, the Catholic parties, and the Democratic party. These parties

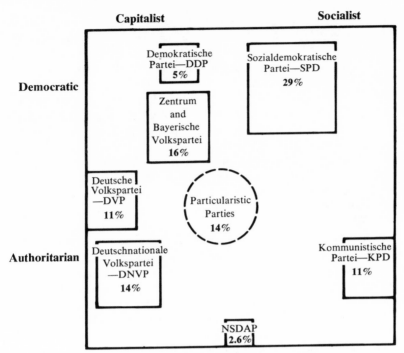

Figure 1. Germany Party Structure in 1928

could compromise on social and economic issues but not on constitutional and foreign policy issues. This led to a situation in which a coherent policy became impossible for any government. Both types of coalition had been tried: the democratic coalition was chosen during five years, the bourgeois coalition during two years. For seven years neither was attainable and minority or presidential cabinets were in office.

The development of the German party system before the advent of the Nazi movement had led to a disaggregation of interests within the parties. The mediation of political, economic, and social interests could not be achieved within parties and had to be secured on the level of the formation of a government coalition. This caused extreme instability in the governments of the Republic, as continuous tension management had to be maintained by means of government alterations. In the period from 13 February 1919, the date of the formation of the first parliamentary government, to 30 January 1933, when Hitler became chancellor, there were twenty cabinets. In only about half of these fourteen years did the governments have a parliamentary majority. This liability of the political process led to a complicated process of government by issue. For any major political issue a separate coalition and cabinet had to be formed. The governments did not rest on firm coalitions of parties on a common platform for a certain period of time but on short-term negotiations on policy actions for specific issues. The coherence of a government was achieved by the interaction of a few personalities who could exert influence within their parties to make them tolerate the government from issue to issue. This caused an alienation between government and Parliament quite in contrast to the principles of parliamentary democracy. The government became more dependent on the prerogatives of the Reichspräsident and saw itself as an independent agency that had to continue governing by continuous crisis management despite the fragmented Parliament. The parties, however, felt that reluctant toleration of government provided them with veto power on symbolic issues without the necessity of becoming entangled in the ongoing crisis management, which could be used to secure the *Gesinnungsgemeinschaft* within the party and its symbolic mediation into their respective electorates. As a contemporary observer wrote: "What we have today is a coalition of ministers, not a coalition of parties. There are no parties committed to the government any more, only opposition parties. That we have arrived at such a situation is a more severe hazard to the democratic system than ministers and parties foresee."[11] This is the clear perception of the crisis of the parliamentary regime under the conditions of the existing party system in 1929, at a time where neither the economic crisis nor the impact of the Nazi movement were dominating the political scene.

An awareness of the malfunctioning of the parliamentary system grew rapidly. It led to widespread resignation within the democratic camp and to a widely encouraged search for new forms of government, thereby revitalizing the authoritarian critique of democracy. A simultaneous development of disaffection with parliamentarianism and a quest for government authority came into being independent of the Nazi agitation against the political system. Even defenders of democracy lost their belief in its effectiveness. "In the entire period there was no government with real authority. It was a philosophy of 'somehow one must govern' which guided, and given the circumstances, had to guide political action but simultaneously led to a complete resignation, deadly to the vitality of a parliamentary democracy."[12]

Ferdinand Hermens, whose judgment we just quoted, pointed out as early as 1932 that one of the causes of the disintegration of the party system was of an institutional kind. He held that the electoral system of unrestricted proportional representation was crucial for the political crisis of the *Parteienstaat*. It facilitated the formation of small parties and the foundation of ever more by giving them the chance of winning a few seats in the Parliament. With about 60,000 votes out of an electorate of thirty-five million voters a splinter group could count on one seat. In 1930 there were nineteen parties that polled less than 100,000 votes each, some of them having the character of politicized sects, like the party against alcohol, which received 1,170 votes. It is obvious that such parties were without any influence, but they reduced the strength of the parliamentary system. After the election in 1928 there were eighty-eight members of Parliament elected by parties polling less than 5 percent of the national vote each. If one assumes only a modified proportional representation system by which no party polling less than 5 percent of the total vote gets seats, 18 percent of the members of Parliament in 1928 would have been excluded. Hermens suggested a majority system which would not only have inhibited the creation of new parties but would also have forced the traditional party system to reorient itself and try to aggregate diverse particularistic interests. While it is quite true that the electoral system of the Weimar Republic facilitated the disintegration of the party system, it did not, of course, originate it. However, it was a condition for the parliamentary crisis that had been widely discussed since 1924, but no alteration of the election system could be achieved by a Parliament that was paralyzed on so many issues.[13]

By 1930, the situation had worsened, and the party system changed. The disintegration of the party system, already clearly visible in 1928, had developed into a regime crisis under the impact of the severe economic crisis. None of the traditional parties, entrenched in old boundaries, was able to reintegrate the substantial segments of the population that were drifting out of the established political order either by voting for particularistic groups or by increased abstention.

Three major components of the traditional party system moved to the right; the conservative Deutschnationale Volkspartei under its new leader, Hugenberg; the Deutsche Volkspartei, after the death of its leader, Stresemann, in 1929, and the Catholic Zentrumspartei, under the more conservative chairmanship of the prelate Kaas.

The DNVP and DVP, which until 1928-29 could be regarded as the semiloyal opposition to the democratic system, now became disloyal. In the Socialist camp the strength of the disloyal opposition of the Communists was likewise growing. The Social Democrats, loyal to the democratic process to the very end, were unable to absorb the drifting voters of 1928. They had nothing to offer these voters, primarily peasants and those of middle-class origin, as they reinforced the traditional labor movement goals in order to defend their basic constituency against the competition of the Communists.

The main event, however, was the breakthrough of the Nazi movement. It became by far the strongest party and reversed the process of slow disintegration into a rapid reintegration of the party structure. The Nazis succeeded in absorbing the unattached and ambivalent voters of the splinter parties and former supporters of the Protestant middle-class and conservative parties. They pulled a substantial number of voters, who were still bound by semiloyal and even loyal parties prior to 1930, into a movement of uncompromising disloyalty to the democratic system. Together with the Communists, the Nazis made the disloyal opposition in 1932 a majority—a majority, however, which was internally antagonistic and unable to form a government (see table 3).

The crisis of the democratic regime was closely connected with the nature of the German party system—its fragmentation and its reluctance to accept the functions of parties in a parliamentary government.[14] To be sure, the tasks with which a German government was confronted in the postwar period and the subsequent economic crisis were extraordinary. The weakness of the democratic potential, furthermore, put severe limits on the formation of governments and loyal oppositions. But while continuous crisis in the years 1919-23 (adjustment to the lost war, assassinations, rightist putsches and leftist upheavals, occupation of the Ruhr, and inflation) could be overcome, the less threatening problems of 1928 to 1930 overburdened the party system. To reiterate, even without the threat of Hitlerism and the consequences of the mass unemployment of 1931 and 1932, the democratic parties were prepared to suspend the democratic procedures and resort to a presidential rule. By early 1930 they had accepted the government of Chancellor Heinrich Brüning, which rested on presidential power rather than on parliamentary majority. This signals the degree of frustration and timidity which became so dominant by the end of the Republic in 1932.

It is likely that the combination of presidential rule, politics of issue coalition, and short-term crisis management could have been carried on for a longer time and that the total collapse of democracy could have been avoided, despite the economic crisis that was further weakening the traditional structure of the German society and polity. There might also have been a chance for a revitalization of the party structure in 1934 or 1935 when the international economy recovered. However, the fragmentation of the party system and the strategy of temporary retreat from government participation and crisis management by emergency decrees were certainly preconditions for the breakdown of democracy.

Table 3. Strength and Composition of the Disloyal Opposition to the Democratic Regime, 1928-33

| | Votes in Reichstag Elections (in percentages) | | | | |
	1928	1930	1932₁	1932₂	1933
DNVP	14.2	7.0	5.9	7.2	8.0
NSDAP	2.6	18.3	37.2	33.0	43.9
KPD	10.6	13.1	14.2	16.8	12.3
Disloyal opposition	27.4	38.4	57.3	57.0	64.2

3. The Constitutional Framework

Any political process is influenced by the constitutional framework in which it takes place. In the case of the breakdown of the Weimar Republic the constitutional framework deserves special attention, as the breakdown and the seizure of power by Hitler has a curious double character. It is a regime change observing legal provisions while using revolutionary means.

In this context a systematic analysis of the Weimar constitution is not to be given, but a few remarks concerning the prerogatives of the Reichspräsident and the famous Article 48 must be made.[15] The constitution basically endorsed parliamentary rule but granted special rights to the president of the Republic. This duality of a parliamentary and a presidential rule was deliberately introduced into the constitution, partly influenced by the former imperial constitution and partly as a means of strengthening the authority of the state and counterbalancing the power of the parties and the Parliament. The president could claim greater personal legitimacy than the chancellor, as the former had a plebiscitarian basis and the latter only an indirect legitimation by Parliament. The president could bring a government into office without active participation of the Parliament as long as the Parliament was not casting a vote of no confidence. The president could dissolve the Parliament without its consent. The president could issue decrees in states of emergency to restore public order with the endorsement of the chancellor, which the Parliament later could revoke or merely tolerate by not casting a vote against the decree. Taken together, the presidential prerogatives allowed for government without active participation of the Parliament. The Parliament could fall back on a passive role of toleration and resort to its veto powers without being forced to formulate a political course of action of its own. There is a certain correspondence between the party structure and the constitution. This could be seen as functional, given the fragmented party structure; it could, however, also prolong a party structure dysfunctional for a parliamentary democracy.

In the first years (1919–24) of the presidency of Friedrich Ebert the emergency powers of the president became widely used to cope with upheavals and revolts within the narrow sense of the constitutional definitions. However, by 1923 and 1924 the presidential prerogatives were also used to cope with economic matters that had no relation to any state of emergency or public disorder. They were, however, only used for a short period of time, since the Parliament always retained its ultimate authority. President Ebert, a Social Democrat who was deeply committed to a democratic form of government, never intended to abuse the emergency powers in order to change the power distribution between the legislative and executive branches of government.

With the appointment of Chancellor Brüning on 30 March 1930, a new situation was created. His government was put into office by the Reichspräsident without consultation with the parties and was declared deliberately to be a nonparliamentary government resting on the authority and the constitutional power of the president. The right to issue emergency decrees was now used as a permanent substitute for formal legislation. Its precondition was the internal paralysis of the Parliament, which would only agree not to pass a vote of no confidence. When in July 1930 an emergency decree on the budget was not tolerated by the Parliament, the president resorted to his right to dissolve the Parliament. The emergency decree was issued again, now not faced with any acting Parliament to resist its legality. Sixty days later, however, new elections had to take place. By combining the three constitutional rights of the president, a government could be kept in power without the explicit endorsement of Parliament, distorting the nature of the constitution. The countervailing powers of the president became the dominant focus of political authority. A shift of power from the legislative to the executive branch took place, which changed parliamentary rule into presidential rule. To hold a national election in September 1930, at the start of the economic crisis and with a Nazi movement already on the way to mobilize and radicalize the electorate, was a politically fatal decision. Its only result was to increase the incapacity of the Parliament. The Nazis, who had had 12 deputies in the Reichstag of 1928, returned now with 107; the Communists enlarged their faction from 54 to 77. However, the decision to dissolve the Parliament was not taken with the aim of restoring parliamentary rule but of prolonging presidential rule. The party crisis had led to an extension of the constitution. The government was no longer conceived as an agent of the Parliament but of the presidential authority. The awareness of the parliamentary crisis became now an awareness of a constitutional crisis. Conservative forces, opposed to parliamentary democracy, saw their opportunity gradually to transform the political system into a semiparliamentary rule with a government "above the parties" and responsible only to the president legitimated by the plebiscite. The more reactionary circles thought the time for exclusion of the labor movement from the political process and a reduction of social legislation had come, restoring not only the prewar political order but its social order as well. Presidential rule became a new form of legal government, opening up a chance for permanent dictatorial rule. As long as Brüning was chancellor, the latter possibility was not contemplated by the government. He aimed at an eventual return to a parliamentary regime.[16] It was only after his dismissal by Reichspräsident von Hindenburg on 30 May 1932 that the essence of the constitution was violated.

The new chancellor, von Papen, appointed by Hindenburg on 1 June 1932, did not even have a chance to be tolerated by the Parliament. Before even a vote of no confidence could be cast, the Parliament was dissolved by presidential decree. New elections were to take place within the constitutional limits of sixty days. This caused an election at the peak of the economic crisis, which could only lead to an enormous increase of Nazi strength in the Reichstag. There had already been three nationwide elections in 1932 that Hitler had used for a continuous campaign. The new Reichstag saw the NSDAP, with 37.2 percent of the votes, as by far the largest faction. However, the Reichstag elected on 31 July 1932 was immediately dissolved on 12 September and a fifth election was called for 11 November, again observing the constitutional provision of the sixty days. The rationale for the two dissolutions and elections of Parliament, however, was an abuse of the constitution, namely, to install a presidential government without parliamentary support. Neither von Papen nor General von Schleicher, who became chancellor on 3 December 1932, were committed to a democratic regime. They were, however, unable to establish an authoritarian rule by either an enforced permanent dismissal of Parliament or a military coup d'état. They succeeded in further discrediting parliamentarism, in providing new occasions for agitation and mobilization of the population by useless elections and in unintentionally justifying Hitler's claims that the present system was rotten and that Germany could only be saved by a truly authoritarian leadership based on his own mass support.[17] Table 4 indicates the breakdown of parliamentarism well before the Nazi seizure of power.

With the gradual shift of power from the Parliament to the president, the arena of decision-making became confined, and legal procedures were replaced by personal relations. The leadership of the parties and factions lost influence. The mediation of interests in the political arena shifted from organized procedures between agencies to obscure informal conferences and confidential agreements. The personal likes and dislikes of Hindenburg, his understanding of the political situation, and his physical health became of utmost importance to the political fate of the country. Rooted in the tradition of the imperial army, living in a world of conservative national commitments, he had no clear understanding of a democratic parliamentary system. Overburdened by the decisions he had to make or at least to justify by his signature, eighty-five years of age and in poor health, he was placed in the center of the remaining arena of legal decision-making,[18] Personal access to Hindenburg rather than constitutional procedures defined political events. The appointments and dismissals of Brüning, Papen, and Schleicher, and finally also the appointment of Hitler, were effected in the influence on Hindenburg of a very small and publicly irresponsible group of people. A process of gradual denaturation took place, covering up even the most obvious violations of constitutional rights. The depossession of the Prussian government by the

Table 4. Erosion of Parliamentary Power

	1930	1931	1932
Laws passed by Parliament	98	34	5
Emergency decrees by the president	5	44	66
Days in parliamentary session	94	41	13

Papen government on 20 July 1932 could still pretend to be legally justified by a presidential decree.[19] This blurring of the categories of legality and legitimacy also served to make the seizure of power by Hitler look legal.[20] He was appointed by the president but could not win a vote of confidence in Parliament. Therefore, the Reichstag was dissolved once more two days after his appointment, and new elections were scheduled for 5 March 1933. Hitler had five weeks without a constitutional basis to establish his rule and in particular to take over the police in Prussia, suppressing leftist forces and intimidating all opposition. On 28 February 1933 an emergency decree was issued, which pretended to be constitutionally legal while it suspended the very basis of the constitution with no Parliament to cast a vote on the decree. The election on 5 March 1933, conducted under the unrestricted impact of Nazi propaganda, using all the suppressive powers of the government, brought the Nazis 43.9 percent of the vote and, only by the coalition with the Deutschnationale Volkspartei and their 8 percent of the vote, a narrow majority. Pseudo-legality was transformed into a nominal legitimacy, which in turn was used to destroy constitutional legality and to establish an undemocratic rule.[21]

Attitudes are formed and actions are taken within an institutional framework. This framework is not neutral but gives rise to a dynamic of its own. It not only defines the normal procedures but makes certain alternatives more accessible than others. The constitution and the election system, both hailed as most democratic, did not cause the breakdown of the Weimar Republic. However, they did not serve to strengthen the democratic political process. The imperial regime, with its authoritarian political order, remained an alternative preferred by many parts of the elite—the civil servants, the military, the professors, the industrialists, and of course, the landed aristocracy. Democratic procedures and institutions did not gain consensual legitimacy with the population, either. Open interest mediation was mistaken for efficiency. At best, the Germans became *Vernunftrepublikaner,* at worst they were longing for a restoration of the monarchy or a charismatic *Führergestalt.*

4. Economic Situation and Social Structure

The impact of the economic depression on the rise of Nazism and the breakdown of democracy in Germany cannot be overestimated. It has often been stated, and the assumption is very plausible, that without the disruption of the economic situation, the political system would not have entered a prolonged crisis, nor would a large segment of the population have been mobilized by the Nazi movement. The rise of the Nazi movement and the unemployment curve show a close similarity. Germany was hit particularly hard by the world depression. Next to the United States, she suffered most, much more than France, Great Britain, the Scandinavian countries, Holland,

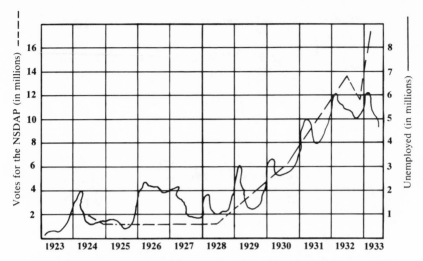

Figure 2.   Unemployment Rate and Vote for the National Socialist Party. Reprinted from Werner Kaltefleiter, *Wirtschaft und Politik in Deutschland* (Cologne and Opladen: Westdeutscher Verlag, 1968), p. 37

and Belgium. This severe economic crisis, which led to a decrease of the gross domestic product in 1932 to 63 percent of its 1928 level, and to the unemployment of six million people in the first months of 1932 and 1933, was caused by the international depression, structural domestic problems, and political factors.[22] The main cause, however, rested in international economic developments and was external to the German political and social system. However, the question of whether the economic crisis was aggravated by German actions and why the economic crisis led to a breakdown of the total political system must be raised.

After a disastrous inflation in 1923, the German economy recovered quickly. Foreign, particularly American, loans provided short-term investment funds; these were used to modernize the industrial production system,

Table 5. National Income, 1929–32 (1929 = 100)

	1929	1930	1931	1932
Germany	100	92	75	61
United States	100	94	78	60
United Kingdom	100	98	87	85
France	100	99	93	84
Sweden	100	107	108	100

Source: League of Nations, *Economic World Survey 1933–34* (Geneva, 1934), p. 158.

Table 6. Unemployment, 1928–33 (Annual average as percentage of labor force)

	1928	1929	1930	1931	1932	1933
Germany	8.6	13.3	22.7	34.3	43.8	36.2
United States	4.4	3.2	8.9	15.9	23.6	24.9
United Kingdom	10.8	10.4	16.1	21.3	22.1	19.9
France	4.0	1.0	2.0	6.5	15.4	14.1
Sweden	10.8	10.2	11.9	16.8	22.4	23.3

SOURCES: The figures for Germany, the United Kingdom, and Sweden are from Walter Galenson and Arnold Zellner, "International Comparisons of Unemployment Rates," in *The Measurement and Behavior of Unemployment,* National Bureau of Economic Research (Princeton, N.J.: Princeton University Press, 1957), p. 455. The figures for France are estimated rates among wage and salary earners in manufacturing, mining, and construction. This represents the total unemployment picture adequately. See Galenson and Zellner "International Comparisons of Unemployment Rates," p. 523. The figures for the United States are from Stanley Lebergott, "Annual Estimates of Unemployment in the United States, 1900–1954," in *The Measurement and Behavior of Unemployment,* p. 215.

which, due to the war, had a ten-year backlog of demands for new equipment. The internal war debts were liquidated by the currency reform of 1923/24, diminishing large sums of private savings, thereby impoverishing the middle classes and causing a lasting, psychological trauma.

The reparations demanded by the Allies became the great political issue; they were thought of as the cause of the German economic difficulties. At first undefined in their amount, they were the subject of continuous negotiations leading to the Dawes Plan of 1924, which regulated the procedures and amount of the annual payments, and later to the Young Plan of 1930, which set up a definitive schedule of payments to end in 1988. The capitalized present value of all payments was computed at just below 37 billion marks, which was a remarkable reduction from the sum of 132 billion marks set up by the Reparations Commission in 1921. In addition to the financial and economic burden, the reparations played an enormous symbolic role in the German political scene. The sum was regarded as totally unjust, much more than what was needed to compensate for the war damage caused by the German army in occupied territories. It was seen as being a means for the permanent enslavement of Germany by France and as a basis for direct intervention in German affairs. A severe limitation of national sovereignty was clearly perceived in the occupation of the Ruhr area as a sanction for alleged German noncompliance in 1923, in the setup of an Allied control commission in Berlin, and in the imposition of foreign experts on the board of the *Reichsbank,* the German central bank, and the national railways. Their controlling power was to secure a guarantee for the reparations payments. By the

provisions of the reparations agreements, the German authorities saw themselves as hampered in embarking on any policy of credit expansion to counteract the depression.[23]

The German reparations were linked with the regulation of French and
British war debts to the United States, and this interdependence caused a fatal
immobility in the international fiscal system and contributed to the enormous
decline in international trade during the world depression. In the German
political scene the reparations became the overriding issue, as the depression
was seen as an ideal opportunity to achieve an international agreement to
abolish the reparations altogether. The Brüning government concentrated all
its efforts on this goal regardless of the repercussions on the domestic economic and political situation. The strategy was first to prove to the Allies the
German incapacity to pay reparations and only then to embark on a policy of
public works and credit expansion. And indeed as the Reparations Conference
in Lausanne from 16 June to 8 July 1932 brought about the final settlement,
Brüning had already been dismissed.

The nationalistic opposition had denounced the policy of compliance and
gradual negotiations on the reparation question from the very beginning in the
early twenties. The NSDAP embarked on a violent campaign against the
reparations and the Versailles treaty, both symbols of national degradation,
both alleged tools of an international conspiracy of world capitalism and in
particular Jewish manipulations against the German people. The experience of
misery served as proof for these allegations, which converted economic problems into ideological commitments of a mythical character.

The domestic economic difficulties started with an agrarian crisis in 1927–
28. Violent demonstrations, particularly in Schleswig-Holstein, gave rise to a
peasant movement directed against the Parteienstaat and demanding special
legislation that would keep agriculture outside the market economy (berufsständische Ordnung). Its basis was a delayed adaptation of agriculture to
the new market conditions. The war and the postwar period had been boom
years for the peasantry because of the shortage of food. The annulment of
debts by the inflation that took place until 1923 and the currency reform had
secured a period of ten years during which agriculture in Germany had not had
to face the conditions of the market. A high renewed indebtedness (partly for
new machinery, partly for consumption, as the harvest of 1923 was sold for
the old, inflated currency) and falling agricultural prices had put certain agricultural areas, particularly those in the north and east, in a severe slump.
Public sales of farms (because of failure to pay interest or taxes) aroused the
peasant population against the perceived immorality of the economic and
political system.

The Landvolkbewegung became a violent populist movement with strong
anti-Semitic overtones. The outburst of violent protest in 1928 led first to the
formation of regional agrarian protest movements and to the erosion of the

voter basis of the Protestant middle-class and conservative parties. By 1930 the agrarian protest movement had turned to the NSDAP. Agrarian voters in Protestant areas provided the Nazis with their first success, in the national elections of 1930. In Schleswig-Holstein the NSDAP won 27 percent of the vote, and in 1932 this was the only district in which the Nazis polled more than 50 percent of the vote. This development took place on a local level and within the regional agrarian subculture. The new leaders of the spontaneous Landvolkbewegung converted to the NSDAP rather than the NSDAP going out to win them.[24]

The party did not react to the agrarian protest until late in 1930. Walther Darré, the agrarian expert, was put in charge of a special organization on 1 August 1930; the first party meeting with representatives of the peasantry convened on 9 February 1931. It must be noted that the alliance of the Landvolkbewegung with the NSDAP was not the result of a special propagandistic effort on the side of the Nazis nor of the personal experience of mass rallies conducted by Hitler. Rather, the Nazi party, being in a state of rapid, disorganized growth, was open for the most diverse activists' particularistic interests and protest moods. The vague reference to a *berufständische Ordnung,* the radical attack on the political system and its open hierarchy made it attractive as a nationally unifying body for regional and social protest, opening up political careers for young activists. The mediation between the agrarian structural crisis and the Nazi movement was provided by the breakdown of traditional intermediary organizations and the unavailability of alternative political organizations in Protestant areas. The Socialists never really managed to care for the peasants; they concentrated on the working class and, via some unions, on the agricultural day laborers. The independent farmer was supposed to die out and become transformed into a new agricultural worker in a Socialist society. As late as 1927 the first agrarian program was proclaimed by the SPD.[25] Only the Catholic milieu, always concerned with the peasants as faithful Catholics, was able to absorb the unrest of the peasants, but, of course, the Catholic Center party was no alternative for the Protestant sectors of the peasantry.

The large landowners in East Elbia, also caught in an economic crisis of long standing, were accustomed to political and economic protection from the aristocratic elite of prewar Prussia. They felt threatened by the new political order and particularly by the Social Democrats, who proposed to nationalize their estates. With the election of Hindenburg as the president of the Republic, a new avenue to state subsidies became available. Hindenburg, belonging to the old Prussian elite and a landholder himself (an estate was presented to him as a gift in 1927), became an advocate of the demands of the landowners. When Hindenburg appointed Brüning as chancellor of the presidential government in 1930, he made it quite clear that a special relief program for the East German estates had to be enacted by the government, the Osthilfe. The dismissal of Brüning in 1932 again was influenced by distrust in Brüning's willingness to continue the Osthilfe. It is remarkable that throughout the severe economic crisis from 1930 to 1932, the government paid 170 million marks to the approximately 13,000 large landowners, much more than was given to industry in direct or indirect subsidies.[26] This curious one-sidedness can only be explained by the specific mediation of the interests of the Junkers, which was easier to achieve in the presidential than in the parliamentary regime.

The structural crisis in agriculture had different political results. The landowners found an avenue to meet their interests and stayed conservative. The peasants did not see an avenue for relief and special treatment via the affiliation with the traditional parties, so they deserted them and formed regional protest movements of their own. As these proved ineffective, they shifted to the Nazis, who in turn, after 1931, skillfully infiltrated the agrarian interest organizations and converted them to supporters of the NSDAP.[27]

The international financial crisis following the crash of the New York stock market in October 1929 caused the stop and recall of the foreign loans in Germany. The German banking system was, due to the inflation, very limited in capital and relied heavily on foreign loans. The investment boom in German industry, as well as in German cities, was financed by short-term loans from the banking system, but these loans were placed on long-term projects. Only 58.6 percent of the total credit volume was financed with long-term credits, as compared with 91.5 percent in 1913. The German banking system, therefore, was more endangered by the international financial crisis than other banking systems. The breakdown occurred in July 1931, when the international financial system did not succeed in saving the Austrian *Kreditanstalt,* and its insolvency reached the German banks. The failure of the international banking and credit system was related to rivalries between France and Great Britain, triggered by a plan to create a tariff union between Austria and Germany, which was preceived by the French as a violation of the peace treaties.

Chancellor Brüning and the president of the Reichsbank, Hans Luther, in close cooperation with the leaders of the major German banks, solved the crisis by more or less nationalizing the banks. Though the handling of the banking crisis can be considered a great success for the government, the crisis itself was most unfortunate for the economic and political situation. The dysfunctions of the credit system led to a further weakening of trust in the economic development. The central bank rate was raised from 5 percent to 8 percent, tightening the credit market further, discouraging the investments vital for a recovery of the economy. The political consequences were equally negative. The bank crisis heightened the distrust in the existing system. The bank managers saw themselves in close dependency on the government and feared direct state control, particularly in case of a Socialist regime. Some of them began to establish relations with Hitler to secure future autonomy.[28]

By 1930 industrial production had declined sharply (see table 7). German industry relied heavily on exports. International trade, however, was falling even more than domestic consumption. From an index of one hundred in 1929, the total imports of seventy-five countries, measured in millions of gold dollars, declined to an index of forty in 1932.[29]

Big industry in Germany had two major interests. The export industry advocated a policy by which it could retain its position on the world market. It favored lower production costs to meet the devaluation of the pound sterling. Since the relative position of the German export industry could not be bettered by an alteration of the exchange rate, as Germany had to observe the gold standard due to reparation treaties, a lowering of wages was thought to be the only remedy. The export industry, particularly the big corporations in the chemical and electrical industry, therefore supported the deflationary policy of the Brüning cabinet, hoping that eventually the international economy would recover. The minister of economics during the period of October 1931 to January 1933, Warmbold, was a former board member of the I. G. Farbenindustrie, a huge chemical corporation created in 1925.

The steel industry, on the other hand, was more oriented toward the domestic market and in general less liberal in economic persuasion. Its leaders were inclined to see a long-term solution only in government spending, particularly in the rearmament of the German army. Nationalistic stands were taken by some leading managers and particularly by Hugenberg, the leader of the Deutschnationale Volkspartei, a former member of the board of Krupp. Their interests were also directed toward a definitive cutback in social legislation and union influence; they were fiercely antisocialistic and opposed the Brüning government for its conciliatory policy toward labor. Representatives of the coal and steel industries, notably Fritz Thyssen and Emil Kirdorf, were among the first industrialists to establish close relations with Hitler. The majority, however, remained ambivalent and preferred to support the truly conservative and authoritarian politics of men like Papen.[30]

Small business, retail trade, and small artisans were under great pressure. They found themselves in a structural crisis, faced with the need to change from the productive trades to the repair and service trades, as well as to cope with the rising trend toward department stores and chain stores. The cause of

Table 7. German Industrial Production (1928 = 100)

	1929	1930	1931	1932	1933
Total industrial production	100.1	87.0	70.1	58.0	65.7
Production goods	102.4	84.3	62.3	47.3	56.1
Consumption goods	96.6	91.0	81.7	74.1	80.0

SOURCE: Ernst Wagemann, ed., *Konjunktur-Statistisches Handbuch 1936* (Berlin: Hanseatische Verlagsanstalt, 1935), p. 49.

their difficulties was seen to be the double attack from capitalist big business and Socialist labor. These segments developed the classic attitude of the struggle against the class struggle, activating all the moral sentiments of the prewar world. Moral indignation and the feeling of political powerlessness had already radicalized them before the advent of the economic crisis. The coincidence of a structural adjustment crisis with the general depression made them particularly vulnerable and ready to believe in Nazi propaganda.[31]

As the effects of the depression on the self-employed do not clearly show up in the unemployment figures, it must be kept in mind that the situation of the population was even worse than the unemployment figures make evident. Germany suffered the worst unemployment of any country during those years (see table 8).

There was already an average of 1.3 million people unemployed in 1927 and 1928, before the depression occurred, which was an unemployment rate of about 9 percent. According to present standards, this would be considered severe structural unemployment. As the unemployment rate went up to 22.7 percent in 1930 and 43.8 percent in 1932, the situation became disastrous. A total disruption of everyday life occurred for about half of the industrial working class. But the white-collar workers were also hit severely, and although they retained a better relative degree of employment, they were less accustomed to unemployment than the working class and felt emotionally more degraded by being out of work.[32]

On 31 January 1933, the day Hitler became Reichskanzler, there were 6,014,000 unemployed: 578,000 white-collar workers and 5,436,000 blue-collar workers, one-quarter of whom were below twenty-five years of age.[33] Many young people never made the transition into a stable working life. They were particularly easy to mobilize into militia-like organizations and were always available for street demonstrations and fights at party rallies. These militia-like organizations threatened public security and on occasion created an atmosphere of civil war, especially the storm troops (SA) of the Nazis and the *Rote Frontkämpferbund* of the Communists. For the young and unemployed men they provided clothing, food, and most of all, a feeling of belonging and comradeship that meant a meaningful structuring of their daily life.[34]

Table 8. Employment In Percentage of the Employment Capacity of Industry

	Annual Averages				
	1929	1930	1931	1932	1933
Hourly wage earners	70.4	61.2	50.7	41.9	46.3
Salary earners	87.8	83.2	73.5	61.2	60.5

SOURCE: Wagemann, *Konjunktur-Statistisches Handbuch 1936*, pp. 17 and 38.

The more unemployment rose, the greater became the number of people who had to live on less than a minimum income. In 1932, of the 5.6 million unemployed, 19.4 percent received unemployment insurance, 25.8 percent got support from a special relief fund, 36.6 percent were on welfare, and 18.2 percent did not get any aid.[35] The unemployment insurance program, created in 1927 to handle about 900,000 unemployed, had already become insolvent by 1929. The municipalities, responsible for the welfare payments, were bankrupt or in a severe financial crisis by 1931. Therefore, all relief payments were lowered substantially. But the population still at work also experienced a mood of deprivation and fear of becoming unemployed. By 1932, the situation of the majority of the population was desperate, disrupting life expectations and conceptions of social and political order. This is also reflected in the birth rate, which fell to the level of the war years 1916–18.

As the supply of labor exceeded the demand for labor, the strategic position of the labor unions became weaker. In April 1930 20 percent of union members were unemployed; in April 1932 the figure was about 44 percent, with an additional 20 percent working reduced hours.[36] The capacity of the unions to exert political pressure and, as a last resort, to conduct a general strike, decreased. Unemployment and depression presented the unions with problems for which they had neither an economic program nor a political strategy. Not until 1932 did they adopt a plan for modest credit expansion and public works; they were politically on the defensive, trying to maintain the status quo and preserve their organizations against the attacks of the Communists and the Nazis.[37] On the other hand, the influence of the employers rose steadily because of the labor market situation and their growing impact on the government. They used their strategic advantages to reduce social legislation and to cut back on union influence in general. The changed power relation became clearly visible and politically important as early as 1930, when an attempt to reconstruct the unemployment insurance program failed because labor and industry would not compromise on the proposed increase of the contributions employees and employers should pay. On this issue the last parliamentary government of the Weimar Republic collapsed; the Social Democrats retreated from active participation and left the field to the conservative forces.[38] The economic crisis had changed the distribution of power and the influence structure within the political system.

The white-collar strata were particularly vulnerable in this crisis. This group had expanded very rapidly in the preceding twenty years and was less integrated than the workers. Their interest groups, primarily the Deutschnationaler Handlungsgehilfen-Verband, were traditionally conservative in orientation, representing the aspirations of the white-collar employee to gain in status and to secure a social position like that of the civil servants. Only after the war did the Socialist and democratic orientations gain in influence via the new white-collar unions. The majority, however, became radicalized in favor of nationalistic and authoritarian political ideas, supporting antidemocratic tendencies and, in the end, the Nazi movement.[39]

General economic developments are reflected in the figures in table 9. They show a decline in the gross domestic product, a decline in private consumption, which corresponds to the decline in the wholesale prices, a much greater decline in gross investment, and a decline in state expenditures. The incomes from wages and salaries and from property and proprietorship declined at the same rate. With the reduction in the state income, expenditures for relief payments rose, which led to an increase in the excise tax from 0.8 percent to 2 percent in 1931. This, together with the high level of the central bank rate, was counterproductive for a revival of the economy.[40] The deflationary policy aggravated the economic situation. The hesitation of the Brüning government to put a public works program into action added to the feeling of helplessness and despair.[41]

To return to the question raised at the beginning of this section, it seems that the economic crisis in Germany was aggravated by peculiarities in the German situation. The coincidence of diverse structural strains in the economy produced by an arrested adaptation of some traditional segments of the economy, particularly agriculture, retail trade, and the trades, an enforced modernization of the industrial production apparatus in the years 1924–29, and a crisis of the structurally weak banking system were immensely heightened by the world depression. Excessive concern with the reparations problem led the government to an economic policy that aggravated the depression in search for a solution.

The second question raised was why the economic crisis led to a breakdown of the political regime. A crisis of everyday life of this sort mobilizes the population to a higher degree than any propaganda can possibly achieve. The mobilization activates parts of the population that under normal conditions do not participate in the political process and therefore are not integrated into the

Table 9. Indicators of Economic Development, 1928–33 (1928 = 100)

	1928	1929	1930	1931	1932	1933
Gross national income (includes net export, at market prices)	100	101	93	78	63	65
Private consumption	100	103	99	84	67	68
Gross domestic investment	100	77	60	28	33	41
Government purchases	100	103	90	81	72	74
Income of households:						
Wage and salary incomes	100	101	94	80	62	63
Property and proprietorship income	100	99	89	74	60	62
Public transfer payments	100	113	124	131	122	111

SOURCE: Data from Dietmar Keese, "Die volkswirtschaftlichen Gesamtgrössen für das Deutsche Reich in den Jahren 1925–1936," in *Die Staats-und Wirtschaftskrise des Deutschen Reiches 1929/33,* ed. Werner Conze and Hans Raupach (Stuttgart: Klett, 1967), pp. 43, 49.

structure of intermediary interest groups and parties. It is likely that this nonintegrated population will turn to the most radical parties available. The outcome of the protest mood of the population depends, then, on the nature of the party system. The radical parties available in a given situation may be less radical than the mood of their voters or more radical; they may be loyal to the system or disloyal. The willingness to support a radical party is determined by the power of the moderate parties to absorb the protest mood and the success with which they can produce a plausible interpretation of the situation. The strength of the moderate party structure depends on the capacity of the radical parties to produce a more plausible interpretation of the situation as well as an organizational network that links divergent protest movements into unified political forces.

In the German case, the economic crisis was most influential for the political mobilization. However, there were several filters that channeled the effects of this mobilization. Prior to the economic crisis, there was a firmly institutionalized disloyal opposition to the democratic regime, consisting of Communists as well as conservative nationalists. Any radicalization of the voters would lead to reenforcement of the disloyal opposition. This, however, could take place only when the moderate parties could neither retain their voters and interest organizations nor absorb the respective protest vote reciprocally. While the Catholics and the Social Democrats were fairly successful in the first respect, they were not in the latter. The Protestant middle-class parties, both liberal and conservative, however, were unable to secure their bases—neither the individual voters nor the interest organizations that had been affiliated with them. The farmers' organizations, the trade associations, and a substantial part of the intellectual and white-collar groupings were searching for new alignments. They could not join the Catholics, because of cultural tradition, nor the Social Democrats, because of class interest and status resentment. Nor did either party try to win them. The Communists were unlikely to attract the middle class, and only a few intellectuals switched to them. So the conservative nationalists would have been the most likely choice for the protest orientation. They, however, did not succeed even in retaining their voter basis.[42]

The availability of the vital Nazi movement, uncompromised by former involvement with the governments and rapidly expanding a wide network of devoted young functionaries and organizations, provided the most plausible protest opportunity. It also presented a definition of the situation that corresponded with the irrationality of contemporary life. Action and the power of will would be the means by which the impact of international conspiracy and the impotence of decadence would be crushed, and the German virtues restored.

To assess the overall impact of the Nazi movement on the breakdown of the political system at the peak of the economic crisis, one could try a rough and,

Table 10. Changes in the Protest Vote, 1924, 1930, and 1932

	1924	1930	1932
Percentage unemployed	13.1	22.7	43.8
Percentage of voter turnout	76.3	81.4	79.9
Protest vote of the Right (DNVP and NSDAP)	24.9	25.3	40.2
Protest vote of the Left (KPD and USPD)	13.2	13.1	16.8

of course, very questionable method, and compare the elections in May 1924, September 1930, and November 1932 (see table 10). The election in May 1924 followed the inflation crisis and a period of great internal disruption, including the occupation of the Ruhr by France and upheavals in middle Germany and Bavaria; they showed the highest percentage of leftist and rightist protest votes prior to the depression. By 1930, at the beginning of the depression, the rightist and leftist protest vote had regained its 1924 strength. With the worsening of the situation until 1932, the leftist protest vote grew by about 27 percent, comprising 16.8 percent of the total vote. Assuming that the rate of growth of the rightist protest vote would be comparable, one could project a total growth in the rightist protest vote to about 31 percent. Instead, it gained 40 percent. It can then be argued that the impact of the Nazi movement prompted about 10 percent of the population, which otherwise would have stayed within the realm of the moderate traditional or splinter-party system, to turn to a rightist protest vote. It was due to the particular aggressiveness of Hitler's movement and the weakness of the moderate liberal parties and Protestant middle-class organizations that the regime collapse entered the realm of possibility in 1932.

5. Adolf Hitler and the Nazi Party

The previous sections have dealt with the framework within which the breakdown took place. But none of the factors discussed so far has been of decisive importance for the final outcome. The active and, in the end, fatal role was played by Hitler and the Nationalsozialistische Deutsche Arbeiterpartei. In underlining Hitler's importance for the breakdown of the Weimar Republic we are not resorting to a demonology of Hitler or the conceptions of "*Männer machen Geschichte*," it is men who make history. Rather, we will emphasize the structural aspects of Hitler's role.[43]

The conceptual tools for this attempt are derived from Max Weber's theory of charisma.[44] Weber proposes four dimensions to define charismatic authority. First, there is a belief in the exceptional qualities of an individual. This belief calls for absolute trust in the leader and makes recognition of his legitimacy a duty. Second, the influence of the leader rests on the recognition of his charismatic qualities as proved by his success. The attributed charisma is subject to proof. The chances of a leader to achieve recognition of his assumed charismatic qualities are increased psychologically by complete personal devotion on the side of his followers, arising out of enthusiasm, despair, or hope. Sociologically, they are determined by the definition of the situation in which the charismatic leader is forced to prove his qualities. Third, the realm of authority is a charismatic community, not a firmly institutionalized organization. The administrative staff consists of trusted agents who have either been provided with charismatic authority by the chief or possess charisma of their own. There is no bureaucratic organization, no principle of formal rules, no supervisory or appellate body, and hence no process of rational judicial decision-making. Fourth, the economic basis is not derived from systematic economic activities but rests on voluntary contributions and booty.

In line with these propositions we will first describe the simultaneous development of Hitler's claim on ultimate authority and the belief in his charismatic qualities. We will then discuss the breakthrough of Hitler's "charismatic community" into a mass movement and a dominating force in the German political scene.

Hitler's ascent comprised a series of successful claims on ultimate authority conducted despite high risks to his personal career. The capacity for unscrupulous tactical decisions and hazardous risk-taking is undoubtedly a personal precondition of his success. On 21 July 1921 he forced the then sectarian party to acknowledge him as the leader, unbound by any formal regulations, by declaring his resignation when leading party members suggested a coalition with other racist-nationalistic organizations, or *völkische Verbände*. This first seizure of power put him in the central position of the Nazi party and established for the first time his claim of ultimate and personal authority. After his defeat at the putsch on 9 November 1923, during his trial and imprisonment, he deliberately kept the party organization in a state of disorganization to avoid the establishment of a new leadership. Upon his release from prison he founded the party anew on 27 February 1925, denouncing all organizations that had formed in the meantime. The new party lost many followers and members because of Hitler's rigid actions. But his was the second successful seizure of power, by now already founded on his artificially built-up reputation as the hero of the Munich putsch. The third successful defense of his ultimate authority took place on 14 February 1926, when party leaders in northern and western Germany began close cooperation and proposed a revision of the party program with leftist inclinations and new organizational procedures. Hitler summoned the district chiefs on short notice to a meeting in Bamberg, where, after a speech five hours long, no dissent was aired, and Gregor Strasser as well as Goebbels, both spokesmen of the dissenters, expressed their personal loyalty. With this third seizure of power within the party organization, Hitler's ultimate authority was firmly established; no further serious attempts at ideological specification and formalization of the decision-making process were undertaken. Later conflicts, in 1930 with Otto Strasser and SA leader Stennes, in 1932 with Gregor Strasser, and in 1934 with Röhm, were settled by Hitler's unquestioned authority, the dissenters losing any personal charismatic authority they might have had the moment Hitler turned against them.[45] Every successful claim on ultimate authority was in itself a verification of Hitler's charisma, proof of his extraordinary gifts. The challenge to his authority was converted into renewed personal loyalty.

This process of gradual increase in Hitler's charismatic authority rested on some preconditions which are independent of his personality, his extraordinary ability to persuade and convince people in face-to-face contact. The first of these preconditions lies in the peculiar organizational structure of the party. The *Führerprinzip* as basic rule meant the total abolition of any formal regulations for decision-making and legitimation of authority. There were no collective bodies, no representative mechanisms, no procedural limitations for actions.[46] Ultimate authority rested with the leader of the party, who became legitimized by undefined acts of plebiscitary consent. He in turn appointed the subleaders, who held in their own areas ultimate authority as bestowed upon them by Hitler, independent of the formal consent of their subordinates. Furthermore, Hitler designed an intricate net of competing realms of jurisdiction, thereby placing himself in the all-important position of supreme conflict manager. Personalized rivalries without an institutionalized claim on competence kept the organization of the party in a state of artificially created disorganization, which only Hitler could control by arbitrary decisions without any limitations by procedure or precedent. There is a correspondence between organizational anarchy and need for ultimate authority, which, in a process of circular stimulation, enhanced Hitler's position, and the dependence of the subleaders on personal loyalty. Hitler's extreme autonomy from the demands of the party gave him the chance to take any action, and also to leave conflicts and competing ideologies unresolved, thereby integrating very divergent interpretations of the aims and the ideological basis of Nazism.

This leads to the second precondition of Hitler's charismatic authority: the lack of an officially defined ideology. The party program as expressed in the twenty-five points of 1920 was a rather arbitrary collection of sentiments and particularist demands, lacking intellectual consistency and pragmatic implementation. Hitler declared this program unalterable in 1926, thereby avoiding any intellectual discussion of ideological matters. It was he and only he who could interpret the Nazi ideology. His personal beliefs, therefore, played an extremely important role in the policy of Nazism. *Mein Kampf,* written between 1924 and 1926, expressed in much greater detail his personal beliefs than did the party program.[47]

There is in particular the violent anti-Semitism, a tendency not equally shared by other Fascist movements.[48] It rested on Hitler's racist Darwinism, the core of his belief system. Other guiding ideas were also shaped by Hitler's convictions: the extreme antimodernism and the preindustrial conception of social order as a militarized peasant society whose development rests on soil and space and whose blood is to be sacrificed to gain eternal life.[49] Hitler had no genuine interest in economic problems. He denounced capitalism and socialism alike. His intention was not to create a new economic order but to have an effective production apparatus at his command. He did not care for capitalism but he could compromise with capitalists, as long as they were compliant and efficient. Hitler's affinity with the capitalistic system rested on his conviction that only individual leadership unrestricted by bureaucratic regulations would produce efficiency, not on any general conception of economic and social order in an industrial society. In effect, "Nazi *Weltanschauung* was a meaningless abstraction until personified in Hitler."[50] This left Hitler uncontrolled by ideological interpretations of his actions by the party members, since "no legitimate questions can be raised about the leader's conception or interpretation of an idea" where there is no clearly defined and implemented obligatory program.[51] The followers could incorporate their own anxieties and hopes into the vague values of the movement, whose programmatic emptiness allowed for an identification with an ultimate authority regardless of specific and mutually exclusive interests and particularistic aims. On the other hand, Hitler could adjust the ideology to the short-term tactics he felt suitable and obscure his personal implementation of the ultimate cause. His ultimate authority was enhanced by his position as sole ideological interpreter of Nazism.

Third, it should be noted that Hitler most decidedly avoided any coalition with organizations outside his direct realm of ultimate authority. From the very beginning he fought against any cooperation with other rightist and völkische groupings, even when such coalitions would have promised greater influence in the political arena. Internal autonomy and external independence were the guiding principles he observed, rigidly putting aside considerations of growth, influences, and stability of the organization. It was his influence that was important to him, not the development of the party or its impact on a given political situation. He observed this principle throughout the negotiations in 1931 and 1932, which were intended to integrate the Nazis into the traditional authoritarian camp and thereby to tame Hitler.

The charismatic nature of the Nazi movement was not only the result of specific properties of Hitler's personality, magical capabilities, rhetorical fascination, and ruthless tactics, but also of deliberately advanced properties of organization, ideology, and external independence of the movement. Hitler was quite aware of the requirements of the role he had chosen for himself and spent much time on the elaboration of the image he wanted to create. Perhaps the greatest personal burden he willingly carried was the discipline to conform to his self-created role and public image.[52]

The party was formed as a "charismatic community" pledged to Hitler and managed by his agents in the districts, the *Gauleiter*. The only nationwide organizational bond was provided by the Munich head office, which was in charge of the finances and the central membership file. Otherwise great regional independence and diversity existed.[53] Only the storm troopers, the SA, developed an identity of their own. They were militarily organized outside the jurisdiction of the Gauleiter and directly committed to their leaders. Many SA leaders, mostly former army officers and veterans of the war, were torn between loyalty to Hitler and a commitment to form a militia as an auxiliary to the regular army. With all of Hitler's personal ability to persuade, to subjugate opponents, to destroy definite spheres of competence, he did not succeed in fully integrating the SA until he ordered the execution of its core leadership during the Röhm affair in 1934. The independent organization and clearly defined identity of the SA set institutional limits on Hitler's charisma. The Nazi militia, which Hitler used to produce an atmosphere of civil war in 1932, was at the same time the greatest threat to the unity of the party. However, the SA leaders had no political strategy of their own and had to fall back on Hitler for subsidies and ideological justification. Thus Hitler kept the SA leadership in line until he no longer needed them.[54]

Hitler was reluctant to establish any other specific organization outside the party, which, by the contextual properties of its field of operation, would not be able to function as a charismatic community. There was never a serious attempt to create National Socialist unions or interest groups.[55] There were, however, a multitude of auxiliary organizations for nearly every occupational group within the party. But they served only to attract sympathizers and absorb divergent interests, never developing into service organizations for a clientele outside the party membership.

A charismatic community will very likely remain small and insulated, consuming its energies in continuous internal conflict management and purification of the charismatic qualities. Hitlerism was, therefore, not regarded as a formation with political importance, but as a disturbing nuisance. Until 1928 this judgment seemed justified. The NSDAP polled 2.6 percent of the national vote in the Reichstag election of 28 May 1928. The membership comprised 100,000 people. Its financial means consisted of membership fees, revenues from publications, and occasional gifts from idiosyncratic wealthy people.[56]

The prospects for the Nazis looked dim. Even vigorous campaigning by Hitler in 1927 (he was prohibited from making public speeches in most states until early 1927) did not have an effect. The general political and social situation did not give his apocalyptic visions the necessary resonance. There were not enough anxieties to be directed toward the promises of the new order of the Third Reich. Nazism was an internally highly integrated but externally isolated political sect. It had succeeded in absorbing the radical völkische fringe in the political scene but it seemed to be entrenched in the boundaries of those circles, which had received 6.5 percent of the national vote in the crisis election of May 1924. There was but little hope for a breakthrough into the established party system. The strategy of a putsch had been discredited since the debacle of November 1923 and was disregarded by Hitler. Mussolini's example of a March on Rome was no more realistic an option.

The breakthrough came with changing political circumstances rather than through the activities of the Nazi party. In the summer of 1929 the nationalist opposition in the established party system propagated a referendum against the Young Plan, which they considered a national degradation and an attempt to prolong the dependency of Germany with reparations. Led by the Deutschnationale Volkspartei under their new rightist leader, Hugenberg, nationalistic and conservative groups like the organization of veterans of the war (Stahlhelm) and the agricultural associations (Landbund) formed a national committee for the referendum against the Young Plan and coopted the Nazis. This was the first step by the conservative establishment toward the acknowledgment of Hitler and his party, giving him a chance to gain national reputation by association with respectable organizations and personalities. It also provided access to financial means and the popular press, which to a large degree was owned or directed by Hugenberg, who had established the greatest press concern in Germany. Nazi propaganda became nationally recognized, Hitler personally respectable.

The referendum on 22 December 1929 was a failure. However, the alliance with the conservatives opened the authoritarian camp to the Nazis. The state elections on 8 December 1929 in Thüringen saw the first major Nazi victory. They obtained 11.3 percent of the vote and were invited to participate for the first time in a state government in coalition with other rightist forces.

The circle of the völkische fringe was broken up, and the Nazi party gained a national reputation. While the conservatives thought they could utilize Hitler and his movement as drummer and supporters for their aims, Hitler kept clear of any commitment and played his part with complete independence. It was not he who became absorbed in the national opposition of the establishment but rather they who lost their voters to Hitler. The DNVP suffered through the defection of its conciliatory leaders and was outdone by the much more radical and populist propaganda of Hitler's NSDAP. By the Reichstag election of September 1930 the DNVP had lost half its 1928 vote, while the NSDAP won 18.3 percent of the vote, becoming more than twice as strong as the DNVP.

The strategy of the established conservatives that had proved so disastrous for them in 1929/30, the futile attempt to tame Hitler and incorporate his party into a national front under their leadership, was repeated in the Harzburger Front in October 1931 and finally in the negotiations to form a rightist cabinet in August 1932 and in January 1933. Three times Hitler played the same game: he agreed to join forces yet upheld his claim for ultimate authority and his independence of action. Hitler could increase his demands from time to time as his relative weight in the rightist-nationalist coalition rose. In 1929 he was the underdog, in 1933 the top dog, due to the accelerating economic crisis and gains in voter suppport. Aided by the depression and growing unemployment, the defection of functionaries in middle-class interest groups to the Nazis, and their rapid infiltration by young and active men converted to the Nazi party and mobilized by the skillful propaganda activities of the party nationwide, by the end of 1931 the NSDAP had won 26.2 percent of the vote in the state elections of Hamburg and 37.1 percent of the vote in the state elections of Hessen. Nazism had become a major component of the political system. Its voters were primarily of Protestant and middle-class background. The agrarian protest vote went to the NSDAP in areas where it was not retained by the Catholic organizations. The industrial and urban protest vote shifted to the Nazis in areas where the labor unions were weak. In areas with large-scale industrial plants, the unions were strong and contained the protest within the Socialist and Communist parties. Therefore, the Catholic and working-class segments of the population were strongly underrepresented in the NSDAP vote.[57]

In the spring of 1932 an election for Reichspräsident was due to be held. Brüning tried to avoid an election at the peak of the economic crisis. However, the parliamentary majority needed to enact a special law to prolong the period of office of Reichspräsident von Hindenburg could not be obtained. Hitler played an important role, categorically refusing any attempt to keep Hindenburg in office without an election. Despite the fact that Hindenburg represented the national values for which Hitler was agitating, he turned against the field marshal and became a candidate for Reichspräsident in 1932. Only seventeen days before the election, he obtained the requisite German citizenship by a nominal appointment to the civil service of the state of Braunschweig, where the Nazis held the Ministry of the Interior. Hitler's candidacy against Hindenburg was an attempt to gain the undisputed leadership in the nationalistic, authoritarian camp, uniting all rightist opposition to the democratic system. Hitler gained 36.8 percent of the vote on the second ballot in April 1932. His claim to supreme leadership was clearly documented and caused a radical reorientation within the conservative elites.

The military, through its political spokesman, General von Schleicher, started to negotiate with Hitler in April 1932; leading industrialists established contacts with Hitler; some Protestant clergymen openly endorsed the Nazis; and a member of the royal Hohenzollern family joined the party. The conservative establishment symbolically, financially, and politically opened the door to power. In early 1932 they still thought they could tame Hitler and persuade him to tolerate a regime of their own. By the end of January 1933 they were willing to grant him the chancellorship.

Hitler skillfully played a double strategy: the promise of legality and the threat of civil war. He had the necessary means at his disposal for both. For the legal creation of an authoritarian regime, it was his mass support and parliamentary strength that provided the basis. For the threat of civil war and a violent revolutionary takeover, it was his private army, the SA, that could arouse public disorder any time and at any place. The violence in political fights on the streets and at the party rallies, particularly those of the Nazis and the Communists, increased considerably in 1932. From January to September 1932 155 were people killed.[58] The entire year of 1932 saw the deaths of 82 Nazis.[59] The election campaign in June and July of 1932 saw the greatest number of casualties, with 100 persons dead. Attempts to outlaw political violence, the use of weapons, the wearing of party uniforms, and party armies, the SA in particular, remained ineffective. Numerous lawsuits were conducted but only a few resulted in prison sentences, more often against Communists than Nazis.[60] As the national government became more accessible to conservative politicians, the willingness to embark on a forceful policy to prohibit Nazi violence became weaker. Growing sympathy from the younger officer corps and the strength of the SA, nearly 500,000 members strong, made it unlikely that the army would be willing forcefully to subjugate the SA. The double character of the SA as Nazi party organization and an auxiliary militia for the regular army in case of war inhibited the prohibition of the SA from its very beginning.

Hitler's tactics were aimed at a legal takeover of government, but as he declined any offer short of the appointment as chancellor, he ran high risks. His followers were disappointed that despite all their efforts and their victories in the elections, the seizure of power had not yet been achieved in the summer of 1932. There were two tendencies within the party. One was articulated by Gregor Strasser, the most important leader next to Hitler. He advocated participation in the government even without Hitler in the chancellorship. The other was espoused by the storm troopers, who were in favor of a violent takeover of the government, a "real" revolution, as they saw it. Here again Hitler's unique position in the Nazi party becomes crucial. He was faced with the loss of control of his forces, but Hitler's institutionalized charisma was not damaged. Strasser resigned and could not muster party support for his course of action. Hitler's charisma also kept the SA in a precarious state of obedience. Hitler retained his freedom of action, his capability for waiting until the conservative establishment would invite him to the chancellorship and give him the unrestricted power of government. No decision-making body of the party or the Reichstag faction existed to influence his decisions. But had it not been for the intrigues of Schleicher and Papen, the deadlock they had created, and the final submission of Hindenburg to the advices of Papen and his son, the seizure of power by Hitler on 30 January 1933 might not have been the necessary result of Hitler's strategy. It was his nature to risk an all or nothing game.

There were at least two chances for the decline of the Nazi movement in late 1932 and early 1933. The first would have aimed at a destruction of the belief in Hitler's charisma; the second would have been connected with a change in the political and economic situation by which the perceived need for charismatic leadership as the only solution to a chaotic crisis would have become less plausible.

Charismatic authority and a charismatic community rest on the belief in the extraordinary gifts of the leader. This belief must be verified by signs of his extraordinary abilities. The destruction of such a movement will be unavoidable if the charisma of the leader can no longer be proved in the perception of his followers. Until the summer of 1932 proof of Hitler's extraordinary capabilities was provided by continuous election victories, which kept the party in a state of high enthusiasm and mobilization. The experience of the futility of the election campaigns and the losses in the November election were potentially a severe blow to Hitler's charisma, the more so as the financial means of the party were completely exhausted. Had it not been for his seizure of power at the last moment, in January 1933, elections in 1933 and 1934 would most likely have seen a severe defection of NSDAP voters.

Charismatic authority needs a situation in which extraordinary capacities are expected: ordinary situations do not call for extraordinary means or personal gifts. It was the combination of a political and economic crisis in Germany in the years 1929–33 that created an atmosphere conductive to belief in extraordinary gifts. Hitler's chances consisted in his capacity to define the situations as doomed and his leadership as the last chance for salvation. These chances would have been limited by improvement in the economic situation, which was expected in 1933, and by governmental stability as provided by the Brüning cabinet on the basis of emergency decrees. However, developments in 1932 reduced politics to a single issue: chaos or regeneration of Germany. This allowed Hitler to gain support from very divergent segments of the population with heterogeneous interests and aspirations on the level of ultimate values. The eschatological character of Nazism had a peculiar pseudo-religious fascination, extremely favorable for the belief in charismatic authority.

The unprecedented growth of the NSDAP in membership (see table 11) and votes (see table 12) within three years must be seen in the context of a highly emotionalized and anomic situation. Forces of destiny seemed at work; economic interests and social distinctions were superseded by a hope in the "power of will" and the "vitality of youth." Trust in the institutions of the existing system was exchanged for the commitment to ultimate values of an unknown but new order.

It was Hitler and the NSDAP who were best prepared to capitalize on this mood and the underlying disruption of the social fabric after 1930. There was no political leader in the democratic camp who could match Hitler's demagogy and provide an alternative general definition of the situation, less irra-

Table 11. Membership of the NSDAP, 1925-33

1925 December	27,117
1926 December	49,523
1927 December	72,590
1928 December	108,717
1929 December	176,426
1930 September	293,000
1930 December	389,000
1931 December	806,294
1932 April	1,000,000+
1932 December	1,378,000
1933 August	3,900,000

SOURCE: Hans-Gerd Schumann, *Nationalsozialismus und Gewerkschaftsbewegung* (Hannover and Frankfort: Norddeutsche Verlagsanstalt, 1958), pp. 167 ff.

tional but convincing. Stresemann had died, Otto Braun, the popular prime minister of Prussia, was ill, Brüning was an introverted personality without popular appeal, Hindenburg had become senile. The democratic elites were paralyzed.[61] The men who influenced the final decisions to hand over the government to Hitler were without popular resonance and opportunistic in outlook: Papen and Schleicher, the last chancellors, Otto Meissner and Hindenburg's son Oskar, the closest advisers to the Reichspräsident, Hugenberg and Schacht, the spokesmen of industry and finance. The Communists, uncompromisingly attacking the democratic system, provided another general definition of the situation, the collapse of capitalism, but their new order was less empty than that of Hitler. Communist Russia attracted neither the peasants, the white-collar class, nor even the majority of the working class. Their

Table 12. Popular Support of the NSDAP, 1928-33

1928	28 May Reichstag elections	2.6%
1929	27 October Landtag elections in Baden	7.0
1929	8 December Landtag elections in Thüringen	11.3
1930	22 July Landtag elections in Saxony	14.4
1930	14 September Reichstag elections	18.3
1931	17 May Landtag elections in Oldenburg	37.2
1931	15 November Landtag elections in Hessen	37.1
1932	13 March Reichspräsident elections, first ballot	30.1
1932	4 April Reichspräsident elections, second ballot	36.8
1932	24 April Landtag elections in Prussia	37.1
	Landtag elections in Bavaria	32.9
	Landtag elections in Württemberg	30.5
1932	29 May Landtag elections in Oldenburg	46.3
1932	19 June Landtag elections in Hessen	43.1
1932	31 July Reichstag elections	37.3
1932	4 November Reichstag elections	33.0
1933	5 March Reichstag elections	43.9

very existence, however, seemed proof that there was only one alternative: chaos or Hitler. Hitler's impact was that he persuaded not only his voters but also many of his enemies into accepting his definition of the situation.

Not only Hitler but the NSDAP as an organization was able to capitalize on the anomic situation. Led by young functionaries, it mobilized town and country by continuous rallies, parades, and demonstrations. It spread the rhetoric and liturgy invented by Hitler during the numerous election campaigns throughout the country. It was able to absorb the rapidly increasing and changing membership and to infiltrate local associations and interest groups.[62] Hitler was a new type of political leader, and the NSDAP was a new type of political party. It was flexible enough for rapid expansion, and its internal immobilization allowed Hitler a unique freedom of decision. There was no other party that combined these elements. The Communist party was inflexible for ideological reasons, the Social Democrats limited their leadership by high internal bureaucratization, the Zentrum party was entrenched in the Catholic milieu, and the bourgeois and conservative parties had no vital local organizations. The NSDAP was the appropriate instrument for Hitler's strategy, which was to create a threat of civil war that he would trade in for the handing over of power. Hitler's bargaining power rested in the NSDAP. But as the NSDAP had no organized will of its own, Hitler could bargain at no cost to himself as long as he commanded the party as a charismatic community.

6. The Process of Transfer of Power

The dismissal of Brüning by Hindenburg at the end of May 1932 meant the destruction of the tiny chance for a consensual emergency policy of the democratic forces. With the appointment of Papen a government was put in office that had no popular support. It had to rely either on the support of the Nazis or on the intervention of the military. The options were radically narrowed. As the military would not embark on a policy of a military rule, there was only Hitler left. The Papen government tried to buy Hitler's toleration and increasingly became the executive of Hitler's demands. First it lifted the prohibition on the SA, decreed by the Brüning government in April 1934. Second, the Papen government announced new elections, giving Hitler a chance for renewed mass mobilization and reenforced strength in the Reichstag. Third, it dissolved the government of Prussia, still in the hands of the Weimar coalition, which thereby could command the police forces in two-thirds of Germany. Despite all this, Hitler did not support the Papen government at all. Only a military government seemed capable of preventing the final seizure of power by Hitler. In December 1933 General von Schleicher tried to form a coalition between the military and the conservative elites that would be tolerated by the unions, but these were desperate machinations, without a chance. Schleicher's inclinations toward an authoritarian political regime had played an important role in the dissolution of the moderate Brüning regime, in the appointment of Papen, whom he personally suggested to Hindenburg, and finally in his turn against Papen. But by now he had become discredited. The alternatives were further reduced, since not even the possibility of a military rule remained realistic. The conservative establishment had conducted a policy by which they sold themselves to Hitler and at the same time destroyed their own basis of power. The more their own power became deflated, the more the power of Hitler became inflated. Even Reichspräsident von Hindenburg, who disliked Hitler personally and profoundly, saw the final solution only in the appointment of just this man.

The democratic forces saw no chance for a counterattack. Instrumentally they had lost the majority. In the game of personal intrigues around the now all-important Reichspräsident, they were excluded. They had no access to the military, and had lost control over the police forces in Prussia. The labor unions had a diminished capacity for a political general strike because of the great number of unemployed. The forces of the old Weimar coalition were unable to form a firm and united front for the defense of democracy on ideological grounds. A process of intimidation and an atmosphere of fatalistic hopelessness prevailed. Strategies to secure individual survival under an anticipated period of Nazi rule fragmented the democratic forces even further. In desperation, but inactive, they observed and submitted to the transfer of power to Hitler.[63]

The process of transfer of power started with the dissolution of the Weimar coalition in 1930, gained momentum with the cooptation of Nazism by the conservative camp in 1931, and came to a conclusion with the conviction that no alternative but Hitler remained in 1932. The Weimar coalition was established in 1918/19 and rested on the coalition of the middle-class parties with the Social Democrats in the *Interfraktioneller Ausschuss* to end the war, the Stinnes-Legien agreement between industry and labor to secure the economy in the demobilization period, and the contract between the military and the republican government to guarantee internal security. Its effect was the exclusion of the conservative and authoritarian forces after the armistice. The dissolution of the Weimar coalition started with the end of the industry-labor agreement in 1923 and the attempt of the employers to reduce social legislation and limit the influence of the unions during the depression. It was aggravated by the alienation of the military from the republican state and finally by the weakening of the party coalition between the middle-class parties and the Social Democrats. This led to an exclusion of the labor movement and the reentry of the conservative and authoritarian forces into the government. However, in 1931, and more so in 1932, the distribution of power had changed. The conservative and authoritarian forces thought first to use Hitler, then to tame him, and in the end they had to submit to him.[64]

The turn from parliamentary democracy to government by emergency decree had hollowed the constitution. The installation of the Papen and Schleicher governments had created a deadlock in which Hindenburg was put into the decisive position. His sentiments were with the authoritarian camp but he was not prepared to suspend the constitution altogether. In appointing Hitler he thought to retain the constitution, as only Hitler had promised a government with parliamentary majority. The idea of return to constitutional normalcy by including Hitler in the political process clearly shows a profound misjudgment of Hitler and the Nazis.

Hitler had followed a strategy that advanced such misunderstanding. He had cut down on the Socialist trends within the NSDAP since 1930, he guaranteed industry that the status quo would be maintained, he promised the military its autonomy, he observed a neutrality in regard to the churches. He activated the common resentments in the authoritarian camp against socialism and liberalism, and made its latent anti-Semitism overt. On the other hand, he could threaten industry with state socialism, the military with his SA militia, and the churches with a new Germanic religion. His was a precarious strategy of offering legality and threatening civil war.

The situation was commonly defined as unsolvable. In anticipation of the surrender of power to Hitler, industry, the military, churches, and the labor unions embarked, as early as the summer of 1932, on a course of action directed not at combating Hitler but at negotiating with him to ensure their respective survivals after his takeover.[65]

Hitler changed his strategy the moment he was appointed chancellor, discrediting all who believed his regime would only be transitory because (1) the collapse of capitalism would carry away fascism as well; (2) the incompetence of the Nazis to govern would lead to a return of the rule of traditional elites; or (3) disappointment with Hitler's regime would lead to a dissolution of the Nazi movement. Hitler acted quickly after his appointment on 30 January 1933. On 28 February he issued with Hindenburg's *placet* an emergency decree that suspended constitutional civil rights, using the burning of the Reichstags building as a pretext. In an atmosphere of public insecurity and terror for the Communists and Socialists, the last free elections took place. These gave Hitler a vote of 43.9 percent, and together with the 8 percent polled by the conservatives, he gained a tiny majority. Two days after the opening of the new Reichstag, on 23 March 1933, Hitler succeeded in mustering a two-thirds majority to pass the *Ermächtigungsgesetz,* which was to suspend the constitution for a period of four years and to entitle the government to act unbound by the constitution. The Communist deputies were already being persecuted and most of them had been imprisoned. Only the Socialists opposed him. It took Hitler seven weeks to turn the pseudo-legality of his seizure of power into a revolution of the political system. The last remnant of the old system, the institution of the Reichspräsident, was incapacitated by the senility of Hindenburg. When he died on 2 August 1934,

Hitler had firmly established his rule and could combine the offices of the president and the chancellor. Parties were prohibited, unions dissolved, the army sworn to obey Hitler personally, public opinion intimidated, and the media controlled. The political system was changed entirely.[66]

NOTES

1. Henry A. Turner, Jr., Introduction to *Nazism and the Third Reich*, ed. Henry A. Turner, Jr. (New York: Quadrangle Books, 1972), p. 4.
2. Only a few general references that provide basic information and further bibliographical references will be listed. The work of Karl Dietrich Bracher, *Die Auflösung der Weimarer Republik*, 5th rev. ed. (Villingen: Ring Verlag, 1971) remains the most important attempt at systematic analysis, despite the twenty years since its conception. It should be consulted together with a more recent but less comprehensive study by Karl Dietrich Bracher entitled *The German Dictatorship* (New York and Washington: Praeger Publishers, 1970). Also of basic importance are the following publications: Erich Matthias and Rudolf Morsey, eds., *Das Ende der Parteien, 1933* (Düsseldorf: Droste Verlag, 1960); Thilo Vogelsang, *Reichswehr, Staat und NSDAP* (Stuttgart: Deutsche Verlagsanstalt, 1962); Werner Conze and Hans Raupach, eds, *Die Staats—und Wirtschaftskrise des Deutschen Reiches, 1929/33* (Stuttgart: Ernst Klett Verlag, 1967); Gotthard Jasper, ed., *Von Weimar zu Hitler, 1930– 1933* (Cologne and Berlin: Kiepenheuer and Witsch, 1968); Anthony Nicholls and Erich Matthias, eds., *German Democracy and the Triumph of Hitler* (London: George Allen and Unwin, 1971); Hans Mommsen, Dietmar Petzina, and Bernd Weisbrod, eds., *Industrielles System und politische Entwicklung in der Weimarer Republik* (Düsseldorf: Droste, 1974); Gerhard Schulz, *Aufstieg des Nationalsozialismus; Krise und Revolution in Deutschland* (Frankfort, Berlin, and Vienna: Propyläen, 1975); and Ernst Nolte, *Three Faces of Fascism* (New York: Holt, Rinehart and Winston, 1966).
3. In the present context no further discussion will be directed toward problems of the German modal personality, authoritarian elements in the German socialization process, particularly of the middle classes, and the political consequences of dogmatism and belief systems. References to these problems will be found in Max Horkheimer et al., *Studien über Autorität und Familie* (Paris, 1936), a study conducted in Germany in the early thirties trying to analyze the social and psychological basis for Nazism; and Erich Fromm, *Escape from Freedom* (New York: Farrar and Rinehart, 1941).
4. For an interesting study of the formation of the ideas of a German way to modernity, see Eckart Pankoke, *Soziale Bewegung-Soziale Frage-Soziale Politik* (Stuttgart: Ernst Klett, 1970). For ideas of leadership in the political thought of liberal and conservative intellectuals, see Walter Struve, *Elites against Democracy* (Princeton, N.J.: Princeton University Press, 1973). For a general analysis of German conceptions of society and democracy, see Ralf Dahrendorf, *Society and Democracy in Germany* (Garden City, N.Y.: Doubleday, 1967). There is an extensive literature on the German cultural development, but we refer in this context only to Hans Kohn, *The Mind of Germany: The Education of a Nation* (New York: Scribner's, 1960); Leonard Krieger, *The German Idea of Freedom* (Boston: Beacon Press, 1957); George L. Mosse, *The Crisis of German Ideology: Intellectual Origins of the Third Reich* (New York: Grosset and Dunlap, 1964); Helmuth Plessner, *Die verspätete Nation* (Stuttgart: Kohlhammer, 1959); Fritz Stern, *The Politics of Cultural Despair* (New York: Doubleday, 1961); and Peter Gay, *Weimar Culture: The Outsider as Insider* (London: Seeker and Warburg, 1969).
5. On Prussia, see most recently Hagen Schulze, *Otto Braun oder Preussens demokratische Sendung* (Frankfort, Berlin, and Vienna: Propyläen, 1977).
6. For the development of the KPD and the influence of the Komintern, see Hermann Weber, *Die Wandlung des deutschen Kommunismus* 2 vols. (Frankfort: Europäische Verlagsanstalt,

1969); Hermann Weber, ed., *Der deutsche Kommunismus: Dokumente* (Cologne and Berlin: Kiepenheuer and Witsch, 1963); Ossip K. Flechtheim, *Die KPD in der Weimarer Republik* (Frankfort: Europäische Verlagsanstalt, 1969); Theo Pirker, *Komintern und Faschismus, 1920–1940* (Stuttgart: Deutsche Verlagsanstalt, 1965).

7. Theodor Eschenburg, *Die improvisierte Demokratie* (Munich: Piper, 1963), pp. 11–60.
8. Thomas Mann, *Betrachtungen eines Unpolitischen*, 10th ed. (Berlin: Fischer, 1919), p. 246.
9. For an analysis of the German party system in the *Kaiserreich*, see M. Rainer Lepsius, "Parteisystem und Sozialstruktur," in *Deutsche Parteien vor 1918*, ed. Gerhard A. Ritter (Cologne: Kiepenheuer and Witsch, 1973) and other articles in that volume. See also Sigmund Neumann, *Die Parteien der Weimarer Republik*, 2d ed. (Stuttgart: Kohlhammer, 1965).
10. Johannes Sass, *Die 27 deutschen Parteien 1930 und ihre Ziele* (Hamburg, 1930) gives a detailed description of the particularistic and partly sectarian small parties.
11. This is the judgment of Gustav Stolper, expressed in the journal *Der deutsche Volkswirt* 13 December 1929, p. 333 (translation by the author).
12. Ferdinand A. Hermens, *Demokratie und Wahlrecht* (Paderborn: F. Schöning, 1933), p. 145 (translation by the author).
13. See ibid., pp. 115–70 or the revised American edition, *Democracy or Anarchy?* (South Bend, Ind.: University of Notre Dame, 1941), pp. 161–240. See also Friedrich Schäfer, "Zur Frage des Wahlrechts in der Weimarer Republik," in *Staat, Wirtschaft, und Politik in der Weimarer Republik*, ed. Ferdinand A. Hermens and Theodor Schieder (Berlin: Duncker and Humblot, 1967).
14. For the basic changes in 1929–30 and their importance for the breakdown, see Bracher, *Die Auflösung der Weimarer Republik* pt. 2, chaps. 1–3; also Werner Conze, "Die Krise des Parteienstaates in Deutschland 1929/30," *Historische Zeitschrift*, 178 (1954); and Conze, "Die politischen Entscheidungen in Deutschland, 1929–1933," in Conze and Raupach, *Staats-und Wirtschaftskrise*.
15. There is an extensive literature on the Weimar constitution and Article 48. See especially Bracher, *Die Auflösung der Weimarer Republik*, pt. 1, chap. 2; idem, "Parteistaat, Präsidialsystem, Notstand," *Politische Vierteljahresschrift* 3 (1960); Karl Löwenstein, *Verfassungslehre* (Tübingen: J. C. B. Mohr, 1959); Martin Needler, "The Theory of the Weimar Presidency," *Review of Politics* 21 (1959); Klaus Revermann, *Die stufenweise Durchbrechung des Verfassungsystems der Weimarer Republik 1930–1933* (Münster: T. Aschendorff, 1959); Ulrich Scheuner, "Die Anwendung des Art. 48 der Weimarer Reichsverfassung unter den Präsidentenschaften von Ebert und Hindenburg," in Hermens and Schieder, *Staat, Wirtschaft und Politik in der Weimarer Republik*.
16. On Brüning, see Heinrich Brüning, *Memoiren, 1918–1934* (Stuttgart: Deutsche Verlags-Anstalt, 1970); idem, *Reden und Aufsätze eines deutschen Staatsmannes*, ed. Wilhelm Vernekohl and Rudolf Morsey (Münster: Regensberg, 1968); and Gottfried Reinhold Treviranus, *Das Ende von Weimar, Heinrich Brüning und seine Zeit* (Düsseldorf and Vienna: Econ, 1968).
17. On Papen and Schleicher, see, in addition to the work of Bracher, Thilo Vogelsang, *Reichswehr, Staat, und NSDAP;* idem, *Kurt von Schleicher* (Göttingen: Musterschmidt, 1965); and Eschenburg, *Die improvisierte Demokratie*, pp. 235–86.
18. On Hindenburg, see Andreas Dorpalen, *Hindenburg and the Weimar Republic* (Princeton, N.J.: Princeton University Press, 1964), and John W. Wheeler-Bennett, *Hindenburg, the Wooden Titan* (London: Macmillan, 1967).
19. On the legal aspects of the so-called *Preussische Staatsstreich*, see, in particular, Arnold Brecht, *Mit der Kraft des Geistes* (Stuttgart: Deutsche Verlags-Anstalt, 1967).
20. One of the most influential legal advisers in constitutional law was Carl Schmitt. His publications served to justify the gradual reinterpretation of the Weimar constitution from a parliamentary *Rechtsstaat* toward a plebiscitarian *Massnahmestaat*. See his *Der Begriff des Politischen: Text von 1931 mit einem Vorwort und drei Corollarien* (Berlin: Duncker and Humblot, 1963), and *Verfassungsrechtliche Aufsätze aus den Jahren 1924–1954* (Berlin: Duncker and Humblot, 1958), in particular, "Legalität und Legitimität (1932)" and "Die staatsrechtliche Bedeutung der Notverordnung (1931)."
21. On the destruction of the constitution by the *Verordnung des Reichspräsidenten zum Schutze von Volk und Staat* on 28 February 1933, see Karl Dietrich Bracher, Wolfgang Sauer, and

Gerhard Schulz, *Die nationalsozialistische Machtergreifung: Studien zur Errichtung des totalitären Herrschaftssystems in Deutschland 1933/34* (Cologne and Opladen: Westdeutscher Verlag, 1960), pp. 82–88.

22. There is an extensive literature on the world depression and the German economic development. See especially Charles P. Kindleberger, *The World Depression, 1929–1939* (Berkeley and Los Angeles: University of California Press, 1973); Robert Aaron Gordon, *Economic Instability and Growth: The American Record* (New York: Harper and Row, 1974). An account of the German development is given in Gustav Stolper, Karl Haüser, and Knut Borchardt, *The German Economy, 1870 to the Present* (New York: Harcourt, Brace, 1967), esp. chap. 4, "The Weimar Republic," by Gustav Stolper; Wilhelm Grotkopp, *Die grosse Krise* (Tübingen: J. C. B. Mohr, 1952); Rudolf Stucken, *Deutsche Geld und Kreditpolitik, 1914–1963* (Tübingen: J. C. B. Mohr, 1964); and Rolf E. Lücke, *Von der Stabilisierung zur Krise* (Zurich: Basle Center for Economic and Financial Research, Series B., no. 3, 1958).

23. The problems of the reparations are dealt with in particular in Wolfgang J. Helbick, *Reparationen in der Ära Brüning* (Berlin: Walter de Gruyter, 1962).

24. For the agricultural crisis, see Werner T. Angress, "The Political Role of the Peasantry in the Weimar Republic," *Review of Politics* 21: 530–49; Max Sering, *Die deutsche Landwirtschaft: Berichte über Landwirtschaft 50* (Berlin, 1932). *The Landvolkbewegung* is described in Günther Franz, *Politische Geschichte des Bauerntums* (Celle: Niedersächsische Landeszentrale für Heimatdienst, 1959); Hans Beyer, *Die Landvolkbewegung Schleswig-Holsteins und Niedersachsens 1928–1932* (Eckernförde: Heimatgemeinschaft des Kreises Eckernförde, 1957); Rudolf Heberle, *Landbevölkerung und National-sozialismus* (Stuttgart: Deutsche Verlags-Anstalt, 1963); Gerhard Stoltenberg, *Politische Strömungen im schleswig-holsteinschen Landvolk, 1918–1933* (Düsseldorf: Droste, 1962); and Heinz Sahner, *Politische Tradition, Sozialstruktur, und Parteiensystem in Schleswig-Holstein* (Meisenheim am Glan: Anton Hain, 1972).

25. Sten S. Nilson, "Wahlsoziologische Probleme des Nationalsozialismus," *Zeitschrift für die gesamte Staatswissenschaft* 110 (1954), shows how in contrast in Norway the farmers' protest was absorbed by the Social Democratic party.

26. The special situation of East Elbian estate agriculture is discussed in Hans Raupach, "Der interregionale Wohlfahrtsausgleich als Problem der Politik des deutschen Reiches," in Conze and Raupach, *Staats-und Wirtschaftskrise*. ed. See also Gerhard Schulz, "Staatliche Stützungsmassnahmen in den deutschen Ostgebieten: Zur Vorgeschichte der 'Osthilfe' der Regierung Brüning," in Hermens and Schieder, *Staat, Wirtschaft, und Politik*; and Henning Graf von Borcke Stargordt, *Der ostdeutsche Landbau zwischen Fortschritt, Krise und Politik* (Würzburg: Holzner, 1957).

27. The conversion and infiltration of the agrarian organizations to and by Nazism is discussed in Horst Gies, "NSDAP und landwirtschaftliche Organisationen in der Endphase der Weimarer Republik," *Vierteljahreshefte für Zeitgeschichte* 15 (1967).

28. The best account of the banking crisis is given in Karl Erich Born, *Die deutsche Bankenkrise, 1931* (Munich: Piper, 1967).

29. Kindleberger, *The World Depression, 1929–1939*, p. 172.

30. See Wilhelm Treue, "Der deutsche Unternehmer in der Weltwirtschaftskrise," in Conze and Raupach, in *Staats-und Wirtschaftskrise;* Henry A. Turner, Jr., "Big Business and the Rise of Hitler," in Turner, *Nazism and the Third Reich;* Alfred Sohn-Rethel, *Ökonomie und Klassenstruktur des deutschen Faschismus* (Frankfort: Suhrkamp, 1973); George W. F. Hallgarten, *Hitler, Reichswehr, und Industrie* (Frankfort: Europäische Verlagsanstalt, 1955); Henry A. Turner, "Das Verhältnis des Grossunternehmertums zur NSDAP," and Bernd Weisbrod, "Zur Form schwerindustrieller Interessenvertretung in der zweiten Hälfte der Weimarer Republik," both in Mommsen et al., *Industrielles System und politische Entwicklung in der Weimarer Republik;* Eberhard Czichon, *Wer verhalf Hitler zur Macht?* (Cologne: Pahl-Rugenstein, 1967).

31. See Seymour Martin Lipset, *Political Man* (Garden City, N.Y.: Doubleday, 1960), chap. 5; Herman Lebovics, *Social Conservatism and the Middle Classes in Germany, 1914–1933* (Princeton, N.J.: Princeton University Press, 1969); Theodor Geiger, *Die soziale Schichtung des deutschen Volkes* (Stuttgart: Enke, 1932); idem, "Panik im Mittelstand," *Die Arbeit 7*

(1930); Svend Riemer, "Zur Soziologie des Nationalsozialismus," *Die Arbeit* 9 (1932); Peter Wulf, *Die politische Haltung des schleswig-holsteinischen Handwerks* (Cologne and Opladen: Westdeutscher Verlag, 1969); Ernst-August Roloff, *Bürgertum und National-sozialismus* (Hannover, Verlag für Literatur und Zeitgeschehen, 1961); idem, "Wer wählte Hitler?" *Politische Studien* 15 (1964); and Heinrich August Winkler, *Mittelstand, Demo-kratie, und Nationalsozialismus: Die politische Entwicklung von Handwerk und Kleinhandel in der Weimarer Republik* (Cologne: Kiepenheuer and Witsch, 1972).

32. The disruptive effects of unemployment are analyzed in Marie Jahoda, Paul F. Lazarsfeld, and Hans Zeisel, *Die Arbeitslosen von Marienthal* (Allensbach: Verlag für Demoskopie, 1961). See also Heinrich Bennecke, *Wirtschaftliche Depression und politischer Radikalis-mus* (Munich: Günter Olzog, 1968).

33. See *Statistisches Jahrbuch für das Deutsche Reich 1935* (Berlin: Statistisches Reichsamt, 1935), pp. 322, 323.

34. On the *Wehrverbände* and *Parteiarmeen*, see Bracher, *Die Auflösung der Weimarer Repub-lik*, chap. 5; for the SA, See Andreas Werner, ʳ'SA und NSDAP," (Ph.D. diss., Erlangen-Nürnberg, 1964); and Heinrich Bennecke, *Hitler und die SA* (München: Olzog, 1962).

35. See *Statistisches Jahrbuch für das Deutsche Reich 1933* (Berlin: Statistisches Reichsamt, 1933), p. 297. For a general account of social legislation, see Ludwig Preller, *Sozialpolitik in der Weimarer Republik* (Stüttgart: Franz Mittelbach, 1949), and Hans-Hermann Hartwich, *Arbeitsmarkt, Verbände, und Staat, 1918–1933* (Berlin: Walter de Gruyter, 1967).

36. See *Statistisches Jahrbuch für das Deutsche Reich 1933* (Berlin: Statistisches Reichsamt, 1933), p. 307.

37. On the labor unions, see Michael Schneider, *Unternehmer und Demokratie: Die freien Gewerkschaften in der unternehmerischen Ideologie* (Bonn-Bad Godesberg: Neue Gesellschaft, 1975); idem, *Das Arbeitsbeschaffungsprogramm des ADGB in der Endphase der Weimarer Republik* (Bonn-Bad Godesberg: Neue Gesellschaft, 1975); and Hannes Heer, *Burgfrieden oder Klassenkampf: Zur Politik der sozialdemokratischen Gewerkschaften 1930–1933* (Neuwied and Berlin: Luchterhand, 1971).

38. See Helga Timm, *Die deutsche Sozialpolitik und der Bruch der grossen Koalition 1930* (Düsseldorf: Droste, 1952); Werner Conze, "Die politischen Entscheidungen in Deutsch-land 1919–1933," in Conze and Raupach, *Staats- und Wirtschaftskrise*.

39. See Hans Speier, *Die Angestellten vor dem Nationalsozialismus: Ein Beitrag zum Ver-ständnis der deutschen Sozialstruktur, 1918–1933* (Göttingen: Vandenhoek and Ruprecht, 1977); Jürgen Kocka, "Zur Problematik der deutschen Angestellten 1914–1933," and Larry E. Jones, "The Crisis of White-Collar Interest Politics: Deutschnationaler Handlungsgehilfen-Verband and Deutsche Volkspartei in the World Economic Crisis," both in Mommsen et al., *Industrielles System und politische Entwicklung in der Weimarer Repub-lik*.

40. For more detailed information, see Dietmar Keese, "Die volkswirtschaftlichen Gesamtgrös-sen für das Deutsche Reich in den Jahren 1925–1936," in Conze and Raupach, *Staats- und Wirtschaftskrise*. The Reichs Kredit-Gesellschaft Aktiengesellschaft in Berlin published semiannual reports on the economic conditions in Germany; they present the contemporary evaluations of the economic situation and a great deal of data. A concise account of the development of unemployment by a contemporary author is Robert Wilbrandt, "Ar-beitslosigkeit in Deutschland," in *International Unemployment* (The Hague: International Industrial Relations Institute, 1931). See also Gerhard Bry, *Wages in Germany, 1871–1945*, National Bureau of Economic Research, no. 68. General Series (Princeton, N.J.: Princeton University Press, 1960); Dietmar Petzina, "Hauptprobleme der deutschen Wirtschaftspolitik 1932/33," *Vierteljahreshefte für Zeitgeschichte* 15 (1967).

41. The logic of the economic policy of the Brüning government is discussed by the two leading figures in the policy: Brüning, *Memoiren*, and Hans Luther, *Vor dem Abgrund* (Berlin: Propyläen, 1964). A critical view is presented in Keese, "Die volkswirtschaftlichen Gesamtgrössen für das Deutsche Reich in den Jahren 1925–1936," in Conze and Raupach; *Staats-und Wirtschaftskrise*. A positive view is presented in Ferdinand A. Hermens, "Das Kabinett Brüning und die Depression," in Hermens and Schieder, *Staat, Wirtschaft, und*

Politik, and in Gottfried Reinhold Treviranus, *Das Ende von Weimar* (Düsseldorf: Econ-Verlag, 1968), pp. 170–219. Treviranus was a personal friend of Brüning and a member of his cabinet.

42. Werner Kaltefleiter, *Wirtschaft und Politik in Deutschland*, rev. ed. (Cologne: West-deutscher Verlag, 1969), discusses the effects of the economic crisis on the voting behavior and the differential chances to turn to the NSDAP or the Communists. For an analysis of the appeal of extreme nationalism as advocated by the national opposition, particularly the NSDAP, see also M. Rainer Lepsius, *Extremer Nationalismus* (Stuttgart: Kohlhammer, 1966).

43. There is an ever-growing literature on Hitler. The most recent book with a claim to com-prehensiveness is Joachim C. Fest, *Hitler* (New York: Harcourt, Brace, Jovanovich, 1974). For a new account of the personal life of Hitler, see Werner Maser, *Hitler: Legend, Myth, and Reality* (New York: Harper and Row, 1973). The postwar classic is Alan Bullock, *Hitler: A Study in Tyranny*, 2d ed. (London: Odhams Press, 1965). The most influential prewar study is Konrad Heiden, *Der Führer: Hitler's Rise to Power* (London: Gollanz, 1944).

44. For the ideal type of charismatic authority, see Max Weber, *Economy and Society*, ed. Guenther Roth and Claus Wittich, 3 vols. (New York: Bedminster, 1968), pp. 241–45 and 1111–57.

45. An excellent study on factional conflicts and their resolution by the charismatic authority of Hitler within the authoritarian party organization is Joseph Nyomarkay, *Charisma and Factionalism in the Nazi Party* (Minneapolis: University of Minnesota Press, 1967).

46. A detailed study of the *Führerprinzip* is given in Wolfgang Horn, *Führerideologie und Parteiorganisation in der NSDAP (1919–1933)* (Düsseldorf: Droste, 1972).

47. Adolf Hitler, *Mein Kampf*, 2 vols. (Munich: Franz Eher, 1925, 1927). His second book was published posthumously: *Hitlers Zweites Buch: Ein Dokument aus dem Jahre 1928* (Stuttgart: Deutsche Verlagsanstalt, 1961). See also Werner Maser, *Hitlers Mein Kampf* (Munich: Bechtle, 1966), and Karl Lange, *Hitlers unbeachtete Maximen* (Stuttgart: Kohl-hammer, 1968).

48. See Peter G. P. Pulzer, *The Rise of Political Anti-Semitism in Germany and Austria* (New York: Wiley, 1964), and Werner E. Mosse, ed., *Entscheidungsjahr 1932: Zur Judenfrage in der Endphase der Weimarer Republik*, 2d ed. (Tübingen: J. C. B. Mohr, 1966).

49. See Eberhard Jäckel, *Hitlers Weltanschauung* (Tübingen: Wunderlich, 1969), and Friedrich Heer, *Der Glaube des Adolf Hitler* (Munich and Esslingen: Bechtle, 1968).

50. Nyomarkay, *Charisma and Factionalism*, p. 21.

51. Ibid., p. 22.

52. This is reflected in the total seclusion of his private life from the public, the careful prepara-tion of his public speeches, the elaborate ritual of the mass rallies, the mythological sym-bolism of flags, and the exaltation of his speeches. See Fest, *Hitler*, bk. 6, chap. 2. See also J. P. Stern, *Hitler: The Führer and the People* (Berkeley and Los Angeles: University of California Press, 1975).

53. On the NSDAP and its regional diversity, see Dietrich Orlow, *The History of the Nazi Party: 1919–1933* (Pittsburgh: University of Pittsburgh Press, 1969); Jeremy Noakes, *The Nazi Party in Lower Saxony, 1921–1933* (London: Oxford University Press, 1971); Eberhart Schön, *Die Entstehung des Nationalsozialismus in Hessen* (Meisenheim am Glan: Anton Hain, 1972); Franz Josef Heyen, *Nationalsozialismus im Alltag: Quellen zur Geschichte des Nationalsozialismus im Raum Mainz-Koblenz-Trier* (Boppard am Rhein: Harald Bolt, 1967); William Sheridan Allen, *The Nazi Seizure of Power: The Experience of a Single German Town, 1930–1935* (Chicago: Quadrangle Books, 1965).

54. See Bennecke, *Hitler und die SA;* Werner, *SA und NSDAP;* and Charles Bloch, *Die SA und die Krise des NS-Regimes 1934* (Frankfurt: Suhrkamp, 1970).

55. See Hans-Gerd Schumann, *Nationalsozialismus und Gewerkschaftsbewegung* (Hannover and Frankfort: Norddeutsche Verlagsanstalt, 1958).

56. See Henry A. Turner, Jr., "Emil Kirdorf and the Nazi Party," *Central European History* 1 (December 1968): 324–44, and idem, "Fritz Thyssen und das Buch 'I paid Hitler,'" *Vierteljahreshefte für Zeitgeschichte* 19 (1971): 225–44.

57. On the election results and the propensity to vote for the NSDAP, see Alfred Milatz, *Wähler und Wahlen in der Weimarer Republik* (Bonn: Bundeszentrale für politische Bildung, 1965);

idem, "Das Ende der Parteien im Spiegel der Wahlen 1930–1933," in Matthias and Morsey, *Das Ende der Parteien 1933;* Alexander Weber, "Soziale Merkmale der NSDAP-Wähler" (Ph.D. diss., Freiburg, 1969); Kaltefleiter, *Wirtschaft und Politik in Deutschland;* Karl O'Lessker, "Who Voted for Hitler?" *American Journal of Sociology* 74 (1968–69); Allan Schnaiberg, "A Critique of Karl O'Lessker's 'Who Voted for Hitler?'" *American Journal of Sociology* 74 (1968/69); W. Phillips Shively, "Party Identification, Party Choice, and Voting Stability: The Weimar Case," *American Political Science Review* 64 (1972).

58. Franz Osterroth and Dieter Schuster, *Chronik der Sozialdemokratie* (Hannover: Verlag für Literatur und Zeitgeschehen, 1963), p. 367.

59. Walter M. Espe, *Das Buch der NSDAP* (Berlin: Schönfeld, 1933), pp. 327–34.

60. For the legislation and its results on political terrorism and antidemocratic activities during the Weimar Republic, see Gotthard Jasper, *Der Schutz der Republik* (Tübingen: Mohr, 1963).

61. On the growing paralysis of leadership in the two major parties of the Weimar coalition see Erich Matthias, "Die Sozialdemokratische Partei Deutschlands," and Rudolf Morsey, "Die Deutsche Zentrumspartei" in Matthias and Morsey, *Das Ende der Parteien 1933.*

62. On the membership and the functionaries of the NSDAP, see Wolfgang Schäfer, *NSDAP, Entwicklung und Struktur der Staatspartei des Dritten Reiches* (Hannover and Frankfurt: Norddeutsche Verlagsanstalt, 1956); Peter Merkl, *Political Violence under the Swastika* (Princeton, N.J.: Princeton University Press, 1975); Michael Kater, "Sozialer Wandel in der NSDAP im Zuge der nationalsozialistischen Machtergreifung," and Hans Mommsen, "Zur Verschränkung traditioneller und faschistischer Führungsgruppen in Deutschland beim Übergang von der Bewegungs- zur Systemphase," both in *Faschismus als soziale Bewegung,* ed. Wolfgang Schieder (Hamburg: Hoffmann and Campe, 1976).

63. For the final stage of the breakdown, see Bracher, *Die Auflösung der Weimarer Republik;* Matthias and Morsey, *Das Ende der Parteien 1933;* Vogelsang, *Reichswehr, Staat und NSDAP;* Hermann Pünder, *Politik in der Reichskanzlei* (Stuttgart: Deutsche Verlags-Anstalt, 1961); and Hans Otto Meissner and Harry Wilde, *Die Machtergreifung* (Stuttgart: Cotta, 1958).

64. See Franz Neumann, *Behemoth: The Structure and Practice of National Socialism, 1933–1944* (New York and Evanston: Harper Torchbooks, 1966), Introduction.

65. On the diverse strategies of survival, see Matthias and Morsey, *Das Ende der Parteien,* and Fritz Stern, ed., *The Path to Dictatorship, 1918–1933* (Garden City, N.Y.: Doubleday, 1966). For industry, see Arthur Schweitzer, *Big Business in the Third Reich* (Bloomington: Indiana University Press, 1964), and Ingeborg Esenwein-Rothe, *Die Wirtschaftsverbände von 1933-45* (Berlin: Duncker and Humblot, 1965). For the military, see Robert J. O'Neill, *The German Army and the Nazi Party, 1933–1939* (London: Cassell, 1966); Francis L. Carsten, *Reichswehr und Politik 1918–1933* (Cologne and Berlin: Kiepenheuer and Witsch, 1964); and John W. Wheeler-Bennett, *The Nemesis of Power* (New York: Viking Press, 1967). For the Protestant church, see Günther van Norden, *Kirche in der Krise* (Düsseldorf: Presseverband der evangelischen Kirche, 1963). For the Catholic church, see Hans Müller, *Katholische Kirche und Nationalsozialismus* (Munich: Nymphenburger Verlagshandlung, 1963); Guenter Lewy, *The Catholic Church and Nazi Germany* (New York: McGraw-Hill, 1965); and Ernst-Wolfgang Böckenförde, "Der deutsche Katholizismus im Jahre 1933," *Hochland* 53 (1960/61). For the labor unions, see Gerhard Beier, "Zur Entstehung des Führerkreises der vereinigten Gewerkschaften Ende April 1933," *Archiv für Sozialgeschichte 15* (1975); Hans Mommsen, "Die deutschen Gewerkschaften zwischen Anpassung und Widerstand 1930–1944," in *Vom Sozialistengesetz zur Mitbestimmung,* ed. Heinz Oskar Vetter (Cologne: Bund Verlag, 1975); and Schumann, *Nationalsozialismus und Gewerkschaftsbewegung.*

66. For the change from legality to revolution in the process of the Nazi seizure of power, see Karl Dietrich Bracher, Wolfgang Sauer, and Gerhard Schulz, *Die nationalsozialistische Machtergreifung: Studien zur Errichtung des totalitären Herrschaftssystems in Deutschland 1933/34* (Cologne and Opladen: Westdeutscher Verlag, 1960); and Martin Broszat, *Der Staat Hitlers: Grundlegung und Entwicklung seiner inneren Verfassung* (Munich: Deutscher Taschenbuch Verlag, 1969).

3.
Democracy in the Shadow of Imposed Sovereignty: The First Republic of Austria

Walter B. Simon

Ideologies are formulated through the constant interplay between current contingencies and historical legacies.—Reinhard Bendix, "Industrialization, Ideologies, and Social Structures."

Citizens of a state that has been created against their expressed will may be expected to be at best semiloyal. Yet democratic politics prevailed in the First Republic of Austria for over a decade under the most trying circumstances and might well have withstood even the most severe tests if the moderate factions of the three political camps had only been a little more consistent in their willingness to cooperate with one another in defiance of the antidemocratic extremist factions in their own ranks. Even as matters went, the cooperation of moderates in all three camps did endow democratic institutions with a viability and vitality that suggests that their breakdown was not at all preordained.

The three mutually antagonistic political camps whose interrelation determined the course of politics in the First Republic of Austria and again in the Second have been identified, under a variety of party designations, with the ideologies of international socialism, proclerical conservatism, and German-nationalism.[1] These ideologies have a common origin in that all three arose in the 1880s as a protest against various aspects of Austrian liberalism, which had become dominant in Imperial Austria after enactment of the Constitution of 1867.[2] The proclerical camp stood against the liberal position regarding the separation of church and state, the German-nationalists opposed liberal cosmopolitanism, and all three camps rejected laissez-faire capitalism. Their joint opposition to capitalism had initially even brought the founding fathers of the three camps together, but their ways soon parted because their ideologies were essentially incompatible.[3] The anticapitalism of the proclerical camp and of the German-nationalists involved a denial of class antagonism and a romantic longing for a harmonious past that never was.[4] Proclerical and German-nationalist anticapitalism expressed itself primarily in anti-Semitism. The schism between the three camps was deepened by the militant anticlericalism of the Socialists and the German-nationalists. The German-nationalists, in turn, opposed both the proclerical camp and the Socialists who were conciliatory in their approach to the language conflicts that set the different national or ethnic groups of Imperial Austria against one another.

In an important sense it was issues of language conflict that tore the polyglot empire apart. The German-speaking Alpine provinces of the Danube monarchy that were to form the Republic of Austria were involved only marginally in these language conflicts, because here the Socialists and the proclerical conservatives took conciliatory positions in order to keep the multilingual Danube empire together. The uncompromising extremists prevailed, however, in the mixed-language areas (and, one should insert here, at the institutions of higher learning), where their militant obstructions impeded compromise solutions. Even though outnumbered by the moderates, the extremists succeeded in disrupting democratic politics to the point that the government had to suspend the *Reichsrat* and govern by decree.

The Republic of Austria that emerged as one of the successor states of the defunct empire was 99 percent German-speaking, the only linguistic minority of consequence being in southern Carinthia on the Yugoslav border. The effectiveness of democratic politics depended entirely upon the relationships between the three ideological camps. In spite of the anarchic state of affairs left in the wake of military catastrophe and political disintegration, prospects for the success of democratic policies appeared hopeful because initially the leaders of the three camps worked together, jointly assuming the responsibility of coping with the catastrophic situation in the remnant of empire that had now become their country. On 12 November 1918 Socialist, proclerical conservative, and moderate German-nationalist leaders proclaimed the "Republic of German-Austria" and formed its first coalition government.

In the First Republic of Austria the effectiveness of democratic politics depended upon the balance between the commitments to partisan ideologies and the commitments to parliamentary democracy and constitutional government of all three political camps. This balance had in each case been uneasy and delicate from the very beginning. Yet the effectiveness and the achievements of democratic institutions and constitutional government in a decade and a half of precarious existence indicate that the ultimate extreme polarization in all three camps and the resulting disruption of democratic politics were not inevitable.[5]

The close cooperation between their leaders at the establishment of the Republic indicates that such cooperation was certainly not out of the question.

Later instances will likewise support the thesis that cooperation between the camps might well have forestalled the ultimate breakdown of democratic politics brought about by the subsequent polarization.

A statement of democratic politics and political ethics is here indicated. Democratic politics serve primarily to define and legitimize the means to be employed in the resolution of conflicts; pursuit of specific goals is left to contesting political forces. The essence of the democratic political process is perhaps most succinctly stated in a phrase from the American constitution, "To build a more perfect union." In this sense democratic politics are not directed toward the achievement of an objectively ideal state of affairs but toward the provision of an arena in which the codified pursuit of conflicting aims itself effects the amendment of imperfections. It goes without saying that limitations upon the means to be employed rest upon the consent of the contesting parties with the understanding that these limitations apply equally to all of them—whether in the opposition or in the government. It is obvious that democratic politics also limit in the short run the scope of ends that may be realized. Democratic politics should, instead, facilitate constant and gradual social change and concomitant far-reaching reforms over protracted periods. Democratic politics break down when the contesting parties strive to achieve their objectives by means not countenanced by the rules of democratic political contest and when they endeavor to impose their will upon the others by any and all means.

An understanding of the nature of democratic politics will be advanced by making a distinction between the political ethics of partisanship and the political ethics of constitutional means. The former commit each party to the achievement of partisan objectives by any and all means, while the latter bind the contesting parties to strive for their objectives solely by the means legitimized by the constitution.[6]

The prevalence of one or the other type of political ethics in a political system affects the functioning of democratic politics profoundly. Moreover, shifts in the balance between an ethics of constitutional means and an ethics of partisan objectives in any one segment of a political system is bound to influence the balance in others. This dichotomy was evident in all three Austrian political camps, and the resultant internal competition between those committed to one or the other type of political ethics kept Austrian democracy in a precarious state.

Tendencies toward an ethics of partisanship had in part been bequeathed by traditions of bitter political strife that had left their residue in programs, platforms, and polemics. These tendencies also fed upon the widespread poverty and economic insecurity that had followed the war and the disintegration of the empire.

Ethics of partisanship and political extremism had another source in the dubious legitimacy of the state. The First Republic of Austria is the only state in history upon which sovereignty was imposed by foreign powers against the expressed wish of its people and their leaders.

In view of all the political and economic problems that confronted the young Republic of Austria, it was doubtful that the new state could survive.[7] Nor did the Austrians have the will to survive as a nation. With the empire irrevocably gone, all parties endorsed a union with the German Republic of Weimar. In this spirit, Article 1 of the Constitution of the Republic of Austria stipulated explicitly that "Deutsch-Oesterreich," the German-speaking part of Imperial Austria that had become the Republic of Austria, was part of the Republic of Germany. All parties had endorsed Article 1 and it was passed by the assembled legislators with but one dissenting vote.[8] But when the peace treaty of Saint-Germain forbade Austrian unification with Germany, Article 1 of the constitution had to be revoked, and the First Republic of Austria was thus compelled to exist against the expressed wish of its people.

In protest against the ratification of the peace treaty, the German nationalists resigned from the government and rallied in the pan-German *Grossdeutsche Volkspartei*.[9] At the initiative of this party, plebiscites were held in several autonomous provinces of Austria with results that showed almost unanimous endorsement of unification with Germany. Thereupon the victorious Allies directed Austria, then in dire need of foreign loans, to abstain from further demonstrations against the terms of the peace treaty.[10]

Resigning themselves to their undesired independence, the Austrians gave to their political parties the loyalty citizens usually reserve for their country. Among all countries the world over, the First Republic of Austria remains unique in the extremely intense political involvement of its citizens. Political parties had their own flags, their own anthems, and even their own armed formations. Election days saw 90 percent of all enfranchised Austrians casting their ballots, and the daily lives of a large proportion of these voters were completely dominated by the framework of their political affiliations. Not only did they pay their dues to support the parties of their choice, but they joined social clubs whose members shared their political preferences. Even hiking clubs, glee clubs, and nurseries enrolled their members along ideological lines.

The spokesmen and leaders of the three camps were, on the whole, committed to parliamentary democracy and the maintenance of democratic parties. So too, most of the time, were the overwhelming majority of their followers until the early 1930s. But the pervasiveness of political associations in the lives of the Austrians kept the camps apart, and within the camps political ethics fluctuated. Ultimately, the devotees of ethics of partisanship—the ideological extremists—succeeded in setting the pace in all three camps and tensions escalated to the breaking point. An atmosphere of latent civil war found expression in countless clashes even before the two fateful civil wars of 1934 that marked the ultimate breakdown of democratic politics.

The polarization that led to this breakdown in Austria also brought the country's three ideologies into sharp relief. These ideologies are of special significance because many countries possess political movements committed to analogous ideologies. Variations of Socialist, nationalist, or religious movements often exist side by side, with resulting evolutions of ideological hybrids composed of these basic ideological ingredients. Almost all of these movements have, on occasion, been torn between a tendency toward uncompromising radicalism and a tendency toward moderation and cooperation. Thus the balance between ethics of partisanship and ethics of constitutional means so characteristic of Austrian politics in the twenties and thirties has its counterpart wherever political movements with strong ideological commitments participate in an unstable democratic system. Furthermore, the Austrian political camps gave expression to and developed ideological positions that are significant in their own right.

The Socialist Camp

The policies and programs of the Austrian Socialists reflect an ever shifting balance between ethics of partisanship and ethics of constitutional means that resulted from efforts to create a synthesis of moderate and radical positions. Efforts to create such a synthesis originated with the founding congress of Hainfeld, which brought together a radical faction and a moderate faction in the *Sozialdemokratische Arbeiterpartei*. This fusion, achieved at Hainfeld on 31 December 1889, set a distinctive stamp on Austrian socialism for generations to come. The Hainfeld program combined an unequivocal commitment to achieve, albeit in the remote future, partisan objectives of socialism with a highly qualified commitment to the constitutional means of parliamentary democracy.[11] Parliamentary democracy was explicitly endorsed as a means of somewhat doubtful value rather than as an end in itself. In this vein the program of Hainfeld states: "Without deceiving ourselves about the value of parliamentarism, a form of modern class domination . . . [the Socialist party] . . . fights for universal and equal suffrage . . . as a most important instrument for agitation and organization."[12]

The moderates were satisfied with the commitment to parliamentary democracy in spite of the hedging, because they were mainly interested in achieving such concrete reforms as a ban on child labor, the eight-hour day, a graduated income tax, the establishment of a Chamber of Labor, and above all else, universal and equal suffrage. The radicals were satisfied with the expression of distrust in parliamentary democracy. Radicals as well as moderates accepted the establishment of a classless society and collective ownership of the means of production as their ultimate goal.

Neither in Imperial Austria nor in the Second Republic of Austria did the Socialist commitment to Marxism affect concrete political action. Instead, the quest for a classless Socialist society on the basis of Marxist doctrine remained on a lofty level of sophisticated exegesis. In the First Republic, however, the policies of the Socialist party were influenced by Marxist ideological orientation. The synthesis of commitment to Marxism with participation in parliamentary democracy has since become known as *Austromarxism*. Austromarxism stands out as an effort to reconcile moderate Socialists with radical Socialists, as a principled synthesis of efforts for short-range reforms with aspirations for long-range objectives, and as an endeavor to establish harmony between theory and practice.

Austromarxism was of little consequence in the Second Republic of Austria, but its synthesis of Marxism with participation in parliamentary politics appears today in the practice of several left-wing Socialist parties. The policies and positions of several sizable parliamentary Communist parties hardly differs from those that evolved under Austromarxist efforts to reconcile revolutionary Marxist theory with practices that are necessarily geared to the give-and-take of parliamentary politics.

The Austromarxist synthesis has been articulated in numerous programs,[13] books, and debates,[14] notably in the Program of Linz of 1926 where it was stipulated that the Socialist society was to be achieved by rallying the majority of voters.[15] Recourse to radical means is, however, explicitly countenanced in case the bourgeoisie should not support the Socialist measures that a Socialist Parliament would enact:

But if, however, the bourgeoisie should resist social change which will be the task and objective of the state authority of the working class by such means of sabotage as systematic throttling of the economic life, armed rebellion, or conspiracy with foreign powers, then the working class would be compelled to break the resistance of the bourgeoisie by the means of dictatorship.[16]

The above paragraph expresses succinctly the duality of the Austromarxist approach: political power was to be won by obtaining a majority in Parliament, but the measures to be enacted by such a majority were expected to provoke resistance that would have to be broken by dictatorial force.

It is noteworthy that in the mid-sixties Communist parties that accepted revisionist positions endorsed by the Kremlin issued similar statements that combined commitment to the achievement of a Socialist society with commitment to democracy. The following is taken from a programmatic pronouncement of the secretary of the American Communist party, issued in 1964:

Marxism-Leninism is a science that recognizes no contradiction between the struggle in defense of democratic institutions and democratic rights, and the struggle for socialism. It is our firm conviction that the masses of the working people are the bearers of the new socialist society that makes us uncompromising fighters for democracy. Democratic institutions are not obstacles on the path to socialism. On the contrary, these are the institutions which the people will use for the transition. Hence we want to preserve and extend them both for now and for the future.[17]

The Austromarxist synthesis was not limited to pronouncements and programs but extended to the day-to-day policies of the Austrian Socialist party in the twenties and thirties, where the duality of the commitments of the Austrian Socialists led to some apparent contradictions in their approach to the problem of revolution in theory, practice, and historical perspective. In 1919, while heading the coalition government of Austria, the Socialists effectively thwarted Communist efforts to foment a revolution.[18] A decade later the Socialists themselves discounted the significance of their antirevolutionary stand. At the annual party conference of 1932 the principal spokesman of Austromarxism, Otto Bauer, apologized to impatient young left-wingers for this and explained that unfortunate objective circumstances had rendered a Socialist revolution in Austria impossible at that time. These "unfortunate circumstances" included the country's dependence upon the "victorious capitalist powers" for badly needed essential supplies. The speaker mentioned as a further stumbling block the political strength of Austria's independent peasantry with its "decades of political training and organizations."[19] By so explaining why the time had simply not been "ripe" for a revolution, the Socialists also discounted the merits of their anti-Bolshevist stand in the eyes of the followers of the other two camps. Their use of revolutionary phraseology to justify their party's antirevolutionary action preserved a degree of unity within the Socialist camp but also brought closer together their opponents in the two anti-Socialist camps.

Yet the preservation of Socialist unity in Austria may be considered a major achievement of the Austromarxist synthesis. In all European countries, especially those bordering upon Austria, strong Communist parties competed with democratic Socialist parties for the allegiance of class-conscious workers. Throughout the twenties and thirties we find that the voting strength of the Czechoslovakian Communist party nearly matched the combined strength of the German-speaking and Czech-speaking democratic Socialist parties of this country, both of which were participating in coalition governments. In all Czechoslovakian elections in the twenties the Communists ran neck and neck with the party of the Czech agrarians, the strongest non-Communist party in the country, and continued to poll about 15 percent of the vote. In Germany, Communist voting strength increased from 3.3 million, or 10.6 percent of the vote, in May 1928 to 6.0 million, or 17.7 percent of the vote, in November 1932, while Social Democratic voting strength declined from 9.2 million, or 29.0 percent, to 7.2 million, or 20.4 percent.

In Austria, however, the Communist vote never exceeded 0.5 percent of the total vote, polling only twenty thousand votes in November 1930. By contrast, the vote of the Austrian Socialist party remained steadily at the 40 percent level throughout the twenties. In local elections held in many parts of Austria in the crisis year of 1932, the Communist vote nearly doubled its November 1930 figure but remained infinitesimal compared to the Socialist vote. While the Communist party remained the strongest party in Berlin from 1928 until 1933, the Communist vote in Vienna remained below the 2 percent level in April 1932, while the Socialist party polled about 60 percent.

The Austrian Socialists took pride in their achievement of "working-class unity" at home and even saw it as their sacred mission to advance such unity abroad, notably in their tireless efforts to bridge the gap between the Second, or democratic Socialist, International and the Third Communist International on a world scale.[20] It was this sense of mission that induced a certain ambivalence into statements about the Soviet Union by Austrian Socialist spokesmen, who would deplore the lack of freedom and democracy there while hailing the great achievements of Lenin's revolution. The tendency to explain away defects in the Soviet system became even more pronounced after the catastrophic defeat in the civil war of February 1934. The outlawed underground organ of the suppressed party gratefully acknowledged the generous acts of solidarity on the part of democratic Socialist parties from all over the world and proclaimed the affinity of revolutionary Austrian socialism with the Russian dictatorship of the proletariat: "Austrian socialism has become the natural link between the revolutionary socialism of the East and the democratic socialism of the West."[21]

Another, even more impressive dimension of the ideological unity that rallied moderates and radicals in one Socialist party was the extensive and all-embracing organizational party network whose size also reflected the high degree of political mobilization characteristic of Austrian politics. In a population of slightly over six million, with about four million voters, over seven hundred thousand people paid regular monthly dues to the Sozialdemokratische Arbeiterpartei. In Vienna alone there were four hundred thousand dues-paying members. A dedicated and well-organized staff of thousands of volunteers collected dues and saw to it that the members and their relatives turned out to vote or to attend rallies and meetings.[22]

The number and scope of affiliated organizations was likewise impressive. Socialist unions enrolled the overwhelming majority of Austria's one million wage earners. The Socialist party sponsored numerous educational and cultural societies as well as social clubs for activities of every kind. Also affiliated with the party was the atheistic *Freidenkerbund* (League of Freethinkers) which, in turn, influenced the way the party ran its nursery schools and helped to indoctrinate the party's scout clubs for teenagers. The party even ran its own burial society, which arranged for cremation, a way of burial not countenanced by the Catholic church.[23]

Of great consequence were the lending libraries set up by the Socialist party in a country where free public lending libraries, so characteristic of Anglo-

Saxon countries, were unknown. These libraries were part of a comprehensive program of adult education that contributed a great deal to the lives of the many working men and women who had received but eight years of formal schooling. The educational program of the party also familiarized Austrian Socialists with the values and traditions of free debate. It should be attributed to this tradition of open debate within the ranks of the Austrian Socialist party that Austrian workers proved not amenable to totalitarian appeals that were to be directed at them by Hitler's national socialism and by Stalin's communism.

Of special significance was the *Republikanischer Schutzbund* (Republican Defense League), the Socialist party's army of militant and disciplined volunteers. Though its main function was to maintain order at meetings and rallies, the Schutzbund was known to be armed, and it did fight the battles of the party in small skirmishes and in the civil war of February 1934.

Touching every aspect of its members' lives, the party and its affiliates truly constituted a state within the state. No other political party in any democratic country has ever achieved such a high degree of enduring voluntary participation. This is all the more noteworthy since the party, with its 40 percent of the vote, had remained in the opposition after its defeat at the polls in 1920. The party did control, through its elected representatives, the autonomous city of Vienna and numerous industrial municipalities, but this provided very little leverage in the form of patronage. Nor could the party offer any other form of material inducement to motivate such extensive involvement of the masses.

Dedication to unity for its own sake had initially caused the Socialist party to pursue a moderate policy while indulging in radical rhetoric. The threat of schisms on the Left, however, made it difficult for the party to depart too far from its rhetoric in political practice. We shall see how this dedication to unity affected Socialist policies in the fateful years of 1931 and 1932. These policies have as yet failed to receive the attention they deserve. They are of special interest in view of tangible alternatives that have been explicitly rejected.

The Two Anti-Marxist Camps

Throughout the twenties the two non-Socialist camps joined forces to such an extent that it was, at times, impossible to distinguish between them. Time and again the Socialists were confronted at the polls by anti-Marxist fusion tickets that rallied proclerical conservatives and anticlerical German-nationalists in order to forestall the specter of an Austromarxist regime.

It is noteworthy that the cooperation between the two anti-Socialist camps brought moderate conservatives together with the more moderate German-nationalists without ever obliterating their respective identities, while extremists in both camps fused completely for a while in the ranks of the paramilitary and avowedly fascist *Heimwehr*. Only with the beginning of the thirties did polarization set in within the anti-Marxist camps so that Austria was soon divided into three irreconcilably hostile camps. Before this three-way polarization actually took place, a last chance for cooperation between the moderates in all three camps appeared briefly and was deliberately rejected in the interest of maintaining unity within the camps themselves.

The Proclerical Conservative camp

In the conflict between good and evil, in which great advantage is given to evil by neglect, the Christian cannot be indifferent to so important an area of conflict as that of politics.— Eugene J. McCarthy, Commonweal, 1 October 1954.

The possibility of conflict between church and state is always present when the head of one is not the head of the other. For this reason clericalism versus anticlericalism has always been an issue in Roman Catholic countries. The question of clerical influence is likely to arise in questions regarding the school system and other matters where the private sphere and the public sphere overlap.

The proclerical *Christlichsoziale Partei* originated in Vienna and Lower Austria in the 1880s ''as an expression of the discontent of the masses against the economic and social abuses created by Liberalism. Uncertain of its objectives, it comprised the petty bourgeoisie and those without property.''[24]

Under the leadership of its founder, Karl Lueger, the Christlichsoziale Partei was anticapitalist, anti-Semitic, devoutly Roman Catholic, and loyal to the Habsburg dynasty and the Austro-Hungarian empire. Initially, Leuger's radicalism and his reputation as a populist demagogue led to the crown's refusal to accept him as mayor of Vienna until he had been elected twice consecutively. Soon the party was accepted as one of the bulwarks of the empire, and in 1907 its leaders entered the government of Imperial Austria. In Vienna the proclerical party lost to the Socialist, and in the small nonindustrial towns the anticlerical German-nationalists rivaled the conservatives for the allegiance of the non-Socialist voters. The Christlichsoziale Partei became the party of the devoutly Roman Catholic independent peasantry, thus enabling it to participate in every government of the First Republic of Austria. After the Socialists went into opposition in November 1920 the conservatives became and remained the major government party of he Republic.

The Christlichsoziale Partei maintained close relations with the Roman Catholic church and counted many members of the clergy among its leaders, most prominent among them Msgr. Ignaz Seipel, head of the government for more than half of the twenties. The coalition governments headed by the proclerical conservatives included German-nationalists for all but two months from November 1920 till September 1933. Only from September 1930 until

November 1930 and from May 1932 until September 1933 did the conservative Christlichsoziale Partei share governmental responsibility with the Heimwehr. In September 1933, the Christlichsoziale Partei fused with the Heimwehr to form the *Vaterlaendische Front,* the party of the Dollfuss-
Schuschnigg dictatorship.

Scrutiny of the record suggests that large sectors of the proclerical and
conservative Christlichsoziale Partei would have preferred the preservation of
democratic politics. Of the three identifiable groups in the party, the two
major ones showed reservations about fusion with the Fascists. Many groups
among the Roman Catholic yeomanry, the mainstay of the conservative camp,
favored democracy. So did the small group of devoutly Roman Catholic
workers led by Leopold Kunschak, who was most outspoken in opposing
fusion with the Fascists and articulately in favor of preserving democratic
politics. Unsympathetic to a complete fusion, though willing to accept the
Fascists as allies, were the spokesmen of political Catholicism, among them
Schuschnigg, the subsequent chancellor, and Miklas, president of the Republic.[25] The leader of the Christlichsoziale Partei, Carl Vaugoins, is also on the
record as having made efforts to preserve at least the identity of his party
within the framework of the Vaterlaendische Front.[26]

In Imperial Austria and again in the First Republic the proclerical conservative camp was oriented toward the preservation of the established order of
things. In addition to its base among the Roman Catholic peasantry, the camp
rallied support among the small shopkeepers and craftsmen who had given the
party of Lueger its triumphant start in Vienna before the turn of the century.
Also of note was the small band of proclerical and conservative Roman
Catholic workers who played an important role through their resistance to the
party's drift toward the extreme right and oblivion before democratic politics
came to an end. After the establishment of the autocratic regime in which their
own political camp played a leading role, this group did provide labor with a
legal voice and continued to stand, albeit without telling effect, against authoritarianism in government. While the Roman Catholic workers were outnumbered among their peers by the Socialists, the devoutly Roman Catholic
academicians and intellectuals were outnumbered among their colleagues by
the German-nationalists.

Today, the record of the voluntary fusion of the proclerical conservative
party with the fascistic Heimwehr and the history of the subsequent authoritarian dictatorship constitute a source of mortifying embarrassment for Austrian
conservatives. Examination shows, however, that the other two camps bear a
fair share of responsibility for the disasters that were to disrupt democratic
politics in Austria, wipe Austria off the map completely for seven years, and
usher in ten years of foreign occupation. The disastrous foreign policy and the
oppressive domestic policies of the authoritarian regime from 1933 till 1938
have left conservatives in Austria with an unpalatable legacy. They had,

however, no choice but to yield to extremists in their camp when extremist radicals determined the policies in the two other camps.

The German-Nationalist Camp

When one talks about "nationalism" among Austrians, the qualifier "German" must be added to avoid confusion. Among Austrians it is understood that in Austria "nationalists" are actually German-nationalists who either reject their Austrian identity entirely or at least subordinate it to their encompassing German nationality.

German-nationalism in Austria, like German-nationalism in Germany or, for that matter, nationalism in general, gives expression to diverse and basically irreconcilable impulses. All ideological impulses seem to contain contradictory and mutually exclusive moral sentiments, but in the case of Austrian German-nationalism such dualism is pronounced with greatest clarity.

Originally, German-nationalism contained and inspired humanist and universalist values; cultivation of the cherished German cultural heritage was combined with respect for the national heritage of others. In Austria, as well as in Germany, German-nationalism was at one time a liberal force, the motive power behind the revolution of 1848 with its demands for constitutional government and individual freedom. In opposition to the tutelage of autocratic regimes, nationalism emerged in many places as a humanist force that afterwards shed its humanist impulses in order to advance chauvinist intolerance and imperialism. This development has been especially swift and far-reaching among the German-nationalists of Austria.

For nearly a century, Austrian German-nationalism has been characterized by an extreme chauvinism, intolerance, and ruthless expansionism that finally left its mark on world history through Hitler's nationalist-socialist regime. Yet the original humanist and liberal impulse, albeit hopelessly overshadowed and banished into marginal recesses, has never been extinguished completely. Occasional upsurges of liberal and humanist traditions have provided Austrian German-nationalism with a varied, fluctuating, and extremely complex history.

Furthermore, German-nationalist sentiments in Austria were at no time limited completely to the various German-nationalist parties but rather found repeated expression in the policies of the two major parties, at times even dominating the politics of the German-speaking provinces of Imperial Austria and the politics of the First Republic. Thus in Imperial Austria the Socialists often compromised their internationalism, and the proclerical conservatives the supernational position of their church, when they supported German-nationalist aspirations in the language question. In the First Republic of Austria all three political camps supported unification with Germany. The Socialists as well as the proclerical conservatives endorsed Austrian independence only after Hitler had come to power in Germany; before this they had accepted the Republic's imposed independence only under duress.

The various German-nationalist parties have differed a great deal among themselves and fluctuated widely both in their ideological commitments and in the size of their following, making German-nationalism the most volatile and unstable element in Austrian politics. By the 1880s the German nationalists in Imperial Austria had broken away from the liberal camp with which they had been indentified since the revolution of 1848, motivated partly by their anticapitalism but mainly by their unbending intransigence in matters related to the language policies of the polyglot empire. In the nearly completely German-speaking provinces that were to form the Republic of Austria, the greatest support for the German-nationalists came from students, the intelligentsia, and the anticlerical bourgeoisie. German nationalist parties polled most of their votes in small towns with little or no industry, in enclaves of Protestant farmers, and in the mixed-language area of southern Carinthia.

But although the German-nationalist parties were comparatively small in Imperial Austria as well as in the First Republic, their policies prevailed, after a fashion, in both, to the detriment of democratic politics. In Imperial Austria, the German-nationalists were strong enough in mixed-language areas and at the universities to impede all efforts to achieve harmony between the language groups by compromise solutions that would have given non-German languages a measure of recognition. It is noteworthy that in one of these mixed-language areas, the Sudetenland of Bohemia, there was a National Socialist German workers' party that as early as 1907 had a program containing the principal points of what was to become the program of Hitler's party and the basis for the policies of the Third Reich. A branch of this party appeared in the Republic of Austria in 1918 and competed with the Austrian branch of Hitler's party for two years after its establishment in 1926 before the two joined forces.

The bulk of German-nationalist support in the first thirteen years of the First Republic of Austria rallied under two parties committed to parliamentary democracy under the German republican colors of black, red, and gold, the colors of the German revolution of 1848. The urban Grossdeutsche Volkspartei represented the anticlerical intelligentsia, especially students and their professors, and found its principal support in nonindustrial provincial capitals and county seats as well as among the salaried petty bourgeoisie. The rural *Landbund* rallied the farmers in Protestant enclaves and their neighbors. The Grossdeutsche Volkspartei never ceased to make an issue of union with Germany (as a result of which the party itself at times lost nearly all of its votes since the cogency of this issue fluctuated). The Landbund, which concentrated its efforts upon the representation of agrarian interests and readily compromised on ideological issues, was willing to support the ratification of foreign loans even when they stipulated, as they invariably did, thanks to

French preoccupation with this matter, a clause that committed Austria to forgo unification with Germany, though this had already been prohibited by the peace treaty. Both parties were represented in all coalition governments with the Christlichsoziale Partei from November 1930 until May 1932; at that point the Grossdeutsche Volkspartei went into opposition over the ratification of the so-called Loan of Lausanne, which involved an Austrian reaffirmation of the injunction not to join Germany for another twenty-five years. The Landbund supported ratification of the loan and remained in the coalition government until September 1933, when the proclerical conservatives fused with the Fascist Heimwehr to install the authoritarian dictatorship.

The firm commitment of the two moderate German-nationalist parties to constitutional government and parliamentary democracy brought them into conflict with the Heimwehr, and in September 1930 both went into opposition against the coalition regime of the Heimwehr with the Christlichsoziale Partei. The fusion ticket of these two parties did very well at the elections held on 9 November 1930. Obtaining nearly 12 percent of the total vote and 19 of 165 members of Parliament, the two moderate German-nationalist factions replaced the defeated Heimwehr as the coalition partner of the conservative proclerical party.

Significantly, the fusion ticket of the two German-nationalist parties entered the elections under the designation *Nationaler Wirtschaftsblock und Landbund, Führung Dr. Schober*. Johann Schober had made a name for himself as chief of the Vienna police and then as a statesman of international caliber. Under his leadership a whiff of old-fashioned liberalism appeared once more on the political scene, and the success of his ticket at the polls was among the aspects of the political situation that appeared to give the harassed Republic a new lease on life. It is of interest that Schober's ticket had received the endorsement of *Die Neue Freie Presse*, the organ of the Jewish bourgeoisie of Vienna that had been the paper of the liberal party before its disintegration.

Subsequent local elections showed that the voters of Schober's fusion ticket defected to Hitler's party in such large numbers that by April 1932 nine out of ten of the party's urban voters had become National Socialist voters. The Grossdeutsche Volkspartei members of Parliament who had been elected on Schober's fusion ticket soon followed their voters and went over to Hitler's National Socialist German workers' party.[27] Thus the bulk of Austrian German-nationalists abandoned the German republican colors and went over to Hitler a year before he became chancellor of the Reich.[28]

Fascism

The pressures that came from across the border were ultimately decisive in putting an end to democratic politics in Austria. With the triumph of Fascism in Italy, antidemocratic forces in Austria gained a great deal of vigor, and Hitler's ascent to power in Germany made democratic politics in Austria altogether unworkable.

Mussolini's seizure of power in Rome contributed significantly to the polarization of Austrian politics. For one thing, the triumph of Fascist "law and order" over "the danger of red revolution" served to encourage the extremists in both anti-Socialist camps. Also, the Italian Fascist regime contributed directly and rather openly to Austrian right wing paramilitary organizations. Furthermore, the brutal oppression of the Italian Socialists stiffened the militant determination of the Austrian Socialists and made them more distrustful of Austrian conservatives, whom they perceived—not altogether without reason—as leaning toward the Fascists. It should also be kept in mind that before the emergence of Hitler's Third Reich as a major power Italy was by far the strongest neighbor of Austria.

The influence of Fascist Italy upon Austrian politics was compounded by its close alliance with the conservative-authoritarian Hungarian regime, which, in turn, had cultivated ties with Austrian ultraconservatives that dated back to the good old days of the Austro-Hungarian empire. The alliance of Italy with Hungary aimed primarily at achieving a revision of the peace treaties of Paris. The Hungarian regime refused to accept the allotment of formerly Hungarian territories on all four sides. Large parts of the new successor states of the defunct Habsburg monarch—Yugoslavia, Rumania, and Czechoslovakia— were constituted from territories ceded by Hungary, and the flags at half-mast on all new Hungarian borders testified to revisionist aspirations. The Italian regime aspired to recover from Yugoslavia the former Austrian Adriatic littoral province of Dalmatia that had at one time belonged to the Republic of Venice. The Austrians had little sympathy for Hungarian revisionist aspirations (especially since Austria's easternmost province, the Burgenland, was among the territories ceded by Hungary), and they had even less sympathy for the Italian claims upon Yugoslavia, since they bitterly resented Italy's wartime role and subsequent seizure of Trieste and southern Tyrol. Also, the oppression of the German language in southern Tyrol offended Austrian sensibilities.

All Austrians, regardless of political sympathies, despised the peace treaties imposed at Paris, and they did not think the state of affairs based upon them could endure. The right-wing proclerical conservatives and the right-wing anticlerical German-nationalists, much as they resented Italian denials of language rights to the southern Tyrolians, accepted Mussolini as a sponsor of their opposition to the order of things established by the hated peace treaties of Versailles, Saint-Germain, and Trianon. They also accepted Mussolini as their champion in the fight against the threat of red revolution and against what they despised as effete liberal democracy.

It is of general significance that the coalition of the two anti-Socialist camps went much further among extremists than among moderates. The moderate proclerical conservatives and the moderate anticlerical German-nationalists, both committed to the preservation of democratic politics, retained their separate identities while they worked together against the Socialists. Thus the agrarian Landbund, unlike the less moderate Grossdeutsche Volkspartei, never even entered fusion tickets with the proclerical conservatives. Among the anti-Socialist extremists, the proclerical Fascists and the anticlerical German-nationalists remained all but undifferentiated until the emergence of Hitler's party created an unbridgeable schism between those oriented toward Rome (or Mussolini and the Vatican) and those loyal to the cause of the Third Reich. Anti-Socialist unity most effectively overshadowed all differentiations among the paramilitary right-wing formations that intermittently clashed with the paramilitary formations of the Socialist Republikanischer Schutzbund. The activism of the avowedly antidemocratic anti-Marxists was motivated at least in part by their desire to conceal from themselves the existing fissures and budding conflicts within their ranks. It is quite possible that activist radicalism is often motivated by such a need to avoid confrontation with contradictions and latent conflict within the ranks.

In the Socialist camp, radical phraseology served to reconcile potential revolutionary dissenters with a basically moderate and reformist policy, while on the extreme right feverish activism served to reconcile ultraconservative, authoritarian proclerical Austrian patriots with anticlerical revolutionary pan-Germans who despised everything Austrian.

Throughout the twenties clashes between militant Socialists and militant right-wingers were the order of the day. These clashes took place on the outer margin of the political decision-making that was guided by democratic processes. The clashes, often involving the shedding of blood and not infrequently the loss of lives, provided an ominous background to acrimonious legislative debates over negotiable issues. There can be no doubt that the bloody clashes exacerbated tensions and rendered the issues at stake more serious than differences regarding the economic policies of such a small country warranted.

The policies of the country as a whole and of its nine autonomous provinces and over four thousand incorporated cities, towns, and villages were determined by democratic politics. There is no evidence that the decision-making process in the various legislative bodies of the Republic has ever been determined by violence in the streets. Ultimately, it was the tripartite polarization at the polls, engendered by influences from across the borders and exacerbated by tensions at home, that brought democratic politics to an end. Intermittent violence reflected and at the same time contributed, however significantly, to the ongoing polarization.

In the chronicle of violence, bloody 15 July 1927 stands out as the watershed in the development of Fascist influence in Austria. Its roots lay in one of the episodic armed clashes that were no rarity in the First Republic of Austria. In a small industrial town in the formerly Hungarian province of Burgenland, a long series of clashes between Socialists and their opponents came to a head on Sunday 30 January 1927 when members of a right-wing paramilitary organization fired on Socialists who passed their headquarters after an exchange of verbal threats, challenges, and insults. The shots killed a child and a crippled war veteran and injured several others. In July, a jury acquitted the accused, triggering a protest in Vienna that became completely unmanageable. A disorderly mob set fire to the Palace of Justice and to the publishing plant of the proclerical conservative daily, whose endorsement of the acquittal had appeared under a banner headline reading "Ein Klares Urteil." The police restored order with a maximum show of force, leaving close to one hundred dead (among them four policemen) and several hundred wounded.[29]

From that day on the Socialists were on the defensive. The spokesman of the party had to admit in Parliament that the party had lost rapport with its followers, and he pleaded in vain for amnesty.[30] Within the Socialist party the Left gained ground among the younger members, but in the country as a whole the initiative passed to the extreme Right, whose various paramilitary outfits rallied now in the avowedly Fascist Heimwehr.

In order to intimidate the Socialists, the Heimwehr, protected by large escorts of federal police, paraded through urban working-class districts that had long been Socialist strongholds. The Socialist leadership, afraid of another massacre, endeavored to restrain their followers with a minimum loss of face by drawing them to rallies held in other parts of the towns and districts in question. Their red flags and other party emblems showed the parading Fascists where the sympathies of the people in these districts lay. Those who had hated and feared the Socialists were, however, most favorably impressed by the capacity of the Heimwehr to intimidate the Socialists, and subsidies flowed freely from banks, industrial corporations, and finally from Fascist Italy. In 1929–30 the Austrian banks alone contributed to the Heimwehr a quarter of a million Austrian schillings a month (about fifty thousand dollars, a fairly sizable amount in impoverished Austria) through the offices of the federal chancellor Schober.[31]

The Heimwehr was composed of the most diverse elements, from devoutly Roman Catholic young farmers to rabidly anticlerical German-nationalist urban petty bourgeoisie, with numerous shades in between. Some favored the return of the monarch, others looked to Hitler, whose star was beginning to rise in Germany, and many more set their hopes on Mussolini. The feverish activism of the Heimwehr in the late twenties resulted at least in part from the necessity to avoid confrontation with the issues that threatened to split its ranks. In numerous armed clashes with the Socialists, the Heimwehr appeared clearly as the aggressor, and the leaders of the diverse factions boasted openly of their plans to take over the government by force in order to suppress the Socialists. On 18 May 1930 leaders of the Heimwehr publicly took the famous "Oath of Korneuburg," which contained the following pledge:

. . . we plan to seize the power of the state and to remodel the state and the economy for the benefit of the whole people. . . . We reject western democratic parliamentarism and the party state. . . . We want to replace [Parliament] by the self-determination of the estates ["Staende"] and to provide a strong leadership for the state, not by representatives of the parties but from the leading persons of the big estates ["Staende"] and from the best and most able men of our movement. . . . Every comrade knows three powers: faith in God, his own hard will, and the word of his leader.[32]

Among those who took this oath were several proclerical conservatives whose commitment to parliamentary democracy is beyond doubt. Foremost among them was the leader of the Lower Austrian peasants, Julius Raab, subsequently head of the coalition government of Socialists and conservatives that guided the Second Republic of Austria for twenty-four years, including the decade under Allied occupation. This detail is significant as a characteristic instance of how moderates may be caught in spite of themselves in actions and commitments promoted by radicals. It is my contention that incongruities of this type should be noted rather than overlooked, and they should be examined objectively rather than exploited for facile criticism. The good name of Julius Raab and the memory of his accomplishments is not tarnished in any way by his unfortunate association with the lamentable Oath of Korneuburg, and a study of this matter should contribute to our understanding of politics.

At the time of the Oath of Korneuburg, misgivings about the Heimwehr had begun to develop in both anti-Socialist camps, especially among the moderate German-nationalists who finally broke over this issue with the proclerical conservatives.

From September 1930 till after the elections of 9 November 1930, the Heimwehr participated in a minority coalition with the proclerical conservative Christlichsoziale Partei against the opposition of the moderate German nationalists and the Socialists. The Heimwehr participated in the election under the designation *Heimatblock,* while some of its units in Vienna and Lower Austria fused with proclerical conservatives to form the ticket "Christlichsoziale Partei und Heimwehr." The Heimatblock polled 6 percent of the total Austrian vote and elected 8 of Austria's 165 members of Parliament. Soon after the elections its ministers resigned from the government. It is characteristic of the fissions within the Heimwehr that its ministers in that short-lived coalition regime were to go different ways. Prince Ruediger von

Starhemberg, vice-chancellor and minister of the interior, was to become once more vice-chancellor in the authoritarian regime of Dollfuss in 1934 and had to go into exile when Austria became part of Hitler's Third Reich in 1938. Franz Hueber, brother-in-law of Herman Goering, and minister of justice in the coalition government from September until November 1930, became once more minister of justice on 11 March 1939, when the National Socialists took over Austria, and he then flourished with the Third Reich.

Soon after the elections of November 1930 the Heimwehr began to disintegrate. For a while its leaders continued to threaten that they would emulate Mussolini's March on Rome with a similar march on Vienna, but their increasing isolation from the moderates in both anti-Socialist camps rendered them ineffective. In the meantime, the ranks of the Heimwehr dwindled with the emergence of Hitlerism as a major political force in Austria. The disintegration of the Heimwehr in the spring and summer of 1931 accounts for the phenomenon that democratic politics in Austria actually took a new lease on life even while Austria's economic situation deteriorated. To be sure, the Heimwehr succeeded in making headlines when some of its units staged an uprising in upper Styria the Sunday of 13 September 1931 and in a revolutionary declaration announced the impending march on Vienna and a Fascist takeover. The government forces were very slow in moving against the rebels, but when two unarmed Socialist workers were shot in one of the industrial towns in the disaffected area the Socialist party presented the government with an ultimatum demanding the immediate suppression of the rebellion lest the Socialist party deploy its own armed units. Thereupon the rebels surrendered to the government forces without a further shot being fired, and the leaders of the rebellion were all acquitted in jury trials three months later. When soon after the Styrian Heimwehr and the leaders of this comic-opera rebellion went over to Hitler's National Socialists, the brief respite granted to democratic politices by the disintegration of the Heimwehr came to an end.

Radicalization and polarization did not follow a straight line at all but proceeded in a complex zigzag of a kind easily overlooked in summary historical accounts. Our purpose here will be to throw these patterns into bold relief as an antidote to the mechanistic determinism that presents past developments quite mistakenly as having been inevitable.

Economic Distress

The precarious state of the economy was a source of discontent and unrest that occasioned and compounded political strife throughout the history of the First Republic of Austria. It is, however, of consequence that political tensions did not parallel economic distress. The economic situation affected the political but it did not determine it.

The postwar inflation that reduced the currency to one fifteen-thousandth of its original value wiped out savings, retirement plans, and insurance policies. At the same time, the transfer of German-speaking civil servants and teachers from formerly Austrian parts of the defunct empire to the territory of the Republic, especially to Vienna, deprived the middle class—robbed of their savings by the inflation—of opportunities for employment as well. Thus the members of the older generation faced poverty upon retirement and the members of the young generation found it difficult to get work.

In 1926 the government suspended the acceptance of new candidates for the judiciary and for administrative positions, thereby blocking access to careers that had previously absorbed about two-thirds of all law graduates.[33] The depression worsened the employment prospects for university graduates considerably, and detailed statistics show that from 1930 to 1934 students leaving the Austrian universities and faculties with final degrees outnumbered retiring practitioners several times over in the professions of law and medicine.[34] The same source states that

no detailed statistics could be obtained on the situation amongst arts and science graduates. All observers agree, however, that it is tragic. . . . In so far as these faculties prepare primarily for the teaching profession their graduates are suffering acutely from the economy measures affecting schools . . . even for the year 1932 . . . there were no openings for teachers of mathematics, physics, and modern languages. The combination of economy measures and of an increasing number of students with a degree seeking employment has made the teaching profession one of the most overcrowded of all careers.[35]

The economic condition of Austrian labor was also distressing. From the stabilization of the currency in 1922 until the beginning of the depression in 1929 the proportion of unemployed continued to hover at the 10 percent level.[36] The percentage of unemployed workers then went from 12.3 percent in 1929 to 15.0 percent in 1930, to 20.3 percent in 1931, to 26.1 percent in 1932, and 29.0 percent in 1933.[37] The production index of 1932 was 60 percent of 1929 levels.[38] During the same years the number of suicides in Austria increased from 2,434 in 1929 to 2,605 in 1930, to 2,775 in 1931, and to 3,972 in 1932.[39]

The increasing unemployment hit the young especially hard. Here we have no reliable statistics because those figures we have were compiled from the rosters of employment, from labor exchanges, and from insurance rolls. It is, however, a matter of record that apprenticeships for teenagers became virtually nonexistent, while the completion of apprenticeships frequently led to the dead-end of permanent unemployment. Graduates from schools that prepared students for entry into colleges and universities received upon graduation letters of congratulation from the various professional societies with the advice not to prepare for entry into their respective professions because these were already hopelessly overcrowded. In the meantime, bankruptcies of business establishments and the failures of banks and insurance companies often wiped out modest savings that had been accumulated since the stabilization of the currency after the inflation.

The Brief Respite

The initial effect of the world depression on Austrian politics was a temporary relaxation of tensions. Though it was followed by greatly heightened political tensions, this short hiatus in political strife should warn scholars against excessive reliance upon economic determinism. In the dramatic course of Austrian history crucial choice points have been overlooked because these were marked by a short interval of undramatic relaxation of tensions. This is understandable because the relaxation was necessarily undramatic. Also, a brief interval of genuine cooperation between the major parties bore fruit of enduring value. This suggests that an experiment in closer continuing cooperation between the major parties, proposed by the leader of one of them, might have changed the course of events that ultimately led to the breakdown of democratic politics.

The relaxation of tensions and the increased vitality of democratic politics hardly appears in those chronicles that fail to go below the surface. Violent clashes continued with no real letup while Fascist militancy became, if anything, more strident.

In the meantime, the right-wing extremists were temporarily paralyzed by internal dissensions. The economic crisis continued to worsen. An effort to rally the moderates of all three camps to establish a coalition government failed, and the two antagonistic extreme antidemocratic right-wing movements that emerged from the schism were to triumph in succession, one under the sponsorship of Fascist Italy and the other as vanguard of National Socialist Germany. Yet there was an instance of cooperation between the three camps that demonstrated their prevalent commitment to democratic politics, a commitment that was endorsed effectively by the voters at the polls.

The revision of the constitution. The outcome of the struggle over revising the constitution is testimony to the vitality of democratic politics in the First Republic of Austria.

In 1929 latent civil war, marked by intermittent armed clashes, threatened to erupt into open civil war over the issue of constitutional reform. Initially, spokesmen of the extreme Right enjoyed the support of the entire anti-Socialist camp for their proposed revisions, which were designed to undercut the position of Vienna as autonomous federal province and to undermine the

Socialist position in numerous other ways. But with well over one-third of the seats in Parliament, the Socialists were in a position to veto changes in the constitution by constitutional means. The Heimwehr and its allies hoped to circumvent Socialist parliamentary veto power by submitting the proposed constitutional changes to a popular referendum. The Socialists made it clear that they would meet with force any attempt to impose constitutional reform by such unconstitutional means as a popular referendum.

Johann Schober, leader of the two moderate German-nationalist parties that were to fuse temporarily under his leadership, who was at that time federal chancellor of the Republic of Austria, also opposed the referendum as unconstitutional. Thanks to his good offices, leaders from the moderate factions of all three camps, the Socialists included, succeeded in working out a revision of the constitution that was acceptable to all parties represented in the Austrian Parliament at that time.

It is significant that the constitution enacted by the representatives of all three political camps in 1929 was reenacted in 1945 as the constitution of the Second Republic of Austria and has been in force since then except for constitutionally enacted amendments. The successful constitutional reform of 1929 certainly indicates that cooperation between the three political camps was possible in spite of the tensions between them. The endurance of this constitution as basic law of the Second Republic of Austria testifies to the political acumen of the leadership of the three political camps during the time of the strife-torn First Republic. The men who represented their parties in working out the constitutional reform do not stand out in history. Their names have been overshadowed by those associated with more dramatic developments and events. Their work did not endure at that time even though it had received the overwhelming endorsement of the Austrian electorate.

The elections of 9 November 1930. The results of the elections held on 9 November 1930 appeared to have revivified democratic politics. The outcome certainly did not suggest that these were to be the last free nationwide elections in Austria for many years to come. Endorsed by the electorate were, above all else, the constitutional reform enacted in the preceding year and beyond that, the regime that had prevailed from November 1920 until September 1930 when the proclerical conservatives accepted the Heimwehr as coalition partner in place of the moderate German nationalists.

Throughout the twenties the German nationalist moderates had worked closely with the proclerical conservatives to contain the Socialists, to oppose Socialist economic programs, and to advance a conservative economic policy that involved the solicitation and acceptance of foreign loans, high protective tariffs, a turnover (or sales) tax on consumer goods, measures to cut the costs of welfare programs, and, as far as possible, a balanced budget and a sound currency. The anti-Socialist camps considered the Socialist economic policies in Vienna to be a program of taxing the rich in order to finance extensive low-cost public housing of good quality, a generous welfare program, and other features that made the autonomous province of Vienna into a miniature welfare state. Also, the anti-Socialist camps opposed the Socialists' legal support of the union shop or the "closed shop" that favored unionization. Furthermore, the Socialists backed legislation to protect the working conditions of those employees who, because of their comparative isolation, lacked real bargaining power, e.g., domestic servants, apprentices and journeymen in small shops and stores, and labor in agriculture and forestry. Here the Socialists encountered the opposition of numerous small-scale employers who provided the backbone of the anti-Socialist parties. The issue of rent controls stirred similar opposition from landlords. These differences regarding economic policies motivated formation of fusion tickets between proclerical conservatives and anticlerical German nationalists but they did not undermine democratic politics as such unless the conflicting parties undergirded their positions in ideological terms.

The enduring class character of the lineup of political forces in the First Republic is reflected by the relatively unchanging composition of the parliaments elected by the Austrian votes in five elections (as tabulated in table 1). These parliaments reflect the popular vote fairly well since they were elected by a system of proportional representation that gave slight advantages to the larger parties.

Thus, in November 1930 the three major parties elected 157 out of 165 members of Parliament and received 90 percent of the votes cast in an election in which over 90 percent of those entitled to vote actually cast their ballots.

Table 1. Composition of the Parliament of the Republic of Austria

Year	Socialist	Proclerical Conservative	Moderate German- Nationalist	Other	Total
1919[a]	72	69	26	3[b]	170
1920	69	85	28	1[c]	183
1923	68	82	15	—	165
1927	71	73[d]	21[d]	—	165
1930	72	66	19[e]	8[f]	165

[a]Without the Burgenland ceded by Hungary in 1920.
[b]One Liberal, one Zionist, and one Czechoslovakian.
[c]One Liberal.
[d]In 1927 the anti-Marxist fusion ticket of Die Einheitsliste elected seventy-three proclerical conservatives of the Christlichsoziale Partei and twelve members of the pan-German Grossdeutsche Volkspartei, while the agrarian Landbund elected nine moderate German-nationalists.
[e]Nationaler Wirtschaftsblock und Landbund—Fuehrung Dr. Schober, the fusion ticket of the Landbund and Grossdeutsche Volkspartei.
[f]The (Fascist) Heimatblock, ticket of the Heimwehr.

These three parties had founded the Republic in 1918 and had recently reaffirmed their joint commitment to ethics of constitutional means and democratic politics by their cooperation in revising the constitution. The Socialists had held on to 42 percent of the vote and had increased their representation in Parliament from 71 to 72. The fusion ticket had likewise done well with 12 percent of the votes cast and the election of 19 members of Parliament. Only the proclerical conservative party had suffered significant losses, and with 36 percent of the vote and 66 seats in Parliament it had become the second strongest party.

Among the avowed enemies of parliamentary democracy the Communists had received about twenty-thousand votes or barely 0.5 percent, in contrast with the 13 percent of the vote polled by the Communist party in Germany two months earlier. The Austrian branch of Hitler's National Socialist party polled slightly over one hundred thousand or not quite 3 percent of the votes cast and likewise remained without representation in Parliament. The Heimatblock polled slightly over two hundred thousand votes, or about 6 percent of the votes cast, and elected 8 members of Parliament, whereupon its ministers resigned from the government in which they had served for just over two months. Soon after the elections the Heimwehr and its political agent, the Heimatblock, began to disintegrate. Even its 8 representatives in Parliament separated and went off in different directions.

The proposed all-party coalition. The establishment of a Fascist party with its own electoral ticket strengthened democratic politics even before that party disintegrated because the defection of the Fascists from the established parties strengthened the moderate wings in both anti-Socialist camps. Then the disintegration of the paramilitary Fascist Heimwehr and its party, the Heimatblock, relaxed tensions further.

Msgr. Seipel, leader of the Christlichsoziale Partei, who had already been chancellor for nearly half of the Republic's brief existence, intended to use the respite to bring together all the forces that wanted to preserve democratic politics. He invited the Socialists and both moderate German nationalist parties to form a national coalition that could cope with the crisis. Though himself once an implacable foe of the Socialists and a sponsor of the Heimwehr, Seipel in the spring of 1931 no longer feared the Austrian Socialists and their version of Marxism. It is probable that he had begun to appreciate that the Socialists employed their radical oratory primarily for the benefit of potential left-wing defectors while their policies sustained democratic politics. Also, Seipel was becoming disenchanted with capitalism. In this vein he stated in June 1931 that he had hoped at one time that reliance upon international capitalism would rehabilitate the political and economic conditions in Central Europe sufficiently to facilitate resistance against the threat of communism. Seipel acknowledged this to have been an error and felt that a position was called for from which communism and capitalism could be opposed simultaneously.[40] This change of heart, occasioned by the collapse of the capitalist economy, contributed to Seipel's readiness to welcome the Socialists as a coalition partner.

It was obviously clear to Seipel that the lull in tensions resulting from the disintegration of the Heimwehr was not going to last. The economic crisis worsened all over the world and made itself felt in Austria with disastrous results.[41] Those looking for work were nearly as numerous as those able to hold on to their jobs, and in many small industrial towns the whole labor force was out of work with no prospect of employment in sight. The plight of the young, who had nothing to look forward to but protracted unemployment, became a particular source of serious unrest and an explosive threat to democratic politics. Many young people lost hope and became apathetic. Others swelled the ranks of militant extremist organizations, who offered them a sense of belonging, a source of self-respect, and hope for a better future.

In addition, Austrian politics had previously been affected by developments in Germany, and there democratic politics collapsed under the tidal wave of extremism. The vote of Hitler's party had grown from 800,000 or 2.6 percent of the total in May 1928 to 6.4 million or 18 percent in September 1930. Elections held in several German states and municipalities in the spring of 1931 left no doubt that the National Socialist party had become the strongest in Germany. In one legislative body after another democratic politics broke down when the antidemocratic parties rallied majorities. The National Socialists and the Communists were not able to work together, but their majorities kept democratic institutions from functioning.

The two moderate German-nationalist parties, at that time still united under the leadership of Johann Schober, were prepared to join an all-inclusive coalition. They shared with the proclerical conservatives the conviction that only a broad coalition of all parliamentary parties committed to democratic politics could hope to cope with the mounting crisis and its political consequences.

The Socialists refused to accept Seipel's invitation to enter a coalition government. This refusal appears as the one deliberate step at a clearly identifiable turning point in Austrian history; and that refusal as well as other Socialist policies in the fateful years 1931 and 1932 deserve a great deal more attention than they have so far received—especially in view of the tangible alternatives and fatal consequences.

The significance of the motives behind the Socialist rejection of the coalition offer transcends the scope of our study of Austrian politics because these motives also bear upon the relations between moderate and radical wings within organizations and political parties in general. It seems that the motive of preserving unity of the ranks as an end in itself often inspires radical oratory that may well impede cooperation with political opponents even when such cooperation would be in the best interests of the moderates of both antagonistic camps. The Socialists refused to participate in the coalition in order to preserve the cherished unity of their party. This action facilitated the takeover of political initiative by the extremists in the other two camps as well.

At the subsequent annual congress of the Austrian Socialist party the decision was explained in terms of Austromarxist theory:

Comrades, I have to warn against taking this path [that of entering a coalition government] no less emphatically than against the other of attempting a revolutionary coup.

The mere entry of several Socialists into a government, such as Dr. Seipel had in mind when he made us this offer a few months ago after the fall of the cabinet Ender, changes nothing in the power relationships between the classes.

We would encounter in the government the same resistance, the same bourgeois sabotage, that we now encounter in Parliament.

No, comrades, the mere entry of Socialists into the government at this time in which the disintegration of the capitalist system is approaching would bring us into great peril; in this government we would just have *to participate in administering the affairs of collapsing capitalism* [italics in original text to indicate enthusiastic applause from the delegates] and we would be in no position to really serve the interests of the working class and the ideals of socialism.[42]

It is obvious that the Socialists were motivated by their fear that entry into a coalition government would split their ranks and jeopardize the Austromarxist unity that meant so much to them. This preoccupation with unity is discussed by an American academic observer who may be considered the principal apologist of Austromarxist policies, Charles A. Gulick. In his defense of the Socialist rejection of Seipel's invitation, Gulick states explicitly that participation in unavoidable economy measures would have compromised the party before the electorate and "perhaps even split their party."[43]

The refusal of the Socialists to join a coalition government on the basis of Socialist principles appears in an odd light in view of the success of the Socialist-conservative coalition that governed the Second Republic of Austria from 1945 until 1966 under the Constitution of 1929, a constitution that itself had been conceived and enacted by a coalition effort accomplished by the Socialists with the parties of the two other camps.[44]

Austrians of all three political camps are now burdened with an *unbewaeltigte Vergangenheit,* a past they cannot cope with. Austrian Socialist historians and historians sympathetic to Austrian Socialism simply ignore the matter of the rejected offer.[45] This omission makes it possible to free the Socialists of even a small share of responsibility for the breakdown of democratic politics in Austria and places the whole burden upon the record of the conservatives.[46]

It is probably true that Socialist participation in a coalition government would have split the ranks of the party because this would have led to the breakaway of radical left-wingers, especially among the young. The other coalition partners would undoubtedly have been confronted by protests from the extremists within their respective camps. Developments would ultimately have depended upon the capacity of such a coalition government to cope with the economic crisis.

This is not the place to speculate on the unorthodox economic measures Seipel's all-party coalition regime might have undertaken to cope with the impact of the world-wide depression upon Austria and what measures the Socialist ministers might have sponsored. (It is, after all, probable that such a regime would have had the means for unorthodox economic measures, since its stability would have assured it access to credits in Western countries.) This is, however, the place to take a critical view of the Socialist quest for unity between moderates and extremists as an end in itself. The implications of such a quest are of consequence for political moderates everywhere.

It is, of course, impossible to predict to what extent Socialist participation in such a coalition government might have compromised the Socialists with their voters, as Gulick fears that it might have. We know for certain, however, that the young radicals who would have gone over to the Communists would undoubtedly have come back. This we may assert with a high degree of assurance because Socialists who went over to the outlawed Communist party after their own party had been outlawed did not accept the tutelage of the Kremlin for long, having become accustomed to thinking for themselves and to speaking their minds freely in the best tradition of Austromarxism and democratic socialism. In the words of Otto Bauer:

. . . comrades attracted by the revolutionary character [of the Communist party] re-fused to forgo the right to think critically and to criticize the Soviet Union and the party line. . . . they were soon repelled by the Communist party and attracted to the revolutionary Socialists. [Under the impact of civil war, dictatorship and suppression the Austrian Socialists who refused to become Communists called their underground organization "Revolutionaere Sozialisten."][47]

The acceptance of unity as an end in itself, long characteristic of Austrian socialism, was articulated effectively by Otto Bauer at the annual congress of the Socialist party in Linz in 1926: "A hundred times better to go the wrong way united . . . for mistakes can be corrected, than to split for the sake of the right way!"[48] This pronouncement, received with thunderous applause by the delegates, was quoted again and again in order to inveigh against the feared schism between the Left and the Right that had immobilized Socialist labor in so many countries, especially in Italy and in Germany. Thus the Austromarx-ists appear to have pursued what they sensed to be the wrong way in the expectation that mistakes in policy could be corrected with greater facility than rifts in the unity of their party.

A coalition of the three parties would have brought together the moderates of all three camps and would have rallied them against the extremists of all three camps in a joint undertaking to preserve democratic politics. When the great coalition failed to materialize, a realignment of political forces led to a new constellation that left Austrian politics split into three hostile camps, each irreconcilably antagonistic toward the other two. This development rendered democratic politics in Austria unworkable.

The realignment of political forces. It was to be expected that the growth of Hitler's National Socialist party in Germany would enhance the appeal of his party in Austria. The political composition of the Austrian electorate suggested, however, that the potential for growth was much smaller for Hitler's party in Austria than it had been in Germany. The increase in National Socialist votes in Germany had come primarily from former supporters of Protestant agrarian and middle-class parties and from former nonvoters.[49] In Germany, the total vote of the two Marxist parties and the total vote of the two proclerical Roman Catholic parties had actually increased while the National Socialist vote increased from 0.8 million in May 1928 to 6.4 million in September 1930 and to 13.7 million in 1932. In Austria voter participation had always been at the 90 percent level, compared to the 70 percent level in Germany. Thus Austria did not possess a sizable reservoir of nonvoters. Also, in Austria the proclerical conservatives shared with the Socialist Austromarxists over 80 percent of the votes cast. Considering how well the proclerical parties and the Marxist parties had been able to hold their own in Germany, this too indicated that the potential for growth was smaller for the Austrian National Socialists than it had been for their counterparts in Germany. The provincial and municipal elections held in most of Austria from the country's last parliamentary elections in November 1930 to the last municipal elections in April 1933 left, however, no doubt that Hitler's party had become a mass party in Austria as well.

The provincial and municipal elections in Austria in 1931, 1932, and the spring of 1933 do not provide us with a complete picture of party strength at any one time for the country as a whole. Yet these elections, held at different times in different places, do provide a fairly reliable picture of the changes in the political alignment of the electorate.

There was, first of all, a steep drop in voter participation immediately after the national elections of 9 November 1930. All parties represented in the Austrian Parliament suffered losses. Losses by the two major parties, the Socialists and the proclerical conservatives, tended to be minor compared to those of the moderate German nationalist Grossdeutsche Volkspartei and of the Fascist Heimwehr. At first Hitler's National Socialists registered only minor gains, but later, in the fall of 1931, throughout 1932, and in the spring of 1933, voting participation recovered and went even beyond the 90 percent level, and they became Austria's major third party. They not only attracted the defectors from the Fascist Heimwehr and from the two moderate German-nationalist parties but they also took votes away from the two major parties.

The municipal elections held in Innsbruck in May 1931 and April 1933 reflect this trend with concrete precision: voting participation went from 91 percent in November 1930 to a record low of 75 percent in 1931 and then to an all-time high of 93 percent in 1933, while the National Socialist vote rose from 794 votes to 1,196 and then to 14,996. In the same elections the moderate German-nationalist vote dropped from 9,742 to 5,063 to 828. The results of the Innsbruck elections in 1930, 1931, and 1933 (see table 2) show clearly that the bulk of the new National Socialist voters were not defectors from their former parties to Hitler. Their losses had rather increased the nonvoters.

Of special interest are the elections held in Klagenfurt, capital of Carinthia, in 1931 and the subequent mayoral elections by the city council. The latter provide a revealing instance of collaboration between the Socialists and the proclerical conservatives. Incidentally, Klagenfurt already had a strong Austrian pre-Hitler National Socialist party that was absorbed by Hitler's party when the Austrian branch was set up (see table 2). The city council elected on 8 February 1931 became deadlocked when the Socialist, conservative, and National Socialist councillors could not summon the needed majority for a mayoral candidate. In the municipal elections of 31 May 1931 the National Socialists emerged as the second strongest party in the city council, overtaking the proclerical conservatives by additional gains primarily from the disintegrating Fascist party. It is of historical interest and of some significance for our discussion that the city councillors of the conservative Christlichsoziale Partei then helped elect the candidate of the Socialist party as mayor of

Table 2. Election Data for Upper Austria, Klagenfurt, and Innsbruck

	Upper Austria		Klagenfurt			Innsbruck		
	9 Nov. 1930 [a]	19 Apr. 1931 [b]	9 Nov. 1930	8 Feb. 1931	31 May 1931	9 Nov. 1930	17 May 1931	23 Apr. 1933
Socialist	134	128	5.1	4.1	4.5	13.4	12.0	9.9
Proclerical conservative	218	240	3.6	3.5	3.5	8.1	9.9	9.4
Fascist	40	19	1.3	1.5[c]	—	3.5	—	0.8
Moderate German-nationalist	72	51	3.7	1.7	1.9[d]	9.7	5.1	0.8
Nazi	12	16	1.9	3.0	3.7	0.8	1.2	15.0
Communist	2.2	3.7	0.2	0.4	0.4	0.1	0.4	0.5
Frauenpartei	—	—	—	—	—	—	0.742	—
Other	—	—	—	—	0.2[e]	—	—	—
Total votes cast (in thousands)	478	458	15.8	14.3	14.3	35.7	30.1	36.8

[a]National elections.
[b]Diet elections.
[c]Fusion of Fascists and a minor party.
[d]Fusion of moderate German-nationalists and a minor party.
[e]Splinter group, apparently Fascist.

Klagenfurt. It is noteworthy that the proclerical conservatives, when compelled to choose between a Socialist and a National Socialist, preferred a Socialist. Therefore, the mayoral elections in Klagenfurt support the view that Seipel's invitation to the Socialists to join a coalition had been made in good faith.

The revealing "moment of truth" in the rising tide of national socialism in Austria came with the provincial and municipal elections held in about three-fourths of Austria on 24 April 1932. These elections showed that Hitler's party had absorbed over 90 percent of the vote of the predominantly urban moderate German-nationalist Grossdeutsche Volkspartei, most of the urban vote and a large part of the rural vote of the Fascist Heimwehr, a large part of the agrarian and moderate German-nationalist Landbund, as well as votes from the two major parties. The elections held in the early part of 1931 had all shown a steep drop in voter participation. In the elections of 24 April 1932 voter participation had nearly returned to November 1930 levels. In the latter part of 1932 and in the spring of 1933 voter participation reached a record high.

On 24 April 1932 Austrians cast their votes in elections in Vienna, Lower Austria, Styria, Carinthia, and Salzburg. Cited here are merely the results of the elections in Vienna, where the National Socialist vote increased from 27,000, or not quite 3 percent of the votes cast in November 1930, to 201,000, or about 18 percent, while the number of votes cast was 35,000, or 3 percent below 1930 levels. The bulk of the National Socialist gain came from the Heimatblock, which had received 26,000 votes in 1930 and did not put up a ticket in 1932, and from the German-nationalists, who had polled 124,000 votes in 1930 as part of Schober's fusion ticket and who now polled 8,000 votes as the Grossdeutsche Volkspartei. The Socialists held their own fairly well, their vote dropping from 700,000 to 680,000, while the Communist vote increased from 10,000 to about 20,000. The decline of the proclerical conservative Christlichsoziale Partei from 283,000 to 234,000 accounts for the remainder of the increase of the vote of Hitler's party in Vienna. It is noteworthy that in Vienna as a whole, as well as in twenty of Vienna's twenty-one districts, the National Socialist vote of April 1932 may be figured directly from the election data of November 1930 by adding the 1930 vote of the National Socialist party to the vote then polled by the Heimatblock and by Schober's German-nationalist fusion ticket plus 15 to 20 percent of the vote polled in 1930 by the Christlichsoziale Partei. The only exception to this is the first district of Vienna, where the National Socialist vote in April 1932 remained below what Schober's German-nationalist fusion ticket had polled in November 1930. It appears that in 1930 the latter, endorsed by the liberal *Neue Freie Presse,* had obtained the vote of the Jewish bourgeoisie. Over nine-tenths of Schober's other voters went over to Hitler.

In Austria, unlike Germany, the National Socialists also took votes away from the Socialists and from the proclerical conservatives. These two suffered losses only where they had been weak all along and did well in their own strongholds. Thus the Socialists held their own in Vienna and in the industrial centers and suffered heavy losses in the Tyrol, Vorarlberg, and Salzburg, while the conservatives held firm in the countryside where they had always been dominant but suffered heavy losses in Vienna, industrial towns, provincial capitals, and county seats where they had always been weak. This attraction of Hitler's party for former nonvoters and voters of minor parties suggests that the mass vote of Hitler's party constituted a nonspecific expression of protest rather than a commitment to a program or an ideology.[50] This, in turn, lends support to our thesis that the breakdown of democratic politics in the First Republic of Austria was not at all inevitable.

The lack of firm ideological commitment among the bulk of National Socialist voters is also confirmed by the instability of the vote in the party's strongholds even while Hitler's party increased its vote by leaps and bounds all over the country. Of the nine communities in which the National Socialists had polled more than 20 percent in 1927 (when the National Socialist vote in all of Austria reached a bare 0.8 percent under the designation *Voelkisch-sozialer Block*), there were four in which they polled less than 10 percent in 1932 when National Socialist voting strength in local elections in most of Austria exceeded 20 percent.[51] Thus Hitler's party was losing votes in established strongholds even while his party experienced election victories all over the country hardly equaled in elections anywhere.

This is not the place to devote a great deal more space to election results, but as a curiosity of some importance the vote in the military barracks of Vienna on 24 April 1932 is worthy of note: here the Christlichsoziale Partei polled 2,043 votes, the Socialists 1,705 votes, and Hitler's National Socialist party 1,860 votes.[52] It should be added that the peace treaty of Saint-Germain permitted Austria a volunteer army of thirty thousand men. In 1919–20 a Socialist minister had done his best to fill the ranks of this army with Socialists; later the proclerical conservative minister of the army did his best to recruit men of his own party. The vote in Vienna's military barracks indicated that the minister had been fairly successful in ridding the army of Socialists, but the high proportion of Hitlerites was probably a bequest from the period during which the anti-Socialist paramilitary organizations had rallied German-nationalists and proclerical conservatives indiscriminately.

The elections held on 24 April 1932 in Vienna, Lower Austria, Styria, Carinthia, and Salzburg left no doubt that the Parliament elected on 9 November 1930 no longer represented the political alignment of the voters. The results of these elections as well as of previous local elections suggested that new elections would return the Socialists with somewhat less than 40 percent of the vote, the proclerical conservatives with about 30 to 35 percent, and the agrarian Landbund with about 5 percent. The National Socialists were bound to poll well over 20 percent of the vote.

In response to the elections results the Socialists demanded the dissolution of the Parliament and election of a new one that would represent the voters.[53] Their demand was accompanied by indications that the Socialists would not consider entering a coalition government. In the words of Otto Bauer:

What matters most, however, is that we take into account in all political decisions and considerations the novelty of the situation. The petty bourgeoisie and the proletarian masses which had been following the old bourgeois parties are in motion, stirred by the crisis of capitalism. They may fall for the lures of fascism. They may be won over to us.

If we appear to the masses as co-partner and as sharing the blame [for the state of affairs] of the bourgeois world, then we shall merely push them to fascism and thereby strengthen the Fascist danger. The more resolutely we give expression to the mood of rebellion which has taken over the masses, the more sharply we differentiate ourselves from the capitalist world, the more resolutely we fight against capitalism, its government, its parties, its whole economic, political, and ideological system, the more resolutely we show the masses the great aim of Socialist revolution as a goal to fight for, the greater the part of the masses now in motion we shall attract.[54]

It is very difficult to infer from Socialist pronouncements what developments the Socialists anticipated or hoped for. They refused to indicate what they themselves might do in a Parliament in which none of the parties held a majority. It seems that they hoped to compel the National Socialists and the proclerical conservatives to form a poorly integrated coalition regime so that they might then attract defectors from both of these antagonistic camps after the inevitable failure of their government to cope with the crisis of capitalism. But this is mere inference. We have no Socialist pronouncements on what was to happen in a Parliament that reflected the three-way split that divided Austria's electorate at that time.

The realignment of voters soon affected Parliament even without new elections. The representative of one wing of Schober's moderate German-nationalist fusion ticket, the Grossdeutsche Volkspartei, went into opposition after refusing to support ratification of the Loan of Lausanne, a loan that was to commit Austria to pledge once again that no attempt would be made to move in the direction of union with Germany for another twenty-five years. With this intransigent stand the moderate pan-German members of Parliament narrowed the gap between themselves and the National Socialists to whom their voters had already defected.

The agrarian Landbund, however, remained in the coalition government and compromised its German-nationalist commitment by endorsing ratification of the loan. Inasmuch as the Socialists were adamant in their opposition to ratification of the loan, the defection of the Grossdeutsche Volkspartei left the government without a majority in Parliament. The government considered ratification of the agreement to obtain this loan essential for Austria's economy.

By that time, the summer of 1932, the Heimwehr had disintegrated altogether. Nearly all of their urban voters and many of their rural voters had gone over to Hitler's National Socialists, and many of their paramilitary units had joined the SA or the SS, the paramilitary organizations of Hitler's party. The eight members of Parliament elected on the Fascist ticket likewise failed to stay together. Only three of them went over to Hitler, but the remaining five, who had next to no following among the voters, were to play a decisive role in the breakdown of democratic politics in Austria. It mattered little that they had no followers among the electorate as long as they held the balance of power in Parliament. Only with their support was the proclerical conservative party able to forestall the quest for new elections demanded by Hitler's National Socialists in the streets and backed in Parliament by the Socialists, the pan-Germans, and the three Fascists who had gone over to the National Socialists. They were also badly needed to provide the parliamentary majority for the ratification of the Loan of Lausanne. As the price for their support the Fascists exacted the Ministry of Interior, which controlled the state executive, including the federal police of Vienna, and the ministry of commerce.

Even with the support of the five Fascists, the new government, formed in May 1932, was in a precarious position because of its small margin. Time and again the government was saved from disaster because accidental death or illnesses among members of Parliament resulted in providential tied votes or in one-vote majorities needed to save the regime. The Loan of Lausanne, for instance, was ratified on the basis of a one-vote margin that came about because a fatally ill supporter of the government died in time to have his successor sworn in to cast his vote for the government while a member of the opposition fell ill at an opportune moment. Several votes of no confidence initiated by the Socialists, by pan-Germans, or by Fascists-turned-Hitlerites failed because of tied votes. In the meantime the economic depression worsened and local elections continued to register sizable gains for the National Socialists.

In the fall and winter of 1932 Hitler's party suffered serious setbacks in national and local elections in Germany, and it seemed for a short while that the German National Socialist party was on the verge of disintegration. Had Hitler's party in Germany actually fallen apart, his party in Austria would undoubtedly have fallen apart too, and Austrian democracy might have had another chance. When Hitler came to power in Germany on 30 January 1933 the fate of democratic politics in Austria was definitely sealed.

The final stage.   In the late twenties and early thirties democratic politics broke down in many European countries and were threatened in most others. The triumph of Hitler in Germany cast further doubt on the survival of democracy long before his armies crossed many European borders. This was especially true in Austria, where the victory of Hitler's National Socialist party in

Germany doomed democratic politics even while Hitler's effort to gain power in Austria at that time failed.

In the spring and summer of 1933 the Austrian Hitlerites made a concerted effort to take over political power by force with the moral and financial support of the new regime in Germany. In reprisal for the deportation of German National Socialist agitators, among them a minister of Bavaria, Germany imposed a travel ban designed to injure Austrian tourism, which depended upon German tourists and played a tremendous role in Austria's weak economy. At the same time the Austrian National Socialists engaged in sporadic but intensive terrorism, using explosives that caused extensive property damage as well as injury and death. Most of their attacks were directed at supporters of the government, some at randomly selected Jews. The practice of depositing explosives in telephone booths also inflicted injuries randomly among the general public. National Socialist terrorism reached its peak in June 1933 when Storm Troopers tossed hand grenades from a roof into a marching formation of Roman Catholic athletes. The government proclaimed martial law and reintroduced the death penalty, abolished in 1919, and thus ended the situation in which the terrorists had operated without fear of reprisals since they did not expect to serve the jail sentences handed down to them. In the spring and summer of 1933 the Austrian National Socialists had been certain of instant victory, but the reintroduction of the death penalty and the ban on their party caused terrorism to decline considerably. The outlawed party continued, however, to function underground, thanks to a hard core of enthusiastic and dedicated young people, predominantly students, and the backing of the German Reich.

Although the failure of the efforts of the Austrian National Socialists to take over the government in the spring of 1933 and the subsequent suppression of their party postponed by nearly five years the day on which Austria was to become a part of Hitler's Third Reich, democratic politics were doomed. None of the three camps commanded a majority of the voters, and the fissures between them had by that time become too deep to permit any cooperation. In all three camps the initiative was with the extremists, and efforts on the part of moderates to break down the barriers piling up between the camps were stymied. The constellation of political forces simply rendered democratic politics impossible.

In March 1933 an intramural crisis paralyzed the Austrian Parliament. During a vote taken by the members of Parliament a Socialist committed an error when he cast his ballot. In the ensuing altercation, the speaker of Parliament as well as the first and second deputy speakers resigned from their posts. The government chose to interpret this development as an indication that "Parliament had eliminated itself," since it was without a speaker. From then on the government legislated by emergency decree on the basis of a defunct wartime authority of dubious legality. Among the first of these emergency

decrees was the dissolution of the Republikanischer Schutzbund, the paramilitary organization of the Socialist party, followed by the outlawing of
the Communist party and, soon after, also of the National Socialist party.

The details of the issues involved in the dissolution and elimination of the
Austrian Parliament in March 1933 have been examined minutely by numerous chroniclers, but these details appear to be of little consequence in the
general scheme of things. It actually matters little whether Parliament had
eliminated itself by its own incompetence, as claimed by the government, or
whether it had been the victim of a diabolical Fascist intrigue, as claimed by
the Socialists. Nor does it really matter to what extent the government did or
did not act illegally when it began to legislate by emergency decree on the
basis of a provision promulgated during World War I. In historical perspective
the legality of this provision is largely irrelevant, since the political constellation of that period precluded any "democratic solution" of the crisis. Clearly,
the authority of the government to govern by emergency decree rested not
upon legal claims of dubious validity but upon brute power. The extreme
polarization in Austria's tripartite political alignments had, however, created a
power vacuum that invited authoritarian intervention.[55]

A few moderate conservatives continued their efforts to bring the moderates
from all three camps together, but they had next to no influence upon the
government. It had become a willing captive of the authoritarian and pro-
Fascist wing of the conservative proclerical camp, which had long admired
Mussolini's regime of law and order. The government soon endorsed the
program of the Heimwehr, which called for an "authoritarian" regime and
explicitly discounted parliamentary democracy and democratic politics.

The German-nationalist camp had become identified with national socialism a year before Hitler became chancellor of German; a handful of urban
pan-Germans remined faithful to the German republican colors and ideals
even after Hitler had come to power in Germany. Their refusal to accept
national socialism was, however, of no consequence whatever in the course of
events. We find in this group a few men of outstanding integrity, intellect, and
courage, but their number was very small.

Of some consequence was the moderate German nationalist agrarian
Landbund, which continued to rally a fair following in and around Protestant
farming communities to its German republican colors of black, red, and gold.
The Landbund had readily accepted the ratification of the Loan of Lausanne
despite its clause accepting Austria's imposed sovereignty, and its ministers
remained in the coalition goverment all through the spring and summer of
1933. The sincere dedication of the Landbund to democratic politics brought
it into conflict with the Heimwehr, represented in the government by the
minister of interior and the minister of commerce, which led to the resignation
of its ministers. Except for a brief spell of two months in the fall of 1930 the
Landbund had participated in every Austrian government for thirteen years.
The small but compact party had always been concerned primarily with agra-

rian interests. Its base of support had always been among a few Protestant farming communities but it also traditionally received a great deal of support from the surrounding Roman Catholic farmers. The Landbund in no way added to the drama of turbulent partisan conflict but appears to have contributed considerably to the effectiveness of Austria's democratic politics.[56] The withdrawal of the Landbund from the government in September 1933 marked a further step toward the total eclipse of democratic politics in Austria.

In the German-nationalist camp and in the proclerical conservative camp the developments in Germany in particular and the world-wide trend away from democratic politics in general put the extremist radicals in the ascendancy and inspired them with hopes for the immediate realization of their aspirations. In the Socialist camp both the extremist radicals and the moderates were in despair.

The impact of the catastrophe that had struck the German Socialists demoralized the Austrian Socialists, and in the new constellation of forces they were no longer able to hold their own. From 15 March 1933, the day Parliament was suspended, until 12 February 1934, when their party was outlawed and civil war broke out, the Socialist leadership tried desperately to contain government-sponsored aggression against the party and to restrain their followers from ill-considered action that had no chance of success. During that period the moderate leaders would probably have succeeded in convincing the Socialist party to accept almost any compromise with the conservatives, but the moderate proclerical conservatives were in no position to offer one, because they had lost all influence upon the course of events. The initiative in the proclerical conservative camp had passed beyond recall into the hands of the antidemocratic extremists who meant to put an end to democratic politics, to organized labor, and to the Socialist party in Austria.

The suspension of Parliament and the outlawing of the Republikanischer Schutzbund were followed by major infringements upon the constitutional rights of free speech, free press, and free assembly, which the Socialists had won in hard struggles before the turn of the century. The Fascist minister of the interior deputized members of his Heimwehr as auxiliary policemen and empowered them, as members of the executive forces of the state, to provoke and terrorize the Socialists.

In an effort to contain government terror and provocations within limits, and primarily to restrain radical youth who were spoiling to meet force with force, the Socialist leadership stipulated, at an extraordinary special convention in the fall of 1933, the conditions under which a call for a general strike, and with this a call to arms, was to be issued:

1. If the government imposed a Fascist constitution in violation of the constitution of the Republic;

2. If the government disposed of the constitutionally established and freely elected administration of the city and province of Vienna in order to install a government commissar;

3. If the government dissolved the Socialist party;
4. If the unions were dissolved or their administration taken over by a union sponsored by the government.[57]

The government refrained until February 1934 from taking any of the four steps that would have called forth massive Socialist resistance. They employed instead what has since become known as "salami tactics," a strategy designed to whittle down the position of the opposition in slices too small to motivate militant resistance. Specifically, the government forces went all out to raid Socialist stores of military equipment. The Socialist leadership could not bring itself to call for armed resistance over a few rifles and machine guns—which was the typical yield of such raids. Also, they continued to hope that moderation might yet prevail in the conservative camp because indications abounded that the majority of the conservative supporters were in favor of reconciliation with the Socialists. The leadership of proclerical industrial labor openly called for such cooperation in order to resore democratic politics and safeguard Austrian independence. Those in a position to determine policy preferred, however, to rely upon the guarantee of support from Fascist Italy, and under these circumstances they systematically undercut Socialist positions in order to prepare the ultimate blow. The Socialists were completely stymied by the fact that even a success against the Austrian Fascists would only bring them face to face with the National Socialists, who enjoyed the backing of Hitler's Germany. Furthermore, the forces of the government could count upon ample support from Italy and Hungary. The Socialists were fully aware of the hopelessness of their situation.

Unceasing provocations continued to goad the young Socialists into action, however, against the counsel of their leaders. Young Socialist spokesmen mocked their leaders with ironic references to the government arms raids that were slowly denuding the party of its secret arsenals: "Genossen, wir muessen mit geistigen Waffen kaempfen, denn andere werden wir bald keine mehr haben!"[58] Eager for action, they cited Karl Marx's dictum in reference to France after the collapse of the revolution of 1848: "Better an end with terror than a terror without end."

In the first week of February 1934 the Socialists suffered further humiliation when raiding parties of the Heimwehr, now deputized as auxiliary policemen, simply occupied and appropriated Socialist party headquarters in rural areas, where their party had always been weak. At the same time the homes and offices of Socialist leaders were subjected to extensive searches for hidden arms, and numerous Socialist leaders were placed under arrest.

On Monday 12 February 1934 a unit of the outlawed Republikanischer Schutzbund resisted on its own initiative a raid on the headquarters of the Socialist party in Linz, provincial capital of Upper Austria, which also had a sizable Socialist working-class population. Within a few hours, warfare spread spontaneously across the country and a general strike was called. The strike turned out to be fairly ineffective, but for several days the armed forces of the government, supported by paramilitary organizations of the government party, battled the Socialists in Vienna and numerous industrial towns throughout the country with tanks, artillery, and flamethrowers. The core of government strength was the volunteer army of about thirty thousand and the federal police force of six thousand in the city of Vienna. We only have rough estimates regarding the size of the paramilitary units involved.

Although the oppressive measures instituted by the Austrian dictatorship against the defeated Socialists appear comparatively mild when contrasted with those imposed by totalitarian dictatorship, the actions taken by the government fell far short of civilized standards of justice. The hangings of nine Socialists after summary court-martial proceedings have remained without moral or legal justification. Among the victims of the hanging courts was a member of Parliament who had returned to his constituency only after the fighting had broken out in order to be with his embattled constituents. Similarly unforgivable was the case of a man, injured in battle, who had to be carried to court on a stretcher and was carried to the gallows the same way. The evil memory of these nine hangings foreclosed any possibility of reconciliation between Austria's two major parties when Fascist Italy reneged on its pledge to preserve an independent Austria.

By September 1933 the proclerical conservative Christlichsoziale Partei had voluntarily dissolved itself in order to merge with the Fascist Heimwehr to constitute the Vaterlaendische Front. After the suppression of the Socialist party in February 1934 the Vaterlaendische Front became the party of the dictatorship. It should be noted that this party was itself pluralist in structure, since its constituent parts never completely surrendered their identities. Also, the regime itself became a great deal milder in its oppression of oppositional organizations and soon tolerated publications and organizations that expressed opposition views and rallied adherents of the two camps whose political activities had been suppressed by emergency decree. Numerous superficial observers of the Austrian scene, among them many Austrians, have long viewed the comparative tolerance of the Austrian dictatorship as a sign of weakness. The dictatorship was indeed weak, rent by inner dissensions, confronted by opposing camps that clearly numbered the majority of the population among their sympathizers, and increasingly hard pressed from across its borders. The internal pluralism of the political camp that supported the dictatorship and the dictatorship's tolerance for oppositional activities are, however, characteristic of authoritarian regimes in general.[59]

In July 1934 the Austrian National Socialists attempted an armed coup, but the dramatic occupation of the chancellery by 144 Storm Troopers wearing uniforms of the government executive (of which a fairly large number of the participants were indeed active members), while another troop of 14 men occupied the radio station, was thwarted. It then took the army and the paramilitary organizations of the government several days to suppress the fighting in the provinces. The Italian army massed units on the border, ready to march in case Germany should provide substantial support to the National Socialist rebels, who were getting a great deal of encouragement from the German broadcasting stations along the Austrian border.

Austria remained under an authoritarian dictatorship for another four years. Under comparatively mild police supervision the National Socialists, the Socialists, and the Communists were able to set up rather sizable underground organizations. Although the underground did not affect Austrian politics directly, it was able to infiltrate legal organizations that the government tolerated as "safety valves." The network of underground organizations that distributed illegal literature and held clandestine meetings during that period was probably as extensive as the network of organizations of all kinds that encompassed the lives of Austrians from the cradle to the grave during the First Republic of Austria while democratic politics prevailed.[60]

Throughout the mid-thirties the power and prestige of Hitler's Germany grew tremendously. Also, Mussolini's Fascist Italy moved closer and closer to Germany and eventually became the ally and junior partner of Hitler's powerful Third Reich. A conference between Hitler and the Austrian dictator, Chancellor Dr. Kurt von Schuschnigg, on 12 February 1938 in Berchtesgaden led to something of a false dawn. In compliance with Hitler's request, Schuschnigg took two Austrian members of Hitler's National Socialist party into the government and granted amnesty to the National Socialist prisoners. He went further, however, and pardoned all political prisoners—Socialists and Communists included—and took a man known for his Socialist affiliation into the government. For about two weeks it seemed that democratic politics were to be revived in Austria, but Schuschnigg's efforts to rally Austrians to the defense of the independence of their country came to nothing. The gestures toward the Socialists had come too late. Also, it did not help matters that Schuschnigg had been minister of justice in February 1934. Worst of all, reliance upon Mussolini's support had reduced Austria to a political pawn of Italian power that was now readily surrendered to Hitler.

On the evening of 9 March 1938 Schuschnigg, in a surprise move to thwart Hitler's aspirations and to legitimate Austrian independence, set the date for a plebiscite on Austrian independence for 13 March. A German ultimatum was followed by the triumphant entry of German troops, and to the frenzied cheers of Austria's German-nationalists, Austria became an integral part of Hitler's Third Reich.

Even though democratic politics broke down in the First Republic of Austria, the tradition of free debate and inquiry nourished by them did bear fruit. While a sizable proportion of Austrians had been enthusiastic supporters of Hitler's regime, resistance was a great deal stronger in Austria than in Germany. Among the thousands of Austrians who suffered under the National

Socialist regime because of their opposition to Hitler were Austrians from all three political camps. The success of democratic politics in the Second Republic of Austria is due to the accomplishments of democratic politics in the First Republic, as well as to the lessons learned from its collapse.

NOTES

1. Richard Charmatz, *Oesterreichs Innere Geschichte von 1848 bis 1907* (Leipzig: B. G. Teubner, 1911).
2. Robert A. Kann, *The Multinational Empire* (New York: Columbia University Press, 1950), vol. 1, pp. 95–108.
3. Adam Wandruszka, "Oesterreichische Politische Struktur," in *Geschichte der Republik Oesterreich,* ed. H. Benedikt (Vienna: Verlag fuer Geschichte und Politik, 1954), p. 291.
4. See, for example, Wilhelm Emanuel Ketteler, *Soziale Gerechtigkeit* (Munich: Deuerlein, 1950); August Maria Knoll, *Der Soziale Gedanke im Modernen Kapitalismus: Von der Romantik bis Rerum Novarum* (Vienna and Leipzig: Reinhold Verlag, 1932); idem, *Katholische Gesellschaftslehre: Zwischen Glaube und Wissenschaft* (Vienna, Frankfort, and Zurich: Europa Verlag, 1966); and idem, *Das Ringen um die Berufsständische Ordnung in Osterreich* (Vienna: Osterreichischer Heimatdienst, 1933). See also the references to Carl von Vogelsang in Friedrich Funder, "Vaterland," *Reichspost,* 11 February 1937; and E. Kogon, *Katholisch-Konservatives Erbgut* (Freiburg: I. Br., 1934).
5. Walter Goldinger, "Der Geschichtliche Ablauf der Ereignisse in Oesterreich," in Benedikt, *Geschichte.*
6. Walter B. Simon, "Politische Ethik und Politische Struktur," *Koelner Zeitschrift fuer Soziologie und Sozialpsychologie* 2, no. 3 (1959): 445–59.
7. Siegmund Schilder, *Der Streit um die Lebensfaehigkeit von Oesterreich* (Stuttgart: F. Enke, 1926).
8. Goldinger, "Der Geschichtliche Ablauf," p. 95.
9. To avoid the confusion of variant translations, the names of political parties will be retained in their original language except where there is a precise equivalent in English.
10. See Otto Bauer, *Acht Monate Auswaertige Politik* (Vienna: Brand, 1919); Friedrich Kleinwaechter and Heinz von Paller, *Die Anschlussfrage* (Vienna and Leipzig: Wilhelm Braumueller, 1929); and Anton Rintelen, *Erinnerungen an Oesterreichs Weg* (Munich: Verlag Brueckmann, 1941).
11. Ernst Winkler, *Die Oesterreichische Sozialdemokratie im Spiegel ihrer Programme* (Vienna: Verlag der wiener Volksbuchhandlung, 1964).
12. Ibid., p. 29.
13. Ibid.
14. Norbert Laser, *Begegnung und Auftrag: Beitraege zur Orientierung im zeitgenoessischen Sozialismus* (Vienna: Europa Verlag, 1963).
15. Winkler, *Die Oesterreichische Sozialdemokratie,* pp. 37–59.
16. Article 3, section III of the Program of Linz, ibid., p. 34–59.
17. Gus Hall, *Which Way U.S.A.? The Communist View* (New York: New Century Publishers, 1964), p. 10.
18. Ernst von Streeruwitz, *Springflut ueber Oesterreich* (Vienna and Leipzig: Wilhelm Braumueller Verlag, 1937), p. 213.
19. Otto Bauer, "Faschismus, Demokratie, und Sozialismus" (speech before the annual meeting of the Austrian Socialist party, Vienna, November 1932. *Protokoll des sozialdemokratischen Parteitags* (Vienna: Verlag der wiener Volksbuchhandlung, 1932), p. 34.
20. Otto Bauer, "Diktatur und Demokratie," in *Bolschewismus oder Sozialdemokratie* (Vienna: Verlag der wiener Volksbuchhandlung, 1920).

21. Otto Bauer, editorial in *Arbeiterzeitung*, 25 March 1934. This paper, a fortnightly, was published in Brno, Czechoslovakia, by the exiled leadership of the Socialist party and smuggled across the border in tens of thousands of copies for distribution by the party's underground network.

22. The party organization of the Socialists, with its mass membership, was revived after 1945 and persists to the present, further evidence of the high degree of mobilization in Austria's traditional three political camps even in the remarkably harmonious political climate of the Second Republic today.

23. Most of the Socialist leaders had severed their ties with the Catholic church and were officially registered as *konfessionslos*, i.e., without religious affiliation.

24. Friedrich Funder, *Von Gestern ins Heute* (Vienna: Verlag Herold, 1952).

25. Irmgard Baernthaler, "Geschichte der vaterlaendischen Front" (Ph.D. diss., Oesterreichisches Institut fuer Zeitgeschichte, Vienna, 1964).

26. Anton Staudinger, "Bemuehungen Carl Vaugoins um Suprematie der Christlichsozialen Partei" (Ph.D. diss., Oesterreichisches Institut fuer Zeitgeschichte, Vienna, 1969), pp. 172-82.

27. Franz Langoth, *Kampf um Oesterreich* (Wels: Welsetmuehl Verlag, 1951).

28. The German-nationalist camp remains today a most fluid and volatile force in Austrian politics. Nazi tendencies still exist side by side with traces of genuine liberalism. This camp also continues in its tendency to rally to leaders who appear as strong personalities without regard for their political views. Thus the German-nationalists rallied behind the moderate statesman and faithful civil servant Dr. Johann Schober in November 1930 only to go over to Hitler within seventeen months. After the war the "third camp" reached its peak in the Second Republic when it rallied the voters to its presidential candidate, Dr. Breitner, a former president of the Austrian Red Cross with a reputation as a humanitarian. The Austrian German-nationalists are also flexible in their acceptance of leaders from across the border in what they consider "their country." While Germans had at one time to choose between Bismarck and Kaiser Wilhelm II, the Austrian German-nationalists admired both simultaneously, and they ignored Bismarck's injunction that they should be above all else loyal Austrians. Judging from the press of the "third camp" in present-day Austria, the German-nationalists looked with pride upon the advances made by the Federal Republic of Germany under the leadership of Adenauer, and it appears likely that the upsurge of the Austrian Socialist party at the polls in March 1970 was occasioned to some degree by the victory scored at the polls by the German Socialists in the preceding fall elections. The Austrian German-nationalist camp has, then, always been somewhat enigmatic and unpredictable. It is, however, highly significant for our study that as late as November 1930 most of this camp endorsed parliamentary democracy and constitutional government. The prevalence of political forces in favor of democratic politics at that time supports the thesis that the collapse of democracy in the First Republic was not inevitable.

29. Violent clashes were especially frequent where Socialist industrial towns were surrounded by anti-Socialist rural communities.

30. Otto Bauer, *Der Blutige 15 te Juli* (Vienna: Vorwaerts Verlag, 1927). This is the text of a speech before the Austrian Parliament on 26 July 1927.

31. Franz Winkler, *Die Diktatur in Oesterreich* (Zurich and Leipzig: Orell Fuessli Verlag, 1935). The author was vice-chancellor until September 1933 and one of the leading members of the Landbund.

32. Charles A. Gulick, *Austria from Habsburg to Hitler* (Berkeley and Los Angeles: University of California Press, 1948), pp. 894–95. Gulick is probably the foremost spokesman and advocate of Austromarxism.

33. Walter M. Kotschnig, *Unemployment in the Learned Professions* (London: Oxford University Press, 1937), p. 107.

34. Ibid., pp. 108–9.

35. Ibid., p. 109.

36. *Wirtschaftsstatistisches Jahrbuch, 1929/1930* (Vienna: Kammer fuer Arbeiter und Angestellte, 1930), p. 83.

37. Kurt Rothschild, *Austria's Economic Development between the Two Wars* (London: Frederick Muller, 1947), p. 52.

38. Ibid.

39. *Statistisches Handbuch fuer die Republik Oesterreich* (Vienna: Statistisches Zentralamt, 1933), p. 24.

40. Ernst Karl Winter, *Ignaz Seipel als Dialektisches Problem* (Vienna: Europa Verlag, 1966), p. 64.

41. See above, p. 87.

42. Otto Bauer, "Die wirtschaftliche und politische Lage Oesterreichs," *Protokoll des sozial-demokratischen Parteitags, 13, bis 15, November 1931* (Vienna: Verlag der wiener Volks-buchhandlung, 1931), p. 29.

43. Gulick, *Austria from Habsburg to Hitler*, pp. 939–41. Gulick's defense of the Austromarxist rejection of Seipel's coalition offer is of interest as the one and only such effort undertaken on the Socialist side after 1932. The Austrian Socialists are repressing memories of the policies of their party during that period and do not care to be reminded (see 47).

44. Not to mention the recent Socialist minority government that depended for its survival upon the support of the *Freiheitliche Partei Oesterreich*, the present party of Austria's German-nationalist camp.

45. Thus we find no reference to the Socialist rejection of Seipel's coalition offer in the rather detailed account of developments in the First Republic of Austria by the Austromarxist historian Julius Braunthal in his *The Tragedy of Austria* (London: Victor Gollancz, 1948).

46. Austrian historians sympathetic to the Socialists likewise delete all references to Seipel's coalition offer. For example, Ludwig Jedlicka, "Das Autoritaere System in Oesterreich," *Aus Politik und Zeitgeschichte, Beilage zur Wochenzeitung Das Parlament*, 25 July 1970, pp. 3–115, in a fairly thorough account of Seipel's sponsorship of the Fascist Heimwehr, makes not a single reference to Seipel's role in the work on the compromise of the constitu-tional reform of 1929. Nor is there a single reference to Seipel's coalition offer, which would mar the presentation of Seipel as having held unswervingly to a strictly authoritarian posi-tion.

47. Otto Bauer, *Die Illegale Partei* (Paris: La Lutte Socialiste, 1939), p. 107.

48. *Der Parteitag von 1926* (Vienna: Verlag der wiener Volksbuchhandlung, 1926), p. 128.

49. Most of the analysts of the German National Socialist vote have come to the conclusion that the increase in the Nazi vote from 0.8 million in May 1928 to 6.4 million in September 1930 came primarily from former nonvoters.

50. Walter B. Simon, "Motivations of a Totalitarian Mass Vote," *British Journal of Sociology* 10, no. 4 (December 1959): 338–45. The actual election data have been taken from Vienna's *Neue Freie Presse* the day after the elections. Only the data of the Innsbruck elections, not recorded in the *Neue Freie Presse*, are taken from the Munich *Voelkischer Beobachter*, 24 April 1933.

51. Simon, "Motivations." p. 342.

52. *Salzburger Volksblatt*, 25 April 1932.

53. Otto Bauer, "Der 24 te April," *Der Kampf* 25 (1932): 192. *Der Kampf* was the monthly organ of the Austrian Socialist party.

54. Ibid.

55. The concept of a "power vacuum" was first applied to the collapse of democratic institu-tions in Germany where democratic politics were stymied when legislative bodies became paralyzed by avowedly antidemocratic majorities that would not and could not work to-gether. See Karl Dietrich Bracher, *Die Auflösung der Weimarer Republik: Eine Studie zum Problem des Machtzerfalls in der Demokratie* (Stuttgart and Dusseldorf: Ring Verlag, 1957).

56. Winkler, *Die Diktatur*.

57. Otto Bauer, *Der Aufstand der Oesterreichischen Arbeiter* (Prague: Verlag der deutschen sozialdemokratischen Arbeiterpartei in der Tschechoslowakischen Republik, 1934), p. 13.

58. "Comrades, we have to fight with weapons of the mind and spirit since soon we will not have any others."

59. For a scholarly differentiation between "authoritarian" and "totalitarian" regimes, see Juan J. Linz, "An Authoritarian Regime: Spain," in *Mass Politics: Studies in Political Sociol-ogy*, ed. Erik Allardt and Stein Rokkan (New York: Free Press, 1970), pp. 251–83, 374–81.

60. For details on the Socialist underground organization, see Bauer, *Die Illegale Partei*, and Joseph Buttinger, *The Twilight of Socialism: A History of the Revolutionary Socialists of Austria*, trans. E. B. Ashton (New York: F. A. Praeger, 1953).

4.

The Lapua Movement: The Threat of Rightist Takeover in Finland, 1930-32

Risto Alapuro and Erik Allardt

Between the two world wars the right-wing or Lapua movement, which was opposed to the Finnish parliamentary political system, was relatively strong compared to similar movements elsewhere. It has often been stressed that a breakdown in the existing Finnish political system was a definite possibility in the years 1930–32.[1] Most of the features that are shown in this volume to be related to developments leading to a takeover apply to the Finnish case, i.e., the development of the Lapua movement. The situation in Finland was characterized by an emergent disloyal opposition, problems of public order, ambivalence on the part of neutral powers, and a narrowing of the political arena to a small number of participants across party lines or outside the parties, resulting in loss of power, power vacuums, and crises of resolution.

There was a partial breakdown of the existing parliamentary political system in that all public activities by the Communists were prohibited. The Communist party had been banned, to be sure, after the civil war in 1918, but up until the 1930s groups closely attached to the party had been able to participate in both party politics and the labor union movement. However, no takeover of the type that occurred in Germany, Italy, and several Eastern European countries took place in Finland. After the critical years of the early 1930s, the disloyal opposition of the Right fell into a peripheral position when a president was elected from the Agrarian Union and a coalition of the Agrarians and the Social Democrats in Finland's cabinet began.

The Lapua movement was never a political party, although it was close to and partly overlapped certain established parties. Also, the movement did not develop a distinct ideological profile, as did the Fascist-type parties in a number of countries at that time. These features seem in some respects to have enhanced and in others diminished the probability of rightist takeover in the Lapua years.

A third rather unusual feature in the Finnish case was the role of the Social Democrats. Their line was clearly and consistently revisionist and, for example, went along with the economic policy followed during the depression. This was probably very important in limiting polarization in the society and consequently decreasing the threat of a takeover.

In going back further, one may also emphasize the comparatively strong institutionalization of the existing political system and the impact of the civil war in 1918. The latter, in contributing to the unified bourgeois hegemony in interwar Finland, considerably affected the fact that in Finland the Fascist-type phenomena of 1930–32 were largely without an independent profile and that the interests of the crucial export industry came to be well represented within the existing political system during the depression.

The Civil War in 1918 and Structural Cleavages in Finnish Society

The best single point of departure for understanding the right-wing movement of the 1920s and 1930s in Finland, as in Germany and Hungary, is to be found in the structures and patterns emanating from World War I. In all these countries the bourgeoisie in the period between the world wars could remember a revolutionary attempt to take power, accompanied by a civil war. However, in Germany and Finland, unlike Hungary, the struggle did not result in a rightist dictatorship nor, for that matter, in a triumph for the revolution. As a consequence, there were dissatisfied groups within the bourgeoisies of these countries in the interwar years. In Finland, the crisis of the political system in 1929–32 was related in many ways to the division crystallized in 1918, although by no means predetermined by it. Of importance were both the structural cleavages due to the war in 1918 and developments preceding it, and the interplay of economic and political events in the critical years of the twenties and thirties.

The civil war in 1918 can be seen as a climax of a rapid mobilization of the working class and the rural proletariat and of a sudden change in the political system. Finland's transition from an estate-based system to universal suffrage in 1906 was unique in its suddenness and depth.[2] In the first general elections the Social Democrats gained 80 of the 200 parliamentary seats. In 1916 they gained the majority in Parliament with 103 mandates, and in 1918 the party led an attempt at revolution, suppressed only with difficulty by the bourgeoisie and the peasantry.

These developments were closely tied to developments in the Russian empire, in which Finland was a grand duchy until the end of 1917. The timing and thoroughness of transition to universal suffrage were largely due to the Russian general strike and attempt at revolution in 1905, and the outbreak of the civil war in 1918 was closely connected with the October Revolution of the previous year. The intertwining of radicalization within the Finnish social system and developments in Russia is of primary importance to understanding the structural conditions favorable to the Lapua movement.

The Bourgeoisie and Bourgeois Parties

Finnish linguistic nationalism, the so-called Finnocism, arose in the nineteenth century and became especially influential in university circles, in the church, and among the wealthy peasantry, while it was inimical to the Swedish-speaking upper class. By the end of the century the nationalist culture had been established as an important integrative value system in the country. This development was facilitated by the partial settlement of the cultural conflict within the upper classes due to the steady advancement of the Finnish among them, and by the easing of economic conflicts between the largely Swedish-speaking industrialist and merchant class and the Finnish-speaking wealthy peasantry. Also of immediate importance to the unity of the different upper-class groups were indications of the beginning of the all-Russian integrative efforts in the 1890s.

All these developments contributed to a culture with strong nationalist overtones, overtones approved largely in the different segments of the bourgeoisie and the peasantry. It may be noted that besides the Finnish nationalism there had also been a distinctly Swedish linguistic nationalist movement in Finland at the end of the nineteenth century.

These tendencies were strengthened, not surprisingly, by the enormous success of the Social Democrats after the introduction of universal suffrage in 1906. In the first general elections ever held in Finland, the Social Democrats gained a proportion of mandates equaled by no other European country at that time.[3] In the ten years from 1908 to 1918 the cultural controversies between Finnish-speaking and Swedish-speaking upper-class groups had clearly declined in importance, and nationalist cultural traits common to different bourgeois groups increased in importance. Significantly, the status of the church rose to a great extent.[4] In the years preceding the attempt at revolution there was considerable unity between elite groups, as has often been pointed out.[5]

This is somewhat different from the situation that usually precedes a revolution. No serious cleavages tore the elite, and in this sense Finnish society was not ripe for revolution.[6] But there were other significant factors. As is well known, the ultimate factor that precipitates a revolution is often the loss of unified control over the instruments of violence, particularly the army.[7] Due to Finland's position as part of the Russian empire, the dominant groups lacked an organized military force altogether; there was no army within Finnish society.[8] This was presumably an essential condition for the outbreak of the civil war. The Russian Revolution was not only an immediately precipitating factor. It also meant a sudden disappearance of the forces upholding authority in Finland. When the armed forces in Russia got out of the hands of the ruling groups, the consequences were apparent in Finland, which was totally dependent on Russia for the maintenance of its political and economic system.

The revolution in Finland was suppressed with great difficulty and with substantial support from German troops. It was also conceived differently by different groups in the population. On the Red side the war clearly was perceived as a class war, but among the Whites it was seen as a liberation war against Russian influence. The superimposition of national feelings on class conflict strengthened antagonisms and added to the cruelty of the revolution. Extremely bloody repression was practiced by the victorious Whites: 8,400 people were executed and about 10,000 people died of disease and starvation in prison camps.[9]

It can be argued that due to the civil war and developments preceding it, the bourgeoisie in Finland was more united after the war than is usually the case in postrevolutionary situations. The civil war was conceived as a national struggle by the victorious Whites, and throughout the 1920s and 1930s it was officially called the Liberation War. One telling feature of the situation after the civil war was the nature of the civil guard; unlike many armed unofficial groups elsewhere, it was a force supported by all bourgeois groups.[10] In contrast to the situation in Germany and Austria, all non-Socialist parties in Finland backed this one armed organization, which was also to become loosely tied with the state machinery. Its significance can be seen in the fact that in the early 1920s there were 100,000 armed men in the civil guard while the corresponding number in the army was between 20,000 and 25,000.[11] Another feature was the comparatively overwhelming domination of one nationalist organization, the Academic Karelia Society, among the students and the young educated class.[12]

This background presumably accounts for the fact that in Finland between the two world wars, a strong but very united nationalistic political culture existed—a more unified bourgeois hegemony than is found in most countries with a history of insurrections.

This cultural unity had consequences important for the development of the Lapua movement. Juan J. Linz states in his introductory essay that the legitimacy question is often tied more to symbolic problems than to conflicts of interest. In Finland's case one can assume that there were large segments of the bourgeoisie who would react similarly and sensitively to all threats against some symbolic national values. Second, it seems quite clear that symbolic conflicts between non-Socialist groups were extremely unlikely. Third, it can be assumed that in the event of a threat from the extreme Right, the borderline between a disloyal opposition and other bourgeois groups would be very vague—a trait that, according to Linz, is apt to increase the possibilities of success for the disloyal opposition.

The above statement hints at a considerable rightist potential in the bourgeoisie in the interwar decades. On the other hand, underscoring the cultural unity of different bourgeois groups is just another way of indicating the absence of a strong, clearly discernible reactionary group in the bourgeoisie. Certainly one central background factor contributing to this absence was the small size and relative weakness of the Finnish elite in the nineteenth century and prior to the civil war. Finland had no dominant landowning upper class in the first phase of its modernization, as did Germany and the Eastern European countries. In Finland the rising nationalistic movement in the nineteenth century had been associated with a quest for support from the wealthy peasantry. Presumably the flexibility of the upper classes after World War I was greater in Finland than in Germany and the Eastern European countries, where the oligarchic social structures existed until the recent past.

There are at least three developments generally related to this background and contributing to the viability of the parliamentary political system established after the civil war. One of them is the fact that the competitive political system had taken root long before the civil war; there was a clear institutional continuity. The same political parties and their corresponding social groups that had been important in the formative years 1906–17, when Finland was a grand duchy in the Russian empire, continued to be crucial after World War I.[13] The biggest of the bourgeois parties was the Coalition party, also called the Conservative party in the following pages. It was backed by the majority of the clergy and by many high-ranking civil servants. The commercial and industrial groups, especially the timber and paper concerns (the main export industry), openly supported it. Another clearly bourgeois postwar party was the Swedish People's party, representing not only the Swedish-speaking bourgeoisie but also other Swedish-speaking groups in the country. Unlike the small, liberal Progress party, these parties tried in 1918 to make Finland into a monarchy, an effort that failed only because of the German defeat in the war.

This initial situation for a parliamentary political system was quite different from the one that prevailed in the Eastern European countries. In Rumania and Poland the new constitutional forms remained in clear conflict with the oligarchic structure of society, and the old social relationships prevailed despite the new constitutions.

The other two important factors contributing to the viability of the political system concern the character of the Left and of the Agrarian Union.

The Working Class and the Social Democrats and Communists

The civil war, and the political mobilization that had developed rapidly and easily prior to it, had a great impact on the position and structure of the Left in

Finland in the 1920s and 1930s. The rapid electoral advance of the Social Democrats after the fundamental change in the political system in 1906 seems to have given some of their leaders a vested interest in the newly established political system. To be sure, explicitly revisionist ideas were not dominant in the party, but they did have a considerable number of supporters.[14] Indicative of the vagueness of ideological controversies within the Social Democratic party is the fact that the leadership had no defined or concrete revolutionary program. Political success seems to have fed the idea that revolution is predetermined, something that would come about through the necessity of nature.[15] In addition, there were nationalist elements in the party, which existed largely due to the strengthening of the all-Russian integrative efforts before and during the world war.[16] This nationalism reduced the gap between the bourgeoisie and a segment of the Social Democrats.

This was the internal situation in the Social Democratic party before the collapse of the Russian empire and before the dominant groups in Finland had lost the opportunity to invoke the armed forces. This sudden loss of the forces maintaining authority presented the revolutionary forces with an opportunity of the utmost importance. The revolutionary forces were undeveloped and weak and would hardly have provided a sufficient base for a serious attempt at revolution. Even revolutionary leaders admitted that the revolution was something of a surprise to the revolutionaries.[17] The bulk of the party leadership was drawn into rather than making the revolution. The revolutionary course was largely due to irresistible pressure from the masses, who were without food; and with the lack of armed forces to control the situation, conditions became rather chaotic in 1917.[18] Moreover, some active politicians in the party, among them several members of Parliament, dissociated themselves from the revolution and remained passive.[19]

The leaders of the defeated revolution founded the Communist party of Finland in Petrograd in 1918, and the revisionists who had kept at a distance from the revolutionary attempt carried on the activities of the Social Democratic party, participating in the general elections in 1919. So, in Finland as elsewhere, the Social Democratic party was divided after the Russian Revolution, but in Finland the gap was markedly increased both by the unpreparedness of party for revolution, which resulted in a deep cleavage within the party, and subsequently by the proximity of revolutionary Russia. The division between the Social Democrats and the Communists was to be reinforced by the division at the national level between Finland and Soviet Union.

Accordingly it seems justifiable to say that Finnish society was not ripe for a revolution when the favorable moment came. The aftermath of the revolutionary attempt was increased cultural unity among the bourgeois groups and a large and deep gap within the ranks of the Social Democrats. Presumably, this had a lasting impact on the nature of Social Democracy in Finland and its relations with Communists, not the least of it being in the critical years of the early 1930s.

The Peasants and the Agrarian Union

In addition to the bourgeoisie and the largely working-class Left, one must consider the peasants when analyzing the structural preconditions of the success and limits to success of the right-wing movement in the interwar period. The civil war and its preceding developments were also significant to the peasants, who were the rank and file of the White army. Going beyond its role in the critical juncture of 1918, the structure of the peasantry and the changes in its position seem to be of significance in its stand in the Lapua years. In Finland the peasants represented a stratum which had gained enormously from the democratization of the political system in 1906, and they developed into a mighty political force. In the first Parliament, elected in 1907, there were nine peasantist representatives out of two hundred; in 1916 the peasant party, the Agrarian Union, had nineteen seats; and in the first general elections after the civil war it gained forty-two mandates. It advanced further in the 1920s, being then the second largest or largest party represented in the Parliament. Thus, the position of the peasants in the Finnish parliamentary system clearly differed from the position of the peasants in the Eastern European countries.[20]

These differences probably reflect differences in the pattern of modernization and its structural consequences. Barrington Moore has argued that fascism was especially strong in those countries in which capitalism had developed in cooperation with the dominant landed upper class. In these countries—Poland, Hungary, and Rumania, for instance—there was a strong homogeneous elite. Therefore, the capitalist transformation could be brought into effect while maintaining intact the preexisting peasant society. In these labor-repressive systems, as Moore calls them, agriculture was adjusted to the market economy by preserving the traditional peasant society but by squeezing more surplus out of it. In these countries the peasants were still heavily tied to the traditional agrarian social structure during the 1920s and 1930s. The crisis of the market economy during the Great Depression hit them very hard and made them very susceptible to Fascist appeals. In these countries, unlike Finland, there was during the 1920s a relatively unstructured and unmobilized base that contributed to the weakness of the political center.[21]

Finland did not have a strong landed aristocracy in the initial stages of industrialization. The commercialization of agriculture did not occur through labor-repressive methods but essentially came about through reliance on the labor market. This, without doubt, contributed to the fact that in Finland the peasant stratum became a part of and a strong adherent of the parliamentary system.[22]

The Situation in the 1920s

It has been argued above that a considerable part of the cultural unity of the non-Socialist groups and the split within the Left were both ultimately connected with the international position of Finland. This connection became clearer still in the 1920s. The proximity of the Soviet Union preserved the close connection between internal and foreign policy questions in post–civil war Finland. For example, in justifying the civil guard, foreign policy and internal arguments were often given side by side.[23]

Within the Left this state of affairs probably deepened the gap between Social Democrats and Communists. In the early 1920s the left-wing Socialists and Communists tried to act within the Social Democratic party, but without success. Väinö Tanner was the leading figure in the attack on the left-wing representatives of the party. Under his leadership the party became in the 1920s an essentially reformist parliamentary party, consistently seeking cooperation with the centrist parties and displaying nationalist overtones. This can be seen especially in the sharp distinction drawn between "Russian" and "Western" traditions of the working-class movement.[24] The contrast was without doubt strengthened by the foundation of the autonomous Soviet Karelia on the Russian side of the Finnish border, headed by many central figures of the defeated revolution in Finland.

The left-wing Socialists formed a new party, which was connected with the Finnish Communist party in the Soviet Union. This party was able, with difficulty, to carry on its political activities in the 1920s and it had between eighteen and twenty-seven deputies in the Parliament while the Social Democrats at the same time gained between fifty-three and sixty parliamentary mandates. Left-wing Socialist representatives had central positions in the trade union movement.[25]

In discussing the developments in the non-Socialist groups, the strength of the civil guard has already been mentioned. Another organization, whose strength indicates the firm position of the bourgeois groups in the society, was the employer-financed strike-breaking organization, Vientirauha (Export Peace). It helped employers to win many labor conflicts, including the great dock strike that lasted from the summer of 1928 to the spring of 1929. The weak trade union movement was at its strongest in the late 1920s, due to the rapid economic growth of Finland in this decade. In explaining the small number of antiparliamentarian demonstrations among the bourgeois circles in the 1920s attention has sometimes been given to this economic growth.[26] This development, based mainly on the export of the products of the paper and timber industry forming 86 per cent of the worth of the exported goods in 1920–29, was of course extremely sensitive to changes in the international market, as would be seen at the end of the decade.

The Lapua Movement, 1929–32: Developments in the Political Arena

The Lapua movement in Finland from 1929 to 1932 was a disloyal opposition, according to the definition presented in Juan J. Linz's introductory essay. Its immediate aim was the destruction of "communism"—taken in a very diffuse sense—and the movement did not care about the rules of the political system in achieving its goals. Generally, the movement held the whole political system based on political parties in contempt, attacked it without scruples, and made demands contrary to the very essence of the party system.[27] Furthermore, on some occasions in those years a Fascist-type seizure of power by the movement and its supporters was not at all out of question. The most serious point appears to have been reached in the summer of 1930. By that time the Lapua movement had gone a long way toward provoking the disintegration of the political system, and the situation displayed many of the features typical of the period preceding the final takeover described by Linz.

The Rise of the Movement

The origin of the Lapua movement is usually dated from the end of 1929, when anti-Communist riots broke out, with farmers as the foremost participants. One cause of the riots was the depression, which had begun to hit the Finnish farmers in 1928. Thus, in Finland as elsewhere, the unsolved problems created by the depression formed a basis for the rise of the agrarian-based right-wing movement.

The strongest immediate support was given by the Coalition party. It is not surprising that within another political party, namely, the Agrarian Union, there also was immediate and substantial support for the movement. When the movement appointed its leaders in March 1930, among those elected was, in addition to two banking directors and two well-known industrialists, the chief editor of the leading Agrarian newspaper. The most visible leader of the movement, Vihtori Kosola, was a member of the Agrarian Union. Consequently, the rise of the Lapua movement might perhaps be characterized roughly by saying that there had been a certain potential for extremism in the Right after the civil war, but the crisis did not explode until there was also a popular movement and both these elements were linked together.

From the summer of 1929 to the summer of 1930 Finland had a minority government composed of the Agrarian Union and the liberal Progress party. From the end of 1929 on it constantly gave in to the demands made by the Lapua movement. The freedom to form associations was denied to Communists by law, and the government stopped all press activity among the Communists after riots and pressures. It summoned the Parliament to meet in the summer of 1930 in order to enact further laws aimed at suppressing Communist activity in correspondence with demands from the Lapua movement and in order to give exceptional powers to the president in cases of civil emergency.[28]

The Summer of 1930 and the Peasants' March

The influence of the Lapua movement reached its peak in the summer of 1930. During that summer and autumn three people were killed, and over a thousand members of local government bodies, Social Democratic party branches, public agencies, trade unions, staffs of newspapers, candidates and former members of Parliament, including the deputy speaker, and even the first president, K. J. Ståhlberg, were the victims of abduction.[29]

The moderate forces more or less withdrew from political responsibility. The sympathies of the president—traditionally a neutral power above the parties—toward the extraparliamentary forces contributed to this withdrawal. The political arena shrank to a very small group of people, and the crucial decisions were made in small circles of politicians and representatives of the Lapua movement. Such traits are a sign of the disintegration of the political system.

The situation developed during the summer of 1930 in such a way—under pressure of the continuing violence and disturbances of the Lapua movement—that the movement succeeded in getting its favorite candidate appointed to the position of prime minister. He was P. E. Svinhufvud, a strong conservative, who together with Mannerheim symbolized White Finland and the victorious Liberation War. It is obvious that in the beginning Svinhufvud was regarded within the Lapua movement as one of its own men. He had been chief executive—an office that preceded the office of the president—after the declaration of independence in 1917, and he had been a monarchist in 1918. As a symbol and figurehead of victorious White Finland he had enormous prestige. Svinhufvud offered two seats in the cabinet to the movement, but apparently because of internal conflicts it was not able to accept this offer. His cabinet arranged for the arrest of all Communist deputies, and with strong pressure from Svinhufvud and the Lapua movement all the anti-Communist laws proposed earlier were forced through. This was effected by insuring a sufficiently large non-Socialist majority in the Parliament through new elections, held under heavy pressure from the Lapua movement, while the government hindered Communists and related groups from running for office.[30]

Some conclusions on the strength of the Lapua movement during the election campaign can be drawn from the election results in table 1. The increase in the total vote was considerable but benefited essentially the non-Socialist parties, particularly the Conservatives. The vote gained by the Social Democrats in 1930 was no larger than the total vote for the Left in the previous year, and it resulted in just seven additional mandates. This change had no impact on the course followed by the Social Democrats. To be sure, they firmly opposed the demands of the Lapua movement, but basically their efforts during the years 1929–32 were concentrated on the defense of the existing political system, an approach markedly different from the Communists' line.[31] It was not until the next general elections in 1933, when the total vote again dropped somewhat, that they were able to increase considerably the number of Social Democratic mandates.

In the summer and fall of 1930 the disloyal opposition in the form of the Lapua movement had gone far toward achieving a disintegration of the political system. The culmination of its efforts was probably reached in the summer of 1930 when twelve thousand members of the Lapua movement, mainly farmers, marched on the capital, apparently inspired by the famous march of the Fascists to Rome in 1922. The Peasants' March, as it was called, was carried out under the auspices of the civil guard, and Mannerheim, Svinhufvud, and the Agrarian president, Relander, were present at the main demonstration, listening to the demands of the movement.

Table 1. Results of the Finnish General Elections of 1929, 1930, and 1933

| Parties | Distribution of Mandates and Popular Vote (in thousands) | | | | | |
| | 1929 | | 1930 | | 1933 | |
	Mandates	Votes	Mandates	Votes	Mandates	Votes
National Coalition party	28	138	42	204	18	188[a]
Patriotic People's movement	—	—	—	—	14	
Swedish People's party	23	109	21	123	21	115
National Progress party	7	53	11	66	11	82
Agrarian Union	60	249	59	308	53	250
Social Democratic party	59	260	66	386	78	414
Socialist Workers' party[b]	23	128	—	12	—	—
Others	—	14	1	32	5	59
Total	200	951	200	1,131	200	1,108
National turnout		55.6%		66.9%		62.2%

SOURCE: Official election statistics.

[a]The semi-Fascist Patriotic People's Movement and the National Coalition party formed party alliances in almost all constituencies.
[b]Communists and left-wing Socialists.

There is some indication that support for the Lapua movement among the Conservatives began to decline after the prohibition of all activities of the Communists and related groups in the fall of 1930. The Lapua movement had raised Svinhufvud to prime minister in 1930 as their own man. But friction between him and the movement arose almost immediately after he assumed office. More distinct differences emerged in 1931 when Svinhufvud was elected president as the candidate of the Conservative party. The Lapua movement, to be sure, supported him strongly during the electoral campaign, and it is also evident that the civil guard exercised pressure on the members of the electoral college, and especially on the Agrarian electors, before the final vote.[32] But a consensus was forming among a group of Conservatives as to who constituted the disloyal opposition, and this divergence in the Coalition party surfaced in the so-called Mäntsälä revolt in 1932. In the general elections in 1933 the divergence became institutionalized with the founding of a new, semi-Fascist party (see table 1).

The Mäntsälä Revolt

The leadership of the Lapua movement gave its support to a revolt in Mäntsälä, a community in the vicinity of the capital, and attempted to mobilize large groups from the civil guard behind its demands.[33] Among these demands was a call for the resignation of the government and the establishment of a new, "unpolitical," "patriotic" government. The aim was apparently to make Mannerheim a leader of the state and to make the conservative industrialist, ex-general, and member of the leadership of the Lapua movement, Rudolf Walden, the prime minister. Many important leaders of the Conservative party, a large part of the leadership in the civil guard, including its commander, and many officers in the armed forces rallied behind these demands.

The Lapua movement failed, however, and a decisive factor in its defeat was undoubtedly the stand of both Svinhufvud and the commander in chief of the armed forces against the demands of the Lapua movement. At the decisive moment the Lapua movement could not mobilize the masses of the civil guard, in which rural elements constituted a clear majority of the rank and file. Also, the commercial and industrial elite had apparently withdrawn much of its support for the movement.[34]

Besides the disengagement of some important conservative factions from the Lapua movement after the anti-Communist laws had been forced through, the attitudes of the other bourgeois parties underwent marked changes as well. This was obviously of utmost importance during the Mäntsälä revolt but it was also significant earlier in 1930–32. As early as late 1930, the so-called lawfulness front had begun to emerge, numbering the Social Democrats, the majority of the Agrarian Union, the Progress party, and the majority of the Swedish People's party as its foremost supporters. This development certainly facilitated Svinhufvud's independent policy toward the Lapua movement from late 1930 on.

Political Parties and the Lapua Movement

The Non-Socialist Parties

One outstanding feature of the Lapua movement has emerged very clearly in the above discussion Unlike the rightist/Fascist disloyal oppositions in most European countries betwen the two world wars, the Lapua movement was not a political party. It might be characterized as a pressure group or perhaps more appropriately as a faction overlapping certain parties, notably the Conservative party and, to a lesser extent, the Agrarian Union. There was also a minority group close to the movement in the Swedish People's party. Differences in attitudes, however, began to crystallize in the course of the movement; as stated above, acceptance and even enthusiasm was general, although it was not the only reaction, in all bourgeois parties in the initial stage of the Lapua movement.

The fact that the movement encountered positive response so rapidly in the form of mass meetings all over the country at its inception has led some to conclude, not without justification, that the initial riots ripened similar demands already nurtured among the Conservatives.[35] The movement encompassed well-known Conservatives, even though the visible leadership of the movement displayed a clear rural image. Most of the leaders appointed in March 1930 were members of the Coalition party and Agrarian Union. It is also noteworthy from a comparative point of view that the Lapua movement never had an anticapitalist ideology, not even of the type of the Fascist movement in Italy. The basic outcome of the Lapua movement was a prohibition of all activities by Communists, along with the emasculation of the trade union movement. The least one can say beyond reference to an important symbolic change in the political system is that the outcome greatly benefited certain rightist groups, especially in the business sector.[36] Furthermore, the weakness and irresoluteness of the official peasantist leadership of the movement can be seen as one more indication of the lack of a distinctive ideological profile in the Lapua movement.

Presumably, the close connection between the movement and the different political parties, especially in the initial stages, is indicative of the relatively strong cultural unity among the non-Socialist groups in Finland. On the other hand, it has also been argued above that symbolic victories were important for the Finnish right-wing movement. It seems that both Svinhufvud's appointment as prime minister and the proscription of Communists from any public activity had just such a strong symbolic significance. Finally, the election of

Svinhufvud as president highlighted a development in which the political system acquired a more conservative flavor but during which the actual changes in the political system were nevertheless limited.

Not until these features had become evident did the Lapua movement acquire a clearer fascistic tone.[37] In other words, not until the basic climate of the political system had become clearly conservative did boundaries within the political Right begin to crystallize. At this point the differences between conservatism and fascism began gradually to emerge.

While the Conservatives continued to collaborate with the Lapua movement after 1930, the Agrarian Union dissociated itself from it in the years 1930–31. Reference was made earlier to the strong and stable position of the farmers in the Finnish political system as compared with the situation of their counterparts in Eastern European countries, which was largely due to a different kind of adjustment to capitalism. In Finland the farmers were fully mobilized long before the thirties and had an institutionalized channel for expressing grievances caused by the depression and reacting to them. In some Eastern European countries, however, the peasants, strongly tied to the structures of traditional agrarian society until recently, were mobilized by the depression in a way benefiting distinctly fascistic parties.[38]

At the level of immediate political developments, the Finnish farmers were hit by the initial stages of the depression at least as badly and probably worse than other social groups. Information on the decline in the level of income of different social groups and on profit rates of agriculture makes understandable the agrarian enthusiasm in 1929–30 for anti-Communist outbursts with strong populist overtones.[39] On the other hand, the final establishment of Agrarian opposition to the Lapua movement and the simultaneous dissociation from collaboration with the Conservatives was apparently also a part of the reaction to the impact of the depression, which sharpened the conflict between agricultural and commercial-industrial interests. It has been pointed out that although the Lapua movement contributed substantial support for depression-hit agricultural production, it did not do so by relieving the indebtedness of farmers. The number of compulsory auctions of farms increased until 1933. This problem apparently had an effect on the course chosen by the Agrarians from 1931 on. It is not without importance, for instance, that in this year the first unorganized and transitory outbursts, the so-called "Depression movements," grew up. Their immediate cause was the problem of indebtedness, and they remained outside the Lapua movement.[40]

The Social Democrats

The cultural unity of non-Socialist groups as a limitation on the success of the Lapua movement has been emphasized above, but it certainly was not independent of the role taken by the Social Democrats. The latter concentrated lar contact with President Relander in 1930, and the party consistently avoided clashes with the movement on the most delicate occasions.[41] Perhaps more important still, the Social Democrats went along with an economic policy that was largely classically liberal in its orientation and was very painful to the working class.[42]

Their role was different in interesting ways from the role of Social Democrats in Spain and Austria in the critical years of the 1930s. In these countries the Socialists obviously accelerated or essentially contributed to the breakdown process by going further to the left in the period preceding the final takeover (see Linz's and Simon's chapters). Unlike Finland, in these countries the boundary between Communists and Social Democrats was unclear. The weakness of the Communist parties allowed the Marxists to stay within the Socialist parties and to consider the Communists as a minor ally rather than as a powerful and dangerous competitor. In Finland this possibility was excluded from the outset. There was an extremely wide gap between two working-class parties after the civil war, while the Communists were considered an enduring threat. As a matter of fact, the orientation of the Social Democrats toward the political center was strengthened considerably in the Lapua years.[43]

The Causes of Government Stability

The conditions and developments contributing to or hampering the success of the Lapua movement have been discussed above mainly at two levels. On the one hand, structural conditions deriving from the civil war and earlier developments have been considered. Undoubtedly they were significant in producing the idiosyncratic relationship between the movement and the political parties, and also, in part, the attitude of the Social Democrats. On the other hand, immediate developments in 1929–32 in the political and, to some extent, the economic arena have also been discussed. These different factors by no means predetermined the limits for the success of the Lapua movement and are certainly not exhaustive in explaining it. There was a real possibility of a rightist takeover at several moments during these critical years. But it remains important to note that certain features typical of the Finnish case, discussed here, decreased the probability of a takeover even in the situations most favorable for the movement.

In the foregoing discussion reference has been made to those dangers that, according to Juan J. Linz, tend to emerge when the boundaries between the conservative groups and the disloyal opposition become diffuse—when there is no consensus on how the disloyal opposition should be defined, when the conservatives begin to cooperate with the disloyal opposition, and when, finally, the disloyal opposition is given an opportunity to share legitimate power. For instance, the Nazi rise to power had all these traits: the upper-class conservative groups wanted to exploit Hitler, but the servant became the master when the opportunity came.

In Finland there were similar features. In the initial phases of the Lapua movement, which led to the prohibition of Communist activities and to Svinhufvud's rise to the position of foremost political personality, the movement had wide bourgeois support. But when the movement attacked a system in which the Communists were no longer a part and in which Svinhufvud was the main symbolic figure, it got support only from some of the Conservatives and a portion of the civil guard. Consequently, it failed to reach its objectives. It seems as if the comparatively strong ideological consensus in the Finnish bourgeoisie and the importance of symbolic victories had at first enhanced the possibilities of a takeover, but after certain processes had taken place, they decreased these same possibilities.

While in Germany the cooperation between the Conservatives and the Nazis led to Hitler's rise to power, in Finland the right-wing movement played out its role and could therefore be dispersed. Put in another way, the semiloyal groups in the Coalition party and the Agrarian Union were not coopted by the disloyal opposition but, instead, first coopted and then neutralized the latter.

In this characterization it is implicitly asserted that the goals of the semiloyal groups had basically been achieved and that, given the prohibition of Communists' activities and the attitude of the Social Democrats, i.e., given the lack of a defensive revolutionary mobilization of the working class, there was no need to count on the activated violence of the Lapua movement; the bourgeoisie was strong enough without its collaboration.

This assertion can also be put forward in economic terms. The fact that the commercialization of agriculture did not occur through labor-repressive methods but essentially through reliance on labor market already suggests (if we follow Barrington Moore) that Finland never developed problems as acute as those of Germany or many Eastern European countries, pushing their industrial and commercial groups to support a fascistic solution. At a more immediate level, we can start with the point made in the beginning of this chapter: in Finland the struggle in the aftermath of World War I eventuated in neither a victory for revolution nor a rightist dictatorship. Discussions of Fascist phenomena in interwar Europe often point out that in many countries the democratized political system from the 1920s on left the capitalists in control of the economy but at the same time afforded the working class a share in political power and the freedom to organize and agitate for the achievement of its own ends. Consequently, fascism, according to this interpretation, once it had proved its right to be taken seriously, came to be looked upon as a potentially valuable ally against both the workers within the country and the capitalists of foreign countries.[44]

It has already been mentioned that before the rise of the Lapua movement the trade union movement was clearly disintegrating. But it remained for the Lapua movement to strengthen and finally confirm this development. The wages of workers decreased in Finland during the depression more, for example, than in Scandinavia, and this was basically due to the weakness of the Finnish trade unions. In the mid-1930s wages generally were less than half the corresponding wages in Sweden or England.[45] On the other hand, it has been pointed out that the extremely rapid industrial growth in Finland between the world wars was largely due to this low level of wages, which allowed the export industry to maintain its ability to compete in the international market.[46]

Consequently, it is not inappropriate to say that the Lapua movement was an ally for the capitalists both against the workers in Finland and against the capitalists in the foreign countries. But it seems that the interests of the export industry in particular came to be very well accounted for in the framework of the existing political system. Therefore, the conflicts within the economy and the accompanying turmoil in the labor market and in the whole of society could never polarize the population in Finland as they did in Germany, where they contributed to the urgency of the search for an agent to restore order.

A Note on Legitimacy, Efficiency, and Effectiveness in the Finnish Case

The use of the concepts of legitimacy, efficiency, and effectiveness usually involves difficult conceptual problems. When these concepts are applied to Finland between the two world wars this difficulty seems to be particularly salient, since the basic issue, the perception of a Communist threat and its elimination, relates to the very nature of the democratic process.

As regards legitimacy it ought to be remembered that in the civil war of 1918 Finland had been sharply divided. For some groups, notably those who supported the Communists, the Finnish political system was not regarded as legitimate during the period between the two world wars. The Communists have not been discussed here because in a historical perspective they seem to have been too weak to threaten the system effectively. For political parties and groups with political significance, notably the bourgeoisie and the rural population, it seems reasonable to say that the prevailing political system maintained an image of legitimacy in spite of the threats from the right-wing Lapua movement.

Many of the incidents and cases described above testify to the existence of a clear conception of the system as legitimate. One could refer to the fact that the Lapua movement did not become clearly Fascist until a distinct boundary between it and the Conservatives had arisen. A belief in the legitimacy of the system seems to have existed, and this was presumably one of the conditions for avoidance of a fascistic dictatorship. On the other hand, there existed a definite threat to the system, a threat that was not averted until the government came to be considered efficient and effective. Evidently, legitimacy alone provides a rather tenuous basis for stability if efficiency and effectiveness are not guaranteed.

The issues related to efficiency and effectiveness, however, are also problematical in the Finnish case. The efficiency of the government was measured in terms of how well it could eliminate the perceived Communist threat. The problem lies in the fact that efficiency here is defined in terms of matters related to the democratic process itself instead of in terms of some independent goals such as standard of living, food distribution, housing, etc. In this chapter it has been shown that the government in the final phase was considered both efficient and effective in hindering Communist activities. In fact, by its own standards it clipped the wings of the Lapua movement. In succeeding, the government also, however, curtailed the democratic process, since the Communists were no longer granted the freedom of association and speech. This relates to the concept of legitimacy. The conception of the government as legitimate was probably not based on very strong beliefs in the democratic process but rather on the simple belief that the present system was the best for maintaining law and stability. The Finnish experience represents a strong case for maintaining an open and historically specific definition of the concept of legitimacy.

Analytically it seems possible to regard legitimacy, efficiency, and effectiveness as separate categories. In practice, however, this conceptual differentiation seems more doubtful. Both efficiency and effectiveness are, so to speak, component parts of legitimacy. A belief that an organizing political authority or a regime is good and should command the obedience of the citizens can hardly be sustained unless there are proofs of its goodness in terms of efficiency and effectiveness.

NOTES

1. E.g., Anthony F. Upton, "Finland," in *European Fascism,* ed. S. J. Woolf (London: Weidenfeld and Nicolson, 1968), p. 184.
2. See Stein Rokkan, *Citizens, Elections, Parties* (Oslo: Universitetsforlaget, 1970), p. 86.
3. See, e.g., Erik Allardt, "Institutionalized Radicalism and Decline of Ideology," in *Decline of Ideology?,* ed. Mostafa Rejai (New York: Aldine and Atherton, 1971), p. 119.
4. Eino Murtorinne, *Taistelu uskonnonvapaudesta suurlakon jälkeisinä vuosina* (Porvoo-Helsinki: WSOY, 1967), pp. 90–104, 222, 229, 231.
5. See, e.g., Juhani Paasivirta, *Suomi vuonna 1918* (Porvoo-Helsinki: WSOY, 1957), pp. 62–64.
6. See Barrington Moore's and Charles Tilly's analyses: Barrington Moore, Jr., *Reflections on the Causes of Human Misery and upon Certain Proposals to Eliminate Them* (London: Allen

Lane, The Penguin Press, 1972), pp. 170–75; Charles Tilly, "Revolutions and Collective Violence," in *Handbook of Political Science*, ed. Fred I. Greenstein and Nelson W. Polsby (Reading, Mass.: Addison-Wesley, 1975), vol. 3.

7. E.g. Moore, *Reflections*, p. 175.

8. The Finnish army had been abolished in 1901 by the grand duke, i.e., the tsar.

9. Jaakko Paavolainen, "Vuonna 1918 teloitettujen punaisten lukumääräongelma," in *Oman ajan historia ja politiikan tutkimus*, ed. Lauri Hyvämäki et al. (Helsinki: Otava, 1967), pp. 210–11; Jaakko Paavolainen, *Vankileirit Suomessa 1918* (Helsinki: Tammi, 1971), pp. 234–48. Different sources present different figures for the number of Reds executed. According to material collected by the Central Statistical Office the number executed was 4,870. See Tor Hartman, "Dead and Missing Persons in the Civil War in 1918," *Tilastollisia tiedonantoja, julkaissut Tilastollinen päätoimisto—Statistiska meddelanden, utgivna av Statistiska Centralbyrån 46* (Helsinki, 1970), p. 18. There are some uncertainties in all the estimates, but the figures given by Paavolainen are in all likelihood closest to the truth. The total population of Finland in 1918 was three million people.

10. On the civil guard, see Marvin Rintala, *Three Generations: The Extreme Right Wing in Finnish Politics* (Bloomington: Indiana University Press, 1962), pp. 147–55.

11. Krister Wahlbäck, *Mannerheimista Kekkoseen: Suomen politiikan päälinjoja 1917–1967* (Porvoo-Helsinki: WSOY, 1968), p. 119.

12. On this organization, see Marvin Rintala, "Finnish Students in Politics: The Academic Karelia Society," *East European Quarterly* 6 (1972):192–205, and Risto Alapuro, "Students and National Politics: A Comparative Study of the Finnish Student Movement in the Interwar Period," *Scandinavian Political Studies* 8 (1973):113–40.

13. Cf. Erik Allardt and Pertti Pesonen, "Cleavages in Finnish Politics," in *Party Systems and Voter Alignments: Cross-National Perspectives*, ed. Seymour M. Lipset and Stein Rokkan (New York: The Free Press, 1967), pp. 328–29.

14. Hannu Soikkanen, "Miksi revisionismi ei saanut kannatusta Suomen vanhassa työväenliikkeessä?" in Hyvämäki et al., *Oman ajan historia*, pp. 184, 187, 191, 196–97; John H. Hodgson, *Communism in Finland: A History and Interpretation* (Princeton, N.J.: Princeton University Press, 1967), pp. 5–19.

15. Soikkanen, "Miksi revisionismi," pp. 196–97.

16. Hodgson, *Communism in Finland*, pp. 15–16, 22.

17. E.g., O. W. Kuusinen, *The Finnish Revolution: A Self-Criticism* (London: The Worker's Socialist Federation, 1919).

18. See Hodgson, *Communism in Finland*, pp. 29–52.

19. Hannu Soikkanen, "Työväenliikkeen jakautumisongelma itsenäisyyden alkuvuosina," *Turun Historiallinen Arkisto* 15 (1960):266–67.

20. See, for example, Henry L. Roberts's illuminating account, *Rumania: Political Problems of an Agrarian State* (New Haven: Yale University Press, 1951), pp. 89–91, 337–38.

21. Barrington Moore, Jr. *Social Origins of Dictatorship and Democracy: Lord and Peasant in the Making of the Modern World* (Boston: Beacon Press, 1966), pp. 433–38.

22. Cf. Moore, *Social Origins*, p. 422.

23. It was of importance, for instance, that because of the outcome of World War I expansionist efforts to annex the eastern Karelia into Finland, which in 1918–19 had seemed real enough to many in the Right—especially in the Coalition party—remained unsuccessful in the end. The Treaty of Dorpat with Soviet Russia in 1921 confirmed the situation and was in the following years attacked by the Right. This component of irredentism and expansive nationalism parallels the case of the Versailles settlement for Germany in many respects, as has been pointed out by Marvin Rintala. See Rintala, *Three Generations*, pp. 99–100.

24. Soikkanen, "Työväenliikkeen jakautumisongelma," pp. 267–71; Ilkka Hakalehto, *Väinö Tanner, Taipumattoman tie* (Helsinki: Kirjayhtymä, 1973), pp. 56–68, 81–100.

25. Hodgson, *Communism in Finland*, pp. 121–29.

26. Jorma Kalela, "Right-Wing Radicalism in Finland during the Interwar Period," *Scandinavian Journal of History* 1 (1976):111–12.

27. See Rintala, *Three Generations*, pp. 165, 166, 183–86.

28. Ibid., pp. 167, 174–75.

29. On violence, see Upton, "Finland," pp. 200-202. On the stand of President Lauri K. Relander, see his diary: *Presidentin päiväkirja II. Lauri Kristian Relanderin muistiinpanot vuosilta 1927-1931*, ed. Eino Jutikkala (Helsinki: Weilin+Göös, 1968), pp. 450-54.

30. See Rintala, *Three Generations*, pp. 174-84.

31. Hakalehto, *Väinö Tanner*, pp. 103-4, 107-8.

32. Rintala, *Three Generations*, pp. 177, 189. See also Paavo Hirvikallio, *Tasavallan Presidentin vaalit Suomessa 1919-1950* (Porvoo-Helsinki: WSOY, 1958), pp. 62-63.

33. On the Mäntsälä revolt see Rintala, *Three Generations*, pp. 191-94.

34. Cf. Upton, "Finland," pp. 209-10.

35. Upton, "Finland," pp. 195-96; Kalela, "Right-Wing Radicalism," pp. 113-15.

36. Kalela, "Right-Wing Radicalism," p. 121.

37. See Upton, "Finland," pp. 203-4.

38. Cf. Moore, *Social Origins*, pp. 437-38, 448-50. Illustrative of the sharp difference sketched here is the rise of agrarian-based fascism in Rumania, which at that time was still, at least formally, a parliamentary democracy. See Eugen Weber, "The Men of the Archangel," in *International Fascism, 1920-1945*, ed. Walter Laqueur and George L. Mosse (New York: Harper Torchbooks, 1966), pp. 110-18.

39. A rough comparison shows that in the initial stages of the depression the decrease in income among the farmers was greater than among the workers, whose real income even rose in 1929. See Klaus Waris, *Kuluttajain tulot, kulutus ja säästäminen suhdannekehityksen valossa Suomessa vuosina 1926-1938* (Helsinki: Kansantaloudellisia tutkimuksia XIV, 1945), pp. 123, 134, 153. The profit rate in agriculture was at its lowest in 1929-30; see Kosti Huuhka, *Talonpoikaisnuorison koulutie* (Forssa: Historiallisia tutkimuksia XLIII, 1955), p. 191.

40. Paula Oittinen, "Pulaliikkeiden alueellinen levinneisyys" (Master's thesis, University of Helsinki, 1975).

41. Relander, *Presidentin päiväkirja II*, pp. 424-25, 507, 521.

42. See Kalela, "Right-Wing Radicalism," pp. 121-22.

43. Hakalehto, *Väinö Tanner*, pp. 115-16. That the stand of Social Democrats cannot alone explain the failure of the takeover becomes clear in a comparison with Germany, where the Social Democratic party was also strongly reformist. Other factors differentiating the Finnish and German situation, at least those sketched above, must be taken into consideration.

44. See, e.g., Paul M. Sweezy, *The Theory of Capitalist Development* (New York: Monthly Review Press, 1968), pp. 329-30, 334.

45. Carl Erik Knoellinger, *Labor in Finland* (Cambridge, Mass.: Harvard University Press, 1960), p. 85.

46. Wahlbäck, *Mannerheimista*, p. 80.

5.

From Great Hopes to Civil War: The Breakdown of Democracy in Spain

Juan J. Linz*

The death of Spanish democracy was the last in a chain of breakdowns in Europe that occurred in Italy, Portugal, Germany, and Austria. This circumstance accounts for many of the distinctive features of the crisis of the Spanish Republic between 1931 and 1936, including foreign intervention in the civil war. That the Spanish democracy survived the rise of fascism in other countries helps explain Spanish socialism's unique response. The Republic was the most short-lived and unstable of the European democracies that failed.[1] It is the only case in which the final breakdown led to a civil war, and Spain and Portugal are the only countries in which the regimes then established have survived until, respectively, 1976–77 and 1974.

In these two countries on the Iberian peninsula the army played a direct rather than an indirect role in the breakdown, which brings their experience closer to the Latin American pattern. The high level of political mobilization in Spain, however, contrasts with the Portuguese and even more with most Latin American cases, and in this respect it resembles European models. Perhaps more than in any other case except the Italian, deep social cleavage and conflict lay beneath the political crisis. Class, religious, and regional conflicts combined and interacted with unique intensity. Spain was the only democracy outside Eastern Europe in which regional, cultural, and linguistic cleavages played a role in the breakdown of democracy. Regional tensions were certainly important in the Austrian crisis, and to some extent in the German crisis, but they did not approach the effect of emerging peripheral nationalisms against an established state conceived by most Spaniards as a nation-state.[2] While religious issues and sentiment were relevant to the crises of Weimar and Italy, and were important in Portugal and Austria, they were never so bitter—so central—as in Spain.

*In writing this essay I have benefited enormously from the critical reading of Edward Malefakis.

The cumulative effect of the problems faced was staggering, but it is notable that major divisions over foreign policy and war responsibilities were not contributory. The colonial wars of the late nineteenth and early twentieth century in Cuba, the Philippines, and Morocco were a closed chapter except for the size of the officer corps and the divisions within the army residual from that time. The world depression had affected Spain, but the agrarian, mixed economy and relative isolation from world trade reduced its impact.[3]

The Republic was a new regime, but perhaps in contrast to the Weimar and Austrian republics, the legitimacy of the monarchy had been more seriously undermined in Spain, and the loyalty of the officer corps to the crown was less intense.[4] Let us not forget that Spain had had a republican regime in the nineteenth century, that dynastic wars had weakened the monarchy after its restoration, but above all, that the king's support for the dictatorship of Primo de Rivera in 1923, in breaking with constitutional rule, had alienated the political class of the Restoration. The army had not been fully sympathetic to the coup of 1923, had turned largely against the dictator because of his arbitrary policies in military matters, and ultimately contributed to his fall, which left the monarchy in an ambiguous position. A significant minority of the army had even conspired against the crown, and after the surprise success of Republican candidates in the municipal elections of 1931, the army stood passively by, large numbers of officers ready to recognize the Republic, while the king left the country. In contrast to the *Reichswehr,* the number of aristocratic officers was small. The supporters of the dictatorship were certainly not enthusiastic about Alphons XIII, who had abandoned their hero. The challenge to the legitimacy of the new regime did not arise out of loyalty to its predecessor, even though a small group of committed monarchists was to become a disloyal opposition. It was a sign of a past crisis that the monarchists formulated their goals in terms of instoration of an authoritarian monarchy rather than restoration of the liberal constitutional monarchy.

The new regime was the result of neither external defeat by a Versailles peace treaty nor violent revolution, but an incredibly peaceful transfer of power, smoothly worked out by the elites. If the new regime had not challenged many values and interests, a large number of conservative Spaniards would have been neutral to, or even welcomed, the change of regime, without having a clear idea of what it involved but without regrets for the one that had fallen. The overthrow of the monarchy was more the result of a vacuum of support than of the organized strength of its Republican opponents, who benefited nonetheless from a widespread and diffused feeling that a change was necessary.[5] Except for the Socialist labor movement, support for the Republic was more an expression of sentiment than of a long, continuous build-up of the strength of antimonarchist parties. For the Anarcho-syndicalist labor movement, the CNT (Confederación Nacional del Trabajo), monarchy or republic made little difference, since its opposition was directed against any bourgeois regime and ultimately against the state itself. It is important to keep in mind, in analyzing the accelerated crisis of the thirties, that the regime initially enjoyed a wide margin of legitimacy, and many of those who had not supported Republican candidates in the elections of April 1931 maintained an expectant, potentially favorable, or passive attitude that could have been used to assure compliance and even to build legitimacy.[6] At that time, the regime faced the active disloyal opposition only of the traditionalists, or Carlists, who had been a passive principled opposition to the liberal monarchy; the supporters of the dictatorship, which served the Republicans as a symbol of political degradation for the country; a small number of loyal monarchists; and the anarcho-syndicalist labor movement, which posed a more serious threat, but having been freed from recent persecution, was still in an expectant mood. It shall be our task to analyze how, in the course of five years, the supporters of a Republic which had been inaugurated so hopefully in April 1931 could become an embattled minority.

In a Europe where fascism and communism had been the leading oppositions to democratic regimes since the early 1920s, the first Spanish fascist group was founded only a month before the proclamation of the Republic, and the Communist party was a sectarian group with few members or followers.[7] Fascism would never achieve an electoral success comparable even to that of the Rexists in Belgium; nevertheless, in the spring of 1936, without a single deputy, it was to emerge as a powerful symbol. The Communist party would exercise considerable influence on the internal struggles of the Socialist party and, through the fusion of their youth organizations, control an important mass organization. Paradoxically, while fascism and communism were weak and were latecomers to Spain, the tensions that the struggle between them had created elsewhere had an impact in Spain that should not be underestimated. The case of Spain is a good example of how the process of breakdown in one country cannot be understood apart from the crises in other democracies in the same period of history. The weakness of fascism in Spain also must be taken into account to understand why the outcome of the crisis was decided by the army, and why the Italian and German models of pseudo-legal takeover of power in Spain did not hold. The CEDA (Confederación Española de Derechas Autónomas), though ambivalent about democracy even to the point of considering an unconstitutional takeover of power, would have attempted this only with army support, not through a combination of violent street action with legal parliamentary action at the elite level. It is an indication of the internal divisions within the army and the desire of many officers for disengagement from politics after the experience of the Primo de Rivera dictatorship that feelers extended in that direction, in late 1934 and before and immediately after the 1936 election, proved unsuccessful.

In the thirties, Spain, like the other European democracies in crisis, was characterized by an increased level of political mobilization, although this was not fully reflected in the rate of electoral participation, partly because of an active syndicalist abstentionism. But that mobilization had been achieved in a short time, rather than as a result of the slow, continuous organizational effort that had taken place in Germany, Austria, and even Italy. Consequently, the level of socialization in the ideology of different parties was lower, as was the degree of stability of loyalties and the discipline of the membership. This fact should be taken into account in explaining the instability of leadership, the bitterness of factional fights (particularly within the Socialist party), the incertitude of the leadership about followers' responses to their policies, and the movement of organized blocks of supporters to more radical positions, particularly in the spring of 1936. This higher level of mobilization differentiates the Spanish crisis from the Portuguese and accounts for the relatively bloodless and slow transition from the Republic to the *Estado Novo* in Portugal as compared to the revolutionary upsurges in October 1934 and in 1936 in Spain. Such rapid mobilization is particularly striking given Spain's economic underdevelopment and brings the Spanish case closer to the Italian between 1918 and 1923. The problems created by underdevelopment in these two countries partly explain the maximalist radicalization of the Socialist labor movement and the ultimate inability of the moderate Socialists to contribute effectively to the consolidation of a progressive democracy. In Spain, however, maximalist strength emerged only after 1933, even though its roots lay further back, whereas in Italy it appeared immediately after the war. Because of the internal divisions in the Spanish Socialist party, its support of the October 1934 revolution, its unwillingness to share the responsibilities of governing after the Popular Front electoral victory in 1936, and its extremist rhetoric and actions from 1933 to 1936, the PSOE (Partido Socialista Obrero Español), a factor of stability in the first period of the Republic, became a major, if not the decisive, factor leading to the breakdown. The similarities and differences in the response of Marxist-Socialist parties to democracies in crisis is central to our study.

The Spanish party system clearly fits the Sartori model of an extremely polarized multiparty system.[8] In terms of the number of parties, their centrifugal tendencies, ideological polarization not only between parties but within parties, and the politics of irresponsible outbidding, the system resembles those of pre-breakdown Italy and Germany. (For the party composition of the Republican legislatures and the vote in 1936, see table 1.) But in the Spanish case these characteristics were sharpened because of the initial constitution of the Republic and its interpretation by the Left Republicans as excluding the full loyalty of anyone to their right. This exclusivistic interpretation was applied even to parties willing to define themselves unequivocally as Republicans, resulting in the delegitimization of the old Radical party because

Table 1. Party Composition of the Legislature during the Second Republic (1931–36)

Party	Constituent Assembly Elected June 1931	Legislature Elected November 1933	Legislature Elected February 1936		Percentage of Vote, 16 February 1936 Election
			Seats	% of Seats	
Sindicalista	—	—	1	0.21	0.13
Bloque Unificación Marxista	—	—	1	0.21	0.17
Partido Comunista	—	1	17	3.6	2.5
PSOE	114	59	100	21.3	16.4
"maximalists"[a]			(49)		
Esquerra (Catalan Left; Companys)	37	22	36	7.6	4.1
Acción Republicana (Azaña)	31	5	—	—	—
Izquierda Republicana (IR)	—	—	87	18.5	13.7
Organización Republicana Gallega Autómata (ORGA)	18	3		included in IR	
Radical Socialista Independiente	2	2			
Radical Socialista	55	1			
Unión Republicana (Mtnez. Barrio)	—	—	38	8.1	5.9
Partido Federal	13	1	—	—	—
Progresistas	8	3	6	1.3	0.9
Agrupación al Servicio de la República (Ortega y Gasset)	13	—			
Republicanos Conservadores	—	16	3	0.64	0.8
Derecha Republicana	14	—	—	—	—
Republicano Liberal Demócrata	2	10	1	0.21	0.8
Partido Radical (Lerroux)	89	102	4	0.85	3.6
Centro (Portela Valladares)	—	—	16	3.4	5.1
Lliga Regionalista (Catalan Right; Cambó)	4	26	12	2.5	2.8
Partido Nacionalista Vasco	—	12	10	2.1	1.4
Minoría Vasco-Navarra (includes four Traditionalists)	15	—	—	—	—

Independents of the Center-Right and the Right	18	13	15	3.2	3.1
Agrarios	24	32	12	2.5	2.6
Acción Nacional	5	—	—	—	—
Acción Popular, CEDA, Derecha Regional Valenciana (Gil Robles)	—	115	88	18.7	23.2
Renovación Española (Calvo Sotelo)	2	15	included in Bloque Nacional		
Bloque Nacional (same)	—	—	13	2.8	3.8
Tradicionalistas (Carlists)	2	21	9	1.9	3.4
Nacionalista (Fascists)	—	1	—	—	—
Falange	—	1	—	—	0.08
Unidentified	3	5	2	0.42	5.6
Vacant seats	—	8	3	—	—
	469	474	474	100.25	100.08

NOTE: The party identifications in the 1931 legislature were very imprecise. The *Anuario Estadístico de España* of 1931 (pp. 487, 489) lists sixty-two members as having been elected on "different Republican lists" in the election of 28 June 1931 and the by-election in November. The *Lista de los Señores Diputados* published by the Cortes in 1932 does not give information on party identification. The sources disagree even on the number of seats in the 1931 legislature: the *Anuario Estadístico* gives 470; the official *Lista de los Señores Diputados*, arranged by districts, gives 469, but includes only 461 names; and Ramón Tamames, in *La República: La era de Franco*, p. 58, gives 484. We have opted to use the figure 469 from the *Lista de los Señores Diputados* of December 1932. On the basis of a variety of sources, party histories, etc., we have attempted to give a figure for each party, even when at any point in the legislative period some deputies changed parties. This explains the discrepancy between sources and with the data in table 22 in Linz, "The Party System of Spain," p. 260.

Table 1. (*continued*)

For the 1933 legislature we have used the information given in the *Boletín de Información Bibliográfica y Parlamentaria de España y el Extranjero* 1, no. 6 (November–December 1933): 1054–71, on party affiliation. It includes the names of 9 more deputies than does the *Lista de los Señores Diputados* of March 1935, which gives 455, but it is not complete. In the case of some deputies, party identification could be obtained from other sources, in order to complete the information, at the risk of some errors due to changes during the course of the legislative session.

Figures for the legislature elected in 1936 were taken from the official *Lista de los Señores Diputados* published by the Cortes in 1936, which lists the parliamentary groups. This list is dated June 1936 and therefore takes into account the results of the "second round" elections that took place in districts where none of the candidates had obtained the required minimum or where the first election had been voided. Since those elections were held after the Left had taken power in February 1936, they were particularly controversial. Some of the discrepancies between these figures and those given in other sources are due to this.

In the 16 February 1936 election, voters were basically confronted with two great coalitions: the Frente Popular and Frente Anti-revolucionario, except in some provinces where the Centro and the PVN ran their own tickets. It is therefore impossible to determine the number of votes the different parties would have obtained if competing with each other (as would have been the case under a system of proportional representation). Assuming that the placing of candidates of different parties on the coalition tickets reflects their appeal in each district, and considering the fact that the voter could split his ticket and give preference to one or another candidate, we have calculated the votes obtained by candidates of different parties compared to the total number of votes cast. Coalition discipline was generally high and probably benefited weaker parties represented on the coalition lists. There are also some missing data and contested returns. Therefore, these data should be considered as indicators of the approximate strength of parties in the electorate. In the comparison between votes and seats it should be kept in mind that the data on seats refer to the final composition of the chamber after the runoff, where required, and in the case of voided returns. Before the debate for admission of election certification, according to initial returns, the CEDA would have had ninety-six instead of eighty-eight deputies, the PSOE eighty-eight instead of one hundred, and the Izquierda Republicana seventy-nine instead of eighty-seven. The debate on the fairness of the election hinges on these highly controversial decisions by the legislature.

The figures for the 1936 vote have been calculated on the basis of the returns for different coalitions and candidates in Javier Tusell, *Las elecciones del Frente Popular* (Madrid: Edicusa, 1971), vol. 2, Appendix 1, pp. 265–97, in Juan J. Linz and Jesús M. de Miguel, "Hacia un análisis regional de las elecciones de 1936 en España," *Revista Española de la Opinión Pública*, 48, April–June 1977, pp. 27–68. Given the electoral law, the attribution of votes to parties rather than to large and heterogeneous coalitions required making certain assumptions and complex calculations presented in the article.

[a]The division of the Socialist (PSOE) deputies into "maximalists" and "moderates" was not institutionalized, but manifested itself in the 49 to 23 vote on the organization of the parliamentary group in March 1936 (Ricardo de La Cierva, *Historia de la Guerra Civil Española* [Madrid: San Martín, 1969], p. 678) and in the 49 to 19 vote in the caucus of 12 May against participating in any sort of government coalition (Stanley G. Payne, *The Spanish Revolution* [New York: Norton, 1970], p. 195).

of its collaboration with the Catholic CEDA. In contrast to the Weimar Republic, in which the constitution was a compromise between Social Democrats, Democrats, and the Zentrum, the Spanish constitution was drafted and supported by a much narrower coalition of Radicals, Left Republicans, and Socialists. But by the fall of 1933, the shift of the Radicals toward the right and the discontent of the Left Socialists under Largo Caballero would break even that relatively narrow coalition. This contrasts with the relative permanence, particularly in Prussia, of the initial Weimar coalition.

That the regional nationalist parties of both the Right and Left would make only a conditional commitment to the regime, and gave priority to their distinctive national interests instead, further complicated the definition of regime-supporting parties. With the exception of minor parties, all parties, even the less radical ones, were loyal to a democratic regime and constitutional procedures only so long as certain values they held higher than democracy could be pursued within the democratic framework. Even the system parties were unwilling to make a clear break with disloyal oppositions on their side of the spectrum.

It is difficult to say whether this basic ambivalence toward the central democratic regime was the result of ideological predispositions or to competition for the same social base in a very fluid and unstructured political situation. It could also be argued that it was a by-product of an electoral system that gave an inordinate advantage to broad coalitions and made it nearly impossible for those not entering them to aspire to a majority in Parliament. During three legislative elections and a number of regional elections in Catalonia, this contributed to distrust between parties that might otherwise have been closer to each other than to extremists on their own sides.[9] Hermens attributes much of the crisis of democracy in Europe to proportional representation;[10] but an electoral system that necessitated coalition with extremists and produced overrepresentation in Parliament of the winning coalition, led to a fragmented and polarized situation that was probably more dangerous to democracy than proportional representation would have been.[11]

There can be no question that Spanish democracy in the thirties faced economic and social problems that exceeded the resources of a liberal democratic regime, but the political leadership added to those problems others that were even more disruptive. In April 1931, however, the strictly political legacy of the past was less of a burden than the memory of Imperial Germany for Weimar or the ghost of the Habsburgs in Austria. In fact, the discontinuity of political development under the constitutional monarchy from 1876 to 1923 was in someways a disadvantage for the Spanish Republic. While in Germany and Austria the regime parties and their leadership represented a continuity of political experience acquired in Parliament and were stable organizations under the old regime, in Spain, except for the top leadership of the Socialist party and the Radical party politicians with municipal political experience, the elite consisted only of new men with little political or administrative experience who had not worked together in Parliament before. This applied to much of the leftist Republican leadership as well as to that of the new mass party of the Right, the CEDA.[12]

Paradoxically, some of the politicians most concerned with constitutional, liberal, democratic legality were men who had occupied legislative and cabinet posts in the liberal monarchy. The nonradical, almost loyal leaders of the Republic at the end of 1935 were a president of the Republic, Niceto Alcalá Zamora, two prime ministers, Chapaprieta and Portela, and a president of the chamber, Santiago Alba, all of whom had been cabinet members under the monarchy. In the spring of 1936, the less strident voices of the opposition were those of men linked by family and career to the old political elites, such as the bourgeois politicians of the Catalan Lliga. Many with political experience under the liberal monarchy made a better adjustment to the Republic than the newer leaders of the Right, who, after the 1931 debacle, had taken the place of the old oligarchic leadership. This raises an interesting question: does a newly established democracy really gain by eliminating from political life those who participated in the previous regime? Might not the new leaders of the same interests be more radical in their opposition than the old leadership would have been?

In terms of the main parties, particularly the system parties, and of political personnel, the republican regimes in Germany and Austria enjoyed greater continuity than did the Spanish Republic. This would explain their greater capacity for compromise, particularly between the social democrats and the Catholic parties, which for several years insured an apparent stabilization that has no equivalent in the Spanish case.

The Problems of Spain and the Crisis of the Republic

The breakdown of Spanish democracy could be viewed as the result of the serious and basically unsolvable problems inherent in Spanish society. It could be argued that the Republic could not overcome all these problems, which had to one degree or another led to the fall of preceding regimes. The argument would be that the structural problems of Spanish society were beyond the capabilities of even the most able democratic elite, and perhaps of any ruling elite. I would be inclined to reject this interpretation, stated in this way. Certainly previous regimes had experienced deep crises, but most managed to last longer than the Republic, and their breakdown cannot be directly and immediately linked with persistent problems in the social structure. The Isabeline monarchy fell in 1868 because of political and conjunctural factors; the First Republic, which was in any case an accidental and highly artificial creation, fell because of disunity within the small elite groups that genuinely believed in it. The most durable regime in Spain after 1800, the Restoration monarchy, survived serious crises for nearly fifty years. The pronunciamento of Primo de Rivera, triggered partly by the Moroccan War crisis (rather like the Fourth Republic's fall because of the Algerian War), ultimately brought it down, but its fall was not exclusively or even primarily due to the basic unsolved social and political problems which had so clearly manifested themselves in 1917. The same is true for the dictatorship of Primo de Rivera and the brief effort at reequilibration of the Restoration before the advent of the Republic in 1931. Certainly the deep crisis in Spanish society lay beneath all these breakdowns of political institutions, but the immediate cause was never a major mobilization of conflicting social groups, never a revolution or a real counterrevolution, and none of these crises of regimes divided society to the point of civil war.

The new regime, therefore, must have exacerbated the problems of the Spanish society to an impossible limit, certainly compounded by the European atmosphere in general. If we had asked various Spanish elites at different moments to name the basic problems that needed solution, their ranking of those problems and their confidence that solutions would be found within the framework of the established regime would have produced very different lists. If we remember, however, that agenda-setting is the result of a complex interaction between the decisions of the elite and pressures from the society, we might be able to understand better the accumulation of problems confronting the new rulers. When so many problems accumulate and find expression under conditions of political freedom, political leaders confront real difficulty in setting priorities among them, for different considerations produce very different outcomes. Regime institutionalization and regime stability might not always be given priority over the realization of other values. In order to consolidate itself, a new regime must do two things: implement policies that will satisfy a large number of potential supporters and link them to the regime, with negative effect on the smallest possible number of opponents; and follow policies that will satisfy the leadership of the coalition which installed the new regime, avoiding policies that would provoke dissent and splits in the coalition.

For the Spanish Republic these two goals were, to a considerable extent, incompatible. In the short run, the second seems to have taken precedence over the first, at the cost of the long-run stability of the regime. In addition, the first goal was unsuccessfully managed because of lack of resources, technical and administrative incompetence, and ideological preconceptions and rigidity.

The agenda of the new regime was dictated by a combination of pressures originating from the social structure (mainly the Socialist party and the labor movement, particularly the new agrarian socialism) and the ideological commitments of the participants in the pact of San Sebastian (largely derived from a conception of political problems that dated back to an older, radical Republican tradition). An agenda derived solely from the structural conditionings would have coped with its first problem, inequality in landownership, with a redistributive agrarian reform in the *latifundia* areas, yielding immediate benefits to tenant farmers, small farmers, and masses of farm laborers. A second problem, unemployment and underemployment, would have been handled next, probably with a large-scale public works program to create jobs. The first would have required a revolutionary will; it might have been possible to implement against the wishes of a relatively small group of noble and bourgeois landowners; additionally, if formulated in nonideological terms, it might have been acceptable to large segments of the population. A public works policy and government-sponsored or government-supported industrialization, however, was not feasible within the parameters of economic thinking at the time of the world-wide depression and the financial resources of the Spanish state. A third structural problem was posed by the popular demands for regional cultural and linguistic autonomy, particularly in Catalonia. A fourth major structural need that exceeded the financial capacity of the state was the rapid expansion and qualitative improvement of mass education. Fifth, these structural problems all demanded a thorough revamping of the fiscal system and reallocation of budgetary resources.

The agenda of the leadership of the Republican coalition coincided in part with the previous structurally determined agenda, but the Left bourgeois parties placed them in a different order and gave priority to other problems, chiefly the reduction and political neutralization of the army and the secularization of the society. Events made the Catalan problem more urgent. The central problem in the minds of the Republican policy-makers was to raise the educational level of the country, which led to an immediate effort to expand primary education in particular. However, these lofty ambitions encountered economic and technical difficulties compounded by the additional strain of attempting in a short period of time to replace the religious orders in the field of secondary education, where they had long dominated. Even the powerful personality of Largo Caballero could not place pro-labor and pro-welfare state policies on the agenda immediately, except for measures such as those on Términos Municipales and Jurados Mixtos, which gave labor unions advantages they had never before enjoyed and increased their size and bargaining power immeasurably. While agrarian reform was on the agenda from the beginning, serious efforts to legislate and implement a redistribution of rural wealth and power found little enthusiasm among the bourgeois Republican parties until later.[13] Even very secondary issues, like the responsibilities of the king and the Primo de Rivera dictatorship, absorbed considerable time on the agenda of the constituent Cortes.

The constituent period was the "honeymoon" of the new regime—a time that could have been used to promote policies creating a strong basis of support, particularly among the workers and peasants; clearly, the ordering of the agenda was not the best. Antimilitarism and anticlericalism received wide support among strata that resented the dominance of the military and the church in Spanish life. However, within the nonrevolutionary conception of the Republic held by its founding coalition, neither of these policies could really destroy or even seriously weaken the hold of the army and church over social power and influence. Both policies, but particularly anticlericalism, created deep resentments that mobilized large sectors of the population who had initially felt apathetic or expectant about the new regime rather than actively negative.[14] Once the immediate emotional gratification that those policies provided the regime-supporters had passed, they did not bring tangible benefits to the masses, and in fact appeared as only a bourgeois diversion from more immediate and pressing social demands. They did not serve to bring the Socialist working class, much less the masses organized in the CNT, into the bourgeois Socialist coalition. The way in which they were implemented, particularly through the retirement of officers at full pay and the proposed substitution of secular schools for the educational system of the religious orders, absorbed economic resources that might have been used to enact social policies benefiting the masses.[15] In addition, the bitter tenor that Azaña and others gave even to the necessary and acceptable army reform was perceived as ressentiment politics and alienated many officers who might have identified themselves with the new regime.[16] Many of the changes in this area, as in others, were more symbolic than pragmatic, creating discontent without benefiting anyone.

The same is even more true of many aspects of the anticlerical legislation and policies. The effort to secularize the society by decree inevitably mobilized a mass Catholic reaction against the new regime, particularly since these policies were accompanied by irresponsible acts by small groups, such as the burning of convents in May 1931, which the authorities were intially unable, or unwilling, to stop.[17] The high priority given to the secularization policy perverted what might otherwise have been an effective educational policy, and it interfered with attention to the Catalan and Basque problems. Catholic grievances were soon to be reinforced by the economic woes of the wheat-growing peasants of north-central Spain after ill-advised grain imports and an extraordinarily large harvest caused a fall in prices. In addition, certain provisions of the Agrarian Reform Law, such as the expropriation of many small and medium-sized land holdings under the *ruedos* provision and the inclusion in the inventories of expropriable land of properties in areas where agrarian reform would not be applied in the foreseeable future, reinforced peasant and small-town Castilian opposition. This opposition would manifest itself first in the April 1933 municipal elections and later in the November 1933 parliamentary victory of the Center Right.[18]

A less demagogic, cooler, and more pragmatic religious policy, taking advantage of compromise with the Vatican if not with the Spanish hierarchy, combined with the longer-range policy of secularization of education through the creation of an inexpensive and high-quality system, would certainly have created fewer opponents. A quickly and effectively implemented agrarian reform centered on a small number of very large landowners, both aristocratic and bourgeois, in areas of the country with serious unemployment problems and social discontent, would have alienated fewer people and gained considerable support for the regime. Ideological preconceptions, combined with lack of adequate information, legalistic constraints, bureaucratic inefficiency, and misconceptions, led the Republican leadership to miss these opportunities and contributed to the disillusionment of the Socialist leadership with the coalition, as well as the shift of the more conservative Republicans toward the right. Some particular aspects of the Socialists' policies in the agrarian labor field added to the growing discontent of the Anarcho-syndicalists.

Ideological rather than pragmatic policy formulation also prevented the regime from presenting those policies in a favorable light to those not directly affected by them, like the industrial middle classes. In the absence of any real commitment to create a socialist economy to substitute for the incipient capitalism of the industrialized regions, ideological debates about worker control and the rights of property could only create distrust of the regime. Agrarian reform should have been presented as an opportunity for industrial sectors to find new markets among the masses as they acquired a better economic position and improved buying power. If public secondary education capable of competing in cost and quality with that of the religious orders had been created, and if fair policies for institutional standards had been set up, the dominant position of the orders could have been displaced without creating the hostility that the outlawing of their teaching aroused.[19] Furthermore, the fact that such legislation could not be immediately implemented because of limited personnel and economic resources could only contribute to the discrediting of the regime.

The injudicious ordering of priorities and the ineffectiveness of the governments of the first bienio created immense problems and expectations that would remain unsatisfied. It also mobilized broad segments of the population, not just against the ruling parties, but against the regime, which those parties had identified with themselves by constitutionalizing what might have been ordinary laws. This meant that change required the mobilization of majorities sufficient to amend the constitution, not simple legislation. The search for such a qualified majority, together with the exigencies of the electoral law, pushed the possibilist sector of Spanish Catholicism into an alliance with the extreme Right. This alliance contributed to the division of those Republicans in the Radical party, who preferred to integrate the Right into the system and were opposed to some of the policies of the first two years, but would soon be disaffected by the revision of the anticlerical policies advocated by the Center Right with whom they had to cooperate to govern. The way in which the policy-making process was conceived by many Republicans, particularly Azaña, almost inevitably led to the splintering-off of the Republican parties more to the right and to the disappointment of the Socialist labor movement with the tangible fruits of the change of regime.

The regime-building phase of the Republic achieved placement of Spain's major problems on the agenda, and the good will of the Republican leadership during that period cannot be doubted. However, the specific formulation of those policies and the failures of their implementation, perhaps in part because of the personality of Azaña, left an unfortunate heritage: the mobilization of opponents, the disillusionment of a key supporter, the Socialist party, and the continuing and intensified hostility of the Anarcho-syndicalists. Only the Catalan policy worked out between Azaña and Companys, and crystallized in the *Estatuto* despite the opposition of Castilian intellectuals and nationalists, can be considered an important contribution to the stabilization of the regime. Even though the events of October 1934 endangered that solution, the relative stability of Catalonia in the spring of 1936 and the growing willingness of the Esquerra (the Catalan Left) and the Lliga (the Catalan conservative party) to play the roles of government and loyal opposition in support of moderate solutions in Madrid can be considered permanent fruits of those initial decisions.

Regional Politics and the Breakdown of Democracy

The peripheral nationalisms, particularly the Catalan, that have contributed to so many crises in modern Spain were also a factor in the crisis of the Republic.[20] Though not a major factor in the immediate causes of the military uprising in July 1936, they contributed to the alienation of the army and other sectors of the society from the regime. Franco propaganda during the civil war constantly referred to the struggle against the *rojo-separatistas,* or "reds and secessionists." The breakdown of federal or regionally decentralized democratic regimes, and of countries with cultural-linguistic minorities, is central neither to our model nor to the cases analyzed in this volume, even though it figured in the cases of the Weimar Republic, Austria, and to some extent, Argentina and Brazil. We shall, therefore, devote some attention to it here in an attempt to draw some general inferences.

The emergence of Catalan and, later, Basque nationalism posed a problem that appeared unsolvable to many Spanish politicians.[21] Decentralized, regional self-government was difficult to reconcile with the tradition of a unitary centralist state that had emerged in the eighteenth and nineteenth centuries. It was even more difficult to reconcile the idea of Spain as a nation-state with that of Spain as a multilingual and even multinational state. For most Spaniards, their country was a nation-state, but for important minorities on the periphery it was only a state compatible with a regional national identification. These two contradictory concepts of the state, complicated by the ambiguous demands of the regional political movements, erupted as inescapable problems after the proclamation of the Republic.

The repressive policies of the Primo de Rivera dictatorship against Catalan nationalism, and the democratization of what had been an upper-class bourgeois movement, led in 1931 to the proclamation of Catalonia as a state integrated in an Iberic Federation. One of the immediate tasks of the provisional government of the Republic, therefore, was to find a formula for bringing the Catalans into the regime. It was the great achievement of Azaña, against the opposition of the Right and of many Republicans, to find an institutional solution to the demands for regional autonomy in the Estatutos. The ensuing debates on the linguistic question, in which the prominent Castilian-speaking intellectuals intervened, aroused the Castilian Spanish nationalists. On the other hand, the anticlerical policy and the initial weakness of a nationwide Catholic conservative opposition helped to strengthen the Partido Nacionalista Vasco (PNV), which represented Catholic sentiment in the Basque country and had vain hopes for separate regulation of relations between church and state in that region. But Catalonia, thanks to the understanding established between Azaña and Companys, was to have an autonomous government in the *Generalitat*. In the Basque country, the disagreements between the Basque nationalists and the Carlists, and the lack of sympathy of the Left for their aspirations, which initially appeared as proclerical and hostile to the Republic, prevented the creation of an autonomous regional government.

Regional nationalism contributed indirectly to the crisis of the Republic by arousing the Spanish Castilian nationalism of the authoritarian Right, symbolized by Calvo Sotelo or Pradera, and shared by many supporters of the more moderate Right. Given the background of much of the officer corps, such sentiments must have been strong in the army. The weakness in Catalonia and the Basque country of the nationwide moderate Center-Right parties, the CEDA and the Radicals, deprived those parties of a solid base among the more modern, urban bourgeoisie and of the leadership such a base could have provided.

More directly, Catalan nationalism and the Barcelona rebellion contributed to profound crisis in October 1934. Companys's statement on 6 October represented a coup d'état by the head of the regional autonomous government and a break with the constitutional legality of the Republic. Let us quote him:

In this solemn hour in the name of the people and the Parliament, the government that I preside over assumes all the faculties of power in Catalonia, proclaims the Catalan State of the Spanish Federal Republic and, to reestablish and fortify the relationship with the leaders of the general protest against fascism, invites them to establish in Catalonia the provisional government of the Republic, which will find in our Catalan people the most generous impulses of fraternity in the common desire to build a Federal, free, and magnificent Republic.

The government of Catalonia will at all times be in contact with the people. We aspire to establish in Catalonia the indestructible redoubt of the essences of the Republic. I invite all the Catalans to obedience to the government and ask that no one shall disobey its orders.[22]

The coup d'état proclaimed a new regime, a Federal Republic in whose name Companys demanded obedience from the military authorities. Their refusal and their loyalty to the Madrid central government, plus Companys's failure to mobilize the Catalan population, quickly brought an end to the hopes of the rebellion.[23]

The October crisis in Barcelona in 1934 involves many of the variables of our model as well as others that are specific to the relationship between central and regional governments. In this last respect, the situation had analogies in Weimar. The coexistence of two governments, the regional one of the Generalitat and the central one in Madrid, the delegation of some of Madrid's powers to the Generalitat, with two parliaments, the national and the Catalan, created complex constitutional problems. In a fully consolidated regime, such conflicts between federal and state governments can be resolved by the decisions of the constitutional tribunal. This procedure was foreseen in the Spanish constitution of 1931, but because of its lack of tradition and the bias of its composition, the tribunal's decision on the competence of the Catalan Parliament to legislate on agrarian contracts lacked authority.[24] The effort to juridify a political issue, so characteristic of weak governments, backfired. In this case, the constitutional issue was complicated by the overlap between national and class cleavages. After the proclamation of the Republic, the Esquerra had become the dominant party in opposition to the traditional, bourgeois, conservative Lliga. While the November 1933 elections had brought to power Radical Republican minority governments with CEDA support in Madrid, the January 1934 elections for the Catalan Parliament had reaffirmed control by the Esquerra. Therefore, the central and regional governments came to represent opposing class interests. When the Esquerra-dominated Parliament enacted a rural tenancy law that favored the supporters of Companys and tended to expand Catalan autonomy, the Catalan landlords turned to the central government to question the authority of the Catalan Parliament to enact such a law.

The issue produced a mass mobilization in Catalonia, bitter debates in the Spanish legislature, the reenactment of the law after its constitutionality had been rejected by the Tribunal of Constitutional Guarantees, and actions by the Catalan authorities against the judiciary. Against this background, two other factors became decisive: the radicalization of the Esquerra youth organization, and the emergence of the Estat Català radical nationalist group under the leadership of Josep Dencàs, which, with its fascist characteristics and its representation in the Catalan government, exercised pressure on Companys. The central government was willing to compromise on the issue, a decision that contributed to its imminent fall. The growing polarization of Lliga and Esquerra interests led to the withdrawal of the Lliga from the Catalan Parliament. The result was a situation in which a powerful regional interest group could turn to the central government for support while the regional government transformed a local class conflict into a nationalistic issue.

At the same time, the generalized distrust of the CEDA and the reaction to its entry into the government of the Center Left, Republicans and Socialists alike, prompted Companys's ambiguous actions in October and the proclamation quoted above. The central government and many Spaniards saw in that proclamation an anticonstitutional act, if not secession. Even though it could also be interpreted as a defense of the Republican regime against a potential threat, Catalan nationalists hoped to use it to change the relationship between the Spanish state and Catalonia. In June 1934, during a parliamentary debate on the thirteen to ten decision of the constitutional court, Azaña stated that "Catalonia is the last rampart left to the Republic. The autonomous power of Catalonia is the last republican power standing in Spain."[25] The statement poses an important question for the analysis of crisis and breakdown of democracies, particularly since it often has been argued that a more strongly federal Germany would have been an obstacle on the path of Hitler to power. It is noteworthy that in the last phase of the *Machtergreifung* the Bavarian government entertained ideas similar to those of Companys in 1934. During the debate, Cambó, the leader of the Catalan Lliga, posed the problem in the following terms:

They speak always as if Catalonia has to be the bulwark of the Left in Spain and of the leftist orientation of the Republic. Within Catalonia parties have the right to express whatever sympathies they may wish; Catalonia collectively, and in its name, its government, has no right to make statements which might endanger the respect that the freedoms of Catalonia deserve of all those governing Spain. Catalonia, collectively, and specially the representative institutions of Catalonia, should not be the bulwark of anyone; they should only be the bulwark of Catalonia.[26]

Cambó rightly stressed how the combination of nationwide cleavages with center versus periphery cleavages threatened the consociational compromise achieved with the Republic. The regional government, by siding with the nationwide opposition and using powers delegated to it by the central government, broke with the consociational solution. The same would be true if the central government were to side with the regional opposition, as it did indirectly by taking the issue of legislative competence before the constitutional court. There is, however, a basic difference between the ill-advised transformation of the political conflict into a legal issue and the proclamation of a Catalan state in a Spanish federal republic by the Catalan regional government.

This crisis demonstrates many of the variables of our model. We find disloyal opposition to the Spanish state in the Catalan extreme nationalists of the Estat Català and other minor groups. Paramilitary groups, the *escamots,* emerged with their distinctive shirts and nationalist social revolutionary mystique. Semiloyalty to the 1931 constitutional pact of elements in Companys's party pushed him to his 6 October decision. The ambivalent relationship between a major party, the Lliga, and the interest group of the landlords, the Instituto San Isidro, prevented them from acting in a politically more constructive way. Azaña's presence in Barcelona made him suspect of semiloyalty, even though it seems clear that he disapproved of the proclamation. However, he did not communicate his knowledge of the intentions of the Catalanists to his political enemy, Lerroux, the head of the Madrid government, and this action would certainly not be covered by our strict definition of loyal opposition.[27] The destructive efforts of the Radical-CEDA governments to link Azaña with the rebellion later contributed to his leadership of a broad Popular Front coalition as well as to the hostility of many Republicans against those governments. This undermining of the personal legitimacy of potentially powerful and respected leaders, so characteristic of the crisis of regimes, was another result of the Barcelona rebellion. Perhaps the inevitable but politically unwise measures against Catalan autonomy, rather than against those responsible for the events, fanned the upsurge of nationalism there and made post-1934 reequilibration of the regime difficult by straining the relationship between Cambó and Gil Robles. Another consequence was the legitimization of the role of the army in deciding political crises, in this case under the intelligent and prudent leadership of a Catalan general in Barcelona, who in July 1936 would be put to death for failing to join the Franco rebellion. It is interesting to note that on 4 October Companys made an unsuccessful attempt to establish contact with the president of the republic, Alcalá Zamora (that is, in our model, with the neutral power) to try to prevent the formation of the new government.

The situation in Barcelona in 1934 exemplifies a special and complex pattern of semiloyal opposition: regional authorities acting beyond constitutional limits to defend a regime against what they perceive as its betrayal by the central government. In a real crisis, rather than a perceived crisis, such an act could serve to defend democracy; but when unjustified, as in this case, it serves only to deepen its crisis. Since the regional government represented a peripheral nationalism, such actions were inevitably perceived as a threat to the unity of the state. This analysis casts doubt on the thesis that the federal structure could serve as an instrument for the defense of democracy by creating regional bulwarks to serve as a basis for the reconquest of democratic institutions. On these grounds, a defense of democracy against Hitler on the basis of Bavarian particularism had little chance.[28] On the other hand, the different political alignments at the regional and national levels in a highly divided society are likely to create a constitutional crisis when the central government intervenes against the regional government, as in the action of the Papen government against Prussia. Those who place so much faith in regional autonomies as stabilizers of Italian democracy should not lose sight of these experiences. Certainly, in multinational societies, the defense of democracy by either the central or the regional government is not likely to help safeguard democratic institutions, since large segments of the population will perceive the conflict as one between nationalities.

It should also be noted that when the Esquerra deputies abandoned the Spanish Parliament to protest the decision of the constitutional court, the Basque nationalists also left their seats. In September 1934 they convened an assembly of municipal representatives to which the Catalans sent a delegation, but which was dissolved by the minister of the interior. The activities of the Catalans to create a coalition based on regional nationalism under the label "Galeuzca" was perceived by the Spanish Right as part of a conspiracy, especially after the Catalan rebellion converged with the Socialist revolution. Their perception was inaccurate but understandable, as it was a projection of their own conspiratorial activities. In 1934, the Basque nationalists, who had been courted by monarchist military conspirators in the first bienio, started their rapprochement with the Left, under the tactical guidance of Prieto. Their commitment to nationalism above all ultimately found them on a side where they did not belong in terms of class and religious outlook—a fact that ultimately embittered the Right against demands for regional autonomy and strengthened the authoritarian opposition to the Republic.

While the complex interaction between regional nationalism, class, and religious issues contributed significantly to the crisis of the thirties, in the spring of 1936 class and ideological conflict became dominant in the final breakdown. For, after the failure of the Estat Català group and in view of the unsympathetic attitude of the Right toward regional aspirations, the Esquerra and the Lliga in Catalonia developed relations that fitted the model of government and loyal opposition and made the region a focal point of relative stability.

Loyalty, Disloyalty, and Semiloyalty

In the Spanish case any attempt at meaningful delimitation of loyalty, disloyalty, and semiloyalty presents almost insuperable difficulties. The main actors do not include a mass Fascist party that explicitly rejects liberal democracy, or an electorally strong Communist party committed to revolution, but rather the Socialist party (PSOE) and the Catholic conservative party (CEDA), whose statements and actions could be characterized at one moment as loyal to democratic institutions and at the next as disloyal. The basic statements—and even more, the perceptions—of these major actors contributed to ambiguous decisions by parties that in other democracies would have been unambiguously loyal. Actions like the break with the institutions by Izquierda Republicana and Unión Republicana on 5 October 1934 can only be understood in that context. Suspicion of the intentions of the CEDA, within the frame of reference created by Hitler's *Machtergreifung,* and particularly the Austrian crisis in February 1934, explain Izquierda Republicana's revealing statement that "the monstrous fact of turning over the government of the Republic to its enemies is a treason. [We] break all solidarity with the present institutions of the regime and affirm [our] decision to turn to all means in defense of the Republic."[29] Such a statement would have been an appropriate expression of loyalty to democratic institutions in the case of a Fascist takeover. But the question here was the formation of a government, still under the leadership of Lerroux, a Radical party prime minister of Republican tradition, and concerned the appointment of three representatives of the CEDA (the largest party in Parliament, with 105 of 474 deputies) to the ministries of agriculture, labor, and justice. This crucial change in a fifteen-man cabinet took place in a parliamentary framework, not as a result of mass pressure on the streets, and two of the three CEDA ministers certainly could not be characterized as antidemocratic or even anti-Republican. In view of the public record after the October Revolution, but not perhaps if one takes into account the more informal feelers CEDA extended toward the army, the reaction of Izquierda Republicana must be defined as semiloyal.

This raises the question of "Loyalty to what?" If loyalty is defined in terms of the commitment to democratic institutions, it means loyal to whoever, under those formal procedures, is entitled to govern regardless of policies pursued, assuming, of course, that the government maintains respect for civil liberties, democratic processes, and the right to free elections. According to these terms, few political forces were unconditionally loyal, and even those coming closest to that standard acted toward democratic governments in ways that are at least dubious. For example, Lerroux, the leader of one of the great parties of Spanish Republicanism, conspirator against the monarchy, leading figure in the coalition governments of the first two years, was apparently not unaware of the sentiments that led to the Sanjurjo pronunciamento, but he only indirectly warned the prime minister, Azaña, of the growing danger.[30] Similarly, years later, Azaña, although he knew of the plans of the Socialists and the Catalan regional government, did not feel obliged to warn the prime minister, Lerroux, nor to publicly dissociate himself from his party's ambiguous support of Socialist revolution and Catalan rebellion.[31] An independent Republican and highly civil politician like Chapaprieta recounts in his memoirs that when asked for advice in March 1936 by the president of the Republic, he recommended appointing a new government (an act within his constitutional prerogative), which, with the support of the armed forces, would reestablish order and authority.[32] He justified his position by arguing that the elections had given the Left only a small majority—he obviously did not take into account the dubious returns of the second round—and that a large number of the electorate had not cast their vote, so that one-third of the electorate was imposing its will on the rest of Spain. Presidential intervention would then pave the way for a new election. Certainly such advice ran counter to a strict definition of loyalty to parliamentary majority rule.

The definition of loyalty to the institutions of the new regime was even more restricted. Its founders were inclined to define as loyal only those who had participated in the establishment of the Republic; that is, those whose politics ranged from Radical on farther to the left. Irrespective of proper democratic behavior, the intention to modify the substantive content of the constitution was defined as disloyal. After 1933, the Socialist party defined as disloyal any party that advocated revoking or changing the policies enacted in the first bienio. Such positions tended to narrow the basis of legitimacy for the new regime.

The system of forces and parties will perhaps be more clearly understood if identified in terms of my definitions of loyal, semiloyal, and disloyal. The Anarcho-syndicalist CNT (Confederación Nacional del Trabajo) and the activists of the FAI (Federación Anarquista Ibérica) in control of the great trade union federation constituted a sincere disloyal opposition to a parliamentary regime, even under a Left-dominated government.[33] The CNT's antagonism to the Socialists and the actions of its followers, particularly the sporadic violence in the first bienio, provoked the regime to repressive actions like the events of Casas Viejas. These were cynically exploited by the opposition (including the Center Republicans) and contributed to Azaña's loss of prestige. The effect could be compared to that of the Spartakist and local Communist uprisings in the postwar years of the Weimar Republic.

The initially insignificant Communist party, the PCE, was a permanent disloyal opposition, which participated as a minor actor in the Asturian Revolution and afterward exercised an overt or covert influence on the maximalization of the Socialist party.[34] The fusion of the Socialist and Communist youth organizations in the spring of 1936 represented a major step in the polarization process and the centrifugal tendencies of the Left. Even though it had few adherents, nonorthodox communism in Catalonia—consisting of the Bloc Obrer i Camperol, the Partit Català Proletari, the later Partido Socialista Unificado de Cataluña (PSUC), the independent Communist leadership, and the Partido Obrero de Unificación Marxista (POUM)—assumed the role of a disloyal opposition combining nationalist and revolutionary appeals in Catalonia.[35] Those minor Catalan extreme leftist parties combined under competent leadership to create the revolutionary Alianza Obrera and played a role in the events of October 1934 in Barcelona, proclaiming a general strike and contributing to popular mobilization in support of the Catalan nationalists. Congruently with our model, the period after the November 1933 elections and even more after the October revolution strengthened centrifugal tendencies in the PSOE and the UGT (Unión General de Trabajadores, the Socialist trade union federation) that ranged from semiloyal to disloyal. In contrast to Germany, Finland, and even Austria and Italy, the line between a system-supporting Socialist party and the revolutionary opposition in Spain was continuously eroded. The competition between political movements on the left for the support of the working class and the context created by the rise of fascism brought the Socialists closer to the revolutionary, antidemocratic forces.[36]

On the other side of the political spectrum, the Traditionalists had always been a principled, disloyal opposition, even to the conservative liberal oligarchic monarchy.[37] Indirectly, they contributed much to the failure to integrate peripheral nationalism into the system. They also provided a historical ideological link for the turn toward authoritarianism of the Alphonsine monarchists.[38] In spite of equivocal appeals by the king for moderation, and the lack of cooperation of many monarchist notables and caciques willing to make peace with a conservative Republic, monarchism under the Republic underwent a process similar to that of the DNVP (Deutschnationale Volkspartei) under the leadership of Hugenberg. Hugenberg's Spanish equivalent, Calvo Sotelo, radicalized by persecution and intellectual contact with the Action Française during his Paris exile, became a pole of attraction to disloyalty and violence on the right.[39] Just as the Communists, orthodox and heterodox, represented a minority on the left, modern fascism was a minority force on the right, not comparable in strength even to the Finnish Lapua.[40] However, its presence in the heated political climate of the thirties contributed to the defensive violence of the Socialists and the retaliatory acts of Fascist violence; and finally to the exaltation of violence by its leaders, all of which fed into the process of breakdown of civil peace. Once again the boundaries between disloyalty and acceptance with reservations of the new regime by the Center Right, particularly the CEDA, were more blurred in Spain than in Germany, where the Zentrum and even the DVP (Deutsche Volkspartei) emphasized the distinctions between themselves and the NSDAP. That the supporters of Calvo Sotelo belonged socially to the same groups as many supporters of the CEDA, and thus did not represent a challenge to Catholicism, enhanced the ambiguity despite the disagreement of the CEDA and Calvo Sotelo about tactics. Participation in the Parliament and the government from 1933 to 1935 seriously strained the relationship between the Center Right and the extreme Right. In that period the Center Right began to move from semiloyalty to loyalty to the democratic regime.[41] However, as the Socialist party moved toward maximalist semiloyal, if not clearly disloyal, positions, and the CEDA faced the competition of the extreme Right and the Falange, particularly among its youth and student supporters, it could not avoid a turn to semiloyalty, even though some of its leaders expressed interest in last-minute reequilibration efforts.

It is difficult in our terms to define the Partido Nacionalista Vasco (PNV) as either loyal or semiloyal. Its actions, with minor exceptions, would place it in the loyal opposition, but the ambiguities of its nationalism, some of its organizational activities, such as paramilitary youth groups, its rhetoric, and its occasional withdrawals (*retraimientos*) from the parliamentary process led some participants at one point or another to perceive it as semiloyal. In Catalonia, minorities within the Catalan nationalist movement, particularly the fascistic activists of the Estat Català, can be considered another disloyal opposition; in 1934 they exercised a centrifugal attraction on the Esquerra, particularly its youth organization. Once more, the boundaries between disloyalty and loyalty, in this case to the Spanish state, were blurred. The effort to create paramilitary organizations and the rhetoric of violence was again present in a three-pronged attack against the conservative Catalans of the Lliga, the central government, and the CNT. If loyalty to the new regime were construed strictly and narrowly, the initial Catalanist interpretation of what the agreement of San Sebastian (on which the founding coalition of the Republic had been based) and the latter efforts to reinterpret the autonomy granted in 1932 could have been perceived by many Spaniards as semiloyal. However, until 1934 and again in the spring of 1936, the Esquerra could be considered one of the basic regime-supporting parties.[42] The same was true of the Lliga throughout the Republic, despite the belated rallying of Cambó to the monarchy in the period 1930–31, the temporary *retraimiento* from the Catalan Parliament dominated by the Esquerra, and local electoral coalitions with the extreme Right. Had it not been for a minority of extreme nationalists and the complexities of working-class politics in Catalonia, the two great Catalan parties, Lliga and Esquerra, could have been important regime-supporting forces. The Center Right, Radicals and CEDA, failed, partly under the pressure of the Castilian-nationalist-oriented Agrarians, in not working more closely with a regime-oriented party like the Lliga.

It is worth emphasizing once more that except for the Anarcho-syndicalist CNT, the openly disloyal oppositions in Spain were, almost to the end, weak in comparison with others in Europe. Neither communism nor fascism had a strong appeal to the Spanish electorate. Even the monarchists of Renovación were probably electorally weaker than the DNVP and were less well-connected with the industrial bourgeoisie, the army, and the bureaucracy. Their rhetoric notwithstanding, minority nationalist groups were less disloyal to the state than similar minorities in Eastern Europe. Ultimately, the breakdown of Spanish democracy must be blamed on the semiloyalty of parties that in other European countries tended clearly to define their allegiance to a democratic regime and their distance from disloyal oppositions, the Socialists, and the demo-Christians or Catholic parties. Blame also falls on the bourgeois Left, Center-Left and Center-Right Republicans, and the Esquerra, and this is the most complex problem. These parties, the regime's founding forces, acted, sometimes with the best intentions, in ways that contributed to the crisis of the regime. Their positions throughout those years would not have been called semiloyal; in retrospect, however, certain actions at some critical junctures, particularly in October 1934, could be defined as semiloyal to democracy, though not to the Republic as conceived by them, for loyalty to the regime established in 1931 is much more limited than loyalty to democracy.

The inability of Azaña and Lerroux, the two most outstanding Republican leaders, to continue working for the institutionalization of the regime, and the resultant fractionalization of the Center Republican parties, were both a sign and a cause of the crisis. It might be tempting to attribute that incapacity to personality differences, but that would be incorrect, since the policies of the Radicals and of the leftist Republicans (initially Acción Republicana, and later, Izquierda Republicana) represented two basic policy options. Azaña's was an effort to combine a bourgeois revolution with social reforms that would incorporate the Socialists into a democratic regime at the risk of losing conservative Republican support. Technical inadequacies, misjudgment in timing and priorities of reforms, pressure from sporadic violence of the Anarcho-syndicalists, the ressentiment policies of petit bourgeois politicians, and an ideological shift within the Socialist party all worked against the noble attempt.[43]

Lerroux, faced with Azaña's decision, the hostility those policies had created in a broad middle class that supported the Republic, and perhaps personally frustrated in his ambitions, attempted another strategy: the incorporation of the Catholic conservative masses, peasants, and middle classes into the Republic, luring them away from an ambiguous semiloyalty.[44] Though an inadequate solution to the social problems of an underdeveloped agrarian country, that policy, in view of the Socialists' tendency toward withdrawal from the responsibilities of the regime, represented a grand design in political terms. Its failure can be blamed on the disloyal revolution by the Socialists and the rebellion of the Catalan Generalitat, the semiloyalty of the Left bourgeois Republicans, the rigidity of the Right and of the interests it represented after 1934, and ultimately on the personal discrediting of Lerroux because of the corruption within the Radical party. The persistent veto of the neutral power of the president of the Republic, Alcalá Zamora, made Lerroux's design impossible. In a regime faced with unsolvable problems like conditional legitimacy, low levels of institutionalization of such conflict-solving mechanisms as a constitutional court, and disloyal oppositions engaging in violence or appealing to it, centripetal tendencies were bound to fail.

There was a third alternative in 1933, represented with more or less coherence by Gordón Ordás and Martínez Barrio. It was based on a broad centrist coalition of Republicans that would have isolated Socialists and clericals, pursued a policy of bourgeois political and cultural reformism, and de-emphasized the solution of pressing social problems.[45] Such a policy, which would have required a different attitude on the part of Lerroux and Azaña, might have been supported by the president and most of the army and have been able to face the opposition of the Right, but it would have encountered decided hostility from the working class, especially the Socialist party. Historically, it would have been a sterile solution, but it might have assured continuity of the regime at about the efficacy level of the Third Republic in France, given the social tensions. It would have been based on a solid core of parties loyal to a democratic regime and, with minor modifications, loyal to the constituent acts of the Republic in the fields of religious, military, and regional policy. Even some of the necessary social reforms would have continued at a slow pace. It would have been an embattled but persistent, if not stable, regime.

The great question that remains almost unanswerable and will be clarified only by more monographic research is why centrifugal tendencies rather than centripetal tendencies were reinforced in the major parties so that possible boundaries between disloyal opposition and conditional support of the regime became blurred. Paul Preston, polemicizing with Richard Robinson, has provided us with a good description of the strong semiloyalty in the CEDA that almost inevitably was perceived by the Socialists and many Left Republicans as a sign of potential disloyalty.[46] Stanley Payne, Edward Malefakis, and earlier, Salvador de Madariaga, have documented the radicalization of the Socialist party toward semiloyalty and even overt revolutionary disloyalty to a democratic republic. The problem is identifying the factors that led to those tendencies, their relative weight, and even more, their timing. Undoubtedly the mutual perceptions and misperceptions of key actors initiated a complex process of feedback that makes it difficult to place the blame on either side, even when the responsibility in terms of overt action of the maximalist Socialist leadership cannot be questioned.

If considerations of weight and timing are put aside, however, an enumeration of the most obvious factors is possible. Foremost is the accidentalism and consequent attentism toward democracy in both the Marxist and the Catholic ideological heritages. Democracy and a bourgeois parliamentary republic are of only instrumental value for a labor movement whose ultimate goal is a better society for the working class and can be abandoned for the dictatorship of the proletariat if perceived as necessary to achieve the goal. Only a full commitment to the long-run Marxist view of social development and the awareness of the limits for revolutionary action in a particular society can make a strictly Marxist view compatible with a negative integration into democracy. This accounts for the position of the only intellectual Marxist in the Spain of the thirties, Besteiro, who opposed participation in the Republican coalition government as well as the October revolution. The more pragmatic, "ouvrieriste" position represented by Largo Caballero allowed Socialist collaboration with the Primo de Rivera dictatorship, his acceptance of the Ministry of Labor in the bienio governments, and the maximalist turn after disillusionment with Republican and Socialist sponsored reformism. The ideological pragmatism that some would label opportunism and Prieto's realistic evaluation of the possibilities for reform and revolution were closer to the realities of the Spanish situation and to the traditional positions of Western European social democrats.[47] However, in the context of the thirties, given the rise of fascism, the unsolvable social problems, the rapid and massive mobilization of the working class, particularly by the Socialists in the countryside, and the competition with the Anarcho-syndicalists and orthodox and heterodox Communists, the appeal of such a position was limited. Besteiro's stance, in line with orthodox prewar Marxism, had been feasible in a stable nondemocratic regime like imperial Germany but was not politically viable for a democratic republic in a society like Spain.[48] In that context, the maximalist voluntarist interpretation of the ideological heritage appealed to most intellectuals in the party and to a large mass of new followers who had not been socialized in the social democratic tradition.[49]

A similar ideological ambiguity in the Catholic heritage operated on the right, compounded by both the Spanish and the international situations. The Catholic church as an institution sees itself as permanent and independent of political change, capable of compromise with any regime, as long as it is a powerful regime or one that respects the vital interests of the church. The stabilization of democracy in Europe, and the need to use its instrumentalities to defend the church's interests even in a hostile climate of bourgeois laicism and anticlericalism, led the papacy to formulate an accidentalist position toward changes in regime. This was quickly picked up in April 1931 by the lay leaders of Spanish Catholicism and was effectively supported by the Vatican, sometimes in conflict with certain leaders of the Spanish hierarchy, who were emotionally identified with the monarchy that had favored both them and the church.[50] This accidentalism was not easy to defend when faced with what many Catholics considered to be the outrageously anticlerical and even antireligious policies of Left Republicans in coalition with the Socialists. Certainly, there were strains of democratic commitment within the Catholic tradition. But the relative political neutralization of the church after the Restoration and the cultural isolation of Spanish Catholicism weakened those tendencies. The far-reaching secularization of the Spanish working class in the nineteenth and early twentieth centuries, and the complex interdependency between the church and the ownership class, had limited the strength of the Christian social movement except in some peasant areas. The sudden mobilization of the Catholic masses by the religious policies of the Republic became more defensive and therefore more conservative than either the Christian Democratic or Christian Social tendencies, and aroused the fear and suspicion of the Left Republicans and all working-class forces.[51] The emergence of a mass party without cadres socialized in the Catholic political and social ideology posed some of the same problems for the CEDA as did the expansion of the Socialist labor movement. The centrality of a single issue— the revision of the anticlerical policies—combined with the narrow-minded defense of the interests of a middle class insecure in its status and economic position, did not help to integrate the Catholic position into the Republic. The Catholic ideological tradition contained concepts incompatible with pluralist liberal democracy, such as corporativism, which in central and northern Europe, and even in France, nevertheless fused with secular non-Fascist intellectual traditions and practices but that in Spain were associated with the anti-revolutionary Carlist heritage and fascism. The example of Dollfuss's struggle with the Socialists in Austria made that ideological heritage particularly threatening.

These basic ideological ambiguities were reinforced by certain practical consequences of the electoral system: the disproportionate number of seats allotted to a relative majority; the need for a minimum quorum to qualify to obtain seats and to avoid a runoff in which divided opponents could unite to gain a disproportionate advantage; and the large districts that weakened the appeal of notables. These, combined with the parties' newness and uncertainty about their strength, obliged major parties to court minor parties by including their candidates in joint lists and to deemphasize the distinctions between allies, at least at the national level. In 1933, for instance, the Right maintained its ambiguity on the issue of monarchy versus republic. In parts of the country where it felt weak, it entered into alliances based on social conservatism with the clearly Republican Radicals, and in others, when more assured of victory, it emphasized its distinctiveness from the extreme Right.[52] Such ambiguity of electoral alliances in the campaign inevitably produced an image that justified accusing the Right of semiloyalty to the regime. These accusations gained strength through the later recriminations by the extreme Right when it felt betrayed by the Center's cooperation with Radicals and with the system generally.

Another effect of the electoral rules in the November 1933 elections was that their lack of cooperation weakened the representation of the Socialists and, particularly, the Left Republicans. This alone, even if no other reason had existed, would have precluded a post-election coalition between Center Right, Center Left, and Left Republicans of the type so well known in the Third French Republic.

In 1936 the same dynamics contributed to a popular front coalition that ranged from the Communists to the Center Left Republicans and forced the regime-supporting parties to appear to the electorate as though they had opened the door to semiloyal and disloyal forces.[53] This increased the difficulty of asserting their authority against their erstwhile allies. In turn the strains within the Right made the formation of joint electoral policies in 1936 difficult, thereby giving the Left an excess of confidence in its strength.

The electoral system had similar consequences for Catalonia's many parties. It forced moderate parties into alliances with nationalist extremists that allowed their opponents to question their loyalty to the Spanish state, or at least to the 1931 compromise on regional autonomy. It also obliged the Lliga to cooperate electorally with the nationwide parties on the Right that were hostile to demands for regional autonomy.[54] The system also tended to deprive parties appealing to the non-Catalan Castilian-speaking minority of a distinct representation. This created a false impression of unanimity in the support of peripheral nationalism.

On the basis of the experience of Germany and other democracies in crisis, Hermens has argued that proportional representation tends to make the fractionalization of parties permanent and permits crisis support for extremist parties to create patterns of representation in parliaments that soon become unworkable. In ways not yet fully clear, the Spanish system seems to have combined the disadvantages of extreme multipartisan, centrifugal polarization and confrontation of two major blocs, causing a bimodal distribution and the elimination of the Center, and assuring minor extremist groups of a disproportionate number of candidates because of the marginal utility of those additional votes. Unfortunately, the Spanish case was not included in the systematic analysis of the political and social effects of electoral systems, but as mentioned earlier, it should give pause to those who attribute too great a share in the breakdown of democracies to proportional representation.

During the course of the Republic, certain leaders were aware of the dysfunctional consequences of the electoral system, particularly the Lliga leadership and, judging by its programmatic statements, the CEDA.[55] But none of the major parties made a serious effort to reform the system. Hopes for a majoritarian victory became part of the maximalist syndrome and were incompatible with any centripetal and consociational tendencies characteristic of major parties.

Neither ideological ambiguity nor the ambiguous image and commitments fostered by the electoral system would have been so important if external events had not reinforced the fears of all major participants. Knowledge of semi- or pseudo-legal power takeovers in Italy, Germany, and Austria must have been an important factor in the defensive radicalization of the Socialists, the Esquerra, and the Left Republicans that crystalized in the October 1934 crisis. That changed European atmosphere also influenced the creation of a broad popular front, which finally included the Communists, despite their numerical weakness. The search for proletarian unity between Socialists and Anarcho-syndicalists, which would have been inconceivable in the first two years of the Republic, also reflected the changed climate. It also accounted for a certain mimicry of fascist styles by the CEDA's youth movement, the Juventud de Acción Popular (JAP), including provocative mass rallies.[56] The creation and success of partisan paramilitary organizations did not have roots in the Spanish past, but were a reflection of external influences. The violence of such organizations and the unwillingness of moderate leaders to dissociate themselves publicly from their activities became a major variable in the climate of distrust.

Counteracting these centrifugal tendencies and the semiloyalty, apparent or real, of parties and leaders would have required increased informal communication within the elite; this would have aided efforts toward political reequilibration of the type that operated in France in 1934 and 1958. However, the enormous discontinuity and inexperience of the political personnel of the regime precluded the establishment of such patterns before the critical years and even during the three legislative periods of the Republic (see table 2).[57] Of the 992 persons elected in those three legislatures, only 116 (11.7 percent) had been members of the lower house or the Senate between 1916 and 1923. In Germany in 1922, 27 percent of the elected officials had been deputies before 1918. Only 7 of the 105 PSOE deputies in 1931 had served under the monarchy, compared to the 48 veterans of the 108 SPD deputies in 1922. Again, in the 1933 legislature, only 10 of 105 followers of Gil Robles had pre-1931 parliamentary experience. This surely contributed to the lack of solidarity within the political class and the tense style of the parliamentary process. The electoral system reinforced those tendencies in the course of the five years of the Republic, since only 71 of the 992 deputies (representing 213 of the 1384 incumbencies) sat in the Cortes throughout the three legislatures. Six hundred seventeen of the 992 would meet their fellow legislators only during one legislative period. Despite the relatively similar quantitative

Table 2. Parliamentary Representation in the Three Legislatures of the Republic (1931, 1933, and 1936)

Legislature Elected	Elected to All 3 Legislatures	Elected to 2 Consecutive Legislatures	Elected in 1931 and 1936, but not in 1933	Elected to 1 Legislature	Total Number in Each Legislature [a]
	Number of Deputies				
1931	71	67	68	258	464
1933		115		197	450
1936				216	470
Total	71 (7.1%)	182 (18.3%)	68 (6.9%)	617 (67.8%)	992
Total number of incumbencies held by those deputies	213 (15.6%)	364 (26.1%)	136 (9.8%)	671 (48.3%)	1384

[a]Based on 1384 seats. The deputies included in this analysis are only those who appear on the *Lista de los Señores Diputados* published by the Cortes in December 1932, March 1935, and June 1936. Those lists do not include all deputies, due to vacancies and contested seats. The actual number of incumbencies and individuals occupying them is therefore somewhat larger. For an analysis of those data see Juan J. Linz, "Continuidad y discontinuidad en la élite política española: De la Restauración al Régimen actual (Franco)," in *Libro homenaje al Prof. Carlos Ollero: Estudios de ciencia política y sociología* (Guadalajara: Gráficas Carlavilla, 1972), pp. 361–412. These data show the extent to which the crisis in the parties and the electoral system deprived the regime of a stable and experienced elite accustomed to working together in Parliament.

strength of the Socialist party representation in 1931 and 1936, only 29 percent of those elected in 1931 and 52.5 percent of the smaller parliamentary group of 1933 returned in 1936. This high turnover within the Socialist party reflects and in part explains the changed political outlook of the PSOE.

Our model emphasizes the significance of the questioning of the moral and political integrity of key leaders as a contributing factor to crisis and breakdown. Certainly, in the case of Spain, this process affected two prominent leaders of the regime forces. This was exemplified by the hateful campaign against Azaña on the occasion of the Casas Viejas incident and later on the basis of his unproved participation in the Barcelona rebellion. The very early questioning by the new Republicans of Lerroux's role in opposition to the monarchy, combined with the suspicion of corruption surrounding him and his party, led many to push the old leader aside and ultimately brought about his painful downfall.[58] The animosity in the polemics within the Socialist party between Largo Caballero and Prieto after 1934, or within the Right between Calvo Sotelo and Gil Robles, and the widespread derision among all political groupings toward the president, Alcalá Zamora, were other instances in which the personal legitimacy of the leading actors was undermined.

Unfortunately, we know very little about the degree to which legislatures and leaders were prevented from taking responsible, system-oriented political action by their dependence on specific interest groups. How much truth is there, for example, in the often alleged role played by Masonry in producing splits and dissension within the Republican parties. Dependence on economic interests, particularly the large landowners, certainly contributed to the rightward turn of the CEDA in May 1935; further, Gil Robles's refusal to support the tax reforms of Chapaprieta contributed to the disintegration of the last Center-Right governments in the fall of 1935.[59] The previously described role of the Catalan landlords in provoking the crisis of 1934 is another example.[60] In Spain, as in the other cases, the dependency of parties on special interest groups and the incapacity or unwillingness of the leadership to oppose them, sometimes against their better judgment, are both a symptom and a cause of the crisis.

In summary, at one point or another, and with varying intensity, the variables we have just discussed contributed to a situation in which few of the leaders of even the most system-oriented parties were willing to place the maintenance of the system ahead of their other commitments to ideology, interest groups, or personal vetoes.

The Role of the Neutral Powers: Defenders of the Constitution or Obstacles to the Democratic Political Process?

Our model illustrates how certain moderating powers outside or above parties—kings, presidents, and courts—become, in crisis democracies, independent influences rather than mere cogs in the democratic machinery. In

Table 3. Cabinets of the Republic, 14 April 1931 to 19 July 1936

				Ministers	
Period	Prime Minister	Date Constituted	Duration (in days)	Total Incumbents	Newcomers to Cabinet Level
I Provisional governments					
1	Alcalá-Zamora	14 April 1931	183	12	11
		Constituent Assembly election 28 June 1931			
2	Azaña Díaz	14 October 1931	63	11	1
II Left Republican-Socialist coalition					
3	Azaña Díaz	16 December 1931	543	11	2
4	Azaña Díaz	12 June 1933	92	11+1	4
Periods I and II			881	(average duration, 220 days)	
III Transition governments					
5	Lerroux García	12 September 1933	26	13	10
6	Martínez Barrio	8 October 1933	69	13+1	6
		Legislative elections 20 November 1933			
IV Radical party-dominated governments with CEDA tolerance					
7	Lerroux García	16 December 1933	77	13+2	5
8	Lerroux García	3 March 1934	56	12+1	3
9	Samper Ibáñez	2 May 1934	159	13	2
Periods III and IV			387	(average duration, 77 days)	
V Radical-CEDA governments					
10	Lerroux with 3 CEDA ministers	4 October 1934	181	15+2	9
11	Lerroux with "experts"	3 April 1935	33	13	6
12	Lerroux with Gil Robles	6 May 1935	142	13	7
13	Chapaprieta Torregrosa with Lerroux, Gil Robles	25 September 1935	34	9	2
14	Chapaprieta Torregrosa without Lerroux	29 October 1935	46	9	2
			436	(average duration, 87 days)	
VI Interim governments					
15	Portela Valladares	14 December 1935	16	10	6
16	Portela Valladares majority nonparty	30 December 1935	51	9	3
Periods IV, V, and VI—called "bienio negro" by its opponents			795	(the two black years) (average duration 79 days)	
		Legislative elections 16 February 1936			
VII					
17	Azaña Díaz	19 February 1936	47	13	7
18	Azaña Díaz	7 April 1936	36	13	
	Barcia Trelles	28 May 1936			
		substitute due to Azaña's presidential candidacy			
		Presidential election 26 April 1936			
19	Casares Quiroga	13 May 1936	66	13	—
Left-bourgeois governments after Popular Front election			149		

17–18 July—military uprising; One-day government of Martínez Barrios, 19 July 1936, first civil war government under José Giral

NOTE: To summarize, during the period from 14 April 1931 to 18 July 1936 (1920 days), the Republic saw nineteen governments and eight prime ministers. The average duration of cabinets was 101 days.

studying a single case, it is tempting to attribute the impact of such offices to the personal idiosyncrasies of their incumbents rather than to structural factors. The personality of President Alcalá Zamora—his touchiness, his jealousy of other political leaders, his outdated political style, his personal preference for weak political leaders, and the role of his entourage—is a particular case in point.[61] The pattern of his relationship with parties, party leaders, Parliament, and extra-parliamentary opinion resembled that maintained by King Alphons XIII prior to 1923. Alcalá Zamora's dissolution of the legislature in 1933 and again on 1 January 1936, his efforts to influence the cabinet formation process, his selection of prime ministers in crisis periods, and his veto of certain leaders were certainly debatable aspects of the political process. Such actions were possible because of weakness or stalemate in Parliament, suspicion of the semiloyalty of parties and their leaders, his own sensitivity to opinion and other pressures outside of Parliament, and his use of information obtained informally. The president reacted to the unstable situation that had arisen by the summer of 1933 by broadening the interpretation of his powers and acting as an arbiter of legitimacy in the system, which led to the alienation and hostility of practically all major political forces and made his ouster before the expiration of his term an event regretted by few despite its ambiguous legality and serious consequences. In attempting to play his role as a defender of the constitution, he unwittingly contributed to a power vacuum and ultimately to breakdown.

The president's misinterpretation of his role in 1935, particularly in connection with the *straperlo* scandal, was manifest in his formation of governments that included his friends and excluded important party leaders, his persistent veto of Gil Robles, and the formation of the two Portela governments. (For data on cabinets of the Republic, see table 3.) The last of these, on 30 December 1935, included no representatives of any of the major parties, only individuals close to the president. It was similar in some respects to the Hindenburg presidential cabinets in that it was unable to present itself before Parliament and its purpose was to organize the elections in the vain hope of creating a new Center from above. All these were actions that contributed to the breakdown of parliamentary democratic government. The defenders of the president might argue that the potential semiloyalty or even disloyalty of Gil Robles and many others in his party justified the actions of the president as a defense of the Republican democratic government. Conversely, it could be argued that if that were true, Gil Robles had had ample time for a coup in the period between 6 May and 14 December 1935, when he was minister of the army.

A neutral power whose role during the Republic has not yet been studied is the Tribunal of Constitutional Guarantees; in addition, there is no analysis of the role of the judiciary as a whole in the handling of social unrest and political violence. Certainly, as noted first by La Cierva,[62] efforts to juridify political conflicts—the Catalan rural tenancy law, for example—and to reform the judiciary for political reasons—a policy advocated by the Center Right in 1935 and by the Popular Front in 1936—indicate that the crisis of democracy was accompanied by an increase in the political significance of the judiciary, and consequently of governmental efforts to exercise influence upon it.

Certain leading intellectual figures, particularly Ortega y Gasset, could also be considered to constitute a kind of neutral power. Written from a vantage point outside partisan strife, his brilliant critique of the Republic between 1931 and 1933 contributed to the alienation of many intelligent Spaniards from the system.[63]

In our model the neutral power of presidents or kings also plays a major role as well in the final power vacuum or crisis that legitimizes the transfer of power to antidemocratic forces, as with Hitler and Mussolini, or effects a reequilibration, as in the cases of Coty in France in 1958 and Svinhufvud in Finland. In Spain the situation was somewhat different. Perhaps it was in view of the role played by other presidents in Europe that the Republican-Socialist coalition decided to use its power in the legislature to oust Alcalá Zamora.[64] Politically, this was a paradox, since the new Left-dominated legislature existed only because of the presidential dissolution three months earlier of the legislature dominated by the Center Right. This decision was to be a significant factor in delegitimizing the regime. It must have been based in part on a fear that Alcalá Zamora might have legitimized a state of emergency, the formation of a provisional government, and the calling of new elections. The Left Socialists and Indalecio Prieto played a major role in this technically dubious and politically irresponsible act, perhaps in the hope that Azaña would move to the presidency. Prieto probably hoped to become prime minister in place of Azaña if the latter were elected to the presidency. But Azaña's election only served to neutralize the most prestigious and effective leader of the Republican Left, who enjoyed high personal legitimacy among the Socialists and other parties. Because the social democratic Prieto failed to gain the support of his party, having been vetoed by the maximalist followers of Largo Caballero, and given the fact that Azaña did not enthusiastically back him, the prime ministership went instead to Casares Quiroga, a close personal collaborator of the president who might have thought he would be just a presidential caretaker. There seems to be general agreement that Casares's was the kind of weak and ambivalent administration so often found in minority governments in the final stage of crisis. In contrast with other cases surveyed in this volume, and somewhat paradoxically, considering his previous, forceful role, in the tragic spring of 1936 Azaña had little effect on the political process, despite an eloquent speech in which he stressed a note of moderation and appealed for consensus.

The Intellectuals and the Republic

Students of the breakdown of the Weimar Republic have emphasized both how the thinking of different types of intellectuals contributed to its crisis by provoking alienation from the regime and how few and weak the so-called *Vernunftrepublikaner* were in German academia. They point out that experts in constitutional law helped to subvert the meaning of the constitution by interpreting it in a way that opened the door to authoritarian tendencies and questioned the role of political parties in a democracy. Right-wing literati added to the mood of crisis by formulating antidemocratic ideologies. Historians and educators contributed hypernationalism and the receptivity to *völkisch* ideas. On the left, literati and artists like Tucholsky did their share by ridiculing politicians and party officials, including the social democrats, and by keeping alive the radical utopian protests. In Italy, Salvemini, and before him, Mosca, have admitted regretfully that they had a share in undermining the Giolittian experiment in democracy with their critique of the failures of parliamentarism and their merciless exposure of the failings of the system. Like D'Annunzio with his rhetoric, the futurist intelligentsia did its share to create the climate in which fascism was born.

It would seem that in the Spanish case things were different. The Republic was often called a republic of professors. Rallied by the *Delenda est monarchia* of Ortega y Gasset, intellectuals of high and low standing played a decisive role in the crisis of the Primo de Rivera dictatorship and the fall of the monarchy. Many leading intellectuals and professors were to be found on the benches of the constituent assembly. According to the Right, the Institución Libre de Enseñanza was the moving force behind the new regime and was the source of its anticlerical policies.[65] Teachers and professors in public secondary schools were among the strong supporters of the new regime, in contrast to Germany, where the nationalist and *völkisch* inclinations of these groups made them pathbreakers of the Right and later often active supporters of the Nazis. In Spain, the right-wing intelligentsia was numerically small and few of its members enjoyed national prestige and influence. Ramiro de Maeztu, who had started as a radical in the milieu of the "98 generation," was not comparable to Mosca and Pareto, Maurras, Spengler, or Carl Schmitt, and was certainly no equal to Ortega or Unamuno. The young writers, journalists, and poets on the periphery of fascism were no match of those identified with the Left.[66]

Even so, intellectuals did not contribute to the consolidation of the Republic, and some of the positions taken by leading figures, largely against their intent, helped to alienate many Spaniards from the new regime. Their critique was often justified in substance, but its form must have contributed to the distrust and withdrawal of allegiance among the youth. None of them can be looked on specifically as a father of Spanish fascism, but some of their positions earned the sympathy of the Fascists, and some of their responses to the modern world and the Spanish situation helped the Fascists formulate their ideas. The Republicans, on the other hand, came to feel very ambivalent toward the intellectuals they had initially welcomed into their ranks as intellectual fathers of the new regime. It is no accident that few of the professors and leading intellectuals who sat in the Constituent Cortes returned either in 1933 or in 1936. Contrary to what might have been expected, the leading intellectuals of the older generation in 1936 were not ready to identify themselves with the Republic and its struggle against Franco. Some were even ready to accept a moderate counterrevolution, while others chose to stay or go abroad, rejecting both sides in the civil war. Among the younger generation, some took a decided stand on one side or the other, but this often led to a disappointing conclusion.

Turning Points

Continuing Crisis: Opportunity for Reequilibration?

The Spanish Republic started life with widespread support. Outside of Syndicalist CNT hostility in 1931, its only opposition was a disorganized and demoralized Right. Later it was to face not only guerrilla warfare by the disloyal opposition but semiloyalty from large parties and social forces that could have been integrated into the system. It would be challenged frontally twice before the final breakdown.

First was the ill-fated, poorly planned, and short-lived coup of 10 August 1932, the *Sanjurjada,* which was even more of a fiasco than the Kapp putsch and was defeated by the police without necessitating a massive general strike or the turning over of power to the army as an arbiter.[67] In fact, the period after the Sanjurjada represented one of stabilization of the system. The revitalized majority carried out the agrarian reform and other important constituent legislation of the regime, which had been floundering before the coup.[68]

The second and much more serious challenge to legal legitimacy was the proletarian revolution in Asturias and the ambiguous challenge to the authority of the Spanish state by the Catalan Generalitat in October 1934. Both were defeated by the government, which was able to invoke the support of the army without transferring power to it.[69] Why, then, did not the defeat of that revolutionary challenge lead to reequilibration of the system, once the temptation to use the crisis to establish an authoritarian rule had been rejected or proved unfeasible? One answer might be that the civil war of 1936 had really started in October 1934. After the major regime party, the PSOE, broke with legality and expressed its unwillingness to accept any system in which the Center Right would have a legitimate place, even though the latter had not used its power to establish an authoritarian corporative system, it was only a question of time before the Republic of 1931 would be declared defunct. A different perspective would argue that the defeat of the revolution provided a unique opportunity for a reequilibration and stabilization of the system, once revolutionary hopes, demonstrated to be weak in many parts of the country, had been defeated, and the bourgeois, conservative clerical forces had shown their unwillingness or inability to abandon Republican legality. From that perspective the period October 1934 to February 1936, particularly the year 1935, constituted an all-too-perfect example of the conditions that prevent successful reequilibration of democracies.

The crisis of the Center-Right coalition of Radicals, CEDA, and other minor parties in 1935 led to the premature parliamentary dissolution of 7 January 1936, and the subsequent election brought bipolarization to its height by destroying any workable Center. All in all, the political events of 1935 pinpoint some of the elements of our model: the role of the neutral powers, specifically the president of the Republic; the impact of the delegitimation of political leaders by scandals adroitly used; the interference of interest groups in the political process; and above all, a crisis in the efficacy of policy formulation combined with the dubious legitimacy of CEDA, the major party, in the eyes of a large part of the society, which was sustained by the moderating power of the president in his refusal to grant the premiership to Gil Robles, the CEDA leader. These were the difficulties the Spanish democracy faced in attempting reequilibration after a serious challenge to its authority; there were also others in the areas of repression, justice, and amnesty for its opponents.

The February 1936 victory of the Popular Front coalition under the leadership of Azaña can be seen in retrospect as the beginning of the end, given the ideological commitments, rhetoric, and actions of the maximalist leadership of the Socialist party and many of its followers, particularly after the PSOE refused to participate in the responsibilities of government and left it to the weak minority Left bourgeois parties. But the electoral victory can also be seen as a lost opportunity to reintegrate the Socialists into the Republican system and to take a more realistic attitude toward the Center Right. The latter had demonstrated between 1933 and 1936, and in the elections themselves, its strength throughout the country and its potential for disengaging itself from the extreme Right to participate in the system.

Under what conditions was reequilibration possible? When could the Republic have reaffirmed its democratic legal authority against the romantic revolutionary climate of the Left and the putschist conspiratorial climate of the extreme Right before the last desperate call of Maura and Sánchez Román for the Republican dictatorship had been made in June 1936?[70] To pose the question in these terms might sound unreal, almost ridiculous, but if we start to analyze the policies that might have led to the persistence of a democratic system from our basic heuristic position, and look at the critical junctures of March and April of 1936 in that light, the question is not so absurd.

As a good example of the problems in the study of crises and breakdowns of regimes, the point of no return might be placed in the first phase of the Republic, when its constitution created a "Republic for the Republicans" in which identification with democracy was possible only for those who accepted not only the institutions of democracy but also the laicism of the constitution. It was a period in which the regime-supporting forces permanently alienated the church, a large part of the officer corps, a diffuse Castilian nationalist sentiment, and important sectors of the landowning peasantry. On the other hand, these forces failed to make the "constituent reforms" that would have assured the loyalty of working-class Marxists and the poor peasantry and definitely linked the Socialist party and the Republicans of the Left in a firm policy of reformist social change. From that perspective, which emphasizes the structural, social, economic, cultural, and political problems, the Republic was doomed because it was not moderate enough on the religious issue or revolutionary enough on social issues to please the Marxists. Legions of sociological political analyses, particularly from the Marxist, and to some extent, the Fascist viewpoint, would see all liberal, democratic, and ideologically radical, but actually moderate, bourgeois reformist or revolutionary regimes of the twentieth century as doomed in advance.

Another point of view might argue that the cost in legitimacy and support resulting from the first bienio—under Azaña—would have been overcome with the incorporation of large part of the Right into the regime, after its electoral success in 1933. This was the perspective from which Lerroux entered into an electoral collaboration with the Right in 1933, governed with its acquiescence, and slowly aimed at obtaining its cooperation, bringing the Catholic Center Right into the government and into support for the regime.[71] From that point of view, the period 1933–35 can be seen as the reequilibration of the latent crisis provoked by the one-sidedness of the constitution-making period dominated by the Left Republicans and the Socialists and an effort on the part of the Radicals to prevent and undermine the disloyal opposition of the extreme Right. The latter found itself increasingly isolated and in the long run would have been unable to penetrate the masses of the conservative electorate. In this view, the crisis of October 1934 becomes the starting point of the breakdown, and the most central question is to account for the radicalization after 1933, and even before the election, of the Socialist party.

As noted before, overcoming the revolution of 1934 without a break in the essence of constitutional legality demonstrated the strength of the Republican regime and its symbols, and the legitimacy of the institutions, especially for the army. In that view, the crisis of December 1935 was a critical moment. It saw the premature dissolution of a parliament that still had the potential to produce majoritarian governments. Even if these had lacked popularity, encountered considerable hostility in the population, and demonstrated limited efficacy in solving the real problems of the country, in the long run they would probably have proved capable of gaining compliance. In contrast to most historians, with the exception of Pabón, we are inclined to pay special attention to that process of disintegration in the political mechanisms at the end of 1935 as well as to the president's blindness to the polarization that would inevitably accompany a general election held under the existing electoral law, given the repression of the working-class unrest and the economic conditions of the country at the time. Our argument would be that dissolution was not necessary and under the circumstances did nothing to reequilibrate, stabilize, and consolidate the regime as a political system. This is not to deny that the basic underlying problems of the country in the long run would not have been solved by the leadership of the Center Right, due to its sterility and narrow-minded selfishness. It is no accident that even Azaña, the great leader of the Republicans of the Left and of the Popular Front, should have confided to his diary in February 1936 a fear of victory.[72] As he foresaw, the democratic Left-bourgeois politicians would be exposed to overwhelming pressures by their maximalist and Communist allies, who were more concerned with achieving their demands than with the stability of the regime.

The acceleration of the crisis in the spring of 1936 makes it difficult to say at what point there was still a chance for reestablishment of public order that would have satisfied both the moderates and the military leadership. The latter was increasingly placing its hopes on a putsch aimed at stopping the mobilization of demands by the working-class parties and the increasing violence of many political organizations and individuals.

From the perspective we have taken, each of the situations, crises, and efforts at stabilization described can be seen as either an opportunity or an irreparable loss in legitimacy, efficacy, and effectiveness for the democratic Republican regime. All were steps in the loss of legitimate, authentic, and effective power, despite their appearance of having strengthened the regime in power by proving that it could defeat its opponents. The whole history of the Republic can be seen as a continuous decline, reflected in the increase in number and strength of disloyal and semiloyal oppositions ready to cooperate with disloyal positions rather than join in the effort to stabilize the regime. In that perspective the successful overcoming of the more acute crises constitutes only minor reversals of a downward trend.

There were, of course, critical junctures at which that trend could have been effectively reversed. At those points the regime could have defeated its opponents, functioned with a certain degree of efficacy by formulating some important policies and institutions (as it did after 10 August 1932), and reaffirmed the continuity of institutions without turning to extreme solutions. In that perspective, moments of crisis and stabilization appear more as part of a cyclical process. Indicators like the number of victims and the range and persistence of disturbance of public order reveal that the crisis increased in intensity and scope as the years passed. The cumulative memory amplified the propaganda which created an overwhelming fear of civil war, a readiness to preventive violence which only further fed the fear and led to ever more constant readiness to resort to violence by the other side. This vicious cycle led in the spring of 1936 to an atmosphere of undeclared civil war, attested to in statements by all the leading politicians. When the military uprising against the regime and the subsequent popular revolution by the working-class organizations occurred in July 1936, it was no surprise to anyone in Spain.

Perhaps more than any other, the case of the Spanish Republic exemplifies the risks that are run when a democratic regime is identified by its founding fathers with a specific political content rather than with a procedural system that legitimates decision-making in response to the changing will of the electorate. The constitutionalization of the ideology of the Left Republican-Socialist coalition, particularly laicization (Article 26, for example, prohibited teaching by religious orders), forced the opposition to make constitutional revision its program. The situation was reflected in the constant use of the term "republic" by the regime-maintaining parties and the relatively infrequent appeals to democracy or law. The expression "The Republic for the Republicans" reflects this emphasis on content rather than form. The Right's counterslogan of "Long live Spain" is another indicator.

It is interesting to speculate on how such a situation came about. One factor was central: the sudden installation of a new regime by a small conspiratorial group and the Socialist party after the disintegration of a dictatorship. This event, occurring in an underdeveloped, nonmobilized society, created an upsurge of support for the regime that was amplified by the electoral system and created overconfidence in its strength and unity of purpose, as well as dangerous ignorance and scorn for its conservative and clerical opponents. That opposition was able to organize its massive support, which, along with other factors, gave it and the Center-Right Republicans who were willing to collaborate an unexpected strength that could not be fully incorporated into the regime, given its identification with substantive content rather than a procedural framework.

There is a lesson in the Spanish case and in the Weimar Republic after its constituent election (which has some similar features): it is possible for new regimes to be built after a serious crisis by majorities which attempt a basic change in social structure and political outlook, even if they turn out to be temporary. But if the rapidly instituted changes remain more symbolic than real, they may outrage the temporarily weak opposition without satisfying the expectations of the supporters of the new regime. In this respect the failure of the Spanish Republic to effect agrarian reform rapidly, thereby disaffecting a small privileged stratum but benefiting large masses of landless persons, was particularly costly in legitimacy. A new regime based on a pragmatic consensus concerning institutions to serve as a procedural framework that left the substantive changes to the ordinary legislative process might ultimately have been more stable.

This points up a clear difference in the atmosphere surrounding the regime installation between post-World War II Italy or Germany and Weimar, and the Spanish constituent assembly. Perhaps the Italians who complained that the "Wind from the North" (the demands for basic reforms that arose in the more politically conscious northern Italy) was not incorporated into the constitution and protested that the Fascists' agreements with the church were constitutionalized in agreement with the Communists, should consider that this probably contributed to the stability of Italian democracy. The process of regime installation in the "North Italian" sense and in a democratic framework probably differs. An authoritarian regime can use the upsurge of support that might accompany its establishment to carry through decisive changes and destroy its opponent's basis of strength without long-run danger to stability of the regime. This is so because its unwillingness to share power with anyone in the first years gives the regime time to consolidate power and makes it impossible for opponents to recoup or realign their forces. A democracy, in which the constituent period is inevitably followed by elections, allows and almost encourages principled opposition to the newly installed regime and its content. Great political skill, which is not always available, is needed to distinguish the democratic institutional framework from the substantive content it has produced in the installation process. In Spain, many antidemocrats would not have been antidemocrats, but conservative or moderate Republicans, had the Constitution been shaped differently. This is especially important because many Republicans were not really democrats, but Republicans first of all.

The Aftermath of the 1934 Revolution:
The Failure of Reequilibration

It has been argued that the October 1934 crisis marked the beginning of the civil war, and that consensus within a democratic regime after that date was impossible. On the other hand, the outcome of that crisis could have led to the stabilization of the regime. This must have been the hope of many politicians of the Center Right and even of the moderate Right who assembled in the Cortes on 9 October to give a vote of confidence to the Lerroux government. Why was it inevitable that October should have poisoned the political atmosphere forever, particularly when, in spite of ambivalence toward the Republic and strong undercurrents of antidemocratic corporativism and authoritarianism, the CEDA and its leader could not bring themselves to use their popularity to establish a moderate authoritarian state with the collaboration of the army, as the clericals in Austria had done shortly before? In fact 1935 saw the incorporation of Catholic, conservative mass support of the CEDA into the Republic (even though not in the "Republic of the Republicans" enacted by the 1931 constitution) and increasing tension between Gil Robles and the extreme Right led by Calvo Sotelo and the few but noisy Fascist followers of José Antonio. Why did the second part of the "black two years," the *bienio negro*, lead to the bitterness of the Spain of 1936 and the recriminations that brought on civil war? Under what conditions would a reequilibration have been possible—granted that an immediate turn to an authoritarian solution had been ruled out?

No one ever questions whether the Left Republicans, and even more the Socialist party, could have reconsidered the positions they adopted in October 1934, or whether, as a loyal opposition, they might not have recognized a Center-Right government in the course of 1935. The question seems preposterous, considering the vengeful actions of the victors.[73] The Left Republicans and the Socialists certainly were not likely to put themselves in the place of the victors. Therefore, the question becomes, Why did the Center-Right government—which had all of the initiatives—ultimately fail? The literature has offered four basic explanations.

The answer provided by the extreme Right would be that the Center and the moderate Right did not use their power effectively to repress the disloyal opposition, specifically the responsible leaders of the Socialist party. This was the position of Calvo Sotelo, when he pointed out that the establishment of the Third Republic and the decades of subsequent stability in France were the fruits of the repression of the Commune.[74] Gil Robles rejected that position, and the government won a vote of confidence with the monarchists and traditionalists abstaining. Actually, such a solution was not possible because of the president's opposition and the probable lack of support among the centrist Radicals and other minor parties. But above all, repression was not feasible against popular mass party and trade union movements like the PSOE and the UGT. Reequilibration by outlawing and persecuting a disloyal opposition is possible only against smaller sectarian groups.

Another approach might have been generosity after victory: an effort to integrate the defeated into the system. This solution implies a different policy, at least toward those who had been caught in a semiloyal position by events not of their making. This would have meant a totally different attitude toward the unfairly and unsuccessfully persecuted Left Republican leader Azaña, who would, as a result, become the engineer of the Popular Front and its undisputed leader in February 1936. This might have worked, but Azaña's initial ambiguity in October, combined with hostility he had aroused during the first bienio and the personal antagonism between him and Lerroux, made such a farsighted and generous policy improbable. On the same political level, a more generous attitude toward the rights of Catalonia (as advocated by the

Lliga leadership), distinguishing the responsibilities of Companys from those of the Catalan people, might have been constructive. Unfortunately, Castilian-based Spanish nationalism had been aroused and could not overcome its distrust of Catalonia. In fact, in view of such predispositions, the response to 6 October in Barcelona was relatively moderate, as indicated by the increased transfer of functions to the Catalan authorities at the end of 1935 and the withdrawal of the anti-Catalanist, Royo Villanova, from the cabinet.

Indeed, a serious indictment can be made against the Center Right for its repression of the proletarian revolution, in both its legal and illegal aspects. The facts reveal the illegal, brutal behavior of government officials, the assassination of prisoners (particularly of a journalist who had reported brutalities), bad treatment of prisoners, delay in freeing those who had limited responsibility or were innocent, and unwillingness to discuss publicly the responsibility of those who had abused their authority and had been dismissed. All this proved an enormous advantage for the opposition, and would be used in the spring of 1936 to excuse revolutionary violence and threats of violence.[75]

The impolitic and unjust persecution of the Syndicalist CNT leaders, who had not participated in any way in the uprising, was particularly inexcusable. The issue of amnesty for those responsible contributed to a constitutional crisis within the cabinet and over the relationship between prime minister and president. While leniency ultimately prevailed for all top leaders, the execution of four relatively minor figures in the uprising, whatever their guilt in acts of violence, consumed political energies unnecessarily and aroused a moral reaction against the government. The rigid position in this case was particularly illegitimate in view of the amnesty granted participants in the putsch of August 1932 by the same parties.

Paradoxically, the nonavailability of the death sentence might have been an advantage for the democratic regime in crisis periods. It would have kept it from falling between the Scylla and Charybdis of appearing either too lenient, by giving in to humanitarian (as well as self-interested) demands for amnesty, or appearing too harsh, particularly toward the less prominent rebels (more easily established as responsible for more obvious crimes), while leaving the main leaders unpunished due to lack of evidence or broader political considerations.

It would, in fact, have been unrealistic to expect a generous reaction to a revolution, and this might not have changed the future behavior of the opposition leadership. The real hope for reequilibration, however, lay in government response to the grievances that had led to the revolutionary situation with a progressive and effective social policy. Let us note, however, that the main strength of the October uprising did not come from the most underprivileged sectors of the working class, and they would not have been the immediate beneficiaries of a more progressive policy. Nevertheless, the situation might have offered an opportunity to neutralize working-class opposition, if not to win its support. The main accusation against the governments between 1934 and late 1935, particularly those constituted after the fall in March 1935 of Giménez Fernández, progressive minister of agriculture of the CEDA, is that they did not enact progressive legislation on agrarian, labor, and tax problems. In fact, the parliamentarians of the coalition parties rejected even the most moderate reforms proposed by the governments which were, in principle, accepted by the leadership. An even stronger case can be made against the government's inability to check the reactionary response of employers and landlords against the defenseless working-classes and farmers, or at least its tolerance of such response. It is debatable whether this basically reactionary social policy was the result of the small size of the progressive wing of the CEDA, its lack of support from the leadership, or its inability to obtain parliamentary support. Contributing factors were that the CEDA did not have a significant working-class base in a Christian trade union movement and that social consciousness had not developed over time in Spanish political Catholicism.

Another significant aspect was the extraordinary venom and distortion in accounts of the Asturian revolution in the bourgeois press. This served to intensify the fears of the bourgeoisie and fuel their hatred against the defeated. That propaganda was to be first paralleled on the opposite side abroad and then at the time of the 1936 elections. Rigid censorship after October 1934 abetted this dual distortion.

The preceding obstacles to reequilibration, or at least to reintegration of the political system, were compounded by the internal crisis of a leading partner in the government coalition, the Radical party. It started with the replacement under pressure of two Radical ministers, by a vote of 161 to 13, on 16 November 1934. The decisive issues surfaced in 1935, however, when the infamous *straperlo* and Nombela affairs led to the incrimination of leading Radical party politicians, the resignation of Lerroux, exonerated of responsibility but affected by that of his political friends and relatives, and the resultant formation of two governments under Chapaprieta, a financial expert without party affiliation, on 15 September and 14 December. This crisis of confidence in a leading Center-Right Republican of undisputed legitimacy in the Republican system, and the weakness and corruption of his party, inevitably made the Center-Right CEDA, claiming 105 of the 238 deputies needed for a majority (particularly in view of the fractionalization of the other parties constituting it), the pivot of any parliamentary government.

Even admitting the lack of political generosity and flexibility, the failure of a progressive social legislative program to face the problems created by the economic crisis for the working-class and peasants, the inability to control the reactionary response of employers and landlords, and the crisis of confidence in and within the Radical party, we still can raise the question of whether dissolution was inevitable, necessary, or desirable, on 1 January 1936. This brings up one of the key variables in our model of the breakdown process in a crisis democracy: the role of the neutral powers. In this case the neutral power was the president of the Republic, Alcalá Zamora, with his unbreakable veto to a CEDA government, his readiness to appoint a government without representatives of the major parties that could not obtain parliamentary support and yet had the right of dissolution, and his effort to control the election under the mistaken illusion that it could produce a new Chamber with a new Center.[76]

If only structural, social, and economic dimensions of the crisis were emphasized, this point would be almost irrelevant. Sooner or later, the Center Right, dominated by the Right, would have failed and been replaced by a Popular Front type of coalition. From our perspective, however, the constitutional crisis of December 1935–January 1936 and the role of the president in it cannot be easily ignored. If we assume—and this is a difficult *if*—that the CEDA, with the cooperation of the Agrarios, the Lliga, minor parties of the Center, and the reconstructed Radical party, could have continued governing, even ineffectively, and maintained order without moving toward a dictatorship until the normal dissolution date in 1937, events could have worked out differently. The memory of revolution and repression might have faded, the impact of the scandals in the Radical party weakened, the economic situation improved, and the international tension in Europe might have contributed indirectly to recovery and unity. And what is perhaps equally important, a reform of the electoral law might have reduced the polarization of 1936. As we know from the Weimar Republic, anticipated elections in a society in crisis do not serve as an agent of reequilibration. Furthermore, the exercise of governmental responsibilities by the Center Right was deepening, and would have deepened even further, the personal and ideological conflict between Gil Robles and the fascistic monarchists who followed Calvo Sotelo, but an election under the law of 1931 inevitably brought them closer together and thereby exacerbated the polarized radicalization.

To explore even further the possibilities of reequilibration, let us ask whether the outcome would have been different if the CEDA leadership had been more enlightened. Certainly a more reasonable policy toward the Anarcho-syndicalists of the CNT, and even a somewhat Machiavellian tolerance for that union federation at a moment when its antagonists in the UGT were defeated, might have prevented an Anarcho-syndicalist turnout for the Popular Front against the formal declarations of its leaders. Even with such tolerance, the CNT could not have attempted any major or effective subversion. Another Machiavellian policy might have been to attract the PNV into the government's sphere of influence by facilitating Basque autonomy, ignoring the ambivalent role of the party in 1934, and rejecting the antiregionalist extremism of the Right. The Catholic Aguirre could have been a partner to Gil Robles as Companys was for Azaña, but unfortunately the Castilian Right lacked an understanding of the peripheral nationalists. An effort by the CEDA to penetrate the Catalan electorate was another folly of the times. Putting aside social reforms benefiting the working class, the regime might have pursued consolidation of its peasant and middle-class support. From that perspective, some of the economic measures affecting the civil servants were ill-conceived even when they were rational.

Assuming that the Center Right could have pursued a more generous policy toward its political and class enemies, would reequilibration of the system have been assured? Had the parties of the Republican Left, under the leadership of Azaña and his Izquierda Republicana—the Esquerra and the Organización Republicana Gallega (ORGA)—along with the Unión Republicana, led by Martínez Barrio, and other minor but prestigious groups, formed a coalition but refused to enter a Popular Front with the PSOE, the PCE, and other parties of the Left, there might be grounds for a positive answer.[77] Given the electoral law and the defeat sustained by both the Left Republicans and the Socialists in 1933, however, this does not seem plausible. Another possible consequence might have been the slowing down or the reversal of the radicalization of the working-class parties, particularly the PSOE, either by a change of view on the part of Largo Caballero or by a victory of his opponents within the party. Again, it seems dubious, in the context of the Europe of the thirties and in the presence of fascism, that the maximalist wing of the party could have changed gears or lost control (though the latter possibility cannot be ignored). After all, its radicalization began at the end of the Left Republican-Socialist coalition rule and was based on disillusionment over the possibility of reform, even with the collaboration of the bourgeois parties of the Left.[78] Excluding the possibility that a more enlightened policy might have prevented the formation of the Popular Front or a reversal in the ideological position and style of the PSOE, there would have been important positive consequences.

First of all, it would have tempered the political climate, lowered the intensity of class antagonisms, weakened the appeal of the amnesty issue, and reduced the distrust middle class sectors felt about the aims of Gil Robles. The Anarcho-syndicalists might have followed the traditional abstentionist posture and thereby weakened the Left electorally. It is difficult to say if it would have affected the vote for the Marxist parties, but it might have reduced the appeal to bourgeois voters of a Popular Front-type coalition. Even so, after the crisis of the Radical party, a Center coalition dominated by a Catholic party might have found it difficult to attract them. The scenario on the other side ignores the effect on the more rightist voters of a more progressive and moderate policy of the CEDA, given the competition of the extreme Right. Such a policy might have led to the loss of some votes and the defection of some of the CEDA deputies to Calvo Sotelo. It would have compounded the difficulty of any coalition for electoral purposes from the Center to the Right. A more generous policy toward Catalonia would certainly have benefited the Lliga and Cambó. Even when a different policy in 1935 would have reduced the polarization, and particularly its intensity, without a change in the electoral law, it is difficult to see how confrontation between these two blocs could have been avoided.

The real difference would have been that a more constructive policy, a less vindictive reaction, and support for the more progressive positions in the party (like those of Giménez Fernández) would have facilitated the cooperation of the CEDA with the Center parties, particularly the Lliga and the Basque PNV. Above all, it might have softened the distrust and hostility of President Alcalá Zamora toward Gil Robles.[79] A reduction of the tensions between those two men, as Chapaprieta and Cambó already knew, might have prevented the crisis at the end of 1935 and the premature dissolution of the Chamber. It is, however, unclear whether such reduction would have required Gil Robles to abandon, at least temporarily, his demands for the premiership and leadership of the party, if we assume that the conflict between the two men was more than political. If assumption of a more constructive position by the CEDA had reversed the presidential veto, facilitated Center-oriented coalitions, and isolated the monarchist anti-democratic Right, new elections might not have been called. Enough time would have been gained to heal the wounds of October, and time would have allowed the Socialist party congress to reverse the Largo Caballero line or a split between maximalists and reformists. Democracy would have been the beneficiary.

Violence, Disorder, and Regime Crises

The maintenance of public order and personal safety is a central function of any political system, though the threshold for tolerance of violence and the meaning assigned to it may vary. Obviously, violence, which in some countries is defined as common crime, acquires in others a political character because the violators of the law (and often the authorities as well) attach political significance to it. Rather than disengage themselves from the criminal acts, the leaders justify them in terms of social and political grievances and blame the government for having created the conditions that provoked them. It is not easy to say at what point the amount, intensity, visibility, and cumulative impact of violence transforms it into an unsolvable problem for the authorities. Any discussion of violence in a society in crisis is blurred by allegations and counterallegations as to who initiated it as well as exaggerations and denials of the evidence. In the present case, whether the acts of violence actually happened as they were described at the time is to some extent unimportant, since the reactions of the participants were more a function of their perceptions than of reality, and therefore absolute certitude about the objective facts becomes less central for the social scientist than for the historian. (See table 4.)

There can be no doubt that the Spanish Republic was characterized by a relatively high rate of social and political violence, that the October revolution and its aftermath represented a trauma that perhaps has no parallel in the other

Table 4. Deaths in Political Conflicts, 15 April 1931–17 July 1936

Year	Occurrences of Violence	Number of Deaths
1931	Incident with monarchists, anarcho-syndicalist violence	10
1932	Conflicts in the villages of Castilblanco and Arnedo between peasants and the police	9
	Sanjurjo pronunciamento (August)	10
1933	Anarchist unrest in Barcelona (January)	37
	Casas Viejas, Andalusian village uprising, and police repression	18
	Anarchist unrest and labor conflicts (December)	89
1934	National farm strike	13
	Falangist violence and counterviolence (June)	2
	Assassination of ex-director of security by Falangists	1
	Asturian Revolution	189
	(October)	

Deaths	Official Data	Data of Aurelio del Llano	
Civilians	855	940	
Police	144	168	
Army	85	88	
	1084	1196	1196
Estimated number of victims of repression		156–210; average: 183	
Barcelona and surrounding area		50	
Spain other than Asturias and Barcelona		42	
Total, October 1934			1471

1935	Executions	2	
	Varios incidents	43	
1936	Fights and assassinations between 3 February and 17 July		
	Madrid	45	
	Barcelona	3	
	Seville, Malaga, and Granada	35	
	Other provincial capitals	54	
	Other cities	13	
	Total urban centers		150*
	Rural towns in 13 agrarian reform provinces	34	
	Villages in 13 agrarian reform provinces	32	
	Rural towns in other provinces	25	
	Villages in other provinces	28	
	Total rural centers		119*
	Grand total for the period (can only be considered an approximation, subject to revision, probably upward)		1929

NOTE: Information on political violence, including number of incidents, the casualties, and even more, the responsibility for them and the political identification of the victims, is obviously a subject for bitter polemic, particularly in the case of the October 1934 revolution and its aftermath, and the period after the 16 February 1936 elections. The topic deserves monographic analysis. On the Asturian Revolution we give the official figures and those assembled by Aurelio Llano Roza de Ampudia in *La revolución en Asturias, Octubre de 1934* (Oviedo: Talleres Tipográficos Altamirano, 1935) that Díaz Nosty in *La Comuna asturiana* considers more accurate. And Díaz Nosty's rough estimate of casualties during the postrevolutionary repression. This table includes information from a variety of sources; for 1935 from *El Sol*, for the period 16 February to 17 July 1936 we have used the data collected by Edward Malefakis. We have coded all the crises of democracy in our study, and that the social tensions which accompanied it increased almost consistently throughout the period, particularly in the "tragic spring" of 1936.[80] Certain acts of violence acquired strong symbolic significance: the burning of convents in May 1931, less than a month after the proclamation of the Republic; the cold-blooded assassination of peasants in Casas Viejas by the police in January 1933; the outrages in the repression of the Asturian Revolution; and the chain of assassinations in Madrid in the spring of 1936, culminating in the death of Calvo Sotelo, one of the two principal opposition leaders, on 12 July 1936, in reprisal by policemen for the assassination of one of their comrades.

In numerous speeches, Azaña, and other political leaders as well, emphasized that fear had become a major political factor.[81] This is reflected in less easily measured results of nonfatal violence, like the burning of churches or attempts to do so, the destruction of property and crops, the intimidation of political opponents, and the brutality that characterized the agents of order. Nor is it possible to weigh the impact of structured violence in social relations, the refusal to give work to farm laborers or the expulsion of tenants with phrases like "go eat Republic" after 1934, and the threats against landowners and even wealthy peasants after February 1936. In a situation of crisis of authority, even the behavior of hooligans and common criminals takes on political significance, is justified in political terms, and is excused as a result of social injustice.[82] What strikes the reader of the political literature of the time—the newspapers and the speeches, even in Parliament—is the constant reference to the willingness to announce or encourage the use of force to achieve goals, the assertion of readiness to die for a cause, the frequent description of the situation as one of latent civil war. This atmosphere became intolerable and led participants to believe that the solution lay only in defeating and outlawing their opponents and establishing their own order.[83]

Could the leadership of different political forces have avoided the emergence of this climate of violence and diminished its political impact? Some violence could certainly have been avoided, while other events resulted from such deep-seated tensions in the society that they erupted beyond control of the leadership. At what point decisive action by the government could have

---

events reported in *El Sol,* the leading Spanish newspaper; for the extended periods of press censorship, we have used *La Prensa* and *La Nación* of Buenos Aires, both known for the quality of their reporting on Spain. The accuracy of the figures is almost irrelevant, since each side was ready to believe much higher figures, irresponsibly manipulated, in the absence of fully reliable information. Ramiro V. Cibrián has analyzed the data for 1936 in detail in an unpublished paper, calculating different indices and ratios that show the changes over time, the geographic distribution in relation to the strength or presence of different parties, and the different patterns of antireligious and other form of violence.

*Total number of deaths in the period 3 February to 17 July 1936 was 269. Among these, 57 were caused by the authorities. Gil Robles gives a higher total of 330 (La Cierva, *Historia de la Guerra Civil . . .* pp. 689–90).

prevented or stopped the cycle of violence is not easy to ascertain. There is no doubt that the political impact of the events could have been reduced by intelligent political and legal handling of the problem. The wave of church burnings in May 1931, for example, might well have been prevented by a quick show of authority, a course which the anticlerical members of the government opposed initially, even against the better judgment of a man like Prieto.[84] In other cases, greater concern for the rights of the victims, investigation of what had happened, and more honest, public disclosures of the acts of subordinates would have cleared the political air of suspicions, exaggeration, and distortion, and would have curtailed their political use in creating a climate of hatred and fear. One such case was Casas Viejas;[85] another, on a grand scale, the unwillingness of the Radical and CEDA governments in 1934 and 1935 to investigate responsible accusations against the army, police forces, and authorities in charge of the repression of the revolution in Asturias.[86] Even when the government indicated that it did not approve those acts, its persistent censorship of the opposition press both in that period and after the 1936 election contributed to the climate of suspicion and fear. Exploitation of embarrassing situations by the disloyal and even semiloyal oppositions in order to undermine the prestige of government leaders and ultimately the regime characterized the situation. During the parliamentary debate on Casas Viejas some extremely destructive phrases were coined about the government's performance during the first two years. In another context, we have noted the political importance of debates about persecution and amnesty of leaders and unknowns alike who were involved in revolutionary events and tragic violence, and the way in which these debates helped to delegitimize the political system, provide opportunities for intervention of the president's neutral power, and strain relationships within the political elite.

The Anarcho-syndicalists' revolutionary tradition provided the basis for both sporadic outbreaks of peasant violence and more-or-less uncoordinated local outbreaks, like those in January 1933 in Catalonia that produced thirty-seven casualties and the one in December 1933 that left 89 dead.[87] The participation of the Socialists in the government during the first years of the Republic and the hope for social reform kept strikes and other forms of conflict at a tolerable level, and the unfortunate events in Casas Viejas had already demonstrated the political dangers of any uncontrolled government response to anarchist violence. The Sanjurjo uprising in this period caused little bloodshed (ten dead and eighteen wounded), a fact that might have to be taken into account in understanding the pressures for leniency, the indignation of the Right at certain aspects of the punishment, and the later amnesty for those responsible. From a legal and moral point of view, this insurrection of the Right is no different from that of the Left in 1934, but the differences in the amount of fighting and bloodshed make the two difficult to compare.

The first massive politico-social action officially supported by the Left was the great rural strike in 1934, instigated by the Federación de Trabajadores de la Tierra in alliance with the Socialist party. In the view of the minister of the interior it represented a threat to the harvest.[88] The spring and summer of that year saw the first mass rallies of the European type: meetings were organized by the CEDA in El Escorial and Covadonga, which contributed so unfortunately to the fascistic image of the party among its opponents and provoked a preventive mobilization on their part.[89] This form of mass mobilization inevitably led to misunderstanding, in view of the events of the year before in Germany, Vienna, and Paris. The mass demonstration in April in support of the Generalitat in Barcelona had the same effect. It was during this period that the violence between Fascists and the Left began, which led to the assassination of a former Director General of Security. By the spring of 1933, the Socialist party had begun to organize its youthful militia, and in April 1934 it started talking about a revolutionary army.[90] Mass rallies, like that of the Alianzas Obreras in September 1934, those of the CEDA, and later of the Popular Front, contributed to the unrealistic sense of power among the leadership.[91]

It was, however, the Asturian Revolution that created the real trauma. Eleven hundred ninety-six people were officially listed as dead, and 2,078 as wounded, including 256 police and 639 military.[92] In addition, 100 participants on each side were assassinated outright or condemned with undue haste, though only four death sentences were actually carried out. There were all too numerous incidents of torture, mistreatment, and illegal executions reported by observers like Gordón Ordás, who were not sympathetic to the revolution; the government refused to investigate them. Estimates of the number of arrests all over the country ranged from 10,000 by La Cierva to 30,000 in the official account by the Communist party. If we consider the number involved in the struggle—4,214 from the local garrison of the army and police and a mobilized working class of some 30,000 individuals—we can sense the impact on public opinion. By contrast, the crisis in Barcelona had few casualties on the government side, 4 military dead and 26 wounded.

The post-1934 situation was unique in democratic regimes, for it involved a revolution and a confused attempt at secession (or at least, what was perceived as such) that led not to the establishment of an authoritarian regime but to continuation of democratic legal institutions using emergency powers of repression and allowing an election less than a year and a half later in which the disloyal oppositions won. The psychological impact on the counter-revolutionaries, who felt threatened by the electoral victory of their opponents and their desire to turn the tables, was a situation without parallel in countries with democratic regimes.

It should be noted that the Fascist party in Spain was unable to gain a mass following (or even to organize a significant number of activists of the storm trooper type). Certainly, the preemptive violence of the Left against fascism, the lack of sympathy of the Radical-CEDA governments for the new movement, and the lack of real support by the conservative interests who preferred to rely on the army, cut down Fascist violence and kept the size of the party insignificant by European standards.[93] In 1936 the only nonmilitary mobilized political threat came from the proletarian masses, mainly the Socialist party and its youth organization, which was soon to fuse with that of the Communists. They were confident that they had the strength to cope with any threat from the army, and in this respect the Spanish Socialists acted quite differently from their comrades in France as well as from the German social democrats who had joined the Reichsbanner against the aggressive Nazi squads.[94] The youth of the CEDA, the Juventud de Acción Popular, despite the ideological and symbolic ambiguities which gave it a pseudo-Fascist character, were not involved in street fighting and terror, even though the group had lost twenty-six members to violence before 1936. Other groups, like the Requeté of the Traditionalists and the Escamots of the Estat Català, acted as paramilitary groups with training by professional officers. The paramilitary forces of the Right were never of a size, organization, or discipline capable of threatening a government effectively. They became relevant only as auxiliaries of the army after the uprising in 1936, a factor that explains much of the later political development of Franco's Spain. Furthermore, the leaders of the Falangist party, including José Antonio, were under arrest from March 1936 on, and party activities were officially suspended.[95]

Little is known of the role of the civilian judiciary in handling political violence in those years, but there are indications that both sides of the political spectrum were dissatisfied and urged reform of the judiciary in order to gain greater political influence upon those decisions of which they disapproved.[96] This would seem to indicate that the Spanish judiciary probably was fairer during crises than its counterpart in Germany or even Italy. The increased tension of the period is reflected in the continuous growth of the police and security forces, which by February 1936 numbered some 34,000 *Guardia Civiles* and 17,000 *Guardias de Seguridad* and *de Asalto,* plus 14,000 *Carabineros.* This is in contrast to a total nominal army strength of 169,819 men in July 1936, (actually reduced by leaves, etc.) of which between 30,000 and 45,000 were in Africa.

There is no accurate information on the amount of violence and disorder in the spring of 1936.[97] According to accusations by the Right in parliamentary debate, 204 were killed and 1,057 wounded between the February elections and mid-May; in the following month another 65 were killed and 230 wounded. These figures would indicate that the high point of violence was in the period right after the election rather than in the late spring, but they do not jibe with the accelerated pace of violence and counterviolence between political groups in Madrid against prominent political figures and the leftist advisers of militias. In that context, the prime minister stated that the government was in belligerent opposition to fascism, a statement which can be understood only by realizing that the entire Right, including the CEDA, was labeled fascist by its opponents. Between the elections and mid-July 1936, the Right estimated the total number of deaths at 343. If correct, these figures contrast unfavorably with the 207 deaths reported in Italy in 1921 between 1 January and 14 May 1921, considering the populations of the two countries.[98] In summary, a figure of 2,000 killed in civil strife during the five and one-half years of the Republic does not seem an unreasonable estimate.

The social and political tension was manifest as well in the frequency and intensity of strikes. It is not always easy to distinguish strikes based on economic and social demands from those whose purpose is fundamentally political. In some cases the strikers' demands were presented first to the government authorities rather than to the employers; for example, in the farm labor strike of 1934, the Socialist farm federation sought legislative decisions against employers rather than utilizing collective bargaining. Then, too, the ideological commitment of the CNT, which tended to transform all strike activity into political protest, must be taken into account. The conflict of the two large-scale labor movements, the UGT and the CNT, both committed to radical social change and both competing for the same constituency or hoping to absorb or fuse with the other, also tended to politicize normal labor conflicts. The rigidity of employers like the small marginal entrepreneurs whose position was so precarious that they could not afford concessions, and the possibility of lockouts in a society suffering from unemployment and underemployment, particularly in the countryside, inevitably drew the government into labor conflicts. As strikes often accompanied violence and tension, they became a matter of public order and therefore a problem for the Ministry of Interior as well as the Ministry of Labor. Socialist domination of the labor arbitration machinery in the first years of the Republic made transactions feasible but at the same time alienated the followers of the CNT.

Unfortunately, the strike statistics for the period are far from complete or accurate.[99] It is therefore difficult to trace the fever curve of labor conflict as distinct from other forms of unrest and tension, such as church burnings, invasions of land by landless farmers, spontaneous clashes, and political crimes and assassinations.[100] There are indications, however, that the causes of these various manifestations of crisis coincided at some times and at others did not, but all combined to create a prerevolutionary atmosphere and growing fear, not only among the privileged but in broad segments of the middle class, including the land-owning peasantry, as well. The society might have tolerated one or another of these manifestations of tension if those responsible had clearly distinguished between legitimate and illegitimate forms of expression, but the rhetoric and symbolic acts, even of the top leadership, tended to make this impossible. Whether this pattern of violence and social tension is beyond the limits of democratic politics would be hard to assert. But certainly the cumulative psychological impact, particularly considering the acceleration of the process of violence, the exaltation of violence by many of the leading political actors, and the ambivalent, if not irresponsible, attitude of governments toward the violence of their partisans, could not but create an unsolvable problem.

It is significant that the late spring of 1936 saw decided efforts at reequilibration of the system and warnings of doom,[101] such as the famous speech by Prieto less than two and one-half months before the outbreak of civil war:

A country can survive a revolution, which is ended one way or another. What a country cannot survive is the constant attrition of public disorder without any immediate revolutionary goal; what a nation cannot survive is the waste of public power and economic strength in a constant state of uneasiness, of anxiety and worry. Naive souls may say that this uneasiness, this anxiety, this worry, is only suffered by the upper classes. In my judgment that is incorrect. The working class itself will soon suffer from the pernicious effects of this uneasiness, this anxiety, this worry, because of the disarray and possible collapse of the economy, because though we aspire to transform the economic structure, so long as it does exist. . . .

Let it not be said, to the discredit of democracy, that sterile disorder is only possible when there is a democratic government in power, because then such disorder would mean that only democracy permits excesses, and that only the lash of dictatorship is capable of restraining them. . . . If disorder and excess are turned into a permanent system, one does not achieve socialism, nor does one consolidate a democratic republic—which I think is our advantage—nor does one achieve communism. You achieve a completely desperate anarchy that is not even advocated by anarchist ideology. You achieve disorder that can ruin the country.[102]

The Army and the Breakdown

A comparative view of the breakdown of Spanish democracy might find that the military pronunciamento in July 1936 was its cause, which would bring the Spanish case closer to a rather simplified Latin American model. However, we feel that, taking into consideration the role of the army, the process of crisis and breakdown in the thirties was more like that of Italy in the twenties. For a long time the army tended to play a role not unlike that of the *Reichswehr* in the crisis of the Weimar Republic rather than that of the "moderating power" of the pre-1964 Brazilian model.[103] Ortega y Gasset, who was anything but sympathetic to the tradition of the Spanish military interventionists, in his only published statement about Spanish politics after 1933 stressed that the army uprising in 1936 was not a classic pronunciamento of the type he had so well defined.[104]

Certainly, military intervention as a moderating power was the model in the minds of many politicians and army officers throughout the years of the Republic. The August 1932 uprising was the last pronunciamento in Spanish history, and it failed dismally as a valid model for the civilians as well as for the majority of the military. In 1934, after the October revolution, in late 1935, and immediately after the 1936 election, the politicians of the extreme Right, like Calvo Sotelo, and Gil Robles himself, explored with trusted high-ranking officers whether the army was ready to play the traditional role of a "moderating power," but they could not effect a favorable response among the officer corps.[105] The army was not ready to act on its own at the urging of the politicians unless the latter assumed responsibility for the action. And to that point the politicians themselves were not ready to go.

The fact was that the army was divided internally as to both its political role and its ideological outlook.[106] Throughout the history of the Republic there were undoubtedly officers, particularly self-retired officers, conspiring against the regime. However, the majority of the senior generals were legalists with no ideological commitments who supported the constitutionally formed legitimate government. Even in July 1936, out of sixteen generals with command of a division and the heads of the two police forces, only four joined the rebellion.[107] Despite professional grievances created by many aspects of the Azaña reforms, and by the style with which they were carried out, the bulk of the officer corps opted for an attentist position. Given the definition of the "Republic for the Republicans," this meant a nonpartisan attitude rather than commitment to the regime, but it did not preclude such officers from having close ties and sympathies with certain more committed officers and political leaders. As long as the institutionalized authorities functioned with some legitimacy and effectiveness, such officers were ready to support them in performance of their duties, as they did during the August 1932 putsch and the 1934 October crisis.

It is symbolic that General Batet, who intelligently defeated the insurrection of the regional government of Catalonia, should have been shot by the rebels in Burgos. It is equally symbolic that López Ochoa, commanding general of the army in Asturias in 1934, opponent of Primo de Rivera, a Mason who attended the funeral of Pablo Iglesias (the founder of the Socialist party), and who had named his daughter Libertad, should be shot in Madrid by the Popular Front. Lerroux was basically right, at least before 1936, when he wrote: ". . . the Spanish army has a frankly liberal spirit; a majority of the officers are indifferent to the form of government and the minority are Republican, or more frequently, Monarchists."[108]

There were other forces at work, of course: the conspiratorial activities of some monarchical generals and officers, both retired and in command; the emergence of the Unión Militar Española as a professional activist organization courted by different political factions; the attraction after October 1934 of Yagüe and a number of younger officers to fascism; and the success on the other side of the spectrum as the Left (especially the Communists) found support among a minority, particularly in the police and the air force and among some noncommissioned officers. The links between military professionals and the paramilitary organizations of all political colors, the public appeals to the army as the backbone of the nation by the extreme Right, particularly Calvo Sotelo, and the aggressive anti-militarism of the Left inevitably contributed to politicization of the officer corps. This link affected decisions concerning command assignments, a highly political matter, arousing the suspicions of the politicians and creating tensions within the officer corps. It seems impossible to imagine in such a highly politicized and polarized society, with political groups advocating violence and preparing to use it, that the armed forces could remain apolitical, committed to supporting the constituted government irrespective of its political color.

Given the double threat of social revolution and regional nationalism perceived as separatism from the Spanish state after 1934, army officers were increasingly open to the notion of an independent political role. In this context, it is important to realize how far the army had moved from the nineteenth-century model of the moderating power. In November 1934, in the middle of the conflict with the president of the Republic about amnesty for officers who had sided with the October rebellion—a dispute which threatened a presidential dissolution of the Chamber and an electoral victory of the Left—the CEDA leader, Gil Robles, explained the situation to the military in the following terms:

For us it was impossible to take the initiative to provoke an exceptional situation even though we do not oppose the army's making known to the president its strong desire to prevent his violating the fundamental norm of the nation, as he was at the point of doing. If I maintain the position of the ministers of the CEDA, there will be no way out of the crisis. Alcalá Zamora will be obliged to give power to a Left government and dissolve the legislature. It will be a true coup d'état, and who shall prevent it?[109]

In spite of the ambiguities of the situation, this message was intended to test the response of the army to an appeal that it use its moderating power. The response was negative. The army did not feel that it had the capacity for the task, and the Center-Right politicians, unlike those of the extreme Right, were not ready to call openly for military support in a coup. On 11 December 1935, when Parliament was on the verge of dissolution by the president, the minister of war, Gil Robles, received a proposal for a coup d'état from his undersecretary, a general. He refused to assume that responsibility and suggested that if the army, united around its natural leadership, felt it had to take power temporarily to save the spirit of the constitution and "prevent a gigantic falsification of revolutionary sign," he would not oppose it. After consultation with fellow officers, the leading generals rejected the suggestion. A letter from Franco to Gil Robles in March 1937 explained the situation in these terms:

. . . Neither the duty of discipline nor the situation of Spain—difficult, but not yet of imminent peril—nor the carefullness with which you proceeded during your whole tenure in the Ministry—which did not authorize me for such a task—permitted me to propose what at that time would have seemed to lack justification or belief in the possibility of success, since the Army, which can rebel when such a sacred cause as that of the Fatherland is in imminent danger, cannot give the appearance of arbiter in political disputes nor define the conduct of parties or the powers of the chief of state. Any action at that time would have been condemned to failure as unjustified had the Army undertaken it; and the latter, which now has rebelled to save Spain, was hoping that, if possible, she would be saved through legal channels that would prevent grave and . . . painful upheavals.[110]

When the results of the election began to be known on 16 February, General Franco contacted the head of the *Guardia Civil* to ask the minister of war of the interim centrist Portela government to declare a state of emergency—a request which he later made directly to the prime minister, who refused after consulting with the president, since the latter approved a state of alarm only. The prime minister, who, hours later, before the final results of the elections were known or the legislature convened, was to give power to Azaña to avoid facing the pressures of the Popular Front masses, explored the possibility of an independent action by the army. Franco, still head of the General Staff, responded that the army did not yet have the moral unity necessary to undertake the task.[111] After the deposition of President Alcalá Zamora on dubious constitutional grounds, and before the election of Azaña, officers under the leadership of López Ochoa proposed that Alcalá Zamora dissolve the legislature and install a military cabinet. This would have been the second dissolution to which he was entitled, according to one interpretation of the constitution. He rejected the idea but apparently hinted that he would not discourage the officers from acting on their own initiative.[112] Again the conspirators could not bring themselves to act without some sort of constitutional mandate.

In all these situations either the politicians or the military considered intervention, but on each occasion the leading officers agreed that action as the moderating power by a relatively united army was possible only if legitimized by civilians holding office constitutionally.

There is no point in recounting here the progress of the various groups of conspirators in the spring of 1936, the slow convergence of the nonpartisan generals with the more political conspirators of the UME, the involvement in May and June of prestigious generals who had heretofore remained aloof from conspiracy, nor the broad support mobilized by the rebels after Franco's commitment and the assassination of Calvo Sotelo on 13 July. What is important for our analysis is to note that the top leadership, particularly General Mola, wanted at all costs to avoid linking what was to be a purely military rebellion to any particular political faction or program and to insure that any civilians joining the uprising were subordinate to the military authority. It is also significant that the leadership deliberately planned the coup to appear Republican, using Republican symbols, an indication of the degree to which monarchical legitimacy no longer served as a rallying symbol. The uprising on 17, 18, and 19 July bore no resemblance to those of the nineteenth century or those taking place in Latin America until quite recently, in which the politicians incite the military to act and then to transfer power to them. In this case the military assumed power themselves, relying on civilian supporters only because of the weakness of the military organization and the need to rally popular support. Faced with what they perceived as a prerevolutionary situation, the military in Spain assumed what Stepan has described as a new professionalism, or at least some elements of it, by abandoning the old role of the moderating power that the semiloyal politicians of the Republic (and many moderates, in the spring of 1936), were ready to assign to them.[113]

Out of the Spanish experience arises the question of whether in a democracy experiencing intense constitutional and social crisis, the intervention of the army as a moderating power, including intervention via an interim military dictatorship, might not sometimes provide greater hopes for the future restoration of democracy than does a total break with the existing institutions by the professional military and the subsequent creation of an authoritarian regime.

Although the army became the ultimate cause of the breakdown, the crisis and loss of legitimacy of the regime and the polarization in the society had progressed to great extremes before the army acted.[114] It would be a mistake to consider this insurrection the main cause. In more than one sense, the regime had already broken down.

BIBLIOGRAPHIC NOTE

The literature on the Republic and the origins of the civil war is large and often highly partisan. Among the major works in English are: Raymond Carr, *Spain, 1808–1939* (Oxford: Oxford University Press, 1966); Gabriel Jackson, *The Spanish Republic and the Civil War, 1931–1939* (Princeton, N.J.: Princeton University Press, 1965); Hugh Thomas, *The Spanish Civil War* (New York: Harper and Row, 1977), a revised and enlarged edition; and Salvador de Madariaga, *Spain: A Modern History* (New York: Praeger, 1958) by a liberal Spanish intellectual who refused to identify in exile with either side (pp. 377– 498 on the Republic). The most comprehensive and best-documented work in Spanish is Ricardo de La Cierva, *Historia de la Guerra Civil española, Antecedents: Monarquía y República, 1898–1936* (Madrid: San Martín, 1969). From a different perspective, see Ramón Tamames, *La República: La era de Franco,* 6th rev. ed. (Madrid: Alianza Editorial, 1977), the work of an economist, and Manuel Tuñon de Lara, *La II Republica,* 2 vols. (Madrid: Siglo XXI, 1972), a short work by a well-known social historian. The collection of essays edited by Manuel Ramírez Jiménez, *Estudios sobre la II República Española* (Madrid: Tecnos, 1975), brings together the most recent work of a group of Spanish scholars on aspects often neglected. Ramírez is also the author of *Los grupos de presión en la segunda República Española* (Madrid: Tecnos, 1969), the best monograph on interest groups. In addition to a number of monographic studies on political parties, the following give an overview and rich documentation: Miguel Artola, *Partidos y programas políticos, 1808– 1936,* vol. 1, *Los partidos políticos,* and vol. 2, *Manifiestos y programas políticos* (Madrid: Aguilar, 1974–75). On political parties in the Republic, see vol. I, pp. 598–700. See also Juan J. Linz, "The Party System of Spain: Past and Future," in *Party Systems and Voter Alignments: Cross-National Perspectives*, ed. Seymour Martin Lipset and Stein Rokkan (New York: Free Press, 1967), pp. 197–282. On the Left, see Stanley G. Payne, *The Spanish Revolution: A Study of the Social and Political Tensions That Culminated in the Civil War in Spain* (New York: Norton, 1970), and Raymond Carr, ed., *The Republic and the Civil War in Spain* (London: Macmillan and St. Martin's Press, 1971). The latter includes chapters by Edward Malefakis on the Left, R. Robinson on the Right, and Stanley Payne on the army.

Edward E. Malefakis, *Agrarian Reform and Peasant Revolution in Spain: Origins of the Civil War* (New Haven: Yale University Press, 1970), covers much more than the title would indicate. The concluding chapters, "The Destruction of the 'Bourgeois' Republic" and "Could the Disaster Have Been Avoided," should be read in conjunction with this essay since they deal with important questions, particularly in relation to the class conflict in Spain, which we have decided to neglect rather than repeat his work.

A collection of documents that should be consulted and that could serve to support points we are making is found in Ricardo de La Cierva, ed., *Los Documentos de la Primavera Trágica: Análisis documental de los antecedentes inmediatos del 18 de julio de 1936* (Madrid: Ministerio de Información y Turismo, Secretaría General Técnica, Sección de Estudios Sobre la Guerra de España, 1967).

Henry Landsberger and Juan J. Linz, "El caso chileno y la España do los años 30: Contraste y similitud," in *Chile 1970–1973: Lecciones de una experiencia*, ed. Federico G. Gil, Ricardo Lagos E., and Henry A. Landsberger (Madrid: Tecnos, 1977), pp. 399–458, is an attempt to point out some of the similarities and differences in the processes leading to the tragic breakdown of democracy in both countries.

NOTES

1. The low performance of the Spanish Republic, measured operationally, stands out among the countries compared in Ted Robert Gurr and Muriel McClelland, *Political Performance: A Twelve-Nation Study* (Beverly Hills, Ca.: Sage, 1971), which include the Weimar Republic and Yugoslavia. Their summary score for Spain between 1932 and 1936 (p. 72) was −7.80, compared to −6.01 for Germany between 1923 and 1932, −3.95 for Yugoslavia between 1921 and 1929, and −2.57 for France between 1879 and 1940. The depth of the crisis is also reflected in the fact that the linear trends (regression coefficients) in the aggregate returns in seven polarized polities between the two world wars and the present postwar period show Spain to be the most polarized. The sum of the coefficients of extreme Right and extreme Left in Weimar Germany was 6.16, while in Spain it reached 15.9. The weakening of the representation of the Center (respectively, −3.65 and −7.3) is particularly noticeable. For the definition of the coefficients method and data used, see Giovanni Sartori, *Parties and Party Systems: A Framework for Analysis* (Cambridge: Cambridge University Press, 1976), pp. 164–73.

   Data on cabinet instability in the period between 14 April 1939 and 17 July 1936 confirm the pattern: average cabinet duration in Spain was 101 days (148 for the Catalan regional governments). The figure for Austria in the early thirties was 149; for Weimar Germany before the Depression (1918–30) it was 210, rising to 258 after 30 March 1930. Average cabinet duration was 260 days in Italy before Mussolini (1918–22), compared to 166 days in Spain during a comparable period (1918–23).

2. Juan J. Linz, "Early State Building and Late Peripheral Nationalisms against the State," in *Building States and Nations: Analysis and Data Across Three Worlds*, ed. S. N. Eisenstadt and Stein Rokkan (Beverly Hills, Ca.: Sage, 1973), vol. 2, pp. 32–116.

3. Pedro Voltes Bou, *Historia de la economía española en los siglos XIX y XX*, 2 vols. (Madrid: Editora Nacional, 1974). The economic history of the period has not yet been thoroughly studied. Leandro Benavides, *Política económica en la II República española* (Madrid: Guadiana, 1972), presents a brief overview with reference to contemporary sources. See also Alberto Balcells, *Crisis económica y agitación social en Cataluña*

(1930-1936) (Esplugues de Llobregat: Ariel, 1971). Balcells, while agreeing on the less dramatic situation in Spain in terms of economic indices and unemployment, rightly notes how that impact was more severe in the absence of unemployment benefits and other social programs.

4. Unfortunately, we have no systematic data to prove this point, since there were no surveys at the time. Indirectly, the small electoral support and membership of monarchist parties, the fact that even the uprising of the army in 1936 was under a Republican flag with manifestoes closing "Live the Republic," the lack of support for monarchical forms of government revealed by surveys in Franco's Spain despite the official reinstauration of a monarchy, the low prestige of the aristocracy, etc., would support our statement.

5. Nothing can better convey a feeling for the vacuum of support for the monarchy after the resignation of Primo de Rivera (January 1930) and particularly in its last hours (April 1931) than the review essay by Jesús Pabón, "Siete relatos de tres días (Estudio preliminar para un libro sobre la crisis de la Monarquía)," in *Días de ayer: Historias e historiadores contemporáneos* (Barcelona: Alpha, 1963), pp. 367–431.

6. On the 1931 municipal elections, see Juan J. Linz, "The Party System of Spain: Past and Future," in *Party Systems and Voter Alignments: Cross National Perspectives,* ed. Seymour M. Lipset and Stein Rokkan (New York: Free Press, 1967), pp. 231–36.

7. On the late founding and weakness of fascism *(strictu sensu)*, see Stanley Payne, *Falange: A History of Spanish Fascism* (Stanford, Ca.: Stanford University Press, 1961); his chapter on Spain in Stein Ugelvik Larsen, Bernt Hagtvet, and Jan Peter Myklebust, *Who Were the Fascists* (forthcoming), with more recent bibliographic references; and Juan J. Linz, "Some Notes Toward a Comparative Study of Fascism in Sociological Historical Perspective, in *Fascism, A Reader's Guide,* ed. Walter Laqueur (Berkeley and Los Angeles: University of California Press, 1976), pp. 3–121. See also the synthesis in Ricardo de la Cierva, *Historia de la Guerra Civil española* (Madrid: San Martín, 1969), chap. 12, pp. 507–75.

8. See reference to Giovanni Sartori's articles and the scholarly discussion provoked by them in our introductory essay.

9. The course of the Republic was punctuated by frequent elections that contributed to the high level of tension, particularly three national elections in less than five years, and the lack of synchronism between the political developments in Catalonia and the rest of Spain. To them we have to add the referenda on the local autonomy statutes. See Javier Tusell, *Las elecciones del Frente Popular,* 2 vols. (Madrid: Edicusa, 1971); idem *La segunda república en Madrid: Elecciones y partidos políticos* (Madrid: Tecnos, 1970); and idem, *Sociología electoral de Madrid (1903–1931)* (Madrid: Edicusa, 1967). See also Miguel M. Cuadrado, *Elecciones y partidos políticos de España (1868–1931)* (Madrid: Taurus, 1969), vol. 2, pp. 853–57, on the 1931 municipal elections, and Jesús de Miguel and Juan J. Linz, "Hacia un análisis regional de las elecciones de 1936 en España," *Revista Española de la Opinión Pública,* 48 (1977): pp. 27–68.

10. See Ferdinand A. Hermens, *Democracy or Anarchy? A Study of Proportional Representation* (Notre Dame, Ind.: Review of Politics, 1941), and his follower Helmut Unkelbach, *Grundlagen der Wahlsystematik: Stabilitätsbedingungen der modernen Demokratie* (Göttingen: Vandenhoeck and Ruprecht, 1956). An early critic who mentioned the Spanish case was Sten S. Nilson, "Wahlsoziologische Probleme des Nationalsozialismus," *Zeitschrift für die gesamte Staatswissenschaft* 110 (1954):279–311, esp. pp. 282–84. For a recent reexamination of the thesis passionately defended by Hermens, see Hans Fenske, *Wahlrecht und Parteiensystem: Ein Beitrag zur deutschen Parteiengeschichte* (Frankfurt: Athenaeum, 1972), pp. 30–35. For a balanced analysis, see Giovanni Sartori, *Parties and Party Systems: A Framework for Analysis* (Cambridge: Cambridge University Press, 1976), vol. 1.

11. The Spanish electoral system is similar in this respect to the Argentinian system that created the impossible game in the post-Perón period: coalitions with parties like the Peronists were inevitable and were perceived as a disloyal opposition.

There is a need for a systematic analysis of the possible alternative outcome of elections with different electoral systems for those years. The failure to enact proportional representation, advocated in principle by the CEDA and strongly favored by the Lliga and other minor parties in 1935, remains unexplained.

12. Juan J. Linz, "Continuidad y discontinuidad en la elite política española, de la Restauración al Régimen actual," in *Estudios de ciencia política y sociología: Homenaje al Profesor Carlos Ollero* (Guadalajara: Gráficas Carlavilla, 1972), pp. 361–423.

13. Fortunately, on the agrarian problem and the failure to tackle the agrarian reform in a politically and technically viable way we have the outstanding monograph by Edward E. Malefakis, *Agrarian Reform and Peasant Revolution in Spain: Origins of the Civil War* (New Haven: Yale University Press, 1970). The low ranking of agrarian reform on the agenda of the leadership of the Republic is reflected in the fact that until May 1932 no serious discussion occurred in the Constituent Cortes and that the obstruction of agrarian reform measures until September by a small minority of the Right would have been defeated if the majority had so desired (Malefakis, *Agrarian Reform*, p. 389).

14. There is no fully adequate history of the church and the Catholic lay movement in the twentieth century, nor is there an adequate treatment of anticlericalism. José Manuel Cuenca, *Estudios sobre la Iglesia española del siglo XIX* (Madrid, 1973), provides some historical antecedents. M. Batllori and V. M. Arbeloa, *Iglesia y Estado durante la Segunda República española: 1931–1936*, is forthcoming. In English, José M. Sánchez, *Reform and Reaction: The Politico-Religious Background of the Spanish Civil War* (Chapel Hill: University of North Carolina Press, 1962), provides an overview. In Spanish, see the chapter in La Cierva, *Historia de la Guerra Civil Española*, pp. 462–81. Even though centered on the civil war period, Antonio Montero Moreno, *Historia de la persecución religiosa en España: 1936–1939* (Madrid: Biblioteca de Autores Cristianos, 1961), provides an overview for the prewar years, including the church burnings, the Asturian Revolution, and the popular anticlericalism in 1936. A good local study based on diocesan documents is Juan Ordóñez Márquez, *La apostasía de las masas y la persecución religiosa en la provincia de Huelva, 1931–1936* (Madrid: Consejo Superior de Investigaciones Científicas, 1968). The sociological study by Severino Aznar, *La revolución española y las vocaciones eclesiásticas* (Madrid: Instituto de Estudios Políticos, 1949), shows the impact of the October revolution on the number of seminarians. For the declarations of the hierarchy, see Jesús Iribarren, ed., *Documentos colectivos del episcopado español, 1870–1974* (Madrid: Biblioteca de Autores Cristianos, 1974). On the other hand, we have the biographies of bishops, including Anastasio Granados, *El Cardenal Gomá: Primado de España* (Madrid: Espasa Calpe, 1969); Ramón Muntanyola, *Vidal i Barraquer, cardenal de la pau* (Barcelona: Estela, 1970); and the book by Juan de Iturralde, *El catolicismo y la cruzada de Franco* (n.p.: Egui-Indarra, n.d.), focused on the links of the church with reactionary elements. Ramón Comas, *Isidro Gomá, Francesc Vidal i Barraquer: Dos visiones antagónicas de la Iglesia española de 1939* (Salamanca: Sígueme, 1977), shows the divergent outlook of two leading churchmen.

To get a feel for the secularizing and anticlerical positions—at their most dignified—see the speeches of Azaña, particularly in the Cortes debate, included in his *Obras completas,* ed. Juan Marichal, 4 vols. (Mexico: Oasis, 1967). See also those of Gordón Ordás in *Mi política en España,* 3 vols. (Mexico D.F.: Imprenta Fígero, 1961–63). There is no sociological-sociopsychological study of popular anticlericalism, nor of the popular manifestations of religiosity in response to it.

On lay Catholicism, the writings of Angel Herrera Oria, director of El Debate, *Obras selectas de Angel Herrera* (Madrid: Biblioteca de Autores Cristianos [BAC], 1943), and Martín Sánchez Juliá, *Ideas claras: Reflexiones de un español actual* (Madrid: BAC, 1959), are revealing. All the works dealing with the CEDA are also relevant to an understanding of the contribution of the religious conflict to the crisis.

15. See Stanley G. Payne, *Politics and the Military in Modern Spain* (Stanford, Ca.: Stanford University Press, 1967), pp. 266–91, on the Azaña reforms (some of them enacted by the provisional government eleven days after the founding of the regime).

16. See Ignacio Hidalgo de Cisneros, *Memorias 2: La república y la guerra de España* (Paris: Editions de la librairie du Globe, 1964), pp. 91–99, on military reactions to Azaña's reforms. The future head of the Republican Air Force in the civil war (a Communist)

documents well the kind of reforms—for instance, retroactively voiding honor court decisions—that even he could not accept.

17. On those unfortunate events and the failure of the government to react effectively, see the memoirs of the minister of the interior at the time, Miguel Maura, *Así cayó Alfonso XIII* (Barcelona: Ariel, 1966), pp. 240–64.

18. Malefakis, *Agrarian Reform*, chap. 8, pp. 205–35, describes in detail how the provisions of the Agrarian Reform Law unnecessarily increased the number of opponents to the regime, yet had no chance, within any reasonable time—given budgetary constraints—to benefit anyone. In addition, they overloaded the bureaucratic machinery with work. Of the 879,371 farms affected by the reform, only 154,716, or 17.6 percent, lay in the eleven latifundio provinces, to which another 11.5 percent were added in the areas of application of the law. The remaining 70.9 percent were affected in their status without, however, any prospect of being actually included in the reform. Had the reform been limited to the eleven principal latifundio provinces, only 20,460 owners would have been affected, even after all the small and medium-sized farms encompassed by the *ruedo* and lease provisions were taken into account. As the law was written, 79,554 owners were forced to register their property.

The enemies of the reform were increased fourfold: more than two thirds of all inventory owners came from northern and central Spain, where land redistribution could not take effect until an enabling law had been passed by the Cortes (pp. 216–17).

19. Carlos Alba Tercedor, "La educación en la II República: Un intento de socialización política," in Ramírez, *Estudios sobre la II República Española*, pp. 49–85.

20. See Linz, "Early State Building," and idem, "Politics in a Multi-lingual Society with a Dominant World Language: The Case of Spain," in *Les États Multilingues: Problèmes et Solutions*, ed. Jean-Guy Savard and Richard Vigneault (Quebec: Université Laval, 1975), pp. 367–444, for an analysis and bibliographic references.

An excellent monograph on the conservative Catalan party is Isidre Molas, *Lliga catalana: Un estudi d'Estasiologia*, 2 vols. (Barcelona: Edicions 62, 1972), that includes an analysis of the party system of Catalonia (2:231–98) and election data for the period (2:267–94), as well as information on Lliga membership, social composition of elites, etc. An overview is provided by Jaume Rossinyol, *Le problème national catalan* (Paris: Mouton, 1969). Jesús Pabón, *Cambó*, 3 vols. (Barcelona: Alpha, 1952–69), is a basic work. For the Catalan Left, see Roger Arnau, *Marxisme català i qüestió nacional catalana, 1930–1936*, 2 vols. (Paris: Edicions Catalanes de Paris, 1974). An earlier overview is contained in Maximiano García Venero, *Historia del nacionalismo Catalán*, 2 vols. (Madrid: Editora Nacional, 1967). Galician regionalism was not a disruptive factor. See Alfonso Bozzo, *Los partidos políticos y la autonomía en Galicia, 1931–1936* (Madrid: Akal, 1976). On the Catalan Estatuto, its origins, enactment, and application, see the excellent study by Manuel Gerpe Landin, *L'estatut d'autonomia de Catalunya í l'estat integral* (Barcelona: Edicions 62, 1977).

21. On Basque nationalism, the most recent comprehensive history is Stanley G. Payne, *Basque Nationalism* (Reno: University of Nevada, 1975). See also Javier Tusel Gómez, *Historia de la Democracia Cristiana en España* (Madrid: Edicusa, 1974), vol. 2, pp. 11–119, particularly on the relations with the CEDA.

22. Quoted in Catalan in La Cierva, *Historia de la Guerra Civil*, p. 378.

23. For an account of the events, see ibid., pp. 369–86, and two contemporary narratives: L. Aymami i Baudina, *El 6 d'Octubre tal com jo l'he vist* (Barcelona: Atenea, 1935), and Jaume Miravitlles, *Crítica del 6 d'octubre* (Barcelona: Libreria Catalonia, 1935).

24. On the case, see Albert Balcells, *El problema agrari a Catalunya 1890–1936: La qüestió rabassaire* (Barcelona: Nova Terra, 1968); Jesús Pabón, *Cambó, Parte segunda: 1930–1947* (Barcelona: Alpha, 1969), pp. 339–60; and the memoirs of the lawyer who argued the case before the constitutional court: Amadeu Hurtado, *Quaranta anys d'advocat: Historia del meu temps* (Esplugues de Llobregat: Ariel, 1967), chap. 10, pp. 256–98.

25. Manuel Azaña, in a parliamentary debate on 25 June 1934. See his *Obras Completas*, vol. 2, p. 981.

26. Quoted in Pabón, *Cambó, Parte segunda*, pp. 335–36.

27. The basic source is the personal defense by Manuel Azaña himself. See Azaña "Mi rebelión in Barcelona (1934–1935)," first published in 1935, reprinted in *Obras Completas,* vol. 3, pp. 25–179.

28. See Karl Dietrich Bracher, Wolfgang Sauer, and Gerhard Schulz, *Die Nationalsozialistische Machtergreifung* (Cologne: Westdeutscher Verlag, 1960), pp. 136–44, the relevant studies by Karl Schwend, and the memoirs of Frhr. von Aretin.

29. The statements of Izquierda Republicana and Unión Republicana on 5 October 1934 are quoted in La Cierva, *Historia de la Guerra Civil,* p. 429. The Partido Republicano Conservador, Partido Federal Autónomo, and Izquierda Radical Socialista made similar statements. Given the legitimizing of the revolution by the bourgeois parties with those statements, a historical study of their formulation would be important. If we consider the CEDA as a potentially legitimate participant in the political process—which those parties did not—these official notes were at best a semiloyal behavior.

30. On the Sanjurjo uprising, see Payne, *Politics and the Military in Spain,* pp. 277–91, and Alejandro Lerroux, *La pequeña historia: Apuntes para la historia grande vividos y redactados por el autor* (Buenos Aires: Cimera, 1945), pp. 143–46, the latter for his account of a conversation with Sanjurjo and his transmittal of the information to Azaña (without, however, revealing names).

31. In his memoirs (*Obras Completas,* vol. 4, pp. 649–52), Azaña describes in detail a conversation on 2 January 1934 with Fernando de los Ríos, former Socialist minister, on the revolutionary plans of the Socialist party. He later had a similar conversation with Largo Caballero. While he tried forcefully to dissuade them, he does not mention any thought of informing the Lerroux government.

32. Joaquín Chapaprieta, *La paz fue posible: Memorias de un político,* with an introductory essay by Carlos Seco Serrano (Esplugues de Llobregat: Ariel, 1971), pp. 407–13.

33. On the anarcho-syndicalist movement, see José Peirats, *La CNT en la revolución española* (Toulouse: Ediciones de la CNT, 1953). A recent analysis is Antonio Elorza, *La utopía anarquista bajo la Segunda República* (Madrid: Ayuso, 1973). On Anarcho-syndicalism and spontaneous peasant protest, see Malefakis, *Agrarian Reform,* chap. 11, pp. 284–316. For additional references, see Stanley G. Payne, *The Spanish Revolution: Study of the Social and Political Tensions That Culminated in the Civil War in Spain* (New York: Norton, 1970).

34. The official history is Partido Comunista de España, *Historia del PCE,* abbreviated version (Havana: Editora Política, 1964). See also the anti-Communist work by Eduardo Comín Colomer, *Historia del Partido Comunista de España,* 3 vols. (Madrid: Editora Nacional, 1967). On the PCE and dissident Communist parties, see also La Cierva, *Historia de la Guerra Civil,* pp. 352–63, and Guy Hermet, *Les communistes en Espagne: Etude d'un mouvement politique clandestin* (Paris: A. Colin, 1971), pp. 17–34.

35. On the Catalan revolutionary parties and groups, see Arnau, *Marxisme català,* and Isidre Molas, *Lliga catalana,* vol. 2, pp. 277–98. For additional references, see Payne, *Spanish Revolution.* On the POUM—Partido Obrero de Unificación Marxista—see Andrés Nin, *Los problemas de la revolución española,* with a Preface by Juan de Andrade (Paris: Ruedo Ibérico, 1971), and Victor Alba, *El marxisme a Catalunya, 1919–1939,* vol. 1, *Historia del B.O.C.,* vol. 2, *Historia del P.O.U.M.,* vol. 3, *Andreu Nin,* and vol. 4, *Joaquím Maurín* (Barcelona: Portic, 1974–75).

36. A definitive history of the Socialist party, particularly in the years from the death of Pablo Iglesias (1925) to the civil war, remains to be written. Today, we must still rely on the scanty memoirs of participants, collections of speeches by different leaders, polemical tracts, and valuable secondary accounts based on limited evidence. Much monographic research is under way, and the provisional synthesis of developments in the PSOE during the thirties in Malefakis, *Agrarian Reform,* will certainly lead that author to write the work needed. The description of the three main tendencies in the party centered around key personalities like Besteiro, Prieto, and Largo Caballero will be insufficient until we know more about their respective bases of support and are able to place their positions in a comparative ideological analysis of Socialist politics. The terms often used to characterize those three positions—reformism, pragmatism, and maximalism—are in part a misleading

shorthand. Except for Besteiro and Fernando de los Ríos, Spanish Socialist leaders did not articulate their positions intellectually in Marxist terms, as did many of their colleagues abroad. Only a more thorough analysis of their statements and actions over the years, i.e., their intellectual roots, would help us to understand more systematically and comparatively their positions in those fateful years.

Such analysis would also limit excessive emphasis on personality conflicts and enable us to interpret as consistent apparently contradictory positions taken in the course of time, which we suspect—given the personalities of some of the actors—responded to an implicit code. From this perspective, Largo Caballero's collaboration with the dictatorship, his ministerial role in the first bienio, his rejection of further collaboration with the Left-bourgeois parties in 1933, his shift to a clearly revolutionary insurrectionist position which led to the events of October 1934, his rejection of the party's participation in the government in 1936 after the Popular Front victory, and his revolutionary voluntarism might ultimately be as consistent as the "orthodox" Marxism of Besteiro's rejection in principle of party participation in bourgeois political alliances (in 1917, 1923, 1930, and 1931) and the inarticulate but obviously socio-democratic stance of Prieto, which had been maintained since the days of Primo de Rivera. Certainly Besteiro's position was politically non-viable in the 1930s, since the PSOE and the UGT were the two best-organized political forces to the left of center, and there was a divided and far from outstanding bourgeois Left and Center political leadership. Outside support and the personal participation of leaders without the commitment of their parties, could not strengthen a progressive Republic nor satisfy the deprived working-class masses. It would perhaps have made sense if Azaña and Lerroux had worked together against both the Right and the proletarian Left, as the bourgeois forces in the Third French Republic sometimes did. But the non-social democratic position of Largo Caballero, whose roots in the early years of the party need to be traced, would only have made sense if the PSOE had been supported by the whole urban and rural proletariat—divided between Socialists and the syndicalists of the CNT, in addition to minor radical parties—and if the society had for one reason or another found itself in a really prerevolutionary situation after its defeat in the war, in a sudden deep economic crisis rather than a structural crisis aggravated by the depression, and with a much weaker urban and rural middle class ready to defend its interests. It is no accident, as La Cierva has noted (*Historia de la Guerra Civil,* pp. 315–20), that Largo Caballero should have embraced the ideas of the working-class alliances (initially formulated by dissident Communists in Catalonia), since only the united action of all proletarian organizations could aspire to revolutionary action. Under the circumstances the chances for victory in a real revolution, even a well-planned one, were considerably less than even. Only the preemptive counterrevolution of 1936 made possible the unity of revolutionary forces and a civil war.

Besteiro's supporters accused Largo of being a "practical reformist who sometimes can take the appearance of an extreme radicalism" and of a "transition from collaborationist opportunism to bolshevik opportunism."

37. Martin Blinkhorn, *Carlism and Crisis in Spain, 1931–1939* (Cambridge: Cambridge University Press, 1975).
38. Paul Preston, "Alfonsist Monarchism and the Coming of the Spanish Civil War," *Journal of Contemporary History* 7, nos. 3 and 4 (July–October 1972):89–114.
39. For a hagiographic biography, see Felipe Acedo Colunga, *José Calvo Sotelo* (Barcelona: AHR, 1957). For a good example of his disloyal opposition, see the speech of 12 January 1936 appealing for a military insurrection (La Cierva, *Historia de la Guerra Civil,* pp. 628–29).
40. See Payne in his writings on Spanish fascism, particularly *Falange.* In contrast, a fascisticized, monarchical, conservative Right had support among certain elites and intellectuals, and the Carlists retained their local strongholds. See Stanley G. Payne, "Spain," in *The European Right,* ed. Hans Rogger and Eugene Weber (Berkeley and Los Angeles: University of California Press, 1965), pp. 168–207, for additional references. It was this sector of the Right that was most active in stimulating military conspiracies, and that established, in March 1934, contacts with the Italian government to buy arms. It is difficult to estimate the electoral appeal the Carlists and Renovación would have had

running candidates separately, but it certainly would have been below that of the DNVP, except in its worst showing. In 1936 the vote going to the candidates of both parties who appeared on coalition lists was 7.2%.

41. In 1933 the extreme Right had gone into the elections in many (but not all) districts allied with the CEDA; soon, however, it would find the collaboration between that party and Radicals as distasteful as did the Radicals, who followed Martínez Barrio in his split with Lerroux. The attacks became increasingly bitter in late 1934 and continued well into the election campaign of 1936, which the extreme Right led under the slogan "Let us vote so that some day we can stop voting." The CEDA, on the other hand, was optimistic about the potential electoral success, overestimating the effect of its organizational and financial resources. From a pro-Bloque Nacional point of view, see Santiago Galindo Herrero, *Los partidos monárquicos bajo la Segunda República* (Madrid: Rialp, 1956), pp. 259–65, which contains correspondence between Gil Robles and Calvo Sotelo. Gil Robles, *No fue posible la paz* (Esplugues de Llobregat: Ariel, 1968), pp. 406–23, describes in detail the tension in the course of the campaign. See also La Cierva, *Historia de la Guerra Civil,* pp. 497–501 and 619.

42. Unfortunately, there is no monographic study on the Esquerra and no scholarly biography of Companys comparable to that of Cambó. See, however, Angel Ossorio Gallardo, *Vida y sacrificio de Companys* (Buenos Aires: Losada, 1943); Josep M. Poblet, *Vida i mort de Lluís Companys* (Barcelona: Pórtic, 1976); Joan B. Culla i Clarà, *El catalanisme d'esquerra (1928-1936): Del grup de "L'Opinió" al Partit Nacionalista Republicà d' Esquerra (1928-1936)* (Barcelona: Curial, 1977); and J. M. Poblet, *Història de l'Esquerra Republicana de Catalunya* (Barcelona: Dopesa, 1976). On the Catalan elite, see Ismael E. Pitarch, *Sociologia dels Polítics de la Generalitat (1931-1939)* (Barcelona: Curial, 1977). The sources of Catalan politics quoted above all deal extensively with the role of the Esquerra.

43. In English, see Frank Sedwick, *The Tragedy of Manuel Azaña and the Fate of the Spanish Republic* (Columbus: Ohio State University Press, 1963). However, the best biographical interpretative sketch is Juan Marichal, *La vocación de Manuel Azaña* (Madrid: Edicusa, 1968). Marichal also edited the monumental four-volume collection, *Obras completas* (see n. 14).

44. There is no scholarly biography of the Radical leader. The following volumes were written without access to archives but are informative and personal: Lerroux, *La pequeña historia;* idem, *Mis memorias* (Madrid: Afrodisio Aguado, 1963). On the Radical party, see Octavio Ruiz Manjón, *El Partido Republicano Radical, 1908-1936* (Madrid: Tebas, 1976).

45. There is no monograph on the Radical-Socialist party, one of the largest in the Constituent Cortes. However, the collection of writings of one of its leaders—Gordón Ordás, *Mi política en España*—gives much information and conveys its style and ideology. The party split into three tendencies in 1933. In later years some of its members would end in the "Center-Right of the Left"—the Unión Republicana. See Manuel Ramírez Jiménez, *Las reformas de la II República* (Madrid: Tucar, 1977), pp. 91–169.

46. Richard A. H. Robinson, *The Origins of Franco's Spain: The Right, the Republic and Revolution, 1931-1936* (Pittsburgh, Pa.: University of Pittsburgh Press, 1970) has been the object of severe criticism by Paul Preston. See Paul Preston, "The 'Moderate' Right and the Undermining of the Second Republic in Spain, 1931-1933," *European Studies Review* 3, no. 4 (1973):369-94. On the polemic, see R. M. Blinkhorn, "Anglo-American Historians and the Second Spanish Republic: The Emergence of a New Orthodoxy," *European Studies Review* 3, no. 1 (January 1973):81-87.

47. There are no published memoirs of Indalecio Prieto, but many interesting and insightful autobiographical articles are included in his *Convulsiones de España,* 2 vols. (Mexico: Oasis, 1967), which include his civil war memoirs.

A prime example of the elimination of real leaders from positions of responsibility and the substitution of second-rate men as stand-ins occurred with the pushing of Azaña into the presidency. The Left Socialists vetoed Prieto as a prime minister, and Casares Quiroga (whose lack of qualifications is almost as much a matter of agreement as his dependency on Azaña) was appointed instead. See the account by Juan Marichal, based on an interview with Araquistain, in Azaña, *Obras,* vol. 3, pp. XXXI–XXXII. Prieto, for his part, later expressed doubt that Azaña was really displeased with his inability to assume the premiership. See La Cierva, *Historia de la Guerra Civil,* p. 667.

48. Emilio Lamo de Espinosa, *Política y filosofía en Julián Besteiro* (Madrid: Edicusa, 1972); Andrés Saborit, *Julián Besteiro* (Buenos Aires: Losada, 1967). On 5 August 1933 Besteiro cautioned the young Socialists who said, "Democracy does not serve us for anything; let us stop (talking) and go toward dictatorship." Besteiro responded, "Many times one is more revolutionary resisting one of those collective madnesses than letting oneself be carried away by the drift of the masses to harvest immediate success and assured applause, at the risk that later the masses will be the ones harvesting the disappointments and suffering" (quoted in Saborit, *Julián Besteiro,* p. 240; see also p. 232).

49. The maximalist position is articulated in Largo Caballero, *Discursos a los trabajadores: Una crítica de la República, Una doctrina socialista, Un programa de acción,* with Foreword by Luis Araquistain, 2d ed. (Madrid: Gráfica Socialista, 1934). Araquistain was also the editor of *Leviatán: Revista Mensual de Hechos e Ideas,* the intellectual organ of that position. The critique by Gabriel Mario de Coca, *Anti-Caballero: Crítica marxista de la bolchevización del partido socialista (1930–1936)* (Madrid: Editorial Engels, Foreword dated March 1936). Indalecio Prieto, R. González Peña, Toribio Echevarría, Amador Fernández, Alejandro Jaume, Antonio Llaneza, etc., *Documentos Socialistas: Colección inquietudes de nuestro tiempo* (n.p.: Gráficas Sánchez, n.d. [probably 1935]), represent the other side in the split of the party.

On the radicalization of the Socialists, the best account is still Malefakis, *Agrarian Reform,* pp. 317–42. The more moderate wing of Spanish socialism perceived the dilemma posed by maximalism when it stated, in the spring of 1936: "The revolutionary verbalism is not, by far, the revolution, but it can be the counterrevolution if it precipitates events of uncorrectible imprudence, the worst of which is the division of the party." See Miguel Artola, *Partidos y programas políticos 1808–1936,* 2 vols. (Madrid: Aguilar, 1974–75), vol. 1, pp. 668–69.

50. See the sources quoted in note 14, particularly Angel Herrera.

51. For an excellent analysis of some of the "constraints" in the 1930s and the "defensive" character of the CEDA that distinguished it both from other European Christian-Democratic movements born more slowly and in more auspicious times and from the Partido Social Popular (founded just before the dictatorship), see Oscar Alzaga, *La primera democracia cristiana en España* (Esplugues de Llobregat: Ariel, 1973), pp. 305–21. The failure of the social policies of the Center Right is treated, with emphasis on the agrarian policies, in Malefakis, *Agrarian Reform,* pp. 342–63. It is handled with restraint in the memoirs of Chapaprieta and viewed critically by Paul Preston in *The Spanish Right under the Second Republic: An Analysis* (Reading: Occasional Publication no. 3 of the University of Reading, Graduate School of Contemporary European Studies, 1971), and in José R. Montero Gilbert, "La CEDA: El partido contrarrevolucionario hegemónico de la II República" in *Estudios sobre la II República Española,* ed. Manuel Ramírez (Madrid: Tecnos, 1973), pp. 89–128. It is a brief summary of his excellent two volume work, *La CEDA: El catolicismo social y político en la II República* (Madrid: Ediciones de la Revista de Trabajo, 1977).

The complex problem of loyalty, semiloyalty, or disloyalty is answered very differently by authors of different ideological persuasions. In our view no answer is possible for the role of the party over the whole period, since changing situations and pressures affected its stance. Obviously in the late spring of 1936 its position could not be that of 1935. On its semiloyalty/disloyalty after 1936, see La Cierva, *Historia de la Guerra Civil,* pp. 740–44. The basic sources are the two volumes by the leader of the party, Jose María Gil Robles, *No fue posible la paz,* and *Discursos Parlamentarios* (Madrid: Taurus, 1971). The latter contains an introductory essay by Carlos Seco Serrano (pp. vii-1).

52. William J. K. Irwin, "The CEDA in the 1933 Cortes Elections" (Ph.D. diss., Columbia University, 1975), and Javier Tusell, *Las elecciones del Frente Popular* (for the 1936 election). La Cierva, *Historia de la Guerra Civil,* pp. 615–19, and the memoirs of Gil Robles and Chapaprieta all convey a sense of the ambiguities, contradictions, and compromises in the coalitions made across the electoral map by this major party.

53. The origins, formation, and meaning of the Popular Front are complex issues, partly obscured for partisan purposes. One detailed account is contained in La Cierva, *Historia de la Guerra Civil,* pp. 579–610. The basic sources are the memoirs and speeches of Azaña

and Gordón Ordás, the small book by Diego Martínez Barrio, *Páginas para la historia del Frente Popular* (Buenos Aires: Publicaciones del Patronato Hispano Argentino de Cultura, 1943), Prieto, *Posiciones socialistas,* pp. 13ff., and José Díaz for the Communists. The initial idea was a Frente Republicano, but a variety of circumstances led to the heterogeneous final coalition, whose program, proclaimed on 15 January 1936 included references to some points of disagreement between Republicans and the Marxist parties. For the program, see Artola, *Partidos y programas,* vol. 2, pp. 454–55.

54. On the negotiations to form electoral tickets in the Catalan provinces, see Isidre Molas, *Lliga catalana,* vol. 1, passim; for the electoral results, see pp. 267–94.

55. Strangely enough, many party leaders were aware of the dangerous implications of the electoral system. For example, Ventosa of the Lliga declared: "For the reform of the electoral system is essential; without proportional representation and with the bonus that is now given to the majority, political stability will never be achieved. It will provoke the alternative crushing of one block of parties by another and nothing else" (ibid., vol. 2, pp. 197–202).

56. A problem faced by Gil Robles, and one which he recognized, was the antidemocratic position of the Juventud de Acción Popular (JAP). (See *No fue posible la paz,* pp. 189–203.) This created many difficulties for him. However, it could be argued that the pseudofascist rhetoric of the JAP deflected the youthful potential for fascism into channels which in practice proved to be nonviolent.

57. Juan J. Linz, "Continuidad y discontinuidad en la élite política española," tables on pp. 395, 397, and 398.

58. The image of public immorality associated with the Radical party, which ultimately destroyed this Center force (in the straperlo and Nombela affairs, though these were *pecata minuta* compared to the Stavisky affair), must be seen in the context of a relatively high level of personal honesty in the politicians of the monarchy and Republic. Without taking those affairs into account, the crisis of late 1935, after a limited reequilibration of the political system after October 1934, cannot be understood. On the affairs and the dubious role of Alcalá Zamora in their political exploitation, see La Cierva, *Historia de la Guerra Civil,* pp. 502–5; Chapaprieta, *La paz fue posible,* pp. 243–91; Gil Robles, *No fue posible la paz,* pp. 295–313; and Lerroux, *La pequeña historia,* chaps. 13–19, passim. Pabón, *Cambó,* vol. 2, pp. 433–58, also contains an excellent account. Philip Williams, "The Politics of Scandal," in *Wars, Plots, and Scandals in Postwar France* (Cambridge: Cambridge University Press, 1970), pp. 3–16, analyzes the political dynamics of scandals in a way that could be applied to this case.

59. There is general agreement that in 1935 not only the extreme Right and the Agrarios, but a considerable number of CEDA deputies, opposed the more progressive social and tax policies of the CEDA ministers and Chapaprieta, even though Gil Robles gave them his support. The specific pressure-group politics involved and their links with the parties deserve further study. See Gil Robles, *No fue posible la paz,* pp. 279–80, 349–51, 355–58, and Chapaprieta, *La paz fue posible,* pp. 292–305. On interest-group politics in the Republic, see Manuel Ramírez Jiménez, *Los grupos de presión en la Segunda República Española* (Madrid: Tecnos, 1969).

60. Balcells, *El problema agrari a Catalunya.*

61. There is no scholarly biography of Niceto Alcalá Zamora, the first president of the Republic, and our views of his role are inevitably colored by the accounts of his opponents, particularly Lerroux and Gil Robles. For his defense, see *Los defectos de la Constitución de 1931* (Madrid: Imprenta de R. Espinosa, 1936), and Niceto Alcalá Zamora, *Memorias (Segundo texto de mis memorias)* (Barcelona: Planeta, 1977) Appendix 5, "Los Ataques de Lerroux," pp. 478–535. Before the formation of the presidential governments at the end of 1935, he had established the custom of receiving cabinet members without the knowledge of the prime minister and of forcing on prime ministers his personal friends in the formation of cabinets. See Largo Caballero, *Mis recuerdos: Cartas a un amigo* (Mexico: Ediciones Unidas, 1954). In his memoirs, Azaña, in addition to Lerroux and Gil Robles, comments on these tendencies and their impact on the political process.

62. La Cierva, *Historia de la Guerra Civil,* pp. 609, 659, and 702–3; Chapaprieta, *La paz fue posible,* pp. 378–81. From the complaints of both the Right and Left about the behavior of the courts, one could think that they were less biased than in Weimar Germany.

63. José Ortega y Gasset exemplifies in a paradigmatic way the dilemmas of a detached, passionately patriotic, politically sophisticated, but vocationally intellectual man witnessing the breakdown of a regime he had helped found and continued to support as the only alternative. His brilliant critical analysis of the fatal errors of all participants contributed inevitably to an alienation from the regime but could not become—in spite of his own faint hopes—a rallying point for a constructive alternative. No one optimistic about the viability of the regime can ignore his analysis, which can be found in *Obras Completas,* vol. 11, *Escritos políticos II (1922–1933)* (Madrid: Revista de Occidente, 1969). Symbolic of that tragedy was that after 3 December 1933, except for an epilogue to his *Rebellion of the Masses* for English readers, published in 1937, he would remain silent on Spanish politics.

64. For the text of the constitution, and Article 81, see Nicolás Pérez Serrano, *La Constitución Española (9 Diciembre 1931), Antecedentes, Texto, Comentarios* (Madrid: Revista de Derecho Privado, 1932) with commentary on each article. Let us not forget that the normal six-year term of office of Alcalá Zamora would have lasted until 10 December 1937. Similarly, the legislature elected on 14 July 1931 could have lasted legally until the same date in 1935, had it not been dissolved by the president in a call for new elections. The legislature constituted after these elections, on 8 December 1933, if it had exhausted its term, would have lasted until the same date in 1937, rather than until 7 January 1936. In view of the Spanish experience, one might ask if premature dissolution in a polarized and tense society, even when it allows the expression of changes in public opinion, does not do a disservice to the stability of democratic institutions and allow parties to escape their responsibilities.

65. There is no systematic analysis of the role of the intellectuals in politics and society in this period that covers the whole ideological spectrum and the role of magazines and of the press. Two important contributions are Carlos M. Rama, *La crisis española del siglo XX* (Mexico: Fondo de Cultura Económica, 1960), and Manuel Tuñón de Lara, *Medio siglo de cultura española (1885–1936)* (1971). Particularly useful on Marxist thought is J. C. Mainer, *Literatura y pequeña burguesía en España (Notas 1890–1940)* (Madrid: Edicusa, 1972). On Miguel de Unamuno, see Elías Díaz, *Revisión de Unamuno: Análisis crítico de su pensamiento político* (Madrid: Tecnos, 1968). On José Ortega y Gasset, see Gonzalo Redondo, *Las empresas políticas de Ortega y Gasset, "El Sol," "Crisol," "Luz" (1917–1934),* 2 vols. (Madrid: Rialp, 1970). In addition, see Juan Marichal, *La vocación de Manuel Azaña,* and José L. García de la Serrana, "Los intelectuales en la II República," in *Estudios sobre la II República Española* ed. Manuel Ramírez, pp. 131–40. Very revealing on the political climate among the intellectuals and the impact of events is Julio Caro Baroja, *Los Baroja (Memorias Familiares)* (Madrid: Taurus, 1972), pp. 255–340. It is important to note that at the end of the dictatorship the intellectual community, despite its ideological differentiation, seems to have had some common ground, but with the civil war it was forced to take sides and in part disperse into exile.

On the presence of university professors in the legislatures of the Republic, and their party affiliation, see Juan J. Linz, "Continuidad y discontinuidad en la élite política española," pp. 402–5. In 1931 there were thirty-nine professors among the 464 deputies, in 1933, twenty, and in 1936, twenty-nine, but only eight served in all three Cortes and only fifteen in the first and third legislatures. In view of these data it appears that while the new regime might initially have deserved the name "the Republic of professors," it did not deserve it by 1936. Of the fifty-two professors who were deputies, eight were Socialists, fourteen were followers of Azaña, and four were followers of the Agrupación al Servicio de la República, but there were also seven of the CEDA and at least six more who were members of the parties supporting the governments of 1933–35.

66. For the thinking of the extreme Right, see Ramiro de Maeztu, *Obra* (Madrid: Editora Nacional, 1974). The intellectual organ of the extreme Right, *Acción Española,* was not founded until December 1931 and apparently had a limited circulation.

67. The Sanjurjada was the last of the pronunciamentos in Spain, if we define them as Ortega y Gasset did in his *Invertebrate Spain* (New York: Norton, 1937), chap. 9. It was also a total failure of planning; it rallied neither broad military nor civilian support, and its rapid defeat showed that at that point the regime could consolidate itself. It also convinced the leadership of the Center Right and the more moderate rightist masses that their efforts had to be directed at an electoral victory. It unfortunately created in the bourgeois Left a certain

disdain for the threats that might come from the army; this might have contributed to the false sense of security that characterized Casares Quiroga in 1936, which in turn led him to disregard the complaints of the Right. It also left as a heritage to the second bienio of Lerroux-Gil Robles after 1933 the issue of amnesty of the participants, which in turn undermined the legitimacy of their response to the October revolution. For an account of events see Payne, *Politics and the Military in Modern Spain,* chap. 15, and the bibliographical references there.

68. See Malefakis, *Agrarian Reform,* pp. 203–4, on the renewed spirit of Republican unity that facilitated the passage of the agrarian reform.

69. The bibliography on the October revolution in Asturias and the attempts to support it elsewhere is extensive. Recent works published in Spain include Bernardo Díaz-Nosty, *La comuna asturiana: Revolución de octubre de 1934* (Madrid: ZYX, 1974); J. A. Sánchez G. Saúco, *La revolución de 1934 en Asturias* (Madrid: Editora Nacional, 1974), with a Foreword by Vicente Palacio Atard, also published in his book, *Cinco historias de las república y de la guerra* (Madrid: Editora Nacional, 1973); and Francisco Aguado Sánchez, *La revolución de Octubre de 1934* (Madrid: San Martín, 1972). However, contemporary writings are more useful in understanding the impact of those events on the participants and the society. See Manuel D. Benavides, *La revolución fue así: Octubre rojo y negro* (Barcelona, 1937); and Manuel Grossi, *La insurrección de Asturias (Quince días de revolución socialista)* (Barcelona: Gráficas Alfa, n.d. [1935]). (There is a French translation of the latter, published in Paris by Etudes et Documentation Internationales in 1972.) See also Antonio Ramos Oliveira, *La revolución española de octubre: Ensayo político* (Madrid: Yunque, 1935); Reporteros Reunidos, *Octubre Rojo (Ocho días que commovieron a España),* Manual de Historia Política de España (Madrid: Rubiños, 1935); Aurelio de Llano Roza de Ampudia, *Pequeños anales de quince días (La revolución en Asturias) Octubre de 1934* (Oviedo: Talleres Tipográficos, 1935); and Ignacio Núñez, *La revolución de octubre de 1934,* 2 vols. (Barcelona: José Vilamala, 1935). The account by General Eduardo López de Ochoa, *Campaña militar de Asturias en octubre de 1934* (Madrid: Yunque, 1936), is very revealing.

70. A motion on 25 May 1936 by Sánchez Román's National Republican Party (PNR), which had initially supported the formation of a Left Republican coalition but finally refused to join it when the Popular Front included the Communists, called for emergency measures to prevent further deterioration of the situation. Miguel Maura's articles in *El Sol* between 18 and 27 June were also calling for a "national republican dictatorship." The PNR proposals were an excellent example of the kind of measures that might defuse a situation which would otherwise lead inevitably to one or another type of dictatorship or civil war, and initiate a process of reequilibration. For the texts, see Payne, *Spanish Revolution,* pp. 202–4.

71. That policy was the natural alternative when Azaña maintained his commitment to the Socialists, and the relations between the two leaders became more difficult. The composition of the legislature elected in 1933 made it inevitable, but it should not be forgotten that the Radicals and the CEDA had already cooperated in the elections in many provinces. See Irwin, "The CEDA in the 1933 Cortes Elections," passim.

72. On Azaña's fear of victory, see Juan Marichal's Introduction in Azaña, *Obras Completas,* vol. 3, pp. xxvii–xxix, which quotes the relevant texts from a conversation with A. Ossorio and Azaña's diary (entry of 19 February 1936).

73. The mismanagement of the aftermath of the October crisis is well summarized in La Cierva, *Historia de la Guerra Civil,* pp. 435–56.

74. See Calvo Sotelo's speech on 6 November, quoted in ibid., p. 422. Julián Soriano Flores de Lemus, *Calvo Sotelo ante la II República: La reacción conservadora* (Madrid: Editora Nacional, 1975), covers only part of the period and is not the monographic study we need of Renovación Española and its leader.

75. On the problem of the repression of those responsible for the revolution, and the political implications of that repression, see the lengthy discussions in the memoirs of all the participants. For a summary, see La Cierva, *Historia de la Guerra Civil,* pp. 441-42, 443–44.

76. On the last two cabinet crises of 1935—so central to our analysis of the creation of a power vacuum by the intervention of Alcalá Zamora, which could only be filled by a new election of plesbiscitarian character that would polarize the society (not unlike those after weak

presidential cabinets under Hindenburg)—see the memoirs of two participants: Chapaprieta, *La paz fue posible*, pp. 328-83, and Gil Robles, *La paz no fue posible*, pp. 358-403. See also the account by Pabón, *Cambó*, pp. 459-67, which sees the problem through the eyes of the great Catalan leader who had warned Gil Robles of the dangers of a conflict with the president "that would oblige him to sacrifice his party or enter into a campaign that could lead the country into anarchy" (p. 460).

77. It might be noted that between January and April of 1935 the bourgeois Left, under the leadership of Azaña, started to articulate a position that included the moderate Socialists and might have offered another platform for reequilibration, but the inevitable constraints of electoral arithmetic demanded formation of a much broader alignment, i.e., the Popular Front, for the 1936 election. See La Cierva, *Historia de la Guerra Civil*, pp. 587-88.

78. In this context the dating of the change in the Socialist movement—PSOE, UGT, and the agrarian trade union (FNTT)—is of more than historical interest. Was it a response to the disintegration of the Socialist-Republican Coalition, Hitler's ascent to power, the electoral success of the anti-Azaña coalition, the perception of the CEDA in the light of the events of 1934 in Austria, or the articulation of latent ideological tendencies whose expression had been submerged under the dictatorship and the instauration of the Republic?

On the change in orientation of the Socialist party, see Paul Preston, "Los orígenes del cisma socialista: 1917-1931," *Cuadernos de Ruedo Ibérico* 49-50 (January-April 1976):12-40, which traces the divisions of the thirties back to positions taken earlier, particularly the Primo de Rivera dictatorship. See also Marta Bizcarrondo, "La crisis del partido socialista en la II República," *Revista del Instituto de Ciencias Sociales de la Diputación de Barcelona* 21 (1973), and David Ruiz, "Aproximación a Octubre de 1934," *III Coloquio de Pau* (1972).

For an analysis of the evolution of the maximalist Socialist leader, see Blas Guerrero, "La radicalización de Francisco Largo Caballero: 1933-1934," *Sistema* 8 (January 1975):73-83. See also Marta Bizcarrondo, *Araquistain y la crisis socialista en la II República Leviatán (1934-1936)* (Madrid: Siglo XXI, 1975). Paul Preston has edited a selection of texts with an introductory essay: *Leviatán (Antología)* (Madrid: Turner, 1976). See Santiago Carillo, *Demain l'Espagne: Entretiens avec Régis Debray et Max Gallo* (Paris: Seuil, 1974), pp. 31-35 and 42-48, on the radicalization of the Socialist youth organization and the cooperation and later fusion with the Communist youth.

For a collection of contemporary texts, manifestoes, analyses, and a long introductory essay demonstrating the ideological convergence and contacts between minor revolutionary groups like the BOC (Bloc Obrero y Camperol) with the PSOE even before and immediately after the 1933 election, see Marta Bizcarrondo, *Octubre del 34: Reflexiones sobre una revolución* (Madrid: Ayuso, 1977). These contacts encountered the hostility of the USC (Unió Socialista de Catalunya), which supported the regional Esquerra government. Bizcarrondo also discusses Largo Caballero's subsequent trip to Barcelona in February 1934.

The maximalist view is well reflected in a statement made by Luis Araquistain in *Claridad*, 13 February 1936: "The historical dilemma is fascism or socialism, and only violence will decide the issue." The statement concluded that since what passed for "fascism" in Spain was weak, socialism would win.

79. On the failure to be generous with Catalonia as region and to distinguish the people and institutions from the error of its government, see Pabón, *Cambó*, pp. 415-21. Such a policy would also have reinforced the ties with the Lliga, a participant in late 1935 governments, and its position in Catalan politics. Such a policy was advocated by Hurtado, *Quaranta anys d'advocat*, vol. 3, pp. 322-25.

80. For the violence from 31 January to 17 July, reported in *El Sol* of Madrid and in *La Nación* and *La Prensa* of Buenos Aires, see tables. The two Argentine papers were used to cover periods in which censorship prevented publication of news. The data probably underestimated the violence; certainly, use of more sensationalist papers on both sides of the political spectrum would raise the figures. The type of violence reported changes over time as the gravity increased. The data were collected by Margaret Scobie for Edward Malefakis; they were coded by Rocío de Terán, and the calculations were made by Ramiro Cibrián.

81. This point is brilliantly stated by Manuel Azaña in the politico-literary dialogue "La Velada de Benicarló" (written in 1937), included in *Obras Completas,* vol. 3, pp. 379–460. The theme had already appeared in a speech on 3 April 1936; see *Obras Completas,* vol. 3, p. 304.

82. While it is possible roughly to quantify the political and social violence, particularly the number of deaths, and to emphasize the psychological and political impact of some assassinations or attempts on the life of political leaders, we cannot fully assess the impact of the rhetoric of violence from Parliament to the daily newspaper and or the politicization and violence in daily social interaction. A good description of the kind of day-by-day occurrences that led to fear and hatred can be found in an article by the great writer Miguel de Unamuno in *Ahora,* 8 June 1936, quoted in La Cierva, *Historia de la Guerra Civil,* pp. 691–92.

83. This atmosphere of violence extended to the Cortes, from the opening session after the election to the last dramatic meeting of the Diputación Permanente after the assassination of Calvo Sotelo. See the text of the dramatic June–July parliamentary debates in which a Communist deputy said that Gil Robles would die with "his shoes on." For the text, see Fernando Díaz-Plaja, ed., *La historia de España en sus documentos: El siglo XX—La guerra (1936–1939)* (Madrid: Faro, 1963), pp. 13–148.

84. See Maura, *Así cayó Alfonso XIII,* pp. 240–64, esp. pp. 251–53.

85. On the Casas Viejas massacre, see Malefakis, *Agrarian Reform,* pp. 258–61. The parliamentary debate on that tragedy and the notes in Azaña's diary at the time are extremely illuminating. They illustrate how isolated revolutionary acts (so characteristic of the Anarchists), the brutality of the forces of order, insufficient information on such events, slowness in perceiving the political danger, and cynical manipulation by disloyal and semiloyal oppositions contribute to the erosion of the legitimacy of a regime and personal authority of its leaders. (For Azaña's interventions in the debate, see *Obras Completas,* vol. 2, pp. 531–45, 574–665; for his diary, see idem, vol. 3, pp. 447–74.) Undoubtedly the dangerous distance between Lerroux and Azaña—two founders of the regime—was increased by those developments. On this last phase of the first bienio, see La Cierva, *Historia de la Guerra Civil,* pp. 239–42.

86. The problem of the repression of the revolution, especially the illegal actions in Asturias, its serious political implications, and the political incapacity to face the problem honestly are well treated by La Cierva, *Historia de la Guerra Civil,* pp. 447–56; the author is a historian who cannot be suspected of leftist bias. The parliamentary and public campaign of Gordón Ordás in particular deserved more serious attention from the government. That lack of response and the censorship prevailing at the time allowed the Left to build an enormous emotional response that lasted until the outbreak of the civil war and even manifested itself in the debate in the Diputación Permanente of the Cortes over the assassination of Calvo Sotelo.

87. The anarcho-syndicalist revolutionary rhetoric and sporadic, more-or-less ill-coordinated uprisings in Catalonia, Zaragoza, and isolated villages were politically important in the first two years of the Republic, because they contributed to a crisis of authority and tensions in the government coalition. See Peirats, *La CNT. en la revolución española;* Elorza, *La utopía anarquista;* Malefakis, *Agrarian Reform;* and John Brademas, *Anarcosindicalismo y revolución en España (1930–1937)* (Barcelona: Ariel, 1974). However, since it was the expected behavior of this principled opposition, which was absent from Parliament and any public office, given its spontaneous and romantic or primitive character, the political significance was different from the actions of the Socialist party in 1934 and 1936. The PSOE and the UGT were seen as responsible and disciplined organizations, which had not been outlawed even under the dictatorship; their leaders sat in Parliament and had just been cabinet members, PSOE members controlled local governments, etc. In addition, our ecological analysis suggests that the violence in 1936 was mainly in traditionally Socialist regions of the country (even though some conflicts were probably caused by the CNT-FAI and took place between their members and the Socialists and other Marxist groups), while some Syndicalist areas—like Catalonia—were relatively quiescent.

88. The Radical minister of interior from 31 March to 4 October 1936, Rafael Salazar Alonso gives an interesting, even when perhaps exaggerated, account of the social tension

in 1934; see *Bajo el signo de la revolución* (Madrid: San Martín, 1936). On that semirevolutionary strike, see Malefakis, *Agrarian Reform*, pp. 335–40. The strike was defeated by a mixture of concessions, lack of support by many workers, and by the security measures of the government. The dead numbered only thirteen, mostly victims of conflicts between strikers and those refusing to join. There were 7,000 arrests, but except for the leaders, most were detained only for short periods of time. Four Cortes deputies were briefly arrested, but only one for more than a night. The strike had catastrophic consequences for the morale of the farm workers' federation.

In any discussion of the rural revolutionary or semirevolutionary outbreaks of Anarchists and Socialists, it should not be forgotten that a large part of the peasantry was made up of small property holders and stable tenants who were either moderate Republicans, CEDA supporters, or even Carlists. See Edward Malefakis, "Peasants, Politics, and Civil War in Spain, 1931-39," in *Modern European Social History*, ed. Robert Bezucha (Lexington, Mass.: D. C. Heath, 1972), pp. 194–227.

89. Mass rallies and demonstrations organized by the parties as shows of strength contributed much to the crisis atmosphere. A good example was the rally organized on 22 April 1934 by the CEDA youth organization—Juventud de Acción Popular—on which La Cierva comments, "It was morally impossible that the Spanish left would not mistake the demonstration of El Escorial for a Fascist rally. The general strike called in Madrid was not able to prevent the ceremony, but clearly marked an expression of resentment and protest" (*Historia de la Guerra Civil*, p. 260). The same would be true for the massive gathering on 6 September 1934 in the Asturian religious sanctuary of Covadonga and for the march of 100,000(?) persons during six hours through Barcelona on 29 April in support of the Generalitat in its conflict with the central government and the Constitutional Court. On the JAP—its organization, relation to the CEDA, ideology, and style—see Montero, *La CEDA*, vol. 1, pp. 582-656.

90. See La Cierva, *Historia de la Guerra Civil*, for the 2 April 1936 appeal in *Claridad* to create people's militias.

91. Cambó, one of the real moderates of the Right, wrote: "The excitement of the masses is the indispensable preparation for a fascist coup or a proletarian revolution . . . these mass rallies can never be used by a party that wants to maintain a center position" (quoted in Pabón, *Cambó*, p. 433).

92. The data on the casualties of dead and wounded in the Asturias Revolution are given in La Cierva, *Historia de la Guerra Civil*, pp. 425–26, who quotes the research in Llano y Roza de Ampudia. *Pequeños anales de quince días*, p. 206ff.

93. On the violence and persecution of the Falange, see the account in La Cierva, *Historia de la Guerra Civil*, pp. 692–96. An ecological analysis of the provinces with higher violence rates, particularly those where socioeconomic structural conflicts do not seem to have been important, suggests that the presence of the Falange contributed to the violence. The same is probably true for the PCE presence (using candidacies in the February elections as an indicator of presence).

94. Ivan Maisky, in his *Spanish Notebook* (London: Hutchinson, 1966), reports that when Alvarez del Vayo visited him (as Soviet ambassador in London) on 11 July he told him that "The Socialist youth league has created its own militia" and concluded that the Republic was "not in serious danger. There are forces in the country sufficient to avert or in any event crush any attempt at a military coup." Asked about the size of the Socialist militia, he said: "In Madrid it numbers up to 15,000 or so. . . . Not at all badly trained . . . as to arms, things are not too good. . . . But the people are with us." This is a good example of the excessive self-confidence that paramilitary forces can inspire. A week later the civil war started. We do not know if the existence of such militias and the plans for a purge of the army was one of the factors precipitating and strengthening the military resolve against the regime.

95. Let us not forget that the Falange, while not formally outlawed, was persecuted not only by the Socialist militia but by the government, which closed its headquarters (27 February 1936). Its leader, José Antonio Primo de Rivera, was under arrest after March 1936 and had been condemned to prison from April onward. We should also not forget that none of its leaders had parliamentary immunity. On this period, see Payne, *Falange*, pp. 101–15; La Cierva, *Historia de la Guerra Civil*, pp. 692–96.

96. It should not be forgotten that Largo Caballero went free in November 1935 for lack of proof of his leadership of the October revolution, and that Azaña, despite the eagerness of the government to implicate him, also went free in April 1935.

97. See table. From a sociological-political point of view, the absolute level is perhaps less important that the universally shared perception, the geographic spread, and the intensity and dramatic nature of cases which occurred in the national capital.

    Another indicator of the political breakdown—also found in Italy—is the substitution of elected municipal authorities by the Ministry of Interior. For data, see Rafael Salazar Alonso, *Bajo el signo de la Revolución*. Casares Quiroga made 270 substitutions between 1931 and 1933 (pp. 116-21), and Salazar Alonso 193 during his own tenure as minister (pp. 122-29); there were a total of 1,116 substitutions out of the 8,346 elected municipal authorities in the country after the October revolution (p. 129).

    Another sign of the impending crisis and the prevailing climate of fear and violence is the fact that 270,000 new gun licenses were taken out in the thirty-six months between mid-1933 and 1936, according to official figures. See Payne, *Spanish Revolution*, p. 195.

98. The figures are given in Renzo de Felice, *Mussolini il fascista: La conquista del potere* (Turin: Einaudi, 1966), p. 87. See also his data on violence, pp. 35-39.

99. Manuel Ramírez, "Las huelgas durante la II República," *Anales de Sociología* 1 (1966):76-88. The number of strikes was: 734 (1931), 681 (1932), 1127 (1933), 594 (1934), 181 (1935), and 1108 between January and July 1936. The monthly figures of the *Boletín del Ministerio de Trabajo* for 1936 are: 26, 19, 47, 105, 242, 444, and 225 until July 17.

100. On farm invasions and accelerated agrarian reform in 1936, see Malefakis, *Agrarian Reform*, pp. 364-87. The settlement from March to July involved 110,921 peasants and the occupation of 572,055 hectares.

101. An example of such strange eleventh-hour efforts to establish bridges between impossible allies are the contacts in May 1936 between Prieto and José Larraz (a man close to the CEDA), perhaps in search of support for a centrist alternative after a possible split of the PSOE and the thought of a split of the CEDA to support such a solution (La Cierva, *Historia de la Guerra Civil*, p. 669-70; Gil Robles, *No fue posible la paz*, pp. 615-627; Tusell, *Historia de la Democracia Cristiana*, vol. 1, pp. 357-59). The last such effort to formulate a program that could lead to a compromise with the military, which had already begun its rebellion, led to the formation on the night of 18 July of the Martínez Barrio cabinet. See the account in Maximiano García Venero, *Madrid, Julio 1936* (Madrid: Tebas, 1973), pp. 334-41 and 345-47, based on the recollections of a leading participant, and the memoirs of Azaña, *Obras completas*, vol. 4, p. 714.

102. Prieto, in a speech in Cuenca on 1 May 1936. Quoted in Payne, *Spanish Revolution*, p. 197. The complete text is in Indalecio Prieto, *Discursos Fundamentales* (Madrid: Turner, 1975), pp. 255-73, with an introductory essay by Edward Malefakis.

103. Alfred Stepan, *The Military in Politics: Changing Patterns in Brazil* (Princeton, N.J.: Princeton University Press, 1971). See part 2, "The 'Moderating Pattern' of Civil-Military Relations: Brazil, 1945-1964," pp. 57-66.

104. José Ortega y Gasset, *Invertebrate Spain*, trans. M. Adams (London: Allen and Unwin, 1937).

105. See Gil Robles, *No fue posible la paz*, pages quoted below.

106. Ramón Salas Larrazábal, *Historia del Ejército Popular de la República*, 4 vols. (Madrid: Editora Nacional, 1973), is an excellent analysis of the structure of the armed forces, including the police, under the Republic and of the political orientations of the officers. Larrazábal provides very detailed information on the response of different services and units to the uprising in July, and calculates the number of officers and enlisted men on both sides. On the basis of those data, he concludes that some 20 percent of the officers sided with the government, and others who were in principle undecided made their choice depending on the winner in the area in which they were located. Many who would have rallied to the government or served it probably changed their minds once the proletarian revolution had started. He also notes that the cleavage lines were largely ideological rather than social, since members of military families frequently fought on opposite sides.

107. Ibid., pp. 186-90. The following table, which gives the alignment of eighty-two generals on 18 July 1936 by location at the beginning of the conflict, is based on his data.

	Government Area	Rebel Area	Total
Serving	22	17	39
Expelled or sent to the reserves	7	10	17
Exiled	1	—	1
Gone over to the enemy	2	2	4
Executed	15	6	21
	47	35	82

108. Lerroux, *La pequeña historia*, p. 346. This view is confirmed in Hidalgo de Cisneros, *Mis memorias*, p. 98, when he writes: "At the advent of the republic there was a minority of republicans in the army and another minority of bitter reactionaries; the remainder, that is, the great majority, were neutral or indifferent, felt no hate nor love for the new regime, but accepted it and obeyed it." But he also notes the change in the course of the years for the reasons he points out; causes that "seen in isolation might appear of little weight, but which were intelligently used by the enemies in a predisposed milieu." Let us note the very different initial climate of opinion in Spain from that in the Weimar Republic. An excellent analysis of the social structure of the armed forces is found in Julio Busquets, *El militar de carrera en España: Estudio de sociología militar* (Barcelona: Ariel, 1967).

109. On the consultations between Gil Robles and the army leadership in November 1934, see Gil Robles, *No fue posible la paz*, p. 147, and La Cierva, *Historia de la Guerra Civil*, pp. 445–46.

110. The feelers put out by Gil Robles toward the army leadership after the president vetoed any possibility that he might form a government, and decided to dissolve the legislature instead on 11 December 1935, are described by him in *No fue posible la paz*, pp. 364–67 and 376–78. For Franco's letter on those events, see Payne, *Politics and the Military in Modern Spain*, pp. 308–9 and 505. For a description of similar explorations after the election returns came in in 1936, see Gil Robles, *No fue posible la paz*, pp. 492–502.

111. See La Cierva, *Historia de la Guerra Civil*, pp. 639–40.

112. Chapaprieta, *La paz fue posible*, pp. 407–13.

113. Alfred Stepan, "The New Professionalism of Internal Warfare and Military Role Expansion," in *Authoritarian Brazil*, ed. Alfred Stepan (New Haven: Yale University Press, 1973), pp. 47–65; see particularly table 2.1, p. 52. Accounts of the conspiracy, the negotiations of military leaders, like Mola, with the leaders of the extreme Right and the refusal to commit themselves to any particular politico-ideological program, the tone of the manifestoes of the rebels, the declaration of the Burgos military junta against all partisan activity (in theory including that of those actively supporting the uprising), the late creation (1938) of the first civilian government, etc., all support our interpretation. This was not the role of the military as a moderating power considered by many politicians in the spring of 1936 (see Chapaprieta, *La paz fue posible*, note 112) or even the type of intervention considered by Gil Robles.

114. Another "explanation" of the breakdown of the democratic Republic has been foreign intervention. The Left and many liberals blame Hitler and Mussolini, and Franco propagandists blame international communism. Both quote false documents, make wrong inferences from circumstantial evidence, give excessive significance to the activities of foreign agents, and have in their favor facts of minor significance in the total picture. Undoubtedly, the international climate and the foreign intervention in the civil war, once initiated, made those interpretations plausible. For our argument here—the breakdown of democracy—it is irrelevant who would have won the civil war if military aid had not been forthcoming to one or the other side at key junctures. Once a civil war had started, after the failure of the military uprising in many parts of Spain and given the inability of the government to defeat it without the support of the revolutionary proletariat, the outcome could not have been continuity with the democracy established in 1931. A Republican victory could perhaps have led to the reestablishment of democracy in the shorter run as it might have brought Spain into World War II; and it might have encouraged, after liberation

by the Allies, a postwar political development similar to that of other European nations. But too many "ifs" are involved to be even mentioned here.

For our analysis, the relevant fact is that the potential foreign support, the contacts established with foreign states and movements, were not sufficiently important to determine the course of action followed either by the counterrevolutionary forces (particularly the army) or for those hoping or talking of revolution.

On this problem, see the outstanding scholarly monograph by Angel Viñas, *La Alemania Nazi y el 18 de julio* (Madrid: Alianza Editorial, 1974), which contains new documentation and extensive critical references to the literature. The efforts by the extreme Right to buy arms from the Italian government in 1934 had not led very far; the Falange received some funds from the Italians, but neither of those developments was of central importance in leading to the final crisis. See John F. Coverdale, *Italian Intervention in the Spanish Civil War* (Princeton, N.J.: Princeton University Press, 1975), pp. 37–65.

Biographical Notes

RISTO ALAPURO received his doctorate from the University of Helsinki in 1973. He pursued postdoctoral studies at the University of Michigan during 1973 and 1974 and has been a lecturer in sociology at the University of Helsinki since then. Dr. Alapuro has published books and articles on the student movement and peasant mobilization in Finland.

ERIK ALLARDT is a Research Professor at the Academy of Finland and Chairman of the Finnish Political Science Association. He received his doctorate from the University of Helsinki in 1952 and has been a Visiting Professor at the University of California at Berkeley, the University of Illinois, and the University of Wisconsin. From 1968 to 1971 he was editor of *Acta Sociologica*. With Stein Rokkan he edited *Mass Politics: Studies in Political Sociology* and with Yrjö Littunen, he edited *Cleavages, Ideologies, and Party Systems*. His book, *Sociologi,* is currently in its sixth edition in Finnish.

PAOLO FARNETI received his Laurea in Jurisprudence from the University of Turin in 1960 and his doctorate in sociology from Columbia University in 1968. He is currently a Professor of Political Science at Turin and Director of the Centro Studi Scienza Politica, Turin. Formerly he was the Lauro de Bosis Lecturer at Harvard University. His publications include *Theodor Geiger e la coscienza del la società industriale, Sistema politico e società civile,* and *L'Italia contemporanea*.

M. RAINER LEPSIUS is Professor of Sociology at the University of Mannheim and has been President of the German Sociological Association since 1971. He received his Ph.D. degree in the social sciences from the University of Munich in 1955. He has published over twenty monographs and essays on such themes as the sociology of intellectuals, industrial sociology, radical nationalism, inequality, regime change, and democracy in Germany as a historical and sociological problem.

JUAN J. LINZ is Pelatiah Perit Professor of Political and Social Science at Yale University. He received his doctorate from Columbia University in 1959 and has taught at Columbia University, Stanford University, the University of Madrid, and the Universidad Autónoma of Madrid. He is Chairman of the Committee on Political Sociology of the International Sociological and Political Science Associations. His publications include "Totalitarian and Authoritarian Regimes," in *Handbook of Political Science*, ed. F. Greenstein and N. Polsby; "Some Notes toward a Comparative Study of Fascism in Comparative Sociological Perspective," in *Fascism,* ed. W. Laquer; and numerous monographs and essays on Spanish elites and entrepreneurs, quantitative history, and parties and elections in Spain and Germany.

WALTER B. SIMON received his M.S. degree in social psychology from the University of Washington in Seattle and his doctorate in sociology from Columbia University. He has taught sociology at several North American universities and is presently teaching at the University of Vienna. His published work deals with the concept of the authoritarian personality, the phenomenon of social movements, aspects of socialization and pedagogy, language politics, and the political implications of cultural pluralism.

ALFRED STEPAN is Professor of Political Science at Yale University and frequently serves as Chairman of Yale's Council on Latin American Studies. He received his doctorate from Columbia University in 1969 and has taught at Yale since then. He has been a Guggenheim Fellow and, from 1978 to 1979, will be a Visiting Fellow at St. Antony's College, Oxford University. He has published *The Military in Politics: Changing Patterns in Brazil* and *The State and Society: Peru in Comparative Perspective*. He is the editor of *Authoritarian Brazil: Origins, Policies, and Future* and co-editor, with Bruce Russett, of *Military Force and American Society*.

III.

The Breakdown
of Democratic Regimes

LATIN
AMERICA

Edited by
Juan J. Linz and Alfred Stepan

The Breakdown
of Democratic Regimes
LATIN AMERICA

1.

The Breakdown of Democracy in Argentina, 1916-30

Peter H. Smith*

Democracies are not expected to break down. Most contemporary theoretical formulations depict democracy (however defined) as the *culmination* of political development (however defined). Studies of political change accordingly tend to focus on the presumed transition from some sort of traditional order through an intermediate phase, perhaps authoritarian, to the creation of a modern polity—that is, a democratic one. And here the analysis stops. The implicit assumption seems to be that democracy, once achieved, will be stable and self-sustaining. The notion is almost analogous to Walter Rostow's concept of an economic takeoff; when political systems lift off the ground, they commence their drive toward maturity.[1]

Like the other countries discussed in this volume, Argentina challenges and even contradicts this formulation. Between 1916 and 1930 Argentina had a political system which met the definition of democracy as a government that "supplies regular constitutional opportunities for peaceful competition for political power (and not just a share of it) to different groups without excluding any significant sector of the population by force."[2] As a result of electoral reform in 1912, instituting universal male suffrage for Argentine citizens and the secret ballot, voter turnout leaped from approximately 20 percent to more than 65 percent, thereafter oscillating between 50 and 80 percent.[3] While the popular base of authority broadened, parliamentary procedure and political parties acquired crucial roles in the articulation and aggregation of group interests. Civilians continued their domination of the political scene. In 1916 presidential power passed smoothly from long-entrenched Conservatives to Hipólito Yrigoyen, leader of the largely middle-class Radical party; another Radical, Marcelo T. de Alvear, won the election of 1922; in 1928 Yrigoyen, at the age of seventy-four, returned to office with a thumping 67 percent majority. But in 1930 the armed forces, in collaboration with civilian ele-

*The author would like to thank the Graduate School at the University of Wisconsin–Madison and the American Philosophical Society for helping to support this research.

ments and with the apparent support of the populace, pulled off a military coup.[4] Argentine democracy was overthrown.

What could have led to this result? Aside from its intrinsic interest, the question draws theoretical significance from the fact that Argentina would seem to have satisfied the commonly considered socioeconomic prerequisites for democratic development.[5] Economic growth was strong: spurred by massive immigration and the exportation of beef and wheat, the gross national product increased by roughly 4.5 percent a year from 1900 to 1930, while per capita income—despite the immigration—grew at an annual average rate of 1.2 percent. In 1914 the absolute level of per capita GNP came to approximately $480 in U.S. dollars (of 1950), a very impressive figure for that era (and I would guess that it was twice this high in the coastal regions and in Buenos Aires, then the center of national politics).[6] Social mobilization was pronounced: the census of 1914 showed that 65 percent of the adults were literate, 36 percent of the population lived in urban areas (20,000 or more inhabitants), and the rate of migration was high. Occupational data reveal that about one-third of the economically active population in 1914 belonged to the middle class—a category that would claim nearly 40 percent by 1947.[7] In short, Argentina presents a case of democratic breakdown in a relatively developed society.

A second characteristic of the situation, particularly important for comparative purposes, is the quality of Argentine democracy. My definition (borrowed from Juan Linz) suggests that democracy is a relative concept, susceptible to various refinements by degree. Robert A. Dahl has argued that pluralism partakes of two dimensions: participation, which is the extent to which people are entitled to take part in the political process; and competitiveness, or contestation, which refers to the extent of effective political opposition.[8] To establish a rough classification table 1 divides both dimensions into three-point scales: high, medium, and low. By these standards Argentina during 1916–30 would, in my judgment, rank high on competitiveness but

Table 1. Classifying Argentine Democracy

Degree of Participation	Degree of Competitiveness		
	Low	Medium	High
Low			
Medium			Argentina, 1916–30
High			

only medium on participation. Elections were hotly contested and winners rarely emerged with more than 60 percent of the vote; but for reasons spelled out below effective suffrage was extended to less than one-half of the adult male population—and women were excluded entirely (although they were not then seeking access either).

Our task, then, is to explain the breakdown of a functioning but limited democracy in a relatively prosperous society. In an effort to do so I shall first consider the possibility that the political system was overwhelmed by external forces, especially the economic depression that began in 1929 (Argentina was not involved in any wars or other cataclysmic events at this time). Then I shall explore the internal and structural characteristics of the political system which might account for its evident debilitation.

Short-Run Economic Causes

One of the standard explanations for the collapse of Argentine democracy maintains that the worldwide depression threw the country's vulnerable export-import economy into a downward spiral which, in turn, discredited the Yrigoyen regime. Governmental inaction—due partly to the aged president's infirmities—outraged a desperate populace and prompted the military to act in the name of efficiency and economic recovery. This same process seems to have occurred throughout Latin America, where governments tumbled like dominoes in 1930; Argentina furnished no exception to the rule.[9]

This argument finds partial support in a sudden decline in GNP per capita between 1929 and 1930. On the other hand, figure 1 also demonstrates that the drop in income only *began* in 1930. One wonders whether its effects would have been strong enough to produce a violent reaction by the early part of the year, when anti-Yrigoyenist plotting commenced; a revolt of 1931 or 1932 might be better explained by these data. Besides, according to this index World War I had plunged the country into an economic crisis of equal or greater severity, and Yrigoyen weathered that storm without major threats. Gross GNP data do not provide a conclusive case for the short-run economic argument.

We might learn more by trying to determine which groups suffered most from the 1929–30 decline. Figure 2 reveals that the crisis hit the export sector: the value of exports dropped sharply, and continued importation produced the most negative balance of trade in decades. But the fall in exports cannot be traced to the market for meat, where prices and values held firm up to September 1930 (figure 3). Since civilian participants in the coup were closely involved in the production of cattle and beef, this situation cannot account directly for their political action.[10]

The wheat market presents another picture, one in which export values

Figure 1.   Per Capita Gross National Product, 1914-32 (in 1950 dollars)

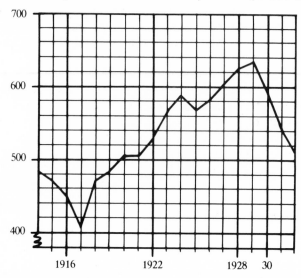

SOURCE: United Nations, Economic Commission for Latin America, *El desarrollo económico de la Argentina*, mimeographed (Santiago de Chile, 1958), E/CN.12/429, Add. 4, p. 4.

Figure 2.   Exports and Balance of Trade, 1914-32 (in millions of pesos)

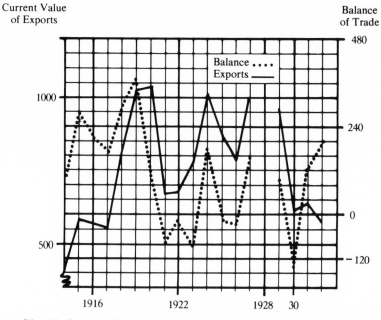

SOURCE: Dirección General de Estadística de la Nación (DGE), *Informes* nos. 11, 24, 33, 34, 40 (Buenos Aires: DGE, 1924-33). Data for 1928 are incomplete.

Figure 3.   Monthly Prices and Exports of Chilled Beef, 1927–31

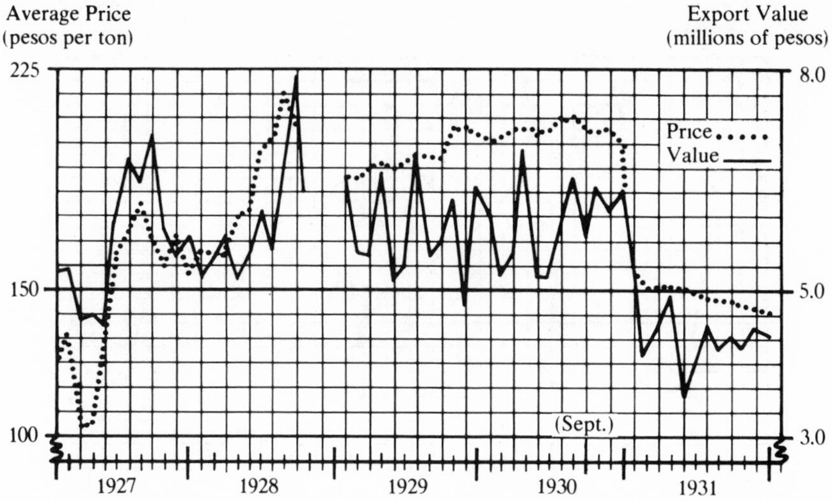

SOURCE: DGE, *Informes* nos. 33, 34, 40 (Buenos Aires: DGE, 1928–33). Data for 1928 are incomplete.

dropped steeply in 1930 (figure 4). Yet this does not explain the revolution. In the first place, this crisis was due mainly to reduction in supply because of drought, not because of Yrigoyen's policy (note how prices maintained their level up until the coup). Second, wheat farmers and other agriculturalists had very little political strength, partly because so many still retained foreign citizenship (about 70 percent in 1914); nor did they make many effective demands in 1930.[11] Undoubtedly there was economic hardship on the grain belt, and some politicians were deeply concerned. But the situation does not appear to have become really intolerable by 1930.[12]

Nor did the onset of the depression generate much pressure from the working class. After a steady rise from 1918 to 1928, a drop in real wages hurt middle- and lower-class consumers. But this reversal did not lead to labor agitation. According to both the number of strikes and the number of strikers, union activism dropped sharply after World War I and stayed fairly low throughout the late 1920s. During the period of democratic politics, real wages were at their lowest and strikes were at their highest from 1918 to 1920, when Yrigoyen crushed the labor movement with military force; by comparison, his second administration was tranquil indeed.[13] It is extremely unlikely that fear of a proletarian revolt or some sort of Red scare could have prompted revolutionaries to throw Yrigoyen out of office.

Generally speaking, the economic impact of the depression does not furnish a convincing causal explanation for the 1930 coup. To be sure, there were problems, particularly regarding foreign exchange and public finances,[14] but

Figure 4.   Monthly Prices and Exports of Wheat, 1927-31

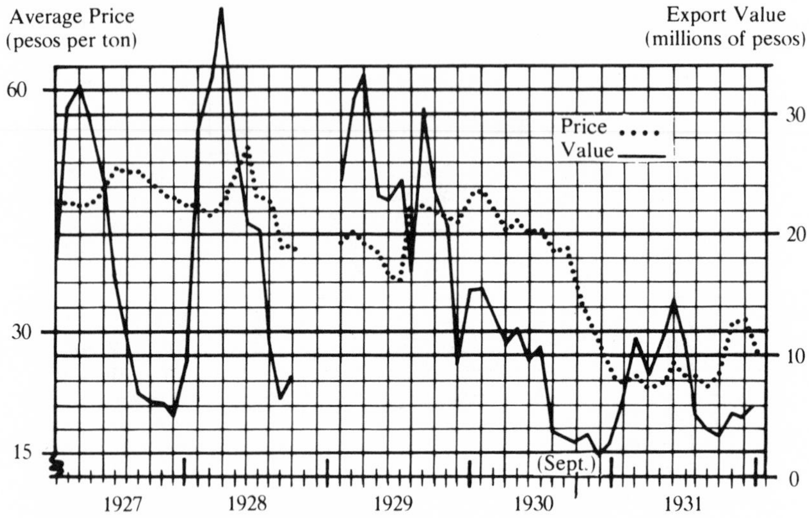

SOURCE: DGE, *Informes* nos. 33, 34, 40 (Buenos Aires: DGE, 1928-33). Data for 1928 are incomplete.

quantitative measures do not show truly startling dislocations or politically "unsolvable problems." And the most significant piece of qualitative evidence is negative. While some civilian members of the anti-Yrigoyen conspiracy referred to "economic crisis" as one reason for their action, most participants failed to mention it or gave it very low priority.[15]

In brief, the economic depression might have emphasized weaknesses within the political system and thus been necessary for the revolution, but it was not itself a sufficient cause. Dahl has neatly summarized the situation: "As it did for most other countries, the onset of the Great Depression in 1929 created serious problems for Argentina [though not in 1929]. But other polyarchies were also hit by economic crisis. Some that were also highly dependent on international trade, like Sweden, and even some that were heavy exporters of agricultural products, like Australia and New Zealand, nonetheless met the crisis with actions that retained, restored, perhaps even enhanced the confidence of their citizens in the effectiveness of their government. In Argentina, things went differently."[16] The question is why. In search of an answer, let us turn to the political arena.

A Crisis of Legitimacy

Political explanations for the downfall of Argentine democracy have frequently been partisan, *ad hominem,* and superficial. One argument stresses

Yrigoyen's age, illness, and possible senility; his government is viewed as leaderless, inept, and riddled with corruption. Another claims that a scheming alliance among all anti-Yrigoyen forces led to a partisan deadlock, denied the will of the people, and provided rationalization for a long-planned overthrow. Still another asserts that Yrigoyen's intention to nationalize petroleum deposits antagonized foreign oil companies, who retaliated by supporting the revolution. Without dismissing these possibilities—though they seem more symptomatic than fundamental—I would prefer to examine some basic structural features of Argentine politics. Democratic systems have withstood inept leadership, *empleomanía,* partisan bickering, and foreign pressure before. What made Argentine democracy so weak?

One way of dealing with this question is to employ the concept of "crisis" as formulated by the Committee on Comparative Politics of the Social Science Research Council. According to this view, political change can be understood as the sequential appearance and resolution (or nonresolution) of political crises in five separate problem areas: identity, legitimacy, participation, penetration, and distribution. Crisis occurs when problems in one or more of these areas require institutional change, and in this case two kinds of crisis are pertinent: crises of participation, which appear when sizable elements of the population, heretofore excluded from the system, demand effective participation in the political process; and crises of legitimacy, which appear when sizable portions of the politically relevant population challenge or deny the normative validity of claims to authority made by existing leadership.[17]

With regard to Argentina between 1916 and 1930, my proposition is this: the electoral reform of 1912 constituted an effective short-run response to a crisis of participation; but its unforeseen consequences created a crisis of legitimacy which ultimately prompted the 1930 coup.

Elaboration of this argument begins with an appreciation of the sequential relationship between economic and political development. In Argentina the formation of a landowning aristocracy *preceded* the establishment of constitutional rule in 1853-62. This was the elite which, while in the process of expansion and consolidation, founded and directed the country's parliamentary system. Throughout the late nineteenth and early twentieth centuries an exclusive circle of aristocrats, epitomized by the Generation of 1880, simultaneously held the keys to economic, social, and political power.[18] They gained control of the army; they openly rigged elections; they made the only major political party (Partido Autonomista Nacional, or PAN) a tool of the administration; and they restricted the decision-making process to their own circles. Congress was not widely used as a forum for the expression of interests, and most significant decisions were made by *acuerdo*—literally by informal "agreement" with members of the executive branch, not by presenting the issues and alternatives to the public.

As these aristocrats continued to consolidate their power, the centralization of authority gave paradoxical emphasis to the fundamentally passive relationship between politics and Argentine society at large. By the late nineteenth century, the distribution of political power had become essentially dependent upon, and derivative from, the distribution of social and economic power. Mobility was unidirectional: socioeconomic prominence was a necessary, and sometimes sufficient, precondition for the attainment of political influence. And though aristocrats built up the strength of the state and used it for promoting economic policies, the political system did not provide—nor was it intended to be—an autonomous power resource.

Expansion of the export-import economy eventually gave birth to middle-class groups which challenged the political supremacy of the landed elite. Allying these new social sectors with *nouveaux riches* landowners and some discontented aristocrats, the Civic Union launched an armed revolt against the government in 1890. After some supporters came to terms with authorities, the predominant wing—the "Radical" Civic Union, or Unión Cívica Radical (UCR)—boycotted elections in protest against fraud and led open rebellions in 1893 and 1905.

Thus emerged a crisis of participation. No doubt these events also raised some questions about the legitimacy of the system, but this does not (in my view) necessarily point to the existence of a "legitimacy crisis" as such. Most opponents of the regime, including the Radicals, seem to have believed in the propriety and desirability of popular elections and constitutional government. Their complaint concerned the faithless violation of the rules, not the substance of the rules themselves. Fundamentally, they wanted to take part.

In time, the Conservative leaders of the old elite found a strategy to meet the situation: in 1911–12 they put through an electoral reform designed to give Radicals a share of power, coopt them into the system, and maintain political stability. Despite the mountains of praise which have been heaped upon President Roque Sáenz Peña for this generous and "democratic" act, it was a calculated maneuver to salvage the prevailing system. Concerned about labor unrest and the apparent threat of violence, Sáenz Peña may have realized that the decision would yield power to the opposition, as it did when Hipólito Yrigoyen was elected president in 1916, but he seems to have understood the underlying commitment of the middle classes to the existing political and economic structure and did not regard their Radical leaders (many of whom were from the aristocracy) as a threat to it.[19]

Two aspects of the Sáenz Peña law underscore the limits of reform. First was the seemingly innocuous requirement that adult males must hold Argentine citizenship in order to vote. Given the large number of unnaturalized immigrants, however, the law actually offered voting rights to less than 50 percent of the adult male population; and since immigrants comprised about one-half of the expanding middle class and an even greater share of Argentina's working class (around 60 percent in urban areas), this meant that suffrage was effectively extended from the upper class to selected segments of the middle class, to the distinct disadvantage of the lower class, especially the urban working class. Second was the so-called "incomplete list," a rule which stipulated that parties could present candidates for only two-thirds of the available seats in the Chamber of Deputies and that individual voters could cast ballots for two-thirds of the vacancies. In practice this regulation usually meant that the first-place party in each provincial election won two-thirds of the province's places in the Chamber; the second-place party got the remaining third; and all other parties were shut out entirely. Thus the incomplete list discriminated sharply against small parties, discouraged the formation of new movements, favored the established interests, and set forth a paradoxical principle: the greater the degree of competition, particularly multiparty competition, the less representative the delegation.[20] In the meantime, national senators continued to be elected by the provincial legislatures rather than by direct vote. Despite the electoral reform, this was to be a limited democracy indeed.

The pattern of challenge and response in the appearance and resolution of this crisis of participation provides a basis for this paper's fundamental argument: that the electoral reform and consequent redistribution of political strength were meant—at least by Conservatives—to uphold and comply with longstanding rules of the Argentine political game.[21] Central to this code was the idea of a balance of power and government by consensus, or what Argentines called the *acuerdo*. Whereas power had previously been parceled out to competing factions *within* the landed aristocracy, it would now be shared *between* the aristocracy and rising middle-class groups (to the virtual exclusion of the lower class). As a result of this understanding, political conflict would retain several traditional features: (1) fluid party allegiance instead of intense partisan loyalty, (2) intraclass fighting instead of class struggle, and (3) continued dependence of the distribution of political power upon the distribution of economic power.[22]

Though it is doubtful that Radicals struck a conscious bargain of this sort, there is no sign that they determined to violate the code. They drew many of their leaders from the same social ranks as did Conservatives, and Radical rhetoric constantly emphasized "morality" in government rather than changes in structure, policy, or procedure.[23] These challengers were seeking power, not alteration of the social system.

More crucial to my argument is the importance which Conservatives attached to the rules of the game. Congressional debates on the 1912 electoral reform reveal discernible traces of these latent assumptions. Discussion of the provision for guaranteed minority representation in the Chamber of Deputies under the incomplete list, for instance, showed the constant conviction that Conservatives would have the majority and direct a kind of coalition government.[24] Thus the reform would guarantee and institutionalize the central tenet of the code: power would be shared among competing factions that would reach decisions by consensus.

Proponents of the reform also appeared to believe that the specific characteristics of traditional conflict would persist. Many looked forward to the reinvigoration of political parties, by this time in disarray, but not to clashes drawn inflexibly along party lines. Legislators should serve the nation, they said more than once, not the interests of party or region. There would be no class warfare: disagreements under the new system ought to be muted, controlled, undemagogic, settled gracefully by "gentlemen." And the retention of Conservative majorities, of course, would ensure that the socioeconomic elite would continue to run the political system. All the rules would stay intact.

Thus many aristocratic Conservatives regarded the maintenance of these norms as essential to the legitimacy of the cooptation strategy and electoral politics in general. To them, democracy would be acceptable only so long as the rules of the game were upheld.

I might point out that these prescriptions concerned the behavior of political leadership, not the actions of rank-and-file citizens. In stressing this code I am choosing to emphasize the role of elites, or leaders, in Argentina's political system. This is not to deny the importance of masses. It merely reflects my view of Argentine politics during this period as an interplay among elites in which the populace, through voting, could strengthen one side or the other. But the crisis of Argentine democracy eventually emerged on the elite level, not because of pressure from below.

While the electoral reform brought immediate changes in voting patterns of the electorate,[25] Radical and Conservative leaders seem to have complied with traditional forms of political practice until the mid-1920s—and then the rules collapsed. By the end of the decade the Radicals, whose consecutive victories at the polls stunned complacent Conservatives, were not sharing power with anybody; they held almost all of it. This was partly due to expansion of the electorate, which roughly doubled in size from 1916 to 1930 and gave the Radicals a mass constituency.[26] In the Chamber of Deputies they possessed a clear majority by 1920; after a split between the "Personalist" Yrigoyen wing and the "Antipersonalist" Alvear faction in 1924, the Yrigoyenist UCR held two-thirds of the seats by 1930. Though Conservatives managed to prolong their hegemony in the Senate, and thus maintain a power base, time was running out; by 1930 Yrigoyenists had a substantial delegation in the upper chamber and they threatened to gain a full majority in upcoming elections.

As these alterations took place within Congress, relationships were also changing between the executive and legislative branches. During the first two Radical administrations there were significant challenges to presidential power. Congressmen often subjected cabinet members to grueling interpellations, questioned government policies, ignored or scrapped executive proposals in favor of bills by senators or deputies. By the later twenties, though, this practice had declined. According to one indicator of legislative "resistance" or "compliance" with presidential demands, there was a sharp and cyclical

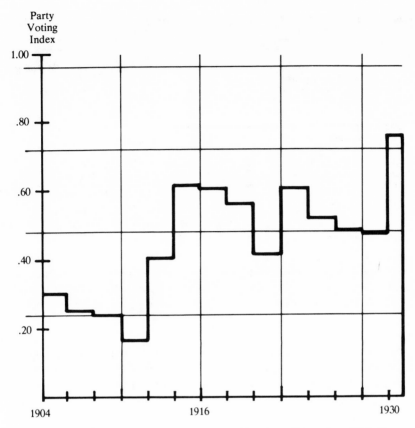

Figure 5.   Degrees of Party Voting in the Chamber of Deputies, 1904-30

transition from compliance before 1916 to resistance in 1916-25 to almost total compliance in 1926-29.[27] Not only were the Conservatives losing out in Congress; parliamentary politics were giving way to centralized presidential power, now in the hands of Radicals.

Intense partisanship also came to replace the loose party affiliations of the early Yrigoyen years. Figure 5 shows how a Party Voting Index, based on roll-call voting in the Chamber of Deputies and ranging from 0 to 1.0, climbed from low levels in the period prior to electoral reform, oscillated between high and moderate levels after 1916, and reached a peak in 1930.[28] By 1928-30 the Yrigoyenist UCR and its opposition were almost always voting against one another. Deviations from the party line had nearly disappeared.

Moreover, party conflict acquired perceptible social overtones. Table 2 indicates that upper-class aristocrats figured prominently among both Radicals

Table 2. Aristocrats Elected to the Chamber of Deputies

	1916–18		1922–24		1928–30	
Party Affiliation	Number of Deputies	Percentage Aristocrats	Number of Deputies	Percentage Aristocrats	Number of Deputies	Percentage Aristocrats
Conservative bloc	39	77.0	33	57.6	28	57.2
All Radicals	75	48.0	100	27.0	111	19.8
(Personalists)			(49)	(14.3)	(100)	(19.0)
(Antipersonalists)			(29)	(41.4)		
(Unclassified)			(22)	(40.9)	(11)	(27.3)
Other or unknown	20	45.0	33	18.2	21	19.0
Entire Chamber	134	55.9	166	31.3	160	26.2

and Conservatives elected to the Chamber of Deputies in 1916–18 (about 48 percent against 77 percent). The break between Yrigoyen and Alvear then divided the Radicals along social as well as regional lines; in the mid-twenties the Personalist group contained proportionately one-third as many aristocrats as the Alvear faction (14 percent against 41 percent). And by 1928–30 the UCR, almost completely Yrigoyenist, was only 19 percent aristocratic while the Conservatives still recruited 57 percent of their leaders from the upper class.[29]

Despite the implications of this finding, the heterogeneous quality of Argentina's middle class makes it necessary to examine closely the specific social characteristics of Radical leaders in the late 1920s. They do not seem to have been merchants, farmers, or industrialists who viewed politics as an avocation. They comprised a special breed: they were professional politicians. Biographical data for Yrigoyenist senators and deputies in 1928–30 show that their average age was around 45, meaning that this was not the same generation which had guided the Radical movement prior to 1916; that they were usually university-trained lawyers; and that they had taken up politics while still in their twenties. There was very little lateral mobility from Argentina's socioeconomic elite into Yrigoyen's political elite during his second administration. As one observer recalled with disgust, "the Congress was full of rabble and unspeakable hoodlums. The parliamentary language used up to then had been replaced by the coarse language of the outskirts of the city and the Radicals' committees. . . ."[30] At least regarding leadership, it began to look as though the political system no longer reflected the distribution of power within the economic system.

While political authority passed into the hands of new social groups, the power of the central government expanded as well. As one expression of this trend, Radical presidents resorted to federal "intervention" in the provinces much more than did previous leaders (in effect, interventions meant federal takeovers of provincial governments). Of ninety-three such actions from 1862 to 1930, thirty-four took place during the fourteen year period of Radical rule, and during his own two terms Yrigoyen intervened at least once in every single province.[31] The economic impact of political decision-making also increased. In the decade from 1920 to 1929 federal expenditures climbed from 9 percent of GNP to nearly 19 percent.[32] This fact alone helps explain the intensification of political pressure as the decade wore on: by 1930 there was more at stake than in 1916.

This acceleration in the centralization of power underscores the importance of Argentina's constitutional structure, which gave great authority to the president and to the majority party. It was not quite a winner-take-all system, and the incomplete list made explicit provision for minority representation in the Chamber of Deputies. But winners took an awful lot: Yrigoyen had nearly total control over patronage; he (and his cabinet) could make many key decisions; and—to take an example—he was well within his legal rights when intervening in the provinces.

Finally, Yrigoyen and his followers made ambiguous use of their power. There is substantial evidence that his economic policies would have been acceptable and even favorable to rural landed interests.[33] This was not the issue. What mattered was the distribution of political power. Typical in this regard was Yrigoyen's excessive use of the power of intervention, which he appears to have employed in order to eliminate pockets of Conservative strength. Debates over the electoral credentials of deputies consumed an inordinate amount of time; in 1930—as a result of such bickering—the legislature passed no laws at all. Though Yrigoyen's physical infirmities and the bureaucracy's ineptness undoubtedly slowed down the decision-making process, concern with the allocation of political power brought the parliamentary machinery to a total halt. This stalemate and publicity about it no doubt engendered public frustration and may help account for popular approval of the September revolution.

In summary, all the traditional rules of Argentina's political game had been seriously violated, particularly after 1928. The Radicals' steady accretion of votes destroyed any balance of power. Intense partisan struggles replaced fluid party allegiances. Subtle social alignments on the elite level, and possibly among the voters too, threatened to end intraclass maneuvering.[34] The political system came to represent an autonomous threat to the socioeconomic system, both through Yrigoyen's recruitment of professional politicians and through the accumulation of independent political power. Understandably enough, in view of their initial expectations, Conservatives came to see democracy as dysfunctional and therefore illegitimate.[35]

Despite the depth of their discontent Conservatives could not oust Yrigoyen by themselves. They found some eager allies in another institution: the armed forces, some of whose members started planning a coup of their own as early as 1929.

The Military

Argentina's nineteenth-century liberals regarded a professional army as an essential part of national development. Only a well-trained military establishment, they reasoned, could crush provisional caudillos, maintain order, and thus provide conditions for the kind of economic growth they sought.[36]

Acting on this perception, Domingo Sarmiento began the trend toward professionalization by founding the Colegio Militar (1870) and the Escuela Naval (1872), still the basic training schools for officers in present-day Argentina. A few years later President Julio Roca, himself a general, greatly encouraged the trend. During the 1890s his colleague and protégé, General Pablo R. Riccheri, negotiated large-scale purchases of new German weaponry. In 1899 Roca and Riccheri engaged a German mission to train staff officers in modern methods and military technology, thereby inaugurating a forty-year period of service collaboration between the two nations. In 1900 the Escuela Superior de Guerra was created by the Ministry of War.

This emphasis on expertise precipitated fundamental alterations in the structure and outlook of Argentina's officer corps. By 1910 the criteria for promotion had changed from political favoritism to seniority and, more particularly, to the mastery of modern warfare. Related to this was a shift in control of promotions from the presidency to an all-military committee composed of commanders of army divisions and headed by the highest-ranking general. As the army developed a common esprit, based partly on a sense of its own efficiency, it also acquired substantial institutional autonomy.

Eventually the possibilities for advancement by merit opened careers to members of the middle class. Specifically, as various studies have revealed, many of the newly promoted generals were sons of immigrants, most notably from Italy.[37] For a considerable portion of Argentina's top-echelon officers, military careers provided avenues to upward social mobility. Gratified by such an opportunity, they forged a strong allegiance to the institution as a whole—and a jealous regard for its independence, honor, and professional reputation. Deeply resentful of intrusions by outsiders, especially "politicians," they often viewed civilian officials with a mixture of scorn and apprehension.

Throughout the twentieth century the Argentine armed forces, particularly the army, steadily gained in importance. By 1930 the armed forces consisted of around fifty thousand men; by 1943 this number had doubled, and by 1955 it had doubled again. In the meantime the military share of the national budget climbed from around 20 percent in the 1920s to approximately 50 percent in 1945.[38]

In short, the process of professionalization gradually turned the Argentine military, especially the army, into a formidable political force quite apart from, and sometimes antagonistic to, the country's constitutional apparatus.

To one degree or another, there was constant tension between military and civilian authorities. And as the legitimacy crisis developed in the 1920s, many officers came to look on politicians with outright contempt.

In this context Yrigoyen adopted the ultimately disastrous policy of turning the army into a source of patronage, promoting officers on the basis of partisan allegiance rather than seniority or merit (partly in order to repay accumulated debts among the military men who had supported his attempted coups in 1893 and 1905). Such maneuverings naturally angered many officers who were intensely proud of the army's professional autonomy and honor and who, largely for this reason, took part in or abetted the 1930 coup. But most striking is the sequence of events: Yrigoyen intervened in military affairs *before* the army intervened decisively in politics, and the officers responded in *reaction* to his interference.[39]

Responding to Yrigoyen's infringement upon the armed forces and to the general process of political decay, military leaders, like the Conservatives, came to view his rule as illegitimate. There were some fundamental disagreements, but Yrigoyen's opponents in the army concurred on one basic point: somehow the traditional rules of the game should be restored.

One group, led by General Agustín P. Justo—himself an Antipersonalist Radical—sought a return to pre-1916 politics. This faction thought the Yrigoyenists had grossly abused electoral and parliamentary procedures. With the Personalists out of the way, power would revert to the aristocrats, conflict would be restrained, the possibility of class struggle would disappear, *gente bien* would rule once again. Thus the democratic structure would reassume its normal, proper, and legitimate functions.[40]

Another group, led by General José F. Uriburu, had a more drastic solution: the creation of a semi-Fascist corporate state. The problem was not Yrigoyen but the system itself. Combining Catholic precepts with admiration of Mussolini's Italy, Uriburu sought to establish a hierarchical order based on social function. He thought the vote should be "qualified" so that the most cultivated members of society would have the predominating influence on elections, and he wanted to reorganize Congress in order to take power away from political professionals—"agents of political committees," as he disdainfully called them. In his "functional democracy" legislators would represent not parties but corporate interests—ranchers, farmers, workers, merchants, industrialists, and so on. A vertical structure of this sort would create a basis for rule by consensus, eliminate class conflict, and perhaps most important—in the Argentine case—reintegrate the political system with the economic system. Once more, and now by conscious design, the political arena would reflect the distribution of power within the economic arena; the pre-1916 rules of the political game would be restated and put into law.[41]

As time wore on, two important elements thus came to regard Argentine democracy as illegitimate: Conservative civilians and segments of the military (this latter group containing two main camps). Conditions for the coup were ripening.

The Coup

The pace of events rapidly quickened during 1930.[42] Signs of trouble appeared in the congressional elections early in the year, when the UCR lost its hold on the federal capital (Buenos Aires) for the first time in fourteen years. And Yrigoyenists did poorly in other major provinces: the great majorities of 1928 were reduced in Buenos Aires and Santa Fe, and reversed in Córdoba and Entre Ríos. As though to underscore the nature of the legitimacy crisis, Congress quarreled from May until August about the legality of key provincial elections. The UCR was flaunting its superiority, and the opposition, badly outnumbered despite the election results, could only boycott sessions in an effort to prevent quorums. As Yrigoyen's critics denounced his use of power, word spread that he would perpetrate another intervention, this time in Entre Ríos.

On 9 August legislators from the opposition parties published the "Manifesto of the Forty-four," protesting Yrigoyen's "arbitrary and despotic" rule and proclaiming the need to "save Argentina's democratic institutions and prevent the ruin of the country." Because of its explicit statement of political grievances, the manifesto merits extensive quotation. "Whereas," the signers proclaimed,

...the system of republican, representative, and federal government of our Constitution has been de facto annulled by the Executive Power, whose arbitrary and despotic will is today the only force which exerts control on public affairs.

The Executive Power has subverted and deformed the rule of provincial autonomy and has violated the law of primary education, the law of secondary education, the organic laws of the army and the navy ... [a series of other laws] and international agreements accepted by this country.

Public funds are squandered without any criteria other than the caprice of the President and the electoral needs of the *oficialista* party [the UCR], precisely at the time that government resources are declining and taxpayers are suffering the effects of a growing economic malaise.

While the country is experiencing greater and greater difficulty in selling its products abroad, the President ignores, with unconscionable negligence, the public outcry in behalf of agrarian interests.

Added to this institutional crisis is a serious economic crisis resulting from the devaluation of our currency, the lack of positive action by the government and the manifest lack of direction [*desorbitación*] in the acts of the Executive Power.

It is urgent to denounce and change this state of affairs by a united, energetic, and patriotic parliamentary and popular action by all men who wish to save Argentina's democratic institutions and prevent the ruin of the country, though this should not mean the pursuit of electoral ends, the abdication of partisan beliefs, or the creation of artificial political conglomerations.

We hereby resolve:

To coordinate parliamentary action in both chambers in order to require the Executive Power to comply with the national Constitution, to spend public funds properly and to faithfully execute fundamental organic laws.

To coordinate the opposition outside of Congress, to publicize . . .the illegal acts of the Executive Power and the ruling party [oficialismo] and to stimulate a civic spirit of resistance. . . .

To develop a plan of action conducive to the achievement of these goals and, if necessary, to solicit the support of all citizens who desire for this Republic a constitutional and democratic government. . . .[43]

The Manifesto of the Forty-four reflects the fundamentally political quality of Argentina's crisis on which I have based my argument. True, the legislators made some reference to economic problems, but these complaints were slightly wide of the mark: precisely in order to stimulate rural exports the Yrigoyen government had negotiated a bilateral trade agreement with Great Britain—the so-called D'Abernon Pact, not yet ratified by the paralyzed Congress (nor would it ever be). Even so, the general thrust of the statement was political. Yrigoyen was abusing his power, he was disregarding laws, he was spending money for partisan reasons, he was negating provincial autonomy— and something had to be done.

A few days later, on 13 August, military members of the Uriburu faction (which included some civilian collaborators) signed a pledge to overthrow the Yrigoyen government, in accordance with their "patriotic duty." Emphasizing the political character of the crisis, the officers solemnly observed:

The institutions of government have reached such a level of corruption that the country will soon be wallowing in misery and bankruptcy.

Parliament no longer exists: under the orders of the President, a disciplined and obedient majority has crushed the rights of the minorities . . . with the insolent insensitivity of preponderance.

The people already see, with indifference, the gradual process of social decomposition resulting from a system which must be brought to an end, cost what it may.

Ignorance and crime have replaced efficiency and respect for law, respect for tradition, and respect for all the moral values which we have received as a dear inheritance from our elders.

As Argentines who love our country, we pledge to save it from final ruin or die in the attempt.[44]

A series of public assemblies to rally support for the Manifesto of the Forty-four then took place in several of Buenos Aires' major theaters. On 20 August the Antipersonalist leaders—former members of the UCR—became outspoken in their opposition: "We must rise up, not only in alliance but also in solidarity with all the other organic forces of action and opinion, in order to save . . . our ideals, and cooperate in the defense of our embattled democracy."[45] Antipersonalist leaders in Entre Ríos issued yet another declaration.[46]

As rumors of a coup began to circulate, Yrigoyen became ill and took to bed. His minister of war, General Luis Dellepiane, urged him to take decisive action by arresting suspected conspirators and shaking up his cabinet. Yrigoyen failed to respond—perhaps because of his illness—and Dellepiane quit in frustration on 2 September. Publication of his letter of resignation, alluding to corruption and irregularities within the government, encouraged the conspirators. Other military officers, seeking a way out of the crisis, urged the resignation of the president and his entire cabinet. Then came the final sequence of events.

3 September: Matías Sánchez Sorondo, a civilian member of the Uriburu clique and later Uriburu's minister of the interior, meets with political leaders of the anti-Yrigoyen parties.

4 September: Student demonstrations at the University of Buenos Aires lead to violence and casualties.

5 September: Because of his illness Yrigoyen delegates power to Vice-President Enrique Martínez. Members of the military conspiracy, which included both the Uriburu and Justo groups, meet with political party leaders to assure civilian presence at Buenos Aires military bases the following day.

6 September: Columns start advancing early in the morning. Vice-President Martínez, possibly anticipating his own elevation to the presidency, takes little action; within eight hours he resigns. A few hours later Yrigoyen, who had left his sickbed in an effort to secure support from the military garrison at La Plata, also resigns. Uriburu steps in as provisional president, and news of the coup prompts a jubilant celebration in downtown Buenos Aires.[47]

Thus the coup. "As a politico-military effort," Robert Potash has said, "this coup was the product of a prolonged period of exploratory talks, a three-month organizing effort, and a high degree of last-minute improvisation. Its success was attributable not to its physical strength—600 cadets and 900 other troops comprised the force that marched on the government—but to its psychological impact on the general public and the rest of the military, and to the paralysis of its opponents."[48]

Although Uriburu directed the provisional government, the Justo group eventually won out. Elected to the presidency in 1931, General Justo and his supporters concocted an elitist and fraudulent pseudo-democracy. While rigging elections and profiting from a Personalist boycott, he governed through a multiparty Concordancia. Conflict was limited, partisanship lax, tension fairly low. It seemed as though the rules of the game were again in effect, but the image proved to be illusory. During the 1930s industrial growth and internal migration led to the appearance of an articulate, mobile, aggressive, urban proletariat—which the Concordancia proceeded to ignore. In time the self-consciously elitist structure of parliamentary politics became increasingly obsolete, so the masses finally turned to an authoritarian solution: the populist dictatorship of Juan Perón. Democracy would not be tried again till 1973, and even then it would not last for long.[49]

Summary and Speculations

The breakdown of democracy in Argentina was the product of a crisis in legitimacy. The crisis was essentially due to the abandonment of longstanding political norms. There remain two fundamental questions: why were the norms abandoned? and could Yrigoyen have acted to avert the crisis?

Some critical factors defied manipulation or resolution by short-run political strategies. Insofar as they caused apprehension, for instance, impending economic difficulties came from outside the system. One-sided election results—which heightened Conservative fears—reflected the collective will of voters, and as a political competitor Yrigoyen could hardly have been expected to surrender electoral gains.

The decisive nature of the Radical triumphs, especially in 1928, points up one of the most fascinating aspects of Argentina's political scene: the utter inability of the Conservatives to cope with the realities of electoral politics. Having created the system, Conservatives promptly lost control of it, and the extent of their demise all but beggars belief. Prior to the Sáenz Peña law Conservatives had a near-monopoly on the vote; in 1916, after the reform, they won about 42 percent; in 1922 and 1928 they slipped to less than 25 percent.[50] This situation contrasts sharply with that in Sweden and Britain, for instance, where traditional elites continued to dominate systems after the extension of the suffrage. The understanding of the failure of Argentine conservatism will require intensive research,[51] but part of the explanation surely involves two related variables: first, the absence of a sedentary peasantry, which has furnished the base of Conservative strength in many other societies; and second, the high degree of urbanization, which placed a large proportion of the electorate beyond the reach of traditional landed elites.

Despite external restraints of this kind, however, it still appears that Yrigoyen might have alleviated the legitimacy crisis through one or more of the following actions:

(1) Yrigoyen might have taken the advice of his war minister and shuffled his cabinet. Specifically, he could have invited some distinguished Conservatives to take portfolios, perhaps three of the total of eight, and created a national government (as Ramsey MacDonald did in Britain). This measure might have done a great deal to ease the legitimacy crisis

because it would have reinstated, in part, the traditional rules of the game.[52]

(2) Yrigoyen could have tried to heal the intraparty split between the Personalists and the Antipersonalists, perhaps inviting one or two Antipersonalists into the cabinet as well. This cleavage helped precipitate the legitimacy crisis because it divided the party along social lines, as shown in table 2, and hastened the virtual expulsion of aristocrats from positions of political power.

(3) Yrigoyen could have stopped his practice of intervening in the provinces; in particular he could have announced his intention *not* to intervene in Entre Ríos, then an Antipersonalist stronghold, and to respect the integrity of senatorial elections in 1931.

(4) Similarly, he could have instructed Radical deputies to approve the credentials of recently elected members of the opposition.

(5) Finally, Yrigoyen might have announced his intention not to tamper with the military, as an institution, and to utilize purely professional criteria in the matter of promotions.

Even though these tactics might not have prevented the coup, especially if they had been implemented as late as August 1930, Yrigoyen's failure to adopt them calls for an explanation. His alleged near-senility and his illness might well have clouded his judgment, but the problem was much more basic than that; had Yrigoyen been in total command of his faculties, I suspect he would have done just what he did.[53] For it does not appear that Yrigoyen or the Radicals purposely betrayed a conscious agreement with Conservatives, or simply changed their minds along the way. What is most striking, in fact, is the very consistency of the Radicals' behavior, since they continued to act like an opposition party once they were in power. The attitudes and tactics which helped them *acquire* power before 1916 did not help them *solidify* power after 1916. Catering to military factions served the interests of an opposition, for instance, but undermined the authority of a president; disputes over congressional credentials could dramatize the plight of an opposition but obstruct the administrative need for policy output; intransigence might allow an opposition to bring attention to key issues but, in leading to the defection of the Antipersonalists, would weaken a government coalition. It is difficult to say why the UCR maintained this inflexible posture, but I might suggest that (1) for Yrigoyen's own generation, the twenty-six-year experience as an "out" group from 1890 to 1916 had created a firm and antagonistic "oppositionist" mentality;[54] and (2) for the new generation of Radical party professionals, political power represented upward social mobility, and they were unwilling to share such a precious commodity with other groups.

More important than the Radicals' unchanging stance, however, was the changing structure within which they operated. Almost by definition, democratic politics after 1916 were incompatible with the traditional rules of the game: quite naturally the exercise of universal suffrage gave great power to the mass party; public campaigning and conflict hardened party lines; the exigencies of electoral politics gave rise to nonaristocratic professional politicians; and popular focus on politics produced demands for an autonomous and powerful government. Moreover, the presidential structure of the Argentine system gave overwhelming power to the majority party and discouraged coalition politics. Conservatives wanted democracy to uphold the rules of the game; but the structure was unsuited to this function, and the pursuit of democratic practice led to the violation of those rules. For Conservatives and their military allies, in brief, democracy became dysfunctional and therefore illegitimate.

Such a process suggests two general conclusions about the breakdown of democracy. First, the inherent tendencies of democratic structures can lead to a crisis of legitimacy and eventual decay. In this case, the electoral and parliamentary apparatus stopped serving its originally intended purposes and created new functions of its own. For key sectors of society the unacceptability of these functions delegitimized the structure, which they promptly overturned. Economic problems may have intensified the urgency of the situation, but they did not bring about the 1930 revolution. The political system had already been gravely weakened by its dysfunctional abandonment of traditional rules. To present the argument in Juan J. Linz's terms: the inefficiency and ineffectiveness of the democratic structure in upholding tacit political norms led to a legitimacy crisis which prevented any efficient or effective response to an unsettling (but not recognizably unsolvable) economic situation, and this paralysis further compounded the legitimacy crisis.

Second, Argentine democracy did not break down despite the level of economic development. In a way, it broke down—or, more precisely, failed to increase its responsive capability—because of the *kind* of socioeconomic development which took place in Argentina and the *sequence* between socioeconomic and political change, since these factors conditioned both the shape of political crises and the nature of elite response. The growth of a beef-and-wheat export economy concentrated socioeconomic power in the hands of a landed elite which believed that the political order should reflect the socioeconomic order, rather than provide some sort of counterweight to it. By taking place *prior* to the establishment of democratic institutions, these processes helped lay down the traditional rules of the political game—rules which democratic structures went on to break in 1916-30, provoking some sectors to seek salvation (and restoration) in a corporate society.

Furthermore, the high proportion of immigrants among the urban laborers made it possible for the country's leadership to meet the pre-1912 participation crisis, and establish competitive politics, without having to effectively enfranchise the working class. These economic and demographic conditions thus gave rise to a *limited* crisis in 1912; they also permitted a response which would ultimately prove to be severely limited in its flexibility and capability. Paradoxically, the same conditions which facilitated the 1912 solution also aggravated further crises after 1930.[55] Suddenly the sons of immigrants, now native Argentines and members of the working class, swelled the ranks of eligible voters—but the traditional parties except for the Socialists, offered no effective representation of their needs. Frustrated by this situation, workers understandably accepted an authoritarian solution when it came. What had facilitated the rise of Argentine democracy, *de facto* exclusion of the working class, also helped bring about its downfall. In the long run, Argentina's pattern of socioeconomic development may have been more conducive to authoritarian, corporatist, and even Fascist politics than to a lasting democracy.

NOTES

1. These assumptions have been so prevalent, especially in the literature of the 1960s, as to defy citation. For some recent alternative views, see Phillipe C. Schmitter, "Paths to Political Development in Latin America," in *Changing Latin America: New Interpretations of Its Politics and Society,* ed. Douglas A. Chalmers, *Proceedings of the Academy of Political Science* 30, no. 4 (August 1972): 83–105; and Guillermo A. O'Donnell, *Modernization and Bureaucratic-Authoritarianism: Studies in South American Politics* (Berkeley: Institute of International Studies, University of California, 1973) esp. chaps. 1 and 2.

2. The definition is taken from Juan J. Linz, "An Authoritarian Regime: Spain," most easily consulted in *Mass Politics: Studies in Political Sociology,* ed. Erik Allardt and Stein Rokkan (New York: The Free Press, 1970), pp. 254–55. Robert A. Dahl also writes of Argentina in this period as a "polyarchy" or *relatively* democratized regime. See his *Polyarchy: Participation and Opposition* (New Haven: Yale University Press, 1972), esp. pp. 132–40.

3. For an excellent analysis of this electoral reform, see Darío Cantón, "Universal Suffrage as an Agent of Mobilization" (paper delivered at the Sixth World Congress of Sociology, Evian, France, 4–11 September 1966). Voter turnout figures appear on pp. 13 and 16.

4. I shall use the terms *coup* and *revolution* interchangeably in this paper, since the 1930 movement meets my definition of a revolution: an illegal seizure of political power through the use or threat of violence by groups seeking to make structural changes in the distribution of political, social, or economic power.

5. See the controversial chapter by Seymour M. Lipset on "Economic Development and Democracy" in his *Political Man: The Social Bases of Politics* (Garden City, N.Y.: Doubleday, 1963), pp. 27–63.

6. Estimates of GNP per capita are in United Nations, Economic Commission for Latin America, *El desarrollo económico de la Argentina*, mimeographed (Santiago de Chile, 1958) E/CN. 12/429. Add. 4, p. 4; the conversion to dollars is based on data in Carlos Díaz Alejandro, *Essays on the Economic History of the Argentine Republic* (New Haven: Yale University Press, 1970), p. 485.

7. See the tables in my article on "Social Mobilization, Political Participation, and the Rise of Juan Perón," *Political Science Quarterly* 84, no. 1 (March 1969): 33, and the data in Gino Germani, *Estructura social de la Argentina: Análisis estadístico* (Buenos Aires: Raigal, 1955), pp. 198 and 220–22.

8. Dahl, *Polyarchy,* Chap. 1.

9. For expressions of this widespread view, see Arthur P. Whitaker, *Argentina* (Englewood Cliffs, N.J.: Prentice-Hall, 1964), pp. 81–82; and Darío Cantón, José L. Moreno, and Alberto Ciria, *Argentina: La democracia constitucional y su crisis* (Buenos Aires: Paidós, 1972), pp. 121–23. The most recent (and sophisticated) version of this argument appears in David Rock, *Politics in Argentina, 1890–1930: The Rise and Fall of Radicalism* (Cambridge: Cambridge University Press, 1975), pp. 252–64. Rock clearly demonstrates that there were economic pressures on the government in 1930, but his assertion that they comprised "the great factor" behind the coup is unconvincing for at least two reasons: first, he does not pay sufficient attention to the *timing* of events (specifically regarding the emergence of pro-coup sentiment, which antedated most of the economic problems); second, as he himself acknowledges (p. 262 n.), he does not analyze the coup from the viewpoint of the elite groups that perpetrated and supported it.

10. Peter H. Smith, *Politics and Beef in Argentina: Patterns of Conflict and Change* (New York: Columbia University Press, 1969), pp. 48–49, 137.

11. Carl Solberg, "Rural Unrest and Agrarian Policy in Argentina, 1916–1930," *Journal of Inter-American Studies and World Affairs* 13, no. 1 (January 1971): 18–52.

12. Ricardo M. Ortiz, "El aspecto económico-social de la crisis de 1930," *Revista de historia* 3 (1958): 63–64.

13. For data on strikes, strikers, and real wages, see Peter H. Smith, *Argentina and the Failure of Democracy: Conflict among Political Elites, 1904–1955* (Madison: University of Wisconsin Press, 1974), pp. 16, 101.

14. Cantón et al., *Argentina*, p. 122; and Rock, *Politics*, pp. 252–64. Rock emphasizes the way that budgetary limitations restricted the growth of the bureaucracy and, consequently, the distribution of patronage; the point is well taken, but in my view, he carries it much too far.

15. See José María Sarobe, *Memorias de la revolución del 6 de septiembre de 1930* (Buenos Aires: Gure, 1957); José Félix Uriburu, *La palabra del General Uriburu*, 2d ed. (Buenos Aires: Roldán, 1933); and statements by various participants in the *Revista de historia* 3 (1958): 95–138.

16. Dahl, *Polyarchy*, pp. 134–35.

17. Leonard Binder et al., *Crises and Sequences in Political Development* (Princeton, N.J.: Princeton University Press, 1971).

18. An aristocracy is here defined as a group of people who hold predominant shares of both economic and social power, who recognize a common bond with other members of the group, and who regulate admission to the group. Whether or not to pursue political power is a matter of choice. For further discussion see Smith, *Argentina*, Appendix A.

19. See his comment in Ministerio del Interior, *Las fuerzas armadas restituyen el imperio de la soberanía popular* (Buenos Aires: Ministerio del Interior, 1946), vol. 1, p. 9; and the discussion in Darío Cantón, *Elecciones y partidos políticos en la Argentina. Historia, interpretación y balance: 1910–1966* (Buenos Aires: Siglo XXI, 1973), chap. 4.

20. Smith, *Argentina*, pp. 11–12.

21. Documentation for this sort of statement is virtually impossible, since people rarely announce their adherence to "codes" which (in many instances) might not have been consciously perceived. In this case I am imputing attitudes from contemporary behavior and from indirect statements made during *and after* the fact (some of which are quoted).

22. This is a little different from Dahl's version of the credo, which is: "I believe in elections as long as I can be sure that my opponents will not win" (*Polyarchy*, p. 140). The fact is that Conservatives *did* accept Radical triumphs in 1916, 1922, and 1928; it was only when these rules were broken that the opposition's victory became intolerable.

23. For narrative background on the Radicals, see Gabriel del Mazo, *El radicalismo: Ensayo sobre su historia y doctrina*, 3 vols. (Buenos Aires: Gure, 1957); Manuel Gálvez, *Vida de Hipólito Yrigoyen: El hombre del misterio*, 5th ed. (Buenos Aires: Tor, 1959); and Félix Luna, *Yrigoyen* (Buenos Aires: Raigal, 1964). On the social background of early Radical leaders, see Ezequiel Gallo and Silvia Sigal, "La formación de los partidos políticos contemporáneos: La U.C.R., 1890–1916," in *Argentina, sociedad de masas*, ed. Torcuato S. di Tella, Gino Germani, and Jorge Graciarena (Buenos Aires: Editorial Universitaria de Buenos Aires, 1965), pp. 124–76; Smith, *Argentina*, chap. 2, esp. table 2-2; and Rock, *Politics*, esp. chap. 3.

24. See the debates in Ministerio del Interior, *Las fuerzas armadas*, vol. 1, pp. 36–303; one specific reference to "coalition government" is on p. 74.

25. Cantón, "Universal Suffrage," esp. pp. 16–22.

26. Darío Cantón, *Materiales para el estudio de la sociología política en la Argentina*, 2 vols. (Buenos Aires: Instituto Torcuato di Tella, 1968); Smith, *Argentina*, p. 10.

27. Smith, *Argentina*, pp. 18–19. For an impressionistic statement about the vigor of the Argentine Congress in 1916–22, see Matías G. Sánchez Sorondo's comment in the *Revista de historia* 3 (1958): 103.

28. Because of its construction I would construe an index of .50 as being very high. The computational procedures were as follows: for each legislative session, I first factor-analyzed all contested roll-call votes, with each deputy obtaining an individual score on each factor; second, I found the maximum proportion of variance in factor scores explained by the optimal dichotomous party grouping; third, I computed the mean proportion of variance explained (R^2), weighted by the statistical importance of the factors. For an extended discussion of this methodology, see Smith, *Argentina*, Appendix B.

29. Here the operational distinction between Personalists and Antipersonalists is based on the roll-call vote for president of the Chamber of Deputies; see Cámara de Diputados, *Diario de Sesiones, 1924* 1 (12 June): 430; a different procedure appears in Smith, *Argentina*, pp. 77–78, with "aristocrats" defined in Appendix A.

30. Mariano Bosch, *Historia del Partido Radical: La U.C.R., 1891–1930* (Buenos Aires: by the author, 1931), p. 214.

31. Rosendo A. Gómez, "Intervention in Argentina, 1860–1930," *Inter-American Economic Affairs* 1, no. 3 (December 1947): 55–73. Interventions were permitted by Article 5 of the constitution, which stated: "The federal government shall have the right to intervene in the territory of the provinces in order to guarantee the republican form of government or to repel foreign invasions; and when requested by the constituted authorities, to maintain them in power, or to reestablish them if they shall have been deposed by sedition or by invasion from another province."

32. Cámara de Diputados, *Diario de Sesiones, 1932* 7 (1 December): 142.

33. Smith, *Politics and Beef*; Solberg, "Rural Unrest." In the prevailing atmosphere of mutual distrust, however, Conservatives may well have feared that Yrigoyenist policies would become detrimental to them in the future—especially in the event of serious economic crisis.

34. Cantón makes this point in *Elecciones*, principally on pp. 149–52. I construe this argument as tentative, however, since Cantón uses rank-order correlation coefficients to measure relationships between conceptually imprecise variables *on the provincial level* (with fifteen observations or less).

35. In a telling expression of Conservative disenchantment with democratic procedure, Joaquín Costa declared—even while accepting his party's nomination to the Chamber of Deputies—that the secret ballot was like "a subterranean mechanism which belongs . . . to sanitation works—it is a water-tight master pipe which carries impassible currents of all parties mixed with the debris of the social organism, among which gloriously stand out the human refuse, the most apt for fertilization of the soil" (*La Nación*, 31 March 1928; quoted in Cantón, "Universal Suffrage," p. 26).

36. Important studies of Argentine military history can be found in Marvin Goldwert, "The Rise of Modern Militarism in Argentina," *Hispanic American Historical Review* 48, no. 2 (May 1968): 184–205; Robert A. Potash, *The Army and Politics in Argentina, 1928–1945* (Stanford, Ca.: Stanford University Press, 1969); Darío Cantón, *La política de los militares argentinos, 1900–1971* (Buenos Aires: Siglo XXI, 1971); and Marvin Goldwert, *Democracy, Militarism, and Nationalism in Argentina, 1930–1966: An Interpretation* (Austin: University of Texas Press, 1972).

37. Potash, *Army*, p. 20; José Luis de Imaz, *Los que mandan* (Buenos Aires: Eudeba, 1964), pp. 56–57.

38. Peter G. Snow, *Political Forces in Argentina* (Boston: Allyn and Bacon, 1971), p. 53; Potash, *Army*, pp. 8, 34, 99; and George I. Blanksten, *Perón's Argentina* (Chicago: University of Chicago Press, 1953), p. 311.

39. In particular see Goldwert, "Rise of Modern Militarism."

40. Evidence for this interpretation is indirect and circumstantial since (to the best of my

knowledge) Justo and his colleagues issued no clear public statement of political purpose; the best available account is in Sarobe, *Memorias*.

41. Sarobe, *Memorias*, pp. 19–38, 44–50, 56–78; Uriburu, *La palabra del General Uriburu,* esp. pp. 22–23, 95–100, 167–68.

42. For descriptions of these events, see J. Beresford Crawkes, *533 días de historia argentina: 6 de septiembre de 1930—20 de febrero de 1932* (Buenos Aires: Mercatali, 1932); Sarobe, *Memorias;* and Potash, *Army,* pp. 39–54.

43. Sarobe, *Memorias*, pp. 271–72. Rock quotes only the clauses relating to economic difficulties, thus removing them from their broader political context (*Politics,* p. 262). In support of his argument he also cites the statement by Enrique Martínez, Yrigoyen's vice-president, to the effect that "The economic crisis was the great factor that made the revolution possible . . . " (p. 262 n.). But this declaration must be interpreted with great caution, not to say skepticism, since it would be natural for prominent Radicals to insist that the coup was due to uncontrollable external forces rather than a failure of the party or the system that they led. And I myself would agree that the economic crisis made the revolution possible; what I would deny, and what Rock concludes, is that the crisis was the primary and determining cause of the coup.

44. Sarobe, *Memorias,* facsimile reproduction between pp. 144–45.

45. Ibid., pp. 273–74.

46. See del Mazo, *Radicalismo,* vol. 2, pp. 149–50.

47. Unfortunately we know very little about the social composition of the crowds which hailed the coup.

48. Potash, *Army,* pp. 42–43.

49. I would not call the electoral interlude of 1958–66 democratic because the Peronists were not allowed to run their own candidates—except in 1962, when the armed forces annulled the results and seized power.

50. See the figures in Cantón, *Elecciones,* pp. 267–69. I have counted votes for local pro–status quo parties as part of the "Conservative" total; otherwise the decline in party strength would appear to be even more drastic.

51. A preliminary analysis of this phenomenon appears in Oscar Cornblit, "El fracaso del Conservadorismo en la política argentina," Trabajo Interno no. 14 of the Centro de Investigaciones Sociales, Instituto Torcuato di Tella, 1973.

52. Actually, Dellepiane did not suggest a coalition cabinet; he merely warned Yrigoyen to replace apparently disloyal aides.

53. It is not at all clear that Yrigoyen was in fact senile: see Rock, *Politics,* pp. 260–61.

54. As Yrigoyen said near the end of his first presidential term: "I did not expect to end up here. I expected to remain in the agreeable role of an opponent [*el papel simpático de opositor*] . . ." (Luna, *Yrigoyen,* p. 182).

55. For discussion of post-1930 crises see Smith, *Argentina,* chap. 6.

2.

Conversations among Gentlemen: Oligarchical Democracy in Colombia

Alexander W. Wilde*

The truth is that the Conservatives have officially terminated the negotiations [for peace], in spite of our having made known, through several very respectable channels, our desire to continue them. That is the absolute truth, and if I do not give you publicly more facts and evidence to corroborate it, it is because I want to be true to the confidentiality that it was appropriate to maintain in a conversation among gentlemen. Carlos Lleras Restrepo, October 1949.

In the 1940s, when the world still seemed divided into democracies and dictatorships, Colombia loomed larger to those studying politics than it does now. It had a two-party system, regular elections, and a record of democratic reforms in the depression of the thirties. Diplomats and political scientists called Bogotá the "Athens of the Americas." They considered Colombia an outpost of Western political culture in a region that in general seemed politically pathological.[1] Hence, the shock was great when that democracy came to an end in November 1949, to be followed by a quasi-corporatist dictatorship (Laureano Gómez, 1950–53) and a Peronist-style military regime (Gustavo Rojas Pinilla, 1953–57). And there was horror and disbelief as what had seemed one of the most democratic of nations fell, over the course of a decade, into the greatest political violence in the hemisphere since the Mexican Revolution.

The basic questions about these events are as alive today as they were then,

*The research on which this chapter is based was completed in March 1974 and made possible in part by a grant from the Ibero-American Program, University of Wisconsin–Madison. A book-length version of this chapter, with fuller documentation, will be published as *Conversaciones de caballeros* (Bogotá: Universidad de los Andes, 1978). The author is grateful for critical comments on earlier drafts from the editors and from Charles W. Anderson, R. Booth Fowler, Richard Weinert, James Scott, Leon Epstein, Thomas Bossert, R. Van Whiting, and especially from Francisco Leal.

28

because they involve problems not only of politics but of political analysis. What is "democracy" in the first place? How is democracy created and sustained? What are its requisites—what social and economic conditions, what political structures, bargains, and leadership? How does democracy break down? What is the role of socioeconomic change? What is the impact of more "political" factors—of the perceptions and choices of politicians, of the character of institutions they operate, of the specific rules of their own democratic game? What kinds of changes would permit a democracy that has broken down to be reestablished? And what, finally, might the study of such a case contribute to our broader understanding of the nature of democracy?

Democracy in Colombia

There are various traditions in democratic theory. One conceives of "democracy" as a kind of civilization, which allows the development of rational, autonomous, and fulfilled individuals. A narrower approach, in part in reaction to the first, defines democracy primarily as a kind of political system—a method for regulating conflict and power.[2] The problem with the former as a standard is that all polities that have existed inevitably fall short. The latter allows us to make a relatively clear distinction between historical cases, with some falling above the threshold of democracy and others below, rather than merely at varying distances from an ideal. Although it can be debated that the latter approach neglects an element that is quintessentially "democratic," it does at least make possible the comparative analysis of historical "democracies."

"Democracy" can be defined in more restricted, procedural terms as those rules that allow (though they do not necessarily bring about) genuine competition for authoritative political roles. No effective political office should be excluded from such competition, nor should opposition be suppressed by force.[3] More specifically, such rules would include freedom of speech, press, and assembly, and the provision of regular institutional mechanisms for obtaining consent and permitting change of political personnel (normally, elections).

Colombia shared with the rest of Latin America the usual supposed impediments to democracy: a high rate of illiteracy, widespread poverty, a powerful Catholic church, a dominant landowning class, poor national integration, and a nineteenth-century heritage of political violence second to none. Despite the lack of the appropriate "requisites,"[4] however, she managed to achieve, between 1910 and 1949, a political system of notable stability, openness, and competitiveness.[5]

Elections were held regularly throughout the period at national, departmental, and municipal levels. The opposition party twice won presidential elections, in 1930 and 1946, and twice took office. Until the breakdown process of 1948–49, all significant political actors regarded elections as the legitimate source of authority. Colombia was one of only two countries in all Latin America (the other was Uruguay) not to suffer a single successful military coup throughout this period. All elections were direct, except senatorial elections (which were made so in 1945); the president appointed departmental governors, who in turn appointed municipal mayors. Literacy restricted the franchise for national elections until 1936. Even so, perhaps half the adult males participated in national elections as early as 1922, and this proportion had risen sharply to nearly three-quarters by the 1940s.[6]

Colombia can be conceived as having evolved from the competitive oligarchy it was in 1910 to the more inclusive "oligarchical democracy" it had become by the 1940s. Figure 1 depicts this evolution in terms of Dahl's schematic classification of political systems.

Even for such a simple, dichotomous characterization, however, considerable qualifications must be entered. Concerning contestation, even a cursory survey of presidential elections during the period shows four—1914, 1926, 1934, and 1938—in which there was only one serious candidate because the opposition refused to run. There are, in addition, two other elections—1918 and 1942—that were competitive only because the governing party nominated two candidates. Indeed, during the period only three presidential elections were fought between nominees of the two parties—1922, 1930, and 1946. These variations in contestation produced parallel variations in electoral participation. The episodic character of participation means that the "inclusive-

Figure 1.   The Evolution of Democracy in Colombia, 1910–49

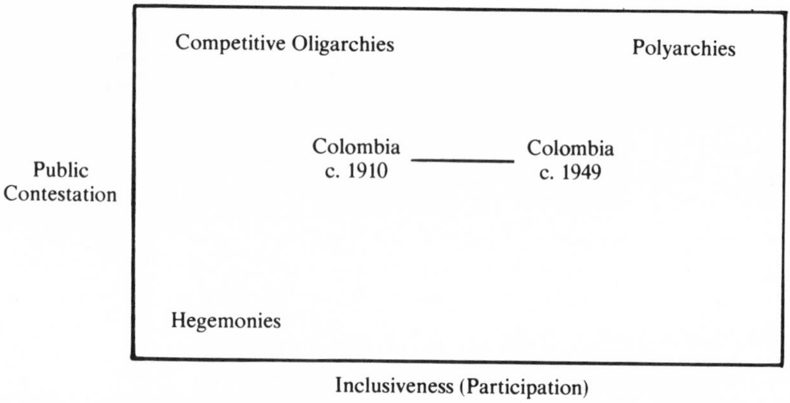

SOURCE: Adapted from Robert Dahl, *Polyarchy* (New Haven: Yale University Press, 1971), figure 1.2, p. 7.

Figure 2.   Competition and Participation in Presidential Elections, 1910–49

Turnout
(in thousands)

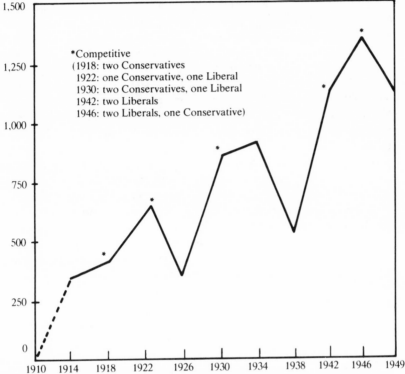

*Competitive
(1918: two Conservatives
1922: one Conservative, one Liberal
1930: two Conservatives, one Liberal
1942: two Liberals
1946: two Liberals, one Conservative)

SOURCES: DANE (Departamento Administrativo Nacional de Estadística), *Colombia política: Estadísticas 1935–1970* (Bogotá: DANE, 1972), table 8.1.1, for data from 1936–49; data from earlier elections are from Jesús María Henao and Gerardo Arrubla, *Historia de Colombia*, 8th ed. (Bogotá: Librería Voluntad, 1967), pp. 838–98 *passim* (from figures gathered from the *Archivo del congreso, Diario oficial*, etc.).

ness" of the system cannot be inferred directly from the formal franchise or electoral laws.

Fraud was always present, as was periodic coercion against the opposition.[7] On balance, however, neither should be taken as reason to deny Colombia its place among historical "democracies." Fraud was, at least, more than a matter of spurious electoral accounting. Peasants were actually mobilized to vote in substantial numbers, and traditional kinds of influence decreased in importance as the society became more urban in the 1930s and 1940s. There were elements in both parties that aspired to permanent hegemony, but the competition of elites over electoral capabilities prevented it. Fraud and coercion never destroyed the institutional framework that permitted two alternations of the parties in power and the significant expansion of participation over time.

The abstention of one party from the polls is a special case. Such *retraimiento* ("retirement"), as it was called in Spain, was indeed a kind of denial by the opposition of the legitimacy of the system. It may demonstrate what Linz calls "semiloyalty," or qualified commitment to democracy—either on the part of the opposition or of the government. But it is important to realize that such a boycott does not in itself demonstrate that the opposition has been excluded by force. Abstention was a recurrent political tactic in Colombia and many Latin societies. It was meant to cover with the banner of righteous protest a multitude of political debilities. When Liberals abstained in the 1920s, or Conservatives in the 1930s, they stayed out as much for reasons of internal party division, disorganization, and a lack of spirit (*mística*) as because of any harassment by the government.

Retraimiento represented a complex calculation by the leaders of the "out" party that it would be better served by abstention than defeat. Party appetites for office would grow keener and might produce the unity that an unsuccessful campaign, making internal difficulties manifest, could render unattainable. This assessment rested on the belief, throughout this period, that the opposition party would *continue to exist* and *at some point* be given the opportunity by division within the government party to regain power. This indeed happened in 1930 and in 1946. The tradition of electoral abstention does suggest that democratic competition was less than fully institutionalized, but in a paradoxical way it also demonstrates a faith that the system would continue to be electoral and competitive.

With several qualifications, then, there was a kind of democracy established and operating in Colombia before November 1949. The foundations constructed in those years proved more durable than most would have believed possible through the breakdown, widespread violence, one-party dictatorship, and military rule that prevailed from 1949 to 1958. In the generation since 1958, the two traditional parties have returned and continued to dominate a political system that has been, despite some restrictions on competition, relatively open and democratic.[8] This regime (the "National Front") has had many shortcomings and failures, but these mean less that it has been undemocratic than that procedural democracy is no panacea.

Colombian Politics and "Infra-Democracy"

When democracy was lost in 1949, much of Colombian politics did not change. The system remained oligarchical, the economy capitalist, the institutions republican, the military civilianist. Above all, party politicians (albeit of only one party) continued to reign. Similarly, the democracy that emerged in the decades after 1910 was not a tabula rasa, but incorporated many elements of previous politics. The convulsive traumas of European democracies, which succeeded or gave way to quite different kinds of regimes, did not suggest such continuities. Analysis of them tended conceptually to equate "democracy" with the "political system" of the given case. In more developmental perspective, for a country without such sharp regime shifts, one should distinguish between the two. The democratic era in Colombia can be seen as a phase of a larger, continuing political system.[9]

When democracy breaks down anywhere, it is because certain rules concerning competition and consent, which we regard as inherent in the general definition of the concept, no longer hold. When democracy breaks down in any particular instance, it is because the specific rules for *that* democracy no longer obtain and have, as a consequence, removed the foundation for the more universal rules. These more specific rules are a product of the historical conditions and agreements that surrounded the creation of democracy in that country, and also of those that existed during subsequent crises when democracy was tested and sustained. To understand the breakdown of democracy in any particular case, we should focus our analysis first on the level of these more specific rules.

Democracy, within the overall development of a political system, is supported by a special configuration of that system—an "infra-democracy"—which makes it possible. Infra-democracy is specific to a particular system; there are many different infra-democracies underlying the different systems we would call "democratic." Part of an infra-democracy is structural. It might associate democracy with a particular kind of economy, a certain distribution of power within society, a particular set of political institutions, a specific kind of social structure. A democracy founded with a two-party system might be threatened by its transformation into a three-party system, or it might survive such change. If politics has any autonomy at all as a social activity, it must be possible for the initial assumptions of a system to be modified, and for the "rules" of the infra-democracy to be amended.

The other part of infra-democracy is experiential. A democracy is created and maintained by people who, for a variety of reasons, are committed to its rules of competition and consent. In a given case that commitment is to a series of historical, often quite specific, memories, understandings, symbols, and experiences.[10] They represent modifications or qualifications to the more general rules of democracy that permit *that* democracy to operate. Whether a democracy breaks down or survives in crisis depends not only on structural considerations but also on the experiential rules of infra-democracy—the expectations and perceptions that political actors have of one another.[11]

For Colombia the most important of the experiential rules was that democracy must be, in Lijphart's useful term, "consociational" between the two traditional parties.[12] Though some fraud and coercion would be accepted from the party in government, it was not expected to rule as a party government, but rather to share power with the elites of the other party. Majoritarianism was qualified. Neither party expected to be a permanent minority without at least some participation in government. In moments of crisis, this tacit norm would often be voiced explicitly, particularly by the opposition. Then it could lead to the strongest sort of consociational mechanism, a bipartisan coalition government. Partisan symbols would be muted, and moderate elites of both parties, emphasizing their common stakes in democracy, would swing party troops behind the fusion ticket.

Oligarchical democracy had its origins in such a coalition, the "Republican Union" of 1909.[13] Both parties had been brought into government by Rafael Reyes in 1904, following the last of the great party civil wars (1899–1903; 100,000 dead) and the loss of the Panamá state. When Reyes ruled as a dictator, civilian politicians composed their ideological differences and forced him out.[14] Although the coalition did not endure, Liberals continued to receive a share of the portfolios in succeeding Conservative governments.[15] The benefits of the interparty peace were abundant. Coffee receipts and foreign investment fueled a surge of rapid economic growth; Colombian exports increased in value more than ten-fold between 1905 and 1928.[16] Elites had strong economic incentives to prevent the renewal of fratricidal warfare.

In 1922 the Conservatives employed all the resources of government to maintain their hegemony, but by 1930 they had split, and a Liberal came to power. In the political and economic crisis of that year, party elites found a new basis for *convivencia* in the National Concentration coalition of Enrique Olaya Herrera, who had been part of the earlier Republican Union of 1910–14. In 1946, a similar division in the ruling Liberals allowed Conservative Mariano Ospina Pérez to become president at the head of the National Union coalition. None of these arrangements was really intended to become a new party; they were, rather, attempts to give a share of power to those committed to the system.

The consociational character of Colombian democracy was clearly oligarchical. It assumed the continuing control of mass mobilization by traditional party elites. Convivencia was primarily a matter of agreement between national factional leaders and depended to a great degree on personal relationships among them. They had to recognize when intra-elite conflict had gone too far and to forge a new consensus when it did. Making that operative, in turn, depended on their ability to retain control of the party machinery and, more generally, of party followers. There were characteristic tensions here: the pull on one side toward compromise with the extremes within one's own party, toward the solidarity that was the basis of political success in normal times; and the pull on the other side toward the more moderate elements of the other party, toward the consensus that made preservation of the system possible in a crisis. They were tensions that could be exacerbated by changes in the other parameters of the infra-democracy.

The most important structural element of the infra-democracy was the party system. The two historical parties, the Liberals and the Conservatives, were the central, inescapable basis of political life for over a century. They defined and shaped nearly all conflict. They were, in some sense, the most fundamental national institutions in society. They were more significant structurally, culturally, and behaviorally than other social groupings (such as regions, classes, and strata) and other national institutions (such as the army, the church, or even the state itself). They possessed, in Anderson's terms, the greatest range of "power capabilities," including symbols, violence, electoral mobilization, and economic resources (patronage).[17]

The dominance of the two parties antedated oligarchical democracy. In contrast to virtually all other Latin American countries (except for Chile), elections were from the very beginnings of the republic significant for transferring political leadership. By the 1850s parties had developed amazing capabilities for electoral mobilization.[18] A parallel capacity, one used as often in these times, was the ability to mobilize considerable violence. Most of the many civil wars of the nineteenth century consisted of conventional battles fought between irregular civilian party armies—a violent extension of electoral conflict.[19]

Thus, when party politicians created a democratic system after 1910, they were accustomed to standing at the center of politics to an unusual degree.[20] They commanded a traditional, largely rural, society. Bogotá in 1912 had a population of 121,000; Medellín, the next largest city, 71,000.[21] Modernization and economic change had barely begun to make society more differentiated, to throw up new forces, new elites, and new organizations to challenge them.

The traditional institutional rivals to parties in more praetorian politics had been thoroughly subordinated. Even in the civil conflicts of the nineteenth century, which frequently had religious aspects, the Catholic church demonstrated little independence or monolithic strength. It was deeply divided over party politics until 1886, when a new constitution gave it a series of public guarantees. Its institutional interests thus protected, the church then confined its political activities largely within the Conservative party until the 1940s.[22]

In contrast to the role of its counterparts in Brazil or Venezuela, the army was ineffectual militarily and marginal politically.[23] It had been reduced by the Liberals to a force of some five hundred men around 1850 (just at the time the parties were formed). As late as 1899 it was disgraced by Liberal party irregulars (led by trained Liberal officers) in the War of 1,000 Days.[24] It gradually became professionalized in the twentieth century; it was 1943 before the first graduate of the *Escuela Militar* reached top rank. The army fought and won an international war with Peru in 1933 and was proud that it was not used for internal police functions. A support for elected government, it arrogated no autonomous "moderating power" to itself. Party politicians for their part almost never knocked at the barracks door.[25] The solution in a crisis was not to provoke a military coup but to find a new consociational convivencia.

The potential for severe party conflict remained, in part because the stakes were high. As in much of nineteenth-century Latin America, the Colombian economy only slowly created new career possibilities for the upwardly mobile. In this context, government offered an unparalleled source of advancement.[26] In Eduardo Santa's memorable phrase, "the budget is the only industry in a country without industries."[27] The Colombian state, in the tradition of the Spanish empire, had an extensive administrative apparatus. It dispensed salaries, licenses, exemptions, profits, privileges, contracts—opportunities, in short, available nowhere else.

Control of this bounty turned on the capture of the national presidency.[28] The president appointed governors, who in turn appointed mayors, and each of these controlled the police at his respective level. Almost every administrative position at all levels of government was filled through patronage, down to the humblest municipal employees.[29] The state was the prize of the parties; it was important for what the parties could obtain from it. In itself it was little institutionalized; it lacked, in Huntington's term, "autonomy."[30] Like Neustadt's weak American president, it was an indispensable clerk.[31] Its own structures and institutions, its own potential public values, were subordinated to the collected particularistic goals of the clientelistic party. One of the assumptions of infra-democracy was that the state had limited capacities, but what resources it did possess were the rightful property of the party of government.

Parties, not government, formed the most significant links between the top and bottom of society.[32] They did so in spite of a lack of strong formal organization. National party bureaucracies began to appear only at the very end of the nineteenth century and remained nascent throughout the period of oligarchical democracy. The parties consisted of various national factions, each of which was a kind of diffuse, vertical hierarchy of various brokers forming a pyramid from local *gamonales* to regional bosses to national elites. Lower-level brokers furnished bodies for battles, both electoral and martial, and their superiors, when in power, responded with jobs and favors from the government. The quest for these stakes tied together the most diverse groups and strata of the society within both of the parties. They could not readily be distinguished from one another on the basis of their social followings; both were "poly-class."

The stakes of the party battle were apparent not only to elites but also to the masses who composed their shock troops. Party mobilization for elections, and particularly for the many internal wars of the nineteenth century, had produced a deep party identification at the grass roots. Although it would be excessive to call the resultant groupings "subcultures," partisan identification was a primary element of social cleavage.[33] Children were socialized into the antagonism of the preceding generations, and recurring armed conflicts reinforced these "hereditary hatreds."[34] By the end of the nineteenth century geography had come to reflect these political and social cleavages: the countryside was increasingly divided between communities that were nearly uniformly Liberal or Conservative. Neighboring villages, often socioeconomically indistinguishable, were often bitterly hostile to one another because of different party loyalties.[35]

It is a mistake to read too much specific content into party identities, especially at the mass level. Among elites something akin to "ideologies" did affect nineteenth-century conflict—particularly over the whole Spanish colonial heritage—but such differences had played themselves out by 1910.[36] The consociational bases of the oligarchical democracy were founded on the muting of such ideology. The identification of the elites with the parties, and their capacity to activate their followers, were based instead on a kind of mística—a "party spirit" that might invoke certain symbols that were part of the history of a band. This identity was of a traditional sort not closely related to existing social or economic distinctions.

Events and Indicators of the Breakdown

The period of political decay for oligarchical democracy began with the second presidency of Alfonso López Pumarejo (1942-45).[37] A triumphant Liberal reformist in the 1930s, López received the presidential sash in 1942 only after a bitter split in his own party of government. It was wartime, and social reform came to an end, replaced by wild speculation and the making of private fortunes.[38] Laureano Gómez, the leader of the opposition Conservatives, talked openly of the need for revolution and justified such acts as the bombing of the Palace of Justice. At one point Gómez was jailed for slandering the interior minister; the judge who sentenced him was nearly assassinated by a seminarian.[39] In 1944 the president was seized and held by an army garrison, in the first attempted military coup in generations, and this was followed by an attempted general strike.[40] The instability of cabinets rose sharply (and would increase further in the subsequent period).

In an atmosphere of intrigue and plotting, of rumor and scandal surrounding his whole government (and including even his family), López resigned from office in 1945. A makeshift government was put together under Liberal Alberto Lleras Camargo to fill the remainder of his term. Lleras took several Conservatives into his cabinet, the bipartisan gesture usual in such a crisis.

Figure 3.   Cabinet Changes, 1930–70

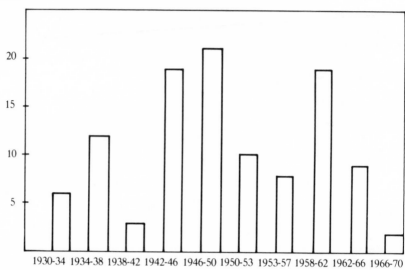

Resignation
Crises

SOURCE: Richard Hartwig, University of Wisconsin–Madison, unpublished paper, 1972, from data collected by the Departamento de Ciencias Políticas, Universidad de los Andes, Bogotá.

NOTE: The simultaneous resignation of several ministers is designated a "resignation crisis." Serious crises, in which five or more ministers resign, are weighted by a factor of three; less serious crises, involving three or four resignations, by a factor of two.

Almost immediately his government faced the most serious strikes in the nation's history, tying up its transportation system and its oil supplies. He survived and held the 1946 elections as scheduled.

The 1946 presidential campaign marked a milestone in the development of democracy. It witnessed the brilliant rise of the populist demagogue, Jorge Eliécer Gaitán, who ceaselessly attacked the corruption and bankruptcy of the whole oligarchical system. Running as a dissident Liberal, Gaitán finished third but became presumptive leader of his party soon after the elections. His candidacy split the majority Liberal vote and gave victory to the Conservative, Mariano Ospina Pérez, who formed a coalition National Union government. There were massive strikes before the end of his first year. The army had to be called in to deal with a riot in Bogotá in October 1946 and another in Cali in November. In the countryside violence broke out in many different regions as Conservatives gradually assumed control of the administrative apparatus.[41]

Gaitán walked an uneasy line between cooperation and opposition. Several times he forced the resignations of Liberal ministers who had participated, as individuals, in the National Union. A general strike was called by the Liberal

Colombian Workers' Federation (CTC) in May 1947, and Gaitán equivocated before finally disassociating his party from it. The urban police seemed unable (or unwilling) to deal with riots in the cities, just as their rural counterparts (with the opposite affiliation) were unable to deal with the growing violence in the countryside. The Liberals blamed the government for repressing dissent; the Conservatives blamed the Liberals for supporting subversion. The Liberal majority in Congress tried to wrest control of the National Police from the executive, and the interior minister replied that the government would defend itself with "blood and fire" if necessary.[42] In January 1948 the Liberals presented the government with a long petition of grievances, listing dozens of incidents of violence against their fellow party members, and in March they left the government.

The crisis of oligarchical democracy began when Gaitán was assassinated, by a lone gunman, in April 1948.[43] His death set off the riot called the *bogotazo*, which destroyed most of the center of the capital and left perhaps thousands dead. Violence spread to other cities, and a general strike was called. The country appeared to be on the edge of collapse. The army, at the urging of Gómez, suggested a military government. Instead, Ospina declared a state of siege and brought the Liberals back into coalition. As the process that had become known as *la Violencia* continued to mount in the countryside, Congress spent its energies for the rest of the year on a complete reform of the electoral system, changing the dates for the next election and ordering a complete new registration of voters.

Despite the efforts of the coalition government, violence was rapidly becoming an "unsolvable problem" for the system.[44] The final phase of the process of breakdown began when the Liberals left the National Union for the last time in May 1949. In June the Liberals won another congressional majority, in the largest voter turnout in Colombian history. From this base they launched a systematic attack on the powers of the president, including reorganization of the police, congressional approval of cabinet ministers, and election of governors and mayors. Most significantly, they introduced yet another electoral reform, which advanced the presidential election to November 1949. The legislature and the executive were locked in constitutional crisis.

All institutional norms were lost in the face of escalating violence and party polarization. Insults, epithets, and threats filled the halls of Congress. Gómez called it the "center of subversion" in the country and demanded that Ospina close it. Deputies came to debates drunk and armed. In September 1949 the Liberal deputy Gustavo Jiménez was killed in a gun battle on the chamber floor in which more than one hundred shots were fired. Four former Liberal presidents attended his funeral; Gómez seated the deputy who had killed the Liberal on his right at a gala dinner. The "neutral powers" in government (in Linz's term)—the Supreme Court, the Council of State, the national Electoral

Registrar—were all politicized along straight party lines. The desperate, behind-the-scenes negotiations between the parties to save the system had failed by October, and the Liberals announced they were boycotting the elections. On 9 November Ospina, in the face of a pending congressional motion for his impeachment, declared a state of siege, closed Congress and the provincial assemblies, and suspended civil liberties. These decrees were essentially just formal confirmation that the system had already broken down.[45]

Backdrop to Breakdown: Structural Change

Beneath these events lay a changing structure of infra-democracy. The presuppositions of the game were shifting. Democracy had begun and had long operated in a traditional, rural economy. Now urbanization had altered the relations between elites and masses. Economic development was creating new sources of power in society. Traditional politics had been limited in its complexity and scope, but now modernization was making possible much greater participation and a much more extensive state. Both resources and demands increased. The pace of change quickened greatly. The place of politics, and of political elites, in national life, became something different. The breakdown of oligarchical democracy occurred, in the last analysis, because political elites decided it would not work. But that decision, that perception, that event, was significantly shaped by change in the whole structure of the situation. Ultimately, it was politicians who acted, but many of the parameters of that choice had been set for them.

Much of existing social science literature about breakdown—theories of revolution, for example—tends to see social and economic factors as the "underlying" causes, as somehow more "fundamental" than politics, which is perceived as reactive and dependent.[46] Other theory in recent years (such as Linz's) has insisted that political factors—institutional quality, leadership, ideology, coalitional skills—are variable quite independently of socioeconomic factors.[47] In reality the two are often difficult to separate.

Naturally, socioeconomic change imposes certain "loads" on a political system, but these loads interact with the political system—they do not simply flow into it. They are defined and redefined over time by this interaction. The Colombian case is one in which political factors clearly made an important and independent contribution to breakdown.

That vast societal process, modernization, came later to Colombia than to much of Latin America. It began in the 1920s, with the first large foreign investments made in Colombia.[48] The economy grew very rapidly.[49] Extensive public investments began to create the communications and infrastructure for a truly national society.[50] A process of urbanization began, which, with some fluctuations, was sustained at a high level through the subsequent decades. Between 1918 and 1953, the urban population grew at an annual rate of 4.2 percent (the rural rate was 1.2 percent), while the urban proportion of the total population rose from 21 to 43 percent.[51] However, Colombia never received the massive influx of European immigrants whose presence had so changed countries like Argentina and Brazil.

These processes, slowed by the depression, accelerated again in the 1940s. Transportation indices of railroads and particularly of airlines, considered indicators of national integration, increased spectacularly during the decade.[52] The gross product generated in the transport sector went from an annual average of 166 million pesos in 1939–45 to 394 million pesos in 1946–53.[53] Economic growth was held back by the war but spurted ahead immediately afterward. The GNP rose 2.2 percent annually between 1939 and 1944, and 6.2 percent annually between 1945 and 1949.[54] The economy was increasingly oriented toward the external market, with exports (led by coffee) nearly doubling from 592 million pesos in 1939–44 to 1,000 million in 1945–53 (in 1950 pesos).[55]

Other kinds of modernization were greatly quickened by la Violencia, the initial origins of which were primarily political. The percentage of the labor force engaged in agriculture, which had declined from 70 percent to 62 percent between 1925 and 1945, dropped more sharply as peasants fled the land, and had reached 55.5 percent by 1951.[56] Between 1945 and 1953 the urban population grew at a rate of 5.2 percent annually, while the rural population grew at 0.4 percent.[57] Bogotá was a city of 650,000 in 1951; Medellín had a population of 360,000. Employment in the secondary sector of the economy increased from 15.2 percent in 1945 to 18.8 percent in 1951.[58] Labor union membership grew rapidly, from 42,678 in 1935 to 94,190 in 1941 to 165,595 in 1947.[59]

The large-scale strikes, the urban riots, and the rural violence of the late 1940s seem to reflect these underlying processes. They represent, in their inchoate way, greater "demands" on the political system. But the political system was also changing. Political change accompanied social and economic change—as a response to it, as a cause of it, and in interaction with it. Late in the process of disintegration, in the periods of "crisis" and "breakdown," some of the changes in the structure of politics were activated and others became more acute. To get at this we need a dynamic analysis of process, of sequence, of dialectics. But the structural changes in the rules, which underlay the whole process, must first be understood.

These changes involved the beginnings of a modern state and the rise of populist politics. The former greatly affected the stakes of politics; the latter, the character of participation. Both altered the scope and style of the political game, shifted the cleavages on which conflict was fought, and challenged the adequacy of traditional mechanisms.

After Conservative governments of the 1920s had laid the foundations, the Liberal administration of Alfonso López Pumarejo (1934–38) began in earnest the construction of the modern state.[60] This meant, above all, the extension of central political authority. The state assumed new functions; it began to regulate the organization of labor, agrarian property relations, and the electoral franchise. It strengthened its controls over commerce and banking, and in the world crisis of the 1930s it asserted its primacy in the direction of the economy. To administer these new functions it created new structures—public agencies and semipublic institutes. And to finance this structural expansion, it laid a solid fiscal groundwork of new direct taxation.

The result, by the time of the crisis in the 1940s, was a state far more extensive than that which had existed during much of the period of oligarchical democracy. On one hand, government had more resources than ever before to meet growing demands. National revenues nearly quadrupled between 1941 and 1949, doubling between 1945 and 1949. Particularly impressive were the gains in revenues obtained through direct taxation, which by 1949 nearly equaled the level of all revenues in 1945 (see table 1). There was no fiscal crisis of the state in the background to breakdown.

On the other hand, however, the differentiation of the state undercut the influence of the parties. They still stood at center stage, but now the apron was filling up with new characters. Bureaucratic agencies, interest groups, and *gremios* were organized, which both expressed and satisfied demands that had been channeled through the parties in simpler times. Even nominally "private" bodies (such as the National Federation of Coffee Growers) characteristically possessed a corporatist kind of relationship to government, with a guaranteed direct representation, support, and often authority.[61] Although it was probably not until the 1960s that they came to constitute what amounted to a parallel government for social and economic affairs, the "decentralized institutes" of many stripes had a significant impact on total public policy much earlier.[62] They insulated many of the new economic functions of government from the party struggle. This may well have removed a major incentive for nongovernmental elites to try to save democracy in the 1940s.[63]

The rise of populist politics was a more direct and obvious challenge to the parties.[64] Unprecedented numbers were drawn into the political system. Voter turnout reached 60 percent of adult males in the presidential election of 1946 and 73 percent in the congressional elections of 1949 (see table 2).[65]

This increase was by no means restricted to urban areas. The rural violence represented, in its own way, another manifestation of the explosion of participation—and an inescapable part of the backdrop to breakdown.

In one sense the traditional parties responded to this opportunity with great success; they recruited the new participants to their old labels.[66] But the sheer size of the increase threatened their oligarchical presuppositions, and changed the character of participation. What the parties were able to establish with the

Table 1. Government Revenues through Direct Taxation, Selected Years, 1935–49 (in millions of Colombian pesos)

	1	2	3	4	5	6	7
Year	All Revenues, Public Sector	All Revenues, National Government	Direct Taxes, National Government	Indirect Taxes, National Government	All Revenues, Public Sector (1950 pesos)	Direct Taxes, Public Sector (1950 pesos)	Indirect Taxes, Public Sector (1950 pesos)
1935	118.7	61.8	5.3 (9%)	41.8	292.7	23.5	269.3
1936	135.8	73.1	14.0 (19%)	45.7	329.6	54.2	275.4
1940	156.8	82.2	25.0 (31%)	45.7	333.1	81.0	252.0
1945	309.2	165.1	67.1 (34%)	75.9	376.1	126.8	249.3
1946	381.3	227.5	87.6 (32%)	93.9	428.5	151.5	277.0
1947	520.0	305.5	130.1 (34%)	123.6	499.9	193.5	306.3
1948	584.6	335.2	155.7 (39%)	126.7	498.8	204.0	294.6
1949	670.0	379.0	187.6 (46%)	133.2	543.6	227.1	316.5

SOURCE: CEPAL (Comisión Económica para América Latina), *El desarrollo económico de Colombia: Anexo estadístico*. From the "Análisis y proyecciones del desarrollo económico," reprinted by the Colombian Departamento Administrativo Nacional de Estadística (Bogotá: DANE, n.d.), tables 46, 47, 50.

NOTE: All amounts given in current pesos except where noted. "Public Sector" revenues include taxes and other revenues at all levels of government. Columns 3 and 4 do not add up to 2 because national revenues include more than taxes. Adjusted revenues—columns 5, 6, and 7—downplay the effects of direct taxation because they include departmental and municipal government, where direct taxation was almost nonexistent. Figures adjusted for inflation were not available for the national government alone.

Table 2. Electoral Participation in the 1940s

Years	Type of Election [a]	Adult Males	Total Votes	Electoral Participation [b]	Registered Voters	Electoral Participation [c]
1935	C	1,834,314	430,728	23.5	1,288,441	33.4
1937	C	1,906,551	550,726	28.9	1,692,004	32.5
1938	P	1,943,729	513,520	26.4	1,700,171	30.2
1939	C	1,981,632	919,568	46.4	—	—
1941	C	2,059,381	885,525	43.0	—	—
1942	P	2,099,227	1,147,806	54.7	2,056,366	55.8
1943	C	2,141,017	882,647	41.2	—	—
1945	C	2,225,570	875,856	39.4	2,279,510	38.4
1946	P	2,260,304	1,366,272	60.2	2,450,596	55.7
1947	C	2,313,038	1,472,689	63.7	2,613,586	56.3
1949	C	2,403,421	1,751,804	72.9	2,773,804	63.1
1949	P	2,403,421	1,140,646	47.4	2,856,339	39.9
1951	C	2,497,905	934,580	37.4	—	—
1953	C	2,632,792	1,028,323	39.0	—	—

SOURCE: DANE (Departamento Administrativo Nacional de Estadística), *Colombia política: Estadísticas 1935-1970* (Bogotá: DANE, 1972), table 8.1.1.

[a] C = congressional, P = presidential.
[b] Votes as percentage of adult males.
[c] Votes as percentage of registered voters.

new participants, urban and rural, were linkages of label, sentiment, and symbol. What they found much more difficult to extend were mechanisms of control. Colombia stood, in some sense, between oligarchical democracy and a more modern, participatory democracy. Its society was still relatively undifferentiated and lacking in intermediate structures. Its participation was more "activated," in the short run, by the political crisis, than "mobilized," for sustained involvement, by social change long underway.[67] Political organization was still primitive. The populist style of politics was indeed new, but the old continued to coexist alongside it.

The rise of trade unions illustrates the extent to which populism challenged oligarchical democracy, and the extent to which it was resisted. The CTC national labor federation, founded in 1936, was involved in party politics from the beginning. Initially, it was clearly a new "power capability" of the Liberals, and to some extent it remained so. The ambiguity of its relationship with the party, however, had emerged by 1945. With Law 6 of that year, the caretaker coalition of Alberto Lleras Camargo consolidated labor gains and prohibited formation of any competing federation. But later that year the same government dealt a crippling blow to the CTC as a national organization when it used the army to break a strike called by the Magdalena River workers.[68]

This was a sign from the "oligarchical" leaders of the Liberal party (above all, López) that they recognized the potential dangers of this new organization. They said to the Conservatives, in effect, that they remained fundamentally committed to the old game. There were others in the party who wanted to use the unions, and all the new participants in the political process, to rewrite the rules in the Liberals' favor. They encouraged the direct action tactics of the CTC as a way of putting continuing pressure on party leadership. The "oligarchical" line prevailed, however, particularly after the death of Gaitán in 1948. The party directorate did not support union desires at several key points—as in the general strike calls of 1947 and 1948 (after the bogotazo, when Echandía led the party back into coalition with the Conservatives).

Nevertheless, the unions did contribute to the breakdown of oligarchical democracy. They did not do this by transforming the nature of politics, as they might have done. They did not decisively shift the cleavages of the system nor become the new base of the Liberal party, for their organization was too weak. They were torn apart in struggles between Liberal and Communist leadership, and they never in this period organized more than a minuscule proportion (perhaps three percent) of the labor force.[69]

Their presence, however, was constantly unsettling. The CTC could compromise the Liberals, they could force the party leadership to choose to support or repudiate them, and could strain party commitment to oligarchical convivencia in a situation of obviously changed conditions. Conservatives distrusted Liberal leaders who professed loyalty to the system on one hand and seemed to take advantage of threats to it on the other. However credible they found the Liberal retreat from the unions after 1945, Conservatives could still doubt the extent to which their oligarchical counterparts actually controlled their movement, particularly in the deteriorating situation of 1948–49.[70]

The rise of populism also meant the reintroduction of ideology, in a broad sense, into politics. After the self-proclaimed "Revolution on the March" of Alfonso López in 1934–38, slogans of class, revolution, and socialism came easily to the lips of Liberal politicians. Conservatives opposed this with increasingly reactionary appeals for the defense of a traditional, orderly, Catholic Colombia. Symbols that had historically separated the two parties (such as the church) were recalled in a new setting of world ideological polarization. As in the Spain of the 1930s (a parallel consciously invoked in Colombia), political conflict could be presented as Armageddon.

Ideology exacerbated weaknesses already present in oligarchical democracy. The system was predicated on the assumption that one party would not become a permanently excluded minority. Liberal governments in the 1930s seemed to challenge that assumption. In the face of Conservative abstention after five years of participation in the executive, López welcomed the "Liberal Republic" as a "convenient, new, obligatory fact."[71] He extended suffrage and completely reformed the system of electoral registration. This made rural fraud more difficult and greatly expanded the urban vote. As Conservatives saw it, the Liberal motive was a highly partisan—one preventing the "true Conservative majority" of the country from being heard. Worse yet, inexorable demographic change supported Liberal designs. As Colombia became more urban, the Liberals' historical strength in the cities would assure their continuing dominance.[72]

Ideology was a fillip on top of this cup. The mainstay of consociational sharing was faith between the elites of the two parties. That faith was subject to very tangible tensions due to the changing structure of the situation: fears of exclusion, temptations to hegemony. An increasingly ideological style put a further burden on these personal relationships. It strengthened the mística of the party, and by strengthening party solidarity, it weakened identification with the larger system.

It is typical, finally, of populist politics that the parties did not significantly modernize as organizations. They remained vertical collections of factions, coordinated at the national level, and dependent on consensus between elites there. They possessed no more ability to discipline rebels at any level in the party than they ever had.

The changed conditions of the 1930s and 1940s—the rapid growth of participation, the rise of new political entrepreneurs within the old parties, and eventually the Violencia—exposed the vulnerability of the traditional structures.

The *Bogotazo* and the Crisis

The assassination of the populist Liberal leader Gaitán on 9 April 1948, was a watershed for oligarchical democracy. The bogotazo which followed the act was the greatest urban riot in the history of the Western hemisphere, a revolution that died in the agonies of birth. After it, Colombian politics would never look the same. To Laureano Gómez it was the end of politics and the beginning of civil war;[73] he called for a military junta and fled the country. To Mariano Ospina Pérez and to the Liberal leaders, it was more ambiguous. On the one hand both could see it as an attack on the president's authority (either justified, for the Liberals, or illegitimate, for Ospina). On the other hand they perceived it as a threat to the system in which they both had a stake. For the great "semiloyal" social institutions—the church and the military—the bogotazo accelerated a dynamic that thrust them deeper into politics.

Politics since the victory of Ospina in 1946 had been dominated by the question of coalition. Violence had begun between Liberals and Conservatives in the countryside, as it had in the past, over administrative spoils. The bipartisan National Union faced a dilemma on an almost daily basis in trying to control it, as the reports of massacres and atrocities reached the capital: were the police the instrument of governmental authority (i.e., "neutral") or of partisan advantage (i.e., Conservative)? This tension was heightened by the Liberal control of Congress, which they retained in the 1947 elections.[74]

There were elements in both parties who wanted an end to Liberal participation in the Ospina government. For the *laureanista* Conservatives, Liberal participation made reconquest of the administration painfully slow[75] and prevented the elimination of the corrupt basis of Liberal electoral success—some 1,800,000 false registrations, they alleged.[76] For the *gaitanista* Liberals, participation meant collaboration in their party's own demolition, as they saw the government gradually destroying the bases for political competition. The antiparticipation line had won out by March 1948, and the Liberals left the first National Union.[77]

Less than a month later, the bogotazo made politicians realize that the system itself was at stake. The Violencia had seemed earlier a traditional, rural sort of partisan conflict; now it threatened to turn into something much more dangerous and immediate. Gaitán's death had removed the figure most menacing to the Conservatives (and to oligarchical Liberals). He was replaced as Liberal leader by Darío Echandía, a man of reserved charm, much less abrasive than Gaitán.[78] Against the desires of the CTC labor federation, Echandía led his party into the second National Union coalition the day after Gaitán's assassination. He received the key post of minister of the interior (*Gobierno*) in the Ospina government, with authority over the country's internal order. Liberals were named to other cabinet posts and various governorships. At lower levels in the administration a pattern of *cruce* ("crossover") was to be instituted. Ministers, governors, and mayors were to name secretaries of the opposite party—a way of giving both parties stakes in the system, with checks on each other.

The elements of both parties that composed the second National Union perceived consociational guarantees as the central problem of politics. The government spent most of its energies during 1948 on one key to that problem, electoral reform.[79] In 1947 the Liberal congressional majority had not supported Gaitán, who wanted electoral reform;[80] they felt confident of their dominance of the old system. By 1948 they were willing to give up the local electoral juries, most of which they controlled, in favor of municipal registrars, whose posts would be split between the two parties and rotated.[81] They agreed to a new registration of voters, with a new, impartial, national registrar. There was to be a National Electoral Court, composed of prestigious and moderate members of both parties, and congressional and municipal elections were to be postponed from March to June of 1949. Soon after the reform finally passed Congress, in December 1948, Ospina lifted the state of siege.

The second National Union came to an end a few months later, however, in May 1949, and the electoral engineering did not save democratic competition. One reason it failed was another reform that the government did *not* make, that of the police. There was no central control over the six different kinds of police forces that existed in the late 1940s.[82] By 1947 the Liberals had tried, unsuccessfully, to remove the control of governors and majors over their own police forces, which Liberals believed were used against them. The bogotazo in 1948, during which many of the police had joined the mobs, made clear that the traditional police system, based on partisanship and patronage, could threaten Conservatives as well.

No nonpartisan reorganization of the police resulted, however, despite a foreign technical mission sent to assist in the effort. Instead, the police were simply gradually purged of Liberals by the executive. A parallel kind of winnowing occurred within the Conservative party, as the more collaborationist, moderate officeholders were forced out in favor of more sectarian types.[83] Violence in the countryside escalated. Armed Liberal bands confronted Conservative *pájaros* and *chulavitas,* the departmental guards that the Liberals called the "political police."[84] Much of this violence from both sides must have been condoned and even actively supported by party elites.[85]

The factional character of the parties undermined the second National Union and subsequent attempts at convivencia. On the Liberal side the leadership situation was confused and competitive; no single figure could dominate the national party as a whole. Much of the weakness and vacillation of the Liberals during 1948 and 1949 can be traced to this. Echandía assumed leadership of the party-in-government but never established his hold over the party machinery throughout the country—the brokers and bosses, clienteles and *militantes.*[86] In government he faced great pressure from Liberals in the provinces, who felt themselves victims of governmental violence, either to protect them or to get out. He was never able to protect them, though he was interior minister, because he could not control the Conservative governors and mayors nominally under his authority. The Liberals eventually left the coalition in May 1949, over no great event but simply over the continued failure of the executive to institute the agreed-upon consociational cruce in several localities. With congressional elections approaching in June 1949, there was probably no other way the leadership could have held troops in line at the grass roots, where the party battle was most devastating.[87]

On the Conservative side, Mariano Ospina commanded the party-in-government as chief executive. He represented the party's "moderate" elements, those with some commitment to the system. He stood, in some sense, for the class interests of the oligarchy—as did the Liberals López and Santos, by this time—against the *país político,* those who could only understand the deepening conflict as a clash of party interests. Contrary to later Liberal allegations, his presidency is replete with evidence of a sincere desire for party cooperation.[88] If he could not make provincial officials responsive to Echandía, it was probably largely because he himself lacked authority over them; they were primarily loyal to Laureano Gómez.

Gómez dominated the Conservative party machinery from 1939 on. Despite his periodic absences from the country, he remained the *jefe único,* hero of the militants and friend of the uncounted *gamonales* who were the backbone of the party's electoral strength. He could not himself run for president in 1946, for fear of uniting the Liberals, but Ospina never threatened his hold over the party, even though he commanded all the political resources of the executive. The Conservatives were in opposition, in fact or in spirit, until the breakdown, and Gómez was the ideal opposition politician. As much as Ospina may have asked his officials to maintain institutional authority, Gómez was always able to appeal to their deeper loyalty to their party.

The bogotazo thrust the church back into politics more deeply than it had been since the civil wars of the nineteenth century. The archbishop's palace, the Nunciatura, the old *colegio* of LaSalle, and the Pontifical Bolivarian University of Medellín were all burned by the mob. In the continuing violence in the countryside priests were murdered and sanctuaries sacked. The church felt itself caught in a civil war waged by a people it was accustomed to considering, in its complacent triumphalism, *"culto y cristiano."*

In its reactions, the church was divided within itself. A significant part, the most visible, reverted, as in past crises, to alliance with the Conservative party. The violence was not for them so much a threat to be overcome as an opportunity to conquer; death to terror and to enemies of the church. At the grass roots there were *párrocos* who mobilized their flocks against Liberals, who called for holy war, who swore "safe-conduct" passes for certified Conservatives in zones of violence.[89] They found considerable support among their bishops, led by Miguel Ángel Builes of Santa Rosa de Osos. Builes, in his Lenten message of 1949, called the Liberal party "communist... the enemy of Christ and his Church." No Colombian, he said, could at the same time be a Catholic and a Liberal. He was joined by many of his fellow bishops in forbidding Catholics to vote for Liberal candidates in the 1949 congressional elections.[90]

The archbishop, Ismael Perdomo, led the forces that opposed this polarization. He encouraged the clergy who attempted to mediate between the warring parties and to minister to the sick and needy. He forbade priests to issue safe-conducts or even to mention party in sermons or sacraments.[91] "The immense majority of Conservatives and Liberals," he wrote in his April 1949 pastoral, "... defends the same creed, is educated under identical moral norms, and feels equal veneration for the spiritual jurisdiction of the Catholic religion."[92] With a principal episcopal ally, the bishop of Manizales, Luis Concha Córdoba (significantly, later to become Archbishop of Bogotá under the National Front), Perdomo had good political, as well as religious, reasons for his stand. In 1949 he already understood the threat the Violencia posed to the institutional church. He perceived that it could be torn apart if convivencia between the parties—guarantor of the whole public order with which the church identified—were not preserved.

Although Perdomo moved the Episcopal Conference gradually to his view, the church, on balance, probably made some contribution to breakdown.[93]

The Collective Pastoral of 3 October 1949 and the archbishop's final plea for peace on 23 October had no visible effect on the course of events.[94] That triumphalist part of the church represented by Builes, on the other hand, fed the Violencia. They reactivated the traditional cleavages separating the parties, which undoubtedly exacerbated local conflict. It is important to note, however, that this invocation of the old místicas does not seem significantly to have affected elite relationships at the political center during the breakdown. The church was not the controverted symbol between them it had been in the past century. Indeed, the Liberals made clear both in the nomination of Echandía and in private negotiations in October 1949 that they accepted the public role of the church as one of the common principles shared by the parties.[95]

For the army, the bogotazo gave added impetus to a politicization that had begun earlier. The military as an institution was created during the long Conservative hegemony (1886–1930). In the 1930s and 1940s, Liberal governments had tried in various ways to neutralize its Conservative sentiment by creating the new National Police, by favoring Liberals in promotions, and above all by emphasizing its nonpartisan professionalism. López praised the army for remaining loyal during the attempted coup of 1944 and stressed that the large number of (Conservative) officers retired were being punished strictly as individuals (despite the fact that many so treated were in no way linked to the conspiracy).[96]

The army faced strong Conservative pressures intended to reinforce its long-standing partisan feeling. Conservative politicians were implicated in the Pasto coup of 1944 and the earlier conspiracy of 1936.[97] After the bogotazo, during Ospina's presidency, known Liberals were purged from the officer corps. Party polarization and the mounting violence, to which the police had contributed, pushed the army further into politics. By 1946 military men had been appointed to nearly one-quarter of the mayoralties in the country.[98] In 1948 one general was made minister of war, another was appointed head of the National Police, and several were made governors of departments.[99] In May of the following year three military men were included in the cabinet following resignation of all the Liberals (after requesting military replacements for various Conservative provincial officials).

Despite some professionalist resentment at this politicization, and despite rapid growth in the size of the institution,[100] the army played no autonomous role in the breakdown of 1949. Indeed, military loyalty to the regime had allowed Conservatives to persecute Liberals as harshly as they did without feeling the need to maintain consensus with other moderate civilians they might have felt if the army had been institutionally more self-confident. In the years after 1949 Gómez systematically tried to ensure that recruitment of officers and men was wholly Conservative (at the same time that junior officers were cooperating with Liberal guerrillas).[101] It was not until 1953 that military resistance to being used in partisan fashion finally pushed the army past the limits of its traditional deference to civilian control.[102]

Breakdown

The backdrop to the drama played out from May to November 1949 was in some ways unexpected. Traditional rural society was disintegrating, the political arrangements of generations were collapsing, and yet much in Colombian life went on as before. Government revenues were rising in a prosperous economy (see table 1). Per capita income was increasing at an unprecedented rate.[103] Exports were little affected through the end of 1949, either in the quantities that could be exported through the ports or in the receipts for the goods. Total kilo weight for exports was considerably higher in 1949 than ever before in Colombian history, and their value was more than twice that of 1945. Vital coffee exports, which composed between 70 and 80 percent of export earnings, were slightly lower in weight in 1949 than in some previous years, but receipts were the greatest ever, the result of a high market price (see table 3). If there had been a crisis in 1948, by 1949 the economy was bullish.[104] The collapse of 1949 was not economic but political.

The overriding concern in the process that took place between May and November was control of the national executive—retention for the Conservatives, recapture for the Liberals. Lacking the presidency, the Liberals used Congress as a power base. After leaving the coalition government in May, they were able to retain their congressional majority in the June elections.[105] From there they launched, in July, a series of "heroic projects" intended to

Table 3. Export Capacity and Earnings: Selected Years, 1940–49

Year	Value[a]	Index for (1) (1930 = 100)	Weight (millions of tons)	Index (1930 = 100)	Coffee, Value[a]	Coffee, Quantity (thousands of bags)
1940	126.0	121	3.57	115	—	—
1942	170.9	164	1.36	44	144.9	4,310
1944	227.1	218	2.99	97	164.7	4,924
1945	246.2	236	3.13	101	183.2	4,924
1946	351.8	338	2.92	94	274.4	5,149
1947	446.3	428	3.17	102	344.8	5,339
1948	504.9	484	3.10	100	412.1	5,588
1949	625.9	601	3.89	125	473.3	5,410

SOURCES: All information except for the last two columns is from *Anuario general de estadística, 1949* (Bogotá: DANE, 1949), table 129; data on coffee were calculated from idem, 1945, table 187, and idem, 1949, table 179.

[a] In millions of Colombian pesos.

enable them to win the next presidential election. To do this they had to circumvent a Conservative president and the system that gave him such great power. They introduced bills calling for nationalization of the police under congressional aegis, the elections of governors and mayors, the institution of a parliamentary style of cabinet, and above all, yet another electoral reform. This "counterreform" (as the Conservatives called it) in effect negated the hard-won accord of the previous year. It moved up the presidential election to November 1949 (instead of June 1950), a time when Congress was still in session and could, presumably, offer some protection against possible abuses. Moving up the date would, however, make it impossible to complete reform of the electoral register, which had been the major Conservative goal in the previous reform.

This offensive was intended by the Liberal leadership as an answer to the charges of "ingenuousness" that had been leveled at them by more partisan *copartidarios* during the second National Union.[106] It was accompanied by a new posture of truculent opposition—ranging from calculated slights of protocol when the president opened Congress in July to expressions of solidarity with the "political prisoners" jailed during the riots of the bogotazo.[107] While all of this was more a matter of style than of substance, it had very real consequences.

For Ospina and the Conservatives, what the Liberals played was a "two-faced game" (*un juego doble*).[108] On one hand they pretended to support democratic institutions, while on the other they fomented rebellion against legitimate authority for their own partisan purposes.[109] They were, at best, "semiloyal." But the Conservatives played a double game as well.[110] The government wanted to wear the cloak of constitutional authority while it allowed its provincial officials and police to try to perpetuate Conservative power by force. Gómez, who had returned to the country from Spain in June, denied that Congress had any legitimacy whatsoever and demanded that the president close it.[111] His son distributed whistles to drown out Liberal speakers in debates. Both sides were guilty of trading on the authority of their institutional bases, thereby undermining whatever autonomy those structures possessed. They were less and less institutions with values of their own, arenas where the parties could resolve differences, and more and more instruments subordinated to "higher" (i.e., partisan) ends.[112]

The eminently political issue of the electoral "counterreform" was debated in constitutional terms (thereby reserving the ultimate decision to the Supreme Court, one of Linz's "neutral powers"). The Conservatives contended that the law it affected, the electoral law of 1948, was a code and required a two-thirds congressional majority for amendment. The Liberals, with less than such a majority, held that the previous reform was an ordinary law and its amendment required only a simple majority plus one. The law was passed by Congress at the end of August with a simple majority and vetoed by Ospina a few days later.

While conflict occurred in the legislature and between Congress and the president, the process Linz calls "the reduction of the arena" had already begun. Moderates interested in achieving convivencia between the parties had begun to realize that the formal, public sites were inadequate. A bipartisan "Pro-Peace Committee," with strong representation from business and financial elites (and the blessing of the archbishop of Bogotá), took the first step in mid-August.[113] On 23 August Ospina responded to them by sending out a general statement of principles, presumably a basis for discussion. He asked that, while conversations were being held, Liberals hold up electoral reform, then being debated. The Liberals saw no definite guarantees to them in the president's message and believed the reform would strengthen their bargaining position. They put it through, and it was vetoed.

On 6 September Ospina told the National Conservative Directorate that he would accept the Liberal electoral reform if it were held to be constitutional by the Supreme Court. His stand was rejected by the *laureanista* directorate, which attacked, both in Congress and in public posters, all other Conservatives who declared themselves in favor of an acuerdo.[114] Ospina went further on 12 September and offered the Liberals a bipartisan Commission of Guarantees charged with examining the state of the country, particularly the activities of "lower authorities" of the government. But the shooting of the Liberal deputy, Gustavo Jiménez, on 8 September, had embittered party relations. Senate Liberals rejected the president's offer and repassed the electoral reform on 13 September. But informal conversations continued.

On 23 September, in what was openly a straight party vote, the Supreme Court accepted the constitutionality of the new Liberal electoral reform. Gómez's *El Siglo* called the court "a contemptible political committee,"[115] but the presidential election was fixed for 27 November. The dialectic of events public and private then developed very rapidly, the two spheres spilling over into one another. The pressures eventually proved too great for the crisis mechanisms of oligarchical democracy, but the defenders of the system made one last attempt to save it.

On 7 October Ospina proposed a sweeping constitutional reform, rather like the one on which the subsequent National Front (1958–74) would be based. Presidential elections would be postponed for four years, with the country ruled in the interim by a bipartisan four-man government council. The Supreme Court, Council of State, and the Electoral Court would be shared equally between the parties, and a two-thirds majority would be required to pass legislation. The reform was discussed privately between four party leaders: Gómez and Urdaneta Arbeláez for the Conservatives, López and Echandía for the Liberals.[116] The first stage of these conversations (another of Linz's "small c's") failed.

The proposal must have been difficult for the Liberal leaders to take entirely seriously. It did not come from Ospina directly but was relayed through Gómez, who later clearly indicated his disagreement with it. Though an apparent concession from the government, it was contradicted by other evidence at about the same time of hardening partisanship, as Gómez exerted his influence more and more directly. At the end of September the key Interior Ministry was given to a hard-line laureanista (a former editor of Gómez's *El Siglo*). On 2 October the governors of six departments were replaced with (in the words of a Conservative commentator) "the most radical personages that could be found in the Conservative party."[117] On 7 October, the same day Ospina's proposal was made, the new Interior Minister on his own initiative retired one Liberal general from the general staff, sent another to Europe, and promoted the notorious anti-Liberal, Gustavo Rojas Pinilla.[118]

The Liberals were confused about the best course. On one hand the "heroic projects," which were still in the legislature, suggested that the party saw defeat as almost inevitable. They implied that only extraordinary steps, which broke with the institutions of oligarchical democracy, could preserve a Liberal victory.[119] But in a contradictory way the Liberals also seemed overly confident. They had, after all, left the government before the congressional elections in June and had won them anyway; surely things could get no worse. "There is no reason to doubt victory," Carlos Lleras Restrepo told a party meeting.[120] The later official party report passes very quickly over this first stage of discussions, in early October, noting simply that "no resolution was reached" and that López called the presidential arrangement "dictatorship by covenant."[121] It may well have been the Liberals who torpedoed agreement at this point, because they thought they could win or because any partisan course—fighting the election or even "retiring"—would at least unite the deeply divided party, while another coalition with the Conservatives threatened to tear it apart from within. They seemed caught between two opposed postures in a crisis in which the rules were rapidly changing.

The situation became increasingly clear after the nomination of Gómez as the Conservative standard-bearer on 12 October. The Liberals finally realized that their only hope, short of revolution, lay in some kind of accord; the Conservatives did not want one. The conversations were renewed, now enlarged to include four more leaders (Lleras Restrepo among them). The Conservatives stalled, making and breaking several appointments. Finally the Liberals decided to make the whole matter public. On radio on 21 October Echandía presented a "peace formula" which closely corresponded to Ospina's earlier proposal. The Pro-Peace Committee, accepting the formula as a solid base for progress, asked the president to mediate a truce between the parties.

This Ospina attempted to do, naming on 24 October a bipartisan committee of senators who were also members of their respective party directorates to study the Echandía plan and to report to him in two days. But on 22 October the police had made an unprovoked attack on the Liberal headquarters in the city of Cali, killing twenty-four and wounding sixty.[122] On 23 October the national electoral registrar, a distinguished moderate Liberal, protested to the government that local violence made his task impossible and that the upcoming election would be a "bloody farce."[123] On 24 October the Council of State (another "neutral power") was consulted by the government about declaring a state of siege. It replied in the negative, in a party vote, blaming much of the violence on the government's own officials.[124] On 26 October the Liberal members of the bipartisan committee on Ospina's proposal suggested an agreement including not only constitutional mechanics but also broad principles shared by the two parties (e.g., the special place of the Catholic church in Colombian society). The Conservatives did not sign, finally arguing that the decision rested not with them but with Laureano Gómez.[125]

There were other eleventh-hour attempts to reach some accord (including a personal call by López on Gómez at his home), but the die was cast. On 28 October Lleras Restrepo announced on the floor of the Senate that the Liberals were withdrawing from all the bipartisan electoral machinery, from the national to the local level, and breaking off all relationships, even personal ones, with all Conservatives:

No relation will we have from now on with the members of the Conservative party; while they do not offer us a different Republic, guarantees that put an end to this infamy, the relations between Liberals and Conservatives, already broken in the public sphere, must be so also in the private sphere as well.[126]

On 29 October and again more emphatically on 2 November Gómez publicly rejected any possibility of an accord.[127]

Facing the impending state of siege, the Liberals were desperate. They came to the decision, formalized in their statement of 7 November, to abstain entirely from the election. They explicitly denied any legitimacy to the government that came to power in them:

Colombian Liberalism will never recognize as legitimate, in any form, the result... and declares that the electoral farce that they intend to carry out on the 27th of November will never give anyone the right to exercise power with valid title nor to be obeyed nor respected by a free people.[128]

There were dark threats about a battle just beginning and fights to the death.[129] The Liberals laid their case before the United Nations in New York, and in the Colombian Congress they prepared to impeach the president. Ospina's reaction on 9 November—the declaration of state of siege, the closing of Congress and the provincial legislatures, the banning of public meetings, and the censorship of press and radio—formally established that the oligarchical democracy was at an end.

Need this have happened? What, in the last analysis, caused the conversations between the parties to fail? Are there any conditions under which they might have produced an accord? And when no agreement could be reached, did the Liberals have no choice but to abstain? Could they have gone to the polls? These are questions for which there are no definitive answers, but in historical retrospect, some plausible guesses can be made.

The only way that informal negotiations might have worked would have been if moderates, committed to the defense of the system, had been able to control both parties. The informal, factional structure of the parties— accompanied by the depth of party identification—made this very difficult. Factionalism within the parties—rather than the existence of multiple separate parties—blurred distinctions between who was and was not loyal to the system. Factions did not put forth competing programs, did not represent recognizable social groupings. Claiming only to act in the "true interests" of the larger party, "disloyal" extremists always knew they had a great resource in the traditional partisan loyalties of the masses. The organizational weaknesses of the parties—particularly under conditions of the Violence—allowed such forces considerable security from any real discipline.[130]

On the Conservative side all these forces were concentrated in Gómez, who worked long and assiduously to put himself into the presidency. He was the unquestioned leader of the party machinery. His weak support for the institutions of democracy had long been evident, not only in his flamboyant encomiums to the Spanish *Falange* but in his deeds. It was Gómez who was ready to give up democracy during the bogotazo in 1948 in favor of a military junta and who left the country immediately when Ospina resolutely remained in office.[131]

It was Gómez who sabotaged all efforts by Ospina to achieve convivencia with the Liberals.[132] It was Gómez's *El Siglo* that editorialized, on the eve of the elections, "We have not destroyed the myth of Liberal majorities in order to halt in a whirlpool of words. . . . We look not for peace but for victory."[133] It was Gómez who stood behind the Conservative National Directorate in October 1949 and proclaimed, six weeks before the election: "let the nation be saved, though democracy be lost in the saving"[134] Democracy was probably not a great historical evil for Gómez, as more ideologically inclined commentators sometimes argue. He once said of himself: "I don't know how to do anything but foul things up" (a somewhat euphemistic rendering of *poner pereques*).[135] Democracy, in 1949, was simply in his way.

There is still the question, however, of why he got his way. Ospina gave many signs throughout his presidency of wanting to preserve intact the system he had inherited. In addition, he had good reason to fear and dislike Gómez, who had deserted him in April 1948, in his moment of greatest need. But when the sticking point was reached, in September and October 1949, Ospina capitulated. His radical initiative of 7 October might have found a much more positive response from the Liberals if he had not preceded it by naming hard-line laureanistas to the Interior Ministry and six governorships. If he had been able, at that point, to name military officers to those positions—as he had done in his cabinet before the June congressional elections—the Liberals would have been much more persuaded of his neutrality. By taking away with one hand what he had given with the other, Ospina undercut those within the Liberal party who wanted somehow to save the system.

Assuming that he did share that desire, why could Ospina not handle Gómez? Why, with all the resources of the presidency at his disposal, was he unable to control the Conservative party? Aside from personal factors, the answer is in part that he could *not* command all the resources of the presidency. Liberal control of Congress and many of the provincial and local assemblies would not allow him to be as partisan as he might otherwise have wished. He chose a strategy of conciliation and coalition. What this meant in very concrete terms was that Liberals demanded and received much of the patronage available at all levels. Ospina could not deliver the administrative spoils that parties were accustomed to receiving upon conquest of the executive. He faced continuous pressure from within his own ranks. He was undermined as party leader by his position as coalition president.[136]

He was also undercut by the Liberals. Their implicit denial of his authority as a "minority president" did nothing to facilitate his potential for arbitration between the parties. More directly, their whole strategy of the electoral counterreform played into the hands of the most sectarian elements in the Conservative party. It moved up the date of the election and prevented a thorough, neutral renovation of registration. It said to the Conservatives, in effect, that the game would be played under the rules the Liberals had written over four successive governments, which included a generous cushion of fictitious registrations.[137] Ospina, who ultimately accepted the Liberal counterreform, was unable to protect his party through the laws. If they wanted to win the presidential election, the Conservatives had strong incentives to use more direct methods to eliminate what they regarded as a "phantom majority."

For the Liberal leadership, the "heroic projects" offensive represented an attempt to build the most militant strategy possible within the limits of the constitution. Still directed essentially toward winning power through the election, it was intended to answer those within the party who urged armed insurrection. But the leadership could maintain neither control of the party nor confidence in the president. It could not bring itself to condemn manifestations of Liberal disloyalty (in Linz's sense), but neither could it stand by, ultimately, as its fellow party members were persecuted by the police and army.[138] At the end of October 1949, as the last interparty negotiations collapsed, as reports of preelectoral violence reached the capital, party loyalty prevailed:

How are we going to accept being called tomorrow to erect national *convivencia* upon this bloody base? No! There will not be *convivencia* this way; because the dead upon which one tried to build it would rise to cry out to the Liberal leaders, "Don't be cowards! Don't be so accommodating! We perished for the ideas that you defended;

we fell in the battle to which you invited us. Over our dead bodies and the grief of our memory one cannot make a pact with the supreme author of the deed. . . ." Our fellow party members who are falling under the hail of bullets and daggers are not victims of isolated individuals but victims of a party and of a system.[139]

It was not sheer humanitarianism, of course, that made the Liberal leaders decide to abstain, but realistic political calculation. With no representation in the electoral machinery, they were defenseless at the polls. If the Conservatives were to eliminate their majority by brute force, better not to lend the undertaking the legitimacy of their participation. Despite their frequently radical, sectarian rhetoric, the Liberal leaders put little that was concrete behind it.[140] Thus, when agreement could not be reached with the Conservatives, revolution was really no alternative to abstention.

Democracy broke down in Colombia in 1949 because the mechanisms upon which it rested were too informal, personalistic, and narrowly based. When governmental institutions offered no solution in a crisis, leaders from the two parties had to find some new basis for ad hoc consensus. This was a typically oligarchical mechanism, created in simpler times in a much less mobilized society. During the National Union period, "conversations among gentlemen" produced pacts between the parties in August 1947, April 1948, and April 1949.[141] None of them had any lasting effect, and the last efforts, which took place between August and October of 1949, did not even result in documentary agreement. The weight of saving the whole system rested on a few men, with uncertain control over their own subordinates and fellow elites,[142] in conditions of considerable general violence.[143] When the Liberals broke off personal relations with Conservatives at the end of October—even before the declaration of abstention and the state of siege—the last fragile support for oligarchical democracy was removed.

Reestablishing Democracy

Following the loss of democracy in November 1949, Colombian politics went through three phases before the National Front was installed in August 1958. The first consisted of the remainder of Ospina Pérez's term and the presidency of Laureano Gómez, from 1950 to 1953. It was a period of increasing violence and deepening dictatorship. It was ended by a widely welcomed military coup, led by Gustavo Rojas Pinilla. In this second phase, from 1953 to 1957, Rojas gradually alienated virtually all those who had exercised power in the previous regime and failed to establish an alternative base for his own authority. After lengthy negotiations, leaders of the political parties assumed the leadership of the opposition to Rojas and ousted him in May 1957.

In the third and final phase, presided over by a military junta from May 1957 to August 1958, the parties reestablished their former primacy in politics. A national plebiscite in December 1957 overwhelmingly endorsed the consociational National Front, which shared all legislative and administrative posts equally between the parties while alternating the presidency. Despite an abortive military coup in May 1958, a refurbished version of oligarchical democracy was successfully reinstalled by the presidency of Alberto Lleras Camargo (1958–62). Whatever its manifold faults and weaknesses, it endured, throughout its constitutional term of sixteen years, until 1974.

What explains this remarkable reincarnation? In the years from 1950 to 1958 both Gómez and Rojas—supported by significant elements within the church, the military, and the Conservative party—attempted to create new corporatist alternatives to oligarchical democracy. There were others who believed the Violencia could be made the catalyst for social revolution. They all failed. What enabled the politicians of the two parties to reconstruct the old game, very much on their own terms? And what brought them together in a common effort after the bitter divisions that led to breakdown?

The central social phenomenon of the period was the Violence. Although even today its historiography remains confusing and incomplete, the ways in which the Violence was understood and the way it affected contemporary events are fairly clear.[144] The dialectic of Liberal support for the guerrilla rebels and Conservative government repression had produced a situation, by the early 1950s, that had escaped from the hands of the political parties. Violence spread and intensified. Despite official optimism, government efforts to control it were of no avail. It increasingly took on the character of an incipient social revolution, a danger against which Alfonso López began to warn in 1952.[145] Rojas Pinilla offered amnesty to those who would lay down their arms, and for some time in 1953 and early 1954 hostilities lessened.

There was a sharp economic downturn in mid-1954, as world coffee prices plummeted, and the Violence flared up again. Pressures for a return to normalcy and to the previous regime began to appear among economic elites, who previously had had little incentive for opposition to either the Gómez or Rojas governments. Although the rural guerrillas never achieved a self-sustained revolutionary insurrection or even a unified command, they were a continuing source of disorder and insecurity in society. The army alone could not eliminate them. In the face of this failure, the arbitrary actions of the Rojas government in the cities—against the parties, newspapers, unions, students, and church—became progressively less tolerable. The return to oligarchical democracy was in part the result of the failure of other kinds of government to solve the fundamental social problem of the era.

There was also a decisive shift within the central social institutions that had previously been, in Linz's term, only "semiloyal." The church had nursed a long hostility to the Liberal party. It was, at best, divided and wavering in its support of democracy. But in the 1950s, the church tried to maintain some autonomy from both Gómez and Rojas, despite the fact that both courted it assiduously. With its traditional *Realpolitik,* the church accepted the Rojas government after the coup of 1953, and in Gómez's choleric reaction from exile in Spain, it may have recognized more clearly than ever before the dangers of close identification with any partisan force.[146]

The church began to become a more coherent, national organization in the course of the 1950s. The Jesuits pushed forward initiatives in several new fields of social action, notably the UTC labor federation. The National Bishops' Conference self-consciously examined contemporary events and their implications for the church's whole mission. The continuing Violence destroyed its triumphalist pride in a people *culto y cristiano* and threatened its institutional existence with the specter of revolution. It became specifically alienated from Rojas, who had fired on student demonstrators from the Jesuit Javeriana University, challenged the UTC with his own labor federation, and tear-gassed a packed Mass on Palm Sunday. The church was squarely behind his overthrow in May 1957. More fundamentally, it gave full support to the National Front, which, besides enshrining the church as the "religion of the nation," also guaranteed future Liberal governments. With an institutional coherence absent heretofore, it gave a significant endorsement to oligarchical democracy.[147]

The military had traditionally put a low value on its own status and competence vis-à-vis civilian politicians.[148] Professionalization had complemented this attitude by explicitly defining institutional functions within a limited sphere. Populist politics and the spread of the Violencia had challenged that valuation. As politics became more partisan, the army became more politicized; as politics became more violent, the army became more important. Its institutional professionalism threatened by Gómez's overt partisanship, the army under Rojas felt called upon to deliver the nation from the tragedy of its party hatreds.

That it was not able to do, in part because it was badly led. Rojas began by making the army the primary guarantor of order. He incorporated the police into its structure—neutralizing a key instrument of the old partisanship—and used the army initially as a broker between existing political forces. But he failed when he tried more actively to realign the bases of the polity. His quasi-Peronist "Third Force," characterized by a mixture of populism and corporatism, frightened almost all those who had benefited from oligarchical democracy without ever gaining the organizational strength to resist them. At the same time Rojas's personalist stance, with its cronyism and corruption, threatened the institutional unity of the armed services.[149] As civilian opposition grew and the Violencia continued, the officer corps came to believe that Rojas himself was a major cause of disorder. The junta that removed him in 1957 saw itself as a surgeon and then as a caretaker: order was primarily a political problem and the military would need party politicians to solve it.[150] In return, officers received assurances that any failings or excesses committed by the army in the past would be considered Rojas's personal responsibility, not that of the military institution.[151] The army and the National Front needed each other.

The National Front was the product of negotiations between the two historical parties beginning in 1956. To get to that point, politicians on both sides had to learn to recognize, between 1950 and 1956, their common stake in oligarchical democracy. In the early years Ospina and Gómez rebuffed the attempts of the Liberals to begin a return to democracy by reconvening Congress. By 1952, when police stood by while urban mobs burned down the offices of the Liberal daily *El Tiempo* and the homes of López and Lleras Restrepo, it had become clear that there would be no easy restoration. At the same time Gómez moved seriously toward installing a new corporatist order in his National Constituent Assembly (ANAC). This would have been a break not simply with liberal institutions but, perhaps most importantly, with the historical presumption of oligarchical politics against *continuismo*. Gómez's corporatist constitution was perceived as a thinly disguised means of keeping himself in power. It created opposition not only among the demoralized Liberals but—more dangerously—within his own party of government, above all from Ospina Pérez. Anti-laureanista Conservatives were a key support for the coup of 1953.[152]

Rojas frightened oligarchical politicians with his Peronist gestures and his attempts to bypass the parties altogether and forge a new kind of mechanism linking "the people" directly with the armed forces. But it was probably his determination to remain in office, his continuismo, that contributed the critical mass to the coalition that ousted him. Construction was begun by Alberto Lleras Camargo, the old López protégé, and Laureano Gómez.[153] Lleras used his prestige as a figure above the divisive intraparty battles of the 1940s to assume the leadership of the Liberals in 1956. His predominance was made easier by changes in the party in the intervening years: the old gaitanistas had scattered; the labor movement had been split and debilitated; and, with the changes in the Violencia, paramilitary forces were no longer key cadres to return the party to power. On the other side Gómez, surprisingly, was the obvious counterpart. Any movement to restore oligarchical democracy would have to begin with a common party opposition to Rojas. But in 1956 the *ospinista* Conservatives worked with and supported the Rojas government. Gómez, who still commanded great reserves of sentiment within his party, remained in exile in Spain.

From the Pact of Benidorm, which Lleras Camargo and Gómez signed in Spain in July 1956, to the so-called Civic Front statement of March 1957, to the Pact of Sitges of July 1957, there was a consistent development of the understandings that resurrected oligarchical democracy.[154] They represented lessons learned throughout the whole process of breakdown, both before and after November 1949. Their central theme was consociational guarantees. The principal cause of the sad plight of the nation, of the violence and dictatorship, was seen to have been each party's fear of exclusion and repression by the other.

Their understandings were reflected in the plebiscite of December 1957, overwhelmingly approved by the electorate,[155] which became part of the restored 1886 constitution. The parties were incorporated into the constitution itself, recognized as fundamental elements of the polity. A whole series of mechanisms implemented parity between the parties as a check on partisanship. Both parties were to receive half the membership of all legislative bodies, whatever their vote in a given district or election. A special majority of two-thirds was required for ordinary legislation. In addition, parity was to be maintained in the cabinet, the Council of State, the Supreme Court, governorships and mayoralties, and the whole administrative and bureaucratic apparatus of the executive.[156] These mutual checks within institutions were supplemented by those between them, notably in the effort to strengthen congressional (vs. presidential) controls over the executive (a lesson learned from the Liberal experience of the 1940s as well as from opposition to Rojas).

The National Front gave institutional substance to what, in the previous infra-democracy, had depended upon personal relationships. It represented a solution to one critical problem of the old oligarchical democracy, that of guaranteeing that neither party would be excluded from the stakes available in the state. What was most remarkable was that it represented little more than that. It was essentially an institutionalized elaboration of the old system, despite all the changes that had taken place in the society and the economy. The structural changes had unsettled politics and contributed to breakdown, but they never found the leadership or the organization to force a fundamental transformation. Those who aspired to channel the new currents in society fell before the combined forces of the oligarchical parties.

The Pact of Sitges had called the National Front "*convivencia* for a generation," an "ordered and respectable democracy for those to come." It did solve the most basic problem of the nation, political order; the Violence gradually came to an end. But it was a conservative victory. Minority guarantees were more important than majority rule. The majority Liberals coopted their Conservative opposition, in a sense, but at the potential cost of casting the system in concrete.[157] It remains for future historians to decide whether this form of "democratic convalescence" made possible—or actually prevented—a fuller democracy, with a broader distribution of the power and wealth of society.[158]

Conclusion: Alternative Perspectives on Breakdown

Oligarchical democracy broke down because traditional party solidarity was strengthened at the expense of identification with the system—but without a concomitant increase in party organization and discipline. It did not break down, despite the claims of most existing commentaries, primarily because of the malevolent intentions of one party or the other.[159] Nor did it collapse, with some inevitable determinism, simply because social and economic change were so massive.[160] Rather, breakdown was a complex process of interaction between the structures of society and politics that reduced the options of the political elite and undermined the mechanisms of consensus between them. It was shaped most fundamentally by the character of the instruments operated by political elites—above all, the parties—and the experiential rules of the game within which they tried to make them work.

This analysis owes much to Juan Linz's general theoretical framework. It encountered many correspondences to the sequence of events he suggests precede a breakdown. More broadly, it found in his emphasis on the *politics* of breakdown—the explicitly political institutions and arenas, the political actors and their perceptions—the most persuasive explanation for why breakdown occurred in Colombia.[161] Thus this case study lends plausibility to Linz's scheme both by being consistent with it and by finding it demonstrably more useful than various alternative approaches to why breakdown occurred. Several of those rejected alternatives should be considered briefly here.

One perspective increasingly in use in studying Latin American politics is class analysis. A class-oriented interpretation might see breakdown as the result of pressures on the system from below, from masses mobilized by the modernization of the 1930s and 1940s whose needs (or "demands") were not met within the oligarchical democracy. The political expression of these pressures would be populism, and its instrument, Gaitán. The defeat of his social and economic reforms in 1947 and his assassination in 1948, in such a view, unleashed the tremendous popular frustration that became the Violencia. In confronting this popular rebellion, the ruling class was divided between strategies of cooptation and of repression. The breakdown, class analysts would argue, was the result of the failure of the ruling class to unite to protect their common interest.[162]

Such an interpretation would be most plausible if oligarchical democracy had collapsed in 1948, following the bogotazo, and not 1949. Significant inflation accompanied the gains in real wages in 1946 and 1947. When inflation accelerated in 1948, as real wages fell, there were very sharp increases in the cost of living in March 1948 in the major cities (see table 4).[163] The urban rioting that broke out all over the republic following Gaitán's death unquestionably expressed genuine popular suffering and anger against the system. It was the high point of populism, if populism is understood as a class phenomenon.[164] From that point on it declined rapidly as a significant force in politics. The gaitanista movement had been largely personalist, but now the *persona* was removed. Perhaps it was also undercut by the improving economy in 1949, when the material conditions of the masses were getting better (see table 4). The demands pressed from below on Liberal leaders in the second

Table 4. Cost of Living and Real Wages, 1940–50

	1	2	3	4	5	6
	Cost of Living Index, Working Class		Real Wage Index, Working Class			Real Salary Index, Nat'l Govt. Employees (1961 = 100)
Year	Bogotá (1937 = 100)	Medellín	Manufacturing		Industrial/Service	
1940	—	—	102	102	—	77
1941	113	99	101	100	—	80
1942	123	106	101	101	—	100
1943	142	124	107	108	—	86
1944	171	139	106	107	—	n.a.
1945	191	162	108	110	—	n.a.
1946	208	187	112	115	107	n.a.
1947	246	218	118	120	110	93
1948	287	262	109	112	107	89
1949	306	278	116	120	124	104
1950	—	—	114	119	142	98

SOURCES: Data for columns 1 and 2 from *Anuario general de estadística, 1945* (Bogotá: DANE, 1945), table 187; idem, 1949, tables 180 and 185. Data for columns 3, 4, and 6 from Albert Berry and Miguel Urrutia, "Salarios reales en la industria manufacturera y en el sector gobierno, 1915–1963," in *Compendio de estadísticas históricas de Colombia,* ed. Miguel Urrutia and Mario Arrubla (Bogotá: Dirección de Divulgación Cultural, Universidad Nacional de Colombia, 1970), tables 13 and 15. Data for column 5 from Economic Commission for Latin America (ECLA), *The Economic Development of Colombia,* vol. 3 of *Analyses and Projections of Economic Development* (Geneva: United Nations, 1957), table 75.

NOTE: Except where noted, 1938 = 100. Column 4 index includes various government-guaranteed fringe benefits (*prestaciones sociales*) not taken into account in column 3. Columns 3 and 4 apply to manufacturing workers in the departments of Cundinamarca, Boyacá, Norte de Santander, and Santander. The majority of the sample was probably drawn from Bogotá (Cundinamarca).

National Union coalition (April 1948–May 1949) were political in nature, not social. They concerned above all the need for protection from partisan government persecution (hence, the call for electoral and police reform). The Violence could never have taken on the scope it did if there had not been significant earlier social change, but in 1948 and 1949 it was still an escalation of the traditional party struggle more than any new kind of class warfare.

Events from 1950 to 1958 confirm the weakness of class as an explanation for breakdown. The Violence never became a social revolution. It consisted essentially of groups of peasants killing one another. The antigovernment guerrillas were never brought together under a unified command; the Liberal rebels resisted incorporation with Communist bands and retained the "false consciousness" of their historical partisan identification. Class unquestionably became more prominent in the Violencia of the 1950s, but the phenomenon as a whole remained ambiguous and contradictory. The localization of violence in the prosperous coffee regions and the seizures of land by peasant bands suggest one thing; the absence of violence from regions which lacked historical grass-roots party competition (as on the Caribbean coast) and the use of peasants by one landlord to seize the lands of another suggest something quite different.[165] In general these years demonstrate that, whatever its very real sufferings, *el pueblo* never became a self-conscious class. In December 1957 it voted overwhelmingly to return to oligarchical democracy.

Another perspective on the Colombian breakdown would have given greater prominence to the role of ideology. According to such an approach, the fundamental source of the breakdown would be seen as the redefinition of partisan cleavage in the 1930s and 1940s in socioeconomic terms, away from the old issues which had been largely depoliticized. A simple version of this approach—based on many of the parties' explicit statements about each other—might see the two collectivities as representing diametrically opposing views about society, with breakdown simply the showdown between them. It would take the rhetoric of politicians as a serious indication of what each of the parties wanted and intended to bring about, given the opportunity. More concretely, it would assume that what was at stake in the struggle between the parties in the late 1940s was the choice between (in their opponent's eyes) a godless, foreign, socialistic mobocracy and a reactionary, repressive, theocratic dictatorship. A more sophisticated version of this interpretation might argue that, in the course of the political crisis, it was the most ideological elements *within* each of the parties that came to the fore, moving each party toward an increasingly ideological self-definition. In either case, polarization and breakdown would be seen as the result of the ideological stakes each party had in the political game.

Political "ideology" implies a fairly coherent body of ideas about the social purposes of politics; it implies, furthermore, that those ideas significantly shape behavior and, more particularly, policy. If any force in Colombian politics should be understood in those terms, it is Laureano Gómez. His whole career as the leader of the Conservative party was shot through with visions of impending apocalypse.[166] No other politician—not even Gaitán— so consistently invoked ultimate ends and Manichean symbolism in his public discourse. His political life was a series of great moral crusades: against Yankee imperialism, against atheistic communism (Liberalism), against majoritarian democracy.

Yet, when he became president in 1950, he did not behave in a particularly ideological way. He did not embark immediately on the construction of a corporate, nondemocratic state. He did not even bother to apologize for his very successful campaign to attract American investment. He did favor a triumphalist Catholic church and persecution of Protestants; he did repress Liberals; he did rule as a dictator. But there was very little in his presidency to suggest a coherent plan or program. Most of what he did can be understood best as opportunism—he did what it took to put him in office and keep him there. What Gómez sought, ultimately, was not power for its social uses, but simply power for its own sake.[167]

Ideology played only a peripheral role in Colombian politics in the 1940s in general. Colombian politics had the appearance of "modern" politics elsewhere—contemporary Europe for example—with parties, organized interests, slogans of class. But the reality was more akin to politics in Renaissance Italy or classical Rome.[168] The operative groupings were more diffuse, the dominant motivations more particularistic, the characteristic style more private and traditional. The elites who excoriated each other so ferociously in public maintained personal relations in private—their *conversaciones de caballeros*—up until the breakdown itself. This atmosphere was encouraged by the lack of a social basis for true class or ideological politics. Like its nineteenth-century liberalism, Colombia's ideology did not grow organically out of indigenous conflict, but was imported from a different environment.[169]

The party factions sometimes clothed themselves in the rhetoric of ideology (for example, the "Left Command" of the 1949 Liberals), but for the most part they were known by personalist designations ("gaitanistas," "lopistas," "santistas," "laureanistas," etc.) after their leaders. Such groupings might well have represented different social interests in some general way, but it would be an overstatement to characterize their differences as ideological. They were not given to manifestoes or programs (in contrast, for example, to Chilean parties in the early 1970s). They did, however, have clear differences over tactical and strategic considerations and, above all, over who would enjoy the fruits of office.

Emotionally charged symbols and perhaps different mentalities did contribute to breakdown by reinforcing the *mística* of each of the parties. But it was ultimately identification with the band per se, devoid of any real ideological content, that mattered. This more traditional sort of identification lay behind the dialectic of the Violencia. The initial battles of 1946, which occurred at the lowest level of the system, principally involved the humble stakes of municipal patronage. Within little more than a year, violence had begotten more violence, in a kind of "defensive feud."[170] In a pattern of attack and revenge, of kill or be killed, the basis of solidarity (and safety) became partisan identification. It is romantic projection, unsupported by the known facts, to claim that the masses, who provided cannon fodder for the conflict, viewed it as a "holy war." It was not the revolutionary ideas of Liberal peasants that threatened Conservative peasants; it was their guns and machetes.[171]

Ultimately the best argument for emphasizing that political institutions and rules (rather than class or ideology) explain the breakdown of 1949 is the way democracy was reestablished in 1958. There were important changes, certainly, during the hiatus. The trauma of the Violençe made the value of order, for its own sake, apparent to virtually the whole society. It is significant, however, that the National Front represented (1) solutions that had been perceived (though not implemented) in 1949; (2) almost exclusively political guarantees, with no notable social character; and (3) an enduring settlement engineered by party politicians—in fact, even the same generation—intimately involved in the breakdown. This does not mean, necessarily, that there would never have been a breakdown if the Ospina plan of October 1949 had been accepted; it could have failed at some later point, just as the second National Union coalition had earlier. But the political content of the National Front, and the way the system was established by party politicians in 1957 and 1958, do suggest quite clearly that it was *political* factors (and political failures) that were central to the breakdown in 1948 and 1949.

Conclusion: Democracy and the Colombian Breakdown

Democracy in Colombia died as it had lived, oligarchical, and so it rose again. Founded in a society that comparative aggregate analysis would argue was unpropitious for its survival, it nevertheless worked for a considerable period of time. It broke down when it could not make the transition from its informal, diffuse, particularistic mechanisms to ones that were broader and more institutionalized. It was undone by the way modernization reactivated old problems on a scale unanticipated by the traditional rules. Colombia thus stands as an important case among a small number of democracies in societies with little modern differentiation—the oligarchical democracies.

Crisis in the system had to be handled oligarchically, by ad hoc agreement among party leaders. Elites committed to the system did exist in the 1940s and they understood very well the specific mechanisms that could have regulated their conflict.[172] Their failure tells us something about the limits of such political engineering. It can be vitiated if there are other leaders who lack such commitment to the system present, particularly if they are not clearly identifiable as "disloyal" and are able to use the same partisan identifications as the "loyal" leaders. More generally, political engineering encounters difficulty if there is competition and conflict among the top leaders within each of the negotiating collectivities.

To the degree that such competition exists, elites may not be able to control nonelites, neither masses nor middle-level brokers; but such control must exist before convivencia can be realized among leaders. Colombian democratic politicians, particularly the Liberals, showed many signs of insecurity in their party leadership. The problem was not simply, as Linz sometimes seems to imply, that "moderates" were lacking in courage or resolve. It was rather that, given the depth of partisan identifications, any conciliatory gesture could be the occasion of a deep split in the party or a repudiation of the leadership. On the other hand, the temptation to achieve party goals by domination rather than cooperation was high. Becoming the hegemonic "majority" was easy to envision when the only significant political cleavage simply divided the polity in two.[173] Trying to stay at the head of their own troops, anxious party leaders (especially the Liberals) may well have transferred the hostilities they felt toward internal challengers to a more acceptable target, the other party.[174]

Over the course of the oligarchical democracy, leaders had controlled followers essentially through a clientelistic system of concrete rewards. They had also been able to count on the traditional deference and apoliticism of much of the population.[175] Some of the new structures of incipient modernization—such as the trade unions—challenged these mechanisms. The Violencia destroyed traditional social controls. But none of the changes in the structure of politics was enough, ultimately, to effect a transition to a new level of organization. When oligarchical party elites reasserted their predominance over the new social forces by forming the National Front, they did so without any significant mass organization.[176] That oligarchical democracy survived is a tribute not only to the skill of these leaders but at least as much testimony to the weakness of the challenge they faced—the lack of explicit and organized alternatives to their system.[177] How much longer the system can continue on such foundations is an open question.

Another open question is the value of "democracy" for such a country as Colombia. There is a strong presumption among students of democracy that a democratic political system is fundamental to the realization of other social values, such as freedom, justice, and equality.[178] Clearly, democracy has not brought such blessings to Colombia in any great measure. It has not notably helped the country to identify and deal with its most important problems.[179] It has served to maintain stability in a social structure that the Catholic church, among others, has come to believe is highly exploitative and unjust.[180] In the breakdown of 1949 it was not clear even to elites, to say nothing of the masses, that a consociational democracy was preferable to various authoritarian possibilities of the Right or Left.

By 1957 it had become so. In the Hobbesian war of the Violencia, the value of order for its own sake became apparent. The National Front did bring about basic social peace, in a society that had long demonstrated an extraordinary capacity for unrevolutionary self-destruction. It did so with a political system of relatively low repressiveness. Latin America and the world have surely experienced many far worse regimes in the past twenty years. The oligarchical democracy is, at least, an open political system; it retains some capacity for change that has been lost in most of the rest of the continent. Whether Colombia can tolerate meaningful change will surely be tested in the near future. The results will be another piece of evidence as to whether "democracy" is a historically specific stage of Western political development or a more permanent, universal form of polity to which peoples will always aspire.

NOTES

1. John Gunther described Colombia in 1941 as "one of the most democratic and progressive nations in the Americas" (*Inside Latin America* [New York: Harper and Row, 1941], p. 161). Cf. the survey of "expert" opinion done by Russell H. Fitzgibbon, "Measurement of Latin American Political Phenomena: A Statistical Experiment," *American Political Science Review* 45 (1951): 517–23, which concluded that Colombia was the fourth most democratic country in the region in 1945.

2. The classic example of a more restricted, procedural definition is Joseph Schumpeter, *Capitalism, Socialism, and Democracy,* 2d ed. rev. (London: George Allen and Unwin, 1947), pt. 4. Recent works that stress the importance of participation for individual and social development are Peter Bachrach, *The Theory of Democratic Elitism* (Boston: Little, Brown, 1967), and Carole Pateman, *Participation and Democratic Theory* (Cambridge: Cambridge University Press, 1970).

3. Marxists have long argued that the conditions that can prevent free competition go much beyond overt force. Historically they pointed to the undemocratic nature of the control of information, an argument updated in sophisticated form by Herbert Marcuse, as in, e.g., (with Robert Paul Wolff and Barrington Moore, Jr.) *A Critique of Pure Tolerance* (Boston: Beacon Press, 1965).

4. The landmark article on the "requisites" of democracy (usually misread as the "prerequisites" for its creation) is Seymour Martin Lipset, "Some Social Requisites of Democracy: Economic Development and Political Legitimacy," rptd. in *Empirical Democratic Theory,* ed. Charles F. Cnudde and Deane E. Neubauer (Chicago: Markham Publishing, 1969), a very useful collection of the evidence on this and related questions.

5. Although voting for the presidency was made direct in 1910, the first election affected was that of 1914.

6. Colombian women first voted in 1957.

7. Before the late 1940s, the election campaign that involved the greatest violence against the opposition was that of the Conservative government of 1922. The Liberals produced a whole book of incidents, entitled *Los partidos en Colombia* (Bogotá: Editorial "Águila Negra," 1922).

8. The requirement that candidates adopt the label of one of the two traditional parties was an insignificant limitation in practice. The lack of party discipline made it possible for anyone

who wished to run to appropriate a Conservative or Liberal label. National Front governments defended themselves by force from revolutionary opponents, such as guerrillas. They did harass critics like Camilo Torres and may have deprived Rojas Pinilla of the presidency in 1970 by fraud. (The final margin was small and the trend of early returns reversed itself in middle-of-the-night counting—a scenario rather like that of Illinois in the U.S. election of 1960.) On the whole these governments permitted a comparatively wide range of civil liberties, though they became observably more arbitrary and repressive after 1970.

9. Such an analysis comes easily to those who study Latin America and are forced to reconcile the "instability" of its politics at one level with its many examples of continuity at another. The most influential description of the "Latin American political system" that exists beyond shifting appearances was Charles W. Anderson, *Politics and Economic Change in Latin America* (Englewood Cliffs, N.J.: Van Nostrand, 1967) chap. 4.

10. Dankwart Rustow emphasizes these specific historical circumstances in "Transitions to Democracy," *Comparative Politics* 2, no. 3 (April 1970): 337–63. A more general, comparative treatment of the creation of democracies is the sensitive and insightful study by Eric A. Nordlinger, *Conflict Regulation in Divided Societies,* Occasional Papers in International Affairs, no. 29 (Cambridge, Mass., Harvard University, January 1972).

11. The "rules of the game" as used here are imputed partly on the basis of expressed sentiments and partly on regularities in behavior. Such an analytical characterization attempts to go beyond the conscious norms of contemporary actors to include latent assumptions that later became manifest. It is not intended to describe an elite "political culture" (in the sense of general background dispositions) so much as an operative code growing out of the way political actors have perceived past problems and attempted to solve them. Cf. Daniel H. Levine, *Conflict and Political Change in Venezuela* (Princeton, N.J.: Princeton University Press, 1973) esp. pp. 231–54; and Philippe Schmitter, "O Sistema," in *Interest Conflict and Political Change in Brazil* (Stanford, Ca.: Stanford University Press, 1971), pp. 376–86.

12. Cf. Arend Lijphart, "Consociational Democracy," *World Politics* 21, no. 2 (January 1969): 207–25.

13. There were similar coalitions in the nineteenth century, of which the most important was the so-called National Party of Rafael Núñez in the 1880s. It brought together moderate elements of both parties around a new Conservative consensus, which was subsequently reflected in the 1886 constitution.

14. In 1909 an agreement was signed by key leaders of both parties that established a common set of principles on formerly divisive issues (e.g., the place of the church in national life). See Francisco de Paula Pérez, *Derecho constitucional colombiano,* 5th ed. (Bogotá: Librería Voluntad, 1967), pp. 230–31.

15. See Jesús María Henao and Gerardo Arrubla, *Historia de Colombia,* 8th ed. (Bogotá: Librería Voluntad, 1967), pp. 818–61 passim.

16. Jorge E. Rodríguez R. and William P. McGreevey, "Colombia: Comercio exterior, 1835–1962," in *Compendio de estadísticas históricas de Colombia* ed. Miguel Urrutia M. and Mario Arrubla (Bogotá: Universidad Nacional de Colombia, 1970), table 9, following p. 208. Coffee rose from 39 percent of export earnings in 1905 to 75–80 percent in 1924–26, after which oil also became a significant exchange earner.

17. Anderson, *Politics and Economic Change.*

18. Some 210,000 votes were cast in the 1856 presidential election, in which universal male suffrage prevailed. This figure represented perhaps 40 percent of the adult male population, certainly very high by world standards of the day. See David Bushnell, "Elecciones presidenciales colombianas 1825–1856," in Urrutia and Arrubla, *Compendio,* p. 310. On the origins of the parties and on electoral organization in this period, see Eduardo Santa, *Sociología política de Colombia* (Bogotá: Ediciones Tercer Mundo, 1964), pp. 39–70; Orlando Fals Borda, *Subversion and Social Change in Colombia,* trans. J. Skiles (New York: Columbia University Press, 1969), pp. 67–92; and Germán Colmenares, *Partidos políticos y clases sociales* (Bogotá: Ediciones Universidad de los Andes, 1968). Although corruption and fraud were commonplace, local electoral organization had continuing significance. See the good description by Helen Delpar in "The Liberal Party of Colombia, 1863–1903" (Ph.D. diss., Columbia University, 1967).

19. The 1876–77 conflict, for example, may have involved as many as 62,000 men, and the 1885 rebellion more than 50,000. See Luis Eduardo Nieto Arteta, *Economía y cultura en la historia de Colombia,* 2d ed. (Bogotá: Tercer Mundo, 1962), p. 383. Julio Holguín Arboleda, *21 años de vida colombiana* (Bogotá: Ediciones Tercer Mundo, 1967), p. 248, and William P. McGreevey, *An Economic History of Colombia, 1845–1930* (Cambridge: Cambridge University Press, 1971), p. 88, give lower estimates. A traditional *copla* from the nineteenth century runs: "In Colombia, that is the land/ of singular things,/ soldiers bring peace/ and civilians war". Quoted by Víctor M. Salazar, *Memorias de la guerra (1899–1902)* (Bogotá: Editorial ABC, 1943), p. 361.

20. Latin American parties in general have had a peripheral role in politics compared, say, to their European counterparts. See Robert Scott, "Parties and Policy-Making in Latin America," in *Political Parties and Political Development* ed. Joseph LaPalombara and Myron Weiner (Princeton, N.J.: Princeton University Press, 1966), pp. 331–67.

21. Edward Friedel and Michael F. Jiménez, "Colombia," in *The Urban Development of Latin America, 1750–1920* ed. Richard M. Morse (Stanford, Ca.: Stanford University Center for Latin American Studies, 1971), p. 62.

22. Alexander W. Wilde, "A Traditional Church and Politics: Colombia" (Ph.D. diss. Columbia University, 1972), chaps. 4 and 5. *Politics and the Church in Colombia* (Durham, N.C.: Duke University Press, 1979), is an expanded and revised version.

23. In Brazil or Venezuela, the military antedated political parties both as institution and as central political actor. See Ronald Schneider, *The Political System of Brazil* (New York: Columbia University Press, 1971), esp. chap. 2; Alfred Stepan, *The Military in Politics: Changing Patterns in Brazil* (Princeton, N.J.: Princeton University Press, 1971); Robert Gilmore, *Caudillismo and Militarism in Venezuela* (Athens: Ohio University Press, 1964); and Winfield Burggraaff, *The Venezuelan Armed Forces in Politics, 1935–1959* (Columbia: Missouri University Press, 1972).

24. See James L. Payne, *Patterns of Conflict in Colombia* (New Haven: Yale University Press, 1968), pp. 111–33, for an insightful analysis of the relation between the parties and the military, with a good short bibliography. See also Anthony Maingot, "Colombia: Civil-Military Relations in a Political Culture of Conflict" (Ph.D. diss., University of Florida, Gainesville, 1967); Richard Maullin, *Soldiers, Guerrillas, and Politics in Colombia* (Lexington, Mass.: Lexington Books, Heath, 1973); Francisco Leal Buitrago, "Política e intervención militar en Colombia," *Revista Mexicana de Sociología* 32, no. 3 (May-June 1970): 491–538.

25. There were reportedly attempts to have Conservative president Miguel Abadía Méndez call in the army in 1929 to prevent a Liberal government from coming to power in 1930. Abadía Méndez refused. See J. A. Osorio Lizarazo, *Gaitán: Vida, muerta, y permanente presencia,* 2d ed. (Buenos Aires: Ediciones Negri, 1952), p. 133. Of the various plots against Liberal governments between 1930 and 1946, the abortive Pasto coup of 10 July 1944 went furthest. President Alfonso López was held prisoner for several days, until it became clear that the army as a whole remained loyal. After this, however, the military was in some sense discredited and was doubly anxious to avoid intervention, despite Liberal overtures from 1949 on.

26. Cf. Merle Kling, "Toward a Theory of Power and Political Instability in Latin America," *Western Political Quarterly* 9, no. 7 (March 1956): 21–35.

27. Cited from Santa's *Sociología política de Colombia* (1955 edition), p. 73, by Germán Guzmán, *La violencia en Colombia: Parte descriptiva* (Cali: Ediciones Progreso, 1968), p. 358.

28. Malcolm Deas sees an important shift in this game with the great increase in central governmental resources that occurred beginning in the 1920s. See his rich, sensitive article on the structure and stakes of parties until the 1930s, "Algunas notas sobre la historia del caciquismo en Colombia," *Revista de Occidente* [Madrid] no. 127 (October 1973), pp. 118–40.

29. See Payne, *Patterns of Conflict,* pp. 51–73 and 185–237, for a provocative (though sometimes perverse) treatment of stakes and factions in Colombia. Payne estimated that posts based on merit comprised less than 4 percent of the total bureaucracy in the 1960s (p. 64).

30. Samuel P. Huntington, *Political Order in Changing Societies* (New Haven, Conn: Yale University Press, 1968), pp. 20–22.

31. Richard Neustadt, *Presidential Power* (New York: Wiley, 1960), Chap. 1.
32. See Fernando Guillén Martínez, *Raíz y futuro de la revolución* (Bogotá: Tercer Mundo, 1963), especially pt. 2, "Los modos de preferir."
33. The followings of the Conservative and Liberal parties were not fully comparable to, say, the Austrian *Lager* or the Weimar *Weltanschauungs gesinnungsgemeinschaften* because partisan identification did not reinforce a whole range of other social, economic, and status distinctions. Nevertheless, the strength of party identification down through society did make these followings the functional equivalent of Lijphart's "subcultures"—the vertical social groupings that had to be manipulated by elites to make consociational agreements work. See Lijphart, "Consociational Democracy."
34. The phrase is that of the nineteenth-century Conservative intellectual and president, Miguel Antonio Caro, himself often blamed for causing the 1895 civil war by his sectarian exclusion of Liberals from his administration. Certainly the most vivid and perhaps the most percipient description of Colombia's traditional political violence is in Gabriel García Márquez's magnificent novel, *One Hundred Years of Solitude*, trans. Gregory Rabassa (New York: Harper and Row, 1970).
35. See Orlando Fals Borda, *Campesinos de los Andes* (Bogotá: Facultad de Sociología, Universidad Nacional; Editorial Iqueima, 1961), pp. 260, 297–302. He writes of the village of Saucío, "open warfare caused each locality [within the area] to strengthen its internal political bonds as a way to survive in social conflicts. In this way, politics became for the *saucita* as important as life itself, since it was identified with his struggle for existence" (p. 299). See also Robert H. Dix, *Colombia: The Political Dimensions of Change* (New Haven: Yale University Press, 1967), pp. 213–14, where several other village-level studies on this point are cited. The feud, in the absence of any significant governmental penetration to most of the countryside, seems the most persuasive explanation of Colombia's singular pattern of vertical cleavage at the village level. Comparably intense party identification in other Latin American countries seems almost always to have had a regional basis—e.g., the Colorados and Blancos in Uruguay, the Apristas in Peru.
36. Even among the causes of the nineteenth-century civil wars, ideology was frequently less important than material stakes. See, e.g., Guillén Martínez, *Raíz*, p. 134. For a more general discussion of the nature of nineteenth-century political conflict, see Wilde, "A Traditional Church," pp. 132–41.
37. On "political decay" see Huntington, *Political Order*, chaps. 1, 4.
38. See Antonio García, *Gaitán y el problema de la revolución colombiana* (Bogotá: M.S.C., 1955), pp. 286–91, for a vivid description, and also *Los elegidos* (Bogotá: Tercer Mundo, 1967), a novel by Alfonso López Michelsen, son of the wartime president and himself president from 1974 to 1978.
39. Abelardo Patiño B., "The Political Ideas of the Liberal and Conservative Parties in Colombia during the 1946–53 Crisis" (Ph.D. diss., American University, 1954), p. 66: Gilberto Zapata Isaza, *¿Patricios o asesinos?* (Medellín? Editorial Ital Torino, 1969), pp. 119–20.
40. Maullin asserts, on the basis of an unpublished manuscript, that the coup attempt was jointly plotted by officers and Conservative politicians (*Soldiers in Colombia*, p. 58). Leal Buitrago, however, argues on the basis of his own interviews that the officers involved acted on their own initiative, reacting against what they regarded as López's politicization of the army. The president had some months earlier—amid constant rumors of coups—broken with civilianist tradition and appointed a trusted officer as his minister of war, ("Política e intervención," pp. 505, 533, n. 58).
41. This violence mirrored that which occurred in 1930–32, when Liberals replaced Conservatives in public administration. The major difference between it and that of the later period is that in the 1930s violence remained localized in only three departments and exhausted itself within a few years. Conservatives later claimed that it was the basis of their policy of abstention, but tactical considerations, primarily the need to allow Laureano Gómez to assert sole control over his badly divided party, were probably more important. On the party violence, see the good summary in Guzmán, *Violencia*, pp. 15–39, and Laureano Gómez's *Comentarios a un régimen*, 2d ed. (Bogotá: Editorial Centro, 1935). On the state of the Conservative party during this period, see Augusto Ramírez Moreno, *La crisis del partido conservador* (Bogotá: Tip. Granada, 1937) and the extremely valuable biography

of the Antioqueño Conservative politician, Fernando Martínez Gómez, *Don Fernando* (Medellín: Editorial Granamérica, 1963), by Pedronel Giraldo Londoño.

42. The interior minister's statement, interpreted as justification for repression, became a powerful cry of Liberals against any cooperation with Conservatives. The logic of the minister's full argument—as distinct from its political context—seems admirable enough on the face of it. See Rafael Azula Barrera, *De la revolución al órden nuevo* (Bogotá: Editorial Kelly, 1956), p. 292.

43. "Crisis" is used here in the sense employed by Douglas Chalmers in "Crisis and Change in Latin America," *Journal of International Affairs* 23, no. 1 [1969]: 78, i.e., to denote a period of emergency of which political actors are contemporaneously aware. This is in contrast to the usage of the influential Committee on Comparative Politics of the Social Science Research Council, which employs the term as equivalent to "structural problem." See, e.g., Leonard Binder et al., *Crises and Sequences in Political Development* (Princeton, N.J.: Princeton University Press, 1971).

44. Linz appears to define the "unsolvable problem" more narrowly, as one dealing with substantive policy and usually "created" in some sense by politicians. In Colombia the "unsolvable problem" was the problem of guarantees of the opposition and authority for the government—the problem of order itself.

45. "The die was already cast": "La suerte estaba ya echada..." (Carlos Lleras Restrepo, *De la república a la dictadura* [Bogotá: Editorial Argra, 1955] p. 306). The identical phrase is used to characterize this point at the beginning of November in two additional first-person accounts, that of the prominent laureanista Conservative, Joaquín Estrada Monsalve, *Así fué la revolución,* 2d ed. (Bogotá: Editorial Iqueima, 1950), p. 113; and that of the moderate Liberal congressman, Guillermo Fonnegra Sierra, *El parlamento colombiano* (Bogota: Gráficas "Centauro," 1952 [1953]), p. 250. These three accounts, with Azula Barrera, *De la revolución,* are all valuable for their insights into events and perceptions among the elite. So, too, is the political biography by Giraldo Londoño, *Don Fernando.* The most useful secondary accounts in English are John Martz, *Colombia: A Contemporary Political Survey* (Chapel Hill, N.C.: University of North Carolina Press, 1962), which draws heavily on contemporary journalistic sources; Vernon Fluharty, *Dance of the Millions* (Pittsburgh, Pa.: Pittsburgh University Press, 1957) by an author who was in Colombia for some of the events; Patiño, "Political Ideas," which also uses primary sources extensively; and Dix, *Colombia: Political Dimensions.*

46. Many authors could be cited, but Chalmers Johnson, *Revolutionary Change* (Boston: Little, Brown, 1966) is a convenient example. See, e.g., pp. 64–70, 106.

47. In addition to Linz one might list Huntington, *Political Order;* Nordlinger, *Conflict Regulation;* Rustow, "Transitions to Democracy"; Gabriel Almond, Scott C. Flanagan, and Robert J. Mundt, eds., *Crisis, Choice, and Change* (Boston: Little, Brown, 1973); John R. Gillis, "Political Decay and the European Revolutions, 1789–1848," *World Politics* 22, no. 3 (April 1970): 344–70; and Mark Kesselman, "Over-institutionalization and Political Constraints: The Case of France," *Comparative Politics,* 3, no. 1 (October 1970): 21–44.

48. Miguel Urrutia, a Colombian economist, argues that in 1913 there was probably less American capital in Colombia than in any other Latin American country. See *The Development of the Colombian Labor Movement* (New Haven: Yale University Press, 1969), p. 85. Between 1923 and 1929 U.S. investments increased from $4 million to $280 million; see J. Fred Rippy, *The Capitalists and Colombia* (New York: Vanguard Press, 1931), p. 152.

49. Colombia's per capita exports more than doubled in the 1920s, from 52.7 million pesos in 1922 to 132.5 million in 1928; see Urrutia, *Colombian Labor,* p. 84. The national budget increased from 43.5 million pesos to 107.5 million between 1923 and 1928, as the GNP grew at an annual rate of 7.3 percent between 1925 and 1929; see García, *Gaitán,* p. 241; and Dix, *Colombia: Political Dimensions,* p. 32, citing a Colombian economic plan.

50. The length of railroad track increased from 1,511 km. in 1921 to 3,122 in 1931 (still only a small fraction of the track at that time in Brazil, Argentina, or Mexico). Telephone line mileage increased from 5,095 in 1913 to 34,680 in 1927, while the number of phones went from 11,860 to 20,066; Fluharty, *Dance* p. 32.

51. ECLA figures, cited by Juan Luis DeLannoy and Gustavo Pérez, *Estructuras demográficas y sociales de Colombia* (Bogotá: CIS, 1961), p. 72.
52. The number of airline passengers increased from 6,685 in 1933 to 103,136 in 1944 to 775,812 in 1949. Air freight grew from 0.7 million kg. in 1933 to 12.6 in 1944 to 139.4 in 1949. See DANE (Departamento Administrativo Nacional de Estadística), *Anuario general de estadística* (Bogotá: DANE, 1949) The airplane also made the Bogotá dailies a national press for the first time.
53. ECLA (Economic Commission for Latin America), *Analyses and Projections of Economic Development; 3, The Economic Development of Colombia* (Geneva: United Nations, 1957), p. 369.
54. Cited in Dix, *Colombia: Political Dimensions,* p. 32.
55. ECLA, *Economic Development of Colombia,* pp. 11, 32, 33.
56. DeLannoy and Pérez, *Estructuras,* p. 93. Figures are actually for employment in the primary sector, but mining can for all practical purposes be ignored here.
57. DeLannoy and Pérez, *Estructuras,* p. 70. Camilo Torres pointed out that peasants sought the cities in these times for the same reason that they had in the Middle Ages: security. See "Social Change and Rural Violence in Colombia," *Studies in Comparative International Development* 4, no. 12 (1968–69).
58. DeLannoy and Pérez, *Estructuras,* p. 93.
59. Cited in Urrutia, *Colombian Labor,* p. 183, from a government labor census.
60. The best analysis is found in Francisco Leal Buitrago, *Análisis histórico del desarrollo político nacional, 1930–1970,* vol. 1 of "Estudio del comportamiento legislativo en Colombia" (Bogotá: Tercer Mundo, 1973). See also Dix, *Colombia: Political Dimensions,* and Fluharty, *Dance.*
61. Leal provides a brief but provocative description of what he calls the "oligarchical corporativist system" in *Desarrollo político,* pp. 48–52. A convenient survey of the most relevant structures created by the Liberals is given by Carlos Lleras Restrepo, "La obra económica y fiscal del liberalismo," in *El liberalismo en el gobierno,* vol. 2, *Sus realizaciones, 1930–1946,* ed. Plinio Mendoza Neira and Alberto Camacho Angarita (Bogotá: Editorial Minerva, 1946), pp. 9–80. On the coffee growers' federation, see Christopher Abel, "Conservative Politics in Twentieth-Century Antioquia (1910–1953)," (Latin American Centre, St. Antony's College, Occasional Paper 3 (Oxford, 1973), pp. 15–16.
62. See Lynton K. Caldwell, "Technical Assistance and Administrative Reform in Colombia," *American Political Science Review* 47, no. 2 (June 1953): 503–5. The best study of this development is a private document not for citation.
63. It may be significant that the National Federation of Coffee Growers, the most powerful economic interest group in the country, did not take part in the initiative by economic elites in August-October 1949, represented by the "Pro-Peace Committee." Mariano Ospina Pérez, who had been the president of the federation for four years, said in 1946, "The coffee industry is neither Liberal nor Conservative. . . . Party politics have never penetrated into the Federation of Coffee Growers" (cited by Hugo Velasco A., *Mariano Ospina Pérez* [Bogotá: Editorial Cosmos, 1953], pp. 81–82).
64. It should be pointed out explicitly that the concept "populism" is used differently in Latin America than elsewhere, particularly in that it refers to *urban* mass-based movements. See Torquato di Tella, "Populism and Reform in Latin America," in *Obstacles to Change in Latin America,* ed. Claudio Véliz (London: Oxford University Press, 1965); and Alistair Hennessey, "Latin America," in *Populism,* ed. Ghita Ionescu and Ernest Gellner (London: Weidenfeld and Nicolson, 1969). There has been much popular and polemical literature on "populism" in Colombia in recent years.
65. The first "Electoral Participation" column in table 2 is more meaningful than the second because of corruption. By the late 1940s registration substantially exceeded eligible population.
66. The greatest challenge by new parties to Liberal and Conservative electoral dominance was registered in the 1945 congressional election, when the Communists and all other parties together received 3.5 percent of the vote. See *Colombia política: Estadísticas 1935–1970* (Bogotá: DANE, 1972) p. 154.

To found a new party was seen in time as essentially a device to enhance one's power within one of the traditional parties. Compare, e.g., Liberal Jorge Eliécer Gaitán's UNIR (Unión Nacionalista Izquierdista Revolucionaria), 1932–35, and Conservative Gilberto Alzate Avendaño and Silvio Villegas' reactionary ANP (Acción Nacionalista Popular), 1936–39. A more recent example is that of the MRL (Movimiento Revolucionario Liberal) of Liberal Alfonso López Michelsen in the 1960s. Both Gaitán and López Michelsen were eventually Liberal presidential nominees (López becoming president in 1974). Alzate would have had a strong bid to a Conservative candidacy in the 1950s if Gómez had not been overthrown.

67. The distinction is made by Chalmers in "Crises and Change," p. 78.

68. See Urrutia, *Colombian Labor,* and the Communist account of Edgar Caicedo, *Historia de las luchas sindicales en Colombia* (Bogotá: Ediciones CEIS, 1971), chap. 3.

69. Calculated from Urrutia, *Colombian Labor,* p. 183.

70. The creation of the Jesuit-sponsored UTC labor federation in 1946, to parallel the Liberal-Communist CTC, seems to have had little immediate effect on Conservative perceptions or strategies. There was still much opposition within the party in the 1940s to any kind of labor organizing. Although Ospina's government tolerated the UTC, illegal under Law 6 of 1945, it did not extend legal recognition until late 1949. With its tactics of economic unionism, the UTC never became a political arm of the Conservative party in the way the CTC was to the Liberal party in the 1930s. See Urrutia, *Colombian Labor;* Abel, "Conservative Politics"; and James Backer, "La historia de las influencias de la Iglesia sobre el sindicalismo colombiano," *Razón y fábula* [Bogotá], no. 22 (November-December 1970), pp. 6–27.

71. Cited in García, *Gaitán,* p. 272. A table listing the proportion of ministries and governorships for each party and for the military, by year, from 1930 to 1958, is given in Leal, *Desarrollo político,* Appendix.

72. The Liberal dominance of the cities was augmented only slightly between 1933 and 1949, although it may have accelerated between 1946 and 1949. See Richard S. Weinert, "Violence in Pre-Modern Societies: Rural Colombia," *American Political Science Review* 60, no. 2 (June 1966): 341, table 1. The proportion of the population residing in the departmental capitals had grown from 31 percent in 1933 to 39 percent in 1951. (See DANE, *XIII Censo nacional de población* [*Julio 15 de 1964*]; *Resumen General* [Bogotá: Imprenta Nacional, 1967], p. 31.) But one should not exaggerate the demographic side of the "permanent minority" danger for the Conservatives. Registration continued much lower in the cities than the countryside. Urban registration constituted less than 19 percent of the total at the end of 1947. See DANE, *Anuario general de estadística, 1947* (Bogotá: Imprenta Nacional, 1948), pp. 732–33. Despite the visibility of the new urban populism, the game was still won or lost in the *campo.*

73. "I compare this moment in Colombia with that of Spain during the revolution of '34. I think that, as [it was] here, civil war is inevitable. May God grant that we win" (Laureano Gómez, in Spain, August 1948, cited in Lleras Restrepo, *De la república,* p. 509).

74. As Conservative Roberto Urdaneta Arbeláez (later to become acting president under Gómez) remarked of the event, "Liberalism believe[d] that it ha[d] lost nothing, and Conservatism that it ha[d] gained everything" (Azula Barrera, *De la revolución,* p. 177). Azula's own analysis at this point, from a Conservative perspective, is cogent.

75. See Conservative complaints in, e.g., Velasco, *Ospina,* pp. 105, 118, 145.

76. The figure of 1,800,000 false Liberal registrations was frequently repeated by Laureano Gómez (see, e.g., Velasco, *Ospina,* pp. 176–77). For the most colorful description of electoral corruption, the plume must go to Conservative Gilberto Alzate Avendaño: "in Colombia, due to the voting of the absent and the dead, elections look more like a gathering in the Valley of Jehoshaphat!" (Estrada Monsalve, *Así fué,* p. 88).

77. Gaitán submitted a lengthy "Memoria de Agravios," documenting incidents of violence against Liberals, to the Ospina government in January 1948 and held a gigantic silent rally of protest in February. The text of his address on the latter occasion is reprinted in *Gaitán: Antología de su pensamiento económico y social* (Bogotá: Ediciones Suramérica, 1968), pp. 411–15, and an earlier "Memorial de Agravios," from April 1947, at pp. 399–410.

78. Echandía had been Santos's representative in negotiating a new Concordat with the Vatican

between 1938 and 1942. Even in Rome the Liberal impressed the Curia with his daily attendance at Mass and his knowledge of the Latin classics (see Giraldo Londoño, *Don Fernando,* pp. 136–37). The initial expectations of the Conservatives, and their later disillusion, is reported in Estrada Monsalve, *Así fué,* pp. 9–10.

79. The only other significant legislation of 1948 granted emergency economic powers to the president.

80. Azula Barrera, *De la revolución,* p. 279.

81. Part of the Liberals' willingness to consider reform may have been based on their losses to the Conservatives in municipal elections. Conservative municipal councils rose from 194 to about 350 after the 1947 elections, while the Liberals dropped from 607 to some 450. See Azula Barrera, *De la revolución,* p. 283.

82. Guzmán, *Violencia,* p. 366. On the organization of the police, see also Special Operations Research Office, *U.S. Army Handbook for Colombia,* 2d ed. (Washington, D.C.: Government Printing Office, 1964), pp. 396–97. The police were not fully nationalized until 1953, when Rojas Pinilla, in one of his first acts in office, removed them from the Interior Ministry and put them under the Armed Forces Ministry.

83. See Abel, "Conservative Politics," pp. 34 ff.

84. Army officers keenly felt a difference between their professionalism and the partisan character of the police. See the review by Col. Alvaro Valencia Tovar of the first edition of Guzmán, *Violencia,* "Informe sobre el libro, 'La Violencia en Colombia,' " *Revista la nueva prensa,* nos. 85–86, (January-February 1963). It is interesting to note the confirmation of this view from within the police. See the judgment of a police captain quoted in Guzmán, *Violencia,* pp. 367–68.

85. Alberto Lleras Camargo, later president under the National Front (1958–62), spoke of the Violencia as "unleashed, ordered, stimulated, without any risk, by remote control," consuming the countryside with the "flames of madness," fed by fuel "dispatched from urban offices" (Azula Barrera, *De la revolución,* p. 231). There were many allegations of urban direction and supply of the guerrillas (see, e.g., Guzmán, *Violencia,* passim) but available evidence seems to indicate that this became significant only after the Liberals dropped out of the 1949 election.

86. After the 1946 election, Gabriel Turbay, the other Liberal in the race against Gaitán and Ospina, left the country and soon died in exile. Older oligarchical leaders, such as López, had undercut their position within the Liberal party by supporting Ospina against the Liberal candidates. Although Gaitán had control of the party machinery by 1947, he never commanded the party-in-government. In any case, he was removed from the scene in 1948. The lack of Liberal unity, even under very threatening conditions, was demonstrated in the 1949 congressional elections. The Liberals ran an average of 2.2 competing lists per department, the Conservatives only 1.1. See Payne, *Patterns of Conflict,,* p. 202.

87. See Lleras Restrepo, *De la república,* pp. 154–55.

88. Ospina opened Congress in July 1948, against the explicit demands of the Conservative party convention of that year, and in 1949 he resisted his party's repeated calls to close Congress from July on. On the first, see Martz, *Colombia,* p. 71.

89. See Martz, *Colombia,* p. 92. Most of the priests in novels about the Violencia are of this partisan type. See Gerardo Suárez Rondón, *La novela sobre la Violencia* (Bogotá: Ed. Luis F. Serrano A., 1966) pp. 61–80, for a discussion of various perspectives.

90. Cited in James E. Goff, *The Persecution of Protestant Christians in Colombia, 1948–1958* (Cuernavaca, Mexico: CIDOC, Sondeos No. 23, 1968), chap. 2, p. 47. Martz, *Colombia,* p. 84, lists at least five other bishops besides Builes who took this action.

91. Germán Arciniegas, *The State of Latin America* (New York: Knopf, 1952), p. 167. Examples of good and nonpartisan priests are found in Guzmán, *Violencia,* pp. 65–66, and Zapata Isaza, *¿Patricios?,* p. 278.

92. *El Catolicismo,* 30 April 1949, cited in Martz, *Colombia,* pp. 83–84.

93. The first response of the Episcopal Conference to the bogotazo was narrow and institutional—a protest against such attacks on its buildings and personnel. Its later collective pastoral of 1948 had long refutations of "Doctrinaire Liberalism" and of communism, and an implicit warning against the Colombian Liberal party. See *Conferencias episcopales,* vol. 1 (1908–1953) (Bogotá: Editorial El Catolicismo, 1956), pp. 464–67, 469–

87. See also the Jesuit view, in an article published soon after the bogotazo, Francisco José González, S. J., "Persecución religiosa en Colombia en el golpe terrorista de Abril 9, 1948," *Revista Javeriana* 29, no. 145, (June 1948). Red-baiting articles in this publication are conveniently indexed in this issue, pp. 268–72.

94. The bishops expressed the hope that 1950 would bring peace to their land, torn apart "by passion and hatreds which are not only anti-Christian but antihuman, drenched with the blood of fratricidal battles... " (*Conferencias episcopales*, vol. 1, p. 492).

95. Lleras Restrepo, *De la república,* pp. 190–91, 295.

96. See Leal Buitrago, "Política e intervención," esp. pp. 502–3, and Gonzalo Canal Ramírez, *Del 13 de Junio al 10 de Mayo en las fuerzas armadas* (Bogotá: Editorial Antares, 1955), p. 18.

97. Maullin, *Soldiers in Colombia,* p. 58, and General Amadeo Rodríguez, *Caminos de guerra y conspiración* (Barcelona: Gráficas Claret, 1955), bk. 2.

98. Cited in Maullin, *Soldiers in Colombia,* p. 58.

99. The alternative of a military junta after the bogotazo was rejected by both Ospina and the Liberal leaders as contrary to Colombia's civilianist traditions. See Azula Barrera, *De la revolución,* pp. 386, 400–404; and Leal Buitrago, "Política e intervención," p. 507 and n. 68.

100. Leal Buitrago claims it had reached 20,000 men by 1949 ("Política e intervención," p. 508), while Maullin puts the figure at 15,000 (*Soldiers in Colombia,* p. 82), up from some 10,000 in 1944.

101. Guzmán, *Violencia,* pp. 372–73; Maullin, *Soldiers in Colombia,* p. 59; and Eduardo Franco Isaza, *Las guerrillas del llano* (Bogotá: Librería Mundial, [1959]), pp. 94, 145–46, and passim.

102. See Canal Ramírez, *Las fuerzas armadas,* pp. 22–25. Martz argues that even in 1953 intervention hinged on personal factors and was not inevitable (*Colombia,* pp. 167–69). This view is supported, from a perspective favorable to Gómez, in Camilo Vázquez Cobo Carrizosa, *El frente nacional: Su origen y desarrollo* (Cali: Carvajal, n.d.), pp. 83–124 passim.

103. The average increase was 5.8 percent annually between 1945 and 1954. See ECLA, *Economic Development of Colombia,* p. 12.

104. See, for example,the "Comentarios económicos" of Humberto Mesa González in the section on "The Month" in the *Revista Javeriana* 32, no. 159 (October 1949): (173–86), and idem, vol. 33, no. 161 (January 1950): 44–49, in which he concluded that, despite the political and social upheaval, the economy was in good shape and getting better.

105. A Liberal perspective in the final break with the National Union government is found in Fonnegra Sierra, *El parlamento,* pp. 213–16. The Conservative view is given in Estrada Monsalve, *Así fué,* pp. 47–57. Ospina, who had often resisted pressures from his own party, blamed the Liberal ministers and parliamentarians for giving in to those from their own.

106. Fonnegra Sierra, *El parlamento,* p. 218.

107. A Liberal congressman had suggested in 1947 that Ospina deserved the same fate as Bolivian president Villarroel, who had been hanged on a lamppost by a mob in 1946. Ospina later wrote that the Liberal salutation to the bogotazo prisoners, the "*nueveabrileños,*" finally convinced him of their disloyalty to democratic norms. See República de Colombia, *La oposición y el gobierno* (Bogotá: Imprenta Nacional, 1950), pp. 36–37.

108. "With one hand, [Liberalism] was throwing rocks, while with the other waving the white flag of peace." Of the 1947 general strike: "In spite of collaborating with the government, the Liberal party supported and was pleased by preparations for the strike" (Velasco, *Ospina Pérez,* pp. 196, 125). The phrase "*juego doble*" was often invoked by Conservatives.

109. Liberal leaders frequently condemned the Violencia. See, e.g., Lleras Restrepo, *De la república,* pp. 115–22.

110. "In many places the agents of authority have believed that in order to achieve institutional stability they should put force at the electoral service of the party of government" (Council of State, October 1949, cited in Fonnegra Sierra, *El parlamento,* p. 264).

111. Lleras Restrepo, *De la república,* p. 275; Fonnegra Sierra, *El parlamento,* 230–32.

112. There is a clear sense of this in the account of Fonnegra Sierra, *El parlamento*, pp. 231, 238. Whether either of the parties might have been justified in doing so is a question that this analysis does not try to answer. Nor does it attempt definitively to apportion historical blame or responsibility between the two sides.

113. The names of the most prominent of the committee's members are given by Ospina in his letter to them, reproduced in Mariano Ospina Pérez, *Historia de un proceso político*, vol. 6 of "El gobierno de Unión Nacional" (Bogotá: Imprenta Nacional, 1950), p. 236. This volume and Lleras Restrepo, *De la república*, offer the most useful documentation of the offers and counteroffers by the two sides during the "reduction of the arena."

114. Lleras Restrepo, *De la república*, p. 278.

115. Cited in "Vida Nacional," *Revista Javeriana* 32 (July-November 1949): (212).

116. Ospina Pérez, *Historia*, pp. 241–43; Lleras Restrepo, *De la república*, pp. 292–93; Giraldo Londoño, *Don Fernando*, pp. 301–3. Martz is incorrect in stating that the proposal came only after Echandía's withdrawal (*Colombia*, p. 93).

117. "The [Conservative] color blue became black in the persons of these individuals" (Giraldo Londoño, *Don Fernando*, p. 299). Bogotá's Liberal *El Tiempo* (4 October 1949) called the designation of the new governors "the most evil-tempered and unlimited demonstration of sectarianism that a government has ever dared in the Republic of Colombia" (cited in "Vida Nacional," *Revista Javeriana* 32 (July-November 1949): (208).

118. Lleras Restrepo, *De la república*, p. 279.

119. Cf. the editorial of *El Tiempo* of 25 September 1949, cited in "Vida Nacional," *Revista Javeriana*, 32 (July-November 1949); (214).

120. *De la república*, p. 182. Cf. p. 189, and the judgments of Giraldo Londoño (*Don Fernando*, p. 303) and Fonnegra Sierra (*El parlamento*, p. 217).

121. "Dictadura pactada": Lleras Restrepo, *De la república*, p. 292.

122. Daniel Caicedo's novel, *Viento seco* (Bogotá: Cooperativa Nacional de Artes Gráficas, 1954), which describes the agonies of the Liberal party in the Valle del Cauca during this period, devotes a large section to the massacre at the Casa Liberal. See also Zapata Isaza, *¿Patricios?* pp. 280–83.

123. Lleras Restrepo, *De la república*, pp. 280—81. Ospina replied, with some justification, that the registrar had made no protest when the Liberal electoral "counterreform" had greatly shortened the time available for reregistration. See "Vida Nacional," *Revista Javeriana* 33, no. 161 (February 1950): (18).

124. Fonnegra Sierra, *El parlamento*, p. 264. Cf. Lleras Restrepo's description of the government's characteristic "technique of the Violence," using thugs to intimidate Liberals after first replacing local military troops with sectarian police; *De la república*, p. 207.

125. Fonnegra Sierra, *El parlamento*, p. 248; Lleras Restrepo, *De la república*, p. 298.

126. Lleras Restrepo, *De la república*, p. 212.

127. Ibid., pp. 292–303; Giraldo Londoño, *Don Fernando*, 306-7.

128. Lleras Restrepo, *De la república*, p. 304.

129. Cf. ibid., p. 305, and editorials from *El Tiempo* cited in Fonnegra Sierra, *El parlamento*, pp. 256–57.

130. It is important to note that "disloyal opposition" to democracy may be present *within* the government (and in the party organization of an executive) as much as outside it. Linz seems to concentrate principally on the latter, drawing mainly from the European experience.

131. See Azula Barrera, *De la revolución*, pp. 384–86, and Giraldo Londoño, *Don Fernando*, pp. 276–77.

132. Cf. Guzmán, *Violencia*, p. 73, citing a Conservative source. It was very much the *exaltado* sentiment of Lucio Pabón Núñez: "Conservatism is ready to fight with force and to die as Christians and sons of Bolívar. . . . our motto is to triumph with the Government [of Ospina Pérez] or in spite of the Government" (cited in Patiño, "Political Ideas," p. 144).

133. Cited in Patiño, "Political Ideas," p. 150.

134. Ibid., pp. 200–201.

135. Ramírez Moreno, *La crisis*, p. 25.

136. Actually, Ospina was probably able to provide a very large number of Conservatives with government jobs without displacing many Liberals, due to the great expansion of revenues

that occurred in these years. This should have contributed to the possibilities of convivencia between the parties, and probably did. It may not have been enough in the end because both parties continued to *think* in terms of a zero-sum—rather than an expanding-sum—game.

137. The official figures of DANE, the national office of statistics, show that registrations exceeded the number of eligible voters (males over twenty-one) by nearly 20 percent by 1949. See table 2, above.

138. For examples of Liberal extremism, see Guzmán, *Violencia,* pp. 352–53, and the discussion on pp. 358–59 of the fanatical pamphlets (of perhaps dubious authenticity). Note the tacit admission by Lleras Restrepo concerning the congressional elites: *"in general* the *authorized* leaders of the party in the chambers did not propose nor accept but very moderate formulas..." *(De la república,* p. 267, emphasis added).

139. Lleras Restrepo, *De la república,* pp. 211, 212.

140. Consider the brilliant excoriation by Juan Lozano y Lozano of the "eminent public men of Liberalism... until yesterday so valiant, demanding, and dissatisfied," who failed to support the resistance of country people to "official violence" and instead "either hid themselves in their houses and private occupations or chose circumspection, moderation, good manners, cool heads, friendly approaches and respectful petitions" ("Prólogo" in Franco Isaza, *Las guerrillas del llano,* p. iv).

141. The phrase is from Lleras Restrepo, reporting on negotiations with the Conservatives, *(De la república,* p. 188). It was also used by *El Tiempo* concerning the Gómez-Gaitán agreement of 1947 ("Vida Nacional," *Revista Javeriana* 29, no. 141 [February 1948]: (10)). A notable feature of this early pact was a provision for a bipartisan tribunal of guarantees. The text of this accord is given in the *Revista Javeriana* 28, no. 139 (Octubre 1947): (146–52). That of the later two pacts is in Lleras Restrepo, *De la república,* pp. 91–93, 115–22.

142. See Lleras Restrepo, *De la república,* pp. 283–84, 300, for documents that reflect the existence of such problems in the Liberal party.

143. It was the *relationship* between the Violencia and the political parties—rather than the presence of massive violence *per se*—that led to breakdown. Elite consensus would have been affected very differently by equally great mobilization and conflict associated, say, with *fidelista* guerrilla revolutionaries instead of identifiably Liberal and Conservative partisans.

144. A convenient descriptive survey on the Violencia, particularly sensitive to its military aspects, is Russell W. Ramsey, "Critical Bibliography on La Violencia in Colombia," *Latin American Research Review* 8, no. 1 (Spring 1973): 3–44.

145. Cited in Leal Buitrago, *Desarrollo político,* p. 88.

146. Wilde, "A Traditional Church," pp. 246–47.

147. Ibid., pp. 251–53.

148. Maingot, "Civil-Military Relations."

149. Maullin, *Solders in Colombia,* pp. 61–64 and 139 (n. 33); and *El proceso contra Gustavo Rojas Pinilla ante el congreso de Colombia* (Bogotá: Imprenta Nacional, 1960), passim.

150. The failure of a pro-Conservative coup from within the army in May 1958, during the period of junta government, confirmed for the officer corps the dangers of rule for the military institution.

151. Dix, *Colombia: Political Dimensions,* p. 128. Cf. the "theory of *desvínculación*" in Canal Ramírez, *Fuerzas Armadas.*

152. Leal Buitrago, *Desarrollo político,* pp. 87–90.

153. The most intimate account of the negotiations between Alberto Lleras and Laureano Gómez and subsequent negotiations between the parties is Vázquez Carrizosa, *Frente nacional,* the memoirs of a Conservative politician who served as an important intermediary, particularly in the early stages.

154. The central passages of all these agreements are conveniently gathered in Jorge Cárdenas García, *El frente nacional y los partidos políticos* (Tunja: Imprenta Departamental, 1958 [1959]), pp. 93–115. Fuller versions of the pacts of Benidorm and Sitges are given in Vázquez Carrizosa, *Frente nacional,* pp. 164–65, 277–83.

155. The vote was some four million in favor, two hundred thousand against. The text of the plebiscite is given in Cárdenas García, *Frente nacional y los partidos,* pp. 117–23; Cárdenas García also provides a useful constitutional analysis, passim.

156. Articles 2 and 4 of the reform anticipate the problems that would be faced in implementing parity, given the unstable, factional character of the parties. See Cárdenas García on *"lentejismo"*: *Frente nacional y los partidos,* pp. 70–71.

157. Cf. Levine's analysis of the reestablishment of democracy in Venezuela after 1958.

158. The phrase is from the party pact of 3 March 1957.

159. Cf. most of the Colombian commentaries; Arciniegas, *State of Latin America,* and Martz, *Colombia,* are probably the most influential accounts in English.

160. Cf. Fluharty, *Dance,* and Orlando Fals Borda, "Violence and the Break-up of Tradition in Colombia," in *Obstacles to Change in Latin America,* ed. Claudio Véliz (London: Oxford University Press, 1965).

161. Cf. Charles Tilly, "Does Modernization Breed Revolution?" *Comparative Politics* 5, no. 3 (April 1973): 425–47, esp. pp. 436–44.

162. A variant class interpretation might stress changes *within* the dominant classes, especially between commercial, agricultural, and industrial groups. See Francisco Leal Buitrago, Social Classes, International Trade, and Foreign Capital in Colombia" (Ph.D. diss., University of Wisconsin-Madison, 1974).

163. The cost of living index for the working class in Bogotá rose from 262 to 284 from January to March 1948; in Medellín it rose from 235 to 257 from January to April. The urban riots occurred in early April. See DANE, *Anuario general de estadística, 1948* (Bogotá), tables 178, 182.

164. There has been little serious social science research done on populism in Colombia, or even on the bogotazo. I could find no account of the fate of Gaitán's economic reforms in the Liberal-dominated 1947 Congress. The program is reproduced in *Gaitán,* pp. 257–328. This volume and *Los mejores discursos de Jorge Eliécer Gaitán, 1919–1938,* 2d. ed., ed. Jorge Villaveces (Bogotá: Editorial de Jorvi, 1968), are useful collections of documents.

165. Cf. Guzmán, *Violencia,* and John Pollock, "How Violence and Politics are Linked: The Political Sociology of *La Violencia* in Colombia," Livingston College, Rutgers University, 7 February 1972 (mimeographed).

166. Patiño, "Political Ideas," is replete with examples.

167. We lack a good political biography of this fascinating central figure. A psychological study that tried to link his own peculiar personality to his party and times might be quite fruitful. Among the available works are: Alfredo Cock Arango, *Las víctimas del doctor Laureano Gómez* ([Bogotá]: no publisher, 1959); Felipe Antonio Molina, *Laureano Gómez: Historia de una rebeldía* (Bogotá: Editorial Librería Voluntad, 1940); and Antonio J. Vélez M. and Domingo Jaramillo H., *El paradigma* (Medellín: Librería Nueva, n. d.).

168. Cf. Lily Ross Taylor, *Party Politics in the Age of Caesar* (Berkeley and Los Angeles: University of California Press, 1949). A focus on ideology may be deceptive in attempting to understand even those polities in which it is most apparent. See the perceptive comment by Eric Nordlinger, "Democratic Stability and Instability: The French Case," *World Politics* 23, no. 1 (October 1965): 143.

169. See Wilde, "A Traditional Church," pp. 86–88, 153–60.

170. Payne, *Patterns of Conflict,* pp. 161–77.

171. This is not to claim that changes in the countryside—e.g., in the concentration of land ownership—did not also contribute to expanding the Violencia beyond its origins in party rivalry and feuding. It is only to say that *ideological explanations* for such changes do not seem to have played a significant part in motivating the conflict. Thus, I disagree with Richard Weinert's important analysis of the Violencia, which turns on the assumption that "peasants rose to the defense of a traditional order personified by the Conservative party, against Liberal peasants whose party affiliation identified them with modernization" ("Violence in Pre-Modern Societies," p. 346). There is no evidence, however, that Conservative peasants perceived themselves as "the sector being threatened by" the modernization policies of the Liberal party—as opposed to being threatened by more traditional party hostilities.

172. Cf. Nordlinger, *Conflict Regulation,* pp. 20–41.

173. Lijphart points out that such a dual cleavage of subcultures seems inherently more unstable than a multiple one, in which the various parties were forced to bargain with each other to form majorities ("Consociational Democracy," pp. 217–18).

174. For a very provocative analysis of how the political security of leaders may affect their attitudes toward conciliation, see Nordlinger, *Conflict Regulation,* pp. 54–72.
175. See Nordlinger, *Conflict Regulation,* pp. 73–87.
176. This contrasts sharply with, say, the Austrian and Venezuelan cases, in which party elites can impose compromises upon supporting social forces and interest groups.
177. The Colombian leaders faced nothing like, for example, the strong post-Peronist trade union movement in Argentina, which made it impossible to reestablish democracy on anything resembling the old assumptions.
178. For a brief empirical exploration of the relationship, see Robert Dahl, *Polyarchy* (New Haven: Yale University Press, 1971), chap. 2.
179. For the view that National Front governments avoided all significant problems, in part because of aid from the United States, see U.S. Senate, Subcommittee on American Republics Affairs, Committee on Foreign Relations, *Colombia—A Case History of U. S. Aid,* part of *Survey of the Alliance for Progress,* 91st Cong., 1st sess. (Washington, D.C.: U. S. Government Printing Office, 1 February 1969).
180. The Colombian church has been among the most timid in Latin American in assuming a "prophetic" stance against social injustice. Nevertheless, see Conferencia Episcopal de Colombia, *La Iglesia ante el cambio,* XXV Asamblea Plenaria, (Bogotá: Secretariado Permanente del Episcopado Colombiano, 1969), esp. pp. 34–38, and idem, *La justicia en el mundo* (Bogotá: Secretariado Permanente del Episcopado Colombiano, 1972), esp. pp. 105–14.

3.

Venezuela since 1958: The Consolidation of Democratic Politics

Daniel H. Levine*

In politics as in everything else, it makes a great difference whose game we play. The rules of the game determine the requirements for success.
E. E. Schattschneider, *The Semi-Sovereign People*

In the early morning of 23 January 1958, General Marcos Pérez Jiménez fled from Venezuela. His hurried departure brought an end to ten years of military rule, permitting the reestablishment of mass democracy, a form of political life Venezuelans had only begun to know in the postwar period. The nation's single prior experience with democratic politics, from 1945 to 1948, had been brought down by the military regime now ended with Pérez Jimenez's flight.

Since throwing off dictatorship in 1958, Venezuelans have built a strong and effective democracy.[1] Their success is particularly striking given the historical record. With only three years of civilian rule in the first fifty-seven years of this century, Venezuelans have achieved one of the few stable competitive political orders in Latin America. Divided by intense conflict and widespread political violence throughout the early 1960s, they have managed four peaceful transitions of power through free elections (1958, 1963, 1968, 1973). These are the first consecutive transfers of power through popular elections in Venezuelan history. Moreover, in 1968 power passed to an opposition party, also for the first time in national history. Burdened with a long and bloody tradition of military rule, Venezuelans have nevertheless produced a complex and powerful system of mass political parties—organizations which penetrate and shape all facets of political life.

Examination of the successful transition to democracy in Venezuela, and of

*This chapter was first written in mid-1973 and substantially revised in 1974. The author is particularly indebted to Guillermo O'Donnell, Alexander Wilde, and the late Kalman H. Silvert, steadfast friend of Latin American democracy, for their careful readings, criticism, and suggestions.

82

its roots in history and social structure, fits nicely with comparative study of the breakdown and survival of democracies. First, the historical record is both recent and relatively clear. A notable change is apparent in the norms and methods of political leadership during the two periods of democratic rule in this century. Although substantially the same people guided organizations and dealt with problems from 1945 to 1948 as did so after 1958, the way they acted and their basic understandings of politics are dramatically different. Second, the form in which elites redefined problems and possible solutions after 1958 is strikingly similar to the experience of other nations. Although the content of conflicts is of course determined by the peculiarities of national history, the form in which they have been resolved is common to many nations. Finally, the study of Venezuelan politics lends itself to the combination of two analytical perspectives all too often kept apart: first, a focus on structural variables (social structure, mobilization patterns, organizational change) and the way in which their evolution sets up likely points of conflict; and second, a set of variables closer to the explicitly political arena, involving the norms, beliefs, and actions of leaders. The close interrelation of structural and normative elements in Venezuela is central to the evolution of the political system in its present form and to its ability to survive the sorts of crises which wrecked the initial democratic experiment of the postwar years.

Structural and normative elements come together in the study of two central and related themes: conflict and legitimacy. In the course of Venezuelan history, basic lines of conflict have undergone major shifts, whose sources must be sought in changing social and economic structures and the way in which groups emerged from them. A further question concerns the creation of institutions to deal with these conflicts. The institutionalization of conflict, providing regular and routine channels for the expression and conciliation of interests, is of course central to any society's ability to manage disputes, allowing diverse interests to coexist. It is perhaps even more important to democracies, committed by definition to the *open* expression of conflict.

Successful institutionalization depends heavily on the degree to which common political processes, criteria of power, and institutions become legitimate to key sectors of the population. An essential question facing political leaders in a new system (or in an existing system where balances and rules have undergone sudden and drastic change) then becomes how, and at what cost, are potentially disloyal oppositions neutralized, incorporated into the system, or excluded and defeated? Here, "legitimacy" means more than mere adherence to a regime or set of authorities. Conflicts over legitimacy are not only disputes over words and symbols—whole systems of action are at stake. Thus, "legitimacy" is used here in a broad sense, to refer to the evolution of shared criteria of power (e.g., money, divine sanction, force, votes, etc.), proper methods of political action, and appropriate arenas for political action and decision.[2]

The development of common norms of behavior among Venezuelan political elites is perhaps the single most important factor differentiating the abortive postwar experiment in democracy from more recent experiences. The consolidation of democracy after 1958, I would argue, is best understood not in terms of the balance among forces (whereby, for example, groups favoring democracy overwhelmed its opponents), but rather in terms of changing definitions of the proper relations among social and political forces. These changes then made possible the development of broadened support for democracy, and the isolation and defeat of opponents on the Right and the Left.

Before going into the historical roots of change in Venezuela, let me outline briefly some major characteristics of the political system established after 1958. Briefly, Venezuelan democracy is a party system. The basic tools of political action are mass parties, the crucial resources of politics are mass mobilization and votes, and power is transferred through elections in which proportional representation and closed party list voting magnify the impact of party organization.[3] Parties are the principal agents for the expression of political conflict, and most political transactions are filtered through the net of party leadership and organization.

Working within these structures, after 1958 a self-consciously prudent leadership set out to redefine the problems of politics in such a way as to make the institutionalization of conflict possible. An operational code of coexistence was developed, marking off acceptable limits and methods of conflict. In this vein, decisions were taken to reduce the level and intensity of conflict, emphasize common interests, and exclude consideration of areas of irreconcilable differences. The establishment of such common understandings made coexistence possible by making the limitation of disputes feasible. For if such agreements are not reached, conflicts easily get beyond the capacity of settlement the parties possess. Moreover, they are likely to be defined in terms which challenge the legitimacy of the system and call into question the survival of competing groups. In such circumstances, the threat of all-out conflict is visible just below the surface of every particular dispute. This is what political elites sought to avoid.

The interaction of normative and structural factors cannot be emphasized too much. Party structures in Venezuela bring people into the political arena, mobilizing large, heterogeneous groups into competing alignments. The potential created in this way can be put to many uses. In recent years, political conflict has been expressed in forms ranging from sporadic street violence and open civil war to elections, parliamentary maneuver, and interelite bargaining and negotiation. The actual form and intensity of conflict depends on the perspectives of elites. As we shall see, party leadership in Venezuela has been able to assert an independent and relatively autonomous role, making general political needs and values prevail over the more limited demands of different sectors of the party such as students, workers, peasants, or teachers. These structural factors make changes in elite norms particularly important. Through their control of organizations, elites are able to shape mass behavior, as the rank and file accept new patterns of action because of a general faith in the leadership of organizations to which they belong. Mass behavior then changes in response to new leadership perspectives. The linkage between the two is structural—the nature of party organization. But the motivating force is normative, as the transformation of elite norms triggers other, related changes.[4]

The analysis which follows is organized in terms of structural and normative changes. In structural terms, the nature of social structure prior to the emergence of mass parties will be considered, to assess the impact of social change on party formation. In other words, how did social structure shape political structures in Venezuela? In normative terms, changing definitions of problems and solutions, and the development of trust, tolerance, and mutual guarantees between competing elites will be examined in the context of specific cases and kinds of conflict.

Origins and Breakdown

From 1908 to 1935, Venezuela lived under the powerful and repressive dictatorship of Juan Vicente Gómez. Under his regime, the administrative and political unification of the country was accomplished. Reinforced by growing oil revenues, Gómez created a permanent national army and an effective state bureaucracy for the first time in Venezuelan history. With these tools in hand, his regime was able to eradicate completely the heritage of civil wars and regional and party conflict which had characterized the nineteenth century. The day of the isolated *caudillo* was ended forever, and regional uprisings passed from the scene.[5]

The dominant central state built in this way had a tremendous impact on a weakly integrated society. In political terms, the affiliations and inherited loyalties which might have carried over to help organize groups within the society were shattered. The traditional parties (Liberals and Conservatives) which had dominated politics throughout the nineteenth century simply disappeared, as their social basis in regional militarism was destroyed.[6] Indeed, it was difficult for any kind of political organization to exist under Gómez—political organization per se was suspect.[7]

Moreover, since the mid-nineteenth century, political leadership in Venezuela has rested not with a stable socioeconomic aristocracy, but rather with a succession of armed caudillos.[8] The landed aristocracy was decimated in nineteenth-century civil wars: property and position depended heavily on political power, not the reverse. The absence of a stable aristocracy was complemented by the weakness of many other institutions which often reinforce social hierarchy. Religious sanctions, for example, were negligible, as the Catholic church barely existed in most of the nation, being particularly weak in the countryside, where most Venezuelans still lived. This is not to argue, of course, that there was no social hierarchy and no inequality. Inequalities were very great, but the important point here is that bonds of loyalty and felt obligation tying upper and lower groups together were in general weak and fragile.

Important social and economic changes also began during the Gómez period. The already weak ties binding social strata together were further weakened by the impact of oil. While helping create a dominant state, oil also contributed to social change by depressing traditional agriculture and stimulating massive population movements. Until the 1920s, Venezuela was an agricultural export economy. After World War I, however, a sharp drop in production was accompanied by a decline in exports of agricultural products, both as a share of total exports and in absolute terms as well. The rapid commercialization of agriculture and the exaction of ever-increasing burdens from the peasantry further contributed to change, by stimulating migration out of the countryside and creating a pool of grievances later crystallized in a powerful peasant movement.[9]

As agricultural production and exports declined, so did rural population. As table 1 shows, the rural-urban mix of the population has been more than reversed since 1936. In addition, urban population has grown much faster than rural population. These data reflect massive internal migration which still continues to pull many Venezuelans out of their native states and regions.[10] The proportion of the work force employed in agriculture also dropped, from 71.6 percent in 1920 to 33.5 percent in 1961, while employment in industry more than doubled, and services (public and private) jumped from 7.6 percent to 24.8 percent in the same period.[11]

The weakness of traditional social ties, combined with an intensive and widespread experience of change, magnifies the impact of new organizations once the repressive lid is removed.[12] This relation, between loose traditional ties and a powerful penetration of society by new organizations, is fundamental for Venezuela. All across the social spectrum, and in all regions as well, people became available for new jobs, exposed to new experiences, and beset by new problems. But the loyalties, organizations, and identities which might have provided some continuity in a period of change were largely absent. Thus, when parties began to organize after 1936, they expanded into an organizational vacuum full of potential recruits. The broadly based nature of change made heterogeneous, multi-class parties quite effective. Moreover, political parties themselves became a central organizing principle in the society. Party affiliation links members of disparate social groups (e.g., workers, peasants, students, professionals), while at the local level, party organization serves many functions—club, social center, employment office, and political movement.[13]

Table 1. Population Distribution, 1936–71

Year	Rural	Urban
1936	71%	29%
1941	69	31
1950	52	48
1961	37	63
1971	27	73

SOURCE: Adapted from "Cuadro 7, Pobloción clasificada segun areas urbana, intermedia, y rural y aumento sobre el censo anterior, censos de 1971, 1961, 1950, 1941, y 1936," *Censo de Población y Vivienda Resúmen Nacional Características Generales,* (Caracas: Ministerio de Fomento, 1974), vol. 1, p. 53. The Venezuelan census classifies persons living in centers of over 2,500 inhabitants as "urban." "Rural" as used here combines censal definitions of "rural" (under 1,000 inhabitants) and "intermediate" (1,000 to 2,500 inhabitants).

In this way, the stage was set for a massive expansion of political organizations once the Gómez regime passed from the scene. The tremendous growth of political organization, from zero in 1935 to the present situation in which party ties penetrate and organize many spheres of life, is in good measure due to Gómez's effective destruction of old structures and ties, and his unwitting stimulation of underlying social change.

With the death of Gómez in December 1935, the political landscape began to change rapidly. While limitations of space preclude any detailed examination of the events beginning in 1936, the long-term significance of this period is clear. The years immediately following the death of Gómez saw the initial foundation of mass political organizations, the introduction of a new political resource (mass pressure), and the beginnings (under party auspices) of secondary associations of all kinds, most importantly industrial and peasant unions. Here the potential noted above begins to be realized, as organizations are created and, along party lines, begin to penetrate many areas of life. Although student leaders returning from exile played an important part in the process, the most significant political development of these years is precisely the growth of mass organizations—often directed by ex-students, but seeking power through mass organization, going far beyond the traditional bounds of student action.

Gómez was followed in office by General Eleazar López Contreras, previously minister of war. At first, López moved cautiously against the new political forces being formed. But soon new political groups had been dissolved, incipient trade unions broken up, and a major strike in the oil fields thoroughly repressed. By March 1937, most leaders of these groups were either in exile, in prison, or in hiding, preparing to begin a long struggle underground. Although the new political forces failed in their immediate goals of social and political change, they clearly found roots in society. Thus, they were able to go underground and survive, forming leadership groups, making contracts, building organizational networks, and elaborating programs for the future.

Throughout López's term in office (1936–41), there was no change in the system of power. Power continued to rest on control of the army and state machine, and politics remained closed to mass participation of any kind. López Contreras was succeeded by his minister of war, General Isias Medina Angarita. Once in power, Medina began a gradual process of political liberalization and organizational expansion, giving open expression to the sources of power nurtured underground in previous years. Seeking a base of support independent from López, and perhaps influenced by the climate of democratic struggle in World War II, he opened the doors to massive political organization. With these changes in the air, an amalgam of groups applied for legal status, and the new party was formally constituted as Acción Democrática (AD) in September 1941.

Upon formation, AD immediately began a vigorous organizational drive destined to build a comprehensive national party structure.[14] AD pioneered the development of a new kind of political party in Venezuela—a permanent organization, existing at all levels and integrating many groups into the party structure. All major parties in Venezuela have followed this basic pattern. They are vertically integrated, with organizational structures reaching from block and neighborhood to the national level; and horizontally integrated, with functional groups such as labor, students, professionals, and the like represented within the party organization. These groups, of course, are themselves divided by competing party groups.

It is important to realize that while many organizations were created after 1936, these were mainly leftist in orientation, representing new seekers after power. Traditional sectors of society did not enter the organizational race, relying instead on continued control of the army and administration to guarantee power and privilege. Economic and social elites felt effectively represented under the old system, and religious elites also failed to build mass organization, depending instead on a network of elite schools and the general sponsorship of other power groups.[15] Such groups were not oriented toward the creation of mass organizations, which indeed must have seemed superfluous in a system which rewarded regional cliques, kinship ties, and personal influence networks more than mass organization.

During the Medina period, AD created a vigorous, effective, and closely knit organization. The party began to penetrate the society on a large scale, as organizers helped to set up and mobilize industrial and peasant unions. By

1945, AD had the upper hand in these areas. But the limited and tantalizing nature of political change was profoundly frustrating to the party.

Although the potential for participation had expanded greatly, the political system remained restrictive of actual participation. Indirect elections remained the rule, female suffrage was denied, and in general mass organization yielded little in the way of effective power. In the political market then in effect, mass organization was simply not a recognized currency. Politics was structured to reward other kinds of resources, and the chances for evolutionary change seemed slim.

This context helps explain the party leadership's acceptance of an invitation to join a military conspiracy against the Medina government. They saw this as a chance to initiate rapid, far-reaching change. The coup was launched on 18 October 1945. After several days of fighting, a provisional revolutionary government was formed, with four members from AD, two military officers, and one independent civilian. The three years which followed, commonly known in Venezuela as the *trienio,* marked the introduction of a party system into Venezuela, abruptly ushering in an experiment with mass political democracy.

Politics in the trienio was characterized by a great expansion of organization set against a pattern of intense and bitter conflict. In electoral terms, all qualifications for suffrage aside from age and citizenship were eliminated. In a nation with many illiterates, this made for an instant expansion of the electorate, from 5 percent of the population before 1945 to 36 percent immediately thereafter.[16] In addition, direct election was instituted at all levels, from municipal councils and state legislatures to deputies, senators, and president. New parties were also formed, most importantly COPEI (a Christian Democratic party) and Unión Republicana Democrática (URD), a party representing the non-Communist left wing of forces that had backed Medina. In general, avenues for the expression of interests were broadened and the costs of organization cut back. The case of labor is particularly notable. Both industrial labor and peasant unions expanded greatly in terms of numbers of unions and total membership. A national Peasant Federation was organized in November 1947, forming part of the Confederation of Venezuelan Workers also organized at that time.[17]

Democracy in the trienio was flawed by the absence of a sense of trust and mutual guarantees among major social and political groups. The nature of political conflict in the period bears witness to this. Many were threatened, in material and symbolic terms, by AD and its regime. Indeed, trienio politics offers a classic example of the problems new democracies face in gaining legitimacy among established groups and institutions. I would argue that conflicts over legitimacy were inevitable in Venezuela. A revolutionary regime had taken power, committed to a radical program of union organization, control over the oil companies, agrarian reform, expanded public education, and the like. Moreover, a new set of political rules was imposed which placed a premium on mass organization. This sudden change in the "rules of the game" left previously secure groups both open to question as to their own legitimacy and ill-equipped to defend themselves, since they possessed few mass organizations.

Such an encounter of new forces with already existing groups and institutions is bound to raise basic questions concerning the form of institutions and the proper means of generating and allocating political power. Moreover, in Venezuela the same factors that gave political parties such deep popular roots also fed the fires of extreme conflict. Among new groups, organizational loyalties reinforced the commitment to struggle. The organization itself became a rallying point, a symbol of action and commitment. Meanwhile, for weakly organized traditional groups, like the church, lack of organization meant inability to control the consequences of action. Without a regular net of organization, extreme appeals may be needed to reach and activate a potential clientele not normally within the reach of organization.[18] Thus, conflicts begin at a more intense and general level, and people join them at a crisis pitch. Conflict is intensified even further, and the stakes magnified even more, by the way in which sudden change in the rules of the game cut the ground from under traditional elites. Conventional expectations of deference and understandings of effective strategies become outmoded overnight. The consequence in Venezuela was a rising sense of powerlessness and persecution, particularly among Catholic, rural, and business interests.

In this way, AD managed in three years to alienate many important power factors in Venezuela, ultimately stimulating an opposition coalition broad enough to overthrow the government of Rómulo Gallegos on 24 November 1948. A brief examination of AD's relations with several major groups will illustrate the point.

Consider the case of the church and the Catholic sector in general. Intense religious-political conflict first arose in 1946, in a dispute over educational policy. AD clashed with the Catholic church, which saw the regime's attempt to expand public education while putting tighter controls on private schools as a direct attack on the church by a Socialist, atheist political regime. For Catholic elites and their sympathizers, the legitimacy of the regime and of the political system it represented was called into question. Catholic elites asserted their right to represent the interests of the (by definition) "Catholic majority," while AD based its claim to legitimacy on the "majority of the voters." These incompatible formulae symbolize the problem of AD-Catholic relations at this time. Catholic leaders did more than attack a set of policies: they questioned the legitimacy of any political system that could produce a result which so clearly distorted the "true" interests of the Catholic majority.

In this context, negotiations, bargaining, and compromise were likely to fail, for such strategies depend on the acceptance of a common frame of reference within which groups negotiate. But the nature of this common ground was itself at issue.

AD also aroused the enmity of many former members of the Gómez, López Contreras, and Medina regimes through its unprecedented trials of former public officials for illegal enrichment while in office. The vigorous expansion of trade union organization brought opposition from economic elites, particularly in the important oil industry, where AD-led unions were very active. Meanwhile, an ambitious land reform program was begun, and the entire structure of rural power was turned around as peasant unions, backed by now-sympathetic government officials, started to push for change.

Those who stood to lose naturally moved into opposition. Opposition from such groups, threatened in positions of power and privilege, was made more effective by the alienation of competing electoral elites. Responding to its traditional critics, AD insisted that its legitimacy arose from popular elections. This overwhelming base of support was demonstrated again and again during the trienio, as a series of elections returned large AD majorities at all levels. Insisting on electoral legitimacy, how then did AD lose legitimacy in the eyes of others committed to the same principles?

In the first place, competing electoral elites despaired of ever winning power by playing according to AD's rules. The party's mass support was too great. In practice, if not in theory, the system excluded all but AD. Moreover, it is important to realize that most previously successful influence strategies (involving informal cliques, family ties, or regional sentiments) were replaced by party networks—in effect, by AD. At the local level, the close integration of party and sectors meant that in the application of programs AD used party-based, exclusive criteria. This strategy, while securing AD's own base, destroyed its legitimacy among competing electoral groups.[19]

As other electoral elites moved toward opposition, more traditional groups felt reinforced, never having accepted the legitimacy of AD in the first place. For the church, and (more gradually) the military, the criteria of power and legitimacy espoused by AD were rejected outright. The church dismissed the idea that the majority of voters could thwart the inherent interests of Catholic majorities. The military was unimpressed by AD's claim to electoral legitimacy—in their view, governments always won elections. Moreover, military leaders became increasingly concerned by reports of armed labor battalions controlled by AD.

During the trienio, AD made little attempt to soften its relations with other parties or to formulate coalitions or working agreements with them on particular issues.[20] The political actions of AD and its leadership were instead marked by the promotion of programmatic and sectoral interests over the restraint of these interests in the pursuit of more broadly based support. Few in AD spoke as did Rómulo Betancourt, at the height of the conflict with the church over education:

... the Revolutionary Government guarantees categorically that it will not go back or stop in its path of democratic achievements. At the same time, however, it invites this sector [within AD] to serene reflection, through which it may distinguish the secondary from the basic and principal. Seeking a conciliatory formula in a problem is a method which prudence and a sense of responsibility always counsel; incompatible with simple stubbornness.[21]

The overthrow of AD thus stemmed ultimately from the threat its continued rule had come to pose to a wide range of social interests. Politics in the trienio was an all-out affair. Organizations were created and new forces mobilized without the development of common rules of democratic coexistence and norms to limit conflict. In all the cases cited, more detailed analysis reveals that AD failed to establish relations of trust and to extend mutual guarantees with major groups. Not all of the blame rests with AD, but clearly the possibility of offering compromise was within its power and was not pursued. For AD, arriving on the scene in 1945 with a young, inexperienced leadership and overwhelming power, incentives to moderation, concession, and compromise were few. Backed by immense electoral majorities and secure in its alliance with the military, AD leadership on the whole saw dissent and opposition not as normal and legitimate aspects of a plural society but rather as evidence of a potential counterrevolutionary conspiracy. Secure in their majorities, AD's leaders discounted the need to compromise with intense minorities, no matter how small in size. Incentives to trust and the extension of guarantees were weak on all sides. Older elites felt threatened in their values, ways of life, and survival, while new elites saw a challenge to the revolution in any opposition. The result of this mistrust and continuous mutual provocation was that the military coup of 1948 was greeted in many sectors as a deliverance from persecution.[22]

A cursory examination of the new military regime's acts indicates that the conflicts examined above were indeed crucial to the fall of AD. Some early measures included the derogation of two major laws passed near the end of the previous regime, the Organic Law of Education and the Agrarian Reform Law. The new educational statute restored private (largely Catholic) education to its pre-1945 position. In the subsequent decade, private education grew rapidly at all levels, while official schools stagnated and their number declined. New laws on agrarian reform made expropriation and distribution of land much more difficult. In addition, previously expropriated land (along with land earmarked for distribution) was returned to private owners, while peasant families were evicted. Unions were dissolved, both in industry and in agriculture, and political party organizations, especially those of AD and the

Communist party (PCV), were suppressed. All this was backed up by a growing apparatus of terror and repression.[23]

Reestablishment and Consolidation

The dictatorship that began in 1948 had a major impact on the subsequent conduct of democratic politics. The experience of resistance to military rule gradually forced cooperation on the political parties, and many who had been bitter enemies during the trienio came to work together, both underground and in exile, against the regime. Top leadership in exile, reflecting on recent events, recognized the role intense unabated conflict had played in weakening trienio democracy. As military rule grew more harsh and personalistic, the costs of these conflicts seemed all the greater and the incentive to avoid such conflicts in the future all the more compelling.

With the overthrow of military rule, steps were taken to correct the errors of the past. The most striking feature of Venezuelan politics after 1958 is the conscious, explicit decision of political elites to reduce interparty tension and violence, accentuate common interests and procedures, and remove, insofar as possible, issues of survival and legitimacy from the political scene. This new orientation took concrete form in an agreement signed between AD, COPEI, and URD in October 1958—the Pact of Punto Fijo. As Rómulo Betancourt noted, this pact reflected a belief that extreme partisanship and intense conflict during the trienio had opened the doors to military intervention. After 1958,

Inter-party discord was kept to a minimum, and in this way leaders revealed that they had learned the harsh lesson which despotism had taught to all Venezuelans. Underground, in prison, in exile, or living a precarious liberty at home, we all understood that it was through the breach opened in the front of civility and culture that the conspiracy of November 24, 1948—unmistakably reactionary and supported by some with naive good faith—was able to pass, a conspiracy which overthrew the legitimate government of Rómulo Gallegos.[24]

The Pact of Punto Fijo contains a series of points worth examining in some detail. First, the three parties explicitly recognized the existence of various parties and of differences between them as normal and legitimate, calling for the depersonalization of political conflict and the elimination of violence. Moreover, they pledged support for a common program, emphasizing mutual interests and shelving more controversial items which might lead to renewed bitter conflict. This commitment to a common program was reinforced by agreement to participate in a coalition government after the 1958 elections, *regardless of their outcome*. In this way, all parties were committed to the defense of the system. The pact further bound the parties to defend the democratic system in case of emergency. The votes received by all three were to be considered as support for the system. In addition, the principle was established that should a party leave the coalition, it did not therefore pass automatically into all-out opposition, but rather remained tied and committed to democratic institutions.

The Pact of Punto Fijo was an attempt to begin building a set of rules of the game acceptable to major groups, committing each to the survival of all through acceptance of the same set of political processes. Thus, the issue of survival was tacitly removed from politics, at least for the signers of the pact and the forces they represented. The possible problems posed by diverse interests and intense oppositions were to be overcome through the use of coalitions, the redefinition of key substantive issues, and the reworking of procedures so as to reduce the intensity of conflict. In these measures, one begins to see a reversal of trienio patterns—now the trade-off of sectoral interests versus compromise and system stability is to be resolved in favor of the latter. During the trienio AD was seen as a threat to religious, military, business, agrarian, and competing electoral elites. After 1958, party leaders set out to bury these fears. Examination of a series of cases, parallel to those prominent in the trienio, reveals striking difference in forms of action and guiding political norms.

The church presents an interesting case. After 1958, relations of the church and the Catholic sector in general to the political system underwent fundamental change. AD mended fences, substantially increasing official subsidies to the church and sponsoring the revision of legal arrangements which had subordinated the church to the state in previous years. In the sensitive area of education, the government, while remaining committed to expansion of public education, tried to avoid raising the potentially explosive issues of organizational principles and ideological justifications for education, thus avoiding trienio-style conflicts. Emphasis was placed instead on redefining the question in technical terms.

When educational reform did arise as an issue, the way in which it was handled is revealing. A lengthy series of secret negotiations was held between the coalition parties and the church—negotiations which were intended from the beginning as a means to compromise. The talks were structured to promote compromise, by emphasizing technical issues and separating them from more intractable questions of philosophy and orientation. A potentially explosive issue was thus redefined in a manageable fashion, procedures were developed for dealing with it (the negotiations), and great efforts were made to keep the conflict in the hands of elites, out of the public eye where leaders on all sides agreed that passions could easily be inflamed, allowing the conflict to get out of hand. Privacy, centralization, and control were the watchwords.

A key factor in the reconciliation of AD and the Catholic sector was a change in the role of the Christian Democratic party, COPEI. During the trienio, COPEI was caught up in a wave of religious opposition to AD. Recently formed at the time, COPEI was not sufficiently differentiated from the rest of the Catholic sector, by virtue of being a political party with political interests and values, to serve as a mediator between Catholics and the regime. After 1948, however, many of the party's most vociferous activists abandoned COPEI, leaving party leaders feeling that they had been used by reactionary opponents of AD, people not really interested in COPEI or its program. These perspectives help explain COPEI's willingness to serve as mediator and buffer between the sectors, often restraining more militant defenders of the church with arguments as to the need for political compromise.

This mediating role was facilitated by COPEI's role in government. The party's membership in governmental coalition from 1959 to 1963 provided an implicit guarantee of survival to the Catholic sector. Moreover, under the sponsorship of COPEI, many leading Catholics participated in government. Thus, in education, labor, agriculture, and other sensitive areas, many who had been bitter enemies in the trienio began to work together on common problems.

The evolution of AD-Catholic relations is a good example of the development of a sense of trust and mutual guarantees between old enemies. As the church and Catholic leaders discovered the willingness of AD to accept initiatives of compromise and offer concrete benefits in return, they began to realize that gains could be made within the system at a cost lower than that associated with all-out conflict. As Catholic elites discovered a disposition within AD to offer and accept initiatives of compromise within a framework of felt guarantees, the old sense of exclusion and powerlessness was replaced by the hope for real possibilities within the system. Catholic elites now felt that they too could win by playing according to AD's rules. A similar feeling helped mend fences between AD and competing political groups.

After 1958, AD moved from a position of absolute electoral dominance to the status of a major party, one among several key groups in the system. As tables 2 and 3 show, in the elections held from 1958 to 1968, opposition parties gradually increased their share of the total vote in both presidential and congressional races. This greater balance is also reflected in congressional representations (see table 4). The decline in AD's vote, plus subsequent divisions of the party which cut into its congressional strength, made coalitions both feasible (as forces were more evenly distributed) and necessary to the operations of government.

Coalition strategies may be followed for several sorts of reasons. As we have seen, it may be in the interest of stability to increase the numbers of groups committed to the system and benefiting from it.[25] Coalitions are also a common response to situations of fragmentation and intense, cumulative conflict. Elite decisions to counter the effects of division often take the form of

Table 2. Percentages of the Vote in Presidential Elections, by Party (1947–73)

Year	Party				
	AD	COPEI	URD	PCV	Other
1947	74.5	22.4	—	3.2	—
1958	49.2	15.7	30.7	3.2	—
1963	32.8	20.2	17.5	—	27.8[b]
1968	28.2	29.0	22.2[a]	—	20.3[c]
1973	48.8	36.8	3.0	—	11.4[d]

SOURCE: Data for 1947, 1958, and 1963 are drawn from Boris Bunimov-Parra, *Introducción a la sociología electoral Venezolana* (Caracas: Editorial Arte, 1968), "Cuadros Anexos." Data for 1968 are from David Myers, *Democratic Campaigning in Venezuela: Caldera's Victory* (Caracas: Editorial Natura, 1973), appendix B, table 24. Data for 1973 from *Latin America*, 21 December 1973.

[a] URD in coalition with two other parties, FND and FDP.
[b] This figure includes votes for Arturo Uslar Pietri (FND), Wolfgang Larrazábal (FDP), and several minor groups.
[c] This figure includes votes for Luis Beltrán Prieto (MEP) and several minor parties.
[d] Includes 4.2 percent for MAS, 5.1 percent for MEP, and 2.1 percent for minor parties.

Table 3. Percentages of the Vote in Congressional Elections, by Party (1958–73)

Year	Party									
	AD	COPEI	URD	PCV	FND[a]	FDP[b]	PRIN[c]	MEP[d]	CCN[e]	Other
1958	49.5	15.2	26.8	6.2	—	—	—	—	—	2.4
1963	32.7	20.8	17.4	—	13.3	9.6	3.3	—	—	2.7
1968	25.7	24.2	9.3	2.8	2.6	5.3	2.3	13.0	11.1	—
1973	44.3	30.3	3.2	1.2	—	1.2	—	5.0	4.3	5.2

SOURCE: Data for 1958 and 1963 drawn from Boris Bunimov-Parra, *Introducción a la sociología electoral Venezolana* (Caracas: Editorial Arte, 1968), "Cuadros Anexos." Data for 1968 drawn from David Myers, *Democratic Campaigning in Venezuela: Caldera's Victory* (Caracas: Editorial Natura, 1973), appendix B, table 28. Data for 1973 are from *Latin America*, 21 December 1973.

[a] FND (Frente Nacional Democrático) is a conservative party formed around the 1963 presidential candidacy of Arturo Uslar Pietri.
[b] FDP (Fuerza Democrática Popular) is a party based on the candidacy and appeal of Wolfgang Larrazábal, head of the provisional government which followed the overthrow of Pérez Jiménez in 1958.
[c] PRIN (Partido Revolucionario de Integración Nacionalista) is a product of a division of AD in 1962.
[d] MEP (Movimiento Electoral del Pueblo) is the product of a division of AD in 1967.
[e] CCN (Cruzada Cívica Nacionalista) ran in the name of ex-president Marcos Pérez Jiménez.

Table 4. Congressional Representation, by Party (1958–73)

Party	1958 Deputies	1958 Senators	1963 Deputies	1963 Senators	1968 Deputies	1968 Senators	1973 Deputies	1973 Senators
AD	73	32	66	22	66	19	102	29
COPEI	19	6	39	8	59	16	64	14
URD	34	11	29	7	18	3	5	1
PCV	7	2	—	—	5	1	2	—
FND	—	—	22	5	4	1	—	—
FDP	—	—	16	4	10	2	—	—
MEP	—	—	—	—	24	5	8	2
CCN	—	—	—	—	21	4	7	1
Other	—	—	7	—	7	1	12	2

SOURCE: Data for 1958, 1963, and 1968 from Juan C. Rey, "El sistema de partidos Venezolano," *Politea* 1 (1972): 216, 219, 223. Data for 1973 from *Semana,* 3–9 January 1974 (Caracas).

coalitions, both limited and all-inclusive. The experience of many smaller European countries, where subcultural fragmentation has been contained through a delicate network of coalitions, speaks directly to this point.[26]

AD assumed power in 1959 in coalition with URD and COPEI. URD left the coalition in 1960, in disagreement over policy toward Cuba, while COPEI decided to pursue an independent line in the next governmental period. But despite changes in composition, the orientation to coalition on the part of AD remained firm, and a different group of partners formed the government for the 1963–68 period.

Relations with military, business, and agrarian sectors reveal a similar cautious pattern. A careful policy of compromise with the military was followed. Many real benefits were provided in training, equipment, housing, pay, and the like. Meanwhile, a purge of old-line interventionist officers was combined with a campaign of persuasion, by President Betancourt and others, to convince the military that AD was the only solution. A right-wing military coup, it was argued, would only lead to a general antimilitary coalition, producing a Cuban-style revolution and the liquidation of the traditional military, as in Cuba.[27]

To conciliate business elites, strikes were restrained and the more Socialist elements of AD's party doctrine were toned down. In the agrarian sector, a radical program of immediate large-scale expropriation and distribution of land was, on the whole, shelved in favor of a more "integral" program, stressing heavy capital investment and colonization, always less controversial than the expropriation of land already under cultivation. A clear indication of changing styles within AD is visible in the process followed in the preparation of a new Agrarian Reform Law. As with education, a law which in the trienio had been largely produced by one party now grew out of extended consultations among many groups.[28] Powell sums up the general issue well:

Should the leadership of the Peasant Federation, through land invasions and demonstrations, militate for a more rapid and drastic agrarian reform program, which might threaten the reformist government by strengthening the hand of its political opponents on the right, who opposed land reform? Or should the leadership use restraint in the pace of its demands and cooperate with the government in solving the administrative problems of the agrarian reform program, which might enhance the long-term probability of success and minimize political opposition to land reform, but at the same time might hazard the loyalty of the militant elements among the peasant masses? It was a replay of the tension from 1945 to 1948 between authority legitimation and interest articulation.[29]

The immediate result of these tensions was a major purge of radical leaders within the peasant movement, a purge conducted by AD party leadership and ratified by elections within the Peasant Federation and the general labor federation in late 1961 and 1962. Purges of radicals, combined with restraint in the tone and content of the agrarian reform program, clearly gained greater legitimacy for AD among traditional and competing elites. Traditional elites had less to fear, and competing electoral groups were able to survive within the unions, since after 1958 most unions and professional associations instituted a policy of proportional representation in order to eliminate the organizational parallelism characteristic of earlier periods.

In all these cases, legitimacy was won through restraint. Restraint, in turn, was achieved through open pressure by party elites on sectoral leadership to moderate demands in order to avoid arousing intense opposition and severe conflict. But why was a policy of restraint followed in the first place? First, AD leaders believed that more groups *should* be involved in the system (e.g., through coalitions), because it would strengthen the system and because it was right. This perspective was born of the experience of exile and reflection on the errors of the trienio. Second, leaders in AD and other democratic parties were afraid—they feared renewed conflict with the Right, and more importantly, they feared the extreme Left and the possibility of a Cuban-style revolution in Venezuela. Fear of the Left was widespread and was used by AD to keep the military, the church, and others lined up in support of the system. The threat of guerrilla warfare helped transform AD, in the eyes of others, from the Antichrist and extreme radical of the 1940s to a bulwark of moderation and stability in the 1960s.

Perhaps more than any other single factor, the development of a leftist strategy of insurrection in the early 1960s consolidated Venezuelan democracy, by unifying Center and Right around AD in response to a common threat. The alienation of the Left is so important that its origins deserve careful attention here. The decisions to reduce the scope and level of conflict after 1958 were made by top party leadership in exile and were later rejected by many who had led the underground struggle against military rule. This division, which often pitted younger leaders with experience underground against older exiles, was particularly notable in AD and URD. Young leaders saw the restoration of democracy in 1958 as an opportunity to push forward quickly with radical programs of change. Naturally, they rejected Betancourt's policy of coalitions and compromise with traditional elites, as these required the sacrifice of radical programs.

Moreover, during the resistance to military rule, AD and URD had cooperated as a matter of course with the Communists. Underground leaders saw no reason to exclude Communists from government and the administration of programs. The issue was joined from the very beginning, for the policy of coalition and compromise described above always excluded the Communist party, defined by Betancourt as a disloyal opposition.

The alienation of the Left took various forms. On the level of opinions and attitudes, the Left was isolated—Center and Right were close in attitudes, and both held positions far removed from those of the Left. In addition, the Left was much more divided internally than other opinion groups.[30] This division at the level of attitudes set the stage for AD's overall strategy—jettisoning the Left in order to reach compromise agreements with more conservative sectors. AD's leaders paid the price of their pursuit of compromise in a series of party divisions throughout the 1960s. In each case, more radical and Socialist elements split off after being expelled. The first and most serious split arose in April 1960, when the Movement of the Revolutionary Left (MIR) was formed. The MIR split was based on the generational-ideological cleavages already noted; and on formation, the new party took from AD its entire youth wing, some trade union groups, one senator, and seventeen deputies. The MIR immediately became a powerful force on the Left, posing a sharp, direct challenge to the legitimacy of AD's policies and procedures.

The first major clashes between the Left and the government arose over methods of political action. The government banned all unauthorized street demonstrations, and the Left replied by asserting that "the streets belong to the people," arguing that the regime should leave methods of popular struggle involving mass mobilization essentially untrammeled. President Betancourt rejected this position, arguing that the true reality of "the people" lay in their representative organizations:

The thesis that the streets belong to the people is false and demagogic . . . the people in the abstract does not exist . . . the people are the political parties, the unions, the organized economic sectors, professional societies, university groups. Whenever any of these groups seeks authorization for a peaceful demonstration, in a building or in the streets, there will be no difficulty in granting it. But as often as uncontrolled groups jump into the streets, under whatever pretext, they will be treated with neither softness nor lenience, for a country cannot live and work, acquire culture and forge riches, if it is always threatened by the surprise explosions of street violence, behind which the historical enemies of democracy, totalitarians of all names and colors, seek to engineer its discredit.[31]

In this speech, as often in action, Betancourt insisted on two central points: organizational concentration and the autonomy of politics. Limiting political methods by concentrating action in common organizational vehicles reflects a desire to avoid situations where conflict can get out of hand and to maintain a great deal of control over the consequences of action. Opposition and conflict are tolerated, and indeed built into the system, but are required to work within common forms and processes—parties, elections, congress, official agencies, and the like. Forms of action difficult to control, such as street demonstrations, land invasions, and private violence, are discouraged and suppressed. The autonomy of politics is affirmed by insisting that politics be left to professional politicians. Once leaders are elected by constitutional means, it was argued, they should be given considerable autonomy and not be subjected to a continuous barrage of demands. Betancourt's insistence on the concentration of political action in a limited range of organizations and arenas offers a clear alternative to "praetorian" politics, in which, according to Huntington, "social forces confront each other nakedly; no political institution, no corps of professional political leaders are recognized or accepted as the legitimate intermediaries to moderate group conflict. Equally important, no agreement exists among the groups as to the legitimate and authoritative methods for resolving conflicts." [32]

Conflict between the government and the Left escalated rapidly. Leftist parties were soon cornered and defeated on many fronts—their press was shut down, their labor leaders expelled from the trade union confederation, and their parliamentarians arrested. All this drove the Left to a strategy of insurrection, while poor economic conditions and apparent divisions within the government made them believe that any guerrilla war would be short and easy. The decision to launch an insurrection, taken in late 1961, represents the most basic challenge hitherto posed to the party system—a total rejection of its institutions as illegitimate, its methods as inefficient for identifying and resolving national problems, and its claims of democracy as a hollow shell for compromise with entrenched privilege.

The guerrilla movement failed. Although intense fighting continued into late 1964, the prospects for success were never very good, for the Left misjudged the nature of Venezuelan society. Their efforts to establish a base in the countryside were thwarted by previous organization and established loyalties. The untapped potential of the 1930s and 1940s was now occupied ground. For these reasons, the guerrilla movement was defeated politically before a shot was fired. It was isolated, unable to make alliances with other groups, and was gradually reduced to a shrinking core of die-hard militants.

The first to pull out were the Communists, who called a tacit truce in April 1965 and began to withdraw from armed struggle, opening renewed contacts with other political groups. Despite bitter criticism from the MIR, the Communist party Central Committee, meeting in 1968, concluded that the party should return to electoral politics. By this decision, the Communists implicitly accepted the rules of the game imposed by AD and its partners and began to seek reentry into national politics on their terms. This was accomplished by a front organization, Unión Para Avanzar (UPA), through which Communist candidates participated in the 1968 elections. The Communist party itself was legalized once again in 1969 by the new Christian Democratic regime. The changing position of the Left through the 1960s is very important for the political system. Insurrection was finally rejected by the Communists because it did not work. Furthermore, Communist leaders acknowledged that a strategy of armed struggle was inappropriate in Venezuela. To win power in a highly mobilized political order like Venezuela, it was necessary to organize masses and not to get mired down in vanguard strategies.[33]

The 1968 elections, while marking the reincorporation of the Left into the political system, were important in other ways as well. Power was turned over to an opposition party for the first time in Venezuelan history, as COPEI took office with only a slight plurality. In addition, by clarifying and reinforcing previous trends to a political system with a dual center (in AD and COPEI), these elections posed a potentially grave problem for the future. Given their key position in the political system, cooperation between AD and COPEI is clearly crucial to future stability. But direct, permanent coalition (on the model of the National Front between Liberals and Conservatives in Colombia) is difficult, if not impossible, given the need of both parties to maintain separate identities.[34] Rafael Caldera, the successful COPEI candidate for president in 1968, posed the issue this way:

... the union of Acción Democrática and COPEI would form an absolute majority in both Chambers. How could such a union be brought about? Could a governmental coalition really be established? On the one hand, Acción Democrática has as its immediate objectives internal reorganization and struggle for the conquest of power, which is its legitimate right within the law, and through the channels which the Constitution and our institutions have provided. This is probably incompatible, and they have expressed this to me, with participation in my government. On the other hand, I was elected as part of a national movement for change, and the nation would not understand my governing through a political coalition, which although perfectly respectable, has held power for ten years now.[35]

Although no formal coalition was put together during Caldera's administration, COPEI arranged a series of informal working agreements in the Congress with AD and other parties, ensuring sufficient cooperation to allow government to proceed. In this way, stability is guaranteed by continued moderation in the relations of government and opposition, without the need for institutionalization of such agreements in formal terms.

Conclusions: Norms and Structures

In analyzing the changing structure of conflict and its implications for political legitimacy and the survival of democracy in Venezuela, several factors might be emphasized. Consider first the role of prudent leadership.

From recent Venezuelan experience, it is clear that elites made conscious decisions to restrain and modify partisan conflict after 1958. This sort of decision, is, of course, rarely taken at any one time, but rather inferred, *post hoc,* from examination of events. In Venezuela, however, it is remarkable how easily one can pinpoint specific events in this pattern of decision: the Pact of Punto Fijo, formation of coalitions, negotiations with the church, restraint in programs, defeat of the Left, etc.

These decisions were part of the creation of a method for the institutionalization of conflict. Political elites in Venezuela did not set out to eliminate conflict. Rather, they recognized it as the legitimate expression of social diversity and invented means by which a variety of groups and interests could live together, without requiring the prior sacrifice of diversity as the price for stability. A central element of the method is its emphasis placed on common procedures, common forms of action, and mutual guarantees. In this context, "consensus" is a much more limited affair than is often implied by the use of that term—an operational code of coexistence, a delimitation of common ground, rather than an expression of identical substantive interests or beliefs.

The decision to accept and live with diversity deserves more extended comment. In studies of the breakdown of democracies, the argument is often encountered that democracy failed because traditional oppositions were not rooted out and a new social harmony instituted. It is similarly alleged that nations with patterns of cumulative cleavages, where social conflicts reinforce one another, are poor bets for survival, because of the nature of conflict itself. However, Venezuela, like many European cases, points up the potentially independent role of leadership decisions in counteracting social and political fragmentation or polarization.[36] In Venezuela, as we have seen, incentives to moderation and compromise, expressed through coalitions and a general reduction in partisan hostility, had a major, independent effect on the structure of conflict.

Venezuelan political leaders built a new political methodology, a set of procedures for handling conflict. The success of this method hinges on the central role of political parties. The great strength of party organization has provided elites with sufficient leverage to impose settlements on rank and file members. The role of leadership is reinforced by the fact that in Venezuela politics has clearly become a matter for specialists, a monopoly of the party organizations and their leaders. Parties play a key double-edged role in Venezuela. On the one hand, they manage the mobilization and incorporation of large masses of people into politics. On the other hand, by virtue of their broad and heterogeneous character, the parties per se have acquired an autonomous position with respect to any single sector. This development of a "public" perspective allows party leaders to aggregate many diverse interests, often restraining group demands in the name of overall political needs.

In normative terms, a profound learning experience occurred among Venezuelan leaders. Learning centered on the notion that politics really is what the cliché says: the art of the possible. Elites began to look at politics in terms of concession and compromise, and not merely as the all-out insistence on program and doctrine. Living in exile during the 1950s, AD leaders began to attribute their fall in 1948 to having pushed too many groups too far too fast. Thus, in marked contrast to their behavior during the trienio, political elites after 1958 exhibited several qualities essential to stability: restraint in goal-setting, restraint in the choice of means, and attention to intensities. Let us examine these points more closely.

Elsewhere in this series, Linz argues that what often seem to be unsolvable problems are not intrinsically so, but rather are produced by politicians who define problems in such a way as to create oppositions and conflicts that are themselves insoluble. In Venezuela, the devotion of leadership to redefining problems, methods of action, and relations among groups is very prominent. For example, the school issue, often a source of major conflict, has been resolved in Venezuela as a conflict over legitimacy.[37] The basic sense of guarantees between the Catholic sector and AD made possible lengthy negotiations over education. In this process, fundamental ideological differences were accepted and set aside, while talks concentrated on common ground. With agrarian reform, redefinition of the problem led to restraint in policy-making and implementation, concentrating on the search for less conflictive methods of agrarian reform. In the crucial area of methods of political action, the dominance of elections as a legitimate source of power is notable, as is the basic agreement among all groups to work within the commonly defined limits of the party system.

Structural and normative factors combined in Venezuela to favor what Etzioni has called the "encapsulation of conflict."[38] Encapsulation of conflict refers to the development of a self-enforcing set of rules and norms, whose constant use makes the system stronger by committing groups to act within already established processes. What were once innovations in intergroup relations become, through continuous, routine use, conventional expectations of common treatment. The successful implementation of these rules and norms rests, of course, on the viability of the structures through which they work. In Venezuela this means the political parties, whose deep social roots and powerful internal structure make the implementation of elite agreements possible.

The argument as presented to this point has an air of inevitability about it. But of course, no real social process ever proceeds quite as automatically as hindsight might lead one to believe. Rather, a wide range of situationally specific elements enters the process, and their impact must be taken into account. The key role of prudent leadership has already been emphasized. In addition, the structural and normative elements contributing to democratic stability received a powerful boost from the common threat posed from the Left. The exclusion of the Left from post-1958 political arrangements clearly helped legitimate AD in the eyes of its old enemies, making it a stable bulwark against repetition of the Cuban Revolution in Venezuela.

In this context, it is instructive to compare the evolution of the Catholic sector after 1958 with the fate of the Left. The Catholic sector was incorporated into the system. It accommodated itself to the system, acknowledged the legitimacy of political processes, and offered, sought, and accepted mutual guarantees of survival. The regime abandoned more radical elements in its program in order to secure the loyalty of Catholic groups, while the church, in turn, refrained from raising basic challenges and buried the hatchet of religious-political conflict. For the Left, however, already organized along mass lines, alienation from the regime resulted from precisely the kinds of bargains through which Catholics and others were incorporated into the system. But with the Left, no compromises were made until defeat was ensured. The extension of mutual guarantees was contingent on the abandonment of legitimacy conflicts in both cases, but the procedures differed notably: concession and compromise with the Catholics; and defeat and acquiescence in the system for the Left.

The difference between these cases deserves further reflection, because it contains, in microcosm, much of the explanation for the survival and stabilization of Venezuelan democracy. So far I have emphasized legitimacy conflicts and their resolution. But legitimacy conflicts are not all the same, and their resolution has different consequences for different groups. In Venezuela the regime incorporated traditional and established groups through compromise, convincing them of the benefits of organization and action according to the new system's rules. In this process, the system's rules do not change: rather, they are frozen, and the substantive limits of action are set in such a way as to avoid fundamental conflict. The incorporation of radical challenging groups, however, was contingent not on negotiation and mutual benefits, but rather on defeat. Here, incentives to compromise were rare, for radical challengers have little to gain from mere incorporation into the system. To achieve their goals, they must expand the system, broaden its scope, and mobilize new and hitherto excluded groups. But the bargains struck with traditional sectors exclude just this kind of strategy, ruling out immediate revolutionary change.

In cold strategic terms, then, it may be easier for democracies to incorporate traditional oppositions than radical ones. The Venezuelan experience presents a strategy of incorporating conservative groups first, and then defeating and reincorporating (on modified terms) the radical opposition. To those who decry such a strategy as a betrayal of the goals for which democracy was established in the first place, Venezuelan leaders might reply that it is better to reduce immediate demands and concentrate on establishing institutional continuity. In this way, the possibility of future change remains open, as institutions survive and acquire broadly based legitimacy. Immediate pressure for radical change might stimulate powerful opposition leading to a reactionary coup and the liquidation of all reform. In other words, half a loaf is better than none.

While, in strategic terms, this approach may pay off in consolidation of the system, it is important to realize that such results have a price—programs shelved, alternatives excluded, and change postponed. In closing I would like to consider some of the costs and consequences of the pattern of change in Venezuela in the 1960s and speculate briefly on the future.

Conclusions: Costs and Benefits

In the terms employed in these pages, Venezuela is clearly a "success." Democracy was consolidated in the face of determined opposition from both Right and Left. Mass participation has been maintained and combined with competition and stability, legitimate political institutions were built, and social progress has been achieved. But because Venezuela opted for success in the form described here, it represents to many not success, but rather an example of all that is wrong with Latin American development—increasing gaps between rich and poor, continued dependence on foreign economic control, and a reformist orientation which sidesteps basic issues of change. The costs of stabilization are alleged to be too great—the success of elites is viewed as a failure to implement "real change."[39]

Let us consider the costs of stability in Venezuela. A striking feature of Venezuelan politics is what might be called a structural coercion, operating at all levels of the political system. This coercion requires all groups and interests to work through the matrix of party if they are to be effective. A major factor preventing complete ossification has been party competition. The need to compete for support, and the increased balance among major parties, has helped avoid some of the dangers common to more hegemonic systems, such as riding roughshod over minorities.

Nevertheless, the current evolution of the system toward a dual center, shared between AD and COPEI, raises important questions about the fate of weaker groups. AD has convinced others of the benefits of working within the system. But if instead of a one-party hegemony, minor groups face a permanent duopoly, may they not feel equally frustrated? With little chance of ever achieving power or seeing their programs translated into action, will they feel the temptation of conspiracy or insurrection?

Furthermore, one important sustaining aspect of the system has been weakened. A major source of strength has been the ability of party leaders to control sectoral groups. But group interests are not infinitely malleable, and the long history of party splits in Venezuela bears witness to the rejection by some groups of these attempts at restraint. The tight linkage of party to sector remains, but multiple party splits have produced a division of control in trade unions, peasant syndicates, and other party-related groups. Instead of two or three major party lines, many sectors are divided into six or seven groups. This multiplication of divisions makes reliable and predictable coordination between levels of action less certain, and reduces the ability of government to control sectoral action.

A final problem for the future of the party system is perhaps a tribute to its own success. Since 1958, social change has proceeded apace, and Venezuela has developed an infrastructure of roads, transport, and electricity, while extending health and educational services in the nation. Population has grown, particularly in the cities, and the development of a national highway network has reduced the isolation of previously peripheral areas. But political parties remain closely tied to the geographical-demographic patterns of previous years. AD and COPEI are still largely based on the periphery of Venezuela, with most of their support in small towns and rural areas.[40] Despite tremendous migration to the cities (about one-fifth of the population now lives in Caracas), these parties have so far failed to organize support in the cities; urban voters have chosen instead to support nonparty, personalistic appeals.[41] In the long run, then, the key elements in the system may be based on a permanently declining share of the population.

The first version of this chapter was completed in September 1973, shortly after the overthrow and death of Salvador Allende in Chile. In conclusion, it is worth considering Chile and Venezuela together. Chilean politics from 1970 to 1973 bears a sharp resemblance to the trienio in Venezuela. Issues were increasingly defined in all-or-nothing terms, and many came to see their very survival threatened by the continued existence of the regime. All kinds of social groups were polarized and split apart, and the nation was engulfed in a rising tide of private and public violence. As a result, military action in both nations came in response to the calls of many political actors caught up in struggles which made the system seem illegitimate.

The experience of Chile is a sobering one and makes the costs and sacrifices entailed in the stabilization of Venezuelan democracy perhaps more acceptable.[42] For elites clearly saw these as necessary to ensure stability. Political leaders in Venezuela sought to build institutions first, believing that only with firm, legitimate institutions, and a broad commitment of diverse groups to their existence, could any reform policies be implemented. A set of authentic political traditions and the expectations created by action within common democratic processes had to be established first.

Perhaps Venezuela represents a middle ground. Since 1958, politics has been marked by the caution, prudence, and care appropriate to a period of transition and institution-building. The danger in such an approach is that decisions taken in response to the problems of a given situation may be transformed into permanent limits to change, and it becomes difficult for policy-makers in one period to break free of the restraints imposed in another. Perhaps now, with twenty years of experience in democracy, with a stable and skilled set of leaders occupying the Center, and the defeat of Right and Left alike, the scope of policy in Venezuela can be expanded to deal more directly with the pressing challenges and problems visible in the nation today.[43]

NOTES

1. This paper draws heavily on the ideas and data presented in my book, *Conflict and Political Change in Venezuela* (Princeton, N.J.: Princeton University Press, 1973). Given this general debt, no further reference will be made to the book, except to indicate the location of more extended discussions of particular points raised below.

2. A useful discussion of legitimacy in these terms is Charles W. Anderson, *Politics and Economic Change in Latin America* (Princeton, N.J.: Van Nostrand, 1967), pp. 90ff.

3. A useful discussion of the proportional representation system employed in Venezuela is David J. Myers, *Democratic Campaigning in Venezuela: Caldera's Victory* (Caracas: Editorial Natura, 1973), pp. 72–77.

4. The role of changing leadership norms in altering mass behavior is examined for Cuba by Richard Fagen in his *The Transformation of Political Culture in Cuba* (Stanford, Ca.: Stanford University Press, 1969), p. 150. For a general analysis of the role of leaders in shaping the political world of followers, see Murray Edelman, *The Symbolic Uses of Politics* (Urbana: University of Illinois Press, 1967), esp. chap. 1.

5. See Robert L. Gilmore, *Caudillism and Militarism in Venezuela, 1810–1910* (Athens, Ohio: Ohio University Press, 1964), for a study of regionalism and civil war in nineteenth-century Venezuela. A very good account of the transition to a new system at the turn of the century is Ramón J. Velásquez, *La caída del liberalismo amarillo*, 2d ed. (Caracas, 1973).

6. Velásquez, *La caída*, gives a brilliant account of the social basis of nineteenth-century militarism.

7. See A. Arellano Moreno, *Mirador de la historia política de Venezuela* (Caracas: Ediciones Edime, 1967), esp. pp. 19–21. In *La caída*, pp. xix–xx, Velásquez notes that "By 1935, younger generations doubted if struggle between parties had ever existed in Venezuela, in any stage of her history. . . . The regime founded by Cipriano Castro in 1899 and consolidated by Juan Vicente Gómez in his 27 years of absolute power had cut down the century-old trees of the political parties, and not even the memory remained of that political landscape. Venezuela was like ploughed land, waiting for the seed."

8. A useful account of the impact of nineteenth-century civil wars on the aristocracy is Domingo A. Rangel, *Los andinos en el poder* (Caracas: Talleres Gráficos Universitarios, 1964) esp. chaps. 1–4.

9. The best source on the peasant movement is John D. Powell, *Political Mobilization of the Venezuelan Peasant* (Cambridge, Mass.: Harvard University Press, 1971). Data on the decline of traditional agricultures are drawn from Powell, pp. 15–27, and María De Lourdes Acedo de Sucre and Carmen M. Nones Mendoza, *La generación venezolana de 1928: Estudio de una élite política* (Caracas: Ediciones Ariel, 1967), pp. 54–55.

10. José Silva Michelena, *The Politics of Change in Venezuela,* vol. 3, *The Illusion of Democracy in Dependent Nations* (Cambridge, Mass.: MIT Press, 1971), p. 79.

11. Silva Michelena, *Politics of Change,* p. 55, table 3.1.

12. This point is discussed in general terms in Samuel Huntington, *Political Order in Changing Societies* (New Haven: Yale University Press, 1968), p. 407.

13. The many roles of party organization in urban *barrios* are discussed in Talton F. Ray, *The Politics of the Barrios of Venezuela* (Berkeley and Los Angeles: University of California Press, 1969), p. 103.

14. AD's initial attempts at organization are described in Rómulo Betancourt, *Venezuela: Política y petróleo*, rev. ed. (Caracas: Editorial Senderos, 1967), esp. chap. 3.
15. This is a common pattern in the traditional Latin American church. See Ivan Vallier, *Catholicism, Social Control, and Modernization in Latin America* (Englewood Cliffs, N.J.: Prentice-Hall, 1970), pp. 25–28.
16. Powell, *Political Mobilization*, p. 68.
17. Data on the growth of the Peasant Federation are provided in Powell, *Political Mobilization*, p. 79. The growth of the trade union confederation is reviewed in John D. Martz, *Acción Democrática: Evolution of a Modern Political Party in Venezuela* (Princeton, N.J.: Princeton University Press, 1966), p. 260.
18. For a general discussion, see James S. Coleman, *Community Conflict* (New York: The Free Press, 1957).
19. Powell, *Political Mobilization*, pp. 83 ff.
20. AD's attitude toward other parties during the trienio is discussed in Martz, *Acción Democrática*, pp. 321–22.
21. Speech by Betancourt on 12 June 1946, reprinted in *Trayectoria democrática de una revolución: Discursos y conferencias*, 2 vols. (Caracas: Imprenta Nacional, 1948), vol. 2, p. 22.
22. A Jesuit magazine greeted the fall of AD with an editorial entitled "God Has Saved Us." See *SIC (Revista de Orientación)*, no. 110 (December 1948).
23. Changes in education in this period are discussed in Levine, *Conflict*, pp. 94–98. On the agrarian situation, see Powell, *Political Mobilization*, pp. 87–94. A general account of military repression is José V. Abreu, *Se Llamaba SN*, 2d ed. (Caracas: Editor, José Augustín Catalá, 1964).
24. Rómulo Betancourt, *Tres años de gobierno democrático*, 2 vols. (Caracas: Imprenta Nacional, 1962), vol. 1, p. 13.
25. This process works at several levels. Speaking of lower class urban groups, Talton Ray points out that "The proportionate size of the minority can grow, of course, as a result of a coalition arrangement which allows persons affiliated with the coalition parties to identify with the in group and therefore to share, in spirit if not in fact, the benefits of government attention. As more persons are brought under the coalition's umbrella, the ranks of malcontents are weakened and partisan contention eases off" (Ray, *Politics of the Barrios*, p. 167).
26. Two very useful general discussions are Arend Lijphart, "Consociational Democracy," *World Politics* 21, no. 2 (January 1969): 207–23; and Val Lorwin, "Segmented Pluralism: Ideological Cleavages and Political Cohesion in the Smaller European Democracies," *Comparative Politics* 3, no. 2 (January 1971): 141–76.
27. Betancourt's relations with the military are discussed in Robert J. Alexander, *The Venezuelan Democratic Revolution: A Profile of the Regime of Rómulo Betancourt* (New Brunswick, N.J.: Rutgers University Press, 1964), pp. 105–17, and Edwin Lieuwin, *Generals vs. Presidents: Neomilitarism in Latin America* (New York: Praeger, 1964), pp. 86–91.
28. The politics surrounding the Agrarian Reform Law of 1960 are described in Powell, *Political Mobilization*, pp. 106–12.
29. Ibid., p. 105.
30. For data on this point, see José Silva Michelena, "Desarrollo cultural y heterogeneidad cultural en Venezuela," *Revista Latinoamericana de Sociología* 3, no. 2 (July 1967), especially pp. 191–93.
31. Betancourt, *Tres años*, vol. 1, p. 245.
32. Huntington, *Political Order*, p. 196.
33. It is interesting to note that since 1968, the Communists themselves have suffered a major division. Younger and more radical elements were expelled and formed a new party. Here, as previously with AD and the MIR, conflict centered on the insistence of top leadership on hierarchy, discipline, and the need to save the party organization, even at the cost of sacrificing more direct and immediate revolutionary goals. Despite the nature of their critique, this group, now organized as the Movement to Socialism (MAS), also operates according to the rules of the game—actively building a trade union base while conducting a vigorous campaign for the presidency and other offices in the 1973 elections.
34. There is some evidence that President Betancourt wanted to explore the possibility of AD

and COPEI backing one presidential candidate in the 1963 elections. His initial efforts were rejected by his party. See Powell, *Political Mobilization,* pp. 196–97.

35. Quoted in Juan C. Rey, "El sistema de partidos venezolano," *Politea* 1 (1975): 225.

36. See Lijphart, "Consociational Democracy," and Lijphart, *The Politics of Accommodation Pluralism and Democracy in the Netherlands* (Berkeley and Los Angeles: University of California Press, 1968).

37. The school issue as a persistent conflict in Western European development is discussed by Seymour Martin Lipset and Stein Rokkan in the Introduction to their *Party Systems and Voter Alignments* (New York: The Free Press, 1968). See also Kalman H. Silvert, "Conclusions," in *Churches and States: The Religious Institution and Modernization,* ed. Kalman H. Silvert (New York: American Universities Field Staff, 1967), esp. pp. 216–17.

38. See Amitai Etzioni, "On Self-Encapsulating Conflicts," *Journal of Conflict Resolution* 8, no. 3 (September 1964): 242–55.

39. A sharply critical perspective is visible in Silva Michelena, *Politics of Change,* and also in Frank Bonilla, *The Politics of Change in Venezuela,* vol. 2, *The Failure of Elites* (Cambridge, Mass.: MIT Press, 1970).

40. See David Myers, "Urban Voting, Structural Cleavage, and Party System Evolution: The Case of Venezuela," *Comparative Politics* 8, no. 1 (October 1975): 119–51, for detailed ecological data which support this analysis.

41. A recent study of urban voting patterns in Venezuela is John D. Martz and Peter B. Harkins, "Urban Electoral Behavior in Latin America: The Case of Metropolitan Caracas, 1958–1968," *Comparative Politics* 5, no. 4 (July 1973): 523–50.

42. The late President Allende defined his differences with parties like AD and leaders like Betancourt in a revealing interview with Regis Debray. See Debray, *The Chilean Revolution: Conversations with Allende* (New York: Vintage Books, 1971), p. 70. As Arturo Valenzuela points out in his essay, the economic straits of the Allende regime made political solutions more difficult. (See Arturo Valenzuela, *The Breakdown of Democratic Regimes: Chile* [Baltimore: The Johns Hopkins University Press, 1978].) It is often argued that the great wealth of Venezuela is really what made political reconciliation possible—everyone could be paid off. But the Venezuelan state has enjoyed great wealth for many years, years which have seen bloody dictatorship and attempts at mutual extermination by political groups, as well as democratic reconciliation. Certainly wealth helps. But in Venezuela, it is clear that the political choices which made for democratic consolidation were *prior to and independent from* the use of money as a tool of reconciliation. The Venezuelan case makes a strong argument for the relative autonomy of political leadership, institutions, and choices—an argument all too visible, with different consequences, in the other cases considered in this volume.

43. I have speculated at length on the likely future prospects of Venezuelan democracy. See my "Venezuelan Politics: Past and Future," in *Contemporary Venezuela and Its Role in International Affairs,* ed. Robert Bond (New York: New York University Press for The Council on Foreign Relations, 1977), pp. 7–44.

4.
Political Leadership and Regime Breakdown: Brazil

Alfred Stepan*

On 31 March 1964 the Brazilian military overthrew the president of the country, João Goulart, and after assuming power themselves began to construct an authoritarian political regime.[1] Until that time, by almost any criteria, Brazil had not experienced a fully functioning democratic regime. However, from 1945 to 1963 electoral participation had become freer and had greatly expanded. Four presidential elections had been held on schedule in this period, and in each case the electoral victor had been installed in office. Though military intromission in politics was high throughout the period—a military overthrow of the elected president in 1954, a military coup in favor of the newly elected president in 1955, and an abortive coup attempt in 1961— the military nonetheless had not violated until this time a twentieth-century tradition that had kept them from assuming office themselves.

After the coup of 1964, however, despite frequent assertions by successive military governments of their intention to prepare the way for a return to civilian rule (as well as initially high civilian expectation that this would occur), military authoritarian control of Brazilian society steadily widened. Thus the acts of 1964 by which the military came to power saw the end of a quasi-democratic political system, and 1964 can be characterized as not merely a coup against a government but a breakdown of regime.

This breakdown was the end result of a long and complex process in which many factors played a part, a process whose complete treatment is beyond the scope or intention of this chapter.[2] In order to fit this study within the framework of the wider comparative study of the breakdown of regimes, the case of Brazil will be approached here from two levels. The first is the "macro-political" level, which examines strains within the political system of a social, economic, and ideological kind predisposing the regime to breakdown. However, it is clear that in Brazil these generalized strains in the

*An earlier version of this paper was first presented as part of the project on the Breakdown of Democratic Regimes at Varna, Bulgaria, in 1970. Because I found the approach useful I subsequently developed the argument in much greater detail in part 3 of my *The Military in Politics: Changing Patterns in Brazil* (Princeton, N.J.: Princeton University Press, 1971). I wish to thank Princeton University Press for permission to borrow heavily from that book for this chapter.

regime were not sufficient cause for its actual breakdown. Specific political strategies and acts, many of them the result of decisions or nondecisions by the chief executive, João Goulart, were also determinants in the final outcome of the crisis. The second level of analysis is thus the "micro-political" level, which takes us into a study of the quality and style of political leadership, especially in the crucial period immediately before the final breakdown of the regime. This area of inquiry allows us to get close to some of the most important variables in the breakdown of regimes, such as the ability or inability of a president to capitalize on existing supports and to avoid contributing to the consolidation of effective opposition.

The first part of this chapter, in accordance with the above schema, analyzes the changing social and economic context in which a sense of crisis arose in Brazil before 1964 and examines the ways in which this sense of crisis contributed to a belief among important military and civilian elites that the regime possessed neither legitimacy nor the internal ingredients for survival. The second part argues, however, that these broad political and social changes, and the declining value attached to the quasi-democratic regime in Brazil, did not in themselves bring about a breakdown of the regime. Many factors tended, until the very last days before the final coup of 1964, to support a continuation. What brought the regime to the breaking point was the quality of the political leadership of President Goulart, whose acts in the last months of the regime crucially undermined existing supports. The critical role that the sequence of political events and the quality of the individual political leader can play in shaping political outcomes has been relatively neglected in recent studies in comparative politics. In regard to the functioning of democracies, works such as Dankwart Rustow's on the emergence of democratic regimes, Juan Linz's on the breakdown of democratic regimes, and the writings of Arend Lijphart and Eric Nordlinger on conflict regulation in democracies redirect attention to the role of political choices and the sequence of political events in the formation, breakdown, or consociational consolidation of democratic regimes.[3] Brazil provides an interesting case study of the specifically political aspects of regime breakdown.

Social and Economic Loads on the Brazilian Regime

The strategies and actions of President Goulart can only be understood within the wider context of broad changes occurring within Brazil that contributed to a heightened sense of regime crisis. At the broadest level we can categorize the changes in the Brazilian political system in the years before the regime breakdown and especially between 1961 and 1964 in the following manner: (1) an increasing rate of political and economic demands made on the government, (2) a decreasing extractive capability due to the decline in the growth of the economy, (3) a decreasing political capability to convert demands into concrete policy because of fragmentation of support, and (4) an increasing withdrawal of commitment to the political regime itself.[4]

Some of these trends may in fact have been "cyclical" rather than "secular." Politically, however, the important fact is that in the crisis atmosphere that dominated Brazil from 1961 to 1964 these trends were perceived by much of the political elite as evidence of a structural crisis.

Social Mobilization and Economic Decline

One of the factors putting new loads on the political system was the rate and composition of population growth. Brazil's population doubled in the twenty-five years preceding the breakdown of the regime. Brazil had an average annual population increase of 3.0 percent, one of the highest in the world. In terms of comparative "loads" on the different economic systems, it compared with 2.4 percent for India, 1.2 percent for France and West Germany, 1.0 percent for Japan, and less than 1.0 percent for Bulgaria, Denmark, and England.[5]

The growth of the politically relevant population capable of making demands on the output functions of the government increased at an even faster rate than the population growth rate indicates. In the decade 1950 to 1960, Brazil's rural population grew from 33 million to 39 million, while the urban population grew much more rapidly, from 19 million to 32 million.[6] This new, rapidly expanding urban population created a whole series of increased requirements for transportation, jobs, and distribution of food and housing.

In the atmosphere of increasing social mobilization and inflation, growing demands were made on the regulative and distributive capabilities of the government. Strikes increased sharply and the government became more and more involved in strike arbitration. In 1959, for instance, government labor tribunals were involved in 524 labor conflicts; by 1963 this figure had risen to 1,069.[7]

In addition to the rapid escalation of demands from the urban sector of the political system, significant elements of the rural population itself shifted in the early 1950s from "parochial" status to "subject" status, or even "participant" status.[8] In March 1963 rural workers were granted the right to form rural unions and for the first time came under the protection of the minimum wage laws.[9] These laws hastened the competition between individual political leaders, the Catholic church, and the government's highly political land reform agency (SUPRA) to organize the peasants into cooperatives, peasant leagues, and rural unions. It is true that the revolutionary nature and class consciousness of Francisco Julião and the peasant leagues were overrated and overpublicized.[10] Nonetheless, viewed historically, a major change was occurring in the quality and quantity of political demands that the peasants and their political mentors were making on the political system.[11]

A final indicator of increasing social mobilization is the electoral system. The total number of voters increased sharply from 6,200,805 in the 1945 presidential election to 14,747,321 in the 1962 congressional and gubernatorial elections.[12] More importantly, the political intensity and ideological polarization in the 1962 elections was much greater than in previous elections, as numerous leftists staged vigorous campaigns and were opposed by militant free enterprise and anti-Communist business groups.[13] This increasing political competition both reflected and created a rising level of demands upon the political system.

At the same time, the political system showed a decreasing extractive capacity. In part this was due to a decline in the rate of growth of the Brazilian economy. Many of the demands in the 1950s had been satisfied by the rate of growth in the per capita gross national product (GNP), which for most of the decade was one of the highest in the world. In 1962, however, the growth rate began to decline sharply, and in 1963 there was an actual decline in the per capita GNP (see figure 1).

In terms of political capability, the increasing social mobilization and later the downturn in economic growth increased the demands made on the "dis-

Figure 1.   Percentage Change in Real Per Capita GNP, 1957–63

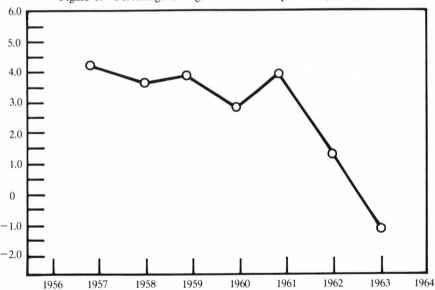

SOURCE: International Monetary Fund, *International Financial Statistics: Supplement to 1966/67 Issues*, p. 28.

tributive'' ability of the government in regard to goods, services, and payments. In response to these demands and in a populist effort to generate greater support, the Goulart government (in office between 1961 and 1964) increased government expenditure. The percent of gross domestic product (GDP) allocated to current account expenditure of the federal government—operational costs of the bureaucracy, subsidies, and transfers—rose from 10.9 in 1959 to 14.4 in 1963. At the same time, however, government tax receipts, which had risen from 17 to 23 percent of the GDP from 1955 to 1959, fell to 20 percent by 1963.[14] Thus in Almond and Powell's vocabulary of governmental capability we can characterize the Brazilian situation in 1962–64 as one in which the government's ability to extract resources such as revenue was declining while the loads on its distributive capability were increasing.[15]

One result was a rapid increase in the government's budget deficit, which accelerated the inflation. Brazilian inflation, always chronic, became acute after 1961 as prices rose by over 50 percent in 1962, 75 percent in 1963, and at a rate of over 140 percent in the three-month period before the collapse of the Goulart government (see figure 2).

The sense of crisis in the economic system was intensified by some indications that the industrialization process was not merely temporarily slowing but facing possible secular decline. The argument was raised that the import substitutions that had been a vital ingredient of Brazil's rapid industrialization in the 1950s were approaching the exhaustion point by the early 1960s.[16] Also, Brazil's export stagnation contributed to serious foreign exchange difficulties and import constraints.

The pressure on Brazil's economy was intensified because it coincided with a declining capacity to extract resources from the international environment.

Figure 2.   Cost of Living Price Index, 1957–63

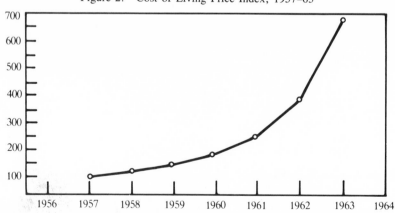

SOURCE: International Monetary Fund, *International Financial Statistics: Supplement to 1966–67 Issues,* p. 27.

Both private and public resources were drying up, due to fears of (and reprisals for) Brazil's inflation, economic nationalism, and political radicalization.[17] By mid-1963, the U.S. government had begun to curtail new development aid contracts with the Brazilian central government. In 1963, debt repayment obligations were so staggering that the finance minister reported to the cabinet that amortization and interest payments already scheduled for the years 1963–65 would amount to $1.8 billion, or about 43 percent of the expected export revenues for that period.[18]

Decreasing Capacity to Convert Demands into Policy: Fragmenting Patterns of Support

In the early 1960s, Brazilian politicians spoke increasingly of the systemic crisis facing the country because of the increased level of demands and the decreased capacity of the economic system to satisfy them. From the early 1950s on, each president had attempted to formulate a coherent development plan, but in each case the plans were abandoned because the president was unable to aggregate political support and because Congress either vetoed the plan or was so divided that it was incapable of allocating resources according to any development priorities. The period before the breakdown of the regime in 1964 was one of increasing fragmentation of the political party system. No single party since 1945 had significantly increased its percentage of nonalliance votes. In fact, the percentage of party alliance votes had been growing at every congressional election (see table 1). The growth of short-term alliances had a disaggregating effect on any program the parties may have stood for at the national level, because the alliances were normally local or state alliances entered into only for the purpose of winning a seat in the federal Congress. Parties standing for different policies in the Congress formed temporary alliances at the local level.[19] The alliances normally disappeared after the election and were unrelated to sustained aggregated support for any program. For example, none of the twenty-six alliances made for the 1958 elections were among the thirty-two formed for the 1962 elections.[20] This steady growth of temporary alliances made it increasingly difficult to make the representatives responsible either to the party or to the wishes of the electorate and has been characterized as a process of "progressive unauthentication."[21]

Within the party system the major source of aggregation under the Vargas and Kubitschek governments in the 1950s was the uneasy coalition between the rural bosses and nationalist entrepreneurs of the PSD party (Partido Social Democrático) and the urban labor leaders of the PTB (Partido Trabalhista Brasileiro). The Brazilian political scientist Hélio Jaguaribe, in his formulation of various possible models of Brazilian growth, termed this coalition "a party of development" and implied that it was an intrinsic part of the success

**Table 1. Growth of Electoral Alliances in
Congressional Elections, Percentage of Party Vote; 1945–62**

Year	PSD	UDN	PTB	Party Alliances
1945	42.3	26.3	10.1	—[a]
1950	22.2	14.0	13.6	16.7
1954	22.0	13.6	14.9	25.7
1958	18.4	13.2	14.7	33.3
1962	15.6	11.2	12.1	41.0

SOURCE: Ronald Schneider, "Election Analysis," in Charles Daugherty, James Rowe, and Ronald Schneider, *Brazil Election Factbook: Number 2, September 1965* (Washington, D.C.: Institute for the Comparative Study of Political Systems, 1965), p. 60.

[a] In 1945, no party alliances were allowed.

of the pragmatic "neo-Bismarckian model" he considered the most appropriate for Brazil's development.[22] The growing radicalization (both Left and Right) within the Brazilian polity, the differential attitudes of the PTB and PSD toward industrial strikes and especially agrarian reform—with its emotional side issues such as rural unionization, land invasion, and constitutional change allowing for expropriation of land without prior payment of cash—increasingly fragmented this major source of aggregation. In 1960, these two parties had allied in eight out of eleven states in which gubernatorial elections were held. In 1962, they were not allied in any of the eleven gubernatorial races.[23]

Withdrawal of Civilian Commitment to the Political Regime

One of the purposes of this volume is to redirect attention to the attitudes and beliefs of the loyal opposition and the defenders of the regime in accord with our premise that these groups are often more important for the survival of democracy than the beliefs and actions of the disloyal opposition which have received so much more attention in social science literature.[24] Significantly, those most empowered to defend the regime, the last two presidents in power before the breakdown in 1964, Quadros and Goulart, were both pessimistic about the chances of the political system working effectively, and it could be argued that they both worked harder at attempting to change the regime than at achieving more limited goals within the existing framework.[25] Quadros in fact resigned in the hopes of being given a Gaullist mandate to rule and implement changes without the normal constitutional constrictions. His successor, Goulart, frequently talked of his powerlessness to govern the country and indeed appeared to allow some problems to worsen in order to strengthen his claim that the system required basic change.[26]

In addition to presidential ambiguity over the effectiveness of the political system, the near civil war that occurred after Quadros's resignation in 1961 and Goulart's assumption of the presidency greatly increased the mobilization of forces within Brazil on both the Left and the Right. In both groups the resignation strengthened the feeling that Brazil was entering a revolutionary stage that called for a new political order. Politicians from the Left and the Right made attempts to resolve the political crisis by extraparliamentary means. The curtailment of the powers of the office of the president before Vice-President Goulart was allowed to assume the presidency in 1961 was in essence an attack on the regime by centrist and conservative civilians and military officers. Many frustrated democratic leftist reformers who had been proregime became antiregime and argued that reform could only come through massive pressure and plebiscitary democracy, or even revolution. President Goulart's adviser, Leonel Brizola, spoke of the need to form "Grupos de Onze" (clandestine groups of eleven armed revolutionaries). Conservatives prepared to defend themselves by force. In the countryside, landowners armed themselves in preparation for civil war. In the cities, especially São Paulo, right-wing vigilante units proliferated.[27]

This sense that the regime was doomed and that Brazil was at the threshold of revolution dominated much of the political dialogue in the period from 1961 to 1964. A few months before the coup of 1964 the right-wing authoritarian nationalist Oliveiros S. Ferreira, a leading columnist for *O Estado de São Paulo,* argued characteristically:

With the renunciation of President Jânio Quadros there opened a crisis of regime— perhaps the most grave in the entire history of the Republic—a power vacuum which must be filled or we will be plunged into the chaos of a civil war. The question that was placed before all lucid men after the renunciation was how to surmount the crisis; that is, what conception of historical process, which types of organizations, and what forms of popular associations should replace the conceptions, parties and regime which have demonstrated themselves incapable of resolving . . . the great national problems.[28]

Celso Furtado, a prominent member of the reformist democratic Left, the first director of SUDENE (Superintendency for the Development of the Northeast), and the chief designer of the Three-Year Development Plan formulated in 1963 for Goulart, writing before the breakdown of 1964 also described the situation as a crisis of regime:

The country's economy, at the mercy of a series of structural constrictions, is by the very nature of its problems in an unstable situation. The primary forces of development—population growth, urbanization, desire for improved living conditions . . . are piling up like political energy in the waters of a river that has been dammed. The disturbing action of these pressing forces tends to increase with the reduction of the economy's rate of growth. We have seen that this reduction led to an aggravation of the inflationary process, which indicates that these forces are increasingly sterile. However, the tension created by these dammed-up forces has led to the awakening of a wide number of groups who have become aware that development is threatened by structural obstacles that are beyond the capacity for action by the present ruling groups. . . . Situations of this kind lead, almost inevitably, to the disruption of the existing balance of forces and the abandonment of conventional political methods.[29]

An analysis of newspaper editorials in the period preceding the coup of 1964 reveals that the crisis was essentially one of regime, in contrast to the preceding crises of 1954, 1955, and 1961, which all essentially concerned individual governments. Before these latter crises, in each of which the military executed or attempted coups, the major theme of newspaper editorials in Brazil was the illegitimacy of the chief executive. This element was of course present in the crisis of 1964. But the editorials in 1964 even more emphatically voiced fear of social disintegration and political "subversion." There was an overtone of elite panic that was absent in editorials relating to the crises in the earlier period.

The *Jornal do Brasil,* for example, believed "the state of law has been submerged in Brazil" and stressed that it was in such situations that "revolutions like that of Russia in 1917" emerged.[30] The *Diário de Pernambuco* ran an editorial entitled "Fruits of Generalized Madness" and warned readers that Brazil faced an hour of "desolation" unless the situation was basically altered.[31] Even the normally moderate *Correio da Manhã* feared that with each incident "indiscipline was getting uncontrollable" and apocalyptically concluded that it was impossible "to continue in this chaos in all areas."[32]

A number of other indicators reveal the atmosphere of regime crisis. The level of civilian arming on the Right and Left was unquestionably much higher than in the periods before the other coups between 1945 and 1964. (The only comparable civilian arming was that in anticipation of the crisis of regime at the end of the Old Republic in 1930.) The coup of 1964 was also preceded by unprecedented crises of authority within the army and by mutinies among the enlisted men.

Another symptom was the quickened pace of elections, plebiscites, and extraparliamentary attempts to change the political rules of the game.[33] Normally in Brazil the presidential election, held every five years, is the only political contest in which national power is perceived to be in the balance. In the three and one-half years between October 1960 and March 1964, however, the country experienced the turmoil of six major political contests, all relatively inconclusive. These contests began with the presidential election in October 1960 and subsequent resignation of Quadros in August 1961; this was followed by a near civil war which was resolved only when Goulart accepted the presidency under a new prime-ministerial form of government. Then came the fiercely contested congressional and gubernatorial elections of 1962, President Goulart's bitter campaign to hold a plebiscite to regain former presidential powers, and the plebiscite itself in January 1963. In October of that year

President Goulart requested Congress to rule by state of siege. Finally, there was the March 1964 drive for "Basic Reforms" with the implicit threat to close Congress and hold a new plebiscite.

The Impact of Political and Economic Crises on the Military: The Growth of Institutional Fears and New Military Ideologies

The military atmosphere leading up to the civil-military crisis of 1964 was in a fundamental way unlike that before the crises of 1945, 1954, 1955, and 1961. One of the key aspects of civil-military relations as they existed before 1964 was that influential civilians and military officers believed that civilian political groups as a whole could rule within the parliamentary constitutional framework and that the political demands emerging from social and economic changes could be transformed into acceptable outputs by the political system. This was an essential element in the return of executive power to civilians following the military coups in Brazil in 1945, 1954, and 1955. Belief in civilian capacity to rule was also instrumental in maintaining a boundary or restraint on the extent of military activity in politics. It was generally understood in the traditional "moderator pattern" of civil-military relations that existed prior to 1964 that the military in times of temporary crises could overthrow a government but would restrain from assuming power and destroying the democratic regime itself.[34] However, in the generalized political and economic crises between 1961 and 1964, numerous factors tended to weaken military perception of the desirability of maintaining this traditional boundary to their political activity.

Especially significant was the development among groups of military officers of a fear that politics was at such a radicalized stage, and the existing political parties and groups so fragmented, that no single group within the polity was competent to rule the country. The rhetoric of mobilization and radicalization, coming in the wake of the Cuban Revolution, was feared by many officers as the prelude to the destruction of the traditional army. The increasing politicization of the enlisted ranks, most marked in the sergeants' revolt in Brasília in September 1963, intensified this fear among officers and was seen to threaten military discipline. Finally, the growing use of political criteria for promotions in the army in order to create an armed force loyal to the president (always a factor in the Brazilian military) was perceived by many officers to have reached alarming proportions.[35] Many felt it not only endangered the hierarchical structure of the military and the personal career expectations of the officers but was also destructive to the nonpartisan role of the military institution itself.

All these factors contributed to the development of attitudes within the officer corps that were no longer consistent with the traditional role of the military, in which the military "moderated" the political system during times of crisis but never actually assumed governmental power itself. At the military's Superior War College (*Escola Superior de Guerra,* ESG), an ideology developed that both questioned basic structural features of the political system and implicitly envisaged a new political role for the military, in which the military would become the "director" and not merely the "moderator" of the entire political system. The fact that the military developed such an ideology, at a formal level, was a factor in the crisis of regime in Brazil, just as the military development of revolutionary warfare doctrines in France, Indonesia, and Peru was an intrinsic part of the crisis of regime in those countries.[36]

Thus by early 1964 important elements within the Brazilian military were becoming increasingly apprehensive about the threats to the military institution, while at the same time groups within the military began to feel that the military possessed, through the work of the Superior War College, the development doctrines, as well as the personal and organizational strengths to rule Brazil. It is not surprising then that numerous small civil-military groups throughout Brazil were openly discussing the overthrow of President Goulart and even the possibility of establishing a new regime in Brazil long before March 1964.

Political Leadership and Regime Breakdown in Brazil: The Realm of the Noninevitable

A working hypothesis that this chapter brings to the analysis is one also stressed by Linz, namely that while powerful economic, political, and ideological strains normally contribute to the breakdown of a regime, these macrosociological factors do not in themselves lead inevitably to its fall. The diffuse generalized factors that are placing a strain on the system have to be brought to a crisis point by the interaction of actors and issues at the micropolitical level.

In fact, there were many factors tending to support the regime as it existed under President Goulart, or at least to inhibit any coup initiatives by military officers. It was in the erosion of existing regime supportive factors that the quality of individual leadership, problem-solving behavior, and political strategies of the chief executive played an extremely important role. Indeed, the analysis of democratic regimes that survive severe crises may well demonstrate that the political leaders paid close attention to reinforcing and relying upon the regime supportive factors.[37] Alternatively, in the case of breakdown, political leaders all too often, wittingly or unwittingly, contribute to the unnecessary erosion of regime support.

There were a number of factors that as late as the beginning of March 1964 tended to support the survival of the Goulart government and to inhibit military attempts to overthrow the regime. First was the vested interest of numerous politicians—Center, Right, and Left—in the maintenance of the regime in order to continue their careers. Many of the most important civilian governors, who had traditionally played a key role in central power decisions, had a stake in the continuation of the formal functioning of the political system because they were themselves prominent candidates for presidential elections slated for October 1965. Adhemar de Barros, governor of the most powerful state of the union, São Paulo, with a state militia of over thirty thousand men at his command, was an active candidate of the Populist PSP party. Carlos Lacerda, governor of Guanabara state, and Magalhães Pinto, governor of Minas Gerais, were not only men with strong state militias but also contenders for the presidential nomination of the UDN party. On the Left, President Goulart could not, by the terms of the Constitution of 1946, succeed himself, and since a relative of the president was also constitutionally barred from running, Leonel Brizola, former governor of Rio Grande do Sul, was also denied the opportunity to run. This meant that the most powerful governor of the Left, Miguel Arraes of Pernambuco, also had a strong vested interest in Goulart's remaining in office and the election being held on schedule. Lacerda, Magalhães Pinto, and de Barros all knew of the formulation of a plan to overthrow Goulart in case Goulart attempted a coup to extend his own powers, but none of these governors committed themselves to this plan until late March 1964. The antiregime plotters felt that without the support of these key governors, however, Goulart could not be overthrown.[38]

Another factor inhibiting the overthrow of President Goulart was that regardless of the distrust in which he was held by many people, he was nonetheless the constitutionally elected president of Brazil. From this fact flowed both the legalistic support acquired from his mere occupancy of this office and the power to appoint civilians and military officers most loyal to him to positions of importance. Here was another source of regime support which had to be taken into account in any political strategy.

From the military viewpoint, there were also several reasons why the emergence of new attitudes—such as institutional fear, declining confidence in civilians, and increased confidence in the military's own abilities to rule—were nonetheless insufficient reasons for assuming power. While small groups of military officers formed, in Linz's terms, a "disloyal opposition" after 1961 and were looking for an excuse to overthrow Goulart and the regime, the military institution as a whole had been badly divided by the abortive attempt to block Goulart from assuming the presidency in 1961. The fear of splitting the military again acted as a major inhibition to any attempt to overthrow Goulart without unanimous military support. In an interview with General Golbery do Couto e Silva, a major participant in the military movement to overthrow Goulart, Golbery noted that "1961 was a disaster for the Army. We decided that we would attempt to overthrow Goulart only if public opinion was in our favor."[39] Speaking of the obstacles to a military coup, Golbery also argued that in 1963 the activists in the military planning a revolution represented only 10 percent of the higher officer corps, while another 70 percent to 80 percent were "legalists" or simply nonactivists. While many of this latter group were becoming increasingly apprehensive about the state of affairs in Brazil, and especially about the question of military discipline and unity, nonetheless they would follow the president in his formal capacity as commander in chief of the army. The other 10 to 20 percent of the officer corps were pro-Goulart activists, many of whom Goulart had appointed to key troop commands and administrative posts.

As late as February 1964 there was widespread fear that Goulart still had sufficient active support that an attempt to overthrow him could lead to civil war lasting two or even three months.[40] As long as Goulart was acting constitutionally there was no loud demand by civilians for the military to intervene. Without this demand, the military activists could not get a "winning coalition" together to take an aggressive first step against Goulart.

Given these various inhibiting factors, a strong case could be made that President Goulart could have completed his term of office without being displaced by the military and without the complete breakdown of the political regime. It is difficult to speculate on the course of events if a military coup had not occurred in April 1964. One possibility is that the widespread consciousness of governmental powerlessness and the need for structural reform could have been capitalized on in the presidential elections scheduled for October 1965, and a victorious candidate for the Left, or a victory by the still enormously popular ex-president Kubitschek, could have mobilized a mandate for democratic reform. Another option was that the more radical forces in such groups as AP, MEB, peasant leagues, and some trade unions could have had more time to develop into a genuine national force. But 1964 was too soon for them. Both of these options have been completely foreclosed for the last fourteen years by the events that Goulart himself helped set in motion. Let us turn to these events.

If we accept that, as late as February 1964, there were powerful inhibitions to the overthrow of Goulart, why then was Goulart actually overthrown, and with such relative ease? Clearly the economic and political crisis had generated, for the military and for many national and international elite groups, the "chemical reagents" capable of producing a breakdown of the regime: the necessary components existed well before 31 March 1964. But they were not sufficient cause for a regime change: the reagents had to be brought to a critical "temperature" and "pressure" for reaction actually to occur.[41] Here the question of the quality and style of Goulart's political leadership became critical, for it was in the strategies and tactics he used in his efforts to "reequilibrate the political system" that in fact crucial support was eroded and a crisis situation brought to the breakdown point.

Goulart's Strategies—Crisis Intensification

In mid-March of 1964 Goulart came to a decision to resolve the political crisis by attempting to change the balance of power in his favor. This decision was to alter profoundly the future of Brazilian politics. It is thus legitimate to analyze his action as a strategy and, since Goulart was deposed a little more than three weeks later, to look for weak points in it. A step-by-step account will show the crisis moving toward resolution.

The final stages of the crisis began on 13 March with a massive rally held in Rio de Janeiro. The president and his trade union supporters had organized the rally knowingly, in the sense that they considered it the first step toward resolving a crisis. On the morning of the rally, Goulart told an interviewer:

Today I am going to run all the risks. The most that can happen to me is that I will be deposed. I will not renounce or commit suicide.[42]

The interviewer remarked that the situation in Brazil did not call for either renunciation or suicide. Goulart replied:

I know. I am only imagining the worst that could happen, following my decision to push reforms and obtain greater powers from Congress. But nothing will happen because my military support [dispositivo militar] is excellent. Assis Brasil has guaranteed me that at my command, the army will follow. . . . From here on forward, I am only going to govern with the support of the people. And what everyone is going to see today [at the rally] is that the people have changed. They are awakened, they are ready for the grand problems of the country.[43]

Goulart was counting on mobilizing the political power of the masses and demanding reforms by plebiscite, by decree, or by pressuring, or even closing, Congress. To do this he implicitly recognized his need for not merely the passive support of the army but the active, aggressive support of key Goulart-appointed generals. The strategy, to be effective, would have required that federal army troops give protection and backing to the mass demonstrations and strikes Goulart was planning throughout the country. It would also probably have involved key army leaders threatening Congress in order to pass the "Basic Reforms." If Congress refused, the army would be the essential factor in any attempt by Goulart to insist on a national plebiscite for these reforms. Likewise, active support of the three service chiefs would be required if Goulart was to attempt to declare a state of siege.[44]

This strong reliance by Goulart on the loyal military activists he had appointed to important positions is consistent with the "moderating pattern" of civil-military relations until 1964. In this system, a weak executive ruling a divided country will attempt to use the military to augment his power. One of Goulart's close associates described the president's attitude toward the military as he entered the crisis period: "Goulart felt he had good relations with the army. . . . He wanted to put the military in as many key positions as possible. It was a form of power and had to be used. . . . He felt he had to pressure Congress by mobilizing mass opinion and by use of the military.''[45] This approach is consistent with Goulart's behavior as president in the period from 1961 to 1963, in regard to his use of the military to force an early holding of the plebiscite, to request a state of siege, and to keep opponents in check.[46]

Thus, Goulart's assumption that he could use the military was not without precedent. However, his tactic of appointing new service chiefs when the old ones did not agree with him—he had had four such chiefs since assuming the presidency—cut him off from accurate feedback about military feeling. Officers closest to him, who urged him forward on his course of increasing pressure on Congress, were more and more out of touch with the bulk of military sentiment. Moreover, his strategy of mobilizing the masses by using leftist activists in the country, while expecting to balance the Left with the military who would also help push the reforms through, had inherent points of tension and weakness.

The inherent danger in regard to military support was that a diffuse, personalist mobilization of the masses, if it were to succeed in pressuring Congress, could go beyond most military officers' tolerance of internal disorder. Also, Goulart's attempts to use the Communist organization ran the risk of diminishing the intensity of support of those officers who endorsed his reforms on nationalist and leftist grounds but who disliked the institutional connection with the Brazilian Communist party.

A serious weakness of Goulart's strategy in regard to the Left was that the Left was too fragmented and too unmobilized to support it; moreover, Goulart himself was unable to lead the Left effectively because, in the past, he had made ambiguous turns both to the Left and the Right. Goulart was not trusted by a number of the most prominent figures of the left. Miguel Arraes, the most important leftist candidate for the upcoming presidential elections, feared that Goulart might upset the election schedule. Arraes also knew that Goulart had always attempted to keep him under control by appointing strong, anti-Communist generals to command the Fourth Army, based in his state capital of Recife. In addition, Arraes was aware that Goulart had attempted to depose both him, the major leftist governor, and Lacerda, the major rightist governor, in 1963 in order to solidify his position. Arraes told various people that he feared that if Goulart executed a coup, Arraes himself would be one of the first to suffer.[47]

The leader of the Communist party, Luís Carlos Prestes, was also deeply ambivalent about Goulart. Prestes wanted to use Goulart to mobilize the country, but he feared that a premature attempt to radicalize the country and eliminate the bourgeoisie from a reform coalition would precipitate a countercoup in which the Communists would be destroyed.[48] Prestes also feared that if Goulart in fact carried off a leftist coup, Goulart might very possibly not keep his promise to make the Communist party legal.[49]

Francisco Julião, the most famous leader of the peasant leagues in the northeast, was hostile to Goulart, whom he accused of trying to turn him into a rural trade union boss, controlled by the Ministry of Labor. Julião felt that Goulart had not backed him in his last election campaign.[50]

Brizola, the most volatile member of the Left, was constantly charging Goulart with being a bourgeois and an opportunist. Brizola's mouthpiece, *Panfleto*, published in February and March of 1964, often criticized Goulart's policies. In early March, Brizola went so far as to say that he would never stand on the platform with Goulart again, because Goulart had so many conservatives in his cabinet.[51]

Finally, the basic ambivalence of the trade unions toward Goulart was illustrated by their refusal to back his request for the state of siege in September of 1963.

The Goulart strategy of forcing the system to a crisis resolution was successful in that it intensified the crisis. Within nineteen days of the rally on 13 March the Brazilian political system had been fundamentally transformed. The results, however, were the opposite of what Goulart had intended. Let us analyze why.

The 13 March Rally and Civil-Military Aftermaths

The two decisive steps for civil-military relations that precipitated the 1964 breakdown were the rally on 13 March and a mutiny of sailors on 27–29 March.

At the 13 March mass rally, widely televised and broadcast, Goulart launched a campaign for broad structural and political reforms that came to be known as the "Basic Reforms." He announced he had just signed a land reform decree which declared subject to expropriation all underutilized properties of over 1,200 acres situated within six miles of federal highways or railways, and lands of 70 acres located within six miles of federal dams or drainage projects. He also nationalized all remaining private oil refineries in Brazil and outlined future plans to enfranchise illiterates (by which means he would almost double the electorate) and legalize the Communist party.

He demanded that the Constitution be reformed because it was obsolete, since it "legalized an unjust and inhuman economic structure." His brother-in-law, Leonel Brizola, went further and declared that Congress had lost "all identification with the people"; he urged the establishment of a "Congress composed of peasants, workers, sergeants, and nationalist officers." Both Brizola and Goulart posed the threat of a plebiscite, using the enlarged electorate to bypass Congress if Congress posed an obstacle to these plans.

Goulart followed up the promise of his rally by presenting his Basic Reforms to Congress on 15 March with a pointed reminder that the three armed services ministers had seen and approved the program. It was announced that a series of mass demonstrations would be held throughout the country. The legally unrecognized high command of labor, the CGT (*Comando Geral dos Trabalhadores*), threatened a general strike if Congress did not approve the constitutional changes by 20 April and also recommended that Goulart declare a unilateral moratorium on the repayment of the foreign debts. May Day loomed as the day of resolution if the political elites remained intransigent.[52]

In terms of strategy and the tactics of political leadership and political survival, what can be said about the effectiveness of Goulart and his allies? Without attempting to discuss the merits of the goals themselves, it can be argued convincingly that Goulart's tactics diminished his support and tended to increase the possibility of a military coup backed by strong civilian opinion.[53]

First, in the euphoric atmosphere that pervaded the Left after the 13 March rally, great hope was placed on the mobilization of groups that had previously been marginal to the political process. Despite the fact that Goulart launched a major attack on existing power-holders, he had not first organized sufficient support to make such an attack feasible. As even one of his own staff acknowledged, "Goulart wanted to make more reforms than he really had the strength to do. He had no organized support for the big reforms he announced."[54] Almost no effort was made to retain as allies the moderate Left and Center, who had in the past cooperated on some reform issues. For Goulart, as well as for a number of other rhetorical nationalists such as Sukarno and Nkrumah, the emotional power of revolutionary symbols and the physical presence of the masses appears to have had a debilitating effect on the capacity to make the normal "political survival calculation," i.e. judging actions in terms of strategically located allies gained versus strategically located enemies created. One of Goulart's closest allies in this crisis period later commented that the mass rally had disoriented Goulart's political perceptions: "Friday, the thirteenth, was the beginning of the President's drive for power. It carried him to a delirium of ephemeral glory . . . [in which] he underestimated his adversaries and overestimated the strength of the masses."[55]

A characteristic example of the almost willful disregard for winning or retaining potential allies was the frequent utterances by major leftist activists that the composition of a future strong reforming government (which the new power of the masses was "certain" to generate shortly) should not include any "bourgeois reformers," such as San Tiago Dantas, a widely respected and influential politician of the moderate Left. Even a newspaper such as *Diário Carioca,* which had strongly supported the programmatic reforms demanded by Goulart, was offended by such tactics.[56]

In addition to alienating potential allies, it is clear that the 13 March rally, by simultaneously raising numerous fundamental problems to crisis level, tended to maximize the number of Goulart's opponents among those strategically located in the power structure. Between 13 March and 15 March, Goulart's demands for fundamental reforms threatened elements among the landowners, military officers, congressmen, foreign capitalists, anti-

Communists, and industrialists. The rhetoric of revolution, coupled with the soaring inflation, created increasing fear and insecurity among the middle classes. On many issues the above groups were hostile to one another, but the Goulart offensive brought them together and minimized their differences.[57] Many people who were "progovernment" shifted to a position we previously referred to as "proregime but antigovernment." "Antigovernment" groups increasingly became "antiregime."

The justice minister later wrote from exile about this counterproductive aspect of the massive rally for the Goulart government. He acknowledged reluctantly that the March 13 rally "came to be the touchstone of the opposition in combating the government. The rally created the expectation of a crisis, of a 'coup,' raids, riots, mutiny, or general subversion in the country. . . . After 13 March, the opposition was galvanized."[58] Indicative of this galvanization of the opposition was the even larger rally of many middle-class people in São Paulo on 19 March to demonstrate against Goulart and in favor of legality.[59] The rhetoric of "resentment politics" gained Goulart a few supporters but also won him some powerful and strategically located enemies. An example is Brizola's calling General Muricy a "gorilla" to his face on a public platform. General Muricy, a commanding general in the north, was one of the first to go into armed revolt against Goulart. Frequent ridicule of Congress was another tactic that was not conducive to getting Congress to cooperate in passing the basic reforms that the Goulart government needed.

A more general example of Brizola's attempts to win marginal additional support at the cost of creating powerful enemies in the center of the political system was his repeated call for the formation of "Grupos de Onze." Private appeals might have been just as effective and would not have created fear among the landowners and the middle class—nor have caused some military officers to shift from a position of neutrality to active conspiracy against Goulart.

Reaction to 13 March—Erosive Effects on Factors Impeding a Coup

Goulart's attack, during the 13 March rally, on the Constitution as archaic and obsolete weakened his own claim, as the constitutional president, to obedience from the military. This point was made a number of times in public statements and newspaper editorials. The *Diário de Notícias* editorialized:

It is undeniable that subversive forces exist clearly aimed at making an attempt to overthrow the regime and existing institutions. . . . These forces seem to have coopted the President himself and have placed him for the first time in the forefront of the subversive process of opposition to the law, to the regime and to the Constitution.

If the Supreme Executive authority is opposed to the Constitution, condemns the regime, and refuses to obey the laws, he automatically loses the right to be obeyed . . . because this right emanates from the Constitution. The armed forces, by Article 177 of the Constitution, are obliged to "defend the country, and to guarantee the Constitutional power, law and order." . . . If the Constitution is "useless" . . . how can the President still command the armed forces?[60]

The 13 March rally also generated for the first time a widespread fear that the drive of the Goulart government might result in postponement of national elections, scheduled for October 1965, or a sharp change in the electoral rules (such as making Goulart, or his relative Brizola, eligible). This had an important impact on civilian-military opinion toward displacing Goulart. The military had been badly divided in their 1961 attempt to displace Goulart unilaterally without prior civilian sanction or support. A number of the key conspirators against Goulart decided that any attempt to oust him had to be initiated by the governor of a major state who had the backing of his own state militia.[61] The two most likely states were São Paulo and Minas Gerais. Both were governed by men who were suspicious of Goulart yet nonetheless had a vested interest in his remaining in office and elections being held on schedule. However, when it appeared that Goulart was trying to restructure the political system, an attempt which might preclude their attempts at the presidency, the two governors began to plot actively against Goulart.

Governor Magalhães Pinto reacted quickly, issuing a manifesto on 20 March on national television that promised Minas Gerais would resist any "revolution commandeered from above." The next day he made arrangements with the governor of the neighboring state of Espírito Santo to use the port of Vitória and railroads to get supplies into Minas in the event of a civil war in which Minas Gerais stood armed against the federal troops of Goulart.[62] Such a war, the governor felt, might last as long as three months. He is reported to have felt that any discussion of the presidential elections was by this time "surrealistic."[63]

The governor of São Paulo, Adhemar de Barros, went on television the night of 20 March to make an impassioned, three-hour address condemning the Goulart government for fomenting revolution. He emphasized his willingness to resist by force and said the São Paulo state militia had 30,000 troops, as well as airplanes to transport them. He pointed out that this force was twice as large as the federal army garrisoned in São Paulo, in which there were a number of pro-Goulart generals.[64]

The armed forces were deeply affected by the rally of 13 March, and their internal divisions over whether they should attempt to displace Goulart began to be reduced. The change of position of the governors of Minas Gerais and São Paulo greatly strengthened the military conspirators.

The rally also resulted in a changed atmosphere in the press. Before 13 March, no editorials directly charged the military with the responsibility for resolving the crisis. The rally, however, raised such issues as changing the Constitution, holding a constituent assembly, and closing Congress. After 13 March appeals began to be made to the constitutional role of the military to guarantee all three branches of government—the legislative and the judicial as well as the executive. Editorials requested the military not to give protective backing to government-sponsored threats to order. This loud public response to the rally of 13 March facilitated the role of the conspirators within the military.

An editorial in *O Jornal,* entitled "Defense of Illegality," appearing two days after the rally, illustrates the new mood of open condemnation of the military for continuing to obey the "illegal" order of the president: "The armed forces say they participated in the illegal and revolutionary rally . . . in obedience to the order of the President! No one is obliged to accept and obey an abusive order!"[65]

In addition to these specific reactions, the rally had more general effects on civil-military relations. Implicit in Goulart's appeal for settlement of the crisis outside traditional political channels was the threat of force. Many different groups began to arm themselves. More importantly, from a political standpoint, it was widely believed by key civilian and military officers that the nation was taking to arms. To this extent, the arena was rapidly becoming one in which the dominant idiom was one of violence, rather than politics. Since the military considered itself to have a monopoly on the legitimate use of arms, and perceived maintenance of internal order as one of its primary functions, it began to move to the center of the arena and assume a dominant position within the political system, thus underlining the relevance of Lasswell and Kaplan's dictum: "The balancing of power is particularly affected by the expectations that prevail about the probable mode by which conflicts will be settled. . . . An arena is *military* when the expectation of violence is high; *civic* when the expectation is low."[66]

The rally greatly increased expectations of force and preparations for a showdown by the forces of the Left and Right. On both sides there were multiple movements, with no central organization. Anti-Goulart factions in the military were getting a more receptive hearing for their articulation of the need for preparation for a countercoup, but they were still far from unified over the necessity of backing a coup of their own. For many military men, a coup attempt still spelled civil war—disaster for the country and for the military as an institution.

The Resolution of the Crisis—The Enlisted Men's Naval Mutiny

It was at this point that the next decisive step in the breakdown process occurred. Despite the build-up of pressure by the active anti-Goulart civilians and military forces, as late as twelve days after the 13 March rally no "winning coalition" existed to overthrow Goulart. Goulart had a number of strategically located officers who both favored the reform program and stood by him. The bulk of the remainder of the officers were legalistic, in the sense of being nonactivists. But arguments expressed in a letter by General Castello Branco were beginning to make a powerful impression on these men, as they began to ask themselves whether their "legalism" entailed loyalty and obedience to the president, and whether obedience to him was still an obedience "within the limits of the law."

Given this lack of unity among the opposition forces, an attempted coup by one sector of the military would have risked splitting the military at this time. The active plotters within the military were convinced that Goulart was intent on becoming a dictator but felt they must wait until he made such a blatant move that they could mobilize support against him easily.

The probable intention of Goulart's strategy was to build up pressure among the masses for reform without losing the passive obedience of the legalistic officers and the active support of key military officers, supporters Goulart needed if he were to bypass Congress and rule by decree. Holding these forces together was made especially difficult because to a great extent Goulart was spurred on by the highly emotional and often contradictory forces of the Left, which he found difficult to unify and direct. The movement was at an explosive point. There was risk of its getting out of control as an effective tactical instrument. The risk lay in the loss of a delicate balance between the increasingly radical civilians and the increasingly threatened officer corps.[67]

The naval mutiny of 26 March occurred against this background. More than one thousand sailors and marines barricaded themselves in an armory in Rio de Janeiro. The naval minister attempted to quell the mutiny. Goulart, instead of backing the minister, in effect dismissed him and allowed the trade unions to participate in the choice of a new minister in his place.

At the time of the mutiny, Goulart was extremely indecisive about his course of action. The mutiny made him face a decision he did not want to make—to punish the enlisted men for the mutiny and risk losing their active support or to treat the mutineers lightly and greatly risk increasing fears among those officers who saw leniency as a threat to the principle of military discipline. Goulart's minister of justice, Abelardo Jurema, wrote that most of the advice that the Goulart government received from civilian activists was to side with the sailors, since Goulart did not have much support to lose among naval officers in any case.[68] Their argument overlooked the crucial factor of the *intensity* of the opposition to Goulart, which was greatly increased by Goulart's action and by the symbolic impact it had on all three services, each of which felt threatened.

In the last moments Goulart vacillated and, according to his chief army aide, General Assis Brasil, abdicated the decision, saying to the new naval minister: "The problem is yours, Admiral. You have a blank check with which to resolve it. If you wish to punish or expel [the mutineers], the decision is yours." The admiral reportedly replied, "I intend, President, to grant an amnesty."[69]

Repercussions within the officer corps were profound. The issue of institutional self-preservation by means of control over military discipline was one over which ideologically divided military officers had the highest internal agreement. The naval mutiny caused a shift in position that hurt Goulart among all three major groups within the military—the active plotters, the legalist uncommitted officers, and the pro-Goulart officers.[70]

The naval mutiny galvanized the active plotters, both civilian and military, into action against Goulart. The operations order issued on the night of 31 March 1964 by General Guedes, commander of the infantry division that first moved against Goulart in the effort to remove him from the presidency, clearly indicates the way in which Goulart's handling of the mutiny acted as a catalyst in the revolutionary drama. The general's order explained to his division that he and Governor Magalhães Pinto had decided it would be a mistake to move against Goulart without profound provocation. In his opinion, and the governor's, any attempt to displace Goulart before Goulart expressly challenged the law would have given Goulart an air of legality and would have been counterproductive. "It would have attracted to his side a forceful sector of the armed forces who lack confidence in politics and are committed to legal formalism." It was necessary to assemble a defensive conspiracy and wait until Goulart stepped beyond the bounds of the law. His slogan, the general explained, was: "He who breaks the law first is lost!" What happened in the mutiny, he felt, showed that he was correct. With the naval mutiny the military had "arrived at the moment for action, and had to act quickly lest it be too late."[71]

Among the legalistic officers, who comprised the majority of the military officers and who were reluctant to take a bold step against the constitutionally elected president, Goulart's sanctioning of indiscipline and disorder allowed the question of legalism to be reformulated. Obedience was owed to the president "within the limits of the law." To many officers, the president's actions now seemed to lie outside the law.

The impact of the naval mutiny of 26 March upon the strong Goulart supporters was powerful. Juan Linz has correctly noted in his introductory essay that the intensity of the belief in the legitimacy of a government is most important for those who participate in a crisis from within the authority structure. Their passive support is not enough; they must feel that the government is so legitimate that it commands their *active* support.

For Goulart, his staff was his *"dispositivo militar,"* his hand-picked men in key locations throughout the country, who in the past had been his active supporters in crises. Goulart's minister of justice, Abelardo Jurema, described, however, an angry meeting between himself and a military officer, Colonel Lino Teixeira, following the mutiny, which illustrates how seriously the issue of military discipline had weakened active support for Goulart:

I was eating in a restaurant in the city . . . when I was approached by Colonel Lino Teixeira. He was furious. . . . He did not understand the situation. He passionately declared his feelings of revolt, anger, and surprise, feelings he said that the pro-Jangistas [military favorable to Goulart] shared. He stressed that the government had lost substantially all of its military *dispositivo*.... He, who only yesterday had been fighting on the side of the President and the reforms, was now ready to fight alongside Carlos Lacerda [a chief plotter against Goulart] to maintain military discipline, which in his view had been irreparably wounded.[72]

A member of the general staff of the army, who did not join the conspiracy against Goulart and who was subsequently purged from the army commented: "The thing that finally was most important in moving military opinion against him [Goulart] was the 'inversion of hierarchy'! Even strong 'Jangistas' broke with him after the mutiny and his speech to the sergeants."[73]

Most of the strong Goulart supporters in the military did not actively join the opposition, but what was crucial was that when the government was actively challenged by the plotters, the intensity of military support for Goulart was not sufficient to prevent Goulart's displacement. Not one officer died defending the Goulart government.

Conclusion

Obviously, this paper cannot cover all the important factors influencing the course of events that led to the regime's breakdown in Brazil in 1964. I have barely touched on the growth of military ideology and education, via the Superior War College, which contributed greatly to military confidence to assume full political power in 1964. Another important factor was the role played by the United States in contributing to the destabilization of the Goulart government and to the shoring up of the military coup. The U.S. government cut back economic and other aid to the Goulart government, moved a task force in the direction of Brazil that could have been ready in case the anti-Goulart coup force encountered heavy resistance, and extended strong political and economic support to the military government after the coup.[74]

Nonetheless, this study of the micro-political events as they took place within the broad context of changing social, economic, and ideological conditions tending to lead to a generalized expectation that the regime was at a critical turning point does illuminate, I believe, the special role that a political leader can play in bringing a regime to a final breakdown point. A number of interesting questions about Goulart's political style and his fall from power remain for further analysis and research. Why, for instance, did Goulart overestimate his political strength? I have already mentioned as one element of his misreading of this strength the exhilaration and consequent disorientation he experienced after speaking to large crowds. Another clue to the extent of Goulart's estrangement from the realities of politics lay in the nature of his political advisers. Goulart had surrounded himself with men who identified with him so personally that they were unrepresentative of the institutions they came from and uninfluential within them. General Assis Brasil, chief of the Casa Militar and therefore one of the key liaisons between the government and the military, is a classic example of a military man who urged Goulart forward to action even though he himself had lost touch with the military institutions he supposedly represented.

A more difficult field of inquiry concerns Goulart's *style* of politics. Goulart talked of the need for revolution, but in the early moments of the coup against him, when it was still by no means certain that he would be overthrown, he personally cautioned his own military commanders to avoid bloodshed. His ambiguity and indecisiveness enraged and demoralized his military supporters.

One other area needs examination—the area of political personality. Goulart had always been the subject of a "whispering campaign" of innuendo, even among his own associates. It was often hinted he was personally and politically ineffectual. Undoubtedly his bravado leadership of the masses filled some personal need. The pattern of confrontation and capitulation that characterized his career suggests that a psychological analysis would be valuable for a fuller understanding of Goulart's political performance.

At the political level, the outcome of his political acts, strategies, and style of politics was to finally erode existing supports to the regime. Combined with structural weaknesses in the regime, Goulart helped pave the way for the final breakdown of the Brazilian regime in 1964.

Indeed, this analysis confirms the conclusion of Alberto Guerreiro Ramos, a leading politician on the Left at the time of the breakdown of the regime, and a distinguished social scientist, who described Goulart's actions in the following terms:

In 1964 he seemed to lose his sense of reality. . . . To a certain extent, one could say that Goulart's fall occurred on March 31, 1964, because he *wanted* it so. He deposed himself by letting himself be deposed. It is clear that Goulart had ways of stabilizing his power, but it appears that he behaved as if he preferred the actions which led to his downfall. . . . Goulart could have finished his presidential period had he decided to behave according to its objective possibilities; Goulart's downfall was not inevitable.[75]

NOTES

1. This regime is analyzed in Alfred Stepan, ed., *Authoritarian Brazil: Origins, Policies, and Future* (New Haven: Yale University Press, 1973).
2. The Brazilian case has been examined from a number of different perspectives. Philippe C. Schmitter, in his *Interest Conflict and Political Change in Brazil* (Stanford, Ca.: Stanford University Press, 1971), argues that the coup was in part a restoration movement endeavoring to reestablish the semicorporatist structure that was being challenged in the years leading

up to 1964. His emphasis thus is not on "breakdown" but rather on "continuity." Fernando Henrique Cardoso in his "Associated-Dependent Development: Theoretical and Practical Implications," in Stepan, *Authoritarian Brazil*, pp. 142–76, argues that the coup brought the political system into alignment with the new economic changes induced by the associated-dependent development process. For a seminal effort to place the 1964 breakdown in Brazil and the 1966 breakdown in Argentina in an analytic framework in which competitive political populism, within the confines of dependent import-substitution industrialization, precipitates a ceiling effect crisis, which in turn contributes to the emergence of a bureaucratic-authoritarian coalition that endeavors to impose a new development model, see Guillermo O'Donnell, *Modernization and Bureaucratic-Authoritarianism: Studies in South American Politics*, Institute of International Studies, University of California, Politics of Modernization Series, no. 9 (Berkeley: 1973). With some qualifications and modifications, I use a variant of this framework to analyze the background to the "exclusionary installation attempts" that began in Brazil in 1964, Argentina in 1966, and Chile in 1973 in chap. 3 of my *The State and Society: Peru in Comparative Perspective* (Princeton, N.J.: Princeton University Press, 1978). Both the "corporatist continuity" and the "structural crisis" arguments are useful: corporatist elements were indeed very strong throughout the 1945–64 semidemocratic interregnum, and the breakdown has in fact facilitated the repression that has played such an important part in the current economic model. Nonetheless I do not feel that either the corporatist continuity or the new repression was inevitable. There remained a small margin of maneuverability within which the process of increasing democratization and participation could have been expanded. How the leaders of the electoral regime contributed to the elimination of this margin remains an important topic and is the subject of this chapter.

3. See Dankwart Rustow, "Transitions to Democracy: Toward a Dynamic Model," *Comparative Politics* 2, no. 3 (April 1970): 337–64; Arend Lijphart, "Consociational Democracy," *World Politics* 21, no. 2 (January 1969): 207–25; Eric A. Nordlinger, *Conflict Regulation in Divided Societies*, Harvard University Center for International Affairs, Occasional Papers in International Affairs, no. 29 (Cambridge: 1972); and the introductory essay by Juan J. Linz.

4. This framework owes much to the suggestive analysis of the capabilities of political systems in Gabriel A. Almond and G. Bingham Powell, Jr., *Comparative Politics: A Developmental Approach* (Boston: Little, Brown, 1966), especially pp. 190–212; and in Gabriel A. Almond, "Political Development: Analytical and Normative Perspectives," *Comparative Political Studies* 1, no. 4 (January 1969): 447–70.

5. All growth rates are for the years 1958 to 1966, as cited in United Nations, *Demographic Yearbook 1966*, pp. 104–111.

6. Brasil, *Anuário estatístico do Brasil—1962*, p. 27. Figures are rounded off to the nearest million.

7. See the section on "Conflitos do trabalho" in ibid., p. 271, and the 1966 edition., p. 339. While a four-year time span is too short to assert that this was a secular trend, the dominant impression in Brazil was clearly one of spiraling labor conflict.

8. For the political differences between parochial, subject, and participant status, see Gabriel Almond and Sidney Verba, *The Civic Culture* (Princeton, N.J.: Princeton University Press, 1963), chap. 1.

9. For a discussion of the law, see Caio Prado Júnior, "O estatuto do trabalhador rural," *Revista Brasiliense*, no. 47 (May-June 1963): 1–13.

10. For an analysis of the nonrevolutionary aspects of Julião, see Anthony Leeds, "Brazil and the Myth of Francisco Julião," in *Politics of Change in Latin America*, ed. Joseph Maier and Richard W. Weatherhead (New York: Praeger, 1964), pp. 190–204. Benno Galjart, in "Class and 'Following' in Rural Brazil," *America Latina*, no. 7 (July-September 1964); pp. 3–24, emphasizes the traditional and mutually competitive aspects of the peasant leagues.

11. The most extensive treatment of the overall growth of rural activism is Neale Pearson, "Small Farmer and Rural Worker Pressure Groups in Brazil" (Ph.D. diss., University of Florida, 1967).

12. *Anuário estatístico do Brasil—1966*, p. 535. For a general discussion of the expansion of voter participation in Brazil, see Joseph L. Love, "Political Participation in Brazil, 1881–1969," *Luso-Brazilian Review* 7, no. 2 (December 1970): 3–24.

13. Two collections of articles concerning the 1962 elections at the local, state, and national

levels are the issue of *Revista Brasileira de Estudos Políticos,* no. 16 (January 1964), and Themistocles Cavalcanti and Reisky Dubnic, eds. *Comportamento eleitoral no Brasil* (Rio de Janeiro: Fundação Getúlio Vargas, January 1964).

14. See Joel Bergsman, *Brazil: Industrialization and Trade Policies* (London: Oxford University Press, 1970).

15. For their definitions of "extractive capability" and "distributive capability," see Almond and Powell, *Comparative Politics,* pp. 195–98.

16. An influential article advancing this thesis was Maria Conceição Tavares et al., "The Growth and Decline of Import Substitution in Brazil," *Economic Bulletin for Latin America* 9, no. 1 (March 1964): 1–59. A variant of this theme also runs through O'Donnell, *Modernization and Bureaucratic-Authoritarianism,* chap. 2.

17. Private capital also reacted negatively to the 1962 profit remittance law. Werner Baer estimates that the inflow of private foreign capital declined from 108 million U.S. dollars in 1961 to 71 million in 1962 to 31 million in 1963. See Werner Baer, *Industrialization and Economic Development in Brazil* (Homewood, Ill.: Richard D. Irwin, 1965), p. 200.

18. The finance minister's report is reprinted in *Correio da Manhã,* 5 July 1963, cited in Thomas Skidmore, *Politics in Brazil, 1930–1964* (New York: Oxford University Press, 1967), p. 257.

19. See Ronald Schneider, "Election Analysis," in Charles Daugherty, James Rowe, and Ronald Schneider, *Brazil Election Factbook: Number 2, September 1965* (Washington, D.C.: Institute for the Comparative Study of Political Systems, 1965), p. 64.

20. Pompeu de Souza, "Eleições de 1962: Decomposição partidária e caminhos da reforma," *Revista Brasileira de Estudos Políticos,* no. 16 (January 1964); pp. 10–11.

21. Ibid., p. 7.

22. Hélio Juaguaribe, *Desenvolvimento econômico e desenvolvimento político* (Rio de Janeiro: Editôra Fundo de Cultura, 1962), pp. 83–84, 101.

23. Schneider, "Election Analysis." See also Skidmore, *Politics in Brazil, 1930–1964,* pp. 229–33.

24. This argument is developed more fully in the introductory essay by Linz.

25. The almost universal reaction of Quadros's close advisers to his sudden resignation was a bitter fury that measures they felt could have been taken within the limits of the existing political framework were aborted; talk and interview with Cândido Mendes, New York, spring 1965. (Cândido Mendes had been an adviser to President Quadros.) Likewise, Goulart abandoned the Furtado Plan of development and various other policies shortly after the attempt to implement them began.

26. For a particularly striking case of Goulart's emphasis on his helplessness, see the interview he gave to *Manchete,* 30 November 1963.

27. In an interview with former officials of a São Paulo vigilante unit, they asserted that as early as June 1963 they had held massive private meetings and were arming themselves.

28. Oliveiros S. Ferreira, *As fôrças armadas e o desafio da revolução* (Rio de Janeiro: Edições GRD, 1964), pp. 13–14. Ferreira himself was active in a civil-military group attempting to overthrow Goulart and impose an authoritarian nationalist solution to the Brazilian impasse.

29. Celso Furtado, *Dialéctica do desenvolvimento* (Rio de Janeiro: Editôra Fundo de Cultura, 1964), p. 134.

30. Front page editorial in large type, 29 March 1964.

31. Editorial, 31 March 1964.

32. Editorial, 31 March 1964.

33. In his introductory essay Linz argues that this is a characteristic feature of the breakdown process.

34. I develop the theoretical and empirical aspects of the "moderator model" of civil-military relations in my *The Military in Politics: Changing Patterns in Brazil;* see especially pp. 62–66.

35. A study of the *Almanaque do Exército* for 1964 reveals that of the line officers promoted to general grade during President Goulart's tenure, only five out of twenty-nine (17.2 percent) had graduated first in their class in any of the three major service schools. This contrasts with the thirty-four out of seventy-three (46.5 percent) of those officers promoted to general before Goulart came to the presidency.

36. This argument is more extensively developed and documented in my "The New Professionalism of Internal Warfare and Military Role Expansion" in Stepan, *Authoritarian Brazil*, pp. 47–65.

37. As the chapter in this volume by Daniel Levine documents, this was a central part of President Betancourt's strategy in Venezuela during the critical years of 1958–63.

38. A number of key coup organizers stressed this point in interviews with the author.

39. Interview with General Golbery do Couto e Silva, Brasília, 18 September 1967.

40. Numerous military men I talked to mentioned this.

41. Chalmers Johnson, *Revolutionary Change* (Boston: Little, Brown, 1966), pp. 90–94, makes a similar distinction between the necessary revolutionary preconditions and final causes of a revolution, which he calls the "accelerator." I prefer not to use this term because it (although not the body of Johnson's analysis) implies that we are only concerned with the speeding up of the "inevitable" breakdown.

42. Quoted in Antônio Callado, "Jango ou o suicídio sem sangue," in Alberto Dines et al., *Os idos de Março* (Rio de Janeiro: José Alvaro, 1964), p. 256. The reference to resignation is to the renunciation of President Jânio Quadros in August 1961; the reference to suicide refers to the suicide of President Vargas in August 1954.

43. Ibid., pp. 256–57. "Dispositivo," as used in the Goulart period, meant more than "support" (*apoio*). It meant senior officers who were personally loyal and actively committed to implementing the president's policies. The "dispositivo" in theory included all the military officers and troops under the command of these key senior officers.

    General Assis Brasil was the chief of the president's military household and, as such, one of the president's chief liaison officers with the military.

44. Since Goulart was overthrown by elements of the military shortly after the 13 March rally that began the deliberate intensification of the crisis, this scenario was never put into effect. Nonetheless, for even the outside observer, the broad outlines of the government's attempt to move the political system toward resolution were clear. The author was in Brazil in this period and wrote an article a week before the coup entitled, "Brazil: Mend or End," *Economist*, 4 April 1964, p. 31, that reflected this sense of imminent crisis.

45. Interview, 11 October 1968, Rio de Janeiro, with Raúl Riff, President Goulart's press secretary, who later had his political rights cancelled by the military government.

46. This is discussed in greater detail in my *The Military in Politics*, pp. 67–72.

47. See Fernando Pedreira, *Março 31: Civis e militares no processo da crise brasileira* (Rio de Janeiro: José Alvaro, 1964), p. 13; also Dines, *Os idos de Março*, pp. 31, 83.

48. See Skidmore, *Politics in Brazil*, p. 278, and his long bibliographic footnote on p. 414. Since the coup, the Communist party has published several reevaluations, in which they are critical of the "immature strategy" that precipitated the counterrevolution.

49. Dines, *Os idos de Março*, p. 30.

50. See Julião's interview with Antônio Callado, in *Tempo de Arraes: Padres e comunistas na revolução sem violência* (Rio de Janeiro: José Alvaro, 1965), pp. 59–60.

51. Dines, *Os idos de Março*, p. 19.

52. For the 13 March rally, and its immediate aftermath, see the author's "Brazil: Mend or End," p. 31. For a description written by the justice minister of the Goulart government, see Abelardo Jurema, *Sexta-Feira, 13: Os últimos dias do Govêrno João Goulart* (Rio de Janeiro: Edições O Cruzeiro, 1964), pp. 139–49. Also, Dines, *Os idos de Março*, pp. 195–219, 249–62.

53. I personally feel that most of the goals were desirable in some form.

54. Interview with Raúl Riff.

55. Jurema, *Sexta-Feira*, p. 149.

56. See their angry editorial, "Frente ampla ou frente estreita?" *Diário Carioca*, 24 March 1964.

57. Given the widespread feeling that Brazil was in need of fundamental reforms, and the lack of unity among the elites, a potentially more fruitful reform strategy could have been to reform sequentially, attempting to build the biggest possible constituency for each reform, each time reconstituting coalitions for new reforms. For a discussion of this reform strategy, see the last two chapters in Albert Hirschman, *Journeys toward Progress* (New York: Twentieth Century Fund, 1963); see especially his "Model 1: Engineering Reform with the Help of the Perspective of Revolution," pp. 277–85.

58. Jurema, *Sexta-Feira*, pp. 144–45.
59. A detailed study of this counter-rally does not yet exist and would be worthwhile.
60. Front page editorial, *Diário de Notícias*, 23 March 1964.
61. For example, General Mourão Filho, the general who finally initiated the coup, has written that he would have attempted a coup earlier if he had received a manifesto to the nation from four major governors. See his official account, published as an army order, "Relatório de revolução democrática iniciada pela 4a RME, 4a DI em 31 de Março de 1964." *Commando de 4a Região Militar, 4a Divisão de Infantaria e Guarnição de Juiz de Fora* (9 May 1964).
62. See the extremely interesting chapter by Pedro Gomes on the role of Minas Gerais in the coup, "Minas: Do diálogo ao 'front,' " in Dines, *Os idos de Março*, pp. 87–89.
63. Ibid., p. 91.
64. See the chapter on the role of São Paulo in the coup by Eurilo Duarte, "32 mais 32, Igual a 64," in Dines, *Os idos de Março*, pp. 125–60.
65. "Defesa da ilegalidade," *O Jornal*, 15 March 1964. Complete text reproduced in Dines, *Os idos de Março*, pp. 392–93. Original order is in the *Arquivo do Marechal H. A. Castello Branco*, located in the library of the General Staff School (ECEME) in Rio de Janeiro.
66. Harold D. Lasswell and Abraham Kaplan, *Power and Society: A Framework for Political Inquiry* (New Haven: Yale University Press, 1950), p. 252.
67. An example of the lack of governmental discretion or control over the left that was endangering this balance was the ministry of education's deliberate showing to a militant sailors' organization the Russian film *The Battleship Potemkin*, in which the parallel between the role of the Russian sailors in the Russian revolution and the possible role of sailors in Brazil was made in a complementary running commentary. See "Provocações," *O Jornal*, 24 March 1964, p. 4. Two days after the article was published, the sailors rebelled and presented Goulart with an undesired crisis of military discipline.
68. See Jurema, *Sexta-Feira*, pp. 151–58. For a detailed account of the mutiny, see Mario Victor, *Cinco anos que abalaram o Brasil* (Rio de Janeiro: Editôra Civilização Brasileira, 1965), pp. 493–514.
69. See the testimony of General Assis Brasil at a military investigating tribunal after the coup, reprinted in *O Estado de São Paulo*, 2 and 3 July 1964.
70. The naval mutiny was so obviously counterproductive that two generals who were later purged from the military even argue that it must have been deliberately instigated by right-wing officers. Interview with General Luiz Tavares da Cunha Mello and General Nicolau Fico, 10 October 1968, Rio de Janeiro.
71. General Bda Carlos Luiz Guedes, *Boletim da Infantaria Divisionária/4 NR 58*, 31 March 1964, p. 2 (copy in possession of author). For a similar account by General Maurão Filho, another key military officer, see *Relatório da revolução democrática iniciada pela 4a RM E 4a DI em 31 de Março de 1964*, p. 3.
72. Jurema, *Sexta-Feira*, pp. 162–63.
73. Interview with General George Rocha, 5 October 1968, Rio de Janeiro.
74. On the role of the United States, see my *The Military in Politics*, pp. 123–33, and my commentary to the article "From Counterinsurgency to Counterintelligence," in Julio Cotler and Richard Fagen, eds., *Latin America and the United States: The Changing Political Realities* (Stanford, Ca.: Stanford University Press, 1974), pp. 361–67. Documentation concerning the ordering on 31 March 1964 of U.S. naval, air munitions, and fuel support to the coast off São Paulo is contained in recently declassified material in the Lyndon B. Johnson Library in Austin, Texas. For a brief discussion of this material, see Jan Knippers Black, *United States Penetration of Brazil* (Philadelphia: University of Pennsylvania Press, 1977), pp. xi–xii. These archives represent a major new source of material on U.S. involvement in Brazil and still await serious scholarly research. Detailed selections from the archives were printed in the *Jornal do Brasil* in December 1976. For U.S. involvement in Brazil in this period also see Moniz Bandeira, *Presença dos Estados Unidos no Brasil* (Rio de Janeiro: Editôra Civilização Brasilera, 1973).
75. From his "Nationalism in Brazil: A Case of Political Breakdown" (unpublished manuscript, 1969, pp. 32–33, 35). In a book written before the breakdown of the regime, he cautioned that the revolutionary Left was dealing with intellectual abstractions rather than actual reality and might endanger the possibility of a fundamental revolution from developing. See Guerreiro Ramos, *Mito e verdade da revolução brasileira* (Rio de Janeiro: Zahar Editôres, 1963).

5.

Permanent Crisis and the Failure to Create a Democratic Regime: Argentina, 1955-66

Guillermo O'Donnell*

On 28 June 1966, military officers "acting as representatives of the armed forces" ousted Arturo Illía, the constitutionally elected president of Argentina. They did not bother to take the usual steps for prevention of popular disorder—which did not occur. Foreign correspondents reported a surprising lack of opposition from the public at large.[1] Their impression was confirmed by survey data, which showed that 66 percent of the respondents approved of the coup and only 6 percent disapproved.[2] All major groups (except the ousted political party and a few minor parties, as well as university students) expressed support for the coup and for the new military government. The Junta Revolucionaria, formed by the chiefs of staff of the army, navy, and air force, ousted the president and the governors of the states, dissolved Parliament, dismissed the judges of the Supreme Court, and enacted an Estatuto Revolucionario whose regulations prevailed over the national constitution. All political activities were banned, political parties were dissolved, and elections were postponed *sine die*. The junta appointed retired general Juan Carlos Onganía as president. Communiqués from the junta and the new president stated the reasons for the coup. The most important of these were: (1) the lack of harmony and solidarity in and among the major social groups, which had led to anarchy, subversion, and neglect of the public interest; (2) the inability of previous civilian governments to solve the national problems of economic stagnation, inflation, lack of authority, widespread social unrest, and loss of international prestige; (3) the unrepresentativeness of the leadership of the political parties and of most organized groups; (4) the irresponsible behavior

*An earlier version of this chapter appeared in my *Modernization and Bureaucratic-Authoritarianism: Studies in South American Politics* (Berkeley: Institute of International Studies, University of California, Berkeley, 1973). I wish to thank the Institute of International Studies for permission to use that material.

138

of political parties, which had led to the polarization of public opinion and inefficient governmental performance; and (5) the danger of a breakdown of the cohesion of the armed forces, the only solid institutions remaining after a long period of national crisis.[3]

This was certainly not the first coup in Argentine history.[4] But it differed from all the others in that it was the first time that the armed forces, with a high degree of internal cohesion, had decided to take political power directly into their own hands for a long and indefinite period, with no intention of convoking elections or returning government to political parties in the foreseeable future. The preceding period, 1955–66, had been punctuated by numerous attempts (successful and unsuccessful) at military coups, but none had changed the existing political system. Rather, the continued political instability of that period was a characteristic feature of the workings of a pseudo-political democracy that denied electoral access to the first plurality (i.e., the largest single political party in a multiparty system) of the electorate.[5] The importance of the June 1966 coup is that it was a conscious effort to change the existing political system by the inauguration of a bureaucratic-authoritarian regime. This "culminating" event ("culminating" in terms of the focus of this chapter) was the result of manifold factors, among them the recurrent political instability of the years between 1955 and 1966.

It is important to bear in mind here certain important distinctions. This chapter is intended to contribute to the explanation of the 1966 change in the Argentine political system by analyzing the crucial step that brought about that change. Thus it is not focused on the examination of the political instability that prevailed between 1955 and 1966, except insofar as this seems to have contributed to the final breakdown.

It is always difficult to decide how far back one should go in examining the factors that seem to have effected the event or phenomenon being analyzed. In the present case it is evident that limiting the examination to the factors that were immediately related to the 1966 coup, such as the military's decision to intervene, the high degree of cohesion among the coup leaders, and the goal of inaugurating a different type of political system, would be too restrictive. Consideration of these factors immediately raises questions concerning the reasons for the military decisions and the lack of public opposition to the coup.

In this way the focus of analysis is broadened; but such a broadened perspective involves problems. First, the conceptual neatness of an explanation centered on only the most immediate factors is sacrificed. Second, it is impossible to avoid simplifying the broad historical and social factors that are thought to have exerted an important influence on factors more immediate to the coup. Why did the military change the goals of its intervention in 1966? Why was this coup decided upon by military officers who had shortly before taken a very explicit *legalista* (i.e., anti-coup) stand? Why was the 1966 coup executed with such an unusual degree of cohesion among the armed forces? Why did most organized groups in Argentine society hasten to express support for the coup and the military government? And in what ways did these circumstances relate to the attempt to inaugurate and consolidate a new type of political system in Argentina?

However, even with its pitfalls, a broad analytical perspective is desirable because it alone will allow a search for answers to these questions. The strategy I intend to follow here will begin with a brief examination of some aspects of Argentine history. Next, I shall study aspects of the general social context of the 1955–66 period. The first phase will provide the main outlines of a "longitudinal" perspective, while the second will give a detailed picture of Argentina immediately before the 1966 coup. These two sections will establish the coordinates within which the factors most directly related to the coup will be studied, which will be done in the final section of the chapter.

Some Aspects of Argentina's Historical Legacy

The analysis here of the historical aspects that preceded the 1966 coup (some of them by many years) will of necessity be very selective. There is no pretense here to write history. The aim is to identify some social problems that emerged during certain historical periods and have remained as "constants" in Argentine society. The historical discussion will be limited strictly to those developments which seem indispensable for this purpose.[6]

"Constants," as used here, are characteristics of Argentine society that have remained as persistent problems or constraints, limiting the possibilities of political action. The persistence of certain historical constants and the emergence of new ones is, during each historical period, a major part of the constellation of problems that must be faced. Each such constellation is made up of the constants and the cluster of more specific problems that confront the political actors in each particular period. These constants could have been eliminated by previous governments, but the fact that they have not has—to borrow Weber's analogy—loaded the dice more and more against formation of an effective political system in Argentina. This failure has in turn fostered the persistence and accumulation of an increasing number of constants.

National Unification and the Landed Oligarchy

Two constants have persisted from a very early period. The first is a high degree of incongruence between actual political behavior and political behavior as prescribed by formal institutions and dominant ideologies.[7] The second is a strong disaffection of vast sectors of the population vis-à-vis the existing political system and the holders of political power, based on salient cleavages around important issues and on an unequal distribution of political resources.[8]

During Spanish colonial rule two very different patterns of settlement prevailed in what would later be Argentina. The central and northern regions were economically part of the Peruvian Viceroyalty, and the conquistadors established a patriarchal rule over largely self-sufficient societies, which they found fit quite well with the hierarchical world-view they had brought from Spain. In contrast, Buenos Aires was very much a secondary settlement; the lands around it were sparsely populated by nomadic Indians and lacked any economic value. The village, although a port, was too distant to benefit from the more affluent Peruvian region, and it had been prohibited by Spain from engaging in international trade. But the expansion of British commerce brought Buenos Aires into conflict with Spain, and soon it became a major center for smuggling. The legislation that the Spanish enacted to prohibit commerce and smuggling in Buenos Aires was utterly ineffective (as was the legislation to protect the Indians of the Peruvian regions). The famous dictum that "the will of the King is obeyed but not executed" accurately reflected the reality.

The movement toward independence from Spain, which originated in Buenos Aires, triggered sixty years of convulsion and anarchy. The civil wars of independence were almost a continuous civil war. On one side of the struggle were the *unitarios,* based in Buenos Aires and heavily involved in international trade. Eager to absorb all European ideological trends, they drafted laws and constitutions for a nation that did not yet exist and that would successfully resist their claims to rule. Their opponents, based in the central and northern regions, sought to preserve their patriarchal, precapitalist way of life. At stake were two very different ideologies and economic interests: the philosphy of the Enlightenment as opposed to that of late Spanish scholasticism, and the incorporation of Argentina into the world market as opposed to the persistence of the closed, subsistence economies of the interior. After they gained independence, the Spanish colonies were, as Richard Morse puts it, "a decapitated patrimonial state" in quest of a legitimacy formula.[9] For the unitarios, outwardly oriented and without traditional legitimation, "government" meant some form of constitutional government in the fashion of Western Europe or the United States. The obvious difficulty was that the context in which the newly independent Spanish colonials operated was not at all the type of society presupposed by those models, and the difference between the two was too great to be ignored. One possibility would have been to try to establish institutions better adapted to the actual conditions, but many unitarios believed that imposing the forms of constitutional government, for the sake of "progress" and at any cost, would necessarily push social reality toward a resemblance to the model societies. Transplanted institutions would shape a social reality that would be compatible with them. After many failures, a constitution was enacted in 1852 that has endured (at least nominally) until the present. The representative who formally proposed the text to the constitutional convention said:

There are only two ways of building a nation: to take her behavior, her character and her habits as they are, or to give her the code that must create the proper behavior, character and habits if the country does not have them. Since this is the case, since the country is in chaos, this constitutional project is the only way to save her.[10]

During the civil wars the words "constitution," "liberalism," and later on, "democracy," *belonged* to the unitarios; but the incongruence between institutional and formal prescriptions of behavior and the actual performance of government was as great as it had been under Spanish rule. In addition, these terms became the symbols of a minority that denied the traditional culture and destroyed the social structures and forms of government of a large proportion of the population.[11] The privileged location of Buenos Aires as a port meant that its inhabitants could act as middlemen for the introduction of European (mainly English) manufactured goods. Because the craft industries of the interior could not compete with these imports, the territorial expansion of the hegemony of Buenos Aires resulted in the extinction of many domestic economic activities. This helps to explain the stern resistance of the interior against Buenos Aires.

When the pace of the industrial revolution accelerated in England during the second half of the nineteenth century, Buenos Aires was able to acquire economic resources and warfare technology that firmly established its hegemony over the interior. But even after 1870, when the country was relatively peaceful, the transplantation of democratic political institutions continued to create major problems. In particular, maintenance of these institutions required that elections be held, when the supporters of the central government were frequently in a minority. Since there was no possibility of allowing the *barbares* to rule, electoral fraud, as well as violence and openly arbitrary exercise of the central government's powers, became a frequent occurrence.

At this point a third Argentine constant became clearly evident. The democratic "rules of the game" were to be given only limited and conditional adherence by the ruling sectors; the application of these rules was subject to the proviso that it produce the "correct" government.[12] If this requirement were not met, the rules were suspended to the extent and for the period necessary to assure that the "correct" government would attain power. As would happen in succeeding periods, since "playing democratically" endangered democracy (as defined by the ruling sectors), the only solution was to act in a blatantly undemocratic fashion while asserting that such action was necessary "for the sake of democracy." Given the consistently high level of popular disaffection toward rulers and institutions, it is not difficult to understand how this constant bred cynicism, instead of helping to establish the legitimacy of the system and its institutions.[13]

At the end of the nineteenth century the ruling sectors eagerly adopted the new ideas emanating from Europe, mixing positivism with Darwinian and Spencerian concepts. The struggle previously defined as "civilization against barbarism" could now be "scientifically" interpreted. Ruling sectors maintained that there was no hope until the remnants of Spanish culture and the "degraded races" were replaced by European immigration.[14] At the turn of the century, during a period of rapidly growing need for labor because of export expansion, the national government actively encouraged Europeans to immigrate.[15]

Another constant, which initially had favorable consequences, manifested itself in this period—i.e., the dependence of the Argentine economy on international trade and capital movements, with limited capabilities for domestic control of their effects. Since the end of the eighteenth century, a basic tenet of the unitarios had been free trade, under which Argentina would export agrarian goods and import most of the industrial products it needed. When British industry expanded rapidly around 1870, so did its need for the exports that Argentina was in a particularly good position to provide. The vast pampas around Buenos Aires, which could provide the cereals (and later, the beef) for export, became essential in the new international trade situation; the economic center in Argentina shifted decisively from the central and northern regions to Buenos Aires. Great efforts were exerted to establish the financial and transport structure required to open the pampas to capitalist exploitation. The extent and rapidity of this expansion into the pampean land can be seen in the data presented in table 1.

Under this external inducement the Argentine economy grew rapidly in the years between 1870 and 1914. The country won an international reputation for prosperity. The standard of living—at least in the Buenos Aires area—was

Table 1. Selected Economic Indicators: Argentina, 1870–1914

	1865–69	1890–94	1910–14
Total length of railroad track (kilometers)	503	—	31,104
Total merchandise exports (millions of gold pesos)	38	—	410
Total area sown with crops (millions of hectares)	0.58	—	20.62
Total wheat exports (annual averages, millions of gold pesos at 1910–14 values)	0.2	28.1	78.1
Total corn exports (same measure as wheat)	0.3	6.0	72.4
Total frozen beef exports (same measure as wheat)	0.0	0.1	49.7

SOURCES: Carlos Díaz Alejandro, *Essays on the Economic History of the Argentine Republic* (New Haven: Yale University Press, 1970), pp. 2–5; and Ernesto Tornquist and Co., *The Economic Development of the Argentine Republic in the Last Fifty Years* (Buenos Aires, 1919), pp. 26, 116–17, 139–40.

high as a result of the advantages that Argentina enjoyed in the international market for the exportation of cereals and beef. But the rest of the country lagged far behind Buenos Aires and the surrounding pampas region. Furthermore, millions of hectares of the best pampean land were appropriated by a tiny sector of the population: Argentina never had an open frontier.[16] The resources from which Argentine prosperity derived were monopolized by the very few, the beneficiaries taking for granted that this was the only road to progress. As one president of the period, Juárez Celman, stated: "With *latifundio* we have achieved the present progress and our outstanding economic and productive capacity. The system of big property has made us rich."[17] Perhaps more important, this privileged stratum consisted, by and large, of less-than-efficient entrepreneurs who showed very little interest in industrial activities.[18] These factors combined to restrict what would otherwise have been an unusual opportunity for building a solid economy and a more open society.

The Middle Class

By the end of the nineteenth century (especially in Buenos Aires), the expanding economy had created an important middle sector, formed by merchants, professionals, civil servants, and owners of the primitive industries that typically appear in the large export-sites of agrarian-export economies. Recent investigations have shown that sheer distance from central, industrial-good exporting economies and some tariff protection for certain products stimulated the growth of some industry, but such industry was owned largely by foreign nationals. This, combined with a preference on the part of the government and ruling sectors for open trade policies, prevented the emergence of a numerically important and politically active national industrial bourgeoisie. Instead, within the middle class the salaried, nonentrepreneurial sectors prevailed overwhelmingly. This middle class fully accepted the existing socioeconomic policies and, if anything, were more anti-industry and more pro–free trade than the oligarchy. Their political demands were limited to fair elections and open access to high-ranking national government positions.[19] However, their road to political power was not easy. Only after three unsuccessful civil-military revolts was a law passed providing for honest electoral registrations, secret ballots, and custody by the military of the urns in which the ballots were deposited.

This long delay in the admission of the middle class into the political arena reflects another constant: the strong resistance by established political actors to the expansion of political participation to include new actors, even when favorable economic circumstances and almost total policy consensus minimized the "risks" of such expansion. When these favorable circumstances later changed, and new political actors disagreed sharply on policy matters, outright opposition to further expansion became the rule.

As Peter Smith argues elsewhere in this volume, neither the oligarchy's concession to the claim for clean elections nor the election in 1916 of the Partido Radical leader, Hipólito Yrigoyen, meant genuine commitment of the oligarchy to democratic rules of the game. The new government operated under conditions of "uncertain legitimacy,"[20] subject to a satisfactory (as defined by the old rulers) handling of national affairs. The oligarchy retained control of crucial political resources—social prestige, economic power, influence on the army, control of the press and the university. Throughout the *Radicales* period the old rulers demonstrated contempt toward the parvenus, whom they saw as inefficient and unreliable people who, after all, were only following the old socioeconomic policies of the ruling sectors.[21]

The Radicales governments were not entirely free of fraud and arbitrary interventions of the central government into the affairs of the states, but on the whole they made remarkable progress in electoral practices and in extending the rule of law. It was particularly unfortunate for Argentina that the British economy began to decline after 1914. Because of this decline and less than skillful government policies, economic growth slowed. Finally, with the impact of the world crisis that began in 1929, the economic situation became very serious. The oligarchy saw in these conditions a confirmation of their belief that only they could govern. In 1930 an oligarchy-backed military coup ousted the Radicales government.

The old oligarchy, then generally called the *Conservadores,* attempted to govern in the midst of the economic crisis. They undertook a program of industrialization designed to save badly needed international currency and provide an internal market for agrarian production.[22] The severe impact of the crisis in the interior of the country, combined with governmental efforts to industrialize in Buenos Aires, drew large numbers of people into urban life.[23] These new migrants were to form the basis of a large urban proletariat, remaining close to their agrarian origins and bringing with them a long record of grievances against the central government. The Conservadores were faced with the old predicament: since they were "democratic," sooner or later they had to call elections. They first tried a gubernatorial election in Buenos Aires State in 1931, which resulted in a Radicales victory. Since the "correct" candidate had not won, the election was annulled, and a federal delegate appointed in place of the elected governor. Later, when former Radical president Marcelo de Alvear tried to run in presidential elections, his candidacy was vetoed by a decree. As a result, under the motto of "Intransigence," the Radicales abstained from electoral participation and organized several unsuccessful civil-military rebellions. Even with the abstention of the Radicales, the Conservadores could not risk honest elections. Systematic "patriotic fraud" was practiced, on the grounds that it was the only way to avoid the disasters that would follow if a majoritarian government were elected.[24] To quote Whitaker:

As the Presidential election of 1937 approached, the rising Radical tide made Justo [the president, elected by fraud in 1932] himself uneasy over the chance of passing electoral control to the right people. Accordingly, he and his followers simply stole the elections by fraud and force. . . . For the political health of the country the effect was disastrous. Coming on top of all that had gone before it seemed to confirm what non-conformists had been saying for years past: that in Argentina democracy was only a snare to facilitate dominion and exploitation of the nation by a privileged few.[25]

For the Radicales and for the still inarticulated groups that rapid industrialization and urbanization had given rise to, this was the "infamous decade." This label reflected, among other things, the outrage produced by the huge concessions that the Conservadores, attempting to preserve part of the original export market, made to British interests. Nationalist sentiment against both Conservadores and British influence increased.

The 1930s saw sweeping political and social changes. The new import-substituting industrialists sought to increase their sway over government decisions. The military saw industrialization as the path to international power and British influence as the major obstacle to industrialization. Ideological alternatives to democracy were being tried in Europe in the 1930s with apparent success. Moreover, the church, particularly after the beginning of the Spanish civil war, was ready to grant ideological legitimacy to antidemocratic movements. From all these elements a nationalist-industrialist ideology with strong authoritarian components began to develop. It had a wide appeal against which the old ruling sectors could oppose only a mockery of democracy and a dependent association with England.[26]

The Urban Popular Sector

During the 1930s the urban popular sector (i.e., the working class and segments of the lower middle class) went through a process of rapid political activation. But none of the existing political parties was willing to absorb a sector formed largely of recent rural migrants—not even the Socialists and Communists, whose basic constituencies were skilled workers and European migrants.[27] World War II further complicated the domestic political situation. The demands for autarchy and industrialization, as well as the diffusion of pro-Axis ideologies, clashed with British interests and with the pro-Allied international policies that most of the ruling sectors favored. Like the rural migrants, the new industrialists and many military officers could find no political parties through which to channel their preferences. The new issues and ideologies had a profound impact on the military, and for the first time the oligarchy could not count on its firm allegiance. In 1943, when it became evident that the 1944 elections were to be decided by "patriotic fraud," the military ousted the Conservadores government. In the resulting military government, Colonel Perón emerged as the leader best able to pull together all the dissident elements that the Conservadores period had generated.[28] Against this coalition, the Radicales, Conservadores, Socialists, and Communists formed a "Democratic Union," but they were defeated (in honest elections) by Perón in 1946.[29]

This is not the place for a study of *Peronismo*.[30] It included authoritarian components which were a blend of the ideologies of the 1930s with a traditional (for Argentina) style of leadership.[31] Perón's policies of income distribution in favor of industry and the popular sector, the enactment of comprehensive labor and welfare legislation, and the introduction of numerous economic controls gained an enthusiastic response from the popular sector, but were very much at odds with the preferences of the recently displaced ruling sectors. As a consequence, and for the sake of "defending democracy," very early in Perón's government the old parties engaged in "disloyal opposition," reinforcing the authoritarian tendencies inherent in Peronismo.[32] The personalities of Perón and his wife appealed to the masses, particularly urban and rural workers. In addition, during Perón's government the standard of living of these sectors rose significantly, many of the rights of labor were effectively protected, and workers could feel that they had gained some influence in national affairs. When attacked, Perón did not miss an opportunity to emphasize his opponents' past behavior as a support for his argument that the "return to democracy" they advocated was a trick for establishing a dictatorship to oppress the people. To say the least, Perón had a strong argument when he observed that his opponents had never practiced the liberal advice they were now giving.

The effect of these developments was to increase the conflict between Peronistas and anti-Peronistas, and to decrease the chances that the formally democratic institutional framework could operate. Both sides helped to create a situation that is well summarized by Floria:

Perón's period was not only the period of Peronismo; it was also the period of anti-Peronismo. This polarization, as it was afterwards called, was the result of the articulation of power and opposition according to rules that were not shared. There were not two parties; there were "two countries": one whose inhabitants could only conceive of Argentina with Perón, and another that could only accept Argentina without Perón and, in terms of power, without Peronismo.[33]

By 1950 the broad coalition that Perón had formed began to disintegrate. Crop failures, misallocation of resources, unfavorable trends in international trade, and the increasing need for foreign currency to sustain advancing industrialization led to an economic crisis. Simultaneously, the authoritarian and repressive components of Peronismo were significantly reinforced. Though unwilling to oppose agrarian interests by pursuing a program of land reform, and unwilling to force industry to absorb the costs of the economic crisis, Perón's government had to protect the gains achieved by the urban workers, its staunchest supporters. After 1949 the industrialists started to withdraw their support and align themselves with the opposition, and in 1954 Perón became involved in a serious conflict with the Catholic church. The armed forces also began to waver in their support, and when, after two abortive attempts to stage coups in 1951 and June 1955, they found that the only remaining solid support for Perón came from the popular sector, they finally ousted him in September 1955.

During the provisional government of General Eugenio Aramburu (1955–58), with the support of the now bitterly anti-Peronista armed forces, the old leaders of the old parties returned to power. The point to be emphasized here is that by 1955 two fundamental and overwhelmingly salient cleavages had coincided: the political division of Peronistas and anti-Peronistas, and the socioeconomic division of the popular sector (constituted largely of the working class) and the labor unions against the rest of society. The result was intense and cumulative polarization.[34]

After 1955 a program of "democratization" was undertaken which resulted in a drastic decrease in the share of wage income in the GNP, numerous attempts to weaken labor unions, and the electoral proscription of the Peronista party. If to these are added the effects of economic stagnation and inflation, it is hardly surprising that the Peronistas maintained their allegiance to Peronismo.[35] The fact that the legal road to political power was closed to them, memories of recent times in which they had been much better off, the need to fight constantly for their shares of income, the vengefulness of the provisional government's policies—all of this hardened the Peronistas' opposition. Widespread social unrest followed.[36]

For anti-Peronistas any return to the pre-1955 political situation was totally out of the question. This view was shared by the armed forces, from which all officers suspected of Peronista leanings had been purged. The military leaders had not forgotten that shortly before being ousted, Perón had seemed determined to organize workers' militias. When a rebellion by Peronistas failed in 1956, the anti-Peronista military officers, breaking an unwritten rule, ordered the leaders of the rebellion shot, thereby increasing the existing polarization.

All the constants described above were still very much a factor in Argentine life. The Peronistas had been removed from government in the name of "democracy." This meant elections would be necessary, but the "wrong" party—the *Peronista* bloc—controlled the largest share of electors. Under these circumstances, political activity was severely constrained: it could serve neither as a means for the return of Peronistas to government, nor as a channel for the implementation of socioeconomic policies favored by Peronistas and the labor unions.[37] The discrepancy between the outwardly expressed democratic beliefs of the ruling sectors and the actual workings of the political system was almost beyond measure. In addition, the severe socioeconomic crisis (which will be analyzed further below) had accentuated the rigidities in the social structure and was creating new patterns of stagnation and dependence. Finally, no matter how great the economic, social, and political costs, the ruling sectors were determined to close any significant political access to the politically activated urban popular sector.

Here I have tried merely to underline political and social constants "extracted" from historical sequence, without attempting the task, impossible here, of explaining their emergence. Despite the pitfalls inherent in a highly condensed description, it was essential to discuss these constants. They refer to historical factors whose more immediate effects, whether on the social processes studied in the section immediately following or on those connected with the 1966 coup that are the subject of the final section of this chapter, are difficult to measure. But insofar as they determine a persistent and pervasive political climate, these constants form the broad base of reference without which it seems impossible to achieve an understanding of more specific factors.

The focus of this chapter turns now toward a more "horizontal" perspective: an analysis of the social context of the 1955–66 period. This analysis is provided on the assumption that this context, to a large extent influenced by the historical constants, exerted a direct influence on the military intervention of June 1966.

The Social Setting of the 1966 Coup

In 1966 the average per capita income in Argentina was $818 (in 1966 U.S. dollars).[38] In 1960 unionized workers numbered around 2,600,000.[39] Agriculture and industry contributed 16.6 and 34.0 percent respectively, to the GNP while 21.4 percent of the working age population was employed in agriculture and 28.0 in industry.[40] Clearly, Argentina was far from being an underdeveloped "traditional" agrarian society. But these data must be considered from the perspective of a long period of slow growth.[41] In 1929 the average per capita income in Argentina was about $700 (1960 U.S. dollars).[42] At that time the Argentine per capita income was slightly below that of Australia, a country remarkably similar to Argentina in terms of production and relations with the world market. Today, Australia's per capita income is almost twice that of Argentina.

From 1925–29 to 1961–65, the average per capita growth rate in Argentina has been 0.8 percent yearly. Díaz Alejandro offers this description of the situation:

Since 1930 . . . the growth rate has been so small, the cyclical fluctuations so violent, and the swings in income distribution so pronounced that it is easy to believe that during some years several groups have been worse off than they, or their parents, were during 1925–1929. Furthermore, in some public services (e.g., telephones, railroads, the post office, statistical services) and in some import-substituting manufactures, quality has deteriorated so that a quality-corrected growth rate would be even smaller. . . . Although time-series for the Argentine terms of trade are of doubtful reliability, it is likely that they declined between 1925–1929 and recent years; correcting the growth rate for this decline would further shave it.[43]

If we take the Perón period (1946–55) as the baseline, the per capita income reached in 1947 was not surpassed until 1965, and the per capita real wages of 1947 were surpassed only in 1958 and in 1965, to fall below the 1947 level in the following years.[44] The characteristics of this arrested development require closer examination:

(1) When the GNP time-series since 1946 are considered, it can be seen that within the average low growth rate, wild fluctuations have taken place from year to year. As column 1 of table 2 shows, in the years 1948, 1949, 1950, 1952, 1956, 1959, 1962, 1963, and 1966 net losses in per capita income were registered, and in some cases losses were substantial.

(2) The average rate of inflation has been 26.5 percent annually between 1946 and 1966, but it was substantially higher in the 1955–66 period *and* in the years of negative growth (see column 2 of table 2).

(3) After reaching a maximum of 46.9 percent in 1952, the salary and wage share in the GNP declined to 39.8 percent in 1965 (see column 3 in table 2), even though the productivity per worker in 1961 was 23 percent above the 1953 level.[45]

(4) During the 1949–66 period Argentina suffered a chronic foreign exchange shortage (see column 4 of table 2), which was aggravated in the years of economic recovery.

Many economists agree that the foreign exchange shortage has been the single most important factor in retarding economic growth in Argentina. This shortage has been closely related to other factors. First, as table 3 shows, the quantum index of Argentine exports declined from 1925–29 to 1960–64 not only in per capita but also in *absolute* terms, reflecting lagging agricultural productivity (see column 2 of table 3). During most of this period the domestic terms of trade discriminated against agrarian products (see column 3 of table 3). In addition, of the net increase in national capital stock between 1929 and 1955, only 1.0 percent went to the rural sector.[46]

Second, from the 1930s nearly until the end of Perón's government, Argentine industry expanded ''horizontally'' by putting heavy emphasis on consumer goods import substitution. But the exhaustion of these ''easy'' stages of import substitution placed serious strains on Argentina's declining import

Table 2. Annual Measures of Various Key Economic Indicators, 1946–66

Year	1 Annual Changes in GDP per Capita (percent of previous year's level in constant pesos)	2 Yearly Inflation	3 Wages and Salaries as Percentage of GNP	4 Change in Net Foreign Exchange Reserves (in mil- lions of current U.S. dollars)
Perón's government				
1946	6.4%	17.7%	38.7%	—
1947	11.9	13.5	37.3	—
1948	-0.7	13.1	40.6	—
1949	-6.5	31.1	45.7	-269
1950	-0.3	25.5	45.9	166
1951	2.1	36.7	43.0	-333
1952	-8.2	38.7	46.9	-173
1953	5.1	4.0	44.8	279
1954	1.9	3.8	45.6	-33
1955	5.0	12.3	43.0	-175
1955–66 period				
1956	-0.2	13.4	42.6	-19
1957	3.6	24.7	41.4	-60
1958	5.3	31.6	43.3	-217
1959	-7.7	113.7	37.8	113
1960	6.1	27.3	38.4	161
1961	5.1	13.5	39.9	-57
1962	-3.7	28.1	39.1	-234
1963	-5.5	24.1	39.1	202
1964	6.2	22.1	38.2	-11
1965	6.7	28.6	39.1	139
1966	-2.4	32.3	39.8	53

SOURCES: Column 1: Banco Central de la República Argentina, *Origen del producto y composición del gasto nacional: Suplemento del Boletín Estadístico, n. 6* (Buenos Aires: Banco Central, 1966), p. 18, and Díaz Alejandro, *Essays*, p. 352. Column 2: Díaz Alejandro, *Essays*, p. 528 (Buenos Aires cost of living). Column 3: UN-ECLA and CONADE, *El desarrollo económico y la distribución del ingreso en la Argentina* (New York: United Nations, 1968), p. 164. Column 4: Díaz Alejandro, *Essays*, p. 353.

Table 3. Economic Indices, 1925–64

Years	1 Quantum Indices of Merchandise Exports (1951– 54 = 100)	2 Index of Agrarian Production (1960 = 100)	3 Internal Terms of Trade (ratio of rural prices to industrial prices) (1935–39 = 100)
1925–29	179	—	100 (1935–39)
1930–39	167	—	72 (1940–45)
1940–44	135	86	77 (1945–49)
1945–49	133	85	83 (1950–55)
1950–54	106	87	93 (1956–58)
1955–59	124	99	96 (1959–61)
1960–64	160	102	103 (1962–64)

SOURCES: Column 1: Díaz Alejandro, *Essays,* p. 76. Column 2: Banco Central, *Origen del producto,* p. 36. Column 3: Díaz Alejandro, *Essays,* p. 89.

capacity. Domestic industrial expansion was hindered by problems of high costs and distorted schedules of supply, as well as severe financial, technological, and managerial limitations. Under such conditions, the need for critical inputs of intermediate and raw materials, as well as of capital goods, grew at a time when exports were lagging. There were growing demands for capital and technology transfers from abroad, indicating a need for (as well as the great difficulties to be faced in) making significant advances toward more mature industrialization; i.e., a more vertically integrated industrialization, with a better structure of costs and supply. Furthermore, increases in the domestic fabrication of capital goods were almost entirely at the level of relatively simple equipment, and Argentine production was not able to satisfy the growing demand for more complex equipment. The yearly average of machinery imports was 198 million U.S. dollars in 1951–55, 352 million in 1956–60, and 498 million in 1961–65.[47] An observation made by Díaz Alejandro neatly summarizes this situation: the income elasticity of Argentine demands for imports was 2.6, which meant that, when and if national income grew by one unit, it generated a demand for 2.6 units of imported goods; therefore, the foreign exchange positions of the country was worsened by positive rates of growth.[48]

The effects of the factors cited—particularly the pressure of the growth years on the foreign exchange position of Argentina—led to drastic devaluations of the peso, usually combined with programs aimed at restricting internal demand and eliminating "marginal" industrial producers. By making imports and exportable agrarian goods more expensive, devaluations fed inflation at the same time that the effects of internal policies drastically decreased output and demand. As can be seen in table 1, the years of negative growth were usually also those of higher inflation and negative income redistributions. One major goal of the devaluations was to increase, by the restriction of domestic demand and income transfers, short-run available exports and, in the long run, to improve agrarian productivity. These effects were supposed to be produced by improving the domestic agrarian terms of trade and the dollar value of rural exportable commodities. But these policies meant severe income losses for the urban-industrial sector, which led to the intense social conflict that marked the 1955–66 period. As a consequence of this conflict, the redistributive policies were soon relaxed, and the presumably beneficial consequences that would have followed from them were never realized.[49]

An important effect of inflation and devaluations has been a wild fluctuation in income shares. As a UN-ECLA and CONADE study says:

The effect of these devaluations on income distribution occurs in two stages. In the first, a horizontal distribution takes place when relative prices change in favor of agriculture, consisting of inter-sectoral income changes from the urban sectors to the agrarian sector or, more specifically, to agrarian producers. But since the effect of devaluation on relative prices is combined with policies of salary restriction or increased unemployment, to some extent the horizontal redistribution is transformed into a vertical redistribution. This means that, in the final analysis, the main income changes (produced by devaluations) are harmful to urban workers and beneficial to agrarian producers, while the relative position of urban entrepreneurs is damaged only to the extent that the effects of devaluation are more intense than the effects of salary (restriction) policies.[50]

In short, devaluations benefit the agrarian sector, but as inflation proceeds and no new devaluation takes place, the urban sector (however its share is allocated between workers and entrepreneurs) recovers its losses. At some point, the effects of devaluation are annulled or even reversed, domestic economic activity increases again, a new foreign exchange crisis is produced, and a new devaluation is made. The magnitude of the shifts of income for several Argentine sectors during 1958–65 can be seen in table 4.

It is difficult to exaggerate the political consequences of this turbulent economic situation, particularly in a setting combining a low level of political legitimacy and a high degree of popular disaffection. Note that the combination of constantly high inflation (aggravated in negative growth years) with drastic devaluations and slow growth meant that to remain at the same level of monetary income would have involved heavy losses in real income. Thus, gains made by all sectors were extremely unstable, and the situation created by slow and erratic economic growth served to raise the stakes of the conflict.

Before going any further, let us look at some more disaggregated data. As previously noted, the real wage income in 1965 was about the same as in 1945. However, as table 2 showed, the share of salaries and wages in the GNP decreased during the 1955–66 period. This apparent discrepancy disappears at the level of more disaggregated data. First, the recurrent attempts to eliminate "marginal" industrial producers, combined with the introduction of more

Table 4. Intersectoral Income Variations Expressed as Percentage of Income Participation of Each Sector, 1958–65

	Average of Absolute Variations	Maximum Yearly Positive Variation	Maximum Yearly Negative Variation
Rural			
Agrarian	12.1%	34.8%	−20.8%
Urban			
Industry	4.8	10.1	−8.5
Construction	7.8	37.5	−11.1
Commerce	6.2	7.8	−22.0
Transport and communications	4.4	12.7	−6.7
General government	8.1	14.3	−17.0
Electricity, gas, and water	10.1	37.5	−20.0

SOURCE: UN-ECLA and CONADE, *El desarrollo económico*, p. 217.

capital-intensive techniques, produced a large pool of urban unemployed, especially in the early 1960s.[51] Since real wage data reflect only the incomes of those lucky enough to find work, they give only a partial picture of the income position of the popular sector. Second, among those employed, there were wide differences in the real income positions of those workers who were well organized and those who, as members of the less dynamic sectors of the economy, lacked the degree of organization necessary to obtain satisfaction of their economic demands.

The source of data for table 5 does not discriminate between wage and salary earners, but census data show that an important proportion of the "Industry and Mining" and "Construction" categories consists of blue-collar workers. The "Commerce and Finance" category is formed largely by white-collar workers, while "Services" (which includes government workers) is a very mixed category. It is important to note that while industrial workers fared relatively well, other blue-collar and apparently most white-collar employees did not. This circumstance surely underlay the disaffection shown by these latter groups during the 1955–66 period, their initial willingness to support the military government, and their responsiveness to a "law and order" appeal. However, no matter how badly they fared, the nonindustrial workers did better than those sectors even less capable of exerting effective pressure on the national government. As table 5 shows, pensioners and *rentistas* in particular were heavy losers.[52]

In other words, at the national level the economic "game" was quite close to zero-sum, and the better organized (and perhaps in the short-run, economically more indispensable) sectors of urban entrepreneurs, agrarian entrepreneurs, and industrial workers could increase their shares of real income at the expense of other, less organized, politically weaker sectors and regions.

The government as an institution was another loser. In terms of gov-

Table 5. Average Real Income of Families in Selected Years (1953 = 100)

	1946	1949	1953	1959	1961	1965
Salary and wage earners						
Industry and mining	88	119	100	90	115	**146**[a]
Construction	106	**137**	100	98	108	118
Transport and communication	106	**128**	100	95	106	110
Commerce and finance	85	**111**	100	94	**111**	**112**
Services	84	**113**	100	91	103	109
Entrepreneurs						
Agriculture	111	82	100	**143**	89	117
Industry, mining, and construction	115	**148**	100	124	135	143
Commerce	162	**175**	100	161	169	155
Transport	86	104	100	150	143	**170**
Services	109	**132**	100	98	105	109
Social security pensioners	105	130	100	79	96	97
Rentistas	**150**	122	100	56	49	39
TOTAL	103	116	100	108	112	124

SOURCE: UN-ECLA and CONADE, *El desarrollo económico,* p. 130.

[a] Year of maximum real income in boldface throughout.

ernmental resources (i.e., the pool of human and economic means at its disposal for the making and implementation of policies), there was a steady deterioration in the 1955–66 period. In Lasswell's terminology, poor governmental performance and diminished resources resulted in a serious "power dis-accumulation" that hampered governmental problem-solving capabilities.[53] This reduced capability reflected the general social situation but also contributed significantly to its worsening and to the final breakdown in 1966.

In 1965 the tax revenues of the national government amounted to 13.2 percent of the GNP, which decreased to 11.9 percent in 1960 and to 10.9 percent in 1965. The income of the social security system amounted in the same years to 5.0, 3.5, and 4.8 percent of the GNP.[54] (The deterioration of governmental income can be seen clearly in table 6, where comparable data for other countries have been included.) The substantial decline in personal income taxes (see table 7) was partially compensated for by increases in indirect taxes but the impact on income distribution was regressive. The drop in governmental income generated huge budget deficits, which were met by highly inflationary increases in the money supply.[55] The proportion of government expenditures allocated to public works dropped from 20.9 percent of the national budget in 1955–59 to 14.5 percent in 1965.[56] A partially overlapping category—public capital investments—declined by 8.6 percent between 1955–60 and 1960–65.[57] Although the data are incomplete, it is very probable that real salaries of government employees declined throughout this period, partially recovering during 1964–66, but never returning to the 1949 level. Perpetual political crisis resulted in a constant turnover of cabinet members

Table 6. Taxation Data for Argentina and Selected Other Countries

	Percentage of Working Age Population Filing Income Tax Returns	Declared Taxable Income as a Percentage of Total Personal Income
Argentina		
1953	10%	18%
1959	9	10
1961	5	9
Other countries		
United States (1950)	89	77
England (1952–53)	90	80
Australia (1958–59)	80	68

SOURCE: UN-ECLA, *Economic Bulletin for Latin America* 9, no. 1 (April 1966).

and high-ranking civil servants, and in the few government activities which can be measured for productivity, a decline is evident.[58]

The general process can be summarized as follows: devaluations benefited agrarian producers and were paid for by the urban sector. This situation was reversed by the inflation and economic reactivation that took place between devaluations. Within the urban sector another game was played for the allocation of gains and losses among different categories of entrepreneurs and workers: the gains that could be appropriated by some of the organized categories were paid for by other less organized sectors and areas. Inflation meant that anyone could lose, on the average, one-fourth of his real income in a year.[59] As a consequence of this situation a "catching-up game" developed, in which only a few sectors were able to influence public policies in order to stay ahead in the constantly changing distribution of income shares. In this sense, a "powerful sector" was one that was able to maintain or improve its real-income position by ensuring the implementation of favorable government

Table 7. Direct Taxes as Percentage of Total Government Income in Argentina, 1946–64

Perón Government		*1956–64*	
1946	38.5%	1956	34.1%
1947	46.3	1957	37.9
1948	49.8	1958	39.3
1949	46.9	1959	29.1
1950	47.3	1960	32.8
1951	43.0	1961	33.0
1952	47.3	1962	30.6
1953	45.0	1963	30.6
1954	41.7	1964	28.3
1955	41.8		

SOURCE: *Panorama de la Economía Argentina*, no. 3, 1967, pp. 23–24.

policies—such as urban and rural entrepreneurs or industrial workers. (In this sense not even the government could be considered powerful.)

An important part of this game consisted of determining strategies that would enable sectors to gain power. First, since rapid inflation continued, a sector that was trying to catch up had to do so in a relatively short time. Second, the focus of demands for policies that would permit "catch-up" was not on institutions such as Parliament, the political parties, and state governments, which played at best a marginal role in the reallocation of economic resources. These demands were concentrated on the presidency, with the result that it became increasingly unlikely that other political institutions could play a meaningful role. Third, the focus on the presidency increased the importance of channels of access that enabled actors to exercise power over the president.[60] Thus, the military became the most effective channel for the satisfaction of sectoral demands; civilian groups sought to influence military factions which could exercise power over the presidency. This fractionalized the military and resulted in more and more numerous and changing demands being channeled through them.

The channeling of demands through the military involved a very real threat of ouster to the government.[61] This danger was evident in the numerous *planteos* (demands from the military backed by the threat of force if they were denied), as well as in the many coups and attempted coups between 1955–66. Those sectors that could induce threats of coups from the military had a definite advantage in playing the catching-up game. These inducements could be obtained through direct access, as in the case of the urban and rural entrepreneurs. For the better-organized urban workers, indirect strategies could produce similar results. By promoting social unrest, as well as by paralyzing production through strikes and the occupation of factories, they could make a government appear unable to maintain even minimal levels of law and order, and thus put it in immediate danger of being ousted. That is, the situation benefited those workers in the better-organized and wealthier unions that could threaten governments with sustained disruptions. (This is reflected in the income figures in table 5.)

It should be borne in mind that the legitimacy of the governments of this period was widely questioned, and that there was generalized political disaffection. Under these conditions threats were very real, and any government that valued survival in office could not ignore them. Hence the governments tended to adopt whatever policies best satisfied the sector that was most threatening at a given time. But the zero-sum conditions meant that each such policy decision raised new threats from other powerful sectors. Frequent policy changes resulted from each governmental decision to placate one sector and the new threats that each such decision generated. (The fluctuations in the preceding tables reflect this pattern)

The resulting situation is well characterized by Huntington's concept of mass praetorianism.[62] In a situation where the primary political aim was control of the means for threatening the survival of the government, political institutions designed for more consensual problem-solving could hardly survive. And where the "threat" strategy prevailed, the most effective way for a sector to have its demands met was to be more threatening than the other sectors. Thus, there was a tendency to escalate the levels of threats. The only effective strategy for each sector was to play according to the actual rather than the institutionally prescribed rules. An "idealistic" sector would have lost heavily in a struggle in which, because of stagnation and inflation, the stakes were very high. A dynamic process had begun that would be very difficult to stop: praetorianism breeds more praetorianism until the conditions for systemic breakdown are reached.

Praetorian politics at high modernization become very complex in two ways. First, social differentiation leads to a greater number of highly activated political actors playing—at several levels simultaneously—a catching-up game based on threats to the government. Second, the combination of high stakes and weak constraints means that formally prescribed patterns become very poor indicators of actual political behavior. The influence of the constants identified earlier in the chapter created the initial conditions of dubious legitimacy, a high degree of popular disaffection, and intense rigidity of the established sectors. The Peronista period accelerated social differentiation and political demands well beyond social integration and social performance. Developmental bottlenecks diminished possible payoffs and made the competition for the allocation of social resources close to a zero-sum game. Under these conditions, government personnel had little opportunity for effective decision-making and policy implementation beyond what was demanded by the more threatening political actors. The steady deterioration of government strength aggravated the social situation. In the catching-up game, most political actors and sectors pursued the vitally important goal of at least keeping pace with inflation, using whatever strategies were most effective. Unfortunately, the most effective strategies for the individual actors were also the most damaging to overall social performance. Each actor was trapped in a situation he could not attempt to change by his own actions without losing heavily and was forced to act in ways that led to even further deterioration of the social context upon which the satisfaction of his demands largely depended. Given the historical heritage and the intensity of social conflict, it was very unlikely that these actors could have reached agreements among themselves that would have channeled their competition into less damaging patterns. This should have been accomplished by governmental action, but the government's low level of legitimacy and limited resources prevented any serious efforts in this direction. This situation fits perfectly the general framework proposed by Juan Linz in his introductory essay: the decaying legitimacy of the regime is compounded by its increasing inefficacy in deciding and implementing policies that can satisfy a significant part of the politically relevant population.

The continued crises generated by this situation annul most individual and sectoral gains. But since there is no way for individuals or sectors to change the institutional parameters (the rules of the game), the only course is to continue along the same lines, hoping in each case that the social deterioration can be minimized. Slowly the possibility of another course emerges. After they have played a "loser's game" for some time, it becomes evident to most actors that the majority lose consistently while a few gain, only to have most of their gains annulled shortly thereafter. Once this pattern is recognized, the parameters of the situation are widely questioned. It is concluded that the rules of the game ought to be changed, and with them the political institutions that have been unable to conduct the game in ways more beneficial to the participants. When this assessment becomes general, what might be termed a "ceiling consensus" is reached, and most sectors agree that the political system should be changed and new parameters for competition established. Of course, such a "consensus" is limited strictly to this point: the actors disagree as much as ever about what the new rules should be. Given a previous history of mass praetorianism, it is likely—when the political system changes—that there will be an authoritarian imposition of new "rules" by whatever coalition succeeds in gaining the governmental power.

This is the "power vacuum" described in the Bracher-Linz model of breakdown of political regimes. Authorities have evidently failed to overcome praetorianism in a way that would have supported their legitimacy and even minimally enhanced the efficacy of their rule. From that point on, the only unknown factor is a matter of how long it will take for a winning coalition to emerge from the set of political actors that have reached the "ceiling consensus."

Political Opinions and Attitudes

Observers see many so-called paradoxes in Argentine politics. For example, Kalman Silvert finds the following paradoxical attitudes: (1) "zero-sum mentality" and "lack of responsible entrepreneurship"; (2) "the almost universal view . . . that no public measure can be good for almost everybody"; (3) "the narrowness of loyalty horizons . . .[and] the failure to accept the state as the ultimate arbiter of secular disputes."[63] I would argue that while Silvert is correct in his perception of attitudes, he is wrong in believing that these attitudes are paradoxical. They may be so from the point of view of Argentina's relatively high level of development (gauged by static criteria that do not allow for consideration of the circumstances and processes analyzed in the preceding pages), but these attitudes are hardly surprising given the social context from which they stem.

Table 8. Positive Response to the Survey Question, "Does the Government Have a Great Effect on Your Daily Life?"

United States	41.0%
Germany	38.0
England	33.0
Italy	23.0
Mexico	7.0
Argentina	41.0
Upper class (N = 157)	52.2
Middle class (N = 960)	40.3
Lower class (N = 721)	39.9

SOURCES: For Argentina: Jeane Kirkpatrick, *Leader and Vanguard in Mass Society: A Study of Peronist Argentina* (Cambridge, Mass.: M.I.T. Press, 1971), p. 159. For other countries: Gabriel Almond and Sidney Verba, *The Civil Culture* (Princeton, N.J.: Princeton University Press, 1963).

NOTE: For Argentina, N = 2,000.

Survey data, unfortunately scant, provide support for Silvert's perceptions. In a nationally representative sample (which did not include the sparsely populated Patagonian states) taken three months before the 1966 coup, respondents were asked several of the questions used by Almond and Verba in *The Civic Culture*.[64] Table 8 shows the measure of one important component of political activation—political awareness—indicating that the impact of government on daily life, as perceived by the Argentine respondents, was very high. Only 20 percent of the respondents declared themselves supporters of a political party; 54 percent did not even lean toward any party.[65] In another survey taken shortly before the 1966 coup, to the question "Do you think that Argentine politics needs new men?" 83 percent answered "Yes," and only 4 percent, "No."[66] In Kirkpatrick's survey 42 percent agreed with the statement "A few leaders would do more for the country than all the laws and talk."[67] A similar percentage expressed the belief that the government is controlled by influential people and groups who do not care at all about people's needs—an attitude reflected in perceptions of the social structure, as shown in table 9. The sectors perceived as most influential are the least "acceptable" groups—i.e., 71.6 percent of the respondents would not back a military supported party, 58.4 percent a church supported party, and 89.7 percent a landowner supported party.[68]

As these data indicate, economic concerns are by far the most salient. The answers to the question "What do you consider the most important problems this country is facing at present?" reported in table 10, clearly reflects this primacy.

The relationship of the concerns reported in table 10 to political opinions is evidenced by the 96 percent positive answers given to a question asking if respondents would support a party that "promised to stamp out corruption and inefficiency from government"; further documentation of this relationship is

Table 9. Response to the Survey Question, "Who Has the Greatest Influence over Government?"

Military	33.8%
Church	14.6
Landowners	10.0
Peronistas	8.3
Labor unions	8.3
Entrepreneurs	4.5
Other, Don't know	20.5

SOURCE: Kirkpatrick, *Leader and Vanguard in Mass Society,* p. 161.

NOTE: N = 2,000.

Table 10. Responses to a Survey Question Concerning Argentina's Most Important Problems

	Income Groups			
	All	Low	Medium	High
Socioeconomic concerns				
High cost of living	35%	32%	38%	10%
Inflation, general economic situation	27	22	27	60
Housing shortage	7	6	7	10
Various social and economic problems	7	8	7	4
Wages (low, inadequate)	3	5	2	—
Pensions	3	5	2	—
Unemployment	7	12	4	—
Political concerns				
Bad government, corruption in politics	7	8	7	4
Trade union, corporation problems	2	1	2	6
Other				
Other answers	3	3	2	17
No problems	2	2	2	—
Don't know, No answer	8	9	8	2

SOURCE: Gallup Survey, *Polls* 2, no. 3 (Spring 1967).

NOTE: N = 1,000 residents of the Buenos Aires area. Questions were open ended; multiple answers were permitted.

found in the answers given to the question "What classes, in your opinion, profit most from the government of President Illía—laborers, middle classes, or upper classes?" (see table 11). If one considers as "favorable" those responses that indicate that the respondent's own sector plus "All" benefit from the Illía government, less than 15 percent of the low and middle income respondents express favorable opinions. Even high income respondents are far less satisfied than would be expected. (Note the sharp rise of "No one" answers among high income respondents.)

With respect to the economic situation, there was broad recognition of the zero-sum conditions (see table 12). As may be obvious, a prediction that the

Table 11. Response to the Survey Question "Who Profits Most from the Illía Government?"

	All Respondents	Income Group of Respondent		
		Low	Middle	High
Laborers	3%	4%	2%	4%
Middle classes	6	4	8	4
Upper classes	53	63	50	27
All, everyone	7	5	7	15
No one	17	9	19	35
Don't know	14	16	13	14

SOURCE: Gallup Survey, *Polls.*

NOTE: N = 1,000 residents of the Buenos Aires area.

Table 12. Response to the Survey Question "Do You Think That Argentina's Economic Situation Will Improve, Remain the Same, or Deteriorate in the Next Months?"

Improve	24%
Remain the same	19
Deteriorate	48
Don't know	9

SOURCE: Kirkpatrick, *Leader and Vanguard in Mass Society,* p. 181.

NOTE: N = 2,000 residents of Argentina.

Argentine economy would remain the same is a pessimistic view. The responses reported in tables 13 and 14 are a good indication of the perceived efficiency of the government for coping with major problems.

The data in tables 9–14 reflect a politically informed population, conscious of the inefficiency of government, skeptical about political parties, hostile in their intersectional perceptions, and aware of the zero-sum character of the national wealth. A very weak commitment to the survival of the existing political system—even when menaced by unpopular sectors—is indicated by the large segments of the population that agree on the desirability of "throwing the rascals out" and the need for a "strong man." Even though the military is unpopular, by 1966 the way was paved for a military takeover that would not meet popular resistance.

Unhappily, interview data are almost totally lacking for other social sectors and groups. Except for entrepreneurs, there are no interview data on the elite's political opinions and attitudes.[69] Not surprisingly, entrepreneurs show hostility toward labor and its leaders, fears of labor's eventual access to political power, and receptivity to "law and order" appeals.[70] Government is per-

Table 13. Response to the Survey Question, "Do You Think the Government Will Be Able to Check Inflation?"

Yes	20%
No	67
No opinion	13

SOURCE: Gallup Survey, *Polls* 2, no. 3 (Spring 1967).

NOTE: The sample consisted of 1,000 residents of the Buenos Aires area.

ceived by them as the epitome of red tape and inefficiency, and the major business organizations openly welcomed the ouster of presidents Perón (1955), Frondizi (1962), and Illía (1966).

As has been suggested earlier in this chapter, discussion of the politics of labor unions is, to a very large extent, discussion of Peronismo. The events of 1955–66 could hardly inspire labor union allegiance to government, and—in agreement for the first time with the ruling sectors (but for different reasons and with very different expectations)—the unions and Peronista leaders welcomed the 1966 coup.[71]

Very little is known about the underpaid and overstaffed government bureaucracy, but it seems evident that low salaries, widespread patronage, and the lack of a civil service career prevented the emergence of a public service that, in the midst of crisis, could have maintained a reasonably high level of problem-solving.

A general, socially diffuse factor which provides a common basis for the different attitudes of the various sectors should be mentioned. In contrast to what might be expected in a so-called developing country, contemporary Argentina has lacked a feeling of "emergence"—a sense that the present, whatever its shortcomings, is better and more promising than anything that has gone before. Argentina's history and literature and, more generally, its intellectual climate are pervaded by the memory (or imagination) of lost opportunities and of periods in which the country is seen to have been better off than it is today. There is also a pervasive search for a historical

Table 14. Response to the Survey Question, "According to the Government, the Recently Authorized Rise in Prices Will Raise the Cost of Living Only Some Two Percent. Do You Think This Is Correct or That It Will Be More?"

Correct	4%
More	86
No opinion	10

SOURCE: Gallup Survey, *Polls* 2, no. 3 (Spring 1967).

NOTE: N = 1,000 residents of the Buenos Aires area.

scapegoat—for the identification of actors and sectors to whom the responsibility may be attributed for a history perceived largely as failure. Even today, the nineteenth-century struggles between unitarios and federales are recalled with bitterness. The failure to achieve a more congenial social context has led to the cynical belief that political and sectoral competition takes place in a Hobbesian world. This view was confirmed for Argentine intellectuals, on both the right and the left, by the problems described in the preceding sections, and what they had to say about the political and social situation made the final breakdown of the pre-1966 political system even more likely.

Due to the linearity of language, I have been able to provide only a very limited account of the highly complex interactions among the political history, the socioeconomic context, and the attitudinal dimensions of pre-1966 Argentina, but what has been presented should suffice to indicate the general setting within which the factors immediately connected to the 1966 coup should be examined.

The Coup of 1966

As one Argentine sociologist has observed, at one time or another "Argentine politicians have all gone 'to knock on the door of the barracks.' "[72] Between the overthrow of Perón (in 1955) and 1962, the armed forces were controlled by *gorila* military officers, with various factions alternating in control, in different moments and in different services, reflecting the high degree of fractionalization of Argentine politics.[73] From these circumstances grew shifting alignments and intense internal conflict in the armed forces. When there is conflict inside the military, it is essential to study the internal alignments, their origins, their connections with other political forces, and their political consequences. Only in this way is it possible to examine the military as a political actor, subject to various inducements but responding to these inducements in special ways that depend to an important extent on factors relating to military organization. This means looking behind public statements and into details of organization virtually inaccessible to empirical research. I cannot claim any substantial advantages over others in this matter, but on the basis of informal interviews I had with leading military officers during the 1955–66 period, as well as published evidence, I propose the preliminary analysis that follows.[74]

By ousting Perón, undoubtedly a majoritarian dictator, the armed forces made an appeal to the need for restoration and preservation of political democracy. Subsequently, their anti-Peronista stand was strongly reinforced by a climate of great social unrest and the effects of the cold war and the Cuban Revolution. Peronista unions and the armed forces came to personify the opposite poles of an intense social conflict. The poor performance of civilian governments created much dissatisfaction among military officers. The army chief of staff, General Toranzo Montero, said that the armed forces were "the guardians of the republican way of life against any extremism or totalitarianism" and were ultimately responsible, due to the "failure of civilian authorities," for solving the problems allegedly caused by Peronismo and "subversion" and for "restoring the values of national unity and public order."[75] This assumption of the role of custodian of basic values opened wide the door for a long series of planteos and coups, especially after President Frondizi came to power in 1958 by means of an electoral "covenant" with Perón. The military's definition of its own role made it the interpreter of the content of the basic values it had been assigned to protect, as well as the interpreter of when and how the basic values were being threatened—paving the way for the electoral proscription of Peronismo and the political parties suspected of being façades for it. Since it could be argued that the basic values were involved in practically all governmental decisions, the military became the most effective channel through which various sectors could have their demands satisfied by the government. Thus, the military became a reflection of all the anti-Peronista sectors of Argentine society. This direct involvement in partisan and sectoral issues destroyed vertical patterns of military authority, led to numerous internal putsches, and shortened the careers of many officers.

By supporting the traditional political parties while remaining verbally committed to what they considered to be democracy, the military officers found themselves in the old predicament: the "correct" parties and candidates could not win fair elections.[76] When they ousted President Frondizi in 1962, the military officers made it clear that they intended to establish a long-term dictatorship, which they presumed to be what was needed to restore "order and authentic democracy" to Argentina. But within the army and the air force a strong reaction had taken place. Many officers protested against the deleterious effects on careers and military organization of the high fractionalization caused by direct political involvement. They proposed that military men should withdraw from politics and "return to their specific duties." In retrospect, it is clear that this was an argument for organizational survival.[77] The suspension of direct political involvement would necessarily mean rejecting military plans to eliminating political parties and elections. The argument for organizational survival and career preservation had wide appeal within the military; in addition, its "back to the barracks" implication evoked immediate support from many civilian sectors alarmed by the prospect of a military dictatorship. The intramilitary conflict was perceived as one between the dictatorial gorilas and the more democratic, professionalist military officers.[78] The factions clashed twice (September 1962 and April 1963), and the upshot was a decisive legalista victory. During the short frays, the legalistas issued persuasive communiqués stating that they were fighting for democracy, for a professionalist, apolitical army, and for the right of the people to cast their ballots "without exclusions" (which necessarily meant lifting the electoral ban on Peronistas). After their victory, however, the legalistas found that despite agreement on the professionalism issue, they were as divided as ever concerning the question of whether or not to allow Peronistas to run (and very likely win) in the next elections. After some internal debate the opinion that "totalitarian parties could not be granted the benefits of democracy" prevailed—i.e., the electoral arena remained closed to Peronistas. The legalistas presided over the messy presidential elections of 1963 in which Illía, the candidate of the old Radicales, was elected by less than one-fourth of the total vote.[79]

After the legalistas won control of the armed forces in 1963, important organizational changes took place. The navy, stronghold of the gorilas, had been decisively defeated, and the army established its clear hegemony over the navy and the small air force. The armed forces, under the strong leadership of General Onganía, the army chief of staff, and aided by U.S. advisory missions, were able to reestablish vertical authority and to foster professionalization markedly. This resulted in restoration of more normal authority and career patterns, increased organizational capabilities, new modes of military training that emphasized both the study of modern technology and of "contemporary problems," steady absorption of U.S. and French "antisubversive" and "civic action" doctrines, a marked decline in personal contacts with political party personnel, and a corresponding increase in personal contacts with those I have called "incumbents of technocratic roles."[80] The resulting feeling of achievement within the military contrasted sharply with the general social situation described earlier in this chapter.

The high organizational costs of fractionalization were fresh in the military memory, and the officers were determined to avoid situations that might risk reintroducing it. As a consequence, the channeling of sectoral demands, and planteos in particular, were explicitly rejected by the new military leadership (and the 1963–66 period was by and large free of them).[81] Professionalism entailed redefining the role of the armed forces as "above politics." As General Onganía repeatedly observed, the armed forces should abstain from political intervention except "under extreme circumstances." (The definition of "extreme circumstances" was of course left to the armed forces.) First, military disengagement from direct political involvement would not only facilitate professionalism but also make possible a much more general and severe condemnation of civilian authorities: their failures could no longer be attributed to military intervention. Second, a role that was above politics would mean a refusal to take sides in purely "civilian" conflicts, but not a loss of interest in whatever national affairs the military deemed deserving of its attention. This was clearly indicated in a speech in which General Onganía stated his conception of the military role:

[The armed forces exist] to guarantee the sovereignty and the territorial integrity of the state, to preserve the moral and spiritual values of Western civilization, to ensure public order and internal peace, to promote general welfare, and to sustain the Constitution, its essential rights and guarantees, and the republican institutions it has established. . . .[In order to achieve those goals] two fundamental premises must hold: the need [of the armed forces] to maintain its aptitude and capability for the custody of the highest interest of the nation, and the economic and social development of the country.[82]

The functions of the armed forces, according to this conception, are even broader than those envisioned by the gorila leaders. It was quite clear that the main practical difference between the two factions consisted in the legalistas' refusal to engage in planteos and direct partisan involvement.

But perhaps of greater significance were the requirements referred to by General Onganía as "fundamental premises." If the armed forces were to perform their functions properly both their organizational strength and the steady socioeconomic development of the country were necessary conditions. Consequently, anything that menaced or hindered the achievement of either condition could be construed as impeding the fulfillment of military functions. Since the performance of these functions was so essential, anything that threatened their necessary conditions was a threat to the most fundamental interest of the nation. Since governments could jeopardize, by action or by omission, these necessary conditions, it was obvious—given this conception of the military role—that government personnel could not receive the allegiance of the military. In the same speech, General Onganía went on to say:

Obedience is due, in the last analysis, to the Constitution and its laws, never to men and political parties that may eventually hold power. If this were not the case, the fundamental mission of the armed forces would be subverted. They would not be apolitical any more; they would become a praetorian guard at the service of some persons or groups.

The fact that the Radicales had supported the defeated military faction tended to increase the likelihood of systemic breakdown. In addition, the persistence of the socioeconomic problems described earlier in this chapter could be interpreted as an indication that the "basic premise" of socioeconomic development was not being met. This, combined with the consistently high degree of social unrest, contributed to fears of the spread and final victory of "subversion," which would implant "totalitarian extremism" and eliminate the armed forces. Government inefficiency and a low rate of socioeconomic development interacted to generate this so-called subversion. The elimination of subversion was part of the "specific duties" of the military (the custody of "national security"), and according to this interpretation, it was at the socioeconomic and governmental levels that the fundamental causes of subversion could best be attacked and eliminated. Thus the military saw the whole set of social problems (everything that could be subsumed under ''achieving socioeconomic development'' and ''ensuring governmental efficiency'') as within the range of its responsibility to maintain national security.[83] The scope of these social problems suggested that their solution could only be achieved by direct control of government, and since their existence was interpreted as a threat to national security, it followed that the armed forces would not have fulfilled their duties until the problems had been ''solved.''[84] Hence direct control of the government by the military would be necessary for the indefinite period required for achieving these solutions.[85]

These conclusions were based on the military's conviction of its own superior capacity to deal with the problems of a slow rate of socioeconomic development and government inefficiency. This conviction stemmed in part from the poor performance of government authorities and the deteriorating social conditions under continued conditions of mass praetorianism that obtained after the legalistas won control of the armed forces, but it was probably mainly the result of the successful professionalist drive. Through professionalization, the military had established clearly defined authority patterns, and military training had greatly improved. The armed forces had been able to solve their problems while civilian sectors continued in a situation of crisis, which could not help but greatly enhance the military's perception of its own superior ability for dealing with problems.[86] The ultimate conviction on the part of the military of the legitimacy of its rule would derive from the anticipated historical demonstration of its superior capacity to govern (as compared with previous civilian governments).[87]

Of course, the military's concern for the state of the society included more direct organizational considerations. The aggravation (or even the persistence) of the social conditions prevailing under mass praetorianism might reintroduce fractionalization within the military, whatever the effects of its efforts at professionalization. Since, according to the legalista conception, fractionalization would hinder the fulfillment of essential military functions, any risk in this respect would also be interpreted as a threat to the highest interests of the nation. Thus military intervention to eliminate threats to its internal cohesion would be justified to whatever extent might seem necessary to the military itself.[88]

Local elections held in 1965 showed that the Peronistas retained the first plurality of the electorate. Aside from the formerly overthrown Peronistas and Frondizistas, the governing Radicales were the only party that could attract more than 10 percent of the total vote. By this time there were abundant indications that a ''ceiling consensus'' had been reached by most of the civilian sectors, and consequently the inducements for a new military intervention became very strong. Social unrest was high, with numerous strikes, occupations of factories, and manifold acts of less organized violence. President Illía had acquired the reputation of being a slow and ineffective decision-maker, while Parliament seemed to have been reduced to a forum for personal quarrels which produced no legislation. Meanwhile the military had greatly enhanced its own abilities (and even more greatly enhanced its assessment of those abilities).

In short, the conditions for a final systemic breakdown had reached a critical stage when, in 1965–66, the organizational evolution of the military gave it the internal cohesion and sense of its own ability that made intervention possible without apparent risk of failure and fractionalization. The situation pointed strongly to a coup that would try to implant an entirely different system, rather than attempt to repair the existing one. This tendency was reinforced by the fact that all the major political parties in Argentina had already been given a chance and had failed, and thus "had" to be ousted by the military.

General elections were scheduled for 1967, and it was evident that the legalista military (as well as many other sectors in Argentine society) were as divided as ever on the question of Peronista electoral participation. Given the social conditions, the organizational evolution of the military, and the fact that all the political parties with more than a minimum share of the vote had been given a chance, it is not an exaggeration to say that by the end of 1965 the major matter of speculation had become the timing of the coup, not its perpetration or its goals.[89] The timing was largely determined by the risk of military fractionalization around the old Peronismo issue: the coup had to occur late enough for many of the officers to perceive clearly the risk of organizational fractionalization, but it could not occur after the electoral campaigns had started. In this way the military leadership would simultaneously increase the probability of a high degree of military cohesion in support of the coup and a minimum of civilian opposition (particularly Peronista, if they were allowed to run in the 1967 elections) to their decision to intervene.[90] On 28 June 1966, the army chief of staff, General Pistarini, declared:

[The achievement] of efficiency, cohesion, and high professional capabilities [by the armed forces] has taken time and great sacrifice. . . . Any attempt to put the army at the service of secondary interests, or to identify it with political, economic, or social sectors, is an attempt against the [military] institution, because it seeks to create internal division and conflict. For this very reason it is also an attempt against the nation.[91]

Soon afterward the coup took place smoothly, and a new political system was inaugurated.

Well before June 1966, numerous civilian sectors had reached a "ceiling consensus," the legitimacy and efficacy of the regime were at a minimum, and almost every sector had been pleading for a military intervention that would drastically change the existing political system. However, for this to occur it was also necessary that the social situation pose new threats to highly valued military organizational achievements and that the process of military professionalization be substantially advanced. The gorila officers had intervened many times, but always for the purpose of pressing relatively limited demands and with the stated intention of returning power to civilians. When in 1962 these officers attempted to assume control for a long period, they were hindered by their precarious hold over a deeply fractionalized and scarcely professional military institution. The new professionalist military leaders—the somewhat ironically labeled legalista officers—intervened only when they were prepared to take government into their own hands for a long time with the aim of achieving very ambitious goals. For long-term intervention to be possible, two conditions lacking in 1962 had to be present in 1966: first, the social crisis necessary for a "ceiling consensus" and, second, the organizational-level variables (the degree of internal cohesion and the feeling of enhanced capabilities) that resulted from the process of professionalization and constitution of "apolitical" armed forces.

It seems ironic that those military leaders who epitomized professionalism and an anti-interventionist stand were those who led the coup that liquidated the existing political system.[92] But this apparent inconsistency must be seen in the light of the preceding circumstances. Mass praetorianism and a high degree of modernization induced the fractionalization of the military, who had collaborated in the extreme political instability that had characterized a good part of the period in which praetorianism prevailed. This situation adversely affected the military, leading to a period of withdrawal from direct political involvement and to concerted efforts at enhancing military organization. The continuation of mass praetorianism led many civilian sectors to reach a ceiling consensus, but the final systemic breakdown had to wait until the military felt that it could intervene again.[93] This discrepancy in the timing of the civilian and military decisions made the period that immediately preceded the final breakdown essentially a political vacuum, in which almost everything had been determined except the exact moment of military intervention.

In the period of withdrawal from direct political involvement, the military enhanced its capabilities—and enhanced even more its self-assessment of those capabilities. In addition, military personnel increased their personal contacts with the technocrats, who would participate in the coup coalition and occupy most of the high civilian government positions in the post-coup regime.

The continuation of mass praetorianism, and with it, the further deterioration of the social context, contrasted with the military's conviction of its enhanced capabilities. It also happens that whatever precautions are taken to isolate the armed forces from the social situation, sooner or later they create problems that threaten to reintroduce military fractionalization. The combination of these two factors led to goals for military intervention that were far more drastic than those envisioned by the military during its interventionist period.

Thus, the "apoliticism" and professionalism of the armed forces during a time of mass praetorianism in a society that had attained a high level of modernization significantly raised the threshold for military intervention; the hectic pattern of coups and planteos ended. Once that threshold had been reached, however, military intervention reoccurred—but it was more cohesive, much more ambitious, and aimed at a far more complete political domination than anything that had gone before. Contrary to what many analysts and policy-makers have expected since the 1950s, apoliticism and professionalism have not solved the endemic problems of militarism. They merely trade off a higher threshold for a far more comprehensive military invervention.

NOTES

1. See, e.g., *Washington Post,* 30 June 1966.
2. Survey (sample and methodology unknown) taken by *Primera Plana,* reported in Carlos Astiz, "The Argentine Armed Forces: Their Role and Political Involvement," *Western Political Quarterly* 22, no. 4 (1969). This article provides useful information and an analysis complementary to this chapter. In another survey, taken in July 1966 (N = 1,000 respondents of the Greater Buenos Aires area, methodology unknown), to the question "Do you think that the revolution of June 28th [1966] was necessary?" 77 percent answered "Yes" (*Correo de la Tarde,* 6–12 June 1967).
3. See, among others, the following official publications: "Mensaje de la Junta Revolucionaria al Pueblo Argentino" (1966); "Mensaje al País del Presidente de la Nación Teniente General Juan Carlos Onganía" (1966); "Mensaje del Teniente General Juan Carlos Onganía con motivo de asumir la Presidencia de la Nación" (1966); and "Mensaje del Presidente de la Nación en la reunión de camaradería de las Fuerzas Armadas" (1967). All were printed by Presidencia de la Nación, Argentina.
4. The best analyses of Argentine civil-military relations, although they do not cover all the main historical events, are Darío Cantón, *La política de los militares argentinos: 1900–1971* (México, D.F.: Siglo XXI, 1971), and Robert Potash, *The Army and Politics in Argentina* (Stanford, Ca.: Stanford University Press, 1969). See also Guillermo O'Donnell, "Modernización y golpes militares: Teoría, comparaciones y el caso argentino," *Desarrollo Económico* 17 (December 1972).
5. This question will be considered in more detail below.
6. For greater detail, the reader is referred to the various sources hereafter cited. An excellent general political history of Argentina is Carlos Alberto Floria and César García Belsunce, *Historia de los argentinos,* 2 vols. (Buenos Aires: Editorial Kapelusz, 1972).
7. It scarcely need be noted that this discrepancy has been repeatedly observed by students of Latin American history; see, for example, Stanley Stein and Barbara Stein, *The Colonial Heritage of Latin America* (New York: Oxford University Press, 1970). For an assessment of more recent evidence, see Federico Gil, *Instituciones y desarrollo político en América Latina* (Buenos Aires: INTAL, 1966).
8. On "political resources," see Robert A. Dahl, *Modern Political Analysis* (Englewood Cliffs, N.J.: Prentice-Hall, 1969).
9. "The Heritage of Latin America," in *The Founding of New Societies,* ed. Louis Hartz (New York, 1966).

10. Speech by José M. Gutiérrez to the constitutional convention (1862).

11. This temporal sequence of national unification is very different from that of earlier European modernizers. In those countries the harsh task of national unification had been largely completed before constitutionalism and democracy became an issue. Significantly, the only clear-cut South American exception to the sequence depicted in the text is Chile.

12. Other authors have observed this "constant" in Argentine society; see Carlos Alberto Floria, "Una explicación política de la Argentina" (Buenos Aires: Centro de Investigaciones y Acción Social, 1967), pp. 33-34; Robert A. Dahl, *Polyarchy: Participation and Opposition* (New Haven: Yale University Press, 1971), pp. 132-40; Eldon Kenworthy, "The Formation of the Peronist Coalition" (Ph.D. diss., Yale University, 1970).

13. An excellent theoretical analysis of legitimacy is Natalio Botana's *La légitimité: Problème politique* (Louvain: Université de Louvain, 1968). See also his "La crisis de legitimidad en la Argentina y el desarrollo de los partidos políticos," *Criterio*, no. 1604 (1970).

14. This has been labeled the "period of self-incrimination" by Albert O. Hirschman ("Introduction" to *Latin American Issues*, ed. Albert O. Hirschman [New York: Twentieth Century Fund, 1960]). But the incrimination was one-sided: it was directed by the ruling sectors at the majority of the population. Naturally, the response was bitter. The ruling sector's perception of the rest of the population was partly a process of selective borrowing; after a visit to Argentina, Lord Bryce noted: "The books most popular among those few who approach abstract subjects are those of Herbert Spencer. [Argentines] are unwilling to believe that he is not deemed in his own country to be a great philosopher" (cited in Arthur P. Whitaker, *Argentina* [Englewood Cliffs, N.J.: Prentice-Hall, 1964], p. 61).

15. On the great wave of European migration of this period, see Gino Germani, *Política y sociedad en una época de transición* (Buenos Aires: Editorial Paidós, 1962), pp. 179-216; Oscar Cornblit, "European Migrants in Argentine Industry and Politics," *The Politics of Conformity in Latin America*, ed. Claudio Veliz (Oxford: Oxford University Press, 1967); and Carl Solberg, *Immigration and Nationalism: Argentina and Chile, 1890-1914* (Austin: University of Texas Press, 1970).

16. For a description of this situation and an analysis of the factors that led to it, see Horacio Giberti, *El desarrollo agrario argentino* (Buenos Aires: Eudeba, 1964); James Scobie, *Revolution on the Pampas* (Austin: University of Texas Press, 1969); Roberto Cortés Conde and Ezequiel Gallo, *La formación de la Argentina moderna* (Buenos Aires: Editorial Paidós, 1967); and Roberto Cortés Conde, "Algunos aspectos de la expansión territorial en Argentina en la segunda mitad del siglo XIX," *Desarrollo Económico* 29 (1968).

17. Cited in Oscar Cornblit, E. Gallo, and Arturo O'Connell, "La generación del 80 y su proyecto: Antecedentes y consecuencias," in *Argentina: Sociedad de masas*, ed. Torcuato di Tella et al.(Buenos Aires: Eudeba, 1965), p. 54. This is an excellent monographic study of the period under consideration here.

18. See Scobie, *Revolution*. Only a small proportion of the industrialists were Argentine. A very small proportion of European migrants opted for Argentine citizenship, and most of them were politically inactive. See Cornblit, *European Migrants;* Germani, *Política*; and Carlos Díaz Alejandro, *Essays on the Economic History of the Argentine Republic* (New Haven: Yale University Press, 1970), chap. 1, for valuable data and good analyses.

19. On the socioeconomic background and policy preferences of this middle sector and its main political expression, the Radical party, see Cornblit *European Migrants;* E. Gallo and Silvia Sigal, "La formación de los partidos políticos contemporáneos: La Unión Cívica Radical (1800-1916)," in di Tella, *Argentina*; and Peter Smith, *Politics and Beef in Argentina: Patterns of Conflict and Change* (New York: Columbia University Press, 1969).

20. The expression is from Floria.

21. For expressions of this contempt, see Darío Cantón, *El parlamento argentino en épocas de cambio: 1880, 1910 y 1946* (Buenos Aires: Editorial del Instituto, 1966).

22. For an excellent analysis of these economic policies, see Díaz Alejandro, *Essays*. A review of the pertinent literature and an analysis of the sociopolitical implications of the policies can be found in Miguel Murmis and Juan Carlos Portantiero, "Crecimiento industrial y alianza de clases en Argentina, 1930-1940" (Instituto Torcuato di Tella, Centro de Investigaciones Sociales, *Documento de Trabajo*, 1968).

23. Using Karl Deutsch's concept, Peter Smith argues that "social mobilization" took place in

Argentina during this period (see his "Social Mobilization, Political Participation, and the Rise of Juan Perón," *Western Political Quarterly* 34, no. 1 [1969]).

24. This expression was coined by Manuel Fresco, a Conservador governor of Buenos Aires State, elected by fraud in the 1930s.

25. Whitaker, *Argentina*. For valuable information on Argentina from the 1930s until 1963, see Tulio Halperín Donghi, *Argentina en el callejón* (Montevideo: Editorial Arca, 1964).

26. The perception by the growing numbers of urban workers of the "democracy" they saw in operation could only reinforce their assessment of the political system and the ruling sectors.

27. The ruling sectors referred to the new migrants as "the shirtless," "the blackheads," "the zoological landslide," and other intentionally derogatory terms. Perón wisely responded by appropriating most of these terms to underline the popular character of his following. This was primarily the language of Conservadores and Radicales supporters, but the reactions of Socialists and Communists toward the new and increasingly active migrants were not noticeably better; see, among other discussions of the reactions of the "traditional" Argentine Left, Jorge Adelardo Ramos, *Revolución y contrarevolución en la Argentina* (La Reja, 1961), and Juan José Hernández Arregui, *La formación de la conciencia nacional* (Hachón, 1964). For a general analysis of this period, see Alberto Ciria, *Partidos y poder en la Argentina moderna (1930-1946)* (Jorge Alvarez Editor, 1964).

28. Kenworthy, "Formation," provides an interesting analysis of the formation of the populist Peronista coalition.

29. As an indication of the degree of misperception of the national mood by the "Democratic Union" (to say the very least), the Union allowed Spruille Braden, the U.S. ambassador, to campaign for them openly. Perón capitalized on this fact, presenting the election as a choice between "Braden or Perón."

30. A useful survey of interpretations of Peronismo is found in Carlos Fayt, ed., *La naturaleza del Peronismo* (Buenos Aires: Editorial Viracocha, 1967).

31. On the ideology of Peronismo during the period in which the movement was in power, see Alberto Ciria, *Perón y el justicialismo* (México, D.F.: Siglo XXI, 1971).

32. This concept is based on the work of Juan J. Linz, as developed in his introductory essay to *The Breakdown of Democratic Regimes,* ed. Juan J. Linz and Alfred Stepan (Baltimore: Johns Hopkins University Press, 1978). From the beginning the opposition tried to oust Perón illegally and engaged in very obstructionist parliamentary strategies.

33. Floria; "Una explicación política" (my translation).

34. The concept of polarization is discussed in Robert A. Dahl, "Some Explanations," in *Political Oppositions in Western Democracies,* ed. Robert A. Dahl (New Haven: Yale University Press, 1966), pp. 380ff.; it is further analyzed below. For a sense of the saliency of this cleavage, see (among many others) Dardo Cúneo, *El desencuentro argentino* (Buenos Aires: Pleamar, 1965); Floria, "Una explicación política"; Mariano Grondona, *Argentina en el tiempo y en el mundo* (Buenos Aires: Editorial Primera Plana, 1967); Augusto Morello and Antonio Tróccoli, *Argentina ahora y después* (La Plata: Editorial Platense, 1967); G. Merkx, "Politics and Economic Change in Argentina from 1870 to 1966" (Ph.D. diss., Yale University, 1968). For evidence from survey data, see José Luis de Imaz, *Motivación electoral* (Buenos Aires: Instituto de Desarrollo Económico, 1962), and Peter Snow, "Argentine Political Parties and the 1966 Revolution" (Laboratory of Political Research, University of Iowa, 1968).

35. For the relevant data on the economy, see tables 2-7.

36. For information concerning the high degree of domestic political violence in Argentina, as indicated by data from this period, see Bruce Russett et al., *World Handbook of Political and Social Indicators* (New Haven: Yale University Press, 1964).

37. This theme is examined in more detail in Guillermo A. O'Donnell, *Modernization and Bureaucratic-Authoritarianism: Studies in South American Politics* (Berkeley: Institute of International Studies, University of California, 1973), pp. 166-96.

38. University of California, *Statistical Abstract for Latin America* (Berkeley and Los Angeles: University of California, 1966).

39. Martin Needler, *Political Development in Latin America,* p. 96.

40. International Labour Organization, *Yearbook of Labour Statistics* (Geneva: ILO, 1967).

41. In my examination of economic aspects, I have relied heavily on the excellent *Essays* of Díaz

Alejandro. Other important sources are Carlos Díaz Alejandro, *Exchange Rate Devaluation in a Semi-Industrialized Country: The Experience of Argentina, 1955–1961* (Cambridge, Mass: MIT Press, 1965); Aldo Ferrer, *La económia argentina: Las etapas de su desarrollo y problemas actuales* (México, D.F., and Buenos Aires: Fondo de Cultura Económica, 1963); Guido di Tella and Miguel Zymelman, *Las etapas del desarrollo argentino* (Buenos Aires: Eudeba, 1967); J. Villanueva, "La inflación argentina," mimeographed (Instituto Torcuato di Tella, 1964); United Nations, Economic Commission for Latin America, "El desarrollo económico de la Argentina," 5 vols., mimeographed (New York: United Nations, 1959); United Nations, Economic Commission on Latin America and Consejo Nacional de Desarrollo (CONADE), *El desarrollo económico y la distribución del ingreso en la Argentina* (New York: United Nations, 1968).

42. Díaz Alejandro, *Essays*, p. 55.
43. Ibid., pp. 69–70.
44. Computed from Banco Central de la República Argentina, *Boletín Estadístico* several issues.
45. UN-ECLA and CONADE, *El desarrollo económico*, p. 193.
46. Diáz Alejandro, *Essays*, p. 75.
47. Computed from Dirección Nacional de Estadísticas y Censos, *Boletín Estadístico*, several issues, and Díaz Alejandro, *Essays*, Statistical Appendix.
48. Díaz Alejandro, *Essays*, p. 356.
49. Analysis of these and related aspects of economic policy can be found in Aldo Ferrer et al., *Los planes de estabilización en la Argentina* (Buenos Aires: Editorial Paidós, 1969).
50. UN-ECLA and CONADE, *El desarrollo económico*, p. 264 (my translation).
51. Jorge M. Katz, "Características estructurales del crecimiento industrial argentino," *Desarrollo Económico*, no. 26 (1967). An excellent exploration of the sociopolitical consequences of these changes is in Fernando Henrique Cardoso and Enzo Faletto, *Dependencia y desarrollo en América Latina* (México, D.F.: Siglo XXI, 1969), pp. 103 ff. For discussion of the urban unemployed, see UN-ECLA and CONADE, *El desarrollo económico*, pp. 123, 193 ff., and the Introductions to the "Planes de desarrollo" for 1965–69 and 1970–74 (Buenos Aires: Consejo Nacional de Desarrollo, 1965, 1970).
52. Consistent with this general point, many regions of the interior, also incapable of exerting effective pressure on the national government, were also heavy losers (see Consejo Nacional de Desarrollo, Introduction [1970]).
53. See Harold D. Lasswell and Daniel Lerner, ed., *Policy Sciences* (Stanford, Ca.: Stanford University Press, 1951).
54. Computed from Consejo Nacional de Desarrollo, *Plan Nacional de Desarrollo* (1965). For useful data on and analysis of this topic, see Oscar Ozlak, "Inflación y política fiscal en la Argentina: El impuesto a los réditos en al período 1956–1965" (Instituto Torcuato di Tella, Centro de Investigaciones en Administración Pública, *Documento de Trabajo*, 1970).
55. For data on this point, see Oficina de Estudios para la Cooperación Económica Internacional, *Argentina económica y financiera* (Buenos Aires: FIAT, 1966), p. 366.
56. See ibid., p. 351.
57. UN-ECLA and CONADE, *El desarrollo económico*.
58. See Eldon Kenworthy, "Coalitions in the Political Development of Latin America," in Sven Groennings et al., eds., *The Study of Coalition Behavior* (New York: Holt, Rinehart and Winston, 1970). For the decline in productivity, see Oficina de Estudios, *Argentina económica*, pp. 351 ff.
59. This situation could be described as one of "fluid scarcity." It is certainly very different from that in more traditional and more developed societies, where income shares (albeit by different mechanisms) are more stable in the short run. The political correlates of fluid scarcity are not likely to be similar to those of more stabilized allocations of economic goods. (An interesting examination of this aspect of Argentine politics can be found in Merkx, "Politics.")
60. Used here in the sense defined by Harold Lasswell and Abraham Kaplan in *Power and Society* (New Haven: Yale University Press, 1950)—i.e., the ability to impose severe deprivations.
61. Charles Anderson considers threat-capabilities a major asset in Latin American politics; see

his *Politics and Economic Change in Latin America* (New York: Van Nostrand, 1967), chap. 2. In a similar vein, see the interesting discussion of a "dual currency" (votes and control of means of violence) in Argentine politics in Kenworthy, "Coalitions," and idem, "Formation."

62. See Samuel Huntington, *Political Order in Changing Societies* (New Haven: Yale University Press, 1969), esp. pp. 192–237.

63. "Liderazgo político y debilidad institucional en la Argentina," *Desarrollo Económico,* no. 3 (1963). (Reprinted in idem, *The Conflict Society: Reaction and Revolution in Latin America* [American Universities Field Staff, 1966].)

64. Jeane Kirkpatrick, *Leader and Vanguard in Mass Society: A Study of Peronist Argentina* (Cambridge, Mass.: MIT Press, 1971); Gabriel Almond and Sidney Verba, *The Civic Culture* (Princeton, N.J.: Princeton University Press, 1963).

65. For other similar data, see Snow, "Argentine Political Parties."

66. Gallup survey, sample of the Greater Buenos Aires area (N = 1,000); reported in *Polls* (1967), pp. 21–31.

67. Snow reports a survey, taken in Buenos Aires before the 1966 coup, that showed 60 percent of the respondents in complete agreement with the statement "We have too many platforms and political programs; what we need is a strong man to lead us!" Another 23 percent agreed to some degree, and only 17 percent were in complete disagreement ("Argentine Political Parties," p. 42).

68. Kirkpatrick, *Leader and Vanguard in Mass Society.*

69. The best study of the Argentine elite—de Imaz, *Los que mandan*—has no interview data.

70. See Dardo Cúneo, *Comportamiento y crisis de la clase empresaria* (Buenos Aires: Editorial Pleamar, 1967); John Freels, *El sector industrial* (Buenos Aires: Eudeba, 1968); and Fernando Henrique Cardoso, *Ideologías* (México, D.F.: Siglo XXI, 1971).

71. See, e.g., the enthusiastic remarks about the coup by union and Peronista leaders in *La Prensa,* 29 and 30 June 1966. It soon became obvious to these leaders that these remarks expressed quite unrealistic hopes that they would have greater political access under the military government.

72. De Imaz, *Los que mandan,* p. 84.

73. The nickname *gorila* was a derogatory allusion to the strong anti-Peronista views of these military officers.

74. The prevailing trend in the study of civil-military relations in "developing" countries has been to endow the military with sets of attitudes and high decision-making capabilities based on taking at face value its organizational charts and public statements concerning its ethos. The military is then assigned a crucial developmental role, and assertions that the military is the only group able to exercise effective governmental power in "developing" societies are "explained." A good example of this approach, applied to Latin American countries, is in John Johnson, *The Military and Society in Latin America* (Stanford, Ca.: Stanford University Press, 1964). But, as Robert Price says, in a good critique of this literature, the empirical evidence does not support these analyses ("A Theoretical Approach to Military Rule in New States," *World Politics* 23, no. 3 [1971]). In contrast to this approach, several authors have argued (correctly, I think) that the political behavior of the military can only be understood in relation to the characteristics of the society in which it operates. They further argue (again correctly) that the middle class in modernizing societies may attempt either to increase or to diminish its participation in the political system, depending on whether it is still striving for its own political incorporation or has already achieved it. A link between these middle-class attitudes and military behavior is presumed to exist because of the predominantly middle-class origins of military officers. The most important statements of this interpretation are Jose Nun, "The Middle Class," in Veliz, *Politics of Conformity*; Huntington, *Political Order*; Needler, *Political Development*; and E. Nordlinger, "Soldiers in Mufti: The Impact of Military Rule upon Economic and Social Change in the Non-Western States," *American Political Science Review* 64, no. 4 (1970). But according to this line of interpretation, the political behavior of the military (in particular, the goals of their intervention) depends *entirely* on variables at the societal level. As I hope to show, though these variables are very important, they do not eliminate the need to consider *empirical* variations in organization (as contrasted with the organization the military attributes to itself). These "intervening" var-

iables mediate the effects of societal variables and the differences may lead to quite different patterns of political behavior in the military. Although the author does not explicitly discuss the issue in these terms, the two-level focus I am proposing has been fruitfully applied to the Brazilian case in Alfred Stepan, *The Military in Politics: Changing Patterns in Brazil*: (Princeton: Princeton University Press, 1971). For a detailed study of the theoretical and empirical questions raised by the behavior of the military in the Argentine case, see Guillermo O'Donnell, "Modernización y golpes militares: Teoría, comparaciones y el caso argentino," *Desarrollo Económico*, October–December 1972.

75. *La Prensa,* 7 April 1959.

76. For further analysis of this theme, see below.

77. Several authors have emphasized this factor; See Edwin Lieuwen, *Generals vs. Presidents: Neomilitarism in Latin America* (New York: Praeger, 1964), pp. 107 ff. An Argentine author, José M. Saravia, also argues that, in this case, organizational concerns—not democratic allegiance—were the major determinants of the actions of the legalista military officers. This interpretation is endorsed in a prologue to Saravia's book by General A. López Aufranc, one of the most influential military officers during these events; see *Hacia la salida* (Buenos Aires: Emecé, 1968).

78. The latter were given the denomination *legalistas,* a term with obvious positive connotations.

79. For further discussion of this election, see below.

80. The results I have described here are reasonably well-supported by the literature. The one exception is the reference to the changes in patterns of personal contacts; for this matter I have relied mainly on my own impressions as a participant-observer during the period.

81. For an interesting statement of the "orthodox" legalista position (and its manifold unresolved ambiguities), see General Benjamín R. Rattenbach, *El sector militar de la sociedad* (Buenos Aires: Círculo Militar Argentino, 1966).

82. *La Prensa,* 6 August 1964 (my translation).

83. This analysis was clearly the basis of the military's perception of its role, its appraisal of the social situation, and its justification for intervention, as is evident in the informal interviews and the military publications of the period. See, e.g., Colonel Mario Orsolini, *Ejército argentino y crecimiento nacional* (Buenos Aires: Editorial Arayú, 1965), and General Osiris Villegas, *Guerra revolucionaria comunista* (Buenos Aires: Pleamar, 1963). For a useful survey of the period, see Carlos Fayt, *El político armado: Dinámica del proceso político argentino, 1960–1971* (Buenos Aires: Ediciones Pannedille, 1971).

84. For a comprehensive statement of this position, see General Osiris Villegas, *Políticas y estrategias para el desarrollo y la seguridad nacional* (Buenos Aires: Pleamar, 1969). Villegas was the secretary of the National Security Council between 1966 and 1968.

85. For some of the many statements of this position, see the official publications cited in n.3.

86. The illogicality of this perception should have been clearly evident, considering that the military had means for solving its internal problems rarely available to civilian sectors (e.g., purges and open combat).

87. The discovery that the military's expectations were largely wrong, as well as of the resistance of social problems to military-style decision-making, are part of a study of the evolution of the political system inaugurated in 1966, which will not be undertaken here.

88. In this examination of military perceptions and motivations, I have limited myself to what seem to be the more important facets, as expressed in informal interviews and published sources. Using this type of information, I have not been able to determine to what extent these conceptions were sincerely held and to what extent they were "covers" for less apparent motivations. (It is my general impression that in most cases they were sincere.) As to the origins of these perceptions and motivations, in addition to the historical-contextual factors analyzed here, it seems very likely that other factors frequently suggested ("antisubversive doctrines," U.S. training missions, secondary socialization) also exerted an important influence. But with the type of information at hand, it is not possible to assess the actual relative contribution of each of these factors.

89. For references to the open discussion of these factors in the months prior to the coup, see Astiz, "Argentine Armed Forces."

90. In the pre- and post-coup interviews upon which I base these impressions, the opinion was

repeatedly expressed that the fate of the Radicales government had been decided long before the coup, but that it was convenient to postpone the decision until it became evident to most civilian sectors and military officers that a new coup was unavoidable. At the same time, there was concern that the coup not occur too close to the 1967 elections, for the reasons indicated in the text.

91. *La Prensa,* 29 June 1966 (my translation).
92. This observation and the others that follow apply to a large extent to the other two bureaucratic-authoritarian systems inaugurated in the 1960s in highly modernized countries: Brazil and Greece. With reference to the evolution of the military, they also apply to another highly "professionalist" coup—the one in Peru. However, the differences that result from a similar level of professionalization in the military but a lower level of social modernization generated, in the Peruvian case, important differences in the composition of the military coalition. This combination also resulted in variation in the politically incorporating and economically expanding goals of the resulting authoritarian system.
93. It should be recalled that for the inauguration of a bureaucratic-authoritarian system few economic and psychological payoffs are available, to most of the population, and that consequently coercion is indispensable for inaugurating and implementing the socioeconomic policies characteristic of that type of political system.

6.

A Structural-Historical Approach to the Breakdown of Democratic Institutions: Peru

*Julio Cotler**

Many of the articles in this volume analyze the breakdown of democracy mainly at the superstructural level and concentrate to a large extent on the immediate events leading up to the final crisis. It is my contention that such an emphasis is not sufficient to explain the collapse of representative institutions. Rather, only through a historical analysis of the class structure in a society can one explain the nature of political institutions and therefore elucidate the fundamental reasons for their breakdown and change.

This distinction should not be taken as an example of economic determinism. Quite the contrary, the development of ideologies and the nature of specific events and personalities are of crucial importance in any political crisis. But these developments take place within the context of larger socioeconomic structures, and it is ultimately this larger framework that defines the alternatives open to political groups.

For these reasons, I have used a historical-structural approach in my analysis of the breakdown of democratic forms in Peru. The main argument advanced in this essay is that, given the nature of Peru's economic development and its continued dependence on the industrialized nations, democracy developed in form but not in content. Peru's role as a provider of raw materials to the industrialized world limited the development of an internal market and therefore blocked all possibilities for independent industrialization. Consequently, the country did not witness the rise of a national bourgeoisie that could partially incorporate the demands of the lower classes and establish a democratic political system.

Such an analysis suggests the hypothesis that the 1968 military coup in Peru

*I would like to thank both Florencia Mallon for her help in translating and editing this chapter and Alfred Stepan for his comments and suggestions. For a more detailed analysis of the Peruvian case see my *Clases, estado y nación en el Perú* (Lima: Instituto de Estudios Peruanos, 1978).

was not the breakdown of democracy at all, but rather the final collapse of an oligarchy that had used democratic forms to maintain control over the population. But one cannot assume that a similar situation obtained in every dependent country. While the history of all Latin American countries has been characterized by some degree of dependence on the world capitalist system, the effect of such a relationship on socioeconomic and political development was particularly pronounced in the Peruvian case. And it is only through a structural-historical analysis that the specific nature of this effect can be fully explained.

In an attempt to incorporate all the necessary levels of analysis, I have divided my essay into two parts. The first sets the historical-structural context for subsequent events. The second analyzes the actual crisis of the political superstructure.

More specifically, part one traces the historical development of the Peruvian oligarchy, its relations with foreign capital, and the mechanisms utilized to deal with popular mobilization. The first section examines the period from independence to the 1920s, when foreign investment was concentrated mainly in the primary sector of the economy. The second considers the 1950s and early 1960s, when foreign investment increased and was extended to both the secondary and tertiary sectors. The third focuses more particularly on the reaction of the lower sectors to the changes set in motion by the new influx of foreign capital, and the oligarchy's attempts to deal with this reaction. The fourth treats the effect of these transformations on attitudes within the church and the army, institutions which had previously provided important support for the regime.

In part two, I deal with the superstructural aspects of the political crisis, referring when necessary to the historical-structural background. The first section examines the changing nature of ideologies and political alliances from 1962 to 1965. The second narrates the events leading up to the October 1968 coup, focusing on the way in which structural and superstructural developments combined to close off all other alternatives.

Part I: The Historical-Structural Context

The Formation of the Dependent Oligarchy

Much of Latin America's history after independence has been characterized by the persistence of a "colonial heritage." In essence, this heritage is defined by the reestablishment of relations between the Latin American nations and the emerging metropolitan bourgeoisies in Europe, but without a reform of the socioeconomic and political structures that had existed in the former during the colonial period. Rather, the renewal of relationships was founded on an exchange of raw materials for manufactured products and on the provision of loans by the Europeans to facilitate the production and transport of these raw materials. But more important was the fact that the "unequal exchange" was based on the exploitation of American labor tied to a precapitalist system of social relations of production, resulting in the formation of extremely stratified societies.

Production and marketing were organized under a government which functioned as a *rentier*, subject to the authority of regional oligarchies and their *caudillos*. This government distributed privilege among the *caciques* and *gamonales*, hoping to reestablish the system of colonial domination. Such a pattern made the growth of a free labor market impossible; consequently, it blocked the rise of a national bourgeoisie and a proletariat, and doomed all attempts at national integration.

In some Latin American countries, it was possible for the national oligarchy, with the help of foreign capital and the local government, to establish some form of hegemony over the population. In these cases, the elite retained a part of the surplus extracted from the precapitalist labor force and used this capital in the development of an internal market and a system of state power. But in other countries, such as Peru, this did not happen. Instead, the renewal of relationships with the world capitalist system went through two stages. The first, characterized by the emergence of a sector within the dominant class which was able to accumulate capital during the guano boom and invest it in agriculture, served to strengthen the precapitalist nature of social relations of production. The second, distinguished by the massive and direct investment of foreign capital in the productive sector, resulted in the formation of a system of enclave economies.[1]

During the crisis of the colonial system, which began at the end of the eighteenth century and culminated in the Wars of Independence of the 1820s, Peru entered a process of political feudalization. During this period a number of regional oligarchies, working through caudillos, attempted to establish territorial hegemony but lacked the resources to succeed. Once relations were broken with the Spanish crown, the colonial aristocracy lost its economic and political basis for control, leaving the political arena open to these many nuclei of local power.

In the mid-nineteenth century, Peru renewed economic relations with Europe. This renewal was founded on the export of guano, a fertilizer rich in organic matter and destined to revolutionize European agricultural productivity. The guano trade gained such importance that, between 1850 and 1865, Peru led Latin America in volume of exports to Europe. For this reason, Peru was able to gain an excellent credit rating on the international financial market, indebting itself especially to the English banks.

The monopoly of income from the guano trade facilitated the rise of an oligarchical sector that invested in agriculture and mining. But this sector was unable to control the state by centralizing the political system and reducing the influence of the regional oligarchies. There were two reasons for this weakness. First, while the income generated by the export of guano increased internal demand, no expansion in internal production resulted, for under a system of free trade, the law of comparative advantage militated against such expansion. Secondly, investment in agriculture and mining occurred without a modification of the precapitalist and servile system of labor relations, thus reinforcing the colonial nature of Peruvian society.

Under such conditions, the development of a free labor market became impossible, thus stunting the growth of an internal market with capitalist nuclei. Traditional social relations remained intact, and no challenge was presented to the regional elites. Quite the contrary, the local power groups maintained control and blocked all measures taken by the new guano elite. The ongoing tension produced by such a conflict resulted in the persistence of *caudillismo* and civil war; consequently, the income from guano was spent in maintaining a military.[2]

In order to finance this continuing struggle and involve the population in a system of patronage and clientelism, the governments supported by the various regional oligarchies were forced to turn to the international banking system. They financed loans of ever-increasing proportions against future income from the guano trade. During the 1870s, this vicious cycle reached a climax, due both to a crisis in the European financial system and to a decline in the volume and quality of guano exports. Thus began the decline into bankruptcy of the Peruvian economy, which became inevitable after the War of the Pacific (1879–1884).

After this last debacle had left the country in a state of economic and political prostration, the foreign bondholders demanded that the government pay off the external debt accumulated over the previous thirty years. Pressure from the bondholders and the European nations forced the Peruvian government to sign the Grace Contract, transferring control of the railroads for ninety-nine years to the bondholders' representative, the Peruvian Corporation. These railroads had been built with foreign capital to facilitate exports. In addition, the Peruvian government gave up the rights to all customs revenue and to a million hectares in the jungle region.

From this point on, foreign capital began to gain control of all the country's main economic resources, initiating the second stage in Peru's renewal of relations with the world capitalist system. The railroad concession made possible the organization in the late 1890s of the Cerro de Pasco Corporation, financed by the Morgan group, in the central part of the country. English capital exploited petroleum, the wool industry, and shipping. All of the country's productive sectors—mining, foreign trade, banking, export agriculture, public services, and even the incipient industrial sector—fell into the hands, or under the influence, of foreign investors.[3]

The control of the national economy by foreign capital led to an abrupt concentration of property and rationalization of production, which in turn resulted in the displacement of small agricultural and industrial producers and petty merchants. Under these conditions, the Peruvian oligarchy was forced to assume a secondary role. Although its members were able to carry out their own consolidation of lands, mines, and industries, they had to accept financial, marketing, and transportation assistance from the foreign sector. Thanks to the increment in international demand, these native groups enriched themselves in the first two decades of this century, convinced that this was the correct road toward political dominance. But as soon became apparent, their role was merely to ensure and maintain imperialist domination, for their alternatives were limited by the enclave nature of the country's economy. The national elite came increasingly to accept these limitations.

The modes of production employed by foreign capital and its native associates continued to be based on the exploitation of dependent labor, limiting the development of a free labor market and therefore of the consumer market. In the same way as the traditional haciendas tied their peons and the Indian communities their members, the new companies involved in the commercialization of raw materials developed the *enganche* system and assured the survival of the *tambo*. Through *enganche,* the company's representatives would advance a sum of money to prospective workers, thus obligating them to work for the firm until the debt had been paid, and reviving the colonial practice of debt-bondage. The isolation of the plantation or mine forced the workers to buy all food, medicine, and tools in the tambo, which was, of course, controlled by the company. These items, like the machines, were imported by the enterprises which obtained a new source for the extraction of profits, impeding the propagation of the capitalist system. In this manner, "dualism" was introduced into Peruvian society: "modern" plantations and mines did not create economic linkages, thus insuring that the manual labor at their disposition remained cheap, because it originated in a basically precapitalist countryside.

In addition, these companies extended their landed property, incorporating some traditional haciendas; they then used the hacienda workers to produce the foodstuffs that would be sold, at market prices, in the tambos. In this way, the new firms were able to extract surplus at two levels: directly, from the workers; and indirectly, from the hacienda peons. Increased demand for foodstuffs, both in these developing productive centers and on the external market, also prompted the traditional *hacendados* to recapture their lands, demanding more work from the dependent labor force, in order to take advantage of new commercial opportunities.[4]

Possibilities for accumulation of capital within the country were, however, limited by the enclave nature of the imperialist firms. These companies had as their goal the export of raw materials, which would then be transformed into manufactured goods abroad. Moreover, the profits from exports were remitted to the countries of origin, leaving in Peru nothing but low wages and minimal taxes, the latter thanks to a policy of tax breaks that was passed to "contribute to national development."

But the implantation of enclave economies and reorganization of the traditional haciendas did send a tremor through Peru's traditional social structure. Thousands of tenant farmers and small proprietors were proletarianized by the expansion of plantations and mining areas. The dependent rural labor force was tied more firmly to the land by the hacendados. And both sectors forged new patron-client relationships with members of the Indian communities.[5] These changes combined to modify the status not only of peasant groups but also of the rural and urban middle classes and the regional oligarchies.

It was within this framework that Peru witnessed the rise of the first antioligarchical political groups, particularly APRA (Alianza Popular Revolucionaria Americana) and the Socialists.[6] The former, under the direction of Víctor Haya de la Torre, became the most important antioligarchic party in Peru until the mid-1950s. Its platform was based on a structural-dualist analysis of Peruvian society that saw the country as divided into a feudal sector and a capitalist-imperialist sector. Both sectors were united in common exploitation of the nation, blocking its development and oppressing both the middle and the lower classes. Political mobilization through an alliance of all the oppressed would allow for the creation of a strong anti-oligarchical and anti-imperialist state, which would then negotiate with foreign capital for the financing necessary to promote nationalist development.[7]

The Socialist movement, led by José Carlos Mariátegui, proposed the construction of a popular front that would bring together all the classes dominated by imperialist capital and its domestic allies with the goal of realizing a Socialist revolution which would carry out the democratic reforms. Mariátegui was firmly convinced that the creation of a native and autonomous capitalism in Latin America was impossible. He argued that the real consequence of the development of capitalism in Latin America would be to condemn the region to an intensified semicolonial dependence on the imperialist centers, therefore impeding both the liberation of the popular classes and the attainment of national development. Thus, owing to the dependent character of the local bourgeoisie, only socialism could resolve the problems of democratic construction in Latin America.[8]

The death of Mariátegui in 1930, the reputation of the Soviet revolution, and the control of the Communist party in Peru by the Comintern thwarted the chances that the movement, as envisioned by Mariátegui, could be realized. This made it possible for APRA to remain the standard-bearer of the antioligarchical and anti-imperialist struggles.

Faced with increasing Aprista pressure, particularly after the crisis of the 1930s, the dominant groups found that they did not possess the means to meet demands for social reform. This was true precisely because the profits from the enclave economies were not retained within national borders. It therefore became necessary to establish an alliance with the army and embark on a policy of violent repression. While in other Latin American countries the crisis produced by the intensification of class struggle was being averted through the development of a policy of import substitution based on the expansion of the internal market, Peru was enmeshed in a violent confrontation between APRA and the army. This confrontation was to define the political framework within which all subsequent national events were to unfold. Throughout the period between 1930 and 1945, APRA sought to penetrate the military, endeavoring to undermine this pillar of the oligarchical order. This effort caused the military hierarchy to redouble its opposition to APRA.

In 1945, popular pressures and a new democratic atmosphere stemming from the Fascist defeat prompted the political system to open itself to popular representation, and the first experiment in democracy in the history of the Peruvian republic was inaugurated. APRA managed to obtain significant representation in the legislative chambers. While APRA, in order to contribute to the solidification of electoral democracy, sought an understanding with the owners—their traditional enemies—the masses exercised pressure to increase economic and political benefits. These pressures, which threatened to destroy the oligarchical model of social domination, led to the resolute opposition of capital. Thus there emerged a political impasse whose only solution was violence. In 1948, the radicalized sectors of APRA began plans to carry out a popular revolution, and the bourgeoisie began to organize a military coup that would put an end to these dangers and politically consolidate their position. While the Aprista revolt miscarried, the military coup headed by General Odría triumphed, putting an end to the short and precarious experiment in democracy.

Once again the pattern of 1930 was repeated: the oligarchical bourgeoisie proved structurally incapable of attending to even the most modest popular demands and to make democratic development possible. For this reason General Odría dedicated himself with special fury to the destruction of the popular political organizations and to the persecution of political, union, and student leaders.

New Forms of Dependency

In 1950 Peru entered a period of substantial economic growth that lasted until 1965, averaging 6 percent a year or 3.5 percent annually per capita. This increase was based mainly on exports, which grew at 8.7 percent a year, as opposed to an average of 4.3 percent in Latin America as a whole. In addition, the terms of trade were favorable, since an increase in the prices of copper and fish meal meant an 8 percent yearly increase in the real value of exports. This growth resulted in a change in the composition of the national economy. While the relative contribution of agriculture dropped from 22 percent to 17 percent of the GNP, the fishing industry—a newcomer to the export sector in the mid-1950s—made up for this loss. Mining and industry, taken together, increased their contribution to GNP from 18 percent to 24 percent over this period, averaging an annual growth rate of 8 percent. The annual rate of growth for agriculture was much lower: it amounted to 2.7 percent a year for export agriculture and 0.8 percent a year for production consumed internally. Thus in 1960 Peru was forced to import 13 percent of the foodstuffs consumed within the country, and this proportion had risen to 24 percent by 1966. Politically, these changes meant the relative dislocation of the old agricultural exporters and their hacendado allies, and their replacement by the groups involved in mining, fishing, and industry.

The increase in exports, and the growth of the capitalist sector in general, was due largely to the participation of foreign capital. From the beginning of Odría's dictatorship in 1948 until the collapse of the experiment with democratic institutions in 1968, foreign investment was provided with special incentives, so that by 1964 foreign participation constituted 47 percent of the total amount invested in exports. In certain sectors, such as petroleum and iron, foreign investment was 100 percent; in copper, it was 88 percent; in zinc, 50 percent; in lead and silver, 50 percent; in fishing, 30 percent; in sugar, 23 percent; and in cotton, 8 percent. And between 1960 and 1966, due both to the 1959 and 1963 laws promoting industry and to special incentives provided in the automobile and chemical industries, U.S. investment in the industrial sector rose from $35 million to $92 million. In fact, three-fourths of the 9 percent annual rate of industrial growth was due to foreign investment.

A similar increase in foreign investment occurred in the financial sector. Between 1960 and 1966, the proportion of foreign capital in the banking system rose from 36 to 62 percent of the total. Thus, while the national banks were growing at a rate of 1 percent a year from 1962 to 1969, the foreign banks grew at an annual rate of 4 percent. This assault of foreign capital on the financial sector seems to have been connected with the rise in direct foreign participation in the dynamic sectors of the economy, especially in industry. The establishment of new industrial firms was increasingly financed by national savings: in 1966, national loans to foreign companies rose by 36 percent in relation to the previous year, while foreign loans fell by 6 percent. And finally, 34 percent of all bank loans were given to industry in 1966, in comparison with 27 percent in 1960.[9]

As had been true of the first two decades of the twentieth century, the period between 1950 and 1968 was characterized by the further concentration of property in foreign hands. Unlike the earlier period, however, this new phase of concentration occurred in both the primary sector and the industrial and banking sectors. Thus from 1950 on, the structure of the Peruvian economy began to lose its enclave nature. Not only did import substitution proceed at a fairly rapid pace, but raw materials also began to be at least partially processed before export.

Yet in contrast to what had occurred in other Latin American countries after the crisis of the 1930s, participation of foreign capital increased both relatively and absolutely, resulting in a further loss of wealth and autonomy by the national bourgeoisie. And while this process had been going on since the beginning of the twentieth century, its intensification during the 1950s sharpened the contradictions between the capitalist mode of production and the precapitalist forms which had been associated with it. Indeed, if until 1950 capitalist development had been closely connected to the survival of precapitalist relations of production, especially in the sierra, industrialization and urban growth began increasingly to transform this relationship into a historical anachronism.

This new phase of dependent-capitalist development led to a substantial modification in the Peruvian occupational and demographic structures. The penetration of new forms of social and labor relations into areas previously dominated by the traditional hacienda meant the relative erosion of the hacendado's power base. In association with these and other factors, migration from rural to urban areas and from the sierra to the coast increased markedly. Between 1940 and 1961, for example, Lima's population grew five-fold. And in the last decade of this period, the annual rate of growth in Lima reached 8 percent, due mainly to the influx of rural migrants.

Over the same intercensus period, the proportion of the population employed in the primary sector fell from 63 percent to 52 percent, while the proportion employed in the tertiary sector rose from 17 percent to 27 percent. The percentage of workers in the secondary sector held steady at 17 percent of the population, which is surprising, given the fact that the 1950s was a decade of industrial growth. Although a part of this discrepancy can be explained through faulty collection of data, most of it had to do with the structural transformation of the industrial sector. Many of the small and medium-sized industries closed down, to be replaced by larger, more capital intensive firms with a reduced capacity to absorb labor.

The rapid changes in the structure of production, property, and employment resulted both in a split within the elite and in the strengthening of popular political mobilization. Odría's government had been brought to power by the Alianza Nacional (National Alliance), which was made up predominantly of exporters. In its first years, therefore, this regime functioned in a typically oligarchical fashion. But socioeconomic diversification soon brought Odría under increasing pressure, both from new groups seeking admission into the oligarchy and from the growing lower- and middle-class movement still being led by APRA.

Odría responded to this pressure by using state revenues—which had expanded due to the growth in exports—in a bid for political autonomy, establishing programs of state aid for the lower classes. During the first six years of the 1950s, government spending, most of which was directed toward public works, rose. This strategy provided the masses with a share in the benefits of economic growth, in the form of employment, hospitals, and schools. But it also allowed Odría to forge important alliances with rising political groups through the careful allocation of construction contracts.

Odría also attempted to attack APRA's political base in a more direct fashion. He organized the Partido Restaurador (Party of Restoration), using the urban masses, and more particularly recent rural migrants, in an effort to forge a populist coalition. He further strengthened this coalition by increasing the scope of social security and workers' benefits and giving women the vote. Odría's combined policy of providing assistance to the lower sectors while allying himself with new groups in the bourgeoisie prompted a number of political observers to compare him with Perón.

But the oligarchical nature of Peru's economy and society put definite limits on Odría's bid for autonomy, since it was impossible to obtain access to the resources necessary for a long-term populist experiment. Even the timid populist pretensions demonstrated by Odría brought down on him the opposition of the oligarchy. Speaking through *La Prensa,* the oligarchy labeled the regime excessive and "arbitrary," and called for a return to duly elected government. In a sense, the nineteenth-century pattern of confrontation between the *civilistas* (civilian politicians of the oligarchy) and the military was reemerging. Within this pattern, the army was useful in the repression of popular discontent and of the divisions produced within the oligarchy. But once the intrinsic weakness of the elite led the military caudillos to use public funds in an attempt to create their own power base, the military regime came to be seen as a threat by the groups that had originally supported it.

A successful urban middle-class mobilization, set into motion by *La Prensa* in alliance with the APRA underground, forced Odría to call a high-level meeting at the convent of Santo Domingo. This meeting was essentially a conference with the oligarchy on the presentation of a common candidate for the forthcoming elections. At the conference it became clear that the winning candidate in any election needed to be able to count on the Aprista vote. Thus, instead of unification, the conference had an unusual outcome: the two factions of the oligarchy attempted to negotiate with APRA to obtain its support. Hernando de Lavalle, Odría's designated successor, offered to legalize APRA after a victory at the polls. Manuel Prado, leader of the opposing faction and a zealous persecutor of APRA during his previous presidential term (1939–45), offered this party cogovernment. This political alliance came to be known as *convivencia* (coexistence).

The New Nature of the Class Struggle

Prado's electoral triumph in 1956, with the support of APRA, marked the beginning of a new political era in Peru. As a basis for this new alliance, Prado's oligarchical faction promised to share political power with the Apristas as long as the latter continued to constitute a "loyal opposition." This meant that APRA relinquished all claim to a radical stance, favoring instead the expansion of existing channels for change, which would permit the modernization of the country without endangering the power structure.

Both groups had become convinced that in order to continue to exist and to further their particular political goals, it was necessary to reach a modus vivendi with the opposition. For the Pradista faction, this was the only way to ensure the existence of the stable political institutions necessary for the creation of a "climate of confidence for investment." In exchange for their quota of political participation, the Pradistas hoped, APRA would check popular unrest and keep the specter of communism under control. If APRA failed in its mission, the army could always be called in once more.

As for the Apristas, they had grown tired of the virulent military repression they had suffered because of their insistence that "Only APRA can save Peru." Moreover, Haya de la Torre had modified his position on the United States, insisting that the latter had changed, since its capital was now contributing to the abolition of Peru's feudal-capitalist dualism. It was now necessary to "popularize" the expanding capitalist system by making it more redistributive or risk the spread of international communism. Not only did APRA agree with the Pradista oligarchy on the dangers of communism, but it also hoped to "democratize" this oligarchical faction to the point that it would support APRA's bid for electoral power.

As soon as this "democratic coexistence" was established, however, it was called into question by new political groups wishing to appropriate APRA's old position on the Left. Structural changes in the socioeconomic system had created important new middle sectors, both technical and professional, as well as a new working-class generation, and these groups were eager to take up the anti-oligarchical banner dropped by APRA. Moreover, APRA's new "sellout" policy (*entreguismo*) generated the first wave of deserters among its youthful members, who hastened to join the ranks of the new movement. In a very short time, therefore, Peru witnessed not only the resurgence of the Communist party but also the creation of three new anti-oligarchical groups: the Christian Democrat party, the Movimiento Social Progresista (Progressive Social Movement), and Acción Popular (the Popular Action party). The last of these proved to be the most important, for in the space of a few weeks it managed to join together all the progressive forces previously sympathetic to APRA and to record an impressive one-third of the 1956 popular vote for its candidate, Fernando Belaúnde.[10]

In addition to this new anti-oligarchical struggle—which was a great deal less radical than APRA's initial mobilization in the thirties—two essentially new forces entered the political arena during this period: the peasantry and the urban shantytown dwellers.[11] The development of capitalism and its penetration into rural areas weakened the traditional hacendados' hold over the peasants, creating favorable conditions for the latter to initiate a sustained struggle to regain the land. The poorer urban sectors organized on two fronts: those faced with chronic underemployment and poor living conditions invaded empty urban lands to dramatize the housing problem; and those belonging to the labor force reorganized their unions and intensified their fight for participation in the national income. Thus land, housing, and employment became the central issues in the contest between pro- and anti-oligarchical forces.

It was within the context of this intense mobilization by both lower and middle sectors that Peru underwent a new process of profound politicization (i.e., the definition of particular interests within, and the struggle between, the different sectors and classes of society). With these new political tensions came the rise of "developmentalist" ideology, which emphasized the need for "structural" changes in Peruvian society in order to bring it out of its "underdeveloped" state. And within the dominant class, pressure from below combined with the rise of developmentalism to cause a split over the definition of a correct government policy.

The essence of the struggle between the two main factions of the elite was well captured in the polemic that arose between *La Prensa* and *El Comercio*, newspapers supported by different sectors of the oligarchy. Both publications agreed that the basic problem was communism, defined as the attempt of the lower sector to gain political power. They also agreed that the only solution to the problem was "development," seen as the expansion of national income and greater participation in this income by the lower classes. But they disagreed radically over the best way to stimulate economic growth and over the optimal mechanisms for income redistribution.

La Prensa, backed by the oligarchical group involved in exports and directly linked to international capital, espoused a policy best defined as laissez faire. The role of the state was seen exclusively as the provision of the necessary infrastructure and the lifting of all economic controls. In this way, the national bourgeoisie and the foreign capitalists could join in bringing new dynamism to the Peruvian economy. The problem of land could be solved by providing the necessary incentives for colonization of the jungle. The problems of housing and employment could be solved by lifting all fiscal restraints on rent and sale of housing and by creating organizations capable of channeling national savings into the construction industry. The increase in construction would not only take care of the housing shortage but would also provide employment for the urban population.

El Comercio, on the other hand, emphasized the need for structural reforms that would do away with the two basic contradictions in Peruvian society: the persistence of "feudalism" within the context of capitalist development and the increasing subordination of national to foreign capital. The most urgent priorities, therefore, were an agrarian, urban, and fiscal reform, and the creation of a powerful state that could control the economic sectors most important for nationalist development. A centralized state could organize production along modern lines and redistribute income to the masses so that their share of profits was in line with their participation in the productive process. It was hoped that this policy would favor the rise of a nationalist industrial bourgeoisie which, in alliance with the state, would lead the country forward to the realization of its economic potential.

These different economic policies implied extremely diverse political positions. *La Prensa* argued that only the institutionalization of "democracy" could provide the necessary base for its economic program. Without "democratic" institutions, military repression would lead to the rise of extremist movements. Furthermore, foreign capital, faced with uncertain long-term conditions, would not invest in Peru under a dictatorship. It was for these reasons that *La Prensa* favored the APRA-Prado coalition and its new policy of coexistence.

In contrast, *El Comercio* combined a reformist and anti-oligarchical economic stance with an extremely traditional political orientation. Economic reform by a centralized state was supported not for its own sake, but as the only way to maintain internal and external security. Peru was seen as threatened on two fronts: international communism on the one hand and Chile's "inveterate expansionist tendencies" on the other. Popular unrest, generated by poverty and exploitation, not only led to the diffusion of extremist ideologies but also prevented the creation of a national consciousness. And without a state to plan the economy, redistribute income, and solve the conflict between capital and labor, Peru would never develop a national identity to protect itself from Communist expansionism and Chilean "threats."

El Comercio's line of reasoning became increasingly attractive to certain sectors of the army. This sympathy was strengthened by the fact that the army and the *Comercio* group shared a profound hatred for APRA, both because of the type of popular participation this party had advanced in its early years and because of APRA's past attacks on the army and the church. Therefore, as time went on, *El Comercio* began to speak more and more directly to the army in its attacks on the APRA-Prado "democratic" experiment, calling for "structural changes" but always emphasizing the importance of maintaining the proper hierarchy of authority.

Then in 1957–58, a rapid fall in exports spawned a new political and economic crisis. President Prado offered the prime ministry to Pedro Beltrán, editor of *La Prensa*. In keeping with his liberal economic policies, Beltrán freed the exchange rate—which led to the devaluation of the currency—and lifted all controls on the movement of capital. In addition, he attempted to gain official approval for a hike in the price of gasoline, which was produced by the International Petroleum Company. This attempt initiated a violent debate in the legislature, not over the price itself but over the legality of IPC's operations in Peru. The controversy quickly spread to the pages of *La Prensa* and *El Comercio,* with the former defending the company and the latter attacking it on a daily basis. A growing nationalist trend emerged in support of *El Comercio*'s position, and this movement was joined by a large number of army officers.

Thus the socioeconomic diversification of Peruvian society facilitated the rise of new political sectors who openly questioned the hegemony of the dependent oligarchy. This polarization of class interests extended itself into the army and the church, permeating all sectors of society. In the 1950s, therefore, the dependent oligarchy found its privileged position under attack, a position it had been able to maintain exclusively because of the aid it had been receiving from the army.

The Roles of Army and Church in the Oligarchical Crisis

The Catholic church in Peru had traditionally been associated with the elite and had constituted one of the institutions through which the oligarchical state legitimized its power. With the mobilization of the 1950s the church responded by importing clergy and capital from other countries—especially from France and the United States—and initiated a strong anti-Communist campaign.[12]

Within the context of this campaign, elements of the clergy nonetheless began to perceive the dominant class as the true anti-Christian force, for they saw the continued exploitation of the masses as the underlying source of the country's discontent. This analysis was strengthened at the international level in the 1960s by the declarations of Vatican II and by the pope's explicit and emphatic censure of imperialism. Within Latin America, the conferences of bishops lent further support to this new trend.[13]

The church's progressive orientation soon gained the support of a majority of the clergy, not only in Peru but in other countries as well. The acceptance of progressivism led to an emphasis on new theological interpretations which helped to modify the image of the church and facilitate communication with the poor. And as a complement to the new ideology, a number of ecclesiastical groups became involved with the ongoing movements among peasants, urban squatters, urban unions, and student organizations.

In addition to participating in the mobilization of the lower sectors, the church organized a series of *cursillos de cristiandad* for members of the armed forces and for urban professionals. These courses were apparently designed to develop a militant Christian conscience within the new technocratic elements in the military and economic elites. In this way, the church hoped to initiate a reform from above by changing the ideas of people in positions of authority and influence. The final goal was the extension of a communitarian orientation throughout Peruvian society, which would help to quiet class struggle without major changes in class structure. This general plan meshed perfectly with the aspirations of the Christian Democrat party, whose members also hoped to eliminate social conflict by integrating all class interests into a single and organic body politic.

In a similar fashion and over the same period, the army underwent a series of ideological and institutional changes that helped to free it from oligarchical control and predispose it toward political intervention in order to insure national development. Up until the moment that a sector of the Peruvian elite, with the help of foreign investment, had managed to gain political control of the country, the Peruvian army had been little more than an armed group whose leaders were divided in their loyalties to different caudillos and the oligarchical factions they represented. But once the newly dominant dependent oligarchy controlled the state, the army united around an identification with this group and began to professionalize.

From the beginning, the function of the military was defined as the provision of support for the dependent oligarchical system. This meant not only political intervention whenever it became necessary to arbitrate conflicts within the oligarchy, but also the repression of political mobilization by the lower classes. Thus from the very moment of its establishment as a professional group, the army identified with the elite and developed a strong anti-Aprista policy.

Yet at the same time and throughout its history, the army found itself infiltrated by Apristas and by the anti-oligarchical ideology being formulated by APRA. As long as it was possible for most army officers to see their principal interests served by an alliance with the elite, the pro-oligarchical tendency continued to dominate. But the tension produced by this difference generated a technocratic-nationalist tendency within the ranks that later became responsible for the creation of the Centro de Altos Estudios Militares (CAEM).[14]

After World War II, the Peruvian army established strong connections with the United States army, purchasing military supplies and receiving extensive technical assistance. Accompanying this modernization was the development of a strong anti-Communist spirit, which combined easily with existing anti-Aprista feeling. And as a result of the introduction of new techniques, the Peruvian army initiated studies in military strategy based on actual conditions within the country, not on outmoded French manuals.

Within this framework, CAEM began a study of Peru's potential for national defense against a possible Communist or Chilean attack, paying special attention to the country's economic structure and the development of its educational, health, and communications facilities. When the results of this study were compared with the known potential of other Latin American countries, particularly those with which Peru shared borders, CAEM concluded that Peru was profoundly underdeveloped in terms of the resources it could mobilize in its own defense. CAEM therefore began immediately to investigate the causes for this state of affairs and to consider policies that would spur improvement of national defense. The developmentalist tone arising from this investigation was similar to the orientation of the new political parties created in 1950 but meshed especially well with the line being advanced by *El Comercio*. CAEM's findings can be summarized in the following sentence: "The sad and desperate reality is that, in Peru, real power is not Executive, Legislative, Judicial or Electoral power, but that which is held by landowners, exporters, bankers, and North American companies."[15]

A series of events then conspired to strengthen this analysis of Peru's dependency on foreign interests. The first of these was the support openly provided to the International Petroleum Company by the U.S. government, to the detriment of Peru's national interests. The second was the refusal by the United States to sell the country supersonic jets and its general reluctance to provide modern arms to Peru while giving them freely to other Latin American countries. Last was the U.S. refusal to give Belaúnde's government economic aid at a time of desperate need while continuing to provide it to Frei in Chile. These three events, along with a few less publicized occurrences, forced the military to conclude that national development was being limited by U.S. political and economic interests who were in association with the national oligarchy. As a result, many Peruvian officers reacted favorably to the theories of dependency being elaborated by Peruvian and other Latin American intellectuals.

While anti-imperialist sentiment developed in CAEM, the army as a whole carried out a reorganization of its institutional structure at the end of the 1950s. This reform had as one of its goals the strengthening of the army's section for military intelligence, prompted by the intensification of social conflict within the country. Careful observation of the Algerian and Vietnam wars, the Cuban Revolution, and popular movements within Latin America convinced military intelligence that the problem of national defense could no longer be seen solely as an external problem but was now also a question of internal security. This analysis was clearly based on anti-Communist considerations. The Soviet Union and China were thought to be creating subversive *focos* within the lower classes and intellectual groups of the Western nations in an attempt to destroy their institutions. And while the United States could be expected to counter any conventional attack these countries might attempt, it was up to Peru and to its army to insure social peace within national borders.

Studies carried out not only by CAEM but also by the army's intelligence service then led to the conclusion that the extreme poverty and exploitation characteristic of the countryside were the main causes for peasant movements. It was the traditional system of dominance, exemplified in the traditional haciendas, that generated agrarian movements, and through these, possible guerrilla focos. The conclusion was clear: it was necessary to ameliorate the conditions of life of the lower sectors in order to prevent the spread of the conflict that was threatening order in Peru.

For these reasons, therefore, an increasing section of the army came to support joint civil and military action for development, particularly the program of community development advanced by Acción Popular, and programs of jungle colonization and agrarian reform. The engineering divisions of the armed forces dedicated themselves to opening roads into the jungle in order to expand the agricultural frontier. The 1962 military junta, established to deal with the political crisis of that year, decreed an agrarian reform law for La Convención (in Cuzco), a center of peasant mobilization since the late 1950s.

But it was not until the outbreak of guerrilla activity all over the country in 1964 and 1965 that the army became truly alarmed about the potential danger the guerrillas could represent. Despite the fact that the guerrilla activity was quickly eliminated, the armed forces were left with the fear that these focos could reappear at any time and present an even more powerful challenge to institutionalized government. As a publication from the Ministry of War explained:

Although it is true that the guerrillas have been defeated, this does not mean that the "revolutionary" war in Peru has ended; the virus of subversion is latent in the universities and schools, unions and offices, clubs and homes. . . . The enemy is everywhere and the citizens should understand as much, and should therefore take an active part in the struggle, each within his own sphere of action and according to his own possibilities.[16]

From this time on the ideology developed by CAEM and the intelligence unit gained increasing acceptance within the army as a whole. Peru's status as a dependent nation was seen as the major cause for underdevelopment, for the impossibility of forming a national consciousness, and consequently for the rise of revolutionary movements. Thus national development became an urgent priority for the army, since it was intimately connected with national defense and internal security. Unless the army took an active and leading role in the elimination of Peru's oligarchical-dependent structures, the result would be a state of profound political disorganization and would lead, as it had done during the War of the Pacific, to a Chilean invasion. Thus the new military orientation came to agree closely with new tendencies in the church, and especially with the policies that had been formulated by *El Comercio* since the middle of 1950.

PART II: The Crisis of the Political Superstructure

The Political Crisis

Class conflict, and the polemic around its nature and solution, intensified greatly as the 1962 elections approached. One of the main reasons for this intensification was the rise of a peasant movement in the south of the country, led by Hugo Blanco. Centered in La Convención, Cuzco, this movement was widely perceived as an example of what could happen on a much larger scale if "traditional structures" were not quickly and completely reformed.

The three main candidates presenting themselves for the elections were Haya de la Torre, representing APRA; Fernando Belaúnde Terry, for Acción Popular; and General Manuel Odría, who represented the oligarchy's most traditional faction—including exporters and traditional landowners—but also had his own following among the poorer urban sectors to whom he had provided services during his last term in power. *La Prensa* backed both Odría and Haya de la Torre, while maintaining a clear preference for the latter. *El Comercio,* on the other hand, given its strong anti-Aprista stand, supported both Odría and Belaúnde but declared its preference for the Acción Popular candidate.

The electoral campaign was fierce, and the results promised to be close. Anticipating the possibility of an Aprista triumph, *El Comercio* began a strong campaign directed at the army, emphasizing the fraudulent nature of the electoral process. As was feared, the returns gave Haya de la Torre the victory by a close margin. The army, assured of support from *El Comercio* and repulsed by the thought of surrendering its autonomy to a mass party government, prepared a coup. A few days before the end of his term, Manuel Prado was exiled.

In 1962, therefore, the first institutional military government in Latin America was installed in Peru. A triumvirate of generals assumed control of the country and attempted to put into practice the new policies being formulated at the Centro de Altos Estudios Militares. The first measures taken included the organization of a national economic planning agency (Instituto Nacional de Planificación), the agrarian reform in La Convención, and the incarceration of several hundred workers, peasants, political leaders, and students. But the lack of political cohesion and ideological maturity among the officers combined with an increase in political unrest to force the junta to seek new elections in 1963. For the new elections, however, it was necessary to support a candidate who would be willing to carry out sweeping reforms without stirring up class conflict in such a way as to cause institutional chaos. For this reason the army, along with the church, supported Belaúnde in 1963.

The new electoral campaign was as heated as that of the year before. Because of popular pressure, all candidates were forced to present anti-oligarchical platforms, promising agrarian and industrial reform and a restructuring of the state. In addition, Belaúnde stated publicly that he would solve the ongoing conflict over the International Petroleum Company within ninety days of being elected, a promise which prompted the American ambassador to state his support for Haya de la Torre; this prompted the military government to request a replacement from Washington.

A close victory by Belaúnde launched the country into a state of uncontrolled euphoria. A university professor and architect who had personally campaigned throughout the country was now to become president and bring about the "conquest of Peru by Peruvians." In keeping with this general tone, the peasant masses anticipated the coming agrarian reform by invading haciendas and taking land for themselves. Thousands of students flocked to the Cooperación Popular (Popular Cooperation) movement to help the peasants "develop their communities," and professional and intellectual groups urged Peruvians to participate in the task of national development.

Six months into his term, Belaúnde called for municipal elections, which had been outlawed for almost fifty years. His party scored an impressive victory, raising their percentage of the vote from the 34 percent received in the presidential elections to 47 percent. Despite this popular support, however, the new government had inherited an unmanageable political system. Before stepping down, the junta had passed a new electoral law which, while neglecting to change the literacy requirement, established the principle of proportional representation. This meant that future presidents would not have a majority in Congress and would therefore have to look for support among opposing groups, because proportional representation would almost invariably mean a pluralistic government.[17]

Congress had been split in such a way that the largest group was formed by APRA, followed by the Acción Popular–Christian Democrat coalition (AP-DC), which supported the president, and the Unión Nacional Odriísta (UNO), which was led by Odría. Under these conditions, the main political problem was establishment of a coalition to facilitate relations between the executive and legislative branches. From the very beginning Manuel Seoane, APRA's second-in-command, along with a number of the Acción Popular leaders, began negotiations to establish a coalition between these two parties. Despite tactical conflicts within APRA, an important group of leaders continued to uphold its original position and could count on the support of its popular base. An equally reformist position was held by the majority of Acción Popular leaders.

But ideological affinities proved to be outweighed by other considerations. If the AP-DC alliance joined forces with APRA, it stood to lose its main basis of support in the army and the backing of *El Comercio*. Furthermore, a section of Acción Popular which would later be called the *termocéfalos* felt that APRA had ''sold out'' to the oligarchy, since it had supported Prado and Beltrán, director of *La Prensa*; therefore they felt that any alliance with them would mean giving up the reformist goals of Acción Popular. Within APRA there existed a feeling that AP was a treacherous competitor, since it had attempted to rob APRA of its reformist banners and appropriate the militancy which ''naturally'' belonged to the latter. Belaúnde was also perceived as siding with the Communists because of the radical tone of his proposals. And finally, Haya de la Torre felt a deep resentment for Belaúnde, for he saw the new president as having stolen from him the position of popular leader, a position Haya had held for thirty years.

Faced with the impossibility of conciliating the two main reformist forces, and the consequent loss of an alliance which would have brought them nearly 70 percent of the popular vote, APRA once again committed the unforgivable: it allied with the Odriístas. If the previous coalition with Prado had meant the loss of a large group of reformists who then swelled the ranks of new political parties, APRA's new ''sell out'' policy proved even more expensive. Numerous Apristas now entered the Movimiento de Izquierda Revolucionaria (MIR), an alliance of members from APRA Rebelde and other leftist groups who were attempting to follow the Cuban model in Peru.

The APRA-UNO coalition resulted, predictably enough, in a parliamentary block of all the reformist proposals being advanced by the executive. Prompted by the rash of land invasions occurring simultaneously with the discussions of the Agrarian Reform Law, APRA-UNO and *La Prensa* accused the government of promoting these ''illegal'' actions through Cooperación Popular. They demanded immediate repression of the peasants and cut the Cooperación Popular budget. These events caused the fall of Belaúnde's first cabinet.

Moreover, the Agrarian Reform Law presented by Acción Popular was sufficiently modified during the discussion in Parliament that it became completely ineffective. The three main points of contention were the type and size of property to which the law would apply, the mechanisms through which the law would be implemented, and the way in which the project would be financed. As to the first point, the coalition managed to exclude all property producing rice, sugar, and cotton, thus maintaining intact the nucleus of all important and powerful agricultural interests. Parliament then gained control of the financing, channeling it through a bureaucratic procedure so extended and complicated as to make rapid action on affected lands virtually impossible. And finally, although the coalition accepted payment for expropriation through government bonds, it also reduced the budget for the Office of Agrarian Reform, thus cutting off the funds necessary for the issue of these bonds.

In this way, APRA-UNO managed to block both of Belaúnde's main reformist programs from the beginning: Cooperación Popular, a movement designed to promote community development through public works and the joint action of the lower classes and the student population, and agrarian reform. This was not surprising, since the political structure allowed the legislature to control the executive:

The strength of the Congress derives from powers granted in the 1933 Constitution. First in importance is the power to *interpellate* (question) *and remove* ministers. With this power, Congress can censure ministers at will, but the president does not have the reciprocal power of most parliamentary systems, namely the ability to call new elections when his ministers receive a vote of no confidence. Second, the Congress must approve all taxes or changes in tax rates. In practice, this has allowed the Congress to get the credit for approving new programs but to block their implementation by refusing to finance them. Third, there is no presidential veto; the president may only "promulgate and implement" laws sent to him. In 1939 President Benavides called a plebiscite which approved a veto and limitations on the Congressional control over taxation, but these adjustments were voted out by an *Aprista*-dominated Congress in 1945. There remained a residual veto by compromise: the president could "observe" a law within ten days after receiving it, but no extraordinary majority was required to reinstate the law. Apra's support of Congressional prerogatives during Belaúnde's presidency is not surprising.[18]

The repression of the peasant movement demanded by the coalition provoked within the ranks of Acción Popular a movement to close down the Congress and call a national plebiscite, a move which would certainly have received the support of the military. Belaúnde rejected such an illegal measure and preferred to search out other political alternatives for solving the crisis. This incident marks the moment that APRA began to turn the Parliament into the "first power within the country," hoping to force the executive to surrender. Meanwhile, the coalition attempted to take all the credit for the government's successes and blame all the mistakes on Belaúnde.

Belaúnde proved to be unable to handle this situation, for he neither looked for a confrontation with the opposition parties nor tried to reach a modus vivendi. In addition to rejecting the possibility for a coup with popular and military support, Belaúnde did nothing to counter Parliament's attempts to dismantle his programs by cutting off funds. In fact, he totally dismissed the possibility of organizing popular support around the party system. Instead, he seemed to want to separate himself both from popular pressure and from that of his party, searching secretly for his own solution to the political crisis.

In addition to Belaúnde's personal inadequacies, the alternatives available for action were limited by other factors. One was the previously mentioned problems involved in a possible alliance with APRA. A further complication proved to be Belaúnde's campaign promise to resolve the conflict surrounding the International Petroleum Company, which led to the U.S. government's decision to cut off funds to Peru.[19]

By the end of Belaúnde's first year in power, it had already become clear that there was little hope for the elimination of traditional and oligarchical social structures in Peru. In 1964, this hopelessness manifested itself in the decision of certain sectors of the Left to adopt the guerrilla foco technique. Luis de la Puente, an old Aprista leader, led the MIR in the constitution of four focos of insurgency which were rapidly destroyed. A similar experiment by the Ejército de Liberación Nacional (National Liberation Army) suffered the same fate the next year.[20]

Despite the tactical failure of the guerrillas, the movement as a whole provided Belaúnde's opposition with new ammunition in the political struggle. In 1964, La Prensa initiated a campaign designed to discredit the president by branding him an agent, ally, and "comrade in arms" of the Communists. Belaúnde's first reaction to the guerrillas had been to underestimate their importance, and La Prensa did not allow him to forget it, going as far as to direct an appeal to the army in the hopes of breaking down the alliance existing between the officers and Acción Popular. In this way, La Prensa hoped to force the government to call in Beltrán as economic adviser and bring the period of reformism to an end. The final move in this campaign was a collaboration between Congress and La Prensa in raising a national loan based on "bonds for the defense of national sovereignty," of which Beltrán himself bought the first million.

Faced with the combined influence of this campaign and pressure from the military, Belaúnde had no choice but to institute an openly repressive policy. The guerrilla focos were located and destroyed, and the peasant movement liquidated. Simultaneously, the government struck against the growing union movement that was trying to separate itself from the influence of the Aprista Confederación de Trabajadores del Perú. The overall result of this policy was the breakdown of all unity on the left. Belaúnde's government quickly lost all support from the radicalized popular sectors and was reduced to seeking temporary alliances with political and military leaders.

But the guerrilla movement marked an important turning point in the attitudes within the military. From this point on, CAEM's warnings about the possibility of revolutionary war took on a new immediacy, and heated discussions began on the need to take drastic measures to avoid political disintegration. The military had hoped for structural reform, but Belaúnde's regime had done nothing but cause a continual political crisis that made reform impossible. Increasingly, therefore, the officers of the armed forces began to argue that it was not feasible to rely on political parties and the parliamentary system to carry out such reforms.

A further problem for Belaúnde was the progressive worsening of Peru's economic situation. Public expenditures rose noticeably during the Acción Popular government. This increase was caused in part by the APRA-UNO coalition's attempts to create an independent power base. The coalition had initiated a policy of patronage and clientelism, through which they hoped to maintain the support of their allies and also court the backing of new groups. One of the mechanisms of implementation for this plan was a system of "parliamentary initiatives," which consisted in presenting a set sum of money to each parliamentary member to spend as he saw fit. But part of the increase in public expenditures was also due to Belaúnde's policies. Seeing his attempts at structural reform blocked by Congress, the president began to promote the development of the country's infrastructure and educational system as a substitute for socioeconomic transformation.

Yet Congress refused to finance increased public spending through a reform in the tax system, forcing the government to rely on deficit financing. During the first fiscal year of the regime the budgetary deficit reached 1,618 million *soles*, which increased to 2,535 million in 1965 and 3,012 million in 1966, an annual rate of 96 percent.

Given the continued intransigence of the APRA-UNO coalition, Belaúnde was unable to finance the deficit internally and was forced to rely on international loans. But the United States was maintaining a financial blockade on Peru until the resolution of the problem with the International Petroleum Company. Consequently, the only loans available were short-term, high-interest loans. This led to an increase in the country's external debt from $120 million in 1963 to $670 million in 1967. Expressed in other terms, this debt constituted 8 percent of exports in 1965 but 18 percent in 1968.

To compound these problems, exports and foreign investment began to fall off in 1965. As investment decreased, all productive sectors of the economy—raw materials, manufacturing, and banking—were hard hit. Combined with the problems of budgetary deficit, this decrease in production contributed to an increase in inflation, which reached 14 percent per year between 1963 and 1967. Then in 1966, as exports continued to decrease and the external debt continued to increase, Peru was faced with a problem in the balance of payments. From then on, the Acción Popular government, and with it the oligarchical regime, would begin to see its very existence come into question.

The Denouement

Beginning in 1966, therefore, the economic crisis reached such proportions that it demanded immediate and energetic action.[21] Four aspects of the crisis needed special attention: the balance of payments, the budgetary deficit, financing of the external debt, and the revitalization of the export sector. In all cases, the alternatives were limited. The balance of payments problem could be solved in one of two ways: through a devaluation of the currency, which would put the burden on the consumer, or through exchange rate and import controls, which would generate strong opposition from the oligarchy and foreign interests. In the case of the budget deficit, the choices were similar. The burden of balancing the budget could be placed on the lower and middle sectors through a reduction in expenditures, thus lowering employment, consumption, and investment, or it could be placed on the foreign capital and oligarchy through new direct taxes on income.

The financing of the external debt and the provision of funds for the export sector were dependent on the ability of the government to reach a new agreement with sources of foreign capital. This ability depended, in turn, on working out the continuing problem with IPC, since, without a solution to this impasse, the United States would not provide assistance to Peru. Yet despite new incentives for agreement, which consisted of $350 million for the exploitation of new copper deposits, a solution did not seem imminent.

The best course of action, therefore, was to attack those problems that could be solved internally: balancing the budget, increasing direct taxes, and controlling the movement of stock. But Congress continued its policy of intransigent opposition, causing several cabinets to fall. Almost through default, a 50 percent official devaluation of the *sol* was announced in August 1967.

A month later, elections were called in the department of Lima to replace a deceased AP representative. These elections had the character of a plebscite, for the department of Lima contained nearly half of the national electorate. The APRA-UNO candidate, who ran on the slogan "No More Taxes," won the election, but a candidate for the unified Left also managed to obtain 18 percent of the vote. Not only did this election demonstrate the AP's loss of its popular base, therefore, but it also pointed to the existence of an important sector capable of uniting the Left around a series of common goals.

Faced with these results, the political forces decided to regroup. Acción Popular, controlled by the termocéfalos, separated itself from the president and reaffirmed the AP's original platform, calling for tax reform, administrative reform of government, careful economic planning, and—most important of all—agrarian and industrial reform. Belaúnde, cut off from his political base, began negotiations with Haya de la Torre and Odría. And the Christian Democrats not only dissolved their alliance with the Acción Popular but also broke off from their own conservative wing.

Faced with a worsening economic and political crisis, Belaúnde invited an "independent" to be his minister of economics and to attempt a solution. When this move failed, the minister accused APRA of manipulating the situation to bring about a second monetary devaluation, thus discrediting the president even further and strengthening their own position in the upcoming elections. This accusation was widely believed, and APRA, seeing tensions rise, especially within the ranks of the military, reconsidered its strategy.

Then in February 1968, a high-level smuggling ring was exposed, implicating important members of the Ministry of Economics and the armed forces. Scandal spread throughout the country, discrediting all national institutions and bringing the military directly into the fray. The ensuing investigation was carried out by an Aprista congressional representative, which presented an immediate threat to the image and prestige of the army. At the same time Belaúnde, hoping to maintain the support of the military and force the congressional opposition to solve the economic crisis, requested the appointment of an army officer as minister of economics. But the measures proposed by the new minister turned out to be the same as those presented by the two previous ministers, for they were based on the recommendations of the Alliance for Progress, which advocated the strengthening and piecemeal reform of existing structures.

Within this framework, *La Prensa* redoubled its attack on the regime, this time generalizing its criticism to include the technocrats, the United States government and the Alliance for Progress. In this way, the newspaper hoped to present its stance as a nationalist one. The new minister of economics then resigned rather than risk an open confrontation with Parliament. The rest of the cabinet followed suit almost immediately.

In June 1968, Belaúnde made one last attempt to salvage the situation by installing a cabinet that was headed by another "independent," Oswaldo Hercelles, and a new minister of hacienda, Manuel Ulloa. Several of the ministers in this cabinet were marginal Apristas, and others belonged to the faction of Acción Popular that had recommended alliance with APRA from the very beginning. This cabinet therefore began its activities by "conversing" with the opposition and became known in the political folklore as the "conversed" cabinet.

The new conformation of alliances, along with the growing Aprista fear that the military might intervene in the 1969 elections if things got much worse, contributed to the decision to grant Hercelles extraordinary powers. This allowed the cabinet to govern without parliamentary regulation for sixty days. Ulloa was therefore able to initiate a strong policy of stabilization, signing more than three hundred decrees in two months.

Over this period, Ulloa put into practice a series of measures that Parliament had systematically blocked for over five years. He taxed inheritance and personal income. He reformed the laws on ownership of stock, facilitating the circulation of shares and making it more difficult to avoid paying taxes on them. He limited participation by foreign capital in Peruvian banks to 33 percent and prohibited foreign banks from opening branches that could take over internal savings. Not only was this last measure a nationalist one, but it also helped open up sources of credit to the national bourgeoisie. In addition, Ulloa increased state participation in the Central Reserve Bank and gave representation on its board of directors to the Confederación de Trabajadores del Perú (Union of Peruvian Workers) and the Federación de Campesinos del Perú (Federation of Peruvian Peasants), both controlled by APRA, and to the Sociedad de Minería (Mining Society), controlled by the oligarchy and foreign capital. Finally, Ulloa ruled that industries strategic to the development of the country should be owned only by the state, or at least that two-thirds of their stock must be in the hands of Peruvians.

Complementing these domestic measures was an agreement on the refinancing of the external debt and a successful bid for more foreign investment. Moreover, the imminent arrival of North American funds for the exploitation of the Cuajone deposits was announced. Ulloa's supporters maintained that these successes were due to his energetic domestic measures. His detractors, especially the termocéfalos, argued that he had received such favorable terms because he had once been an executive in a company financed by U.S. capital. Either way, however, the solution of Peru's economic crisis seemed assured. The only missing step was the working out of an agreement with IPC.

Ulloa's rapid success was a result of his alliance with APRA. This alliance also led to a new regrouping of the country's political groups, with Acción Popular and the radical wing of the Christian Democrats uniting behind Edgardo Seoane as a presidential candidate for 1969. APRA had, in the meantime, also separated from UNO, which itself had split into two groups.

The interesting question then becomes: why did APRA change its position again, and why so rapidly? The most plausible answer seems to lie in the proximity of the presidential elections. APRA needed a new ally with which it could govern the country, an ally acceptable to the national and foreign capitalists and capable of neutralizing the army. Moreover, Ulloa knew that without APRA he would only be acceptable to the personal supporters of Belaúnde. The termocéfalos, Odriístas, and *La Prensa* would be opposed in any case, and the army and *El Comercio* could be appeased with a nationalist stance; thus APRA was Ulloa's best ally, and Ulloa was APRA's best candidate for the coming election.

Starting in July, however, all hopes for new political alliances were dashed by a crisis over an agreement with IPC. At that point IPC decided to negotiate, and indicated that it was willing to accept the terms that had been presented by the Peruvian government five years earlier. Under these terms, IPC agreed to turn over to the government a number of semidepleted oil wells but demanded that in return the government retract all other claims. In addition, the much-disputed refinery at Talara would stay in the hands of IPC, and their concession on the distribution of gasoline would be extended for forty years, with an option to renew at the end of this period for another forty. Finally, IPC wanted exploration rights to a million hectares in the jungle.

On 28 July 1968, Belaúnde addressed the nation, promising that the country's problems with IPC were over. He invited parliamentary leaders and high-ranking military officers to assist in the signing of the agreement. In this way, Belaúnde hoped to make this "triumph" a national occasion, not a partisan one, and to regain favor with the nationalist forces.

Temporarily, Belaúnde's attempt at national unity seemed a success. Even *El Comercio,* which in principle objected to the terms of the agreement, toned down its criticism when faced with the government's first triumph in the midst of failure. But it did not take long for a new scandal to emerge, this time over the definition of the ongoing relationship between the state, new owner of the national oil wells, and the foreign-owned refinery.

In September, the director of the Empresa Petrolera Fiscal (the state oil company) announced over national television that someone had stolen the last page of the Act of Talara, as the agreement had come to be called. This was the page that defined the price that IPC would pay EPF for the petroleum the latter was forced to sell. Once again, scandal spread rapidly. Seoane and Acción Popular publicly denied any connection with the president, and Belaúnde attempted to regain control of AP headquarters through the use of police and hired gunmen. APRA also denied any connection with the agreement and the scandal, and left Ulloa and the cabinet to their own devices. *El Comercio* attacked the government vehemently in its editorials and the army felt the shock of public immorality and political disorder.

By the end of September, the whole cabinet was forced to resign. After several unsuccessful attempts, the president managed to organize a new one on 2 October. But this last cabinet did not survive for more than twenty-four hours. The army had been planning a coup since February, and it now took place ahead of schedule. An armored division on maneuvers forty kilometers from the capital cut short its practice and marched on the presidential palace.

Conclusion

To sum up, then, my main points are the following. Because of the dependent relationship forged between the Peruvian oligarchy and foreign capital, there developed in Peru a system of enclave economies. This prevented the rise of an independent national bourgeoisie which could have developed the economy and controlled enough resources to give in to some of the demands of the popular sectors. Consequently, when faced with popular mobilization in the 1930s, the oligarchy was forced to rely on the army and follow a policy of intense repression.

When foreign investment extended to the industrial and banking sectors in the 1950s, Peru's economy began to lose its enclave nature. Yet it was precisely this expansion of international capital which reaffirmed the extreme precariousness of the Peruvian bourgeoisie and state, sealing the fate of both. The ensuing changes in the country's demographic and occupational structures intensified and extended the class struggle, and new lower-class groups entered the political arena. In an attempt to maintain control in this situation of social-structural transformation, the Peruvian oligarchy began an experiment with democratic institutions in 1956. This experiment was carried on between 1963 and 1968 with the Acción Popular regime of Fernando Belaúnde. But the two mass parties—APRA and Acción Popular—were unable to agree on a coalition because of their differing historical backgrounds and their differing bases of political support. In effect, the fact that the modern section of the bourgeoisie, together with the army and the church, supported Acción Popular and its program of reforms and not APRA stemmed from their fear that APRA would modernize the country by means of a popular mobilization. They saw such mobilization as a threat, because it might set into motion a process which would end up destroying their autonomy and special interests. Thus APRA allied itself with the traditional UNO group in Congress, and through continual blockage of Belaúnde's reformist proposals brought Acción Popular to its knees. The army, fearful of the threat to internal security presented by the political crisis, and convinced that the only road to stabilization was through structural reform, stepped in to institute the reformist policies that the Acción Popular government had been unable to put into practice. As carried out by the army, however, these reforms had a clear technocratic and administrative character designed to obviate any possibility that the masses might take the initiative and develop politically in an autonomous manner. Thus the revolutionary government of the armed forces realized a good part of the program of the Acción Popular and of the original plans of APRA, but without direct participation of the political parties or of the popular classes.

NOTES

1. Fernando Henrique Cardoso and Enzo Faletto, *Dependencia y desarrollo en América Latina* (Mexico City: Ed. Siglo XXI, 1969).
2. Shane Hunt, "Growth and Guano in Nineteenth Century Peru," Discussion Paper no. 34, Research Program in Economic Development (Princeton, N.J.: Woodrow Wilson School of Public and International Affairs, February 1973).
3. William Bollinger, "The Rise of U.S. Influence in the Peruvian Economy, 1869–1921," (M.A. thesis, University of California, 1972); James C. Carey, *Peru and the United States, 1900–1962* (Notre Dame, Ind.: University of Notre Dame Press, 1964); Rosemary Thorpe and Geoff Bertram, "Industrialization in an Open Economy, 1870–1940," manuscript (Oxford University, 1974).

4. Aníbal Quijano, "El Perú en la crisis de los años treinta," in *La crisis de los años treinta en América Latina,* ed. Pablo Gonzáles Casanova (Mexico City: UNAM, forthcoming); De-Wind Adrian, "De campesinos a mineros," *Estudios Andinos,* no. 2, 1974–76, pp. 1–32.

5. Julio Cotler, "The Mechanics of Internal Domination and Social Change in Peru," in *Masses in Latin America,* ed. Irving L. Horowitz, (New York: Oxford University Press, 1970), pp. 407–44.

6. Peter F. Klarén, *Modernization, Dislocation and Aprismo: Origins of the Peruvian Aprista Party, 1870–1932,* Latin American Monographs no. 2, Institute of Latin American Studies (Austin: University of Texas Press, 1973).

7. Víctor Raúl Haya de la Torre, *El Antimperialismo y el APRA,* Cuarta Edición (Lima: Editorial-Imprenta Amauta, 1972).

8. For Mariátegui's thought see his *Siete ensayos de interpretación de la realidad peruana* (Lima: Biblioteca Amauta, 1971), and his *Ideología y política* (Lima: Biblioteca Amauta, 1971.)

9. Rosemary Thorpe, "The Expansion of Foreign Ownership in Peru in the 1960's: A Perspective on the Military's Economic Policy," manuscript (Oxford University, 1976).

10. See François Bourricaud, *Power and Society in Contemporary Peru* (New York: Praeger Publishers, 1970), pt. 2, chap. 4; pt. 3, chap. 1.

11. Hugo Blanco, *Tierra o muerte* (Mexico City: Ed. Siglo XXI, 1973); Julio Cotler and Felipe Portocarrero, "Peru: Peasant Organizations," in *Latin American Peasant Movements,* ed. Henry A. Landsberger (Ithaca, N.Y.: Cornell University Press, 1969), pp. 297–322; Wesley Craig, "From Hacienda to Community: An Analysis of Solidarity and Social Change in Peru," Latin American Studies Program, Cornell University (Dissertation Series no. 6, 1967); David Collier, *Squatters and Oligarchs: Authoritarian Rule and Policy Change in Peru* (Baltimore, Md.: Johns Hopkins University Press, 1976).

12. Luigi R. Einaudi et al., "Latin American Institutional Development: The Changing Catholic Church" (Santa Monica, Ca.: Rand Corporation, 1969).

13. Primera semana social del Perú, *Exigencias sociales del catolicismo en el Perú* (Lima: agosto, 1959).

14. Víctor Villanueva, *El CAEM y la revolución peruana* (Lima: Instituto de Estudios Peruanos, 1972).

15. CAEM, *El Estado y la política general* (Chorrillos: CAEM, 1963), p. 92.

16. Ministerio de Guerra, "Los guerrillas en el Perú y su represión" (Lima: Ministerio de Guerra, 1966).

17. Guillermo Hoyos Osores, "Crisis de la democracia en el Perú," *Cuadernos Americanos* (México: enero-febrero, 1969), pp. 7–31.

18. Jane Jaquette, "The Politics of Development in Peru" (Ph.D. diss., Cornell University, 1971), pp. 139–40.

19. Richard Goodwin, "Letter from Peru," *The New Yorker,* 17 May 1969.

20. Richard Gott, *Guerrilla Movements in Latin America* (New York: Doubleday and Co., 1971), pp. 307–94; Hector Béjar, *Peru 1965: Notes on a Guerrilla Experience* (New York: Monthly Review Press, 1969).

21. For a detailed discussion of this and other aspects of the development, see Julio Cotler, "Political Crisis and Military Populism in Peru," *Studies in Comparative International Development* 6 no. 5 (1970–71): 95–113; and Jaquette, "Politics of Development."

Biographical Notes

JULIO COTLER is Senior Researcher at the Instituto de Estudios Peruanos, in Lima, and has been a Professor at the University of San Marcos and at the Universidad Nacional Autónoma de México. He received his doctorate in sociology from the University of Bordeaux in 1960. He has just completed *Clases, estado, y nación en el Perú,* is co-editor, with Richard Fagen, of *Latin America and the United States: The Changing Political Realities,* and has published extensively on peasant movements, corporatism, military populism, internal domination, and dependency.

DANIEL LEVINE is Associate Professor of Political Science at the University of Michigan and, during 1978–79, Visiting Fulbright Professor at the National University of Guatemala. He received his doctorate from Yale University in 1970. He is the author of *Conflict and Political Change in Venezuela* and has published widely on Venezuelan politics, the Catholic Church, Latin American social change, and political culture.

JUAN J. LINZ is Pelatiah Perit Professor of Political and Social Science at Yale University. He received his doctorate from Columbia University in 1959 and has taught at Columbia University, Stanford University, the University of Madrid, and the Universidad Autónoma of Madrid. He is Chairman of the Committee on Political Sociology of the International Sociological and Political Science Associations. His publications include ''Totalitarian and Authoritarian Regimes,'' in *Handbook of Political Science,* ed. F. Greenstein and N. Polsby; ''Some Notes toward a Comparative Study of Fascism in Comparative Sociological Perspective,'' in *Fascism,* ed. W. Laquer; and numerous monographs and essays on Spanish elites and entrepreneurs, quantitative history, and parties and elections in Spain and Germany.

GUILLERMO O'DONNELL is Director and founder of CEDES (Centro de Estudios de Estado y Sociedad) in Buenos Aires. He did advanced studies in law and political science at the National University of Buenos Aires and Yale University and has been a Visiting Professor at the University of Michigan and a Fellow of the Institute for Advanced Study, Princeton. His publications include *Modernization and Bureaucratic-Authoritarianism: Studies in South American Politics,* and, with Delfina Linck, *Dependencia y Autonomía.* He is currently completing a book on the ''bureaucratic-authoritarian'' period in Argentina between 1966 and 1973.

PETER H. SMITH is Chairman of the Department of History, University of Wisconsin at Madison. He received his doctorate from Columbia University in 1966. Among his many publications are *Politics and Beef in Argentina: Patterns of Conflict and Change; Argentina and the Failure of Democracy: Conflict Among Political Elites, 1904–1955;* and *Labyrinths of Power: Political Recruitment in Twentieth-Century Mexico.*

ALFRED STEPAN is Professor of Political Science at Yale University and frequently serves as Chairman of Yale's Council on Latin American Studies. He received his doctorate from Columbia University in 1969 and has taught at Yale since then. He has been a Guggenheim Fellow and, from 1978 to 1979, will be a Visiting Fellow at St. Antony's College, Oxford University. He has published *The Military in Politics: Changing Patterns in Brazil* and *The State and Society: Peru in Comparative Perspective*. He is the editor of *Authoritarian Brazil: Origins, Policies, and Future,* and co-editor, with Bruce Russett, of *Military Force and American Society.*

ALEXANDER WILDE is a Research Associate in the Woodrow Wilson International Center for Scholars in Washington, D.C. He received his doctorate in political science from Columbia University in 1972 and has taught at the University of Wisconsin at Madison and at Haverford College. He is the author of various articles on politics and religion, as well as the book, *Politics and the Church in Colombia*. With Arturo Valenzuela he has written studies on budgetary politics in Chile. He has just completed a monograph, *Conversaciones de caballeros: La democracia oligárquica en Colombia.*

IV.

The Breakdown
of Democratic Regimes

CHILE

Arturo Valenzuela

Introduction

On the morning of 11 September 1973, jet aircraft of the Chilean Air Force bombed and strafed La Moneda, the palace of the president and the most vivid symbol of Chile's historic institutions. The smoldering debris marked the downfall of Salvador Allende, a Socialist who had firmly believed he could lead his country down the path of greater social justice within the framework of democratic, pluralist, and libertarian traditions. Allende's tragic death, on the ruins of his experiment, marked not only the demise of the Popular Unity government but also the violent breakdown of one of the world's oldest democracies. What happened? Why did political institutions much admired around the globe cease to function?

Coups d'état and military rule, common in other Latin American countries, had been almost completely absent in Chile since the 1830s. From that date Chilean elites had been able to fashion a viable set of institutions which permitted the vast majority of Chilean presidents to serve out their terms and make way for their duly elected successors.[1]

That process was facilitated by the fact that Chilean elites did not divide sharply along social and economic lines. Both the traditional landed elites and the newer mining and commercial interests shared a similar stake in Chile's export economy.[2] Divisions emerged primarily over a series of issues related to the expansion of a centralized secular state. By the mid-1850s, local notables and the church had become increasingly alarmed over the central state's penetration of society. The revolt of 1891 was aimed in large measure at returning autonomy to local leaders.[3] Though the revolt undermined presidential authority, it did not destroy the commitment to representative institutions. The Parliament grew in prestige and influence, in turn contributing to the expansion of stable political party networks. Unlike their neighbors in Argentina, by the turn of the century Chilean middle-class parties had become full participants in the governing process. They emerged before the development of a strong bureaucracy and the push for mass participation and became the key brokers tying political clienteles to the emerging state apparatus.[4]

Though parties were instrumental in channeling and controlling mobilization and moderating political conflict among elites, it must be stressed that

This study was first presented at the conference on "Breakdowns and Crises of Democratic Regimes," Yale University, 10–15 December 1973.

i

Chilean democracy was hardly characterized by social peace. Large portions of the population were excluded from active citizenship and the incipient working-class movement was at times brutally repressed.[5] Political democracy never really meant social democracy, as sharp inequality and a meager standard of living for the vast majority of the population continued to be important features of Chilean society. Nevertheless, the openness of the rules of competitive politics and the legitimacy of institutions did allow for the rise of Marxist electoral parties with roots in the urban and mining proletariat. In turn, the support of the Left gave middle-class parties the necessary impetus to achieve control of the government and to bring about a whole array of reforms that benefited the working class. The rise of a strong Left clearly polarized Chilean politics, but the Marxist parties abided by Chilean rules of the game, gaining considerable electoral strength by mid-century.[6] In the 1960s significant reforms, particularly in the rural areas, further consolidated the growing gains of previously excluded elements.

The purpose of this study is to analyze why and how Chilean democracy broke down. In so doing, it will describe in as much detail as strictly necessary the political events during the period just before the coup d'état—stressing the positions of the key actors and the impact of political as well as economic developments on the final outcome. The study, however, cannot restrict itself merely to a review of the important events in the months before the breakdown. A description of the Allende years must be preceded by a careful analysis of the principal characteristics of Chilean politics at mid-century. Only with a prior understanding of the main features of the political system is it possible to draw on the Chilean experience to make meaningful observations about the functioning and crises of competitive democratic regimes. This is true for three reasons. In the first place, without knowledge of the nature of the system which broke down, it is difficult to judge whether the breakdown constitutes a fundamental crisis of regime or is merely another in the series of recurring "crises" which continually characterize some political systems. Secondly, a description of the system is a prerequisite to a full understanding of the principal factors or developments which are at the root of the breakdown. Is it underlying stress in the political system itself which precipitates or exacerbates the crisis? Or is the crisis primarily the result of socioeconomic difficulties around the time of military intervention? Alternatively, is the crisis due to the mistakes and irresponsibility of key political personalities? If several factors are involved, how do they relate to one another? It follows that it is only with a thorough consideration of the principal dimensions of the political system that one can ascertain the extent to which they define or shape the actions of individuals and groups, leaders and followers. In the final analysis, we need to know what range there is for human choice. To what extent were the actors in the human drama destined to live out their fate—or to what extent could they have chosen a different denouement?

It soon became clear in completing the research for this project that while the background of the Chilean system could be presented in essentially static terms, the process of breakdown could only be analyzed in a dynamic fashion. This is the reason for the largely chronological organization of the work. In the fast-moving and changing context of Chilean politics the principal factors and characteristics of the system could change significantly at any point in time. The process was dialectical. Actions by one set of actors within the framework of rules and institutions at time A were followed by counter-actions by others which not only affected the correlation of forces but changed the very rules of the game for time B. The system which had existed in 1971 was a different one after the October 1972 strike and the incorporation of the military into the cabinet. There was also a fundamental change after the March 1973 elections and the 29 June 1973 coup attempt. Unfortunately for those wishing to avoid a much more devastating ''fate'' than a representative democratic regime, as the system evolved the range of choice was also diminished and the outcome became more and more certain.

It is the principal thesis of this work that the main characteristic of the Chilean system by mid-twentieth century was a marked political polarization. Conflict and confrontation were mediated by a web of institutions and through the verdict of an electoral system which defined the power capabilities of political groups. Polarization was initially restricted to elites; as time went on it became increasingly pervasive. Polarization was aggravated by the loss of a pragmatic Center coalition and the rise of an ideological Center party under the Christian Democrats. Political competition preceded and indeed accelerated class competition. In turn, the economic crisis followed the political crisis, rather than vice versa. Certain characteristics of the Chilean institutional arena, including winner-take-all elections, contributed to a centrifugal tendency (to use Giovanni Sartori's term) which placed great stress on the whole system.

The Chilean case supports Juan Linz's contention that it is not the actions of the extreme forces on the Right and Left per se which have brought down democratic regimes.[7] Certainly their actions were profoundly disruptive and created extraordinary difficulties for those who believed that change could be brought about within traditional institutional parameters. But the extremes were a constant in the political system. The actual breakdown was more the result of the inability of centrist forces—of democrats on both sides of the divided political system—to see the logic of escalating crisis, or for that matter, foresee the dire consequences of a repressive authoritarian regime. As group stakes, narrow stakes, prevailed, the room for maneuvering was drastically reduced. The outcome that all secretly dreaded, but refused to face, came to pass.

This study challenges some fashionable assumptions about the Chilean case and democratic regimes in general. The fact that centrist elements did not succeed in structuring agreements to save the system does not mean that the outcome was inevitable. The constraints were often formidable and became increasingly so. But there was room for action to save the system at critical junctures. It is a myth that the outcome would have been different had Allende taken the advice of the maximalists within his own coalition and sought to accelerate a violent class confrontation. Such a strategy would merely have hastened the coup d'état by undermining the traditional system even sooner. It is also a myth that change and progressive policies would have been impossible within the framework of ongoing institutions. Certainly the kinds of fundamental transformations that some sectors sought would have been impossible. But they would have been extraordinarily difficult to achieve, given the short time span, in any regime, even the most progressive. The sad irony is that today not only has the hope of fundamental transformation vanished for the foreseeable future, but much of the genuine progress which Chile made over the years has been severely undermined. The worst myth of all is that the working class in Chile had not made any real progress. Much blood and suffering went into the accumulation of the victories of the Chilean working class. Though narrow in scope, those victories loom as monumental ones in the context of a regime which today deprives the population of fundamental human rights and has led the country back into the early twentieth century in social rights.

But is is also a myth that democracy is a failure because it inevitably allows for the rise of progressive forces capable of consolidating substantial electoral support. Those who condemn Chilean institutions and procedures for having allowed "foreign" influences to enter Chilean political life fail to see how integral those forces were in Chilean society and how great a stake they had in the system. By interpreting the breakdown of democracy as inevitable, these sinister forces can more easily justify the injustices and abuses of the present. This author hopes that other observers, in other times and places, will draw the basic lesson from the Chilean case. Democracy is a system difficult to create, perhaps more difficult to preserve. Given the alternative of authoritarianism, every effort to maintain democracy is well worth the price.

I have benefited greatly from the help of many people in completing this study. My greatest debt is to the many Chilean politicians, officials, and observers who gave freely of their time to tell me their versions of what happened. For many the process of thinking about and remembering what happened in Chile is a painful one. I am deeply grateful for our open and candid conversations which enabled me to piece together aspects of the tragic puzzle, even if incompletely. Several of my sources will, and already have, disagreed strongly with some of the judgments in this study. I am, of course, solely responsible for these judgments.

Interviewees ranged from a former president and former cabinet officers in the Frei and Allende administrations, to ex-middle level leaders such as congressmen, agency heads and sub-heads, and labor leaders, to former municipal and local party officials in Santiago and in a sample of eight communities in southern Chile. In addition the author benefited from numerous conversations with colleagues in Chile, the United States, and Europe who have followed Chilean developments closely for years. The interviews in Chile were conducted in July 1972, February 1974, and during a longer stay in Chile from July 1974 to January 1975. The first part of the study also draws extensively on field research conducted in Chile during 1969. Many of the interviewees requested anonymity. Because of the brutality of repression under the military junta, I have decided for the time being not to reveal the names of those interviewed. At least one of those interviewed was brutally assassinated and others have been arrested or harrassed. Sections of the study which draw primarily from interview sources have been identified. Because so much of the Chilean political debate was reported openly and fully, if not accurately, by the free press, it has been possible to use public sources for the bulk of the study.

I would like to acknowledge publicly the continued guidance which I have received from J. Samuel Valenzuela in the long and arduous process of writing this book. His keen judgment, his genuine concern, and his candid appraisals have been invaluable assets. He shares with me whatever there is of value in this work but is exonerated from any shortcomings. My father, Raimundo Valenzuela, also provided indispensable encouragement. His incisive reading of an earlier draft of the manuscript and his encyclopedic knowledge of Chilean affairs saved me from numerous serious errors. From the very inception of this project, Juan Linz and Alfred Stepan have provided help and support. The Chilean case reveals how accurate and perceptive were many of Juan Linz's generalizations about the nature of crisis in democratic regimes. Alfred Stepan not only provided intellectual advice but also ensured that the project of which this study is a part reached publication. Henry Y. K. Tom of the Johns Hopkins University Press has been patient and understanding.

The completion of this book would have been difficult without the generous support of the Committee on Latin America of the Social Science Research Council, which enabled me to spend several months in Chile in 1974, and the continuous support of the Duke University Research Council, which made it possible to complete much of the quantitative analysis.

The Breakdown
of Democratic Regimes
CHILE

)

1.
Chilean Politics at Mid-Century

The Party System

Students of Latin American politics have often observed that Chile's political system was significantly different from those found on the rest of the continent. As Federico Gil has noted, in his basic work on Chilean politics, this distinctiveness was due in large measure to Chile's party system, "where political forces [were] clearly and distinctly aligned, as in many European countries." As Gil says, "the resemblance of the Chilean party system to that of much of Europe, and particularly to the system which existed in France during the Third and Fourth republics, is striking."[1] Chile's party system was everywhere, not only determining the political recruitment process for important national posts but also structuring contests in such diverse institutions as government agencies, professional and industrial unions, neighborhood organizations, and even local high schools. Parties were so much a feature of national life that in a survey conducted in Santiago, only 22.2 percent of Santiago residents felt parties could be dispensed with in governing the country.[2]

An important characteristic of the Chilean party system was its high degree of competitiveness. In the 1930s there were over thirty party organizations. Changes in the electoral law and the consolidation of party strengths had reduced that number to ten by 1970.[3] Despite the decline in the number of parties, no Chilean party has received more than 30 percent of the vote in either a congressional or a municipal election since the adoption of the 1925 constitution.[4] The only exceptions occurred in the 1965 and 1967 congressional and municipal elections, in which the Christian Democrats obtained 42.3 percent and 35.6 percent respectively, only to see their percentage of the vote decline in subsequent contests. These national figures mask the fact that parties structured competition even in the smallest and most backward municipalities. Analysis of aggregate data shows that the fractionalization of the vote did not vary much, controlling either for size or level of socioeconomic development of communities. Furthermore, the contest for local office was as intense and competitive as the contest for the national legislature.[5]

3

In 1970, this system was composed of five major parties and several minor parties spanning the ideological spectrum. The Right comprised the National party, formed in 1966 by a fusion of the traditional Conservatives and Liberals in an effort to overcome a steady erosion of their electoral fortunes. Though committed to the Chilean rules of the democratic game (which they had helped to shape), the Nationals were also clearly committed to the prevailing Chilean socioeconomic system, which had given their leaders positions of wealth and status in society.[6] The Left in Chile was dominated by the Communist and Socialist parties. The former was the largest Communist party in Latin America outside Cuba, and it adhered closely to Moscow's directions. The Socialist party, which had been racked by dissension since its creation, had a more heterogeneous base than the Communists. After years of bitter rivalry, interrupted by occasional agreements, the two Marxist parties instituted an alliance in 1956 known as the Frente de Acción Popular (FRAP), which backed Salvador Allende's unsuccessful candidacy for the presidency in 1958. The FRAP served as the immediate forerunner of the Popular Unity coalition, which in 1970 finally succeeded in electing Allende to the nation's highest office.[7]

The Center was occupied by the anticlerical Radicals—once the dominant party of the Chilean political system—which saw its role diminish markedly, first with the rise of Carlos Ibañez's populism in the 1950s and then with the rise of the Christian Democratic party in the 1960s. The Christian Democrats surged into prominence as a reform movement of the Center, advocating a "revolution in liberty." Fear of Allende's Marxist supporters contributed to a heavy Christian Democratic vote in the 1964 presidential election. However, the party's strength quickly eroded as both Right and Left increased their share of the electorate toward the end of Eduardo Frei's term in office.[8]

It is apparent that Chile's party system was not only highly competitive but also highly polarized. A substantial portion of the electorate either supported parties committed to a radical transformation of the social and political structures or parties vehemently opposed to any change in the status quo. The 1958 Santiago survey cited earlier revealed that 31.4 percent of the respondents classified themselves as rightists, and 24.5 percent classified themselves as leftists. A smaller number, 17.8 percent, placed themselves in the center of the political spectrum, while a quarter of the respondents gave no specific answer. As table 1 shows, with the exception of the small upper-class group, all of the class categories showed evidence of significant polarization. James Prothro and Patricio Chaparro have compared the Hamuy findings with more recent survey data and concluded that this distribution of public opinion on a Left-Right continuum remained markedly stable from 1958 to 1970.[9] The polarization of Chilean politics is also clearly evident in the verdict of the electorate. Under the proportional representation system of the 1925 constitution, the Socialist and Communist parties made steady headway, particularly

Table 1. Self-identification of Chileans as to Political Preference and Social Class

SOCIAL CLASS

Political Preference	Upper		Upper-Middle		Lower-Middle		Working		No Answer		Total	
	N	%	N	%	N	%	N	%	N	%	N	%
Right	11	78.6	67	33.0	98	32.8	60	29.4	17	54.8	253	31.4
Center	3	21.4	63	31.0	59	19.7	19	9.6	0	0.0	144	17.8
Left	0	0.0	37	18.2	58	19.4	100	31.1	3	9.7	198	24.5
Other	0	0.0	4	2.0	4	1.3	3	0.7	1	3.2	12	1.5
No answer	0	0.0	32	15.8	80	26.8	78	29.2	10	32.3	200	24.8
Total in sample	14		203		299		250		31		807	

SOURCE: International Data Library and Reference Service, Survey Research Center, ''1958 Presidential Election Survey in Santiago, Chile'' (University of California, Berkeley).

in urban and mining communities, while the Right continued to dominate Chile's backward rural areas and maintain the allegiance of many groups of the growing middle-class sector. Over the last thirty years the Right obtained an average of about 30 percent of the vote to the Left's 20 percent—though by 1973 increasing support for the Left had reversed those proportions. Table 2 shows divisions of the Chilean electorate in all congressional elections from 1937 to 1973, underscoring the continued polarization. The table shows that parties of the Center surged at the expense of both Right and Left; but, except in the 1965 contest, they never received more than 50 percent of the suffrage. Over time, three important centrist tendencies can be noted. The first was that of the Radical party, which dominated Chilean politics from 1938 to 1952. Though it allied with the Left to gain the presidency in the 30s and 40s, it became increasingly concerned over the rising strength of the Communists, particularly after the 1947 municipal election.[10] As a result, the Communist party was declared illegal and the Radical party veered sharply to the Right. This event, and many years in the presidential palace, took its toll on the increasingly weak centrist party.[11] The Radicals were replaced as the Center by the dramatic ascendancy of former-president Carlos Ibañez, who won the presidency in 1952 at the head of a disparate coalition of groups ranging from the radical wing of the Socialist party to elements tied closely to the Chilean Nazi movement. Ibañez's centrist movement, however, did not survive his own directionless administration, and by the end of his term the Left, including the now-legal Communist party, had regained its electoral strength.[12] With the demise of the Ibañez coalition, the Christian Democrats became the new centrist movement, this time drawing primarily on support from the Right. As noted above, by the end of the 1960s its impressive support had also withered.

Table 2. Percentage of Vote Received by Parties on the Right, Center, and Left in Chilean Congressional Elections, 1937 to 1973

DIPUTADO ELECTIONS

Percentage of Total Vote

Party	1937	1941	1945	1949	1953	1957	1961	1965	1969	1973	Mean
Right (Conservative, Liberal, National after 1965)	42.0	31.2	43.7	42.0	25.3	33.0	30.4	12.5	20.0	21.3	30.1
Center (Radical, Falangist, Christian Democrats, Agrarian Laborist)	28.1	32.1	27.9	46.7	43.0	44.3	43.7	55.6	42.8	32.8	39.7
Left (Socialist, Communist)	15.4	33.9	23.1	9.4	14.2	10.7	22.1	22.7	28.1	34.9	21.5
Other	14.5	2.8	5.3	1.9	17.5	12.0	3.8	9.2	9.1	11.0	8.7

SOURCE: Dirección del Registro Electoral, Santiago, Chile.

Giovanni Sartori, drawing on his studies of Italian politics, has stressed the importance of polarization and the role of centrist parties in understanding the dynamics of a multi-party system.[13] Sartori argues that in a highly polarized context, with a clearly defined Right and Left commanding substantial percentages of the electorate, the principal drive of the political system will be centrifugal. This means that a polarized system has a tendency to move toward the extremes—toward greater divisions in the society. Unlike party systems which have avoided the emergence of clearly opposing tendencies, a polarized party system has no strong centripetal drive—no dominant centrist consensus. Ironically, polarized systems do have Center poles occupied by one or more parties. However, Sartori argues, under such circumstances the Center does not represent a significant political tendency in itself but tends to be composed of fragments emanating from both the Left and the Right poles. Sartori notes that the "center is mainly a feedback of the centrifugal drives which predominate in the system" and is "more a negative convergence, a sum of exclusions, than a positive agency of instigation."[14] Sartori's analysis is extremely helpful in understanding the Chilean case, because it explains the repeated surge of centrist movements in Chilean politics which rose at the expense of both Right and Left. Since these centrist movements only minimally represented a viable centrist tendency and were in fact primarily reflections of the erosion of the two extreme poles, they have crumbled, only to make way for a new centrist coalition. The instability of centrist movements, in turn, contributed to difficulties in structuring common public policies because of the resulting fragility of centrist consensus at the decision-making level. The erosion of centrist consensus would accelerate dramatically during the Allende years and contribute directly to the crisis culminating in regime breakdown.

It is important to stress that the polarized party system had a different impact in Chile's presidential system than it did in the Italian parliamentary system which Sartori studies. Despite competitiveness, polarization, and the instability of centrist options, the government in Chile was not in danger of "falling" if it failed to gain, or lost, majority support in the legislature. By the same token, coalitions, which were formed in the legislature after a parliamentary election in Italy, had to be structured before the presidential election in Chile. As noted above, no single party or tendency was capable of winning the presidency on its own. Either the presidency was won by a small plurality or shifting centrist groups became the key to the election. Candidates of the Center were elected with support from the Left in the presidential elections of 1938 and 1946; with support from the Right in 1932 and 1964; and with support from both sides in 1952. Only on two occasions during that period did the presidency go to a candidate representing the Right or Left; in 1958, when the Conservative Jorge Alessandri was elected, and in 1970, when the Marxist Salvador Allende won. In both cases the poles rejected compromise and the parties of the Center mistakenly thought they would succeed on their own. The Chilean political system was able to cope successfully with Alessandri's rightist presidency, for soon centrist groups joined his administration. As will be seen below, a centrist coalition was never successfully structured during the Allende years.

Since preelection coalitions were constituted primarily for electoral reasons, in an atmosphere of considerable political uncertainty, they tended to disintegrate after a few months of the new administration. Ideological disputes were often at the root of coalition changes, as partisans of one formula would resist the proposals of other partisans. But narrow political considerations were also important. The president could not succeed himself, and it soon became apparent to the leadership of other parties in his own coalition that they could best improve their fortunes in succeeding municipal and congressional elections by dissociating themselves from the difficulties of incumbency in a society fraught with economic problems. For in the final analysis, only by proving electoral strength in subsequent elections in which parties ran on their own could a party demonstrate its value to future presidential coalitions. Erosion of preelection coalitions inevitably led to new temporary alliances with parties and groups willing to provide congressional and general political support to the executive in exchange for presidential concessions. President Gonzalez Videla turned to the Liberals after he dissolved his alliance with the Communists. Carlos Ibañez also turned to the Right when he accepted the support of the Conservative party at a critical point in the mid-1950s. President Alessandri, elected by the Right, was finally forced to make an agreement with the centrist Radicals to maintain a workable administration. Elections were clearly characterized by the politics of outbidding, since the fate of a government did not hang on a lost vote. Parties went out of their way to criticize incumbents and would seize on every inflationary increase, every incident of police repression, every allegation of partisan or corrupt practice in an effort to pave the way for a better showing at the polls. The rhetoric of the party-controlled press and of the skilled orators of the party leadership occasionally reached frenzied proportions. In such an atmosphere, centrist parties with basically pragmatic orientations, who shifted from support to opposition and then again to support of an incumbent, suffered politically. Perhaps even more than in a parliamentary system, the forces of "polarized pluralism" contributed to further polarization with their centrifugal tendencies.

Paradoxically, in light of this discussion of competitiveness and polarization, the Chilean party system was also characterized by the central importance of particularistic transactions involving small rewards and payoffs for political support. Elected officials from all groups and factions spent a major part of their waking moments obtaining pensions for widows, jobs for school teachers, higher salary increases for unions or trade associations, bridges for local municipalities, and a host of other favors either by acting directly or by serving as intermediaries before the complex and ubiquitous state bureaucracy. In Chile, the advent of the politics of ideology and program did not erode the particularisitc politics of earlier years; it merely added a new dimension to the political system.

In analytical terms, we can think of the party system as being divided into two distinct arenas.[15] In the central arena, with its primary locus in the capital city, major controversies over matters such as redistributive legislation, the survival of presidential cabinets, and the structuring of new presidential alliances clearly predominated. The principal actors were ministers, high-level bureaucrats, party officials, youth leaders, and congressmen. Many of these leaders owed their careers either directly or indirectly to support from the small group of party activists and militants who controlled party organizations. Some national figures, such as Eduardo Frei and Salvador Allende, operated almost exclusively in this arena, paying little attention to the more mundane side of politics. Others, including most congressmen not occupying major party roles, straddled both arenas, often with considerable difficulty.

By contrast, in the local arena, at the grass-roots of the political system, payoffs and political favors were the primary stuff of politics. Indeed, much of the Chilean style of electoral campaigning depended on the face to face contact between candidates and supporters aimed at translating particularistic favors into votes and party loyalty. Candidates for congressional offices with large constituencies made widespread use of lower-level brokers such as municipal councillors in consolidating their own support. In return, local brokers could expect that the congressman or senator would help to satisfy his own client's needs, either directly, by acting as an intermediary with the bureaucracy, or by congressional action. The local arena was not restricted only to individualistic demands. It also included the demands of a multitude of organized groups, most of which had close party ties. In Chile, private sector groups ranged from professional associations, business organizations, and student and youth groups to labor unions, church groups, and local neighborhood councils.

Most of these groups were organized into national confederations. For example, professional societies created the Confederation of Professional Associations, which was mandated to defend the interest of all university-trained professionals before the government and the public at large. The powerful Society for Industrial Advancement (SOFOFA) included many regional industrial groups as well as individual members and claimed to represent most of Chilean private industry.[16] Labor unions of private and public employees and farm workers were also organized into various national confederations, most of which were in turn affiliated with the *Central Unica de Trabajadores*.[17] The agrarian reform process begun during the Frei administration added a whole new array of rural unions, cooperatives, and *asentamientos* to this vast institutional structure.

Whether it was a particular business seeking tax relief, a union organization seeking the establishment of a pension fund, a professional association after legal recognition, or a municipality after a new dam, political leaders and officials were continuously besieged by an overwhelming number of petitions. Parties were without question the key networks for processing demands, often by channeling them up through different levels of the party hierarchy. As noted above, congressmen were the most important national brokers and were the primary link between the two arenas.[18]

This dual system, with roots in the patron-client politics of the parliamentary republic at the turn of the century, was continually reinforced by the highly centralized nature of the Chilean political and administrative system and the very scarce resources of its weak economy.[19] The system was also reinforced by various aspects of the electoral system, notably the absence of cumulative voting in Chile's modified version of the D'Hondt proportional representation system. Though each party presented a list, which could include as many candidates as there were seats, voters could cast their votes for only one candidate. The total vote for all candidates on each list was used to decide how many seats a particular party could fill. If a party was entitled to one or more seats, those candidates receiving the highest individual vote would take those seats.[20] Candidates were thus running not only against candidates of opposition parties but against candidates on their own party list, attempting to insure the highest plurality. Followers, committed to a party for ideological or traditional reasons, often chose their particular candidate over others on the party slate, depending on his or her ability to deliver the particularistic goods.

In the absence of adequate survey data, it is difficult to ascertain the relative importance of particularistic services and ideological commitments in cementing party loyalty and determining electoral behavior. Undoubtedly, both elements interacted with others, such as traditional party identification and reference group influence, and had differing effects on different voting groups. What is important to stress, given the central role of particularistic transactions in Chilean politics, is that party polarization was not due solely to underlying ideological cleavages in society. A very important factor in shaping and perpetuating continued polarization was the sharp ideological polarization characteristic of the central arena. It was the highly ideological political elites, in control of powerful party organizations, who structured the options of the electorate. Small parties, independent candidates, and fractions of former parties had little chance of surviving. Many citizens were committed to particular options, either because of clientelistic politics, ideological proclivities, or both. For that reason alone, the structuring of new options would have been enormously difficult. What made it virtually impossible to break out of the polarized system was the increased polarization among party activists, who in turn, and in a somewhat circular fashion, further polarized the system at the mass level. Thus, for example, the decline of the Christian Democrats was not due only to loss of support among the populace because the party represented a dubious centrist tendency. It was also reinforced by repeated party splits at the elite level, followed by actual defections by elements who wanted to identify more closely with Marxist parties. This undermined any possibility of capitalizing on the party's fragile strength in order to become a viable Center. The sharp polarization in the 1960s among activists in the Radical party, which made the two principal factions practically indistinguishable from the two extreme poles of the party system and led to the formation of two parties, the Radical and the Radical Democracy parties, helped to preclude any comeback of the Radicals as either a centrist tendency or a Center pole.

This description of the Chilean party system parallels in some respects Duncan MacRae's description of the French system under the Fourth Republic. MacRae maintains that the sharp divisions in French politics were not simply a reflection of sharp societal divisions. Certainly latent divisions existed and exist today in French society, but as MacRae notes, they "constituted a permissive but not sufficient condition for political division." Actual political divisiveness depended on other factors and especially on "the existence of sets of intermediate political leaders divided on national issues, talking of national problems in different terms from one another, and not interpenetrating with one another."[21] In Chile, as in France, the polarized group of activists sought to channel the latent divisions in society with both programmatic and particularistic strategies, reinforcing polarization of the entire system.

The importance of particularistic transactions and the attachment of many voters to parties because of a traditional identification that often spanned several generations helps to explain a final feature of the Chilean party system: its heterogeneous base of support. In turn, the heterogeneous base of support further reinforced the important role of particularistic transactions, as party leaders sought to retain the allegiance of sectors actively being wooed by elements claiming to better represent their interests. Clearly the Socialist and Communist parties received a significant portion of their support from organized working-class elements. This was due to growing class consciousness as well as the simple fact that leftist parties were the first to move in and provide services and benefits to previously disenfranchised urban and mining groups. By the same token, the National party drew the strongest support from the most privileged sectors of society. And yet survey research shows that most parties, particularly the centrist and rightist parties, had cross-class support, drawing substantial votes from both urban and rural low income sectors. Thus Alejandro Portes, in his study of squatter settlements in Santiago in 1969, found that the Christian Democratic party received as much support from low income groups as did the Communists and Socialists combined.[22] The Hamuy survey, conducted in 1958, reported similar findings: a substantial portion of the population in working-class categories supported the Right. And yet the Hamuy data, presented in table 3, also reveal a sizable proportion of university-trained professionals and middle-level managers who were more likely to support the Left than the Right. Only unskilled workers, small businessmen, and managers of large business concerns indicated political leanings more consistent with expected class interests. Aggregate data analysis, while confirming that the Left drew more from working-class sectors and the Right from upper-class groups, also lends support to the finding that much of the support was quite heterogeneous. As table 4 notes, working-class categories did not explain a substantial amount of the variance in party vote for any party, with the exception of the Communists, whose vote was heavily determined by the mining population.[23] These findings further support the notion that polarization in Chile, though channeling and to a great degree reflecting latent societal cleavages, was more directly influenced by the polarization of options as structured by the elites and party militants.

The Institutional Context and the Rules of the Game

Chilean politics was characterized by a highly competitive and polarized party system. In such an atmosphere, centrist consensus was always fragile, and coalitions disintegrated with ease, as parties and groups struggled to

Table 3. Distribution by Occupational Categories of Preference for the Political Right, Center, or Left of a Sample of Chileans in 1958

Political Preference	Domestic Servants		Unskilled Workers		Self-employed Workers		Skilled and Semi-skilled Workers		White-Collar Workers		Small Business-men		Middle Manager and Professionals		Large Company Managers		Not Ascertained		Total	
	N	%	N	%	N	%	N	%	N	%	N	%	N	%	N	%	N	%	N	%
Right	13	38.2	26	22.4	71	40.1	26	27.1	67	37.7	23	37.7	15	20.5	10	58.8	2	66.7	253	31.4
Center	2	5.9	11	9.5	22	12.4	9	9.4	58	25.2	19	31.1	20	27.4	3	17.6	0	0.0	144	17.8
Left	6	17.6	44	37.9	36	20.3	35	36.5	49	21.3	4	6.6	21	28.8	2	11.8	1	33.3	198	24.5
Other	0	0.0	1	0.9	2	1.1	1	1.0	3	1.3	2	3.3	3	4.1	0	0.0	0	0.0	12	1.5
Other and Not ascertained	13	38.2	34	29.3	46	26.0	25	26.0	53	23.0	13	21.3	14	19.2	2	11.8	0	0.0	200	24.8
Total	34	4.2	116	14.4	177	21.9	96	11.9	230	28.5	61	7.6	73	9.0	17	2.1	3	0.4	807	100.0

SOURCE: International Data Library and Reference Service, Survey Research Center, "1958 Presidential Election Survey in Santiago, Chile," (University of California, Berkeley).

Table 4. Variation in the Vote for Each Major Chilean Party or Alliance in a National and a Local Election Explained by Socioeconomic Indicators (in percentages)

Election	Nationals	Radicals	Christian Democrats	Communists	Socialists
Congressional election of 1969	28.3	8.5	18.5	22.6	9.8
Municipal election of 1967	22.8	13.5	17.1	40.0	12.2

SOURCE: Electoral data from the Dirección del Registro Electoral, Santiago, Chile.

NOTES: N = 287 communes.

Coefficients of determination (R²) expressed in percentage form. All multiple correlation coefficients (R) significant at .001 level.

The independent variables are medical assistance, homes with bathrooms, school attendance, population in industry, population in construction, population in services, population in mining, instruction, and population size. The dependent variables are the percentages of the vote which each party or alliance received in each election and in each commune.

outbid each other in gaining the favor of the electorate. Yet it would be seriously misleading to describe Chilean politics only in terms of parties and groups, leaders and followers. Ideological confrontations and group demands should not obscure the fact that the Chilean political system was also highly institutionalized. Strong governmental institutions played key roles in the public policy-making process, and most relevant political actors accepted the validity of both codified rules and procedures and a host of informal practices which had evolved over generations to rationalize the political process.

The Chilean state consisted of an awesome set of structures and institutions. Even before the election of Salvador Allende to the presidency, the state played a greater role in the nation's economy than it did in the economy of any other Latin American country with the exception of Cuba. By the end of the 1960s direct public investment represented well over 50 percent of all the gross investment, and the state controlled over 50 percent of all credit. Furthermore, the government accounted for 14 percent of the GNP and 13 percent of the economically active population.[24] A state agency, the *Corporación de Fomento de la Producción* (CORFO), owned shares in eighty of the country's most important enterprises and institutions, and majority shares in thirty-nine of the same.[25] Most private groups and institutions were closely regulated by the state and relied on its favorable dispensations. Not only did it chart the course for economic growth and control prices, it also ran the major social security programs and had a dominant role in collective bargaining.

But the important point about the Chilean institutional system is not only its size. The key point is that Chilean politics were not praetorian politics. Unlike the politics of some of its neighbors, Chilean politics did not involve the naked confrontation of political forces, each seeking to maximize its own stakes through direct action in the face of transitory authority structures incapable of guarding, even in the most elementary fashion, the public good.[26] Elected and nonelected officials, if not party militants, were able to put aside the acrimonious verbal assaults of afternoon political rallies and come together to structure compromises during the evening hours, whether in a congressional committee room or over a late meal in a Santiago restaurant. Bitter exchanges on the nature of the Cuban Revolution, the Vietnam War, the exploitation of workers, or copper nationalization gave way to hard-nosed bargaining on the next wage readjustment or budget supplement bill, or a joint strategy to obtain a new hospital for the community of Mulchen. At the same time, powerful state structures, largely insulated from political control and partisan battles, exercised important governmental functions drawing on formal authority and institutional clout. Thus the comptroller general could obtain the arrest of the mayor and all the municipal councillors of the city of Ancud for granting a Christmas bonus from a budget item designated for another purpose;[27] or the *Dirección del Trabajo* could institute a formidable array of rules and procedures for "conciliation" in order to resolve a labor dispute.[28]

It is beyond the scope of this work to provide a detailed description of the Chilean institutional context.[29] However, before turning to a discussion of the "rules of the game," noting the key role of the legislature in the political process, a brief mention of the most prominent institutions is in order.

In addition to the president and Congress, the Chilean constitution specified two additional branches of government, the court system and the *Contraloría General de la República*. The courts had a long tradition of independence from the executive and constituted a bulwark for the protection and interpretation of a highly detailed legal code dedicated in large measure to the preservation of traditional institutions and economic relations. Appointments at all levels of the hierarchy were based on seniority and merit and were determined by the institution itself, as the executive could choose the appointee only from lists submitted to him by the courts. Supreme Court justices were appointed for life, and the court alone had the power to remove judges for malfeasance. Though the court's power of judicial review was limited in comparison to that of the U.S. Supreme Court, the court could declare unconstitutional a legislative act as applied to a specific case.[30]

One of the most unusual branches of the Chilean government was its independent *Contraloría*. An agency with a career staff composed of over 750 civil servants and a director appointed for life, the Contraloría was charged with a variety of functions, ranging from audits of public accounts to ruling on the legality of executive decrees and issuing advisory opinions on the constitutionality of proposed congressional legislation. Unlike the courts, which intervened once litigation was instituted, the Contraloría gave its opinions in response to informal requests by elected officials of opposition groups and private parties. A prestigious organization, the Contraloría commanded respect from most Chilean civil servants, who feared its scrupulous championship of legalism and frugality, sometimes maintained at the expense of rationality and fairness. A public official who erred in the expenditure of public funds could be suspended by the Contraloría and asked to replace misapplied monies. If there were any criminal, as opposed to administrative, wrongdoing, the functionary could be prosecuted in the courts by the Contraloría.

The president, with the unanimous concurrence of his cabinet, could insist on implementing any decree declared illegal by the Contraloría (decree of insistence), except in matters of public expenditures. But this was done only very rarely as it left cabinet members open to possible congressional accusations which could result in removal from office. In a society with numerous and complex laws and sharp ideological divisions, an agency such as the Contraloría had evolved as an interpreter of existing legislation as well as a "guarantor" of legalism.[31]

Perhaps even more important for the purposes of the argument at hand than the autonomy of the other "coequal" branches of government was the marked autonomy of many agencies and organizations within the executive branch itself.[32] What was striking about the Chilean bureaucracy was not how much power it gave the chief executive but how difficult it was for him to control its day-to-day activities. This was so because most public institutions lay outside the executive chain of command in the "decentralized agencies." Such entities determined much of their own budgets and controlled their own hiring practices even though they were nominally controlled by one of the fourteen government ministries. Forty percent of all public employees in Chile worked for the more than fifty semiautonomous bureaus. They generally provided the bulk of economic and social services in areas such as agriculture, housing, social security, and economic development. While they willingly accepted any efforts by the administration to increase their jurisdiction and functions, they strongly resisted attempts to decrease them or to change in any dramatic way the nature of programming and the style of action. Many of the Christian Democrats' innovative programs in housing and urban development were thwarted by the unwillingness of semiautonomous agencies to follow changed guidelines for programming and investments.[33]

By law a president could not remove civil servants in order to replace them with a new cadre more congenial to his policy objectives. New presidents were thus forced to create new agencies to carry out their programs. Often a new agency would duplicate the tasks of an older one, further complicating the problem of coordination and intensifying the competition for a share of the limited governmental budget.[34]

Another characteristic of Chilean institutions which simultaneously reinforced this autonomy and contributed to the "institutionalization" of decision-making was the formal inclusion of private interests in state boards and agencies. The result was that key areas of the economy were dominated by essentially "private" governments. The boards of many government agencies included one-third representation from private interests, one-third from technical experts, and one-third from the government. According to one study, during the period 1958–64 the four most powerful business organizations had voting membership in all the major financial and policy institutions, including the Central Bank, the State Bank, and CORFO.[35] Each business group had voting power on the government bureaus relevant to their particular economic sector. Before the Agrarian Reform Law was passed in 1966, it was difficult to carry out any initiatives in rural reform because 30 percent of the vote in the key agencies was controlled by economic interests that would be adversely affected by reforms.[36] The Frei government moved to give more effective representation in these state agencies to organizations of the middle and working classes.

The intermingling of private and public in the state sector was also reinforced by the existence of strong professional associations and union organizations. In several important cases, professional groups had become influential in governmental agencies. Architects, for example, dominated the Ministry of Housing. The Ministry of Public Works was the almost exclusive fiefdom of civil engineers, and the Ministry of Agriculture was staffed by agronomists and a few veterinarians. A university degree in a particular field was sometimes a prerequisite for appointment or advancement in a given agency, thus guaranteeing privileged employment opportunities for a small group of individuals. The professional standards and outlooks of a particular association, in addition to its vested interests, contributed to the formation of public policy that was often quite different from that being advocated by the political executive and his allies.[37]

But the other countries in Latin America had also seen the rise of strong state institutions and a fragmented policy-making process without a lessening of praetorian political tendencies. The key to the Chilean system, which differentiated it sharply from that in countries like Argentina, was the continuing importance of political party networks and the existence of viable arenas of accommodation, notably the Parliament.[38] At first glance the parties seem to have been merely another layer of organization in the complex Chilean political pluralism. In fact, the party structures which permeated all levels of society were the crucial linkage mechanism binding organizations, institutions, groups, and individuals to the political center. Local units of all parties were active within each level of the bureaucracy, each labor union, each student federation, and each professional association. Parties often succeeded in capturing a particular organization or in setting up a rival one. Once an issue affecting the organization or group arose, the party structures were instrumental in conveying the demands of the organization or group to the nucleus of the policy-making process, where the legislature played a funda-mental role.

The Chilean Congress, as early as the 1850s, began to establish a tradition of independence from the executive when it delayed approval of the presiden-tial budget in exchange for concessions on other legislative matters.[39] Though it lost its position as the preeminent institution, which it had enjoyed for thirty years around the turn of the century, by mid-century it still was one of the strongest legislative bodies in the world. The Congress retained final authority over the approval of laws. It could create new programs, abolish old ones, and reduce or modify budgets. The legislature was instrumental in the creation of the complex and unwieldy social security system, and until the constitutional reforms of 1970 it was the key arena for negotiation on the all-important question of salary readjustment. The Senate could even block the president from traveling abroad, as it did during the Frei administration. Congressional committees not only played important roles in the drafting of legislation but served as investigatory bodies. It was in the halls of Congress or through the good offices of deputies or senators from all parties that key compromises were structured between the executive and the opposition on major policy matters such as agrarian reform and copper nationalization. And even more significantly for the stability of the system, it was in the legislature that disparate party factions reached compromises on less important issues of mutual benefit to constituents.

While the conciliation and compromise which took place in the chambers and meeting rooms of the Chilean Congress can be attributed in part to socialization of "institutional norms," shared norms were far less important in explaining the functioning of the system than were other factors. The continuing relevance of the legislature as an arena of compromise was due to the fact that no party or coalition was capable of displacing another. There simply were no giants in the system, and it was clearly to the benefit of all to work within the ongoing mechanisms rather than attempt to destroy them. This was the case because in the final analysis electoral success was the most important measure of a party's power. Additionally, each party and coalition required concrete benefits for supporters in order to maximize their electoral fortunes. The deadlock of political forces was thus accompanied by a strong need to process a whole array of favors for individuals and groups through party networks. The pragmatism of some of the parties of the Center facili-tated this process, but all parties had congressional specialists dealing in the mundane side of politics. As noted earlier, benefits were obtained not only through logrolling in the legislature but through direct appeals by individual legislators capable of approaching a bureaucracy sensitive to the influence of the Parliament and its leaders over budget allotments and staff positions. The overwhelming majority of legislators were convinced that they had to pay significant attention to this ''casework'' in order to ensure their own political careers and the viability of the electoral support of their parties.[40]

The fundamental issue around which much of the politics of conciliation revolved was the attainment by groups and individuals of their *reivindicaciones*, or just demands.[41] For the most part these involved wage readjustments, which are critical in an economy plagued by a high rate of inflation. Table 5 shows the annual variation of the consumer price index from 1952 to 1970. During the first three years of the decade inflation was relatively low, but it reached 46 percent in 1964 and averaged 25.7 percent over the ten-year period.[42] At the same time, Chile experienced a generally slow economic growth rate, with the per capita growth of the national product amounting to an estimated 1.6 percent from 1915 to 1964, though the industrial growth rate was 4.3 percent in the same period.[43] The latter index rose 7 percent in the early 1960s, only to decline to an average of 2.4 percent from 1967 to 1970. The distribution of income also remained sharply skewed, with 60 percent of the population commanding 28 percent of the national income and 14 percent commanding 42 percent. Indeed, the top 2 percent of the Chilean population enjoyed 12.5 percent of the nation's income. Consequently, the main preoccupation of labor unions and other private and public groups was the attainment of income readjustments commensurate with or possibly above the estimated increase in the cost of living. Inflation, therefore, set the basic parameters for the bargaining system. Since the government and its agencies regulated both salary and price increases, the battle over *reajustes* was fought in the public arena and the principal compromises were hammered out in the legislature.

Given the intensity of party polarization in Chile, it is quite likely that an institution like the Congress could not have been created in the mid-twentieth century. But the legislature as an arena of accommodation and as the principal focus of party politics had emerged before the polarization of the party system. It also predated the development of strong state institutions and a centralized bureaucracy.

This had a profound effect on future development. It meant that even with the development of bureaucratic agencies designed to foster economic development and redistribute wealth, political parties with legislative linkages continued to be the principal political networks of the system. Though legislators would increasingly be limited in their ability to generate resources in the Congress itself, they would continue to be the key brokers between constituents and the bureaucracy. By implication, this reinforced the viability of representative institutions. Where a strong bureaucracy emerged before a strong party system, as in Brazil and Argentina, the prospect for the development of informal or officially sponsored linkage networks without popular representation was much greater. Under such circumstances, the chances of maintaining or fostering democratic institutions was severely undermined.[44]

Table 5. Yearly Rates of Inflation, 1952 to 1970 (in percentages)

	Consumer Price Index, Retail		Consumer Price Index, Wholesale	
Year	Variation from December-December	Yearly Average Variation	Variation from December-December	Yearly Average Variation
1952	12.1	22.2	20.9	24.0
1953	56.1	25.3	35.2	23.0
1954	71.1	72.2	65.3	56.9
1955	83.8	75.1	82.8	76.3
1956	37.7	56.1	45.9	63.1
1957	17.3	26.8	34.5	43.2
1958	32.5	25.9	25.3	25.5
1959	33.3	38.6	25.2	30.0
1960	5.4	11.6	1.6	5.3
1961	9.7	7.7	1.6	0.8
1962	27.7	13.9	26.8	8.3
1963	45.4	44.3	45.4	53.7
1964	38.4	46.0	43.7	50.6
1965	25.9	28.8	24.5	24.4
1966	17.0	22.9	19.7	22.9
1967	21.9	18.1	19.8	19.3
1968	27.9	26.6	33.1	30.5
1969	29.3	30.6	39.4	36.5
1970	34.9	32.5	33.7	36.1

SOURCE: Data from Dirección de Estadística y Censos, found in Ricardo Ffrench-Davis, *Políticas económicas en Chile, 1952–1970* (Santiago: Ediciones Nueva Universidad, 1973), pp. 242–46. Ffrench-Davis has made some minor corrections in these figures. The official figures are being used for comparison purposes with the figures of the Allende years.

The existence of a viable legislature with a long tradition, the continuing polarization and competitiveness of Chilean politics, and the need to accommodate particularistic demands contributed to the perpetuation of a politics of accommodation and compromise. The polarization and competitiveness of Chilean party politics made accommodation necessary. The "clientelism" of electoral politics made it possible.

It was inevitable that in such a system of accommodation, change could only be incremental. Depending on the coalition, and the position of the centrist party of the moment, policies would be either reformist or oriented toward the status quo. Constant demands for particular rewards with the availability of resources for only a small number of new programs made it almost impossible to find adequate funding for long-range projects or dramatic new initiatives. A disparity existed in Chile between calls for structural change and transformation and the realities of an incrementalist bargaining system.[45] This disparity problably contributed to the pervasive feeling of permanent crisis in Chilean politics. And yet, because of the acceptance of votes as the key political currency of the system, the necessity of bargaining in a highly competitive, though polarized, atmosphere, and the weight of incrementalist decision-making itself, Chilean elites had been able in the past to conciliate their differences when serious confrontations seemed imminent.

Chilean Politics and the Chilean Military

In the comings and goings of Chilean politics, the armed forces were at the periphery of the political process. Not since the period 1924–31 had they actively intervened to determine the fate of governments. Even then, the armed forces ruled directly for a very short period of time. The administration of General Ibáñez from 1927 to 1931 was an elected government which relied on the tacit rather than the active support of the military. It was based more on the political figure of the leader than on the organized participation of the institution in the governing process.[46]

For the most part the officer corps interacted little with the leadership of social, economic, and political institutions.[47] Though respected as professional soldiers and as bearers of a glorious military tradition, they were generally looked down upon by other elites, who considered them narrow and uneducated.[48] That does not mean, however, that the military did not have influence over important policy areas, particularly those dealing with military affairs. Historically, the military has fared well in Chile. In recent years Chile ranked sixth in Latin America in per capita military expenditures and fifth in the size of the armed forces relative to the size of the population.[49]

A tradition of nonintervention in political affairs, however, should not be taken as proof that the Chilean military was above conspiratorial politics. In fact, in practically every administration since the 1930s there have been military incidents which revealed that sectors within the officer corps would have been happy to throw the politicians out. As recently as the mid-fifties a strong movement (the *Linea Recta*) developed in the army to obtain direct military rule with the support of President Ibáñez.[50] Historically, there has been continuous tension between the so-called *golpista* elements, who desire direct intervention, and "constitutionalists," who support the "neutrality" of the armed forces.

During the administrations of Jorge Alessandri and Eduardo Frei, civil-military relations deteriorated significantly. Military expenditures as a percentage of the national budget declined sharply from over 15 percent to an average of 9.8 percent in the Alessandri years and an average of 5.3 percent in the Frei years.[51] Open dissatisfaction with the government's "neglect" of the armed forces led to the resignation of the commander in chief of the navy in 1967. And on 21 October 1969 General Roberto Viaux moved troops from his Tacna regiment on the presidential palace, the first such act of direct military insubordination in decades. Though the movement was quickly put down, it clearly reflected the state of discontent within the military. Viaux, the commander in chief of the navy, and the head of the Santiago garrison of the army would later play important roles in a coup attempt staged shortly after Allende's election to prevent the Popular Unity government from taking office.[52]

For the most part, military officers in Chile probably shared the views of the former commander in chief of the Chilean army who noted that

not only the army, I guarantee, but all of the armed forces have a clear doctrine: military power is consciously subordinated to the political power, the Constitution and the laws. . . . Never could we intervene on our own, because we are disciplined. Furthermore, history demonstrates to us that never has that intervention been necessary, because our governors have a common sense and good judgment.[53]

The final remark is extremely instructive. Nonintervention was conditional on the performance of civilian elites, not on a clear principle of allegiance to civilian rule. Chilean military officers saw themselves as guardians of the constitution. In a survey conducted in 1967 among retired generals, 84 percent agreed (64 percent strongly) that the "military is necessary for the country even if there is no war in order to act as a guardian of the constitution in case a government tries to violate it." Only 16 percent of the officers interviewed disagreed with the statement.[54]

2.

The Late 1960s and the Election of Allende: Socioeconomic Change and Political Crisis

As Juan Linz has noted, the literature on the requisites for stable democracy and the causes of breakdown of democratic regimes has focused on underlying socioeconomic problems as the key independent variables. Without denying the importance of socioeconomic or structural factors, Linz has cautioned against this simple sociological determinism, which views politics as static and neglects to consider variables like leadership or to analyze the dynamics of the political process in explaining complex phenomena such as political breakdowns. Linz holds that the "structural characteristics of societies, the actual and latent conflicts, constitute a series of opportunities and constraints for the social and political actors, men and institutions, which can lead to one or another outcome. We shall start from the assumption that those actors have certain choices that can increase or lower the probability of the persistence and stability of a regime."[1]

This study has already described some of the principal structural characteristics of the Chilean political system at mid-century. It has noted the extent of party competitiveness and polarization, with its tendency to erode a working Center. It has highlighted the differentiation and autonomy of the institutional sector and described the accommodationist politics which resulted from political deadlock and the need to redistribute to diverse social forces the finite resources of a relatively poor society. In doing so, it stressed the precariousness of a political process in a situation where high levels of inflation had resulted from group demands which taxed the economic capabilities of the system. But Chile had survived for decades with such a system and had turned accommodationist politics into a fine art. Is it possible that a severe socioeconomic crisis had finally overwhelmed Chilean politics? Keeping in mind Juan Linz's warning, we cannot proceed without evaluating the socioeconomic dimensions of Chilean society in the period immediately preceding the election of Salvador Allende.

The literature suggests that at least two seemingly contradictory dimensions of economic change should be kept in mind in evaluating potential economic strains. In the first place, a marked decline in the economy, especially one following a period of significant improvement in standards of living, could contribute to a degree of societal frustration capable of undermining political authority.[2] Conversely, the second perspective argues that a sharp improvement in economic development could also disrupt political order. By undermining traditional social relations and encouraging new forms of mobilization, rapid economic change places demands on political institutions which exceed their capacity to respond.[3]

In examining the evidence for the Chilean case it will not be possible to present definitive conclusions about the impact of economic change on the political process. The theoretical literature in question has drawn primarily on retrospective analysis and provides no precise indication as to which of the many possible variables available are most important. Nor does it possess clear criteria on how much change must take place in the value of different indicators to reach the threshold of political breakdown. For this reason, much of the literature is tautological. Socioeconomic factors can be shown to be intense enough to cause a crisis only when a crisis has in fact occurred. Such a formulation leaves open the real possibility that other variables not considered in the analysis contributed to the final denouement.[4]

A resolution of these methodological and theoretical difficulties will of necessity entail further synchronic, and particularly diachronic, cross-national research. That does not mean, however, that in a case study such as this one we cannot come to a good judgment about the relative importance of economic versus political variables. By using time-series data we can evaluate whether changes in the values of certain indicators were greater in the period preceding the breakdown of regime than in previous periods not followed by political breakdown.

The Economic Evidence

An examination of a series of economic indicators for the six-year period preceding the election of Salvador Allende gives little indication of either serious economic decline or of explosive economic growth, with its disruptive potential. It is true that there was a mild recession in 1967, followed by slower rates of growth during the next two years than in the inaugural years of the Christian Democratic administration. However, what is striking about the Chilean data is how positive the Christian Democratic years were in relationship to previous years. As table 6 shows, there was in fact a secular decline in per capita GNP from 1953 to 1959, and it was not until 1963 that the per capita index surpassed that of 1953. Not only was the decline reversed in 1960, but the increase in per capita GNP was clearly better during the course of the Frei administration (1965–70) than it had been during the Alessandri

Table 6. Selected Economic Indices for the Period 1952–1970 (1969 = 100)

Year	Per Capita GNP	Government General Expenditures	Government Investment Expenditures	Government Revenues, Mining Excluded	Government Revenues From Mining	Percentage Readjustment of Real Minimum Wage with Respect to Previous Year	Readjustment of Real Wages and Salaries with Respect to Previous Year	Balance of Payments in 1969 Dollars
1952	79.7	43.0	32.9	30.2	42.8	—	—	-21.5
1953	82.7	48.4	24.8	32.5	25.6	-0.1	—	-27.4
1954	80.8	45.4	25.8	30.7	35.9	-2.1	—	-19.3
1955	80.9	48.3	28.9	32.0	44.2	-10.9	—	0.4
1956	79.8	44.6	29.6	31.4	59.0	-11.1	—	-54.4
1957	78.5	47.9	25.4	35.1	41.6	-4.0	—	-34.2
1958	78.4	45.6	28.5	36.9	27.9	-4.9	—	32.4
1959	77.7	46.4	38.0	38.4	43.6	1.0	—	35.8
1960	78.5	55.9	46.6	45.4	42.0	-6.6	—	-52.2
1961	81.1	60.8	49.2	52.5	33.7	20.9	11.8	-138.7
1962	83.5	69.7	60.2	55.0	45.4	5.5	3.6	-54.7
1963	84.5	61.5	62.4	52.3	45.3	-16.5	-8.7	15.1
1964	86.4	61.6	59.9	52.2	46.7	-2.6	-5.3	63.1
1965	89.6	73.3	84.5	66.4	57.2	7.2	13.9	81.3
1966	96.4	82.8	100.4	77.3	91.4	1.3	10.8	94.3
1967	95.5	88.1	89.3	86.2	87.5	-2.8	13.5	-31.6
1968	96.7	94.6	97.6	93.6	84.2	-4.9	-2.0	109.7
1969	100.0	100.0	100.0	100.0	100.0	-5.2	4.3	80.7
1970	101.4	121.2	102.6	111.4	123.5	-4.5	8.5	—

SOURCE: Ricardo Ffrench-Davis, *Políticas económicas en Chile, 1952–1970* (Santiago: Ediciones Nueva Universidad, 1973), tables 35, 51, 68, and 75.

administration (1959–64); the year 1970 ended in a historic high. Though the minimum wage suffered a decline in the last few years of the Frei administration, overall real wages increased substantially during the same years. A glance back at table 5, which depicts the rate of inflation from 1952 to 1970, presents a similar picture. Though inflation remained high during the Christian Democratic administration, in no year did it reach the high of 45.4 percent experienced in the Alessandri administration or the 83.8 percent rate of the Ibañez administration. Finally, the relatively better economic situation of the late 1960s was accompanied by a positive balance of trade, again a situation with no parallel during the previous two decades.

Table 6 goes beyond merely presenting data on the economy; it also provides information about governmental performance and capability. Not only was the economy in relatively better shape during the Frei years but both government revenues and government expenditures increased dramatically, affording an opportunity for the state to provide a level of services as well as capital and investment improvements unmatched in previous administrations. In real terms, expenditures on health, housing, and education increased 136 percent, 130 percent, and 167 percent, respectively.[5] Nor was investment shortchanged, as both public and private investment grew significantly.

By all indications, then, the period immediately preceding the advent to power of the *Unidad Popular* (or U.P.) was not characterized by a mounting and unprecedented secular crisis in the Chilean economy. The mid-fifties were far worse in every respect from an economic point of view. And during that period, governmental capabilities, measured in terms of taxation and expenditures, also experienced decline or stagnation. Nor is there any indication that economic transformations in the late 1960s were too dramatic or strong. Increases in standards of living were modest, but better than before, and government capability, measured strictly in terms of available resources, clearly stayed ahead.

Under such conditions, one would have to say that social mobilization resulting directly from economic deprivation, relative deprivation, or economically induced social dislocation would have been less in the 1960s than in previous years. Paradoxically, many observers have noted that in fact social and political mobilization increased substantially during the late 1960s. What were the dimensions of that mobilization? If it was massive, how did it come about, given the analysis of the economic situation? Could social and political mobilization, developing independent of a severe economic crisis, have had a destabilizing impact on the system?

Political and Social Mobilization in the Late 1960s

Observers of Latin American politics have noted that in the early 1960s Chile may have ranked first in democratic stability in Latin America, but it ranked fourteenth in electoral participation.[6] As figure 1 shows, voter partici-

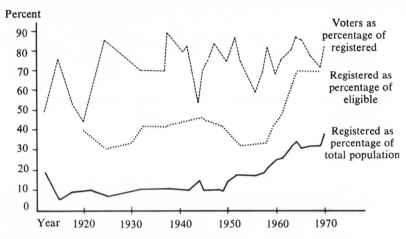

Figure 1. Political Participation, 1912–70

Source: Electoral data from the Dirección General del Registro Electoral, Santiago, Chile. Demographic information from Dirección de Estadística y Censos, "Población total por provincias de Chile, 1885–60" (Santiago, 1964); idem, "Población del país" (Santiago, 1964); and *El Mercurio*, 4 September 1970, pp. 11, 12.

pation was restricted during the parliamentary republic in the early part of the century, so that it was not until the 1950s, with the adoption of female suffrage, that the electoral participation rate exceeded that of 1912. This reduced voter participation was primarily the result of electoral laws which restricted voting to the literate population and made it necessary to register periodically in order to stay on the electoral rolls. Low mobilization was reinforced by the fact that Marxist parties did not turn to the countryside to seek electoral bases. In fact, rural unionization was illegal until 1967. Marxist parties concentrated on gaining support among the growing industrial proletariat. Reduced participation was also reinforced by the clientelistic electoral system favored by both the Right and the Center, which in turn undermined populist appeals until the rise of Carlos Ibañez in the 1950s. Underlying this state of affairs was a tacit agreement between rural and urban elites. Rural elites were willing to endure the hardship of price controls on agricultural goods imposed by an industrially oriented middle class which relied, during the Radical years, on support from the parties of the Left with similar interests. In turn, centrist and leftist parties did not alter the basic political and social structure of the landed elite.[7]

An important turning point in electoral mobilization came with the electoral reforms of 1958 and 1962. These reforms not only did away with periodical registries but also established rules requiring voter registration and mechanisms to enforce those rules. Thus a citizen who failed to register and vote could be punished by a prison term. Even more significantly, since prison terms were rarely imposed, government agencies and banks were required to ask for the electoral registration certificate to process any service.[8] These requirements, and the increased activities of the parties, meant that the electorate expanded from 1.25 million, or 16 percent of the population, in 1960, to 2.84 million, or 28.3 percent of the population, in 1971.[9]

Dramatic as these increases in voter turnout are, it must be cautioned that voter participation is perhaps not the best indicator of destabilizing mobilization. Quite to the contrary, voting is not a very demanding act, and increased turnout can be taken as an indicator of increased participation within the framework of the ongoing system. It is necessary to turn to other indicators of mobilization to better evaluate the extent of social demands on the Chilean system in the late 1960s.

Henry Landsberger and Tim McDaniel have argued that "uncontrolled" mobilization or "hypermobilization" began in Chile "not in 1970, but in 1965, by the assumption to power of the PDC. A flood was released and further stimulated, as manifested by rising union membership and a rising rate of strike activity. This flood did not lead on to 'fortune,' because it could not even be rechannelled, let alone contained...."[10] Unionization and strike activity clearly are better indicators of "uncontrolled" mobilization than is electoral turnout. Our task will be to analyze the evidence on the extent of mobilization and attempt to evaluate the character of that mobilization.

Table 7 presents information on the growth of industrial and craft unions from 1937 to 1970. It is immediately apparent that during the Frei period the absolute rate of growth for these unions was substantial. Industrial unions grew by 38 percent and craft unions grew by 90 percent. At first glance it would appear that this was an unprecedented development in Chilean history, signaling a dramatic change in the mobilization of the urban working class. More detailed examination, however, reveals that the upward trend in the 1960s was primarily a period of recuperation from a decline in union membership both in real and relative terms during the 1950s. What is striking about the information presented in the table is that despite the increased level of unionization in the Christian Democratic administration, the percentage of the industrial population organized in industrial unions was still lower in 1970 (35.1 percent) than it had been in 1953 (38.3 percent). And despite the dramatic increase in craft union membership in the late 1960s, the percentage of organized workers in the nonagricultural sector rose from only 19.3 percent in 1953 to 19.4 percent in 1970. The union population kept pace with general changes in society, but did not exceed those changes in any dramatic way. This can be appreciated by surveying the growth of industries eligible for unionization. Between the 1957 and the 1967 industrial censuses the number of industries employing more than twenty workers (an industry was required to have twenty-five to form an industrialized union) rose from 1,875 to 3,468,

Table 7. Growth of Industrial and Craft Unions in Selected Years, 1932 to 1970

Year	Number of Industrial Unions	Number of Members in Industrial Unions	Active Population, Industry	Percentage of Industrial Population Unionized	Number of Craft Unions	Number of Members in Craft Unions	Total Nonagricultural Work Force	Total Nonagricultural Work Force Unionized	Percentage of Work Force Unionized
1932	168	29,442	205,000	14.4	253	25,359	801,000	54,801	0.07
1934	266	42,617			414	38,468		81,085	
1936	275	51,185			315	35,514			
1938	333	78,989			599	46,983			
1940	629	91,940	298,100	33.9	1,259	70,357	965,100	180,497	18.7
1942	602	122,688			991	71,641			
1944	596	143,860			1,056	103,221			
1946	591	148,276			1,115	103,498			
1948	607	151,633			1,250	112,043			
1950	626	147,306			1,270	111,994			
1952	635	155,054	405,100	38.3	1,393	128,329	1,489,700	288,131	19.3
1954	667	165,888			1,372	132,161			
1956	788	170,689			1,563	144,303			
1958	641	154,650			1,225	119,666			
1960	608	122,306	406,000	30.1	1,144	107,687	1,605,900	229,981	14.3
1962	598	134,478			1,154	110,669			
1964	632	142,951			1,207	125,926			
1966	990	179,506			1,679	161,363			
1968	1,261	189,815			2,163	222,212			
1970	1,440	197,651	562,900	35.1	2,569	239,323	2,256,200	436,974	19.4

SOURCE: Union data for 1932–58, James O. Morris and Roberto Oyaneder, *Afiliación y finanzas sindicales en Chile* (Santiago: INSORA, 1962), pp. 18–20; for 1960–68, Instituto Nacional de Estadísticas, *Finanzas, bancos, cajas sociales año 1969* (Santiago, The Institute, 1969), p. 153; for 1970, *Mensaje del Presidente Allende ante el Congreso Pleno*, 21 May 1972, pp. 859–61. Census data for 1930, Universidad de Chile, Instituto de Economía, *Desarrollo económico de Chile, 1940–1956* (Santiago: Editorial Universitaria, 1956), table A25. Census data for 1940 and 1952, Dirección de Estadísticas y Censos, *Cifras comparativas de los censos de 1940 y 1952 muestra del censo de 1960* (n.d.) p. 9. Population figures for 1970, ODEPLAN, *Plan de la economía nacional* (1971) p. 62. Population data are provided only for census years.

a rise of 85 percent.[11] During the same period the number of unions rose 83 percent. Since the number of unionized workers in the same period rose 23 percent, the average size of unions declined as more small industries became organized. In 1958 the average union had 248 workers, while in 1967 it had 162.

It must be noted further that the total number of union members has been overstated in table 7. This is so because many of the craft union members are also members of industrial unions. In 1967, for example, about 20 percent of the craft union members were also members of a plant union. Furthermore, it is likely that during the 1960s the proportion of craft union members holding dual membership increased rather than decreased. Legislation was enacted during the Frei government to upgrade the classification of several industrial crafts from *obrero* (blue-collar worker) to *empleado* (white-collar worker), which meant an increase in status and government benefits for those favored. In order to guarantee the new status and benefits, workers would routinely petition to form a craft union. The fact that unionization seemed merely to keep pace with general trends in Chilean society, and that much of the unionization which took place during this period was the result of legislation, detracts considerably from its value as an indicator of "uncontrolled mobilization." In fact it can be argued, as Clotario Blest, the founder of the Chilean labor federation, has done, that the growth of craft unions is an indicator of potential weakening of the labor movement as a militant force rather than of increased strength.[12] The empleado status of many craft unions drives a sharp wedge into the solidarity of the working class by dramatizing social distinctions. Furthermore, craft unions are weak in terms of collective bargaining rights, meaning that empleado status is often sought despite the fact that it might lower the ability of the group in question to carry out trade union functions.[13]

The 1960s, then, saw a resumption of the secular pattern of growth which began with the Popular Front government elected in 1938. The decline of the labor movement in the 1950s was due to economic crisis and the repression of labor by the Ibañez administration. (Ibañez maintained the ban on the Communist party until 1958.) It was also due to the sharp divisions and disarray in the leadership ranks of the movement. The 1960s, and especially the Frei administration, marked not only a period of labor organization but also a period of substantial reform and active government encouragement of the union movement.

Perhaps the most dramatic indicator of the favorable attitude of the government toward reform was its active organization of the heretofore unorganized rural workers. Over two hundred rural unions were organized before the passage of legislation in 1967 allowing the formal establishment of rural unions. As table 8 shows, by November of 1970 136,984 rural workers were unionized, whereas only five years earlier there were a mere 2,118 organized

Table 8. Growth of Agricultural Unions

Year	Number of Unions	Total Number of Members
1925	10	5,000
1953	15	1,042
1958	28	2,030
1960	18	1,424
1961	22	1,831
1962	22	1,860
1963	22	1,500
1964	24	1,658
1965	32	2,118
1966	201	10,417
1967	211	42,474
1968	371	78,419
1969	421	104,666
1970 (through November)	476	136,984

SOURCE: For 1925, Alan Angell, *Politics and the Labour Movement in Chile* (London: Oxford University Press, 1972), p. 37; for 1953, Servicio Nacional de Estadísticas, *Estadística Chilena, Sinopsis 1958;* for 1960–68, Instituto Nacional de Estadísticas, *Finanzas, bancos y cajas sociales año 1969,* (Santiago: The Institute, 1969); p. 153; for 1969–70, Dirección de Presupuestos, *Balance consolidado del sector público de Chile años 1969–1970 y período 1964–1970,* p. 41.

workers in the countryside. This meant that by 1970, 18 percent of the active population in agriculture was organized, an unprecedented organizational effort for such a short period of time. It is here that one finds the best indicator of significant mobilization during the late 1960s prior to the advent of the government of Salvador Allende.[14]

Yet even this mobilization must be kept in perspective. By 1970 organized rural workers represented less than 5 percent of the active population, so that in terms of society as a whole the organizational effort was not great. Furthermore, over 80 percent of the population in the countryside remained unorganized. More importantly, rural unionization was rarely the result of spontaneous, uncontrolled mobilization. It was a deliberate policy, sanctioned by legislation and conducted primarily by government agencies. The fact that toward the end of the period political parties became active in the unionization effort, and that some agencies of the government were less willing to move fast in the countryside than others, does not detract from the main point that the process of rural unionization was a highly organized and controlled one.[15]

Turning to another possible indicator of mobilization, the incidence of strikes by the labor movement, we see that the 1960s and in particular the Christian Democratic administration witnessed a dramatic increase in strike activity (see table 9). Whereas in 1960 the country experienced 245 strikes, in 1966 that number had increased to 1,073. If we compare the penultimate years of the Alessandri and Frei administrations we can see that the incidence of strikes as well as the number of workers affected by strikes went up 135

Table 9. Evolution of Strikes, 1947–69

Year	Number of Unions	Number of Strikes	Average Strike per Union	Number of Strikers	Percentage of Strikers over Active Population	Number of Workers per Strike	Total Man-days Lost in Strikes	Man-days Lost per Strike	Days per Strike per Worker
1947–50	1858	121	.07	44,603		369	1,194,885	9,875	26.8
1952	1982	215	.11	151,715	.10	706	1,766,827	8,218	11.6
1954	2049	305	.15	74,696		246	905,849	2,970	12.1
1956	2351	147	.06	105,438		717	1,657,194	11,273	15.7
1959	1732	204	.12	82,188		403	869,728	4,263	10.6
1960	1752	245	.14	88,518	.06	361	—	—	—
1963	1830	416	.23	117,084		281	—	—	—
1965	2010	723	.39	182,359		259	—	—	—
1966	2669	1073	.40	195,435		182	2,015,253	1,878	10.3
1969	3749	977	.26	275,406	.12	281	972,382	995	3.5
Percentage change, 1959–69	105	135		135					

SOURCE: For 1947–50, Universidad de Chile, Instituto de Economía, *Desarrollo económico de Chile, 1952–56* (Santiago: Editorial Universitaria, 1956), p. 7; 1952–56. Servicio Nacional de Estadística, *Estadística de Chile Sinopsis 1958* (Santiago: Dirección Nacional de Estadística y Censos, 1958); 1959–69, *Mensaje Presidencial, 1970*, p. 366.

percent. Increased strike activity closely paralleled the increase in number of unions (105 percent) in the same two years. This suggests that the increase in strike activity was probably stimulated more by the proliferation of new organizations than by the addition of members to old ones. This observation is supported by the evidence that the average number of workers per strike decreased substantially from the 1950s to the 1960s. In the earlier period there were fewer unions to call strikes, but they involved a proportionally larger number of workers in each strike. Likewise, it can be noted that while the average number of strikes called per union shot up in 1965 and 1966, in 1969 it was at a level similar to that of 1963. Finally, column five helps to place the significance of strike activity in perspective. It shows that for the census years of 1952, 1960, and 1970 the proportion of strikers to total active population varied little—from 10 percent to 6 percent to 12 percent, respectively.[16]

But if strike activity is merely a reflection of the increasing number of unions, and, as we noted earlier, the increased number of unions did not lead (except in the rural areas) to substantial new mobilization, relative to growth in the society, how significant is the increased strike activity as an indicator of "uncontrolled" mobilization? Neither the number of strikes nor the number of strikers seems to be an indicator of *massive* change. And yet the size and number of strikes may be less important in judging mobilization than the *intensity* of strike activity. Did strikes become more intense in the late 1960s? Table 9 reports the total man-days lost in strikes, which is an indicator of strike intensity, since it suggests the number of days strikers were willing to stay off the job. In Chile this was a particularly good measure because of the severe lack of adequate strike support funds, which rendered any strike a real hardship for the workers involved. The evidence reported is noteworthy, but it contradicts what might be expected. The absolute number of days lost per year to strikes was substantially higher in *absolute* terms in the early 1950s than in the late 1960s. This was the case despite the fact that the active population in the early 1950s was 50 percent smaller than in the late 1960s. Likewise, the average duration of a strike was considerably higher in 1947–50, when the figure was 26.8 days, than in 1969, when it was 3.5.

What is important about these figures is that strikes were of longer duration and were much more costly both to the country and to the workers in a period when the government was much more likely to repress workers. The short duration of strikes in the Frei administration is a clear indicator of a deliberate government policy aimed at settling labor disputes in the worker's favor. The restrictive and antilabor Labor Code, with its ludicrous definition of what constituted a legal strike and its penalties for so-called illegal strikes, was applied less in favor of the employers and more in favor of the workers. Ironically, it was this same favorable predisposition toward workers, rather than mass alienation, which stimulated the increase in unionization and strikes. With the relaxation of government repression, workers were much freer to take the initiative, secure in the knowledge that their actions would receive favorable government response. As Alan Angell notes, "the sharp increase in strikes since 1965 need not be interpreted as a Marxist attempt to heighten the class war. It was more likely due to the fact that the government was more sympathetic to unions; that the number of unions and unionists increased considerably; that a larger labour inspectorate meant more attempts at conciliation and less use of police repression; and, of course, to national strikes, especially in 1967–68, against national-income policies."[17]

This interpretation of the origins of increased strike activity is similar to the one advanced earlier to explain worker unionization, particularly rural unionization. It was a response to a deliberate policy on the part of the government to include people who had been left behind. It was part of the same strategy which led to "popular promotion" schemes with other disenfranchised elements, namely the urban slum dwellers and urban squatters. Though government figures on the success of the *juntas de vecinos* and *centros de madres* are exaggerated, many new neighborhood organizations sprang up initially under government sponsorship (promoción popular) and later under the sponsorship of rival political parties, primarily on the Left.[18]

The Late 1960s: Political Crisis

The previous analysis helps to explain how participation increased despite the lack of dramatic changes in the economy. Political factors, rather than simple economic ones, were the critical variables in explaining the change in mobilization patterns. After a period of deliberate governmental demobilization, which undermined many of the gains that the working class had achieved during the Popular Front period, the government once again adopted a favorable attitude toward popular involvement in the political economic life of the nation. Both through relaxation of governmental repression and a deliberate policy of popular mobilization, which extended for the first time into the countryside, the Christian Democratic administration was able to match and surpass previous rates of popular mobilization.

Precisely because Chilean mobilization did not tax the economic system, and because it developed in response to deliberate governmental policy, one could advance the proposition that it presented a good example of what Gabriel Almond has called "responsive performance." As Almond notes, "participation in and of itself tends to be a valued activity and may be viewed as a demand. And when a political system legitimates participatory activity on the part of different groups of the population, it may be said to be responding to these demands."[19]

Mobilization was not in itself a threat. It represented increased participation which could easily have been absorbed by the Chilean political system, had not the system experienced an important transformation. But that qualifier is extremely important and is the key to understanding the role of social mobilization in the Chilean crisis. It is a mistake to identify the mobilization of the late 1960s as an example of "responsive performance," not so much because of the nature of mobilization per se, but because of basic changes in Chilean politics, which transformed any kind of mobilization into a potentially destabilizing force. Nor was the gap between mobilization and the ability of the system to cope with mobilization simply a matter of the erosion of key political institutions such as Chile's strong political parties. In fact, during the late 1960s Chilean parties became stronger and more institutionalized than ever before. What changed were the traditional rules of the game and accommodationist politics, revolving around the legislature, that had made it possible for strong political actors and institutions to compromise and to structure a working consensus. According to this interpretation, the political crisis preceded the social mobilization of new groups and the more dangerous countermobilization of established interests. There is no doubt that during the Allende administration both types of mobilization would get out of hand and have seriously destabilizing effects. But initially, mobilization in Chile was less a cause of impending crisis than a symptom of crisis at the center of the political system. And though that crisis came to a head in the Allende years, its roots must be sought earlier, particularly in the Christian Democratic administration of Eduardo Frei.

One of the most important factors contributing to a qualitative change in the nature of the political system was the first appearance of a relatively cohesive centrist movement with an ideological rather than a pragmatic outlook. The largely pragmatic Radicals had been challenged earlier by the surge movement of Carlos Ibañez and the "apolitical" conservatism of Jorge Alessandri. But it was not until the emergence of the Christian Democrats as the new Center in Chilean politics that the Radicals clearly lost ground as a major political force.

Unlike the fragmented and poorly organized Ibañistas, the Christian Democrats had a talented and cohesive leadership group with the resources and energy to try to capture the Center of the political spectrum with an unprecedented organizational effort. Arguing that Christian Democracy provided an alternative to liberal capitalism and Marxist socialism, they consciously sought to break the polarization of Chilean politics by capturing the Center pole and turning it into a new centrist tendency. From 9.4 percent of the vote in the congressional election of 1957 (as the *Falange Nacional*), the Christian Democrats captured 15.4 percent in 1961 and finally overtook the Radicals with 22 percent (to the Radical 20.8 percent) in the municipal elections of 1963. As table 10 shows, the rise of the Christian Democrats paralleled the slower but steady rise of the Left. It is important to note that the success of the Christian Democrats was not gained at the expense of the Radicals, but rather

Table 10. Percentage of the Vote Received by Major Chilean Parties, 1937–73

Political Preference	1937	1941	1945	1949	1953	1957	1961	1965	1969	1973
Right										
Conservatives	21.3	17.2	23.6	22.7	14.4	17.6	14.3	5.2	—	—
Liberals	20.7	14.0	20.1	19.3	10.9	15.4	16.1	7.3	—	—
Nationals	—	—	—	—	—	—	—	—	20.0	21.3
Center										
Radicals	18.7	23.0	19.9	27.7	15.6	22.1	21.4	13.3	13.0	3.7
Christian Democrats or Falangists	—	3.4	2.6	3.9	2.9	9.4	15.4	42.3	29.8	29.1
Democrats	9.4	5.7	5.4	6.8	5.6	5.0	6.9	—	—	—
Agrarian Laborists (Ibañista)	—	—	—	8.3	18.9	7.8	—	—	—	—
Left										
Socialists	11.2	22.1	12.8	9.4	14.2	10.7	10.7	10.3	12.2	18.7
Communists	4.2	11.8	10.3	—	—	—	11.4	12.4	15.9	16.2
Other	14.5	2.8	5.3	1.9	17.5	12.0	3.8	9.2	9.1	11.0
Total	100.0	100.0	100.0	100.0	100.0	100.0	100.0	100.0	100.0	100.0

SOURCE: Calculated from data available in the Dirección del Registro Electoral, Santiago, Chile.

at the expense of the Conservative and Liberal parties and fragments of the Ibañista movement. Support for the rightist party declined from 29.2 percent of the vote in 1957 to 23.6 percent in 1963.

The new strength of the Christian Democrats put them in a very good position for the 1964 presidential election. When each of the major parties had presented candidates in 1958, Allende, representing the Communist and Socialist alliance, had lost the election by 33,416 votes (of 1,235,552 cast). When a candidate presented by the alliance of Radicals, Liberals, and Conservatives lost a crucial by-election to the Left in the months before the 1964 presidential contest, the Liberals and Conservatives threw their support to Eduardo Frei, the Christian Democratic candidate. He proceeded to win the election by a comfortable margin of 56.1 percent of the vote to 38.9 percent for Salvador Allende, the candidate of a united Left.[20]

The Christian Democrats in Chile were not the only ones interested in a third alternative for Chile. The Kennedy administration's Alliance for Progress called for changes that would benefit new industrial groups to the detriment of the more traditional elites with ties to the land. Significant reforms would help to undermine the potential for another Cuba in Latin America. The Christian Democrats in Chile were the logical group to receive strong support for a preemptive effort to undermine the threat of the Left while bringing about a measure of development. The 1964 election saw an unprecedented interference in Chilean politics from external sources. The Central Intelligence Agency channeled three million dollars to the Frei campaign, which also received substantial sums of money from European and private business sources. The CIA also undertook to support the Frei effort by mounting a massive propaganda campaign. The campaign, referred to in Chile as a "campaign of terror," sought to depict the Allende candidacy as one that would institute a repressive and bloody regime in which, among other things, children would be taken away from their mothers. There is little doubt that that vituperative propaganda campaign contributed to the sharp rise in conflict and mistrust in Chilean politics.[21]

Once in office the Christian Democrats moved ahead vigorously to implement their program. They made it clear from the outset that a major component of the program would be the incorporation into the nation's political life of sectors that had previously been excluded. With overt and covert support from the United States, they embarked on a massive effort to organize what were referred to as "marginal" segments of society.[22] All other political forces in the country, ranging from Conservatives to Communists, were put on the defensive as the Christian Democrats made it clear that they intended to break the deadlock of electoral strength by capturing the allegiance of a majority of the population. Indeed Frei's victory had suggested that the party already had an unprecedented degree of majority support. From the outset the Radicals came in for harsh criticism.[23] Christian Democrats soon moved to challenge that party's hold over much of the bureaucracy. Radicals were accused of being the party of expediency and compromise and of responsibility for the decay of institutions and the lack of progress in meeting the social crisis. The Center had been taken over by a party which openly disdained the political maneuvering of clientelistic politics that for so long had kept the system going. What is even more important, however, is that the Center was able to win not only the presidency but majority support in one chamber of the Congress. In the 1965 congressional elections, for the first time in memory, a single party captured a majority of the Chamber of Deputies with an impressive 42.3 percent of the vote. From that position of strength, exerting considerable discipline over its legislators, the Christian Democrats proceeded to rule as a "single party" (partido único). On major issues such as agrarian reform or copper nationalization, compromises were struck with opposing forces.[24] However, on much of the day-to-day running of the government, with the support of its majority in the Chamber, the government was able to undermine significantly the politics of clientelism.[25] Item vetoes of the executive, upheld in the Chamber of Deputies, cut back on congressional ability to logroll public works bills and to influence salary readjustments. Arguing against the incrementalism which had impeded reform, government technocrats sought to institute more "rational" planning schemes which would dispense with the "distortions" of the political process. Opposition parties and legislators were progressively excluded from many of the particularistic deals of the past. Congress lost some of its earlier importance as an arena of accommodation. The Senate, "refuge" of the opposition, became a largely negative force, going so far as to take the unprecedented step, noted in chapter 1, of barring President Frei from visiting the United States.

The plebiscitarian policies of President Frei would culminate, at the end of his term, in the adoption of constitutional reforms specifically aimed at curbing the role of Congress within the system. The legislature's jurisdiction over budgetary and salary readjustments, in particular, was strongly reduced. Ironically, in light of future developments, the Left, which had always drawn strength from its position in the legislature, voted against most of the reforms. The Right, convinced that former-president Alessandri would be an easy winner in the 1970 race, voted for the reforms.[26] Both the Christian Democrats and the Right would thus inherit a Congress which could serve either as a rubber stamp or a negative force. Even before the election of Allende the institutional mechanisms for accommodation had become weaker and more rigid.

The mobilization of the late 1960s must be understood in light of this "*partido único*" strategy of the Christian Democrats. Their efforts at mobilization and their disdain for some of the traditional clientelistic mechanisms encouraged as never before a frantic race among all sectors to prevent the centrist party from obtaining majority support. The Left moved quickly, if belatedly, into the countryside and *poblaciones* to accelerate its effort to broaden its base among the working class. The Conservatives and Liberals responded to their disastrous 12.5 percent of the vote in the 1965 race by fusing into a National party and turning to the magic name of Alessandri to curb the party which was expropriating their lands and robbing them of electoral strength. While the mobilization per se did not exceed the capabilities of the system, the goal of the mobilization was not only to incorporate new sectors into the political process but to ensure that this incorporation would lead to partisan advantage.

The problem with the Christian Democrats, and with the country, was that they did not succeed in their goal of depolarizing Chilean politics by establishing a new majority. The support for Frei in 1964 and the impressive showing in the congressional election of 1965 merely illustrated the workings of a polarized system. The Center had succeeded with support from the two sides of the political spectrum (with most of the strength coming from the Right) and not through a fundamental shift in political allegiances in the system. The 1969 congressional election vividly illustrated this problem. The Christian Democratic vote dropped to 29.8 percent of the total. The National party made a strong comeback, obtaining 20 percent of the vote, while the Left continued to make headway. The pragmatic Radicals proved to be the only real casualties, dropping to 13 percent of the vote, their lowest level in this century. The Christian Democrats had attempted to govern as if they had become a new political force with widespread support for its claim of representing a "third" way in Chilean politics. But this conviction proved to be an illusion. In fact the Christian Democrats never succeeded in becoming a genuinely new orientation in Chilean politics—a viable centrist tendency capable of eroding the strength of both Right and Left. In Sartori's terms, they continued to represent an unstable pole in the center of the political spectrum. As a convenient option, their support had come about more through a "sum of exclusions," primarily from the Right. With the rapid defection of voters from the Right, and the failure to pick up voters from the Left, the party's strength withered quickly. In the process, the *partido único* stand alienated other political groups and heightened political tensions. The Christian Democrats temporarily broke the deadlock of Chilean politics but failed to restructure the polarized system which had created the deadlock in the first place. By undermining, however unintentionally, the fragile understanding of Chilean politics without altering the traditional correlation of forces they simply aggravated polarization and worsened the deadlock. It is no wonder that it would prove impossible to structure a Center-Right or Center-Left coalition in the coming presidential race of 1970—thus opening the way for a three-way race in which the Right or the Left could win without support from the Center.

This study has stressed the role of the Christian Democrats because of the important role which a strongly ideological Center plays in undermining the fragile consensus of a polarized democratic system. However, that should not be taken to mean that other factors were unimportant even if not decisive. In particular, it is important to stress that the technocratic Christian Democrats were not the only group to question the implications of the old bargaining system. The Left in Chile, during the same period, began to feel a direct challenge from numerically small but increasingly vocal groups who rejected the system of party politics and called for revolutionary transformations through violent means. They drew their inspiration from the Cuban revolution, the Uruguyan Tupamaros, and the struggle of Vietnamese revolutionaries who caught the imagination of students and others in their guerrilla war against the most powerful nation on earth. The most important of these groups was the *Movimiento de Izquierda Revolucionaria* (Revolutionary Left Movement—MIR) founded by students at the University of Concepción.[27] By the late 1960s organizational efforts in the countryside and in working-class neighborhoods began to produce modest results.

The challenge from the Center and the far Left and the adoption of a more revolutionary line within the Socialist, Communist, and even Radical parties, particularly their youth sectors, inevitably heightened the militancy of leftist organizations. The traditional "bourgeois" bargaining system had not only lost much legitimacy but was also less acceptable as a mechanism for ensuring gains—albeit partial ones. The reduction of the effectiveness of those mechanisms would further reinforce such a conclusion. Although erosion of support for the traditional system from the Right would become more visible after the 1970 election, the October 1969 military move by General Viaux had also demonstrated that powerful sectors were tired of the comings and goings of democracy, despite the fact that Jorge Alessandri was widely viewed as the certain winner of the 1970 election. In this atmosphere of heightened competition and political crisis, Chileans prepared for the 1970 presidential contest.

The 1970 Election: The Problem of a Minority President

The election of Salvador Allende to the presidency of Chile in 1970 was not the result of a dramatic shift of the Chilean electorate to the Left. The stark reality is that the significant increases in popular participation and electoral registration during the late 1960s were not channeled, in proportionally higher terms, to the parties of the Left. In fact, as table 11 shows, Allende obtained a smaller percentage of the total vote in that election than he had in the previous presidential election. If we assume that leftist voting patterns for 1964–70 were stable, then Allende was supported by only 55,467, or 13.3 percent, of the 416,731 new voters registered between those years. Since the vote for the Christian Democratic candidate declined dramatically between the two elections, it is quite probable that the conservative Alessandri was the principal beneficiary of the newly mobilized vote. Perhaps more than any other statistic, this one reveals that heightened radicalism was not a principal characteristic of Chilean electoral politics in 1970. Instead, Salvador Allende's election was the result of the inability of Chile's polarized political system to structure a winning majority coalition before the election and was further evidence of erosion of traditional mechanisms of political accommodation.

According to coalition theorists, a coalition situation occurs when three or more actors with actual or perceived preferences which are dissimilar coordinate their actions in order to achieve an outcome which is preferable to that which could be achieved by acting alone.[28] In 1964 such a coalition was structured when the rightist conservatives and liberals backed Eduardo Frei after the disastrous showing of a conservative candidate in a local by-election. The Right feared that the united Left would achieve the victory which they had missed by a narrow 33,416-vote margin in 1958. By 1970, however, sentiment had changed and the Right felt it would be better served by going it alone, supporting the candidacy of independent conservative Jorge Alessandri. Though the Christian Democrats as a group were probably closer in ideological distance to the National party as a whole, and the election of a Marxist was still a clear possibility, conservatives felt a strong contempt for the Frei government, both for its reforms in the countryside and its *partido único* stand. Furthermore, the Christian Democratic candidate for president, Radomiro Tomic, openly sought an alliance not with the Right but with the Left, expressing the prevailing feeling that in a three-way race the conserva-

Table 11. Results of the 1958, 1964, and 1970 Presidential Elections in Chile

	1958			1964			1970	
Candidate	Vote	%	Candidate	Vote	%	Candidate	Vote	%
Allende	356,493	28.5	Allende	977,902	38.6	Allende	1,070,334	36.2
Bossay	192,077	15.4	Frei	1,409,012	55.7	Tomic	821,801	27.8
Frei	255,769	20.5	Duran	125,233	5.0	Alessandri	1,031,159	34.9
Alessandri	389,909	31.2						
Zamorano	41,304	3.3						
Blank and void	14,798	1.1	Blank and void	18,550	0.7	Blank and void	31,505	1.1
Total vote	1,250,350	100.0	Total vote	2,530,697	100.0	Total vote	2,954,799	100.0
Total registration	1,497,902		Total registration	2,915,121		Total registration	3,539,747	
Percent of abstentions	16.5		Percent of abstentions	13.2		Percent of abstentions	16.5	

SOURCE: Compiled from materials in the Dirección del Registro Electoral, Santiago, Chile.

tive candidate would win.[29] However, the Left was not about to accept an alliance with the Christian Democrats, particularly when such an alliance would have involved a Christian Democratic standard-bearer. The Left was dissatisfied with the *partido único* stance and the unwillingness of the Christian Democrats to move further in their reforms and was hopeful that it might be able to pull an upset in a race which divided the opposition into two separate candidacies.[30] Counter to some of the assumptions made in coalition theory, each of the major actors in Chilean politics sought to maximize its position, after a complex set of internal struggles, following the dictates of ideology and its perceptions of past as well as future political events. They were not responding to a narrow set of utilities of a material sort, nor did they have a clear conception of the shifting and contradictory preferences of other actors or a clear vision of what the final outcome would be.[31]

In the three-way contest, the miscalculations of the Right became immediately apparent. Alessandri ran a dismal race and confounded most pollsters by trailing Allende's 36.2 percent of the vote with 34.9 percent—a 39,175-vote difference.[32] What had almost happened in 1958, when centrist parties also ran their own candidates, finally took place in 1970. For the first time in Chilean history, a candidate of the Left, not one merely supported by the Left, had won the highest office in the land.

The results of the race clearly illustrate that the Christian Democrats had been primarily a Center artificially created by the polarization of the system. With the support of the Right, Frei had gained 55.7 percent of the vote in 1964. In 1970, Tomic obtained a mere 27.8 percent of all ballots cast. Table 12 shows the importance of erosion of rightist support for the Christian Democrats over the previous six years. The simple correlation coefficient between the vote for Frei in 1964 and Alessandri in 1970 is actually higher than the correlation between the vote for Frei and Tomic. At the same time the correlation between the vote for Alessandri in 1970 and the Christian Democratic vote in the congressional elections of 1965 and 1969 declined sharply while the correlation between the 1970 vote for Tomic and Christian Democratic support in those elections increased.

The basic fact of the Allende presidency from the very outset was that it constituted a minority presidency. Though Tomic's platform was similar in many ways to Allende's, it would be a serious mistake to argue that Allende's program for dramatic social change received the backing of a majority of the population.[33] The combined votes that Tomic and Allende received in 1970 amounted to more than 50 percent of the total vote cast. However, aggregate data suggest that Tomic was more likely to draw support from areas where Alessandri was strong than from areas where Allende had electoral strength. The simple correlation between the vote for Tomic and the vote for Alessandri in all Chilean communes was .31. By contrast, the same correlation with the Allende vote was -.64, similar to the correlation of -.77 between Allende and Alessandri. Furthermore, survey data suggest that many Tomic voters, reflect-

Table 12. Simple Correlation Coefficients between the 1970 Votes for Tomic and Alessandri and the Vote for Frei in 1964 and for the Christian Democrats in the 1965 and 1969 Congressional Elections

Candidate	Frei, 1964	Christian Democrats, 1965	Christian Democrats, 1969
Tomic, 1970	.53	.50	.64
Alessandri, 1970	.67	.31	.18

SOURCE: Calculated from electoral returns from the Dirección del Registro Electoral, Santiago, Chile.

ing the ambiguities of their centrist position, would have preferred Alessandri over Allende. This is vividly illustrated by the results of a survey taken shortly before the election and reported in table 13. Respondents were asked which candidates they would not vote for under any circumstances. As the table shows, 56.6 percent of those surveyed rejected the Allende candidacy, as opposed to 43.7 percent against Tomic and 40.1 percent against Alessandri. From the table we can deduce that 46 percent of the lower socioeconomic group would refuse to vote for the "popular" candidate, and only 48 percent would refuse to vote for the candidate identified with the economic elite. The latter group was clearer in its preferences, with 74 percent rejecting the Allende candidacy and only 22 percent rejecting the Alessandri candidacy. Allende simply would not have received a majority of the vote in a two-way race. The sharp polarization of the Chilean political system which was so clearly apparent in the 1970 vote is further underscored by the survey data presented in table 14. Voters were asked their reasons for refusing to vote for any one of the three candidates. Large proportions of the respondents rejected the candidates on the extremes for ideological reasons. Thus 61 percent of those rejecting Allende and 48 percent of those rejecting Alessandri cited unfavorable characteristics of the candidate's ideological posture. By contrast, only 9 percent of those rejecting the centrist candidate gave ideological reasons.

A brief analysis of the correlates of the 1970 presidential vote with several indicators of the urban and rural working class provides a further understanding of the different appeals of each of the candidates. The strongest simple correlations are the negative ones between the vote for Allende and agricultural workers (-.48) and the positive one between the Popular Unity candidate and miners (.50). Though table 15 shows that the president also did better than his adversaries among sectors of the urban working class, both the simple correlations and partial regression coefficients are substantially weaker. Nevertheless, the table does reveal a clear contrast in the base of support for Allende and his two contenders and a substantial similarity in the voting base of the two losing candidates. Both Tomic and Alessandri were strong in the rural areas. Analysis of scattergrams reveals that the stronger correlation between rural votes and Tomic than between rural votes and Alessandri is somewhat misleading. Alessandri in 1970 still had a clear edge over Tomic in

Table 13. Percentage of Voters, by Socioeconomic Group, Refusing to Vote for Allende, Tomic, or Alessandri in 1970 under Any Circumstance

	CANDIDATE							
	Allende		Tomic		Alessandri		Total	
Socioeconomic Group	Number of Responses	%	Number of Responses	%	Number of Responses	%	Number of Responses	%
Upper	89	73.6	61	50.4	27	22.3	121	12.0
Middle	239	66.4	140	38.9	124	34.4	360	35.8
Lower	241	45.9	239	43.8	253	48.2	525	52.2
Total	569	56.6	440	43.7	404	40.1	1,006	100.0

SOURCE: Sales-Reyes Survey, July–August 1970. The author is grateful to James Prothro and Patricio Chaparro for making the results of the survey available to him.

NOTE: The number of responses and the total number in sample do not agree since some respondents rejected more than one candidate.

areas with the highest percentage of agricultural workers. However, since his support was also stronger in some communities with few agricultural workers, the correlation coefficient is slightly smaller. At the same time, the Left had made some inroads in communities with high concentrations of industrial workers. Even so, electoral analysis of the 1970 election shows that the social base of party politics in Chile remained quite heterogeneous. Indicators of the urban working class explain 36, 26, and 19 percent of the variance in the vote for Allende, Alessandri, and Tomic, respectively.

The Allende triumph drew international attention, not only because it represented the first free election of a Marxist head of government firmly committed to a fundamental transformation of his country's existing socioeconomic order but also because of the new government's promise to institute its revolutionary transformations in accord with Chilean constitutional and legal precepts. Indeed, Allende would refer to his experiment as one ranking in importance with the Russian Revolution. In a different historical context, Chile would pioneer in the establishment of a second model for the construction of a Socialist society, a model based not on the violent destruction of the old order

Table 14. Percentage of Respondents Rejecting the Candidacies of Allende, Tomic, or Alessandri in 1970 on Ideological Grounds

	JUSTIFICATIONS				
Candidate	Ideological	%	Non-ideological	%	Total Number of Responses
Allende	346	61.0	222	39.0	569
Tomic	38	8.6	402	91.4	440
Alessandri	194	48.0	210	52.0	404

SOURCE: Same as table 13.

Table 15. Simple and Partial Correlations between the Vote for Presidential Candidates in 1970 and Indicators of Working Classes

Nonagricultural Working Class	Allende		Alessandri		Tomic	
	r	Beta	r	Beta	r	Beta
Miners	.50	.45	−.47	−.45	−.31	−.27
Industrial artisans and workers	.25	.14	−.17	−.11	−.19	−.10
Urban wage laborers	.30	.12	−.19	−.05	−.28	−.16
Domestic and personal service workers	.10	.04	−.03	−.01	−.10	−.04
Office workers	.31	.23	−.17	−.10	−.31	−.27
Commercial workers and salespeople	.13	−.06	−.09	.04	−.09	.09
	R.60	R^2.36	R.51	R^2.26	R.44	R^2.19
Agricultural workers	−.48		.31		.39	

SOURCE: Calculated from 1970 census data and electoral data from the Dirección del Registro Electoral, Santiago, Chile.

but on its peaceful replacement according to democratic, pluralist, and libertarian traditions.[34]

Salvador Allende's stand would immediately raise the issue of whether a minority candidate committed to fundamental change would actually rule or would have to settle for merely reigning. The Congress was dominated by the Christian Democrats and the Right, and after the reforms of 1970 it was more of a confrontational than an accommodationist body. Key institutions such as the Contraloría and the courts were outside the executive chain of command. Indeed, Allende's "victory" led to an even more immediate question as to whether he would be allowed to take office in the first place. The Chilean constitution specified that if no candidate received an absolute majority of the votes, the actual election of the president had to take place in the Congress. A coalition which had failed to form before the election could very well be structured in the congressional arena.

In assessing the political climate of the country and the potential for the formation of the coalition that would enable Allende to take office and actually rule, it is important to specify more clearly the concrete dimensions and manifestations of polarized politics by identifying the positions of major political groups in Chilean society. In so doing, reference will not be made to the myriad individual issues which any society faces, but to two fundamental and overriding matters which Chile confronted in 1970: commitment to the ongoing socioeconomic order and commitment to the institutions and procedures of Chile's long-standing political democracy. These were general questions, often more symbolic than substantive and not easily disaggregated, which nevertheless involved extremely high stakes having to do with the survival of rules of the game themselves.

As noted above, Allende took a position on both, arguing that radical change could be instituted without disturbing the procedures of Chilean democracy. However, only a small fraction of the political elites strongly supported both values. This is the case because it is extremely difficult to isolate support for the rules and procedures of democratic politics from institutions and socioeconomic structures which have been long identified with the same rules. For some, the dismantling of the old order meant that the rules and procedures that permitted the dismantling would lose their legitimacy. Their stake in the social and economic benefits of the status quo was more important than their stake in democratic rules and procedures. By contrast, other factions placed greater value on the destruction of the old order than on the rules of the game which were thought to perpetuate the status quo. A second set of actors may have placed a high value on the rules and procedures but were equally divided on the desirability of change in the institutional and economic order. Support for rules and procedures is severely tested as the other value is put in jeopardy.

Figure 2 summarizes the placement of key Chilean political parties and groups on these two dimensions: support for rules and procedures and support for institutions. As the figure suggests, in 1970 those groups could be divided into anti-rules and pro-rules groups.

It is clear that in 1970 there were two different kinds of disloyal groups fulfilling Juan Linz's definition of those "willing to abandon competitive politics between parties and civil liberties required to maintain competition."[35] The first group rejected the prevailing socioeconomic order. It was made up primarily of the Movement of the Revolutionary Left (MIR). The MIR believed that the only way a Socialist society could be brought about was through a violent uprising of peasants and workers. This group was skeptical of the Allende candidacy and only reluctantly gave it support, signaling at the same time that they would continue their effort to organize and provoke a real confrontation as soon as possible. They presented a challenge from the Left to the proposition that change could come about through legal channels. The MIR position was shared by a rather sizable element of Allende's own party, the Socialists. Shortly before the election, this faction gained control of the party and made it clear that in the final analysis the transformation of the system would be achieved not by playing along with bourgeois elements but by pushing for a fundamental confrontation.[36] Both groups stressed the importance of bringing about a Socialist society and creating a new man. Allende's fundamental premise—that Chile could institute a Socialist order within the framework of democratic legality—was severely challenged by important elements within his own party.

The second group of disloyal elements came from the small sector of the

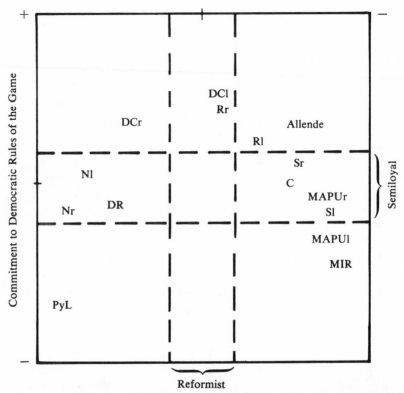

Figure 2. Placement of Key Political Groups in 1970 on Two Dimensions: Commitment to the Socioeconomic Order aid Commitment to the Democratic Rules of the Game

LEGEND: r = rightist; l = leftist; DC = Democracia Cristiana; DR = Democracia Radical; N = Nacional; PyL = Patria y Libertad; S = Socialista; C = Comunista; MAPU = Movimiento de Acción Popular Unitario; MIR = Movimiento de Izquierda Revolucionario.

society which had clearly reaped enormous social and economic rewards from the status quo. As members of the economic Right, many were openly hostile to Chilean democratic institutions and from the outset sought to bar the election of Allende or forcefully remove him from office. In general, the disloyal Right counted on the support of only a handful of activists in late 1970. They were powerful, and they counted among their number elements within the armed forces with close links to U.S. intelligence sources intent on destroying the Popular Unity government. The disloyal rightist ranks would swell considerably as time went by, drawing individuals not only from the wealthy economic groups but also from middle-class and military sectors. Much of the leadership of the nation's industrial and commercial federations were clearly more sympathetic toward the antidemocratic Right than they were toward the more traditional political Right, which had a greater stake in partisan politics. From the outset, then, it was clear that on both sides there were elements whose commitment to their preferred socioeconomic order was greater than their commitment to the democratic process.

The pro-rules group was composed of elements who were loyal to the principles underlying the democratic rules of the game. However, this group was also sharply divided on the desirability of a radical transformation of the socioeconomic structures of society. The president, who had been a member of the Chilean Congress for decades and was a former president of the senate and an author of numerous pieces of social welfare legislation, was joined in his belief that fundamental change could be achieved legally by several other groups in the Popular Unity coalition. First and foremost among these was the Communist party, which argued strongly that the only possible strategy in Chile was a gradual consolidation of power within the framework of traditional institutions. The Radical party, which included outstanding Chilean political personalities such as Senators Luis Bossay and Alberto Baltra, was also convinced that Chilean socialism could become a reality without revolutionary violence. The moderate sector of the Socialist party, of which Senator Aniceto Rodriguez was a prominent spokesman, concurred with that thesis, as did some elements in the progressive wing of the Christian Democrats, including Radomiro Tomic. It must be noted, however, that even within these groups there were substantial differences. The Communists, and, to a degree, Allende himself, argued that eventually the process would lead to the creation of new institutions and procedures. Fundamental transformation would be political as well as socioeconomic. Indeed, even on the question of the future viability of traditional electoral procedures, the Communists were hesitant.[37] By contrast, other groups, including many Radicals and Socialists, were more interested in the inauguration of fundamental socioeconomic changes without the radical transformation of Chile's social democratic political framework. The progressive Christian Democrats envisioned a different kind of socialism, one with much less central control than the socialism envisioned by Communists.[38] While desiring more popular input, they too were more committed to the main outline of traditional institutional arrangements.

Though there were important divisions between leaders and groups who, in broad terms, shared the president's goals, there was a sharp division between them and those sectors who believed in the institutions and rules of the game but were antagonistic to accelerated social and economic transformations. This sector was made up of those elements of the National party who had a long history of political involvement and took great pride in the democratic rules their forefathers had fashioned. Most of them held comfortable positions in commercial, industrial, and agricultural circles, and feared the further erosions in their status which would result from continued challenges to the capitalist system. Many Christian Democrats, identified with the more conservative policies of the last year of the Frei administration, shared these views. Though perhaps more willing than the Nationals to consolidate some reforms, such as those initiated in the countryside, they were much less willing to accept fundamental challenge to a progressive capitalism than were the moderate sectors of the Popular Unity coalition or the progressive sectors of their own party.[39]

The pro-rules sectors were under enormous pressure because of the inherent contradictions within their own amorphous ranks. Those favoring dramatic change faced the clear prospect of having their hopes thwarted. Those favoring the economic or political status quo faced the possibility of loss of privilege and the erosion of traditional institutions. Broad sectors of both groups were capable of falling into the category of "disloyal opposition" as their attachment to the rules faltered. Both would be tested by the constraints of the Chilean system and by the pressures of increasingly mobilized sectors. Eventually the contradictions, coupled with the strong pressure from anti-rules groups, would lead to a characterization of the tradeoffs as zero-sum tradeoffs. And yet Allende, and many others, were confident at the outset that history was on their side, and that it would not be necessary to choose between established rules and a fervent commitment to greater social justice.

This analysis suggests that the number of politically relevant groups and leaders who shared Allende's position on both major issues was very small. Ideological polarization was at an all-time high. It also suggests the enormous predicament which Allende faced in the Chilean Congress. To be elected president he needed a majority, and yet with eighty-three seats in both houses his coalition was eighteen seats short of a majority.

But the Nationals and Radical Democrats, intent on stopping Allende, commanded only forty-three seats in the legislature, a number far too small to engineer the election of Jorge Alessandri. The divided Christian Democrats at the Center of the political spectrum held the balance of power with their seventy-four seats.[40] The pressure on the Christian Democrats was enormous, not only from within the country but from the United States.[41]

Already, U.S. corporations, with the tacit support of the U.S. government, had added their weight to the financial panic instigated by Chilean big business as soon as Allende won the election. In the most blatant intervention in the history of Chilean politics, President Nixon ordered the CIA to stop Allende's election. It soon became clear to U.S. agents, however, that it would not be possible to bribe Christian Democratic legislators. Furthermore, President Frei would have nothing to do with a scheme to have the Congress vote for Alessandri with the understanding that Alessandri would then resign, thus paving the way for a new election in which Frei would be eligible to run for office again. With the approval of the top authorities of the United States government, the CIA then tried to convince key figures of the Chilean military to stage a coup. When the pro-American general, René Schneider, commander in chief of the army, refused to think about such an alternative, foreign and domestic conspirators kidnapped the general in the mistaken hope that the act would produce a coup.[42] In the first political assassination of a prominent Chilean leader since 1837, Schneider was shot to death by his would-be kidnappers. The plot clearly backfired, as most of the conspirators were identified and convicted. President Frei and president-elect Allende marched side by side in the funeral cortege attended by a broad spectrum of civilian and military leadership.

The struggle within the Christian Democratic party over the election of Allende was intense. Tomic, the losing candidate, had already gone on record supporting the Allende victory. Shortly after the ballots were counted, he had embraced his "old friend" and pledged full support. But even though the Tomic wing of the party controlled the more important leadership positions, distrust of Allende was pervasive. A decision to vote for Allende threatened the weak unity of the party.

The impasse was finally resolved when Allende agreed to support a constitutional amendment that would require him to respect civil liberties, elections, and freedom of the press, all of which had been understood to be cornerstones of Chilean democracy for generations. The so-called *Estatuto de Garantía* (Statute of Guarantees) was a vivid illustration of the serious polarization of Chilean politics and the severe erosion of the traditional rules of the game. Those rules in the final analysis are based on a degree of trust, and the need to extract a formal declaration from Allende that he would preserve the constitution showed the deterioration of confidence between political leaders who had been close for decades and for whom a respect for the rules of the game had been implicit. It was also clear evidence of fear that the game of winning support at the expense of other sectors, which had been accelerated during the Christian Democratic period, would continue with renewed strength.

Unlike the Pact of Punto Fijo in Venezuela, which marked the beginning of a period of détente between antagonistic groups and was a mutual agreement to respect the outcome of elections, the Estatuto de Garantía, extracted as a condition for political support, marked a breakdown in mutual understanding signaling the fragility of Chilean institutions.[43] Allende began his administration in an atmosphere of profound crisis. Financial panic, political confrontation, and the resolute attempts by military conspirators and foreign intelligence agents to prevent him from coming to office did not augur well for the government. Many individuals openly questioned the legitimacy of the system which made his election possible, and others, while providing support, showed a profound distrust in the new president's good faith and a real fear for the future of the country's institutions.

3.

The Move to a Socialist Society and the Erosion of the Political Center

Upon his inauguration, Allende moved swiftly and with great political skill to enact a program which he hoped would eventually lead to a socialist society with genuine popular control over economic and political life.[1] His early programs of distributing milk to children and the relaxed style of the *"compañero presidente"* who would mix with the population in his shirt-sleeves brought significant personal support.[2] The Christian Democrats continued their tacit support by agreeing to vote for Popular Unity leadership in one of the houses of Congress. Allende, a genuine idealist, was sure that he would quickly overcome his minority election as the people became convinced that his government was a true popular government. When Regis Debray asked him what he would do if the Congress blocked some of his proposals, he did not hesitate to answer that he would call a plebiscite to override congressional opposition.[3]

The economic policy of the Allende administration involved a four-pronged strategy of income redistribution, expansion of government programs and services, state control of key industries, and extension of land reform. The ultimate goal was to transform class and property relations and to institute a new economic development scheme along Socialist lines.

The policy of income redistribution was aimed not so much at reducing differentials between categories of wage and salary earners as at increasing labor's share of the national income in relationship to the private corporate and *rentier* sectors of the economy. Chilean policy-makers believed that this policy was perfectly viable in conventional economic terms. By increasing income, new demand would be generated, in turn inducing a rise in production in a sluggish economy operating well below capacity. Since much of the new demand would come from low income wage earners, it would spur demand in the labor-intensive sector of the economy, which produced the bulk of the goods consumed by low income people. Unemployment would be further reduced, spurring production.[4]

The fact that the economic policy was based on standard economic calculations does not mean that government officials and planners were oblivious to the political consequences of the strategy. Quite to the contrary, they were hopeful that the potential risk of accelerated income distribution would be offset by clear political gains for the Popular Unity coalition. Economic objectives were not sought merely as an end in themselves, but as tools to broaden the admittedly weak support which Allende had received in his narrow electoral victory. Pedro Vuskovick, the minister of economy and principal architect of the economic program, stressed forcefully that the basic program of the government was not merely reformist but revolutionary. He added:

if that is our starting point, what is involved in economic policy is not a set of technical problems, but rather an essentially political problem, serving primarily, and that is its central objective, as an instrument to broaden and consolidate the positions of power of the workers . . . economic policy is determined both by a desire to realize an economic program fully and completely and by a need to secure in the economic sphere the appropriate political conditions to develop the overall program. That is the reason for the simultaneous existence of programmatic and strategic objectives in economic policy.[5]

In sum, it must be stressed that the policies followed by the Allende government in the crucial first year were not simply a response to uncontrolled popular pressure for a greater share of the finite goods of Chilean society but were the result of a deliberate policy with clear economic and political objectives. Certainly the Popular Unity government raised great expectations, and its policies would subsequently encourage ever-increasing pressures. The fact is, however, that income redistribution and price controls were set in motion as a concerted and calculated policy initiated from above.

The record shows that the process of income distribution exceeded governmental goals. The government raised the basic wage by 66.6 percent and the basic monthly salary by 35 percent. By July of 1971 average income per employee had increased by 54.9 percent rather than the 40 percent to 45 percent programmed.[6]

Income redistribution was accompanied by a dramatic increase in government spending, particularly on social services such as housing, education, health, and sanitation. By the end of 1971, fiscal expenditures had increased 70 percent, from 19 to 33 billion *escudos*. Ten billion of this amount was financed by Central Bank credits, as opposed to only 1.8 billion the previous year. At the same time, as table 16 shows, credit expanded substantially; the public sector's share of total bank credit increased from less than one-third to almost 60 percent.[7] For the twelve-month period between December 1970 and December 1971, the money in circulation increased by 110.5 percent as the government sought to meet the financial demands of its new programs and obligations.[8]

Table 16. Total Amount of Credit Granted by the Banking System, December 1970–
December 1971 (millions of escudos)

	Public Sector			Private Sector	Total
	Treasury	Other	Total		
End of December 1970	916	1,152	2,068	6,777	8,845
End of July 1971	6,487	2,634	9,121	8,512	17,633
End of December 1971	9,301	6,814	16,115	10,785	26,900

SOURCE: Banco Central, *Boletín Mensual*, no. 537, November 1972, p. 1362; cited in Stefan de Vylder, *Allende's Chile: The Political Economy of the Rise and Fall of the Unidad Popular* (Cambridge: Cambridge University Press, 1976), p. 57.

Initially, the Popular Unity government's economic policies had very positive effects. In 1971 the gross domestic product increased by 8.6 percent, the best single year in decades, with moderate to strong increases in all major sectors.[9] Unemployment declined as employment in areas such as construction, public utilities, manufacturing, and services increased 11.7 percent, 7.6 percent, 7.1 percent, and 5.1 percent, respectively.[10] Increased production led to increased demand, primarily for basic goods such as agricultural products. Agricultural production did register an increase of 8.6 percent in crop-farming and 1.8 percent in livestock production. This increase, however, was not enough to meet the burgeoning demand, and the government was forced to increase its imports of foreign goods sharply. In the short run such a measure was feasible because of the ample reserves which had accumulated due to the rise in copper prices in the last years of the Frei administration. Finally, the ability of the economy to respond to government stimulation meant that inflation actually dropped from 34.9 percent in 1970 to 22.1 percent in 1971.[11]

The government also moved swiftly in its effort to create a Socialist economy. By nationalizing major industries, government planners hoped to be able to channel profit not only into further investment but also into subsidies for government programs. Likewise, nationalization of the banks would give the government control over credit for the same purposes. Both banks and industries were taken over by purchasing shares of their stock or by employing existing legislation permitting authorities to intervene in a firm which for some reason was not providing essential services.[12] Workers sympathetic to the Popular Unity coalition often forced a plant or enterprise to cease operations, opening the way for government takeover. By December 1971 the number of industrial establishments controlled by the state had risen from thirty-one to sixty-two, not including thirty-nine more under government seizure.[13] A major accomplishment for the government was the nationalization of the United States copper interests after the Chilean Congress, controlled by the opposition, unanimously approved the necessary legislation. Though nationalization of the copper industry would aggravate the dispute between the government and the foreign enterprises, it must be stressed that many other foreign firms were taken over on mutually agreeable terms.[14]

The takeover of banks and business enterprises generally proceeded without much violence. The opposite was true in agricultural areas, where landowners resisted government expropriation or workers took over the land. Members of the MIR made significant inroads in some rural areas, providing organizational support and, in some cases, arms for rural confrontations. As table 17 shows, rural strikes continued to increase in 1971, but there was a real explosion of land seizures, which increased by 180 percent over 1970. The administration was reluctant to repress such activities and thus tacitly encouraged them, asserting that disputes occurred in only .02 percent of all properties.[15] Spurred in part by farm workers, the Allende government seized over 1,300 properties during its first year, 300 more than the number expropriated in the six years of the preceding administration.[16]

Government planners, hoping for popular approval of their policies, were not disappointed with the outcome of the first nationwide test of political strength after the 1970 election, which was the 1971 election of municipal councils. As table 18 shows, the Popular Unity parties received a slightly higher percentage of the total vote than did the opposition parties. In a slightly smaller electorate than the one participating in the previous year's presidential election (despite an increase in registration, which included for the first time illiterates and eighteen–twenty-one-year-olds), the opposition parties received 486,980 fewer votes, while the government gained 307,375 votes. In particular, President Allende's own Socialist party did extremely well, with an increase in support of 95 percent over the 1967 municipal election. This compared favorably to the increase of 83 percent which President Frei's party had gained in the 1967 municipal elections by comparison with the 1963 contest. Whereas the 1967 election had given the opposition a clear advantage, by 1971 the Left had pulled abreast, with a net increase of nine percent over the previous municipal election.[17] Preliminary analysis of the 1971 municipal election suggests that the increase in support came from diverse sectors of the active population. As will be analyzed more closely below, the social bases of the vote in 1971 for all the Popular Unity parties did not change dramatically with respect to the vote for Allende in 1970.

Table 17. Number of Rural Conflicts Resulting in Strikes or Land Seizures (*Tomas*), 1967–71

	1967	1968	1969	1970	1971
Strikes	693	648	1,127	1,580	1,758
Tomas	9	26	148	456	1,278
Total	702	674	1,275	2,036	3,036

SOURCE: Stefan de Vylder, *Allende's Chile: The Political Economy of the Rise and Fall of the Unidad Popular* (Cambridge: Cambridge University Press, 1976), p. 204.

Table 18. Results of Municipal Elections, 1967 and 1971

Party	1967 Number of Votes	%	1971 Number of Votes	%
Popular Unity				
Socialists	324,965	13.9	663,367	22.3
Communists	346,105	14.8	477,862	16.9
Radicals [a]	252,640	10.8	228,426	8.1
Social Democrats [b]	17,457	0.1	38,054	1.3
Total	941,167	40.0	1,377,709	48.6
Opposition				
Christian Democrats	834,810	35.6	729,398	25.7
Nationals	334,656	14.3	513,074	18.1
Radical Democrats [a]	124,434	5.3	110,021	3.9
Padena [b]	38,859		13,487	0.5
Total	1,332,759	57.0	1,365,980	48.2
Others, blank and void	69,361	3.0	128,967	3.0
Grand Total	2,343,287	100.0	2,835,402	100.0
Total registered	3,073,992		3,792,682	
Percentage of abstentions	23.7		23.7	

SOURCE: Calculated from data available in the Dirección del Registro Electoral, Santiago, Chile.

[a] The Democracia Radical had not been created in 1967. The Radical vote was arbitrarily divided between Radicals and Radical Democrats, assuming that the relative strength of the two factions was the same in 1967 as it was in 1971, the first election after the split.

[b] The Social Democrats and PADENA, which were combined in 1967, have been arbitrarily separated, assuming that the relative strength of the parties was the same as it was in the 1969 congressional election, the first election after the split.

One of the most important characteristics of the 1971 vote is that it reflected further political polarization. Because the electorate perceived the contest to be between a Popular Unity coalition and a more status quo-oriented opposition, it threw more of its support to the two parties on the extremes, the Socialists and the Nationals. All of the centrist parties, including the Christian Democrats and the two Radical fragments, lost support in absolute terms with respect to the previous election. Their combined percentage of the vote declined from 52 percent to 40 percent.

Though the short-term policies of the Popular Unity coalition contributed to economic and political success in 1971, it would be misleading to imply that serious difficulties did not surface in that same year, difficulties that presaged new problems. Government economists were aware of the potentially explosive consequences of an overstimulated economy. As Minister Vuskovic himself noted in an October 1971 seminar, two very serious consequences of government policy were the drastic reduction in investment and the almost complete depletion of foreign reserves.[18] Despite increases in public investment, domestic investment outside of construction dropped 71.3 percent.[19]

The policy of accommodating demand with imports resulted in a critical shortage of foreign reserves as copper prices dropped and production in the largest copper mines decreased. The $343.4 million in reserves the country had in 1970 had dwindled to $32.3 million by December of 1971.[20] The priority given to the importation of foodstuffs, which rose from 14 percent to 24 percent of total imports, meant a corresponding decline in other items, including a decline of 22 percent in imported machinery.[21] These figures suggest that by the end of 1971, increased demand stimulated by the government had already reached a level which exceeded the short-term capability of domestic production and import capacity. Vuskovic himself underscored this, noting that "bottlenecks" could only be avoided by increased investments and production. He also warned that because of these potential difficulties "it is difficult to visualize for next year a policy of wage increases with the same likelihood that those increases would not be translated, automatically, into higher prices."[22] He further envisioned a period of consolidation rather than expansion of the income gains of 1971.

Unfortunately for the government and for the country, the year 1972 would not be a year of consolidation, and the economic picture would contrast unfavorably with that of 1971. By July 1972, as table 19 shows, inflation had increased sharply to 45.9 percent and by the end of the year had quadrupled to a record high of 163.4 percent. By December 1972 Chile's reserve situation showed a net deficit of $288.7 million and its balance of payments deficit had increased four-fold over the previous year to $538 million.[23] Bottlenecks developed at an ever-increasing rate as black market operations and hoarding

Table 19. Yearly Rates of Inflation, December 1970–September 1973

Period	Percentage Increase in Prices
December 1970–December 1971	22.1
June 1971–June 1972	40.1
July 1971–July 1972	45.9
August 1971–August 1972	77.2
September 1971–September 1972	114.3
October 1971–October 1972	142.9
November 1971–November 1972	149.8
December 1971–December 1972	163.4
January 1972–January 1973	180.3
February 1972–February 1973	174.1
March 1972–March 1973	183.3
April 1972–April 1973	195.5
May 1972–May 1973	238.4
June 1972–June 1973	283.4
July 1972–July 1973	323.2
August 1972–August 1973	303.6
September 1972–September 1973	286.0
October 1972–October 1973	528.4
April 1973–April 1974	746.2

SOURCE: Instituto Nacional de Estadística, mimeographed reports.

became common practices and production was unable to keep pace with demands for essential items. In order to prevent a dramatic cutback in government programs, money was printed at an even faster rate; consequently, by 1972 the percentage of the budget covered by emissions had increased from 30 or 40 percent over the previous year.[24]

The Popular Unity government's problems were compounded by sharp cutbacks in international aid and credit. The hostility which greeted the Allende election victory in U.S. governmental and financial circles was soon translated into a policy of cutting off support for the Popular Unity government. The Chilean nationalization of the copper industry further hardened this policy. U.S. officials used their influence with international lending agencies such as the World Bank and the Inter-American Development Bank to cut off aid. The World Bank eliminated all new aid and the IDB approved only small loans to private organizations. At the same time the U.S. Export Import Bank denied credit for purchasing U.S. jetliners, and governmental aid and loan programs were discontinued. Private banks, whose short-term credits are often vital in international transactions, also reduced loan programs with the Chilean government.[25] During the Frei administration, an average of $300 million in short-term credits was available to Chile. By 1972, that figure had dwindled to $30 million.[26] Table 20 summarizes the actions of major U.S. and international lending and aid agencies before and during the Popular Unity administration.

It is crucial to stress that in absolute terms the decline of aid to Chile did not represent a severe cutback in resources. But given the sharp drop in copper prices, the dramatic increases in the importation of food, and the huge indebtedness which the Allende government inherited from its predecessor, restrictions on aid and credits seriously complicated the government's predicament. This was particularly true for aid from U.S. sources. Since tools and machinery of U.S. origin were so important to the Chilean economy, the difficulties which Chile faced in obtaining spare parts contributed to dislocations in the productive sector. For example, in the transportation sector, the value of machinery and equipment of U.S. origin dropped from $152.6 million in 1970 to $110 million in 1971, and by late 1972, according to some estimates, 30 percent of private buses, 33 percent of state buses, and 21 percent of all taxis were out of commission due to lack of parts. One estimate is that the value of the U.S. share of total Chilean imports dropped from 37.2 percent in 1970 to about 10 percent in 1972.[27] Though the Chilean government was able to establish commercial links with other countries and obtain alternative credits, these were often tied to specific items and projects and could not completely substitute for American-made products. A dramatic indication of this was the Chilean government's decision in 1972 to purchase a Boeing jetliner with cash rather than accept credit to purchase two Soviet airliners which would have necessitated a complete revamping of the whole support and maintenance infrastructure.[28]

Table 20. Foreign Aid to Chile from U.S. Government Agencies and International Institutions—Total of Loans and Grants (in millions of dollars)

	FISCAL YEAR													
	1953–61	1962	1963	1964	1965	1966	1967	1968	1969	1970	1971	1972	1973	1974
Total U.S. economic aid	339.7	169.8	85.3	127.1	130.4	111.9	260.4	97.1	80.8	29.6	8.6	7.4	3.8	9.8
AID	76.4	142.7	41.3	78.9	99.5	93.2	15.5	57.9	35.4	18.0	1.5	1.0	.8	5.3
Food for Peace	94.2	6.6	22.0	26.9	14.2	14.4	7.9	23.0	15.0	7.2	6.3	5.9	2.5	3.2
Export-Import Bank	169.0	.8	16.2	15.3	8.2	.1	234.6	14.2	28.7	3.3	—	1.6	3.1	98.1[a]
Total U.S. military aid	41.8	17.8	30.6	9.0	9.9	10.1	4.1	7.8	11.8	.8	5.7	12.3	15.0	15.9
Total U.S. economic and military aid	381.5	187.6	115.9	136.1	140.3	122.0	264.5	104.9	91.8	30.4	14.3[b]	21.3[b]	21.9	123.8[b]
Total international organizations[c]	135.4	18.7	31.2	41.4	12.4	72.0	93.8	19.4	49.0	76.4	15.4	28.2	9.4	111.2
IBRD (World Bank)	95.2	—	—	22.6	4.4	2.7	60.0	—	11.6	19.3	—	—	—	13.5
Inter-American Development Bank	5.7	15.1	24.4	16.6	4.9	62.2	31.0	16.5	31.9	45.6	12.0	2.1	5.2	97.3

SOURCE: "U.S. Overseas Loans and Grants, Obligations and Loan Authorizations, 1 July 1945 to 30 June 1971," pp. 39, 175. Prepared by Statistics and Reports Division, Office of Financial Management, Agency for International Development, and printed in U.S., Senate, "Hearings, before the Select Committee to Study Governmental Operations with respect to Intelligence Activities," vol. 7 (4 and 5 December 1975), p. 181.

[a] Includes $57 million from the Export-Import Bank and $41.1 million from other sources.

[b] Total per chart plus Export-Import Bank.

[c] U.S. contributions to International organizations included above; therefore U.S. aid and international aid should not be added.

Because of the dependent nature of the Chilean economy, the dwindling of the Chilean government's international reserve position made the country extremely vulnerable to international retaliation. Though Chile's economic difficulties cannot be attributed solely to an international economic "blockade," that blockade did contribute to a spiral of increasing economic difficulties.

These mounting economic difficulties soon posed a substantial political threat to the government. In December 1971, middle-class women staged the much-publicized march of the empty pots. By August 1972 it was clear that the government's economic policies were seriously affecting the upper and middle classes. Table 21 presents the results of a survey taken in August 1972. The survey reveals that 99 percent of the upper classes felt that it was difficult to buy supplies—a feeling shared by 77 percent of the middle classes. While the policy of the government was clearly perceived as threatening by approximately 60 percent of the population, 75 percent of the lower classes felt that it was now easier to obtain goods. These figures reflect considerable discontent in the petit bourgeois group that the Popular Unity government had considered important to the success of its program.

In the political sphere, the government experienced some reversals after the 1971 municipal election. Popular Unity candidates were defeated by a united opposition in three out of four congressional by-elections. In April 1972, the government's candidate was defeated in the crucial election for the rectorship of the University of Chile. The results showed that the Popular Unity lost ground not only among the usually conservative sectors of the faculties but also among segments of the university that had for years provided majorities to Marxist candidates. Finally, in the first fully democratic popular elections of the Chilean Labor Federation, the Christian Democrats did surprisingly well, actually winning majorities in one of the large copper companies which had traditionally selected leftist labor leaders. At the same time, the government found that its plans to enact a unicameral legislature and popular courts were stalled, while the effort to institute a system of genuine worker participation in industrial decision-making, with a few interesting exceptions, never really got off the ground.

Further political difficulties for the Allende administration arose in confrontations with other institutions and forces in the complex Chilean institutional arena. On several occasions government actions were stymied by objections from the Contraloría or from the courts. However, the most ominous confrontation was posed by the opposition in Congress. In his first year, Allende had shuffled his cabinet only once, to resolve internal disputes within his coalition. By the end of 1972, he had instituted two full and six partial cabinet changes involving seventeen ministerial posts—several in response to attempts by the Congress to impeach his ministers. In January and again in July of 1972 his minister of the interior was impeached by Congress. Congress

Table 21. Response to the Survey Question, "In Your Opinion, is Buying Essential Products at This Time for Your Home Easy or Difficult?"

| | SOCIOECONOMIC GROUPS | | | |
	Upper	Middle	Lower	Total
Easy	1%	17%	75%	47%
Difficult	99	77	19	48
Neither	0	6	6	5

SOURCE: *Ercilla*, 13–19 September 1972, p. 10.

used its veto power to deny tax increases which could have helped to alleviate the fiscal crisis. In February of 1972 both houses of Congress approved legislation that called for a constitutional amendment to regulate the areas of the economy. If adopted, it would mean that Allende would have to modify significantly his program of creating a Socialist sector of the economy.[29] The amendment would permit the takeover of industries only by legislative approval and, because of a retroactive provision, would require the executive to place in the hands of Congress the entire policy of his first months in office. Passage of the provision on the economy was to engender the most significant confrontation of the Allende regime. Its importance lies in the fact that it marked the clear breakdown of the tenuous centrist consensus which had enabled Allende to reach the presidency. What happened? How did an auspicious beginning turn so sour? Why was the government unable to consolidate the gains of 1971? Why did the fragile Center collapse?

Internal and External Constraints:
The Problem of a Minority Coalition
Intent on Change in a Highly Polarized Society

The early failures of the Popular Unity government and the eventual breakdown of Chilean democracy cannot be explained by accusing one side or the other of destroying the system. It was not merely the result of erroneous economic policies or a deliberate strategy on the part of elements in the government to accelerate the collapse of bourgeois institutions. Nor was it simply the result of reactionary forces, aided and abetted from abroad, who sought to preserve privilege at all cost. Certainly these elements were present in varying degrees. But the breakdown of democracy in Chile must be understood in broader terms. It must be understood as the failure to structure a viable Center in a highly polarized society with strong centrifugal tendencies. As noted earlier, key sectors in both the government and the opposition were committed to the possibility of change within the context of ongoing institutional processes. But it was not only a matter of choice. Actions and decisions were subject to the powerful constraints and limitations of the ongoing system's electoral and institutional dimensions. Both those in the government and those in the opposition who were committed to a peaceful resolution of conflict were buffeted by pressures from both extremes. The pressure was so great that the long-term advantage of structuring working agreements was continously set aside in favor of the short-term requirement of preserving immediate political strength. The government found itself incapable of shifting away from its income distribution policies or imposing order on the working class for fear not only of the opposition but of rival elements within its own coalition. Its initiatives were blocked in the rambling bureaucracy and questioned by the courts, the Contraloría, and the Congress. The fundamental structural transformations it sought to achieve were blocked by a constitution it could not amend for lack of votes in Congress. Likewise, for the fragmented Christian Democrats, ideological pressures and electoral considerations, dictated by the continuous challenge of the National party for leadership of the opposition, made it increasingly difficult to continue with a policy of tacit support for the government. The politics of outbidding, as much within each coalition as between coalitions, carried the day.

It is crucial to stress that this process was a dialectical one. Government actions, taken to overcome political constraints and open opposition, often resulted in greater and more intense opposition, in turn forcing the government to take additional actions which could only worsen the political climate. The fragmentation of elites, the independence of a highly vocal and partisan media, the continuous mobilization of mass support by both camps and by elements within each camp added further to the confusion and made it hard to arrive at the minimum consensus necessary to preserve the regime. In time, many centrist elements on both sides would move increasingly into semiloyal or disloyal positions.

Does this mean that the outcome was inevitable? Though the political constraints provided the critical parameters defining the limits and potentials for political choice and action, it does not follow that the outcome was inevitable. In Chile there was room for choice. Class consciousness was not such that the working class in Chile would have settled for no less than total revolution—for surely compromise would have meant that. Neither were large segments of the middle class so reactionary that they would settle for only a Fascist government. At certain key junctures in the unfolding Chilean drama different choices would have led to different results, though as the process unfolded itself, and as polarization became more extreme, the range of the possible was dramatically reduced. It is the task of this section to analyze both the government and the opposition, pointing out some of their constraints and opportunities. Because of the unfolding evolution of a complex process, the analytical argument will of necessity be combined with a description of the changing parameters of the system over time.

The Popular Unity Government

Juan Linz has argued that many of the problems faced by governments during a crisis relate to their inability to solve major problems. Unsolvable problems are in part the responsibility of policy-makers themselves, who are unable to provide an adequate response due to a lack of means or knowledge, or the incompatibility of necessary actions with those that have greater priority.[30] The economic crisis during the Allende period clearly became the government's chief unsolvable problem. Though opposition groups must bear much of the blame for economic sabotage, government policies created strong reaction and its counterpolicies simply did not succeed in avoiding economic catastrophe.

The stark reality of the Allende years was that it proved to be politically impossible to cut back on the policy of increasing the income of poorer sectors of society and of those sectors affiliated with the Left. The strike at the El Salvador mine early in the Allende period, though resolved in the government's favor, presaged many more, including the crippling strike at El Teniente in the winter of 1973. What made the situation intolerable, however, was that wage increases for those sectors whose increases had traditionally been postponed were not accompanied by a parallel cutback in the portion of the national economic pie going to the more privileged groups. By February 1972 across-the-board wage increases were granted to make up for heightened inflation. Important groups such as the armed forces, radio operators, and Chuquicamata miners managed to get readjustments substantially higher than official inflation figures. By October 1972 wages and salaries for all but the wealthiest elements had increased by 99.8 percent over the previous year.[31] Like previous governments, the Popular Unity government did not succeed in deviating from the traditional policies of patronage and reajuste. "The income policy of 1971 was based on the principle of overall expansion rather than distribution. Quite consciously, the UP decided to favor not only the poor majority (which in percentage terms received a little more than average) but the comparatively well-to-do middle classes as well."[32] When the newly mobilized sectors sought their due on the same basis as everyone else, the Chilean economy was severely taxed.

The favorable predisposition of the government to the economic betterment of practically everyone in the society contributed to a dramatic rise in strike activity. Whereas in 1969 there were 977 strikes, in 1972 the figure had jumped to an all-time high of 3,287. In the first two years of the Allende government strike activity increased by 170 percent, far exceeding the increase of 45 percent in the 1964–66 period. As table 22 shows, strike activity far outstripped any new unionization. In fact, in 1972 the unionized industrial population continued to be slightly smaller than it had been in 1952. (See tables 7 and 9 for a comparison with earlier years.) A breakdown of this strike

Table 22. Growth of Industrial, Craft, and Agricultural Unions During the Popular Unity Years

Year	Number of Industrial Unions	Number of Members in Industrial Unions	Average Size of Industrial Unions	Number of Craft Unions	Number of Members in Craft Unions	Average Size of Craft Unions	Number of Agricultural Unions
1964	632	142,951	226.2	1,207	125,926	104.5	24
1970	1,440	197,651	137.3	2,569	239,323	93.2	510
1971	1,605	205,894	128.3	2,881	252,924	87.8	632
1972	1,781	213,777	120.0	3,511	282,181	80.4	709

SOURCE: For 1964, see tables 7 and 9. For 1970, see *Mensaje del Presidente ante el Congreso Pleno*, 21 May 1972, pp. 859, 860, and 861. For 1971 and 1972, see *Mensaje del Presidente ante el Congreso Pleno*, 21 May 1973, pp. 793 and 794. The author is grateful to Henry Landsberger for making these reports available to him.

activity shows that in 1971 the agricultural sector, with only 12.3 percent of the unions, experienced 38.6 percent of the strikes. By 1972, however, most of the strike activity had shifted to the urban areas. Strikes by public employees accounted for some of this shift, increasing from 132 in 1971 to 815 in 1972, a jump of 145 percent. In dialectical fashion, groups from all walks of life responded to government attempts to ameliorate their situation by making further demands.

There is little doubt that by 1972 mobilization had gotten out of hand, often to the chagrin of the president, who tried to obtain more discipline by cajoling the populace. Yet the government continued to encourage indiscipline by its policies. This was the case not only because of the goal of redistribution but also because many strikes were encouraged by government officials and Popular Unity political groups in order to accelerate the process of takeover of industries.

To many government officials, it seemed that the takeover of industries, spurred by worker initiatives, would in turn contribute to the solution of the problem of heightened demand. By controlling key sectors of the economy they would be able to make the decisions necessary to manage inflation and spur production. Table 23 provides information on interventions and requisitions, including temporary ones, through November 1972. These accelerated in times of political crisis such as late 1971 and September and October of 1972. By the end of 1972 approximately one-fourth of industrial production was in state hands.[33]

The trouble was that state intervention in industry posed unanticipated problems which aggravated rather than lessened the economic difficulties. Some were political and some were economic. Thus, the takeover was met by a strong and hostile reaction among both large and small businessmen and their allies. The vast majority were in no danger of government takeover. Nevertheless, they feared that they too would be expropriated. Sabotage and hoarding became the order of the day. In January 1972 the *Partido de Iz-*

Number of Members in Agricultural Unions	Average Size of Agricultural Unions	Number of Strikes	Number of Strikes per Union	Number of Workers on Strike	Number of Workers per Strike	Man-days Lost	Days per Strike per Worker	Year
1,658	69.1	564	.31	138,474	245	869,728	10.6	1964
114,112	223.7							1970
127,782	202.2	2,709	.52	304,530	112	1,414,313	4.6	1971
136,527	192.6	3,289	.55	397,142	121	1,654,151	4.2	1972

quierda Radical (PIR), still a member of the Popular Unity coalition, urged that the government issue a clear statement of its policy of economic regulation so as to permit small and middle-sized industries to return to normal operations. They noted that the uncertainty caused by the takeover of firms had led to an 8 percent decline in total investment and a 20 percent decline in private investment.[34] Sabotage from the Right, economic uncertainty, and disruption of plant operations contributed to production difficulties by the second year of Allende's term, compounding the problem of meeting demands.

But sabotage and labor indiscipline were only part of the problem. Many firms had been mismanaged or neglected, and on entry into the public sector they proved to be more of a burden than an asset.[35] Furthermore, and ironically, the very policy of wage increases and price freezes which were to be supported by substantial government control of the economy actually hurt the state industries and corporations as much as they did the private ones. Many government-controlled industries found themselves close to bankruptcy and were forced to turn to the Central Bank for loans in order to remain solvent. The Central Bank, bypassing normal budgeting procedures, lent enormous sums of money to nationalized industries as well as other government agencies. This proved to be an important factor in spurring increases in currency emissions, as table 24 shows, in turn further fueling inflationary pressures. During the fiscal year 1971–72 the government deficit rose from 10 to 26 billion escudos.

It is important to stress that the growing pattern of agencies turning toward the Central Bank in order to make ends meet had serious political as well as economic effects. It contributed to the government's loss of control and centralized authority over the general financial structure, thereby making it more difficult to reverse policies. The Office of the Budget and the Ministry of Finance found it increasingly difficult to coordinate the budget of the state sector and keep tabs on the vast state apparatus. During the Allende years the Ministry of Finance lost not only the initiative over general economic policy to the Ministry of Economics under Vuskovic's direction, but substantial control over the budgetary process. In the crisis atmosphere of the Allende

Table 23. Number of Requisitions and Interventions by Time Periods, November 1970–November 1972

Period	Interventions	Requisitions	Total
November–December 1970	37	1	38
January–February 1971	23	—	23
March–April 1971	1	5	6
May–June 1971	12	12	24
July–August 1971	9	6	15
September–October 1971	24	7	31
November–December 1971	21	9	30
January–February 1972	13	6	19
March–April 1972	14	7	21
May–June 1972	16	3	19
July–August 1972	7	18	25
September–October 1972[a]	23	48	71
November 1972	2	4	6
Total	202	126	328

SOURCE: Based on Instituto de Economía, *La economía chilena en 1972*, pp. 116 ff; cited in Stefan de Vylder, *Allende's Chile: The Political Economy at the Rise and Fall of the Unidad Popular* (Cambridge: Cambridge University Press, 1976), p. 146.

[a] During the "October events" a large number of enterprises were subjected to intervention or requisition for participation in the general lockout. Most of these companies were later returned to their owners.

years, the already cumbersome and decentralized Chilean public sector became more and more unmanageable. The bold effort to gain control of essential sectors of the economy did not help to counteract the ill effects of the early expansionist policies but only created more difficulties which further precluded extrication.

At the root of the difficulties in economic policy and state management were more basic political problems which can be traced to the coalition nature of a government operating within the rules of traditional Chilean politics. The Popular Unity parties were intent not only on bringing about change in Chilean society, often in different directions, but on maximizing their own party fortunes, according to the precepts of traditional Chilean party politics. Despite the parties' recourse to demonstrations and occasional violence, in the final analysis their "power capability" was measured by electoral success. This continued to be paramount in Chilean politics, and indirectly all groups, including the MIR, would turn to the ballot box and concern themselves with patronage and electoral considerations. This made it very difficult to impose any kind of centralized control over, or clear direction on, the government program. Not only did the president have to spend an enormous amount of time dealing with strikes and disputes by public employees and private unions and associations, he also had to contend with orchestrating an enormously complex coalition government.

From the outset the Popular Unity parties implemented a complex quota system to give each party organization access to a wealth of government patronage. From the level of ministers down through the undersecretaries to

Table 24. Increases in Money Supply and in Prices, December 1970 to July 1973 (in percentages)

Period	Percentage Increase in Money Supply	Percentage Increase in Prices
December 1970–December 1971	110.5	22.1
December 1971–December 1972	164.9	163.4
January 1972–January 1973	190.5	180.3
February 1972–February 1973	198.2	174.1
March 1972–March 1973	198.2	183.3
April 1972–April 1973	210.9	195.5
May 1972–May 1973	230.2	238.5
June 1972–June 1973	257.4	283.4
July 1972–July 1973	286.7	323.6

SOURCE: *El Mercurio,* 26 August 1973.

the lowest officials in the public bureaucracy, elaborate schemes were instituted to divide up public employment and responsibility. By and large the quota system was determined by the electoral strength of each political party. Conflicts and disputes were common. For example, when the *intendente* of Valparaiso resigned, the Radicals feared they would be denied the post, which they felt was theirs. They were particularly concerned since they had lost considerable ground in the municipal election of 1971. After much frustrating debate, Allende opted for appointing a "neutral" military officer to the post—a harbinger of things to come.

Cleavages also arose in government agencies. Not only the weight of bureaucratic practices but party cleavages cut down on the effectiveness of agency actions in implementing change. For example, the Socialist vice-president of INDAP, one of the key organizations of the agrarian reform movement, was attacked publicly by leaders of the Movement of Popular United Action (MAPU) in a power play that shook the organization.[36] Coalition difficulties were compounded by the further fractionalization of the parties of the Center, who were clearly caught in the centrifugal tendencies of Chilean politics. After the municipal elections the Radical party split, with a sizable faction arguing that the party leadership was too close to the Marxist position. Though the PIR remained temporarily in the government coalition, it was a new political entity to be reckoned with. The MAPU also split when a fragment of the Christian Democratic party broke away and formed the *Izquierda Cristiana*. Fractionalization made the complex task of allocating patronage to different elements of the coalition even more time-consuming. Allende argued that "there are more forces now supporting the government... but its base has been weakened by the internal problems of the parties."[37] In spite of his calls for the creation of a single party out of the Popular Unity coalition, the tradition of "going it alone" proved too strong.

The problems of patronage and quotas became even more demanding with the takeover of industries. The *interventores* (receivers) were appointed, particularly in later stages, largely as a reward for party activity and to insure that particular parties and factions had industries "of their own." Many interventores were very competent and dedicated. Others became notorious for their lack of knowledge of the industry they were supposed to regulate and for the element of political corruption that they introduced. In March 1972 the Communist party issued a strong criticism of the interventores, noting that they often simply replaced the old managers, living in the same houses and driving the same cars. It called for a clear and concise plan for the development of the country.[38]

Finally, the politics of quotas and political appointments led to a significant loss of authority in government agencies as well as state operated industries. Workers simply would not take orders from managers who belonged to other parties.[39] Often the simplest decisions in factories had to be resolved by party meetings or orders from party authorities on the outside. In the early years of the Allende administration perhaps the most significant example of this problem took place in the copper mines when Communist managers were appointed. Unions under the direction of the Popular Socialist party, a leftist party not in the coalition, took strong issue with the direction provided by the Communist managers. The party released the following statement in January 1972.

The USOPO believes, and makes it public, that the Communist party, when it comes to Chuquicamata, must change its attitude in its treatment of the workers....We have seen that it is its clear intent to exercise party predominance at all costs, without hesitating as to the means employed and the consequences which might result to the interests of the workers and the economy of the country.[40]

The political competition and quota system thus not only cut down on the efficiency of the government and led to serious political divisions and conflicts, but it also reinforced the decentralized and autonomous tendencies of much of the Chilean state, making it more difficult for those in the top policy-making positions to impose authority and chart the general direction of the government.

While this study has stressed the importance of patronage and electoral considerations in accounting for much of the difficulty of coordination and management, it would be a serious mistake to ignore the profound ideological disagreements and differences wihin the coalition. Both elements interacted, contributing not only to the lack of direction of the governmental effort but to its failure to respond in a unified and forceful way when decisive action was called for. In fact ideological disagreements often meant that sectors within the Popular Unity government worked at cross-purposes with one another. The Socialists stressed mobilization and worker participation, while the Communists argued for a slower course of action aimed at consolidating gains in the control of the productive sectors of the economy. Some elements of the

Socialist party and minor parties such as the MAPU pressed for radical mobilization and forced expropriation, stressing the need to prepare for armed conflict. The Left knew that it had to act together if any progress was to be made, but serious policy differences undermined concerted action.[41]

Particularly after the negative consequences of early policies became apparent, both the president and the Communist party became increasingly critical of the strategy of taking over the economy as fast as possible. Clear strains became public in December 1971 when some parties of the Popular Unity coalition, supporting a by-election candidate, issued a platform statement calling for nonpayment of landowners for expropriated lands. The Communist party condemned this statement in very strong terms.

One of the most serious evidences of a clear split in the parties came in the city of Concepción in the fall of 1972 when regional members of the Popular Unity coalition, in alliance with the MIR, sought forcibly to prevent an authorized demonstration by opposition elements. They argued that such marches gave comfort to Fascist elements and undermined the Popular Unity government. In the ensuing struggle, the police were forced to intervene, and one student, a member of an extreme leftist group, was killed.

The reaction to the death of the student and the confrontation in Concepción was immediate and widespread. With the exception of the Communist party, the regional organizations of the governing coalition called for an immediate dismissal of the intendente of the province, a Communist, and the dissolution of the police antiriot unit. Demonstrators in the capital expressed their anger by yelling slogans such as "Reformism opens the door to fascism" and "Down with politics of conciliation." The regional organization of the coalition issued a statement in which it argued that the events of Concepción showed that there were two currents among the people:

One [group] believes that it is possible to get along with the enemies of the people, which in practice means forgetting the existence of a class struggle, which seeks to rely on the apparatus of the State and not on the power of the people and the masses and even seeks a repression of those sectors of the left which don't share their policy of conciliation . . . .
The other policy affirms the conviction that it is not possible to conciliate with the enemies of the working class. It holds that the contradictions between exploiters and exploited remain and are becoming more intense. It holds that it is necessary to rely on the forced and organized mobilization of the masses, rejecting all dogmatism and sectarianism in the bosom of the people . . . . This policy rejects the tendency to assign in fact a neutral posture to the popular Government and requires that the force of the Government be joined with the force of the people to spur and channel the Chilean revolution.[42]

The Communist party, in a press conference held by its secretary general, strongly condemned the events in Concepción and argued that the other parties of the Popular Unity and the MIR had taken "an erroneous path." He added:

Let it be clear that we are in favor of recognizing the rights of the opposition when it is manifested through legal channels . . . . We believe that there is no possibility today, in the current moment, to modify that legality, that institutional structure, by any means, neither through legal means nor through extralegal means . . . . We feel that there is urgency in closing the ranks around the program of the UP, the government of the UP and the President of the Republic, and that it is possible to have a correlation of forces since it is not true that those who are not with the government are fascists . . . . To be a revolutionary is not to take over things because that is easy when one knows that the government will not repress you. To be a revolutionary is to win the battle of production . . . unfortunately not everyone agrees with this.[43]

This debate clearly illustrates the dilemma faced by Allende and the more Center-oriented elements of the coalition. Because of electoral and patronage obligations and because of significant disagreements as to the course of action, Allende had little control over the actions of many officials and parties within the government. A superb politician, he was adept at resolving the day-to-day disputes which arose, but he was unable to steer a clear course, either one which provoked a clear and rapid confrontation, which he argued against, or one of moderation, which he advocated but could not consistently follow. As a master of the art of the possible, Allende was being driven further and further into an impossible situation. Radomiro Tomic expressed Allende's dilemma clearly in August 1971 when he said, "The UP finds itself obligated to live on daily expediencies at the service of limited objectives, which are the only ones within its reach . . . ."[44] Ironically, had the matter merely been one of different ideological perspectives, it might have been possible to reach accommodation and set new directions (as the coalition tried more or less successfully to do in several famous "self-criticism" sessions). But the political problem involved more than overall strategy. It also involved the more mundane politics of a disparate coalition, and as will be noted below, it involved a cyclical and escalating confrontation with the opposition which further reduced possible options.

As time went on the problem of violence became increasingly important. Yet it, along with the mounting difficulties in the economy, was a basically unsolvable problem for Allende. He could cajole and try to persuade, as he did in an open meeting in Concepción and in a face-to-face debate with the MIR, but he could not repress the revolutionary Left and those sectors within the coalition bent on spontaneous acts. Allende had too much respect for the symbols of the Cuban Revolution and the guerrilla struggles elsewhere in Latin America to be identified as a betrayer of a "revolutionary" cause.[45] In 1969 a few *pobladores* had been killed in a confrontation with the police and it became an immediate national disaster, with the minister of the interior and President Frei himself held responsible for the massacre. A president of the people could simply not risk such a confrontation—particularly in view of the past political significance of such tragedies. Indeed, when a poblador was killed by the police, Allende went in person and virtually alone to apologize for the incident. The position of the government on this matter was repeatedly stressed by the head of the Communist party in his critique of the Left: "Neither the President of the Republic, Salvador Allende, nor the parties of the UP and in the first place the Communist party, believe, even remotely, that repressive measures can be taken against groups of workers, farmers, and students who violate the law. The MIR knows this well and takes advantage of it."[46] Yet leftist violence was often simply a response to rightist violence, which, toward the end of the Allende years, would eventually overshadow leftist violence in an increasingly ominous vicious circle of action and reaction.

That violence itself would become an important issue on its own right is dramatically illustrated by a poll taken in August 1972. As table 25 indicates, 83 percent of Chileans agreed that the country was living in a climate of violence. Though 98 percent of the highest socioeconomic group concurred with that judgment, it was shared by 75 percent of the nation's lowest socioeconomic group. What is even more important, however, is the distribution of blame for violence. Table 26 shows that Chileans blamed both sides, the government as well as the opposition, for encouraging violence. Predictably, the highest socioeconomic group placed the blame primarily on the government, while the lowest socioeconomic group blamed the opposition. What is most significant, however, is that a majority of individuals thought that the government was either primarily responsible for the violence or shared the responsibility for it. Even 18 percent of the lowest socioeconomic category believed that the government was at least partially to blame for the climate of disorder. This clearly posed a severe problem for the legitimacy of authority in Chile. Not only was the government viewed as being unable to control violence, but a significant portion of the population believed that it was responsible for violence. As Juan Linz notes, the problem of order is one of the most vexing ones for a democratic regime. It is even more vexing for a

Table 25. Responses to the Survey Question, "At This Time in Chile, Do You Think That There Is a Climate of Violence?"

| | SOCIOECONOMIC GROUPS | | | |
	Upper	Middle	Lower	Total
Yes	98%	92%	75%	83%
No	2	8	25	17

SOURCE: *Ercilla*, 13–19 September 1972, p. 11.

Table 26. Responses to the Survey Question, "If You Think That There Is a Climate of Violence in Chile at This Time, Do You Think That It is Encouraged by the Government or the Opposition?"

	SOCIOECONOMIC GROUPS			
	Upper	Middle	Lower	Total
Government	36%	27%	18%	23%
Opposition	7	20	35	27
Other sectors	54	44	22	33
No climate of violence	2	8	25	17

SOURCE: *Ercilla*, 13–19 September 1972, p. 11.

democratic regime attempting to carry out significant transformations of society with a diverse and disorganized coalition and a multiplicity of institutional political constraints in a climate of growing economic difficulty.[47]

The Opposition

Political and economic problems of the government were compounded by serious difficulties with the opposition. The process was dialectical: objections of the oppostion were due in part to government policies and government policies were due in part to the reactions of the opposition. Hoarding and sabotage in certain industries, both national and foreign, worsened the situation and forced the government to take a stronger and more aggressive stand. Foreign funds were used in a massive propaganda barrage aimed at discrediting the government through the right-wing press. Every incident of violence, every confrontation, every negative economic item was magnified, further polarizing the political atmosphere and undermining the economy.

The National party had opposed governmental initiatives from the outset, when its congressmen refused to vote for Allende's election. The only exception of importance was the unanimous vote in favor of the government's constitutional amendment nationalizing the copper mines. In addition, the ultra-right *Patria y Libertad* did not hesitate to engage in violent harrassment.[48] What was crucial, however, was the role of the Christian Democratic party. As the key centrist party the Christian Democrats had made Allende's election possible, and their continued support was needed lest the government run afoul of the Congress. As noted earlier, this understanding did break down as the Christian Democrats sponsored resolutions on areas of the economy, passed by the Congress, as a direct challenge to the president.

The tenuous Christian Democratic agreement with the government worked out around the Statute of Guarantees had actually begun to erode some months earlier. In July 1971 an agreement between the government and the Christian Democrats, through which the latter would control the leadership of the Senate while the Popular Unity coalition would control the Chamber of Deputies, broke down. At the same time the Christian Democrats joined the National Party in running an opposition candidate against the government in a by-election, voted against the government plan for a unicameral legislature, and finally, after three earlier refusals, joined the Nationals in the impeachment of José Toha, the minister of the interior. The loss of the Christian Democrats in Congress would pave the way for a series of impeachment attempts and maneuvers between the executive and the Congress that would sorely try the institutional stability of the country. Economic and fiscal difficulties would be compounded by the refusal of the legislature to consider new taxes to meet governmental deficits.

The difficulty was that, like Allende, the left-wing faction of the Christian Democratic party was subject to pressure not only from the right-wing faction of the party but from other parties.[49] Pressures were not only ideological but narrowly political in origin, stemming from the requirements of electoral survival in a competitive party system. Though many Christian Democrats shared the broad goals of the Allende administration, as members and leaders of an opposition party they had different stakes and interests. Above all, they needed to protect the autonomy and integrity of their party and see to it that it maintained its strength, defined primarily in terms of electoral success. As a centrist party, the Christian Democrats were particularly aware of the potential for erosion of support from either side. As party interests took on added importance, the progressive wing of the party began to lose its controlling influence in party affairs. Two factors were contributory in enhancing the importance of narrow party stakes for the leadership and the position of the more conservative elements. In the first place, the disorder and violence accompanying the early changes had had a significant impact on the party. Rural violence and the takeover of industries had created an atmosphere of uncertainty further (and ably) exaggerated by the right-wing press. Of particular significance was the assassination of Edmundo Perez Zujovic, a close friend of President Frei and a former minister of the interior, who had been widely attacked and accused of the "murder" of the pobladores of Puerto Montt. Though Allende immediately condemned the assassination, many Christian Democrats felt that the media, much of which was affiliated with government parties, had great responsibility for intensifying the public attacks on Perez and other members of the party. Furthermore, elements in the party connected with Chile's private economic sector had reacted with horror at the government's attempts to take over industrial, commercial, and financial institutions. As early as September 1971, the moderate Christian Democratic senator Renán Fuentealba suggested that the government might be violating the Statute of Guarantees. He specifically mentioned attacks on key figures of his party in the government press, attempts to curb the Christian Democratic media, and incidents of uncontrolled urban violence.[50]

Concern over uncontrolled violence, attacks by the press, and the speed with which the government was pushing its program were not, however, the only issues that affected the position of the Christian Democrats and undermined the leverage of the progressives or moderates. Just as important was the dilemma of survival for an electoral party of the Center in a highly polarized context. The April 1971 municipal elections were thus an important turning point. In those elections the government did very well, while the Christian Democrats continued to lose their share of the electorate. Under such circumstances any accommodation policy with the government appeared to be politically risky.

The gravity of these political problems came to the fore in a by-election for a congressional seat on 18 July 1971. Since only one seat could be filled, the contest would of necessity be a zero-sum game in which only one candidate could win. If both the National party and the Christian Democrats put up a candidate against the Popular Unity coalition, the latter stood a good chance of winning as it had in the presidential election. Strong pressure came to bear, both inside and outside of the Christian Democratic party, for the formation of a coalition to prevent a government victory.

In these difficult circumstances, and at the initiative of youthful elements of the party, Christian Democrats proposed to Allende that an agreement be worked out to prevent a race that would further polarize Chilean politics. According to the proposal, the government would recognize that the seat should be a Christian Democratic seat, since it had been held earlier by a Christian Democrat, and would present no candidate. The Christian Democrats, in turn, would run a candidate acceptable to the president and abide by the same principle in future by-elections.

The proposal, however, never got off the ground, mainly because of opposition from the Socialist party. Failure to avoid a polarized race led to a joint candidacy between the Christian Democrats and the Nationals and to a political alliance which would survive through the Allende years.[51] In the bitter race which followed, the opposition candidate won. The race clearly added to the polarization of Chilean politics, not only because of its high visibility and the barrage of attacks and counterattacks but also because the opposition alliance led to a split in the ranks of the Christian Democrats. The formation of the Christian Left, which pledged support to the government, further undermined the viability of the Christian Democrats as a viable Center option by adding to the strength of the party's right wing. Elements on both sides of the political spectrum closest to the Center, who had been instrumental in structuring the agreement which made the Allende presidency possible, were abandoning their coalitions. As fragments of the established parties, they were heading for political oblivion, with little role to play in a more rigid and confrontational politics.

The Failure of Centrist Compromise

The increased polarization and loss of support from Christian Democratic circles eventually led to the adoption, in a joint session of Congress on 20 February 1972, of a constitutional amendment, designed to regulate the government's role in the economy. For the first time in decades, Chile faced a serious constitutional crisis threatening the survival of the regime.

In narrowly legal terms, confrontation between government and opposition resulted from the opposition's claim that the president could not veto the proposed reforms and that the only way out of an impasse, short of presidential capitulation, was the submission of the measure to a national plebiscite. Allende, in turn, argued that he indeed could veto the constitutional legislation and that his item vetoes would stand unless rejected by a two-thirds vote of the Congress. Allende insisted that a constitutional amendment required the same stringent procedures called for in the adoption of a simple law. The opposition maintained that the 1970 constitutional reforms established the procedure of a plebiscite precisely in order to resolve an impasse between the president and a majority of Congress. In this highly formalized system, where very specific legal clauses were of the utmost importance, the reforms lent themselves to differing interpretations of the fundamental law of the land.[52] Underlying the dispute were certain political realities. The congressional role had been strongly reduced in Chilean politics. The Christian Democrats, who had supported such a reduction, had hoped that they would still be in the presidency. Ironically, they were now the largest single party in a legislature whose only powers were negative ones. It could reject or approve, but no longer could it bargain and compromise. The arena of accommodation had disappeared, and to counteract a president intent on pursuing his program it was necessary to have enough votes to override a veto. The congressional opposition was short of two-thirds majority, and Allende clearly had the upper hand. With the power of the presidency it was possible to institute major governmental initiatives without legislative concurrence. And yet Allende and his advisers realized that he could probably not win a plebiscite involving a simple yes or no answer on a basic issue if a plebiscite were forced. The president's early confidence that a majority of the people would support his position had disappeared.

On two separate occasions in 1972, direct talks were opened between the Christian Democrats and government officials in an attempt to resolve the impasse over the constitutional amendment. Centrists on both sides noted that the reforms adopted by Congress incorporated some ideas congruent with the Popular Unity platform. But it was not only ideological questions that had to be resolved: practical political questions were also at stake. The government did not want the opposition dictating the terms for each nationalization; the

Christian Democrats were fearful that if too many nationalized industries fell into the hands of government parties, their political position would be severely undermined.

The first set of talks, in March 1972, entrusted by Allende to the centrist Partido de Izquierda Radical, ran into immediate difficulties after the minister of economy, who was skeptical of the compromise attempt, set out forcibly to expropriate major industries designated by the government for the social sector. The PIR and the Radical party objected, claiming that the action had not been sanctioned by the parties in the government coalition. The minister, Pedro Vuskovic, with the backing of other sectors of the government, notably the Socialists, was trying to present the bargainers with a *fait accompli*. The Vuskovic actions and Socialist opposition led to the cancellation of the talks in early April. Pressure from the Left also contributed to the erosion of the government's Center position as the PIR decided to resign from the cabinet and join the opposition, arguing that the government was not serious about wanting to avoid a clash between constitutional powers. Their action further undermined the chances for success of future compromise attempts. The departure of the PIR severely challenged the government's oft-repeated contention that the Popular Unity was a broad coalition including non-Marxist middle sectors and meant the loss of a group which included respected political leaders such as Senators Luis Bossay and Alberto Baltra. Allende, unwilling to break with his own Socialist party, interpreted the exit of the PIR as a personal betrayal and accepted its ministers' resignations "with pleasure."[53] While the Socialists noted that the PIR had been a representative of the ruling class all along, the Communist party expressed deep regret at the erosion of government support. Just as the decision to ally with the Nationals had stripped the Christian Democrats of elements on its Left, so the attempts to compromise contributed to a further erosion of a center posture, this time from the right wing of the government. The possibility of a centrist consensus was being rendered even more difficult by the tendency of Chile's centrifugal forces to fragment the Center. The fragmentation of the Center had now become a cause as well as a symptom of profound crisis.

The breakdown of the talks was followed in the next few weeks by enormous mass demonstrations in the streets of Santiago organized by government and opposition, strikes by doctors, an accusation by the MIR that the military was planning a coup, strikes in the copper mines, and a tense election for rector of the University of Chile in which the government candidate lost by a substantial margin.

In early June, in this atmosphere of political conflict, amid a deteriorating economic situation, the Popular Unity parties met for another round of "self criticism." Allende, with support primarily from the Communist party, sought to stem the tide of anarchy by attempting a change in direction. He relieved Vuskovik of his central role in economic policy-making and named Orlando Millas, a leading Communist intellectual, to the important post of minister of finance. The government also called for renewed efforts to reach an accommodation with the Christian Democrats over the smoldering constitutional impasse. Secret talks, later made public, were initiated in June 1972, with the minister of justice, a Radical, representing the government. Millas, for one, noted that "it would be deadly to continue to widen the group of enemies and, to the contrary, it will be necessary to make concessions, and at least neutralize certain social sectors and groups by remedying tactical mistakes."[54] However, once again the position of the Communist party was not fully supported by the Socialist party, whose leadership gave reluctant approval to the talks. Vuskovic expressed Socialist sentiment when he said: "It is not possible to consolidate what has been done so far when the enemies of the workers maintain important bases of support. To complete the social area is a requisite not only to advance to socialism, but also to defend what has been accomplished."[55]

On the side of the opposition, centrist elements once again signaled the need to reach an accommodation. Senator Fuentealba of the PDC stated:

Aside from the legal conflict, there exists the danger of confrontation which can result from the legal conflict. Open fighting will come if this continues and no agreements are reached; fighting in the streets, fight for power, concentrations, manifestations, forums.... A period of agitation will result whose consequences may be very grave for the tranquility of the country and the normal development of our democratic processes.[56]

But Fuentealba and his colleagues were strongly attacked by the Right for not being aware of the "Communist threat,"[57] and the General Confederation of Production and Commerce, representing large economic interests, issued a statement "expressing concern that the experience so far makes it necessary, unfortunately, to view with skepticism this new dialogue, at the congressional level, without the participation of the private sector organizations [gremios]."[58]

Considerable progress was made in the talks and a basic agreement in principle was worked out. It involved seven main points:

1. The transfer to the state sector or a mixed sector of approximately eighty of the most strategic industries, both foreign and domestic. The agreement included norms for compensation.

2. A requirement that in future a specific law of Congress would be required to pass industries into the state or mixed sectors.

3. Restrictions on the executive's ability to intervene on a temporary basis in private firms.

4. Specific norms for worker participation in the administration of mixed

enterprises, especially banks, several of which would remain in the hands of a majority of their workers.

5. Creation of worker-managed enterprises.

6. Creation of a judicial body to decide complaints of discriminatory treatment of enterprises not in the state sector.

7. Allocation of a substantial portion of public funds for publicity to newspapers, radio, and television stations in private hands.[59]

The agreement was long and complex, and involved significant concessions on both sides, but particularly on the side of the president. It allowed for the possibility of worker-controlled industries not tied in with a state network and restricted the future ability of the president to bring private enterprises into the public sphere. It committed the president to a subsidy of the opposition press with state funds. Some matters were not resolved, including the difficult issue of whether the paper monopoly would be allowed into the public sector, which would have given the government potential control over the availability of newsprint. Nevertheless, fundamental issues were settled. These issues were at the core of the primary disputes between the government and the largest opposition party and their resolution would have helped to defuse much of the confrontation. Even if elements on both extremes, Right and Left, had balked, an agreement by the Center could have gone a long way toward consolidating a process of change, albeit more gradual.

And yet, despite the fact that the leadership of the Christian Democrats supported the compromise, compromise was blocked by the refusal of the more conservative faction of the party to go along. Ignoring the pleas of Agustín Gumucio, an ex-Christian Democrat now serving as a government negotiator who said that "we think that we could reach an agreement on pending matters if we only had some additional time.... We have worked in a climate of mutual respect...," the conservative faction of the party forced an immediate vote in the Senate which ended all compromise efforts.[60] This faction was concerned about the ambivalent posture of the party. While the talks were going on, the Christian Democrats were not only engaged with other opposition parties in another bitter by-election against a government candidate but they also had approved an impeachment accusation against the minister of the interior. The electoral dangers of an ambivalent posture were underscored by a third event. The Christian Democrats had presented their own candidate for the student federation of the University of Chile, refusing to join the Nationals; as a result the Communist party candidate won. The Conservative faction was determined not to concede anything. It had a high regard for the president's considerable political skills and a low regard for his trustworthiness and felt that in the conversations the leadership had been outmaneuvered by a more experienced politician. They argued that Allende could be dealt with only from a position of unquestioned strength.[61] Though the progressive elements had majority support in the party, they were unable and unwilling to force the issue. As a group the Christian Democrats showed their reluctance to take risks and strike out on a clear middle course.

The irony is that elements on Allende's left also felt that the government should not bargain with the opposition except from a position of unquestioned strength. The presence on both sides of sectors arguing for higher bargaining demands confused and clouded the perceptions of moderates on the one side and the preferences of the moderate actors on the other, and often contributed to rendering the positions of the actors in the Center hesitant and ambivalent.

By the middle of July 1972, centrist agreement still proved elusive. Though Allende had attempted a policy change, it had been slow in coming, and the Christian Democrats were not prepared to bargain. Above all, they wanted to maximize their goal of electoral viability in the hopes of recapturing the presidency in 1976. The rightist Christian Democrats were confident that they had an upper hand. The government could not win a plebiscite and was unwilling to risk one. They hoped that economic hardship, anarchy, and instability would favor them in the approaching 1973 congressional elections. Why compromise, given all the difficulties and uncertainties of compromise under such circumstances?

At a critical turning point, the lonely voices in the government and the opposition calling for accommodation went unheeded. There was little concern that a crisis of regime might not only lead to the destruction of any hope for a Socialist revolution, but might destroy the very democratic rules of the game. Chileans were generally convinced that they were different—that in spite of all their difficulties they were not like other Latin Americans—and that a breakdown of regime was simply out of the question. Narrow stakes—group stakes—prevailed. As a result, the politics of mobilization and confrontation were exacerbated as everyone looked forward to the March 1973 congressional elections as a way out of the deadlock.

The Politics of Mobilization and Confrontation

When the Popular Unity government was inaugurated, mass marches and rallies, typical of a presidential campaign, did not taper off. They became a vital part of the Chilean political landscape. The government as well as the opposition turned to the mobilization of large crowds, in stadiums and in the streets, in an attempt to demonstrate their power. Thus, after the march of the empty pots in December of 1971, the Popular Unity coalition answered with a mass rally of its own. In cities across the country marches staged by one group were followed by counter-marches by another, as each side tried to prove that true popular support rested with them. When asked whether he thought that mass demonstrations, leading at times to civil disobedience, would allow for the construction of socialism, Luis Corvalán, secretary general of the Communist party, answered:

I think so, provided that our forces are superior, that the presence in the street of masses that on our side is greater than the adversaries', as has been the case up to now. For every time that they have taken the initiative, and have gone out into the streets, we have responded with demonstrations that are much stronger; and this has forced them to retreat.[62]

The failure to compromise in July 1972, however, led to a fundamental and qualitative change in this game of political mobilization. No longer would it be a matter of increasing bargaining stakes by filling more corners of the Plaza Bulnes or more seats in the national stadium. The clear message of the aborted negotiations—that resolution to the Chilean crisis could only come from winning or losing decisively in the 1973 congressional elections eight months later—led to an unprecedented effort by a multitude of political actors to prove *actual* as opposed to *potential* power capability.[63] Political mobilization became political confrontation. As early as August 1972 a rash of confrontations took place between the government and its supporters and groups on both the Left and the Right. These confrontations would continue to escalate to such a point that the country would grind to a halt in October of that year. A feeling of crisis and fear would grip the country. For the first time Chileans talked seriously of civil war.

One of the most important features of the new confrontation was the direct involvement for the first time on a massive scale of the *gremios,* representing thousands of small business associations. On 22 August retail merchants declared a one-day national strike, and in early September the truckers went out on a strike.[64] Acting out of fear of economic threats occasioned both by the faltering economy and government attempts to ration distribution of supplies and regulate transportation, they moved to defend their basic economic interests. Because of the importance of the trucking industry in the Chilean economy, the truckers' strike in particular dealt a serious blow to the government and served to rally other groups and associations who subsequently joined the movement to paralyze the economy. What is important about this movement is that it marked a change from party-directed and party-manipulated mobilization to direct mobilization by both big and small businessmen seeking to protect their stakes in the system. Christian Democratic elements, as well as sectors of the National party who had a role in the organization of these groups in the late 1960s, found that they acted increasingly on their own, often at cross-purposes with party leadership. Their independence in turn aggravated the problem of competition between the Christian Democrats and the Nationals, further forcing the Christian Democrats to harden their position lest they lose their perceived support among large sectors of the middle class.[65] Spokesmen for both parties rushed to express solidarity with the myriad striking groups.

The government and parties of the Left moved swiftly to counteract the effects of the mobilization of the petite bourgeoisie. The *Juntas de Abastecimientos y Precios* (JAPs), originally set up to channel goods and food to poorer neighborhoods, were extended to create a vast, government-run network to ration supplies. The government, with the cooperation of the Central Labor Federation (CUT), sought to keep industries open and functioning, and enlisted the support of students, workers, and professionals sympathetic to the government coalition in counter-strikes. But the actions of the opposition also gave renewed impetus to more revolutionary elements both in the Popular-Unity coalition and outside it, who moved to set up *comandos comunales*, *comandos campesinos*, and *cordones industriales* with paramilitary characterisitics to defend communities, farms, and factories. Like the gremios, these organizations acted on the fringes of the established leadership of political parties, forming the base of a small, though increasingly radicalized sector of the working class. Their actions would have political consequences similar to those resulting from the actions of the gremios. They would drive a further wedge in the unity of the Popular Unity coalition and put great pressure on established parties increasingly to radicalize the process of transformation.[66] Ironically, it was the counter-mobilization of the petite bourgoisie responding to real, contrived, and imaginary threats which finally engendered, in dialectical fashion, a significant and autonomous mobilization of the working class. Aside from a few scattered initiatives by groups such as the MIR, prior to October 1972 the established government parties had maintained political control over their followers and the bulk of Chile's workers. It took the massive onslaught of the *huelgas patronales* to begin to consolidate a degree of class consciousness and autonomous action. Even so, throughout the Allende period radicalized sectors of the working class remained a minority, and the most significant destabilizing and uncontrolled mobilization would continue to be the counter-mobilization of the middle class. The breakdown of Chilean democracy was more the result of counter-mobilization against perceived threats than excessive mobilization of sectors demanding their due.[67]

As it had from the very beginning, the mass media played a key role in this period of escalating confrontation. The media, which saturated every corner of the small country, became the principal exponent of the most extreme views. It was hard to separate the real battle from the symbolic battle of the newspapers, radio, and television screens. Events were exaggerated and distorted. Lies and character assassination were the order of the day. Everything took on political significance, and even the most insignificant event became a crucial and more ominous turning point. Opposition papers, and in particular the influencial *El Mercurio*, which had received large sums of money from U.S. intelligence, were particularly skillful in rallying the vast array of opposition groups and organizations. For the most part the wielders of information acted independently of the political leadership, and their strident accusations and counter-accusations contributed to further polarization in the already volatile atmosphere. With the erosion of regular bargaining channels, leaders on each side were forced to rely more and more on a medium which did not always convey with accuracy the positions of leaders on the other side. Symbolic politics increasingly replaced "real" politics, further undermining the possiblity of creating institutionalized channels for accommodation. Leaders of the Popular Unity government and of the Christian Democrats both expressed their despair at the excesses of their respective media organizations, some going so far as to say that the media was now the tail wagging the national dog.[68]

It soon became clear that confrontation politics had moved the fulcrum of the Chilean political system outside the realms of traditional decision-making institutions. The political leadership had lost, in large measure, control over its own followers. Political elites on both sides had resorted to the politics of mobilization and manipulation of the media in an effort to strengthen their own position vis-à-vis the opposition. As long as the leadership of both sides had continued to work through established institutional mechanisms of accommodation, mobilizational politics remained a tool of the leadership. However, as soon as accommodationist mechanisms faltered—as soon as the most salient and serious crisis of Chilean politics could no longer be resolved through the structuring of a Center consensus—mobilizational politics took on a life of its own. Political elites who strove for maximum political influence found themselves losing their preeminent positions in Chilean politics. For the government the matter was even more serious; not only did it have less and less influence over the actions of its many followers on the Left, but to a large degree it had lost authority over Chilean society. The economy, already on the brink of collapse, was buffeted further. By December 1972 inflation was at a record 150 percent.[69] And once again, these developments further constrained the options for the future. The failure of the compromise attempt in mid-1972 had been a further blow to those sectors of the Popular Unity coalition who had pressed for the moderate and conciliatory approach in a secret meeting at *Lo Curro* a few weeks earlier. It was also a serious setback for the progressive sector of the Christian Democrats, which had placed its prestige and energy in the compromise attempt. The politicians had had their day. There was only one other institution which could fill the political vacuum and make it possible for the 1973 elections to take place at all. That institution was the Chilean military.

4.

The Chilean Military, the 1973 Election, and Institutional Breakdown

The failure to compromise, the resultant decline in the role of traditional mediating institutions and procedures, mobilization politics, and the steady erosion of leadership's control over its followers was accompanied by a resort to what Juan Linz calls "neutral" powers in order to resolve disputes.[1] The Contraloría, the courts, the Constitutional Tribunal, and finally the armed forces steadily became more involved in highly political and controversial disputes which clearly belonged in the legislative arena and required bargaining and compromise to achieve resolution.

The Contraloría was repeatedly asked to determine the legality of a host of government and opposition actions, including industrial and farm takeovers. Though the Contraloría's rulings at times favored the government, on many volatile questions it ruled against government actions. In August 1971, for example, it ruled against the attempts of an agency head to take over a textile firm. This case and others like it led to strong attacks on the Contraloría from the government press. The comptroller general responded in an unusual news conference by decrying the nation's polarization, which had forced an agency such as Contraloría to be either "revolutionary or reactionary."[2] Similar attacks were levied against the courts, who were also called upon to rule on the legality of controversial actions. For the most part, the conservative Chilean judiciary, faithfully interpreting existing law, did not hesitate to defend the rights of proprietorship, condemning the government's attempts to subordinate property rights to human rights and the requirements of a Socialist order. In particular, the refusal of government officials to use the police to throw invaders off private property led to serious clashes with the judicial branch.[3] The Constitutional Tribunal, in turn, was called on to rule on whether the majority in Congress or the president was right on the procedure for adopting constitutional amendments.

The involvement of these organizations in the heat of political controversy, a symptom of the failure of leaders to agree, contributed to the open politicization of previously "neutral" forces and the further deterioration of the legitimacy of the system. They came under heavy attack from the Left as representatives of bourgeois social order and were vehemently defended by the Right as the bulwarks of tradition and legality. For both sides the symbolic level had become paramount, and it became impossible to separate the rules and procedures of democracy from the institutions which in Chile embodied those rules.

Thus, in the final analysis, the only "neutral" power with any real legitimacy and a capacity to mediate between contending forces was the military. But it was not until the chaotic and dangerous confrontation of October 1972, with its threat of civil war, that the armed forces intervened directly as political buffers. On 5 November, Allende brought the commander in chief of the army into his cabinet as minister of the interior. Along with military men at the head of the Ministry of Mines and the Ministry of Public Works, General Carlos Prats was charged with helping to restore order and guarantee the neutrality of the approaching congressional elections of March 1973.

When Allende took office he realized fully the importance of military neutrality if he were to carry out major aspects of his program. The government went out of its way to accommodate the armed forces' material and salary requirements.[4] Incorporation of a military man into the cabinet as minister of the interior was, however, a desperate measure of last resort that carried with it extremely grave risks. Once before, in April 1972, Allende had brought a general into the cabinet when internal disputes in the Popular Unity coalition made it difficult to name a minister of mines. That experience did not provide good precedent. The minister had complained that he lacked authority and that policy was executed according to political requirements at lower levels. He was unwilling to sign decrees of insistence in order to overrule the Contraloría, thus thwarting several government initiatives. When Allende reorganized his cabinet in June, the general did not stay on.

The incorporation of the commander in chief of the army into the cabinet could not but help to bring out latent generational, service, and political cleavages within the military institutions. It would increase tension between the elements who abhorred the Popular Unity government and were prepared to move against it with force and the "constitutionalists" who preferred not to take the enormous risks such an act would entail.

Underscoring their dependence on the military as a buffer, many leaders in both the government coalition and in the opposition went out of their way effusively to praise the military, stressing that they were basically on the military's side. However, the military was strongly criticized by a few, particularly those on the extremes of the political spectrum. Elements of the Socialist party did not hide their frustration when the military refused to sign decrees of insistence which would enable more firms to be brought into the social sector. Likewise, right-wing elements in the opposition bitterly criticized the military for initiatives aimed at stopping the wave of strikes and restoring order.[5] The officers were constrainted from both sides. On the one hand, they were not given enough authority; political cadres in the ministries continued to call the shots, as Admiral Ismael Huerta, the minister of public works, revealed with frustration. Yet the Left criticized them for blocking the Popular Unity program. On the other hand, they were criticized for legitimizing the government by an opposition banking on the government's failure to obtain a majority in the approaching congressional elections. These pressures clearly took their toll within military ranks. Particularly affected was General Carlos Prats, who made a heroic attempt to preserve the constitutional order and was accused of sympathizing with the government. (Resentment against him would surface after the March 1973 elections.) Politicians had turned to the military to resolve their problems, and in the process they had contributed to the further politicization of military institutions. When brought in to solve political problems, the military simply could not act as a "neutral" force— that is a contradiction in terms. Prats could only hope that the congressional election of 1973 would provide a solution and they could turn the whole thing back to the politicians.

The March Election: Stalemate, Renewed Confrontation, and Power Deflation

With the commanding general of the army serving as minister of the interior, the contending political forces in Chile channeled all of their energies and resources into the electoral campaign. The electoral contest would mark the culmination of the process of polarization begun years earlier, as each side joined together in structuring joint lists. Formed in July 1972, the Federation of the Popular Unity and the Democratic Confederation became concrete, tangible indicators of the total loss of any middle ground in the turbulent drama of Chilean politics. The structuring of federated parties not only indicated that each side wanted to prove it commanded majority support in the country, but it also demonstrated that individual parties on both sides feared the loss of support which they might experience at the hands of their own coalition partners. Though voters would still be able to vote for candidates identified with particular parties, lists were jointly structured, giving the voters a clear choice between mutually exclusive alternatives.[6]

For several long months the electorate was bombarded by a flurry of speeches, declarations, rallies, charges, and counter-charges of an intensity rarely seen in Chilean politics. Personal vilification became the order of the day, as the ever-present broadcast and print media sought to tarnish the images of leaders and contenders.[7] Funds from abroad and from moneyed sectors of Chilean society flowed freely into the opposition press and the campaigns of Nationals and Christian Democrats.[8]

The opposition forces argued that the election was a final and definitive plebiscite on the conduct of the Popular Unity government.[9] Both the Christian Democrats and the Nationals bitterly criticized the government's performance in the economic field and condemned what they saw as anarchy and chaos that would further damage Chilean institutions.[10] The Nationals, more than the Christian Democrats, emphasized that the struggle was a fundamental one between Marxism and democracy and that the election was merely a step in a broader and more fundamental confrontation.[11] Elements in both parties called for a concerted attempt to gain a two-thirds majority in the legislature in order to give the opposition the constitutional authority to impeach the president.[12] Further to the right, the paramilitary Patria y Libertad organization vociferously led an ever-increasing chorus of voices calling not only for a clear electoral victory but for a final solution involving armed intervention and the military defeat of the Left.[13]

The government parties were united in arguing that the Popular Unity Federation would do well in the election, but they rejected any suggestion that a parliamentary contest could be considered a plebiscite on government performance.[14] With the help of the military, the government sought to ensure order and to make the best of the serious economic situation. Efforts to distribute supplies and foodstuffs to the *poblaciones* were increased. However, on critical issues the Left demonstrated less cohesion and unity than did the opposition. For the opposition the issue was clear—the government should be soundly defeated. For the Popular Unity coalition it was a matter not only of winning an election but of continuing to govern a country while maintaining a commitment to revolutionary transformations. The Communist party, and Allende himself, repeatedly called for conciliation and directed its appeal not only to elements of the working class but also to the broad middle sectors of society. The Communists often specifically called on workers of Christian Democratic persuasion to support the government. They condemned the atmosphere of confrontation. The Communist party repeatedly spoke of the danger of civil war, adopting as its principal slogan "No—to the civil war."[15]

But a large sector of the Socialist party, including Carlos Altamirano, its executive secretary, called not for a consolidation of gains but for further acceleration of the class struggle. The Socialists interpreted the October strike as a signal of the power of the business sectors and as confirmation of their repeated arguments for a more rapid and militant mobilization of the working class. They specifically condemned the "reformism" of the Communist party as exemplified by efforts such as those of Minister Orlando Millas to resolve the still-pending question of the legalization of the public sector of the economy.[16] Some Socialists went so far as to call for a resounding victory of the Popular Unity government in order to defeat tendencies within the coalition favoring "conciliation."[17] Other sectors of the Left, both in and out of the coalition, also demanded a renewed confrontation that would accelerate the "contradictions" of Chilean society and prepare the working class for a

Table 27. Comparison of the Vote Received by Opposition and Popular Unity Parties in the 1969 and 1973 Congressional Elections

	1969		1973	
Party	Number of Votes	%	Number of Votes	%
Popular Unity				
Socialists	294,448	12.2	678,674	18.4
Communists	383,049	15.9	595,829	16.2
IC			41,432	1.1
API			29,977	.8
MAPU			90,620	2.5
Radical	313,559	13.0	133,751	3.6
UP List			46,100	1.3
Others	65,378	2.8		
Total	1,056,434	43.9	1,616,383	43.9
Opposition				
Christian Democrats	716,547	29.8	1,049,676	28.5
National	480,523	20.0	777,084	21.1
PIR			65,120	1.8
DR			70,582	1.9
CODE ticket			33,918	.9
Total	1,197,070	49.8	1,996,380	54.2
Other				
USOPO	51,904	2.2	10,371	.3
Blank and Void	98,617	4.0	57,770	1.6
Registered	3,244,892		4,510,060	
Voting	2,406,129		3,680,307	
Abstaining	838,763	16.5	829,753	18.4

SOURCE: Electoral statistics from the Dirección del Registro Electoral.
NOTE: Party names have been abbreviated as follows:
  IC = Izquierda Cristiana
  API = Acción Popular Independiente
 MAPU = Movimiento de Acción Popular Unitario
  PIR = Partido Izquierda Radical
  DR = Democracia Radical
 CODE = Confederación Democrática
USOPO = Unión Socialista Popular

protracted struggle leading to fundamental revolutionary change.[18] Both the government and the opposition had in their midsts political forces seeking not only an electoral victory but further direct confrontation. Their very presence contributed to the "justification" of the arguments of the most extreme elements on both sides. It undermined further the ever more tenuous position of the moderate sectors. From both poles of Chilean politics, political prophecies became self-fulfilling prophecies.

Predictably, the March 1973 congressional elections did not resolve the political crisis. They merely illustrated further how polarized the country was

Table 28. Correlation between Vote and Occupational Category, in Santiago and Nationwide

	Blue-collar Workers[a]				Self-employed Workers[b]			
	Popular Unity		Opposition		Popular Unity		Opposition	
	Nationwide	Santiago	Nationwide	Santiago	Nationwide	Santiago	Nationwide	Santiago
1970 presidential election	.52	.49	−.47	−.50	.13	.33	−.11	−.33
1971 municipal election	.46	.46	−.32	−.34	.15	.39	−.09	−.26
1973 congressional election	.34	.47	−.36	−.30	.08	.36	−.08	−.27

SOURCE: Electoral data from the Dirección del Registro Electoral; 1970 census material from the Instituto Nacional de Estadística.

NOTE: N = 287 communes.

[a]Includes artisans, miners, and industrial laborers.
[b]Includes self-employed sales and service workers.
[c]Includes professional, technical, and office employees.
[d]Includes managers and high-level administrators.

and how equally divided the contending forces were. The opposition came nowhere near achieving a two-thirds majority in the Congress, and in fact lost six deputies and two senators. The Popular Unity coalition, on the other hand, continued to be a minority coalition, receiving 43.9 percent of the votes cast to the opposition's 54.2 percent. As table 27 shows, this represented a sharp decline in the combined vote of the opposition and an increase in the vote of the Popular Unity government compared to the 1970 presidential race. However, the table also shows that, compared with the previous congressional race, the overall change was slight. In fact, with the exception of the Socialists, there was a change of only about 1 percent in the relative strength of the major parties. Only the Socialists, who no doubt inherited some of the support of the Radical party, made significant headway, gaining 6.2 percent in their relative standing. Preliminary analysis of the electoral correlates of the vote of 1973 also suggests a picture of continuity. There was no dramatic shift in the bases of support. Traditional working-class regions and sectors continued their support of the government, while the opposition continued to have strength in the countryside and more affluent areas. There seems to have been some erosion of middle sector support for the Left—with a concomitant strengthening of support in working-class and rural areas. Table 28 provides a few of these correlates, contrasting the support received by the government and the opposition over the three elections of the Popular Unity period in all of the nation's communes and in the communes of Santiago. Scattergrams reveal that the reduction of strength of the coalition among blue-collar workers suggested by the declining correlations did not take place. Rather, the coali-

White-collar Workers[c]				Managers[d]				
Popular Unity		Opposition		Popular Unity		Opposition		
Nationwide	Santiago	Nationwide	Santiago	Nationwide	Santiago	Nationwide	Santiago	
.30	.12	−.28	−.13	−.21	−.22	−.20	.21	1970 presidential election
.25	.13	−.25	−.20	.16	−.25	−.17	−.02	1971 municipal election
.15	−.05	−.13	.18	.09	−.40	−.08	.47	1973 congressional election

tion seems to have increased its strength in areas with smaller concentrations of blue-collar workers.

The eagerly awaited congressional elections did not clear the political air. Instead, they gave renewed impetus to forces eager to accelerate the process of confrontation. The strong showing of the Socialist party within the Popular Unity coalition was interpreted by many as clear evidence that working-class Chileans were ready for an acceleration of the revolutionary program. By the same token, many opposition elements, concerned about the preservation of the status quo and prevailing institutions, saw the election as a signal that the rules of the game were no longer adequate to protect their goals and interests, and that unconstitutional means would have to be employed to curb the government. Violent and seditious acts escalated; military officers plotted. Important elements in the semiloyal group identified in chapter 2 moved into the disloyal category, including members of the National party and even some Christian Democrats. In this impasse Allende faced three options.

In the first place, he could have sought the continuation of a military cabinet. This would have had the obvious advantage of continuing to legitimize his minority government. The problem was that the Left in the coalition had become increasingly upset about the military presence and its dampening effect on the revolutionary program. At the same time the military officers in the cabinet were conscious of the awkward position they were in. Criticism from the Left was accompanied by strong criticism from the Right that they were serving to legitimize government policies, policies over which they often had little control.

The second strategy would have entailed a final truce with the Christian Democrats. The issue of the "areas of the economy" was the key question on the political agenda, and some kind of compromise would have had to be worked out to avoid the much-postponed final constitutional crisis. A cabinet of national unity, including Christian Democrats or prominent men with the confidence of both sides, would have been a step in this direction. This strategy was again criticized by both extremes of the political spectrum. It would have had to overcome much of the bitterness engendered by the congressional campaign. If the level of trust had been low in July 1972, the intervening months had worsened rather than improved the level of consensus.

The third strategy, one advocated by many elements within the Popular Unity, particularly on the Left, was for the government to forge ahead with renewed determination. The verdict at the polls had been encouraging—this was a good time to press ahead with the strategy of the *fait accompli*, they felt. The government had done well in maintaining popular support despite the economic crisis; if it could find new determination and direction it might increase its support and gain more victories.

Salvador Allende had great difficulty making up his mind. At first, he seriously considered the first option. His inclination was to continue a middle ground that would enable him to further implement his program with the continued support and legitimacy provided by military ministers. But it was not only the Left in the Popular Unity coalition who opposed this course: the military men themselves were simply not prepared to continue in the cabinet.[19] The experience of serving as a buffer in the highly polarized Chilean environment had taken its toll. Now that a political defeat of the government was no longer a possibility, many elements within the armed forces began to press with renewed vigor for a military solution. The constitutionalists, and particularly General Prats, were on the defensive. To avoid the harsh criticism of complicity with the government and to stave off increasing sedition in the officer corps, it was best, they felt, to allow the military to return to its professional responsibilities.

Faced with the need to form a new cabinet, Allende appointed a civilian cabinet drawn from moderate elements in the Popular Unity coalition. It was unclear whether the government planned to press for dramatic new moves or would attempt to enter a conciliatory period. At the swearing-in ceremony of the ministers, the president stressed the importance of institutional legality and pluralism. And yet, at a rally at the CUT that very evening, many of the same ministers attacked the opposition and the Christian Democrats with strong words and called for closure of the Congress.[20] Once again, the coalition and its president projected an ambivalent posture.

The Christian Democrats continued to refer to themselves as the biggest party in the country and stressed the importance of "opposition at all costs." In a meeting preparatory to the upcoming Christian Democratic Convention, Eduardo Frei noted that opposition to the government had to be categorical and total "because this position stems from an attitude of opposition to the Marxist attempt to implant totalitarianism in Chile. . . . I am being threatened by a spiritual death by Marxism and dictatorship. I don't even want to live in a Marxist country."[21]

In this tense atmosphere, the opposition was able to seize on a critical issue which once again put the government on the defensive and for the first time aligned the Catholic hierarchy openly with critics of the government. The controversy involved a government proposal, long under study, to create a Unified National Schooling System (Escuela National Unificada).[22] One of the fundamental goals contemplated in the reform was the strengthening of vocational training in the secondary school system, which was primarily designed as a preuniversity course of study.

Though the substance of the reforms was generally accepted by different sectors of the government coalition, the actual draft prepared by technical-political sectors of the Ministry of Education led to considerable government controversy.[23] Jorge Tapia Valdés, the minister of education, with backing from his Radical party, was concerned that the proposed timing of the reforms and the wording of the draft would create serious problems for the government. The reforms were to take effect in June 1973, and the draft contained highly partisan language. With the support of the president of the republic, the minister sought to delay implementation of the plan and to have a new draft proposal drawn up which could be more widely circulated for consultation before final approval. Elements of both the Socialist and Communist parties within the ministry, without adequate party consultation, pressed for the original proposal. It was that draft which came to light after the congressional elections and became the basis for a strong attack on the government's alleged goal of turning the educational system into a massive indoctrination program. Most of the original goals of the project were lost in the heated and acrimonious debate which ensued. As on previous occasions, the inability of the government to present a unified program, and the insistence of middle-level militants on rhetoric which would clearly inflame the opposition, presented the government with a serious political predicament. Not only did the church object to the proposal, which gave the opposition considerable legitimacy, but the issue served as a rallying point for opponents of the government within the armed forces.[24] All of the commanding officers of the armed services met with the beleaguered minister of education in April 1973 to protest the ENU reforms. It was clear from the meeting that they were not interested in hearing the substance of the reforms; they were primarily interested in conveying to the government that they agreed with the tone of the opposition's criticism of the entire conduct of governmental policy. The highest-ranking officers were now openly conveying their lack of neutrality on policy matters not normally in their sphere of competence or responsibility.

Clearly stung by the massive outcry against the ENU proposal, President Allende was forced to withdraw the proposal and give assurances that it would not be enacted without broad consultation. The political motivations of the opposition were further evidenced by the fact that despite the withdrawal, opposition parties continued to encourage mass demonstrations in the streets.

This incident, coming on the heels of the congressional election in which the government's performance was commendable, was extraordinarily damaging to the government. It not only provided the opposition with an issue capable of mobilizing further sectors against the government, but it also sapped the government of the momentum it needed to continue ruling the country until the 1976 presidential contest. And, to make matters worse, Allende's capitulation on the issue aggravated its already deteriorating relations with the left wing of the coalition.

In an attempt to recapture the offensive, and in a renewed attempt to show the increasingly skeptical left wing of the coalition that it had not given in, Allende's cabinet moved officially to take over forty firms which had been occupied during the October strike. This was done by a decree of insistence, with all cabinet officers signing an order to overrule the objections of the comptroller general. Predictably, that action led to immediate cries for impeachment of the entire cabinet and allegations that the government had become illegitimate.

The postelection period had once again brought a sharp renewal of the politics of confrontation. On the critical constitutional reform issue, Allende argued that the Constitutional Tribunal should and could rule on whether or not the president's position was the correct one. The inability to reach a consensus on procedural matters had led to the involvement of yet another "neutral" institution in the hope that the impossible could be arbitrated. The opposition promptly noted that the tribunal did not have jurisdiction over the matter and that it would not abide by an unfavorable decision. At the same time, the legal confrontation escalated when Congress approved another constitutional amendment to "regularize" the "reform" process by barring expropriations of rural plots under forty acres and giving titles to those who lived on the land.

Outside the halls of Congress the media escalated its rhetoric. The Communist party and the Christian Democrats traded bitter accusations after the Communist newspaper, *El Siglo*, attacked the Frei administration for receiving money from the CIA in 1964, further embittering the relations between the two groups. Renán Fuentealba, the president of the Christian Democratic party, noted that Chile was experiencing the worst totalitarian threat in its history: "The government has declared war on Chilean Democracy. War is War. We will know how to respond." Fuentealba went on to attack Allende personally for not disavowing the charges: "It was the ignoble and improper attitude of a man who says he is a man."[25]

The Christian Democratic response to the takeover of additional firms was equally bitter. Senator Patricio Aylwin, who would soon be elected to the presidency of his party in a close and heated convention, remarked that "with this decision the government of Mr. Allende has taken to extremes the almost continuous policy of doing whatever he pleases with absolute contempt for juridical norms regulating the exercise of power in a state of laws."[26] The government press countered with strong attacks criticizing opposition leaders and the Senate for "selling out."

In the midst of these charges and counter-charges a small but significant incident took place. General Carlos Prats, commander in chief of the army and former minister of the interior, spoke before a closed meeting of eight hundred officers of the Santiago garrison. His remarks, arguing for respect of the constitutional government, were met by a chorus of coughs. The "constitutioñalists" within the armed forces were now clearly on the defensive.[27]

By May the government had imposed a state of emergency in Santiago, as organized groups from both sides clashed in the streets. These demonstrations came on the heels of a rash of strikes in public transportation, in the state steel mill, and in government agencies—all demanding higher wages and government guarantees against economic hardship. On top of this, miners struck at the critical El Teniente copper mine, starting a strike that would last for weeks and would force the government to cut off deliveries of copper to key customers.[28]

With the military out of the cabinet, and in an atmosphere of renewed confrontation, the government had lost its authority over the country. Displaying even greater determination than in October 1972, private economic groups of the revolutionary Left struck out on their own. The maximalists were now openly arguing for a strategy of arming the workers for the final confrontation. More than ever, the opposition parties could not keep up with the demands of their former bases and of the gremios who took most of the initiative in fighting the government.

The Supreme Court now openly criticized Allende, arguing that the country faced "a crisis of the rule of law." Police were no longer capable of controlling violence—the courts were no longer being obeyed. Allende personally exchanged a series of letters with the members of the Supreme Court, defending his government and accusing the justices of siding with order at the expense of social justice.[29] The reduction of the political arena was also evidenced by an unprecedented exchange of letters between the president and a group of retired military officers who made a public declaration deploring the effects which the economic crisis and social agitation might have on the country's national defense. Allende also went in person to engage in a bitter "dialogue" with extreme leftist employees of the Ministry of Public Works who had occupied the ministry and shut it down. When he engaged in personal conversations with striking miners in an attempt to settle the El Teniente strike, both the Socialist party and the Communist party attacked his recognition of the legitimacy of what they referred to as "opposition" workers. An increasingly lonely figure, Allende was now finding that his skilled efforts at persuasion were falling on deaf ears.

Any attempt at reopening a dialogue with the Christian Democrats, a course Allende and some of his cabinet officers urged privately and publicly, received a further setback in the third week of May when the Christian Democratic party elected a "hard line" slate to preside over the party's fortunes. In a skillfully orchestrated set of political maneuvers, former-president Frei succeeded in convincing the convention to adopt the thesis that Chile faced the prospect of a Marxist dictatorship, and that the party's response could only be one of continued and invigorated opposition. This position won by a narrow 55 percent to 45 percent margin over the thesis maintaining that Chile's problem was not too much authority, but too much anarchy. According to the progressive wing of the party, the nation's chaos could only be overcome through a policy of rapprochement and accommodation. The election of Patricio Aylwin to the presidency of the organization signaled the determination of a narrow majority to refuse to take any initiatives at finding a political solution unless the president was genuinely willing to capitulate to its demands.[30] Earlier fragmentations of the party, which had seen the left wing gradually split off, first to form the MAPU and then to form the Christian Left, had contributed to shifting the balance in favor of the party's right wing.

The election of officers from the more conservative faction had created serious structural impediments to any centrist agreement. Previously the conciliators in both the Popular Unity coalition and the Christian Democrats dominated their respective authority positions. Allende headed the government and was titular leader of his coalition; Fuentealba had represented the more progressive elements in the opposition party. Now, official attempts at an understanding between the two groups would have to be channeled through the more conservative Aylwin leadership. Any unofficial contacts with the progressive wing of the Christian Democrats would only aggravate the prospect of a settlement by raising Christian Democratic fears that any split in the party would work to the disadvantage of the fragment not identified with the official leadership, and therefore would not contribute to a political solution.[31] If a workable settlement between contending forces were to be arrived at, the Christian Democrats, through their official leadership, would have to be a party to it. The shift of power to the right would escalate the bargaining demands of the opposition and make any agreement considerably more costly to the president.[32]

Shortly after the Christian Democratic convention, the question of a compromise took on renewed urgency. In the first week of June the Constitutional Tribunal ruled that it was not competent to judge the lingering constitutional dispute between the president and Congress. The conflict was finally left without a single referee. Both sides attempted to adopt that version of the constitutional amendment which they favored, though the Contraloría ruled against the president. Congress then moved to impeach four of Allende's cabinet ministers and eight of the twenty-five provincial intendants. On 18 June the opposition Democracia Radical party issued a statement which cried, "Enough declarations—the effective fight on all fronts must begin."[33] A prominent National senator declared on nationwide television, "The president of the Republic is at present an illegitimate head of state."[34] And *El Mercurio* featured an article declaring:

It is the categoric duty of sensible people to put an end to looting and disorder stimulated by an inept and crazy government which smothers us. . . . In order to accomplish this task of political salvation, we have to renounce all political parties, the masquerade of elections, the poisoned and deceitful propaganda, and turn over to a few select military men the task of putting an end to political anarchy.[35]

The government responded to this upsurge of seditious talk by holding a huge mass rally to demonstrate the people's continued support for the government. It marked the beginning of the end of the Chilean "way to socialism," for a week later, on 29 June, a garrison of the Chilean military attempted a coup d'état. The coup was put down swiftly by the decisive action of General Prats. Garrisons that had hesitated were prevented from joining the revolt. But, despite the cheers from the Left, the government's "victory" proved illusory. The fate of the country was no longer merely in the hands of politicians; it had now also fallen into the hands of a divided and highly politicized military.

Efforts at Compromise:
The Abdication of the Democrats

The attempted coup of 29 June 1973 marked the final turning point in the unfolding tragedy of Chilean politics. It provided President Allende with further evidence that the military could no longer be counted on as a neutral arbiter. When he called the fourteen generals of the army into his office to obtain support, only four offered categorical backing. He realized that his days as president were numbered unless he could regain political authority. He rejected the advice of the maximalist forces in his coalition who continued to press for widespread arming of workers. The president felt armed confrontation was naive and suicidal. "How many masses does one need to stop a tank?" he reportedly asked Senator Altamirano.[36] If Allende had been ambivalent before, his actions after the attempted coup clearly indicated that he was prepared to come to some kind of agreement with the Christian Democrats in a last effort to structure a compromise that would defuse the political opposition. The Christian Democrats were still the largest party in the country, and their leaders commanded great respect among vast sectors of the opposition. Even though many people were no longer interested in preserving the traditional system, a compromise between the president and the principal opposition party would have made any coup attempt, or for that matter any attempt to spark armed confrontation by the masses, extremely costly.[37]

Prominent members of the Christian Democratic party shared these sentiments and called on the party to reach an understanding with the government. Fernando Castillo, one of the most distinguished members of the progressive wing of the party and rector of the Catholic University, spoke in the name of all of the country's university presidents, saying that it was crucial that a consensus be found to defend democratic institutions. He warned, "as the danger increases, a minimum loyal consensus becomes more urgent."[38]

The situation was extraordinarily delicate. The military commanders were unwilling to join a cabinet, reflecting the unusual unrest in the ranks.[39] Since military commitment to neutrality had suffered seriously, it was Allende's hope that an agreement among politicians would help to strengthen those factions in the military who were still reluctant to violate the basic canons of traditional Chilean civil-military relations.

But compromise among the centrist forces still faced the perennial constraints of the last two and one-half years; both government and opposition faced the virulent opposition of the extreme Right and the extreme Left. Furthermore, the leadership of the Christian Democrats had shifted to the conservative side. The level of trust was at an all-time low. Group stakes and individual stakes took precedence over the stakes which most Chileans had in the ongoing system. Everyone sought to impose his own solutions; debatable issues had all but disappeared.

Efforts at compromise were immediately attacked by Altamirano, who noted:

There are those who pretend to urge "democratic dialogues" with Christian Democracy. As Socialists we say that a dialogue is possible with all those forces who clearly define themselves as against exploiters and against imperialism. We foster and will develop dialogue at the level of the masses, with all the workers, whether they are our militants or not, but we reject all dialogues with reactionary and counter-revolutionary leaderships and parties.[40]

Echoing this theme, the secretary general of the MIR claimed that it was "the ruling classes that need a truce to develop their tactic of obstructionism. Nothing would be more dangerous or suicidal today than to give up the positions that have been achieved and initiate a truce."[41]

Pressures on the Christian Democrats from the Right were also clear. In a cable sent from Rome, Senator Fuentealba warned against these pressures:

There are sectors bent on producing the fatal outcome, involving the fall of the government in the shortest possible time. They are criminals. I have faith that my party will be able to abide by the principles and ideals that inspire it, ignoring those who today approach as friends, when in the past they sought the party's destruction.... [42]

From the very outset, attempts to reach a *modus vivendi* ran into difficulties.[43] When Allende asked the Christian Democrats to support a declaration of state of siege in the aftermath of the coup, the Christian Democratic Council met to consider the request. Some members argued that the party should give Allende an affirmative response and then qualify it by asking for certain guarantees against the abuse of power. This conciliatory stand received only four votes to the fourteen received by the harsher demand for a rejection of the government request until certain guarantees could be offered. Like a sovereign state receiving a delegation from another sovereign state, the council informed three of Allende's ministers of the decision. They did not return as scheduled to bring the government's reply. The published declaration of the Christian Democrats concluded by noticing that "once again, Christian Democracy thinks it necessary to stress before the people of Chile that the responsibility for bringing to an end the climate of disorder, insecurity and chaos to which the country has come and the extremely grave crisis in which it finds itself is primarily the responsibility of the President of the Republic."[44]

The president moved swiftly, however, to institute a new cabinet, relieving the ministers who had been impeached—a painful move for the Communist party. He worked hard at attempting to construct a cabinet of prestigious individuals, such as Felipe Herrera, the former president of the Inter-American Development Bank. He also sought out opposition figures such as Fernando Castillo.

The Christian Democrats, however, expressing the fear that Allende was trying to divide the party, refused to grant permission for their members to join the cabinet. Having failed to put together a bipartisan "blue ribbon" ministry, Allende proceeded to form one of a decidedly moderate character. As minister of the interior he named Carlos Briones, an independent Socialist considered to be a "man of law" in many circles. As minister of foreign relations, he kept Clodomiro Almeyda, one of the few Allende ministers to escape impeachment consistently. Senator Volodia Teitelboim, the leading ideologue of the Communist party, called the cabinet a "unity cabinet" designed to bring together all Chileans who wished to avoid the catastrophe of civil war, adding that the cabinet was an opening to dialogue.[45] At considerable risk to the unity of his own coalition, which was already experiencing significant erosion from the far Left, Allende continued to pursue the strategy of establishing a "minimum consensus" with the largest opposition party.

The leadership of the Christian Democrats did not respond readily to the president's overtures. It felt that Allende was being less than honest—that he was not really prepared to break with his extreme Left—and was merely buying time to implement his full program. At the same time, the leadership was under considerable pressure from a rightist faction intent on undermining Allende as much as possible. These elements were prepared to foster and join the escalating chorus of demands for the president's resignation. Party-affiliated gremios, unions, and local organizations added their numbers and voices to the crippling strikes which were rapidly reappearing. Many party members were in contact with military officers, giving tacit approval to plans for direct military action.

In late July, however, the cardinal, Raúl Silva Enriquez, employing all of the prestige of his office, urged a renewal of conversations between the antagonistic factions. Allende, in an emotional speech before the CUT, responded with a renewed appeal for talks. Defying many of the members of his party, who booed him at a mass meeting at party headquarters, Senator Patricio Aylwin, the Christian Democratic president, agreed to the conversations. The strong pressure on him was further evidenced by attacks on "dialogue" printed in the party paper, *La Prensa*.

Attempts were also being made behind the scenes to ensure the success of the talks. Gabriel Valdés, the highly regarded foreign minister in the Frei government, returned temporarily to Chile during July from his post at the United Nations.[46] After meeting with President Allende and top leaders of the Christian Democratic party, he was invited to a dinner at the home of Aniceto Rodriquez, a prominent leader of the moderate wing of the Socialist party. There he met with several cabinet ministers and prominent leaders of the Popular Unity coalition, who were anxious to hear from Valdés his views on a possible resolution of the crisis. They expressed real interest in establishing links at levels other than the highly public and formal dialogue of the president and the leader of the Christian Democrats. They also seemed willing to entertain the idea that a settlement might mean the incorporation of Christian Democrats in the cabinet, even at the risk of losing the support of a segment of the Socialist party. In turn, the Christian Democrats would have to respect much of the basic outline of the government program, even if in modified form. There seemed to be agreement that the crisis had reached a point where only drastic measures should be taken against all odds. And yet that very conversation was interrupted by a phone call summoning the minister of the interior. He was given the shocking news that Allende's own naval attaché had been assassinated. The fury of charges and counter-charges which followed in the press and the quickening pace of events drowned out further progress behind the scenes. The formal conversations were begun the following Monday, with little groundwork having been done and with enormous obstacles to success. The entire nation watched and waited.

The Christian Democratic leaders went into the talks with the conviction that Allende would have to abandon much of his program and cut his ties with the far Left if an agreement were to be worked out.[47] Allende, in turn, was reluctant to take that final step. After the CUT speech he told Gabriel Valdés that he had experienced the saddest day of his life, and that he had indeed broken with his own party. But shortly afterward he postponed the start of the talks, much to the chagrin of his own minister of the interior, in a last-ditch effort to get Socialist party compliance. The Christian Democrats immediately interpreted this change of heart as evidence of the president's inability to abandon the more extreme elements of his coalition. They did not understand that Allende simply was reluctant to take a step that would have signaled the end of the Popular Unity in the absence of clear assurance that the Christian Democrats would provide him with genuine backing. The president believed that Frei had been meeting with army officers and was in tacit agreement with those supporting a coup. Why should he isolate himself further by severing ties with his own people if important Christian Democrats wanted him out of office anyway? In this confusing atmosphere neither side knew what the other side really wanted; neither side was fully prepared to believe that, even if the other side were sincere, it would be able to keep its word. The political arena had been drastically reduced to a few men attempting to come up with a magic settlement, but these men no longer had full control of the social forces around them. Only a dramatic announcement from the talks might have averted the final denouement; it was not forthcoming.

Senator Aylwin and his colleagues entered the conversations fearing that Allende, with his great reputation for political maneuvering, might outsmart them. They felt an enormous pressure, not only from their constituents but from their adversary, not to give in too much—not to concede essential points. When Allende, in their first meeting, pulled out some fat folders and noted that agreement could be reached on many substantive issues, Aylwin felt that Allende was still stalling. He insisted on pinning the president down with several demands, including a demand that the president bring the military in at all levels of government. The opposition, he noted, needed guarantees of good faith. The president could not accept that; it would have meant a virtual abdication of his role as governor. Allende stressed the many bases for possible agreement, including his willingness to resolve the constitutional question in Congress by accepting most of the opposition's version of the amendment, on the condition that the same procedure not be used again so that Chile would not become a parliamentary regime. He argued further that it was the responsibility of the politicians to structure an understanding, to resolve the political impasse. Then, the military could be brought in as an arbiter.

The non-negotiable demand made by the Christian Democrats for the incorporation of the military into the government was criticized as too extreme by many prominent members of the party, who still felt that Chile's problem was not dictatorship but anarchy. Neither Allende nor the Christian Democratic leadership seemed fully to appreciate the enormous political constraints the other was under. In their dogged opposition the Christian Democrats were more fearful of what Allende might do than what the consequences might be to the entire system on which their party, more than others, depended. Many seemed convinced that the "constitutionalist" Chilean military might simply force the president to leave and turn things back to them again. They seemed to have forgotten the fate of other democrats and centrist groups, in other times and places, who had abdicated at the critical moment.

On 9 August 1973, with the breakdown of formal talks and a new and massive truckers' strike underway, Allende, much to the chagrin of the Left, moved to bring the military into his cabinet. He knew that he no longer had much choice. While trying to save face by taking this action after the talks had terminated, he had in fact given in to most of the opposition's demands. The Christian Democratic leadership was, however, not satisfied. After initially supporting the move, they rebuked the president for not going far enough and replacing officials at all levels of the government. Critics within the party argued that the Christian Democrats were being unreasonable in making further demands before the new cabinet was given a real chance and in the process undermining the position of the military officers who had agreed to join the cabinet under great duress. The politicians had gone beyond the point of no return. They had been unable to come up with a political solution to Chile's political problems, and now it was too late. As the politicians continued to trade charges and counter-charges, the armed forces had in fact assumed authority over the country. It was only a matter of time before the *golpista* factions would be able to consolidate their plans to replace the elected government by force.

The Military on Its Own: The Fear of a Parallel Army and of Insurrection in the Ranks

The 29 June 1973 coup attempt was not the beginning of direct involvement of military officers in politics. From the early coup attempts before Allende took office until the fall of the Popular Unity government elements within the military plotted to overthrow the regime. But it was not until the 29 June incident, when a small tank regiment moved on the presidential palace, that an actual attempt took place. The *tanquetazo* was not a response to a general plan to take over the government. Rather, it was a move by a disgruntled officer, about to be relieved of his command, in the mistaken belief that discontent in the rest of the armed forces would lead to a rapidly escalating military takeover.[48] General Prats was able to move swiftly and easily, with little loss of life, to put down the insurrection, thus demonstrating that the "constitutionalist" sector in the military, particularly in the army, still had the upper hand. Yet the mere fact that a regiment of the highly professional Chilean army would move without direct orders from superiors provided tangible evidence of the mounting discontent among middle-ranking officers. The statements in the government press to the effect that the June coup had been a clear triumph for Allende ignored the depth of discontent in military ranks. It was significant that the dead rebels, as well as the dead loyalists, were buried with full military honors by an institution bent on ignoring the chants of Popular Unity adherents who cried, "Firing squad, firing squad."[49]

The abortive attempt had a profound impact on the armed services. In the political vacuum left by a weakened government struggling to achieve a compromise with the opposition, the military would increasingly strike out on its own in an attempt to control what was perceived to be the growing military threat of the Left. In the process a series of events would lead to the eventual loss of authority of the leading "constitutionalists" and their replacement by officers willing to move against the government.

It must be stressed that while there was conspiratorial planning at various levels, the coup was not a highly coordinated affair arranged weeks in advance. Rather, it was the result of a gradual and haphazard process.[50] This was the case because the Chilean military was a highly professional organization with a tremendous respect for discipline and the hierarchy of rank. It was not possible for middle-level officers of various services to stage a "colonel's coup" by mobilizing a few regiments. The abortive 29 June coup had vividly demonstrated that. For the coup to take place it would be necessary not only to structure a substantial consensus among high-ranking officers but also to see to it that the commanding officer of each service was in agreement with the final action. And, until the very end, in every service, the commanding officers were committed constitutionalists. In particular, General Prats and Admiral Montero strongly, and, for a time, successfully, resisted the pressures of their colleagues. General Ruiz Danyau, while more supportive of the neutrality of the military than most of his other air force colleagues, would bend more readily to pressure. Removal of a commanding officer was a tedious and frustrating process, because in the final analysis it could result only from action by the president of the republic or from a voluntary resignation approved by the president of the republic. It is instructive that it was not until the three generals in question were removed from their posts with presidential consent, albeit grudging, that the golpistas were able to push to a final military solution.

The importance of hiearchy and the respect for rank is illustrated by the formation after the 29 June incident of a committee of fifteen of the highest-ranking officers from the three services to discuss common problems and prepare for the possibility that Allende might invite the military into the cabinet. The three commanders in chief presided, and other officers sat around the table in order of seniority. In the 30 June meeting, General Pinochet, second in seniority to Prats, noted that it would be inappropriate to refer to political matters and that the officers should remain neutral and discuss economic problems. Though the officers drafted a twenty-nine-point memorandum critical of the national situation that was to be submitted to the president for discussion, it was clear that any talk of military insurrection was simply out of the question.[51]

It must also be underscored that the success of the golpistas in undermining the constitutionalists was not merely a response to an intramilitary debate isolated from the evolving situation in the country. In fact two sets of developments had a profound effect on the internal correlation of forces in the military. The first was the already noted failure of the politicians to reach a consensus which would force Allende to structure a new military cabinet in an atmosphere in which direct calls for military takeover were the order of the day. But even more significant was the escalation of *direct* confrontation between the military and elements of the Left. This took the form of growing fear within the armed forces that for the first time the institution itself was threatened. Officers were worried that the Left planned to set up a parallel military force among workers and, even more ominously, instigate widespread insubordination among the troops.[52]

Though elements within the armed forces undoubtedly feared statements coming from the revolutionary Left about armed workers, it was not until after the attempted coup that military men began to show active concern over the development of a parallel army. The government had given wide publicity to the attempt at mobilization of the cordones industriales around Santiago as soon as the tanks started rolling.[53] After 29 June, leftist sectors of the Popular Unity coalition, while criticizing efforts of the government to compromise with the opposition, called for mass mobilization and arming of the workers. In a speech the secretary general of the socialist party noted:

The workers of the whole country have organized in cordones industriales, communal commandos, peasant councils, committees of vigilance and other organizations, which constitute the seeds of an incipient but powerful popular force, and are an unbreakable barrier before any insurrectionary attempts of the bourgeoisie. Workers, peasants, neighborhood dwellers, young people, all are amassing their own power to repel the mutinous power of the bourgeois. And they have the obligation to do just that as a class and as a revolutionary movement.[54]

At around the same time Miguel Enriquez, head of the MIR, observed that

The working class is today a structured army, bent on fighting for its interests and resisting the onslaught of the reactionaries. The working class and the people . . . have given notice to their political leadership that the struggle has left the corridors of parliament and that they will not permit setbacks or concessions.[55]

The leader of the Communist party also argued that "If the reactionary sedition becomes worse, passing into the area of armed struggle, no one should doubt that the people will rise as one man to crush it with speed."[56] At the same time, a widely distributed pamphlet urged the workers to

Develop at an accelerated pace the acomplishment of military tasks in the party and among the masses . . . . Form organizations necessary to assure the self defense of the masses in industries, services, neighborhoods, communes, and cordones, developing "armed popular power" and developing the bases for the construction of the future Army of the People.[57]

Ironically, the militant rhetoric of leaders on the Left was in part due to the fact that the 29 June movement had shown the response of the working class to be less than overwhelming. Only a handful of cordones had taken over factories. Most of the Left had stood by and watched General Prats put down the revolt.[58] In view of the poor showing of the Left, revolutionary elements wanted to accelerate the arming of the workers to be better prepared for another attempted coup. Yet their attempt to ensure a better "defense" of the working class led to a concerted determination on the part of the armed forces to prevent that very development.[59] The weakness of the cordones had also been observed by many officers who, nevertheless, had been rudely awakened to the potential of working-class resistance. They quickly turned to a law, which had been on the books for some time, giving the armed forces authority over control of arms in order to assure themselves that a parallel army would not be created.

The first significant military raid came as early as 8 July in the Metropolitan Cemetery, when the air force led a large raid in search of weapons. The government press immediately attacked the raid and ridiculed the air force for not finding any weapons. In a televised interview the commander of the air force showed his annoyance, particularly against a leftist newspaper partly owned by the minister of defense. At the same time, in a clear demonstration of the rift between the military and the government, he vehemently attacked the undersecretary of the interior's contention that no weapons were found in the raid.

Actions by the air force were followed by similar efforts by the navy in the port city of Valparaíso. In two weeks naval forces carried out over twenty raids in search of weapons. Despite the fact that rightist groups were also armed, the raids were aimed at factories in the social sector and particularly at those in the hands of Socialist party militants. Again the commander in chief of the navy clashed with the undersecretary of the interior. When military officers raided a worker's federation headquarter in Osorno, the secretary general of the CUT sharply criticized the arms control law, calling it the "damned law," a term coined by the MIR.

By August the government no longer controlled the actions of the armed forces. Allende could only observe helplessly as the military broke into government factories and party headquarters. In Concepción the navy conducted a number of raids against suspected leftist arsenals. While dangerous materials were occasionally discovered, more often they were found in agencies such as the Highway Department and the Development Corporation, both of which stored explosives for routine work. Probably the worst incident of military search-and-destroy operations took place in the southern city of Punta Arenas. The army broke into a factory and apparently destroyed machinery and killed a worker in its search for weapons. The attack on the army from the Left became so vehement that Allende personally had to instruct elements of his coalition to keep the criticism down.

The fear of a parallel army also contributed to a refinement of the many contingency plans which the armed forces had long since developed to enable them to act in concert to control domestic insurgency. The air force, fearing possible damage to some of its aircraft from the Los Cerrillos Cordones, which was located near the military airport, obtained the support of marines to guard the planes and transferred many planes to other cities without presidential approval. It would not be difficult to turn the machinery set up to root out illegal arms to the broader goal of destroying the government.[60]

With the 29 June attempted coup, parties of the extreme Left called not only for formation of armed groups which would be prepared to fight the next coup but for the open resistance of enlisted men to those officers who did not fully support the government. All around Santiago, posters went up urging soldiers not to take orders in the event of military action. The head of the Socialist party argued publicly that

Soldiers, marines, air force men, and police can't serve as tools at any time and under any circumstance for the assassination of workers. And if the case should come up again, officers, noncommissioned officers, and rank-and-file soldiers have the obligation not to obey. What is even clearer: not only do they have a duty to disobey orders which would mean shooting at the people... they must actively oppose any such action. We are sure that this patriotic stand, national and revolutionary, will prevail over the desperate maneuvers of the bourgeoisie.[61]

Almost immediately after the attempted coup, officers began to purge the ranks of elements viewed as sympathetic to the government. This was particularly true in the navy. On 7 August the navy denounced a plot, coordinated by the MIR and factions of the Socialist party, to take over several ships. The navy argued that the Left was deliberately fostering insurrection in the ranks. The Left, in turn, argued that this was necessary in order to counter the open plotting among naval officers. The navy accompanied its announcement of internal difficulties with renewed raids all over the Concepción area in search of arms, a call for denial of congressional immunity to top Popular Unity leaders, and the issuance of an order of detention against the secretary general of the MIR. These events placed the government in an untenable situation. It simply could not arrest those who argued that they were doing their best to protect the government from a coup. On the other hand, the activities of leftist leaders among rank-and-file army personnel further reinforced the resolve of those intent on staging a coup and seriously undermined the position of those officers, particularly Admiral Montero, who continued to argue that the armed forces should remain neutral.[62] For a majority of officers, it was no longer a matter of objecting to erroneous government policies but a matter of defending themselves and their institutions from the possibility of destruction.

The Military Cabinet and the Triumph of the Hard Liners

With the failure of the talks with the Christian Democrats, and the failure of his thesis that the politicians should resolve the fundamental difficulties before turning elsewhere, Allende turned to the armed forces to create a cabinet of "national security." In so doing he fully accepted the points prepared by the military committee of fifteen as condition for their entry into the cabinet. In a 6 August meeting, both General Prats and Admiral Montero indicated willingness to join the cabinet. They felt strongly about the need to resolve the political crisis within the framework of the Chilean constitution. For General Ruiz the situation was more difficult; the pressure from his fellow generals not to enter the government was intense. General Prats became defense minister, Admiral Montero went to the Ministry of Finance and General Ruiz to the Ministry of Public Works. The other ministries were filled by moderate leaders of the UP with Orlando Letelier in the Ministry of the Interior.

In inaugurating his new cabinet, the president openly criticized the attempt by elements on the revolutionary Left to infiltrate the armed forces. He also had to intervene personally to break up a strike in the Ministry of Public Works and Transport so that General Ruiz could take over as minister, charged among other things with the difficult task of settling the ongoing and paralyzing truckers' strike. For all intents and purposes Allende had broken with his Socialist colleagues.[63]

But from the very outset the military cabinet was in deep trouble. The chorus of demands for the president's resignation had now become thunderous. The Christian Democrats, instead of interpreting the president's move as fulfilling their earlier demands, criticized it vehemently for not going far enough. The truckers and other striking organizations were clearly no longer interested in negotiating. With ample financial support from external sources, they were content to wait and force a presidential resignation or a military coup.[64] Though the president was willing to dismiss the undersecretary of the ministry, whom opposition groups blamed for the lack of a settlement in the truckers' strike, it no longer made much difference. The Christian Democrats strongly supported the strikers. The military was once again caught in the middle. A deafening outcry from the opposition called on them to be firm and not to give into the government. The National party openly called for a coup. The revolutionary Left, possessed of ample evidence of plotting at middle levels of the military, sought desperately to consolidate a military posture, thereby only aggravating military insecurity. Sabotage from right-wing groups escalated. On 13 August three high-tension pylons outside of Santiago were dynamited, interrupting a presidential speech and cutting off power in the center of the country for an hour. Shortly thereafter General Ruiz resigned and was succeeded as commander in chief by General Gustavo Leigh and as minister of public works and transport by General Humberto Magliochetti. The air force generals made it clear once again that there was little support for the government from their quarter. Doctors, lawyers, teachers, and engineers joined the antigovernment strikes.

The most serious blow yet to the government came on 22 August when General Prats finally resigned. His resignation came after a curious incident in which the wives of many fellow officers demonstrated outside his home. Soon after that a majority of the generals asked him to resign to ensure "unity" in the armed forces. Prominent among the anti-Prats generals were Generals Oscar Bonilla and Sergio Arellano, who were known to have close ties with sectors of the Christian Democratic party. This reinforced the view among Popular Unity leaders that some Christian Democrats, including former president Frei, tacitly supported a military solution.[65]

The same day the Chamber of Deputies, with support from the Christian Democrats, adopted a "sense of the House" resolution which held that the government of President Allende was unconstitutional, all but inviting a military coup.[66] More than ever the opposition seemed to be openly inciting action. To the relief of the president, General Augusto Pinochet, who was closely identified with Prats, gave strong assurances to the government that the army would continue to remain neutral and pledged support to ensure loyalty at all levels. On 28 August Allende named a new and final cabinet with Carlos Briones as the minister of the interior.

What finally sealed the fate of the Popular Unity government, however, was the successful attempt of the navy to obtain the resignation of Admiral

Montero.[67] For some time many of his fellow admirals had been urging him to resign. On 29 August Admiral Jose Toribio Merino, second in command, and Admiral Sergio Huidobro, commanding officer of the naval infantry, went to see Montero to convey the opinion of the Naval Council that he should step down. Montero immediately called the president, who insisted that all three come over to see him. A bitter exchange took place in which the president told Merino that he knew that he was "at war" with the navy. On the first of September all of the admirals were summoned to the office of the minister of defense, Orlando Letelier, to explain one by one why they felt Montero must resign. Finally, after often tearful sessions with his colleagues, Montero asked to be relieved of his post. Allende also relented and agreed to let the admiral give way to a successor on 7 September. (The president would later try fruitlessly for six hours to convince Admiral Merino in person to pledge support for the government.)

The whole political system had been reduced to the president and a few trusted colleagues, moving from crisis to crisis, minute by minute, twenty-four hours a day, attempting to cajole and convince others to postpone what now seemed inevitable. Many of the same officers who later would authorize the merciless persecution of Allende's friends and followers spent hours in personal conversations with the president himself. Allende had also been in touch with the president of the Christian Democrats in a futile attempt to head off the damaging vote in the Chamber of Deputies. At the same time, he was carrying on extensive negotiations with elements of his own coalition in an attempt to forge another political solution. The device decided on was a plebiscite, to be held during the second week of September, calling for the election of a constitutional assembly to resolve the crisis. The Communist party was intent on the move, and secretary general Luis Corvalán supported it vigorously.[68] To Corvalán's irritation, Allende insisted on trying to bring the balking Socialists around to his position, though he was determined to proceed without their support if necessary. Through the good offices of the cardinal, the Christian Democrats were approached directly to obtain their reaction to the plebiscite proposal. General Pinochet and other army generals Allende deemed loyal were informed of his plan on 7 September. Over the weekend the minister of the interior and others worked frantically to come up with the wording for the president's speech, announcing the plebiscite, and they still had legal problems to resolve the night of 10 September.

But the coup was already in progress. Over the same weekend top naval officers met in Valparaíso to coordinate their activities, confident that elements within the army were in favor and that General Pinochet was now willing to go along. To make absolutely certain that the other services were in agreement, two high-ranking naval officers set out for Santiago and, incredibly, had to return to Valparaíso because they had forgotten to take money for the highway toll. After some delay they were able to fulfill their mission. Generals Leigh and Pinochet signed a document prepared by Admiral Merino setting the date of the coup for 11 September 1973.[69]

The shift in the army appeared to be a last-minute shift on the part of General Pinochet. A large number of lower-ranking army officers had that same week personally called Orlando Letelier, the minister of defense, to invite their former colleague from military academy days to a banquet for more than ninety officers the following week. They spoke cordially with the new minister of defense, hardly reflecting the mood of a military organization already geared up to destroy the government and arrest its top leaders, including the minister of defense. With the shift of General Pinochet, however, the professional institution quickly fell into line, sealing the fate of the Popular Unity government.[70]

On Tuesday of the following week, the military moved quickly to depose the elected government. The presidential palace and the president's private residence became the central targets of bombs and army troops. Allende died in his presidential office, the first of many victims of a military coup aimed not at "restoring" institutions and democratic procedures but at dismantling them with brutality and vengeance. The real transformation of Chilean politics began not on 4 September 1970 but on 11 September 1973.

Conclusion

The 1970 presidential election brought into office, for the first time in Chilean history, a minority coalition dominated by Marxist parties dedicated to a fundamental transformation of that country's economic, social, and political structures. From the outset, the experiment of President Salvador Allende encountered a multiplicity of constraints inherent in Chile's highly polarized political system. The government sought to change the economy and redistribute income on short notice, without abandoning the traditional politics of *reivindicaciones*. Government parties struggled over different ideological programs while continuing to engage in competitive electoral politics. In a highly dialectical process, elements wedded to both the social and political status quo reacted with vigor at any encroachment on their privileges. The polarized system became even more polarized as zero-sum elections and the pressure of electoral competition contributed to an erosion of the tenuous Center. Structural constraints were accompanied by symbolic contraints. An escalation of rhetoric on both sides made it difficult for leaders committed to the ongoing system to perceive and understand what was going on. It is clear that this crisis was fundamentally a political crisis, and the political crisis in Chile preceded the socioeconomic crisis. In time mobilization would get out of hand, but it was the counter-mobilization of those who felt threatened in a system which lost authority which finally contributed to the breakdown of Chilean democracy.

Given the characteristics of the Chilean system which structured human action, the Chilean breakdown followed, at an ever-faster pace, the path described by Juan Linz in his analysis of earlier European breakdowns. The challenge from elements openly disloyal to the traditional democratic regime turned out to be less important than the abdication of erstwhile supporters caught in the crossfire from both extremes. Leaders chose to protect narrow personal stakes, defined by the requirements of electoral advantage, refusing to see the importance of preserving the regime itself.

There is little doubt that the pressures on the democrats in the Center to maintain a viable consensus were enormous. Both sides often complained about these pressures and difficulties, and yet each side failed to see the gravity of the pressures on those of the opposite side. Their actions only worsened the situation and, by implication, the prospects for a successful regime-saving compromise.

Allende was often too willing to bow to the pressures from the Left and continuously gave ambivalent cues. He thus undermined, in the early stage of his government, the position of those elements of the opposition who were genuinely interested in reaching an agreement that would not involve a threat to the Popular Unity coalition's basic program. The corruption and disorder in the political process and the "unsolvable problem" of the economy only made things more difficult. The Christian Democrats, in turn, were intimidated by the political threat both from the Right and from many of their own followers, and were obsessed with the notion of presenting a hard-line posture to the very end. They should have realized more fully the necessity of coming to an agreement when the government coalition was willing, in the crucial negotiations of June and July 1972. But, even more seriously, they should have realized that the political game shifted dramatically in the last stage of the Popular Unity government with the outcome of the 1973 elections and the attempted coup of 29 June of that year. In combating the dubious prospect of "Marxist totalitarianism," to the bitter end, they failed to realize how much of a stake they had in the democratic political order they thought they were defending. By not moving forcefully to structure a political solution, they seriously undermined the position of the president and his advisers, who were clearly ready to reach a mutual accommodation. In the chaotic atmosphere of mid-1973 this failure only undermined further the authority of the government and the increasingly powerless leadership of the political elites themselves. The resulting mobilization and countermobilization, used to demonstrate power capabilities, became an indicator of loss of real power. The resort to so-called neutral powers only led to a fatal reliance on the armed forces to "solve" the crisis. And contrary to the expectations of some naive "democrats," including many prominent Christian Democrats, Chile's armed forces did not merely see to it that an "unconstitutional" president was removed from office: they dispensed with the constitution altogether.

But the moderates of the Center were not the only ones who misinterpreted Chilean political reality. The scenario of the revolutionary Left was also an illusory one. The leftists blamed the government for not accelerating the political process in order to force a confrontation that would have led to working-class victory and a genuine Socialist revolution. Ironically, while the Christian Democrats and the Nationals were attacking the government for setting the stage for a dictatorship of the Left, the revolutionary Left was just as vehemently attacking the government for failing to move in that direction. The assumptions of the revolutionary Left were two-fold. In the first place, they were convinced that the working class, given the proper direction, was ready to join in a militant challenge which might involve armed class struggle. And secondly, they assumed that during the first period of the Popular Unity government, the "reactionary forces" were divided and the military was neutral, so that a massive and rapid effort to mobilize the working class would find little resistance. From an analysis of the Chilean case it is clear, however, that it would not have been possible to overcome, in two short years, the basically economic aspirations of the working class and to infuse them with revolutionary class consciousness. Workers in Chile expected to better their lot in life under the new government; they would not have given their lives for a revolution which many of them thought had already come.

But it is quite evident from a study of the Chilean case that the second assumption was also untenable. The opposition was divided in the early years of the Allende administration because progressive sectors of the opposition were willing to support the government; indeed, they enabled the government to come to power in the first place. It is absurd to think that they would have remained supportive or neutral had the government embarked on an unequivocal strategy of accelerating class conflict. The countermobilization which occurred in the end would simply have occurred sooner. Even more significantly, there was no support in the armed forces for a revolutionary strategy which would have tolerated the mobilization of armed workers. The government was able to stave off military interference for as long as it did precisely because it stuck to basic constitutional procedures. Had Allende and his colleagues moved dramatically in 1971 to "consolidate power," the golpista faction in the armed forces would have materialized much sooner. Even if the working class had been more revolutionary than it was, it would have been impossible in 1971 (as it was in 1973) to mount a military force capable of challenging the highly professional Chilean military.

The fact is that the revolutionary Left, by attempting to radicalize the political process, contributed in substantial measure to undermining the very success of the government's so-called *Via Chilena* strategy. By its actions, the revolutionary Left, which had always ridiculed the possibility of a Socialist transformation through peaceful means, was engaged in a self-fulfilling prophecy.

It is clear that any agreement to structure a compromise to preserve the Chilean system would have entailed acceptance by the Popular Unity coalition of progressive changes, many of which would have fallen short of original goals. The Christian Democrats would, in turn, have had to accept a more fundamental transformation of the ongoing system than many would have wanted. It is also likely that an agreement would have involved a curtailment of the activities of some groups of the revolutionary Left.

The key is not that such a development would have precluded a revolutionary transformation. A fundamental and early Socialist revolution in Chile was simply out of the question anyway. The tragic dilemma of Chile today is that it must now live with a third alternative which is far worse for most of the political actors on the Chilean stage and for the bulk of the population: a reactionary military government. Christian Democrats now realize that the threat of the Allende government was nothing compared to the systematic denial of basic political freedoms and human rights under the rule of General Pinochet. Elections have been banned, electoral registers burned, and scores of party leaders arrested, harassed, or exiled. The party has lost its organs of information and is unable to express its views, let alone provide an alternative for leadership. The Left, of course, has suffered much more. Many of its leaders have been tortured and killed. Militants and their followers have been systematically harassed, deprived of their jobs and their livelihoods. Union leaders have been arrested and relieved of their positions. The revolutionary Left has been decimated and some of its most prominent leaders killed in real and alleged confrontations. Certainly their lot is far worse today than it was under political democracy. The courts, who argued so eloquently for human rights when there was no real threat, have shamefully acquiesced in a violation of human rights without precedent in Chile's history as an independent nation.

The Chilean experience has shown how easy it is for a professional and "neutral" military to become a repressive military regime. As soon as the military defined fellow countrymen as enemies against whom all-out war had to be waged, every conceivable repressive measure became justifiable. It is not surprising that the military has acted like an occupation force and treated the whole nation as if it were a giant regiment. It is also natural for an institution that thrives on hierarchy, order, and discipline to consider political democracy anathema to a war effort. In fact, the military leaders have explicitly blamed democracy for allowing "foreign" forces to corrupt a segment of the Chilean people. In order to "heal" the nation they have sought to extirpate all of those policies which in some way can be identified with a weak democracy and Marxist forces. Thus they have gone beyond banning political rights and persecuting people, and have dismantled reforms, not only of the Allende administration, but reforms won democratically over the years by progressive forces. Rights to strike, to job security, to education, and to good health have been severely restricted by a regime so obsessed with national security that the only ones to benefit from its policies are those sectors of the population identified with large Chilean and foreign business enterprises. The absence of political brokers and mechanisms of accountability means that little redress can be obtained, not only for the more flagrant political wrongs but for the everyday injustices that countless Chileans suffer at the hands of faceless and distant public and private bureaucracies. Even the gremios, who so vociferously called for the overthrow of Allende, now find their channels of access blocked and their traditional methods of protest curtailed.

It is still too early to tell what will happen in Chile. In their effort to obtain a better and more just society or to maintain the values they held dear, Chileans contributed to the destruction of a unique system of government. The coup of 1973 was followed by such widespread killing and repression that it will probably be impossible to restructure in quite the same way institutions and procedures which had evolved over generations. The problem is not only that it will be difficult for the military junta to step down because of the inevitable demands for retaliation. The main difficulty may very well be one of structuring the centrist consensus which proved to be so elusive in the last years of Chilean political democracy. So far, representatives of the various Chilean factions seem more intent on vindicating their actions and previous positions than on seeking to build bridges to the future.[71]

Notes

INTRODUCTION

1. Most scholars point to the leadership of Diego Portales, a cabinet minister in the late 1830s, as the most important influence on the development of stable republican institutions in Chile. The literature on the Portales period is very extensive. The reader is referred to the following works as particularly useful ones: Ramón Sotomayor Valdés, *Historia de Chile bajo gobierno del General D. Joaquín Prieto*, 3d ed. (Santiago: Fondo Histórico Presidente Joaquín Prieto, 1962); Francisco Antonio Encina, *Portales*, 2 vols. (Santiago: Editorial Nascimiento, 1964); Diego Barros Arana, *Un decenio de la historia de Chile*, 2 vols. (Santiago: Imprenta Universitaria, 1906); Aurelio Díaz Meza, *El advenimiento de Portales* (Santiago: Ediciones Ercilla, 1932). A classic study of the economy and economic policies during the period is Daniel Martner, *Historia de Chile: Historia económica*, vol. 1 (Santiago: Balcells and Co., 1929). Among the best general works for understanding the period, and which, for the most part, praise Portales, are Alberto Edwards Vives, *La fronda aristocrática* (Santiago: Editorial Ercilla, 1936); and Luis Galdames, *History of Chile* (Chapel Hill: University of North Carolina Press, 1941). Critical assessments of Portales come both from liberal and Marxist historians who condemn the nineteenth-century Chilean state as serving in an autocratic fashion the interests of the landed aristocracy. Among liberal historians, see Ricardo Donoso, *Desarrollo político y social de Chile desde la constitución de 1833* (Santiago: Imprenta Universitaria, 1942); and idem, *Las ideas políticas en Chile*, 2d ed. (Santiago: Editorial Universitaria, S.A., 1967). Among Marxists, see Julio Cesar Jobet, *Ensayo Crítico del desarrollo económico y social de Chile* (Santiago: Editorial Universitaria, 1955). Both critics and admirers of Portales agree that he was responsible for establishing the institutional structure of nineteenth-century Chile. Some authors have recently questioned the view that Portales was singlehandedly responsible for the course of Chilean democracy. For example, see Jay Kinsbruner, *Diego Portales: Interpretative Essays on the Man and Times* (The Hague: Martinus Nijhoff, 1967). Arturo Valenzuela believes that a succession of events, including the war against the Perú-Bolivia confederation and the character of the Bulnes presidency, must be taken into account in analyzing the Chilean "deviant case." See Arturo Valenzuela, *Political Brokers in Chile: Local Government in a Centralized Polity* (Durham, N.C.: Duke University Press, 1977).
2. For a discussion of this thesis see Claudio Véliz, "La Mesa de tres patas," *Desarrollo Económico* 3, nos. 1–2 (April–September 1963): 173–230. This theme is also discussed in Armand Mattelart, Carmen Castillo, and Leonardo Castillo, *La ideología de la dominacíon en una sociedad dependiente* (Buenos Aires: Ediciones Signos, 1970); Norbert Lechner, *La democracia en Chile* (Buenos Aires: Ediciones Signos, 1970); and Julio Samuel Valenzuela, "The Determinants of Suffrage Expansion in Chile: The 1874 Law" (unpublished paper, Columbia University, 1972).
3. An excellent article on the historiography of the civil war of 1891 is Harold Blakemore, "The Chilean Revolution of 1891 and Its Historiography," *Hispanic American Historical Review* 45, no. 3 (August 1965): 393–421. Standard interpretations of the war stress either the ideology and personality of Balmaceda and congressional actors or the institutional conflict between the presidency and Congress. Marxist scholars such as Hernán Ramírez Necochea have put forth a revisionary interpretation. Ramírez argues that Balmaceda was a nationalist intent on placing the nitrate industry in Chilean hands. He was opposed by foreign (British) nitrate interests who, in effect, were able to buy off elements in the Chilean

Congress. See his *Balmaceda y la contrarrevolución de 1891*, 2d rev. ed. (Santiago: Editorial Universitaria, 1969). While both interpretations have considerable merit, this author believes that a third interpretation, stressing the important center-local struggle, deserves much more attention. See Valenzuela, *Political Brokers in Chile*, chap. 8.

4. General discussions of the evolution of Chilean political parties include Galdames, *A History of Chile*; Federico Gil, *The Political System of Chile* (Boston: Houghton Mifflin Co., 1966); Alberto Edwards and Eduardo Frei, *Historia de los partidos políticos chilenos* (Santiago: Editorial del Pacífico, 1949); Germán Urzúa Valenzuela, *Los partidos políticos chilenos* (Santiago: Editorial Jurídica de Chile, 1968); Sergio Guilisati Tagle, *Partidos políticos chilenos* (Santiago: Editorial Nascimiento, 1964).

5. For studies describing the repression of labor, see Hernán Ramírez Necochea, *Historia del movimiento obrero. Siglo XIX. Antecedentes* (Santiago: Talleres Gráficos Lautaro, 1956) and Julio Cesar Jobet, *Ensayo crítico del desarrollo económico social de Chile* (Santiago: Editorial Universitaria, 1955).

6. However, in 1948, the middle-class parties shifted to an alliance with the Right and banned the Communist party, fearing the increased electoral strength of the Left. For references see n. 10, chap. 1.

7. See Juan Linz, *The Breakdown of Democratic Regimes: Crisis, Breakdown, and Reequilibration* (Baltimore, Md.: Johns Hopkins University Press, 1978).

CHAPTER 1

1. Federico Gil, *The Political System of Chile* (Boston: Houghton Mifflin Co., 1966), p. 244.

2. The survey was conducted in Santiago, Chile, in mid-1958 by Eduardo Hamuy. Raw data were obtained from the International Data Library and Reference Service, Survey Research Center, University of California, Berkeley. Chapter 1 of this study draws extensively on the author's "Political Constraints and the Prospects for Socialism in Chile," *Proceedings of the Academy of Political Science* 30, no. 4 (August 1972): 65–82.

3. On Chilean electoral law, see Mario Bernaschina, *Cartilla electoral* (Santiago: Editorial Jurídica, 1958). For the 1962 electoral law and its 1965 and 1968 modifications, see Antonio Vodanovic, ed., *Ley general de elecciones* (Santiago: Editorial Nascimiento, 1969). In 1970 a constitutional amendment was adopted giving illiterates the right to vote and lowering the voting age to eighteen. It took effect in time for the 1971 municipal election. For the legislative history of the amendment and its text, see Guillermo Piedrabuena Richards, *La reforma constitucional* (Santiago: Ediciones Encina, 1970).

4. All electoral information appearing in this chapter is derived from raw data obtained primarily in mimeograph form from the Dirección del Registro Electoral, Santiago, Chile.

5. See Arturo Valenzuela, "The Scope of the Chilean Party System," *Comparative Politics* 4, no. 2 (January 1972): 179–99. Data from Chile lead to a rejection of an influential body of literature in the social sciences which suggests that underdeveloped communities are less politically differentiated. For example, see S. N. Eisenstadt, "Social Change, Differentiation, and Evolution," *American Sociological Review* 29, no. 3 (June 1964): 375–87.

6. On the Chilean Right, see Ignacio Arteaga Undurraga, comp., *Partido Conservador XIV-Convención Nacional-1947* (Santiago: Imprenta Chile, 1947), which includes sketches of all conservative conventions from 1878 to 1947, lists of legislators and cabinet officers belonging to the party from 1831 to 1949, the party platform, and general notes on the 1947 convention. See also Marcial Sanfuentes Carrión, *El Partido Conservador* (Santiago: Editorial Universitaria, 1957), and José Miguel Prado Valdés, *Reseña histórica del Partido Liberal* (Santiago: Imprenta Andina, 1963). A very valuable reference to the numerous parties and party fragments spanning the ideological spectrum is Lía Cortés and Jordi Fuentes, *Diccionario político de Chile* (Santiago: Editorial Orbe, 1967).

7. Books on the Chilean Left are numerous. For a sampling, see Julio Cesar Jobet, *El Partido Socialista de Chile*, 2d ed., 2 vols. (Santiago: Ediciones Prensa Latinoamericana, 1971); Raúl Ampuero, *La izquierda en punto muerto*, 3d ed. (Santiago: Editorial Orbe 1969); Salomón Corbalán, *El Partido Socialista* (Santiago: Imprenta Atenea, 1957); Alejandro

Chelén Rojas, *Trayectoria del socialismo* (Buenos Aires: Editorial Austral, 1967); Hernán Ramírez Necochea, *Origen y formación del Partido Communista de Chile* (Santiago: Editorial Austral, 1965); Luis Corvalán Lepe, *Camino de victoria* (Santiago: Sociedad Impresora Horizonte, 1971); Ernst Halperin, *Nationalism and Communism in Chile* (Cambridge, Mass.: MIT Press, 1965).

8. For studies of the Chilean Radical party, see Luis Palma Zuñiga, *Historia del Partido Radical* (Santiago: Editorial Andrés Bello, 1967); Florencio Durán Bernales, *El Partido Radical* (Santiago: Editorial Nascimiento, 1958); Germán Urzúa Valenzuela, *El Partido Radical: Su evolución política* (Santiago: Academia de Ciencias Políticas y Administrativas, 1961). On the Christian Democrats, see Leonard Gross, *The Last Best Hope: Eduardo Frei and Chilean Christian Democracy* (New York: Random House, 1967); George Grayson, *El Partido Demócrata Cristiano Chileno* (Buenos Aires: Editorial Francisco de Aguirre, 1968); Eduardo Frei Montalva, *Pensamiento y acción* (Santiago: Editorial del Pacífico, 1958); Jaime Castillo Velasco, *Las fuentes de la Democracia Cristiana,* 2d ed. (Santiago: Editorial del Pacífico, 1968); Arturo Olavarría Bravo, *Chile bajo la Democracia Cristiana* (Santiago: Editorial Nascimiento, 1966); Suzanne Bodenheimer, "Stagnation in Liberty," in *North American Congress on Latin America*; *New Chile* (Berkeley: NACLA, 1972): 118–29; Arpad von Lazar and Luis Quiróz Varela, "Chilean Christian Democracy: Lessons in the Politics of Reform Management," *Inter-American Economic Affairs* 21, no. 4 (Spring 1968): 51–72.

9. "Public Opinion and the Movement of the Chilean Government to the Left, 1952–1972," in Arturo Valenzuela and J. Samuel Valenzuela, *Chile: Politics and Society* (New Brunswick, N.J.: Transaction, Inc., 1976), pp. 67–114.

10. President Gabriel Gonzalez Videla conveyed his concern about the Communist electoral success directly to party leader Volodia Teitelboim when he told him, the day after the 1947 municipal election, that "I cannot permit the Communist party to achieve power through democratic channels." See the citation in Ampuero, *La izquierda en punto muerto*, p. 24. A discussion of the outlawing of the Communist party can be found in Chelén Rojas, *Trayectoria del socialismo*, pp. 114–19. A fascinating discussion of the controversial election of 1938 which brought the Popular Front into office is contained in Marta Infante Barros, *Testigos del treinta y ocho* (Santiago: Editorial Andrés Bello, 1972).

11. On the Radical years, see John R. Stevenson, *The Chilean Popular Front* (Philadelphia: The University of Pennsylvania Press, 1942); Alberto Baltra Cortés, *Pedro Aguirre Cerda* (Santiago: Editorial Orbe, 1962); Alberto Cabero, *Recuerdos de don Pedro Aguirre Cerda* (Santiago: Editorial Nascimiento, 1948). See also Arturo Olavarría Bravo, *Chile entre dos Alessandri*, 2 vols. (Santiago: Editorial Nascimiento, 1962).

12. A good account of the Ibañez period remains to be written. See general works such as Gil, *Political System of Chile*; Alberto Edwards and Eduardo Frei, *Historia de los partidos político chilenos*; (Santiago: Editorial del Pacífico, 1949); and Ricardo Donoso, *Desarrollo político y social de Chile* (Santiago: Imprenta Universitaria, 1943).

13. See Giovanni Sartori, "European Political Parties: The Case of Polarized Pluralism," in *Political Parties and Political Development,* ed. Joseph Lapalombara and Myron Weiner (Princeton, N.J.: Princeton University Press, 1966), chap. 5. A preliminary attempt at applying the Sartori model to the Chilean case is Rafael López Pintor, "El sístema de partidos en Chile: Un caso de pluralismo extremo," mimeographed (Santiago: INSORA, 1968). When López wrote his piece the Christian Democrats had not as yet experienced a sharp decline. He thus attributes to Chile a Center more akin to the Italian case of 1963 than to the cases of Weimar and Spain in the 1930s, where the Center was considerably weaker.

14. Sartori, "European Political Parties," pp. 156, 164.

15. For documentation of this characterisitic of the Chilean party system, see Arturo Valenzuela, *Political Brokers in Chile: Local Governemnt in a Centralized Polity* (Durham, N.C.: Duke University Press, 1977), chap. 7.

16. For a discussion of the relationship of business and government, see Constantine C. Menges, "Public Policy and Organized Buisness in Chile: A Preliminary Analysis," *Journal of International Affairs* 2, no. 2 (1966): 343–65. A thorough discussion of business confederations and professional associations can be found in David F. Cusak, "La interacción entre el sector público y los agentes mediadores en el sistema político chileno," part 2, mimeo-

graphed (Santiago: INSORA, 1968); and David F. Cusak, "The Politics of Chilean Private Enterprise under Christian Democracy," (Ph.D. diss., University of Denver, 1970).

17. On Chilean labor, see Alan Angell, *Politics and the Labour Movement in Chile* (London: Oxford University Press, 1972); Jorge Barría Serán, *Trayectoria y estructura del movimiento sindical chileno, 1946–62* (Santiago: INSORA, 1963); James O. Morris, *Elites, Intellectuals, and Consensus: A Study of the Social Question and the Industrial Relations System in Chile* (Ithaca, N.Y.: Cornell University Press, 1966); Henry Landsberger, Manuel Barrera, and Abel Toro, *El pensamiento del dirigente sindical chileno* (Santiago: INSORA, 1963); Hernán Ramírez Necochea, *Historia del movimiento obrero en Chile* (Santiago: Talleres gráficos Lautaro, 1956); Julio Samuel Valenzuela, "The Chilean Labor Movement: The Institutionalization of Conflict," in Valenzuela and Valenzuela, *Chile: Politics and Society*.

18. For documentation of these vertical linkages and the role of the legislature, see Valenzuela, *Political Brokers in Chile*, chaps. 5–7.

19. See ibid. For evolution of the system over time, see chap. 8.

20. For a detailed discussion of elements of the electoral system and reforms of 1958, see Bernaschina, *Cartilla electoral*.

21. Duncan MacRae, *Parliament, Parties, and Society in France, 1946–1958* (New York: St. Martin's Press, 1967), p. 16.

22. Alejandro Portes, "Urbanization and Politics in Latin America," *Social Science Quarterly* 52, no. 3 (December 1971): 697–720. See also his "Occupation and Lower Class Political Orientation in Chile," in Valenzuela and Valenzuela, *Chile: Politics and Society*.

23. For another discussion of Chilean voting behavior which also emphasizes some of the heterogeneous bases of support, see Robert Ayres, "Unidad Popular and the Chilean Electoral Process," in Valenzuela and Valenzuela, *Chile: Politics and Society*, pp. 30–67. It must be stressed again that the Socialists had much more heterogeneous bases of support than the Communists and relied, particularly in earlier periods, primarily on traditional clientelistic politics. For documentation, see Chelén Rojas, *Trayectoria del socialismo*.

24. Oficina de Planificación Nacional, *Plan de la economía nacional: Antecedentes sobre el desarrollo chileno, 1960–70* (Santiago: ODEPLAN, 1971), pp. 7, 170–76, 372, 383. This volume is an excellent summary of the state of the Chilean economy and the role of the public sector as of 1970. For a discussion using many of the same figures and comparative data on other Latin American countries, see Sergio Bitar, "La estructura económica chilena y la transición al socialismo," *Mensaje* 20, nos. 202–3 (September-October 1971): 404–12.

25. See the excellent study "Public Enterprises: Their Present Significance and Their Potential in Development," *Economic Bulletin for Latin America* 15, no. 2 (2d semester 1970): 1–70, for this information and information on other Latin American countries. At the same time the importance of a highly concentrated private industrial and financial sector should not be minimized. See Ricardo Lagos Escobar, *La concentración del poder económico* (Santiago: Editorial del Pacífico, 1961); and Maurice Zeitlin and Richard Ratcliff, "The Concentration of National and Foreign Capital in Chile," in Valenzuela and Valenzuela, *Chile: Politics and Society*, pp. 297–337.

26. For a definition of praetorianism and an influential discussion of political institutionalization, see Samuel P. Huntington, *Political Order in Changing Societies* (New Haven: Yale University Press, 1968), especially chap. 4.

27. For the Chilean Senate debate on this incident, see *El Mercurio*, 27 June 1969, p. 13.

28. See J. S. Valenzuela, "The Chilean Labor Movement," in Valenzuela and Valenzuela, *Chile: Politics and Society*, pp. 135–171.

29. The best single comprehensive description of Chilean institutions before the coup is Gil, *Political System of Chile*.

30. Alejandro Silva Bascuñan, *Tratado de derecho constitucional*, 3 vols. (Santiago: Editorial Jurídica, 1963).

31. For a discussion of the Contraloría, see Enrique Silva Cimma, *Derecho administrativo chileno y comparado*, 2d ed. (Santiago: Editorial Jurídica, 1969), vol. 2. According to Silva Cimma, from 1959 to 1969 Chilean presidents did not issue *decretos de insistencia* aimed at overruling the Contraloría (see p. 368). On Chilean public finances, see Hugo Araneda Dörr, *La administración financiera del estado* (Santiago: Editorial Jurídica, 1966). On municipal finances and the role of the Contraloría, see A. Valenzuela, *Political Brokers in Chile*, chap. 2.

32. Several excellent studies on the Chilean bureaucracy have appeared. These include Germán Urzúa Valenzuela and Anamaría García Barzelatto, *Diagnóstico de la burocracia chilena* (Santiago: Editorial Jurídica, 1971); Germán Urzúa Valenzuela, *Evolución de la administración pública chilena (1818–1968)* (Santiago: Editorial Jurídica, 1970); Rafael López Pintor, "Development Administration in Chile: Structural, Normative and Behavioral Constraints to Performance," (Ph.D. diss., University of North Carolina, 1972) and his *Una Explicación Sociológica del Cambio Administrativo: Chile, 1812–1970* (Madrid: Documentación Administrativa, no. 168, 1975).

33. See A. Valenzuela, *Political Brokers in Chile*, chap. 6.

34. For a discussion of some of these problems from the point of view of the planner, see Osvaldo Contreras Strauch, *Antecedentes y perspectivas de la planificación en Chile* (Santiago: Editorial Jurídica, 1971). This work was heavily influenced by the thinking of Osvaldo Sunkel.

35. See Menges, "Public Policy and Organized Business in Chile."

36. Jacques Chonchol, "Poder y reforma agraria en la experiencia chilena," in Anibal Pinto et al., *Chile Hoy* (Mexico: Siglo XXI, 1970), p. 296. According to Chonchol, when the Christian Democrats came into office agricultural policy was set by twenty-one different agencies dependent on five different ministries. As late as 1966 the Ministry of Agriculture controlled only 11 percent of agricultural credit and only 2 percent of rural investments (see pp. 303–4). This is one of the best treatments available of the complexities of the unwieldly public sector.

37. See the remarks of Carmen Lazo, a popular Socialist deputy, criticizing the excessive technocracy of the public sector during the Allende period and calling for a greater role for the non-specialist, in *Ercilla*, 11 July 1973, p. 11. See also Chonchol, "Poder y reforma agraria en la experiencia Chilena."

38. On the "praetorian" aspects of Argentine politics, see Eldon Kenworthy, "Coalitions in the Political Development of Latin America," in *The Study of Coalition Behavior: Theoretical Perspectives from Four Continents* ed. Sven Groennings, E. W. Kelley, and Michael Leiserson (New York: Holt, Rinehart and Winston, 1970), pp. 103–4. For a fascinating discussion of the "impossible" Argentine political game, see Guillermo O'Donnell, *Modernization and Bureaucratic-Authoritarianism: Studies in South American Politics* (University of California at Berkeley: Institute of International Studies, 1973), chap. 4.

39. On the Chilean Senate, see Weston Agor, *The Chilean Senate* (Austin: University of Texas Press, 1971). An invaluable study of the workings of the Chilean legislature is Jorge Tapia Valdés, *La técnica legislativa* (Santiago: Editorial Jurídica, 1960). For a discussion of the role of the legislature in Chilean politics over time, with particular emphasis on the importance of the parliamentary republic in the institutionalization of Chilean politics, see A. Valenzuela, *Political Brokers in Chile*, chap. 8.

40. This argument is developed in Arturo Valenzuela and Alexander Wilde, "Presidentialist Politics and the Decline of the Chilean Congress," in *Legislatures and Political Development*, ed. Joel Smith and Lloyd Mussolf (Durham, N.C.: Duke University Press, 1978).

41. Derived from Roman law, it means the search for a rightful redress of grievances or the obtension of rightful demands through the legal process.

42. An excellent summary and analysis of the extensive debate on Chilean inflation, which goes back into the nineteenth century, can be found in Albert O. Hirschman, *Journeys toward Progress* (New York: The Twentieth Century Fund, 1963). A classic study of earlier inflation is Frank W. Fetter, *Monetary Inflation in Chile* (Princeton, N.J.: Princeton University Press, 1931). Influential studies of Chilean inflation include Osvaldo Sunkel, "La inflación chilena: Un enfoque heterodoxo," *El Trimestre Económico* 25 (October-December 1958); Luis Escobar, "Desocupación con inflación: El caso chileno," *Panorama Económico*, August 1959; Nicolás Kaldor, "Problemas econónomicos de Chile," *El Trimestre Económico* 26 (April-June 1959).

43. An excellent recent study of industrialization in Chile is Henry W. Kirsh, "The Industrialization of Chile, 1880–1970," (Ph.D. diss., University of Florida, 1973). See also Oscar Muñoz, *Crecimiento industrial de Chile, 1914-1965* (Santiago: Universidad de Chile, Instituto de Economía y Planificación, 1968), p. 26. Among the many fine general treatments of the Chilean economy, see: Francisco A. Encina, *Nuestra inferioridad económica* (Santiago: Editorial Universitaria, S.A., 1955); Anibal Pinto Santa Cruz, *Chile: Un caso de*

desarrollo frustrado (Santiago: Editorial Universitaria, S.A., 1959); idem, *Chile: Una economía difícil* (México: Fondo de Cultura Económica, 1964); Ricardo Ffrench-Davis, *Políticas económicas en Chile, 1952-1970* (Santiago: Ediciones Nueva Universidad, 1973); Oscar Muñoz et al., *Proceso a la industrialización chilena* (Santiago: Centro Estudios de Planificacion Nacional, 1972); Markos Mamalakis and Clark Reynolds, eds. *Essays on the Chilean Economy* (Homewood, Ill.: Richard D. Irwin, 1964); José Cademártori, *La economía chilena* (Santiago: Editorial Universitaria, 1968).

44. Quoted in Valenzuela and Wilde, "Presidentialist Politics." Hans Daalder makes a similar argument in differentiating the political evolution of several European countries. See his "Parties, Elites and Political Developments in Western Europe," in Lapalombara and Weiner, *Political Parties and Political Development*, p. 60.

45. In the United States an ideology of "disjointed incrementalism" seems to be congruent with that of incrementalist decision-making. See Charles E. Lindbloom, *The Intelligence of a Democracy* (New York: The Free Press, 1965). On the ideology of master planning in Chile and other Latin American countries, see Hirschman's provocative analysis in *Journeys toward Progress*.

46. For historical treatments of the Chilean military, see Frederick M. Nunn, *Chilean Politics, 1920-31: The Honorable Mission of the Armed Forces* (Albuquerque: University of New Mexico Press, 1970); and idem, *The Military in Chilean History* (Albuquerque: University of New Mexico Press, 1976).

47. In a survey conducted in 1967 the overwhelming majority of respondents noted that the military did not have a political role. See Roy Allen Hansen, "Military Culture and Organizational Decline: A Study of the Chilean Army," (Ph.D. diss., University of California at Los Angeles, 1968), chap. 4. Basing his observations on a comprehensive survey of retired officers, Hansen notes that military officers picked their five best friends almost exclusively from the ranks of fellow officers.

48. This theme came through very strongly in interviews with Chilean politicians conducted by the author in 1969 and 1974. Hansen, however, notes that his population sample held the military in higher esteem on qualities such as honesty and trustworthiness than they did other elite groups, including politicians (see ibid).

49. Charles Lewis Taylor and Michael C. Hudson, *World Handbook of Political and Social Indicators* (New Haven: Yale University Press, 1972), pp. 35, 39.

50. See the works by Nunn referred to in n. 46. This point is forcefully made in a good article on the Chilean military after the coup by Jorge Neff entitled, "The Politics of Repression: The Social Pathology of the Chilean Military," in *Latin American Perspectives* 1, no. 2 (Summer 1974): 59–63. See also the work by Alain Joxe, *Las Fuerzas armadas en el sistema político de Chile* (Santiago: Editorial Universitaria, 1970).

51. Statistics for the pre-Alessandri period are from Gil, *Political System of Chile*, p. 178. The most recent statistics can be found in Dirección de Presupuestos, Ministerio de Hacienda, *Balance Consolidado del Sector Público* for relevant years.

52. See chap. 2 below.

53. *Ercilla*, 15–21 September 1965, p. 8. Cited in Arturo Valenzuela, "The Chilean Political System and the Armed Forces, 1810–1925" (M.A. thesis, Columbia University, 1967), p. 144.

54. Hansen, "Military Culture and Organizational Decline," p. 254. Thus the Chilean military conceived of their role in similar terms as the Brazilian military and the military in other Latin American countries. For a brilliant discussion of the guardian role in Brazil, see Alfred Stepan, *The Military in Politics: Changing Patterns in Brazil* (Princeton, N.J.: Princeton University Press, 1971), pt. 2.

CHAPTER 2

1. See Juan Linz, *The Breakdown of Democratic Regimes: Crisis, Breakdown, and Reequilibration* (Baltimore, Md.: Johns Hopkins University Press, 1978).

2. See the influential essay by James C. Davies, "Toward a Theory of Revolution," *American Sociological Review*, 27 (February 1962): 5–16. For a thorough review of relative depriva-

tion theories which attempt to explain political disorder and violence, see Ted Robert Gurr, *Why Men Rebel* (Princeton, N.J.: Princeton University Press, 1970).

3. For a recent and important version of this argument, see Samuel P. Huntington, *Political Order in Changing Societies* (New Haven: Yale University Press, 1968), chap. 1. See also Karl Deutsch, "Social Mobilization and Political Development," *American Political Science Review*, 55 (September 1961): 492–502.

4. For an interesting analysis which challenges Huntington's notion that weak institutionalization leads to decay and exposes some of the ambiguities of his argument, see Mark Kesselman, "Overinstitutionalization and Political Constraint: The Case of France," *Comparative Politics* 111 (October 1970): 21–44.

5. See the excellent publication by the Dirección de Presupuesto, Ministerio de Hacienda, *Balance consolidado del sector público de Chile años 1969-1970 y período 1964-1970* (Santiago: Talleres Gráficos del Servicio de Prisiones, 1973), p. 36.

6. See Martin Needler, *Political Development in Latin America* (New York: Random House, 1968), p. 90.

7. For this thesis see Almino Alfonso et al., *Movimiento campesino chileno*, 2 vols. (Santiago: ICIRA, 1970). See also Brian Loveman, "The Transformation of the Chilean Countryside," in *Chile: Politics and Society*, ed. Arturo Valenzuela and J. Samuel Valenzuela (New Brunswick, N.J.: Transaction, Inc., 1976), pp. 238–96.

8. See Mario Bernaschina, *Cartilla electoral* (Santiago: Editorial Jurídica, 1958).

9. Population figures are derived from publications of the Instituto Nacional de Estadística; all voting figures come from the Dirección del Registro Electoral, Santiago, Chile.

10. The excellent article by Landsberger and McDaniel deals primarily with the Popular Unity period. This author agrees with most of their analysis, though he interprets somewhat differently mobilization in the pre-Allende period. See "Hypermobilization in Chile, 1970–73," *World Politics* 28, no. 4 (July 1976): 538.

11. Data for 1967 from Dirección de Estadística y Censos, "Chile industria manufacturera: Número de establecimientos y ocupación en el año 1967," mimeographed, 1968, p. 8. The figures for 1957 are taken from the excellent publication by the Instituto de Economía, Universidad de Chile, *La economía de Chile en el período 1950-1963*, vol. 2 (Santiago: Instituto de Economía, 1963), p. 105. According to the Oficina de Planificación Nacional (ODEPLAN), employment in large firms tripled in the same period. See ODEPLAN, *Plan de la economía nacional Antecedentes sobre el desarrollo chileno, 1960-70* (Santiago: ODEPLAN, 1971), p. 181.

12. Interviews with the author in Santiago de Chile in October, November, and December of 1974.

13. This point is made in Alan Angell, *Politics and the Labour Movement in Chile* (London: Oxford University Press, 1972), p. 67. I am indebted to Samuel Valenzuela for his helpful comments on this section.

14. The three main campesino confederations were: Triunfo Campesino, formed initially by INDAP of the Ministry of Agriculture; Libertad, which grouped organizations connected with the church and the Christian Democratic party; and Ranquil, associated with Marxist parties. In 1969 Triunfo Campesino had almost 50 percent of the affiliates, but by late 1972 Ranquil came to predominate with about half of the unionized rural workers. Data from Dirección del Trabajo, Santiago.

15. See the sources cited in n. 7.

16. In fact, in 1920 there were as many as 270,000 unionized workers, not counting empleados. With an active population of 1,228,000, this meant that as early as that date 22 percent of the active workers were unionized. For the union figures see U.S. Bureau of Labor Statistics, *Bulletin,* no. 461 (October 1928). The figures on active population come from República de Chile, *Censo de la población de chile, 1930*, p. vii. For a revisionary work on the Chilean labor movement which analyzes these findings, see the forthcoming doctoral dissertation by J. Samuel Valenzuela, "The French and Chilean Labor Movements" (Columbia University, 1978).

17. Angell, *Politics and the Labour Movement*, p. 76. See also J. Samuel Valenzuela, "The Chilean Labor Movement: The Institutionalization of Conflict," in Valenzuela and Valenzuela, *Chile: Politics and Society*, pp. 135–71.

18. See the chapter entitled "Participación nacional y popular," in Eduardo Frei, *Cuarto mensaje presidencial*, 21 May 1968, for a discussion of the rationale behind "popular participation." See also the publications of DESAL (Centro para el Desarrollo Económico y Social de América Latina). For an evaluation of the urban effort, see Luis Alvarado, Rosemond Cheetham, and Gastón Rojas, "Mobilización social en torno al problema de la vivienda," *EURE* 3, no. 7 (April 1973): 27–70.

19. Gabriel Almond, "Popular Development: Analytical and Normative Perspectives," *Comparative Political Studies* 1, no. 4 (January 1969): 463.

20. For a good discussion of the 1964 election see Federico Gil, *The Political System of Chile* (Boston: Houghton Mifflin Co., 1966), chap. 7.

21. U.S. intervention in the 1964 election has long been the subject of discussion. For an early treatment see the study, based in part on Eastern European intelligence, by Eduardo Labarca, *Chile invadido* (Santiago: Editorial Austral, 1969), chap. 3. More precise details of the U.S. role were revealed in the staff report of the Select Committee to Study Governmental Operations with respect to United States Intelligence, *Covert Action in Chile* (Washington, D.C.: U.S. Government Printing Office, 18 December 1975), pp. 14–19. A CIA study concluded that "U.S. intervention enabled Eduardo Frei to win a clear majority in the 1964 election, instead of merely a plurality" (ibid, p. 17). Three million dollars was a tremendous amount of money in the Chilean context, amounting to $1.20 per vote. Labarca argues that the Frei campaign received close to $20 million, including money from European and private sources. As a comparison, in 1964 the Goldwater and Johnson campaigns together spent 54 cents per vote. See Congressional Quarterly, *Politics in America*, 4th ed. (Washington, D.C.: Congressional Quarterly, 1971), p. 80.

22. Between 1964 and 1969 the CIA spent $2 million in Chile, not only for electoral support but also to strengthen Christian Democratic support among peasants and slum dwellers. See *Covert Action in Chile*, pp. 17–19. It is an open secret that DESAL, the "think tank" headed by Jesuit Roger Vekemans which drew up most of the blueprints for *"promoción popular,"* was supported by the CIA. Table 20 in chap. 3 provides information on the vast U.S. aid to the Frei government.

23. These observations are based on the author's research experience in Chile in 1969. The argument of this section is elaborated much more fully in Arturo Valenzuela and Alexander Wilde, "Presidentialist Politics and the Decline of the Chilean Congress," in *Legislatures and Political Developments*, ed. Joel Smith and Lloyd Mussolf (Durham, N.C.: Duke University Press, forthcoming). For a good example of the debate of the period, see the special issue on the 1967 municipal elections put out by *Ercilla*, 29 March 1967. The Christian Democrats called for an end to the "old style of give and take and the politics of the political clique" (p. 25). The vice-president of the Radical party bitterly criticized the government's attempt to turn the municipal election into a plebiscite, noting that "a long tradition has been broken as the head of state has cast himself in the role of electoral leader" (p. 3).

24. A good case study of the agrarian reform decision is Robert R. Kaufman, *The Politics of Land Reform in Chile, 1950–1970* (Cambridge, Mass.: Harvard University Press, 1972). On the copper decision, see Theodore Moran, *Multinational Corporations and the Politics of Dependence: Copper in Chile* (Princeton, N.J.: Princeton University Press, 1974).

25. The statistics cited earlier in this chapter show that the government made considerable progress in achieving its objectives. However, it was not necessary for it to adopt an arrogant attitude in attaining that end. At one point the government sought to bar congressmen from granting subsidies to local organizations, a traditional pork barrel which represented an infinitesimal portion of the budget. The consideration was one purely of "efficiency." The political ramifications only became obvious after a storm of opposition was raised. See Valenzuela and Wilde, "Presidentialist Politics and the Decline of the Chilean Congress."

26. Ibid. A thorough legislative history of the reforms can be found in Guillermo Piedrabuena Richards, *La reforma constitucional* (Santiago: Ediciones Encina, 1970). Major essays presenting the government's viewpoint on the reforms can be found in Eduardo Frei et al., *Reforma constitucional 1970* (Santiago: Editorial Jurídica, 1970).

27. The history of the MIR has yet to be written.

28. See the articles by Michael Leiserson, "Game Theory and the Study of Coalition Behavior," and E. W. Kelley, "Bargaining in Coalition Situations," in *The Study of Coalition Behavior: Theoretical Perspectives from Four Continents,* ed. Sven Groennings, E. W. Kelly, and Michael Leiserson (New York: Holt, Rinehart and Winston, 1970).

29. In understanding the potential for coalition-building before the election, it must also be stressed that the Right, in a situation unlike that of 1964, had a very viable candidate in ex-president Alessandri. The Right felt that if there were to be a Right-Center coalition again, it would have to be around their candidate this time.

30. It is also clear from the Christian Democratic Party Congress of 1969 that, despite Tomic's stand, the party was not prepared to move sharply to the left.

31. For some of the limitations of game theory in the study of politics, see Leiserson, "Game Theory and the Study of Coalition Behavior," pp. 270–72. See also the discussion by Scott C. Flanigan in *Crisis, Choice, and Change: Historical Studies of Political Development*, ed. Gabriel A. Almond, Scott C. Flanigan, and Robert C. Mundt (Boston: Little, Brown and Co., 1972), pp. 67–72.

32. For the first time in Chilean politics television was important in a presidential campaign. This clearly hurt Alessandri, who was not able to live up to his image of an austere, nonpartisan, and wise leader. He looked tired and feeble, and he overstressed the theme that workers must work more for less if the country was to prosper.

33. An excellent summary and analysis of the three presidential platforms, using categories derived from the sociology of knowledge, is Frédéric Debuyst and Joan E. Garcés, "La opción chilena de 1970: Análisis de los tres programas electorales," *Revista Latinoamericana de Ciencia Política* 2, no. 2 (August 1971): 279–369. The authors present a detailed side-by-side table of the three platforms in a lengthy Appendix.

34. Allende made this argument repeatedly in his public statements. For a concrete example, see his first speech before the joint session of Congress in Salvador Allende, *Salvador Allende: Su pensamiento político* (Santiago: Empresa Editora Nacional Quimantú Limitada, 1972), p. 112. An English translation of the speech can be found in Regis Debray, *The Chilean Revolution: Conversations with Allende* (New York: Random House, Vintage Books, 1971). The question of a revolution within the ongoing legal system led to a significant intellectual debate in Chilean circles. The foremost articulator of this view is Eduardo Novoa. See his "Vías legales para avanzar hacia el socialismo," *Mensaje*, no. 208 (April 1971), pp. 84–90, which suggests how legislation on the books, dating in some cases from the brief Socialist experiment of 1932, could be used to move legally toward a Socialist economy. The Allende administration would make use of these regulations during its term in office. For a more pessimistic appraisal of the move to socialism within legal frameworks, which stresses the constraints of the legal system, see Eduardo Novoa, "Aspectos constitucionales y legales de la política del gobierno de la Unidad Popular," in *La vía chilena al socialismo*, ed. Gabriel Palma (Mexico: Siglo XXI, 1973). For an excellent series of articles on the same topic, see the special edition on "Revolución y legalidad: Problemas del estado y el derecho en Chile," of *Cuadernos de la Realidad Nacional*, no. 15 (December 1972).

35. See his *The Breakdown of Democratic Regimes*.

36. Though Allende was identified with the more moderate faction of the party, he supported the election of Carlos Altamirano to the party leadership, in large measure because of personal rivalries and disputes. Many in the moderate faction of the party had pushed for the nomination of Aniceto Rodriguez as the presidential candidate of the Left, believing that Allende had had his chance in the past and had failed. The support for Altamirano can also be interpreted as an effort on the part of the president to regain a measure of influence over the left wing of the party. Strained relations with the leadership of his own party was to be an important feature of his government.

37. See the fascinating interview with Luis Corvalán, secretary general of the Chilean Communist party, in Eduardo Labarca, *Corvalán 27 horas* (Santiago: Quimantú, 1972), esp. pp. 109–12.

38. See the study by Debuyst and Garcés, "La opción Chilena de 1970," for a comparison of the party platforms.

39. It should be stressed that this author does not feel that the more conservative wing of the

Christian Democratic party should automatically be lumped with all other "reactionaries." Most of the leadership of this group had and has a strong commitment to democracy. They were clearly "moderates" within the Chilean context.

40. Data on the breakdown of seats in the Congress were obtained from the Oficina de Informaciones de la Cámara de Diputados and the Oficina de Informaciones del Senado.

41. Though traditionally the front-runner had been elected in the Congress, this does not mean that parties supporting the runner-up in the popular election also voted for the front-runner; they usually voted for their own candidate. Thus in 1946 the Conservatives voted for Eduardo Cruz-Coke, in 1952 the Radicals voted for Pedro Alfonso, and in 1958 the FRAP voted for Allende. In 1970 the Christian Democrats found themselves in the peculiar position of commanding the key block of votes in the Congress but having no presidential candidate in contention.

42. For an analysis of U.S. action see the interim report of the Select Committee to Study Governmental Operations with respect to intelligence activities, United States Senate, *Alleged Assassination Plots Involving Foreign Leaders* (Washington, D.C.: U.S. Government Printing Office, 20 November 1975), pp. 225–54. The lengths to which the Central Intelligence Agency went is illustrated by Cable 882, Headquarters to Station, 10/19/70, in which the station was urged to fabricate a justification for a coup. Suggestions included the use of "firm" intelligence that Cubans would reorganize intelligence services along Soviet-Cuban lines and that Allende planned to empty armories to the Communist Peoples' Militia. Station noted that "we are now asking you to prepare intel report based on some well-known facts and some fiction to justify coup, split opposition, and gain adherents for military coup. With appropriate military contact can determine how to 'discover' intel report which could even be planted during raids planned by Carabineros [quotation marks in original]." See p. 234. Nixon himself initiated the action in a meeting that took place on 15 September 1970 with Henry Kissinger, National Security Council adviser; John Mitchell, attorney general; and Richard Helms, director of the Central Intelligence Agency. The president noted that $10 million could be spent on the operation, that the Chilean economy should be made to "scream," and that every effort should be made to "Save Chile" (p. 227). Though the embassy was not involved in the kidnapping plot, Ambassador Korry put great pressure on Frei to stop Allende's bid for the presidency. In a situation report the ambassador noted that he had sent a message to Frei to the effect that "Frei should know that not a nut or bolt will be allowed to reach Chile under Allende. Once Allende comes to power we shall do all within our power to condemn Chile and the Chileans to utmost deprivation and poverty, a policy designed for a long time to come to accelerate the hard features of a Communist society in Chile" (p. 231).

43. See Daniel Levine, "The Role of Political Learning in the Restoration and Consolidation of Democracy: Venezuela since 1958," in Linz and Stepan, *The Breakdown of Democratic Regimes*, vol. 3, *The Problem in the Latin American Context*.

CHAPTER 3

1. The program of the Popular Unity government has been published in Gabriel Palma, *La vía chilena al socialismo* (Mexico: Siglo XXI, 1973), pp. 269–92. The same book includes the platform of the Popular Unity drawn up for the 1973 congressional elections (see pp. 293–322). For an English translation, see Ann Zammit, ed., *The Chilean Way to Socialism* (Austin: The University of Texas Press, 1973).

2. Events referred to in this study were widely reported in the Chilean press. The author relied primarily on *El Mercurio Edición Internacional, Ercilla, Chile Hoy*, and the British periodical *Latin America* for the general chronology. For more in-depth study of important events, such as the conversations of mid-1972 between the government and the Christian Democrats, the daily press was used, including *El Mercurio, La Nación, La Prensa, El Siglo, Las Noticias de Ultima Hora, Mayoría,* and other newspapers. Though *El Mercurio* is an extremely conservative paper and sought from the outset to destroy the Allende government, it was and is the primary newspaper of record, reporting the full texts of statements made by parties and

leaders, and printing official statistics, documents, and Senate debates. Material from interviews with key political actors helped supplement published sources.

3. See Regis Debray, *The Chilean Revolution: Conversations with Allende* (New York: Random House, Vintage Books, 1971).

4. For a general statement of the government economic policy, see the presentation made by the minister of economics, Pedro Vuskovic, in October 1971 and published in Lelio Basso et al., *Transición al socialismo y experiencia chilena* (Santiago: CESO-CEREN, 1972), pp. 99–114. A clear statement of Popular Unity policy, stressing primarily economic factors such as the importance of increased demand to offset idle plant capacity, can be found in Julio López, "La estrategia económica del gobierno de la Unidad Popular," *Cuadernos de la Realidad Nacional*, no. 9 (September 1971), pp. 69–86.

5. Basso et al., *Transición al socialismo*, pp. 101–2. In a seminar held in March 1972, when the economic situation had deteriorated considerably, Vuskovic stressed much more strongly these political goals as the primary criteria for economic policy. See his "La política económica del gobierno de la Unidad Popular," in Palma, *La vía chilena al socialismo*, p. 44. See also the "debate" on pp. 79–99.

6. Stefan de Vylder, *Allende's Chile: The Political Economy of the Rise and Fall of the Unidad Popular* (Cambridge : Cambridge University Press, 1976), p. 54.

7. Ibid.

8. On the money supply see table 24.

9. De Vylder, *Allende's Chile*, p. 63. Allende summarized the first year's economic accomplishments in his message of 4 November 1971. See *Allende: Su pensamiento político,* pp. 260–61, 266–67.

10. Ibid., pp. 70–71.

11. During the first six months of 1971 inflation was 11.1 percent, still very favorable as compared to the last year of the Frei administration, when inflation had reached 34.9 percent. These figures from the Instituto Nacional de Estadística are printed in *Oficina de Informaciones del Senado, Boletín Informativo Económico*, 16 June 1972, p. 1.

12. See the works of Eduardo Novoa, cited chap. 2, no. 34. See also part 4 of Andrés Echeverría and Luis Frei, *La lucha por la juricidad en Chile* (Santiago: Editorial del Pacífico, 1974), vol. 1, for reprints of several additional articles by Novoa, and the declaration of Minister of Economics Orlando Millas and the Comptroller General Héctor Humeres on the "resquicios legales."

13. De Vylder, *Allende's Chile*, p. 145.

14. Most U.S. firms were nationalized with no dispute. This was the case, for example, with RCA Victor, Bethlehem Steel, and all the U.S. bank offices in Chile. There were difficulties with other companies such as ITT and the Ford Motor Company. The Ford plant was accused of illegally shutting down operations and of cutting off the importation of vital parts. It was taken over by workers, and eventually the government intervened. See *El Mercurio Edición Internacional*, 31 May–6 June 1971, p. 8. The ITT became notorious for its attempts to stop Allende's election by urging economic sabotage and attempting to enlist U.S. intelligence in its efforts. ITT's role was first exposed by columnist Jack Anderson in the *Washington Post*, 22 March 1972, p. C23. The ITT documents, incriminating the company in a blatant conspiracy to meddle in Chilean affairs, were published in *Documentos secretos de la ITT* (Santiago: Empresa Editoral Nacional Quimantú, 1972). For further information see the Report to the Committee on Foreign Relations, United States Senate, by the Subcommittee on Multinational Corporations, "The International Telephone and Telegraph Company and Chile, 1970–71," 21 June 1973 (Washington, D.C.: Government Printing Office, 1973).

15. See the speech by Jacques Chonchol, *El Mercurio Edición Internacional*, 15–21 February 1971, p. 6. Page 1 of the same issue reports on sharp exchanges in the Chilean Senate over the issue of violence and expropriations in the countryside. It also contains a statement made by the six leaders of the Popular Unity parties asserting the government's commitment to carry out the agrarian reform process within the law.

16. *Allende: Su pensamiento político*, p. 256.

17. In studying Chilean elections, care must be taken not to compare elections for different offices. Elections for local office so often revolve around local issues and candidates that it is

misleading to compare them with senatorial and presidential elections. Elections for the Chamber of Deputies often combine local and national issues. For a discussion of local campaigning, see Arturo Valenzuela, *Political Brokers in Chile: Local Government in a Centralized Polity* (Durham, N.C.: Duke University Press, 1977), chap. 4.

18. Basso et al., *Transición al socialismo*, p. 107.
19. De Vylder, *Allende's Chile*, p. 66.
20. See *El Mercurio Edición Internacional*, 28 May–3 June 1972, p. 2.
21. These data come from the Superintendencia de Aduanas and the Banco Central, *El Mercurio Edición Internacional*, 23–29 August 1971, p. 2. According to figures projected by the Sociedad de Fomento Fabril, by 1973 food imports would account for 75 percent of copper earnings. See *El Mercurio Edición Internacional*, 30 July–5 August 1973, p. 2. Much of the problem stemmed from the fact that increased demand was not channeled into economic sectors with idle capacity, such as the durable goods industry, but was directed into areas, such as agriculture, that were already incapable of meeting demand. The policy of increasing the wages of working-class elements was simply not conducive to bailing out a consumer-goods-oriented industry that was lagging. For an economic analysis along these lines see *El Mercurio Edición Internacional*, 7–13 June 1971, p. 2. These difficulties were recognized by government economists like López. See his "La estrategia económica."
22. Basso et al. *Transición al socialismo*, p. 107.
23. See n. 21 for the source of these data.
24. *El Mercurio Edición Internacional*, 24–30 July 1972, p. 2.
25. For documentation of the U.S. blockade, see Elizabeth Farnsworth, Richard Feinberg, and Eric Leeson, "The Invisible Blockade: The United States Reacts," in *Chile: Politics and Society*, ed. Arturo Valenzuela and J. Samuel Valenzuela (New Brunswick, N.J.: Transaction, Inc., 1976), pp. 338–73. For a statement by a Chilean official on the rationale behind U.S. policy, see Armando Uribe, *Le livre noir de l'intervention américaine au Chile* (Paris: Editions du Seuil, 1974). Uribe notes that Chilean policy-makers felt that the United States was less concerned about the copper nationalization than the impact a successful Allende experiment might have on the internal politics of France and Italy. The election of leftist governments in those countries would affect the balance of forces between East and West. This view was expressed by Henry Kissinger in a "deep background briefing" (see Uribe, *Le livre noir*, pp. 92–93, 202). It is quite probable that the U.S. State Department was more concerned with Allende's "Communist" policies and his treatment of foreign capital than Kissinger's office was. However, Kissinger's office had largely taken over the foreign policy role of the U.S. government. For documentation of the U.S. role in undermining the Chilean government both through open and covert actions, see the staff report of the Select Committee to Study Governmental Operations with Respect to Intelligence Activities, U. S., Senate, "Covert Action in Chile, 1963–73."
26. U.S., Senate, "Covert Action in Chile, 1963–73," p. 32.
27. De Vylder, *Allende's Chile*, p. 129.
28. The debate over the U.S. blockade has become extensive. Paul Sigmund, by taking the statements of U.S. officials too literally, downplayed the negative effects of the blockade in his "The 'Invisible Blockade' and the Overthrow of Allende," *Foreign Affairs* 52, no. 2 (January 1974): 322–40. For a response to Sigmund see Elizabeth Farnworth's "More Than Admitted," *Foreign Policy*, no. 16 (Fall 1974), pp. 127–41. For Sigmund's rebuttal see his "Less Than Charged," in idem, pp. 142–56. Sigmund's view was also taken to task in Richard Fagen's excellent article "The United States and Chile: Roots and Branches," *Foreign Affairs* 53, no. 2 (January 1975): 297–313. The revelations of the U.S. Senate Select Committee on Intelligence have substantially clarified the U.S. government's concerted attempts to undermine the Popular Unity government.
29. See Echeverría and Frei, *La lucha por la juricidad en Chile*, vol. 3, pt. 2, for the text of the opposition measure and other documents pertaining to its debate.
30. See Juan Linz, *The Breakdown of Democratic Regimes: Crisis, Breakdown, and Reequilibration* (Baltimore, Md.: Johns Hopkins University Press, 1978).
31. Figures from de Vylder, *Allende's Chile*, p. 91. Reajustes for various groups were widely reported in the press during this period.
32. De Vylder, *Allende's Chile*, p. 91. See the article by Andy Zimbalist and Barbara Stallings,

"Showdown in Chile," *Monthly Review* 25, no. 5 (October 1973): 1–24, which stresses the failure to instill a spirit of sacrifice in the workers. They note the efforts of the government to "demobilize" the workers and stress economic gains as the principal strategy. The Socialist party continually stressed the need to maintain and expand mobilization, and criticized the fact that the Popular Unity parties let the Committees of the Popular Unity, which had worked during the campaign, lapse. For example, see the internal party document published in *El Mercurio Edición Internacional*, 13–19 March 1972, p. 5. It is not so clear, however, as Zimbalist and Stallings maintain, that the Communists were the primary force behind the redistributive policy (p. 11). The Socialists continued to support Vuskovic, the primary architect of that policy. The Communists did frown on "mobilization" and expressed concern that the capitalist rules should not be abandoned too quickly while the economy was still essentially capitalist. See for example, Luis Corvalán's comments in Eduardo Labarca, *Corvalán 27 horas* (Santiago: Quimantú, 1972), pp. 26–27. But it is not clear to the author that, if a policy of more rapid mobilization of the masses had been instituted, the Popular Unity could have in fact deviated from a redistributive pattern. To instill notions of economic sacrifice, moral as opposed to economic incentives, would take a long period of time— longer than a six-year presidential term. Further mobilization would probably have heightened the pressure for redistribution, further aggravating the economic situation. Economic policies took effect immediately. Political policies, which some policy-makers thought should accompany economic policies, would have, even in the best of circumstances, taken much longer.

33. *El Mercurio Edición Internacional*, 31 January–6 February 1972, p. 5. A long document from the PIR, stating its position, is reproduced in this issue. It should be noted that the visit of Fidel Castro to Chile in late 1971 undoubtedly had a negative impact on the middle class's perception of the Allende government. Castro stayed in Chile from 10 November to 4 December 1971, and his every move was widely reported. For a compilation of Castro's speeches and press conferences see *Fidel en Chile* (Santiago: Quimantú, 1972).

34. De Vylder, *Allende's Chile*, p. 99.

35. This section is drawn primarily from extensive interviews in Santiago in August 1974 with former high-ranking officials of the Budget Bureau who served during the Allende years.

36. See *Posición*, 4 July 1972, p. 12. Allende sharply attacked these practices. See *Allende: Su pensamiento político*, p. 274.

37. Press conference reported in *El Mercurio Edición Internacional*, 2–8 August 1971, p. 1.

38. *El Mercurio Edición Internacional*, 13–19 March 1972, p. 5. See the same page for Socialist party critiques of the partisan competitiveness between Popular Unity parties. Internal criticism was brought out in several Popular Unity meetings. Important meetings took place in El Arrayán in March of 1972 and Lo Curro in June 1972.

39. For a discussion of Allende's continual exhortations to end labor indiscipline and a review of these problems, see Henry Landsberger and Tim McDaniel, "Hypermobilization in Chile, 1970–73," *World Politics* 28, no. 4 (July 1976): 502–43.

40. *El Mercurio Edición Internacional*, 31 January–6 February 1972, p. 6.

41. For the position of the MIR, see its newspaper, *El Rebelde*. A prestigious magazine of opinion, *Punto Final*, often expressed views close to those of the MIR. The official paper of the Communist party was *El Siglo*, though the party had several other publications, including, for example, *Ramona,* for more popular consumption. The leading Socialist newspaper was *Las Noticias de Ultima Hora*. In addition, weeklies such as *Mayoría* and the first-rate *Chile Hoy* presented views generally in line with those of the Socialist party. *Clarín* and *Puro Chile*, sensationalist tabloids, also supported the government. The official newspaper of the government was *La Nación*.

It should be stressed that the leadership of the Left was not necessarily very close. A very revealing fact is that the secretary general of the Communist party, Luis Corvalán, and Salvador Allende, colleagues in numerous struggles, did not use the familiar "tu" in addressing each other. Also, Communist leaders, in particular, did not often mix with leaders of other leftist parties socially. See Labarca, *Corvalán 27 horas*, p. 199. Corvalán also notes that the rivalries between followers were particularly intense (p. 198).

42. From the *Manifiesto de Concepción* issued on 22 May 1972 and reprinted in several newspapers. For a summary, see *El Mercurio Edición Internacional*, 22–28 May 1972, p. 1.

43. See the transcript of his press conference in *El Mercurio*, 27 May 1972, p. 25. For Allende's criticism of the ultra-leftists, see *Allende: Su pensamiento político*, pp. 211–12.

44. *El Mercurio Edición Internacional*, 9–15 August 1971, p. 5.

45. See Debray, *Chilean Revolution*, especially pp. 72–77.

46. *El Mercurio*, 27 May 1972, p. 25.

47. It must be stressed that much of the violence was blown out of proportion in the press accounts. Large headlines and shrill radio and television accounts conveyed the impression that what had been an isolated incident of violence had engulfed the whole nation. It is clear that with the relaxation of government violence and increased mobilization Chile was facing a level of confrontation not seen since the turbulent 1930s. But the perception of violence no doubt exceeded the real dimensions of violence, thereby having an exaggerated political impact.

48. The position of the Right was amply presented in the media. For the position of the far Right, including Patria y Libertad, see *Tribuna*, *Sepa*, and *PEC*. *El Mercurio*, which moved increasingly to the disloyal opposition and became a principal mouthpiece for the arch-conservative tendencies of the military junta after the coup, often printed ads for the extreme rightist group. See, for example, the full-page ad placed by Patria y Libertad presenting its platform and plan of action in the edition of 17 June 1972, p. 29. The *El Mercurio* company also published other dailies, such as *La Segunda*. *Qué Pasa*, a very informative conservative weekly, began to make inroads on *Ercilla*'s preeminent position in that market. The often inflammatory headlines and accounts of the Right are documented in part in Michele Mattelart and Mabel Piccine, "La prensa burguesa, no sería más que un tigre de papel?" *Cuadernos de la Realidad Nacional*, no. 16 (April 1973), pp. 250–63. As will be noted below, inflammatory headlines from both sides helped to confuse and polarize the political atmosphere.

49. The major Christian Democratic organ was *La Prensa*. As noted earlier, the popular weekly *Ercilla* also had a Christian Democratic orientation. For a moderate and leftist pro-Christian Democratic view, consult *Mensaje*. For a more conservative magazine, see the official *Política y Espíritu*.

50. For his statement, see *El Mercurio Edición Internacional*, 27 September–3 October 1971, p. 1. For a very valuable collection of documents that summarize the views of the Christian Democrats and the opposition by early 1972, see Joan E. Garcés, *Revolución, congreso, y constitución: El caso Tohá* (Santiago: Quimantú, 1972). The book reviews the movement of the Christian Democratic party away from its tentative support for the government and toward its alliance with the Right, culminating in the first successful impeachment vote, that of Allende's minister of the interior, José Tohá.

51. Actually, Christian Democrats had approached the government even earlier with a proposition that the competition between the two groups be kept at a minimum during the 1971 municipal elections. The Christian Democrats wanted to conserve their strength while not attacking the government. The government rejected the overture. The success of the Socialists in the 1971 election gave them electoral reasons (in addition to ideological objections) to striking an alliance with the Christian Democrats. As noted earlier, the Socialists gained strength dramatically to become Chile's first party. Under such circumstances Socialists could understandably perceive the Christian Democratic overtures as self-serving—at least in electoral terms. However, it is clear to this author that elements in the progressive wing of the Christian Democrats were genuinely concerned about the costs of electoral confrontation with the government and foresaw the increasing dangers of further polarization. Much of this analysis is based on interviews with high-level political leaders, primarily Christian Democrats, in Santiago, Chile, during the months of January and February of 1974. Subsequent interviews later that year corroborated the earlier ones.

52. The section of the constitution, adopted in 1970, that dealt with the question of how amendments were to be promulgated, was indeed ambiguous. According to Article 108, paragraph 1, constitutional reforms must follow the same procedures as those followed to adopt an ordinary law, with a few exceptions. The article then proceeds to note that for the adoption of an amendment, an absolute majority of members of both houses must approve the measure on two different occasions. The president cannot reject the bill submitted to him by the joint session of Congress. He can only propose modifications and corrections or

elaborate on items which he had proposed. The last paragraph states that if the president's proposals are accepted by a majority of the Congress, as specified in the second paragraph (that is, an absolute majority), the measure can then be returned to the president for promulgation. The problem is that the last paragraph does not say what happens when the Congress does not approve of the presidential modifications. According to Allende, since the first paragraph says that unless specified otherwise, a constitutional amendment follows the procedures of a simple law, and a simple law requires a two-thirds vote by the Congress in order to override presidential suggestions, a two-thirds vote was required. The president argued that the last paragraph, specifying an absolute majority of the Congress, was inserted in order to insure that a constitutional amendment could not be approved by only a majority of members present, as the constitution specifies for an ordinary law. But this requirement did not mean that the regular procedure requiring a two-thirds vote to override presidential vetoes was waived. The opposition in turn argued that the last paragraph implied not only that an absolute majority was needed to approve presidential vetoes, but that it also meant that by a mere majority the Congress could reject presidential vetoes. As far as the opposition was concerned, the last paragraph was included in Article 108 not only to specify that an absolute majority of Congress is needed for approval, but also to abolish the requirement for the two-thirds vote for overriding presidential modifications. This author, while recognizing the ambiguity, is inclined to think that the president's position was more tenable. The article clearly states that all procedures applied to a simple law must be followed, with specific exceptions. Since the exceptions do not include any reference to procedures for overriding presidential vetoes, merely a modification of the kind of majority needed to ratify those vetoes, all of the procedures for adopting a simple law should be followed. This position is shared by Alejandro Silva Bascuñan in a book published before the controversy. Silva was a prominent member of the opposition. See his "El tribunal constitucional," in Gustavo Lagos et al., *Reforma constitucional 1970* (Santiago: Editorial Jurídica, 1970), p. 262. For the constitutional reform and its legislative history, see Guillermo Piedrabuena Richards, *La reforma constitucional* (Santiago: Ediciones Encina, 1970). Piedrabuena argues that the spirit of the 1970 reforms, which provided for a plebiscite to resolve executive-legislative disputes, suggests that the impasse must be between the president and a majority, not a two-thirds majority of Congress (p. 129). This is a compelling argument, and quite logical, though it does not solve the ambiguity in the text. The Constitutional Tribunal set up to resolve such questions would in June 1973 refuse to clear up the matter. Finally, it must be added that Allende probably exceeded the provisions of Article 108 in his vetoes of the measure, which amounted to an outright rejection of many provisions of the proposed amendment. For an article supporting the position of the opposition, see Jaime Navarrete's "Observaciones del Presidente de la República y reforma constitucional," in *El Mercurio*, 28 March 1972. For an article supporting the president, see Julio Silva Solar, "Diputado Julio Silva demuestra legalidad de tesis presidencial," in *La Nación*, 17 April 1972.

53. For a compilation of documents on these talks, see Oficina de Informaciones del Senado, "Reforma constitucional que crea áreas de la economía nacional," *Boletín de Informaciones General*, no. 99, 17 April 1972.

54. Cited in *Las Noticias de Ultima Hora*, 30 June 1972, p. 4.

55. Ibid. For the position of the Communist party and the Socialist party at this time, see the articles in *Mayoría* 1, no. 37 (28 June 1972): 10–13.

56. *La Prensa*, 25 June 1972.

57. See *PEC*, 30 June 1972, p. 3. The strong feelings are reflected in some remarks which Sergio Onofre Jarpa, the president of the National party, made to Tomás Pablo, a Christian Democratic senator, in a hallway of the Senate. They are reported in *El Mercurio*, 15 June 1972, p. 15.

58. *Ercilla*, 16–22 June 1972, p. 17. The gremios flooded the papers with ads opposing talks. For an example, see *El Mercurio*, 16 June 1972, p. 17. For a good statement of the views of a powerful gremio, see the extensive report presented by Jorge Fontaine, the president of the Confederación de la Producción y del Comercio to the organization's national congress on 6 July 1972. The statement, endorsed unanimously, stresses the importance to the gremios of defending their own position and, by implication, relying less on the traditional party machinery. See *La Prensa*, 8 July 1972, pp. 6, 18.

59. For a valuable discussion of these topics, noting how close the negotiations were after the first round of talks, see the interview with José Antonio Viera-Gallo, assistant secretary in the Department of Justice, published in *La Prensa*, 26 March 1972. The letters and exchanges between the government and the Christian Democrats in July were made public by Jorge Tapia, the minister of justice. The author is grateful to Jorge Tapia for providing him with the summary of the principal themes and for giving him his personal observations on the progress of the talks. In addition to other interviews with people knowledgeable about the negotiations, the author benefited greatly from attending the debates in the Chilean Congress, and particularly the Senate, during this period.

60. *Las Noticias de Ultima Hora*, 30 June 1972, p. 20. For the Christian Democratic statement on the conclusion of the talks, see *La Prensa, 30 June 1973*, p. 20.

61. In fact, in an interview with the author in 1974, a prominent Christian Democratic leader noted that Allende won considerable mileage as a result of the "weakness" of the party leadership.

62. Labarca, *Corvalán 27 horas*, p. 44.

63. For an influential discussion of Latin American politics which elaborates on the concept of "power capability," see Charles Anderson, *Politics and Economic Development in Latin America* (Englewood Cliffs, N.J.: Van Nostrand, 1967), chap. 4.

64. For an excellent discussion focusing on the confrontation dimension see David Cusak, "Confrontation Politics and the Disintegration of Chilean Democracy," *Vierteljahresberichte*, no. 58 (December 1974), pp. 313–53.

65. There is no question that the strengthening of these groups as independent entities capable of independent action was aided by contributions from foreign and domestic business circles and from U.S. intelligence. In fact, shortly before the October strikes, $24,000 was provided to an anti-Allende business organization by the CIA. In all, $8 million was spent covertly in Chile between 1970 and 1973 with over $3 million spent in fiscal 1972 alone. See U.S., Senate, "Covert Action in Chile," pp. 1, 60.

66. Several organizations did very interesting research on the popular movement in Chile during the Allende government. The best work was done on the *poblaciones*. For a sampling, see the articles by CIDU researchers Manuel Castells, Luis Alvarado, Rosemond Cheetham, Adriana Garat, Gastón Rojas, Santiago Quevedo, Eder Sader, Jorge Fiori, and Ignacio Santa Maria in vol. 3, no. 7 (April 1973) of the journal *EURE*. See also the article by the Equipo de Estudios Poblacionales del CIDU, "Reivindicación urbana y lucha política: Los campanmentos de pobladores en Santiago de Chile," *EURE* 2, no. 6 (November 1972): 55–81. Another project deserving mention is the CIDU work on popular justice. See Rosemond Cheetham et al., *Pobladores: Del legalismo a la justicia popular, 2 vols.* (Santiago: CIDU, 1972).

67. Much of the literature cited in n. 66 underscores the economic orientation of the working class. In particular see Manuel Castells, "Movimiento de pobladores y lucha de clases," and Jorge Fiori, "Campamento Nueva Habana: Estudio de una experiencia de autoadministración de Justicia," both in *EURE* 3, no. 7 (April 1973). The campamento Nueva Habana was the most prominent *población* under the influence of the MIR. Even there, concerns with clientelistic matters were important, and, as Fiori notes, militancy subsided as *pobladores* began to see the Popular Unity government as the revolution already arrived. The "reivindicationist" orientation of the working class during the Popular Unity period is also strongly stressed by J. Samuel Valenzuela, "The Chilean Labor Movement: The Institutionalization of Conflict," and James Petras, "Nationalization, Socioeconomic Change, and Popular Participation," both in Valenzuela and Valenzuela, *Chile: Politics and Society*. For the best treatment yet on the role of the miners in the Allende government, which also strongly emphasizes "clientelistic" as opposed to revolutionary behavior, see Francisco Zapata, "Los mineros de Chuquicamata: Productores o proletarios?" (Mexico: Centro de Estudios Sociológicos, El Colegio de Mexico, Cuaderno no. 13, 1975). Since the miners had always constituted the backbone of support for the Left, their position was critical. Zapata shows that they continued to press for bread and butter issues as they had done when the Left was in opposition. (See n. 28, chap. 4.) The cordones formed during the October strike never really became strong enough to channel a mass movement. (On this point, see n. 58, chap. 4.) Earlier work by Henry Landsberger and his associates made similar points. See especially

Henry Landsberger, Manuel Barrera, and Abel Toro, "The Chilean Labor Union Leader: A Preliminary Report on His Background and Attitudes," *Industrial and Labor Relations Review* 17, no. 3 (April 1964): 399–420.

68. Radomiro Tomic, for one, expressed this view in an interparty memorandum, dated 7 November 1973, analyzing the situation after the coup. The opposition press, particularly the influential *El Mercurio*, received substantial covert funds from the United States to support its relentless campaign against the government. Every incident was magnified by a newspaper which reached every corner of the country. See U.S., Senate, "Covert Action," pp. 59–60. In evaluating the role of the media the author benefited from the views of several individuals. Particularly helpful were the views of a person who served in high editorial positions, including that of acting editor, of one of the most important Socialist newspapers.

69. See table 19.

CHAPTER 4

1. See Juan Linz, *The Breakdown of Democratic Regimes: Crisis, Breakdown, and Reequilibration* (Baltimore, Md.: Johns Hopkins University Press, 1978).

2. See the article "Revolucionario o Momio," in *El Mercurio Edición Internacional*, 13–19 March 1971. See also the statement of Contraloría objecting to procedures of the Dirección de Industria y Comercio (DIRINCO) in *La lucha por la juricidad en Chile*, ed. Andrés Echeverría and Luis Frei (Santiago: Editorial del Pacífico, 1974), vol. 1, pp, 311–12.

3. More broadly, the court argued that all it could do was enforce the law, and that if policy changes were sought, it was up to the legislature to modify the law. The government retorted that the court was selective in applying the law, which had considerable room for intepretation. In particular the government criticized the court's zeal in protecting private property and its refusal to curb the most libelous and seditious attacks of the opposition media. For a fascinating exchange of letters which reveals how the same "legality" was approached from different perspectives, see the exchange of letters between the president and the Supreme Court. They are reproduced in Echeverría and Frei, *La lucha por la juricidad*, vol. 3, pp. 168–98.

4. Whereas the percentage of the national budget devoted to military affairs had dropped to 5.3 percent during the Frei period (see chapter 1), it increased to 9.12 percent during the Allende years. At the same time, the government welcomed a continuation of military aid from the United States. While economic aid was reduced sharply, military aid was maintained, as the following table, showing U.S. military assistance to Chile, indicates.

Year	Military Assistance	Military Sales	Military Personnel Trained in Panama
1966	8,366,000	1,490,000	68
1967	4,766,000	1,690,000	57
1968	7,507,000	2,100,000	169
1969	2,662,000	2,147,000	107
1970	1,966,000	9,450,000	181
1971	1,033,000	2,958,000	146
1972	2,227,000	4,583,000	197
1973	918,000	2,242,000	257

SOURCE: United States, Senate, *Hearings before the Select Committee to Study Governmental Operations with Respect to Intelligence Activities*, 94th Cong., 1st sess., 4 and 5 December 1975, pp. 184–85.

5. For a revealing example of the constant effort of leaders on both sides to court the military,

and thus pressure it to subscribe to their own position, see the Senate debate of 26 October 1972, published in *El Mercurio*, 30 October 1972, p. 9.

6. The Unión Socialista Popular, the splinter party of the Socialists, did run candidates on a separate list, but they obtained only 1.6 percent of the vote. It must be stressed that the confederations were for electoral purposes only. Each of the parties continued to run the campaign as a separate organization and, as will be seen below, not without some conflict.

7. The pressure on the Christian Democrats to continue to oppose the government was revealed during the campaign by a sharp attack on party members whom the Nationals said were engaged in "secret talks" with the government to arrange for a common strategy after the election. This pressure was aimed at keeping the progressive wing of the party in line. See the declaration of the acting president of the National party, Carlos Raymond, reported in *La Prensa*, 15 February 1973. This and subsequent citations to the press in this section on the campaign are taken from the thorough step-by-step description of the public debate found in Carmen Barros and Patricio Chaparro, "La campaña de las elecciones de 1973: Chile un estudio de caso," mimeographed (Santiago: Instituto de Ciencias Políticas Universidad Católica, Documento de Trabajo No. 4, June 1974).

8. The Forty Committee, charged with overseeing U.S. covert actions, approved $1,626,666 for support of opposition candidates. See Select Committee on Intelligence, U.S., Senate, "Covert Action in Chile," p. 60. It should be reiterated that the funds went a long way, given the enormous differential between the official and the black market rate for dollars. At one time the official rate was around 40 escudos to the dollar and the black market rate 3000 to the dollar. The author interviewed one, not very prominent, congressman of the Democracia Radical party who received more money for the 1973 campaign than he had received for all previous campaigns put together. Though he was not told where the funds came from, he knew the money came from foreign sources.

9. See, for example, the interview with National party Senate candidate Fernando Ochagavía, *La Tercera de la Hora*, 9 December 1973. For the Christian Democrats see the document of the plenary council of the party, reported in *La Prensa*, 5 December 1972, and the statement of former-president Eduardo Frei, a Senate candidate for the Christian Democrats, in his declaration of candidacy speech, *La Prensa*, 5 December 1972. See also the declaration of Osvaldo Olguín, acting president of the Christian Democrats, reported in *La Prensa*, 14 February 1973. For other similar citations, see Barros and Chaparro, *La campaña de las elecciones*, pp. 59, 88.

10. See Barros and Chaparro, pp. 60–88 and 89–108.

11. For instance, see the speech by the president of the Nationals, Sergio Onofre Jarpa, published in *La Tercera de la Hora*, 14 December 1972.

12. This was a minority position in the Christian Democratic party. Among those who argued this line was Senate candidate Alejandro Noemi. See *La Tercera de la Hora*, 6 January 1973.

13. On the need for victory, see the declaration of the political commission of Patria y Libertad in *Patria y Libertad*, no. 30 (16 November 1972), p. 4. In that same issue, however, the rightist movement argued that the elections would not resolve the question because the Left only respected the force of arms (see p. 16). The utter contempt of Patria y Libertad for "liberal democracy" can be seen in the article in *Patria y Libertad*, no. 37 (4 January 1973), p. 2. These citations are drawn from Barros and Chaparro, pp. 190–92.

14. See the speech the president of the Popular Unity coalition, Senator Rafael Agustín Gumucio, published in *El Siglo*, 6 February 1973. The coalition's platform for the elections can be found in *La Nación*, 6 February 1973.

15. On the need for an alliance with the middle class and workers of other parties, see the speeches of the principal ideologue of the Communist party, Senator Volodia Teitelboim, in *El Siglo*, 30 January 1973 and 2 February 1973. For the injunction against civil war, see the speech by the secretary general of the party, Luis Corvalán, in *El Siglo*, 23 February 1973. See Barros and Chaparro, pp. 121–40.

16. See the well-publicized public letter by Carlos Altamirano published in *La Nacion*, 3 February 1973, condemning the Millas proposal.

17. For example, see the argument of Senator Carrera in *La Nación*, 3 February 1973. The position of the Socialists can be found in Carlos Altamirano, *Tres documentos* (Santiago: Ediciones SCI, 1973), and in Barros and Chaparro, pp. 141–60.

18. For the MAPU, see the electoral platform published in *La Nación,* 4 February 1973, and the declaration of Oscar Guillermo Garretón in *Revista de Frente*, no. 14 (1–15 November 1972). On the MIR position, which held that the elections were simply an artifact of the bourgeoisie and the dominant classes and were consequently a poor arena for confrontation, see the exchange of letters with the Socialist party published in *Punto Final*, no. 176 (30 January 1973), p. 2. On the need to accelerate confrontation, see the two articles by Manuel Cabieses, "Cambia el Gobierno si pierde en marzo," *Punto Final*, no. 174 (2 January 1973), p. 3; and "El dilema de marzo: avanzar o transar," *Punto Final*, no. 178 (27 February 1973), p. 2.

19. *Ercilla*, 14–20 March 1973.

20. *Ercilla*, 4–10 April 1973.

21. *Ercilla,* 11–17 April 1973, p. 10.

22. The controversy over the ENU was widely reported in the press.

23. This section is based on interviews.

24. The church's declaration on the controversy and the answer of the minister of education can be found in Carlos Oviedo, ed., *Documentos del episcopado: Chile 1970–73* (Santiago: Ediciones Mundo, 1974), pp. 151–58.

25. *Ercilla*, 18–24 April 1973, p. 13.

26. *Ercilla*, 25 April–1 May 1973, p. 8.

27. *Ercilla*, 25–31 May 1973, p. 13.

28. The El Teniente strike was a severe blow to the government at a time when it needed more than ever to project an image of unified working-class support. The strike, which began in April and lasted until the first part of July, had its origins in a disagreement between the government and the miners over a wage readjustment approved in October 1972. The opposition declared strong support for the workers even though their demands meant salary increases which far exceeded those of other workers. Though it must be noted that much of the support for the strike came from the professional unions, the strike had a demoralizing effect on the government and divided the workers. Other workers, such as the miners of Chuquicamata, declared "solidarity strikes" with those of El Teniente. At Chuquicamata, a motion supported by white-collar workers won. Blue-collar workers continued to work in extraordinarily difficult circumstances. The strike demonstrated further the essentially economic demands of the elite groups of the working class and their lack of strong revolutionary consciousness.

29. See *Ercilla*, 13–19 June 1973, pp. 7–10. For an article sharply critical of the court, see Victor Vaccaro, "Escándalo en la Corte," *Chile Hoy*, 22–28 June, pp. 16–17. The exchange of letters between the president and the court has already been cited. See n. 3.

30. That Allende was intent on pursuing a dialogue, and that the Christian Democrats, and Frei in particular, were not interested, is also evidenced by some "behind the scenes" developments. In May, Allende sought, through the good offices of the cardinal, to set up a personal conversation with Frei to discuss the serious crisis. Frei refused to participate in any private meeting with the president, arguing that he would only attend a public meeting following a public invitation. Frei did not trust the president. He would not consider the possibility that Allende was making a genuine effort to resolve the country's difficulties and refused to recognize that Allende, like himself, was under enormous political pressures from his own camp. That Allende was even willing to risk a private meeting set up at his initiative is evidence of good faith. These observations, and the section on the Christian Democratic convention, are based on extensive interviews primarily with prominent Christian Democrats.

31. The fragment that retained the strongest claim to a party's traditions had a much better chance of surviving. Both the MAPU and the Izquierda Cristiana, though taking with them important leadership elements of the party, were not able to retain support at the polls. The same was true with the fragments of the Radical party, the Democracia Radical and the Partido de Izquierda Radical, or the fragment of the Socialist party, the Union Socialista Popular. In the 1973 congressional elections the minor parties and all segments of the divided Radical party fared very poorly.

32. According to prominent members of the progressive faction of the Christian Democratic party, in interviews with the author, one of Allende's principal mistakes was not to try to be more accommodating toward the Christian Democratic party during the early years of his

administration. The progressive wing of the party still controlled the party leadership and a defection of the Right might have been possible. This would have been to the advantage of both the government and the leftist and centrist elements in the Christian Democrats. A split, after the leadership had been taken over by the more conservative wing of the party, would act only to the detriment of the more moderate sectors, who would risk becoming politically insignificant.

33. *Chile Hoy*, 6–12 July 1973, p. 11.
34. Ibid.
35. Ibid.
36. Quoted by Regis Debray in "Il es mort dans sa loi," *Le Nouvel Observateur*, no. 462 (17–23 September 1973), p. 37.
37. In interviews with the author, leaders of the Christian Democrats and top officials of the Allende government who were involved in the negotiations concurred with this assessment. They noted that while the air force and the navy might have been ready to move, the army was divided enough that a compromise would have made it difficult to get the vital army support for military action. This is very important. Leaders on both sides were not convinced that a coup was inevitable. And even in retrospect they speculated that it could have been averted as of July 1973. They (particularly the leadership of the Christian Democrats) did not realize at the time that the lack of compromise was in itself an important catalyst for the coup.
38. *Ercilla*, 18–24 July 1973, p. 7.
39. Ibid.
40. *Chile Hoy*, 13–19 July 1973, p. 8.
41. Ibid., p. 6.
42. *Chile Hoy*, 6–12 July 1973, p. 3.
43. This and succeeding sections are also based in part on interviews with former high-level political leaders, primarily Christian Democrats.
44. The statement can be found in Echeverría and Frei, *La lucha por la juricidad*, vol. 3, pp. 123–24. It is instructive that the day of the coup attempt the leadership of the Christian Democratic party met for hours and was unable to decide on an official reaction until after the insurrection had failed.
45. *Ercilla*, 11–17 July 1973, p. 9.
46. This section is based on interviews with Gabriel Valdés in February and March 1974. It was corroborated in interviews with other principals who were at the dinner. Private conversation between the president and C.D. officials were actually officially prohibited by the C.D. leadership, which feared reaction from the Nationals and C.D. supporters.
47. The press carried good accounts of the conversations. This section, however, relies primarily on interviews. For a published account, see *Ercilla*, 8–14 August 1973, pp. 7–10.
48. See the special supplement to *El Mercurio* published on 11 September 1974 entitled "Como llegaron las fuerzas armadas a la acción del 11 de Septiembre de 1973." The author of the twenty-four-page supplement, Arturo Fontaine Aldunate, the associate director of the newspaper, interviewed at length "more than fifteen" high-ranking officers who were "first line protagonists." Despite the fact that the account is self-serving and that Fontaine does not hide his own biases, this report is extraordinarily valuable because it paints a full picture of the gradual move toward a military coup in the three services, particularly in the navy. Another useful, though less informative account based on very well-placed sources is the article by William Montalbano, "How the Chilean Military Toppled Allende," in the *Miami Herald*, 16 September 1973, pp. 1, 22A.
49. For the slogans see *Chile Hoy*, 6–12 July 1973, p. 15.
50. We know that some officers were conspiring from the beginning. Several conspirators were removed in the wake of the Schneider assassination and internal incidents within the armed forces in later periods, such as September 1972. The CIA successfully "penetrated" one group of plotters in January of 1972. The CIA received reports on the group planning a coup through July, August, and September of 1973. See Select Committee on Intelligence, U.S. Senate, "Covert Action in Chile," p. 39. The point is not that plotting did not exist, but rather that the process through which the plotters had to go in order to move the institution toward a coup was a long and tedious one.

51. See Fontaine, "Como llegaron las fuerzas armadas," p.10.

52. In an earlier version of this study, I argued that intervention by Allende in the hierarchy of rank was one of the factors which contributed to military dissatisfaction. Since the writing of that work I have been able to conduct further interviews with high-ranking officials in the Allende government. On the basis of those interviews and a reevaluation of the public record, it seems that the question of disturbance of the hierarchy of rank by the president was not an important one. In fact, Allende scrupulously resisted efforts by many people in his own coalition to obtain more loyal officers. See, for example, the letter by Senator Altamirano to Allende in which the Socialist leader threatened to withdraw the minister of the interior from the cabinet unless the president finally agreed to replace some leaders of the Carabineros. The letter, ironically, is published in the Junta de Gobierno, *Libro blanco del cambio de gobierno en Chile* (Santiago: Editorial Lord Cochrane, 1973), p. 113, as purported evidence of Popular Unity meddling in the armed forces. As will be clear below, it was not only the Socialist who wanted officers replaced; the plotters also wanted the president to move down the hierarchy of rank to ensure the success of their plans. The earlier study is "Il crollo della democrazia in Chile," *Revista Italiana di Scienza Politica* 5, no. 1 (April 1975): 83–129.

53. See the article by Faride Zerán, "El poder popular en acción," *Chile Hoy*, 6–12 July 1973, pp. 6–7. This was one of a multitude of articles which appeared after the coup celebrating the potential of working-class mobilization to fend off a coup by occupation of factories and even armed resistance. For a treatment of the *comandos comunales*, see "Comandos comunales: Órganos de Poder del Pueblo," *Punto Final*, no. 189 (31 July 1973).

54. *Chile Hoy*, 13–19 July 1973, p. 8.

55. Ibid., p. 6.

56. Ibid., p. 7.

57. MAPU Garretón faction, *Boletín Informativo*, no. 5.

58. Despite the enormous publicity to the cordones, they never constituted a massive force. When the government sought to return industries taken over by workers in the attempted coup, many workers resisted. At one point the Cordón Los Cerrillos barricaded themselves inside factories to prevent the devolution of industries. Though perhaps five thousand workers were mobilized, that number was a small fraction of the Santiago working class. In interviews with the author, a sociologist from the University of Chile who was working closely with the Cordón Los Cerrillos put the active members at only a few hundred. The account by Patricia Santa Lucia, "The Industrial Working Class and the Struggle for Power in Chile," in *Allende's Chile*, ed. Philip O'Brien (New York: Praeger Special Studies in International Politics and Government, 1976), pp. 128–66, which paints a picture of a strong movement in the text, reveals the weakness of the cordones in an appendix which attempts to list cordones and their membership.

59. Allende and the Communist party understood this and through their control of the Central Unica de Trabajadores sought to downplay the cordones after an initial period of praise. In turn they left themselves open to charges that they were unwilling to let the working class defend itself. It is clear to this author, however, that there was no way in which the working class could have been mobilized to fight and die in such a short period of time, given the essentially economic outlook of the great bulk of the population and the escalating conspiracy in the armed forces. The maximalist Left was engaged in a self-fulfilling prophecy.

60. On these plans, see Fontaine, "Como llegaron las fuerzas armadas," p. 11. Prats signed the documents.

61. *Chile Hoy*, 3–10 July 1973, p. 8. These statements incensed military leaders; see William Montaldo, "How the Chilean Military Toppled Allende."

62. *Ercilla*, 5–11 August 1973, pp. 7–8.

63. This is derived from conversations with cabinet officers close to Allende. See also Regis Debray, "Il est mort dans sa loi," p. 37.

64. It is quite clear that the strikers were not willing to settle for any satisfaction of their immediate economic demands; they were intent on forcing the president to resign from office or provoking a coup. This view of the strikers' intent was shared by prominent Christian Democrats who spoke out publicly. See Renán Fuentealba's interview in *Chile Hoy*, 17–23 August 1973, p. 28. At this same time the Forty Committee in Washington approved another

$1 million to support opposition groups. The money was not spent as the coup was imminent. See Select Committee on Intelligence, U.S. Senate, "Covert Action in Chile," p. 61.

65. In interviews and correspondence with the author, President Frei strongly denied that he was involved in any coup attempt. It is clear, however, that President Frei thought that a coup was imminent, and more importantly, inevitable, It is also clear that he did have direct contacts with some officers, including his former military aides Generals Bonilla and Arellano. Some of his closest associates, Sergio Ossa and Juan de Dios Carmona, had close ties with military officers and probably knew of the impending coup. This author doubts that the former president was directly involved in any conspiracy. Nevertheless, by his inaction he tacitly supported the coup. Frei was the most important political figure in the opposition and along with Allende the most prominent politican in the country. Had he used his influence to oppose a coup, both privately and publicly, it would have made it extremely difficult for the military to act. Some of Frei's colleagues sensed that. Only ten days before the coup Bernardo Leighton, his former minister of the interior and an old friend who maintained contacts with Allende, urged Frei to talk to Allende in an effort to stave off the coup. Frei once again argued that he would only talk to Allende publicly, failing to appreciate that the situation in September 1973 was very different from what it had been in May of that year when he set down similar conditions. The declaration issued by the Christian Democrats after the coup reflected the thinking of Frei and the leadership. It blamed the government exclusively for the situation in Chile and noted that the armed forces "did not seek power" and that "their institutional traditions and the republican history of the country inspires confidence that as soon as the tasks which they have assumed to avoid the grave dangers of destruction and totalitarianism which threatened the Chilean nation have been completed, they will return power to the sovereign people." When several Christian Democrats, including Bernardo Leighton, issued a public declaration condemning the coup, Frei went out of his way, in an interview with *ABC* magazine, to argue that that group represented a minority in the party and that the military had "saved Chile." The Christian Democratic declaration, that of those who opposed the coup, and a summary of Frei's *ABC* interview can be found in *Chile-America*, no. 4 (1975), pp. 43–49.

That a bold attempt by politicians to avert a coup would have received significant popular support is evidenced by a survey taken in Santiago only days before the coup. Fifty-one and one-half percent of the respondents thought the military should not involve itself in the political sphere, compared to only 27.5 percent who thought it should. The authors of the poll concluded that despite the fact that 72 percent of the sample as opposed to a mere 3 percent thought the country was living in "abnormal times," Chileans still preferred a "democratic solution." For the survey see *Ercilla*, 22–28 August 1973, pp. 18–19.

66. The Chamber's resolution argued, among other things, that from the beginning the Allende government had sought to gain total power, that in so doing it had violated the constitution and laws and had ignored other powers, particularly Congress. It called on the military cabinet members, by virtue of their oath of loyalty to the constitution, to "place an immediate end to all situations referred to that infringe the constitution and laws, in order to channel governmental action through lawful paths and assure constitutional order for our fatherland and the essential bases of democratic conviviality among Chileans." Allende in answering the congressional action noted that it would "facilitate the seditious intentions of certain sectors . . .the deputies of oppositon formally exhorted the Armed Forces and Police to adopt a deliberating posture with respect to executive power, and break their duty to obey the Supreme Government. . . ." See Echeverría and Frei, *La lucha por la juricidad,* vol. 3, pp. 199–211. Allende had tried to stave off the vote in the Chamber. Orlando Letelier pleaded to no avail with Bernardo Leighton to try to stop the vote. Later, both Leighton and Tomic would point to the action of the Chamber as one of the major mistakes of the Christian Democratic party.

67. See Fontaine, "Como llegaron las fuerzas armadas," for the fascinating narrative.

68. On the Communist party position see the summary of a forthcoming book by Eduardo Labarca reported in *Chile-America*, nos. 12–13 (November-December 1975), pp. 75–77.

69. See Fontaine, "Come llegaron las fuerzas armadas," p. 20.

70. The military, however, did go to some length to try to ensure cohesiveness in the armed forces. Shortly after the coup it was announced that the armed forces had moved to prevent

the government from carrying out a Z plan which called for the assassination of a host of military officers during the 19 September 1973 military parade. And yet, according to military spokesmen themselves, the Z plan was only discovered after the coup. Whether the plan was actually one of many plans undoubtedly produced by a host of little groups (this Z plan called for the assassination of Allende himself, thus also raising questions about the military's view that the government was preparing the action), or a fabrication, it was used to instill fear in the army. Top leaders of the Christian Democratic party who supported the military coup when it took place told the author that they had little doubt that the Z plan was a fabrication. For the Z plan, see the official publication which the junta put out shortly after the coup in order to justify their actions, *Libro blanco del cambio de gobierno en Chile*. An English-language version was published and widely disseminated in the United States. According to the U.S. Senate Committee on Intelligence, the CIA paid the travel expenses of pro-junta spokesmen who went abroad to support the military action. See "Covert Action in Chile," pp. 40, 62. In interviews with the author, other participants and observers of the period shortly after the coup also interpreted the severity of the repression as a mechanism used by the armed forces to ensure loyalty. Even on Dawson Island, where there was clearly no possibility of attack, the military was kept in constant fear of an imminent attack. According to one military officer who fled the country shortly after the coup, General Oscar Bonilla had to work hard on 10 September to obtain the loyalty of many officers. See *Chile-America*, no. 5 (31 March 1975), p. 24.

71. For a discussion of over thirty works that have appeared since and reflect previous and current thinking on the Chilean experience by a cross-section of authors, see Arturo Valenzuela and Samuel Valenzuela, "Visions of Chile," *Latin American Research Review* 10, no. 3: 155–75.

Biographical Notes

RISTO ALAPURO received his doctorate from the University of Helsinki in 1973. He pursued postdoctoral studies at the University of Michigan during 1973 and 1974 and has been a lecturer in sociology at the University of Helsinki since then. Dr. Alapuro has published books and articles on the student movement and peasant mobilization in Finland.

ERIK ALLARDT is a Research Professor at the Academy of Finland and Chairman of the Finnish Political Science Association. He received his doctorate from the University of Helsinki in 1952 and has been a Visiting Professor at the University of California at Berkeley, the University of Illinois, and the University of Wisconsin. From 1968 to 1971 he was editor of *Acta Sociologica*. With Stein Rokkan he edited *Mass Politics: Studies in Political Sociology* and with Yrjö Littunen, he edited *Cleavages, Ideologies, and Party Systems*. His book, *Sociologi,* is currently in its sixth edition in Finnish.

JULIO COTLER is Senior Researcher at the Instituto de Estudios Peruanos, in Lima, and has been a Professor at the University of San Marcos and at the Universidad Nacional Autónoma de México. He received his doctorate in sociology from the University of Bordeaux in 1960. He has just completed *Clases, estado, y nación en el Perú,* is co-editor, with Richard Fagen, of *Latin America and the United States: The Changing Political Realities,* and has published extensively on peasant movements, corporatism, military populism, internal domination, and dependency.

PAOLO FARNETI received his Laurea in Jurisprudence from the University of Turin in 1960 and his doctorate in sociology from Columbia University in 1968. He is currently a Professor of Political Science at Turin and Director of the Centro Studi Scienza Politica, Turin. Formerly he was the Lauro de Bosis Lecturer at Harvard University. His publications include *Theodor Geiger e la coscienza della società industriale, Sistema politico e società civile,* and *L'Italia contemporanea.*

M. RAINER LEPSIUS is Professor of Sociology at the University of Mannheim and has been President of the German Sociological Association since 1971. He received his Ph.D. degree in the social sciences from the University of Munich in 1955. He has published over twenty monographs and essays on such themes as the sociology of intellectuals, industrial sociology, radical nationalism, inequality, regime change, and democracy in Germany as a historical and sociological problem.

DANIEL LEVINE is Associate Professor of Political Science at the University of Michigan and, during 1978–79, Visiting Fulbright Professor at the National University of Guatemala. He received his doctorate from Yale University in 1970. He is the author of *Conflict and Political Change in Venezuela* and has published widely on Venezuelan politics, the Catholic Church, Latin American social change, and political culture.

JUAN J. LINZ is Pelatiah Perit Professor of Political and Social Science at Yale University. He received his doctorate from Columbia University in 1959 and has taught at Columbia University, Stanford University, the University of Madrid, and the Universidad Autónoma of Madrid. He is Chairman of the Committee on Political Sociology of the International Sociological and Political Science Associations. His publications include "Totalitarian and Authoritarian Regimes," in *Handbook of Political Science,* ed. F. Greenstein and N. Polsby; "Some Notes toward a Comparative Study of Fascism in Comparative Sociological Perspective," in *Fascism,* ed. W. Laquer; and numerous monographs and essays on Spanish elites and entrepreneurs, quantitative history, and parties and elections in Spain and Germany.

GUILLERMO O'DONNELL is Director and founder of CEDES (Centro de Estudios de Estado y Sociedad) in Buenos Aires. He did advanced studies in law and political science at the National University of Buenos Aires and Yale University and has been a Visiting Professor at the University of Michigan and a Fellow of the Institute for Advanced Study, Princeton. His publications include *Modernization and Bureaucratic-Authoritarianism: Studies in South American Politics,* and, with Delfina Linck, *Dependencia y Autonomía.* He is currently completing a book on the "bureaucratic-authoritarian" period in Argentina between 1966 and 1973.

WALTER B. SIMON received his M.S. degree in social psychology from the University of Washington in Seattle and his doctorate in sociology from Columbia University. He has taught sociology at several North American universities and is presently teaching at the University of Vienna. His published work deals with the concept of the authoritarian personality, the phenomenon of social movements, aspects of socialization and pedagogy, language politics, and the political implications of cultural pluralism.

PETER H. SMITH is Chairman of the Department of History, University of Wisconsin at Madison. He received his doctorate from Columbia University in 1966. Among his many publications are *Politics and Beef in Argentina: Patterns of Conflict and Change; Argentina and the Failure of Democracy: Conflict Among Political Elites, 1904–1955;* and *Labyrinths of Power: Political Recruitment in Twentieth-Century Mexico.*

ALFRED STEPAN is Professor of Political Science at Yale University and frequently serves as Chairman of Yale's Council on Latin American Studies. He received his doctorate from Columbia University in 1969 and has taught at Yale since then. He has been a Guggenheim Fellow and, from 1978 to 1979, will be a Visiting Fellow at St. Antony's College, Oxford University. He has published *The Military in Politics:*

Changing Patterns in Brazil and *The State and Society: Peru in Comparative Perspective*. He is the editor of *Authoritarian Brazil: Origins, Policies, and Future* and co-editor, with Bruce Russett, of *Military Force and American Society*.

ALEXANDER WILDE is a Research Associate in the Woodrow Wilson International Center for Scholars in Washington, D.C. He received his doctorate in political science from Columbia University in 1972 and has taught at the University of Wisconsin at Madison and at Haverford College. He is the author of various articles on politics and religion as well as the book, *Politics and the Church in Colombia*. With Arturo Valenzuela he has written studies on budgetary politics in Chile. He has just completed a monograph, *Conversaciones de caballeros: La democracia oligárquica en Colombia*.

ARTURO VALENZUELA is Associate Professor of Political Science and Director of the Comparative Area Studies Program at Duke University. He was born in Concepción, Chile, and received his doctorate from Columbia University in 1971. During 1977–1978 he was a Visiting Fellow of the Institute of Development Studies, University of Sussex. His publications include *Political Brokers in Chile: Local Government in a Centralized Polity,* and *Chile: Politics and Society,* which he edited with J. Samuel Valenzuela, as well as articles on budgetary politics, political history, and socialism in Chile.

Index to Part I

Index to Part II

Index to Part III

155

Index to Part IV

Library of Congress Cataloging in Publication Data
Main entry under title:

The Breakdown of democratic regimes.

    Includes indexes.
    CONTENTS: pt. 1. Linz, J. J. Crisis, breakdown,
and reequilibration.—pt. 2. Linz, J. J. and
Stepan, A., editors. Europe.—pt. 3. Linz, J. J.
and Stepan, A., editors. Latin America. [etc.]
    1. Europe—Politics and government—20th
century—Addresses, essays, lectures. 2. Latin
America—Politics and government—Addresses, essays,
lectures. I. Linz Storch de Gracia, Juan José,
1926–   II. Stepan, Alfred C.
JN94.A2B72   320.9′4′05   78–584
ISBN 0-8018-2008-1